LEGAL LOOSELEAFS IN PRINT 1992

COMPILED AND EDITED
BY
ARLENE L. EIS

INFOSOURCES PUBLISHING

LEGAL LOOSELEAFS IN PRINT 1992

Printed in the United States of America.

ISBN 0-939486-23-7
ISSN 0275-4088

Price $90

Order from:

Infosources Publishing
140 Norma Road
Teaneck, New Jersey 07666
(201) 836-7072

CONTENTS

INTRODUCTION

This edition of LEGAL LOOSELEAFS IN PRINT marks our twelfth year of publication. The aim of LEGAL LOOSELEAFS IN PRINT was to present for the first time in one compilation a listing and subject index of the legal looseleafs published in the United States that were currently in print. The book won wide critical acclaim and is being used in hundreds of libraries around the world. It gives complete information on about 4100 looseleafs covering all areas of the law, published by 324 different publishers. The following statistics will show how the book has grown:

	1981	1992
Titles listed	1380	4100
Publishers listed	100	324
Pages in book	192 p.	608 p.

The FTC Guides for the Law Book Industry (16 CFR 256.0 (1982)) define a looseleaf as follows: 256.0(e) Looseleaf (binder). A law book or series of law books that consist of ring or post-bound (compression-type) binders used to hold separate looseleaf sheets as opposed to the bound book format wherein pages are permanently attached to the binder.

The looseleaf format was introduced in legal publishing at the beginning of this century, and its popularity has increased greatly since then. Although the looseleaf is such an integral part of legal literature, it has been very neglected in the bibliographic treatment of the law. The standard legal bibliographies omit looseleafs, and as a result, full bibliographic information regarding looseleafs has heretofore been very difficult to locate.

LEGAL LOOSELEAFS IN PRINT 1992, in its listing and subject indexing of looseleafs, fills this void in the bibliographic arena of legal literature. The book has proved to be an indispensable and efficient tool for both the librarian and the lawyer in their research of legal looseleafs. It also serves as an aid in the selection and acquisition of legal looseleafs.

LEGAL LOOSELEAFS IN PRINT 1992 consists of the following sections:

Publishers List — a list of publishers of legal looseleafs, with full names, addresses, telephone numbers and FAX numbers for each publisher. This information is intended to facilitate ordering of books. In addition, each publisher has been assigned an abbreviation which is used in entries throughout the book.

Key to Publishers' Abbreviations — presents the abbreviations in alphabetical order, and matches each with a publisher's name.

Title List — This, the main body of the book, is an alphabetical list of the looseleafs by title. Each listing gives nine uniform points of information.

1. Title
2. Author or editor
3. Publisher
4. Year of original publication
5. Number of volumes
6. Price for the volumes, and whether the price includes any future supplementation

7. Frequency of publication
8. Annual cost of supplementation
9. Library of Congress control number/OCLC control number/LC classification

In each entry, the points of information are numbered as above and are presented in a clear, concise and easy-to-read format. (For a more detailed explanation of these points, see page 35.)

Publisher Index — An index by publisher's abbreviation, to all the looseleafs listed in the *Title List*.

List of Cessations and Deletions — All titles deleted from the 1991 edition are listed here, accompanied by the publisher's name and the latest year the listing appeared.

Subject Index — to all the looseleafs listed in the *Title List*. Library of Congress-type subject headings are used with slight modifications. The index uses "see also" references. For each subject there appears a list of titles of the works on that subject. Every title is further identified by its publisher, and refers you back to the *Title List*.

EDITORIAL POLICIES

LEGAL LOOSELEAFS IN PRINT 1992 omits from its coverage sets of state statutes and regulations, free publications, and newsletters and reports that are simply stored in looseleaf binders. Newsletters and reports are, as of 1985, fully covered in LEGAL NEWSLETTERS IN PRINT. Also omitted are sets of books in which only the index volumes or a minority of the volumes are looseleaf. Looseleafs published by foreign publishers are not included. Selected federal, state and local government publications have been covered. GPO stock numbers have been provided for U.S. government publications for easy ordering. All other legal looseleafs in the English language fall within the scope of this volume.

Prices quoted in this book are per single copy in effect January 1992, and are subject to change.

The Editor invites comments on LEGAL LOOSELEAFS IN PRINT 1992. You are also invited to take advantage of our FREE PHONE CONSULTATION SERVICE available to subscribers only.

Information on new looseleaf publications is also requested. Write to Infosources Publishing, 140 Norma Road, Teaneck, New Jersey 07666. New editions are published each March.

ACKNOWLEDGMENTS

Thanks are due to all my colleagues in the library community who are the devoted users of LEGAL LOOSELEAFS IN PRINT. A special thank you is owed to all of you who have taken the time to write to me over the past twelve years with your comments and criticisms. You are strongly urged to continue writing to me, and together we will further develop and improve LEGAL LOOSELEAFS IN PRINT.

March, 1992 — Arlene L. Eis

PUBLISHERS' LIST

Access Reports, Inc.
417 Elmwood Ave.
Lynchburg, VA 24503
(804) 845-5727
(Access Reports)

Adams-Hall Publishing
3420 Ocean Park Blvd., Suite 3060
Santa Monica, CA 90405
(310) 399-7137; (800) 888-4452
(Adams-Hall)

Alabama Bar Institute for
Continuing Legal Education
Box 870384, Univ. of Alabama
Tuscaloosa, AL 35487-0384
(205) 348-6230
(800) 627-6514; Fax (205) 348-1072
(ABICLE)

Alexander Hamilton Institute
197 W. Spring Valley Avenue
Maywood, NJ 07607
(201) 587-7052
(800) 879-2441; Fax (201) 587-7063
(Alex. Hamilton Inst.)

ALI-ABA Committee on Continuing
Professional Education
4025 Chestnut Street
Philadelphia, PA 19104
(215) 243-1620
(800) CLE-NEWS; Fax (215) 243-1664
(ALI-ABA)

Altman Weil Pensa
P.O. Box 625
Newtown Square, PA 19073
(215) 359-9900; Fax (215) 359-0467
(Altman Weil Pensa)

American Bankers Association
1120 Connecticut Ave., N.W.
Washington, DC 20036
(202) 663-5000; Fax (301) 843-8405
(Am. Bankers)

American Bar Association
750 N. Lake Shore Dr.
Chicago, IL 60611
(312) 988-5555; Fax (312) 988-6281
(ABA)

American Civil Liberties Union
132 West 43rd Street
New York, NY 10036
(212) 944-9800; Fax (212) 869-9065
(ACLU)

American Dental Assn.
211 E. Chicago Ave.
Chicago, IL 60611
(312) 440-2920; (800) 947-4746
(American Dental)

American Horse Council
1700 K Street, N.W., Suite 300
Washington, DC 20006
(202) 296-4031; Fax (202) 296-1970
(AHC)

American Immigration Lawyers Assn.
1400 Eye St., N.W., Suite 1200
Washington, DC 20005
(202) 371-9377; Fax (202) 371-9449
(American Immigration Lawyers Assn.)

American Institute of Architects
1735 New York Avenue, N.W.
Washington, DC 20006
(202) 626-7475; Fax (202) 626-7420
(AIA)

American Institute of Certified
Public Accountants
P.O. Box 1003
New York, NY 10108
(800) 248-0445 (NY); (800) 334-6961
(AICPA)

American Land Title Association
1828 L Street NW, Suite 705
Washington, DC 20036
(202) 296-3671; Fax (202) 223-5843

(ALTA)

American Lawyer Mgmt. Service
625 Polk St., Suite 500
San Francisco, CA 94102
(415) 749-5400
(Am. Lawyer)

American Prepaid Legal Services Institute
541 N. Fairbanks Court
Chicago, IL 60611
(312) 988-5751; FAX (312) 988-5032
(API)

American Society of Corporate Secretaries, Inc.
1270 Avenue of the Americas
New York, NY 10020
(212) 765-2620; Fax (212) 765-8349
(ASCS)

American Stock Exchange, Inc.
86 Trinity Place
New York, NY 10006
(212) 306-1391; Fax (212) 306-1372
(ASE)

Anderson Publishing Co.
2035 Reading Road
Cincinnati, OH 45202
(513) 421-4142
(800) 582-7295; Fax (513) 562-8116
(Anderson)

Arkansas Bar Association
400 West Markham
Little Rock, AR 72201
(501) 375-4605
(800) 482-9406 (AR); Fax (501) 375-4901
(Arkansas Bar)

Arlen Communications Group, Inc.
75 Varick St.
New York, NY 10013
(212) 966-5100; Fax (212) 226-4630
(Arlen)

Aspen Publishers Inc.
200 Orchard Ridge Dr., Suite 200
Gaithersburg, MD 20878
(301) 417-7500
(800) 638-8437; Fax (301) 417-7550
(Aspen)

Assn. of Transportation Practitioners
1725 K St. NW, Suite 301
Washington, DC 20006-1401
(202) 466-2080; Fax (202) 467-4330
(ATP)

Assn. of Trial Lawyers of America
1050 31 Street, N.W.
Washington, DC 20007
(202) 965-3500
(800) 424-2727; Fax (202) 298-6849
(ATLA)

Atlantic Information Services, Inc.
1050 17 St. NW, Suite 480
Washington, DC 20036
(202) 775-9008
(800) 521-4323; Fax (202) 331-9542
(Atlantic Info.)

Atlantic Law Book Company
150 Hartford Ave.
Wethersfield, CT 06109
(203) 563-6881; Fax (203) 721-7588
(Atlantic)

Bancroft-Whitney Co.
P.O. Box 7005 3250 Van Ness Ave.
San Francisco, CA 94120-7005
(415) 929-3500
(800) 848-4000; Fax (415) 929-3746
(Bancroft)

Banks-Baldwin Law Publishing Co.
P.O. Box 1974
Cleveland, OH 44106
(216) 721-7373
(800) 362-4500(OH); Fax (216) 721-8055
(Banks)

Bar Association of the District of Columbia - Young Lawyers Section
1819 H Street, N.W., 12th Floor
Washington, DC 20006

(202) 223-6600; Fax (202) 293-3388
(Bar Assn. of D.C.)

Barclays Law Publishers
400 Oyster Point Blvd., Suite 500
South San Francisco, CA 94080
(415) 588-1155
(800) 888-3600; Fax (415) 244-0408
(Barclays)

Baylor University Press
P.O. Box 6325 Baylor Univ.
Waco, TX 76798
(817) 755-2161
(Baylor Univ. Press)

Bender, Matthew & Co., Inc.
See Matthew Bender & Co., Inc.

Big Foot Press
1720 S. Bellaire St.
Denver, CO 80222
(303) 691-9119; Fax (303) 758-8762
(Big Foot)

Bisel, George T., Company
See George T. Bisel Company

Blais
304 Newbury, Suite 364
Boston, MA 02115
(617) 421-9520
(Blais)

BNA Books
1250 23rd St., N.W.
Washington, DC 20037
(202) 452-4400; Fax (202) 452-9186
(BNA Books)

Board of Governors of the
Federal Reserve System
20th St. & Constitution Ave., N.W.
Washington, DC 20551
(202) 452-3244; Fax (202) 728-5886
(Fed.)

Boardman, Clark Co., Ltd.
See Clark Boardman Callaghan

Book Publishing Company
201 Westlake Ave. N.
Seattle, WA 98109
(206) 343-5700
(800) 537-7881; Fax (206) 343-3038
(Book Pub.)

Bowne & Co., Inc.
345 Hudson St.
New York, NY 10014
(212) 924-5500 x575
(Bowne)

Bureau of National Affairs, Inc.
1231 25th Street, N.W.
Washington, DC 20037
(202) 452-4200
(800) 372-1033; Fax (202) 822-8092
(BNA)

Business & Legal Reports
644 Wall Street
Madison, CT 06443
(800) 727-5257; Fax (203) 245-2559
(BLR)

Business International Corp.
215 Park Avenue South
New York, NY 10003
(212) 460-0600; Fax (212) 995-8837
(Bus. Intern.)

Business Laws, Inc.
11630 Chillicothe Rd.
Chesterland, OH 44026
(216) 729-7996
(800) 759-0929; Fax (216) 729-0645
(Bus. Laws)

Butterworth Legal Publishers
289 E. 5th St.
St. Paul, MN 55101
(612) 227-4200; Fax (612) 224-4714
(Butterworth-St. Paul)

Butterworth Legal Publishers
90 Stiles Road
Salem, NH 03079
(603) 898-9664

(800) 548-4001; Fax (603) 898-9858
(Butterworth-NH)

Butterworth Legal Publishers
Echelon II, Suite 100, 9430 Research Blvd.
Austin, TX 78759
(512) 346-9686; Fax (512) 346-9373
(Butterworth-Texas)

Butterworth Legal Publishers
P.O. Box 5105
Clearwater, FL 33518
(813) 441-8933
Fax (813) 443-1912; (800) 237-9707
(Butterworth-Fla.)

Byram, R. W. & Co.
See R. W. Byram & Co.

California Family Law Report, Inc.
P.O. Box 5917
Sausalito, CA 94966
(415) 332-9000; Fax (415) 332-8381
(CFLR)

California Journal Press
1714 Capitol Ave.
Sacramento, CA 95814
(916) 444-2840; Fax (916) 444-2339
(Calif. Jnl. Press)

Callaghan & Co.
See Clark Boardman Callaghan

Carl Vinson Institute of Government
University of Georgia
201 N. Milledge Ave.
Athens, GA 30602
(404) 542-2736; Fax (404) 542-9301
(Institute-Ga.)

Carroll Publishing Co.
1058 Thomas Jefferson St., N.W.
Washington, DC 20007
(202) 333-8620; Fax (202) 337-7020
(Carroll)

Center for Immigrants Rights, Inc.
48 St. Mark's Place
New York, NY 10003
(212) 505-6890; Fax (212) 995-5876
(Center for Immig. Rights)

Central Publishing Co.
P.O. Box 10866, 200-A Monroe St., Suite 225
Rockville, MD 20849-0866
(301) 424-4132; Fax (301) 762-2663
(Central)

CGL Reporter, Inc.
120 S. Riverside Plaza, Suite 2250
Chicago, IL 60606
(312) 648-4554
(CGL)

Charles D. Spencer & Associates
250 S. Wacker Dr., Suite 600
Chicago, IL 60606
(312) 993-7900; Fax (312) 993-7910
(Spencer)

Chase Manhattan Bank N.A.
1211 Ave. of the Americas, 34th Fl.
New York, NY 10036
(212) 789-5311
(Chase Manhattan)

Chicago Board of Trade
141 W. Jackson
Chicago, IL 60604
(312) 435-3613; Fax (312) 341-3392
(Chicago Bd.)

Chicago Mercantile Exchange
30 South Wacker Drive
Chicago, IL 60606
(312) 930-3452; Fax (312) 466-4410
(CME)

Cincinnati Stock Exchange
205 Dixie Terminal Building
Cincinnati, OH 45202
(513) 621-1410; Fax (513) 621-4963
(Cincinnati)

Claitor's Publishing Division
3165 S. Acadian at I-10
Baton Rouge, LA 70821

(504) 344-0476
(800) 274-1403; Fax (504) 344-0479
(Claitor's)

Clark Boardman Callaghan
155 Pfingsten Rd.
Deerfield, IL 60015
(800) 323-1336
(708) 948-7000; Fax (708) 948-8955
and
375 Hudson Street
New York, NY 10014
(212) 929-7500
(800) 221-9428; Fax (212) 924-0460
(Clark Boardman Callaghan)

Cohasset Associates, Inc.
505 North Lake Shore Drive
Chicago, IL 60611
(312) 527-1550; Fax (312) 527-1552
(Cohasset)

Colorado Legal Publishing Company
1360 S. Clarkson St. #300
Denver, CO 80210
(303) 778-6811; Fax (303) 744-9323
(CLP)

Commerce Clearing House, Inc.
4025 W. Peterson Avenue
Chicago, IL 60646
(312) 583-8500; Fax (312) 940-0113
(CCH)

Commodity Exchange, Inc.
4 World Trade Center
New York, NY 10048
(212) 938-2921; Fax (212) 432-1154
(COMEX)

Commonwealth Publishing Co., Inc.
101 N. Westlake Blvd., Suite 203
Westlake Village, CA 91362
(805) 496-6642
(Commonwealth)

Communication Research Inc.
3954 44 Street, SE
Grand Rapids, MI 49508
(616) 698-0444; Fax (616) 698-0603
(CRI)

Connecticut Bar Association
Continuing Legal Education
101 Corporate Place
Rocky Hill, CT 06067
(203) 721-0025; Fax (203) 257-4125
(Conn. Bar)

Connecticut Law Tribune Co.
One Post Rd., Suite 100
Fairfield, CT 06430
(203) 256-3600; Fax (203) 255-3319
(Conn. Law Tribune)

Continuing Education of the Bar, California
2300 Shattuck Avenue
Berkeley, CA 94704
(510) 642-8000 ext. 001A
(800) 858-4545 ext. 001A; Fax (510) 642-3788
(Calif. CEB)

Continuing Legal Education in Colorado, Inc.
1900 Grant St., Suite 900
Denver, CO 80203
(303) 860-0608; Fax (303) 894-0821
(CLE-Colorado)

Corbel & Co.
1660 Prudential Drive
Jacksonville, FL 32207
(904) 399-5888
(800) 326-7235; Fax (904) 399-5551
(Corbel)

Corporate Reports, Inc.
1101 King St., Suite 400
Alexandria, VA 22314
(703) 739-3745; Fax (703) 683-6974
(Corporate Reports)

Corporate Tax Publishers, Inc.
109 Oaktree Place
Leonia, NJ 07605
(201) 461-6619; Fax (201) 461-6619
(Corp. Tax)

Council of Michigan Foundations

One South Harbor Ave., Suite 3
Grand Haven, MI 49417
(616) 842-7080; Fax (616) 842-1760
(Council of Mich. Fdtns.)

Court Information Services Co.
1823 Avenue O
Brooklyn, NY 11230
(718) 375-4019; Fax (718) 998-8059
(Court Info.)

CRS Inc.
P.O. Box 234
Kents Hill, ME 04349
(207) 685-9090; Fax (207) 685-6091
(CRS)

Daniel Publishing Co.
P.O. Box 2684
Great Falls, MT 59403-2684
(406) 727-1290
(Daniel)

Dearborn Financial Publishing Inc.
520 N. Dearborn
Chicago, IL 60610
(800) 621-9621
(800) 654-8596 (IL); Fax (312) 836-1021
(Dearborn)

District of Columbia Bar, The
1707 L Street, N.W., 6th Fl.
Washington, DC 20036-4202
(202) 331-3883; Fax (202) 223-7726
(D.C. Bar)

Eastern Mineral Law Foundation
West Virginia Univ. College of Law
P.O. Box 6130
Morgantown, WV 26506-6130
(304) 293-2470; Fax (304) 293-7654
(EMLF)

Education Funding Research Council
1611 N. Kent St., Suite 508
Arlington, VA 22209
(703) 528-1082; Fax (703) 528-6060
(EFRC)

Enterprise Publishing Co.
725 N. Market St.
Wilmington, DE 19801
(302) 654-0110
(800) 533-2665; Fax (302) 654-0277
(Enterprise)

Entertainment Business Publishing Co.
8530 Wilshire Blvd.
Beverly Hills, CA 90211
(213) 278-7244
(EBP)

Environment Books Inc.
4905 Smith Rd.
Plano, TX 75094-9556
(214) 881-1331
(Environment Books)

Environmental Law Institute
1616 P St., N.W., Suite 200
Washington, DC 20036
(202) 939-3844; Fax (202) 328-5002
(ELI)

Equity Publishing Corp.
Orford, NH 03777-9797
(603) 353-4351
(Equity)

Executive Press, Inc.
P.O. Box 21639
Concord, CA 94521-0639
(510) 685-5111; Fax (510) 685-4802
(Exec. Press)

Facts & Comparisons
111 West Port Plaza, Suite 423
St. Louis, MO 63146
(314) 878-2515
(800) 223-0554; Fax (314) 878-5563
(Facts)

Farnam Equipment Co.
P.O. Box 34820
Phoenix, AZ 85067
(602) 285-1660
(800) 234-0592; Fax (602) 285-1803
(Farnam)

Fast Eddie Publishing Co.
1155 S. Main St., Suite 100
Willits, CA 95490
(707) 459-3999
(Fast Eddie)

FDIC Corp. Communications Office
550 17 St. N.W., Rm. 6058
Washington, DC 20429
(202) 898-6996; Fax (202) 393-5169
(FDIC)

Fed-Track Publications
P.O. Box 6159
Alexanderia, VA 22306
(703) 780-6844
(Fed-Track)

Federal Bar Association
1815 H Street, N.W., Suite 408
Washington, DC 20006
(202) 638-0252; Fax (202) 775-0295
(FBA)

Federal Home Loan Mortgage Corp.
8200 Jones Branch Drive
Reston, VA 22101
(800) 373-3343
(Freddie Mac)

Federal National Mortgage Assn.
510 Walnut St.
Philadelphia, PA 19106
(215) 575-1400; Fax (215) 575-1481
(FNMA)

Federal Publications Inc.
1120 20th Street, N.W.
Washington, DC 20036
(202) 337-7000; Fax (202) 659-2233
(Fed. Publ.)

Federal Reserve Bank of New York
33 Liberty Street
New York, NY 10005
(212) 720-5216; Fax (212) 720-6767
(Fed.-NY)

Financial Accounting Standards Board
401 Merritt 7
Norwalk, CT 06856
(203) 847-0700; Fax (203) 849-9714
(FASB)

Financial Publishing Co.
82 Brookline Ave.
Boston, MA 02062
(617) 262-4040
(800) 247-3215; Fax (617) 247-0136
(Finan. Pub.)

Florida Bar, The
650 Apalachee Parkway
Tallahassee, FL 32399-2300
(904) 561-5600
(800) 342-8060 (FL); Fax (904) 222-3729
(Florida Bar)

Foreign Tax Law Publishers, Inc.
P.O. Box 2189
Ormond Beach, FL 32175-2189
(904) 253-5785; Fax (904) 257-3003
(Foreign Tax)

Francis Marion, Inc.
130 E. Frederick
Boerne, TX 78006
(512) 249-8705
(800) 662-9025; Fax (512) 249-1891
(Francis Marion)

Fred B. Rothman & Co.
10368 West Centennial Rd.
Littleton, CO 80127
(303) 979-5657
(800) 457-1986; Fax (303) 978-1457
(Rothman)

Gann Law Books
1 Washington Park, Suite 1500
Newark, NJ 07102
(201) 268-1200; Fax (201) 268-1330
(Gann)

George T. Bisel Company
710 South Washington Square
Philadelphia, PA 19106
(215) 922-5760

(800) 247-3526 (PA); Fax (215) 922-2235
(Bisel)

Georgetown University Law Center,
CLE Division
777 N. Capitol St., N.E., Suite 405
Washington, DC 20002
(202) 408-0990; Fax (202) 408-1431
(Georgetown)

Glanville Publishers, Inc.
75 Main St.
Dobbs Ferry, NY 10522
(914) 693-8100; Fax (914) 693-0402
(Glanville Publishers)

Gould Publications
199 State Street
Binghamton, NY 13901-2782
(607) 724-3000
(800) 847-6502; Fax (607) 723-4285
(Gould)

Government Information Services
1611 N. Kent St., Suite 508
Arlington, VA 22209
(703) 528-1082; Fax (703) 528-6060
(GIS)

Government Institutes, Inc.
Four Research Place, Suite 200
Rockville, MD 20850
(301) 921-2300; Fax (301) 921-0373
(Govt. Inst.)

Government Research Service
701 Jackson, Rm. 304
Topeka, KS 66603
(913) 232-7720
(800) 346-6898; Fax (913) 232-1615
(Govt. Res.)

Greenwood Press
88 Post Road West
Westport, CT 06880
(203) 226-3571; Fax (203) 222-1502
(Greenwood)

Griffin Communications, Inc.
1420 Bristol St. N., Suite 220
Newport Beach, CA 92660
(714) 752-1058; Fax (714) 955-1929
(Griffin)

Gulf Publishing Co., Book Division
P.O. Box 2608
Houston, TX 77019
(713) 529-4301
(800) 231-6275; Fax (713) 525-4647
(Gulf)

Harrison Company
3110 Crossing Park
Norcross, GA 30071
(404) 447-9150; (800) 282-9867 (GA)
(800) 241-3561; Fax (404) 729-0265
(Harrison)

Hawaii Institute for Continuing
Legal Education
University of Hawaii School of Law
2515 Dole Street
Honolulu, HI 96822
(808) 956-6551; Fax (808) 956-6402
(HICLE)

Hawkins Publishing Co., Inc.
1207B Central Ave.
Mayo, MD 21106
(301) 798-1677
(Hawkins)

HBJ Miller Accounting Publications, Inc.
465 S. Lincoln Drive
Troy, MO 63379
(314) 528-8110
(800) 543-1918; Fax (800) 235-0256
(HBJ Miller)

Health Industry Manufacturers Assn.
1200 G St., N.W., Suite 400
Washington, DC 20005
(202) 434-7256; Fax (202) 783-8750
(HIMA)

Hein, William S. Co., Inc.
See William S. Hein Co., Inc.

Holding, Laura A.
    See Laura A. Holding

IBL Seminars
P.O. Box 3488
Santa Monica, CA 90408
(310) 450-0500; Fax (310) 450-0132
(IBL Seminars)

Idaho Law Foundation
P.O. Box 895
Boise, ID 83701
(208) 342-8958; Fax (208) 342-3799
(Idaho Law)

Illinois Institute for Continuing Legal
    Education
2395 W. Jefferson Street
Springfield, IL 62702
(217) 787-2080
(800) 252-8052 (IL); Fax (217) 787-5986
(Illinois ICLE)

Indiana Continuing Legal Education Forum
230 East Ohio Street, Suite 300
Indianapolis, IN 46204
(317) 637-9102; Fax (317) 633-8780
(Indiana CLE)

Information Requirements Clearinghouse
5600 S. Quebec St., #250C
Englewood, CO 80111
(303) 721-7500; Fax (303) 721-8849
(IRC)

Institute for Defense & Disarmament Studies
675 Massachusetts Ave., 8th fl.
Cambridge, MA 02139
(617) 354-4337; Fax (617) 354-1450
(IDDS)

Institute of Continuing Legal Education
1020 Greene St.
Ann Arbor, MI 48109-1444
(313) 764-0533
(800) 922-6516 (MI); Fax (313) 763-2412
(ICLE-Michigan)

Institute of Property Taxation
888 17th St., N.W., Suite 1150
Washington, DC 20006
(202) 452-1213; Fax (202) 452-1240
(Inst. of Prop. Tax.)

International Association of Assessing Officers
1313 E. 60 Street
Chicago, IL 60637-2892
(312) 947-2069; Fax (312) 362-2246
(IAAO)

International Conference of Building Officials
5360 South Workman Mill Road
Whittier, CA 90601
(213) 699-0541
(800) 423-6587; Fax (213) 692-3853
(ICBO)

International Franchise Association
1350 New York Ave., N.W.
Washington, DC 20005
(202) 628-8000; Fax (202) 628-0812
(IFA)

International Law Institute
1615 New Hampshire Ave. N.W.
Washington, DC 20009
(202) 483-3036; Fax (202) 835-0894
(Intl. Law Inst.)

International Risk Management Institute, Inc.
12222 Merit Drive, Suite 1660
Dallas, TX 75251-2217
(214) 960-7693
(800) 827-4242; Fax (214) 960-6037
(Intl. Risk Mgmt. Inst.)

Interstate Oil & Gas Compact Commission
900 N.E. 23 Street, P.O.B. 53127
Oklahoma City, OK 73105
(405) 525-3556
(800) 822-4015; Fax (405) 525-3592
(IOCC)

Investment Company Institute
1600 M Street, N.W., Suite 600
Washington, DC 20036
(202) 293-7700; Fax (202) 293-2673
(ICI)

Investor Responsibility Research Center
1755 Massachusetts Ave. N.W., Suite 600
Washington, DC 20036
(202) 234-7500; Fax (202) 332-8570
(IRRC)

Invictus Publishing Corporation
180 South Broadway
White Plains, NY 10605
(914) 949-6550
(Invictus)

Iowa State Bar Association
1101 Fleming Building
Des Moines, IA 50309
(515) 243-3179
(800) 457-3729; Fax (515) 243-2511
(Iowa Bar)

J.J. Keller & Associates
3003 Breezewood Lane
Neenah, WI 54957
(414) 722-2848; (800) 558-5011
(800) 242-6469(WI); Fax (414) 727-7516
(Keller)

James P. Manak
421 Ridgewood Avenue
Glen Ellyn, IL 60137
(708) 858-6392
(Manak)

James Publishing, Inc.
3520 Cadillac Ave., Suite E
Costa Mesa, CA 92626
(714) 755-5450
(800) 882-7855; Fax (714) 549-8835
(James)

Jefren Publishing Co., Inc.
1513 Auburn Ave.
Rockville, MD 20850
(301) 279-7082; (800) 444-0405
(Jefren)

JKP Publications
P.O. Box 1535
Severna Park, MD 21146
(410) 647-0936
(JKP)

John Liner Organization
155 Federal St.
Boston, MA 02110
(617) 423-0978
(800) 682-5759; Fax (617) 482-7820
(John Liner Org.)

John Wiley & Sons, Inc.
One Wiley Drive
Somerset, NJ 08873
(908) 469-4400
(800) 526-5368; Fax (908) 302-2300
(Wiley)

Joint Committee on Continuing Legal Education
School of Law, Univ. of Virginia
Charlottesville, VA 22901
(804) 924-3416
(800) 223-2167); Fax (804) 979-3147
(Jt. Comm. Va.)

Jury Verdict Research, Inc.
30700-H Bainbridge Rd.
Solon, OH 44139
(216) 248-7960
(800) 321-6910; Fax (216) 349-5879
(Jury Verdict)

Kansas Bar Association
1200 Harrison
Topeka, KS 66601
(913) 234-5696; Fax (913) 234-3813
(Kansas Bar)

Keller, J.J. & Associates
See J.J. Keller & Associates

Kluwer Law & Taxation
6 Bigelow Street
Cambridge, MA 02139
(617) 354-0140; Fax (617) 354-8595
(Kluwer)

Knowles Law Book Publishers
P.O. Box 911004
Ft. Worth, TX 76111
(817) 838-0202

(800) 299-0202; Fax (817) 831-4725
(Knowles)

Lambda Legal Defense and
Education Fund, Inc.
666 Broadway
New York, NY 10012
(212) 995-8585; Fax (212) 995-2306
(Lambda)

Lamb's Flight, Ltd.
RR #1 Airport Rd., Box 2055
Johnson City, NY 13790
(607) 770-9901
(800) 338-LAMB (NY); Fax (607) 729-6293
(Lamb's Flight)

Land Development Institute, Ltd.
1401 16th St., N.W.
Washington, DC 20036
(202) 232-2144; Fax (202) 232-4757
(Land Dev.)

Laura A. Holding
100 Norman Drive
Mars, PA 16046
(412) 776-8286
(Holding)

Law Bulletin Publishing Company
415 North State Street
Chicago, IL 60610
(312) 644-7800; Fax (312) 644-4255
(Law Bulletin)

Law Journal Seminars-Press, Inc.
111 Eighth Avenue, Suite 900
New York, NY 10011
(212) 741-8300
(800) 888-8300; Fax (212) 741-3985
(Law Journal)

Law-Arts Publishers, Inc.
159 W. 53 Street
New York, NY 10019
(212) 586-6380
(Law-Arts)

Lawpress
P.O. Box 5024
Westport, CT 06881
(203) 256-1717; (800) 622-1181
(Lawpress)

Lawrence Lame
98-30 67th Avenue
Rego Park, NY 11374
(718) 830-0124
(Lame)

Lawyers Co-operative Publishing Co.
50 Broad Street East
Rochester, NY 14694
(716) 546-5530
(800) 527-0430; Fax (716) 546-5037
(Lawyers Coop.)

Lawyers Weekly Publications
30 Court Square
Boston, MA 02108
(617) 227-6034
(800) 444-LAWS; Fax (617) 227-8824
(Lawyers Weekly)

Legal Research Systems, Inc.
115 Olde Wood Rd.
Glastonbury, CT 06033
(203) 659-0106; (800) 448-4524
(Legal Res. Systems)

Legal-Medical Studies Inc.
P.O. Box 8219, JFK Station
Boston, MA 02114
(617) 742-7959
(Legal-Med.)

Lexikon Services Publications
3241 Boulder Creek Way
Sacramento, CA 95842
(916) 331-9906
(Lexikon)

Little, Brown & Co. Law Div.
34 Beacon Street
Boston, MA 02108
(617) 227-0730
(800) 343-9204; Fax (617) 859-0629
(Little, Brown)

Longshore Newsletter
15 Fowler Court
San Rafael, CA 94903
(415) 499-9105; Fax (415) 472-6823
(Longshore)

Los Angeles Daily Journal
915 East First Street
Los Angeles, CA 90012
(213) 625-2141; Fax (213) 680-3682
(LADJ)

LRP Publications
747 Dresher Rd.
Horsham, PA 19044
(215) 784-0860
(800) 341-7874; Fax (215) 784-9639
(LRP)

M&M Resources Corp.
P.O. Box 15013
Los Angeles, CA 90015
(213) 748-0421; Fax (213) 742-0301
(M&M Resources)

M.L. Smith Publishers & Printers
P.O. Box 2678
Nashville, TN 37219
(615) 242-7395
(800) 866-7729; Fax (615) 256-6601
(Smith)

Maine State Bar Association
124 State Street
Augusta, ME 04330
(207) 622-7523; Fax (207) 623-4140
(Maine Bar)

Manak, James P.
  See James P. Manak

Mariposa Publishing, Inc.
1375 Wolters Blvd., Suite 100
St. Paul, MN 55110
(612) 490-1419
(800) 442-1419; Fax (612) 490-1160
(Mariposa)

Mark A. Stephens, Ltd.
10018 Colesville Road
Silver Spring, MD 20901
(301) 593-0443; (800) 358-8001
(Stephens)

Maryland Institute for Continuing
  Professional Education of Lawyers, Inc.
520 West Fayette St.
Baltimore, MD 21201-1729
(410) 328-6730; Fax (410) 328-8476
(MICPEL)

Massachusetts Continuing Legal Education-
  New England Law Institute, Inc.
20 West Street
Boston, MA 02111
(800) 632-8077 (MA)
(617) 482-2205; Fax (617) 482-9498
(Mass. CLE)

Matrimonial CaseLaw Corp.
585 Stewart Ave. Suite 314
Garden City, NY 11530-9716
(516) 745-1500
(Matrimonial CaseLaw)

Matthew Bender & Co., Inc.
11 Penn Plaza
New York, NY 10001
(212) 967-7707
Fax (212) 244-3188; (800) 223-1940
(Bender)

Medilex Co.
371 E. Monte Vista
Phoenix, AZ 85004
(602) 241-1400; Fax (602) 241-0519
(Medilex)

Meiklejohn Civil Liberties Institute
Box 673
Berkeley, CA 94701
(510) 848-0599
(Meiklejohn Civil Liberties Institute)

Merritt Company, The
P.O. Box 955
Santa Monica, CA 90406
(310) 450-7234; Fax (310) 396-4563

(Merritt)

Metropolitan News Co.
210 South Spring St.
Los Angeles, CA 90014
(213) 628-4384; Fax (213) 687-3886
(Metropolitan News)

Michie Company, The
P.O. Box 7587
Charlottesville, VA 22906
(804) 972-7600
(800) 446-3410; Fax (804) 972-7666
(Michie)

Michigan Legal Services
220 Bagley Avenue
Detroit, MI 48226
(313) 964-4130; Fax (313) 964-1192
(Mich. Legal)

Michigan Trial Lawyers Assn.
501 S. Capital Ave., Suite 405
Lansing, MI 48933
(517) 482-7740; Fax (517) 482-5332
(MTLA)

MidAmerica Commodity Exchange
141 W. Jackson Blvd.
Chicago, IL 60604
(312) 341-3046
(MidAmerica)

MII Publications Inc.
1211 Connecticut Ave. N.W., Suite 402
Washington, DC 20036
(202) 293-1740; Fax (202) 293-0377
(MII)

Minneapolis Grain Exchange
400 Fourth South St.
Minneapolis, MN 55415
(612) 338-6212; Fax (612) 339-1155
(Minneap.)

Minnesota CLE
40 North Milton
St. Paul, MN 55104
(612) 227-8266
(800) 759-8840 (MN); Fax (612) 227-6262
(Minn. CLE)

Minnesota Institute of Legal Education
29 S. Fifth St.
Minneapolis, MN 55402
(612) 339-1128; Fax (612) 339-8573
(MILE)

Missouri Bar CLE
P.O. Box 119
Jefferson City, MO 65101
(314) 635-4128; Fax (314) 635-2811
(MoBar)

Mortgage and Real Estate Investment Guide
P.O. Box 703
Marshfield, MA 02050
(617) 834-8702
(Mortgage)

Mortgage Bankers Association of America
P.O. Box 37236
Washington, DC 20013
(202) 861-6500; Fax (202) 466-2479
(MBAA)

National Asbestos Council
1777 Northeast Expressway, Suite 150
Atlanta, GA 30329
(404) 633-2622; Fax (404) 633-5714
(Natl. Asbestos)

National Attorneys' Publications
P.O. Box 540
Islip, NY 11751
(516) 581-1934; Fax (516) 581-8937
(Nat. Atty.)

National Center for Computer Crime Data
1222-B 17th Ave.
Santa Cruz, CA 95062
(408) 475-4457; Fax (408) 475-5386
(NCCCD)

National Center for Lesbian Rights
1663 Mission Street, 5th Fl.
San Francisco, CA 94103
(415) 621-0674; Fax (415) 621-6744

(Natl. Center for Lesbian Rights)

National Commercial Finance Association
225 West 34th Street
New York, NY 10001
(212) 594-3490; Fax (212) 564-6053
(NCFA)

National Council of Savings Institutions
1101 15th St. NW, Suite 400
Washington, DC 20005
(202) 857-3100; Fax (202) 659-4816
(NCSI)

National Employment Law Institute
444 Magnolia Ave., Suite 200
Larkspur, CA 94939
(415) 924-3844; Fax (415) 924-2908
(NELI)

National Federation of Community
Broadcasters
666 11th St. NW, Suite 805
Washington, DC 20001
(202) 393-2355
(NFCB)

National Fire Protection Assn.
1 Batterymarch Park
Quincy, MA 02269
(617) 770-3000; (800) 344-3555
(Natl. Fire Protection Assn.)

National Health Publishing, a div. of
Williams & Wilkins
428 E. Preston St.
Baltimore, MD 21202
(410) 528-4270
(800) 446-2221; Fax (410) 447-8438
(Natl. Health)

National Lawyers Guild AIDS Network
558 Capp St.
San Francisco, CA 94110
(415) 824-8884
(Natl. Lawyers Guild AIDS Network)

National Legal Publishing Co., Inc.
1360 S. Clarkson St., Suite 300
Denver, CO 80210
(303) 778-6811
(800) 729-1528; Fax (303) 744-9323
(Natl. Legal Publishing)

National Notary Assn.
8236 Remmet Ave.
Canoga Park, CA 91304
(818) 713-4038
(800) 876-6827; Fax (818) 713-0842
(Natl. Notary)

National Obscenity Law Center
475 Riverside Drive, Suite 239
New York, NY 10115
(212) 870-3232
(Nat. Obscenity Law Center)

National Private Truck Council
1320 Braddock Place, Suite 720
Alexandria, VA 22314
(703) 683-1300; Fax (703) 683-1217
(NPTC)

National Tax Training School
P.O. Box 382
Monsey, NY 10952
(914) 352-3634; Fax (914) 352-8138
(NTTS)

National Technical Information Service
(U.S. Dept. of Commerce)
5285 Port Royal Road
Springfield, VA 22151
(703) 487-4630; Fax (703) 321-8547
(NTIS)

National Trust for Historic Preservation
1785 Massachusetts Avenue, N.W.
Washington, DC 20036
(202) 673-4297; Fax (202) 673-4038
(NTHP)

National Underwriter Co.
505 Gest St.
Cincinnati, OH 45203
(513) 721-2140
(800) 543-0874; Fax (513) 721-0126
(Natl. Underwriter)

Nebraska Continuing Legal Education, Inc.
635 S. 14 Street
Lincoln, NE 68501-1809
(402) 475-7091; Fax (402) 475-7091
(Nebraska CLE)

New England Legal Publishers
P.O. Box 425
Weston, MA 02193
(617) 891-6200
(NELP)

New Hampshire Bar Assn. CLE
112 Pleasant St.
Concord, NH 03301
(603) 224-6942; Fax (603) 224-2910
(NH Bar)

New Jersey Institute for Continuing Legal
Education
1 Constitution Sq.
New Brunswick, NJ 08901
(908) 249-5100; Fax (908) 249-2815
(New Jersey ICLE)

New York City Dept. of City Planning
22 Reade St., 1st Floor
New York, NY 10007
(212) 720-3667
(NYC)

New York State Bar Association
1 Elk Street
Albany, NY 12207
(518) 463-3724
(800) 582-2452; Fax (518) 463-8844
(NYSBA)

New York State Office of Court
Administration
P.O. Box 3139, Church St. Station
New York, NY 10008
(212) 417-4912; Fax (212) 417-2022
(NYS OCA)

New York State Trial Lawyers Association
132 Nassau Street
New York, NY 10038
(212) 349-5890; Fax (212) 608-2310
(NYSTLA)

New York Stock Exchange, Inc.
20 Broad Street, 5th fl.
New York, NY 10005
(212) 656-7603; Fax (212) 656-2512
(NYSE)

NILS Publishing Company
21625 Prairie Street
Chatsworth, CA 91311
(818) 998-8830
(800) 423-5910; Fax (818) 718-8482
(NILS)

North Carolina Bar Foundation
1312 Annapolis Drive
Raleigh, NC 27605
(919) 828-0561; Fax (919) 821-2410
(No. Carolina Bar)

NYPER Publications
Box 370
Latham, NY 12110-0370
(518) 786-1654
(NYPER)

Oasis Press
300 N. Valley Drive
Grants Pass, OR 97526
(503) 479-9464; (800) 228-2275
(800) 221-4089 (CA); Fax (503) 476-1479
(Oasis)

Oceana Publications, Inc.
75 Main Street
Dobbs Ferry, NY 10522
(914) 693-8100; Fax (914) 693-0402
(Oceana)

Office of Thrift Supervision,
Communications Services Division
1700 G St. NW
Washington, DC 20552
(202) 906-6155
(Office of Thrift Supervision)

Ohio CLE Institute
1700 Lake Shore Drive

Columbus, OH 43204-9955
(614) 487-8585
(800) 232-7124; Fax (614) 487-8808
(Ohio CLE)

Ohio State Bar Foundation
33 W. 11th Ave.
Columbus, OH 43201
(614) 487-2050
(Ohio State Bar)

Oklahoma Bar Assn. CLE
P.O. Box 53036
Oklahoma City, OK 73152
(405) 524-2365
(800) 522-8065; Fax (405) 524-1115
(Okla. Bar CLE)

On Point Press
P.O. Box 1969
Jackson, MS 39215-1969
(601) 939-3895
(On Point)

Options Clearing Corp.
440 S. LaSalle St., Suite 908
Chicago, IL 60605
(312) 322-2026
(Options Clearing Corp.)

Oregon Criminal Defense Lawyers Assn.
44 W. Broadway, Suite 403
Eugene, OR 97401
(503) 686-8716; Fax (503) 686-2319
(OCDLA)

Oregon State Bar
5200 S.W. Meadows Rd.
Lake Oswego, OR 97035
(503) 620-0222
(800) 452-8260 (OR); Fax (503) 684-1366
(Oregon Bar)

Pacific Law Institute
1088 Bishop St., Suite 706
Honolulu, HI 96813
(808) 524-4155; Fax (808) 524-0573
(Pacific Law Inst.)

Panel Publishers
36 West 44 St.
New York, NY 10036
(212) 354-4545
(800) 457-9222; Fax (212) 302-5119
(Panel)

Pantagraph Printing/Legal Division
P.O. Box 1406
Bloomington, IL 61702
(309) 829-1071
(Pantagraph)

Parker & Son Publications, Inc.
P.O. Box 9040
Carlsbad, CA 92018
(619) 931-5979; (800) 452-9073
(800) 752-9796; Fax (619) 931-7877
(Parker)

Pearson Publications Co.
5910 N. Central Expressway, Suite 1000
Dallas, TX 75206
(214) 891-6332
(Pearson)

Pennsylvania Bar Institute
P.O. Box 1027
Harrisburg, PA 17108-1027
(717) 233-5774
(800) 932-4637 (PA); Fax (717) 233-6082
(Penn. Bar)

Pension Publications of Denver, Inc.
P.O. Box 24127
Denver, CO 80224
(303) 759-1004; Fax (303) 759-5744
(PPD)

Philanthropy Monthly
Box 989
New Milford, CT 06776
(203) 354-7132
(Philanthropy Monthly)

Phillips Publishing, Inc.
7811 Montrose Rd.
Potomac, MD 20854
(301) 340-2100

(800) 722-9120; Fax (301) 424-4297
(Phillips)

Pic's National Law Network
112 Long Road
King of Prussia, PA 19406
(215) 337-3880; Fax (215) 337-4614
(Pic's)

Pike & Fischer, Inc.
4600 East-West Hwy., Suite 200
Bethesda, MD 20814
(301) 654-6262; Fax (301) 654-6297
(P&F)

Practising Law Institute
810 Seventh Avenue
New York, NY 10019
(212) 765-5700
(800) 321-0093); Fax (212) 265-4742
(PLI)

Practitioners Publishing Co.
P.O. Box 966
Ft. Worth, TX 76101-0966
(817) 332-3709
(800) 323-8724; Fax (817) 336-2433
(Practitioners Publishing)

Pratt, A.S. & Sons, Inc.
1117 N. 19 Street
Arlington, VA 22209
(703) 528-0145; Fax (703) 528-1736
(Pratt)

Prentice Hall Law & Business, Inc.
270 Sylvan Avenue
Englewood Cliffs, NJ 07632
(201) 894-8484
(800) 223-0231; Fax (201) 894-8666
(P-H Law & Bus.)

Prentice Hall Legal & Financial Services
1873 Western Ave.
Albany, NY 12203
(800) FILE-UCC; Fax (800) 333-0680
(Prentice Hall Legal & Financial Services)

Privatization Council Inc.
1101 Connecticut Ave., N.W., Suite 700
Washington, DC 20036
(202) 857-1142; Fax (202) 223-4579
(Privatization Council)

Probus Publishing
1925 N. Clybourn St.
Chicago, IL 60614
(312) 868-1100
(800) 776-2871; Fax (312) 868-6250
(Probus)

Professional Development Foundation, Inc.
P.O. Box 1429
Lafayette, CA 94549-9801
(415) 284-9296
(Prof. Dev. Fdtn.)

Professional Publications and Education, Inc.
2303 E. Dartmouth
Englewood, CO 80110
(303) 758-2221; Fax (303) 757-0958
(Prof. Pubs.)

Public Law Education Institute
1601 Connecticut Ave., N.W., Suite 450
Washington, DC 20036
(202) 232-1400
(PLEI)

Public Reporting Services, Inc.
496 Hudson St.
New York, NY 10014
(212) 989-8303
(Public Reporting Services)

Public Securities Association
40 Broad Street
New York, NY 10004-2373
(212) 440-9430; Fax (212) 742-1549
(PSA)

R.C. Simpson Co.
Two Fairview Plaza, Suite 604
5950 Fairview Road
Charlotte, NC 28210
(704) 553-0716; Fax (704) 553-0734
(Simpson)

R.W. Byram & Co.
706 Guadalupe
Austin, TX 78701
(512) 478-2551
(800) 252-3201 (TX); Fax (512) 478-3318
(Byram)

Record Controls, Inc.
1215 National Avenue
Addison, IL 60101
(708) 543-8040; Fax (708) 543-8055
(Record Controls)

Research Institute of America, Inc.
90 Fifth Ave.
New York, NY 10011
(800) 431-2057
(800) 431-9025 (212) 645-4800
(RIA)

Rocky Mountain Mineral Law Foundation
7039 E. 18th Ave., 3rd Floor
Denver, CO 80220
(303) 321-8100; Fax (303) 321-7657
(Rocky Mt.)

Ronin Publishing, Inc.
P.O. Box 1035
Berkeley, CA 94701
(510) 540-6278
(Ronin)

Rothman, Fred B. & Co.
See Fred B. Rothman & Co.

Roytech Publications, Inc.
7910 Woodmont Ave., Suite 902
Bethesda, MD 20814
(301) 654-4281; Fax (301) 907-7773
(Roytech)

RPC Publications
3200 Red River St., Suite 302
Austin, TX 78705
(512) 472-7765
(800) 580-4567 (TX); Fax (512) 472-2232
(RPC)

Rules Service Company
7658 Standish Place
Rockville, MD 20855
(301) 424-9402; Fax (301) 762-7853
(Rules)

Rutter Group
15760 Ventura Blvd., Suite 630
Encino, CA 91436
(818) 990-3260; (800) 747-3161 (CA)
(800) 383-8145; Fax (818) 986-2180
(Rutter)

S&FA Reporting Services, Inc.
1101 King St., Suite 600
Alexandria, VA 22314
(703) 739-0200; Fax (703) 683-2239
(S&FA)

Shafer Books
139 Grand Street
Croton-on-Hudson, NY 10520
(914) 271-6919; Fax (914) 271-5193
(Shafer)

Shepard's/McGraw-Hill
P.O. Box 35300
Colorado Springs, CO 80935
(719) 481-7639
(800) 525-2474; Fax (800) 525-0053
(Shepard's)

Sheshunoff Information Services Inc.
Capitol Station, P.O. Box 13203
Austin, TX 78711-9969
(512) 472-2244
(800) 456-2340; Fax (512) 476-1251
(Sheshunoff)

Simpson, R.C. Co.
See R.C. Simpson Co.

Smith, M.L., Publishers & Printers
See M.L. Smith Publishers & Printers

South Carolina Bar Continuing Legal Education Division
950 Taylor St.
Columbia, SC 29205
(803) 771-0333

(800) 768-7787; Fax (803) 799-4118
(S. Carolina Bar)

Spencer, Charles D. & Associates
See Charles D. Spencer & Associates

Spidell Publishing Co.
1100 North Gilbert Street
Anaheim, CA 92801
(714) 776-7850; Fax (714) 776-9906
(Spidell)

Staffort Hart Publishing Co.
5860 South Curtice
Littleton, CO 80120
(303) 798-7084; Fax (303) 798-8974
(Staffort)

State Bar Association of North Dakota
P.O. Box 2136
Bismarck, ND 58502
(701) 255-1404
(800) 472-2685 (ND); Fax (701) 224-1621
(State Bar of N. Dak.)

State Bar of Arizona
363 North First Avenue
Phoenix, AZ 85003
(602) 252-4804; Fax (602) 271-4930
(State Bar of Ariz.)

State Bar of California
555 Franklin Street
San Francisco, CA 94102
(415) 561-8200; Fax (415) 561-8228
(State Bar of Calif.)

State Bar of Michigan
306 Townsend Street
Lansing, MI 48933
(517) 372-9030
(800) 968-0738; Fax (517) 482-6248
(State Bar of Mich.)

State Bar of Montana
46 North Last Chance Gulch
Helena, MT 59601
(406) 442-7660; Fax (406) 442-7763
(State Bar of Mont.)

State Bar of South Dakota
222 East Capitol
Pierre, SD 57501
(605) 224-7554; Fax (605) 224-0282
(S.D. Bar)

State Bar of Texas
P.O. Box 12487 Capitol Station
Austin, TX 78711
(512) 463-1411; Fax (512) 463-1475
(State Bar of Texas)

State Bar of Wisconsin ATS-CLE
402 West Wilson Street
Madison, WI 53703
(608) 257-3838; (800) 362-8096 (WI)
(800) 728-7788; Fax (608) 257-5502
(State Bar of Wisc.)

Sten-O-Press
P.O. Box 36
San Pablo, CA 94806
(415) 233-1880; Fax (415) 233-1249
(Sten-O-Press)

Stephens, Mark A., Ltd.
See Mark A. Stephens, Ltd.

Tax Form Library
518 West Main Street
Louisville, KY 40202
(502) 589-7466; Fax (502) 589-7095
(Tax Form)

Tax Seminars Institute
5151 N. Harlem, Suite 311
Chicago, IL 60656
(312) 774-8388; Fax (312) 774-8309
(TSI)

Taxwise Giving
13 Arcadia Road
Old Greenwich, CT 06870
(203) 637-4553
(800) 243-9122; Fax (203) 637-4572
(Taxwise)

Thomas Law Book Company, Inc.
1717 Olive Street

St. Louis, MO 63103
(314) 621-2236;(800) 344-2348
(Thomas)

Thompson Publishing Group
1725 K Street, N.W.
Washington, D.C. 20006
(202) 872-4000
(800) 424-2959; Fax (202) 296-1091
(Thompson)

Tower Publishing Company
34 Diamond Street
Portland, ME 04112
(207) 774-9813
(800) 431-2665 (ME);Fax (207) 775-1740
(Tower)

TPLR, Inc.
P.O. Box 1162, Back Bay Annex
Boston, MA 02117
(617) 424-0094; Fax (617) 437-3672
(TPLR)

Transnational Juris Publications, Inc.
P.O. Box 7282
Ardsley-on-Hudson, NY 10503
(914) 693-0089; Fax (914) 693-8776
(Transnational Juris Publications)

U.S. Comptroller of the Currency
Administrator of National Banks
Washington, DC 20219
(202) 874-4700
(U.S. Compt.)

U.S. Government Printing Office
Washington, DC 20402
(202) 783-3238; Fax (202) 275-2529
(USGPO)

U.S. League of Savings Institutions
111 East Wacker Drive
Chicago, IL 60601
(312) 644-3100; Fax (312) 938-2541
(USLSI)

Uniform Boiler and Pressure Vessel Laws
Society, Inc.
308 N. Evergreen Rd. Suite 240
Louisville, KY 40243
(502) 244-6029; Fax (502) 244-6030
(Uniform Boiler)

United Communications Group
11300 Rockville Pike, Suite 1100
Rockville, MD 20852
(301) 816-8950; (800) 487-4824
(United Communications Group)

United States Trademark Assn.
6 East 45 Street
New York, NY 10017
(212) 986-5880; Fax (212) 687-8267
(USTA)

United States Trust Company of New York
114 West 47 St.
New York, NY 10036
(212) 852-3537; Fax (212) 852-3525
(U.S. Trust)

University of Missouri at Kansas City
School of Law CLE
5100 Rockhill Road
Kansas City, MO 64110-2499
(816) 235-1648; Fax (816) 444-6560
(UMKC/CLE)

University of Missouri-Columbia
School of Law CLE
Law Building, Rm. 205
Columbia, MO 65211
(314) 882-7251; Fax (314) 882-9676
(UMC CLE)

University of Wisconsin Law School
Continuing Education and Outreach
905 University Avenue
Madison, WI 53715
(608) 263-2906; Fax (608) 263-3472
(CLE-Wisc.)

University Publications of America
4520 East-West Hwy., Suite 800
Bethesda, MD 20814
(301) 654-1550
(800) 692-6300;Fax (301) 657-3203

(UPA)

University Publishing Group
107 E. Church St.
Frederick, MD 21701
(301) 694-8531;(800) 654-8188
(Univ. Publ.)

Unz & Co.
190 Baldwin Ave.
Jersey City, NJ 07306
(201) 795-5400
(800) 631-3098; Fax (201) 795-0695
(Unz & Co.)

Utah State Bar
645 South 200 East
Salt Lake City, UT 84111
(801) 531-9077; Fax (801) 531-0660
(Utah Bar)

Warren, Gorham & Lamont, Inc.
210 South Street
Boston, MA 02111
(800) 950-1202
(617) 423-2020; Fax (617) 423-2026
(WG&L)

Washington Service Bureau, Inc.
655 15 Street, N.W.
Washington, DC 20005
(202) 508-0600
(800) 221-3184; Fax (202) 508-0694
(WSB)

Washington State Bar Assn. CLE
2001 6th Ave.
Seattle, WA 98121
(206) 448-0433; Fax (206) 448-0309
(Wash. Bar)

West Publishing Co.
3773 Hwy. 149
Eagan, MN 55123
(612) 228-2500
(800) 328-9352; Fax (612) 687-1302
(West)

Wiley Law Publications
P.O. Box 1777
Colorado Springs, CO 80901
(908) 469-4400;(800) 225-5945 x 2497;
Fax (908)302-2300
(Wiley Law)

Wiley, John & Sons, Inc.
See John Wiley & Sons, Inc.

William S. Hein & Co., Inc.
1285 Main Street
Buffalo, NY 14209-1987
(716) 882-2600 (800) 828-7571; Fax (716) 883-8100
(Hein)

KEY TO PUBLISHER'S ABBREVIATIONS

ABA	American Bar Association
ABICLE	Alabama Bar Institute for Continuing Legal Education
Access Reports	Access Reports, Inc.
ACLU	American Civil Liberties Union
Adams-Hall	Adams-Hall Publishing
AHC	American Horse Council
AIA	American Institute of Architects
AICPA	American Institute of Certified Public Accountants
Alex. Hamilton Inst.	Alexander Hamilton Institute
ALI-ABA	ALI-ABA Committee on Continuing Professional Education
ALTA	American Land Title Association
Altman Weil Pensa	Altman Weil Pensa
Am. Bankers	American Bankers Association
Am. Lawyer	American Lawyer Mgmt. Service
American Dental	American Dental Assn.
American Immigration Lawyers Assn.	American Immigration Lawyers Assn.
Anderson	Anderson Publishing Co.
API	American Prepaid Legal Services Institute
Arkansas Bar	Arkansas Bar Association
Arlen	Arlen Communications Group, Inc.
ASCS	American Society of Corporate Secretaries, Inc.
ASE	American Stock Exchange, Inc.
Aspen	Aspen Publishers Inc.
ATLA	Assn. of Trial Lawyers of America
Atlantic Info.	Atlantic Information Services, Inc.
Atlantic	Atlantic Law Book Company
ATP	Assn. of Transportation Practitioners
Bancroft	Bancroft-Whitney Co.
Banks	Banks-Baldwin Law Publishing Co.
Bar Assn. of D.C.	Bar Association of the District of Columbia - Young Lawyers Section
Barclays	Barclays Law Publishers
Baylor Univ. Press	Baylor University Press
Bender	Matthew Bender & Co., Inc.
Big Foot	Big Foot Press
Bisel	George T. Bisel Company
Blais	Blais
BLR	Business & Legal Reports
BNA	Bureau of National Affairs, Inc.
BNA Books	BNA Books
Book Pub.	Book Publishing Company
Bowne	Bowne & Co., Inc.
Bus. Intern.	Business International Corp.
Bus. Laws	Business Laws, Inc.
Butterworth-Fla.	Butterworth Legal Publishers
Butterworth-NH	Butterworth Legal Publishers
Butterworth-St. Paul	Butterworth Legal Publishers
Butterworth-Texas	Butterworth Legal Publishers

Byram	R.W. Byram & Co.
Calif. CEB	Continuing Education of the Bar, California
Calif. Jnl. Press	California Journal Press
Carroll	Carroll Publishing Co.
CCH	Commerce Clearing House, Inc.
Center for Immig. Rights	Center for Immigrants Rights, Inc.
Central	Central Publishing Co.
CFLR	California Family Law Report, Inc.
CGL	CGL Reporter, Inc.
Chase Manhattan	Chase Manhattan Bank N.A.
Chicago Bd.	Chicago Board of Trade
Cincinnati	Cincinnati Stock Exchange
Claitor's	Claitor's Publishing Division
Clark Boardman Callaghan	Clark Boardman Callaghan
CLE-Colorado	Continuing Legal Education in Colorado, Inc.
CLE-Wisc.	University of Wisconsin Law School Continuing Education and Outreach
CLP	Colorado Legal Publishing Company
CME	Chicago Mercantile Exchange
Cohasset	Cohasset Associates, Inc.
COMEX	Commodity Exchange, Inc.
Commonwealth	Commonwealth Publishing Co., Inc.
Conn. Bar	Connecticut Bar Association Continuing Legal Education
Conn. Law Tribune	Connecticut Law Tribune Co.
Corbel	Corbel & Co.
Corp. Tax	Corporate Tax Publishers, Inc.
Corporate Reports	Corporate Reports, Inc.
Council of Mich. Fdtns.	Council of Michigan Foundations
Court Info.	Court Information Services Co.
CRI	Communication Research Inc.
CRS	CRS Inc.
D.C. BAR	District of Columbia Bar, The
Daniel	Daniel Publishing Co.
Dearborn	Dearborn Financial Publishing Inc.
EBP	Entertainment Business Publishing Co.
EFRC	Education Funding Research Council
ELI	Environmental Law Institute
EMLF	Eastern Mineral Law Foundation
Enterprise	Enterprise Publishing Co.
Environment Books	Environment Books Inc.
Equity	Equity Publishing Corp.
Exec. Press	Executive Press, Inc.
Facts	Facts & Comparisons
Farnam	Farnam Equipment Co.
FASB	Financial Accounting Standards Board
Fast Eddie	Fast Eddie Publishing Co.
FBA	Federal Bar Association
FDIC	FDIC Corp. Communications Office
Fed-Track	Fed-Track Publications
Fed.	Board of Governors of the Federal Reserve System
Fed.-NY	Federal Reserve Bank of New York
Fed. Publ.	Federal Publications Inc.
Finan. Pub.	Financial Publishing Co.
Florida Bar	Florida Bar, The

FNMA	Federal National Mortgage Assn.
Foreign Tax	Foreign Tax Law Publishers, Inc.
Francis Marion	Francis Marion, Inc.
Freddie Mac	Federal Home Loan Mortgage Corp.
Gann	Gann Law Books
Georgetown	Georgetown University Law Center, CLE Division
GIS	Government Information Services
Glanville Publishers	Glanville Publishers, Inc.
Gould	Gould Publications
Govt. Inst.	Government Institutes, Inc.
Govt. Res.	Government Research Service
Greenwood	Greenwood Press
Griffin	Griffin Communications, Inc.
Gulf	Gulf Publishing Co., Book Division
Harrison	Harrison Company
Hawkins	Hawkins Publishing Co., Inc.
HBJ Miller	HBJ Miller Accounting Publications, Inc.
Hein	William S. Hein & Co., Inc.
HICLE	Hawaii Institute for Continuing Legal Education
HIMA	Health Industry Manufacturers Assn.
Holding	Laura A. Holding
IAAO	International Association of Assessing Officers
IBL Seminars	IBL Seminars
ICBO	International Conference of Building Officials
ICI	Investment Company Institute
ICLE-Michigan	Institute of Continuing Legal Education
Idaho Law	Idaho Law Foundation
IDDS	Institute for Defense & Disarmament Studies
IFA	International Franchise Association
Illinois ICLE	Illinois Institute for Continuing Legal Education
Indiana CLE	Indiana Continuing Legal Education Forum
Inst. of Prop. Tax.	Institute of Property Taxation
Institute-Ga.	Carl Vinson Institute of Government
Intl. Law Inst.	International Law Institute
Intl. Risk Mgmt. Inst.	International Risk Management Institute, Inc.
Invictus	Invictus Publishing Corporation
IOCC	Interstate Oil & Gas Compact Commission
Iowa Bar	Iowa State Bar Association
IRC	Information Requirements Clearinghouse
IRRC	Investor Responsibility Research Center
James	James Publishing, Inc.
Jefren	Jefren Publishing Co., Inc.
JKP	JKP Publications
John Liner Org.	John Liner Organization
Jt. Comm. Va.	Joint Committee on Continuing Legal Education
Jury Verdict	Jury Verdict Research, Inc.
Kansas Bar	Kansas Bar Association
Keller	J.J. Keller & Associates
Kluwer	Kluwer Law & Taxation
Knowles	Knowles Law Book Publishers
LADJ	Los Angeles Daily Journal
Lambda	Lambda Legal Defense and Education Fund, Inc.
Lamb's Flight	Lamb's Flight, Ltd.
Lame	Lawrence Lame

Land Dev.	Land Development Institute, Ltd.
Law Bulletin	Law Bulletin Publishing Company
Law Journal	Law Journal Seminars-Press, Inc.
Law-Arts	Law-Arts Publishers, Inc.
Lawpress	Lawpress
Lawyers Coop.	Lawyers Co-operative Publishing Co.
Lawyers Weekly	Lawyers Weekly Publications
Legal Res. Systems	Legal Research Systems, Inc.
Legal-Med.	Legal-Medical Studies Inc.
Lexikon	Lexikon Services Publications
Little, Brown	Little, Brown & Co. Law Div.
Longshore	Longshore Newsletter
LRP	LRP Publications
M&M Resources	M&M Resources Corp.
Maine Bar	Maine State Bar Association
Manak	James P. Manak
Mariposa	Mariposa Publishing, Inc.
Mass. CLE	Massachusetts Continuing Legal Education-New England Law Institute, Inc.
Matrimonial CaseLaw	Matrimonial CaseLaw Corp.
MBAA	Mortgage Bankers Association of America
Medilex	Medilex Co.
Meiklejohn Civil Liberties Institute	Meiklejohn Civil Liberties Institute
Merritt	Merritt Company, The
Metropolitan News	Metropolitan News Co.
Mich. Legal	Michigan Legal Services
Michie	Michie Company, The
MICPEL	Maryland Institute for Continuing Professional Education of Lawyers, Inc.
MidAmerica	MidAmerica Commodity Exchange
MII	MII Publications Inc.
MILE	Minnesota Institute of Legal Education
Minn. CLE	Minnesota CLE
Minneap.	Minneapolis Grain Exchange
MoBar	Missouri Bar CLE
Mortgage	Mortgage and Real Estate Investment Guide
MTLA	Michigan Trial Lawyers Assn.
Nat. Atty.	National Attorneys' Publications
Nat. Obscenity Law Center	National Obscenity Law Center
Natl. Asbestos	National Asbestos Council
Natl. Center for Lesbian Rights	National Center for Lesbian Rights
Natl. Fire Protection Assn.	Natl. Fire Protection Assn.
Natl. Health	National Health Publishing
Natl. Lawyers Guild AIDS Network	Natl. Lawyers Guild AIDS Network
Natl. Legal Publishing	National Legal Publishing Co., Inc.
Natl. Notary	National Notary Assn.
Natl. Underwriter	National Underwriter Co.
NCCCD	National Center for Computer Crime Data
NCFA	National Commercial Finance Association
NCSI	National Council of Savings Institutions
Nebraska CLE	Nebraska Continuing Legal Education, Inc.
NELI	National Employment Law Institute
NELP	New England Legal Publishers
New Jersey ICLE	New Jersey Institute for Continuing Legal Education

NFCB	National Federation of Community Broadcasters
NH Bar	New Hampshire Bar Assn. CLE
NILS	NILS Publishing Company
No. Carolina Bar	North Carolina Bar Foundation
NPTC	National Private Truck Council
NTHP	National Trust for Historic Preservation
NTIS	National Technical Information Service (U.S. Dept. of Commerce)
NTTS	National Tax Training School
NYC	New York City Dept. of City Planning
NYPER	NYPER Publications
NYS OCA	New York State Office of Court Administration
NYSBA	New York State Bar Association
NYSE	New York Stock Exchange, Inc.
NYSTLA	New York State Trial Lawyers Association
Oasis	Oasis Press
OCDLA	Oregon Criminal Defense Lawyers Assn.
Oceana	Oceana Publications, Inc.
Office of Thrift Supervision	Office of Thrift Supervision, Communications Services Division
Ohio CLE	Ohio CLE Institute
Ohio State Bar	Ohio State Bar Foundation
Okla. Bar CLE	Oklahoma Bar Assn. CLE
On Point	On Point Press
Options Clearing Corp.	Options Clearing Corp.
Oregon Bar	Oregon State Bar
P&F	Pike & Fischer, Inc.
P-H Law & Bus.	Prentice Hall Law & Business, Inc.
Pacific Law Inst.	Pacific Law Institute
Panel	Panel Publishers
Pantagraph	Pantagraph Printing/Legal Division
Parker	Parker & Son Publications, Inc.
Pearson	Pearson Publications Co.
Penn. Bar	Pennsylvania Bar Institute
Philanthropy Monthly	Philanthropy Monthly
Phillips	Phillips Publishing, Inc.
Pic's	Pic's National Law Network
PLEI	Public Law Education Institute
PLI	Practising Law Institute
PPD	Pension Publications of Denver, Inc.
Practitioners Publishing	Practitioners Publishing Co.
Pratt	Pratt, A.S. & Sons, Inc.
Prentice Hall Legal & Financial Services	Prentice Hall Legal & Financial Services
Privatization Council	Privatization Council Inc.
Probus	Probus Publishing
Prof. Dev. Fdtn.	Professional Development Foundation, Inc.
Prof. Pubs.	Professional Publications and Education, Inc.
PSA	Public Securities Association
Public Reporting Services	Public Reporting Services, Inc.
Record Controls	Record Controls, Inc.
RIA	Research Institute of America, Inc.
Rocky Mt.	Rocky Mountain Mineral Law Foundation
Ronin	Ronin Publishing, Inc.
Rothman	Fred B. Rothman & Co.

Roytech	Roytech Publications, Inc.
RPC	RPC Publications
Rules	Rules Service Company
Rutter	Rutter Group
S&FA	S&FA Reporting Services, Inc.
S. Carolina Bar	South Carolina Bar Continuing Legal Education Division
S.D. Bar	State Bar of South Dakota
Shafer	Shafer Books
Shepard's	Shepard's/McGraw-Hill
Sheshunoff	Sheshunoff Information Services Inc.
Simpson	R.C. Simpson Co.
Smith	M.L. Smith Publishers & Printers
Spencer	Charles D. Spencer & Associates
Spidell	Spidell Publishing Co.
Staffort	Staffort Hart Publishing Co.
State Bar of Ariz.	State Bar of Arizona
State Bar of Calif.	State Bar of California
State Bar of Mich.	State Bar of Michigan
State Bar of Mont.	State Bar of Montana
State Bar of N. Dak.	State Bar Association of North Dakota
State Bar of Texas	State Bar of Texas
State Bar of Wisc.	State Bar of Wisconsin ATS-CLE
Sten-O-Press	Sten-O-Press
Stephens	Mark A. Stephens, Ltd.
Tax Form	Tax Form Library
Taxwise	Taxwise Giving
Thomas	Thomas Law Book Company, Inc.
Thompson	Thompson Publishing Group
Tower	Tower Publishing Company
TPLR	TPLR, Inc.
Transnational Juris Publications	Transnational Juris Publications, Inc.
TSI	Tax Seminars Institute
U.S. Compt.	U.S. Comptroller of the Currency
U.S. TRUST	United States Trust Company of New York
UMC CLE	University of Missouri-Columbia School of Law CLE
UMKC/CLE	University of Missouri at Kansas City School of Law CLE
Uniform Boiler	Uniform Boiler and Pressure Vessel Laws Society, Inc.
United Communications Group	United Communications Group
Univ. Publ.	University Publishing Group
Unz & Co.	Unz & Co.
UPA	University Publications of America
USGPO	U.S. Government Printing Office
USLSI	U.S. League of Savings Institutions
USTA	United States Trademark Assn.
Utah Bar	Utah State Bar
Wash. Bar	Washington State Bar Assn. CLE
West	West Publishing Co.
WG&L	Warren, Gorham & Lamont, Inc.
Wiley Law	Wiley Law Publications
Wiley	John Wiley & Sons, Inc.
WSB	Washington Service Bureau, Inc.

KEY TO TITLE LIST

1. TITLE (and series statement where applicable).

2. AUTHOR or EDITOR (this item is left blank when the author's name is not available, or when the work is produced by a large editorial staff).

3. PUBLISHER.

4. YEAR OF ORIGINAL PUBLICATION and EDITION.

5. NUMBER OF VOLUMES.

6. PRICE FOR THE VOLUMES, and whether the price includes any future supplementation.

7. FREQUENCY OF SUPPLEMENTATION (the term "periodic supp." is used to denote supplementation which is provided at irregular intervals, without any set schedule).

8. ANNUAL COST OF SUPPLEMENTATION (For works with an annual renewal fee, the renewal fee is listed here if it differs from the price in Item 6. If the renewal fee is the same as the price in Item 6, Item 8 is omitted to avoid repetition. For supplemented works, the annual price is provided for the most recent year or two in which there was supplementation, except when this information was not made available by the publisher.)

9. Library of Congress card number/OCLC number/LC classification.

TITLE LIST

1. **AALL ANNUAL MEETINGS: AN ANNOTATED INDEX OF THE RECORDINGS**
2. Houdek, Frank G. and Susan D. Goldner
3. Rothman
4. 1989
5. 1 vol.
6. $37.50
7. annual supp.
8. 1989 - $15; 1990 - $20
9. 89-10120//r902/19672597/Z675.L2H68

1. **ABA/BNA LAWYER'S MANUAL ON PROFESSIONAL CONDUCT**
2. Robbins, Robert A.
3. BNA
4. 1983
5. 2 vols.
6. $570/yr.
7. biweekly supp.
8. renewal - $540/yr.
9. 11801340/KF305.A1A22

1. **ABA LAWYERING SKILLS: COURSE MATERIALS, CLIENT INSTRUCTIONS**
2. Standing Comm. on Continuing Education of the Bar
3. ABA
4. 1982
5. 1 vol.
6. $15
7. no supp. planned

1. **ABA LAWYERING SKILLS: COURSE MATERIALS, PARTICIPANTS' COPY (group A & group B)**
2. Standing Comm. on Continuing Education of the Bar
3. ABA
4. 1982
5. 2 vols.
6. $15/vol.
7. no supp. planned

1. **ABA LAWYERING SKILLS: INSTRUCTOR'S MANUAL**
2. Standing Comm. on Continuing Education of the Bar
3. ABA
4. 1982
5. 1 vol.
6. $70
7. no supp. planned

1. **ABA STANDARDS FOR CRIMINAL JUSTICE, 2nd ed.**
2. Criminal Justice Section
3. ABA
4. 1980
5. 4 vols.
6. $190
7. periodic supp.
8. 1986 - $31
9. 79-91936/7414341/KF9223.A6A5

1. **ABA'S COMPLIANCE SOURCEBOOK**
2. -
3. Am. Bankers
4. 1987
5. 1 vol.
6. $129 - members; $194 - nonmembers
7. no supp. yet

1. **THE ABCs OF LOCAL GOVERNMENT LAW**
2. Wittman, Walter T. et al.
3. New Jersey ICLE
4. 1990
5. 1 vol.
6. $35
7. no supp. planned
9. 21920073/KFN2230.Z9A22

1. **ABC'S OF PRO BONO DIVORCE**
2. -
3. NH Bar
4. 1989
5. 1 vol.
6. $30
7. no supp. planned

1. **ABDOMINAL INJURIES (Courtroom Medicine Series vol. 10 & 10A)**
2. Kalisch, Jules et al.
3. Bender
4. 1973
5. 2 vols.
6. $255 incl. 3 mos. supp.
7. annual supp.
8. 1990 - $169.50; 1991 - $250
9. 73-90330/810604/RA1011.C68

1. **ABOVEGROUND STORAGE TANK GUIDE**
2. -
3. Thompson
4. 1991
5. 1 vol.
6. $397/yr.
7. monthly supp.
8. renewal - $387/yr.
9. 24049878/TP692.5.A26

1. **ACCELERATED DISPUTE RESOLUTIONS**
2. -
3. Indiana CLE
4. 1991
5. 1 vol.
6. $40
7. no supp. planned

1. **ACCESS REPORTS/FREEDOM OF INFORMATION NEWSLETTER AND REFERENCE FILE**
2. Hammitt, Harry A., ed.
3. Access Reports
4. NA
5. 2 vols.
6. $550/yr. incl. newsletter
7. biweekly newsletter & periodic supp.

1. **ACCOUNTANCY LAW REPORTS**
2. -
3. CCH
4. 1938
5. 2 vols.
6. $460/yr.; $420/yr. for 2 yrs.
7. monthly supp.
9. 59-933/1564305/HF5601.C71

1. **THE ACCOUNTANT'S BUSINESS MANUAL**
2. Behrenfeld, William H. & Andrew R. Biebl
3. AICPA
4. 1987
5. 1 vol.
6. $138 - members; $172.50 - nonmembers
7. semiannual supp.
8. 1988 - $70; 1990 - $42.50
9. 87-992/15223414/HF5616.U5B38

1. **ACCOUNTANTS SEC PRACTICE MANUAL**
2. Poloway, Morton & Dane Charles
3. CCH
4. 1976
5. 2 vols.
6. $470/yr.; $425/yr. for 2 yrs.
7. monthly supp.
9. 76-372708/2913059/KF1446.P64

1. **ACCOUNTANT'S WORKBOOK SERIES**
2. Loebbecke J. & E. Luria
3. Bender
4. 1986
5. 20 vols.
6. $410/1 yr. service; $725/2 yr. service
7. periodic supp.
8. renewal-$335/yr.
9. 85-073517/14200445/HF5635.A315x

1. **ACCOUNTING ARTICLES**
2. -
3. CCH
4. 1965
5. 1 vol.
6. $495/yr.; $450/yr. for 2 yrs.
7. monthly supp.
9. 8360734

1. **ACCOUNTING FOR BANKS**
2. Koltveit, James M.
3. Bender
4. 1982
5. 1 vol.
6. $105 incl. 3 mos. supp.
7. periodic supp.
8. 1990 - $84; 1991 - $92
9. 82-61894/9622139/HG1707.K6

1. **ACCOUNTING FOR GOVERNMENT CONTRACTS - COST ACCOUNTING STANDARDS**
2. Anderson, Lane K.
3. Bender
4. 1981
5. 1 vol.
6. $115 incl. 3 mos. supp.
7. periodic supp.
8. 1990 - $96; 1991 - $105
9. 81-69113/8155946/KF849.A83

1. **ACCOUNTING FOR GOVERNMENT CONTRACTS - FEDERAL ACQUISITION REGULATION**
2. Anderson, Lane K.
3. Bender
4. 1985
5. 1 vol.
6. $105 incl. 3 mos. supp.
7. periodic supp.
8. 1990 - $75; 1991 - $110
9. 85-71931/12985106/KF849.A73

1. **ACCOUNTING FOR PUBLIC UTILITIES**
2. Hahne, Robert et al.
3. Bender
4. 1983
5. 1 vol.
6. $110 incl. 3 mos. supp.
7. annual supp.
8. 1990 - $75; 1991 - $85
9. 83-70030/9794477/HF5686.P93H34

1. **ACCOUNTING MALPRACTICE**
2. -
3. MILE
4. 1990
5. 1 vol.
6. $58
7. no supp. planned

1. **ACCOUNTING STANDARDS - ORIGINAL PRONOUNCEMENTS**
2. -
3. FASB
4. 1984
5. 5 vols.
6. $365/yr.
7. periodic supp.
8. renewal - $330/yr.
9. 83-81494

1. **ACCOUNTING SYSTEMS FOR LAW OFFICES**
2. Burke, William J.
3. Bender
4. 1978
5. 1 vol.
6. $105 incl. 3 mos. supp.
7. periodic supp.
8. 1990 - $67; 1991 - $130
9. 79-104226/5051497/KF320.A2B87

1. **ACQUISITIONS AND DISPOSITIONS OF OIL AND GAS PROPERTIES**
2. -
3. EMLF
4. 1990
5. 1 vol.
6. $100
7. no supp. planned

1. **ACQUISITIONS AND MERGERS: NEGOTIATED AND CONTESTED TRANSACTIONS (Securities Law Series Vol. II)**
2. Lorne, Simon M.
3. Clark Boardman Callaghan
4. 1985
5. 2 vols.
6. $215 incl. 3 mos. supp.
7. annual supp.
8. 1989 - $127; 1991 - $135
9. 85-4103/11755878/KF1477.L67

1. **ACQUISITIONS UNDER THE HART-SCOTT-RODINO ANTITRUST IMPROVEMENTS ACT**
2. Axinn, Stephen M. et al.
3. Law Journal
4. rev. 1988
5. 1 vol.
6. $115
7. periodic supp.
8. 1988 - $65
9. 88-26864/18962731/KF1655.A74

1. **ADA COMPLIANCE GUIDE**
2. Montuori, Dan
3. Thompson
4. 1990
5. 1 vol.
6. $239/yr.
7. monthly supp.
8. renewal - $208/yr.
9. 22481768/KF480.A19

1. **ADMINISTERING OREGON ESTATES**
2. Perry, James & Stanton, Allison, eds.
3. Oregon Bar
4. 1991
5. 1 vol.
6. $105
7. periodic supp.
8. no supp. yet
9. 91-60289/24805216/KFO2547.A93

1. **ADMINISTRATIVE HEARINGS**
2. Lewis-Frazee, Hon. Judith et al.
3. MICPEL
4. 1991
5. 1 vol.
6. $42
7. no supp. planned
9. 23948946/KFM1640.A23

1. **ADMINISTRATIVE INTERPRETATIONS OF THE UNIFORM CONSUMER CREDIT CODE**
2. Miller, Fred H
3. Butterworth-NH
4. 1989
5. 1 vol.
6. $110

7. annual supp.
8. 1990 - $30
9. 89-23880/20357483/KF1039.A62A36

1. **ADMINISTRATIVE LAW**
2. Mezines, Basil et al.
3. Bender
4. 1977
5. 6 vols.
6. $570 incl. 3 mos. supp.
7. annual supp.
8. 1990 - $506; 1991 - $550
9. 77-73137/2910568/KF5402.M4

1. **ADMINISTRATIVE LAW**
2. -
3. NH Bar
4. 1988
5. 1 vol.
6. $35
7. no supp. planned

1. **ADMINISTRATIVE LAW**
2. Administrative Law Section
3. Conn. Bar
4. 1989
5. 1 vol.
6. $20
7. no supp. planned

1. **ADMINISTRATIVE LAW, THIRD SERIES**
2. Willis, John W. & James A. Rauen
3. P&F
4. 1989
5. 3 looseleaf vols.
6. $845 incl. 1 yr. supp.
7. biweekly supp.
8. renewal - $845/yr.; $1570/2 yrs.

1. **ADMINISTRATIVE LAW MANUAL**
2. Baker, David H., ed.
3. Bar Assn. of D.C.
4. 2nd ed. - 1989
5. 2 vols.
6. $74.20
7. no supp. yet

1. **ADOPTION LAW**
2. -
3. Indiana CLE
4. 1990
5. 1 vol.
6. $45
7. no supp. planned

1. **ADOPTION LAW AND PRACTICE**
2. Hollinger, J. et al.
3. Bender
4. 1988
5. 1 vol.
6. $110 incl. 3 mos. supp.
7. annual supp.
8. 1990 - $50; 1991- $60
9. 88-72113/18902565/KF545.A93

1. **ADOPTION, PATERNITY AND OTHER FLORIDA FAMILY PRACTICE**
2. -
3. Florida Bar
4. 2nd ed. - 1990
5. 1 vol.
6. $65
7. as needed
8. no supp. yet
9. 80-85264/23255789/KFF94.F55

1. **ADR IN BUSINESS DISPUTES**
2. -
3. MILE
4. 1991
5. 1 vol.
6. $68
7. no supp. planned

1. **ADVANCED BANKRUPTCY INSTITUTE**
2. -
3. MICPEL
4. 2/91
5. 1 vol.
6. $42
7. no supp. yet

1. **ADVANCED BANKRUPTCY INSTITUTE**
2. -
3. Georgetown
4. 1991
5. 1 vol.
6. $101
7. no supp. planned

1. **ADVANCED CHAPTER 11 BANKRUPTCY PRACTICE**
2. Salerno, Thomas J.
3. Wiley Law
4. 1990
5. 2 vols.
6. $210
7. annual supp.
8. 1991 - $70; 1992 - price NA
9. 16688899/KF1527.S25

1. **ADVANCED ESTATE PLANNING**
2. -
3. MICPEL
4. 1991
5. 1 vol.
6. $42
7. no supp. yet
9. 22104918/KF750.Z9A25

1. **ADVANCED ESTATE PLANNING INSTITUTE**
2. -
3. Georgetown
4. 1991
5. 1 vol.
6. $101
7. no supp. planned

1. **ADVANCED PLANNING & ZONING**
2. -
3. Conn. Bar
4. 1991
5. 1 vol.
6. $53
7. no supp. planned

1. **ADVANCED PROBATE LAW**
2. -
3. Ohio CLE
4. 1989
5. 1 vol.
6. $35
7. no supp. planned

1. **ADVANCED REAL PROPERTY INSTITUTE**
2. -
3. MICPEL
4. 1991
5. 1 vol.
6. $250 (incl. tapes)
7. no supp. yet
9. 22104906/KFM1326.A24

1. **ADVANCED SALES REFERENCE SERVICE**
2. -
3. Natl. Underwriter
4. NA
5. 8 vols.
6. $385/yr.
7. monthly supp.
8. renewal - $199/yr.
9. 4170185/HG8051.A3X

1. **ADVANCED UNDERWRITING SERVICE (AUS)**
2. Sheldon, Bill & Georgia Mann
3. Dearborn
4. 1981
5. 8 vols.
6. $315
7. monthly supp. & newsletter
8. renewal - $204/yr.
9. 12396900/KF1160.A38

1. **ADVANCED WORKERS' COMPENSATION LAW**
2. -
3. Ohio CLE
4. 1989
5. 1 vol.
6. $35
7. no supp. planned

1. **ADVANCED WORKERS' COMPENSATION LAW**
2. -
3. Conn. Bar
4. 1990
5. 1 vol.
6. $53
7. no supp. planned

1. **ADVERTISING COMPLIANCE SERVICE**
2. Lichtenberger, John, ed.
3. Greenwood
4. 1981
5. 2 vols.
6. $445/yr. incl. all back issues
7. semimonthly supp. & 6 special reports

1. **ADVERTISING LIABILITY**
2. -
3. MILE
4. 1991
5. 1 vol.
6. $68
7. no supp. planned
9. 24207372/KF1614.Z9A38

1. **ADVISING CLIENTS ABOUT RETIREMENT PLANS**
2. -
3. Minn. CLE
4. 1991
5. 1 vol.
6. $55
7. no supp. planned

1. **ADVISING CLIENTS ABOUT WELFARE BENEFITS**
2. -
3. Minn. CLE
4. 1991
5. 1 vol.
6. $55
7. no supp. planned

1. **ADVISING ELDERLY CLIENTS AND THEIR FAMILIES**
2. -
3. Illinois ICLE
4. 1991
5. 1 vol.
6. $89.95
7. periodic supp.
8. no supp. yet
9. 23726109/KFI1291.A3A38

1. **ADVISING FARMERS**
2. -
3. Illinois ICLE
4. 1987
5. 2 vols.
6. $102.95
7. periodic supp.
8. no supp. yet
9. 9600950/KFI1317.5.A38

1. **ADVISING FINANCIAL INSTITUTIONS**
2. -
3. MICPEL
4. 1991
5. 1 vol.
6. $42
7. no supp. yet
9. 20515657/KFM1365.A98

1. **ADVISING ILLINOIS FINANCIAL INSTITUTIONS**
2. -
3. Illinois ICLE
4. rev. - 1987
5. 2 vols.
6. $142.95
7. periodic supp.
8. 1989 - $29.95
9. 7799502/KFI1365.A93

1. **ADVISING OREGON BUSINESS FORMS VOLUME**
2. Roy, Richard E. & Jere M. Webb, eds.
3. Oregon Bar
4. 1991
5. 1 vol.
6. $85
7. periodic supp.

1. **ADVISING OREGON BUSINESSES**
2. Roy, Richard E. & Jere M. Webb, eds.
3. Oregon Bar
4. 1989
5. 4 vols. projected
6. $320
7. periodic supp.
8. 2 vols. due in 1992
9. 88-61297/20719726/KFO2605.A75A3

1. **ADVISING SMALL BUSINESS**
2. -
3. Minn. CLE
4. 1991
5. 1 vol.
6. $50
7. no supp. planned
9. 24680496

1. **ADVISING SMALL BUSINESS CLIENTS, VOL. 1**
2. Stroud, Robert, ed.
3. Jt. Comm. Va.
4. 1987
5. 1 vol.
6. $57
7. periodic supp.
8. to be supp. in 1992
9. 88-146486/18716178/KFV2634.A93

1. **ADVISING SMALL BUSINESS CLIENTS, VOL. 2**
2. Stroud, Robert, ed.
3. Jt. Comm. Va.
4. 1990
5. 1 vol.
6. $57
7. periodic supp.
8. no supp. yet
9. 81-183608/8133734/KFV2634.A93

1. **ADVISING SMALL BUSINESSES**
2. Alberty, Steven
3. Clark Boardman Callaghan
4. 1989
5. 3 vols.
6. $305 incl. 6 mos. supp.
7. periodic supp.
8. 1990 - $45
9. 89-10039/19845466/KF1659.A94

1. **ADVISING THE EMPLOYER**
2. -
3. MILE
4. 1991
5. 1 vol.
6. $68
7. no supp. planned
9. 24511010

1. **ADVISING THE OLDER CLIENT**
2. Chard, Lynn P., ed.
3. ICLE - Michigan
4. 1991
5. 1 vol.
6. $95
7. periodic supp.
8. 1991 - price NA
9. 90-85065/23036659/KFM4291.A3A38

1. **ADVISING THE SMALL BUSINESS CLIENT**
2. -
3. Wash. Bar
4. 1989
5. 1 vol.
6. $45
7. no supp. planned

1. **ADVISING THE SMALL BUSINESS CLIENT**
2. -
3. Indiana CLE
4. 1990
5. 1 vol.
6. $55
7. no supp. planned

1. **ADVOCATING FOR CHILDREN AND FAMILIES IN CINA PROCEEDING**
2. Leviton, Susan P. & Larry M. Waranch
3. MICPEL
4. 1985
5. 1 vol.
6. $42
7. no supp. planned
9. 12192518/KFM1550.C4L48

1. **AFFIRMATIVE ACTION BRIEFING WORKBOOK**
2. -
3. NELI
4. 1991
5. 2 vols.
6. $150
7. no supp. planned

1. **AFFIRMATIVE ACTION COMPLIANCE MANUAL FOR FEDERAL CONTRACTORS**
2. Sala, Susan J.
3. BNA
4. 1975
5. 2 vols.
6. $270/yr.
7. monthly supp.
8. renewal - $256/yr.
9. 78-507/3382114

1. **AGE DISCRIMINATION**
2. Eglit, Howard
3. Shepard's
4. 1981
5. 4 vols.
6. $240
7. annual supp.
8. 1990 - $82; 1991 - $50
9. 81-16719/8139507/KF390.A4E34

1. **THE AGENDA OF REGULATIONS**
2. Brennan, Robert Francis, ed.
3. Central
4. 1988
5. 1 vol.
6. $45
7. supp. 5x/yr.

1. **AGRICULTURAL LAW**
2. Harl, Neil E.
3. Bender
4. 1980
5. 15 vols.
6. $865 incl. 3 mos. supp.
7. supp. as needed
8. 1990 - $648; 1991 - $750
9. 80-80911/6205325/KF1682.H37

1. **AGRICULTURAL LAW MANUAL**
2. Harl, Neil E.
3. Bender
4. 1985
5. 1 vol.
6. $115 incl. 3 mos. supp.
7. periodic supp.
8. 1990 - $85; 1991 - $100
9. 85-72402/12985622/KF1682.H38

1. **AGRICULTURAL LAW SYSTEM**
2. -
3. Arkansas Bar
4. 1984
5. 1 vol.

6. $75
7. no supp. yet

1. **AIA BUILDING CONSTRUCTION LEGAL CITATOR**
2. Spencer, Whalen & Graham
3. AIA
4. 1982
5. 2 vols.
6. $110
7. no supp. planned
8. 1982 - $66; 1984 - $21.75
9. 83-104473/8638749/KF901.A67A35

1. **AICPA AUDIT AND ACCOUNTING MANUAL**
2. AICPA
3. CCH
4. 1979
5. 1 vol.
6. $120/yr.; $90/yr. for 2 yrs.
7. periodic supp.
9. 79-111789/5708250/HF5667.A55

1. **AICPA TECHNICAL PRACTICE AIDS**
2. AICPA
3. CCH
4. 1975
5. 2 vols.
6. $120/yr.; $90/yr. for 2 yrs.
7. periodic supp.
9. 75-329864/1549249/HF5616.U5A585

1. **AIDS AND FLORIDA LAW**
2. Waters, Robert Craig
3. Butterworth-Fla.
4. 1989
5. 3 vols.
6. $180
7. periodic supp.
8. 1990 - $100.25; 1991 - $36.60
9. 19931770/KFF357.8.A35W38

1. **AIDS AND THE LAW**
2. Cook, Mona et al.
3. MICPEL
4. 1991
5. 1 vol.
6. $62
7. no supp. planned
9. 24236041/KF3803.A54A54

1. **AIDS, HERPES & INFECTIOUS DISEASES**
2. -
3. MILE
4. 1989
5. 1 vol.
6. $58
7. no supp. planned

1. **AIDS IN THE WORKPLACE: RESOURCE MATERIAL**
2. -
3. BNA
4. 3rd ed.-1989
5. 1 vol.
6. $75
7. no supp. yet
8. -
9. 89-9889/19737423/RC607.A26A347A2

1. **AIDS LAW & LITIGATION REPORTER**
2. Collins, Christopher J.
3. Univ. Publ.
4. 1986
5. 4 vols.
6. $1955/yr.
7. quarterly supp. & monthly newsletter
8. renewal - $475/yr.
9. 14877415/KF3803.A5.A65C65

1. **AIDS LEGAL GUIDE: A PROFESSIONAL RESOURCE ON AIDS-RELATED ISSUES & DISCRIMINATION**
2. Rubenfeld, Abby R., ed.
3. Lambda
4. 2nd ed.-1987
5. 1 vol.
6. price NA
7. to be revised in 1992
9. 11366271/KF3803.A2.A32

1. **AIDS PRACTICE MANUAL**
2. Albert, Paul et al., eds.
3. Natl. Lawyers Guild AIDS Network
4. 3rd ed. - 1991
5. 1 vol.
6. $95
7. periodic supp.
9. 24168259/KF3803.A54A957

1. **AIDS REFERENCE & RESEARCH COLLECTION**
2. Hummel, Robert F.
3. Univ. Publ.
4. 1986
5. 4 vols.
6. $550
7. annual supp.
8. $99/yr.

9. 14373916

1. **AIDS REFERENCE GUIDE**
2. Goodwin, Steve
3. Atlantic Info.
4. 1988
5. 2 vols.
6. $335/yr.
7. monthly supp.
9. 88-142335/17766209/RA644.A25A376

1. **AIR AND AVIATION TREATIES OF THE WORLD**
2. Fox, James
3. Oceana
4. 1984
5. 3 vols.
6. $300
7. periodic supp.
8. 1986 - $85
9. 84-10389/10779601/K4093.A35

1. **AIR POLLUTION: FEDERAL LAW AND ANALYSIS**
2. Currie, David P.
3. Clark Boardman Callaghan
4. 1981
5. 1 vol.
6. $110 incl. 6 mos. supp.
7. periodic supp.
8. 1989 - $45; 1990 - $47
9. 81-21566/8034725/KF3812.C87

1. **AIR POLLUTION CONTROL**
2. Joseph, Eileen Z.
3. BNA
4. 1980
5. 1 vol.
6. $630
7. periodic supp. & biweekly newsletter - Air & Water Pollution Control
8. renewal - $580/yr.
9. 80-147/5877912

1. **ALABAMA APPELLATE PRACTICE**
2. -
3. ABICLE
4. new ed. - 1987
5. 1 vol.
6. $50
7. no supp. yet

1. **ALABAMA BUSINESS CORPORATION LAW**
2. Wilson, James C., Jr. et al.
3. ABICLE
4. 1980
5. 1 vol.
6. $47.50
7. periodic supp.
8. 1985 - $7.50
9. 81-178209/8052149/KFA213.W54

1. **ALABAMA DIVORCE SYSTEMS MANUAL**
2. Graves, Patrick H. Jr.
3. ABICLE
4. rev. ed. - 1990
5. 1 vol.
6. $75
7. periodic supp.
8. no supp. yet
9. 84-149471/11260521/KFA100.G7

1. **ALASKA BANKRUPTCY RULES**
2. -
3. Book Pub.
4. 1984
5. 1 vol.
6. $20
7. supp. as needed
8. 1988 - $6.50

1. **ALASKA DIRECTORY OF PERMITS**
2. -
3. Book Pub.
4. 1985
5. 1 vol.
6. $85
7. supp. as needed
8. 1987 - $42
9. 12742493/KFA1525.D57

1. **ALASKA TIME LIMITS: STATUTES AND COURT RULES**
2. -
3. Book Pub.
4. 1986
5. 1 vol.
6. $75
7. supp. as needed
8. 1988 - $35
9. 14197598/KFA1290.L5.A337

1. **ALBERTA-NORTHWEST TERRITORY & YUKON TAX REPORTER**
2. -
3. CCH
4. 1973
5. 1 vol.

6. $275/yr.; $250/yr. for 2 yrs.
7. supp. as needed
9. 74-154350/815778

1. **ALCOHOL AND DRUG ABUSE IN THE WORKPLACE: THE COMPLETE RESOURCE GUIDE**
2. -
3. BNA
4. 1989
5. 1 vol.
6. $95
7. no supp. planned
9. 89-25444/20671508/KF3540.A94

1. **THE ALIEN UNDER AMERICAN LAW: TEXT, MATERIALS, CASES**
2. Mutharika, A. Peter
3. Oceana
4. 1980
5. 2 vols.
6. $170
7. periodic supp.
8. 1984 - $65; 1985 - $75
9. 80-18236/6486992/KF4800.M87

1. **ALIMONY, CHILD SUPPORT AND COUNSEL FEES**
2. Melli, M. et al.
3. Bender
4. 1988
5. 3 vol.
6. $310 incl. 3 mos. supp.
7. annual supp.
8. 1990 - $99; 1991- $170
9. 88-71188/18596965/KF537.A94

1. **ALL ABOUT CABLE**
2. Goodale, James C.
3. Law Journal
4. rev. ed. - 1981
5. 1 vol.
6. $85 incl. 3 mos. supp.
7. periodic supp.
8. 1988 - $39; 1989 - $40
9. 81-14293/7795602/KF2844.H36

1. **ALL-STATE SALES TAX REPORTS**
2. -
3. CCH
4. 1940
5. 5 vols. (with weekly newsletter - State Tax review)
6. $1000/yr.; $910/yr. for 2 yrs.
7. semimonthly supp.
9. 78-6454/4170789

1. **ALLSTATE PERSONAL INCOME TAX FORMS FILE**
2. -
3. NTTS
4. 1984
5. 2 vols.
6. $195
7. periodic supp.

1. **ALL STATES TAX GUIDE**
2. -
3. RIA
4. 1960
5. 1 vol.
6. $595/yr.; $560/yr. for 2 yrs.
7. monthly supp.
8. renewal - $535/yr.

1. **ALMANAC OF THE FEDERAL JUDICIARY, VOL. I (District Judges)**
2. P-H Editorial Staff
3. Prentice Hall Law & Business
4. 1988
5. 1 vol.
6. $170
7. semiannual supp.
8. 1991 - $240
9. 84-80461/12901897

1. **ALMANAC OF THE FEDERAL JUDICIARY, VOL. II (Circuit Judges)**
2. P-H Editorial Staff
3. Prentice Hall Law & Business
4. 1988
5. 1 vol.
6. $130
7. semiannual supp.
8. 1991 - $175
9. 84-80461/12901897

1. **ALTERNATE DISPUTE RESOLUTION**
2. -
3. Florida Bar
4. 1989
5. 1 vol.
6. $50
7. supp. as needed
8. no supp. yet
9. 89-80981/21248289/KFF560.3.A944

1. **ALTERNATIVE DISPUTE RESOLUTION**
2. Bergstein, Melvyn H. et al.
3. New Jersey ICLE

4. 1988
5. 1 vol.
6. $30
7. no supp. planned
9. 18119225/KFN2360.5.Z9A47

1. **ALTERNATIVE DISPUTE RESOLUTION DESKBOOK: ARBITRATION & MEDIATION IN WASHINGTON**
2. Meyers, Bruce F., ed.
3. Wash. Bar
4. 1989
5. 1 vol.
6. $95
7. periodic supp.
8. no supp. yet
9. 88-51557/20130700/KFW560.3.A95

1. **ALTERNATIVE DISPUTE RESOLUTION TECHNIQUES**
2. Hancock, W.A.
3. Bus. Laws
4. 1989
5. 1 vol.
6. $95
7. annual supp.
8. renewal - $44/yr.
9. 89-147011/19934893/KF9084.C59

1. **AMERICAN DISABILITY ACT**
2. -
3. Indiana CLE
4. 1991
5. 1 vol.
6. $40
7. no supp. planned
9. 23361604/KF3469.A75A63

1. **THE AMERICAN LAW OF MINING**
2. Rocky Mountain Mineral Law Foundation
3. Bender
4. 2nd ed. - 1985
5. 6 vols.
6. $600 incl. 3 mos. supp.
7. annual supp.
8. 1990 - $200; 1991 - $345
9. 61-1644/7241556/KF1815.R6

1. **AMERICAN LAW OF PRODUCTS LIABILITY 3D**
2. Publ. Editorial Staff
3. Lawyers Coop. & Bancroft
4. 1987
5. 14 vols.
6. $1365 incl. 6 mos. supp.
7. quarterly supp. & newsletter 8x/yr.
8. 1991 - $494
9. 86-82984/16132121/KF1296.A97

1. **AMERICAN LAW OF REAL PROPERTY**
2. Gaudio, Arthur R., ed.
3. Bender
4. 1991
5. 3 vols.
6. $295 incl. 3 mos. supp.
7. annual supp.
8. no supp. yet
9. 91-72507/24278913/KF566.A53

1. **THE AMERICAN LAWYER MANAGEMENT SERVICE**
2. -
3. Am. Lawyer
4. 1990
5. 3 vols.
6. $545
7. quarterly supp.
8. $125/supp.
9. 11470725

1. **AMERICAN STOCK EXCHANGE COMPANY GUIDE**
2. -
3. ASE
4. rev. - 1983
5. 1 vol.
6. $50 incl. all future supp.
7. periodic supp.
8. supp. included in price
9. 9593239/HG4575.N521

1. **AMERICAN STOCK EXCHANGE GUIDE**
2. -
3. CCH
4. 1960
5. 2 vols.
6. $315/yr.; $285/yr. for 2 yrs.
7. monthly supp.
9. 61-1718/1951579/HG4575.N5213

1. **AMERICANS WITH DISABILITIES ACT**
2. Hallock, Marcy M. et al.
3. MICPEL
4. 1991
5. 1 vol.
6. $42
7. no supp. planned

1. **AMERICANS WITH DISABILITIES ACT**
2. -
3. NELI
4. 1991
5. 1 vol.
6. $75
7. no supp. planned

1. **AMERICANS WITH DISABILITIES ACT**
2. -
3. MILE
4. 1991
5. 1 vol.
6. $68
7. no supp. planned
9. 24465476/KF3469.Z9A6

1. **ANALYSIS OF FEDERAL TAXES: INCOME**
2. RIA prof. editorial staff
3. RIA
4. 1991
5. 14 vols. (part of Federal Tax Coordinator 2d)
6. $655/yr.; $625/yr. for 2 yrs.
7. biweekly supp.
8. renewal - $580/yr.
9. 23232443/KF6285.R5331

1. **ANALYSIS OF FEDERAL TAXES: INCOME, ESTATE & GIFT**
2. RIA prof. editorial staff
3. RIA
4. 1991
5. 16 vols. (part of Federal Tax Coordinator 2d)
6. $800/yr.; 760/yr. for 2 yrs.
7. biweekly supp.
8. renewal - $725/yr.
9. 23966535/KF6285.R533

1. **ANDERSON'S OHIO CIVIL PRACTICE WITH FORMS**
2. McCormack, John et al.
3. Anderson
4. 1972
5. 8 vols.
6. $475 incl. 1 yr. supp.
7. annual supp.
8. 1990 - $125; 1991 - $100

1. **ANDERSON'S OHIO EVIDENCE: CIVIL & CRIMINAL**
2. Blackmore, Josiah H. & Glen Weissenberger
3. Anderson
4. 1980
5. 2 vols. + paperback manual
6. $250 incl. 1 yr. supp.
7. annual supp.
8. 1990 - $97.50; 1991 - $232.50
9. 82-238692/9322859/KFO540.B55

1. **ANDERSON'S OHIO PROBATE PRACTICE AND PROCEDURE**
2. -
3. Anderson
4. 1990
5. 3 vols. + paperback manual
6. $350 incl. 1 yr. supp.
7. annual supp.
8. 1991 - $140
9. 22470410/KFO144.A93

1. **ANNOTATED FINANCIAL INSTITUTION BOND**
2. Tort & Insurance Practice Section
3. ABA
4. 1988
5. 1 vol.
6. $109
7. no supp. yet
9. 17894111//KF1223.A5

1. **ANNOTATED GUIDE TO THE ILLINOIS RULES OF PROFESSIONAL CONDUCT**
2. -
3. Illinois ICLE
4. 1991
5. 1 vol.
6. $99.95
7. periodic supp.
8. no supp. yet
9. 23153271/KFI1276.5.I44

1. **ANNOTATED TAX FORMS**
2. Roberts, Sidney I. et al.
3. RIA
4. 1969
5. 2 vols.
6. $425/yr.
7. bimonthly supp.
9. 69-11444/36057/KF6366.R6

1. **ANNOTATIONS TO SURPLUS LINES STATUTES**
2. -
3. ABA
4. 1990
5. 1 vol.
6. $124
7. periodic supp.
8. no supp. yet

9. 89-82256/21501205/KF1165.A56

1. **ANNUAL BANKRUPTCY LAW INSTITUTE**
2. -
3. No. Carolina Bar
4. 13th annual - 1990
5. 1 vol.
6. $71.40
7. annual institutes

1. **ANNUAL EMPLOYEE BENEFITS**
2. -
3. Minn. CLE
4. 14th - 1991
5. 1 vol.
6. $50
7. annual institutes

1. **ANNUAL ESTATE PLANNING SEMINAR**
2. -
3. Wash. Bar
4. 36th annual - 1991
5. 1 vol.
6. $55
7. annual vol.

1. **ANNUAL FEDERAL CIVIL PRACTICE**
2. -
3. Indiana CLE
4. 1991
5. 1 vol.
6. $60
7. no supp. planned
9. 24044708/KF8840.A2F4

1. **ANNUAL NORTHWEST SECURITIES INSTITUTE**
2. -
3. Wash. Bar
4. 9th annual - 1991
5. 2 vols.
6. $55
7. annual vol.

1. **ANNUAL SURVEY OF CONNECTICUT BUSINESS LAW**
2. -
3. Conn. Bar
4. 1991
5. 1 vol.
6. $53
7. no supp. planned

1. **ANNUAL TAX INSTITUTE MANUAL**
2. -
3. Minn. CLE
4. 50th annual - 1990
5. 1 vol.
6. $75
7. annual institutes

1. **ANNUAL TAX PLANNING INSTITUTE**
2. -
3. Conn. Bar
4. 1990
5. 1 vol.
6. $53
7. no supp. planned

1. **ANNUALS AND SURVEYS APPEARING IN LEGAL PERIODICALS: AN ANNOTATED LISTING**
2. DeLashmitt, Eleanor, comp.
3. Rothman
4. 1987, 1988
5. 1 vol.
6. $37.50
7. annual supp.
8. 1988 - no charge; 1989-1991 - $27.50
9. 87-28393/16831148/KF8.D45

1. **ANTIDUMPING AND COUNTERVAILING DUTY LAWS (International Business and Law Series, vol. 3)**
2. Pattison, Joseph E.
3. Clark Boardman Callaghan
4. 1984
5. 1 vol.
6. $135 incl. 3 mos. supp.
7. annual supp.
8. 1989 - $69.50; 1991 - $89.50
9. 84-14463/10996142/KF6708.D8P38

1. **ANTITRUST: AN ECONOMIC APPROACH**
2. Givens, Richard
3. Law Journal
4. 1983
5. 1 vol.
6. $85
7. periodic supp.
8. 1989 - $84; 1990 - $84
9. 83-9346/9466038/KF1649.G58

1. **ANTITRUST AND RESTRICTIVE BUSINESS PRACTICES: INTERNATIONAL, REGIONAL & NATIONAL REGULATION**
2. Marke, Julius J. & Najeeb Samie
3. Oceana

4. 1982
5. 2 vols.
6. $170
7. periodic supp.
8. 1983 - $85; no further supp.
9. 82-14281/8906589/K3856.A35A75

1. **ANTITRUST AND TRADE REGULATION (Business Organizations vols. 16-16N & Index)**
2. von Kalinowski, Julian O. et al.
3. Bender
4. 1969
5. 16 vols.
6. $825/yr.
7. quarterly supp. & monthly newsletter
8. 1988 - $675; 1990 - $790
9. 70-10836/68741/KF1645.V6

1. **ANTITRUST AND TRADE REGULATION: DESK ED.**
2. von Kalinowski, Julian O. et al.
3. Bender
4. 1981
5. 2 vols.
6. $245 incl. 3 mos. supp.
7. periodic supp.
8. 1990 - $199; 1991 - $260.50
9. 81-162127/7352375/KF1645.V6

1. **ANTITRUST BASICS**
2. Vakerics, Thomas V.
3. Law Journal
4. 1985
5. 1 vol.
6. $85
7. periodic supp.
8. 1989 - $42; 1990 - $42
9. 85-16811/12312507/KF1649.V27

1. **ANTITRUST CIVIL JURY INSTRUCTIONS**
2. Section of Antitrust Law
3. ABA
4. 1980
5. 1 vol.
6. $65
7. periodic supp.
8. 1986 - $30
9. 80-67740/7836025/KF9066.A5A95

1. **ANTITRUST CONSENT DECREE MANUAL**
2. Section of Antitrust Law
3. ABA
4. 1979
5. 1 vol.
6. $15
7. supp. as needed
8. no supp. yet
9. 79-90960/6077939/KF1657.C6A95

1. **ANTITRUST COUNSELING AND LITIGATION TECHNIQUES**
2. von Kalinowski, Julian O., ed.
3. Bender
4. 1984
5. 4 vols.
6. $400 incl. 3 mos. supp.
7. annual supp.
8. 1990 - $339; 1991 - $225
9. 83-73261/10682706/KF8840.A8

1. **ANTITRUST DISCOVERY HANDBOOK**
2. Section of Antitrust Law
3. ABA
4. 1981
5. 1 vol.
6. $35
7. periodic supp.
8. 1983 - $19
9. 80-70442/7432816/KF8900.A75

1. **ANTITRUST DIVISION MANUAL**
2. U.S. Dept. of Justice Antitrust Div.
3. order from USGPO - stock #927-001-00000-4
4. 1979
5. 1 vol.
6. $17/yr.
7. periodic supp.
9. 5880377/KF1653.Z9U58

1. **APPEAL AND REVIEW**
2. Batchelor, Jeffrey M. & Alfred A. Hampson, eds.
3. Oregon Bar
4. 1977
5. 1 vol.
6. $90
7. periodic supp.
8. 1986 - $35; to be rev. in 1993
9. 77-366937/3293273/KFO2955.O7

1. **APPEAL SECURITIES ACT HANDBOOK**
2. -
3. Bowne
4. 5th ed. - 1981
5. 1 vol.
6. $200 incl. 1 yr. supp.

7. 6 supp./yr.
8. renewal - $145/yr.
9. 10407015

1. **APPEALS (Art of Advocacy Series)**
2. Houts, Marshall & Walter Rogosheske
3. Bender
4. 1981
5. 1 vol.
6. $110 incl. 6 mos. supp.
7. periodic supp.
8. 1990 - $74.50; 1991 - $91
9. 10167953/KF8915.H68

1. **APPEALS TO THE ELEVENTH CIRCUIT**
2. Rahdert, George K. & Larry M. Roth
3. Butterworth-Fla.
4. 1984
5. 3 vols.
6. $180
7. periodic supp.
8. 1989 - $79; 1990 - $69
9. 11060470

1. **APPEALS TO THE FIFTH CIRCUIT**
2. Rahdert, George K. & Larry M. Roth
3. Butterworth-Texas
4. 1977
5. 2 vols.
6. $150
7. periodic supp.
8. 1989 - $110; 1990 - $21.50
9. 12061230/KF9054.R33

1. **APPEALS TO THE THIRD CIRCUIT**
2. Wertheimer, Ellen
3. Butterworth-NH
4. 1986
5. 2 vols.
6. $130
7. periodic supp.
8. 1987 - $50; 1990 - $65
9. 86-152334/14002972/KF9054 3rd.A4

1. **APPELLATE ADVOCACY**
2. -
3. Ohio CLE
4. 1990
5. 1 vol.
6. $45
7. no supp. planned

1. **APPELLATE ADVOCACY HANDBOOK**
2. -
3. NH Bar
4. 1990
5. 1 vol.
6. $35
7. no supp. planned
9. 13592364

1. **APPELLATE PRACTICE**
2. -
3. Indiana CLE
4. 1988
5. 1 vol.
6. $50
7. no supp. planned
9. 13205509/KFI3555.A75I57

1. **APPELLATE PRACTICE**
2. -
3. Indiana CLE
4. 1991
5. 1 vol.
6. $65
7. no supp. planned

1. **APPELLATE PRACTICE & PROCEDURE HANDBOOK**
2. Walther, David L. et al.
3. State Bar of Wisc.
4. 1986
5. 1 vol.
6. $115
7. periodic supp.
8. 1988 - $30; 1990 - $48

1. **APPELLATE PRACTICE - VIRGINIA AND FEDERAL COURTS**
2. -
3. Jt. Comm. Va.
4. 1986
5. 1 vol.
6. $52
7. periodic supp.
8. 1988 - $20.90

1. **APPLYING GAAP AND GAAS**
2. Munter, Paul & Thomas Ratcliffe
3. Bender
4. 1985
5. 2 vols.
6. $185 incl. 3 mos. supp.
7. annual supp.
8. 1990 - $139; 1991 - $175
9. 84-72343/11821038/HF5616.U5M83

1. **APPLYING GOVERNMENT ACCOUNTING PRINCIPLES**

2. Dittenhofer, Mortimer A., ed.
3. Bender
4. 1990
5. 1 vol.
6. $110
7. periodic supp.
8. 1991 - $64
9. 90-084110/23109491

1. **APPLYING GOVERNMENT AUDITING STANDARDS**
2. Dittenhofer, Mortimer A.
3. Bender
4. 1990
5. 1 vol.
6. $105
7. periodic supp.
8. 1991 - $64
9. 90-084111/22974446/HJ9801.A62

1. **APPRAISERS' LIABILITY**
2. Levine, Mark Lee
3. Prof. Pubs.
4. 1990
5. 1 vol.
6. $48
7. no supp. yet

1. **ARBITRATION AND MEDIATION**
2. Neil, Carl R. et al., eds
3. Oregon Bar
4. 1987
5. 1 vol.
6. $75
7. to be supp. in 1992
9. 87-60320/16944480/KF02960.5.A93

1. **ARBITRATION OF COMMERCIAL AND CONSTRUCTION DISPUTES**
2. -
3. MILE
4. 1990
5. 1 vol.
6. $58
7. no supp. planned

1. **ARBITRATION PRACTICE**
2. -
3. Illinois ICLE
4. 1989
5. 1 vol.
6. $131.95
7. periodic sup.
8. no supp. yet

1. **ARBITRATOR'S QUALIFICATIONS REPORTS**
2. -
3. Simpson
4. 1956
5. 8 vols.
6. $560/yr. (leased)
7. bimonthly supp.
9. 9591778

1. **THE ARCHITECT'S HANDBOOK OF PROFESSIONAL PRACTICE, 11TH ED.**
2. Haviland, David, ed.
3. AIA
4. 1988
5. 4 vols.
6. $160
7. periodic supp.
8. 1990 - $60; 1991 - $60
9. 16580038/NA2570.A62

1. **ARIZONA APPELLATE HANDBOOK**
2. Haire, L. Ray & Paul G. Ulrich
3. State Bar of Ariz.
4. 1980
5. 3 vols.
6. $225
7. annual supp.
8. 1990 - $25; 1991 - $90
9. 4264734/KFA2955.S7

1. **ARIZONA ATTORNEY'S FEES MANUAL**
2. Gale, C.M. et al.
3. State Bar of Ariz.
4. 1987
5. 1 vol.
6. $45
7. periodic supp.
8. no supp. yet
9. 16577347/KFA2477.5.F4.A7

1. **ARIZONA COURTROOM EVIDENCE MANUAL**
2. McClennen, Crane et al.
3. State Bar of Ariz.
4. 2nd ed. - 1988
5. 1 vol.
6. $90
7. bimonthly or annual supp.
8. 1990 - $35
9. 85-061412/12376322/KFA2940.F43

1. **ARIZONA COURTS MANUAL**
2. Bluff, Guy W.

3. State Bar of Ariz.
4. 1991
5. 1 vol.
6. $65/2 yrs.
7. semiannual supp.
8. no supp. yet

1. **ARIZONA LAND USE LAW**
2. Jorden, Douglas A. & Michael D. House
3. State Bar of Ariz.
4. 1988
5. 1 vol.
6. $85
7. annual supp.
8. 1991 - $35
9. 88-177344/18747658/KFA2858.J67

1. **THE ARIZONA LAW OF MEDICAL MALPRACTICE**
2. Stephan, Robert, Jr.
3. Medilex
4. 1983
5. 1 vol.
6. $88
7. supp. every 18 mos.
8. 1988 - $40
9. 83-60043/9409086/KFA2726.3.S83

1. **ARIZONA LEGAL SERVICES PRACTICE MANUAL, VOL. I**
2. Davis, Ann M.M., ed.
3. State Bar of Ariz.
4. 2nd ed. - 1989 & 1991
5. 2 vols.
6. $130
7. periodic supp.
8. 1991 - $100
9. 20309869/KF390.5.P6A97

1. **ARIZONA PROBATE CODE PRACTICE MANUAL**
2. Geiser, Jeannette K. et al., eds.
3. State Bar of Ariz.
4. 3rd ed. - 1989
5. 1 vol.
6. $90
7. annual supp.
8. no supp. yet
9. 19877080/KFA2544.G45

1. **ARKANSAS CORPORATION SYSTEM**
2. -
3. Arkansas Bar
4. 1987
5. 1 vol.
6. $100
7. periodic supp.
8. no supp. yet

1. **ARKANSAS DOMESTIC RELATIONS SYSTEM**
2. -
3. Arkansas Bar
4. 1981
5. 2 vols.
6. $75/vol.
7. periodic supp.
8. 1986 - $75; supp. in 1992
9. 6899813/KFA3694.A74

1. **ARKANSAS FORMBOOK**
2. -
3. Arkansas Bar
4. 1988
5. 2 vols.
6. $150
7. no supp. yet

1. **ARKANSAS RULES OF EVIDENCE**
2. Gitelman, Mort
3. Francis Marion
4. 1988
5. 1 vol.
6. $70 incl. next supp.
7. annual supp.
8. 1990 - $35; 1991 - $35
9. 17865220/KFA4140.A6G57

1. **THE ARLEN MUTUAL FUND HANDBOOK**
2. Wadsworth, Robert H., ed.
3. Arlen
4. 1986
5. 1 vol.
6. $325/yr.
7. periodic supp.
8. renewal - $225/yr.
9. 86-71930/14397813/KF1078.A6A74

1. **ARMS CONTROL REPORTER**
2. Hardenbergh, Chalmers
3. IDDS
4. 1982
5. 1 vol./yr.
6. $365/yr.-instit. with open access; $550/yr.-business, govt.; $160/yr.-students
7. monthly supp.
9. 85-3055/9160157/JX1974.7.A75x

1. **ARREST, SEARCH AND SEIZURE**
2. -
3. Illinois ICLE
4. 1985
5. 1 vol.
6. $99.95
7. periodic supp.
8. 1990 - $29.95
9. 5107762

1. **ARSON LEGISLATION REFERENCE MANUAL**
2. Young Lawyers Div.
3. ABA
4. 1985
5. 1 vol.
6. free
7. no supp. planned

1. **THE ART OF DISCOVERY**
2. -
3. NH Bar
4. 1990
5. 1 vol.
6. $35
7. no supp. planned

1. **ASBESTOS ABATEMENT RESOURCE GUIDE, 2ND ED.**
2. -
3. BNA
4. 1989
5. 1 vol.
6. $250
7. no supp. planned
9. 89-9950/19722540/KF3964.A73A95

1. **ASBESTOS ABATEMENT RULES: THE COMPLETE RESOURCE GUIDE**
2. -
3. BNA
4. 1988
5. 1 vol.
6. $110
7. no supp. yet
9. 17631681/KF1297.A73A7

1. **ASBESTOS REGULATORY DIRECTORY**
2. -
3. Natl. Asbestos
4. 1991
5. 1 vol.
6. $24.95 - members; $39.95 - nonmembers
7. periodic supp.
8. no supp. yet

1. **ASSET-BASED FINANCING**
2. Ruda, Howard
3. Bender
4. 1985
5. 4 vols.
6. $420 incl. 3 mos. supp.
7. annual supp.
8. 1989 - $177; 1990 - $178
9. 84-72027/11707266/KF1428.A6A87

1. **ASSET BASED LOAN TRANSACTION**
2. Comm. of the Young Lawyers Section
3. Conn. Bar
4. 1988
5. 1 vol.
6. $20
7. no supp. planned

1. **ASSET VALUATION IN DIVORCE**
2. -
3. MILE
4. 1989
5. 1 vol.
6. $58
7. no supp. planned

1. **ATTORNEY ASSISTANCE MANUAL FOR PERSONS WITH AIDS/ARC**
2. -
3. Wash. Bar
4. 1989
5. 1 vol.
6. $25
7. no supp. planned

1. **ATTORNEY FEES IN WASHINGTON**
2. Talmadge, Philip A.
3. Butterworth-St. Paul
4. 1991
5. 1 vol.
6. $85
7. periodic supp.
8. no supp. yet

1. **ATTORNEY GUIDE TO CONDUCTING A DEPOSITION**
2. Lane, Larry
3. NYSTLA
4. 1990
5. 1 vol.
6. $75
7. periodic supp.
8. no supp. yet

1. **ATTORNEY'S DESKBOOK FOR TAKING AND DEFENDING DEPOSITIONS**
2. -
3. UMKC/CLE
4. 1985
5. 1 vol.
6. $45
7. no supp. yet
8. -
9. 13085505/KF8900.A4A8

1. **ATTORNEY'S DICTIONARY OF MEDICINE, 16TH ED.**
2. Schmidt, J.E.
3. Bender
4. 1962
5. 4 vols.
6. $350 incl. 3 mos. supp.
7. annual supp.
8. 1990 - $274; 1991 - $341
9. 62-6520/6007322/R121.S329

1. **ATTORNEY'S DICTIONARY OF PATENT CLAIMS**
2. Aisenberg, I.A.
3. Bender
4. 1985
5. 2 vols.
6. $250 incl. 3 mos. supp.
7. annual supp.
8. 1989 - $142; 1990 - $150
9. 85-71218/12986569/KF3120.A86

1. **ATTORNEYS' FEES: BEYOND THE DOLLARS**
2. -
3. Wash. Bar
4. 1988
5. 1 vol.
6. $35
7. no supp. planned

1. **ATTORNEY'S FEES IN FLORIDA**
2. Hauser, James C.
3. Butterworth-Fla.
4. 1989
5. 3 vols.
6. $180
7. periodic supp.
8. 1990 - $184.80; 1991 - $41.50
9. 90-164594/21907684/KFF77.5.F4H38

1. **ATTORNEY'S GUIDE TO CALIFORNIA PROFESSIONAL CORPORATIONS, 4th ed.**
2. Hargrove, John O., ed.
3. Calif. CEB
4. 4th ed.-1987
5. 1 vol.
6. $105
7. periodic supp.
8. 1989 - $29; 1991 - $35
9. 87-71434//r89/16396976/KFC545.5.A98

1. **ATTORNEY'S GUIDE TO CONDUCTING DEPOSITIONS - AUTOMOBILE NEGLIGENCE CASES**
2. Lame, Lawrence B.
3. Lame
4. 1987
5. 1 vol.
6. $75
7. annual supp.
8. $12/yr.
9. 17634436/KF8900.A3L35

1. **ATTORNEY'S GUIDE TO PENSION AND PROFIT-SHARING PLANS**
2. Gilbert, Richard A. et. al.
3. Calif. CEB
4. 3rd ed. - 1985
5. 1 vol.
6. $150
7. periodic supp.
8. 1989 - $40; 1991 - price NA
9. 85-70006/12154380/KFC575.6.A97

1. **THE ATTORNEY'S GUIDE TO THE HANLESTER EXCLUSION CASE**
2. -
3. United Communications Group
4. 1990
5. 1 vol.
6. $349
7. periodic supp.

1. **THE ATTORNEY'S GUIDE TO THE SEVENTH CIRCUIT COURT OF APPEALS**
2. -
3. State Bar of Wisc.
4. 1988
5. 1 vol.
6. $70
7. periodic supp.
8. 1989 - $20; 1991 - $42
9. 17450781/KF9054.A98

1. **ATTORNEY'S HANDBOOK OF ACCOUNTING**
2. Sellin, Henry

3. Bender
4. 3rd ed. - 1979
5. 1 vol.
6. $115 incl. 3 mos. supp.
7. periodic supp.
8. 1990 - $82.50; 1991 - $85
9. 79-123301/5990030/HF5635.S465

1. **ATTORNEY'S MEDICAL REFFERENCE**
2. Creighton, Smith & Young
3. Parker
4. 1984
5. 1 vol.
6. $75
7. no supp. yet
8. -
9. 84-216325/11866116/RA1018.C74

1. **ATTORNEY'S TEXTBOOK OF MEDICINE, 3RD ED.**
2. Gray, Roscoe N.
3. Bender
4. 3rd ed. - 1949
5. 17 vols.
6. $1500 incl. 3 mos. supp.
7. 3 supp./yr.
8. 1989 - $1155; 1990 - $1335
9. 50-628/9060133/RA1053.G782

1. **ATTORNEYS' TEXTBOOK OF MEDICINE: MANUAL OF TRAUMATIC INJURIES**
2. Various Contributing Authors
3. Bender
4. 1989
5. 3 vols.
6. $300 incl. 3 mos. supp.
7. annual supp.
8. 1990 - $86.50; 1991 - $139
9. 20645318/RA1121.A86

1. **THE ATTORNEY'S UMBRELLA BOOK**
2. -
3. Griffin
4. 1990
5. 3 vols.
6. $525
7. periodic supp.
8. renewal - $155/yr.
9. 90-179640/22346299/KF1215.A97

1. **AUDIT & ACCOUNTING GUIDES**
2. -
3. CCH
4. 1991
5. 2 vols.
6. $360/yr.
7. periodic supp.

1. **AUSTRALIAN FEDERAL TAX REPORTS**
2. -
3. CCH
4. 1969
5. 10 vols.
6. $1765/yr.; $1605/yr. for 2 yrs.
7. weekly supp.

1. **AUSTRALIAN INCOME TAX GUIDE - (without legislation)**
2. -
3. CCH
4. 1981
5. 3 vols.
6. $525/yr.; $475/yr. for 2 yrs.
7. semimonthly supp.
9. 12793870/K4460.4.C663A8

1. **AUSTRALIAN INCOME TAX GUIDE & INCOME TAX LEGISLATION**
2. -
3. CCH
4. 1969
5. 6 vols.
6. $750/yr.; $680/yr. for 2 yrs.
7. semimonthly supp.

1. **AUSTRALIAN SECURITIES LAW REPORTS**
2. -
3. CCH
4. 1972
5. 2 vols.
6. $525/yr.; $475/yr. for 2 yrs.
7. periodic supp.

1. **AUSTRALIAN TAX CASES**
2. -
3. CCH
4. NA
5. 2 vols.
6. $665/yr.; $605/yr. for 2 yrs.
7. semimonthly supp.
9. 3953784

1. **AUSTRALIAN TAX LIBRARY**
2. -
3. CCH
4. 1972
5. 15 vols.
6. $1945/yr.

7. weekly supp.

1. **AUSTRALIAN TRADE PRACTICES REPORTS**
2. -
3. CCH
4. 1974
5. 2 vols.
6. $820/yr.; $700/yr. for 2 yrs.
7. monthly supp.
9. 78-319790/4641070

1. **THE AUTOMATED LAW FIRM: A COMPLETE GUIDE TO SOFTWARE AND SYSTEMS**
2. Robbins, Richard L.
3. Prentice Hall Law & Business
4. 1989
5. 1 vol.
6. $75 incl. 4 mos. supp.
7. periodic supp.
8. 1990 - $60; 1991 - $60
9. 89-27647/20453566/KF320.A9R6

1. **AUTOMATIC TAX PLANNER**
2. -
3. Panel
4. 1985
5. 1 vol.
6. $150 incl. 1 yr. supp.
7. quarterly supp.
9. 85-6528/11969746/KF6297.S3

1. **AUTOMOBILE ACCIDENT HANDBOOK**
2. -
3. UMKC/CLE
4. 1984
5. 1 vol.
6. $63.75
7. no supp. yet

1. **AUTOMOBILE ACCIDENT LAW AND PRACTICE**
2. Miller, Keith C. et al.
3. Bender
4. 1988
5. 4 vols.
6. $420 incl. 3 mos. supp.
7. annual supp.
8. 1990 - $150; 1991 - $248.50
9. 88-71474/18603422/KF1290.A8A83

1. **AUTOMOBILE ACCIDENT RECONSTRUCTION**
2. -
3. MILE
4. 1990
5. 1 vol.
6. $58
7. no supp. planned

1. **AUTOMOBILE INSURANCE HANDBOOK**
2. Baker, Gerald H.
3. New Jersey ICLE
4. 1991
5. 1 vol.
6. $80
7. periodic supp.
8. no supp. yet
9. 23294809/KFN1991.A4B341

1. **AUTOMOBILE LAW REPORTS (insurance cases)**
2. -
3. CCH
4. 1966
5. 1 vol.
6. $980/yr.; $890/yr. for 2 yrs.
7. semimonthly supp.
9. 13118082

1. **AUTOMOBILE LIABILITY INSURANCE**
2. Schermer, Irvin E.
3. Clark Boardman Callaghan
4. 2nd ed. - 1981
5. 3 vols.
6. $315 incl. 3 mos. supp.
7. annual supp.
8. 1988 - $170; 1989 - $208.50
9. 81-15532/7837826/KF1218.S32

1. **AUTOMOBILES**
2. Lovett, James D. & James L. Branton
3. Knowles
4. 1985
5. 1 vol.(avail. in Texas & natl. eds.)
6. $135 incl. 3 mos. supp.
7. annual supp.
8. 1988 - $43; 1990 - $42
9. 12202649/KF8925.T7B73

1. **AVIATION ACCIDENT LAW**
2. Kreindler, Lee S.
3. Bender
4. 1963
5. 3 vols.
6. $340 incl. 3 mos. supp.
7. annual supp.
8. 1990 - $234; 1991 - $382

9. 63-3421/1597975/KF1290.A9K73

1. **AVIATION LAW REPORTS**
2. -
3. CCH
4. 1931
5. 4 vols.
6. $1460/yr.; $1325/yr. for 2 yrs.
7. semimonthly supp.
9. 80-2674/6880641

1. **AVIATION REGULATORY DIGEST SERVICE**
2. Eyler, Carl R.
3. Hawkins
4. 1965
5. 1 vol.
6. $260/yr.
7. monthly supp.

1. **AVOIDING AND DEFENDING WRONGFUL DISCHARGE CLAIMS**
2. Pepe, Stephen P. & Scott Dunham
3. Clark Boardman Callaghan
4. 1987
5. 1 vol.
6. $100 incl. 6 mos. supp.
7. annual supp.
8. 1989 - $36; 1990 - $43
9. 87-10345/15549222/KF3471.P46

1. **AVOIDING LEGAL PITFALLS IN LAND USE AND REAL ESTATE DEVELOPMENT; WATER RESOURCES & REGULATIONS**
2. -
3. Conn. Bar
4. 1991
5. 1 vol.
6. $53
7. no supp. planned

1. **BAD FAITH ACTIONS: LIABILITY AND DAMAGES**
2. Ashley, Stephen S.
3. Clark Boardman Callaghan
4. 1984
5. 1 vol.
6. $98 incl. 6 mos. supp.
7. annual cum. supp.
8. 1989 - $42.50; 1990 - $44.50
9. 84-28489/11532426/KF1301.5.I58A85

1. **BAD FAITH & PUNITIVE DAMAGES: ANNOTATIONS TO FIRST PARTY INSURANCE CASES, STATUTES, AND REGULATIONS**
2. -
3. ABA
4. 1986, 1989
5. 2 vols.
6. $120
7. periodic supp.
9. 86-71258/22129964

1. **BAKER'S OHIO SCHOOL LAW GUIDE**
2. Baker, Robert T.
3. Anderson
4. new ed. - 1990
5. 2 vols.
6. $225 incl. 1 yr. supp.
7. annual supp.
8. 1990 - $50; 1991 - $95
9. 81-211008/8409795/KF0390.B34

1. **BALDWIN'S KENTUCKY PRACTICE**
2. Baker, James M., ed.
3. Banks
4. 1980
5. 4 vols.
6. $240 incl. 9 mos. supp.
7. biennial supp.
8. 1989 - $95
9. 80-117198/6626436/KFK1730.B34

1. **BALDWIN'S OHIO CIVIL PRACTICE**
2. Klein, James M. & James P. Murtaugh
3. Banks
4. 1988
5. 3 vols.
6. $275 incl. 9 mos. supp.
7. annual supp.
8. 1990 - $57.50
9. 88-61264/17865213/KFO529.A2

1. **BALDWIN'S OHIO DOMESTIC RELATIONS LAW**
2. Sowald, Beatrice K. & Stanley Morganstern
3. Banks
4. 1984
5. 1 vol.
6. $175 incl. 9 mos. supp.
7. annual supp.
8. 1990 - $37
9. 10707009/KFO94.Z95B34

1. **BALDWIN'S OHIO SCHOOL LAW**
2. -
3. Banks

4. 1981
5. 1 vol.
6. $225 incl. 9 mos. supp.
7. annual supp.
8. 1990 - $55
9. 75-315469/692735/KFO390.A6S672

1. **BALDWIN'S OHIO TAX LAW AND RULES**
2. -
3. Banks
4. 3rd ed. - 1976
5. 2 vols.
6. $180 incl. 9 mos. supp.
7. annual supp.
8. 1990 - $70
9. 73-160738/1084737/KFO470.A6B322

1. **BALDWIN'S OHIO TOWNSHIP LAW**
2. Shimp, William B.
3. Banks
4. 4th ed. - 1984
5. 3 vols.
6. $185 incl. 9 mos. supp.
7. annual supp.
8. 1990 - $95
9. 77-371433//r894/2937137/KFO430.A3

1. **BALLANTINE AND STERLING CALIFORNIA CORPORATION LAWS**
2. Clark, R. Bradbury, ed.
3. Bender & Parker
4. 4th ed. - 1962
5. 6 vols.
6. $715 incl. 3 mos. supp.
7. supp. 3x/yr.
8. 1990 - $482.50; 1991 - $799
9. 63-47230/1492208/KFC340.B3

1. **BANK ACCOUNTING AND AUDITING SERVICE**
2. Mecimore, Charles D.
3. Sheshunoff
4. 1989
5. 1 vol.
6. $295 incl. 1 yr. supp.
7. monthly supp.
9. 19258445/HG1706.M4

1. **BANK CAPITAL SERVICE**
2. -
3. Sheshunoff
4. 1989
5. 1 vol.
6. $245 incl. 1 supp.
7. periodic supp.
8. 1991 - $190

1. **BANK HOLDING COMPANY COMPLIANCE MANUAL**
2. Beckford, J.G.
3. Bender
4. 1986
5. 1 vol.
6. $120 incl. 3 mos. supp.
7. periodic supp.
8. 1990 - $102; 1991 - $166
9. 86-73032/15545994/KF1017.B43

1. **BANK HOLDING COMPANY SUPERVISION MANUAL**
2. -
3. Fed.
4. rev. - 1986
5. 1 vol.
6. $40 incl. all supp.
7. periodic supp.
8. updated in 1991
9. 8231252/HG2567.B66

1. **BANK REGULATORY REPORTING REQUIREMENTS: A GUIDE TO MEASURING COMPLIANCE**
2. Regulatory Compliance Associates
3. Probus
4. 1989
5. 2 vols.
6. $135
7. periodic supp.
8. no supp. yet
9. 89-60691/20747041/KF974.B218

1. **BANK WAGE-HOUR AND PERSONNEL SERVICE**
2. Buschman, Thomas W.
3. Pratt
4. NA
5. 2 vols.
6. $117/yr.
7. semimonthly supp.

1. **BANKING AND FINANCE**
2. -
3. MILE
4. 1991
5. 1 vol.
6. $68
7. no supp. planned
9. 23126061/KF1035.Z9B357

1. **BANKING AND THRIFT: AN INDUSTRY IN TRANSITION**
2. -
3. MILE
4. 1991
5. 1 vol.
6. $68
7. no supp. planned
9. 23667390/KF974.B36

1. **BANKING CRIMES**
2. Villa, John K.
3. Clark Boardman Callaghan
4. 1987
5. 1 vol.
6. $110 incl. 3 mos. supp.
7. annual supp.
8. 1989 - $59.50; 1991 - $65
9. 87-10333/15549187/KF1030.R3V55

1. **BANKING LAW**
2. Solomon, Frederic et al.
3. Bender
4. 1981
5. 14 vols.
6. $885 incl. 3 mos. supp.
7. periodic supp.
8. 1990 - $744; 1991 - $990
9. 81-127541/7735697/K974.B37

1. **BANKING LAW MANUAL**
2. Norton, Joseph J. & Sherry C. Whitley
3. Bender
4. 1983
5. 1 vol.
6. $105
7. periodic supp.
8. 1990 - $94; 1991 - $72
9. 82-73916/9596263/KF974.N67

1. **BANKRUPTCY**
2. Lee, Joe
3. Clark Boardman Callaghan
4. 1981
5. 1 vol.
6. $94.50 incl. 3 mos. supp.
7. annual supp.
8. 1990 - $44.50; 1991 - $49
9. 79-92367/8199218/KF1524.L43

1. **BANKRUPTCY: ANNOTATED FORMS**
2. Martin, Judge Robert D.
3. Prentice Hall Law & Business
4. 1989
5. 2 vols.
6. $160 incl. 4 mos. supp.
7. periodic supp.
8. 1990 - $75; 1991 - $100
9. 89-23123/20418800/KF1521.M37

1. **BANKRUPTCY: TEXT, STATUTES, RULES**
2. Ginsberg, Judge Robert E.
3. Prentice Hall Law & Business
4. 2nd ed. - 1989
5. 2 vols.
6. $160
7. annual supp.
8. 1990 - $110; 1991 - $125
9. 89-23169/20453681/KF1524.G56

1. **BANKRUPTCY "A BASIC REVIEW"**
2. -
3. Indiana CLE
4. 1991
5. 1 vol.
6. $45
7. no supp. planned
9. 24044700/KF1544.A75B35

1. **BANKRUPTCY AND LENDER LIABILITY LITIGATION**
2. -
3. NH Bar
4. 1990
5. 1 vol.
6. $35
7. no supp. planned
9. 23067248/KFN1421.Z9B36

1. **BANKRUPTCY & WORKOUTS IN THE TROUBLED OIL & GAS INDUSTRY**
2. -
3. EMLF
4. 1991
5. 1 vol.
6. $100
7. no supp. planned

1. **BANKRUPTCY–CHAPTER 13**
2. -
3. Indiana CLE
4. 1989
5. 1 vol.
6. $50
7. no supp. planned

1. **BANKRUPTCY COURT DECISIONS**
2. Hays, Frances P., ed.
3. LRP

4. 1974
5. 3 vols.
6. $675/yr.
7. weekly supp.
9. 75-643806/2241426/KF1519.B34

1. **BANKRUPTCY DESK GUIDE**
2. Travers, Timothy E., mng. ed.
3. Lawyers Coop.
4. 1990
5. 4 vols.
6. $413 incl. 6 mos. supp.
7. semiannual supp.
9. 90-62917/23011130

1. **BANKRUPTCY FOR THE CORPORATE LAWYER**
2. Young Lawyers Section
3. Conn. Bar
4. 1989
5. 1 vol.
6. $20
7. no supp. planned

1. **BANKRUPTCY FORMS MANUAL**
2. Admin. Office of U.S. Courts
3. Hein
4. 1990
5. 2 vols.
6. $125
7. no supp. yet
9. 22198944/KF1521.A43

1. **BANKRUPTCY INSTITUTE**
2. -
3. Minn. CLE
4. 1991
5. 1 vol.
6. $60
7. no supp. planned

1. **BANKRUPTCY LAW**
2. Perris, Hon. Elizabeth L. & Kevin D. Padrick, eds.
3. Oregon Bar
4. 1988
5. 2 vols.
6. $140
7. periodic supp.
8. to be supp. in 1992
9. 87-60319/20282993/KFO2621.B36

1. **BANKRUPTCY LAW AND PRACTICE IN MICHIGAN**
2. Mears, Patrick E.
3. ICLE - Michigan
4. 1987
5. 1 vol.
6. $95
7. annual supp.
8. 1988 - $25; 1990 - $55
9. 87-80722/16662943

1. **BANKRUPTCY LAW & PROCEDURE: A FUNDAMENTAL GUIDE FOR LAW OFFICE PROFESSIONALS**
2. Berger, Steven N.
3. Wiley Law
4. 1989
5. 1 vol.
6. $95
7. annual supp.
8. 1990 - $35; 1991 - price NA
9. 89-185631/19947567/KF1524.3.S25

1. **BANKRUPTCY LAW FOR THE GENERAL PRACTITIONER**
2. -
3. Maine Bar
4. 1989
5. 1 vol.
6. $30
7. no supp. planned

1. **BANKRUPTCY LAW FUNDAMENTALS**
2. Aaron, Richard I.
3. Clark Boardman Callaghan
4. 1984
5. 1 vol.
6. $115 incl. 3 mos. supp.
7. annual supp.
8. 1988 - $47.50
9. 83-27535/10322361/KF1524.A73

1. **BANKRUPTCY LAW REPORTS**
2. -
3. CCH
4. 1929
5. 3 vols.
6. $695/yr.; $630/yr. for 2 yrs.
7. semimonthly supp.
9. 39-444/4668069/KF1520.C65

1. **BANKRUPTCY LITIGATION AND PRACTICE: A PRACTITIONER'S GUIDE**
2. Salerno, Thomas J.
3. Wiley Law
4. 1987

5. 1 vol.
6. $125
7. annual supp.
8. 1990 - $36.50; 1991 - $50
9. 87-142218/16582872/KF1527.S25

1. **BANKRUPTCY LITIGATION CONFERENCE**
2. -
3. MILE
4. 1991
5. 1 vol.
6. $68
7. no supp. planned
9. 23717694/KF1524.3.B28

1. **BANKRUPTCY LITIGATION MANUAL**
2. Cook, Michael L.
3. Prentice Hall Law & Business
4. 1989
5. 1 vol.
6. $95 incl. 4 mos. supp.
7. periodic supp.
8. 1990 - $75; 1991 - $85
9. 88-22484/18225000/KF1527.B273

1. **BANKRUPTCY LOCAL COURT RULES**
2. Pike and Fischer, Inc.
3. Clark Boardman Callaghan
4. 1989
5. 4 vols.
6. $415 incl. 1 yr. service
7. quarterly supp.
9. 89-70888/20800022/KF1527.A2

1. **BANKRUPTCY PRACTICE**
2. -
3. Illinois ICLE
4. 1990
5. 1 vol.
6. $109.95
7. periodic supp.
8. no supp. planned
9. 23183494

1. **BANKRUPTCY PRACTICE DESKBOOK, Rev. Ed.**
2. Maloy, Richard H.W. & David D. Bird
3. Butterworth-NH
4. 1991
5. 3 vols.
6. $285
7. annual supp.
8. 1991 - price NA
9. 90-15031/22420499/KF1524.M26

1. **BANKRUPTCY PRACTICE FOR THE GENERAL PRACTITIONER, 2/E**
2. Drake, W. Homer, Jr.
3. Shepard's
4. 2nd ed. - 1990
5. 2 vols.
6. $195
7. annual supp.
8. 1990 - $33; 1991 - $33
9. 90-39381/21761638/KF1524.D7

1. **BANKRUPTCY PRACTICE HANDBOOK**
2. Ellis, Dale
3. Parker
4. 1992
5. 1 vol.
6. price NA
7. annual supp.
8. no supp. yet

1. **BANKRUPTCY PRACTICE HANDBOOK**
2. Williams, Rosemary E.
3. Clark Boardman Callaghan
4. 1983
5. 1 vol.
6. $95 incl. 6 mos. supp.
7. annual supp.
8. 1989 - $39; 1990 - $41.50
9. 83-21070/10072078/KF1527.W54

1. **BANKRUPTCY PRACTICE MANUAL**
2. -
3. No. Carolina Bar
4. 1991
5. 1 vol.
6. $89.95
7. no supp. yet

1. **BANKRUPTCY SERVICE, LAWYERS EDITION**
2. Publ. Ed. Staff
3. Lawyers Coop. & Bancroft
4. 1979
5. 15 vols.
6. $1150 incl. 1 yr. supp.
7. quarterly supp.
8. 1991 - $740
9. 78-71987/4622752/KF1520.B36

1. **BANKRUPTCY STAY MANUAL**
2. Ralston, Richard
3. Book Pub.
4. 1989
5. 1 vol.
6. $75

7. supp. as needed
8. no supp. yet

1. **BANKRUPTCY STRATEGIES FOR LENDERS**
2. Sutherland, Michael J. & John R. Blinn
3. Wiley Law
4. 1988
5. 1 vol.
6. $105
7. annual supp.
8. 1989 - $28; 1992 - price NA
9. 87-141603/16228390/KF1524.3.B546

1. **BANKRUPTCY TAX**
2. Davidow, William M., Jr. et al.
3. MICPEL
4. 1991
5. 1 vol.
6. $42
7. no supp. planned

1. **BANKS AND THRIFTS: GOVERNMENT ENFORCEMENT AND RECEIVERSHIP**
2. Zisman, Barry S., ed.
3. Bender
4. 1991
5. 1 vol.
6. $100 incl. 3 mos. supp.
7. annual supp.
8. no supp. yet
9. 91-76051/24705082

1. **THE BAR FOUNDATION HANDBOOK**
2. Bar Services Div.
3. ABA
4. 1986
5. 1 vol.
6. $65
7. no supp. yet
9. 22129649

1. **BARCLAYS CALIFORNIA SUPREME COURT SERVICE**
2. Lydon, George, ed.
3. Barclays
4. 1981
5. 1 vol.
6. $395/yr.
7. weekly supp.
9. 88-646219/14253076/KFC45.1.B37

1. **BARCLAYS UNITED STATES D.C. CIRCUIT SERVICE**
2. Gomez, Frank, ed.
3. Barclays
4. 1990
5. 1 vol.
6. $395/yr.
7. biweekly supp.
9. 24676718

1. **BARCLAYS UNITED STATES EIGHTH CIRCUIT SERVICE**
2. Gomez, Frank, ed.
3. Barclays
4. 1987
5. 1 vol.
6. $395/yr.
7. biweekly supp.
9. 89-640249/16852539/KF112 8thU54

1. **BARCLAYS UNITED STATES ELEVENTH CIRCUIT SERVICE**
2. Gomez, Frank, ed.
3. Barclays
4. 1991
5. 1 vol.
6. $395/yr.
7. biweekly supp.
9. 24101248

1. **BARCLAYS UNITED STATES FIFTH CIRCUIT SERVICE**
2. Gomez, Frank, ed.
3. Barclays
4. 1990
5. 1 vol.
6. $395/yr.
7. biweekly supp.

1. **BARCLAYS UNITED STATES FIRST CIRCUIT SERVICE**
2. Gomez, Frank, ed.
3. Barclays
4. 1991
5. 1 vol.
6. $395/yr.
7. biweekly supp.
9. 23885364/KF117.1st.B24X

1. **BARCLAYS UNITED STATES FOURTH CIRCUIT SERVICE**
2. Gomez, Frank, ed.
3. Barclays
4. 1990
5. 1 vol.
6. $395/yr.
7. biweekly supp.
9. 24161650/KF112.4th.1.B37

1. **BARCLAYS UNITED STATES NINTH CIRCUIT SERVICE**
2. Gomez, Frank, ed.
3. Barclays
4. 1985
5. 1 vol.
6. $395/yr.
7. supp. 36x/yr.
9. SN85-15291/11940793/KF112.1 9thU55

1. **BARCLAYS UNITED STATES SECOND CIRCUIT SERVICE**
2. Gomez, Frank, ed.
3. Barclays
4. 1988
5. 1 vol.
6. $395/yr.
7. biweekly supp.
9. SN89-8480/19991459/KF112 2d.U54

1. **BARCLAYS UNITED STATES SEVENTH CIRCUIT SERVICE**
2. Gomez, Frank, ed.
3. Barclays
4. 1988
5. 1 vol.
6. $395/yr.
7. biweekly supp.
9. SN89-8436/19038490/KF112 7th.U54

1. **BARCLAYS UNITED STATES SIXTH CIRCUIT SERVICE**
2. Gomez, Frank, ed.
3. Barclays
4. 1987
5. 1 vol.
6. $395/yr.
7. biweekly supp.
9. 89-640248/15190921/KF112 6th.U54

1. **BARCLAYS UNITED STATES TENTH CIRCUIT SERVICE**
2. Gomez, Frank, ed.
3. Barclays
4. 1987
5. 1 vol.
6. $395/yr.
7. biweekly supp.
9. 89-640250,SN88-1765/17016700/KF112.T45

1. **BARCLAYS UNITED STATES THIRD CIRCUIT SERVICE**
2. Gomez, Frank, ed.
3. Barclays
4. 1990
5. 1 vol.
6. $395/yr.
7. biweekly supp.

1. **BASIC BANKRUPTCY**
2. -
3. Okla. Bar CLE
4. 1990
5. 1 vol.
6. $40
7. no supp. planned

1. **BASIC BOOK OF BUSINESS AGREEMENTS**
2. Goldstein, Arnold
3. Enterprise
4. 1983
5. 1 vol.
6. $69.95
7. periodic supp.
8. 1990 - $19.95; 1991 - $19.95
9. 82-84448/9827342/KF886.G64

1. **BASIC COAL, OIL & GAS LAW**
2. -
3. EMLF
4. 1985
5. 1 vol.
6. $100
7. no supp. planned
9. 14776426/KF1819.A2E27

1. **BASIC CORPORATE PRACTICE**
2. Corporations Committee of the Young Lawyers Section
3. Conn. Bar
4. 1988
5. 1 vol.
6. $20
7. no supp. planned

1. **BASIC CORPORATE PRACTICE**
2. -
3. Conn. Bar
4. 1990
5. 1 vol.
6. $53
7. no supp. planned

1. **BASIC CORPORATE PRACTICE**
2. -
3. Indiana CLE
4. 1988
5. 1 vol.
6. $50

7. no supp. planned

1. **BASIC ESTATE PLANNING**
2. -
3. Illinois ICLE
4. 1990
5. 1 vol.
6. $76.95
7. periodic supp.
8. no supp. yet

1. **BASIC ESTATE PLANNING**
2. -
3. Indiana CLE
4. 1991
5. 1 vol.
6. $40
7. no supp. planned

1. **BASIC ESTATE PLANNING AND ADMINISTRATION**
2. -
3. Jt. Comm. Va.
4. 2nd ed. - 1989
5. 1 vol.
6. $62
7. periodic supp.
8. no supp. yet

1. **BASIC INSURANCE LAW**
2. -
3. Indiana CLE
4. 1990
5. 1 vol.
6. $55
7. no supp. planned

1. **BASIC INSURANCE LAW II**
2. -
3. Indiana CLE
4. 1991
5. 1 vol.
6. $40
7. no supp. planned

1. **BASIC LEGAL FORMS**
2. Hyman, Marvin
3. WG&L
4. 2nd ed. - 1991
5. 1 vol.
6. $96
7. semiannual supp.
8. 1990 - $120; 1991 - $43.50
9. 80-53751/7516875/KF170.H9

1. **BASIC LEGAL TRANSACTIONS**
2. DiLorenzo, Vincent
3. WG&L
4. 1985
5. 1 vol.
6. $88
7. annual supp.
8. 1989 - $102; 1991 - $125.25
9. 85-51424/12715229/KF170.D5

1. **BASIC PROBATE**
2. -
3. Indiana CLE
4. 1991
5. 1 vol.
6. $65
7. no supp. planned

1. **BASIC PROBATE**
2. -
3. Okla. Bar CLE
4. 1990
5. 1 vol.
6. $40
7. no supp. planned

1. **BASIC REAL ESTATE PRACTICE, VOL. 1**
2. -
3. Illinois ICLE
4. 1988
5. 1 vol
6. $78.95
7. periodic supp.
8. 1990 - $24.95
9. 17931900/KFI1326.B37

1. **BASIC REAL ESTATE PRACTICE, VOL. 2**
2. -
3. Illinois ICLE
4. 1988
5. 1 vol.
6. $78.95
7. periodic supp.
8. 1990 - $24.95
9. 17931900/KFI1326.B37

1. **BASIC RESIDENTIAL REAL ESTATE CLOSINGS**
2. Real Property Law Section
3. Conn. Bar
4. 1988
5. 1 vol.

6. $20
7. no supp. planned

1. **BASIC TAXATION OF NATURAL RESOURCES**
2. -
3. EMLF
4. 1986
5. 1 vol.
6. $80 - members; $100 - nonmembers
7. no supp. planned

1. **THE BASICS OF BANKRUPTCIES: CHAPTERS 7 AND 13**
2. -
3. Wash. Bar
4. 1988
5. 1 vol.
6. $35
7. no supp. planned

1. **BASICS OF BUSINESS LAW**
2. -
3. Ohio CLE
4. 1989
5. 1 vol.
6. $35
7. no supp. planned

1. **BECOMING EXPERT WITH WORDPERFECT IN YOUR LAW OFFICE**
2. -
3. Indiana CLE
4. 1991
5. 1 vol.
6. $55
7. no supp. planned
9. 24044699/KF318.B43

1. **BENCH BOOK FOR TRIAL JUDGES - NEW YORK**
2. Assn. of Justices of the Supreme Court of the State of New York
3. Lawyers Coop.
4. 1989
5. 1 vol.
6. $94.50 incl. 6 mos. supp.
7. annual supp.
8. 1991 - $39.50
9. 89-63828/21339470/KFN6025.A83

1. **BENDER'S FEDERAL PRACTICE FORMS**
2. Frumer, Louis R. et al.
3. Bender
4. 1951
5. 16 vols.
6. $1225 incl. 3 mos. supp.
7. semiannual supp.
8. 1990 - $1095; 1991 - $953
9. 51-13295/2023669/KF8836.F78

1. **BENDER'S FEDERAL PRACTICE MANUAL**
2. Hall, Irwin & Marvin Waxner
3. Bender
4. 2nd ed. - 1952
5. 2 vols.
6. $225 incl. 3 mos. supp.
7. annual supp.
8. 1990 - $152; 1991 - $255.50
9. 53-835/2302228/KF8816.A2

1. **BENDER'S FEDERAL TAX FORMS**
2. Lorenzo, Virginia
3. Bender
4. 1990
5. 4 vol.
6. $285/yr.; $510 for 2 yrs.
7. periodic supp.
8. renewal - $470/yr.
9. 89-82462/21437724

1. **BENDER'S FEDERAL TAX SERVICE**
2. Various Contributing Authors
3. Bender
4. 1969
5. 20 vols.
6. $900/year - 1 yr. service; $850/yr. - 2 yr. service
7. weekly supp.
9. 89-60825/20167895/KF6285.B445

1. **BENDER'S FLORIDA FORMS OF PLEADING**
2. Maloy, Richard H.W. & W.S. McDuff
3. Bender
4. 1968
5. 14 vols.
6. $840 incl. 3 mos. supp.
7. semiannual supp.
8. 1989 - $865; 1990 - $798.50
9. 68-29161/449244/KFF68.M3

1. **BENDER'S FORMS FOR THE CIVIL PRACTICE**
2. Frumer, Louis R. et al.
3. Bender
4. 1963
5. 33 vols.
6. $1690 incl. 3 mos. supp.

7. semiannual supp.
8. 1989 - $962.50; 1990 - $1597.50
9. 63-5700/2054377/KFN5995.A65B4

1. **BENDER'S FORMS OF DISCOVERY**
2. -
3. Bender
4. 1963
5. 20 vols.
6. $1140 incl. 6 mos. supp.
7. annual supp.
8. 1989 - $778; 1990 - $990.49
9. 63-3100/9258747/KF8900.A3B4

1. **BENDER'S FORMS OF PLEADING**
2. Warren, Oscar L. et al.
3. Bender
4. 1946
5. 22 vols.
6. $1075 incl. 3 mos. supp.
7. annual supp.
8. 1989 - $801; 1990 - $903
9. 46-15490/2015994/KFN6010.A65B4

1. **BENDER'S I.N.S. REGULATION SERVICE**
2. Publ. Ed. Staff
3. Bender
4. 1989
5. 1 vol.
6. $150 incl. 1 yr. service
7. bimonthly supp.
9. 19700472/KF4821.A2

1. **BENDER'S MODERN UCC LITIGATION FORMS (Bender's Uniform Commercial Code Service vols. 4 & 4A)**
2. Betsos, Peter J.
3. Bender
4. 1969
5. 2 vols.
6. $230 incl. 3 mos. supp.
7. annual supp.
8. 1989 - $139; 1990 - $177.50
9. 75-94373/80903/KF885.B4

1. **BENDER'S NEW YORK EVIDENCE - CPLR**
2. Frumer, Louis R. et al.
3. Bender
4. 1962
5. 7 vols.
6. $780 incl. 3 mos. supp.
7. annual supp.
8. 1989 - $520; 1990 - $643.50
9. 62-6515/10851537/KFN6030.A6F7

1. **BENEDICT ON ADMIRALTY, 7TH ED.**
2. Cohen, Michael Marks et al.
3. Bender
4. 7th ed. - 1973
5. 23 vols.
6. $1250 incl. 3 mos. supp.
7. annual supp.
8. 1989 - $853; 1990 - $1058.50
9. 74-77414/4598929/KF1104.B4

1. **BENEFITS AND RETIREMENT PLAN GUIDE**
2. WG&L staff, ed.
3. WG&L
4. 1991
5. 2 vols.
6. $330/yr.
7. monthly supp.

1. **BENEFITS COORDINATOR**
2. WG&L Prof. Ed. Staff
3. WG&L
4. 1989
5. 7 vols.
6. $675/yr.; $625/yr. for 2 yrs.
7. biweekly supp. & newsletter
8. renewal - $575/yr.
9. 19924025/KF3512.A6R42

1. **BENEFITS REVIEW BOARD - BLACK LUNG REPORTER**
2. -
3. Bender
4. 1981
5. 3 vols.
6. $575 incl. 1 yr. supp.
7. biweekly supp.
8. renewal - $500/yr.
9. 74-29408

1. **BENEFITS REVIEW BOARD - LONGSHORE REPORTER**
2. -
3. Bender
4. 1974
5. 3 vols.
6. $595 incl. 1 yr. supp.
7. biweekly supp.
8. renewal - $500/yr.
9. 74-29408/1363588/KF3613.4.B45

1. **BERGMAN ON NEW YORK MORTGAGE FORECLOSURES**
2. Bergman, Bruce

3. Bender
4. 1990
5. 2 vols.
6. $210 incl. 3 mos. supp.
7. annual supp.
8. no supp. yet
9. 90-0/23752834/KFN5177.F6B47

1. **BERNACCHI ON COMPUTER LAW - A GUIDE TO THE LEGAL AND MANAGEMENT ASPECTS OF COMPUTER TECHNOLOGY**
2. Bernacchi, Richard L. et al.
3. Little, Brown
4. 1986
5. 2 vols.
6. $195
7. periodic supp.
8. 1989 - $69.50; 1991 - $60
9. 85-81394/14055827/KF946.B47

1. **BETTER, EARLIER SETTLEMENTS THROUGH ECONOMIC LEVERAGE**
2. Hermann, Philip J.
3. Jury Verdict Research, Inc.
4. 1989
5. 2 vols.
6. $290 incl. 1 yr. supp.
7. supp. as needed
9. 90-117106//r90/20486063/KF1257.H38

1. **BILINGUAL DICTIONARY OF CRIMINAL JUSTICE TERMS (ENGLISH/SPANISH)**
2. Benmaman, V. et al.
3. Gould
4. 1991
5. 1 vol.
6. $17.95
7. periodic supp.
9. 23867172/K52.S6B45

1. **BILLS OF PARTICULARS IN NEW YORK**
2. Leventhal, Howard G.
3. Lawyers Coop.
4. rev. - 1990
5. 2 vols.
6. $180 incl. 6 mos. supp.
7. annual supp.
8. 1991 - $38
9. 90-2335/21972052/KFN6021.B5G74

1. **BIOLAW**
2. Childress, James F. et al., eds.
3. UPA
4. 1986
5. 2 vols.
6. $350/yr.
7. monthly supp.
9. 9417670/KF3821.A6B56

1. **BIOTECHNOLOGY AND THE LAW**
2. Cooper, Iver P.
3. Clark Boardman Callaghan
4. 1982
5. 2 vols.
6. $225 incl. 3 mos. supp.
7. annual supp.
8. 1989 - $49.50; 1991 - $139
9. 82-12957/8669230/K1519.M5C66

1. **BIRTH LAW/ADOPTION**
2. -
3. NH Bar
4. 1988
5. 1 vol.
6. $35
7. no supp. planned

1. **BLACK'S TEXAS EVIDENCE**
2. Black, Thomas
3. Lawyers Coop.
4. 1985
5. 2 vols.
6. $165 incl. 6 mos. supp.
7. annual supp.
8. 1990 - $55; 1991 - $51.50
9. 85-393/11728241/KFT1740.B58

1. **BLETZACKER'S OBBC STUDY GUIDE**
2. Bletzacker, Richard W.
3. Banks
4. 2nd ed. - 1990
5. 1 vol.
6. $60 incl. 9 mos. supp.
7. periodic supp.
9. 85-233026/12566744/KFO459.A1B55

1. **BLUE SKY COMPLIANCE MANUAL**
2. Palmer, Bobby G., Jr.
3. Butterworth-NH
4. 1987
5. 1 vol.
6. $75
7. annual supp.
8. 1990 - $50
9. 1695988/KF1440.Z95P34

1. **BLUE SKY GUIDE**
2. -
3. ICI

4. 1981
5. 2 vols.
6. $600 incl. 1 yr. supp.
7. 3 supp./yr.
8. renewal - $300/yr.
9. 10204625/KF1435.B58

1. **BLUE SKY LAW (Securities Law Series; Vol. 12 & 12A)**
2. Long, Joseph C.
3. Clark Boardman Callaghan
4. 1985
5. 2 vols.
6. $215 incl. 3 mos. supp.
7. annual supp.
8. 1989 - $124.50; 1991 - $165
9. 85-11377/12103740/KF1070.Z95L66

1. **BLUE SKY LAW REPORTS**
2. -
3. CCH
4. 1928
5. 4 vols.
6. $775/yr.; $705/yr. for 2 yrs.
7. semimonthly supp.
9. 47-2581/1564311

1. **BLUE SKY REGULATIONS (Business Organiz. vols. 11c, pt. 1 & 2)**
2. Sowards, H. L. & N. Hirsch
3. Bender
4. 1977
5. 4 vols.
6. $510 incl. 3 mos. supp.
7. supp. as needed
8. 1989 - $460; 1990 - $485.50
9. 77-365432/3273572/KF1440.Z95S69

1. **BNA ADMINISTRATIVE PRACTICE MANUAL**
2. Cottine, Bertram R.
3. BNA Books
4. 1988
5. 1 vol.
6. $275
7. periodic supp.
8. 1991 - $125
9. 18481188

1. **BNA CIVIL TRIAL MANUAL**
2. Robbins, Robert A.
3. BNA
4. 1985
5. 2 vols.
6. $540/yr.; $486/yr. for 2 yrs.
7. biweekly supp.
9. 11693065/KF8915.B63

1. **BNA CRIMINAL PRACTICE MANUAL**
2. Mroczka, Judith C.
3. BNA
4. 1987
5. 3 vols.
6. $460/yr.
7. biweekly supp.
8. renewal - $410/yr.
9. 15129066/KF9615.B59

1. **BNA PENSION REPORTER**
2. Sayre, David A.
3. BNA
4. 1974
5. 3 vols.
6. $661/yr.
7. weekly supp. & reports
8. renewal - $622/yr.
9. 75-640924//r85/2153735/HD7106.U15B78a

1. **BNA POLICY AND PRACTICE SERIES**
2. Manville, Bill L.
3. BNA
4. 1946
5. 12 vols.
6. $1065/yr.
7. weekly supp. and newsletters
8. renewal - $1,028/yr.
9. sf79-10252/3463998/HD4802.B952

1. **BNA'S PATENT, TRADEMARK & COPYRIGHT JOURNAL**
2. Samuels, Jeffrey M.
3. BNA
4. 1970
5. 2 vols.
6. $880/yr.
7. weekly supp.
8. renewal - $850/yr.
9. 84-42909/2037246/K2.N38

1. **BOARD OF CONTRACT APPEALS BID PROTEST DECISIONS**
2. -
3. Fed. Publ.
4. 1988
5. 1 vol.
6. $452/yr.
7. monthly supp.
9. 17971375/KF846.A2U5

1. **BOHANNON'S NEW MEXICO ENVIRONMENTAL LAW HANDBOOK**
2. Bohannon, Paul M.
3. Butterworth-Texas
4. 1990
5. 1 vol.
6. $95
7. periodic supp.
8. no supp. yet
9. 90-37617/21560979/KFN3954.B64

1. **BOSTON STOCK EXCHANGE GUIDE**
2. -
3. CCH
4. 1970
5. 1 vol.
6. $275/yr.; $250/yr. for 2 yrs.
7. monthly supp.
9. 75-26412/151746/HG5131.B7A5

1. **THE BRAHM COURT INDEX**
2. Brahm, Robert T.
3. Longshore
4. 1988
5. 1 vol.
6. $395 incl. 1 yr. supp.
7. quarterly supp.
8. renewal - $135/yr.

1. **BRÉGY: SELECTED SECTIONS OF PENNSYLVANIA PROBATE, ESTATES AND FIDUCIARIES CODE**
2. Fahrner, K.A. et al.
3. Bisel
4. 1991
5. 1 vol.
6. $89.50 incl. 3 mos. supp.
7. annual supp.
8. no supp. yet
9. 90-84168

1. **BRITISH COLUMBIA CORPORATIONS LAW GUIDE**
2. -
3. CCH
4. 1974
5. 1 vol.
6. $390/yr.; $355/yr. for 2 yrs.
7. monthly supp.
9. 12679119/KEB312.5.B75

1. **BRITISH COLUMBIA REAL ESTATE LAW GUIDE**
2. -
3. CCH
4. 1979
5. 1 vol.
6. $390/yr.; $355/yr. for 2 yrs.
7. monthly supp.

1. **BRITISH COLUMBIA TAX REPORTER**
2. -
3. CCH
4. 1969
5. 1 vol.
6. $250/yr.; $225/yr. for 2 yrs.
7. monthly supp.
9. 75-3525

1. **BRITISH TAX CASES**
2. -
3. CCH
4. 1982
5. 1 vol.
6. $370/yr.; $335/yr. for 2 yrs.
7. semimonthly supp.
9. 83-109488/10457436/KD5355.B74

1. **BRITISH TAX GUIDE**
2. -
3. CCH
4. 1963
5. 2 vols.
6. $560/yr.; $510/yr. for 2 yrs.
7. semimonthly supp.
9. 4401712

1. **BRITISH TAX LEGISLATION**
2. -
3. CCH
4. 1982
5. 3 vols.
6. $395/yr.; $360/yr. for 2 yrs.
7. semimonthly supp.
9. 9241214/KD5359.B77

1. **BROADCAST RULES SERVICE**
2. Emeritz, Robert E. et al.
3. P&F
4. 1986
5. 1 vol.
6. $340
7. bimonthly supp.
8. $248/yr.; $480/2 yrs.
9. 15364443/KF2763.4.P54

1. **BROKER-DEALER REGULATION (Securities Law Series, Vol. 15)**
2. Lipton, David A.
3. Clark Boardman Callaghan

4. 1988
5. 1 vol
6. $125 incl. 3 mos. supp.
7. annual supp.
8. 1989 - $45; 1991 - $62.50
9. 88-14553/17918078/KF1071.L57

1. **BROMBERG AND RIBSTEIN ON PARTNERSHIP**
2. Bromberg, Alan R. & Larry E.
3. Little, Brown
4. 1988
5. 2 vols. (& 1 forthcoming 6/92)
6. $195
7. annual supp.
8. 1990 - $59.50; 1991 - $70
9. 87-82663/18139435/KF1375.B7

1. **BUSINESS AND COMMERCIAL LITIGATION**
2. -
3. Illinois ICLE
4. 1988
5. 1 vol.
6. $91.95
7. periodic supp.
8. 1990 - $24.95

1. **BUSINESS, BANKS, BORROWERS & THE ENVIRONMENT**
2. -
3. Indiana CLE
4. 1991
5. 1 vol.
6. $60
7. no supp. planned

1. **BUSINESS BUY-SELL AGREEMENTS**
2. Howell, Weldon C. et al.
3. Calif. CEB
4. 1991
5. 1 vol. with forms disk
6. $110
7. periodic supp.
8. no supp. yet

1. **BUSINESS CRIME**
2. Arkin, Stanley S. et al.
3. Bender
4. 1981
5. 7 vols.
6. $650 incl. 3 mos. supp.
7. semiannual supp.
8. 1989 - $464; 1990 - $566
9. 80-70544/12707861/KF9350.B87

1. **BUSINESS FORMS FROM ALI-ABA COURSE MATERIALS**
2. -
3. ALI-ABA
4. 1991
5. 1 vol.
6. $100
7. periodic supp.
8. no supp. yet

1. **BUSINESS FRANCHISE GUIDE**
2. -
3. CCH
4. 1980
5. 2 vols.
6. $590/yr.; $535/yr. for 2 yrs.
7. monthly supp.
9. 80-114055/6182787/KF2023.A6C65

1. **BUSINESS IN CZECHOSLOVAKIA: A PRIMER AND OVERVIEW**
2. Barbanel, Jack A. & Lynda L. Maillet
3. Transnational Juris Publications
4. 1991
5. 1 vol.
6. $125
7. periodic supp.
8. no supp. yet

1. **BUSINESS IN HUNGARY: A PRIMER AND OVERVIEW**
2. Barbanel, Jack A. & Lynda L. Maillet
3. Transnational Juris Publications
4. 1991
5. 1 vol.
6. $125
7. periodic supp.
8. no supp. yet

1. **BUSINESS IN POLAND: A PRIMER AND OVERVIEW**
2. Barbanel, Jack A. & Lynda L. Maillet
3. Transnational Juris Publications
4. 1991
5. 1 vol.
6. $125
7. periodic supp.
8. no supp. yet

1. **BUSINESS IN THE SOVIET UNION: A PRIMER AND OVERVIEW**
2. Barbanel, Jack A. & Lynda L. Maillet
3. Transnational Juris Publications
4. 1991
5. 1 vol.

6. $125
7. periodic supp.
8. no supp. yet
9. 91-50747/24627350/KLA920.B37

1. **BUSINESS IN YUGOSLAVIA: A PRIMER AND OVERVIEW**
2. Barbanel, Jack A. & Lynda L. Maillet
3. Transnational Juris Publications
4. 1991
5. 1 vol.
6. $125
7. periodic supp.
8. no supp. yet

1. **BUSINESS INSURANCE LAW & PRACTICE GUIDE**
2. Various Contributing Authors
3. Bender
4. 1989
5. 3 vols.
6. $315 incl. 3 mos. supp.
7. annual supp.
8. 1990 - $53.50
9. 89-60890/22527245/KF1137.B76

1. **BUSINESS INTERESTS IN ESTATES**
2. -
3. Illinois ICLE
4. 1988
5. 1 vol.
6. $104.95
7. periodic supp.
8. 1990 - $15.95
9. 17888007/KFI1340.B8

1. **THE BUSINESS JUDGMENT RULE**
2. Block, Dennis J. et al.
3. Prentice Hall Law & Business
4. 3rd ed. - 1989
5. 1 vol.
6. $125 incl. 4 mos. supp.
7. periodic supp.
8. 1990 - $75; 1991 - $125
9. 89-22959/20320028/KF1423.B585

1. **BUSINESS LAW IN EUROPE**
2. Storm, Paul & Maarten Ellis
3. Kluwer
4. 1990
5. 1 vol.
6. $174 incl. 3 mos. supp.
7. periodic supp.
9. 22301902/KJE2061.B8

1. **BUSINESS LAW MONOGRAPHS**
2. Indiv. authors for each monograph
3. Bender
4. 1984
5. 31 vols.
6. $725 incl. 1 yr. supp.
7. periodic supp. and rev.
8. renewal - 1989 - $580
9. 84-71102/11423996/KF1414.A1B8

1. **BUSINESS LITIGATION: CURRENT ISSUES**
2. -
3. NH Bar
4. 1991
5. 1 vol.
6. $35
7. no supp. planned

1. **BUSINESS LITIGATION IN FLORIDA**
2. -
3. Florida Bar
4. 1989
5. 1 vol.
6. $65
7. supp. as needed
8. no supp. yet
9. 89-83636/20067169/KFF207.B87

1. **BUSINESS LITIGATORS INSURANCE GUIDE**
2. Cotkin, Ralph & Bruce Friedman
3. Parker
4. 1992
5. 1 vol.
6. price NA
7. annual supp.
8. no supp. yet

1. **THE BUSINESS OF LAW - A HANDBOOK ON HOW TO MANAGE LAW FIRMS**
2. Smith, Larry
3. Prentice Hall Law & Business
4. 2nd ed. - 1990
5. 1 vol.
6. $75 incl. 4 mos. supp.
7. annual supp.
8. 1991 - $60
9. 84-11258/10799659/KF318.C67

1. **BUSINESS ORGANIZATIONS WITH TAX PLANNING**
2. Cavitch, Zolman

3. Bender
4. 1963
5. 16 vols.
6. $1330 incl. 6 mos. supp.
7. quarterly supp.
8. 1989 - $1125; 1990 - $1206.50
9. 70-11868/73475/KF1366.C3

1. **BUSINESS STRATEGIES**
2. -
3. CCH
4. 1983
5. 4 vols. (1 vol. newsletter)
6. $595/yr.; $540/yr. for 2 yrs.
7. semimonthly supp.

1. **BUSINESS, TAX & ESTATE PLANNING FOR THE CLOSELY-HELD BUSINESS**
2. Abell, W. Shepherdson et al.
3. MICPEL
4. 1991
5. 1 vol.
6. $42
7. no supp. planned
9. 24236015/KF750.E87

1. **THE BUSINESS TORT OF FRAUD AND MISREPRESENTATION**
2. Freedman, Warren
3. Butterworth-NH
4. 1989
5. 2 vols.
6. $180
7. annual supp.
8. 1990 - $75; 1991 - $75
9. 88-26199/18412446/KF1271.F74

1. **BUSINESS TORTS**
2. -
3. Maine Bar
4. 1990
5. 1 vol.
6. $35
7. no supp. planned

1. **BUSINESS TORTS**
2. Zamore, J.
3. Bender
4. 1989
5. 4 vols.
6. $420 incl. 3 mos. supp.
7. annual supp.
8. 1990 - $70
9. 88-64072/19582303/KF3195.B87

1. **BUSINESS TRANSACTIONS: TAX PLANNING AND ANALYSIS**
2. RIA prof. editorial staff
3. RIA
4. 1991
5. 7 vols.
6. $735/yr.; $700/yr. for 2 yrs.
7. biweekly supp.
8. renewal - $665/yr.
9. KF6464.B885

1. **BUSINESS TRANSACTIONS IN GERMANY (FRG)**
2. Ruster, Bernd, ed.
3. Bender
4. 1983
5. 4 vols.
6. $380 incl. 3 mos. supp.
7. periodic supp.
8. 1989 - $87; 1990 - $127.50
9. 82-73188/9428790/KK2057.B87

1. **BUSINESS VENTURES IN EASTERN EUROPE AND THE SOVIET UNION: THE EMERGING LEGAL FRAMEWORK FOR FOREIGN INVESTMENT**
2. Birenbaum, David E. & Dimitri P. Racklin
3. Prentice Hall Law & Business
4. 1991
5. 2 vols.
6. $170 incl. 4 mos. supp.
7. periodic supp.
8. no supp. yet
9. 91-17630/23690021/KJC6433.B57

1. **BUYING AND SELLING A BUSINESS**
2. -
3. Penn. Bar
4. 1990
5. 1 vol.
6. $65
7. no supp. planned

1. **BUYING AND SELLING BUSINESSES**
2. -
3. Illinois ICLE
4. 1987
5. 1 vol.
6. $97.95
7. periodic supp.
8. 1990 - $24.95
9. 8462801/KFI1415.S3B99x

1. **BY-LAWS AND RULES OF THE CINCINNATI STOCK EXCHANGE**
2. -
3. Cincinnati
4. 1980
5. 1 vol.
6. $100 incl. supp.
7. periodic supp.

1. **CABLE TELEVISION: HANDBOOK AND FORMS**
2. Stein, Ira C.
3. Shepard's
4. 1985
5. 1 vol.
6. $95
7. annual supp.
8. no supp. yet
9. 85-26157/12804721/KF2844.S74

1. **CABLE TELEVISION AND OTHER NONBROADCAST VIDEO**
2. Brenner, Daniel L., and Monroe E. Price
3. Clark Boardman Callaghan
4. 1986
5. 1 vol.
6. $125 incl. 3 mos. supp.
7. annual supp.
8. 1989 - $55; 1991 - $67.50
9. 85-30946/13004536/KF2844.B74

1. **CABLE TELEVISION LAW: A VIDEO COMMUNICATIONS PRACTICE GUIDE**
2. Ferris, Charles D.
3. Bender
4. 1983
5. 3 vols.
6. $345 incl. 3 mos. supp.
7. biannual supp.
8. 1989 - $225; 1990 - $276.50
9. 83-71589/10191830/KF2844.F47

1. **CABLE TV RULES SERVICE**
2. Emeritz, Robert E. & Jeff Tobias
3. P&F
4. 1990
5. 1 vol.
6. $190 incl. 1 yr. supp.
7. bimonthly supp.
8. renewal - $145/yr.; $270/2 yrs.

1. **CAL-OSHA REPORTER**
2. Bell, Anne, ed.
3. Sten-O-Press
4. 1973
5. 1 vol.
6. $185/yr.
7. weekly supp.

1. **CALIFORNIA ARBITRATION HANDBOOK**
2. Niles, Edward I.
3. Parker
4. 1992
5. 1 vol.
6. price NA
7. annual supp.
8. no supp. yet

1. **CALIFORNIA ARBITRATION PRACTICE GUIDE 2D**
2. Toker, John
3. Lawpress
4. 1987
5. 1 vol.
6. $85
7. annual supp.
8. 1990 - $65.50; 1991 - $67.50
9. 87-405348/16922343/KFC1094.T64

1. **CALIFORNIA ATTORNEY PRACTICE**
2. Yen, Mary & Tom Lowe
3. Bender
4. 1986
5. 3 vols.
6. $350 incl. 3 mos. supp.
7. periodic supp.
8. 1989 - $85; 1990 - $135
9. 86-71994/14944623/KF300.C28

1. **CALIFORNIA CIVIL ACTIONS - PLEADING AND PRACTICE**
2. K. Arnold & Publisher's Editorial Staff
3. Bender
4. 1983
5. 5 vols.
6. $475 incl. 3 mos. supp.
7. periodic supp.
8. 1989 - $224; 1990 - $280
9. 83-070207/9946495/KFC1010.A97

1. **CALIFORNIA CIVIL LITIGATION FORMS MANUAL**
2. -
3. Calif. CEB
4. 1980
5. 2 vols.
6. $80

7. periodic supp.
8. 1989 - $20; 1990 - $28
9. 80-65241/6603088/KFC1020.A65C34

1. **CALIFORNIA CIVIL PROCEDURE BEFORE TRIAL**
2. -
3. Calif. CEB
4. 3rd ed. - 1990
5. 3 vols.
6. $195
7. periodic supp.
8. no supp. yet
9. 90-81348/22420457

1. **CALIFORNIA CIVIL TRIALBOOK**
2. Wharton, Richard et al.
3. West
4. 1990
5. 1 vol.
6. $65
7. periodic supp.
8. no supp. yet
9. 90-70912/22909556/KFC1025.Z9W48

1. **CALIFORNIA CLOSELY HELD CORPORATIONS**
2. Wood, Robert W., ed.
3. Bender
4. 1987
5. 1 vol.
6. $300 incl. 3 mos. supp.
7. periodic supp.
8. 1989 - $165; 1990 - $224.50
9. 87-72366/17504366/KFC875.C35

1. **CALIFORNIA COMMISSION OF CORPORATIONS OFFICIAL OPINIONS**
2. -
3. Calif. CEB
4. 1969
5. 13 vols.
6. $70/yr. (vols. avail. back to 1969 - $312)
7. periodic supp.

1. **CALIFORNIA COMMUNITY PROPERTY WITH TAX ANALYSIS**
2. Stein, Joseph J. and Jack Zuckerman
3. Bender
4. 1985
5. 1 vol.
6. $115 incl. 3 mos. supp.
7. periodic supp.
8. 1989 - $48; 1990 - $57
9. 85-71220/12271150/KFC125.C6C35

1. **CALIFORNIA COMPENDIUM ON PROFESSIONAL RESPONSIBILITY**
2. Vapnek, Paul W. ed.
3. State Bar of Calif.
4. 1983
5. 3 vols.
6. $157
7. annual supp.
8. renewal - $40/yr.
9. 83-181138/10019707/KFC76.5.A2C34

1. **CALIFORNIA COMPLEX LITIGATION**
2. Greer, Michael et al.
3. Parker
4. 1991
5. 1 vol.
6. $90
7. supp. as needed
8. no supp. yet

1. **CALIFORNIA CONSERVATORSHIPS AND GUARDIANSHIPS**
2. Johnstone, William S. & Susan T. House
3. Calif. CEB
4. 1990
5. 2 vols.
6. $145
7. periodic supp.
8. 1991 - price NA
9 90-80562/21731266/KFC112.J6

1. **CALIFORNIA CONSUMER CREDIT LAW & REGULATIONS**
2. Gold, Kathi, ed.
3. NILS
4. 1986
5. 1 vol.
6. $95 incl. 3 mos. supp.
7. annual supp.
8. 1989 - $75; 1990 - $75
9. 86-60779/19877251/KFC262.A36C6

1. **CALIFORNIA CORPORATE PRACTICE GUIDE 2D**
2. King, Morgan I.
3. Lawpress
4. 1985
5. 1 vol.
6. $85
7. annual supp.
8. 1989 - $75
9. 82-84615/9148192/KFC345.K56

1. **CALIFORNIA CORPORATE SECURITIES LAW NOTEBOOK**

2. -
3. Calif. CEB
4. 1973
5. 1 vol.
6. $50
7. periodic supp.
8. $30/yr.
9. 73-620159/858603/KFC350.C34

1. **CALIFORNIA CORPORATE SECURITIES LAW OF 1968**
2. Marsh, Harold W., Jr. & Robert Volk
3. Bender
4. 1977
5. 3 vols.
6. $350 incl. 6 mos. supp.
7. annual supp.
8. 1989 - $153; 1990 - $201.50
9. 74-16853

1. **CALIFORNIA COURTROOM EVIDENCE**
2. Haight, Fulton & Joseph Cotchett
3. Parker
4. rev. 3rd ed. - 1988
5. 1 vol.
6. $85 incl. 3 mos. supp.
7. annual supp.
8. 1989 - $30.75; 1990 - $31.50
9. 88-61607/19670444/KFC1030.A333C67

1. **CALIFORNIA CRIMINAL DEFENSE PRACTICE**
2. Publishers Ed. Staff Directed by P. Sallander
3. Bender
4. 1981
5. 6 vols.
6. $710 incl. 3 mos. supp.
7. periodic supp. & monthly newsletter
8. 1988 - $323; 1989 - $403; 1990 - $501
9. 81-155422/7877500/KFC1155.C342

1. **CALIFORNIA CRIMINAL TRIALBOOK**
2. Caldwell, Harry et al.
3. West
4. 1990
5. 1 vol.
6. $77.50
7. periodic supp.
8. no supp. yet
9. 89-52022/21904028/KFC1162.C35

1. **CALIFORNIA DAMAGES: LAW AND PROOF**
2. Johns, Leland
3. Parker
4. 4th ed. - 1990
5. 1 vol.
6. $85 incl. 6 mos. supp.
7. annual supp.
8. 1991 - price NA
9. 85-61141/12212229/KFC100.D3J6

1. **CALIFORNIA DECEDENT ESTATE PRACTICE**
2. Norman, William A. et al.
3. Calif. CEB
4. 1986
5. 3 vols.
6. Vol. I & II - $150; Vol. III - $95
7. annual supp.
8. Vols. I & II: 1989 - $55; 1990 - $60
Vol. III: 1989 - $40; 1990 - $45
9. 86-70193//r872/13541795/KFC210.C356

1. **CALIFORNIA DEPOSITION AND DISCOVERY PRACTICE**
2. DeMeo, J.N. et al.
3. Bender
4. rev. ed. - 1971
5. 3 vols.
6. $350 incl. 3 mos. supp.
7. annual supp.
8. 1989 - $116; 1990 - $149
9. 18805889/KFC1020.D41

1. **CALIFORNIA DEPOSITIONS**
2. Branton, James L. & James D. Lovett
3. Knowles
4. 1984
5. 2 vols.
6. $185 incl. 3 mos. supp.
7. annual supp.
8. 1988 - $55; 1990 - $41
9. 12196408/KFC1020.B7

1. **CALIFORNIA DRUNK DRIVING DEFENSE**
2. Taylor, Lawrence
3. Lawyers Coop.
4. 1988
5. 1 vol.
6. $90 incl. 6 mos. supp.
7. annual supp.
8. 1989 - $30
9. 88-19301/18136818/KFC477.T39

1. **CALIFORNIA DRUNK DRIVING LAW**
2. Kuwatch, Ed
3. Fast Eddie
4. 1991

5. 1 vol.
6. $115 incl. 4 mos. supps., & 2 supps.
7. quarterly supp.
8. 1989 - $125.75; 1990 - $135.75
9. 87-80136/16003989/KFC477.Z9K89

1. **CALIFORNIA ELIGIBLE SECURITIES LIST**
2. -
3. CCH
4. 1971
5. 1 vol.
6. $205/yr.
7. weekly supp.
9. 11766621

1. **CALIFORNIA EMPLOYERS GUIDE TO EMPLOYEE HANDBOOKS & PERSONNEL POLICY MANUALS**
2. Labor Law Dept. - Morrison and Foerster, San Francisco, CA.
3. Bender
4. 1989
5. 1 vol.
6. $95 incl. 3 mos. supp.
7. annual supp.
8. 1990 - $32; 1991 - $45
9. 19705227/KFC556.C35

1. **CALIFORNIA EMPLOYMENT LAW**
2. Wilcox, Kirby
3. Bender
4. 1989
5. 4 vols.
6. $425 incl. 3 mos. supp.
7. annual supp.
8. 1990 - $145
9. 88-64017/19578906/KFC556.C35

1. **CALIFORNIA EMPLOYMENT LAW: A GUIDE TO CALIFORNIA LAWS REGULATING EMPLOYMENT IN THE PRIVATE SECTOR**
2. Emanuel, William J. & Michael L. Wolfram
3. M & M Resources
4. 1989
5. 2 vols.
6. $235
7. annual supp.
9. 90-115511/20644939/KFC570.E47

1. **CALIFORNIA ENVIRONMENTAL LAW & LAND USE PRACTICE**
2. Various Contributing Authors
3. Bender
4. 1989
5. 4 vols.
6. $425 incl. 3 mos. supp.
7. semiannual supp.
8. 1990 - $91
9. 89-81038//r90/20734408/KFC610.C348

1. **CALIFORNIA EXPERT WITNESS GUIDE, 2nd ed.**
2. Kennedy, Raoul D. & James C. Martin
3. Calif. CEB
4. 1991
5. 1 vol.
6. $90
7. periodic supp.
8. no supp. yet
9. 91-71424/24034460/KFC1042.K46

1. **CALIFORNIA FAMILY LAW PRACTICE**
2. Adams, Stephen & Nancy Sevitch
3. CFLR
4. 1980
5. 2 vols.
6. $273.13
7. 3 supp./yr.
8. 1990 - $237; 1991 - $263
9. 13623211/KFC115.A32

1. **CALIFORNIA FAMILY LAW - PRACTICE AND PROCEDURE**
2. Markey, Hon. Christian E. Jr., ed.
3. Bender
4. 1978
5. 7 vols.
6. $610 incl. 3 mos. supp.
7. annual supp.
8. 1989 - $397; 1990 - $486.50
9. 78-70343/4715516/KFC115.A6C3

1. **CALIFORNIA FAMILY TAX PLANNING**
2. Rice, Ralph S. & Terence R. Rice
3. Bender
4. 2nd ed. - 1966
5. 2 vols.
6. $215 incl. 3 mos. supp.
7. annual supp.
8. 1989 - $99.50; 1990 - $119.50
9. 67-30351/900495/KFC861.R52

1. **CALIFORNIA FORECLOSURE: LAW AND PRACTICE**
2. Sheneman, Margaret
3. Shepard's
4. 1991
5. 1 vol.
6. $95

7. annual supp.
8. no supp. yet
9. 91-8972/21377619/KFC177.F6S53

1. **CALIFORNIA FORMS OF JURY INSTRUCTION**
2. Wells, John F.
3. Bender
4. 1985
5. 4 vols.
6. $400 incl. 3 mos. supp.
7. periodic supp.
8. 1989 - $177.50; 1990 - $228
9. 84-73086/12418229/KFC1047.A65W45

1. **CALIFORNIA FORMS OF PLEADING AND PRACTICE-ANNOTATED**
2. -
3. Bender
4. 1962
5. 52 vols.
6. $2500 incl. 3 mos. supp.
7. quarterly supp.; $966
8. 1989 - $1487; 1990 - $1944.50
9. 62-52786/5454954/KFC1010.A65C15

1. **CALIFORNIA INSURANCE DISPUTES**
2. Clifford, Robert C.
3. Parker
4. 1991
5. 1 vol.
6. $90 incl. 3 mos. supp.
7. annual supp.
9. 91-62069/24624956/KFC290.C55

1. **CALIFORNIA INSURANCE LAW & PRACTICE**
2. Syril, P.H. et al.
3. Bender
4. 1986
5. 4 vols.
6. $450 incl. 3 mos. supp.
7. periodic supp.
8. 1989 - $177.50; 1990 - $266
9. 86-71788/15052861/KFC290.C35

1. **CALIFORNIA JUDICIAL COUNCIL FORMS MANUAL**
2. -
3. Calif. CEB
4. 1981
5. 2 vols.
6. $80
7. periodic supp.
8. $30/yr.
9. 81-65171/7530916/KFC995.A65C34

1. **CALIFORNIA JURY INSTRUCTIONS - CIVIL (BAJI)**
2. Committee on Standard Jury Instructions Civil, of Superior Court of Los Angeles County
3. West
4. 1989
5. 2 vols.
6. $135
7. supp. 3x/yr.
8. 1990 - $55.50; 1991 - $19

1. **CALIFORNIA JURY INSTRUCTIONS - CRIMINAL (CALJIC)**
2. Committee on Standard Jury Instructions Criminal, of Superior Court of Los Angeles County
3. West
4. 1989
5. 2 vols.
6. $145
7. supp. 3x/yr.
8. 1990 - $80; 1991 - $31

1. **CALIFORNIA LAND USE PROCEDURE**
2. Ramos, J.R.
3. Shepard's
4. 1991
5. 2 vols.
6. $150
7. annual supp.
8. no supp. yet
9. 91-27020/24107861/KFC810.A65R36

1. **CALIFORNIA LAW OF EMPLOYEE INJURIES AND WORKMEN'S COMPENSATION**
2. Hanna, Warren L.
3. Bender
4. 2nd ed. - 1966
5. 4 vols.
6. $410 incl. 3 mos. supp.
7. annual supp.
8. 1989 - $240; 1990 - $297
9. 68-2549/431248/KFC592.H32

1. **CALIFORNIA LEGAL FILING DIRECTORY**
2. Britton, Patricia A.
3. Shepard's
4. 1988
5. 1 vols.
6. $60

7. annual supp.
8. 1989 - $32; 1990 - $36
9. 88-31776/18742965/KFC77.B757

1. **CALIFORNIA LEGAL FORMS - TRANSACTION GUIDE**
2. Badger, Don J. et al.
3. Bender
4. 1968
5. 29 vols.
6. $1900 incl. 3 mos. supp.
7. biannual supp.
8. 1989 - $1278; 1990 - $1577
9. 68-8572/5454980/KFC68.C36

1. **CALIFORNIA LEGAL SECRETARY**
2. Hazlewood, Marlene
3. James
4. 1986
5. 1 vol.
6. $69.99 incl. 3 mos. supp.
7. annual supp.
8. 1990 - $42.21; 1991 - $44.29
9. 14773280

1. **CALIFORNIA LIABILITY INSURANCE PRACTICE: CLAIMS AND LITIGATION**
2. -
3. Calif. CEB
4. 1991
5. 2 vols.
6. $160
7. periodic supp.
9. 90-84639/23113345/KFC297.C35

1. **CALIFORNIA MARITAL TERMINATION AGREEMENTS**
2. Richmond, Diana
3. Calif. CEB
4. 1988
5. 1 vol.
6. $100
7. periodic supp.
8. 1990 - $20; 1991 - $36
9. 88-70540/18113448/KFC126.R54

1. **CALIFORNIA MECHANICS' LIEN LAW AND CONSTRUCTION INDUSTRY PRACTICE**
2. Marsh, Matthew E.
3. Parker
4. 5th ed. - 1990
5. 1 vol.
6. $80 incl. 3 mos. supp.
7. annual supp.
8. no supp. yet
9. 90-61737/22221296/KFC229.M3

1. **CALIFORNIA MEDI-CAL GUIDE**
2. -
3. CCH
4. 1988
5. 1 vol.
6. $200/yr.; $180 for 2 yrs.
7. monthly supp.

1. **CALIFORNIA PARALEGAL'S GUIDE**
2. Mack, Zella
3. Parker
4. 3rd ed. - 1987
5. 2 vols.
6. $95 incl. 3 mos. supp.
7. annual supp.
8. 1990 - $36.50; 1991 - $31
9. 15996608/KFC77.M3

1. **CALIFORNIA PERSONAL INJURY FORMS**
2. Randall, James Grafton
3. Lawyers Coop.
4. 1987
5. 2 vols.
6. $130 incl. 6 mos. supp.
7. annual supp.
8. 1988-$37.50; 1989 - $39
9. Z77-71561/18146447/KFC77.M3

1. **CALIFORNIA PLEADING AND PRACTICE FORMS**
2. Weissman, Barry Leigh
3. Lawyers Coop.
4. 1986
5. 2 vols.
6. $160 incl. 6 mos. supp.
7. annual supp.
8. 1988-$39; 1989 - $41
9. 86-31036//r88/14906005/KFC1010.A65W45

1. **CALIFORNIA POINTS AND AUTHORITIES**
2. Sallander, Pamela et al.
3. Bender
4. 1965
5. 23 vols.
6. $1190 incl. 3 mos. supp.
7. periodic supp.
8. 1989 - $859; 1990 - $1577
9. 65-3994/10877559/KFC1010.C34

1. **CALIFORNIA PRACTICE GUIDE - BAD FAITH**
2. Kornblum, Guy et al.
3. Rutter
4. 1986
5. 1 vol.
6. $132 incl. 3 mos. supp.
7. annual supp.
8. 1990 - $42
9. 14225519

1. **CALIFORNIA PRACTICE GUIDE - CIVIL APPEALS AND WRITS**
2. Eisenberg, Jon et al.
3. Rutter
4. 1989
5. 2 vols.
6. $175 incl. 3 mos. supp.
7. annual supp.
8. 1990 - $72; 1991 - $77
9. 20518170/KFC1075.E47

1. **CALIFORNIA PRACTICE GUIDE - CIVIL PROCEDURE BEFORE TRIAL**
2. Weil, Judge Robert I. & Judge Ira A. Brown
3. Rutter
4. 1983
5. 3 vols.
6. $220 incl. 3 mos. supp.
7. annual supp.
8. 1990 - $98; 1991 - $98.50
9. 9143209/KFC995.W4

1. **CALIFORNIA PRACTICE GUIDE - CORPORATIONS**
2. Friedman, C. Hugh
3. Rutter
4. 1984
5. 2 vols.
6. $175 incl. 3 mos. supp.
7. annual supp.
8. 1990 - $59; 1991 - $77
9. 11307840/KF1410.F74

1. **CALIFORNIA PRACTICE GUIDE - ENFORCING JUDGMENTS AND DEBTS**
2. Ahart, Judge Alan & Rick Schwartz
3. Rutter
4. 1988
5. 2 vols.
6. $175 incl. 3 mos. supp.
7. annual supp.
8. 1990 - $58; 1991 - $82
9. 18903847/KFC1065.S37

1. **CALIFORNIA PRACTICE GUIDE - FAMILY LAW**
2. Hogoboom, Judge William P. & Donald P. King
3. Rutter
4. 1981
5. 3 vols.
6. $195 incl. 3 mos. supp.
7. annual supp.
8. 1990 - $85; 1991 - $98.50
9. 9638663/KFC126.A6H6

1. **CALIFORNIA PRACTICE GUIDE - FEDERAL CIVIL PROCEDURE BEFORE TRIAL**
2. Schwarger, Judge Wm. et al.
3. Rutter
4. 1989
5. 2 vols.
6. $220 incl. 3 mos supp.
7. annual supp.
8. 1991 - $98
9. 20073689/KFC995.W4

1. **CALIFORNIA PRACTICE GUIDE - LANDLORD-TENANT**
2. Friedman, Terry et al.
3. Rutter
4. 1989
5. 2 vols.
6. $175 incl. 3 mos supp.
7. annual supp.
8. 1990 - $72; 1991 - $87
9. 19890745/KFC145.F75

1. **CALIFORNIA PRACTICE GUIDE - PERSONAL INJURY**
2. Flahavan, William F. et al.
3. Rutter
4. 1984
5. 2 vols.
6. $175 incl. 3 mos supp.
7. annual supp.
8. 1990 - $98; 1991 - price NA
9. 11081216/KFC1028.P4F52

1. **CALIFORNIA PRACTICE GUIDE - PROBATE**
2. Ross, Bruce & Judge Henry Moore, Jr.
3. Rutter
4. 1986
5. 2 vols.
6. $195 incl. 3 mos. supp.
7. annual supp.

8. 1990 - $93.50; 1991 - price NA
9. 14698736/KFC205.A6R61

1. **CALIFORNIA PROBATE PRACTICE**
2. Blaylock, Robert J. et al., eds.
3. Bender
4. 1991
5. 4 vols.
6. $375 incl. 3 mos. supp.
7. annual supp.
8. no supp. yet
9. 91-71678/24254145/KFC205.C32

1. **CALIFORNIA PROBATE PROCEDURE**
2. Marshall, Arthur K.
3. Parker
4. 5th ed. - 1989
5. 2 vols.
6. $160 incl. 3 mos. supp.
7. biannual supp.
8. 1991 - $71.50
9. 89-3347/19520749/KFC205.M3

1. **CALIFORNIA PROBATE WORKFLOW MANUAL, REVISED**
2. -
3. Calif. CEB
4 rev. 1989
5. 2 vols.
6. $120
7. periodic supp.
8. 1990 - $32
9. 79-53359/6783755/KFC205.C34

1. **CALIFORNIA PRODUCTS LIABILITY ACTIONS**
2. Cotchett, Joseph W. & Robert E. Cartwright
3. Bender
4. rev. ed. - 1975
5. 1 vol.
6. $115 incl. 3 mos supp.
7. annual supp.
8. 1989 - $54; 1990 - $58
9. 85-236295/2533515/KFC323.A3C67

1. **CALIFORNIA PUBLIC AGENCY PRACTICE**
2. Ogden, G. et al.
3. Bender
4. 1988
5. 3 vols.
6. $350 incl. 3 mos. supp.
7. annual supp.
8. 1989 - $58; 1990 - $95
9. 88-72180/20055831/KFC780.C354

1. **CALIFORNIA PUBLIC SECTOR LABOR RELATIONS**
2. Labor & Employment Law Section of the State Bar of California
3. Bender
4. 1989
5. 1 vol.
6. $115 incl. 3 mos. supp.
7. annual supp.
8. 1990 - $32
9. 88-64017/20583070/KFC760.C34

1. **CALIFORNIA REAL ESTATE FORMS AND COMMENTARIES**
2. Cheatham, Robert W. and Robert E. Merritt, Jr.
3. Prentice Hall Law & Business
4. 1984
5. 1 vol.
6. $95 incl. 4 mos. supp.
7. annual supp.
8. 1988 - $60; 1990 - $60
9. 84-922/10348683/KFC140.A65C48

1. **CALIFORNIA REAL ESTATE LAW AND PRACTICE**
2. Augustine, Don et al.
3. Bender
4. 1973
5. 16 vols.
6. $900 incl. 3 mos. supp.
7. supp. as needed
8. 1989 - $559; 1990 - $747.50
9. 73-88801/902534/KFC140.B45

1. **CALIFORNIA REAL PROPERTY PRACTICE FORMS MANUAL**
2. Scott, Craig H., ed.
3. Calif. CEB
4. 1988
5. 1 vol.
6. $85; with forms disk - $110
7. periodic supp.
8. 1990 - $22; 1991 - $22
9. 88-61368/18162233/KFC140.A65C34

1. **THE CALIFORNIA STATE GOVERNMENT DIRECTORY**
2. -
3. Calif. Jnl. Press
4. 1977
5. 1 vol.
6. $95 incl. 1 yr. supp.
7. quarterly supp.

8. renewal - $80/yr.
9. 10637045/JK8767.A55

1. **CALIFORNIA TAXATION**
2. Peterson, Robert A.
3. Bender
4. 1983
5. 6 vols.
6. $400/yr. service; $760/2 yrs. service
7. annual supp. & monthly newsletter
8. renewal - $340/yr.
9. 83-71226/10090188/KFC860.P47

1. **CALIFORNIA TAXES, 2nd ed.**
2. Crawford, Roy E. et al.
3. Calif. CEB
4. 1988
5. 2 vols.
6. $130 ($75 each)
7. periodic supp.
8. Vol. I: 1989 - $35; 1990 - $55
   Vol. II: 1989 - $35; 1990 - $55
9. 88-70962/18121580

1. **CALIFORNIA TORTS**
2. Levy, Neil et al.
3. Bender
4. 1985
5. 6 vols.
6. $650 incl. 3 mos. supp.
7. periodic supp.
8. 1989 - $237; 1990 - $331.50
9. 85-61608/13334794/KFC310.C35

1. **CALIFORNIA TRIAL GUIDE**
2. Johnson, Earl
3. Bender
4. 1986
5. 6 vols.
6. $495 incl. 3 mos. supp.
7. periodic supp.
8. 1989 - $170; 1990 - $344
9. 86-72167/KFC1025.C337

1. **CALIFORNIA TRIAL TECHNIQUES**
2. Player, Theresa J. et al.
3. Parker
4. 1991
5. 1 vol.
6. $90 incl. 3 mos. supp.
7. annual supp.
9. 91-62074/24624983/KFC1030.P53

1. **CALIFORNIA UNEMPLOYMENT AND DISABILITY PROGRAMS**
2. O'Brien, Judge David W. & Bernadette M.
3. Parker
4. 1991
5. 1 vol.
6. $85 incl. 3 mos. supp.
7. annual supp.
9. 91-62073

1. **CALIFORNIA UNINSURED MOTORIST LAW**
2. Eisler, Paul A.
3. Parker
4. 4th ed. - 1986
5. 2 vols.
6. $120
7. supp. as needed
8. 1990 - $62; 1991 - $42
9. z78-61135/13842524/KFC298.A86E58

1. **CALIFORNIA WAGE AND HOUR GUIDE**
2. Aubry, Lloyd W., Jr.
3. M & M Resources
4. 1990
5. 1 vol.
6. $150
7. periodic supp.
8. no supp. yet

1. **CALIFORNIA WHITE COLLAR CRIME**
2. Papageorge, Thomas A. & Robert C. Fellmeth
3. Parker
4. 1991
5. 1 vol.
6. $85
7. supp. as needed
8. no supp. yet

1. **CALIFORNIA WILL DRAFTING, THIRD EDITION**
2. -
3. Calif. CEB
4. 1992
5. 2 vols.
6. price NA
7. no supp. yet

1. **CALIFORNIA WILLS & TRUSTS**
2. Hartog, John A. et al., eds.
3. Bender
4. 1991
5. 3 vols.
6. $300 incl. 3 mos. supp.
7. annual supp.

8. no supp. yet
9. 91-73662/24585993/KFC201.C36

1. **CALIFORNIA WILLS & TRUSTS - FORMS**
2. Hartog, John A. et al., eds.
3. Bender
4. 1991
5. 3 vols.
6. $300 incl. 3 mos. supp.
7. annual supp.
8. no supp. yet
9. 91-73678/24586124/KFC201.C362

1. **CALIFORNIA WORKERS' COMPENSATION CLAIMS & BENEFITS**
2. O'Brien, Judge David W. & Bernadette M.
3. Parker
4. 1991
5. 1 vol.
6. $85 incl. 3 mos. supp.
7. annual supp.
8. no supp. yet

1. **CALIFORNIA WORKERS' COMPENSATION LAW**
2. Herlick, Stanford
3. Parker
4. 4th ed. - 1990
5. 2 vols.
6. $140 incl. 3 mos. supp.
7. annual supp.
8. 1991 - price NA
9. 90-61733/22449722/KFC592.H47

1. **CALLAGHAN'S APPELLATE ADVOCACY MANUAL**
2. Cooley, John W.
3. Clark Boardman Callaghan
4. 1989
5. 2 vols.
6. $160 incl. 6 mos. supp.
7. annual supp.
8. 1990 - $38
9. 89-9686/19624040/KF9050.C66

1. **CALLAGHAN'S CRIMINAL LAW IN NY**
2. LCP editorial staff, ed.
3. Lawyers Coop.
4. 1985
5. 2 vols.
6. $180 incl. 6 mos. supp.
7. annual supp.
8. 1990 - $47; 1991 - $50
9. 84-12703/10878443/KFN6100.G77

1. **CALLAGHAN'S FAMILY COURT LAW AND PRACTICE IN NEW YORK**
2. Publisher's editorial staff
3. Lawyers Coop.
4. rev. ed. - 1984
5. 2 vols.
6. $165 incl. 6 mos. supp.
7. annual supp.
8. 1988 - $79; 1989 - $48.50
9. 84-17580/11089505/KFN5116.K47

1. **CALLMANN UNFAIR COMPETITION, TRADEMARKS AND MONOPOLIES, 4TH ED.**
2. Callman, Dr. Rudolf; Rev. supp. by Louis Altman
3. Clark Boardman Callaghan
4. 1981
5. 9 vols.
6. $775 incl. 6 mos. supp.
7. semiannual supp.
8. 1989 - $260.50; 1990 - $276
9. 81-7639//r873/7550998/KF1609.C33

1. **CANADA CORPORATE SECRETARY'S GUIDE**
2. -
3. CCH
4. 1978
5. 1 vol.
6. $285/yr.; $260/yr. for 2 yrs.
7. monthly supp.

1. **CANADA CORPORATIONS LAW REPORTS**
2. -
3. CCH
4. 1949
5. 2 vols.
6. $390/yr.; $355/yr. for 2 yrs.
7. monthly supp.
9. 78-314141/7875764/KE1387.5.C36

1. **CANADA INCOME TAX GUIDE**
2. -
3. CCH
4. 1952
5. 1 vol.
6. $235/yr.; $215/yr. for 2 yrs.
7. 18 supp./yr.
9. 12350630/KE5757.5.C35

1. **CANADIAN COMMERCIAL LAW GUIDE**
2. -

3. CCH
4. 1967
5. 2 vols.
6. $390/yr.; $355/yr. for 2 yrs.
7. monthly supp.
9. 7634166/KE917.5.C3

1. **CANADIAN EMPLOYMENT BENEFITS AND PENSION GUIDE**
2. -
3. CCH
4. 1963
5. 2 vols.
6. $440/yr.; $400/yr. for 2 yrs.
7. monthly supp.
9. 10059081/KE3298.C2

1. **CANADIAN EMPLOYMENT SAFETY AND HEALTH GUIDE**
2. -
3. CCH
4. 1980
5. 3 vols.
6. $485/yr.; $440/yr. for 2 yrs.
7. monthly supp.

1. **CANADIAN ENERGY NEWS**
2. -
3. CCH
4. 1980
5. 1 vols.
6. $320/yr.; $290/yr. for 2 yrs.
7. semimonthly supp.
9. 80-39124/1868706/HD9502

1. **CANADIAN ENERGY PROGRAM REPORTER**
2. -
3. CCH
4. 1982
5. 1 vol.
6. $225/yr.; $205/yr. for 2 yrs.
7. periodic supp.
9. 9473114

1. **CANADIAN ESTATE PLANNING AND ADMINISTRATION REPORTER**
2. -
3. CCH
4. 1979
5. 2 vols.
6. $365/yr.; $330/yr. for 2 yrs.
7. monthly supp.
9. 80-475754/6425809/KE5974.A6C36

1. **CANADIAN FAMILY LAW GUIDE**
2. -
3. CCH
4. 1976
5. 3 vols.
6. $415/yr.; $375/yr. for 2 yrs.
7. monthly supp.

1. **CANADIAN GOVERNMENT PROGRAMS AND SERVICES GUIDE**
2. -
3. CCH
4. 1973
5. 1 vol.
6. $265/yr.; $240/yr. for 2 yrs.
7. monthly supp.
9. 74-165017/934907/JL5.C65

1. **CANADIAN INCOME TAX ACT, REGULATIONS AND RULINGS**
2. -
3. CCH
4. 1976
5. 3 vols.
6. $265/yr.; $240/yr. for 2 yrs.
7. monthly supp.
9. 8817049

1. **CANADIAN INDUSTRIAL RELATIONS & PERSONNEL DEVELOPMENT**
2. -
3. CCH
4. 1971
5. 1 vol.
6. $360/yr.; $325/yr. for 2 yrs.
7. weekly supp.

1. **CANADIAN INSURANCE LAW REPORTS**
2. -
3. CCH
4. 1948
5. 1 vol.
6. $335/yr.; $305/yr. for 2 yrs.
7. monthly supp.

1. **CANADIAN LABOUR LAW REPORTS**
2. -
3. CCH
4. 1946
5. 3 vols.
6. $555/yr.; $505/yr. for 2 yrs.
7. semimonthly supp. & newsletter

1. **CANADIAN PRODUCT SAFETY GUIDE**
2. -
3. CCH
4. 1978
5. 2 vols.
6. $360/yr.; $325/yr. for 2 yrs.
7. monthly supp.
9. 79-308554/5265859/KE3763.A6C17

1. **CANADIAN SALES TAX REPORTS**
2. -
3. CCH
4. 1969
5. 2 vols.
6. $345/yr.; $315/yr. for 2 yrs.
7. monthly supp.
9. 79-433340/46159

1. **CANADIAN SECURITIES LAW REPORTS**
2. -
3. CCH
4. 1966
5. 5 vols.
6. $545/yr.; $495/yr. for 2 yrs.
7. monthly supp.
9. 10182380/KC221.C734

1. **CANADIAN SMALL BUSINESS GUIDE**
2. -
3. CCH
4. 1981
5. 1 vol.
6. $235/yr.; $215/yr. for 2 yrs.
7. monthly supp.

1. **CANADIAN TAX REPORTS**
2. -
3. CCH
4. 1937
5. 10 vols.
6. $855/yr.; $775/yr. for 2 yrs.
7. weekly supp. & newsletter
9. 39-8290

1. **CANCER (Courtroom Medicine Series vol. 13)**
2. Frank, Arthur et al.
3. Bender
4. 1978
5. 3 vols.
6. $335 incl. 3 mos. supp.
7. annual supp.
8. 1989 - $196; 1990 - $242
9. 78-71942/4567419/RA1011.C68

1. **CAPITAL CHANGES REPORTER**
2. -
3. CCH
4. 1928
5. 6 vols.
6. $865/yr.; $785/yr. for 2 yrs.
7. weekly supp.
9. 12128814/HG4061.C36

1. **CAPITAL FORMATION AND INVESTMENT INCENTIVES AROUND THE WORLD**
2. Diamond, Walter H. & Dorothy B.
3. Bender
4. 1981
5. 2 vols.
6. $285 incl. 3 mos. supp.
7. periodic supp.
8. 1989 - $284.50; 1990 - $305.50
9. 81-68262/7953267/K3830.4.D5

1. **CAPITAL REGULATIONS TRAINING MANUAL**
2. -
3. Office of Thrift Supervision
4. 1990
5. 1 vol.
6. $50 - regulated instits.; $75 - others
7. periodic supp.

1. **THE CAPTIVE INSURANCE MANUAL**
2. Robertson, James A.
3. NILS
4. 1989
5. 2 vols.
6. $185 incl. supp. for bal. of calendar yr.
7. supp. as needed
9. 89-063277/23146012

1. **CASE ASSESSMENT AND EVALUATION**
2. Howarth, Don and Suzelle Smith
3. Clark Boardman Callaghan
4. 1989
5. 1 vol.
6. $95 incl. 6 mos. supp.
7. annual supp.
8. 1990 - $30
9. 89-17455/20133984//KF300.H68

1. **CASE EVALUATOR'S MANUAL**
2. Research Dept.
3. Jury Verdict
4. 1987

5. 1 vol.
6. $625/yr.
7. annual supp.

1. **CASEHANDLING MANUAL**
2. U.S. National Labor Relations Board
3. order from USGPO - stock #931-001-00000-1
4. 1989
5. 3 vols.
6. $50/yr.
7. periodic supp.
9. 19790808/KF3372.A36N375

1. **CASES AND MATERIALS ON FLORIDA DOMESTIC RELATIONS**
2. Onoprienko, George
3. Florida Bar
4. 1986
5. 2 vols.
6. $60
7. as needed
8. 1990 - $25
9. 8774127/KFF94.O56

1. **CASEY FEDERAL TAX PRACTICE**
2. Casey, Laurence F. & George T. Donahue
3. Clark Boardman Callaghan
4. 1984
5. 6 vols.
6. $400 incl. 6 mos. supp.
7. annual supp.
8. 1989 - $119; 1990 - $112.50
9. 14282359/KF6310.C3

1. **CATALOGING LEGAL LITERATURE: A MANUAL ON AACR2 AND LIBRARY OF CONGRESS SUBJECT HEADINGS FOR LEGAL MATERIALS, WITH ILLUSTRATIONS**
2. Enyingi, Peter et al.
3. Rothman
4. 2nd ed. - 1988
5. 1 vol.
6. $65
7. periodic supp.
8. 1988 - $50; 1990 - $42.50
9. 88-4362//r89/17548494/Z695.1.L3E65

1. **CCH NASAA REPORTS**
2. -
3. CCH
4. 1986
5. 1 vol.
6. $230/yr.; $210/yr. for 2 yrs.
7. periodic supp.
9. 13727758/KF1068.4.N6

1. **CCH TAX TRANSACTIONS LIBRARY**
2. Advisory Board Members
3. CCH
4. 1987
5. ongoing vols.
6. $545/yr.; $495/yr. for 2 yrs.
7. supp. as needed
9. 15545685/KF6297.A45H45

1. **CFTC ADMINISTRATIVE REPORTER**
2. -
3. WSB
4. 1983
5. 1 vol.
6. $1370/yr.
7. monthly supp.
9. SN83-7783/9274838/KF1085.A6C4

1. **CGL REPORTER - TRIAL AND INSURANCE COUNSEL'S HANDBOOK**
2. Berkeley, Jill B.
3. CGL
4. 1983
5. 9 vols.
6. $225/yr.
7. 2x/yr.
8. renewal - $175/yr.
9. 10684527

1. **CHANCERY AND SPECIAL REMEDIES**
2. -
3. Illinois ICLE
4. 1987
5. 1 vol.
6. $98.95
7. periodic supp.
8. 1989 - $24.95
9. 8227907/KFI1285.C45

1. **THE CHANGING SCENE FOR ALIENS: THE IMMIGRATION ACT OF 1990**
2. -
3. Conn. Bar
4. 1991
5. 1 vol.
6. $53
7. no supp. planned

1. **CHANGING THE SITUS OF A TRUST**
2. Hendrickson, Robert A. & Neal R. Silverman
3. Law Journal

4. 1982
5. 1 vol.
6. $75
7. periodic supp.
8. 1988 - $39; 1990 - $40
9. 81-20722/7999254/KF731.H46

1. **CHAPTER 1 HANDBOOK**
2. Edwards, Charles E., ed.
3. EFRC
4. 1971
5. 1 vol.
6. $157.95/yr.
7. quarterly supp.

1. **CHAPTER 11 REORGANIZATIONS**
2. Anderson, John C.
3. Shepard's
4. 1983
5. 1 vol.
6. $95
7. annual supp.
8. 1990 - $36; 1991 - $36
9. 83-20048/9970218/KF1544.A95

1. **CHAPTER 12: FARM REORGANIZATIONS**
2. Anderson & Morris
3. Shepard's
4. 1987
5. 1 vol.
6. $110
7. annual supp.
8. 1990 - $32; 1990 - $34
9. 87-162960/16468789/KF1546.F35A95

1. **CHAPTER 13 BANKRUPTCY**
2. Lundin, Keith M.
3. Wiley Law
4. 1990
5. 2 vols.
6. $225
7. annual supp.
8. 1991 - price NA
9. 90-62341/22452141/KF1524.L86

1. **CHAPTER 13 PRACTICE AND PROCEDURE**
2. Drake, W. Homer, Jr. & Jeffrey W. Morris
3. Shepard's
4. 1983
5. 1 vol.
6. $95
7. annual supp.
8. 1989 - $32; 1990 - $34
9. 83-18705/9894352/KF1524.D72

1. **CHAPTER 93A RIGHTS AND REMEDIES**
2. Greaney, John M. et al.
3. Mass. CLE
4. 1989
5. 1 vol.
6. $75
7. periodic supp.
8. no supp. yet
9. 89-62762/21107177

1. **CHARGES TO THE JURY AND REQUESTS TO CHARGE IN A CRIMINAL CASE IN NEW YORK**
2. Goodman, Budd G., & H.G. Leventhal
3. Lawyers Coop.
4. rev. - 1983
5. 2 vols.
6. $180 incl. 6 mos. supp.
7. annual supp.
8. 1988 - $127; 1989 - $122.50
9. 83-15323/9893351/KFN6171.G66

1. **CHARITABLE GIVING AND SOLICITATION**
2. Stern, Sue S. et al.
3. WG&L
4. 1981
5. 1 vol.
6. $395/yr.
7. monthly supp.
9. 82-106636/8390102/KF6388.A6S7

1. **CHARITABLE LEAD TRUSTS - EXPLANATION, SPECIMEN AGREEMENTS, FORMS**
2. Teitell, Conrad
3. Taxwise
4. 1983
5. 1 vol.
6. $141
7. annual supp.
8. 1990 - $74; 1991 - $70
9. 83-71107/9808828/KF6449.A65T437

1. **CHARITABLE TRUSTS IN ESTATE PLANNING**
2. -
3. Minn. CLE
4. 1991
5. 1 vol.
6. $35
7. no supp. planned
9. 23318447/KF740.H37

1. **THE CHASE WILL & TRUST FORMS MANUAL**
2. -
3. Chase Manhattan
4. 1982
5. 1 vol.
6. $100 incl. 1 yr. supp.
7. annual supp.
8. $30/yr.

1. **CHECKLISTS FOR TRANSACTIONS IN PENNSYLVANIA RESIDENTIAL REAL ESTATE**
2. -
3. Penn. Bar
4. 1987
5. 1 vol.
6. $75
7. no supp. planned

1. **CHECKLISTS OF FEDERAL AND STATE STATUTES ON INTERLOCKING DIRECTORSHIPS**
2. -
3. ASCS
4. 1984
5. 1 vol.
6. $80 - nonmembers; $40 - members
7. periodic supp. planned
8. 1990 - free
9. 12115355/KF1423.A95

1. **CHECKS, DRAFTS & NOTES**
2. Reitman, Jeffrey B. and Harold Weisblatt
3. Bender
4. 1984
5. 1 vol.
6. $120 incl. 3 mos. supp.
7. annual supp.
8. 1989 - $90.50; 1990 - $100.50

1. **CHEMICAL CRISIS MANAGEMENT GUIDE**
2. Wereley, Linda
3. Keller
4. 1987
5. 1 vol.
6. $75
7. semiannual supp.
8. $60/yr.
9. 87-81370/18292973/KF3958.C48

1. **CHEMICAL PROCESS SAFETY REPORT**
2. Woehrle, Lori, ed.
3. Thompson
4. 1990
5. 1 vol.
6. $349/yr.
7. monthly supp.

1. **CHEMICAL REGULATION REPORTER**
2. Chabel, Bernard S.
3. BNA
4. 1977
5. 6 vols.
6. $1395/yr.
7. weekly supp. and reports
8. renewal - $1345/yr.
9. 79-112036//r842/5289079/KF3958.A15B87

1. **CHEMICAL SUBSTANCES CONTROL**
2. Joseph, Eileen Z.
3. BNA
4. 1980
5. 1 vol.
6. $570/yr.
7. periodic supp.
8. renewal - $520/yr.
9. 80-13525/6559213

1. **CHEST, HEART & LUNGS (Courtroom Medicine Series vol. 11)**
2. Kalisch, Jules et al.
3. Bender
4. 1975
5. 2 vols.
6. $240 incl. 3 mos. supp.
7. annual supp.
8. 1988 - $105; 1989 - $120; 1990 - $177
9. 75-313871/1505354/RA1011.C68

1. **CHICAGO BOARD OPTIONS EXCHANGE GUIDE**
2. -
3. CCH
4. 1973
5. 1 vol.
6. $380/yr.; $345/yr. for 2 yrs.
7. monthly supp.
9. 74-163514/901693/HG5131.C43C5

1. **CHILD CUSTODY & CHILD PROTECTION**
2. Juvenile Justice Comm.
3. Conn. Bar
4. 1990
5. 1 vol.
6. $20
7. no supp. planned

1. **CHILD CUSTODY AND VISITATION LAW AND PRACTICE**
2. Editorial Staff
3. Bender
4. 1983
5. 4 vols.
6. $455 incl. 3 mos. supp.
7. periodic supp.
8. 1989 - $260; 1990 - $311.50
9. 82-84733/10430466/KF547.C47

1. **CHILD SUPPORT REFERENCE MANUAL**
2. Young Lawyers Div./Center on Children and the Law
3. ABA
4. 1990
5. 1 vol.
6. $35
7. no supp. yet
9. 90-6975/21195414/KF549.Z9C47

1. **CHINA HAND: INVESTING, LICENSING & TRADING CONDITIONS TODAY**
2. -
3. Bus. Intern.
4. 1981
5. 1 vol.
6. $1400/yr.
7. monthly supp.
9. 10218211/HF41.C44

1. **CHINA LAWS FOR FOREIGN BUSINESS**
2. -
3. CCH
4. 1986
5. 5 vols.
6. $1810/yr.; $1645/yr. for 2 yrs.
7. periodic supp.

1. **CHINESE FOREIGN ECONOMIC LAW**
2. Rui Mu & Wang Guiguo, eds.
3. Intl. Law Inst.
4. 1990
5. 1 vol.
6. $65 incl. 6 mos. supp.
7. periodic supp.
8. 1991 - free
9. 89-81869/24041513

1. **CHOICE OF BUSINESS ENTITY AND PURCHASE AND SALE OF A BUSINESS**
2. -
3. Maine Bar
4. 1988
5. 1 vol.
6. $30
7. no supp. planned

1. **CITATION SERVICE - MARYLAND RULES OF PROCEDURE**
2. -
3. Rules
4. 1975
5. 1 vol.
6. $65 incl. 1 yr. supp.
7. semiannual supp.
8. renewal fee

1. **CIVIL APPEALS**
2. -
3. Illinois ICLE
4. 1989
5. 1 vol.
6. $98.95
7. periodic supp.
8. no supp. yet

1. **CIVIL COMMITMENT IN MINNESOTA, 2nd Ed.**
2. Janus, Eric
3. Butterworth-St. Paul
4. 1991
5. 1 vol.
6. $95
7. periodic supp.
8. no supp. yet
9. 91-2023/23080283/KFM5491.I5J36

1. **CIVIL DISCOVERY: A GUIDE TO EFFICIENT PRACTICE**
2. Schwarzer, William W. & Lynn H. Pasahow
3. Prentice Hall Law & Business
4. 1988
5. 1 vol.
6. $75 incl. 4 mos. supp.
7. periodic supp.
8. 1989 - $45
9. 88-9818/17732269/KF8900.S388

1. **CIVIL EVIDENCE TRIAL MANUAL FOR TEXAS LAWYERS**
2. Larkin, Murl A.
3. Butterworth-Texas
4. 1986
5. 1 vol.
6. $120
7. periodic supp.
8. 1989 - $112.50; 1990 - $81.50
9. 13523752/KFT1740.L365

1. **CIVIL LIABILITIES: ENFORCEMENT AND LITIGATION UNDER THE 1933 ACT**
2. Hicks, William J.
3. Clark Boardman Callaghan
4. 1989
5. 1 vol.
6. $125 incl. 3 mos. supp.
7. annual supp.
8. 1990 - $89; 1991 - $99
9. 89-17809/20259328/KF1439.H49

1. **CIVIL LITIGATION**
2. Foster, Randolph & J. Webb, et al eds.
3. Oregon Bar
4. 1982
5. 2 vols.
6. $150
7. periodic supp.
8. 1990 - $55; to be rev. in 1993
9. 82-60933/8875956/KFO2938.C58

1. **CIVIL PLEADING AND PRACTICE**
2. Newell, Robert D. et al.
3. Oregon Bar
4. 1991
5. 2 vols.
6. $165
7. periodic supp.
8. 1985 - $217.50; 1991 - $65
9. 91-60291

1. **CIVIL PLEADING AND PRACTICE FORMS, GEORGIA**
2. Editorial Staff
3. Harrison
4. 1989
5. 3 vols.
6. $299.95
7. annual supp.
8. 1989/90 - $29.95; 1990/91 - $62.95
9. 19701687/KFG535.A65H38

1. **CIVIL PRETRIAL PRACTICE**
2. -
3. MILE
4. 1991
5. 1 vol.
6. $79.50
7. no supp. planned

1. **CIVIL RICO**
2. Smith, David B. & Terrance G. Reed
3. Bender
4. 1987
5. 1 vol.
6. $120 incl. 3 mos. supp.
7. supp. as needed
8. 1989 - $51; 1990 - $108
9. 16885823

1. **CIVIL RIGHTS ACTIONS**
2. Cook, Joseph G. & John L. Sobieski
3. Bender
4. 1983
5. 7 vols.
6. $625 incl. 6 mos. supp.
7. periodic supp.
8. 1989 - $346.50; 1990 - $313.50
9. 83-70748/9889113/KF4749.C65

1. **CIVIL TRIAL MANUAL II**
2. McCullough, Ralph C. III & James L. Underwood
3. ALI-ABA
4. 2nd ed. - 1980
5. 1 vol.
6. $180
7. periodic supp.
8. 1987 - $89.50
9. 81-65817/7808132/KF8915.M39

1. **CLA STUDY GUIDE**
2. Florida Legal Assistants, Inc.
3. Butterworth-Fla.
4. 1986
5. 1 vol.
6. $60
7. periodic supp.
8. 1989 - $19.50; 1990 - $19.75
9. 15710530

1. **CLASS ACTIONS**
2. -
3. Illinois ICLE
4. 1986
5. 1 vol.
6. $76.95
7. periodic supp.
8. 1990 - $17.95
9. 18690316/KF8896.C543

1. **CLASS ACTIONS: LAW & PRACTICE WITH FORMS**
2. Aron, Carl R. et al.
3. Clark Boardman Callaghan
4. 1987
5. 4 vols.
6. $380 incl. 6 mos. supp.
7. annual supp.
8. 1990 - $84

9. 87-32552//r88/17106249/KF8896.C545

1. **CLASS ACTIONS: THE LAW OF 50 STATES**
2. Dickerson, Thomas A.
3. Law Journal
4. 1988
5. 1 vol.
6. $75
7. periodic supp.
8. no supp. yet
9. 88-23033/18326613/KF8996.Z95D53

1. **CLEAN AIR ACT**
2. Barrett, Jane F. et al.
3. MICPEL
4. 1991
5. 1 vol.
6. $42
7. no supp. planned

1. **CLEAN AIR ACT**
2. -
3. Indiana CLE
4. 1991
5. 1 vol.
6. $35
7. no supp. planned
9. 23361627/KF3812.A75C53

1. **CLEAN AIR PERMITS: MANAGER'S GUIDE TO THE 1990 CLEAN AIR ACT**
2. -
3. Thompson
4. 1990
5. 1 vol.
6. $298 incl. 1 yr. supp.
7. monthly supp. & newsletter

1. **CLIVE SCHMITTHOFF'S INTERNATIONAL COMMERCIAL ARBITRATION**
2. Simmonds, Kenneth R.
3. Oceana
4. 1974
5. 12 vols.
6. $1147.50
7. periodic supp.
8. 1987 - $100; 1988- $100
9. 80-133095/7008728/K2400.I59

1. **CLOSELY HELD CORPORATIONS**
2. Brode, George Jr., ed.
3. Illinois ICLE
4. 1990
5. 2 vols.
6. $131.95
7. periodic supp.
8. no supp. yet

1. **CLOSELY HELD CORPORATIONS: BUYING - SELLING - MERGING**
2. -
3. MILE
4. 1991
5. 1 vol.
6. $68
7. no supp. planned
9. 23761654/KF1466.C56

1. **CLOSELY HELD CORPORATIONS: FORMS AND CHECKLISTS**
2. Douglas, James A. et al.
3. WG&L
4. 1988
5. 1 vol.
6. $88
7. semiannual supp.
8. 1990 - $42.25; 1990 - $92.25
9. 88-50705//r89/19080697/KF1466.A65.D68

1. **CLOSING ARGUMENTS**
2. Stein, Jacob A.
3. Clark Boardman Callaghan
4. 1969
5. 1 vol.
6. $98 incl. 6 mos. supp.
7. annual supp.
8. 1989 - $37.50; 1990 - $69
9. 68-54723/121915/KF8915.S7

1. **CLOSING OFFICER'S GUIDE (WASHINGTON)**
2. Phillips, Fred B.Jr.
3. Butterworth-St. Paul
4. 1983
5. 1 vol.
6. $70
7. periodic supp.
8. 1989 - $17.50
9. 83-72596/10824503/KFW127.P44

1. **COAL LAW AND REGULATION**
2. Biddle, Timothy M., et. al.
3. Bender
4. 1983
5. 5 vols.
6. $500 incl. 3 mos. supp.
7. periodic supp.
8. 1988 - $98.50; 1990 - $75

9. 82-74106/9517458/KF1830.C6

1. **COALBED METHANE LEGAL ISSUES**
2. -
3. EMLF
4. 1990
5. 1 vol.
6. $80 - members; $100 - nonmembers
7. no supp. planned

1. **CODE AND REGULATIONS**
2. -
3. CCH
4. 1946
5. 6 vols.
6. $445/yr.; $405/yr. for 2 yrs.
7. monthly supp.
9. 4921059/KF6300.A6C6

1. **COFFEE, SUGAR AND COCOA EXCHANGE INC. GUIDE**
2. -
3. CCH
4. 1979
5. 1 vol.
6. $220/yr.; $200/yr. for 2 yrs.
7. monthly supp.

1. **COLLECTED LEGISLATION OF THE USSR AND THE CONSTITUENT UNION REPUBLICS: LEGISLATION AND CONSTITUTIONS**
2. Butler, William E., ed.
3. Oceana
4. 1978
5. 7 vols.
6. $700
7. periodic supp.
8. 1985 - $170; 1988 -$100
9. 78-24391/8824123/KMO.C658

1. **A COLLECTION OF BIBLIOGRAPHIC & RESEARCH RESOURCES**
2. Oceana Editorial Staff
3. Oceana
4. 1984
5. 2 vols.
6. $300
7. periodic supp.
8. 1988 - $150; 1990 - $125
9. 11197330/Z6461.C654

1. **COLLECTIONS**
2. -
3. Indiana CLE
4. 1991
5. 1 vol.
6. $50
7. no supp. planned

1. **COLLECTIVE BARGAINING NEGOTIATIONS AND CONTRACTS**
2. Dunn, Mary P.
3. BNA
4. 1945
5. 2 vols.
6. $714/yr.
7. biweekly supp. and newsletter
8. renewal - $676/yr.
9. 46-1174/1537825/HD6500.B8

1. **COLLIER BANKRUPTCY CASES, 2ND SERIES**
2. Babitt, King et. al.
3. Bender
4. 1979
5. 5 vols. (back vols. avail.)
6. $500/yr.
7. bimonthly supp.
8. renewal - $425/yr.
9. 5777819/KF1524.C641

1. **COLLIER BANKRUPTCY COMPENSATION GUIDE**
2. Bernstein, Stanley B.
3. Bender
4. 1988
5. 1 vol.
6. $115 incl. 3 mos. supp.
7. annual supp.
8. 1989 - $62.50; 1990 - $43
9. 88-70976/18315643/KF1526.B4

1. **COLLIER BANKRUPTCY EXEMPTION GUIDE**
2. King, Lawrence, ed.
3. Bender
4. 1982
5. 1 vol. (also vol. 7 - Collier on Bankruptcy, 15th ed.)
6. $125 incl. 3 mos. supp.
7. annual supp.
8. 1989 - $73; 1990 - $110
9. 82-073555/9776205/KF1524.C56

1. **COLLIER BANKRUPTCY FORMS MANUAL, 3RD ED.**
2. King, Lawrence P. & A.L. Mollar
3. Bender
4. 1979

5. 2 vols. (also vol. 6 - Collier on Bankruptcy, 15th ed.)
6. $210 incl. 3 mos. supp.
7. annual supp.
8. 1989 - $85; 1990 - $111
9. 79-126517//r903/5944455/KF1521.M64

1. **COLLIER BANKRUPTCY MANUAL, 3RD DESK ED.**
2. King, Lawrence P. et al.
3. Bender
4. 1979
5. 3 vols.
6. $355 incl. 3 mos. supp.
7. annual supp.
8. 1989 - $258.50; 1990 - $307.50
9. 54-14498/3275460/KF1524.C59

1. **COLLIER BANKRUPTCY PRACTICE GUIDE**
2. Herzog, Asa & Lawrence P. King
3. Bender
4. 1981
5. 9 vols.
6. $950 incl. 3 mos. supp.
7. periodic supp.
8. 1989 - $528.50; 1990 - $995
9. 81-67269/7831604/KF1524.C63

1. **COLLIER FAMILY LAW AND THE BANKRUPTCY CODE**
2. Sommer, Henry J. & Margaret Dee McGarity
3. Bender
4. 1991
5. 1 vol.
6. $105 incl. 3 mos. supp.
7. annual supp.
8. no supp. yet
9. 91-70557/24368610/KF505.S65

1. **COLLIER FARM BANKRUPTCY GUIDE**
2. Rogers, R.
3. Bender
4. 1989
5. 1 vol.
6. $115 incl. 3 mos. supp.
7. annual supp.
8. 1989 - $61; 1990 - $68.50
9. 88-63648/19174463/KF1546.F35R64

1. **COLLIER HANDBOOK FOR CREDITOR'S COMMITTEES**
2. King, Lawrence P., ed.
3. Bender
4. 1988
5. 1 vol.
6. $70 incl. 3 mos. supp.
7. annual supp.
8. no supp. yet
9. 87-73449/17356566/KF1527.S85

1. **COLLIER LABOR LAW AND THE BANKRUPTCY CODE**
2. Pulliam, Mark S. and Richard A. Conn, Jr.
3. Bender
4. 1989
5. 1 vol.
6. $115 incl. 3 mos. supp.
7. annual supp.
8. 1990 - $70.50
9. 20749610

1. **COLLIER ON BANKRUPTCY, 15TH ED.**
2. King, Lawrence P., Ed.
3. Bender
4. 1979
5. 15 vols.
6. $1445 incl. 3 mos. supp.
7. supp. as needed
8. 1989 - $999; 1990 - $1205.50
9. 79-625372/5944188/KF1524.C6

1. **COLLIER REAL ESTATE TRANSACTION AND BANKRUPTCY CODE**
2. Cherkis, Laurence D., et al.
3. Bender
4. 1984
5. 1 vol.
6. $120 incl. 3 mos. supp.
7. periodic supp.
8. 1989 - $68; 1990 - $85.50
9. 84-70341/10829192/KF1524.C45

1. **COLLIER'S LENDING INSTITUTIONS AND THE BANKRUPTCY CODE**
2. Rosenberg, J. Robert and Lawrence P. King
3. Bender
4. 1985
5. 1 vol.
6. $115 incl. 3 mos. supp.
7. periodic supp.
8. 1989 - $78; 1990 - $86.50
9. 85-73449/13241192/KF1524.R71

1. **COLORADO APPELLATE HANDBOOK**
2. Low, Andrew M., ed.
3. CLE - Colorado

4. 1984
5. 1 vol.
6. $75
7. periodic supp.
8. 1985 - $15; 1987 - $25
9. 12279765/KFC2355.A55C6

1. **COLORADO CORPORATE FORMS**
2. Erickson, David L.
3. Lawyers Coop.
4. 1984
5. 1 vol.
6. $80 incl. 6 mos. supp.
7. periodic supp.
8. 1988 - $38.50; 1989 -$40.50
9. 83-24042/10185355/KFC2013.A65E74

1. **COLORADO CORPORATE FORMS - PRACTICE**
2. Moye, John E.
3. Aspen
4. 1988
5. 2 vols.
6. $269 incl. 3 mos. supp.
7. annual supp.
8. 1989 - $89
9. 87-30777/16980041/KFC2013.A65M69

1. **COLORADO COURT RULES**
2. Publisher's staff
3. Michie
4. 1985
5. 1 vol.
6. $70
7. periodic supp.
8. 1989 - free; 1991 - free
9. 85-62290/12820120

1. **COLORADO DOMESTIC RELATIONS FORMS - PRACTICE**
2. Hinds, Robert T., Jr. & Albert M. Bonin
3. Aspen
4. 1988
5. 1 vol.
6. $159 incl. 3 mos. supp.
7. annual supp.
8. $70-$95/supp.
9. 88-14486/17875944/KFC1894.A65H56

1. **COLORADO ESTATE PLANNING**
2. Colorado Assn. of Legal Secretaries
3. Parker
4. 1991
5. 1 vol.
6. price NA
7. annual supp.
8. no supp. yet
9. 91-65619

1. **COLORADO ESTATE PLANNING FORMS BOOK**
2. Committee of Probate & Trust Section of Colorado Bar Assn.
3. CLE - Colorado
4. 1992
5. 1 vol.
6. price NA
7. no supp. yet
8. -
9. 9834371

1. **COLORADO ESTATE PLANNING HANDBOOK**
2. Huff, William S., et al., eds.
3. CLE - Colorado
4. 3rd ed. - 1985
5. 1 vol.
6. $110
7. periodic supp.
8. 1989 - $85
9. 11868672/KFC1940.C63

1. **COLORADO ESTATE PLANNING, WILL DRAFTING AND ESTATE ADMINISTRATION FORMS - PRACTICE**
2. Stewart, C. Jean
3. Aspen
4. 1988
5. 2 vols.
6. $239 incl. 3 mos. supp.
7. annual supp.
8. $70 - $95/supp.
9. 87-38504/17354237/KFC1940.A65S74

1. **COLORADO ETHICS OPINIONS HANDBOOK**
2. Ethics Comm. of Colorado Bar
3. CLE - Colorado
4. 2nd ed. - 1983
5. 1 vol.
6. $70
7. periodic supp.
8. 1989 - $29; 1990 - $25
9. 9501215/KFC1876.5.A2C6

1. **COLORADO JURY INSTRUCTIONS 3D - CIVIL**
2. Supreme Court Comm. on Civil Jury Instructions

3. Bancroft
4. 3rd ed. - 1989
5. 2 vols.
6. $180 incl. 6 mos. supp.
7. annual supp.
8. 1990 - $22; 1991 - $57.50
9. 88-63229/20218750/KFC2342.6.A65C6

1. **COLORADO LAW OFFICE HANDBOOK**
2. Colorado Assn. of Legal Secretaries
3. Parker
4. 1989
5. 1 vol.
6. $75
7. supp. as needed
8. 1990 - $22
9. 89-63077

1. **COLORADO LOCAL COURT RULES**
2. Tonsing, R.L. & M.E.
3. CLP
4. 1976
5. 1 vol.
6. $55
7. semiannual supp.
8. $27/yr.
9. 5984045/KFC2329.A2

1. **COLORADO PROBATE SYSTEM**
2. Wade, James, R.
3. CLE - Colorado
4. 1982
5. 1 vol.
6. $85
7. supp. as needed
8. 1987 - $35

1. **COLORADO REAL ESTATE FORMS - PRACTICE**
2. Quail, Beverly J.
3. Aspen
4. 1988
5. 3 vols.
6. $299 incl. 3 mos. supp.
7. annual supp.
8. 1988 - $84.95
9. 87-34680/17326977/KFC1926.A65Q35

1. **COLORADO REAL ESTATE PRACTICE**
2. Carpenter, Willis
3. CLE - Colorado
4. 1990
5. 2 vols.
6. $175
7. 1990 - $45; 1991 - $45
9. 20661330/KFC1926.Z9C3

1. **COLORADO REAL ESTATE TRANSACTIONS**
2. Oliver, Owen L.
3. Bancroft
4. 1985
5. 1 vol.
6. $110 incl. 6 mos. supp.
7. annual supp.
8. 1989 - $48; 1990 - $57.50
9. 85-80619/13813941/KFC1926.043

1. **COLORADO RULES OF EVIDENCE (ANNOTATED)**
2. Bucholtz, Alan & Ethan Jacobson
3. CLP
4. 1982
5. 1 vol.
6. $85
7. annual supp.
8. 1990 - $42.50; 1991 - $40
9. 12858904/KFC2340.J3

1. **COLORADO TITLE INSURANCE PRACTICE**
2. Carpenter, Willis V.
3. CLE - Colorado
4. 1987
5. 1 vol.
6. $85
7. periodic supp.
8. 1988 - $35; 1991 - price NA
9. 15737596/KFC1992.T58C27

1. **COLORADO WORKERS' COMPENSATION LAW AND PRACTICE**
2. Jaynes, Ronald C. et al.
3. CLP
4. 1984
5. 1 vol.
6. $108
7. annual supp.
8. 1989 - $42; 1990 - $59
9. 85-115090/12050192/KFC2142.J39

1. **COMEX BY-LAWS, RULES AND REGULATIONS**
2. -
3. COMEX
4. 1978
5. 1 vol.
6. $175
7. periodic supp. (3-4x/yr.)
8. renewal - $150/yr.

1. **COMMERCIAL AND CONSUMER WARRANTIES**
2. McDonnell, Julian B.
3. Bender
4. 1987
5. 3 vols.
6. $325 incl. 3 mos. supp.
7. annual supp.
8. 1989 - $155; 1990 - $176.50
9. 87-71816/16802459/KF919.C6M35

1. **COMMERCIAL ARBITRATION HANDBOOK**
2. Hoeniger, Berthold A.
3. Parker
4. 1991
5. 1 vol.
6. $90
7. annual supp.
8. no supp. yet
9. 90-63234/23210257/KF9085.H563

1. **COMMERCIAL ASSET-BASED FINANCING**
2. Nimmer, Raymond
3. Clark Boardman Callaghan
4. 1988
5. 4 vols.
6. $370 incl. 6 mos. supp.
7. annual supp.
8. 1990 - $49
9. 88-25803/18463386/KF1040.N56

1. **COMMERCIAL BANKRUPTCY**
2. -
3. Maine Bar
4. 1990
5. 1 vol.
6. $30
7. no supp. planned

1. **COMMERCIAL BLANKET BOND ANNOTATED**
2. Tort & Insurance Practice Section
3. ABA
4. 1985
5. 1 vol.
6. $49.95
7. no supp. yet
8. supp. in 1991
9. 85-72949/14091339/KF1223.A53C66

1. **COMMERCIAL, BUSINESS AND TRADE LAWS AND COMMERCIAL LAWS OF THE MIDDLE EAST (COMPLETE SERVICE)**
2. Simmonds, Kenneth R. & Gamal Badr, eds.
3. Oceana
4. 1980
5. 29 vols.
6. $3915
7. peridic supp.
8. no supp. yet

1. **COMMERCIAL BUSINESS & TRADE LAWS OF THE WORLD**
2. Simmonds, Kenneth R., ed.
3. Oceana
4. 1981
5. vols. for 18 countries or regions
6. $150/vol.
7. periodic supp.

1. **COMMERCIAL DAMAGES: A GUIDE TO REMEDIES IN BUSINESS LITIGATION**
2. Knapp, Charles J.
3. Bender
4. 1986
5. 3 vols.
6. $380 incl. 3 mos. supp.
7. periodic supp. & monthly newsletter
8. 1989 - $370; 1990 - $293.50
9. 85-71219/13761064/KF889.C57

1. **COMMERCIAL FINANCE GUIDE**
2. Shifin, Laurel
3. Bender
4. 1990
5. 1 vol.
6. $100 incl. 3 mos. supp.
7. annual supp.
8. no supp. yet
9. 90-81945/22437854

1. **COMMERCIAL LANDLORD/TENANT PRACTICE**
2. -
3. Illinois ICLE
4. 1991
5. 1 vol.
6. $125.95
7. periodic supp.
8. no supp. yet

1. **COMMERCIAL LAW AND PRACTICE GUIDE**
2. Zaretsky, Barry L. et al., eds.
3. Bender
4. 1991

5. 3 vols.
6. $315 incl. 3 mos. supp.
7. annual supp.
8. no supp. yet
9. 91-61859/24031464/KF885.C65

1. **COMMERCIAL LAW ANNUAL**
2. Del Duca, Louis & Patrick Del Duca
3. Clark Boardman Callaghan
4. 1991
5. 1 vol.
6. $70 incl. 3 mos. supp.
7. annual supp.
8. no supp. yet
9. 91-655177/24025701/KF872.C6

1. **COMMERCIAL LAWS OF THE MIDDLE EAST**
2. Keesee, Allen P.K.
3. Oceana
4. 1980
5. 9 vols./9 countries
6. $150/vol.
7. periodic supp.
8. -
9. 80-18047/6447174

1. **COMMERCIAL LAWS OF THE WORLD**
2. -
3. Foreign Tax
4. 1947
5. 31 vols. covering 103 countries
6. $1050 incl. 1 yr. supp.
7. monthly supp. & biweekly bulletin
8. renewal - $400/yr.

1. **COMMERCIAL LEASE LITIGATION**
2. -
3. Conn. Bar
4. 1990
5. 1 vol.
6. $53
7. no supp. planned

1. **COMMERCIAL LEASE NEGOTIATIONS**
2. -
3. Georgetown
4. 1990
5. 1 vol.
6. $75
7. no supp. planned

1. **COMMERCIAL LIABILITY INSURANCE**
2. Gibson, Jack P.
3. Intl. Risk Mgmt. Inst.
4. 1985
5. 2 vols.
6. $256/yr.
7. quarterly supp. & "Executive Briefing" newsletter
9. 86-100424/12998168/KF1215.G53

1. **COMMERCIAL LOAN DOCUMENTATION GUIDE**
2. Norton, J.
3. Bender
4. 1988
5. 1 vol.
6. $105 incl. 3 mos. supp.
7. annual supp.
8. 1989 - $36.75; 1990 - $46
9. 88-71189/18933488/KF1035.C66

1. **COMMERCIAL PAPER AND PAYMENT SYSTEMS**
2. Lawrence, William E.
3. Butterworth-NH
4. 1990
5. 2 vols.
6. $150
7. annual supp.
8. no supp. yet
9. 90-45632/22275061/KF957.L39

1. **COMMERCIAL PAPER UNDER THE UNIFORM COMMERCIAL CODE (Bender Uniform Commercial Code Service, vol. 2 series)**
2. Hart, F.M. & Willier, W.F.
3. Bender
4. 1972
5. 2 vols.
6. $235 incl. 3 mos. supp.
7. annual supp.
8. 1989 - $163.50; 1990 - $196.50
9. 72-81356/589054/KF957.Z95H35

1. **COMMERCIAL PRACTICE INSTITUTE**
2. -
3. MILE
4. 1991
5. 1 vol.
6. $68
7. no supp. planned

1. **COMMERCIAL PROPERTY INSURANCE**
2. Robinson, Linda G.

3. Intl. Risk Mgmt. Inst.
4. 1989
5. 2 vols.
6. $220 incl. 1 yr. supp.
7. quarterly supp.

1. **COMMERCIAL REAL ESTATE FORMS**
2. Saft, Stuart M.
3. Shepard's
4. 1987
5. 3 vols.
6. $240
7. annual supp.
8. 1990 - $81; 1990 - $48
9. 87-28664//r88/16924418/KF593.C6S23

1. **COMMERCIAL REAL ESTATE TRANSACTIONS**
2. -
3. Minn. CLE
4. 1991
5. 1 vol.
6. $50
7. no supp. planned

1. **COMMERCIAL REAL ESTATE TRANSACTIONS PRACTICE MANUAL**
2. Burnham, Becky L., et al, eds.
3. State Bar of Ariz.
4. 1989
5. 2 vols.
6. $90
7. annual supp.
8. no supp. yet
9. 19551308/KFA2526.A7C66

1. **COMMODITIES REGULATION: FRAUD, MANIPULATION & OTHER CLAIMS**
2. Markham, Jerry W.
3. Clark Boardman Callaghan
4. 1987
5. 2 vols.
6. $215 incl. 3 mos. supp.
7. annual supp.
8. 1989 - $139; 1990 - $149
9. 87-12979/16006154/KF1085.M37

1. **COMMODITY FUTURES LAW REPORTS**
2. -
3. CCH
4. 1974
5. 2 vols.
6. $640/yr.; $580/yr. for 2 yrs.
7. semimonthly supp.
9. 75-312697/1419259/KF1085.A6C64

1. **COMMON MARKET REPORTS**
2. -
3. CCH
4. 1962
5. 5 vols. (including Doing Business in Europe & Euromarket weekly newsletter)
6. $1185/yr.; $1075/yr. for 2 yrs.
7. semimonthly supp.
9. 6907067/HC241.2.C6175

1. **THE COMMUNITY REINVESTMENT ACT**
2. Stevenson, T. Herbert
3. Probus
4. 1989
5. 1 vol.
6. $75
7. supp. as needed

1. **THE COMMUNITY REINVESTMENT ACT MANUAL: POLICIES AND COMPLIANCE**
2. Brandel, Roland E. & David E. Teitelbaum
3. Prentice Hall Law & Business
4. 1989
5. 1 vol.
6. $85 incl. 4 mos. supp.
7. periodic supp.
8. no supp. yet
9. 89-37037/20490479/KF1035.B73

1. **COMMUNITY RIGHT-TO-KNOW MANUAL: GUIDE TO SARA TITLE III**
2. Hirschman, Susan, ed.
3. Thompson
4. 1987
5. 2 vols.
6. $324/yr.
7. bimonthly supp.
8. renewal - $294/yr.
9. 16865604/KF3945.Z9E53

1. **COMPANIES AND OTHER LEGAL PERSONS UNDER NETHERLANDS LAW**
2. Warendorf, H.C.S.
3. Kluwer
4. 1989
5. 1 vol.
6. $155 incl. 3 mos. supp.
7. periodic supp.
8. 1990 - $100; 1991 - $148

1. **COMPANY POLICY AND PERSONNEL WORKBOOK**
2. Ramey, Ardella & Carl Sniffen
3. Oasis
4. 1987
5. 1 vol.
6. $49.95
7. supp. every 2-3 yrs.
8. updated 1991
9. 12688839/HF5549.R344

1. **COMPANY POLICY STATEMENTS**
2. Hancock, W.A., ed.
3. Bus. Laws
4. 1987
5. 1 vol.
6. $95
7. annual supp.
8. renewal - $44/yr.
9. 87-410754//r89/17190547/HD60.5.U5C667

1. **COMPARATIVE NEGLIGENCE**
2. Larson, L. et al.
3. Bender
4. 1984
5. 3 vols.
6. $370 incl. 3 mos. supp.
7. annual supp.
8. 1989 - $232; 1990 - $300.50
9. 84-72422/11605446/KF1286.Z95C66

1. **COMPARATIVE NEGLIGENCE MANUAL**
2. Publishers Editorial Staff
3. Clark Boardman Callaghan
4. rev. - 1986
5. 1 vol.
6. $95 incl. 6 mos. supp.
7. annual supp.
8. 1989 - $50; 1990 - $51
9. 85-21297/12557929/KF1286.P35

1. **COMPARISON OF STATE UNEMPLOYMENT INSURANCE LAWS**
2. U.S. Department of Labor Employment & Training Admin.
3. order from USGPO - stock #929-002-00000-8
4. 1988
5. 1 vol.
6. $32/yr.
7. periodic supp.
9. 8224989

1. **COMPENDIUM OF COMMERCIAL FINANCE LAW**
2. -
3. NCFA
4. NA
5. 4 vols.
6. $350 incl. 1 yr. supp.
7. supp. as needed
8. renewal - $275/yr.
9. 10285509

1. **COMPENDIUM OF MASSACHUSETTS FAMILY LAW**
2. Leshin, Michael L.
3. Mass. CLE
4. NA
5. 1 vol.
6. $50
7. periodic supp.
8. no supp. yet

1. **COMPENDIUM OF STATE PRIVATIZATION LAWS**
2. Posternak, Blankenship & Fish
3. Privatization Council
4. 1986
5. 1 vol.
6. $85-sponsors, $125-members, $165-nonmembers
7. biennial supp.
8. 1990 - $50-nonmembers; $40-members
9. 14451234/KF1600.C56

1. **COMPENSATION STRATEGY AND MANAGEMENT**
2. Hansen, Fay, ed.
3. WG&L
4. 1977
5. 1 vol.
6. $376/yr.
7. monthly supp.

1. **COMPETITION LAW IN WESTERN EUROPE & THE USA**
2. Gijlstra, D. J.
3. Kluwer
4. 1980
5. 15 vols.
6. $789 incl. 3 mos. supp.
7. bimonthly supp.
8. 1990 - $600; 1991 - $650
9. 79-309063//r903/2831631/K3856.C66

1. **COMPETITION LAW OF CANADA**
2. Kaiser, Gordon E.
3. Bender

4. 1988
5. 1 vol.
6. $120 incl. 3 mos. supp.
7. annual supp.
8. 1989 - $45
9. 88-176241/18590078/KE1639.K35

1. **COMPETITION LAW OF THE EEC**
2. Van Bael, I. & J. Bellis
3. Bender
4. 1988
5. 1 vol.
6. $120 incl. 3 mos. supp.
7. annual supp.
8. 1990 - $56.50
9. 88-176190/18590074/KJE6456.V363

1. **COMPETITION LAW OF THE UNITED KINGDOM/REPUBLIC OF IRELAND**
2. Allen, W. & G. Hogan
3. Bender
4. 1988
5. 1 vol.
6. $120 incl. 3 mos. supp.
7. annual supp.
8. 1989 - $45; 1990 - $67.50

1. **COMPETITION LAWS OF THE PACIFIC RIM COUNTRIES**
2. Von Kalinowski, J., ed.
3. Bender
4. 1988
5. 1 vol.
6. $120 incl. 3 mos. supp.
7. annual supp.
8. 1989 - $64.50; 1990 - $97.50
9. 90-161155/21872834/K3850.C654

1. **COMPLAINT BOOK**
2. Christiansen & McGuire
3. MTLA
4. 1982
5. 1 vol.
6. $80 (member); $100 (nonmember)
7. no supp. planned

1. **THE COMPLETE BOOK OF CORPORATE FORMS**
2. Nicholas, Ted
3. Enterprise
4. 1980
5. 1 vol.
6. $69.95
7. periodic supp.
8. 1990 - $19.95; 1991 - $19.95
9. 80-67502/7277684/KF1411.N48

1. **COMPLETE FEDERAL TAX FORMS**
2. RIA prof. editorial staff
3. RIA
4. 1966
5. 3 vols.
6. $315/yr.; $285/yr. for 2 yrs.
7. biweekly supp.
8. renewal - $255/yr.
9. 23740589/KF6286.R528

1. **THE COMPLETE GUIDE TO MECHANIC'S AND MATERIALMAN'S LIEN LAWS OF TEXAS, 3RD ED.**
2. Steves, Sterling W. & Brenda T. Cubbage
3. Butterworth-Texas
4. 1990
5. 1 vol.
6. $115
7. periodic supp.
8. 1991 - $57.50
9. 89-98359/13215694/KFT1355.5.S74

1. **COMPLETE NON-PROFIT CORPORATION HANDBOOK**
2. Nicholas, Ted
3. Enterprise
4. 1986
5. 1 vol.
6. $69.95
7. periodic supp.
8. new ed. in prep.
9. 16749224

1. **COMPLETE PERSONNEL ADMINISTRATION HANDBOOK FOR LAW FIRMS**
2. -
3. Altman Weil Pensa
4. 1991
5. 1 vol.
6. $175
7. periodic supp.
8. no supp. yet

1. **COMPLEXITIES OF DIVORCE PRACTICE IN THE 1990's**
2. -
3. NH Bar
4. 1991
5. 1 vol.
6. $35
7. no supp. planned

1. **COMPLIANCE EXAMINATIONS UPDATE FOR FINANCIAL INSTITUTIONS**
2. Tidwell, Drew V. & John H. Mancuso
3. WG&L
4. 1988
5. 1 vol.
6. $235/yr.
7. semimonthly supp.
9. 85-240936/17934608/KF1040.T46

1. **COMPLIANCE GUIDE FOR PLAN ADMINISTRATORS**
2. -
3. CCH
4. 1976
5. 3 vols. plus newsletter binder
6. $595/yr.; $540/yr. for 2 yrs.
7. semimonthly supp.
9. 76-646661/2534539/HD7106.U5C59a

1. **COMPLYING WITH INTERNATIONAL ANTITRUST REGULATIONS**
2. Vogelsohn, J. et al.
3. Bender
4. 1988
5. 1 vol.
6. $105 incl. 3 mos. supp.
7. annual supp.
8. no supp. yet
9. 88-71744/18837110/KF1649.V64

1. **COMPTROLLER GENERAL'S PROCUREMENT DECISIONS**
2. -
3. Fed. Publ.
4. 1974
5. 2 vols.
6. $984/yr.
7. monthly supp.
9. 880309/KC85.U5831

1. **COMPTROLLER'S HANDBOOK FOR CONSUMER EXAMINATIONS**
2. -
3. U.S. Compt.
4. 1983
5. 1 vol.
6. $90/yr.
7. periodic supp.
8. -
9. 9336756/KF996.5.U58

1. **COMPTROLLER'S HANDBOOK FOR NATIONAL BANK EXAMINERS**
2. -
3. U.S. Compt.
4. 1977
5. 1 vol.
6. $90 incl. 1 supp.
7. periodic supp.
8. renewal - $90/yr.
9. 5824536/KF996.5.C6

1. **COMPTROLLER'S MANUAL FOR CORPORATE ACTIVITIES**
2. -
3. U.S. Compt.
4. 1987
5. 2 vols.
6. $105
7. periodic supp.
8. renewal - $30/yr.
9. 15528982/KF996.5.U5395

1. **COMPUTER CONTRACTS**
2. Bigelow, Robert P.
3. Bender
4. 1987
5. 4 vols.
6. $405 incl. 3 mos. supp.
7. annual supp.
8. 1989 - $212; 1990 - $281.50
9. 86-72664//r90/17353841/KF905.C6B53

1. **COMPUTER CRIME LAW REPORTER**
2. BloomBecker, Buck, ed.
3. NCCCD
4. 1989
5. 1 vol.
6. $120
7. annual supp.
8. 1989 - $30; 1991 - $40

1. **COMPUTER FUNDAMENTALS FOR LEGAL PROFESSIONALS**
2. Gurdak, John A.
3. Pearson
4. 4th ed. - 1991
5. 1 vol.
6. $59.95
7. annual supp.
8. 1989 - $29.95; 1990 - $29.95
9. 19210925/KF320.A9G87

1. **COMPUTER LAW - DRAFTING AND NEGOTIATING FORMS AND AGREEMENTS**
2. Brown, Peter & Richard Raysman
3. Law Journal
4. 1984

5. 1 vol.
6. $95
7. periodic supp.
8. 1989 - $84; 1990 - $84
9. 84-4335/10483628/KF390.5.C6R3

1. **COMPUTER LAW: EVIDENCE AND PROCEDURE**
2. Bender, David
3. Bender
4. 1977
5. 3 vols.
6. $310 incl. 3 mos. supp.
7. annual supp.
8. 1989 - $162.50; 1990 - $175
9. 78-50956/10781688/KF8947.B43

1. **COMPUTER LAW INSTITUTE**
2. -
3. Wash. Bar
4. 1991
5. 1 vol.
6. $55
7. no supp. planned

1. **COMPUTER SOFTWARE: PROTECTION, LIABILITY, LAW, FORMS**
2. Kutten, L.J.
3. Clark Boardman Callaghan
4. 1987
5. 2 vols.
6. $195 incl. 3 mos. supp.
7. periodic supp.
8. 1989 - $90; 1991 - $150
9. 87-11763/15629130/KF3024.C6K88

1. **COMPUTER SOFTWARE AGREEMENTS: FORMS AND COMMENTARY**
2. Matuszeski, John et al.
3. WG&L
4. 1987
5. 1 vol.
6. $135
7. semiannual supp.
8. 1989 - $54.50; 1991 - $125.50
9. 87-50238/16092768/KF905.C6R53

1. **COMPUTER SOFTWARE PROTECTION LAW**
2. Sherman, Cary H. et al.
3. BNA Books
4. 1989-90
5. 2 vols.
6. $615
7. periodic supp.
8. 1991 - $325
9. 88-39851/18624237/KF3024.C6S54

1. **COMPUTERS AND THE TRIAL LAWYER**
2. Bernstein, Paul
3. ATLA
4. 1992
5. 1 vol.
6. price NA
7. periodic supp.
8. no supp. yet

1. **A CONCISE GUIDE TO DISCIPLINE IN THE PUBLIC SERVICE**
2. Randall, Harvey and Eric D.
3. NYPER
4. 1986; rev. 1989
5. 1 vol.
6. $95
7. annual supp.
8. 1989 - $35; 1990 - $35
9. 86-60129

1. **CONDEMNATION: TRIAL TECHNIQUES AND RECENT DEVELOPMENTS**
2. McKirdy, Edward D. et al.
3. New Jersey ICLE
4. 1987
5. 1 vol.
6. $40
7. no supp. planned

1. **CONDEMNATION AND EMINENT DOMAIN**
2. Reid, Richard A.
3. MICPEL
4. rev.-1988
5. 1 vol.
6. $21
7. periodic supp.
8. no supp. yet
9. 16538914/KFM1650.R44

1. **CONDEMNATION PROCEDURES AND TECHNIQUES - FORMS (Real Estate Transaction Series, vols. 3 pts. 1 & 2, 3A, 3A pt. 2, 3B, 3B pt. 2)**
2. Rohan, Patrick J. & Melvin A. Reskin
3. Bender
4. 1968
5. 6 vols. (also vols. 7, 8, 8A, 9, 10 Nichols on Eminent Domain)
6. $495 incl. 3 mos. supp.

7. biannual supp.
8. 1989 - $388.50; 1990 - $425
9. 79-5082/19860/KF5599.R6

1. **CONDOMINUM DEVELOPMENT: FORMS WITH COMMENTARY**
2. Buck, Gurdon H.
3. Clark Boardman Callaghan
4. 1990
5. 2 vols.
6. $198 incl. 3 mos. supp.
7. periodic supp.
8. no supp. yet
9. 90-38804/21676609/KF581.A65B8

1. **CONDOMINIUM LAW AND PRACTICE - FORMS (Real Estate Transaction Series, vols. 1, 1 pt. 2 & 3, 1A, 1B, 1C)**
2. Rohan, Patrick J. & M.A. Reskin
3. Bender
4. 1965
5. 8 vols.
6. $615 incl. 3 mos. supp.
7. biannual supp.
8. 1989 - $522.50; 1990 - $558.50
9. 65-5256/522085/KF581.R6

1. **CONDOMINIUMS AND COMMUNITY ASSOCIATIONS IN THE 1990'S: HOW TO REPRESENT THEM AND THOSE WHO DEAL WITH THEM**
2. -
3. Conn. Bar
4. 1990
5. 1 vol.
6. $53
7. no supp. planned

1. **CONFLICTS OF INTEREST IN BUSINESS TRANSACTIONS**
2. -
3. Wash. Bar
4. 1990
5. 1 vol.
6. $40
7. periodic supp.
8. no supp. yet
9. 89-52071/21871766/KF311.C657

1. **CONGRESSIONAL HEARINGS CALENDAR**
2. Reams, Bernard & Kimberly Martin
3. Hein
4. 1988
5. 2 vols.
6. $95/yr.
7. quarterly supp.
8. -
9. 87-2708/16878498

1. **CONGRESSIONAL INDEX**
2. -
3. CCH
4. 1937
5. 2 vols. published biennially
6. $785/yr.; $715/yr. for 2 yrs.
7. weekly supp. when in session

1. **CONGRESSIONAL INVESTIGATIONS: LAW AND PRACTICE**
2. Grabow, John C.
3. Prentice Hall Law & Business
4. 1988
5. 1 vol.
6. $85 incl. 4 mos. supp.
7. periodic supp.
8. no supp. yet
9. 88-23872/18351456/KF4942.G73

1. **CONNECTICUT APPELLATE PRACTICE AND PROCEDURE**
2. Tait, Colin C.
3. Butterworth-NH
4. 1989
5. 1 vol.
6. $105
7. annual supp.
8. 1991 - $70
9. 89-35313/20393673/KFC4155.T34

1. **THE CONNECTICUT CHILD SUPPORT GUIDELINES**
2. Family Law Section
3. Conn. Bar
4. 1989
5. 1 vol.
6. $25
7. no supp. planned

1. **CONNECTICUT CRIMINAL PROCEDURE**
2. Spinella, Paul
3. Atlantic
4. 1985
5. 1 vol.
6. $65
7. no supp. planned
9. 86-101897/12925346/KFC4175.S65

1. **CONNECTICUT EVIDENCE**
2. Holden, Benedict & John Daly
3. Atlantic
4. 1988
5. 2 vols.
6. $125
7. annual supp.
8. 1990 - $60; 1991 - $65
9. 16940860/KFC4140.A53H64

1. **CONNECTICUT LAW ENFORCEMENT HANDBOOK**
2. -
3. Gould
4. 1988
5. 1 vol.
6. $7.95
7. periodic supp.
8. $5 - $10/supp.
9. 89-111474/19811255/KFC4161.Z9C66

1. **CONNECTICUT LAW OF REAL PROPERTY**
2. Burke, Richard, et al.
3. Atlantic
4. 1986
5. 1 vol.
6. $40
7. periodic supp.
8. no supp. yet

1. **CONNECTICUT PRACTICE BOOK**
2. Commission on Official Legal Publications
3. Atlantic
4. 1978
5. 2 vols.
6. $118
7. periodic supp.
8. $24/yr.

1. **CONNECTICUT PROBATE DESKBOOK**
2. Blair Nancy E., et al.
3. Lawyers Coop.
4. 1988
5. 1 vol.
6. $105 incl. 6 mos supp.
7. annual supp.
8. 1989 - $65; 1991 - $75
9. 88-81924/18987257/KFC3744.B55

1. **CONNECTICUT REAL PROPERTY STATUTES**
2. Butterworth's Staff
3. Butterworth-NH
4. 1980
5. 1 vol.
6. $45
7. annual supp.
8. 1990 - $42; 1991 - $45
9. 82-073439/9730843/KFC3712.A3

1. **CONNECTICUT SUMMARY PROCESS LAW**
2. -
3. Conn. Bar
4. 1991
5. 1 vol.
6. $53
7. no supp. planned

1. **THE CONNECTICUT SUMMARY PROCESS MANUAL**
2. Marzinotto, Paul J.
3. Conn. Law Tribune
4. 1985
5. 1 vol.
6. $128.95
7. periodic supp
8. 1988-89 - $55; 1990 - $15
9. 86-219005/15316650/KFC3717.M37

1. **CONNECTICUT TIME LIMITATIONS**
2. Butterworth's Staff
3. Butterworth-NH
4. 1984
5. 1 vol.
6. $40
7. annual supp.
8. 1990 - $30; 1991 - $35
9. 82-071705/9469389/KFC3690.T5C66

1. **THE CONNECTICUT UNFAIR TRADE PRACTICES ACT**
2. Antitrust Section and Consumer Law Section
3. Conn. Bar
4. 1988
5. 1 vol.
6. $25
7. no supp. planned
9. 19564803/KFC3830.A78S46

1. **THE CONSOLIDATED CHEMICAL REGULATION GUIDEBOOK**
2. Waldo, Andrew B.
3. Roytech
4. 1991
5. 2 vols.
6. $580 incl. 3 supps.
7. periodic supp.

1. **THE CONSOLIDATED TAX RETURN**
2. Crestol, Jack et al.
3. WG&L
4. 4th ed. - 1988
5. 1 vol.
6. $155
7. semiannual supp.
8. 1989 - $59.75; 1991 - $134.50
9. 88-62090/18776366/KF6499.C58C68

1. **CONSOLIDATED TAX RETURNS: A TREATISE ON THE LAW OF CONSOLIDATED FEDERAL INCOME TAX RETURNS**
2. Peel, Fred W., Jr., et al.
3. Clark Boardman Callaghan
4. 3rd ed. - 1984
5. 2 vols.
6. $225 incl. 1 yr. supp.
7. quarterly supp.
8. 1989 - $134; 1990 - $142.50
9. 84-23688/11289968/KF6499.C58P43

1. **CONSTITUTIONS OF AMERICAN DENOMINATIONS**
2. Schenck, Robert L.
3. Hein
4. 1984
5. 3 vols.
6. $175
7. no supp. planned
9. 83-82907/11066512/BR517.C66

1. **CONSTITUTIONS OF CANADA: FEDERAL AND PROVINCIAL (English/French)**
2. Wiktor, Christian L. & Guy Tanguay
3. Oceana
4. 1978
5. 4 vols.
6. $350/set
7. periodic supp.
8. 1985 - $150; 1987 - $100
9. 78-62326/4067764/KE4128.C65

1. **CONSTITUTIONS OF DEPENDENCIES AND SPECIAL SOVEREIGNTIES**
2. Blaustein, Albert P. & Eric B. Blaustein
3. Oceana
4. 1975
5. 7 vols.
6. $625
7. periodic supp.
8. 1990-91 - $125; 1991-92 - $125
9. 75-21651/1693963

1. **CONSTITUTIONS OF THE COUNTRIES OF THE WORLD: A SERIES OF UPDATED TEXTS, CONSTITUTIONAL CHRONOLOGIES AND ANNOTATED BIBLIOGRAPHIES**
2. Blaustein, Albert P. and Gisbert H. Flanz
3. Oceana
4. 1971
5. 21 vols.
6. $1,500
7. quarterly supp.
8. 1990 - $135; 1991 - $270
9. 76-141327/251886/K3157.A2B58

1. **CONSTITUTIONS OF THE UNITED STATES: NATIONAL AND STATE, 2nd ed.**
2. Columbia Univ. Legislative Drafting Research Fund & Frank P. Grad
3. Oceana
4. 1974
5. 6 vols. & index binder
6. $520
7. periodic supp.
8. 1990 - $110; 1991 - $210
9. 74-7681/895387/KF4530.C6

1. **CONSTRUCTION AND DESIGN LAW**
2. National Institute of Construction Law, Inc.
3. Michie
4. 1984, 1985
5. 5 vols.
6. $400
7. periodic supp.
8. -
9. 11821441/KF5701.A59C661

1. **CONSTRUCTION BANKRUPTCY**
2. -
3. Wash. Bar
4. 1988
5. 1 vol.
6. $35
7. no supp. planned

1. **CONSTRUCTION INDUSTRY STANDARDS AND INTERPRETATIONS**
2. U.S. Dept. of Labor, Occupational Safety & Health Admin.
3. order from USGPO
4. 1990
5. 1 vol.
6. $32/yr.

7. periodic supp.
9. 7642470

1. **THE CONSTRUCTION INSTITUTE**
2. -
3. MILE
4. 1990
5. 1 vol.
6. $58
7. no supp. planned
9. 13576348

1. **CONSTRUCTION INSTITUTE 1991**
2. -
3. MILE
4. 1991
5. 1 vol.
6. $84.80
7. no supp. planned

1. **CONSTRUCTION LAW**
2. -
3. NH Bar
4. 1988
5. 1 vols.
6. $35
7. no supp. planned

1. **CONSTRUCTION LAW**
2. Alexander, Richard E. & Steven R. Schell eds.
3. Oregon Bar
4. 1989
5. 2 vols.
6. $125
7. periodic supp.
8. no supp. yet
9. 88-60957//r89/19886305/KFO2555.8B8C66

1. **CONSTRUCTION LAW**
2. Stein, Steven G.M., ed.
3. Bender
4. 1986
5. 4 vols.
6. $440 incl. 3 mos. supp.
7. periodic supp.
8. 1989 -$263.50; 1990 - $314.50
9. 86-70262/13880095/KF902.C622

1. **CONSTRUCTION LAW DIGESTS**
2. Acret, James
3. Shepard's
4. 1990
5. 2 vols.
6. $210
7. quarterly supp.
8. 1991 - $26

1. **CONSTRUCTION LIEN LAW HANDBOOK**
2. Martin, Steven W.
3. State Bar of Wisc.
4. 1991
5. 1 vol.
6. $70
7. periodic supp.
8. no supp. yet

1. **CONSTRUCTION LITIGATION**
2. -
3. Illinois ICLE
4. 1990
5. 1 vol.
6. $87.95
7. periodic supp.
8. no supp. yet

1. **CONSTRUCTION LITIGATION**
2. -
3. MILE
4. 1989
5. 1 vol.
6. $58
7. no supp. planned
9. 14706708

1. **CONSTRUCTION RISK MANAGEMENT**
2. Woodward, Jeffrey, et al.
3. Intl. Risk Mgmt. Inst.
4. 1984
5. 3 vols.
6. $198 incl. 1 yr. supp. & newsletter
7. quarterly supp.
9. 18227726/TH438.F371

1. **CONSUMER AND COMMUNITY AFFAIRS HANDBOOK**
2. -
3. Fed.
4. 1981
5. 1 vol.
6. $75/yr.
7. monthly supp.
9. 7816956/HG2560.C66

1. **CONSUMER CREDIT**
2. Lapine, Kenneth M.
3. Bender
4. 1984
5. 4 vols.

6. $340 incl. 6 mos. supp.
7. annual supp.
8. 1989 - $252.50; 1990 - $206.50
9. 80-70891/1109102/KF1039.A8L36

1. **CONSUMER CREDIT GUIDE**
2. -
3. CCH
4. 1969
5. 5 vols.
6. $810/yr.; $735/yr. for 2 yrs.
7. biweekly supp.
9. 79-4093/19798/KF1039.A8C6

1. **CONSUMER CREDIT REGULATIONS**
2. Nicewander, Dan, et al.
3. Wiley Law
4. 1986, updated 1989
5. 1 vol.
6. $105
7. annual supp.
8. 1990 - $35; 1991 - $45
9. 7066271

1. **CONSUMER CREDITORS' REMEDIES**
2. -
3. MILE
4. 1991
5. 1 vol.
6. $68
7. no supp. planned
9. 24465492/KFM5620.Z9C66

1. **CONSUMER LAW**
2. -
3. Indiana CLE
4. 1990
5. 1 vol.
6. $45
7. no supp. planned

1. **CONSUMER PRODUCT SAFETY GUIDE**
2. -
3. CCH
4. 1972
5. 3 vols.
6. $735/yr.; $670/yr. for 2 yrs.
7. weekly supp.
9. 73-159434/623011/KF3945.A6C6

1. **CONSUMER PROTECTION AND THE LAW**
2. Pridgen, Dee
3. Clark Boardman Callaghan
4. 1986
5. 1 vol.
6. $95 incl. 3 mos. supp.
7. annual supp.
8. 1988 - $45; 1989 - $55
9. 86-6825/13358053/KF1609.P75

1. **CONSUMER PROTECTION, ANTITRUST & UNFAIR BUSINESS PRACTICES**
2. Wallis, Richard J. ed.
3. Wash. Bar
4. 5th annual - 1991
5. 1 vol.
6. $35
7. no supp. planned
9. 88-50874/KFW231.W37

1. **CONTEMPORARY CRIMINAL PROCEDURE**
2. Holtz, Larry E.
3. Gould
4. NA
5. 1 vol.
6. $34.95
7. periodic supp.

1. **CONTEMPORARY FAMILY LAW**
2. Wardle, Lynn et al.
3. Clark Boardman Callaghan
4. 1988
5. 4 vols.
6. $250 incl. 6 mos. supp.
7. annual supp.
8. 1989 - $42
9. 88-2912/17507069/KF505.W37

1. **CONTEMPORARY FEDERAL CRIMINAL PRACTICE: A PRACTICAL GUIDE TO THE COMPREHENSIVE CRIME CONTROL ACT OF 1984**
2. George, B. James, Jr.
3. Prentice Hall Law & Business
4. 1986
5. 2 vols.
6. $65 incl. 4 mos. supp.
7. periodic supp.
8. 1990 - $45; 1991 - $70

1. **CONTEMPORARY ISSUES IN FORECLOSURES**
2. Real Property Section
3. Conn. Bar
4. 1989
5. 1 vol.
6. $20

7. no supp. planned

1. **CONTESTED ESTATES**
2. -
3. Illinois ICLE
4. 1985
5. 1 vol.
6. $80.95
7. periodic supp.
8. 1987 - $24.95

1. **CONTRACT APPEALS DECISIONS**
2. -
3. CCH
4. 1956
5. 1 vol.
6. $805/yr.; $730/yr. for 2 yrs.
7. semimonthly supp.
9. 83-460264/9371538/KF846.C65

1. **CONTRACT AUDIT MANUAL**
2. U.S. Defense Contract Audit Agency
3. order from USGPO - stock #708-077-00000-3
4. 1979
5. 2 vols.
6. $27/yr.
7. periodic supp.
9. 5931897

1. **CONTRACT CHECKLISTS**
2. Kritzer, Albert
3. Kluwer
4. 1990
5. 1 vol.
6. $132 incl. 3 mos. supp.
7. periodic supp.

1. **CONTRACT LAW**
2. -
3. Indiana CLE
4. 1989
5. 1 vol.
6. $60
7. no supp. planned

1. **CONTRACT LAW IN OREGON**
2. Birdwell, William A. & Joel S. Kaplan
3. Oregon Bar
4. 1991
5. 1 vol.
6. $85
7. periodic supp.
8. no supp. yet
9. 91-60292/23468377/KFO2550.C66

1. **CONTRACTING WITH THE RTC AND FDIC**
2. Vartanian, Thomas P. et al.
3. Prentice Hall Law & Business
4. 1991
5. 1 vol.
6. $110 incl. 4 mos. supp.
7. periodic supp.
8. no supp. yet

1. **CONTRACTS AND SALES OF GOODS**
2. -
3. Illinois ICLE
4. 1990
5. 1 vol.
6. $98.95
7. periodic supp.
8. no supp. yet

1. **CONTRACTS FOR DEED: USE AND REMEDIES**
2. -
3. Minn. CLE
4. 1991
5. 1 vol.
6. $25
7. no supp. planned
9. 24149027

1. **CONTROLLED SUBSTANCES: A LEGAL AND CHEMICAL GUIDE TO THE FEDERAL DRUG LAWS**
2. Shulgin, Alexander
3. Ronin
4. 2nd ed. - 1991
5. 1 vol.
6. $39.95
7. periodic supp.
9. 24563708/KF3885.S49

1. **CONTROLLING TOXICS**
2. -
3. MILE
4. 1990
5. 1 vol.
6. $79.50
7. no supp. planned

1. **COOPERATIVE HOUSING LAW AND PRACTICE FORMS (Real Estate Transactions Series, vols. 2, 2A, 2B)**
2. Rohan, Patrick J. & Melvin A. Reskin
3. Bender
4. 1967

5. 4 vols.
6. $360 incl. 3 mos. supp.
7. annual supp.
8. 1989 - $251; 1990 - $305.50
9. 70-1350/36418/KF623.R6

1. **COPING WITH FORECLOSURES**
2. -
3. Maine Bar
4. 1991
5. 1 vol.
6. $35
7. no supp. planned
9. 23893450/KF697.F6M352

1. **COPYRIGHT LAW REPORTS**
2. -
3. CCH
4. 1978
5. 2 vols.
6. $455/yr.; $415/yr. for 2 yrs.
7. monthly supp.
9. 78-106071/4011222/KF2991.5.C6

1. **COPYRIGHT LAWS AND TREATIES OF THE WORLD**
2. -
3. BNA Books
4. 1957
5. 3 vols.
6. $665
7. periodic supp.
8. 1987-88 - $180
9. 56-4854/2268837/Z553.U583

1. **COPYRIGHT REGISTRATION PRACTICE**
2. Hawes, James E.
3. Clark Boardman Callaghan
4. 1990
5. 1 vol.
6. $95 incl. 3 mos. supp.
7. annual supp.
8. 1991 - $42.50
9. 90-334/21231818/KF3004.H39

1. **CORPORATE ACQUISITIONS AND MERGERS (Business Organizations vols. 13, 13A & 13B)**
2. Fox, Byron F. & Eleanor M. Fox
3. Bender
4. 1968
5. 4 vols.
6. $580 incl. 3 mos. supp.
7. semiannual supp.
8. 1989 - $496; 1990 - $552
9. 68-7903/435111/KF1477.F6

1. **CORPORATE ACQUISITIONS, MERGERS AND DIVESTITURES**
2. Solomon, Lewis D.
3. WG&L
4. 1983
5. 1 vol.
6. $425/yr.
7. monthly supp. and "ideas" letter
9. 83-196195/11972031/KF1477.A6S66

1. **CORPORATE COUNSEL'S GUIDE TO BUSINESS ETHICS POLICIES**
2. Hancock, W. A., ed.
3. Bus. Laws
4. 1991
5. 1 vol.
6. $95
7. annual supp.
8. no supp. yet
9. 24497694/HF5387.C67

1. **CORPORATE COUNSEL'S GUIDE TO BUSINESS-RELATED IMMIGRATION**
2. Hancock, W.A., ed.
3. Bus. Laws
4. 1986
5. 1 vol
6. $95
7. quarterly supp.
8. renewal - $68/yr.

1. **CORPORATE COUNSEL'S GUIDE TO CONSTRUCTION CONTRACTS**
2. Hancock, W. A., ed.
3. Bus. Laws
4. 1991
5. 1 vol.
6. $95
7. annual supp.
8. no supp. yet

1. **CORPORATE COUNSEL'S GUIDE TO CONSULTING AGREEMENTS**
2. Hancock, W. A., ed.
3. Bus. Laws
4. 1991
5. 1 vol.
6. $95
7. annual supp.
8. no supp. yet

1. **CORPORATE COUNSEL'S GUIDE TO DISTRIBUTION COUNSELING**

2. Hancock, W. A., ed.
3. Bus. Laws
4. 1990
5. 1 vol.
6. $95/yr.
7. annual supp.
8. $44/yr.

1. **CORPORATE COUNSEL'S GUIDE TO EMPLOYEE RELATIONS LAW**
2. Hancock, W.A., ed.
3. Bus. Laws
4. 1991
5. 3 vols.
6. $265
7. quarterly supp.
8. no supp. yet
9. 24148451

1. **CORPORATE COUNSEL'S GUIDE TO EMPLOYMENT CONTRACTS**
2. Hancock, W. A., ed.
3. Bus. Laws
4. 1990
5. 1 vol.
6. $95/yr.
7. annual supp.
8. $44/yr.

1. **CORPORATE COUNSEL'S GUIDE TO ENVIRONMENTAL LAW**
2. Hancock, W.A.
3. Bus. Laws
4. 1989
5. 3 vols.
6. $135
7. annual supp.
8. renewal - $74/yr.

1. **CORPORATE COUNSEL'S GUIDE TO EUROPEAN ECONOMIC COMMUNITY LAW**
2. Hancock, W.A., ed.
3. Bus. Laws
4. 1991
5. 1 vol.
6. $95
7. periodic supp.
8. no supp. yet

1. **CORPORATE COUNSEL'S GUIDE TO GOVERNMENT CONTRACTING & SUBCONTRACTING**
2. Hancock, W. A., ed.
3. Bus. Laws
4. 1991
5. 1 vol.
6. $95
7. annual supp.
8. no supp. yet
9. 23752721

1. **CORPORATE COUNSEL'S GUIDE TO INTERNATIONAL ANTITRUST LAWS**
2. Hancock, W. A., ed.
3. Bus. Laws
4. 1991
5. 1 vol.
6. $95
7. annual supp.
8. no supp. yet

1. **CORPORATE COUNSEL'S GUIDE TO LITIGATION MANAGEMENT**
2. Hancock, W. A., ed.
3. Bus. Laws
4. 1990
5. 1 vol.
6. $95/yr.
7. annual supp.
8. $44/yr.

1. **CORPORATE COUNSEL'S GUIDE TO PROTECTING TRADE SECRETS**
2. Hancock, William A., ed.
3. Bus. Laws
4. 1987
5. 1 vol.
6. $90
7. annual supp.
8. renewal - $39/yr.

1. **CORPORATE COUNSEL'S GUIDE TO THE ROBINSON-PATMAN ACT**
2. Hancock, W. A., ed.
3. Bus. Laws
4. 1991
5. 1 vol.
6. $95
7. annual supp.
8. no supp. yet

1. **CORPORATE COUNSEL'S GUIDE TO UNFAIR COMPETITION**
2. Hancock, W. A., ed.
3. Bus. Laws
4. 1986
5. 1 vol.
6. -
7. annual supp.

8. renewal - $44/yr.
9. 17401012

1. **CORPORATE COUNSEL'S MANAGERIAL GUIDE**
2. Hancock, W. A., ed.
3. Bus. Laws
4. 1988
5. 1 vol.
6. $90
7. annual supp.
8. renewal - $39/yr.

1. **THE CORPORATE COUNSELLOR'S DESKBOOK**
2. Block, Dennis J. et al.
3. Prentice Hall Law & Business
4. 3rd ed. - 1990
5. 1 vol.
6. $95 incl. 4 mos. supp.
7. periodic supp.
8. 1991 - $60
9. 90-6931/21195185/KF1425.C67

1. **CORPORATE CRIMINAL LIABILITY**
2. Brickey, Kathleen I.
3. Clark Boardman Callaghan
4. 1984
5. 3 vols.
6. $240 incl. 6 mos. supp.
7. annual supp.
8. 1989 - $55; 1990 - $59.50
9. 84-9465/10752325/KF9236.5.B74

1. **CORPORATE FORMS**
2. -
3. Nebraska CLE
4. 1991
5. 1 vol.
6. $125
7. periodic supp.

1. **CORPORATE LAW: ROLE OF THE LAWYER**
2. -
3. NH Bar
4. 1990
5. 1 vol.
6. $40
7. no supp. planned

1. **CORPORATE PACKAGE & MINUTE BOOK (CA, FL, TX)**
2. Fink, Kevin et al.
3. Oasis
4. 1987
5. 1 vol.
6. $39.95
7. biannual supp.
8. no supp. yet

1. **CORPORATE PRACTICE INSTITUTE**
2. -
3. MILE
4. 1991
5. 1 vol.
6. $79.50
7. no supp. planned

1. **CORPORATE PRACTICE SERIES**
2. Lempert, Larry
3. BNA
4. 1978
5. 51 + portfolios
6. $1190/yr.
7. periodic supp. and weekly news- letter - BNA'S Corporate Counsel Weekly
8. renewal - $1040/yr.
9. 85-641106/4177937/KF1397.C654

1. **CORPORATE SECRETARY'S GUIDE**
2. -
3. CCH (in coop. with Am. Society of Corp. Secretaries)
4. 1988
5. 4 vols.
6. $405/yr.; $370/yr. for 2 yrs.
7. monthly supp. & semimonthly newsletter
9. 88-141858/17892496/KF1422.A6C67

1. **CORPORATE TAX PLANNING**
2. Kosarek, Chester & Bruce Mantell
3. New Jersey ICLE
4. 1989
5. 1 vol.
6. $40
7. no supp. planned
9. 21863413/KF6465.K67

1. **CORPORATE TAX PRACTICE MANUAL**
2. Anderson, Stephen T.
3. Panel
4. 1989
5. 1 vol.
6. $99 incl. 1 yr. supp.
7. semiannual supp.
9. 90-127096/21296397/KF6464.A83

1. **CORPORATE TAXATION**
2. -

3. Georgetown
4. 1990
5. 1 vol.
6. $101
7. no supp. planned

1. **CORPORATION BUSINESS AND BANKING MID-YEAR**
2. -
3. Wash. Bar
4. 1990
5. 2 vols.
6. $70
7. annual editions

1. **CORPORATION FORMS**
2. -
3. WG&L
4. 1961
5. 2 vols.
6. $381/yr.
7. monthly supp.
9. 6412610/KF1410.P725

1. **CORPORATIONS MANUAL - COLORADO**
2. Mauro, Richard F., ed.
3. CLE - Colorado
4. 1987
5. 1 vol.
6. $85
7. periodic supp.
8. 1989 -$34
9. 16994850/KFC2010.Z9C65

1. **COST ACCOUNTING STANDARDS GUIDE**
2. -
3. CCH
4. 1972
5. 1 vol.
6. $225/yr.; $205/yr. for 2 yrs.
7. monthly supp.
9. 72-194359/496285/KF846.5.C6

1. **THE COST OF PERSONAL BORROWING IN THE UNITED STATES**
2. -
3. Finan. Pub.
4. 1971
5. 1 vol.
6. $129.95 incl. 1 yr. service & newsletter
7. supp. as needed
8. renewal - $75/yr.
9. 10567793/HG1628.C67

1. **COUNSELING LANDLORDS AND TENANTS**
2. -
3. Okla. Bar CLE
4. 1990
5. 1 vol.
6. $60
7. no supp. planned

1. **COUNSELING THE ELDERLY CLIENT IN MICHIGAN**
2. Martin, Katherine, ed.
3. Lawyers Coop.
4. 1991
5. 2 vols.
6. $180 incl. 6 mos. supp.
7. annual supp.
8. no supp. yet
9. 91-29997/24246414/KFM4291.A3M37

1. **COUNTRY HANDBOOKS**
2. Kritzer, Albert
3. Kluwer
4. 1990
5. 1 vol.
6. $111 incl. 3 mos. supp.
7. periodic supp.

1. **COURT AWARDED ATTORNEY FEES**
2. Derfner, Mary F. & Arthur Wolf
3. Bender
4. 1983
5. 3 vols.
6. $370 incl. 3 mos. supp.
7. annual supp.
8. 1989 - $268; 1990 - $312
9. 83-71461/10059852/KF8995.D47

1. **COURT OF APPEALS FOR THE FEDERAL CIRCUIT: PRACTICE AND PROCEDURE**
2. Dunner, D. R. & C. L. Gholz
3. Bender
4. 1973
5. 2 vols.
6. $210 incl. 3 mos. supp.
7. annual supp.
8. 1989 - $40; 1990 - $50
9. 73-82579//r903/1801098/KF3157.D86

1. **COURT OF APPEALS FOR THE FEDERAL CIRCUIT: REVIEW OF PATENT AND TRADEMARK CASES**
2. Dunner, Donald R. and Charles L. Gholz

3. Bender
4. rev. ed. - 1985
5. 2 vols.
6. $210
7. periodic supp.
8. 1989 - $140; 1990 - $50
9. 12929742/KF3157.D862

1. **COURT RULES FOR NORTHERN CALIFORNIA**
2. -
3. LADJ
4. NA
5. 6 vols.
6. $215/yr.
7. monthly supp.
9. 4428849

1. **COURT RULES FOR SOUTHERN CALIFORNIA**
2. -
3. LADJ
4. NA
5. 6 vols.
6. $215/yr.
7. monthly supp.

1. **COURT RULES OF MICHIGAN ANNOTATED**
2. Collins, Lynn M. & Daniel D. Kopka
3. ICLE - Michigan
4. 1991
5. 7 vols.
6. $179 incl. 1 yr. supp.
7. quarterly supp.
8. $75 - $85/yr.
9. 91-75608/11850353/KFM4729.A2

1. **COURT RULES UPDATE**
2. -
3. Court Info.
4. 1988
5. 1 vol.
6. $195/yr.
7. monthly supp.
9. 18850866/KFX2018.S8A4

1. **COURTROOM TOXICOLOGY**
2. Houts, Marshall et al.
3. Bender
4. 1981
5. 7 vols.
6. $505 incl. 3 mos. supp.
7. periodic supp.
8. 1989 - $215; 1990 - $334
9. 81-65437/7947370/RA1228.H68

1. **CRASH LITIGATION**
2. -
3. MILE
4. 1990
5. 1 vol.
6. $58
7. no supp. planned

1. **CREDIT UNION LAW SERVICE**
2. Publisher's Editorial Staff
3. Bender
4. 1985
5. 5 vols.
6. $415/1 yr.; $750/2 yrs.
7. quarterly supp. & monthly newsletters
8. renewal-$375/1 yr.; $675/2 yrs.
9. 84-61522/12349125/KF1008.C74

1. **CREDITOR/DEBTOR RIGHTS**
2. -
3. Okla. Bar CLE
4. 1990
5. 1 vol.
6. $40
7. no supp. planned

1. **CREDITOR-DEBTOR RIGHTS SECTION MID-YEAR MEETING**
2. -
3. Wash. Bar
4. 1990
5. 1 vol.
6. $35
7. annual editions

1. **CREDITOR'S REMEDIES AND BANKRUPTCY**
2. -
3. MILE
4. 1990
5. 1 vol.
6. $63
7. no supp. planned

1. **CREDITOR'S RIGHTS AND REMEDIES**
2. -
3. Oregon Bar
4. 1990
5. 1 vol.
6. $92.50
7. periodic supp.
8. no supp. yet
9. 88-61298/21293916/KFO2620.C74

1. **CREDITOR'S RIGHTS IN BANKRUPTCY**
2. Murphy, Patrick A.
3. Shepard's
4. 2nd ed. - 1988
5. 1 vol.
6. $95
7. annual supp.
8. 1989 - $26; 1990 - $32
9. 88-38822/18833815/KF1524.M87

1. **CREDITORS' RIGHTS IN ILLINOIS**
2. -
3. Illinois ICLE
4. 1990
5. 1 vol.
6. $87.95
7. periodic supp.
8. no supp. yet

1. **CRIME 1991**
2. -
3. MILE
4. 1991
5. 1 vol.
6. $68
7. no supp. planned

1. **CRIMINAL CONSTITUTIONAL LAW**
2. Rudstein, David S. et al.
3. Bender
4. 1990
5. 3 vols.
6. $285
7. annual supp.
8. no supp. yet
9. 90-83943/22730689/KF9219.R82

1. **CRIMINAL DEFENSE**
2. -
3. Indiana CLE
4. 1989
5. 1 vol.
6. $50
7. no supp. planned

1. **CRIMINAL DEFENSE ETHICS: LAW & LIABILITY**
2. Burkoff, John M.
3. Clark Boardman Callaghan
4. 1986
5. 1 vol.
6. $110 incl. 3 mos. supp.
7. annual supp.
8. 1989 - $55; 1991 - $79.50
9. 86-6092/13332832/KF306.B87

1. **CRIMINAL DEFENSE JURY INSTRUCTIONS**
2. Ackley, Harry
3. Knowles
4. 1984
5. 1 vol. (Calif. only)
6. $135 incl. 3 mos. supp.
7. annual supp.
8. 1989 - $36; 1990 - $42
9. 12985716/KFC1171.A76

1. **CRIMINAL DEFENSE PRACTICE**
2. -
3. NH Bar
4. 1991
5. 1 vol.
6. $40
7. no supp. planned

1. **CRIMINAL DEFENSE TECHNIQUES**
2. Eisenstein, Michael, ed.
3. Bender
4. 1969
5. 10 vols.
6. $1010 incl. 3 mos. supp.
7. biannual supp.
8. 1989 - $582; 1990 - $713.50
9. 72-110613/60998/KF9656.C74

1. **CRIMINAL EVIDENCE TRIAL MANUAL FOR TEXAS LAWYERS**
2. Larkin, Murl A.
3. Butterworth-Texas
4. 1986
5. 1 vol.
6. $120
7. periodic supp.
8. 1989 - $86.50; 1990 - $140
9. 14707170/KFT1780.A6L37

1. **CRIMINAL JURY INSTRUCTIONS FOR THE DISTRICT OF COLUMBIA**
2. Young Lawyers Section
3. Bar Assn. of D.C.
4. 4th ed. - 1985
5. 1 vol.
6. $50
7. no supp. yet
8. new ed. in 1992
9. 67-7709/969281/KFD1783.A65B3

1. **CRIMINAL JURY INSTRUCTIONS - NEW YORK**
2. Comm. on Criminal Jury Instructions
3. NYS OCA

4. 1983
5. 4 vols.
6. $100
7. annual supp.
8. 1990 - $7; 1991 - $7

1. **CRIMINAL LAW**
2. Snouffer, Hon. William C. et al., ed.
3. Oregon Bar
4. 1986
5. 2 vols.
6. $135
7. periodic supp.
8. 1990 - $55
9. 86-61478/14564862/KFO2975.C755

1. **CRIMINAL LAW**
2. -
3. Indiana CLE
4. 1989
5. 1 vol.
6. $50
7. no supp. planned

1. **CRIMINAL LAW ADVOCACY**
2. Kadish, Mark J. et. al.
3. Bender
4. 1982
5. 7 vols.
6. $675 incl. 3 mos. supp.
7. periodic supp.
8. 1989 - $358; 1990 - $401
9. 82-70639/8840774/KF9656.C745

1. **CRIMINAL LAW DESKBOOK**
2. McCloskey, Patrick
3. Bender
4. 1984
5. 1 vol.
6. $125 incl. 3 mos. supp.
7. annual supp.
8. 1989 - $63; 1990 - $78
9. 84-71993/11476866/KF9656.M35

1. **CRIMINAL LAW FORMBOOK**
2. Fagan, Tom et al.
3. OCDLA
4. 1982
5. 1 vol.
6. $95-nonmembers; $75-members
7. periodic supp.
8. supp. in 1992

1. **CRIMINAL LAW HANDBOOK**
2. -
3. Arkansas Bar
4. 1985
5. 1 vol.
6. $75
7. periodic supp.
8. 1988 - $5
9. 13905848/KFA4161.A6A7

1. **THE CRIMINAL LAW REPORTER**
2. Goebes, Robert L.
3. BNA
4. 1967
5. 1 vol.
6. $570/yr.
7. weekly supp.
8. renewal - $540/yr.
9. 1565436/KF9615.C7

1. **CRIMINAL PATTERN JURY INSTRUCTIONS**
2. Colquitt, Joseph A.
3. ABICLE
4. 1989
5. 2 vols.
6. $85
7. periodic supp.
8. no supp. yet

1. **CRIMINAL PRACTICE AND PROCEDURE IN THE DISTRICT COURT OF MARYLAND**
2. Kaminkow, Michael E. & R.J. Steinberg
3. MICPEL
4. rev. - 1989
5. 1 vol.
6. $26.25
7. periodic supp.
8. no supp. yet
9. 12632392/KFM1775.C92

1. **CRIMINAL PROCEDURE IN NEW YORK PART 1 & PART 2**
2. Publisher's Editorial Staff
3. Lawyers Coop.
4. rev. ed. - 1987
5. 4 vols.
6. $320 incl. 6 mos. supp.
7. annual supp.
8. 1989 - $135.50; 1990 - $70
9. 82-9425/18928390/KFN6155.J35

1. **CRIMINAL TRIAL PRACTICE**
2. Friedman, Richard, et al.
3. New Jersey ICLE
4. 1988

5. 1 vol.
6. $55
7. no supp. planned
9. 18119139/KFN2379.Z9S451

1. **CRIMINAL TRIAL PRACTICE IN FLORIDA**
2. -
3. Florida Bar
4. 1984
5. 1 vol.
6. $40
7. periodic supp.
8. no supp. yet
9. 83-82210/10592146/KFF579.C74

1. **CRITICAL ISSUES: TRADEMARKS**
2. Publ. Edit. Staff
3. Lawyers Coop.
4. 1990
5. 1 vol.
6. $105 incl. 6 mos. supp.
7. annual supp.
9. 90-63738/23760954/KF3178.4.C7

1. **CROSS BORDER PRACTICE COMPENDIUM**
2. Donald-Little, Dorothy, ed.
3. Kluwer
4. 1991
5. 1 vol.
6. $79 incl. 3 mos. supp.
7. periodic supp.
8. no supp. yet

1. **CROSS-EXAMINATION OF LAY WITNESSES (Art of Advocacy Series)**
2. Durst, John & Fred Queller
3. Bender
4. 1988
5. 1 vol.
6. $110 incl. 3 mos. supp.
7. annual supp.
8. 1989 - $57; 1990 - $74.50
9. 88-71936/18891993/KF8925.PUD87

1. **CROSS-EXAMINATION OF MEDICAL EXPERTS**
2. Houts, Marshall
3. Bender
4. 1982
5. 1 vol.
6. $110 incl. 6 mos. supp.
7. periodic supp.
8. 1989 - $70; 1990 - $75
9. 81-71994/9131662/KF8920.H68

1. **CROSS-EXAMINATION OF NON-MEDICAL EXPERTS (Art of Advocacy Series)**
2. Habush, Robert L.
3. Bender
4. 1981
5. 1 vol.
6. $110 incl. 3 mos. supp.
7. periodic supp.
8. 1989 - $64; 1990 - $75
9. 81-69234/7985747/KF8920.H28

1. **CUMULATIVE CHANGES**
2. Koschei, Jon, ed.
3. RIA
4. 1986
5. 2 vols.
6. $525/yr.; $495/yr. for 2 yrs.
7. quarterly supp.
8. renewal - $475/yr.

1. **CURRENT DEVELOPMENTS IN INTELLECTUAL PROPERTY LAW**
2. -
3. Conn. Bar
4. 1991
5. 1 vol.
6. $53
7. no supp. planned

1. **CURRENT LEASING LAW AND TECHNIQUES - FORMS (Real Estate Transaction Series, vols. 7, 7A, & 7B)**
2. Rohan, Patrick
3. Bender
4. 1982
5. 4 vols.
6. $415 incl. 3 mos. supp.
7. annual supp.
8. 1989 - $267.50; 1990 - $324
9. 82-70468/8584962/KF588.1.R64

1. **CURRENT LEGAL FORMS WITH TAX ANALYSIS**
2. Rabkin, Jacob and Mark H. Johnson
3. Bender
4. 1948
5. 22 vols.
6. $1400 incl. 3 mos. supp.
7. 3-4 supp./yr.
8. 1989 - $955; 1990 - $1053.50
9. 48-19805/194528/KF170.R3

1. **CURRENT PATENT INTERFERENCE PRACTICE**

2. Collins, Bruce M.
3. Prentice Hall Law & Business
4. 1987
5. 1 vol.
6. $85 incl. 4 mos. supp.
7. periodic supp.
8. 1989 - $45; 1990 - $45
9. 87-7302//r88/16578420/KF3124.C65

1. **CUSTOMS LAW AND ADMINISTRATION (INCLUDING CUSTOMS SERVICE DECISIONS)**
2. Sturm, Ruth F. & Eugene M. Wypyski
3. Oceana
4. 3rd ed. - 1982
5. 4 vols.
6. $500/set
7. periodic supp.
8. 1991 - $300
9. 82-8268/8587792/KF6694.S8

1. **CUSTOMS REGULATIONS OF THE UNITED STATES**
2. U.S. Customs Service
3. order from USGPO - stock #948-006-00000-6
4. new ed. due 1991
5. 1 vol.
6. price NA
7. periodic supp.

1. **D.C. CODE OF PROFESSIONAL RESPONSIBILITY AND OPINIONS OF THE D.C. BAR LEGAL ETHICS COMMITTEE**
2. -
3. D.C. Bar
4. 1983
5. 1 vol.
6. $43.75
7. periodic supp.

1. **D.C. FEDERAL COURTS HANDBOOK**
2. P-H Editorial Staff
3. Prentice Hall Law & Business
4. 2nd ed. - 1991
5. 1 vol.
6. $85 incl. 4 mos. supp.
7. periodic supp.
8. 1989 - $45; 1990 - $55
9. 24622957/KFD1729.A2

1. **D.C. RULES OF PROFESSIONAL RESPONSIBILITY**
2. -
3. D.C. Bar
4. 1991
5. 1 vol.
6. $40
7. annual subscription service

1. **DAMAGES**
2. Markley, Charles R. & Ronald G. Stephenson, eds.
3. Oregon Bar
4. 1990
5. 2 vols.
6. $130
7. periodic supp.
8. no supp. yet
9. 90-60402/21919040/KFO2490.D3D35

1. **DAMAGES**
2. Branton, James L. & James D. Lovett
3. Knowles
4. 1987
5. 1 vol. (Avail. in Texas and Natl. eds.)
6. $135 incl. 3 mos. supp.
7. annual supp.
8. 1988 - $56; 1990 - $43
9. 15230430/KFT1290.D3.L68

1. **DAMAGES IN CONSTRUCTION LITIGATION**
2. -
3. Indiana CLE
4. 1990
5. 1 vol.
6. $50
7. no supp. planned

1. **DAMAGES IN EMPLOYMENT CASES**
2. -
3. Conn. Bar
4. 1991
5. 1 vol.
6. $53
7. no supp. planned

1. **DAMAGES IN TORT ACTIONS**
2. Minzer, Marilyn K. et al.
3. Bender
4. 1982
5. 10 vols.
6. $1100 incl. 3 mos. supp.
7. periodic supp.
8. 1989 - $902.50; 1990 - $780.50
9. 81-69913/8227955/KF1250.D35

1. **DAMAGES UNDER THE UNIFORM COMMERCIAL CODE**

2. Anderson, Roy Ryden
3. Clark Boardman Callaghan
4. 1988
5. 2 vols.
6. $170 incl. 6 mos. supp.
7. annual supp.
8. 1989 - $39.50; 1990 - $42.50
9. 88-9517/17674853/KF836.A96

1. **DATA PROCESSING AGREEMENTS (2nd ed.)**
2. Hancock, W.A.
3. Bus. Laws
4. 1990
5. 1 vol.
6. $95
7. annual supp.
8. renewal - $44/yr.
9. 22839283/KF905.C6D38

1. **DEALING WITH FINANCIALLY TROUBLED COMPANIES**
2. Hancock, W.A., ed.
3. Bus. Laws
4. 1987
5. 1 vol.
6. $90
7. annual supp.
8. renewal - $39/yr.
9. 88-415777/17770693/KF1501.C67

1. **DEATH (Courtroom Medicine Series vols. 3, 3A & 3B)**
2. Houts, Marshall, et al.
3. Bender
4. 1966
5. 3 vols.
6. $335 incl. 3 mos. supp.
7. annual supp.
8. 1989 - $162.50; 1990 - $222
9. 66-5679/895087/RA1011.C68

1. **DEBT COLLECTION**
2. -
3. Conn. Bar
4. 1991
5. 1 vol.
6. $53
7. no supp. planned

1. **DEBTOR-CREDITOR LAW**
2. Eisenberg, Theodore, Ed.-in-Chief
3. Bender
4. 1982
5. 10 vols.
6. $880 incl. 3 mos. supp.
7. periodic supp.
8. 1989 - $565; 1990 - $670
9. 81-68420/8259660/KF1501.D42

1. **DEBTORS-CREDITORS SYSTEM**
2. -
3. Arkansas Bar
4. 1988
5. 1 vol.
6. $100
7. periodic supp.

1. **DEEDS IN LIEU OF FORECLOSURE**
2. -
3. Illinois ICLE
4. 1991
5. 1 vol.
6. $99.95
7. periodic supp.
8. no supp. yet

1. **DEFENDING CRIMINAL CASES IN VIRGINIA**
2. Williamson, Richard W., ed.
3. Jt. Comm. Va.
4. 1981
5. 1 vol.
6. $73
7. periodic supp.
8. 1987 - $15; 1989 - $21
9. 81-182081/8033213/KFV2975.D43

1. **DEFENDING DRINKING DRIVERS**
2. Tarantino, John
3. James
4. 2nd ed. - 1986
5. 1 vol.
6. $89.90 incl. 3 mos. supp.
7. annual supp.
8. 1990 - $45.99; 1991 - $42.82
9. 13141825/KF2231.T37

1. **DEFENDING DUI AND TRAFFIC CASES**
2. -
3. Illinois ICLE
4. 1991
5. 1 vol.
6. $99.95
7. periodic supp.
8. no supp. yet
9. 18969933/KFI1497.8.D44

1. **DEFENDING DWIs IN WASHINGTON**

2. Cowan, Douglas L. & Stephen W. Hayne
3. Butterworth-St. Paul
4. 1987 Rev. 1989
5. 1 vol.
6. $115
7. periodic supp.
8. 1989 - $67.50
9. 86-73068

1. **DEFENDING ILLINOIS CRIMINAL CASES**
2. -
3. Illinois ICLE
4. 1988
5. 1 vol.
6. $99.95
7. periodic supp.
8. 1991 - $29.95
9. 18316628/KFI1775.D42

1. **DEFENSE AGAINST A PRIMA FACIE CASE**
2. Publisher's Editorial Staff
3. Clark Boardman Callaghan
4. 1982
5. 1 vol.
6. $95 incl. 6 mos. supp.
7. annual supp.
8. 1989 - $49; 1990 - $80
9. 82-4176/8283611/KF8940.P7D778

1. **DEFENSE OF DRUNK DRIVING CASES: A GUIDE FOR THE GENERAL PRACTITIONER**
2. -
3. Maine Bar
4. 1989
5. 1 vol.
6. $30
7. no supp. planned

1. **DEFENSE OF DRUNK DRIVING CASES: CRIMINAL - CIVIL**
2. Erwin, Richard E. & Marilyn K. Minzer
3. Bender
4. 3rd ed. - 1971
5. 4 vols.
6. $485 incl. 3 mos. supp.
7. annual supp.
8. 1989 - $330; 1990 - $406.50
9. 72-166435/267053/KF8925.T7E7

1. **DEFENSE OF NARCOTICS CASES**
2. Bernheim, David
3. Bender
4. 1972
5. 2 vols.
6. $245 incl. 3 mos. supp.
7. annual supp.
8. 1989 - $171.50; 1990 - $193
9. 72-89203/584106/KF3890.B45

1. **DEFENSE OF SPEEDING, RECKLESS DRIVING, VEHICULAR HOMICIDE**
2. Campbell, James F.
3. Bender
4. 1984
5. 2 vols.
6. $225 incl. 3 mos. supp.
7. annual supp.
8. 1989 - $144; 1990 - $168
9. 84-71307/11574288/KF2231.C36

1. **DEFENSE TECHNIQUES FOR DWI CLIENTS**
2. -
3. Indiana CLE
4. 1989
5. 1 vol.
6. $55
7. no supp. planned

1. **DEFERRED GIVING - EXPLANATION, SPECIMEN AGREEMENTS, FORMS**
2. Teitell, Conrad
3. Taxwise
4. 1971
5. 2 vols.
6. $223
7. annual supp.
8. 1990 - $121; 1990 - $121
9. 84-051582/12310556/KF6449.A65T44

1. **DEFINITION OF SUBDIVISION IN MAINE LAW**
2. -
3. Maine Bar
4. 1990
5. 1 vol.
6. $35
7. no supp. planned

1. **DELAWARE CORPORATION LAW & PRACTICE**
2. Drexler, David A. et al.
3. Bender
4. 1988
5. 1 vol.
6. $105 incl. 3 mos. supp.
7. 1990 - $33
8. no supp. yet

9. 88-71934/11729041/KFD213.D7

1. **THE DELAWARE LAW OF CORPORATIONS AND BUSINESS ORGANIZATIONS**
2. Balotti, R. Franklin & Jesse A. Finkelstein
3. Prentice Hall Law & Business
4. 2nd ed. - 1990
5. 6 vols.
6. $395 incl. 4 mos. supp.
7. periodic supp.
8. 1991 - $160
9. 85-23768/12978894/KFD213.B35

1. **DEMONSTRATIVE EVIDENCE**
2. -
3. Indiana CLE
4. 1989
5. 1 vol.
6. $60
7. no supp. planned

1. **DEMONSTRATIVE EVIDENCE (Art of Advocacy Series)**
2. Lipson, Ashley
3. Bender
4. 1988
5. 1 vol.
6. $110 incl. 3 mos. supp.
7. annual supp.
8. 1989 - $52; 1990 - $74.50
9. 88-71359/18504695/KF8967.L56

1. **THE DEMONSTRATIVE EVIDENCE SOURCEBOOK**
2. Filter, Douglas
3. Staffort
4. 1985
5. 1 vol.
6. $59
7. no supp. yet
8. new ed. in 1991
9. 85-50214/12975192/KF8967.Z9F55

1. **THE DEPARTMENT OF JUSTICE MANUAL**
2. -
3. Prentice Hall Law & Business
4. 1987
5. 13 vols.
6. $1100 incl. 4 mos. supp.
7. periodic supp.
8. 1990 - $395; 1991 - $345
9. 87-20721/16579926/KF5107.D47

1. **DEPOSITION - STRATEGY, LAW AND FORMS**
2. Sann, Alexander & S. Bellman, eds.
3. Bender
4. 1981
5. 10 vols.
6. $750 incl. 3 mos. supp.
7. periodic supp.
8. 1989 - $197; 1990 - $263.50
9. 80-70547/7167354/KF8900.D47

1. **DEPOSITIONS**
2. Branton, James L. & James D. Lovett
3. Knowles
4. 1984
5. 2 vols. (Avail. in Texas & Natl. Eds.)
6. $185 incl. 3 mos. supp.
7. annual supp.
8. 1989 - $51 (TX); $43 (Natl.)
   1990 - $47 (TX); $43 (Natl.)
9. KF8900.B77

1. **DEPOSITIONS: PROCEDURE, STRATEGY AND TECHNIQUE**
2. Lisnek, Paul M. & Michael J. Kaufman
3. West
4. 1990
5. 1 vol.
6. $68
7. periodic supp.
8. no supp. yet
9. 89-27265/21717782/KF8900.L57

1. **DEPRECIATION AND CAPITAL PLANNING**
2. -
3. WG&L
4. 1987
5. 1 vol.
6. $135/yr.
7. semiannual supp.
8. $62.50
9. 88-205862/18661398/KF6386.B46

1. **DEPRECIATION HANDBOOK**
2. Del Negro, John & Harvey Levenson
3. Bender
4. 1983
5. 1 vol.
6. $105 incl. 3 mos. supp.
7. periodic supp.
8. 1989 - $73; 1990 - $131
9. 83-70021/9544564/KF6386.D44

1. **DESIGN AND UTILITY MODELS THROUGHOUT THE WORLD**
2. Greene, Anne Marie, ed.
3. Clark Boardman Callaghan
4. 1983
5. 1 vol.
6. $135 incl. 3 mos. supp.
7. periodic supp.
8. 1989 - $97.50; 1990 - $114.50
9. 82-20738/8954053/K1525.A49D47

1. **DESIGNING EFFECTIVE COMPANY POLICIES: PLUG LEGAL LOOPHOLES AND PUMP UP PRODUCTIVITY**
2. -
3. Alex. Hamilton Inst.
4. 1987
5. 1 vol.
6. $62.25
7. 3 supp./yr.
8. $19.50/supp.
9. 17223343

1. **DETENTION AND CORRECTIONS CASELAW CATALOG**
2. Miller, R.C. & D.J. Walter
3. CRS
4. 4th ed. - 1991
5. 1 vol.
6. $80
7. annual supp.
8. 1990 - $30; 1991 - $40
9. 15079484/KF9730.A59D47

1. **DETERMINING CHILD & SPOUSAL SUPPORT**
2. Smith, Jeanne Wielage & Elizabeth S. Beninger
3. Clark Boardman Callaghan
4. 1986
5. 1 vol.
6. $80 incl. 6 mos. supp.
7. annual supp.
8. 1989 - $39; 1990 - $42.50
9. 87-22411/16468419/KF549.B46

1. **DETERMINING ECONOMIC DAMAGES**
2. Martin, Gerald D.
3. James
4. 1988
5. 1 vol.
6. $69.95 incl. 3 mos. supp.
7. annual supp.
8. 1989 - $38.85; 1990 - $44.95
9. 19806253

1. **DEVELOPMENTS IN SEC DISCLOSURE**
2. -
3. Georgetown
4. 1989
5. 1 vol.
6. $75
7. no supp. planned

1. **DIGEST OF COMMERCIAL LAWS OF THE WORLD – (INCLUDING FORMS OF COMMERCIAL AGREEMENTS AND STATE VARIATIONS OF COMMERCIAL LAW)**
2. Nelson, Lester, ed.
3. Oceana
4. 1966
5. 11 vols. (avail. separately)
6. $850
7. quarterly supp.
8. 1990 - $120; 1991 - $125
9. 65-22163/11300432/K1005.4.D54

1. **DIGEST OF COMMERCIAL LAWS OF THE WORLD – FORMS OF COMMERCIAL AGREEMENTS OF THE WORLD**
2. National Association of Credit Management; Lester Nelson
3. Oceana
4. 1984
5. 2 vols.
6. $200
7. periodic supp.
8. 1986 - $100; 1987 - $100
9. 65-22163/11300432/K1004.35.D5

1. **DIGEST OF COMMERCIAL LAWS OF THE WORLD – STATE VARIATIONS OF COMMERCIAL LAW**
2. National Association of Credit Management
3. Oceana
4. 1984
5. 2 vols.
6. $200
7. periodic supp.
8. 1990 - $25; 1991 - $15

1. **DIGEST OF INTELLECTUAL PROPERTY LAWS OF THE WORLD**
2. Nelson, Lester, ed.
3. Oceana
4. 1990
5. 3 vols.

6. $300
7. periodic supp.
8. 1990 - $155; 1990 - $150
9. 21325287/K1005.D63

1. **DIGEST OF LEGAL ACTIVITIES OF INTERNATIONAL ORGANIZATIONS AND OTHER INSTITUTIONS**
2. UNIDROIT International Institute for the Unification of Private Law
3. Oceana
4. 8th ed. - 1988
5. 1 vol.
6. $150
7. periodic editions
8. -
9. 89-140602/18999167/K612.D53

1. **DIGEST OF MARYLAND CASES ON DISCRIMINATION**
2. Maryland State Bar Assn. Section of Labor Law MCHR Digest Subcommittee
3. MICPEL
4. 1985
5. 1 vol.
6. $57.75
7. periodic supp.
9. 12634129/KFM1534.D57

1. **DIGEST OF MARYLAND UNEMPLOYMENT INSURANCE DECISIONS**
2. Singleton, Judith S.
3. MICPEL
4. 1985
5. 1 vol.
6. $31.50
7. periodic supp.
8. 1987 - $10
9. 12821651/KFM1545.Z9S6

1. **DIGEST OF STATE LAND SALES REGULATIONS**
2. Bloch, Stuart Marshall & Wm. B. Ingersoll
3. Land Dev.
4. 1973; rev. - 1985
5. 1 vol.
6. $220/yr.
7. quarterly supp.
8. renewal - $190/yr.

1. **DIGEST OF UNEMPLOYMENT COMMISSION DECISIONS**
2. -
3. Book Pub.
4. 1984
5. 5 vols.
6. $400
7. supp. as needed

1. **DIRECT EXAMINATION (Art of Advocacy Series)**
2. Baldwin, Scott
3. Bender
4. 1981
5. 1 vol.
6. $110 incl. 3 mos. supp.
7. annual supp.
8. 1989 - $64; 1990 - $50
9. 81-66579/7579926/KF8915.B35

1. **DIRECTOR & OFFICER INSURANCE COVERAGE**
2. -
3. MILE
4. 1991
5. 1 vol.
6. $68
7. no supp. planned

1. **DIRECTOR & OFFICER LIABILITY: INSURANCE & INDEMNIFICATION**
2. Hancock, W.A., ed.
3. Bus. Laws
4. 1988
5. 1 vol.
6. $85
7. annual supp.
8. renewal - $38/yr.
9. 12697216

1. **DIRECTOR OF NURSING MANUAL: FEDERAL REGULATIONS AND GUIDELINES**
2. Ed. Staff
3. National Health
4. 1980
5. 1 vol.
6. $130 incl. 1 yr. supp.
7. quarterly supp.
8. renewal - $105/yr.
9. 80-125106/11495719

1. **DIRECTORS IN THE HOT SEAT**
2. -
3. MILE
4. 1989
5. 1 vol.
6. $58
7. no supp. planned

1. **DIRECTOR'S PORTFOLIO**
2. Goldstein, Arnold S.
3. Enterprise
4. 1987
5. 1 vol.
6. $49.95
7. periodic supp.
8. no supp. yet

1. **DISABILITIES IN THE WORKPLACE: A GUIDE TO FEDERAL AND STATE LAWS**
2. -
3. WG&L
4. 1991
5. 1 vol.
6. $275/yr.
7. monthly supp. & newsletter
9. 24773914/KF3469.A6D5

1. **DISABILITY DISCRIMINATION IN EMPLOYMENT**
2. Coleman, John J.
3. Clark Boardman Callaghan
4. 1991
5. 1 vol.
6. $95 incl. 3 mos. supp.
7. annual supp.
8. no supp. yet
9. 91-22911/24246828/KF3469.C65

1. **THE DISABILITY LAW REPORTER SERVICE**
2. Cooke, Edmund D. & Peter S. Gray, eds.
3. Prentice Hall Law & Business
4. 1991
5. 2 vols.
6. $345/yr.
7. periodic supp.
9. 91-30196/24318898/KF4754.3.C66

1. **DISCOVERY**
2. Branton, James L. & James D. Lovett
3. Knowles
4. 1988
5. 1 vol. (avail. in Texas & Natl. eds.)
6. $135 incl. 3 mos. supp.
7. annual supp.
8. 1990 - $43; 1991 - $42
9. 18905641/KFT1737.L6

1. **DISCOVERY (Art of Advocacy Series)**
2. Miltz, Arthur Ian
3. Bender
4. 1982
5. 1 vol.
6. $110 incl. 3 mos. supp.
7. periodic supp.
8. 1989 - $65; 1990 - $74.50
9. 82-72756/8938958/KF8900.M5

1. **DISCOVERY – HOW TO MAKE IT WORK FOR YOU**
2. -
3. Wash. Bar
4. 1989
5. 1 vol.
6. $35
7. no supp. planned

1. **DISCOVERY TOOLS: HOW TO WIN YOUR CASE BEFORE TRIAL**
2. -
3. Indiana CLE
4. 1988
5. 1 vol.
6. $55
7. no supp. planned

1. **DISCOVERY UNDER THE MARYLAND RULES**
2. Kenny, John J. et al., eds.
3. MICPEL
4. 2nd ed. - 1986
5. 1 vol.
6. $42
7. periodic supp.
8. -
9. 12980990/KFM1737.D5

1. **DISPUTED PATERNITY PROCEEDINGS**
2. Schatkin, Sidney
3. Bender
4. rev. 4th ed. - 1975
5. 2 vols.
6. $250 incl. 3 mos. supp.
7. annual supp.
8. 1989 - $184.50; 1990 - $222
9. 75-21702/2040836/KFN5131.S3

1. **DISTRIBUTING FOREIGN PRODUCED PRODUCTS IN THE U.S.**
2. Hayutin, David L.
3. Bender
4. 1988
5. 1 vol.
6. $105 incl. 3 mos. supp.
7. annual supp.
8. no supp. yet
9. 87-72785/77799540/KF1993.A6H38

1. **DISTRICT COURT FORMS**
2. Project of the Young Lawyers' Section of the Maryland State Bar Assn.
3. MICPEL
4. rev. 1986
5. 1 vol.
6. $26.25
7. periodic supp.
8. 1987 - $10.50; 1988 - $10.50
9. 13655577/KFM1714.D5D57

1. **DISTRICT COURT PRACTICE MANUAL-CIVIL**
2. Blakeslee, Wesley D., ed.
3. MICPEL
4. rev. - 1990
5. 1 vol.
6. $36.75
7. periodic supp.
8. -
9. 11489301/KFM1714.D6

1. **DISTRICT OF COLUMBIA CITATION SERVICE**
2. -
3. Rules
4. 1970
5. 1 vol.
6. $59 incl. 1 yr. supp.
7. semiannual supp.
8. renewal fee

1. **DISTRICT OF COLUMBIA COURT RULES**
2. -
3. Rules
4. 1952
5. 3 vols.
6. $85 incl. 1 yr. supp.
7. periodic supp.
8. renewal fee

1. **THE DISTRICT OF COLUMBIA ESTATES, TRUSTS AND PROBATE LAW DIGEST**
2. Fox, Nancy, ed.
3. D.C. Bar
4. 2nd ed. - 1990
5. 1 vol.
6. $50 - nonmembers
7. annual supp.
8. no supp. yet
9. 90-83575/22763261/KFD1344.A59F38

1. **THE DISTRICT OF COLUMBIA PRACTICE MANUAL**
2. -
3. D.C. Bar
4. 1987
5. 1 vol.
6. $127
7. periodic supp.
8. 1989 - $43.75
9. 87-72672/16903691/KFD1281.D52

1. **DIVORCE**
2. -
3. Indiana CLE
4. 1990
5. 1 vol.
6. $50
7. no supp. planned

1. **DIVORCE: COMMON & COMPLEX ISSUES**
2. -
3. Indiana CLE
4. 1988
5. 1 vol.
6. $50
7. no supp. planned

1. **DIVORCE ORGANIZATION SYSTEM: A SYSTEM FOR MANAGING A DIVORCE PRACTICE IN MARYLAND 2ND ED.**
2. Putzel, Constance K.
3. MICPEL
4. rev. - 1988
5. 1 vol.
6. $63
7. periodic supp.
9. 89-123186/20096260/KFM1300.P87

1. **DIVORCE, SEPARATION AND THE DISTRIBUTION OF PROPERTY**
2. Oldham, J. Thomas
3. Law Journal
4. 1987
5. 1 vol.
6. $85
7. periodic supp.
8. 1989 - $77; 1990 - $84
9. 87-2709/15365333/KF524.Z95O43

1. **DIVORCE TAX PLANNING STRATEGIES**
2. Brown, William J.
3. Shepard's
4. 1990
5. 2 vols.

6. $160
7. semiannual supp.
8. 1991 - $36
9. 90-30428/21039894/KF6333.B76

1. **DIVORCE TAXATION**
2. -
3. Indiana CLE
4. 1990
5. 1 vol.
6. $50
7. no supp. planned

1. **DIVORCE TAXATION**
2. O'Connell, Marjorie A.
3. WG&L
4. 1981
5. 1 vol.
6. $415/yr.
7. monthly supp.
9. 82-155830/8827294/KF6428.A4O25

1. **DOCUMENTARY EVIDENCE (Art of Advocacy Series)**
2. Lipson, Ashley S.
3. Bender
4. 1986
5. 1 vol.
6. $110 incl. 3 mos. supp.
7. periodic supp.
8. 1989 - $70; 1990 - $75

1. **DOCUMENTATION OF REAL ESTATE TRANSACTIONS**
2. Miller, David P. & Robert S. Ball, eds.
3. Oregon Bar
4. 1991
5. 1 vol.
6. price NA
7. periodic supp.
8. no supp. yet
9. 91-52943

1. **DOCUMENTING SECURED TRANSACTIONS: PROBLEM AVOIDANCE AND EFFECTIVE DRAFTING**
2. Hillman, William C.
3. PLI
4. 1987
5. 1 vol.
6. $80
7. annual supp.
8. 1990 - $40; 1991 - $50
9. 87-62040/16969290

1. **DOING BUSINESS IN BRAZIL**
2. Neto, Pinheiro, ed.
3. Bender & Oyez
4. 1979
5. 1 vol.
6. $260/yr.
7. semiannual supp. & monthly newsletter
9. 79-52072/5993084

1. **DOING BUSINESS IN CANADA**
2. Stikeman and Elliott
3. Bender
4. 1984
5. 3 vols.
6. $350 incl. 3 mos. supp.
7. periodic supp.
8. 1989 - $290; 1990 - $292
9. 84-71749/11557156/KE450.B87D643

1. **DOING BUSINESS IN CHINA**
2. Streng, William & Allen Wilcox
3. Bender
4. 1990
5. 1 vol.
6. $105 incl. 3 mos. supp.
7. periodic supp.
8. no supp. yet
9. 89-50424/22454254/KQKO.D63

1. **DOING BUSINESS IN EUROPE**
2. -
3. CCH
4. 1972
5. 1 vol. (included free with Common Market Reports)
6. $775/yr.; $705/yr. for 2 yrs.
7. monthly supp.
9. 1613205

1. **DOING BUSINESS IN FRANCE**
2. Simeon Moquet Borde & Associes
3. Bender
4. 1983
5. 2 vols.
6. $290 incl. 3 mos. supp.
7. periodic supp.
8. 1989 - $253; 1990 - $275
9. 83-70749/10106733

1. **DOING BUSINESS IN IRELAND**
2. Ussher, P. et al.
3. Bender
4. 1987
5. 1 vol.

6. $110 incl. 3 mos. supp.
7. periodic supp.
8. 1989 - $49; 1990 - $52.50
9. 86-72294/15562718/KDK175.B87D65

1. **DOING BUSINESS IN JAPAN**
2. Kitagawa, Zentaro
3. Bender
4. 1980
5. 10 vols.
6. $720 incl. 3 mos. supp.
7. periodic supp.
8. 1989 - $347; 1990 - $451
9. 81-100046/7555533

1. **DOING BUSINESS IN MEXICO**
2. Reiner, S. Theodore, & Ann Reiner, eds.
3. Bender
4. 1980
5. 3 vols.
6. $295/yr.
7. periodic supp.
8. 1988 - $185; 1989 - $195
9. 80-51896/6799663

1. **DOING BUSINESS IN SPAIN**
2. Pombo, Fernando
3. Bender
4. 1987
5. 1 vol.
6. $195 incl. 3 mos. supp.
7. annual supp.
8. 1989 - $43.50; 1990 - $61.50
9. 87-71123/16767352/KKT78.B86P66

1. **DOING BUSINESS IN THE UNITED KINGDOM**
2. Clifford-Turner, City of London Solicitors
3. Bender
4. 1985
5. 3 vols.
6. $340 incl. 3 mos. supp.
7. periodic supp.
8. 1989 - $300; 1990 - $397
9. 85-72018/13334914/KD665.B86.D65

1. **DOING BUSINESS IN THE UNITED STATES**
2. Spires, Jeremiah J. et al.
3. Bender
4. 1978
5. 6 vols.
6. $585 incl. 3 mos. supp.
7. annual supp.
8. 1989 - $372.50; 1990 - $437.50
9. 78-69571/4417632/KF889.S67

1. **DOING BUSINESS WITH EASTERN EUROPE**
2. -
3. Bus. Intern.
4. 1975
5. 10 vols.
6. $3300/yr.
7. monthly supp.
9. 1950253/HF4050.B85

1. **DOMESTIC MAIL MANUAL**
2. U.S. Postal Service
3. order from USGPO - stock #739-003-00000-8
4. 1979
5. 1 vol.
6. $19/yr.
7. quarterly supp.
9. 82-2716/5153904

1. **DOMESTIC RELATIONS (MASSACHUSETTS): THE SUBSTANTIVE LAW**
2. Rotenberg, Hon. Ernest
3. Butterworth-NH
4. 1984
5. 1 vol.
6. $50
7. periodic supp.
8. 1986 - $15
9. 11890518

1. **DOMESTIC VIOLENCE TRAINING MANUAL**
2. House of Ruth Domestic Violence Legal Clinic
3. MICPEL
4. 1989
5. 1 vol.
6. $26.25
7. periodic supp.
9. 16911777/KFM1294.H84

1. **DOMINION TAX CASES**
2. -
3. CCH
4. 1949
5. 1 vol.
6. $390/yr.; $355/yr. for 2 yrs.
7. 3 supp./month
9. 76-30364/2442993/HJ3237

1. **DOMKE LAW AND PRACTICE OF COMMERCIAL ARBITRATION**
2. rev. by Gabriel Wilner
3. Clark Boardman Callaghan
4. rev. - 1984
5. 1 vol.
6. $105 incl. 6 mos. supp.
7. annual supp.
8. 1989 - $45.50; 1990 - $47
9. 83-26207/10277482/KF9085.D6

1. **DRAFTING BANKRUPTCY REORGANIZATION PLANS**
2. Pearson, John K., et al.
3. Wiley Law
4. 1988
5. 1 vol.
6. $125
7. annual supp.
8. 1990 - $55; 1992 - price NA
9. 18268802/KF1544.A65P4

1. **DRAFTING CALIFORNIA IRREVOCABLE LIVING TRUSTS, 2nd ed.**
2. Cohan, John R., ed.
3. Calif. CEB
4. 1987
5. 1 vol.
6. $105
7. periodic supp.
8. 1988 - $27; 1990 - $44
9. 86-72863/16119581/KFC188.D72

1. **DRAFTING EFFECTIVE CONTRACTS**
2. Feldman, R.A.
3. Prentice Hall Law & Business
4. 1989
5. 1 vol.
6. $80
7. periodic supp.
8. 1990 - $50
9. 89-38736/20221463/KF889.F38

1. **DRAFTING ESTATE PLANNING DOCUMENTS**
2.
3. Okla. Bar CLE
4. 1990
5. 2 vols.
6. $120
7. no supp. planned

1. **DRAFTING LICENSE AGREEMENTS**
2. Epstein, Michael A. & Frank L. Politano, eds.
3. Prentice Hall Law & Business
4. 1991
5. 1 vol.
6. $95 incl. 4 mos. supp.
7. periodic supp.
8. no supp. yet
9. 91-11933/23356361/KF3145.D7

1. **DRAFTING MARRIAGE CONTRACTS IN FLORIDA**
2. -
3. Florida Bar
4. 2nd ed. - 1988
5. 1 vol.
6. $45
7. as needed
8. -
9. 77-071497/17868692/KFF95.D73

1. **DRAFTING NEW YORK WILLS**
2. Klipstein, H. D.
3. Bender
4. 1983
5. 2 vols.
6. $210 incl. 3 mos. supp.
8. 1989 - $86; 1990 - $114.50
9. 83-163674//r88/10276949/KFN5201.K55

1. **DRAFTING THE DURABLE POWER OF ATTORNEY: A SYSTEMS APPROACH, 2nd ed.**
2. Collin, Lombard, Moses & Spitler
3. Shepard's
4. 2nd ed. - 1991
5. 2 vols.
6. $165
7. annual supp.
8. 1990 - $32; 1991 - $42
9. 87-21166/16467822/KF1347.D7

1. **DRAFTING THE UNION CONTRACT**
2. Laureau, Peter
3. Bender
4. 1988
5. 1 vol.
6. $105 incl. 3 mos. supp.
7. annual supp.
8. 1989 - $44; 1990 - $62
9. 88-70133/17664059/KF3408.L36

1. **DRAFTING WILLS AND TRUST AGREEMENTS**
2. -
3. Illinois ICLE

4. 1990
5. 1 vol.
6. $95
7. no supp. yet
9. 16829297/KFI1344.A65H8

1. **DRAFTING WILLS AND TRUST AGREEMENTS: A SYSTEMS APPROACH, 2nd ed.**
2. Wilkins, Robert P.
3. Shepard's
4. 2nd ed. - 1989
5. 2 vols.
6. $220
7. periodic supp. & monthly newsletter
8. renewal - $80/yr.
9. 89-5986/19354736/KF748.W55

1. **DRAFTING WILLS AND TRUSTS IN MASSACHUSETTS**
2. Reed, Alette E. et al.
3. Mass. CLE
4. 1990
5. 1 vol.
6. $95
7. periodic supp.
8. no supp. yet
9. 89-64081/21988263/KFM2544.D73

1. **THE DRINKING DRIVER IN MINNESOTA, 2nd Ed.**
2. Nicholas, Donald H., editor
3. Butterworth-St. Paul
4. 1989
5. 1 vol.
6. $88
7. periodic supp.
8. 1990 - $40; 1991 - $40
9. 89-688/19222195/KFM5697.8.N53

1. **DRINKING/DRIVING LITIGATION: CRIMINAL AND CIVIL**
2. Nichols, Donald H.
3. Clark Boardman Callaghan
4. 1985
5. 5 vols.
6. $360 incl. 6 mos. supp.
7. semiannual supp.
8. 1989 - $123; 1990 - $131
9. 85-29890/20526763/KF2231.N53

1. **DRINKING/DRIVING LITIGATION TRIAL NOTEBOOK**
2. Nichols, Donald H.
3. Clark Boardman Callaghan
4. 1987
5. 1 vol.
6. $75 incl. 6 mos. supp.
7. annual supp.
8. 1989 - $30; 1990 - $32.50
9. 16959016/KF8925.T7N52

1. **DRUG ABUSE AND THE LAW SOURCEBOOK**
2. Uelmen, Gerald & Victor Haddox
3. Clark Boardman Callaghan
4. 1983
5. 2 vols.
6. $210 incl. 3 mos. supp.
7. annual supp. and bimonthly reporting service
8. 1989 - $69.50; 1991 - $85
9. 81-21711/8112767/KF3885.U43

1. **DRUG AND ALCOHOL TESTING: ADVISING EMPLOYERS**
2. Turkula, William D.
3. Butterworth-NH
4. 1990
5. 1 vol.
6. $110
7. periodic supp.
8. no supp. yet
9. 90-41925/22004645/KF3540.T87

1. **DRUG & MEDICAL DEVICE LIABILITY**
2. -
3. MILE
4. 1991
5. 1 vol.
6. $68
7. no supp. planned

1. **DRUG PRODUCT LIABILITY**
2. Dixon, Marden G. et al.
3. Bender
4. 1974
5. 3 vols.
6. $340 incl. 3 mos. supp.
7. annual supp.
8. 1989 - $217; 1990 - $255
9. 75-307248/1324848/KF1297.D7D59

1. **DRUG TESTING IN THE WORKPLACE: COMPLYING WITH THE LAW**
2. -
3. Conn. Bar
4. 1991
5. 1 vol.
6. $43
7. no supp. planned

1. **DRUG TESTING LAW, TECHNOLOGY & PRACTICE**
2. Evans, David G.
3. Clark Boardman Callaghan
4. 1990
5. 1 vol.
6. $95 incl. 6 mos. supp.
7. annual supp.
8. no supp. yet
9. 90-15085/22492562/KF3540.E93

1. **DRUG TESTING LEGAL MANUAL**
2. Zeese, Kevin B.
3. Clark Boardman Callaghan
4. 1987
5. 1 vol.
6. $95 incl. 3 mos. supp.
7. annual supp.
8. 1989 - $45; 1991 - $84.50
9. 87-37516/17324392/KF3890.Z44

1. **DRUG TESTING MANUAL**
2. -
3. Keller
4. 1989
5. 1 vol.
6. $75
7. semiannual supp.
8. $50/yr.

1. **DRUG TESTING PROGRAM MATERIALS**
2. -
3. NELI
4. 1990
5. 1 vol.
6. $75
7. no supp. planned

1. **DRUNK DRIVING 1991**
2. -
3. MILE
4. 1991
5. 1 vol.
6. $68
7. no supp. planned

1. **DUI AND OTHER TRAFFIC OFFENSES IN FLORIDA**
2. -
3. Florida Bar
4. 1986
5. 1 vol.
6. $50
7. supp. as needed
8. 1989 - $25
9. 85-82325/14974681/KFF297.8D85

1. **DUII TRIAL NOTEBOOK**
2. Hingson, John H. III et al.
3. OCDLA
4. 1991
5. 1 vol.
6. $145-nonmembers; $110-members
7. periodic supp.
9. 24768650/KFO2697.8.D85

1. **DUNLAP-HANNA, PENNSYLVANIA FORMS**
2. Meyer, Milford J. & Raymond L. Shapiro
3. Bender
4. 1948
5. 12 vols.
6. $995 incl. 3 mos. supp.
7. periodic supp.
8. 1989 - $339; 1990 - $335
9. 49-13527/9345882/KFP68.D81

1. **DUTCH BUSINESS LAW**
2. Schuit, Steven R.
3. Kluwer
4. 1989
5. 1 vol.
6. $203 incl. 3 mos. supp.
7. periodic supp.
8. 1990 - $159; 1991 - $175
9. 88-23070/18441856/KKM920.S38

1. **THE DWI CASE: STRATEGIES AND TECHNICAL CONSIDERATIONS FOR DEFENSE AND PROSECUTION**
2. -
3. NH Bar
4. 1989
5. 1 vol.
6. $35
7. no supp. planned

1. **DWI DEFENSE FORMS**
2. Tarantino, John A.
3. James
4. 1982
5. 1 vol.
6. $89.97 incl. 3 mos. supp.
7. annual supp.
8. 1989 - $42.92; 1990 - $46.99
9. 85-206704/11274863/KF2231.A65T37

1. **DWI - DRAM SHOP**
2. -
3. Indiana CLE

4. 1990
5. 1 vol.
6. $50
7. no supp. planned

1. **EASTERN EUROPEAN STATES AND THE DEVELOPMENT OF THE LAW OF THE SEA: REGIONAL DOCUMENTS, NATIONAL LEGISLATION**
2. Sebek, Victor
3. Oceana
4. 1976
5. 2 vols.
6. $150
7. no supp. planned
9. 77-7734/JX4411.S4

1. **ECKHARDT'S WORKBOOK FOR WISCONSIN ESTATE PLANNERS**
2. Bradley, Mark J., et al.
3. State Bar of Wisc.
4. 1990
5. 1 vol.
6. $225
7. periodic supp.
8. 1991 - $58
9. 90-9405/20935165/KFW2540.E25

1. **ECONOMIC ISSUES IN DIVORCE**
2. -
3. Maine Bar
4. 1990
5. 1 vol.
6. $30
7. no supp. planned
9. 22400772/KF535.Z99M243

1. **ECRA COMPLIANCE**
2. Farer, David B.
3. New Jersey ICLE
4. 1988
5. 1 vol.
6. $65
7. no supp. planned

1. **EDUCATION LAW**
2. Rapp, James A.
3. Bender
4. 1984
5. 4 vols.
6. $375 incl. 3 mos. supp.
7. periodic supp.
8. 1989 - $225.50; 1990 - $277
9. 83-73154/10588158/KF4119.R36

1. **EDUCATION LAW**
2. -
3. MICPEL
4. 1991
5. 1 vol.
6. $42
7. no supp. yet

1. **EEC MERGER CONTROL REPORTER**
2. Van Gerven, G. & S. Kinsella, eds.
3. Kluwer
4. 1991
5. 1 vol.
6. $395/yr.
7. monthly supp.
9. 91-30643/24284310/KJE6467.A38E35

1. **EEO COMPLIANCE MANUAL**
2. Trowers-Crowley, Sharleen, ed.
3. WG&L
4. 1979
5. 3 vols.
6. $382
7. monthly supp.
9. 78-74620/4695450/KF3464.A6E66

1. **EEO IN FEDERAL, STATE AND LOCAL GOVERNMENT CONFERENCE MANUAL**
2. -
3. NELI
4. 1991
5. 1 vol.
6. $100
7. no supp. planned
9. 12968192/KF3464.E44

1. **EEO UPDATE 1990**
2. -
3. Georgetown
4. 1990
5. 1 vol.
6. $75
7. no supp. planned

1. **EEOC COMPLIANCE MANUAL**
2. Sala, Susan J.
3. BNA
4. 1975
5. 2 vols.
6. $180/yr.; $170/yr. for 2 yrs.
7. periodic supp.
9. 84-210562/11551057/KF3464.A6U55

1. **EEOC COMPLIANCE MANUAL**
2. -
3. CCH
4. 1975
5. 1 vol.
6. $195/yr.; $175/yr. for 2 yrs.
7. periodic supp.
9. 2369728/KB1.C7e

1. **EFFECTIVE INTRODUCTION OF EVIDENCE IN CALIFORNIA**
2. Armstrong, William H., et al.
3. Calif. CEB
4. 1989
5. 1 vol.
6. $85
7. periodic supp.
8. 1991 - price NA
9. 89-82625/22240551/KFC1030.E442

1. **EFFECTIVE LEGAL WRITING**
2. -
3. Indiana CLE
4. 1991
5. 1 vol.
6. $35
7. no supp. planned

1. **EFFECTIVE STATE AND MUNICIPAL HEARINGS PRACTICE**
2. -
3. Maine Bar
4. 1991
5. 1 vol.
6. $35
7. no supp. planned
9. 23377495/KF5402.Z99M232

1. **EFFICIENCY AND JUSTICE IN APPEALS: METHODS AND SELECTED MATERIALS**
2. ABA Task Force on Appellate Procedure
3. ABA
4. 1978
5. 1 vol.
6. $15
7. no supp. planned
9. 78-107619/4468704/KF9050.A94

1. **EFFICIENT MARITAL DISSOLUTION**
2. -
3. Minn. CLE
4. 1991
5. 1 vol.
6. $60
7. no supp. planned

1. **EFT REGULATION E COMPREHENSIVE COMPLIANCE MANUAL**
2. -
3. Am. Bankers
4. 1982
5. 1 vol.
6. $253-nonmembers; $169-members
7. periodic supp.
8. 1985 - $20-members; $30-nonmembers
9. 10747589/HG1710.A43

1. **EITF ABSTRACTS (A SUMMARY OF PROCEEDINGS OF THE FASB EMERGING ISSUES TASK FORCE)**
2. Financial Accounting Standards Board
3. FASB
4. 1988
5. 1 vol.
6. $240/yr.
7. bimonthly supp.
9. 18005598/HF5611.F35

1. **ELDER LAW**
2. -
3. Indiana CLE
4. 1991
5. 1 vol.
6. $65
7. no supp. planned

1. **ELDER LAW**
2. -
3. Maine Bar
4. 1989
5. 1 vol.
6. $30
7. no supp. planned
9. 18556213/KF3737.L48

1. **EMERGENCY REPORTING REQUIREMENTS FOR ENVIRONMENTAL SPILLS AND RELEASES**
2. MacBeth, Angus & Stephen D. Ramsey
3. Prentice Hall Law & Business
4. 1989
5. 2 vols.
6. $150 incl. 4 mos. supp.
7. periodic supp.
8. 1990 - $125
9. 88-8730/19850476/KF3958.M33

1. **EMINENT DOMAIN**
2. -
3. Indiana CLE

4. 1991
5. 1 vol.
6. $60
7. no supp. planned
9. 23107471

1. **EMINENT DOMAIN**
2. -
3. MILE
4. 1991
5. 1 vol.
6. $68
7. no supp. planned

1. **EMINENT DOMAIN–STATE AND FEDERAL**
2. Blankenship, A. Hugo, J., ed.
3. Jt. Comm. Va.
4. 1988
5. 1 vol.
6. $36
7. periodic supp.
8. no supp. yet
9. 88-141999/18351550/KFV2850.E47

1. **EMINENT DOMAIN IN ARIZONA**
2. Herrick, Robert V. et al.
3. State Bar of Ariz.
4. 1991
5. 1 vol.
6. $90
7. periodic supp.
8. no supp. yet
9. 24210086/KFA2850.A9K477

1. **EMPLOYEE AND UNION MEMBER GUIDE TO LABOR LAW**
2. National Lawyers Guild
3. Clark Boardman Callaghan
4. 1981
5. 2 vols.
6. $189 incl. 3 mos. supp.
7. annual supp.
8. 1988 - $116.50; 1989 - $65
9. 81-10090/7578067/KF3369.E46

1. **EMPLOYEE BENEFITS CASES**
2. Sayre, David A.
3. BNA
4. 1981
5. 1 vol.
6. $769/yr.
7. weekly supp.
8. renewal - $730/yr.
9. 7437577

1. **EMPLOYEE BENEFITS COMPLIANCE COORDINATOR**
2. WG&L prof. ed. staff
3. WG&L
4. 1979
5. 4 vols.
6. $465/yr.; $425/yr. for 2 yrs.
7. monthly supp. & biweekly newsletter
8. renewal - $385/yr.
9. 80-2872/5177372/KF3509.A6E4

1. **EMPLOYEE BENEFITS COMPLIANCE MADE SIMPLE**
2. -
3. BLR
4. 1988
5. 1 vol.
6. $149.95 incl. 1 yr. supp.
7. quarterly supp.
8. renewal - $89.95/yr.

1. **EMPLOYEE BENEFITS GUIDE**
2. Bacon, David L. et al.
3. Bender
4. 1991
5. 1 vol.
6. $100 incl. 3 mos. supp.
7. annual supp.
8. no supp. yet
9. 91-75895/24672255/KF3512.A73B33

1. **EMPLOYEE BENEFITS LAW**
2. -
3. Illinois ICLE
4. 1987
5. 2 vols.
6. $208.95
7. periodic supp.
8. 1990 - $65.95

1. **EMPLOYEE BENEFITS LAW, ERISA AND BEYOND**
2. Mamorsky, Jeffrey
3. Law Journal
4. 1980
5. 2 vols.
6. $125
7. annual supp.
8. 1989 - $100; 1990 - $120
9. 80-14698/6277426/KF3512.M36

1. **EMPLOYEE BENEFITS MANAGEMENT**
2. -
3. CCH
4. 1990

5. 5 vols.
6. $580/yr.; $525/yr. for 2 yrs.
7. monthly supp.
9. 21547849/KF6410.A6E47

1. **EMPLOYEE BENEFITS UPDATE: INCLUDING SECTION 89**
2. -
3. Indiana CLE
4. 1989
5. 1 vol.
6. $60
7. no supp. planned

1. **EMPLOYEE, BUSINESS AND PROFESSIONAL DEFAMATION**
2. Alexander, Paul & Vanessa Wells
3. Bender
4. 1990
5. 1 vol.
6. $95 incl. 3 mos. supp.
7. periodic supp.
8. no supp. yet
9. 90-84002/22753640/KF1266.A9

1. **EMPLOYEE COMMUNICATIONS GUIDE**
2. -
3. WG&L
4. 1959
5. 1 vol.
6. $279/yr.
7. monthly supp.

1. **EMPLOYEE COMPENSATION IN [YOUR STATE]**
2. -
3. BLR
4. 1987
5. 2 vols.
6. $246/yr.
7. monthly newsletter & periodic supp.

1. **EMPLOYEE DISCIPLINE PRACTICES AND PROBLEMS: AVOIDING THE MENACE OF LEGAL LIABILITY**
2. -
3. Alex. Hamilton Inst.
4. 1987
5. 1 vol.
6. $59.50
7. no supp. yet

1. **THE EMPLOYEE HANDBOOK AUDIT: REDUCING THE RISKS OF UNJUST CLAIMS**
2. -
3. Alex. Hamilton Inst.
4. 1988
5. 1 vol.
6. $62.25
7. 3 supp./yr.
8. $19.50/supp.
9. 16928801

1. **EMPLOYEE NONCOMPETITION LAW**
2. Aspelund, Donald J. & Clarence E. Erikson
3. Clark Boardman Callaghan
4. 1987
5. 1 vol.
6. $110 incl. 3 mos. supp.
7. annual supp.
8. 1989 - $45; 1991 - $65
9. 87-11759/15629124/KF1625.Z95A86

1. **THE EMPLOYEE PROBLEM SOLVER**
2. -
3. Alex. Hamilton Inst.
4. 1991
5. 1 vol.
6. $70
7. supp. 3x/yr.
9. 24562355/HF5549.5E428E55

1. **EMPLOYEE RIGHTS LITIGATION: PLEADING AND PRACTICE**
2. Natl. Employment Lawyers Assn.
3. Bender
4. 1991
5. 3 vols.
6. $325 incl. 3 mos. supp.
7. annual supp.
8. no supp. yet
9. 91-70516/23994335/KF3464.E46

1. **EMPLOYEE STOCK OWNERSHIP PLANS**
2. -
3. MILE
4. 1989
5. 1 vol.
6. $58
7. no supp. planned

1. **EMPLOYEE TESTING: THE COMPLETE RESOURCE GUIDE**
2. -
3. BNA
4. 1988
5. 1 vol.

6. $55
7. no supp. planned
9. 18060926/KF3457.3.E45

1. **EMPLOYER'S GUIDE TO AUDITING PERSONNEL & EMPLOYMENT PRACTICES**
2. Hartstein, Barry A.
3. Bus. Laws
4. 1988
5. 1 vol.
6. $96
7. annual supp.
8. renewal - $44/yr.

1. **EMPLOYER'S GUIDE TO MANDATED HEALTH BENEFITS - THE COBRA HANDBOOK**
2. Hamburger, Paul
3. Thompson
4. 1987
5. 1 vol.
6. $245/yr.
7. monthly supp.
8. renewal - $217/yr.

1. **EMPLOYER'S GUIDE TO THE IMMIGRATION REFORM AND CONTROL ACT OF 1986**
2. Hartsfield, William E.
3. BLR
4. 1987
5. 1 vol.
6. $39.95
7. no supp. yet
9. 17319610/KF4819.3.H37

1. **EMPLOYER'S HANDBOOK - COMPLYING WITH IRS EMPLOYEE BENEFIT RULES**
2. Hevener, Mary B.
3. Thompson
4. 1988
5. 1 vol.
6. $238/yr.
7. monthly supp.
8. renewal - $206/yr.
9. 18738537

1. **EMPLOYER'S IMMIGRATION COMPLIANCE GUIDE**
2. Frye H.M. & R. Klasko
3. Bender
4. 1987
5. 2 vols.
6. $265/yr.
7. monthly supp.
8. 1988 - $195; 1989 - $210
9. 15562477/KF4815.K5

1. **EMPLOYMENT AND TRAINING REPORTER**
2. Morales, Cecilio, ed.
3. MII
4. 1969
5. 2 vols.
6. $684/yr.
7. weekly supp. & reports

1. **EMPLOYMENT-AT-WILL REPORTER**
2. -
3. NELP
4. 1983
5. 1 vol./yr.
6. $465/yr.
7. monthly supp.
9. 83-9197/9614232/KF3471.A6E46

1. **EMPLOYMENT COORDINATOR**
2. WG&L prof. ed. staff
3. WG&L
4. 1984
5. 17 vols.
6. $925/yr.; $860/yr. for 2 yrs.
7. monthly supp. & biweekly newsletter with binder
8. renewal - $795/yr.
9. 85-104721/12079369/KF3315.E47

1. **EMPLOYMENT DISCRIMINATION**
2. Larson, Arthur
3. Bender
4. 1975
5. 5 vols.
6. $655 incl. 3 mos. supp.
7. biannual supp.
8. 1989 - $494; 1990 - $564.50
9. 75-24811/1926215/KF3464.L37

1. **EMPLOYMENT DISCRIMINATION**
2. Cox, Paul N.
3. Butterworth-NH
4. 1987
5. 1 vol.
6. $105
7. annual supp.
8. 1990 - $35; 1991 - $45
9. 87-373/15315842/KF3464.C69

1. **EMPLOYMENT DISCRIMINATION**
2. -
3. Illinois ICLE

4. 1989
5. 1 vol.
6. $109.95
7. periodic supp.
8. no supp. yet

1. **EMPLOYMENT DISCRIMINATION AND CIVIL RIGHTS ACTIONS**
2. Richey, Charles R.
3. Clark Boardman Callaghan
4. 1988
5. 1 vol.
6. $95 incl. 3 mos. supp.
7. periodic supp.
8. 1991 - $90
9. KF3464.R53

1. **EMPLOYMENT DISCRIMINATION COMPLAINTS**
2. Labor & Employment Law Section
3. Conn. Bar
4. 1990
5. 1 vol.
6. $25
7. no supp. planned

1. **EMPLOYMENT DISCRIMINATION COMPLAINTS**
2. -
3. Conn. Bar
4. 1991
5. 1 vol.
6. $53
7. no supp. planned

1. **EMPLOYMENT DISCRIMINATION COORDINATOR**
2. WG&L prof. ed. staff
3. WG&L
4. 1988
5. 8 vols.
6. $740/yr.; $690/yr. for 2 yrs.
7. biweekly supp.
8. renewal - $640/yr.
9. 20577967/KF3464.A6R4

1. **EMPLOYMENT DISCRIMINATION LAW**
2. Pitt & Helveston
3. MTLA
4. 1985
5. 1 vol.
6. $70 (member); $85 (nonmember)
7. no supp. planned

1. **EMPLOYMENT DISCRIMINATION LAW, VOL. II**
2. Stark and Gordon
3. MTLA
4. 1986
5. 1 vol.
6. $70 (member); $85 (nonmember)
7. no supp. planned

1. **EMPLOYMENT DISCRIMINATION LAW UPDATE**
2. -
3. NELI
4. 1991
5. 1 vol.
6. $100
7. no supp. planned

1. **EMPLOYMENT DISPUTES**
2. -
3. NH Bar
4. 1989
5. 1 vol.
6. $20
7. no supp. planned

1. **EMPLOYMENT GUIDE**
2. Manville, Bill L.
3. BNA
4. 1986
5. 1 vol.
6. $396/yr.
7. biweekly supp.
8. renewal - $332/yr.

1. **EMPLOYMENT IN ILLINOIS**
2. Sautter, Maynard G.
3. Butterworth-St. Paul
4. 1983
5. 1 vol.
6. $55
7. periodic supp.
8. 1989 - $22; 1990 - $30
9. 84-100473/9710720/KFI1531.S28

1. **EMPLOYMENT IN IOWA**
2. Sautter, Maynard G.
3. Butterworth-St. Paul
4. 1984
5. 1 vol.
6. $55
7. periodic supp.
8. 1989 - $20; 1990 - $30
9. 84-186299/11260555/KFI4531.S27

1. **EMPLOYMENT IN MINNESOTA**
2. Sautter, Maynard G.
3. Butterworth-St. Paul
4. 1982
5. 1 vol.
6. $55
7. periodic supp.
8. 1990 - $20; 1990 - $35
9. 83-121396/9577301/KFM5731.S28

1. **EMPLOYMENT IN MISSOURI, 2nd Ed.**
2. Summers, Mark S. & William R. Barr
3. Butterworth-Texas
4. 1990
5. 1 vol.
6. $60
7. periodic supp.
8. 1991 - $28.50
9. 90-2466/22181420/KFM8134.S94

1. **EMPLOYMENT IN OHIO**
2. Sautter, Maynard G.
3. Butterworth-St. Paul
4. 1984
5. 1 vol.
6. $55
7. periodic supp.
8. 1989 - $22; 1990 - $30
9. 84-138509/10382083/KFO331.S28

1. **EMPLOYMENT IN OREGON**
2. Butterworths Staff
3. Butterworth-St. Paul
4. 2nd ed. - 1991
5. 1 vol.
6. $55
7. periodic supp
8. no supp. yet
9. 91-30412/24373579/KFO2731.K56

1. **EMPLOYMENT IN TEXAS, 3rd Ed.**
2. Summers, Mark S.
3. Butterworth-Texas
4. 1990
5. 1 vol.
6. $70
7. annual supp.
8. 1990 - $30; 1991 - $27.50
9. 89-70854/20758202/KFT1531.S93

1. **EMPLOYMENT IN WASHINGTON STATE: REV. ED.**
2. Davis, Wright & Tremaine
3. Butterworth-St. Paul
4. 1987
5. 1 vol.
6. $55
7. periodic supp.
8. 1989 - $26.50; 1990 - $35
9. 19966925/KFW331.L38

1. **EMPLOYMENT IN WISCONSIN**
2. Sautter, Maynard G.
3. Butterworth-St. Paul
4. 1983
5. 1 vol.
6. $55
7. periodic supp.
8. 1989 - $22; 1990 - $30
9. 83-235684/10318382/KFW2731.S28

1. **EMPLOYMENT LAW - 7th ANNUAL**
2. -
3. MILE
4. 1991
5. 1 vol.
6. $63
7. no supp. planned
9. 15295419

1. **EMPLOYMENT LAW BRIEFING MANUAL**
2. -
3. NELI
4. 1991
5. 2 vols.
6. $150
7. no supp. planned

1. **EMPLOYMENT LAW CHECKLISTS & FORMS**
2. Jacobs, Louis & Jack Ruzicho
3. Clark Boardman Callaghan
4. 1991
5. 2 vols.
6. $165 incl. 6 mos. supp.
7. annual supp.
8. no supp. yet
9. 91-25359/24068123/KF3369.R89

1. **EMPLOYMENT LAW CONFERENCE MANUAL**
2. -
3. NELI
4. 1991
5. 1 vol.
6. $100
7. no supp. planned

1. **EMPLOYMENT LAW DESK BOOK FOR TENNESSEE EMPLOYERS**
2. Phillips, John B., Jr.
3. Smith
4. 1989
5. 1 vol.
6. $90
7. periodic supp.
8. 1991 - $19
9. 21540264/KFT334.P53X

1. **EMPLOYMENT LAW DESKBOOK**
2. Various Contributing Authors
3. Bender
4. 1989
5. 1 vol.
6. $105 incl. 3 mos. supp.
7. annual supp.
8. 1990 - $42
9. 89-61934/20502084/KF3455.E47

1. **EMPLOYMENT LAW FOR THE GENERAL PRACTITIONER**
2. -
3. Wash. Bar
4. 1989
5. 1 vol.
6. $35
7. no supp. planned

1. **EMPLOYMENT LAW HANDBOOK**
2. -
3. Minn. CLE
4. 1991
5. 1 vol.
6. $125
7. no supp. planned

1. **EMPLOYMENT LAW INSTITUTE**
2. -
3. MICPEL
4. 1990
5. 1 vol.
6. $52.50
7. no supp. yet

1. **EMPLOYMENT LAW UPDATE**
2. -
3. MILE
4. 1990
5. 1 vol.
6. $58
7. no supp. planned

1. **EMPLOYMENT LAW UPDATE**
2. -
3. Wash. Bar
4. 1988
5. 1 vol.
6. $35
7. no supp. planned

1. **EMPLOYMENT LITIGATION IN THE NINETIES**
2. -
3. NELI
4. 1991
5. 1 vol.
6. $100
7. no supp. planned

1. **EMPLOYMENT PRACTICES GUIDE**
2. -
3. CCH
4. 1934
5. 4 vols. (also published as part of Labor Law Reports)
6. $680/yr.; $620/yr. for 2 yrs.
7. semimonthly supp.
9. 65-5463/5128021/KF3464.A6C6

1. **EMPLOYMENT REGULATIONS IN [STATE]: A SURVIVAL KIT FOR [STATE] EMPLOYERS: PROCEEDINGS**
2. -
3. IBL
4. 1991
5. 1 vol. (avail. for 3 states)
6. $99.50
7. annual editions

1. **EMPLOYMENT SAFETY AND HEALTH GUIDE**
2. -
3. CCH
4. 1971
5. 4 vols.
6. $710/yr.; $645/yr. for 2 yrs.
7. weekly supp. & newsletter
9. 74-26093/150150/KF3568.4.C6

1. **EMPLOYMENT SCREENING**
2. Larson, Lex
3. Bender
4. 1988
5. 1 vol.
6. $110 incl. 3 mos. supp.
7. annual supp.
8. 1989 - $41; 1990 - $52.50

9. 88-71888/18572700/KF3457.L37

1. **EMPLOYMENT TERMINATION**
2. -
3. Illinois ICLE
4. 1989
5. 1 vol.
6. $109.95
7. periodic supp.
8. 1990 - $24.95
9. 18121265

1. **EMPLOYMENT TESTING: A NATIONAL REPORTER ON DRUG, POLYGRAPH, AIDS AND GENETIC TESTING**
2. Orthman, Rosemary, ed.
3. UPA
4. 1987
5. 2 vols.
6. $275/yr.
7. biweekly newsletter
9. 15275293/KF3457.3.A6E4

1. **ENCYCLOPEDIA OF FINANCIAL AND ESTATE PLANNING**
2. Roth, Randall W., ed.
3. HICLE
4. 1990
5. 1 vol.
6. $115
7. periodic supp.
8. 1991 - $20

1. **ENCYCLOPEDIA OF MATRIMONIAL PRACTICE**
2. Brown, Ronald L., ed.
3. Prentice Hall Law & Business
4. 1991
5. 1 vol.
6. $95 incl. 4 mos. supp.
7. periodic supp.
8. no supp. yet
9. 91-33578/24373059/KF535.E53

1. **ENCYCLOPEDIC DICTIONARY OF CONTRACT AND PROCUREMENT LAW**
2. Keyes, W. Noel
3. Oceana
4. 5th ed. - 1991
5. 1 vol.
6. $150
7. periodic supp.
8. no supp. yet
9. KF847.5K48

1. **ENERGY LAW & TRANSACTIONS**
2. Muchow, David J. & William A. Mogel
3. Bender
4. 1990
5. 5 vols.
6. $450 incl. 3 mos. supp.
7. periodic supp.
8. no supp. yet
9. 90-158683/21354003/KF2120.E535

1. **ENERGY MANAGEMENT AND FEDERAL ENERGY GUIDELINES**
2. -
3. CCH
4. 1973
5. 7 vols.
6. $1100/yr.; $1000/2 yrs.
7. weekly supp.
9. 73-171091/708341/KF2120.A6C64

1. **ENERGY RESOURCES TAX REPORTER**
2. -
3. CCH
4. 1983
5. 2 vols.
6. $515/yr.; $470/yr. for 2 yrs.
7. monthly supp.
9. 12426278/HD9502.U52E53

1. **ENFORCEMENT OF LIENS AND JUDGMENTS**
2. Ackerly, Benjamin
3. Jt. Comm. Va.
4. 1982
5. 1 vol.
6. $62
7. periodic supp.
8. 1985 - $16; 1989 - $20.90
9. 82-233446/9255369/KFV2576.L5E53

1. **ENFORCEMENT OF MONEY JUDGMENTS ABROAD**
2. Weems, Philip R.
3. Bender
4. 1988
5. 1 vol.
6. $115 incl. 3 mos. supp.
7. annual supp.
8. 1989 - $24; 1990 - $54.50
9. 88-70370/18589120/K7683.E54

1. **ENGINEERING FOR THE PERSONAL INJURY ATTORNEY: THEORY, EXPERTS, EVIDENCE**

2. Kuperstein, Ira S. & Neil L. Salters, eds.
3. Bender
4. 1991
5. 1 vol.
6. $110 incl. 3 mos. supp.
7. annual supp.
8. no supp. yet
9. 91-70096/23588193/TA219.A85

1. **ENTERTAINMENT INDUSTRY CONTRACTS: NEGOTIATIONS & DRAFTING GUIDE**
2. Farber, D.C., ed.
3. Bender
4. 1986
5. 4 vols.
6. $515 incl. 3 mos. supp.
7. periodic supp.
8. 1989 - $301; 1990 - $488.50
9. 86-234209/15428077/KF2932.E57

1. **ENTERTAINMENT LAW**
2. Simensky, Melvin & Thomas Selz
3. Shepard's
4. 1990
5. 4 vols.
6. $260
7. annual supp.
8. 1989 - $56; 1990 - $58
9. 83-432/9217046/KF4290.S44

1. **ENTERTAINMENT LAW AND BUSINESS**
2. Orenstein, Harold and David Sinacore-Guinn
3. Butterworth-NH
4. 1989
5. 2 vols.
6. $180
7. periodic supp.
8. 1990 - $45; 1991 - $45
9. 89-662/19221910/KF4290.074

1. **ENVIRONMENT REPORTER**
2. McClain, Wallis E., Jr.
3. BNA
4. 1970
5. 25 vols.
6. $2180/yr.
7. weekly supp. & reports
8. renewal - $1980/yr.
9. 70-29347/200885/KF3775.A6E49

1. **ENVIRONMENTAL AND LAND USE LAW MID-YEAR MEETING**
2. -
3. Wash. Bar
4. 1991
5. 1 vol.
6. $70
7. annual vol.

1. **ENVIRONMENTAL CITIZEN SUITS**
2. Axline, Michael D.
3. Butterworth-NH
4. 1991
5. 1 vol.
6. $95
7. periodic supp.
8. no supp. yet
9. 90-29187/22983131/KF3725.A989

1. **ENVIRONMENTAL COMPLIANCE MANAGEMENT IN [STATE]**
2. -
3. IBL
4. 1991
5. 1 vol. (avail. for CA, IL, NY, TX, OH, PA, NJ)
6. $99.50
7. annual editions

1. **ENVIRONMENTAL CONSIDERATIONS IN NATURAL RESOURCE AND REAL PROPERTY TRANSACTIONS**
2. -
3. Rocky Mt.
4. 1988
5. 1 vol.
6. $105
7. no supp. planned
9. 19000896/KF3775.A75I56

1. **ENVIRONMENTAL IMPACT REVIEW IN NEW YORK**
2. Gerrard, Michael B., et al
3. Bender
4. 1990
5. 1 vol.
6. $110 incl. 3 mos. supp.
7. periodic supp.
8. 1991 - $55
9. 90-83804/22455206/KFN5610.G47

1. **ENVIRONMENTAL INSURANCE COVERAGE: STATE LAW & REGULATION**
2. Lathrop, Mitchell L.
3. Butterworth-NH
4. 1991
5. 1 vol.
6. $125

7. periodic supp.
8. no supp. yet
9. 90-23012/22732998/KF1220.P5Z955

1. **ENVIRONMENTAL ISSUES CONCERNING FINANCIAL INSTITUTIONS**
2. -
3. MILE
4. 1989
5. 1 vol.
6. $58
7. no supp. planned

1. **ENVIRONMENTAL LAW**
2. -
3. Maine Bar
4. 1990
5. 1 vol.
6. $40
7. no supp. planned

1. **ENVIRONMENTAL LAW**
2. -
3. MoBar
4. 1991
5. 2 vols.
6. $95
7. periodic supp.
8. no supp. yet

1. **ENVIRONMENTAL LAW**
2. -
3. Ohio CLE
4. 1989
5. 1 vol.
6. $35
7. no supp. planned

1. **ENVIRONMENTAL LAW: ALR ANNOTATIONS**
2. Publisher's Editorial Staff
3. Lawyers Coop.
4. 1991
5. 5 vols.
6. $450 incl. 6 mos. supp.
7. periodic supp.
8. no supp. yet
9. 91-62061/24695432/KF3775.A53E58

1. **ENVIRONMENTAL LAW: AN UPDATE FOR THE BUSY NATURAL RESOURCES PRACTITIONER**
2. -
3. Rocky Mt.
4. 1990
5. 1 vol.
6. $125
7. no supp. planned
9. 22534648/KF3775.A75I57

1. **ENVIRONMENTAL LAW AFFECTING REAL ESTATE DEVELOPMENTS**
2. -
3. Georgetown
4. 1991
5. 1 vol.
6. $101
7. no supp. planned

1. **ENVIRONMENTAL LAW FOR ENVIRONMENTAL LAWYERS**
2. -
3. Indiana CLE
4. 1991
5. 1 vol.
6. $50
7. no supp. planned
9. 24785911/KF277.E5E58

1. **ENVIRONMENTAL LAW FOR THE GENERAL PRACTITIONER**
2. -
3. Indiana CLE
4. 1991
5. 1 vol.
6. $50
7. no supp. planned
9. 24786120/KF277.E5G46

1. **ENVIRONMENTAL LAW FOR TRANSACTIONAL ATTORNEYS**
2. -
3. Illinois ICLE
4. 1991
5. 1 vol.
6. $89.95
7. periodic supp.
8. no supp. yet
9. 8061071/KFI1554.E58

1. **ENVIRONMENTAL LAW FORMS GUIDE**
2. Steinberg, Robert E. and Richard H. Mays
3. Shepard's
4. 1990
5. 5 vols.
6. $490
7. semiannual supp.
8. no supp. yet
9. 89-71470/20823874/KF3775.A65M39

1. **ENVIRONMENTAL LAW INSTITUTE**
2. -
3. MILE
4. 1991
5. 1 vol.
6. $79.50
7. no supp. planned

1. **ENVIRONMENTAL LAW REPORTER**
2. Breen, Barry, ed.
3. ELI
4. 1970
5. 7 vols.
6. $925/yr.
7. monthly supp.
8. 1990 - $795; 1991 - $860
9. 85-643063/10271051

1. **ENVIRONMENTAL LAW SYMPOSIUM**
2. -
3. Indiana CLE
4. 1990
5. 1 vol.
6. $75
7. no supp. planned

1. **ENVIRONMENTAL LAW UPDATE FROM VARIOUS PERSPECTIVES**
2. -
3. Okla. Bar CLE
4. 1990
5. 1 vol.
6. $60
7. no supp. planned

1. **ENVIRONMENTAL LIABILITY – LAW AND STRATEGY FOR BUSINESSES AND CORPORATIONS**
2. Schnapf, Lawrence P.
3. Butterworth-NH
4. 1990
5. 1 vol.
6. $110
7. periodic supp.
8. 1991 - price NA
9. 90-44400/22208549/KF3775.S36

1. **ENVIRONMENTAL LIABILITY IN REAL ESTATE MATTERS**
2. -
3. Minn. CLE
4. 1991
5. 1 vol.
6. $25
7. no supp. planned

1. **ENVIRONMENTAL REGULATION OF LAND USE**
2. Malone, Linda A.
3. Clark Boardman Callaghan
4. 1990
5. 1 vol.
6. $110 incl. 3 mos supp.
7. annual supp.
8. 1991 - $49.50
9. 90-267/21197437/KF5698.M264

1. **ENVIRONMENTAL REGULATION OF REAL PROPERTY**
2. Robinson, Nicholas A.
3. Law Journal
4. 1982
5. 1 vol.
6. $90
7. periodic supp.
8. 1989 - $84; 1990 - $84
9. 82-100/8171315/KF5698.R6

1. **ENVIRONMENTAL REGULATIONS FOR [STATE]**
2. -
3. IBL
4. 1991
5. 1 vol. (avail. for CA, IL, NJ, NY, MI, TX, PA, OH)
6. $99.50
7. annual editions

1. **EQUAL EMPLOYMENT COMPLIANCE MANUAL**
2. Ruzicho, Andrew J. & Louis S. Jacobs
3. Clark Boardman Callaghan
4. 1977
5. 1 vol.
6. $290 incl. 1 yr. supp.
7. semiannual supp. & monthly newsletter & special reports
8. 1989 - $255; 1990 - $255
9. 77-14116/3294590/KF3464.A6E65

1. **EQUIPMENT RULES SERVICE**
2. Tobias, Jeff, et al.
3. P&F
4. 1988
5. 1 vol.
6. $355
7. bimonthly supp.
8. $260/yr.; $490/2 yrs.
9. 20293271/KF2810.E64

1. **ERISA CITATOR**
2. -
3. WSB
4. 1985
5. 1 vol.
6. $500/yr.
7. monthly supp.
9. 11924400

1. **ERISA CLAIMS AND LITIGATION**
2. -
3. Minn. CLE
4. 1991
5. 1 vol.
6. $50
7. no supp. planned

1. **ERISA PRACTICE AND PROCEDURE**
2. Cooke, Ronald J.
3. Shepard's
4. 1989
5. 1 vol.
6. $110
7. annual supp.
8. 1991 - $28
9. 89-28938/20595112/KF3512.C65

1. **ERISA QUALIFIED PLAN GUIDE**
2. -
3. PPD
4. 1975
5. 4 vols.
6. $275/yr.
7. bimonthly supp.
8. renewal - $175/yr.
9. 3447895/KF3510.A6E7

1. **ERISA UPDATE**
2. -
3. WSB
4. 1991
5. 1 vol. (1974-1989 vols. avail. - $1470)
6. $850/yr.
7. monthly supp.
9. 4785336

1. **ERISMAN'S REVERSIBLE ERRORS**
2. McColl, Arch & Michael McColloch
3. Knowles
4. 1983
5. 2 vols.
6. $185 incl. 3 mos. supp.
7. annual supp.
8. 1988 - $55; 1990 - $65
9. KFT1775.A53.E7

1. **ERISMAN'S REVERSIBLE ERRORS IN ILLINOIS CRIMINAL CASES**
2. Hartman, Marshall & Joan Pantsios, eds.
3. Knowles
4. 1990
5. 1 vol.
6. $135 incl. 3 mos. supp.
7. annual supp.
9. 90-4633/21524128/KFI1775.A53E75

1. **ESCHEAT AND ABANDONED PROPERTY LAWS**
2. -
3. ASCS
4. 2nd ed. - 1988
5. 1 vol.
6. $100 - nonmembers; $50 - members
7. periodic supp.
8. to be rev. in late 1991
9. 18209053

1. **ESOP FORMS MANUAL**
2. -
3. Corbel
4. 1985
5. 1 vol.
6. $245 incl. 1 yr. supp.
7. supp. as needed
8. renewal - $85/yr.
9. 12483845/KF3496.A65L8

1. **ESSENTIALS OF EVIDENCE**
2. -
3. Wash. Bar
4. 1989
5. 1 vol.
6. $55
7. no supp. planned

1. **ESTABLISHING A CHARITABLE FOUNDATION IN MICHIGAN**
2. Tarnacki, Duane L.
3. Council of Mich. Fdtns.
4. 2nd ed. - 1989
5. 1 vol.
6. $80 incl. 4 yrs. supp.
7. annual supp.
8. incl. in price
9. 87-101985/15429646/KFM4339.C4T37

1. **ESTABLISHING A TRANSNATIONAL FRANCHISE**
2. Pattison, Joseph E.
3. Bender
4. 1988

5. 1 vol.
6. $105 incl. 3 mos. supp.
7. annual supp.
8. no supp. yet
9. 18198940/K3966.P37

1. **ESTABLISHING A U.S. JOINT VENTURE WITH A FOREIGN PARTNER**
2. Detjen, David W.
3. Bender
4. 198
5. 1 vol.
6. $105 incl. 3 mos. supp.
7. annual supp.
8. 1990 - $53
9. 87-72789/17799596/KF1380.5.D48

1. **ESTATE ADMINISTRATION (MASSACHUSETTS): A HANDBOOK WITH FORMS**
2. Riley, Michael H.
3. Butterworth-NH
4. 1985
5. 1 vol.
6. $85
7. periodic supp.
8. 1990 - $35; 1991 - $35
9. 82-73459/13008520/KFM2547.R55

1. **ESTATE & GUARDIANSHIP ADMINISTRATION**
2. -
3. Indiana CLE
4. 1989
5. 1 vol.
6. $65
7. no supp. planned

1. **ESTATE & PERSONAL FINANCIAL PLANNING**
2. Koren, Edward F.
3. Clark Boardman Callaghan
4. 1988
5. 4 vols.
6. $395 incl. 1 yr. supp.
7. quarterly supp. & monthly newsletter
8. 1989 - $275; 1990 - $275
9. 88-22286/18289844/KF6297.K67

1. **ESTATE PLANNING**
2. -
3. Indiana CLE
4. 1991
5. 1 vol.
6. $40
7. no supp. planned

1. **ESTATE PLANNING**
2. -
3. RIA
4. 1954
5. 1 vol.
6. $290/yr.
7. monthly supp.

1. **ESTATE PLANNING**
2. Susman, Gerald S.
3. Law Journal
4. 1980
5. 1 vol.
6. $85
7. periodic supp.
8. 1989 - $84; 1990 - $84
9. 80-20480/6626613/KF6572.R59

1. **ESTATE PLANNING, 5TH ED.**
2. Casner, A. James
3. Little, Brown
4. 1983
5. 9 vols.
6. $595
7. annual supp.
8. 1990 - $110; 1991 - price NA
9. 83-080449/9832662/KF749.C3

1. **ESTATE PLANNING & ADMINISTRATION IN INDIANA**
2. -
3. Indiana CLE
4. 1988
5. 1 vol.
6. $45
7. no supp. planned

1. **ESTATE PLANNING AND BUSINESS TAX SYMPOSIUM**
2. Borteck, Robert D., et al.
3. New Jersey ICLE
4. 1989
5. 1 vol.
6. $55
7. no supp. planned

1. **ESTATE PLANNING AND TAXATION COORDINATOR**
2. RIA prof. ed. staff
3. RIA
4. 1978
5. 9 vols.
6. $760/yr.; $725/yr. for 2 yrs.

7. biweekly supp. & monthly newsletter
8. renewal - $690/yr.
9. SN79-7479/5293401

1. **ESTATE PLANNING – BASICS**
2. -
3. NH Bar
4. 1990
5. 1 vol.
6. $35
7. no supp. planned

1. **ESTATE PLANNING CHECKLISTS/FORMS**
2. -
3. RIA
4. 1954
5. 1 vol.
6. $290/yr.
7. quarterly supp.

1. **ESTATE PLANNING FOR FARMERS & RANCHERS, 2nd ed.**
2. Kelley & Ludtke
3. Shepard's
4. 2nd ed. - 1986
5. 2 vols.
6. $210
7. annual supp.
8. 1989 - $46; 1990 - $48
9. 86-20309/14097979/KF750.K4

1. **ESTATE PLANNING FOR THE AGING OR INCAPACITATED CLIENT IN MASSACHUSETTS**
2. Freedman, Donald, et al.
3. Mass. CLE
4. 1991
5. 1 vol.
6. $95
7. periodic supp.
8. 1992 - price NA

1. **ESTATE PLANNING FOR THE SINGLE PARENT**
2. -
3. Minn. CLE
4. 1991
5. 1 vol.
6. $35
7. no supp. planned

1. **ESTATE PLANNING IN LOUISIANA**
2. Hickey, Maunsel W. et al.
3. Lawyers Coop.
4. 1991
5. 1 vol.
6. $95 incl. 6 mos. supp.
7. periodic supp.
9. 91-60179/24189264/KFL140.H52

1. **ESTATE PLANNING LAW AND TAXATION**
2. Westfall, David
3. WG&L
4. 2nd ed. - 1989
5. 1 vol.
6. $105
7. semiannual supp.
8. 1991 - $100.75
9. 89-50908/20009189/KF6584.W47

1. **ESTATE PLANNING MANUAL FOR TRUST OFFICERS**
2. Adams, Roy M.
3. Am. Bankers
4. 1988
5. 1 vol.
6. $140-members; $210-nonmembers
7. periodic supp.
8. no supp. yet
9. 21172063/KF6584.A73

1. **ESTATE PLANNING PRACTICE**
2. -
3. Calif. CEB
4. 1987
5. 2 vols.
6. $140
7. periodic supp.
8. 1989 - $40; 1991 - price NA
9. 86-73142/16095139/KFC195.E85

1. **ESTATE PLANNING SIMPLIFIED**
2. Moy, Doug
3. Wiley Law
4. 1989
5. 2 vols.
6. $175
7. annual supp.
8. 1990 - $60; 1991 - $65
9. 89-130061/19616189/KF750.M69

1. **ESTATE TAX FREEZE**
2. Freeman, Douglas R.
3. Bender
4. 1985
5. 1 vol.
6. $105 incl. 3 mos. supp.
7. annual supp.

8. 1989 - $55; 1990 - $69.50
9. 84-72696/11818167/KF6572.F74

1. **ESTATE TAX TECHNIQUES**
2. J.K. Lasser Institute, eds.
3. Bender
4. 1955
5. 3 vols.
6. $270 incl. 3 mos. supp.
7. annual supp.
8. 1989 - $170; 1990 - $206.50
9. 55-3159/1153442

1. **ESTATE TAXATION IN MASSACHUSETTS, WITH FORMS**
2. Rosales, Benjamin & Alexander A. Bove Jr.
3. Lawyers Coop.
4. 1987
5. 1 vol.
6. $110 incl. 6 mos. supp.
7. annual supp
8. 1989 - $39; 1990 - $41.50
9. 88-416848/17406965/KFM2882.R67

1. **ESTIMATING AND PROVING PERSONAL INJURY DAMAGES**
2. Tarantino, John A.
3. James
4. 1988
5. 1 vol.
6. $69.96 incl. 3 mos. supp.
7. annual supp.
8. 1990 - $39.87
9. 18456766/KF1256.A7T37

1. **THE ETHICAL OREGON LAWYER**
2. Jarvis, Peter P., ed.
3. Oregon Bar
4. 1991
5. 1 vol.
6. $95
7. periodic supp.
8. no supp. yet
9. 91-60290/24233277

1. **ETHICS & PROFESSIONAL RESPONSIBILITY: A HANDBOOK FOR WISCONSIN LAWYERS**
2. Kaap, Keith J.
3. State Bar of Wisc.
4. 1985
5. 1 vol.
6. $95
7. periodic supp.
8. 1988 - $45

1. **ETHICS IN GOVERNMENT REPORTER**
2. -
3. WSB
4. 1980
5. 2 vols.
6. $520/yr.
7. monthly supp.
9. 81-1909/7016853/KF4568.A6E85

1. **EUROPE 1992**
2. Biles, Blake A.
3. Ohio CLE
4. 1989
5. 1 vol.
6. $45
7. no supp. planned

1. **EUROPEAN COMMUNITY COMPANY LAW**
2. Mead, Philip, ed.
3. Oceana
4. 1991
5. 1 vol.
6. $150
7. periodic supp.
8. no supp. yet

1. **EUROPEAN COMMUNITY LAW & BUSINESS REPORTER**
2. Patterson, Patricia, ed.
3. Legal-Med.
4. 1990
5. 1 vol.
6. $150/yr.
7. bimonthly supp.
9. SN 90-6012/21589280

1. **EUROPEAN PATENTS HANDBOOK, 2nd ed.**
2. Chartered Institute of Patent Agents
3. Bender & Oyez
4. 1978
5. 4 vols.
6. $490 incl. 3 mos. supp.
7. annual supp.
8. 1989 - $367.50; 1990 - $456.50
9. 78-53872/4125953/K1505.4.C46

1. **EVALUATING THE FLUIDIZED BED COMBUSTION (FBC) OPTION, 6th Ed.**
2. Sheahan, Richard
3. Govt. Inst.
4. 1988

5. 1 vol.
6. $95
7. no supp. planned

1. **EVERYTHING ELSE YOU NEEDED TO KNOW ABOUT FAMILY LAW**
2. -
3. Indiana CLE
4. 1989
5. 1 vol.
6. $60
7. no supp. planned

1. **EVIDENCE**
2. Unis, Richard L. et al.
3. Oregon Bar
4. 1986
5. 1 vol.
6. $85
7. periodic supp.
8. to be supp. in 1992
9. 86-61477/15088167/KFO.2940.E83

1. **EVIDENCE (TEXAS & NATIONAL EDITIONS)**
2. Branton, James L. & Jim D. Lovett
3. Knowles
4. 1991
5. 1 vol.
6. $135 incl. 3 mos. supp.
7. annual supp.
9. KFT1740.A59B7

1. **EVIDENCE: KEEPING IT OUT**
2. -
3. Indiana CLE
4. 1988
5. 1 vol.
6. $55
7. no supp. planned

1. **EVIDENCE: SELECTED PROBLEMS**
2. -
3. NH Bar
4. 1989
5. 1 vol.
6. $35
7. no supp. planned

1. **EVIDENCE – A TRIAL MANUAL FOR MICHIGAN LAWYERS**
2. Hackett, Wesley P., Jr.
3. Lawyers Coop.
4. 1981
5. 2 vols.
6. $180 incl. 6 mos. supp.
7. annual supp.
8. 1990 - $62; 1991 - $55
9. 81-3833//r862/7461912/KFM4740.H3

1. **EVIDENCE IN FLORIDA**
2. -
3. Florida Bar
4. 3rd ed. - 1989
5. 1 vol.
6. $50
7. periodic supp.
8. no supp. yet
9. 89-83452/19604030/KFF540.E85

1. **EXAMINATION BEFORE TRIAL AND OTHER DISCLOSURE DEVICES**
2. Publisher's Editorial Staff
3. Lawyers Coop.
4. rev. ed. - 1984
5. 2 vols.
6. $180 incl. 6 mos. supp.
7. annual supp.
8. 1990 - $42; 1991 - $55
9. 84-1903/10459118/KFN6020.K47

1. **EXAMINATION OF TITLE**
2. -
3. Minn. CLE
4. 1991
5. 1 vol.
6. $50
7. no supp. planned

1. **EXAMINATION OF WITNESSES**
2. Gonzales, Richard
3. Clark Boardman Callaghan
4. 1989
5. 1 vol.
6. $95 incl. 6 mos. supp.
7. annual supp.
8. 1990 - $25
9. 89-23998/20420032/KF8915.G66

1. **EXAMINING EYEWITNESSES AND INTERVIEWING WITNESSES**
2. -
3. Conn. Bar
4. 1990
5. 1 vol.
6. $53
7. no supp. planned

1. **EXCESS LIABILITY: DUTIES & RESPONSIBILITIES OF THE INSURER**

2. Magarick, Pat
3. Clark Boardman Callaghan
4. 3rd ed. - 1988
5. 1 vol.
6. $115 incl. 3 mos. supp.
7. periodic supp.
8. 1989 - $139
9. 88-17495/18051856/KF1250.M3

1. **EXCHANGING REAL ESTATE**
2. Levine, Mark Lee
3. Prof. Pubs.
4. 1981 - new ed. in 1991
5. 2 vols.
6. $57
7. annual supp.

1. **EXECUTIVE AND PROFESSIONAL EMPLOYMENT CONTRACTS**
2. Kutten, L.J. and Bernard D. Reams, Jr.
3. Butterworth-NH
4. 1988
5. 1 vol.
6. $105
7. periodic supp.
8. 1991 - $50
9. 88-9543/17732051/KF898.K87

1. **EXECUTIVE COMPENSATION**
2. Kroll, Arthur H.
3. Prentice Hall Law & Business
4. 1985
5. 3 vols.
6. $470/yr.
7. monthly supp.
9. 11613365/HD4965.5.U6K75

1. **EXECUTIVE COMPENSATION AND TAXATION COORDINATOR**
2. RIA prof. ed. staff
3. RIA
4. 1979
5. 3 vols.
6. $445/yr.; $415/yr. for 2 yrs.
7. monthly supp. & monthly newsletter with binder
8. renewal - $385/yr.
9. 80-2871/6909226

1. **EXEMPT ORGANIZATIONS REPORTS**
2. -
3. CCH
4. 1971 (formerly Private Foundations Reports)
5. 3 vols.
6. $720/yr.; $655/yr. for 2 yrs.
7. semimonthly supp.
9. 72-177495/6954886/KF6449.A6C65

1. **EXEMPTED TRANSACTIONS UNDER THE SECURITIES ACT OF 1933 (Securities Law Series, vol. 7, 7A, 7B, 7C & 7D)**
2. Hicks, J. William
3. Clark Boardman Callaghan
4. 1979
5. 5 vols.
6. $595 incl. 3 mos. supp.
7. annual supp.
8. 1989 - $235; 1991 - $361.50
9. 79-15969/5101209/KF1439.H5

1. **EXPORT ADMINISTRATION REGULATIONS**
2. -
3. order from USGPO
 - stock #903-012-00000-5
4. 1988
5. 1 vol.
6. $87
7. supp. by Export Admin. Bulletin
8. -
9. 19033993/KF1987.A329O45

1. **EXPORT ADMINISTRATION REGULATIONS AND EXPORT RESOURCES**
2. -
3. Unz & Co.
4. 1991
5. 1 vol.
6. $275/yr.
7. periodic supp.

1. **EXTRADITION LAWS AND TREATIES OF THE UNITED STATES**
2. Kavass, Igor I. & Adolf Sprudzs, comps.
3. Hein
4. 1980
5. 2 vols.
6. $175
7. periodic supp.
8. 1987 - $42.50; 1989 - $45
9. 79-56183/6159074/JX4301.E97

1. **EXTRANEOUS OFFENSES & UNCHARGED CONDUCT**
2. McColl, Arch & David McCormack
3. Knowles
4. 1986
5. 1 vol. (Texas only)

6. $135 incl. 3 mos. supp.
7. annual supp.
8. 1990 - $62
9. 15123315/KFT1740.M28

1. **EXTRAORDINARY CONTRACTUAL RELIEF REPORTER**
2. -
3. Fed. Publ.
4. 1974
5. 4 vols.
6. $580
7. annual supp.
8. renewal - $230/yr.
9. 975984/KC85.U75E8

1. **THE EYE (Courtroom Medicine Series, vol. 14)**
2. Chapman, Loring F. & Edward A. Dunlap
3. Bender
4. 1981
5. 2 vols.
6. $235 incl. 3 mos. supp.
7. periodic supp.
8. 1989 - $148; 1990 - $177.50
9. 80-85516/7337462/RA1062.5

1. **EYE-WITNESS IDENTIFICATION**
2. Sobel, Nathan R.
3. Clark Boardman Callaghan
4. 2nd ed. - 1981
5. 1 vol.
6. $105 incl. 3 mos. supp.
7. annual supp.
8. 1989 - $49.50; 1990 - $59.50
9. 81-17043/7924220/KF9662.S63

1. **FAIR EMPLOYMENT & HOUSING COMMISSION PRECEDENTIAL DECISIONS SERVICE**
2. -
3. Calif. CEB
4. 1982
5. 1 vol.
6. $90/yr. (back vols. avail.-$200)
7. periodic supp.

1. **FAIR EMPLOYMENT PRACTICES**
2. Sedmak, Nancy J.
3. BNA
4. 1965
5. 3 vols.
6. $761/yr.
7. bimonthly supp.
8. renewal - $665/yr.

1. **FAIR HOUSING - FAIR LENDING**
2. P-H Editorial Staff
3. Prentice Hall Law & Business
4. 1985
5. 1 vol.
6. $410/yr.
7. monthly supp.
9. 85-61994/12366362/KF5740.A6F3

1. **FAIR LABOR STANDARDS HANDBOOK FOR STATES, LOCAL GOVERNMENTS AND SCHOOLS**
2. Ginsburg, Gilbert J. & D.B. Abrahams
3. Thompson
4. 1985
5. 2 vols.
6. $231/yr.
7. monthly supp.
8. renewal - $216/yr.
9. 12594098/KF3455.A33

1. **FAIR POLITICAL PRACTICES COMMISSION NOTEBOOK SERVICE**
2. -
3. Calif. CEB
4. 1975
5. 5 vols.
6. $212 incl. 1 yr. supp.
7. periodic supp.
8. renewal - $95/yr.
9. 76-623002

1. **FAIR POLITICAL PRACTICES COMMISSION'S ENFORCEMENT DECISIONS**
2. -
3. Calif. CEB
4. 1976
5. 1 vol.
6. $300
7. annual supp.
8. $100/yr.

1. **FALSE CLAIMS, ANTI-KICKBACK AND PROGRAM FRAUD CIVIL REMEDIES**
2. -
3. BNA
4. 1988
5. 1 vol.
6. $145
7. no supp. planned
9. 19058106

1. **FAMILY BUSINESS ORGANIZATION**
2. Kelly, Donald H. and David A. Ludtke

3. Shepard's
4. 1990
5. 2 vols.
6. $160
7. annual supp.
8. no supp. yet
9. 90-20022/22629843/KF1466.K45

1. **FAMILY LAW**
2. Baldwin, Richard C. et al., eds.
3. Oregon Bar
4. 1990
5. 2 vols.
6. $140
7. periodic supp.
8. no supp. yet
9. 90-63590/24468549/KFO2494.Z9F35

1. **FAMILY LAW**
2. Branton, James L. & James D. Lovett
3. Knowles
4. 1990
5. 1 vol. (avail. in Texas & Natl. eds.)
6. $135 incl. 3 mos. supp.
7. annual supp.
8. 1991 - $43
9. 89-78225/20931200/KF505.B666

1. **FAMILY LAW: TEXAS PRACTICE AND PROCEDURE**
2. Kazen, Barbara A. et al.
3. Bender
4. 1982
5. 6 vols.
6. $675 incl. 3 mos. supp.
7. periodic supp.
8. 1989 - $390; 1990 - $516.50
9. 81-70957/8215560/KFT1294.F35

1. **FAMILY LAW AND PRACTICE**
2. Rutkin, Arnold H.
3. Bender
4. 1985
5. 4 vols.
6. $440 incl. 3 mos. supp.
7. periodic supp.
8. 1989 - $262; 1990 - $313
9. 85-62785/1297922/KF503.4.F35

1. **FAMILY LAW AND PRACTICE IN VIRGINIA**
2. -
3. Jt. Comm. Va.
4. 1986
5. 1 vol.
6. $73
7. periodic supp.
8. 1989 - $26
9. 15245423/KFV2500.F3

1. **FAMILY LAW CASENOTES AND QUOTES**
2. Bailey, Thomas, et al.
3. State Bar of Wisc.
4. 1990
5. 1 vol.
6. $145
7. periodic supp.
8. 1990 - $42; 1991 - $88
9. 21549642/KFW2494.B34

1. **FAMILY LAW CHECKLISTS**
2. Crouch, Richard & Contributors
3. Clark Boardman Callaghan
4. 1990
5. 2 vols.
6. $150 incl. 6 mos. supp.
7. annual supp.
8. no supp. yet
9. 90-46750/22422540/KF505.C76

1. **FAMILY LAW FORMBOOK**
2. -
3. State Bar of Mont.
4. 1986
5. 1 vol.
6. $60
7. periodic supp.
8. no supp. yet

1. **FAMILY LAW GUIDEBOOK (MASSACHUSETTS): A HANDBOOK WITH FORMS**
2. Ginsburg, Hon. Edward M.
3. Butterworth-NH
4. 1985
5. 1 vol.
6. $50
7. periodic supp.
8. no supp. yet
9. 11561453/KF505.G56x

1. **FAMILY LAW INSTITUTE**
2. Carmel, Alan S.
3. MICPEL
4. 1991
5. 1 vol.
6. $42
7. no supp. yet
9. 21531520/KFM1294.F352

1. **FAMILY LAW LITIGATION GUIDE: DISCOVERY, EVIDENCE AND TRIAL PRACTICE**
2. Hampton, Lawrence P. et al.
3. Bender
4. 1991
5. 3 vols.
6. $295 incl. 3 mos. supp.
7. annual supp.
8. no supp. yet
9. 91-71510/24031470/KF535.F35

1. **THE FAMILY LAW PRACTICE MANUAL**
2. Kindregan, Charles P.
3. Legal-Med.
4. 1988
5. 1 vol.
6. $75
7. annual supp.
8. 1989 - $20; 1990 - $20
9. 87-82717/16878986/KF533.5.K56

1. **THE FAMILY LAW REPORTER**
2. Auerbach, Randy P.
3. BNA
4. 1974
5. 2 vols.
6. $520/yr.
7. weekly supp. & reports
8. renewal - $490/yr.
9. 75-645618/22425501/KF501.A3F3

1. **FAMILY LAW SECTION MID-YEAR MEETING & SEMINARS**
2. -
3. Wash. Bar
4. 1991
5. 1 vol.
6. $55
7. annual vol.

1. **FAMILY LAW TAX GUIDE**
2. -
3. CCH
4. 1985
5. 1 vol.
6. $445/yr.; $405/yr. for 2 yrs.
7. monthly supp.
9. 85-185842/12077957/KF6296.A8F36

1. **FAMILY LAW UPDATE**
2. -
3. Minn. CLE
4. 1991
5. 1 vol.
6. $60
7. no supp. planned

1. **FAMILY TAX PLANNING**
2. Rice, Ralph S. & Terence R.
3. Bender
4. 1960
5. 2 vols.
6. $210 incl. 3 mos. supp.
7. annual supp.
8. 1989 - $99.50; 1990 - $91
9. 60-1695/10779790/KF6296.A8R5

1. **FARM PRODUCTS FINANCING AND FILING SERVICE**
2. Kershen, Drew L. & J. T. Hardin
3. WG&L
4. 1990
5. 1 vol.
6. $295/yr.
7. supp. 3x/yr.
8. -
9. 90-70256/22106364/KF1692.A6K4

1. **FASB ACCOUNTING STANDARDS - CURRENT TEXT**
2. -
3. FASB
4. 1982
5. 2 vols.
6. $255/yr.
7. periodic supp.
8. renewal - $200/yr.
9. 82-50808/8774765/HF5667.A55

1. **FCC RULEMAKING REPORTS**
2. -
3. CCH
4. 1986
5. 3 vols.
6. $765/yr.; $695/yr. for 2 yrs.
7. biweekly supp.
9. 14341702/KF2765.1.A6F3

1. **FCC RULES CURRENT SERVICE**
2. Emeritz, Robert E. et al.
3. P&F
4. 1985
5. 9 vols.
6. $1055
7. weekly supp.
8. $795/yr.; $1510/2 yrs.

1. **FDA COMPLIANCE POLICY GUIDES MANUAL**

2. FDA
3. NTIS - order # PB91-915499/CAU (manual); PB91-915400/CAU (updates)
4. 1990
5. 1 vol.
6. $181
7. monthly supp.
8. $175/yr.
9. 7664020/WA697.F105

1. **THE FDA ENFORCEMENT MANUAL**
2. Levine, Arthur N.
3. Thompson
4. 1991
5. 1 vol.
6. $637/yr.
7. monthly supp.

1. **FDIC ENFORCEMENT DECISIONS AND ORDERS**
2. -
3. Prentice Hall Law & Business
4. 1990
5. 4 vols.
6. $375/yr.
7. monthly supp.

1. **FED-TRACK GUIDE TO ANTIDUMPING FINDINGS AND ORDERS**
2. -
3. Fed-Track
4. 1983
5. 3 vols.
6. $250 incl. 1 yr. supp.
7. monthly supp.
8. $175/yr.
9. 83-197290/9870610/KF6708.D8A5

1. **FED-TRACK GUIDE TO COUNTERVAILING DUTY CASES**
2. -
3. Fed-Track
4. 1984
5. 2 vols.
6. $225 incl. 1 yr. supp.
7. monthly supp.
8. $130/yr.
9. 10854222

1. **FED-TRACK GUIDE TO INVESTIGATION OF UNFAIR TRADE PRACTICES**
2. -
3. Fed-Track
4. 1989
5. 2 vols.
6. $250 incl. 1 yr. supp.
7. monthly supp.
8. $165/yr.

1. **FEDERAL ACQUISITION REGULATIONS**
2. -
3. order from USGPO - stock #922-006-00000-8
4. 1990
5. 1 vol.
6. $146/yr.
7. periodic supp.

1. **FEDERAL AUDIT GUIDES**
2. -
3. CCH
4. 1977
5. 4 vols.
6. $445/yr.; $405/yr. for 2 yrs.
7. periodic supp.
9. 78-106155/4490536/KF6233.4.C6

1. **FEDERAL AVIATION ADMINISTRATION - CODIFIED REGULATIONS**
2. -
3. Rules
4. 1962
5. 6 vols.
6. $300 incl. 1 yr. supp. (parts avail. separately)
7. periodic supp.
8. renewal fee

1. **FEDERAL AVIATION REGULATIONS**
2. U.S. Federal Aviation Admin.
3. order from USGPO
4. 23 vols. covering various parts - avail. separately priced from $14-$59 per vol. incl. supp.

1. **FEDERAL BAIL & DETENTION HANDBOOK**
2. Weinberg, Hon. John L.
3. PLI
4. 1988
5. 1 vol.
6. $70
7. annual supp.
8. 1990 - $25; 1990 - $35
9. 17559680/KF9632.W44

1. **FEDERAL BANK HOLDING COMPANY LAW**

2. Heller, Pauline B.
3. Law Journal
4. 1986
5. 1 vol.
6. $115
7. periodic supp.
8. 1989 - $60; 1990 - $130
9. 86-2809/13215890/KF1017.H435

1. **FEDERAL BANKING LAW REPORTS**
2. -
3. CCH
4. 1914
5. 6 vols.
6. $865/yr.; $785/yr. for 2 yrs.
7. weekly supp.
9. 45-10232/1564320

1. **FEDERAL BANKING LAW SERVICE**
2. Stemler, D. McF.
3. Pratt
4. 1878
5. 5 vols.
6. $220/yr.
7. 35 supp./yr.
9. 37-15762/9747690/KF971.5.F42

1. **FEDERAL BANKRUPTCY HANDBOOK**
2. Ed. Staff
3. Gould
4. NA
5. 1 vol.
6. $18
7. annual supp.
8. 1990 - $6.95; 1991 - $6.95
9. 89-175102/20560751/KF1527.A315A2

1. **FEDERAL BUSINESS LAWS**
2. Hancock, W.A.
3. Bus. Laws
4. 1972
5. 7 vols.
6. $575
7. monthly supp.
8. renewal - $280/yr.
9. 8289850/KF1600.A6F38

1. **FEDERAL CARRIERS REPORTS**
2. -
3. CCH
4. 1937
5. 4 vols.
6. $935/yr.; $850/yr. for 2 yrs.
7. semimonthly supp.
9. 49-2875/1564322

1. **FEDERAL CIRCUIT COURT RULES SERVICE**
2. -
3. Rules
4. 1982
5. 1 vol.
6. $35 incl. 1 yr. supp.
7. periodic supp.
9. 83-128141/10020967/KF9053.A4

1. **FEDERAL CIRCUIT PATENT CASE DIGESTS**
2. Chernoff, Daniel P.
3. Clark Boardman Callaghan
4. 1990
5. 1 vol.
6. $95 incl. 3 mos. supp.
7. annual supp.
8. no supp. yet
9. 90-44464/22208873/KF3106.3.C48

1. **FEDERAL CIVIL LITIGATION**
2. -
3. MILE
4. 9/88
5. 1 vol.
6. $58
7. no supp. planned

1. **FEDERAL CIVIL PRACTICE**
2. -
3. Illinois ICLE
4. rev. - 1987
5. 1 vol.
6. $104.95
7. periodic supp.
8. 1989 - $25.95

1. **FEDERAL CIVIL PRACTICE HANDBOOK**
2. Ed. Staff
3. Gould
4. NA
5. 1 vol.
6. $18
7. annual supp.
9. 1990 - $6.95; 1991 - $6.95

1. **FEDERAL CIVIL PROCEDURE**
2. Niles, Edward I.
3. Parker
4. 2nd ed. - 1990
5. 1 vol.
6. $90 incl. 3 mos. supp.
7. annual supp.

8. no supp. yet
9. 90-62791/22613361/KF8840.N55

1. **FEDERAL CIVIL TRIALBOOK**
2. Matthews, Cari P.
3. West
4. 1991
5. 1 vol.
6. $70 incl. 3 mos. supp.
7. periodic supp.
8. no supp. yet
9. 90-071139/24797947/KF8915.M377

1. **FEDERAL COMMUNICATIONS COMMISSION RULES AND REGULATIONS**
2. -
3. Rules
4. 1963
5. 4 vols.
6. $329 incl. 1 yr. supp. (parts avail. separately)
7. bimonthly supp.
8. renewal fee

1. **FEDERAL CONSUMER CREDIT LAWS & REGULATIONS**
2. Gold, Kathi, ed.
3. NILS
4. 1987
5. 1 vol.
6. $95 incl. 3 mos. supp.
7. annual supp.
8. 1991 - $75
9. 87-62231

1. **FEDERAL CONSUMER PROTECTION: LAWS, RULES AND REGULATIONS**
2. Reams, Bernard D. Jr. & J.R. Ferguson
3. Oceana
4. 1978
5. 5 vols.
6. $500
7. periodic supp.
8. 1990 - $250
9. 78-11285/4498849/KF1604

1. **FEDERAL CONTRACT MANAGEMENT - A MANUAL FOR THE CONTRACT PROFESSIONAL**
2. Steiger, Norman A.
3. Bender
4. 1982
5. 3 vols.
6. $350 incl. 3 mos. supp.
7. periodic supp.
8. 1989 - $308.50; 1990 - $333.50
9. 82-70574/8909276/KF849.F36

1. **FEDERAL COURT PROCUREMENT DECISIONS**
2. -
3. Fed. Publ.
4. 1982
5. 2 vols.
6. $748/yr.
7. monthly supp.
9. 85-641482/8835576/KF845.A2F43

1. **FEDERAL COURTROOM EVIDENCE**
2. Cotchett, Joseph W. & Arnold B. Elkind
3. Parker
4. 1987
5. 1 vol.
6. $85 incl. 3 mos. supp.
7. annual supp.
8. 1990 - $32; 1991 - $32.50
9. 87-62261/16670630/KF8935.C68

1. **FEDERAL CRIMINAL APPEALS**
2. Griffin, Lissa
3. Clark Boardman Callaghan
4. 1991
5. 1 vol.
6. $100 incl. 3 mos. supp.
7. annual supp.
8. no supp. yet
9. 91-21122/23940868/KF9690.G75

1. **FEDERAL CRIMINAL JURY INSTRUCTIONS**
2. Saltzburg, Stephen A. and Harvey S. Perlman
3. Michie
4. 1985
5. 3 vols.
6. $225
7. periodic supp.
8. 1990 - $60
9. 85-210472//r86/12055522/KF9682.A65S24

1. **FEDERAL CRIMINAL LAW AND PROCEDURE: ALR ANNOTATIONS**
2. -
3. Lawyers Coop.
4. 1991
5. 9 vols.
6. $795

7. periodic supp.
8. no supp. yet
9. 91-61452/24430680/KF9210.3.F43

1. **FEDERAL CRIMINAL PRACTICE**
2. -
3. Illinois ICLE
4. 1987
5. 1 vol.
6. $87.95
7. no supp. yet
8. 1989 - $24.95
9. 18130365/KF9619.F4

1. **FEDERAL CRIMINAL PRACTICE**
2. -
3. Mass. CLE
4. NA
5. 1 vol.
6. $50
7. periodic supp.
8. 1989 - $19.50

1. **FEDERAL CRIMINAL PRACTICE HANDBOOK**
2. -
3. State Bar of Wisc.
4. 1987
5. 1 vol.
6. $65
7. periodic supp.
8. 1989 - $21

1. **FEDERAL ELECTION CAMPAIGN FINANCING GUIDE**
2. -
3. CCH
4. 1976
5. 2 vols.
6. $340/yr.; $310/yr. for 2 yrs.
7. periodic supp.
9. 76-371915/2386963/KF4920.A6C34

1. **FEDERAL ENERGY REGULATORY COMMISSION REPORTS**
2. -
3. CCH
4. 1979
5. 6 vols.
6. $935/yr.; $850/yr. for 2 yrs.
7. periodic supp.
9. 84-153382/10949096/KF2120.A6F34

1. **FEDERAL ENFORCEMENT**
2. -
3. Georgetown
4. 1990
5. 1 vol.
6. $101
7. no supp. planned

1. **FEDERAL ENVIRONMENTAL REGULATION**
2. Delogu, Orlando E. and John Henry Davidson, Jr.
3. Butterworth-NH
4. 1990
5. 2 vols.
6. $165
7. annual supp.
8. 1991 - $55

1. **FEDERAL EQUAL OPPORTUNITY REPORTER**
2. -
3. LRP
4. 1979
5. 3 vols.
6. $815/yr. (back vols. avail.)
7. biweekly supp.

1. **FEDERAL ESTATE AND GIFT TAX REPORTS**
2. -
3. CCH
4. 1913
5. 3 vols.
6. $400/yr.; $365/yr. for 2 yrs.
7. weekly supp.
9. 66-2054/3873075/KF6571.A8C65

1. **FEDERAL ESTATE AND GIFT TAXES**
2. -
3. RIA
4. 1926
5. 2 vols.
6. $425/yr.; $395/yr. for 2 yrs.
7. biweekly supp.
8. renewal - $360/yr.

1. **THE FEDERAL ESTATE TAX PREPARATION OF THE 706**
2. Bolton, Raymond N.
3. Prof. Dev. Fdtn.
4. 1990
5. 1 vol.
6. $95 incl. 1 supp.
7. quarterly supp.
8. renewal - $85/yr.
9. 21546136/KF6572.Z9B64

1. **FEDERAL EVIDENCE FOUNDATIONS**
2. Larkin, Murl A.
3. Butterworth-Texas
4. 1988
5. 1 vol.
6. $90
7. annual supp.
8. no supp. yet
9. 88-24274/18379603/KF8935.L37

1. **FEDERAL EVIDENCE PRACTICE GUIDE**
2. McLauglin, J.
3. Bender
4. 1989
5. 3 vols.
6. $315 incl. 3 mos. supp.
7. annual supp.
8. 1990 - $164.50
9. 88-63110/19111236/KF8935.F39

1. **FEDERAL EXCISE TAX REPORTS**
2. -
3. CCH
4. 1913
5. 1 vol.
6. $285/yr.; $260/yr. for 2 yrs.
7. weekly supp.
9. 67-4841/1564324

1. **FEDERAL EXCISE TAXES**
2. -
3. RIA
4. 1956
5. 1 vol.
6. $350/yr.; $310/yr. for 2 yrs.
7. monthly supp.
8. renewal - $275/yr.

1. **FEDERAL GRANTS MANAGEMENT HANDBOOK**
2. Lamomeaux, Denise
3. Thompson
4. 1978
5. 2 vols.
6. $224/yr.
7. monthly supp. & newsletter
8. renewal - $195/yr.
9. 78-112049/4375001/KF6733.A6F42

1. **FEDERAL GUIDE**
2. Wiorski, Robert, ed.
3. USLSI
4. 1953
5. 4 vols.
6. $1200-nonmembers, $750-members incl. 1 yr. supp.
7. monthly supp.
8. 1991-nonmembers - $680; members - $380

1. **FEDERAL INCOME, GIFT AND ESTATE TAXATION**
2. Rabkin, Jacob & Mark H. Johnson
3. Bender
4. 1942
5. 17 vols.
6. $900 incl. 1 yr. supp.; $1650 incl. 2 yr. supp.
7. monthly supp. & newsletter
8. 1988 - $525; 1989 - $605
9. 42-17785/2369475/HJ4652.A7R3

1. **FEDERAL INCOME TAXATION OF BANKS AND FINANCIAL INSTITUTIONS**
2. Rook, Lance W.
3. WG&L
4. 6th ed. - 1990
5. 1 vol.
6. $175
7. quarterly supp.
8. 1991 - $271.50
9. 89-51274/20846172/KF6495.B2F42

1. **FEDERAL INCOME TAXATION OF CORPORATE LIQUIDATIONS**
2. Goff, Neil M.
3. Shepard's
4. 1984
5. 2 vols.
6. $195
7. annual supp.
8. 1985 - $24; 1987 - $30
9. 84-20312/11236092/KF6499.D5G63

1. **FEDERAL INCOME TAXATION OF CORPORATIONS AND SHAREHOLDERS: FORMS**
2. Bittker, Boris I., et al.
3. WG&L
4. 3rd ed. - 1989
5. 2 vols.
6. $195
7. supp. 3x/yr.
8. 1988 - $134; 1991 - $200
9. 89-50253/20647754/KF6462.B5

1. **FEDERAL INCOME TAXATION OF CORPORATIONS FILING CONSOLIDATED RETURNS**

2. Lerner, Herbert J. et al.
3. Bender
4. 1975
5. 4 vols.
6. $385 incl. 6 mos. supp.
7. annual supp.
8. 1989 - $213.50; 1990 - $247
9. 75-750/1952258/KF6499.C58F4

1. **FEDERAL INCOME TAXATION OF DEBT INSTRUMENTS**
2. Garlock, David C.
3. Prentice Hall Law & Business
4. 1991
5. 1 vol.
6. $110 incl. 4 mos. supp.
7. periodic supp.
8. no supp. yet
9. 91-29474/24321048/KF6392.G37

1. **FEDERAL INCOME TAXATION OF INDIVIDUALS**
2. Bittker, Boris I. & Martin J. McMahon, Jr.
3. WG&L
4. 1988
5. 1 vol.
6. $105
7. semiannual supp.
8. 1989 - $46; 1991 - $102
9. 88-50706/18478034/KF6369.B57

1. **FEDERAL INCOME TAXATION OF INVENTORIES**
2. Schneider, Leslie J.
3. Bender
4. 1979
5. 3 vols.
6. $355 incl. 3 mos. supp.
7. supp. as needed
8. 1989 - $287; 1990 - $313
9. 79-63508/5100836/KF6450.S3

1. **FEDERAL INCOME TAXATION OF LIFE INSURANCE COMPANIES**
2. Antes, Richard, et al.
3. Bender
4. 2nd ed. - 1986
5. 3 vols.
6. $330 incl. 3 mos. supp.
7. annual supp.
8. 1989 - $211.50; 1990 - $87
9. 83-73413/10593989/KF6495.I5F42

1. **FEDERAL INCOME TAXATION OF OIL AND GAS INVESTMENTS**
2. Bruen, Alexander J. & W.B. Taylor
3. WG&L
4. 2nd ed. - 1989
5. 1 vol.
6. $175
7. annual supp.
8. 1989 - $59.50; 1990 - $73
9. 88-62149/18967610/KF6482.B78

1. **FEDERAL INCOME TAXATION OF PASSIVE ACTIVITIES**
2. Jennings, Michael N. & Daniel R. Bolar
3. WG&L
4. 1990
5. 1 vol.
6. $110
7. semiannual supp.
8. 1991 - $46
9. 90-70549/22207862/KF6396.J46

1. **FEDERAL INCOME TAXATION OF REAL ESTATE**
2. Robinson, Gerald J.
3. WG&L
4. 5th ed. - 1988
5. 1 vol.
6. $105
7. supp. 3x/yr.
8. 1989 - $145; 1991 - $165.50
9. 87-51572/17898507/KF6535.R62

1. **FEDERAL INCOME TAXATION OF REAL ESTATE: FORMS AND CHECKLISTS**
2. Robinson, Gerald J.
3. WG&L
4. 1989
5. 1 vol.
6. $96
7. periodic supp.
8. 1991 - $49.75
9. 87-51572/20430949/KF6535.R62

1. **FEDERAL INCOME TAXATION OF S CORPORATIONS**
2. Eustice, James S. & Joel D. Kuntz
3. WG&L
4. 2th ed. - 1985
5. 1 vol.
6. $135
7. supp. 3x/yr.
8. 1990 - $57.75; 1991 - $186
9. 85-50357/12183765/KF6491.E84

1. **FEDERAL INFORMATION DISCLOSURE**
2. O'Reilly, James T.
3. Shepard's
4. 2nd ed. - 1990
5. 2 vols.
6. $195
7. semiannual supp.
8. 1991 - $33
9. 90-46754/22422562/KF5753.O74

1. **FEDERAL INSURANCE LAWS**
2. Waldman, Sarita, ed.
3. NILS
4. 1985
5. 1 vol.
6. $165 incl. 3 mos supp.
7. semiannual supp.
8. 1989 - $72; 1990 - $72
9. 85-061984/13396976/KF1151

1. **FEDERAL INSURANCE REGULATIONS**
2. -
3. NILS
4. 1978
5. 1 vol.
6. $165 incl. 1 yr. supp.
7. semiannual supp.
8. 1990 - $148
9. 77-87141/4136714/KF1152

1. **FEDERAL JUDGES AND JUSTICES: A CURRENT LISTING OF NOMINATIONS, CONFIRMATIONS, ELEVATIONS, RESIGNATIONS AND RETIREMENTS**
2. Wildman, Iris J.
3. Rothman
4. 1987
5. 1 vol.
6. $75 incl. 1 yr. supp.
7. monthly supp.
8. 1989 - $75; 1990 - $75
9. 86-2656/14995936

1. **FEDERAL LABOR RELATIONS REPORTER**
2. -
3. LRP
4. 1970
5. 3 vols.
6. $745/yr. (back vols. avail.)
7. semimonthly supp.
9. 80-8956/5933973

1. **FEDERAL LAND USE LAW**
2. Mandelker, Daniel R., et al.
3. Clark Boardman Callaghan
4. 1986
5. 1 vol.
6. $120 incl. 3 mos. supp.
7. annual supp.
8. 1989 - $49.50; 1990 - $65
9. 86-17099/13823408/KF5698.M283

1. **FEDERAL LITIGATION GUIDE**
2. Law Firm of McCutchen, Doyle, Brown & Emerson
3. Bender
4. 1985
5. 4 vols.
6. $550 incl. 3 mos. supp.
7. periodic supp. & monthly newsletter
8. 1989 - $366.50; 1990 - $425
9. 84-73355/12949192/KF8840.F397

1. **FEDERAL LOCAL COURT FORMS**
2. Hollins, Royanne R.
3. Lawyers Coop.
4. 1986
5. 2 vols.
6. $150 incl. 6 mos. supp.
7. semiannual supp.
8. 1990 - $51; 1991 - $61
9. 87-32582/17107922/KF8836.H58

1. **FEDERAL LOCAL COURT RULES**
2. Pike & Fischer, ed.
3. Lawyers Coop.
4. 1964
5. 3 vols.
6. $395 incl. 6 mos. supp.
7. bimonthly supp.
8. 1990 - $280; 1991 - $320
9. 64-20105/13396788/KF8820.A2

1. **FEDERAL MARITIME COMMISSION SERVICE**
2. Eyler, Carl R.
3. Hawkins
4. 1970
5. 1 vol.
6. $260/yr.
7. periodic supp.

1. **FEDERAL MERIT SYSTEMS REPORTER**
2. -
3. LRP
4. 1979
5. 3 vols.
6. $745/yr. (back vols. avail.)

7. weekly supp.
9. 12047606

1. **FEDERAL MOTOR VEHICLE SAFETY STANDARDS AND REGULATIONS**
2. U.S. National Highway Traffic Safety Admin.
3. order from USGPO - stock #950-031-00000-0
4. 1989
5. 1 vol.
6. $134/yr.
7. monthly supp.
9. 3129141/KF2212.A33

1. **FEDERAL ONSHORE OIL AND GAS POOLING AND UNITIZATION II**
2. -
3. Rocky Mt.
4. 1990
5. 2 vols.
6. $145
7. no supp. planned
9. 21059458/KF1853.A75I35

1. **FEDERAL ORGANIZATION SERVICE CIVIL**
2. -
3. Carroll
4. 1974
5. 1 vol.
6. $450/yr.
7. supp. every 6 wks.
9. 83-647321/9837594/JK404.F44

1. **FEDERAL ORGANIZATION SERVICE MILITARY**
2. -
3. Carroll
4. 1974
5. 1 vol.
6. $900/yr.
7. supp. every 6 wks.
9. 83-647321/9837594/JK404.F44

1. **FEDERAL PAY AND BENEFITS REPORTER**
2. -
3. LRP
4. 1974
5. 2 vols.
6. $530/yr. (back vols. avail.)
7. monthly supp.
9. 14255425

1. **FEDERAL REGULATION OF DEPOSITORY INSTITUTIONS**
2. Schott, Paul Allen
3. WG&L
4. 1988
5. 1 vol.
6. $98
7. annual supp.
8. 1989 - $44; 1991 - price NA
9. 88-50707/18765296/KF1017.S33

1. **FEDERAL REGULATION OF INTERNATIONAL BUSINESS**
2. Malawer, Stuart S.
3. Hein
4. 1980
5. 6 vols.
6. $895
7. periodic supp.
8. 1988 - $45; 1991 - $45
9. 80-69834/7422725/KF1976.M34x

1. **FEDERAL REGULATION OF THE CHEMICAL INDUSTRY**
2. O'Reilly, James T. et al.
3. Shepard's
4. 1980
5. 1 vol.
6. $95
7. annual supp.
8. 1989 - $56; 1990 - $60
9. 80-11488/6092625/KF1875.F4

1. **FEDERAL REGULATIONS FOR PRIVATE TRUCK OPERATIONS**
2. -
3. NPTC
4. 1991
5. 1 vol.
6. $165
7. semiannual supp.
8. new ed. due 1992
9. 76-370608/2402416/KF2251.P7

1. **FEDERAL REGULATORY PROCESS: AGENCY PRACTICES & PROCEDURES**
2. Edles, Gary J. & Jerome Nelson
3. Prentice Hall Law & Business
4. 2nd ed. - 1989
5. 1 vol.
6. $85 incl. 4 mos. supp.
7. periodic supp.
8. 1990 - $50; 1991 - $50
9. 89-22777/20218023/KF5402.E34

1. **FEDERAL RESERVE REGULATORY SERVICE**

2. -
3. Fed.
4. 1981
5. 3 vols.
6. $200/yr.
7. monthly supp.
9. 9188924/KF6219.A332

1. **FEDERAL RESERVE SYSTEM COMPLIANCE HANDBOOK**
2. -
3. Fed.
4. 1988
5. 1 vol.
6. $20
7. periodic supp.

1. **FEDERAL RULE BOOK**
2. -
3. Minn. CLE
4. 1991
5. 1 vol.
6. $40
7. no supp. planned
9. 24681530/KF8841.F33

1. **FEDERAL RULES OF BANKRUPTCY**
2. Patchan, Joseph
3. Clark Boardman Callaghan
4. 3rd ed. - 1988
5. 1 vol.
6. $100 incl. 3 mos. supp.
7. periodic supp.
8. 1989 - $45
9. 83-25878/10228851/KF1527.P37

1. **FEDERAL RULES OF CIVIL PROCEDURE**
2. Coyne, Thomas A.
3. Clark Boardman Callaghan
4. 1982
5. 1 vol.
6. $105 incl. 3 mos. supp.
7. annual supp.
8. 1989 - $93; 1990 - $52.50
9. 81-18095/7923564/KF8840.C65

1. **FEDERAL RULES OF CRIMINAL PROCEDURE**
2. Hermann, Michele G.
3. Clark Boardman Callaghan
4. 2nd ed. - 1980
5. 1 vol.
6. $105 incl. 3 mos. supp.
7. annual supp.
8. 1989 - $45; 1991 - $55
9. 80-10646/6016299/KF9607

1. **FEDERAL RULES OF EVIDENCE**
2. Rothstein, Paul F.
3. Clark Boardman Callaghan
4. 2nd ed. - 1978
5. 1 vol.
6. $105 incl. 3 mos. supp.
7. annual supp.
8. 1989 - $45; 1991 - $59.50
9. 78-9296/3913210/KF8935.R65

1. **FEDERAL RULES OF EVIDENCE SERVICE**
2. Pike & Fischer, ed.
3. Lawyers Coop.
4. 1979
5. 31 bound vols.
6. $1085 incl. 6 mos. supp.
7. monthly service
8. 1990 - $525; 1991 - $560
9. 79-119/4591532/KF8935.F4

1. **FEDERAL SECURITIES ACT – ANALYSIS, PROCEDURES AND FORMS (Business Organizations vol. 11, 11 pt. 1, 1A, 2, 2A)**
2. Sowards, Hugh L.
3. Bender
4. 1965
5. 6 vols.
6. $555 incl. 3 mos. supp.
7. semiannual supp.
8. 1989 - $468; 1990 - $529
9. 73-10837/62454/KF1436.5.S6

1. **FEDERAL SECURITIES EXCHANGE ACT OF 1934 (Business Organizations vols. 11A parts 1-2D)**
2. Gadsby, Edward N.
3. Bender
4. 1971
5. 9 vols.
6. $785 incl. 3 mos. supp.
7. semiannual supp.
8. 1989 - $600; 1990 - $748
9. 78-302733/3706485/KF1068.4.G3

1. **FEDERAL SECURITIES LAW REPORTS**
2. -
3. CCH
4. 1933
5. 7 vols.

6. $1080/yr.; $980/yr. for 2 yrs.
7. weekly supp. & newsletter
9. 11872559/KF1436.5.C736

1. **FEDERAL SECURITIES LAWS - REGULATIONS - FORMS**
2. -
3. CCH
4. 1979
5. 5 vols.
6. $375/yr.; $340/yr. for 2 yrs.
7. monthly supp.
9. 80-112909/6604148/KF1436.5.C647

1. **FEDERAL SENTENCING GUIDELINES**
2. -
3. NH Bar
4. 1990
5. 1 vol.
6. $35
7. no supp. planned
9. 21387806/KFN1787.Z9N48

1. **FEDERAL SENTENCING GUIDELINES 1991**
2. Crowe, Thomas L. et al
3. MICPEL
4. 1991
5. 1 vol.
6. $42
7. no supp. planned

1. **FEDERAL SENTENCING MANUAL**
2. McFadden, Gerald, et al.
3. Bender
4. 1989
5. 1 vol.
6. $115 incl. 3 mos. supp.
7. annual supp.
8. 1990 - $92.50
9. 89-85665/20574310/KF9685.M3

1. **FEDERAL TAX ADVISOR**
2. -
3. CCH
4. 1991
5. 35 vols.
6. $1040/yr.; $945/yr. for 2 yrs.
7. weekly supp.
9. 23722231/KF6285.F27

1. **FEDERAL TAX ADVISOR – CONTROL EDITION**
2. -
3. CCH
4. 1991
5. 23 vols.
6. $765/yr.; $695/yr. for 2 yrs.
7. weekly supp.

1. **FEDERAL TAX AND RELATED FORMS**
2. -
3. Tax Form
4. 1979
5. 2 vols.
6. $175/yr.
7. annual editions
9. 11605709/KF6366.F43

1. **FEDERAL TAX ARTICLES**
2. -
3. CCH
4. 1962
5. 1 vol.
6. $420/yr.; $380/yr. for 2 yrs.
7. monthly supp.
9. 65-8518/1564326/KF6285.C73F5

1. **FEDERAL TAX ASPECTS OF BANKRUPTCY**
2. McQueen, C. Richard and Jack Crestol
3. Shepard's
4. 1984
5. 1 vol.
6. $95
7. annual supp.
8. 1989 - $32; 1990 - $32
9. 84-11/10323027/KF6332.M35

1. **FEDERAL TAX ASPECTS OF CORPORATE REORGANIZATIONS**
2. Schneider, Daniel M. & Paul E. Hoelschen, Jr.
3. Shepard's
4. 1988
5. 1 vol.
6. $95
7. annual supp.
8. 1990 - $28; 1991 - $30
9. 88-32695/18779069/KF6499.C6S3

1. **FEDERAL TAX ASPECTS OF REAL ESTATE TRANSACTIONS**
2. -
3. Illinois ICLE
4. 1987
5. 1 vol.
6. $121.95
7. periodic supp.
8. 1990 - $24.95

9. 16115584/KF6540.F25

1. **FEDERAL TAX COORDINATOR 2D**
2. RIA prof. ed. staff
3. RIA
4. 1970
5. 35 vols.
6. $1325/yr.; $1275/yr. for 2 yrs.
7. weekly supp. & weekly newsletter with binder
8. renewal - $1225/yr.
9. 40-33082

1. **FEDERAL TAX DEDUCTIONS**
2. Comerford, Brian E. et al.
3. WG&L
4. 2nd ed. - 1991
5. 1 vol.
6. $98
7. annual supp.
8. no supp. yet
9. KF6385.C65

1. **FEDERAL TAX FORMS**
2. -
3. CCH
4. 1973
5. 3 vols.
6. $325/yr.; $295/yr. for 2 yrs.
7. periodic supp.
9. 798837/HJ4652.C486

1. **FEDERAL TAX GUIDE**
2. -
3. CCH
4. 1917
5. 8 vols.
6. $705/yr.; $640/yr. for 2 yrs.
7. weekly supp.
9. 38-2290/1782059

1. **FEDERAL TAX GUIDE**
2. -
3. RIA
4. 1931
5. 2 vols.
6. $375/yr.; $345/yr. for 2 yrs.
7. weekly supp.
8. renewal - $325/yr.
9. 41-4084/3579680/KF6285.P73x

1. **FEDERAL TAX GUIDE REPORTS (Control Edition)**
2. -
3. CCH
4. 1958
5. 2 vols. (also vol. 1 + 1A of reg. ed. of Federal Tax Guide)
6. $430/yr.; $392/yr. for 2 yrs.
7. weekly supp. - vol. reissued annually

1. **FEDERAL TAX GUIDEBOOK**
2. Prigal, Alan
3. Bender
4. 1972
5. 1 vol.
6. $145 incl. 3 mos. supp.
7. annual supp.
8. 1989 - $101; 1990 - $120
9. 72-92898/609418/KF6335.R3

1. **FEDERAL TAX MANUAL (with monthly reports)**
2. -
3. CCH
4. 1982
5. 1 vol.
6. $225/yr.; $206/yr. for 2 yrs.
7. monthly supp.
9. 83-116258

1. **FEDERAL TAX PLANNING**
2. Westin, Richard A.
3. Shepard's
4. 1990
5. 3 vols.
6. $195
7. annual supp.
8. no supp. yet
9. 90-8966/22243251/KF6297.W47

1. **FEDERAL TAX PRACTICE AND PROCEDURE**
2. -
3. Illinois ICLE
4. 1991
5. 1 vol.
6. $99.95
7. periodic supp.
8. no supp.yet
9. 24316909/KF6320.F43

1. **FEDERAL TAX REGULATIONS**
2. -
3. RIA
4. NA
5. 5 vols.
6. $210/yr.; $195/yr. for 2 yrs.
7. quarterly supp.
8. renewal - $180/yr.

9. 12395317/KF6357.523.A2

1. **FEDERAL TAXATION OF BUSINESS ENTERPRISES**
2. Thompson, Samuel C. Jr. et al.
3. Clark Boardman Callaghan
4. 1989
5. 3 vols.
6. $300 incl. 1 yr. supp.
7. quarterly supp.
9. 88-30260/18629025/KF6450.F43

1. **FEDERAL TAXATION OF CLOSE CORPORATIONS**
2. Hood, Edwin T. & John J. Mylan
3. Clark Boardman Callaghan
4. 1990
5. 2 vols.
6. $160 incl. 6 mos. supp.
7. semiannual supp.
8. no supp. yet
9. 90-45826/22307367/KF6484.H66

1. **FEDERAL TAXATION OF INSURANCE COMPANIES**
2. Partners of KPMG Peat Marwick
3. RIA
4. 1991
5. 1 vol.
6. $490/yr.; $445/yr. for 2 yrs.
7. bimonthly supp.
8. renewal - $400/yr.
9. 24258606/KF6495.I5F36

1. **FEDERAL TAXATION OF INTELLECTUAL PROPERTY TRANSFERS**
2. Olson, Joseph E.
3. Law Journal
4. 1986
5. 1 vol.
6. $70
7. periodic supp.
8. 1987 - $35; 1989 - $37
9. 85-30038/12971368/KF6428.I5O45

1. **FEDERAL TAXATION OF OIL AND GAS TRANSACTIONS**
2. Fiske, Leland E.
3. Bender
4. 1958
5. 2 vols.
6. $225 incl 3. mos. supp.
7. annual supp.
8. 1989 - $81; 1990 - $93
9. 59-25923/6261345/KF6482.F5

1. **FEDERAL TAXATION OF PARTNERSHIPS AND PARTNERS**
2. McKee, William S. et al.
3. WG&L
4. 2nd ed. - 1990
5. 2 vols.
6. $195
7. 3 supp./yr.
8. 1991 - $138
9. 78-109388/4514686/KF6452.M26

1. **FEDERAL TAXATION OF PARTNERSHIPS AND PARTNERS: STRUCTURING AND DRAFTING AGREEMENTS**
2. McKee, William S. et al.
3. WG&L
4. 1989
5. 1 vol.
6. $145
7. semiannual supp.
8. 1989 - $56; 1991 - $68.75
9. 88-51621/19680677

1. **FEDERAL TAXATION OF REAL ESTATE**
2. Samansky, Allan J. & James C. Smith
3. Law Journal
4. 1985
5. 1 vol.
6. $80
7. periodic supp.
8. 1989 - $84; 1990 - $84
9. 85-77/11650164/KF6535.S25

1. **FEDERAL TAXATION OF S CORPORATIONS**
2. Schenk, Deborah H.
3. Law Journal
4. 1986
5. 1 vol.
6. $75
7. periodic supp.
8. 1989 - $75; 1990 - $79
9. 85-18064/12370903/KF6491.S33

1. **FEDERAL TAXATION OF S CORPORATIONS AND SHAREHOLDERS**
2. Bravenec, Lorence L.
3. PLI
4. 1988
5. 1 vol.
6. $45
7. annual supp.
8. no supp. yet

9. 88-62893/18955363/KF6491.B72

1. **FEDERAL TAXATION OF TRUSTS, GRANTORS AND BENEFICIARIES**
2. Peschel, J.L. & E.D. Spurgeon
3. WG&L
4. 2nd ed. - 1989
5. 1 vol.
6. $145
7. annual supp.
8. 1990 - $57.75; 1991 - price NA
9. 89-51608/20621132/KF6443.P4

1. **FEDERAL TAXES, 2ND**
2. -
3. RIA
4. 1913
5. 17 vols.
6. $1195/yr.; $1150/yr. for 2 yrs.
7. weekly supp.
8. renewal - $1085/yr.
9. 27-1499

1. **FEDERAL TAXES AFFECTING REAL ESTATE**
2. Faggen, Ivan, et al.
3. Bender
4. 1978
5. 1 vol.
6. $120 incl. 3 mos. supp.
7. periodic supp.
8. 1989 - $75; 1990 - $89
9. 82-111387/8495309/KF6540.F26

1. **FEDERAL TESTIMONIAL PRIVILEGES**
2. Larkin, Murl A.
3. Clark Boardman Callaghan
4. 1982
5. 1 vol.
6. $105 incl. 3 mos. supp.
7. annual supp.
8. 1989 - $84.50; 1991 - $114.50
9. 82-12958/8669231/KF8958.L57

1. **FEDERAL TRADE COMMISSION: LAW, PRACTICE AND PROCEDURE**
2. Ward, Peter C.
3. Law Journal
4. 1986
5. 1 vol.
6. $85
7. periodic supp.
8. 1989 - $82; 1990 - $84
9. 86-20042/14133895/KF1611.W35

1. **FEDERAL TRADE COMMISSION REGULATORY MANUAL**
2. Kanwit, Stephanie W.
3. Shepard's
4. 1979
5. 2 vols.
6. $190
7. annual supp.
8. 1989 - $70; 1991 - $78
9. 79-20919/6142340/KF1611.K36

1. **FEDERAL TRIAL EVIDENCE**
2. Dombroff, Mark A.
3. James
4. 1986
5. 1 vol.
6. $49.75 incl. 3 mos. supp.
7. annual supp.
8. 1989 - $37.92; 1990 - $39.93
9. 16954408/KF8935.D65

1. **FEDERAL TRIAL EVIDENCE**
2. Wagner, Charles
3. Butterworth-NH
4. 1984 - 1988
5. 2 vols.
6. $80
7. periodic supp.
8. 1988 - $36; 1989 - $40
9. 11619792/KF8935.W336

1. **FEDERAL UNFAIR COMPETITION: LANHAM ACT 43(a)**
2. McKenney, Charles E. & George F. Long III
3. Clark Boardman Callaghan
4. 1989
5. 1 vol.
6. $105 incl. 3 mos. supp.
7. annual supp.
9. 89-32831/19627187/KF3193.M38

1. **FEE AGREEMENT FORMS MANUAL**
2. -
3. Calif. CEB
4. 1989
5. 1 vol.
6. $50 (with disks - $85)
7. periodic supp.
8. no supp. yet
9. 88-63608/19566792/KFC77.5.F43P53

1. **FERC PRACTICE AND PROCEDURE MANUAL**

2. Munro, Stephen
3. Thompson
4. 1983
5. 2 vols.
6. $795/yr.
7. monthly supp. & newsletter
8. $736/yr.
9. 8825630/KF2120.1.A6H35

1. **FIDELITY LAW TOPICAL OUTLINE & BIBLIOGRAPHY**
2. -
3. ABA
4. 1989
5. 1 vol.
6. $67
7. no supp. yet
9. 89-85114/20300576/KF1223.A1F53

1. **FIDUCIARY INCOME TAXES**
2. Sassin, Lynn B. et al.
3. MICPEL
4. 1991
5. 1 vol.
6. $42
7. no supp. planned
9. 23948857/KFM1670.F45

1. **FIDUCIARY TAX GUIDE**
2. -
3. CCH
4. 1990
5. 1 vol.
6. $320/yr.; $290/yr. for 2 yrs.
7. monthly supp.
9. 90-200663/22544839

1. **FIFTY-STATE LEGISLATIVE DIRECTORY**
2. -
3. Calif. Jnl. Press
4. 1987
5. 1 vol.
6. $75/yr.; $120/2 yrs.
7. annual supp.

1. **FINANCIAL AND ESTATE PLANNING**
2. -
3. CCH
4. 1980
5. 4 vols.
6. $670/yr.; $610/yr. for 2 yrs.
7. semimonthly supp. & newsletter "Estate Planning Review"
9. 80-2669/6880623

1. **FINANCIAL AND ESTATE PLANNING FORMS MANUAL**
2. -
3. HICLE
4. 1990
5. 1 vol.
6. $60
7. periodic supp.
8. 1991 - $5

1. **FINANCIAL AND ESTATE PLANNING RESOURCE GUIDE**
2. Rook, Lance
3. Bender
4. 1988
5. 3 vols.
6. $285 incl. 3 mos. supp.
7. annual supp.
8. no supp. yet
9. 88-71360/18950588/HG179.R64

1. **FINANCIAL INSTITUTIONS LAW**
2. -
3. MILE
4. 1991
5. 1 vol.
6. $79.88
7. no supp. planned

1. **FINANCIAL INSTITUTIONS REFORM, RECOVERY & ENFORCEMENT ACT OF 1989**
2. -
3. Indiana CLE
4. 1989
5. 1 vol.
6. $50
7. no supp. planned

1. **FINANCIAL MANAGEMENT AND ACCOUNTING FOR THE CONSTRUCTION INDUSTRY**
2. Construction Financial Mgmt. Assn.
3. Bender
4. 1988
5. 1 vol.
6. $105 incl. 3 mos. supp.
7. annual supp.
8. 1989 - $46.50; 1990 - $60
9. 88-71212/19815169/HF5686.B7F58

1. **FINANCIAL SERVICES AND EEC LAW**
2. van Empel, Martijn, ed.
3. Kluwer

4. 1991
5. 1 vol.
6. $184 incl. 3 mos. supp.
7. periodic supp.
8. no supp. yet

1. **FINANCIAL STATEMENT PREPARATION MANUAL**
2. -
3. CCH
4. 1989
5. 1 vol. (with quarterly reports)
6. $170/yr.; $150/yr. for 2 yrs.
7. quarterly supp.
9. 19489404/HF5658.B2F56

1. **FINANCING FOREIGN OPERATIONS (FFO)**
2. -
3. Bus. Intern.
4. 1957
5. 2 vols.
6. $1375/yr. (avail. also in separate area editions)
7. monthly supp.
9. 2256517

1. **FINANCING FOREIGN OPERATIONS/LATIN AMERICA**
2. -
3. Bus. Intern.
4. NA
5. 1 vol.
6. $850/yr.
7. monthly supp.

1. **FINANCING REAL ESTATE TRANSACTIONS**
2. -
3. Illinois ICLE
4. rev. - 1988
5. 2 vols.
6. $131.95
7. periodic supp.
8. no supp. yet
9. 76-10452/2377771/KFI1330.F5

1. **FINANCING TRANSNATIONAL PROJECTS**
2. Sullivan, Ronald F.
3. Bender
4. 1988
5. 1 vol.
6. $85 incl. 3 mos. supp.
7. annual supp.
8. no supp. yet
9. 87-72786/17744322/KF902.A8S85

1. **FINE'S WISCONSIN EVIDENCE**
2. Fine, Ralph Adam
3. Butterworth-St. Paul
4. 1988
5. 1 vol.
6. $95
7. periodic supp.
8. 1989 - $30; 1990 - $40
9. 88-14594/17953824/KFW2940.F56

1. **FIRE, CASUALTY & SURETY BULLETINS**
2. -
3. Natl. Underwriter
4. NA
5. 5 vols.
6. $455/yr.
7. monthly supp.
8. renewal - $295/yr.
9. 12615408/HG8535.N3

1. **FIRE LITIGATION SOURCEBOOK**
2. Patton, Alexander J. & John C. Russell
3. Wiley Law
4. 1986
5. 1 vol.
6. $135
7. periodic supp.
8. 1992 - price NA
9. 85-25441/12809651/TH9180.P38

1. **"FIRE ME & I'LL SUE" - A MANAGER'S SURVIVAL GUIDE TO EMPLOYEE RIGHTS**
2. Condon, Thomas J.
3. Alex. Hamilton Inst.
4. 1986
5. 1 vol.
6. $68.50
7. 3 supp./yr.
8. $19.75/supp.
9. 14339696/HF5549.5.D55C66X

1. **FIRREA: A LEGISLATIVE HISTORY AND SECTION-BY-SECTION ANALYSIS**
2. Pulles, Gregory, et al.
3. Shepard's
4. 1990
5. 2 vols.
6. $195
7. periodic supp.
8. to be supp. in 1992

9. 22770498/KF975.P8

1. **FLEET SAFETY COMPLIANCE MANUAL**
2. Weiland, Betty Bartel
3. Keller
4. 1978
5. 1 vol.
6. $75
7. semiannual supp.
8. $65/yr.
9. 78-71720/5220599/KF2265.K38

1. **FLETCHER CORPORATE PRACTICE DESKBOOK**
2. Golter, Harry
3. Clark Boardman Callaghan
4. 1988
5. 1 vol.
6. $95 incl. 6 mos. supp.
7. annual supp.
8. 1989 - $25; 1990 - $30

1. **THE FLEX PLAN HANDBOOK**
2. -
3. Thompson
4. 1991
5. 1 vol.
6. $349/yr.
7. quarterly supp.

1. **FLORIDA ADMINISTRATIVE PRACTICE**
2. -
3. Florida Bar
4. 3rd ed. - 1990
5. 1 vol.
6. $65
7. periodic supp.
8. no supp. yet
9. 90-80637/21980050/KFF440.F55

1. **FLORIDA ADMINISTRATIVE PRACTICE MANUAL**
2. England, Arthur J., Jr., & L. Harold Levinson
3. Butterworth-Fla.
4. 1979
5. 3 vols.
6. $240
7. periodic supp.
8. 1989 - $166.25; 1990 - $143.80
9. 79-116944/4954171/KFF44O.E53

1. **FLORIDA APPELLATE PRACTICE MANUAL**
2. England, Arthur J., Jr. & Tobias Simon
3. Butterworth-Fla.
4. 1979
5. 3 vols.
6. $240
7. periodic supp.
8. 1989 - $109; 1990 - $125.75
9. 5786941/KFF555.E53

1. **FLORIDA ATTORNEY'S/SECRETARY'S HANDBOOK**
2. -
3. Mariposa
4. 1990
5. 1 vol.
6. $55
7. annual supp.
8. 1990 - $51; 1991 - $46
9. 18095820/KFF77.W34

1. **THE FLORIDA BAR PROBATE SYSTEM**
2. Kelley, Rohan
3. Florida Bar
4. 2rd ed. - 1990
5. 2 vols.
6. $165
7. periodic supp.
8. no supp. yet
9. 90-84192/23230387/KFF144.A65K44

1. **FLORIDA CIVIL DISCOVERY MANUAL**
2. Butterworth Staff
3. Butterworth-Fla.
4. 1979
5. 1 vol.
6. $80
7. periodic supp.
8. 1989 - $71; 1990 - $57
9. 79-115981/5708778/KFF537.M37

1. **FLORIDA CIVIL PROCEDURE**
2. Hapner, Elizabeth
3. Butterworth-Fla.
4. 1990
5. 3 vols.
6. $120
7. periodic supp.
8. no supp. yet
9. 91-171231/24321189/KFF530.H36

1. **FLORIDA CIVIL TRIAL PRACTICE**
2. -
3. Florida Bar
4. 4th ed. - 1990
5. 1 vol.
6. $70

7. periodic supp.
8. no supp. yet
9. 90-86240/24066024/KFF538.F56

1. **FLORIDA COMMERCIAL LANDLORD-TENANT LAW**
2. Glover, Nicholas C.
3. Butterworth-Fla.
4. 1985
5. 1 vol.
6. $80
7. periodic supp.
8. 1989 - $75; 1990 - $79.75
9. 12498110/KFF117.3.A6G58

1. **FLORIDA CONDOMINIUM LAW AND PRACTICE**
2. -
3. Florida Bar
4. rev. ed. - 1987
5. 1 vol.
6. $80
7. as needed
8. 1990 - $30
9. 82-71807/8774521/KFF114.C655

1. **FLORIDA CONDOMINIUM LAW MANUAL**
2. MacGregor, Douglas S.
3. Butterworth-Fla.
4. 1980
5. 3 vols.
6. $195
7. periodic supp.
8. 1989 - $109.50; 1990 - $136.50
9. 82-234737//r89/9441714/KFF114.C6F54

1. **FLORIDA CONSTRUCTION LAW & PRACTICE**
2. -
3. Florida Bar
4. 2nd ed. - 1991
5. 1 vol.
6. $70
7. periodic supp.
8. no supp. yet
9. 91-70278/24073528/KFF155.8.B8C66

1. **FLORIDA CONSUMER LAW MANUAL**
2. Tennyson, Rod
3. Butterworth-Fla.
4. 1977
5. 3 vols.
6. $240
7. periodic supp.
8. 1989 - $124.50; 1990 - $109.95
9. 79-118388/5751360/KFF230.T46

1. **FLORIDA CORPORATE PRACTICE**
2. -
3. Florida Bar
4. 2nd ed. - 1990
5. 1 vol.
6. $80
7. supp. as needed
8. no supp. yet
9. 90-81378/KFF213.F55

1. **FLORIDA CORPORATIONS**
2. Ross, Howard P.
3. Lawyers Coop.
4. 1980
5. 2 vols.
6. $210 incl. 6 mos. supp.
7. annual supp.
8. 1989 - $64.50; 1990 - $74.50
9. 79-91141

1. **FLORIDA CORPORATIONS – LAWS AND PRACTICE**
2. Hoffman, Larry J., et al.
3. Bender
4. 1985
5. 4 vols.
6. $375 incl. 3 mos. supp.
7. periodic supp.
8. 1989 - $166; 1990 - $212
9. 85-71573/12819130/KFF213.F56

1. **FLORIDA CORPORATIONS MANUAL**
2. Gordon, Michael W.
3. Butterworth-Fla.
4. 1975
5. 5 vols.
6. $320
7. bimonthly supp.
8. 1989 - $237.25; 1990 - $246
9. 79-117607/5616158/KFF213.G67

1. **FLORIDA CREDITORS' RIGHTS MANUAL**
2. Rakusin, Stephen B.
3. Butterworth-Fla.
4. 1975
5. 5 vols.
6. $320
7. bimonthly supp.
8. 1989 - $168.75; 1990 - $189
9. 79-113577/5312372/KFF220.R34

1. **FLORIDA CRIMINAL DEFENSE TRIAL MANUAL**
2. Davidson, Lloyd
3. Butterworth-Fla.
4. 1972
5. 5 vols.
6. $320
7. periodic supp.
8. 1989 - $204.75; 1990 - $227.85
9. 75-307247/1324847/KFF575.B37

1. **FLORIDA CRIMINAL DISCOVERY AND PRE-TRIAL MOTIONS MANUAL**
2. Yetter, John F.
3. Butterworth-Fla.
4. 1979
5. 1 vol.
6. $80
7. quarterly supp.
8. 1989 - $78.50; 1990 - $96.50
9. 82-237314/5525945/KFF537.Y47

1. **FLORIDA CRIMINAL PROCEDURE SERVICE**
2. Yetter, John
3. Butterworth-Fla.
4. 1980
5. 1 vol.
6. $80
7. annual supp.
8. 1989 - $36.75; 1991 - $35.80
9. 83-126813/6508317/KFF575.A4

1. **FLORIDA CRIMINAL RULES AND PRACTICE**
2. -
3. Florida Bar
4. 3rd ed. - 1990
5. 1 vol.
6. $75
7. annual supp.
8. no supp. yet
9. 90-82228/23892917/KFF575.A33

1. **FLORIDA CRIMINAL SENTENCING LAW**
2. Davidson, Lloyd T.
3. Butterworth-Fla.
4. 1984
5. 2 vols.
6. $160
7. periodic supp.
8. 1989 - $118; 1990 - $158.80
9. 10984190/KFF583.2.A6D38

1. **FLORIDA DISSOLUTION OF MARRIAGE**
2. -
3. Florida Bar
4. 3rd ed. - 1990
5. 1 vol.
6. $90
7. supp. as needed
8. no supp. yet
9. 90-80636/21902535/KFF100.F62

1. **FLORIDA ENVIRONMENTAL AND LAND USE LAW**
2. -
3. Florida Bar
4. 1986-1987
5. 2 vols.
6. $150
7. periodic supp.
8. 1989 - $25; 1991 - $75
9. 85-81351/13783278/KFF354.F55

1. **FLORIDA ESTATES PRACTICE GUIDE**
2. Thomas, Thomas A.
3. Bender
4. 1964
5. 4 vols.
6. $410 incl. 3 mos. supp.
7. annual supp.
8. 1989 - $244; 1990 - $297.50
9. 65-616/1251999

1. **FLORIDA EVIDENCE MANUAL**
2. Hughes, Kenneth B.
3. Butterworth-Fla.
4. 1975
5. 4 vols.
6. $280
7. periodic supp.
8. 1989 - $203.75; 1990 - $199.25
9. 80-100568/6329400/KFF540.H83

1. **FLORIDA FAMILY LAW**
2. Abrams, Brenda
3. Bender
4. 1986
5. 6 vols.
6. $500 incl. 3 mos. supp.
7. periodic supp. & monthly newsletter
8. 1989 - $165; 1990 - $219.50
9. 86-71657/14708349/KFF94.A6F2

1. **FLORIDA FAMILY LAW PRACTICE**
2. Schackow, Gerald
3. Butterworth-Fla.
4. 1976
5. 4 vols.

6. $280
7. periodic supp.
8. 1989 - $203.50; 1990 - $218.75
9. 80-108735/6357889/KFF94.S3

1. **FLORIDA FORMS OF JURY INSTRUCTIONS**
2. Various Contributing Authors
3. Bender
4. 1989
5. 4 vols.
6. $400 incl. 3 mos. supp.
7. annual supp.
8. 1990 - $87.50
9. 89-62650/20771483/KFF542.6.A65F58

1. **FLORIDA JUVENILE LAW AND PRACTICE**
2. -
3. Florida Bar
4. 2nd ed. - 1988
5. 1 vol.
6. $60
7. as needed
8. 1989 - $20
9. 87-83666/18307169/KFF596.F57

1. **FLORIDA JUVENILE PROCEDURE**
2. Hapner, Elizabeth
3. Butterworth-Fla.
4. 1985
5. 1 vol.
6. $80
7. periodic supp.
8. 1989 - $64.50; 1990 - $72.50
9. 12934988/KFF595.H36

1. **FLORIDA KEYSTONE, LAWYER'S DESK LIBRARY OF PRACTICE**
2. -
3. Bisel
4. 1990
5. 3 vols.
6. $237.50 incl. 3 mos. supp.
7. annual supp.
8. 1991 - price NA

1. **FLORIDA LAND USE RESTRICTIONS**
2. Juergensmeyer, Julian & James Wadley
3. Butterworth-Fla.
4. 1982
5. 3 vols.
6. $240
7. periodic supp.
8. 1989 - $72.50; 1990 - $101.25
9. 82-235048/9350057/KFF458.J828

1. **FLORIDA LAW OF SECURED TRANSACTIONS IN PERSONAL PROPERTY**
2. Williams, Winton E.
3. Butterworth-Fla.
4. 1979
5. 3 vols.
6. $240
7. annual supp.
8. 1989 - $16; 1990 - $43
9. 82-235077/6372290/KFF175.W55

1. **FLORIDA LAWYER'S GUIDE**
2. Namack, Wm. H. III & W. McKinley Smiley, Jr.
3. Lawyers Coop.
4. 1984
5. 2 vols.
6. $180 incl. 6 mos. supp.
7. annual supp.
8. 1989 - $87.50; 1990 - $90
9. 83-25192/10207858/KFF80.N35

1. **FLORIDA LEGAL FILING DIRECTORY**
2. Hill, Kathleen J.
3. Shepard's
4. 1988
5. 1 vol.
6. $55
7. annual supp.
8. 1989 - $32; 1991 - $36
9. 88-27280/18817312/KFF77.H56

1. **FLORIDA LEGAL RESEARCH AND SOURCEBOOK**
2. Martin, Nikki L.
3. Butterworth-Fla.
4. 1989
5. 1 vol.
6. $50
7. annual supp.
8. no supp. yet
9. 90-164579/21907658/KFF75.M37

1. **FLORIDA LEGAL SECRETARY**
2. Hill, Kathleen J.
3. James
4. 2nd ed. - 1987
5. 2 vol.
6. $89.95 incl. 3 mos. supp.
7. periodic supp.
8. 1990 - $42.90
9. 15814771/KFF77.H55

1. **FLORIDA MECHANICS' LIEN MANUAL**
2. Rakusin, Stephen B.
3. Butterworth-Fla.
4. 1974
5. 4 vols.
6. $320
7. periodic supp.
8. 1989 - $206.25; 1990 - $208
9. 79-109737/5173061/KFF155.5.R34

1. **FLORIDA MOTOR VEHICLE LIABILITY LAW**
2. MacConnell, Marcia
3. Butterworth-Fla.
4. 1981
5. 4 vols.
6. $280
7. periodic supp.
8. 1989 - $149.25; 1990 - $189.90
9. 82-240257/9622112/KFF196.3.A8A93

1. **FLORIDA NEGLIGENCE LAW MANUAL**
2. MacConnell, Marcia
3. Butterworth-Fla.
4. 1986
5. 2 vols.
6. $160
7. periodic supp.
8. 1989 - $151.50; 1990 - $159.80
9. 13264251/KFF196.M29

1. **FLORIDA PARALEGAL SERIES: WILLS, TRUSTS, ESTATES**
2. Butterworth's Staff
3. Butterworth-Fla.
4. 1982
5. 1 vol.
6. $60
7. annual supp.
8. 1989 - $54; 1990 - $29
9. 82-236499/9255575/KFF144.C37

1. **FLORIDA PRACTICE GUIDE: PERSONAL INJURY**
2. Rinaman, James C. et al.
3. Lawyers Coop.
4. 1988
5. 2 vols.
6. $180 incl. 6 mos. supp.
7. annual supp.
8. 1990 - $65; 1991 - $71
9. 88-37616/18778689/KFF539.P4H53

1. **FLORIDA PREMISES LIABILITY**
2. MacGregor, Douglas
3. Butterworth-Fla.
4. 1991
5. 1 vol.
6. $80
7. periodic supp.
8. no supp. yet
9. 23237379/KFF196.3.L3M28

1. **FLORIDA PRETRIAL PRACTICE IN CRIMINAL CASES**
2. -
3. Florida Bar
4. 1986
5. 1 vol.
6. $55
7. periodic supp.
8. 1989 - $15
9. 86-83194/15694603

1. **FLORIDA PROBATE CODE MANUAL**
2. Smith, David T.
3. Butterworth-Fla.
4. 1975
5. 4 vols.
6. $280
7. periodic supp.
8. 1989 - $150.25; 1990 - $97.75
9. 79-113130/755288995/KFF144.S55

1. **FLORIDA PROCEEDINGS AFTER DISSOLUTION OF MARRIAGE**
2. -
3. Florida Bar
4. 1983
5. 1 vol.
6. $45
7. periodic supp.
8. 1988 - $20
9. 83-80870/9648976/KFF100.F63

1. **FLORIDA PUBLIC EMPLOYEE REPORTER**
2. -
3. LRP
4. 1975
5. 1 vol.
6. $595/yr. (back vols. avail.)
7. semimonthly supp.
9. 11131329/KFF332.8.P8A5

1. **FLORIDA REAL ESTATE**
2. Alpert, Jonathan L.
3. Lawyers Coop.
4. 1982
5. 1 vol.

6. $115 incl. 6 mos. supp.
7. annual supp.
8. 1989 - $66; 1990 - $71.50
9. 81-85397/8929136/KFF112.A95

1. **FLORIDA REAL ESTATE CLOSINGS**
2. Rich, Neysa
3. Butterworth-Fla.
4. 1990
5. 1 vol.
6. $50
7. periodic supp.
8. no supp. yet
9. 91-122101/22196523/KFF127.R52

1. **FLORIDA REAL ESTATE CONTRACTS**
2. Holcomb, Charles
3. Butterworth-Fla.
4. 1987
5. 1 vol.
6. $80
7. periodic supp.
8. 1989 - $18.50; 1990 - $87.30
9. 16844238/KFF126.A6H6

1. **FLORIDA REAL ESTATE TRANSACTIONS**
2. Boyer, Ralph E.
3. Bender
4. 1959
5. 4 vols.
6. $475 incl. 3 mos. supp.
7. annual supp.
8. 1989 - $381; 1990 - $436
9. 59-2476/1731075/KFF126.B69

1. **FLORIDA REAL ESTATE TRANSACTIONS**
2. Gibson, Paul C.
3. Butterworth-Fla.
4. 1982
5. 3 vols.
6. $195
7. periodic supp.
8. 1989 - $99.75; 1990 - $129.80
9. 82-240219/8251067/KFF126.G5

1. **FLORIDA RESIDENTIAL LANDLORD TENANT LAW MANUAL**
2. Hauser, James C.
3. Butterworth-Fla.
4. 1983
5. 3 vols.
6. $180
7. periodic supp.
8. 1989 - $119.75; 1990 - $135
9. 84-163252/11186325/KFF117.H38

1. **FLORIDA RULES OF COURT SERVICE**
2. Butterworth's Staff
3. Butterworth-Fla.
4. 1972
5. 2 vols.
6. $120
7. periodic supp.
8. 1989 - $94.25; 1990 - $99.75
9. 15239891/KFF529.A2a

1. **FLORIDA RULES OF CRIMINAL EVIDENCE**
2. Ackerman, John
3. Francis Marion
4. 1990
5. 1 vol.
6. $65 incl. 1 supp.
7. semiannual supp.
8. 1990 - $45; 1991 - $45

1. **FLORIDA SECURITIES LAW**
2. Palmer, Bobby G., Jr.
3. Butterworth-Fla.
4. 1989
5. 1 vol.
6. $80
7. annual supp.
8. no supp. yet
9. 90-181210/22239939/KFF214.A1P35

1. **FLORIDA SMALL BUSINESS PRACTICE**
2. -
3. Florida Bar
4. 2nd ed. - 1991
5. 1 vol.
6. $75
7. supp. as needed
8. no supp. yet
9. 91-70173/23825398/KFF234.F58

1. **FLORIDA STANDARD JURY INSTRUCTIONS IN CIVIL CASES**
2. -
3. Florida Bar
4. 1967
5. 1 vol.
6. $50
7. as needed
8. 1988 - $15; 1989 - $10
9. 67-24732/1974912/KFF542.A65F55

1. **FLORIDA STANDARD JURY INSTRUCTIONS IN CRIMINAL CASES**
2. Supreme Court's Committee

3. Florida Bar
4. 1981
5. 1 vol.
6. $40
7. periodic supp.
8. 1987 - $10; 1989 - $20
9. 81-67759/8431451/KFF583.A65F5

1. **FLORIDA STATE & LOCAL TAXATION**
2. Clark, Millard W., Jr.
3. Butterworth-Fla.
4. 1983
5. 2 vols.
6. $120
7. periodic supp.
8. 1989 - $29; 1990 - $89.95
9. 10089857/KFF470.C52

1. **FLORIDA SUMMARY CLAIMS HANDBOOK**
2. Coleman, Ted P.
3. Butterworth-Fla.
4. 1978
5. 2 vols.
6. $160
7. periodic supp.
8. 1989 - $108.75; 1990 - $99.85
9. 75-330978/1975484/KFF530.C6

1. **FLORIDA TAX SERVICE - 2nd ed.**
2. Hudson, David M.
3. Bender
4. 1985
5. 4 vols.
6. $370/1 yr. service; $680 for 2 yrs.
7. annual supp.
8. renewal - $310
9. 84-72809/11737321/KFF470.F56

1. **FLORIDA TAXATION**
2. Holland & Knight
3. Shepard's
4. 1991
5. 1 vol.
6. $125
7. annual supp.
8. no supp. yet

1. **FLORIDA TORTS**
2. Bender Editorial Staff
3. Bender
4. 1988
5. 5 vols.
6. $550 incl. 3 mos. supp.
7. annual supp.
8. 1989 - $130; 1990 - $157.50
9. 88-71562/18953586/KFF195.F48

1. **FLORIDA TRAFFIC AND D.U.I. PRACTICE MANUAL**
2. MacConnell, Marcia
3. Butterworth-Fla.
4. 1980
5. 2 vols.
6. $160
7. periodic supp.
8. 1989 - $174.50; 1990 - $159
9. 82-237937/9731857/KFF297.8.S38

1. **FLORIDA TRIAL EVIDENCE**
2. Dekle, Hal and Don Beverly
3. Wiley Law
4. 1988
5. 1 vol.
6. $95
7. annual supp.
8. 1990 - $35; 1991 - $40
9. 87-403955/16718621/KFF540.D45

1. **FLORIDA TRIAL GUIDE**
2. -
3. Bender
4. 1990
5. 5 vols.
6. $420
7. periodic supp.
8. no supp. yet

1. **FLORIDA WILL AND TRUST DRAFTING**
2. McCaughan, Russell
3. Florida Bar
4. 1977
5. 1 vol.
6. $55
7. as needed
8. no supp. yet
9. 77-71508/3340977

1. **FLORIDA WORKERS' COMPENSATION MANUAL**
2. Butterworth's Staff
3. Butterworth-Fla.
4. 1979
5. 2 vols.
6. $160
7. periodic supp.
8. 1989 - $92.25; 1990 - $129.30
9. 5356643/KFF342.S54

1. **FLORIDA ZONING LAW MANUAL**
2. Davidson, Lloyd & M. MacConnell
3. Butterworth-Fla.
4. 1980
5. 3 vols.
6. $240
7. periodic supp.
8. 1989 - $128; 1990 - $107
9. 6153823/KFF458.D3

1. **FOLK ON THE DELAWARE GENERAL CORPORATION LAW: A COMMENTARY AND ANALYSIS, 2nd ed.**
2. Folk, Ernest L. III, et al.
3. Little, Brown
4. 1988
5. 3 vols.
6. $195
7. semiannual supp.
8. 1989 - $40; 1990 - $65
9. 87-80499/17346831/KFD213.F59

1. **FOOD AND DRUG ADMINISTRATION REGULATORY MANUAL**
2. O'Reilly, James T.
3. Shepard's
4. 1979
5. 2 vols.
6. $180
7. annual supp.
8. 1989 - $60; 1990 - $65
9. 79-21246/5410778/KF3871.O7

1. **FOOD DRUG COSMETIC LAW REPORTS**
2. -
3. CCH
4. 1938
5. 6 vols.
6. $1780/yr.; $1620/yr. for 2 yrs.
7. weekly supp.
9. 38-39329

1. **FOOTING THE BILL: THE PRICE OF LAND USE REGULATION**
2. -
3. Wash. Bar
4. 1988
5. 1 vol.
6. $35
7. no supp. planned

1. **FORECLOSING SECURITY INTERESTS**
2. Watkinson, John C. ed.
3. Oregon Bar
4. 1971
5. 1 vol.
6. $112.50
7. periodic supp.
8. 1988 - $35; to be supp. in 1992
9. 84-61832/11457797/KFO2575.F67

1. **FORECLOSURE LAW MANUAL**
2. -
3. State Bar of Calif.
4. 1984, rev. - 1985 & 1989
5. 1 vol.
6. $75
7. no supp. planned

1. **FORECLOSURES IN MINNESOTA**
2. -
3. Minn. CLE
4. 1991
5. 1 vol.
6. $60
7. no supp. planned

1. **FOREIGN CORRUPT PRACTICES ACT REPORTER**
2. Hancock, W.A.
3. Bus. Laws
4. 1979
5. 2 vols.
6. $145/yr.
7. quarterly supp.
8. renewal - $145/yr.
9. 5212470

1. **FOREIGN LAW: CURRENT SOURCES OF CODES AND BASIC LEGISLATION IN JURISDICTIONS OF THE WORLD (vol. I: The Western Hemisphere; vol. II: Western & Eastern Europe; vol. III: Africa, Asia, Australia)**
2. Reynolds, Thomas H. & Arturo A. Flores
3. Rothman
4. vol. I - 1989; vol. II - 1991; vol. III - 1992
5. 3 vols.
6. set - $450; per vol. - $175. Set price includes 1990 and 1991 supp. to vol. I and 1991 supp. to vol. II.
7. annual supp.
8. est. $150/yr.
9. 89-10223/19814621/K38.R49

1. **FOREIGN STATE IMMUNITY IN COMMERCIAL TRANSACTIONS**
2. Gordon, Michael Wallace
3. Butterworth-NH
4. 1991

5. 1 vol.
6. $100
7. periodic supp.
8. no supp. yet
9. 90-47938/22422157/JX4173.G59

1. **FOREIGN TAX AND TRADE BRIEFS**
2. Diamond, Walter H.
3. Bender
4. 1951
5. 2 vols.
6. $300/yr.
7. monthly supp. & monthly newsletter
8. renewal - $248/yr.
9. 51-8230/4810391

1. **FOREIGN TRADE AND INVESTMENT**
2. Clasen, Thomas F.
3. Butterworth-NH
4. 1991
5. 1 vol.
6. $95
7. periodic supp.
8. no supp. yet

1. **FORENSIC SCIENCE**
2. Wecht, Cyril H., ed.
3. Bender
4. 1981
5. 3 vols.
6. $315
7. periodic supp.
8. 1989 - $170; 1990 - $252.50
9. 81-69427/8588698/KF8961.F67

1. **FORGOING LIFE SUPPORT: LIVING WILLS AND HEALTH CARE POWERS OF ATTORNEY**
2. -
3. Maine Bar
4. 1991
5. 1 vol.
6. $25
7. no supp. planned
9. 24311307/KF3827.E87M32

1. **FORM DRAFTING CHECKLISTS - AM JUR PRACTICE GUIDE**
2. -
3. Lawyers Coop.
4. 1991
5. 2 vols.
6. $180
7. periodic supp.
8. no supp. yet

1. **FORMS AND AGREEMENTS FOR ARCHITECTS, ENGINEERS AND CONTRACTORS**
2. Dib, Albert
3. Clark Boardman Callaghan
4. 1976
5. 4 vols.
6. $420 incl. 3 mos. supp.
7. biannual supp.
8. 1989 - $252; 1991 - $294
9. 75-37971/1859911/KF902.D5

1. **FORMS AND AGREEMENTS ON INTELLECTUAL PROPERTY AND INTERNATIONAL LICENSING**
2. Melville, L.W.
3. Clark Boardman Callaghan
4. 3rd ed. - 1979
5. 3 vols.
6. $345 incl. 3 mos. supp.
7. annual supp.
8. 1989 - $134.50; 1991 - $174.50
9. 78-17576/3966109/KD1269.M45

1. **FORMS AND PROCEDURES UNDER THE UNIFORM COMMERCIAL CODE (Bender's Uniform Commercial Code service vols. 5, 5A, 5B, 5C, 5D)**
2. Hart, Frederick M. & William F. Willier
3. Bender
4. 1963
5. 5 vols.
6. $590 incl. 3 mos. supp.
7. semiannual supp.
8. 1989 - $416; 1990 - $495
9. 63-24584/5032390

1. **FORMS FOR HANDLING CONDOMINUM AND COOPERATIVE CONVERSIONS**
2. Lambert, Benjamin D. Jr. & William Goldberg
3. New Jersey ICLE
4. 1988
5. 1 vol.
6. $75
7. no supp. planned
9. 18673949/KFN1914.C6L45

1. **FORMS FOR NEW JERSEY DIVORCE PRACTICE**
2. Snyder, Edward S. & L.M. Hymerling
3. New Jersey ICLE
4. 3rd ed. - 1988
5. 1 vol.

6. $75
7. no supp. planned
9. 18240213

1. **FORMS OF BUSINESS AGREEMENTS, VOLS. 1 & 2**
2. -
3. WG&L
4. 1955
5. 2 vols.
6. $425/yr.
7. quarterly supp.

1. **FORMS OF BUSINESS AGREEMENTS, VOL. 3 (Commercial Transactions)**
2. -
3. WG&L
4. 1975
5. 1 vol.
6. $296/yr.
7. quarterly supp. & monthly "Ideas" newsletter

1. **FOUR COUNTY DOMESTIC PRACTICE**
2. -
3. Penn. Bar
4. 1990
5. 1 vol.
6. $50
7. no supp. planned

1. **THE 401(K) HANDBOOK**
2. Ortman, John, ed.
3. Thompson
4. 1991
5. 1 vol.
6. $295/yr.
7. monthly supp.

1. **FRANCHISE & DISTRIBUTION LAW & PRACTICE**
2. Garner, W. Michael
3. Clark Boardman Callaghan
4. 1990
5. 3 vols.
6. $345 incl. 6 mos. supp.
7. annual supp.
8. no supp. yet
9. 90-1421/21077578/KF2023.G37

1. **FRANCHISES**
2. -
3. MICPEL
4. 1990
5. 1 vol.
6. $42
7. no supp. yet

1. **FRANCHISING (Business Organizations vols. 15, 15A, 15B & 15C)**
2. Glickman, Gladys
3. Bender
4. 1969
5. 4 vols.
6. $500 incl. 3 mos. supp.
7. biannual supp.
8. 1989 - $402; 1990 - $473.50
9. 76-10835/69676/KF2023.A6G5

1. **FRANCHISING: REALITIES AND REMEDIES**
2. Brown, Harold
3. Law Journal
4. 1981
5. 1 vol.
6. $90
7. periodic supp.
8. 1989 - $83; 1990 - $84
9. 81-11774/8177766/KF2023.B7

1. **FRANCHISING: REALITIES AND REMEDIES FORMS VOLUME**
2. Brown, Harold
3. Law Journal
4. 1988
5. 1 vol.
6. $80
7. periodic supp.
8. 1989 - $35
9. 88-9117/17775997/KF2023.B7

1. **FRANCHISING AND LICENSING OF PUBLIC SERVICES IN FLORIDA**
2. Little, Joseph W., et al.
3. Butterworth-Fla.
4. 1985
5. 1 vol.
6. $80
7. periodic supp.
8. no supp. yet
9. 12413848/KFF285.L58

1. **FRAUD – CIVIL FRAUD & WHITE COLLAR CRIME**
2. -
3. MILE
4. 1989
5. 1 vol.
6. $58
7. no supp. planned.

1. **FRAUD, WINDOW DRESSING, AND NEGLIGENCE IN FINANCIAL STATEMENTS**
2. Kellogg, Irving & Loren B.
3. Shepard's
4. 1991
5. 2 vols.
6. $165
7. annual supp.
8. no supp. yet
9. 91-15972/23731479/HF5681.B2K37

1. **FRAUDULENT CONVEYANCES**
2. -
3. Indiana CLE
4. 1991
5. 1 vol.
6. $45
7. no supp. planned

1. **FREE TRADE AGREEMENT ANNOTATED**
2. Bernier, Ivan & Benoit LaPointe
3. Blais
4. 1990
5. 1 vol.
6. $165
7. periodic supp.
8. no supp. yet

1. **FREE TRADE LAW REPORTS**
2. -
3. CCH
4. 1989
5. 1 vol. (with monthly newsletter)
6. $265/yr.; $240/yr. for 2 yrs.
7. monthly supp.
9. 20567577

1. **FRIEDMAN, OHIO SECURITIES LAW AND PRACTICE**
2. Friedman, Howard
3. Banks
4. 1987
5. 1 vol.
6. $200 incl. 9 mos. supp.
7. annual supp.
8. 1991 - $71
9. 16663164/KFO179.A6F7

1. **FRINGE BENEFITS TAX GUIDE**
2. -
3. CCH
4. 1985
5. 1 vol.
6. $340/yr.; $310/yr. for 2 yrs.
7. monthly supp.
9. 85-202107/12806056/KF6410.A6C38

1. **FTC FRANCHISING RULE: THE IFA COMPLIANCE KIT**
2. Caffey, Andrew A. Jeffrey E. Kolton
3. IFA
4. 1990
5. 1 vol.
6. $225-nonmembers; $175-members
7. no supp. planned
9. 6130915/KF2023.A6Z84

1. **FUNDAMENTALS OF ESTATE PLANNING**
2. -
3. MICPEL
4. 1990
5. 1 vol.
6. $50
7. no supp. yet

1. **FUNDAMENTALS OF ESTATE PLANNING PRACTICE**
2. -
3. Minn. CLE
4. 1990
5. 1 vol.
6. $50
7. no supp. planned

1. **FUNDAMENTALS OF FAMILY LAW**
2. -
3. MICPEL
4. 1990
5. 1 vol.
6. $185 (incl. tapes)
7. no supp. yet
9. 22104961/KFM1294.F86

1. **FUNDAMENTALS OF FEDERAL CRIMINAL PRACTICE & FEDERAL SENTENCING GUIDELINES**
2. -
3. Conn. Bar
4. 1991
5. 1 vol.
6. $95
7. no supp. planned

1. **FUNDAMENTALS OF HEALTH CARE LAW**
2. -
3. Indiana CLE
4. 1991

5. 1 vol.
6. $50
7. no supp. planned
9. 23361628/KFI3360.A75F85

1. **FUNDAMENTALS OF ORGANIZING MINNESOTA CORPORATIONS**
2. -
3. Minn. CLE
4. 1990
5. 1 vol.
6. $45
7. no supp. planned

1. **FUNDAMENTALS OF PROBATE ADMINISTRATION**
2. -
3. NH Bar
4. 1990
5. 1 vol.
6. $35
7. no supp. planned
9. 11086912

1. **FUNDAMENTALS OF PROBATE PRACTICE**
2. -
3. Minn. CLE
4. 1990
5. 1 vol.
6. $50
7. no supp. planned

1. **FUNDAMENTALS OF QUALIFIED PENSION AND PROFIT SHARING PLANS OUTLINE**
2. Moore, Bruce
3. PPD
4. 1991
5. 1 vol.
6. $100
7. annual editions

1. **FUNDAMENTALS OF REAL ESTATE TRANSACTIONS**
2. Miller, David P. & Robert S. Ball, eds.
3. Oregon Bar
4. 1991
5. 1 vol.
6. price NA
7. periodic supp.
8. no supp. yet
9. 91-52614

1. **FUNDING WASTEWATER TREATMENT FACILITIES: THE COMPLETE RESOURCE GUIDE TO THE NEW STATE REVOLVING FUND PROGRAM**
2. -
3. BNA
4. 1988
5. 2 vols.
6. $260
7. no supp. planned
9. 88-37692/18778770/HD4477.S73

1. **GAAP PRACTICE MANUAL**
2. Afterman, Allan B.
3. WG&L
4. 1985
5. 1 vol.
6. $198/yr.
7. quarterly supp.
8. renewal - $198/yr.
9. 84-62873/12146417/HF5616.U5A4

1. **GAS TRANSPORTATION MARKETING SERVICE**
2. Krehbiel, Greg
3. Thompson
4. 1989
5. 2 vols.
6. $556
7. monthly supp.
8. renewal - $523/yr.
9. 88-193346/16126165/HE199.5.G3G37

1. **GENERAL INDUSTRY STANDARDS AND INTERPRETATIONS**
2. U.S. Dept. of Labor, Occupational Safety & Health Admin.
3. order from USGPO - stock #929-005-00000-7
4. 1989
5. 1 vol.
6. $98/yr.
7. periodic supp.
9. 7972713

1. **GENERIC DRUGS: A GUIDE TO FDA APPROVAL REQUIREMENTS**
2. Beers, Donald O.
3. Prentice Hall Law & Business
4. 1988
5. 1 vol.
6. $85 incl. 4 mos. supp.
7. periodic supp.
8. 1989 - $75
9. 89-25523/20562387/KF3894.G45B44

1. **GEORGIA ARREST SEARCH AND SEIZURE**
2. Davidson, Lloyd T.
3. Butterworth-Fla.
4. 1987
5. 1 vol.
6. $80
7. annual supp.
8. no supp. yet
9. 16825138/KFG576.5.A6D38

1. **GEORGIA ATTORNEY'S/SECRETARY'S HANDBOOK**
2. -
3. Mariposa
4. 1990
5. 1 vol.
6. $55
7. annual supp.
8. 1990 - $51; 1991 - $46
9. 19796243/KFG77.W34

1. **GEORGIA CIVIL PROCEDURE FORMS – PRACTICE**
2. Jenkins, A. Felton, Jr. & Ralph A. Pitts
3. Aspen
4. 1988
5. 2 vols.
6. $229 incl. 3 mos. supp.
7. annual supp.
8. $70-$95/supp.
9. 87-35128/17296339/KFG530.A65J46

1. **GEORGIA COMMERCIAL FINANCING FORMS**
2. Shortridge, Wayne et al.
3. Aspen
4. 1991
5. 2 vols.
6. $239 incl. 3 mos. supp.
7. annual supp.
8. no supp. yet
9. 90-48048/22422417/KFG170.A65S48

1. **GEORGIA CONDOMINIUM LAW MANUAL**
2. MacGregor, Douglas
3. Butterworth-Fla.
4. 1985
5. 1 vol.
6. $80
7. annual supp.
8. 1989 - $19.50; 1990 - $27.50
9. 12379892/KFG114.C6M33

1. **GEORGIA CORPORATE FORMS-PRACTICE**
2. Speer, G. William, et al.
3. Aspen
4. 1988
5. 2 vols.
6. $250 incl. 3 mos. supp.
7. annual supp.
8. 1989 - $220
9. 87-30644/16900081/KFG213.A65S64

1. **GEORGIA CREDITORS' RIGHTS MANUAL**
2. James, Tricia L. Z.
3. Butterworth-Fla.
4. 1987
5. 3 vols.
6. $180
7. periodic supp.
8. 1989 - $37.75; 1990 - $27.50
9. 87-406154/15710759/KFG220.J36

1. **GEORGIA DIVORCE**
2. McGough, Barry B.
3. Lawyers Coop.
4. 1981
5. 1 vol.
6. $115 incl. 6 mos. supp.
7. annual supp.
8. 1990 - $69; 1991 - $55
9. 79-91143/8532415/KFG100.M37

1. **GEORGIA DOMESTIC RELATIONS FORMS - PRACTICE**
2. Bates, Edward E. Jr.
3. Aspen
4. 1988
5. 1 vol.
6. $159 incl. 3 mos. supp.
7. annual supp.
8. 1989 - $65
9. 88-6264/17648995/KFG94.A65B38

1. **GEORGIA ESTATE PLANNING, WILL DRAFTING AND ESTATE ADMINISTRATION FORMS–PRACTICE**
2. Levy, Bertram L., & Benjamin T. White
3. Aspen
4. 1987
5. 2 vols.
6. $239 incl. 3 mos. supp.
7. annual supp.
8. 1988 - $125; 1989 - $89
9. 87-19515/16648112/KFG140.A65LH8

1. **GEORGIA FAMILY LAW MANUAL**
2. Butler, Anita M.
3. Butterworth-Fla.
4. 1985
5. 2 vols.
6. $120
7. periodic supp.
8. 1989 - $18; 1990 - $26
9. 12596773/KFG94.B8

1. **GEORGIA LANDLORD-TENANT LAW**
2. MacGregor, Douglas S.
3. Butterworth-Fla.
4. 1987
5. 1 vol.
6. $80
7. annual supp.
8. 1988 - $14; 1990 - $49.50
9. 87-406156/15232757/KFG117.M33

1. **GEORGIA PROBATE MANUAL**
2. Hapner, Elizabeth
3. Butterworth-Fla.
4. 1985
5. 2 vols.
6. $120
7. periodic supp.
8. 1989 - $26; 1990 - $54.50
9. 13293017/KFG142.A6H3

1. **GEORGIA REAL ESTATE FORMS-PRACTICE**
2. Grove, Russell S., Jr. & Deborah E. Glass
3. Aspen
4. 1987
5. 2 vols.
6. $249 incl. 3 mos. supp.
7. annual supp.
8. $1988 - $86
9. 87-20004/16356718/KFG126.A65G76

1. **GEORGIA STATE RULES OF COURT**
2. Butterworth's Staff
3. Butterworth-Fla.
4. 1986
5. 1 vol.
6. $50
7. periodic supp.
8. 1989 - $26.50; 1990 - $17.50
9. 15233055/KFG529.A2

1. **GERMAIN'S TRANSNATIONAL LAW RESEARCH**
2. Germain, Claire M.
3. Transnational Juris Publications
4. 1991
5. 1 vol.
6. $125
7. periodic supp.
8. no supp. yet
9. 91-16405/23732020/K85.G47

1. **GETTING PAID: EFFECTIVELY USING STATUTORY LIEN AND BOND RIGHTS**
2. -
3. Wash. Bar
4. 1989
5. 1 vol.
6. $35
7. no supp. planned

1. **GIANNELLI, OHIO EVIDENCE MANUAL**
2. Giannelli, Paul C.
3. Banks
4. 1982
5. 1 vol.
6. $125 incl. 9 mos. supp.
7. annual supp.
8. 1990 - $45
9. 82-136787/8139148/KFO540.G52

1. **GIBBER ON ADMINISTERING ESTATES IN MARYLAND**
2. Gibber, Allan J.
3. MICPEL
4. 3rd ed. - 1991
5. 1 vol.
6. $94.50
7. periodic supp.
8. no supp. yet
9. KFM1390.Z9G5

1. **GILBERT CRIMINAL LAW AND PROCEDURE OF NEW YORK**
2. Zett, J. et al.
3. Bender
4. 1974
5. 1 vol.
6. $97.50 incl. 3 mos. supp.
7. annual supp.
8. 1989 - $92.50; 1990 - $97.50
9. 14631686/KFN6100.G372

1. **GILMORE ON MICHIGAN CIVIL PROCEDURE BEFORE TRIAL**
2. Curtis, Judith A. et al.
3. ICLE - Michigan

4. 3rd ed. - 1987
5. 2 vols.
6. $145
7. annual supp.
8. 1990 - $45; 1991 - $55
9. 87-80720/16512832/KFM4737.G54

1. **GITLIN ON DIVORCE: A GUIDE TO ILLINOIS MATRIMONIAL LAW**
2. Gitlin, H. Joseph
3. Butterworth-St. Paul
4. 1991
5. 2 vols.
6. $160
7. periodic supp.
8. no supp. yet
9. 90-24715/22811557/KFI1300.G57

1. **GLOBAL MARKETS**
2. -
3. MILE
4. 1991
5. 1 vol.
6. $79.50
7. no supp. planned

1. **GOING PRIVATE**
2. Borden, Arthur M.
3. Law Journal
4. 1982
5. 1 vol.
6. $90
7. periodic supp.
8. 1988 - $39; 1989 - $42
9. 82-74/8171158/KF1414.B67

1. **GOING PUBLIC AND THE PUBLIC CORPORATION (Securities Law Series vols. 1 & 1A)**
2. Bloomenthal, Harold S.
3. Clark Boardman Callaghan
4. 1986
5. 3 vols.
6. $325 incl. 3 mos. supp.
7. annual supp.
8. 1989 - $107; 1991 - $154.50
9. 86-11386/13793870/KF1439.B538

1. **GOING TO TRIAL**
2. -
3. Conn. Bar
4. 1990
5. 1 vol.
6. $63
7. no supp. planned

1. **GOING TO TRIAL - A STEP-BY STEP GUIDE TO TRIAL PRACTICE AND PROCEDURE**
2. General Practice Section
3. ABA
4. 1989
5. 1 vol.
6. $49.95
7. no supp. planned
9. 88-83250/19133366/KF8915.Z9G58

1. **GOLD MINE FINANCING**
2. -
3. Rocky Mt.
4. 1988
5. 1 vol.
6. $105
7. no supp. planned

1. **GOODS IN TRANSIT**
2. Sorkin, Saul
3. Bender
4. 1976
5. 3 vols.
6. $350 incl. 3 mos. supp.
7. annual supp.
8. 1989 - $253.50; 1990 - $295.50
9. 76-25719/2577491/KF1091.S6

1. **GORDON ON MARYLAND FORECLOSURES**
2. Gordon, Alexander, IV
3. MICPEL
4. 2nd ed. - 1985
5. 1 vol.
6. $90
7. supp. planned
8. 1989 - $25
9. 85-62511/13360543/KFM1330.5.F6G67

1. **GOTHERMAN & BABBIT, OHIO MUNICIPAL LAW**
2. Gotherman, John E. & Harold W. Babbit
3. Banks
4. 1975
5. 3 vols.
6. $260 incl. 9 mos. supp.
7. annual supp.
8. 1989 - $45
9. 75-326786/8667137/KFO431.A6C72

1. **GOVERNMENT CONTRACT ACCOUNTING 2ND ED.**
2. Bedingfield, James & Louis Rosen
3. Fed. Publ.

4. 1985
5. 1 vol.
6. $165
7. periodic supp.
8. no supp. yet
9. 84-81400/12442746/KF849.B44

1. **GOVERNMENT CONTRACT AND PROGRAM FRAUD**
2. -
3. MILE
4. 1991
5. 1 vol.
6. $68
7. no supp. yet

1. **GOVERNMENT CONTRACT BIDDING**
2. Schnitzer, Paul A.
3. Fed. Publ.
4. 3rd ed. - 1987
5. 1 vol.
6. $165
7. periodic supp.
8. no supp. yet
9. 86-81876/16929209

1. **GOVERNMENT CONTRACT DISPUTES, 2ND ED.**
2. Latham, Peter
3. Fed. Publ.
4. 1986
5. 1 vol.
6. $165
7. periodic supp.
8. no supp yet
9. 85-82038/14392299/KF848.L38

1. **GOVERNMENT CONTRACT GUIDEBOOK**
2. Arnavas, Donald F. & Wm. Ruberry
3. Fed. Publ.
4. 1986
5. 1 vol.
6. $165
7. periodic supp.
8. 1991 - $55
9. 85-82367/13340697/KF849.A87

1. **GOVERNMENT CONTRACTS: CYCLOPEDIC GUIDE TO LAW, ADMINISTRATION AND PROCEDURE**
2. McBride, John C. & Thomas J. Touhey
3. Bender
4. 1962
5. 16 vols.
6. $875
7. monthly supp.
8. renewal - $575/yr.
9. 63-24103/1598330/KF849.M25

1. **GOVERNMENT CONTRACTS REPORTS**
2. -
3. CCH
4. 1941
5. 10 vols.
6. $1615/yr.; $1470/yr. for 2 yrs.
7. weekly supp.
9. 58-9005/7925389/KF846.5.C63

1. **GOVERNMENT DISCRIMINATION**
2. Kushner, James A.
3. Clark Boardman Callaghan
4. 1988
5. 1 vol.
6. $110 incl. 3 mos. supp.
7. annual supp.
8. 1989 - $80; 1991 - $59.50
9. 87-34572/17300287/KF4764.K87

1. **GOVERNMENT EMPLOYEE RELATIONS REPORT**
2. Harris, Anthony A.
3. BNA
4. 1963
5. 2 vols.
6. $712/yr.
7. weekly supp. & reports
8. renewal - $676/yr.
9. 68-5192/1751355/HD8008.A1B8

1. **THE GOVERNMENT SECURITIES MANUAL**
2. -
3. PSA
4. 1990
5. 1 vol.
6. $225
7. supp. as needed
8. renewal fee
9. 23227028

1. **GOVERNMENTAL ACCOUNTING AND AUDITING DISCLOSURE MANUAL**
2. Afterman, Allan B. & Rowen H. Jones
3. WG&L
4. 1991
5. 1 vol.
6. $98

7. annual supp.
8. no supp. yet

1. **GOVERNMENTAL IMMUNITY IN MICHIGAN**
2. Baylor, Ronald E.
3. ICLE - Michigan
4. 1991
5. 1 vol.
6. $75
7. annual supp.
8. no supp. yet
9. 91-73441

1. **GOWER FEDERAL SERVICE - MINING**
2. -
3. Rocky Mt.
4. 1962
5. 4 vols.
6. $540 incl. 1 yr. supp.
7. periodic supp.
8. renewal - $315/yr.
9. 11122252/KF1815.M55

1. **GOWER FEDERAL SERVICE - MISCELLANEOUS LAND DECISIONS**
2. -
3. Rocky Mt.
4. 1970
5. 1 vol.
6. $165/yr.
7. periodic supp.
8. renewal - $165/yr.
9. 10693159

1. **GOWER FEDERAL SERVICE - OIL AND GAS**
2. -
3. Rocky Mt.
4. 1948
5. 3 vols.
6. $365 incl. 1 yr. supp.
7. periodic supp.
8. renewal - $215/yr.
9. 9289173/KF1865.A6R65

1. **GOWER FEDERAL SERVICE - OUTER CONTINENTAL SHELF LANDS**
2. -
3. Rocky Mt.
4. 1954
5. 3 vols.
6. $310 incl. 1 yr. supp.
7. periodic supp.
8. renewal - $150/yr.
9. 6747986/KF1856.A6G7

1. **GOWER FEDERAL SERVICE - ROYALTY VALUATION AND MANAGEMENT**
2. -
3. Rocky Mt.
4. 1988
5. 13 vols.
6. $1200 incl. 1 yr. supp.
7. periodic supp.
8. renewal - approx. $500/yr.
9. 18937933/KF1815.R7

1. **GRAND JURY LAW AND PRACTICE**
2. Beale, Sara Sun & William C. Bryson
3. Clark Boardman Callaghan
4. 1986
5. 2 vols.
6. $170 incl. 6 mos. supp.
7. annual supp.
8. 1989 - $40.50; 1990 - $45
9. 86-29164/13533042/KF9642.B43

1. **THE GREENBOOK-SELECTED COLORADO MATERIALS ON WILLS, ESTATES, TRUSTS AND TAXES**
2. Probate & Trust Section
3. CLE - Colorado
4. 1986
5. 1 vol.
6. $65
7. periodic supp.
8. 1989 - $25; 1990 - $25
9. 15243871/KF765.Z99C63

1. **GROUND LEASES AND LAND ACQUISITION CONTRACTS**
2. Halper, Emanuel B.
3. Law Journal
4. 1988
5. 1 vol.
6. $85
7. periodic supp.
8. no supp. yet
9. 88-39957/18625358/KF593.G7H25

1. **GROUND WATER CONTAMINATION**
2. -
3. Rocky Mt.
4. 1991
5. 1 vol.
6. $125
7. no supp. planned

1. **THE GUARDIAN AD ITEM HANDBOOK**
2. Alschuler, J.N. et al.
3. State Bar of Wisc.
4. 1988
5. 1 vol.
6. $80
7. periodic supp.
8. 1989 - $22; 1990 - $35
9. 17160000

1. **GUARDIANS & CONSERVATORS**
2. -
3. MILE
4. 1991
5. 1 vol.
6. $68
7. no supp. planned
9. 23938495/KFM5506.G827

1. **GUARDIANSHIP**
2. -
3. Ohio CLE
4. 1990
5. 1 vol.
6. $45
7. no supp. planned

1. **GUARDIANSHIP**
2. -
3. Indiana CLE
4. 1988
5. 1 vol.
6. $45
7. no supp. planned

1. **GUARDIANSHIP AND CONSERVATORSHIP IN MASSACHUSETTS**
2. Cross, John H. & Robert D. Fleischner
3. Butterworth-NH
4. 1991
5. 1 vol.
6. $85
7. periodic supp.
8. no supp. yet
9. 91-8491/23179908/KFM2506.C76

1. **GUARDIANSHIPS**
2. Strasser, William I., et al.
3. New Jersey ICLE
4. 1986
5. 1 vol.
6. $45
7. no supp. planned

1. **A GUIDE FOR WISCONSIN NONPROFIT ORGANIZATIONS**
2. -
3. State Bar of Wisc.
4. 1990
5. 1 vol.
6. $85
7. periodic supp.
8. no supp. yet
9. 21480369

1. **GUIDE TO ACQUISITIONS AND DIVESTITURES**
2. Hancock, W. A., ed.
3. Bus. Laws
4. 1990
5. 2 vols.
6. $195/yr.
7. annual supp.
8. $54/yr.

1. **GUIDE TO ASSIGNING AND LOANING BENEFIT PLAN MONEY**
2. Hamburger, Paul
3. Thompson
4. 1991
5. 1 vol.
6. $295/yr.
7. monthly supp.
9. 24520956/HD4928.N62G5

1. **GUIDE TO CAFETERIA PLAN DESIGN, ADMINISTRATION & COMMUNICATION**
2. Mayer Hoffman McCann
3. Corbel
4. 1987
5. 1 vol.
6. $495
7. supp. as needed

1. **GUIDE TO CALIFORNIA EVIDENCE**
2. Berger, Moise E.
3. Parker
4. 1988
5. 2 vols.
6. $135 incl. 3 mos. supp.
7. annual supp.
8. 1990 - $57.50; 1991 - $43.50
9. 83-81289/19506901/KFC1030.B47

1. **GUIDE TO COMMERCIAL LENDING LAW**
2. Gotcher, Pamela C.

3. Sheshunoff
4. 1989
5. 1 vol.
6. $245 incl. 1 yr. supp.
7. semiannual supp.
8. 1990 - $190; 1991 - $190
9. 90-229579/20938858/KF1035.G67

1. **GUIDE TO COMPUTER LAW**
2. -
3. CCH
4. 1989
5. 2 vols.
6. $320/yr.; $290/yr. for 2 yrs.
7. semimonthly supp.
9. 89-151962/19718877/KF390.5.C6G85

1. **GUIDE TO CONSUMER LENDING LAW**
2. Williams, Scott C.
3. Sheshunoff
4. 1991
5. 1 vol.
6. $245 incl. 1 yr. supp.
7. semiannual supp.
8. no supp. yet

1. **GUIDE TO CONTRACTING WITH THE RESOLUTION TRUST CORPORATION**
2. Fensterheim, G. David, ed.
3. Thompson
4. 1990
5. 2 vols.
6. $383/yr.
7. monthly supp.
9. 21941678/KF1004.F366

1. **GUIDE TO COUNTERTRADE**
2. Hancock, W.A.
3. Bus. Laws
4. 1986
5. 1 vol.
6. $90
7. supp. as needed
8. renewal - $35/yr.

1. **GUIDE TO EFFECTIVE BANKRUPTCY LITIGATION**
2. Pollard, David W. & Joseph J. Burton
3. Shepard's
4. 1988
5. 1 vol.
6. $95
7. annual supp.
8. 1990 - $24; 1991 - $30
9. 88-31538/18813906/KF1527.P65

1. **GUIDE TO EMPLOYMENT LAW AND REGULATION**
2. Tulac, Gary, ed.
3. WG&L
4. 1943
5. 4 vols.
6. $382/yr.
7. weekly supp.

1. **GUIDE TO ENVIRONMENTAL LIABILITY IN REAL ESTATE TRANSACTIONS**
2. Flynn, David
3. Thompson
4. 1991
5. 1 vol.
6. $475/yr.
7. monthly supp. & newsletter

1. **GUIDE TO EXPORT CONTROLS**
2. Ray, Philip L. & Eric L. Hirschhorn
3. Bus. Laws
4. 1986
5. 1 vol.
6. $85/yr.
7. annual supp.
8. renewal - $44/yr.
9. 13142075/KF1987.R38

1. **GUIDE TO FEDERAL FUNDING FOR ANTI-DRUG PROGRAMS**
2. -
3. GIS
4. 1991
5. 2 vols.
6. $192/yr.
7. quarterly supp. & weekly newsletter

1. **GUIDE TO FEDERAL FUNDING FOR EDUCATION**
2. Edwards, Charles E. ed.
3. EFRC
4. 1975
5. 1 vol.
6. $193/yr.
7. monthly supp.
8. annual editions
9. 81-643087/7238591/LB2805.F29

1. **GUIDE TO FEDERAL FUNDING FOR GOVERNMENTS AND NON-PROFITS**
2. -
3. GIS
4. 1991
5. 2 vols.

6. $193/yr.
7. monthly supp.

1. **GUIDE TO GOVERNMENT CONTRACTING**
2. -
3. CCH
4. 1991
5. 1 vol.
6. $325/yr.; $295/yr. for 2 yrs.
7. monthly supp.
9. 91-199364/24590713/KF846.5.G85

1. **GUIDE TO HOMEOWNERS' ASSOCIATIONS AND OTHER COMMON INTEREST REALTY ASSOCIATIONS**
2. Rutledge, Marilyn Z. & David A. Tolson
3. Practitioners Publishing
4. 1990
5. 2 vols.
6. $109
7. annual supp.
9. 23466992/HD7287.8.G85

1. **THE GUIDE TO IMMIGRATION COUNSELING: A STEP-BY-STEP LEGAL HANDBOOK**
2. Wernick, Allan
3. Center for Immig. Rights
4. 2nd ed. - 1987
5. 2 vols.
6. $55.50-indivs. & libraries; $40.50 - nonprofits
7. periodic supp.
8. 1987 - $25
9. 86-102414/13090305/KF4819.W47

1. **GUIDE TO INTERNATIONAL COMMERCE LAW**
2. Vishny, Paul H.
3. Shepard's
4. 1984
5. 2 vols.
6. $195
7. annual supp.
8. 1989 - $44; 1990 - $48
9. 81-18215/7923883/K1005.4.V57

1. **A GUIDE TO MICHIGAN TORT REFORM**
2. Mather, Lance R.
3. ICLE - Michigan
4. 1987
5. 1 vol.
6. $65
7. periodic supp.
8. 1988 - $35; 1989 - $35
9. 87-80339/15608992

1. **A GUIDE TO MUNICIPAL OFFICIAL STATEMENTS**
2. Daley, Joseph C., et al.
3. Prentice Hall Law & Business
4. 2nd ed. - 1990
5. 1 vol.
6. $95 incl. 4 mos. supp.
7. periodic supp.
8. no supp. yet
9. 80-12106/6087262/KF6775.D34

1. **GUIDE TO PENSION AND PROFIT SHARING PLANS: TAXATION, SELECTION AND DESIGN**
2. Dunkle, David S.
3. Shepard's
4. 1984
5. 1 vol.
6. $95
7. annual supp.
8. 1989 - $30; 1990 - $36
9. 84-22123/11207432/KF6449.D86

1. **GUIDE TO PRACTICAL APPLICATIONS OF THE UN CONVENTION ON CONTRACTS FOR THE INTERNATIONAL SALE OF GOODS**
2. Kritzer, Albert
3. Kluwer
4. 1990
5. 1 vol.
6. $111 incl. 3 mos. supp.
7. periodic supp.
9. 90-33767/21373251/K1030.4.K75

1. **GUIDE TO PURCHASE & SALES FORMS**
2. Hancock, W.A.
3. Bus. Laws
4. 1983
5. 1 vol.
6. $125 incl. 1 yr. supp.
7. annual supp.
8. renewal - $45/yr.

1. **GUIDE TO RECORDS RETENTION**
2. Hancock, W.A.
3. Bus. Laws
4. 1986
5. 2 vols.
6. $145

7. annual supp.
8. renewal - $60/yr.
9. 13495206/KF1357.5.G83

1. **A GUIDE TO REHABILITATION**
2. Deutsch, Paul and Horace W. Sawyer
3. Bender
4. 1985
5. 2 vols.
6. $150 incl. 3 mos. supp.
7. periodic supp.
8. 1989 - $55; 1990 - $68.50
9. 85-72019/12835052/HD7255.5.D37

1. **GUIDE TO STATE LEGISLATIVE AND ADMINISTRATIVE MATERIALS**
2. Fisher, Mary L.
3. Rothman
4. 4rd ed. - 1988
5. 1 vol.
6. $32.50
7. periodic supp.
8. 1985 - $27.50; 1988 - $30
9. 88-23892/KF1.G8

1. **A GUIDE TO TEXAS WORKERS' COMPENSATION REFORM**
2. Montford, John T. et al.
3. Butterworth-Texas
4. 1991
5. 2 vols.
6. $225
7. periodic supp.
8. no supp. yet.
9. 91-361/23143982/KFT1542.M66

1. **A GUIDE TO THE FEDERAL LAW OF BANKING AND INSURANCE**
2. Whiting, Richard M. & James E. Scott
3. Prentice Hall Law & Business
4. 1989
5. 1 vol.
6. $85 incl. 4 mos. supp.
7. periodic supp.
8. 1990 - $50; 1991 - $55
9. 89-8409/19628192/KF1167.S37

1. **GUIDE TO THE INTERNATIONAL SALES OF GOODS CONVENTION**
2. Hancock, W.A., ed.
3. Bus. Laws
4. 1986
5. 1 vol.
6. $90/yr.
7. supp. as needed
8. $39/yr.
9. 15149683/K1028.3198.G84

1. **GUIDE TO TOXIC TORTS**
2. Searcy, M.T.
3. Bender
4. 1987
5. 3 vols.
6. $340 incl. 3 mos. supp.
7. periodic supp.
8. 1989 - $79; 1990 - $141.50
9. 86-073147/15670211/KF1257.G83

1. **GUIDE TO UNCLAIMED PROPERTY AND ESCHEAT LAWS**
2. Andreoli, A.L., et al.
3. Commonwealth
4. 3rd ed. - 1989
5. 2 vols.
6. $349.50
7. periodic supp.
8. 1989 - $145
9. 82-71985/8624637/KF705.Z95A5

1. **GUIDE TO U.S. FOOD LABELING LAW**
2. Flynn, Mara
3. Thompson
4. 1991
5. 1 vol.
6. $485/yr.
7. monthly supp.
8. renewal - $485/yr.
9. 24443652/KF3875.A6H87

1. **GUIDEBOOK TO CHANCERY PRACTICE IN NEW JERSEY**
2. Dreier, Hon. Wm. A. & Jane Castner
3. New Jersey ICLE
4. 1984
5. 1 vol.
6. $55
7. periodic supp.
8. 1989 - $15
9. 11526000

1. **GUIDEBOOK TO SECURITY INTERESTS IN PERSONAL PROPERTY**
2. Reiley, Eldon H.
3. Clark Boardman Callaghan
4. 1986
5. 1 vol.
6. $105 incl. 3 mos. supp.
7. annual supp.
8. 1988 - $45; 1989 - $49.50
9. 85-16673/12286599/KF1050.Z95R43

1. **GUIDEBOOK TO THE FREEDOM OF INFORMATION AND PRIVACY ACTS**
2. Franklin, Justin D. and Robert F. Bouchard, eds.
3. Clark Boardman Callaghan
4. 1986
5. 1 vol.
6. $110 incl. 3 mos. supp.
7. annual supp.
8. 1989 - $89.50; 1990 - $114.50
9. 86-6161/13333482/KF5753.G85

1. **GUIDELINES FOR REVIEWING QUALIFICATIONS OF CANDIDATES FOR STATE JUDICIAL OFFICE**
2. Judicial Administrative Div.
3. ABA
4. 1984
5. 1 vol.
6. $2
7. no supp. planned
9. 85-143308/12666637/KF8785.Z9A48

1. **HANDBOOK FOR INTERNAL AUDITORS**
2. Perry, William E.
3. Bender
4. 1985
5. 2 vols.
6. $185 incl. 3 mos. supp.
7. periodic supp.
8. 1989 - $90; 1990 - $126.50
9. 85-70260/13063523/HF5668.25.P467

1. **HANDBOOK FOR LEGAL SECRETARIES IN VIRGINIA 2ND ED.**
2. Virginia Assn. of Legal Secretaries
3. Michie
4. 1980
5. 1 vol.
6. $50
7. periodic supp.
8. 1988 - $20
9. 67-36/2695272/KFV2477.V45

1. **HANDBOOK OF ANNOTATED FORMS FOR THE SURVEYING PRACTICE**
2. Robillard, Walter & Dr. Knud Hermansen
3. Wiley Law
4. 1989
5. 1 vol.
6. $65
7. annual supp.
8. no supp. yet

1. **HANDBOOK OF COLORADO FAMILY LAW**
2. Whicher, Susan W.
3. CLE - Colorado
4. 1982
5. 1 vol.
6. $105
7. periodic supp.
8. 1988 - $30; 1991 - $35
9. 9275634/KFC1894.W45

1. **HANDBOOK OF FORMS FOR THE CONNECTICUT FAMILY LAWYER**
2. Wynn, Mary Ellen & Ellen Lubell
3. Conn. Law Tribune
4. 1991
5. 1 vol.
6. $135
7. periodic supp.
8. no supp. yet

1. **HANDBOOK OF INSURANCE COVERAGE DISPUTES**
2. Ostrager, Barry R. & Thomas R. Newman
3. Prentice Hall Law & Business
4. 4th ed. - 1991
5. 1 vol.
6. $145 incl. 4 mos. supp.
7. annual supp.
8. no supp. yet
9. 88-8427/18522401/KF1164.079

1. **HANDBOOK OF LEGAL RESEARCH IN MASSACHUSETTS**
2. Botsford, Margot & Ruth Matz, eds.
3. Mass. CLE
4. 1988
5. 1 vol.
6. $35
7. periodic supp.
8. 1991 - $19.50
9. 87-62742

1. **HANDBOOK ON EUROPEAN EMPLOYEE CO-MANAGEMENT**
2. Kolvenbach, Walter
3. Kluwer
4. 1988
5. 2 vols.
6. $184 incl. 3 mos. supp.
7. periodic supp.
8. 1990 - $156; 1991 - $135
9. 87-29711/16901094/KJE2997.K65

1. **HANDBOOK ON INSURANCE COVERAGE DISPUTES**
2. Ostrager, Barry R. & Thomas R. Newman
3. Prentice Hall Law & Business
4. 4th ed. - 1991
5. 1 vol.
6. $135 incl. 4 mos. supp.
7. periodic supp.
8. no supp. yet
9. 91-5101/24380115/KF1164.O79

1. **HANDBOOK ON LEGAL ETHICS FOR SOUTH CAROLINA LAWYERS - 2nd ed.**
2. Haynsworth, Harry J. IV
3. S. Carolina Bar
4. 1990
5. 1 vol.
6. $85
7. no supp. yet
9. 14106333/KFS1876.5.A2H29

1. **HANDICAPPED REQUIREMENTS HANDBOOK**
2. Montouri, Don
3. Thompson
4. 1978
5. 2 vols.
6. $196/yr.
7. monthly supp. & newsletter
8. renewal - $174/yr.
9. 4543183/HD7255.H238

1. **HANDLING CLAIMS IN PROBATE MATTERS**
2. -
3. Minn. CLE
4. 1991
5. 1 vol.
6. $35
7. no supp. planned

1. **HANDLING COMPLEX CRIMINAL CASES**
2. -
3. Georgetown
4. 1990
5. 1 vol.
6. $75
7. no supp. planned

1. **HANDLING DWI CASES, 1991 Ed.**
2. Bernstein, Gary S. et al.
3. MICPEL
4. 1991
5. 1 vol.
6. $52.50
7. no supp. planned
9. 24493212/KFM1497.8.H23

1. **HANDLING FEDERAL TORT CLAIMS: ADMINISTRATIVE AND JUDICIAL REMEDIES**
2. Jayson, Lester S.
3. Bender
4. 1964
5. 3 vols.
6. $350 incl. 3 mos. supp.
7. annual supp.
8. 1989 - $253; 1990 - $280.50
9. 65-599/1597608/KF1325.P3J3

1. **HANDLING GOVERNMENT INVESTIGATIONS**
2. Hancock, W.A.
3. Bus. Laws
4. 1987
5. 1 vol.
6. $90
7. annual supp.
8. renewal - $39/yr.
9. 88-123057/17728543/KF1414.C65

1. **HANDLING MOTOR VEHICLE ACCIDENT CASES: FORMS**
2. Messina, John L., ed.
3. Clark Boardman Callaghan
4. 1990
5. 1 vol.
6. $95 incl. 6 mos. supp.
7. annual supp.
8. no supp. yet
9. 90-1377/21035234/KF1290.A8H36

1. **HANDLING MOTOR VEHICLE ACCIDENT CASES: TREATISE**
2. Messina, John L., ed.
3. Clark Boardman Callaghan
4. 1990
5. 1 vol.
6. $95 incl. 6 mos. supp.
7. annual supp.
8. no supp. yet
9. 89-25234/20561580/KF8925.T7H36

1. **HANDLING OCCUPATIONAL DISEASE CASES**
2. Baron, Frederick M.
3. Clark Boardman Callaghan
4. revised edition - 1989
5. 1 vol.
6. $98 incl. 6 mos supp.

7. annual supp.
8. 1990 - $30
9. 89-678//r89/19262826/KF8925.P4B37

1. **HANDLING THE AUTOMOBILE NEGLIGENCE CASE: A SYSTEMS APPROACH**
2. Bishop, L. Ray et al.
3. ICLE - Michigan
4. 1988
5. 1 vol.
6. $95
7. periodic supp.
9. 83-82390/18800912/KFM4739.T7B57

1. **HANDLING THE BASIC WORKER'S COMPENSATION CASE IN NEW YORK**
2. Magro, Michael V.
3. NYSBA
4. 1985
5. 1 vol.
6. $50
7. no supp. yet
9. 84-60392/14069561/KFN5592.H36

1. **HANDLING THE MEDICAL MALPRACTICE CASE: A SYSTEMS APPROACH**
2. Bishop, L. Ray & Donald E. Shelton
3. ICLE - Michigan
4. 1982
5. 1 vol.
6. $95
7. no supp. planned
9. 82-081490/8442850/KFM4739.M34B57

1. **HANDLING YOUR OWN DIVORCE WITHOUT A LAWYER: A GUIDE TO SELF- REPRESENTATION IN INDIANA**
2. Buckley, William R.
3. Daniel
4. 1986
5. 1 vol.
6. $17.50
7. no supp. yet
9. 86-196214/14378189/KFI3100.Z9B83

1. **HARASSMENT IN THE WORKPLACE**
2. -
3. MILE
4. 1991
5. 1 vol.
6. $68
7. no supp. planned

1. **HARMONIZED TARIFF OF THE U.S.**
2. -
3. Unz & Co.
4. 1991
5. 1 vol.
6. $275/yr.
7. periodic supp.

1. **HARMONIZED TARIFF SCHEDULES OF THE UNITED STATES ANNOTATED**
2. U.S. International Trade Commission
3. order from USGPO - stock #949-007-00000-6
4. 1991
5. 1 vol.
6. $64/yr.
7. periodic supp.
9. 20822302/HF1042.H36

1. **HARRISON'S SAPP. FLORIDA PLEADINGS, PRACTICE & LEGAL FORMS ANNOTATED, 2D ED.**
2. -
3. Harrison
4. NA
5. 12 vols.
6. $520
7. annual supp.
8. 1990 - $142.95; 1991 - $149.95
9. 74-196013/1195706/KFF68.S322

1. **HART-SCOTT-RODINO ANTITRUST IMPROVEMENTS ACT OF 1976: REMERGER NOTIFICATION SOURCE BOOK**
2. Federal Trade Commission
3. order from USGPO - stock #018-000-00328-7
4. 1990
5. 1 vol.
6. $34
7. no supp. planned
9. 17021913/KF1654.A325A164

1. **HAUSSER & VAN AKEN, OHIO REAL ESTATE LAW & PRACTICE**
2. Hausser, Robert L. & W. R. Van Aken
3. Banks
4. 1985
5. 1 vol.
6. $140 incl. 9 mos. supp.
7. annual supp.
8. 1991 - $55
9. 85-226731/13125452/KFO112.H36

1. **HAWAII ADOPTION MANUAL**
2. -
3. HICLE
4. 1984
5. 1 vol.
6. $40
7. supp. planned
8. no supp. yet
9. 11338635/KFH104.5.H39

1. **HAWAII APPELLATE HANDBOOK**
2. -
3. HICLE
4. 1988
5. 1 vol.
6. $95
7. supp. planned
8. no supp. yet
9. 12652802/KFH513.A6H37

1. **HAWAII ARBITRATION SOURCEBOOK**
2. -
3. Pacific Law Inst.
4. 1987
5. 1 vol.
6. $20
7. to be supp. in 1991
9. 16188377/KFH56O.5.H38

1. **HAWAII COLLECTION SOURCEBOOK**
2. Fidell, Jay M. & Emma S. Matsunaga
3. Pacific Law Inst.
4. 2nd ed. - 1990
5. 1 vol.
6. $90
7. periodic supp.
8. 1990 - $42
9. 15434262/KFH220.Z9F54

1. **HAWAII COMMERCIAL REAL ESTATE MANUAL**
2. -
3. HICLE
4. 1988
5. 1 vol.
6. $95
7. no supp. yet

1. **HAWAII CONVEYANCE MANUAL**
2. -
3. HICLE
4. 1987
5. 1 vol.
6. $75
7. periodic supp.
8. no supp. yet
9. 7103625/KFH127.Z9H39

1. **HAWAII CORPORATION SOURCEBOOK**
2. Fonseca, Roger W. et al.
3. Pacific Law Inst.
4. 2nd ed. - 1987
5. 1 vol.
6. $75
7. to be supp. in 1991
9. 15647184/KFH213.A65F66

1. **HAWAII CRIMINAL LAW AND PROCEDURE DIGEST**
2. -
3. HICLE
4. 1989
5. 1 vol.
6. $60
7. periodic supp.
8. 1991 - $25

1. **HAWAII DIVORCE MANUAL: A COOPERATIVE EFFORT**
2. LeClair, Robert J.
3. HICLE
4. 3rd ed. - 1988
5. 1 vol.
6. $50
7. periodic supp.
8. new ed. planned
9. 11338526/KFH100.H38

1. **HAWAII GUARDIANSHIP SOURCEBOOK (vol. I - Property)**
2. Conrad, John & Sandy Nitta
3. Pacific Law Inst.
4. 1988
5. 1 vol.
6. $50
7. to be supp. in 1991
9. 19735041

1. **HAWAII LEGAL PRACTICE MANUAL - CORPORATIONS & REAL ESTATE**
2. -
3. HICLE
4. 1988
5. 1 vol.
6. $50
7. no supp. yet

1. **HAWAII LEGAL PRACTICE MANUAL - LITIGATION**

2. -
3. HICLE
4. 1988
5. 1 vol.
6. $50
7. no supp. yet
8. new ed. in 1991

1. **HAWAII LEGISLATIVE SOURCEBOOK**
2. Toyofuku, Robert
3. Pacific Law Inst.
4. 1987
5. 1 vol.
6. $50
7. supp. as needed
8. to be supp. in 1992
9. 15647151/JK9371.T69

1. **HAWAII PRACTICE GUIDE: NO FAULT LAW**
2. Bell, Roy J. III & Colbert M. Matsumoto
3. Pacific Law Inst.
4. 1989
5. 1 vol.
6. $73
7. to be supp. in 1991

1. **HAWAII PROBATE SOURCEBOOK**
2. Conrad, John R.
3. Pacific Law Inst.
4. 2nd ed - 1986
5. 1 vol.
6. $75
7. to be supp. in 1991
9. 13387520/KFH144.A6C66

1. **HAWAII REAL ESTATE FINANCING**
2. -
3. HICLE
4. 1990
5. 1 vol.
6. $125
7. no supp. yet

1. **HAWAII RULES OF EVIDENCE**
2. Partington, Earle
3. Francis Marion
4. 1989
5. 1 vol.
6. $45 incl. 1 supp.
7. semiannual supp.
8. 1990 - $35; 1991 - $35
9. 23804332

1. **HAWAII SURROGATE COURTS FILING PROCEDURES MANUAL**
2. -
3. HICLE
4. 1991
5. 1 vol.
6. $75
7. periodic supp.
8. no supp. yet

1. **HAWAII WILLS AND TRUSTS SOURCEBOOK**
2. Conrad, John R. et al.
3. Pacific Law Inst.
4. 1986
5. 1 vol.
6. $70
7. to be supp. in 1992
9. 15647117/KFH144.Z9C66

1. **HAZARD COMMUNICATION COMPLIANCE MANUAL: THE COMPLETE GUIDE FOR WORKER RIGHT-TO-KNOW**
2. -
3. BNA
4. 1988
5. 1 vol.
6. $185
7. no supp. planned
9. 17927310/KF3945.A33H39

1. **HAZARD COMMUNICATION GUIDE**
2. -
3. Keller
4. 1987
5. 1 vol.
6. $145
7. semiannual supp.
8. $105/yr.
9. 85-80596//r85/12374009/KF3570.H39

1. **HAZARDOUS MATERIALS GUIDE**
2. McDowell, George
3. Keller
4. 1976
5. 1 vol.
6. $125
7. semiannual supp.
8. $105/yr.
9. 76-40627/3205793/KF3945.K44

1. **HAZARDOUS MATERIALS TRANSPORTATION**

2. Chabel, Bernard S.
3. BNA
4. 1977
5. 2 vols. (included in Chemical Regulation Reporter)
6. $510/yr.
7. monthly supp.
8. renewal - $475/yr.
9. 79-112034/5172961/KF3958.A15B87

1. **HAZARDOUS SUBSTANCES AND THE LAW AT A COMPLEX AQUATIC SITE**
2. -
3. Wash. Bar
4. 1989
5. 1 vol.
6. $35
7. no supp. planned

1. **HAZARDOUS WASTE**
2. Cooke, Susan M.
3. Bender
4. 1986
5. 3 vols.
6. $320 incl. 3 mos. supp.
7. periodic supp.
8. 1989 - $182; 1990 - $222.50

1. **HAZARDOUS WASTE LAW AND PRACTICE**
2. Stensvaag, John-Mark
3. Wiley
4. 1986
5. 2 vols.
6. $190
7. annual supp.
8. 1989 - $25; 1991 - price NA
9. 86-9280/13525829/KF3946.S74

1. **HAZARDOUS WASTE LIABILITY**
2. -
3. MILE
4. 1990
5. 1 vol.
6. $63
7. no supp. planned

1. **HAZARDOUS WASTE MANAGEMENT GUIDE: IDENTIFICATION, MONITORING, TREATMENT AND DISPOSAL**
2. Wereley, Linda
3. Keller
4. 1980
5. 1 vol.
6. $125
7. semiannual supp.
8. $105/yr.
9. 80-82887/7177789/TD811.5.J2

1. **HAZARDOUS WASTE OPERATIONS & EMERGENCY RESPONSE COMPLIANCE MANUAL**
2. -
3. Keller
4. 1990
5. 1 vol.
6. $75
7. periodic supp.
9. 90-62221/22382332/KF3958.H39

1. **HAZARDOUS WASTE REGULATORY GUIDE**
2. Wereley, Linda
3. Keller
4. 1982
5. 1 vol.
6. $119
7. semiannual supp.
8. $95/yr.
9. 81-86200/8903580/KF3945.Z95H39

1. **HEAD AND BRAIN (Courtroom Medicine Series vol. 8, 8A & 8B)**
2. Chapman, Loring F. et al.
3. Bender
4. 1972
5. 3 vols.
6. $350 incl. 3 mos. supp.
7. annual supp.
8. 1989 - $234; 1990 - $283
9. 72-90082/589259/RA1011.C68

1. **HEALTH ADMINISTRATION: LAWS, REGULATIONS AND GUIDELINES**
2. Ed. Staff
3. National Health
4. 1977
5. 2 vols.
6. $195 incl. 1 yr. supp.
7. quarterly supp.
8. renewal - $175/yr.
9. 77-80387/10961947/KF3821.H43

1. **HEALTH CARE FACILITY MANAGEMENT**
2. -
3. CCH
4. 1990
5. 2 vols.
6. $505/yr.; $460/yr. for 2 yrs.

7. biweekly supp.
9. 21979287/KF3825.A6H4

1. **HEALTH CARE FRAUD AND ABUSE: A GUIDE TO FEDERAL SANCTIONS**
2. Cacioppo, Paul C.
3. Clark Boardman Callaghan
4. 1991
5. 1 vol.
6. $95 incl. 3 mos. supp.
7. annual supp.
9. 90-23174/22733310/KF3608.A4C33

1. **HEALTH CARE LABOR MANUAL**
2. Skoler, Martin E.
3. Aspen
4. 1974
5. 3 vols.
6. $550 incl. 1 yr. supp.
7. bimonthly supp.
9. 74-24672/1970442/KF3580.H4M3x

1. **HEALTH CARE LAW**
2. -
3. Illinois ICLE
4. 1988
5. 1 vol.
6. $175.95
7. periodic supp.
8. 1990 - $42.95

1. **HEALTH CARE LAW: A PRACTICAL GUIDE**
2. -
3. Bender
4. 1985
5. 1 vol.
6. $105
7. periodic supp.
8. 1989 - $60; 1990 - $71.50
9. 85-72541/12785267

1. **HEALTH CARE LAW SOURCEBOOK**
2. Weissburg & Aronson
3. Bender
4. 1989
5. 2 vols.
6. $195 incl. 3 mos. supp.
7. annual supp.
8. 1990 - $91
9. 89-150954/20527378/KF3821.A3

1. **HEALTH CARE 1991**
2. -
3. MILE
4. 1991
5. 1 vol.
6. $68
7. no supp. planned

1. **HEIN'S INTERIM DECISION SERVICE**
2. -
3. Hein
4. 1983
5. 2 vols.
6. $65/yr.
7. annual supp.
8. 1990 - $65; 1991 - $65
9. 86-21986/9983419/KF4812.A2U5

1. **HEIN'S LEGAL PERIODICAL CHECKLIST**
2. Hein, William S., Jr. et al.
3. Hein
4. 1991
5. 3 vols.
6. $295
7. annual supp.
9. 91-72808/24201348/K36.H45

1. **HEIN'S STATE REPORT CHECKLIST**
2. Keith Wiese, Compiler
3. Hein
4. 3rd ed. - 1991
5. 1 vol.
6. $49.50
7. annual supp.
8. 1990 - $49.50; 1991 - $49.50
9. 87-35698/17263917/KF3.W54

1. **HERZOG'S BANKRUPTCY FORMS AND PRACTICE**
2. Herzog, Asa S. et al.
3. Clark Boardman Callaghan
4. 8th ed. - 1987
5. 2 vols.
6. $190 incl. 3 mos. supp.
7. annual supp.
8. 1998 - $104.50; 1989 - $49.50
9. 87-20162//r88/16465491

1. **HIMA REGULATORY MANUAL**
2. -
3. HIMA
4. 1988
5. 1 vol.
6. $130 - nonmembers; $80 - members
7. annual supp.

1. **HIP AND THIGH (Courtroom Medicine Series, vols. 7 & 7A)**
2. Kalisch, Jules et al.
3. Bender
4. 1972
5. 2 vols.
6. $245 incl. 3 mos. supp.
7. annual supp.
8. 1989 - $126; 1990 - $177.50
9. 79-178023/298768

1. **HISTORIC PRESERVATION LAW (Real Estate Transaction Series, vols. 11, 11A & 11B)**
2. Boasberg, T. et al.
3. Bender
4. 1986
5. 3 vols.
6. $260 incl. 3 mos. supp.
7. periodic supp.
8. 1987 - $67.50; 1988 - $93.50
9. 87-120223/16130000/KF4310.B63

1. **HISTORY OF THE TARIFF SCHEDULES OF THE UNITED STATES ANNOTATED**
2. U.S. International Trade Commission
3. order from USGPO - stock #949-001-00000-8
4. 1991
5. 1 vol.
6. $64/yr.
7. periodic supp.
9. 7973086/HF1756.A5

1. **HOLDING COMPANIES HANDBOOK**
2. -
3. Office of Thrift Supervision
4. 1990
5. 1 vol.
6. $25
7. periodic supp.

1. **HOME HEALTH AND HOSPICE MANUAL: REGULATIONS AND GUIDELINES**
2. Ed. Staff
3. National Health
4. 1985
5. 1 vol.
6. $125 incl. 1 yr. supp.
7. quarterly supp.
8. renewal - $110/yr.
9. 85-239908/14001918/KF3826.H64H66

1. **HOME MORTGAGE DISCLOSURE ACT: A PRACTICAL APPROACH TO MANAGING COMPLIANCE**
2. Stevenson, T. Herbert
3. Probus
4. 1990
5. 1 vol.
6. $75
7. no supp. yet
9. 90-83202/22393237/KF691.S848

1. **HOMEOWNERS ASSOCIATIONS AND PLANNED UNIT DEVELOPMENTS - LAW AND PRACTICE (Real Estate Transactions series, vols. 6 & 6A)**
2. Rohan, Patrick J.
3. Bender
4. 1977
5. 3 vols.
6. $350 incl. 3 mos. supp.
7. biannual supp.
8. 1989 - $229; 1990 - $283
9. 77-152606/3328720/KF581.R62

1. **HONG KONG REVENUE LAW**
2. Willoughby, Peter G.
3. Bender
4. 1981
5. 3 vols.
6. $295 incl. 3 mos. supp.
7. periodic supp.
8. 1989 - $304; 1990 - $164
9. 81-68260/8805471

1. **HORSE OWNERS AND BREEDERS TAX MANUAL**
2. Davis, Thomas A.
3. AHC
4. new ed. - 1991
5. 1 vol.
6. $90
7. periodic supp.
9. 11422620

1. **HORSE SYNDICATION MANUAL**
2. Wood, Kenneth A.
3. Farnam
4. 1983
5. 1 vol.
6. $65 incl. 1 yr. supp.
7. periodic supp.
9. 83-51790/10665522/KF915.Z93H69

1. **HOSPITAL CONTRACTS MANUAL**
2. Baker & Hostetler
3. Aspen
4. 1982
5. 2 vols.

6. $352 incl. 3 mos. supp.
7. semiannual supp.
8. about $50-100/supp.
9. 82-16344/8764082/KF3825.H67

1. **HOSPITAL LAW MANUAL, ATTORNEY'S VOLUMES**
2. -
3. Aspen
4. 1959
5. 3 vols.
6. $695 incl. 1 yr. supp.
7. quarterly supp.
9. 74-80713/5799285/KF3825.A6A85

1. **HOSPITAL LEGAL FORMS, CHECKLISTS & GUIDELINES**
2. Rowland, Howard S. & Beatrice L.
3. Aspen
4. 1990
5. 2 vols.
6. $282 incl. 3 mos. supp.
7. semiannual supp.
8. $97/supp.

1. **HOSPITAL LIABILITY**
2. Smith, James Walker
3. Law Journal
4. 1985
5. 1 vol.
6. $85
7. periodic supp.
8. 1989 - $84; 1990 - $84
9. 85-19798/12557800/KF3825.3.S55

1. **HOSTILE TAKEOVERS: 1988 UPPER MIDWEST UPDATE**
2. -
3. MILE
4. 1988
5. 1 vol.
6. $63
7. no supp. planned

1. **HOT ISSUES IN EMPLOYMENT LITIGATION**
2. -
3. Indiana CLE
4. 1991
5. 1 vol.
6. $50
7. no supp. planned
9. 24044701/KF3464.A75H68

1. **HOUSING AND DEVELOPMENT REPORTER**
2. -
3. WG&L
4. 1973
5. 4 vols.
6. $725/yr.
7. weekly supp. & reports
8. $695/yr.
9. 73-644880/1787686/KF5729.A1H68

1. **HOUSING DISCRIMINATION: LAW AND LITIGATION**
2. Schwemm, Robert G.
3. Clark Boardman Callaghan
4. 1990
5. 1 vol.
6. $95 incl. 3 mos. supp.
7. annual supp.
8. 1991 - $45
9. 90-42201/22005533/KF5740.S39

1. **HOUSING LAW**
2. -
3. NH Bar
4. 1990
5. 1 vol.
6. $35
7. no supp. planned

1. **HOW INSURANCE COMPANIES SETTLE CASES**
2. Miller, Clint
3. James
4. 1989
5. 1 vol.
6. $79.98 incl. 3 mos. supp.
7. annual supp.
8. 1990 - $36.98
9. 89-146624/19478114/KF1164.3.M55

1. **HOW TO ADMINISTER ESTATES IN ALABAMA**
2. -
3. ABICLE
4. 1987
5. 1 vol.
6. $60
7. no supp. yet

1. **HOW TO AVOID OSHA**
2. Moran, Robert D.
3. Gulf
4. 1981

5. 1 vol.
6. $69
7. no supp. yet
9. 80-39727/7006952/KF3570.M67

1. **HOW TO COMPLY WITH THE DRUG-FREE WORKPLACE ACT**
2. -
3. BLR
4. 1988
5. 1 vol.
6. $189.95
7. periodic supp.
8. $29.95/yr.

1. **HOW TO HANDLE A MOTOR VEHICLE ACCIDENT CASE**
2. -
3. Okla. Bar CLE
4. 1990
5. 1 vol.
6. $60
7. no supp. planned

1. **HOW TO HANDLE PROBLEM CRIMINAL CASES, AND A LOOK AT NEW CRIMES**
2. -
3. Maine Bar
4. 1990
5. 1 vol.
6. $35
7. no supp. planned

1. **HOW TO HAVE A MILLION DOLLAR PRACTICE**
2. -
3. Conn. Bar
4. 1990
5. 1 vol.
6. $53
7. no supp. planned

1. **HOW TO MANAGE YOUR LAW OFFICE**
2. Altman, Mary Ann & Robert I. Weil
3. Bender
4. 1973
5. 1 vol.
6. $115 incl. 3 mos. supp.
7. supp. & revisions
8. 1989 - $70; 1990 - $82.50
9. 73-84686/798008/KF318.A758

1. **HOW TO MARKET AND ADVERTISE YOUR LAW PRACTICE**
2. Lee, Tom L.
3. CRI
4. 1988
5. 1 vol.
6. $49
7. supp. as needed

1. **HOW TO PREPARE FOR, TAKE, AND USE A DEPOSITION**
2. Benson, Robert E. & John C. Tredennick, Jr.
3. James
4. 1990
5. 1 vol.
6. $59.88 incl. 3 mos. supp.
7. annual supp.
8. 1991 - $34.99
9. 90-189906/22092790/KF8900.B39

1. **HOW TO PROBATE AN ESTATE AND HANDLE POST-MORTEM MATTERS**
2. -
3. Wash. Bar
4. 1991
5. 1 vol.
6. $45
7. no supp. planned

1. **HOW TO SAVE TIME AND TAXES IN HANDLING ESTATES (How to Save Time and Taxes Series vol.1)**
2. Clark, John A.
3. Bender
4. 2nd ed. - 1979
5. 1 vol.
6. $120 incl. 3 mos. supp.
7. supp. and/or revisions
8. 1989 - $82; 1990 - $97
9. 79-77168/3598323/KF6572.C552

1. **HOW TO SAVE TIME AND TAXES PREPARING FIDUCIARY INCOME TAX RETURNS-FEDERAL AND STATE (How to Save Time and Taxes Series vol. 2)**
2. Rounds, Stowell & Joseph J. O'Connell
3. Bender
4. 2nd ed. - 1974
5. 1 vol.
6. $115 incl. 3 mos. supp.
7. supp. and/or revisions
8. 1989 - $79.50; 1990 - $94
9. 74-181490/860759/KF6443.R6

1. **HOW TO SAVE TIME AND TAXES PREPARING THE FEDERAL PARTNERSHIP RETURN**

2. Fiore, E.D. Jr., et al.
3. Bender
4. 2nd ed. - 1986
5. 1 vol.
6. $105 incl. 3 mos. supp.
7. periodic supp. and/or revisions
8. 1989 - $50; 1990 - $59
9. 70-77168/3598377/KF6452.F5

1. **HR POLICY AND PROCEDURE**
2. -
3. WG&L
4. NA
5. 1 vol.
6. $376/yr.
7. biweekly supp.

1. **HUD AND CDA FINANCING TECHNIQUES**
2. Coleman, Thomas et al.
3. MICPEL
4. 1991
5. 1 vol.
6. $42
7. no supp. planned

1. **HUMAN RESOURCE MANAGEMENT IN CANADA**
2. -
3. WG&L
4. NA
5. 2 vols.
6. $393/yr.
7. monthly supp.

1. **HUMAN RESOURCES MANAGEMENT**
2. -
3. CCH
4. 1981
5. 5 vols.
6. $1095/yr.; $995/yr. for 2 yrs.
7. monthly supp.
9. 81-216720/7973780/KF3455.A6H85

1. **HUMAN RESOURCES MANAGEMENT – OSHA COMPLIANCE**
2. -
3. CCH
4. 1977
5. 1 vol.
6. $335/yr.; $305/yr. for 2 yrs.
7. monthly supp.
9. 77-154282/8127424/KF3568.4C58a

1. **HUMAN RIGHTS: THE INTER-AMERICAN SYSTEM**
2. Buergenthal, Thomas & Robert Norris
3. Oceana
4. 1982
5. 4 vols.
6. $380
7. periodic supp.
8. 1991 - $250
9. 82-81889/9255764/KD2574.H85

1. **HUMAN RIGHTS: THE INTER-NATIONAL PETITION SYSTEM: A REPERTOIRE OF PRACTICE**
2. Tardu, Maxime & Thomas E. McCarthy
3. Oceana
4. 1979
5. 3 vols. out of 4 projected
6. $300
7. periodic supp.
8. 1985 - $100
9. 79-14453/4932863/K3240.4.T37

1. **HUMAN RIGHTS ORGANIZATIONS AND PERIODICALS DIRECTORY**
2. Ginger, Ann Fagan et al., eds.
3. Meiklejohn Civil Liberties Institute
4. 6th ed. - 1990
5. 1 vol.
6. $30
7. no supp. planned
9. 74-24010/1790837/KF4741.H84

1. **IDAHO APPELLATE HANDBOOK**
2. -
3. Idaho Law
4. 2nd rev. ed. - 1989
5. 1 vol.
6. $125
7. periodic supp.
8. no supp. yet

1. **IDAHO CIVIL JURY INSTRUCTIONS**
2. Idaho Pattern Jury Instructions Comm.
3. Idaho Law
4. rev. ed. - 1987
5. 1 vol.
6. $70
7. periodic supp.
8. 1987 - $10.50

1. **IDAHO PRE-TRIAL CIVIL PROCEDURE**
2. Lewis, Craig
3. Idaho Law

4. 1982
5. 1 vol.
6. $66.95
7. no supp. yet

1. **IDAHO REAL ESTATE PRACTICE HANDBOOK**
2. -
3. Idaho Law
4. 1988
5. 1 vol.
6. $80
7. no supp. yet

1. **ILLINOIS ADMINISTRATIVE LAW**
2. -
3. Illinois ICLE
4. 1991
5. 1 vol.
6. $49.95
7. periodic supp.
8. no supp. yet

1. **ILLINOIS ATTORNEY'S/SECRETARY'S HANDBOOK**
2. -
3. Mariposa
4. 1991
5. 1 vol.
6. $59
7. annual supp.
8. 1990 - $51; 1991 - $50
9. 17222783/KFI1277.I44

1. **ILLINOIS CIVIL DISCOVERY PRACTICE**
2. -
3. Illinois ICLE
4. 1987
5. 1 vol.
6. $104.95
7. periodic supp.
8. 1989 - $25.95
9. 9231697/KFI737.I4

1. **ILLINOIS CIVIL PRACTICE**
2. -
3. Illinois ICLE
4. 1991
5. 3 vols. (avail. separately)
6. $315 ($104.95 per vol.)
7. periodic supp.
8. no supp. yet
9. 8500063/KFI1738.I42x

1. **ILLINOIS CIVIL TRIAL EVIDENCE**
2. -
3. Illinois ICLE
5. 1 vol.
6. $104.95
7. periodic supp.
8. 1989 - $25.95
9. 9908460/KFI1740.I44

1. **ILLINOIS CIVIL TRIAL GUIDE**
2. Howerton, Robert H. et al., eds.
3. Bender
4. 1991
5. 5 vols.
6. $395 incl. 3 mos. supp.
7. annual supp.
8. no supp. yet

1. **ILLINOIS COMMERCIAL FINANCING**
2. Givens, Ronald B. & Mary Fontaine
3. Aspen
4. 1992
5. 2 vols.
6. price NA incl. 3 mos. supp.
7. annual supp.

1. **ILLINOIS CONDOMINIUM LAW**
2. -
3. Illinois ICLE
4. 1987
5. 1 vol.
6. $105.95
7. periodic supp.
8. 1990 - $24.95
9. 1260969

1. **ILLINOIS CORPORATE FORMS--PRACTICE**
2. Jersild, Thomas N.
3. Aspen
4. 1988
5. 2 vols.
6. $249 incl. 3 mos. supp.
7. annual supp.
8. 1989 - $89
9. 88-16688/18015803/KFI1413.A65J47

1. **ILLINOIS COURTS RULE BOOK**
2. Vande Werken, Walter B.
3. Law Bulletin
4. 4th ed. - 1990
5. 1 vol.
6. $55 incl. 1 yr. supp.
7. quarterly supp.
8. renewal - $32/yr.
9. 67-8052/1129493/KFI1729.A2

1. **ILLINOIS CRIMINAL LAW & PROCEDURE**
2. Ed. Staff
3. Gould
4. NA
5. 1 vol.
6. $15.95
7. periodic supp.
8. $5 - $10/supp.

1. **ILLINOIS DOMESTIC RELATIONS FORMS–PRACTICE**
2. Rinella, Bernard B. & Richard A.
3. Aspen
4. 1989
5. 1 vol.
6. $159 incl. 3 mos. supp.
7. annual supp.
8. $79-95/supp.
9. 89-70/19125273/KFI1294.A65R56

1. **ILLINOIS DRAM SHOP ACT PRACTICE**
2. -
3. Illinois ICLE
4. 1988
5. 1 vol.
6. $67.95
7. periodic supp.
8. 1991 - $15.95
9. 17994365/KFI1576.D7I44

1. **ILLINOIS EMINENT DOMAIN PRACTICE**
2. -
3. Illinois ICLE
4. 1989
5. 1 vol.
6. $98.95
7. periodic supp.
8. no supp. yet
9. 19609486/KFI1650.I4

1. **ILLINOIS ESTATE ADMINISTRATION**
2. -
3. Illinois ICLE
4. 1989
5. 1 vol.
6. $109.95
7. periodic supp.
8. no supp. yet
9. 19877543/KFI1347.I52

1. **ILLINOIS ESTATE PLANNING, WILL DRAFTING AND ESTATE ADMINISTRATION FORMS–PRACTICE**
2. Adams, Roy M. et al.
3. Aspen
4. 1988
5. 2 vols.
6. $239 incl. 3 mos. supp.
7. annual supp.
8. 1989 - $89
9. 88-24092/18324202/KFI1340.A65A33

1. **ILLINOIS FAMILY LAW**
2. -
3. Illinois ICLE
4. 1988
5. 2 vols.
6. $164.95
7. periodic supp.
8. 1989 - $38.95
9. 10700260/KFI1294.I433

1. **ILLINOIS FAMILY LAW**
2. -
3. Pantagraph
4. 1984
5. 1 vol.
6. $43.50 incl. 1 yr. supp.
7. quarterly supp.
8. renewal - $39.95/yr.

1. **ILLINOIS FORMS OF JURY INSTRUCTIONS**
2. -
3. Bender
4. 1991
5. 3 vols.
6. $325 incl. 3 mos. supp.
7. annual supp.
8. no supp. yet

1. **ILLINOIS JUVENILE LAW AND PRACTICE**
2. -
3. Illinois ICLE
4. 1990
5. 1 vol.
6. $93.95
7. periodic supp.
8. no supp. yet

1. **ILLINOIS LAND USE LAW**
2. -
3. Illinois ICLE
4. 1989
5. 1 vol.
6. $98.95
7. periodic supp.
8. no supp. yet
9. 3918464/KFI1658.L37

1. **THE ILLINOIS LAW OF CRIMINAL INVESTIGATION**
2. Manak, James P., ed.
3. Manak
4. rev. 2nd ed. - 1986
5. 1 vol.
6. $75
7. annual supp.
8. 1991-92 - $55.50
9. 14048102/KFI1775.N42

1. **ILLINOIS LAWYER'S MANUAL, 3RD ED.**
2. Becker, Benjamin M., et al.
3. Lawyers Coop.
4. 1975
5. 2 vols.
6. $180 incl. 6 mos. supp.
7. annual supp.
8. 1990 - $74.50; 1991 - $77
9. 60-1143//r84

1. **ILLINOIS LEGAL FILING DIRECTORY**
2. Wilber, Wanda K.
3. Shepard's
4. 1990
5. 1 vol.
6. $60
7. annual supp.
9. 90-45091/22240339/KFI1277.5.F4W55

1. **ILLINOIS LIMITATIONS MANUAL, 2ND ED.**
2. Butterworth's Staff
3. Butterworth-St. Paul
4. 1989
5. 1 vol.
6. $50
7. periodic supp.
8. 1990 - $45
9. 19551273/KFI1290.L5I39

1. **ILLINOIS MECHANICS' LIENS PRACTICE**
2. -
3. Illinois ICLE
4. 1986
5. 1 vol.
6. $102.95
7. periodic supp.
8. 1989 - $24.75

1. **ILLINOIS MUNICIPAL LAW**
2. -
3. Illinois ICLE
4. 1987
5. 3 vols.
6. $184.95
7. periodic supp.
8. 1990 - $39.95
9. 3995701/KFI1631.I29

1. **ILLINOIS NON-PATTERN JURY INSTRUCTIONS**
2. Rowley, Carl L. & Jon M. Moyers
3. Lawyers Coop.
4. 1991
5. 1 vol.
6. $130 incl. 6 mos. supp.
7. annual supp.
8. no supp. yet
9. 91-4135/23766470/KFI1742.6.R69

1. **ILLINOIS PRACTICE GUIDE - PERSONAL INJURY**
2. Crowe, Hon. Brian, et al.
3. Lawyers Coop.
4. 1988
5. 2 vols.
6. $180 incl. 6 mos. supp.
7. annual supp.
8. 1990 - $70; 1991 - $76
9. 88-14506/17876089/KFI1739.P4C76

1. **ILLINOIS PRODUCT LIABILITY PRACTICE**
2. -
3. Illinois ICLE
4. 1990
5. 1 vol.
6. $98.95
7. periodic supp.
8. no supp. yet

1. **ILLINOIS PUBLIC EMPLOYEE REPORTER**
2. -
3. LRP
4. 1985
5. 1 vol.
6. $595/yr. (back vols. avail.)
7. semimonthly supp.
9. 11717566/KFI1533.8.P8A49

1. **ILLINOIS REAL ESTATE**
2. Gutstein, Solomon
3. Lawyers Coop.
4. 1983
5. 2 vols.
6. $210 incl. 6 mos. supp.
7. annual supp.
8. 1989 - $86; 1990 - $102

9. 79-92517/9651956/KFI1312.G87

1. **ILLINOIS REAL ESTATE FORMS--PRACTICE**
2. Rudnick, Paul D. et al.
3. Aspen
4. 1989
5. 3 vol.
6. $299 incl. 3 mos. supp.
7. annual supp.
8. $79-95/supp.
9. 88-24182/18350845/KFI1236.A65R83

1. **ILLINOIS REAL PROPERTY SERVICE**
2. -
3. Lawyers Coop.
4. 1988
5. 16 vols.
6. $1527.50 incl. 1 yr. supp.
7. annual supp.
8. 1990 - $65; 1991 - $95
9. 88-82954

1. **ILLINOIS RULES & PRACTICE HANDBOOK, 2ND ED.**
2. -
3. Pantagraph
4. 1982
5. 1 vol.
6. $49.50 incl. 1 yr. supp.
7. quarterly supp.
8. renewal - $49.95/yr.
9. 82-228585/8623398/KFI1729.A2

1. **ILLINOIS STATE AND LOCAL TAXATION**
2. -
3. Illinois ICLE
4. 1991
5. 1 vol.
6. $99.95
7. periodic supp.
8. no supp. yet
9. 23835227/KFI1670.I445

1. **ILLINOIS STRUCTURAL WORK ACT PRACTICE**
2. -
3. Illinois ICLE
4. 1990
5. 1 vol.
6. $59.95
7. periodic supp.
8. no supp. yet
9. 13137035/KFI1475.I44

1. **ILLINOIS TAX SERVICE**
2. Czerwionka, Frederick J., et al.
3. Bender
4. 1985
5. 4 vols.
6. $370 incl. 1 yr. service; $680 for 2yrs.
7. monthly supp.
8. renewal - $310/yr.
9. 13036661/KFI1670.C84

1. **ILLINOIS TRIAL EVIDENCE**
2. Goodman, Lee Hugh
3. James
4. 1986
5. 1 vol.
6. $49.80 incl. 3 mos. supp.
7. annual supp.
8. 1990 - $42.80
9. 86-224384/14715712/KFI1740.G6

1. **ILLINOIS TRIALS: LAW AND STRATEGY**
2. Gillis, Kenneth L.
3. Butterworth-St. Paul
4. 1990
5. 1 vol.
6. $88
7. periodic supp.
8. no supp. yet
9. 89-71325/20932587/KFI1738.G55

1. **ILLINOIS WORKERS' COMPENSATION PRACTICE**
2. -
3. Illinois ICLE
4. 1990
5. 1 vol.
6. $98.95
7. periodic supp.
8. no supp. yet

1. **IMMIGRATION AND NATURALIZATION PRACTICE**
2. -
3. Illinois ICLE
4. 1988
5. 2 vols.
6. $87.95
7. periodic supp.
8. no supp. yet

1. **IMMIGRATION JUDGE BENCHBOOK**
2. -
3. American Immigration Lawyers Assn.

4. rev. - 1988
5. 1 vol.
6. $52.50
7. periodic supp.
8. no supp. yet
9. 20728724/KF8925.E4U5

1. **IMMIGRATION LAW AND BUSINESS**
2. Fragomen, Austin T.
3. Clark Boardman Callaghan
4. 1983
5. 2 vols.
6. $195 incl. 3 mos. supp.
7. annual supp. & monthly reporting service
8. 1989 - $124.50; 1991 - $159
9. 83-11315/9575980/KF4819.F7

1. **IMMIGRATION LAW AND CRIMES**
2. National Lawyers Guild
3. Clark Boardman Callaghan
4. 1984
5. 1 vol.
6. $105 incl. 3 mos. supp.
7. annual supp.
8. 1989 - $84.50; 1991 - $110
9. 84-4281/10483584/KF4819.I472

1. **IMMIGRATION LAW AND DEFENSE, 3rd ED.**
2. National Lawyers Guild
3. Clark Boardman Callaghan
4. 1988
5. 2 vols.
6. $195 incl. 3 mos. supp.
7. annual supp.
8. 1989 - $130; 1991 - $147
9. 87-20163/16525590/KF8925.E4I46

1. **IMMIGRATION LAW AND PRACTICE IN FLORIDA**
2. -
3. Florida Bar
4. 2nd ed. - 1987
5. 1 vol.
6. $65
7. periodic supp.
8. no supp. yet
9. 82-83851/17572842/KF4819.I475

1. **IMMIGRATION LAW AND PROCEDURE: DESK ED.**
2. Gordon, Charles & E. G. Gordon
3. Bender
4. 1980
5. 1 vol.
6. $125 incl. 3 mos. supp.
7. periodic supp.
8. 1989 - $80; 1990 - $93
9. 81-165987/7923324/KF4819.G59

1. **IMMIGRATION LAW AND PROCEDURE, REV. ED.**
2. Gordon, C. & H.N. Rosenfield
3. Bender
4. rev. ed. - 1966
5. 12 vols.
6. $1040 incl. 3 mos. supp.
7. annual supp.
8. 1989 - $767.50; 1990 - $910
9. 59-3484/3103303/KF4819.G6

1. **IMMIGRATION LAW AND PROCEDURE REPORTER**
2. Kaye, Allen E. and Roy J. Watson Jr.
3. Bender
4. 1985
5. 3 vols.
6. $550 incl. 1 yr. supp.
7. 1988 - $425; 1989 - $500
9. 85-71745/12942993/KF4815.I46

1. **IMMIGRATION LAW FOR GENERAL PRACTITIONERS AND HUMAN RESOURCE PERSONNEL**
2. -
3. Conn. Bar
4. 1990
5. 1 vol.
6. $53
7. no supp. planned

1. **IMMIGRATION LAW SERVICE**
2. Publisher's Editorial Staff
3. Lawyers Coop. & Bancroft
4. 1985
5. 9 vols.
6. $760 incl. 1 yr. supp.
7. quarterly supp. & newsletter 8x/yr.
8. 1991 - $570
9. 84-82463/11696045/KF4815.I45

1. **IMMIGRATION LAW UPDATE**
2. -
3. MICPEL
4. 1990
5. 1 vol.
6. $50
7. no supp. yet

1. **IMPROVING CHILD SUPPORT PRACTICE**
2. Natl. Legal Resource Center for Child Advocacy & Protection
3. ABA
4. 1986
5. 2 vols.
6. $45
7. no supp. planned
9. 14052439/KF549.A75I56

1. **INCOME TAXATION: ACCOUNTING METHODS AND PERIODS**
2. Bauernfeind, George C.
3. Shepard's
4. 1983
5. 2 vols.
6. $190
7. annual supp.
8. 1989 - $39; 1991 - $48
9. 83-13575/9686828/KF6314.B38

1. **INCOME TAXATION OF FOREIGN-RELATED TRANSACTIONS**
2. Rhoades, Rufus V. & Marshall J. Langer
3. Bender
4. 1971 (vols. 1 & 2), 1980 (vols. 3 & 4)
5. 5 vols.
6. $675 incl. 3 mos. supp.
7. biannual supp.
8. 1989 - $509; 1990 - $641.50
9. 76-185647/281940/KF6419.R45

1. **INCOME TAXATION OF NATURAL RESOURCES**
2. -
3. RIA
4. 1964
5. 2 vols.
6. $580/yr.; $550/yr. for 2 yrs.
7. monthly supp.
8. renewal - $520/yr.
9. 77-352959/2817375/KF6482.B7

1. **INDEX OF FEDERAL SPECIFICATIONS, STANDARDS AND COMMERCIAL ITEM DESCRIPTIONS**
2. General Services Admin., Office of Federal Supply & Services
3. order from USGPO - stock #022-003-01166-8
4. 1990
5. 1 vol.
6. $30
7. no supp. planned
9. 19341633/JK1679.I53

1. **INDEX TO CHEMICAL REGULATION**
2. Apinis, Inara Z.
3. BNA
4. 1979
5. 1 vol. (included in Chemical Regulation Reporter)
6. $595/yr.
7. weekly supp.
8. renewal - $545/yr.
9. 17853680/KF1875.A3698B8

1. **INDEX TO LAW SCHOOL ALUMNI PUBLICATIONS**
2. Burchill, Mary D.
3. Rothman
4. 1985
5. 2 vols. (1 bound vol. 1980-89; 1 looseleaf vol.)
6. $37.50 - looseleaf; $67.50 - bound
7. semiannual supp.
8. 1989 - $67.50; 1990 - $37.50
9. 85-10900/12107407/KF261.B87

1. **INDIANA ANIMAL AND WILDLIFE LAW**
2. Buckley, William R. & Janet E.
3. Daniel
4. 1985
5. 1 vol.
6. $17.50
7. periodic supp.
8. 1989 - $5
9. 86-185963/12747085/KFI3084.5.A45B83

1. **INDIANA ESTATE PLANNING AND PROBATE PRACTICE**
2. -
3. Bender
4. 1990
5. 4 vols.
6. $400 incl. 3 mos. supp.
7. periodic supp.
8. no supp. yet
9. 90-83077/22486554

1. **INDIANA FORMS OF PLEADING AND PRACTICE**
2. Thompson, Charles A. & Judith Shaw Hostetler
3. Bender
4. 1972
5. 6 vols.
6. $525 incl. 3 mos. supp.
7. annual supp.

8. 1989 - $145; 1990 - $197.50
9. 72-95917/622157/KFI3530.A65T45

1. **INDIANA LAW UPDATE**
2. -
3. Indiana CLE
4. 1991
5. 1 vol.
6. $68
7. no supp. planned

1. **INDIANA PATTERN JURY INSTRUCTIONS - CIVIL**
2. Civil Instructions Comm.
3. Michie
4. 2nd ed. - 1989
5. 2 vols.
6. $160 incl. 3 mos. supp.
7. no supp. yet
9. 89-63956/20834284/KFI3542.6.A65I53

1. **INDIANA PATTERN JURY INSTRUCTIONS - CRIMINAL**
2. Indiana Judges Assn. Comm. on Pattern Jury Instructions
3. Michie
4. 1990
5. 2 vols.
6. $160
7. periodic supp.
8. no supp. yet

1. **INDIANA PUBLIC EMPLOYEE REPORTER**
2. -
3. LRP
4. 1975
5. 1 vol.
6. $365/yr. (back vols. avail.)
7. semimonthly supp.

1. **INDIANA'S NEW GUARDIANSHIP LAW--AN UPDATE**
2. -
3. Indiana CLE
4. 1989
5. 1 vol.
6. $50
7. no supp. planned

1. **INDIVIDUAL EMPLOYMENT RIGHTS**
2. Sedmak, Nancy J.
3. BNA
4. 1986
5. 2 vols. (incl. in Labor Relations Reporter)
6. $531/yr.
7. biweekly supp.
8. renewal - $511/yr.
9. 14239399

1. **INDIVIDUAL JUDGES' RULES**
2. Committee on Federal Courts
3. NYSBA
4. 1986
5. 1 vol.
6. $60
7. quarterly supp.
8. $45/yr.
9. 86-62411

1. **INDIVIDUAL RETIREMENT PLANS GUIDE - IRA, SEP, KEOGH**
2. -
3. CCH
4. 1982
5. 1 vol.
6. $210/yr.; $190/yr. for 2 yrs.
7. monthly supp.
9. 82-2595/8290988/KF3510.A6I5

1. **INDIVIDUALS WITH DISABILITIES EDUCATION LAW REPORTER**
2. -
3. LRP
4. 1979
5. 2 vols.
6. $795
7. biweekly supp.
9. 79-114098/4989388/KF4210.A6E38

1. **INFECTIOUS WASTE: THE COMPLETE RESOURCE GUIDE**
2. Jessup, Deborah H.
3. BNA
4. 1988
5. 2 vol.
6. $370
7. no supp. planned
9. 88-600462/18814363/RA567.7.J48

1. **INFORMAL PROBATE**
2. -
3. Minn. CLE
4. 1991
5. 1 vol.
6. $35
7. no supp. planned
9. 23299366

1. **INFORMATION LAW: FREEDOM OF INFORMATION, PRIVACY, OPEN MEETINGS, OTHER ACCESS LAWS**
2. Braverman, Burt A. & Frances J. Chetwynd
3. PLI
4. 1986
5. 2 vols.
6. $100
7. annual supp.
8. 1990 - $35
9. 85-63252/13295389/KF5753.B73

1. **INFORMATION RETURNS GUIDE**
2. -
3. CCH
4. 1987
5. 1 vol.
6. $220/yr.; $200/yr. for 2 yrs.
7. monthly supp.
9. 87-403976/16005633/KF6314.A6I54

1. **INHERITANCE, ESTATE AND GIFT TAX REPORTS**
2. -
3. CCH
4. 1928
5. 9 vols. (incl. fed. & all states & Fed. Estate & Gift Tax Reports)
6. $910/yr.; $825/yr. for 2 yrs.
7. weekly supp.
9. 8620177

1. **INITIATIVE: A RESOURCE GUIDE TO DEVELOPING SUCCESSFUL MINORITY PROGRAMS**
2. Commn. on Opportunities for Minorities in the Profession
3. ABA
4. 1989
5. 1 vol.
6. $40
7. no supp. yet
9. 24402605

1. **INNOVATIONS IN HEAD INJURY REHABILITATION**
2. Deutsch, Fralish
3. Bender
4. 1988
5. 1 vol.
6. $95 incl. 3 mos. supp.
7. annual supp.
8. 1989 - $45; 1990 - $53.50
9. 88-72055/19452819/RD521.D48

1. **INS AND OUTS OF FORECLOSURES**
2. Apker, Burton M., et al.
3. State Bar of Ariz.
4. 1990
5. 1 vol.
6. $75
7. annual supp.
8. no supp. yet
9. 89-62700/21931290/KFA2530.Y37

1. **INSIDER TRADING REGULATION**
2. Langevoort, Donald C.
3. Clark Boardman Callaghan
4. 1991
5. 1 vol.
6. $110 incl. 3 mos. supp.
7. annual supp.
8. no supp. yet
9. 23129374

1. **INSURANCE AND RISK MANAGEMENT FOR STATE AND LOCAL GOVERNMENTS**
2. Rynard, Thomas W.
3. Bender
4. 1991
5. 1 vol.
6. $100 incl. 3 mos. supp.
7. annual supp.
8. no supp. yet
9. 91-71604/24360048/KF1321.R92

1. **INSURANCE BAD FAITH LITIGATION**
2. Shernoff, William
3. Bender
4. 1984
5. 1 vol.
6. $125 incl. 3 mos. supp.
7. annual supp.
8. 1989 - $75; 1990 - $89
9. 84-70028/10689392/KF1301.5.I58S53

1. **INSURANCE COVERAGE FOR EMPLOYMENT CLAIMS**
2. -
3. Minn. CLE
4. 1991
5. 1 vol.
6. $50
7. no supp. planned
9. 23299577

1. **INSURANCE COVERAGE ISSUES RELATIVE TO NATURAL DISASTERS**

2. Maybank, Burnet R.
3. S. Carolina Bar
4. 1989
5. 1 vol.
6. $50
7. no supp. planned
9. 21067767/HG9979.M29

1. **INSURANCE LAW**
2. -
3. NH Bar
4. 1991
5. 1 vol.
6. $35
7. no supp. planned

1. **INSURANCE LAW**
2. -
3. Minn. CLE
4. 1990
5. 1 vol.
6. $50
7. no supp. planned

1. **INSURANCE LAW REPORTS - FIRE AND CASUALTY**
2. -
3. CCH
4. 1929
5. 1 vol.
6. $775/yr.; $705/yr. for 2 yrs.
7. semimonthly supp.
9. 78-1200/4079910

1. **INSURANCE LAW REPORTS - LIFE, HEALTH & ACCIDENT**
2. -
3. CCH
4. 1929
5. 1 vol.
6. $750/yr.; $680/yr. for 2 yrs.
7. monthly supp.
9. 9836920/KF1160.C6

1. **INSURANCE LAWS (FOR THE 50 U.S. STATES, THE DISTRICT OF COLUMBIA, PUERTO RICO, AND THE VIRGIN ISLANDS)**
2. -
3. NILS
4. NA
5. 1 or 2 vols. per state
6. $103 - $190 incl. 3 mos. supp.
7. periodic supp.
8. 1989 - $75; 1990 - $94

1. **INSURANCE REGULATIONS**
2. -
3. NILS
4. NA
5. 1 or 2 vols. per state
6. $103 (NY, 2 vols.-$145) incl. supp. for bal. of calendar yr.
7. periodic supp.
8. 1989 - $63; 1990 - $68

1. **INSURANCE RELATED REGULATIONS**
2. -
3. NILS
4. NA
5. 1 vol.
6. $50 - 75 incl. supp. for bal. of calendar yr.
7. periodic supp.
8. 1990 - $44

1. **INSURANCE SETTLEMENT HANDBOOK**
2. -
3. James
4. 1990
5. 1 vol.
6. $89.96 incl. 3 mos. supp.
7. annual supp.
8. no supp. yet
9. 91-116851/23177609/KF1164.I57

1. **INSURING REAL PROPERTY**
2. Cozen, S.
3. Bender
4. 1989
5. 3 vols.
6. $305 incl. 3 mos. supp.
7. annual supp.
8. 1990 - $60
9. 88-63745/19372085/KF1190.I57

1. **INTELLECTUAL PROPERTY AND ANTITRUST LAW**
2. Holmes, Wm. C.
3. Clark Boardman Callaghan
4. 1983
5. 1 vol.
6. $110 incl. 3 mos. supp.
7. annual supp.
8. 1989 - $90; 1991 - $110
9. 83-2600/9219294/KF3116.H64

1. **INTELLECTUAL PROPERTY AND COPYRIGHT LAW**
2. Astrachan, James B. et al.
3. MICPEL

4. 1991
5. 1 vol.
6. $26.25
7. no supp. planned

1. **INTELLECTUAL PROPERTY COUNSELING AND LITIGATION**
2. Horwitz, Lester & Ethan Horwitz
3. Bender
4. 1988
5. 5 vols.
6. $520 incl. 3 mos. supp.
7. annual supp.
8. 1989 - $84; 1990 - $351
9. 88-70318/12105399/KF2979.I57

1. **INTELLECTUAL PROPERTY LAW**
2. -
3. Indiana CLE
4. 1989
5. 1 vol.
6. $50
7. no supp. planned

1. **INTELLECTUAL PROPERTY LAW**
2. -
3. MILE
4. 1990
5. 1 vol.
6. $58
7. no supp. planned

1. **INTELLECTUAL PROPERTY LITIGATION**
2. -
3. Minn. CLE
4. 1991
5. 1 vol.
6. $45
7. no supp. planned
9. 23855602/KF2980.Z9I67

1. **INTELLECTUAL PROPERTY PROTECTION IN ASIA**
2. Wineburg, Arthur
3. Butterworth-NH
4. 1991
5. 1 vol.
6. $125
7. periodic supp.
8. no supp. yet
9. 91-7877/23144454

1. **INTERNAL REVENUE CODE & REGULATIONS**
2. RIA prof. editorial staff
3. RIA
4. 1991
5. 7 vols. (part of Federal Tax Coordinator 2nd)
6. $275/yr.; $250/yr. for 2 yrs.
7. biweekly supp.
8. renewal - $190/yr.
9. 24020983/KF6285.R533

1. **INTERNAL REVENUE CODE OF 1986 AS AMENDED**
2. -
3. RIA
4. NA
5. 2 vols.
6. $190/yr.; $165/yr. for 2 yrs.
7. quarterly supp.
8. renewal - $150/yr.
9. 54-4488/823494/KB81.P67

1. **INTERNAL REVENUE MANUAL: ABRIDGED & ANNOTATED**
2. Gates, Bryan
3. Clark Boardman Callaghan
4. 1991
5. 3 vols.
6. $295 incl. 1 yr. supp.
7. quarterly supp.

1. **INTERNAL REVENUE MANUAL - ADMINISTRATION**
2. -
3. CCH
4. 1977
5. 6 vols.
6. $460/yr.; $420/yr. for 2 yrs.
7. periodic supp.

1. **INTERNAL REVENUE MANUAL - AUDIT**
2. -
3. CCH
4. 1977
5. 3 vols.
6. $490/yr.; $445/yr. for 2 yrs.
7. periodic supp.
9. 2914384/KF6301.C73b

1. **INTERNAL REVENUE SERVICE**
2. -
3. MILE
4. 1990
5. 1 vol.
6. $58
7. no supp. planned

9. 20984500/KF6297.Z9I48

1. **INTERNATIONAL AGENCY AND DISTRIBUTION AGREEMENTS**
2. Clasen, Thomas F.
3. Butterworth-NH
4. 1991
5. 4 vols. - avail. separately
6. $425 set; $110 for Analysis & Forms Vol.; $115 ea. for the other 3 vols.
7. periodic supp.
8. no supp. yet
9. 90-20091/22597069/K1021.C553

1. **INTERNATIONAL BENEFITS INFORMATION SERVICE**
2. Spencer, Bruce F. et al., eds.
3. Spencer
4. 1969
5. 1 vol.
6. $690/yr. (Reference materials avail for countries at $150 each. Renewal - $75 each/yr.)
7. monthly supp.
9. 84-7969/5924699

1. **INTERNATIONAL BOYCOTTS**
2. Hancock, W.A.
3. Bus. Laws
4. 1978
5. 6 vols.
6. $345/yr.
7. quarterly supp.
9. 5213009

1. **INTERNATIONAL BUSINESS PLANNING: LAW AND TAXATION - UNITED STATES**
2. Streng, William P. & J.W. Salacuse
3. Bender
4. 1982
5. 6 vols.
6. $535 incl. 3 mos. supp.
7. periodic supp.
8. 1989 - $300; 1990 - $355.50
9. 81-71852/8888112/KF1976.S77

1. **INTERNATIONAL BUSINESS PORTFOLIOS**
2. -
3. Bender
4. 1988
5. 8 vols. (avail. separately at $105/ea.)
6. $380 incl. 3 mos. supp.
7. annual supp.
8. 1990 - $49.50

1. **INTERNATIONAL BUSINESS TRANSACTIONS**
2. Campbell, Dennis
3. Kluwer
4. 1989
5. 3 vols.
6. $313 incl. 3 mos. supp.
7. periodic supp.
8. 1990 - $213; 1991 - $200
9. 19996221/K3943.A23In8

1. **INTERNATIONAL CAPITAL MARKETS AND SECURITIES REGULATION (Securities Law Series, vol. 10, 10A. 10B & 10C)**
2. Bloomenthal, Harold S.
3. Clark Boardman Callaghan
4. 1982
5. 4 vols.
6. $435 incl. 3 mos. supp.
7. annual supp.
8. 1989 - $75; 1991 - $185
9. 82-12959/8669232/K1331.I55

1. **INTERNATIONAL COMMERCIAL ARBITRATION: CASES UNDER THE NEW YORK CONVENTION**
2. Gaja, Giorgio
3. Oceana
4. 1978
5. 3 vols.
6. $300
7. periodic supp.
8. 1989 - $95; 1990 - $95
9. 78-991/3722251/JX6607.G3

1. **INTERNATIONAL COMMERCIAL ARBITRATION: COMMERCIAL ARBITRATION LAW IN ASIA AND THE PACIFIC**
2. Simmonds, Kenneth R. & Brian H.W. Hill
3. Oceana
4. 1989
5. 1 vol.
6. $125
7. periodic supp.
8. 1987 - $125; 1990 - $125
9. 87-23270/16645303/K2400.C66

1. **INTERNATIONAL COMMERCIAL ARBITRATION – INTER-AMERICAN COMMERCIAL ARBITRATION**
2. Norberg, Charles R.
3. Oceana
4. 1988

5. 1 vol.
6. price not set
7. annual supp. projected
9. 18395620

1. **INTERNATIONAL COMMERCIAL ARBITRATION – INTERNATIONAL CHAMBER OF COMMERCE ARBITRATION**
2. Craig, W. Lawrence, et al.
3. Oceana
4. 1984
5. 2 vols.
6. $300
7. periodic supp.
8. 1986 - $100; 1990-91 - $175
9. 84-7465/10751709/K2400.C725

1. **INTERNATIONAL COMMERCIAL ARBITRATION – SOVIET COMMERCIAL AND MARITIME ARBITRATION**
2. Butler, William E.
3. Oceana
4. 1980
5. 1 vol. included in INTERNATIONAL COMMERCIAL ARBITRATION
6. $125
7. periodic supp.
8. 1989 - $95
9. 80-10606/6016205

1. **INTERNATIONAL COMPUTER LAW**
2. Keustermans, Jozef A. et al.
3. Bender
4. 1988
5. 1 vol.
6. $105 incl. 3 mos. supp.
7. annual supp.
8. 1989 - $35; 1990 - $90
9. 88-70942/18908089/K564.C6K48

1. **INTERNATIONAL COPYRIGHT LAW AND PRACTICE**
2. Nimmer, M. & P. Geller
3. Bender
4. 1988
5. 2 vols.
6. $210 incl. 3 mos. supp.
7. annual supp.
8. 1989 - $50; 1990 - $125
9. 88-70402/17887949/K1420.5I5

1. **INTERNATIONAL COURT OF JUSTICE OPINION BRIEFS**
2. International Law Section
3. ABA
4. 1978
5. 1 vol.
6. $15
7. no supp. yet
8. -
9. 78-56268/11092307/JX1971.6.I57

1. **INTERNATIONAL ENCYCLOPEDIA FOR LABOUR LAW AND INDUSTRIAL RELATIONS**
2. Blanpain, R., ed.
3. Kluwer
4. 1977
5. 18 vols.
6. $2626 incl. 3 mos. supp.
7. periodic supp.
8. 1990 - $1000; 1991 - $1000
9. 78-313934/3419153/K1705.I5

1. **INTERNATIONAL ENVIRONMENT REPORTER**
2. Allen, Marlon B.
3. BNA
4. 1978
5. 4 vols.
6. $1405/yr.
7. monthly supp.
8. renewal - $1295/yr.
9. 79-114492/5407507/K3585.4.I57

1. **INTERNATIONAL ESTATE PLANNING**
2. Newton, William H., III
3. Shepard's
4. 1986
5. 2 vols.
6. $195
7. annual supp.
8. 1990 - $68; 1991 - $72
9. 80-28413//r872/7172909/KF6584.N48

1. **INTERNATIONAL EXPORTING AGREEMENTS**
2. Ezer, Shaul
3. Bender
4. 1985
5. 1 vol.
6. $105 incl. 3 mos. supp.
7. periodic supp.
8. 1989 - $24; 1990 - $53.50
9. 85-72292/13259920/K3950.E93

1. **INTERNATIONAL EXTRADITION: U.S. LAW AND PRACTICE**
2. Bassiouni, M. Cherif
3. Oceana

4. 2nd rev. ed. - 1987
5. 2 vols.
6. $200
7. periodic supp.
9. 82-22373

1. **INTERNATIONAL HANDBOOK ON COMMERCIAL ARBITRATION – NATIONAL REPORTS AND BASIC LEGAL TEXTS**
2. van den Berg, J.
3. Kluwer
4. 1984
5. 3 vols.
6. $274 incl. 3 mos. supp.
7. periodic supp.
8. 1990 - $140; 1991 - $94
9. 84-3908/10483165/K2400.I594

1. **INTERNATIONAL HANDBOOK ON CONTRACTS OF EMPLOYMENT**
2. Bradley, John S.
3. Kluwer
4. 1988
5. 1 vol.
6. $184 incl. 3 mos. supp.
7. periodic supp.
8. 1990 - $137; 1991 - $150
9. 88-13583/18417375/K1765.I53

1. **INTERNATIONAL HUMAN RIGHTS INSTRUMENTS**
2. Lillich, Richard B.
3. Hein
4. 1991
5. 1 vol.
6. $95
7. biennial supp.
8. no supp. yet
9. 82-82582/8930810/K3238.A1I536

1. **INTERNATIONAL INCOME TAX RULES OF THE UNITED STATES**
2. McIntyre, Michael J.
3. Butterworth-NH
4. 1989
5. 2 vols.
6. $195; student ed. - $48
7. periodic supp.
8. 1990 - $55
9. 88-24210/18350948/KF6306.M35

1. **INTERNATIONAL JUDICIAL ASSISTANCE (CIVIL AND COMMERCIAL)**
2. Ristau, Bruno A.
3. Intl. Law Inst.
4. 1984
5. 2 vols.
6. $220 incl. 6 mos. supp.
7. biennial supp.
8. 1988 - $35; 1990 - $50
9. 84-63137/12033446/K7624.R57

1. **INTERNATIONAL JUDICIAL ASSISTANCE (CRIMINAL)**
2. Ristau, Bruno A. & Michael Abell
3. Intl. Law Inst.
4. 1990
5. 4 vols.
6. $440 incl. 6 mos. supp.
7. annual supp.
8. no supp. yet
9. 23366485/K7624.I57

1. **INTERNATIONAL LAW**
2. -
3. Indiana CLE
4. 1991
5. 1 vol.
6. $35
7. no supp. planned

1. **INTERNATIONAL LOAN WORKOUTS AND BANKRUPTCIES**
2. Gitlin, Richard A. and Rona R. Mears, eds.
3. Butterworth-NH
4. 1989
5. 2 vols.
6. $160
7. periodic supp.
8. no supp. yet
9. 88-7508/18560576/K1370.I56

1. **INTERNATIONAL OFFSHORE FINANCIAL CENTRES**
2. -
3. CCH
4. 1989
5. 1 vol.
6. $330/yr.; $300/yr. for 2 yrs.
7. quarterly supp.

1. **INTERNATIONAL PATENT LITIGATION: A COUNTRY-BY-COUNTRY ANALYSIS**
2. Meller, Michael N., ed.
3. BNA Books
4. 1983
5. 1 vol.

6. $195
7. $90/supp.
9. 83-8013/9672008

1. **INTERNATIONAL PERSONAL TAX PLANNING ENCYCLOPEDIA**
2. Lawrence, R.C., Cadwalader, Wickersham & Taft, ed.
3. Butterworth-NH
4. 1990
5. 2 vols.
6. $175/set
7. periodic supp.
8. no supp. yet
9. gb90-20211/21292378

1. **INTERNATIONAL PROTECTION OF THE ENVIRONMENT: TREATIES AND RELATED DOCUMENTS 2d Series**
2. Ruster, Bernd & Bruno Simma
3. Oceana
4. 1989
5. 3 vols.
6. $375
7. 1991 - $135
9. 75-24843/1739124/K3585.4.I575

1. **INTERNATIONAL RESOURCES LAW: A BLUEPRINT FOR MINERAL DEVELOPMENT**
2. -
3. Rocky Mt.
4. 1991
5. 1 vol.
6. $125
7. no supp. planned
9. 24356016/K3478.A55I57

1. **INTERNATIONAL SECURITIES REGULATION**
2. Rosen, Robert C., ed.
3. Oceana
4. 1987
5. 3 vols.
6. $375
7. periodic supp.
8. 1990 - $125; 1991 - $125
9. 86-12602//r892/13670366/K1331.I558

1. **INTERNATIONAL TAX GUIDE: U.S. INCOME TAXATION**
2. Cooper, John & Richard Gershon
3. Clark Boardman Callaghan
4. 1991
5. 1 vol.
6. $95 incl. 6 mos. supp.
7. annual supp.
8. no supp. yet
9. 91-3915/23771295/KF6445.C66

1. **INTERNATIONAL TAX PLANNING MANUAL**
2. -
3. CCH
4. 1986
5. 2 vols.
6. $535/yr.; $485/yr. for 2 yrs.
7. quarterly supp.
9. 13470428/K4464.In7

1. **INTERNATIONAL TELECOMMUNICATIONS AGREEMENTS**
2. Wallenstein, Gerd D.
3. Oceana
4. 1977
5. 3 vols.
6. $300
7. periodic supp.
8. 1985 - $100; 1986 - $100
9. 77-72058/3162177/K4305.4.W34

1. **INTERNATIONAL TRADE PRACTICE**
2. Kaye, Hertzberg and Plaia
3. Shepard's
4. 1981
5. 2 vols.
6. $195
7. annual supp.
8. 1986 - $48; 1987 - $52
9. 80-39860/7172389/KF6659.K39

1. **INTERNATIONAL TRADE REPORTER CURRENT REPORTS**
2. Botsford, Linda G.
3. BNA
4. 1947
5. 2 vol.
6. $860/yr.
7. weekly supp.
8. renewal - $760/yr.
9. 84-647805/10882565/HF3000.I57

1. **INTERNATIONAL TRADE REPORTER DECISIONS**
2. Botsford, Linda G.
3. BNA
4. 1980
5. 2 vols.
6. $880/yr.

7. bimonthly supp.
8. renewal - $760/yr.
9. 84-6242/10881494

1. **INTERNATIONAL TRADE REPORTER EXPORT REFERENCE MANUAL**
2. Botsford, Linda G.
3. BNA
4. 1947
5. 3 vols.
6. $550/yr.
7. weekly supp.
8. renewal - $530/yr.
9. 89-7389/19488497

1. **INTERNATIONAL TRADE REPORTER IMPORT REFERENCE MANUAL**
2. Botsford, Linda G.
3. BNA
4. 1984
5. 2 vols.
6. $880/yr.
7. bimonthly supp.
8. renewal - $760/yr.
9. SN89-7399/19488427

1. **INTERNATIONAL TRANSACTIONS**
2. -
3. Florida Bar
4. 1988
5. 1 vol.
6. $80
7. supp. as needed
8. no supp. yet
9. 88-81566/20828307/KFF230.I58

1. **INTERNATIONAL TRANSPORT TREATIES**
2. Claringbould, M.H., ed.
3. Kluwer
4. 1986
5. 1 vol.
6. $261 incl. 3 mos. supp.
7. periodic supp.
8. 1990 - $80; 1991 - $75

1. **INTERNATIONAL WITHHOLDING TAX TREATY GUIDE**
2. Diamond, Walter H.
3. Bender
4. 1974
5. 1 vol.
6. $150/yr.
7. quarterly supp.
9. 74-77413/5224240/HJ3233.D5

1. **INTERPRETATION HANDBOOK**
2. -
3. NYSE
4. 1979
5. 3 vols.
6. $300/yr.
7. periodic supp. (usually 50/yr.) & "Information Memorandum" newsletter
9. 79-128429/6040821/KF1074.N3N48

1. **INTERROGATORIES, DOCUMENTS AND ADMISSIONS**
2. Young, John Hardin
3. Butterworth-NH
4. 1989
5. 1 vol.
6. $70
7. periodic supp.
8. 1991 - $25
9. 89-202846//r90/2041672/KF8900.Y68

1. **INTERSTATE COMMERCE COMMISSION - RULES OF PRACTICE**
2. -
3. Rules
4. 1977
5. 2 vols.
6. $72 incl. 1 yr. supp.
7. periodic supp.
8. renewal fee

1. **INTERSTATE COMMERCE GUIDE**
2. -
3. Keller
4. 1982
5. 1 vol.
6. $125
7. semiannual supp.
8. $97/yr.
9. 81-86201/8806786/KF2167

1. **INTERSTATE MOTOR CARRIER FORMS MANUAL**
2. -
3. Keller
4. 1976
5. 1 vol.
6. $95
7. semiannual supp.
8. renewal - $80/yr.
9. 76-7194/2346029/KF2254.K43

1. **INTRODUCING EVIDENCE: A PRACTICAL GUIDE FOR MICHIGAN LAWYERS**

2. Robinson, James K. and Lynn M. Collins, eds.
3. ICLE - Michigan
4. 1988
5. 1 vol.
6. $70
7. periodic supp.
8. 1990 - $30; 1991 - $35
9. 88-81316/18126345/KFM4740.A75I5

1. **INTRODUCTION TO BANKRUPTCY**
2. -
3. Ohio CLE
4. 1990
5. 1 vol.
6. $45
7. no supp. planned

1. **INTRODUCTION TO CONNECTICUT ENVIRONMENTAL LAW**
2. Conservation & Environmental Quality Section
3. Conn. Bar
4. 1989
5. 1 vol.
6. $20
7. no supp. planned
9. 20450056/KFC3956.A75S45

1. **INTRODUCTION TO CONNECTICUT ENVIRONMENTAL LAW - PART I: POLLUTION CONTROL**
2. Conservation & Environmental Quality Section
3. Conn. Bar
4. 1988
5. 1 vol.
6. $10
7. no supp. planned

1. **INVESTIGATING EMPLOYEE CONDUCT**
2. Hartsfield, William
3. Clark Boardman Callaghan
4. 1988
5. 1 vol.
6. $95 incl. 6 mos. supp.
7. annual supp.
8. 1989 - $30; 1990 - $35
9. 88-26200/18412453/KF3319.H37

1. **INVESTING, LICENSING AND TRADING CONDITIONS ABROAD (ILT)**
2. -
3. Bus. Intern.
4. 1955
5. 3 vols.
6. $1695/yr. (avail. also in separate area editions)
7. monthly supp.
9. 2256543

1. **INVESTMENT ADVISERS GUIDE**
2. -
3. ICI
4. 1984
5. 2 vols.
6. $500 incl. 1 yr. supp.
7. semiannual supp.
8. renewal - $200/yr.
9. 11353571

1. **INVESTMENT LAWS OF THE WORLD: THE DEVELOPING NATIONS**
2. ICSID
3. Oceana
4. 1973
5. 13 vols.
6. $1050
7. periodic supp.
8. 1990 - $110; 1991 - $125
9. 77-72048/3214815

1. **INVESTMENT LIMITED PARTNERSHIPS AND OTHER PASS-THROUGH VEHICLES (Securities Law Series, Vols. 4, 4A, 4B, 4C)**
2. Haft, Robert J. & Peter M. Fass
3. Clark Boardman Callaghan
4. rev, ed, - 1981
5. 5 vols. & newsletter binder
6. $595 incl. 1 yr. supp.
7. biannual supp. & newsletter & annual handbook
8. 1989 - $325; 1991 - $478
9. 81-6179/7552236/KF6415.H3

1. **INVESTMENT PROMOTION AND PROTECTION TREATIES**
2. ICSID
3. Oceana
4. 1983
5. 3 vols.
6. $300
7. periodic supp.
8. 1987 - $100; 1990 - $110
9. 9482559

1. **IOWA ATTORNEY'S/SECRETARY'S HANDBOOK**
2. -

3. Mariposa
4. 1991
5. 1 vol.
6. $51
7. annual supp.
8. 1990 - $49; 1991 - $42
9. 20476903/KFI4277.I68

1. **IOWA BANKRUPTCY**
2. Oppold, Robert S.
3. Butterworth-St. Paul
4. 1984
5. 1 vol.
6. $55
7. periodic supp.
8. 1990 - $50; 1991 - $45
9. 84-199941/11344490/KFI4421.O67

1. **IOWA CIVIL JURY INSTRUCTIONS**
2. -
3. Iowa Bar
4. 1987
5. 2 vols.
6. $65
7. semiannual supp.
8. 1990 - $13.50; 1991 - $15

1. **IOWA FAMILY LAW MANUAL**
2. -
3. Iowa Bar
4. 1988
5. 2 vols.
6. $67.50
7. periodic supp.
8. 1989 - $6

1. **IOWA LAND TITLE EXAMINATION STANDARDS**
2. -
3. Iowa Bar
4. 1985
5. 1 vol.
6. $12
7. periodic supp.
8. 1991 - $4
9. 5236086

1. **IOWA LEGAL FORMS – COMMERCIAL REAL ESTATE**
2. Dietz, Dennis A.
3. Butterworth-St. Paul
4. 1983
5. 1 vol.
6. $50; $85 with disk
7. periodic supp.
8. 1990 - $30
9. 84-151719/11210624/KFI4317.3.A65D54

1. **IOWA LEGAL FORMS – CORPORATIONS**
2. Field, Hugh M.
3. Butterworth-St. Paul
4. 1982
5. 1 vol.
6. $50; $85 with disk
7. periodic supp.
8. 1988 - $34; 1990 - $26
9. 83-131753/9169240/KFI4413.A65F53

1. **IOWA LEGAL FORMS – CREDITORS' REMEDIES**
2. Kelly, Edwin F.
3. Butterworth-St. Paul
4. 1983
5. 1 vol.
6. $50; $85 with disk
7. periodic supp.
8. 1986 - $15; 1990 - $25
9. 83-183548/10432246/KFI4420.A65K44

1. **IOWA LEGAL FORMS – CRIMINAL LAW**
2. Berger, Peter W. & Kermit L. Dunahoo
3. Butterworth-St. Paul
4. 1983
5. 1 vol.
6. $50; $85 with disk
7. periodic supp.
8. 1986 - $20; 1990 - $22
9. 84-109719/10697127/KFI4761.A65B47

1. **IOWA LEGAL FORMS – FAMILY LAW**
2. Parsons, Terry Diane
3. Butterworth-St. Paul
4. 1984
5. 1 vol.
6. $50; $85 with disk
7. periodic supp.
8. 1986 - $15; 1990 - $25
9. 85-132355/12105807/KFI4294.A65P37

1. **IOWA LEGAL FORMS – PERSONAL INJURY**
2. Kirk, Max E.
3. Butterworth-St. Paul
4. 1983
5. 1 vol.
6. $50; $85 with disk

7. periodic supp.
8. 1988 - $15; 1989 - $20
9. 84-109730/10697128/KFI4397.P3K57

1. **IOWA LEGAL FORMS – PROBATE**
2. Lawler, Thomas A.
3. Butterworth-St. Paul
4. 1984
5. 1 vol.
6. $50; $85 with disk
7. periodic supp.
8. 1988 - $20; 1989 - $22
9. 84-201787/11370230/KFI4344.A65L39

1. **IOWA LEGAL FORMS – RESIDENTIAL REAL ESTATE**
2. Dunakey, David D.
3. Butterworth-St. Paul
4. 1982
5. 1 vol.
6. $50; $85 with disk
7. periodic supp.
8. 1988 - $15

1. **IOWA LEGAL FORMS – WORKERS' COMPENSATION**
2. Hanssen, Dennis L.
3. Butterworth-St. Paul
4. 1983
5. 1 vol.
6. $50; $85 with disk
7. periodic supp.
8. 1986 - $18; 1988 - $25
9. 84-151740/10029008/KFI4542.H36

1. **IOWA LIMITATIONS MANUAL, 2ND ED.**
2. Publ. Ed. Staff
3. Butterworth-St. Paul
4. 1989
5. 1 vol.
6. $50
7. periodic supp.
8. 1990 - $35; 1991 - $40
9. 82-150480/8929924/KFI4290.L5M38

1. **IOWA MATRIMONIAL LAW**
2. Bray, Daniel L.
3. Butterworth-St. Paul
4. 1986
5. 1 vol.
6. $88
7. periodic supp.
8. 1989 - $55; 1991 - $40
9. 14204751/KFI4295.B7

1. **IOWA PLEADING AND CAUSES OF ACTION**
2. LaMarca, George A.
3. Butterworth-St. Paul
4. 1989
5. 2 vols.
6. $160
7. periodic supp.
8. no supp. yet
9. 88-35916/19064095/KFI4735.L36

1. **IOWA PRACTICE**
2. Vestal, Allan D. & Philip Willson
3. Lawyers Coop.
4. 1984
5. 2 vols.
6. $175 incl. 6 mos. supp.
7. annual supp.
8. 1990 - $77; 1991 - $71.50
9. 83-23969/10146009/KFI4730.V47

1. **IOWA PROBATE MANUAL**
2. -
3. Iowa Bar
4. 1986
5. 2 vols.
6. $145
7. periodic supp.
8. 1990 - $72.50

1. **IOWA REAL ESTATE MANUAL**
2. -
3. Iowa Bar
4. 1990
5. 2 vols.
6. $87.50
7. no supp. yet

1. **IOWA UNIFORM JURY INSTRUCTIONS - CRIMINAL**
2. -
3. Iowa Bar
4. 1988
5. 2 vols.
6. $65
7. semiannual supp.
8. 1990 - $10.50; 1991 - $15

1. **IRA COMPLIANCE MANUAL**
2. -
3. RIA
4. 1982
5. 2 vols.
6. $300/yr.; $275/yr. for 2 yrs.

7. monthly supp.
8. renewal - $250/yr.
9. 82-2910/8337355

1. **IRAs, SEPs AND SELF-EMPLOYED PLANS COMPLIANCE GUIDE**
2. Scudere, Carmine
3. Bender
4. 1986
5. 2 vols.
6. $220 incl. 1 yr. supp.
7. quarterly supp.

1. **IRS LETTER RULINGS**
2. -
3. CCH
4. 1977
5. 1 vol.
6. $1185/yr.; $1075/yr. for 2 yrs.
7. weekly supp.
9. 77-642257/3270137/KF6282.A2C65

1. **IRS POSITIONS**
2. -
3. CCH
4. 1982
5. 1 vol.
6. $490/yr.; $445/yr. for 2 yrs.
7. weekly supp.
9. 8983989/KF6300.A83

1. **IRS PRACTICE AND PROCEDURES TAX PACKAGE**
2. Davis, La Vaughn T.
3. Stephens
4. 1977
5. 1 vol.
6. $155/yr.
7. monthly newsletter and IRS Directory

1. **IRS PUBLICATIONS**
2. -
3. CCH
4. 1977
5. 3 vols.
6. $275/yr.; $250/yr. for 2 yrs.
7. periodic supp.
9. 2981431/KF6289.A1C65

1. **ISSUES ON ENVIRONMENTAL LAW**
2. Gibbs, Meredith E.
3. MICPEL
4. 1991
5. 1 vol.
6. $40
7. no supp. yet
9. 22104896/KFM1554.I86

1. **THE ITALIAN CIVIL CODE AND COMPLEMENTARY LEGISLATION**
2. Beltramo, Mario et al.
3. Oceana
4. 1991
5. 2 vols.
6. $250
7. periodic supp.
8. no supp. yet
9. 91-7912/23144612/KKH494.31942.A52

1. **IT'S THE LAW: WHAT NONPROFITS NEED TO KNOW**
2. -
3. HICLE
4. 1990
5. 1 vol.
6. $15
7. no supp. yet

1. **JAPANESE INTERNATIONAL TAXATION**
2. Huston, John et al.
3. Bender
4. 1983
5. 1 vol.
6. $130 incl. 3 mos. supp.
7. periodic supp.
8. 1989 - $75; 1990 - $93
9. 82-72215/9539459

1. **JOB SAFETY AND HEALTH**
2. Joseph, Eileen Z.
3. BNA
4. 1977
5. 1 vol.
6. $528/yr.
7. biweekly supp. & bulletin
8. renewal - $475/yr.
9. 78-147/3547682

1. **JOINT VENTURES**
2. MacLaren, Terrence F. and Walter G. Marple, Jr.
3. Clark Boardman Callaghan
4. 1985
5. 2 vols.
6. $215 incl. 3 mos. supp.
7. annual supp.
8. 1989 - $132.50; 1991 - $159
9. 85-10934/12082762/K1309.M33

1. **JOINT VENTURES: STRUCTURING ALTERNATIVES**
2. Nachmias, Carolyn S. & James F. Nasuti
3. Shepard's
4. 1988
5. 1 vol.
6. $95
7. annual supp.
8. 1990 - $24; 1991 - $28
9. 88-33673/18835084/KF6452.N33

1. **JOINT VENTURES WITH INTERNATIONAL PARTNERS**
2. Dobkin, James A. and Jeffrey A. Burt
3. Butterworth-NH
4. 1989
5. 1 vol.
6. $105
7. annual supp.
8. 1991 - $45
9. 89-32640/19626408/K1309.J63

1. **JOINT VENTURES WITH THE SOVIET UNION**
2. Osakwe, Christopher
3. Butterworth-NH
4. 1990
5. 1 vol.
6. $125
7. annual supp.
8. no supp. yet
9. 89-70886/20800007

1. **JUDGES CRIMINAL BENCHBOOK**
2. -
3. Minn. CLE
4. 1988
5. 1 vol.
6. $75
7. no supp. planned

1. **JUDICIAL PROFILES**
2. -
3. LADJ
4. NA
5. 6 vols.
6. $190/yr.
7. quarterly supp.
9. 5308503/KFC980.L6

1. **THE JUDICIAL RESPONSE TO LAWYER MISCONDUCT**
2. Center for Professional Responsibility
3. ABA
4. 1989
5. 1 vol.
6. $19.95
7. no supp. planned
9. 84-177336/11290996/KF308.J83

1. **JURISDICTION AND FORUM SELECTION**
2. Casad, Robert
3. Clark Boardman Callaghan
4. 1988
5. 1 vol.
6. $125 incl. 6 mos. supp.
7. annual supp.
8. 1989 - $29; 1990 - $32
9. 88-23758/18351056/KF8858.C327

1. **JURISDICTION AND SUMMONS IN OREGON**
2. Merrill, Fredric R.
3. Butterworth-St. Paul
4. 1986
5. 1 vol.
6. $45
7. periodic supp.
8. no supp. yet
9. 86-70783/15550138/KFO2932.M47

1. **JUROR MISCONDUCT**
2. Hardwick, Lillian B. & B. Lee Ware
3. Clark Boardman Callaghan
4. 1988
5. 1 vol.
6. $110 incl. 3 mos. supp.
7. annual supp.
8. 1989 - $39.50; 1991 - $49.50
9. 88-26261/18413598/KF8972.H29

1. **JURY INSTRUCTIONS (Art of Advocacy Series)**
2. Baldwin, Scott, et al.
3. Bender
4. 1989
5. 1 vol.
6. $110 incl. 3 mos. supp.
7. annual supp.
8. 1990 - $64
9. 89-85664/20727131/KF8984.B182

1. **JURY INSTRUCTIONS IN CRIMINAL ANTITRUST CASES 1964-1976**
2. Section of Antitrust Law
3. ABA
4. 1978
5. 1 vol.
6. $20

7. periodic supp.
8. 1982 - $35
9. 77-94398/3695836/KF1657.C7A47

1. **JURY INSTRUCTIONS IN INTELLECTUAL PROPERTY CASES**
2. Burton, Duane
3. Big Foot
4. 1980
5. 2 vols.
6. $498
7. annual supp.
8. 1990 - $99.50; 1991 - price NA
9. 80-126501/6326745/KF8984.A67B87

1. **JURY SELECTION (Art of Advocacy Series)**
2. Wagner, Ward, Jr.
3. Bender
4. 1981
5. 1 vol.
6. $110 incl. 3 mos. supp.
7. annual supp.
8. 1989 - $64; 1990 - $73
9. 10971918/KF8979.Z9J87

1. **JURY SELECTION: STRATEGY AND SCIENCE**
2. Blue, Lisa & Jane N. Saginaw
3. Clark Boardman Callaghan
4. 1980
5. 1 vol.
6. $95 incl. 6 mos. supp.
7. annual supp.
8. 1989 - $25; 1990 - $25
9. 86-26855/14519445/KF8978.B57

1. **JURY TRIAL MANUAL FOR CRIMINAL OFFENSES TRIED IN THE DISTRICT COURT**
2. District Court Dept. of the Trial Court Committee on Juries of Six
3. Mass. CLE
4. 4th ed. - 1987
5. 1 vol.
6. $50
7. no supp. planned
9. 17371535

1. **JURYWORK - SYSTEMATIC TECHNIQUES**
2. National Jury Project
3. Clark Boardman Callaghan
4. 2nd ed. - 1983
5. 2 vols.
6. $195 incl. 3 mos. supp.
7. annual supp.
8. 1989 - $95; 1990 - $79.50
9. 82-22635/9018988/KF9680.J875

1. **JUVENILE COURT HANDBOOK FOR MINNESOTA**
2. Walling, Wright S.
3. Butterworth-St. Paul
4. 1984
5. 1 vol.
6. $65
7. periodic supp.
8. no supp. yet
9. 85-110261/11969504/KFM5996.W35

1. **JUVENILE JUSTICE PROCEDURES MANUAL**
2. -
3. ABICLE
4. 1991
5. 2 vols.
6. $85
7. no supp. planned

1. **JUVENILE LAW**
2. -
3. MoBar
4. 1985
5. 1 vol.
6. $55
7. periodic supp.
8. 1988 - $20

1. **JUVENILE LAW**
2. -
3. NH Bar
4. 1990
5. 1 vol.
6. $35
7. no supp. planned
9. 13387426/KFN1786.A75N34

1. **JUVENILE LAW**
2. Welch, Donald, eds.
3. Oregon Bar
4. 1970
5. 1 vol.
6. $110
7. periodic supp.
8. 1988 - $40
9. 84-61883/11338332/KFO2996.J88

1. **JUVENILE LAW AND PRACTICE IN THE DISTRICT OF COLUMBIA**
2. Mlyniec, Wallace & John Copacino
3. D.C. Bar

4. 1988
5. 1 vol.
6. $25.50
7. periodic supp.
8. no supp. yet
9. 89-139499/18917568/KFD596.M59

1. **KANSAS ADMINISTRATIVE LAW WITH FEDERAL REFERENCES**
2. Ryan, David L.
3. Kansas Bar
4. rev. 1991
5. 1 vol.
6. $100
7. periodic supp.
8. -
9. 82-84313/9269847/KFK440.R9

1. **KANSAS APPELLATE PRACTICE**
2. Harman, Hon. Jerome, ed.
3. Kansas Bar
4. rev. - 1984
5. 1 vol.
6. $35
7. no supp. yet
9. 4836783/KFK555.A6K35

1. **KANSAS BANKRUPTCY HANDBOOK**
2. Pearson, John K., est al., eds.
3. Kansas Bar
4. 1986
5. 1 vol.
6. $195
7. periodic supp.
8. 1990 - $110
9. 16123749/KFK221.K36

1. **KANSAS CODE OF CIVIL PROCEDURE 2D ANNOTATED**
2. Gard, Spencer A.
3. Bancroft
4. 1979
5. 2 vols.
6. $150 incl. 6 mos. supp.
7. annual supp.
8. 1989 - $30; 1991 - $34
9. 79-53496/6040363/KFK528.A313G37

1. **KANSAS CORPORATION LAW AND PRACTICE**
2. Logan, James K. & Alson R. Martin
3. Kansas Bar
4. 3rd ed. - 1988
5. 2 vols.
6. $225
7. periodic supp.
9. 88-82764/19047985/KFK213.L63

1. **KANSAS CRIMINAL LAW HANDBOOK**
2. Barbara, Michael A.
3. Kansas Bar
4. 1987
5. 1 vol.
6. $105
7. periodic supp.
8. no supp. yet
9. 16004997/KFK575.Z9B24

1. **KANSAS EMPLOYMENT LAW**
2. Schroeder, E.P.
3. Kansas Bar
4. 1991
5. 1 vol.
6. $150
7. biennial supp.
8. no supp. yet

1. **KANSAS ESTATE ADMINISTRATION**
2. Logan, James K., ed.
3. Kansas Bar
4. 5th ed. - 1986
5. 1 vol.
6. $115
7. periodic supp.
8. to be supp. in 1992
9. 15246173/KFK147.K35

1. **KANSAS EVIDENCE OBJECTIONS WITH EVIDENTIARY FOUNDATIONS**
2. Barbara, Michael A.
3. Kansas Bar
4. 1981; rev. - 1988
5. 1 vol.
6. $75
7. periodic supp.
8. 1988 - $35; to be supp. in 1992
9. 81-80684/7836458/KFK540.B37

1. **KANSAS FAMILY LAW HANDBOOK**
2. Elrod, Linda Henry
3. Kansas Bar
4. rev. - 1990
5. 2 vols.
6. $215
7. periodic supp.
8. 1990 - $48.50 (forms book)
9. 83-80643/10210775/KFK95.E47

1. **KANSAS LAW OF SALES UNDER THE UNIFORM COMMERCIAL CODE**

2. Rasor, Paul B. & Anne Baker
3. Kansas Bar
4. 1981
5. 1 vol.
6. $100
7. periodic supp.
8. 1989 - $85
9. 81-84870/8156151/KFK156.R37

1. **KANSAS LOCAL GOVERNMENT LAW**
2. -
3. Kansas Bar
4. 1991
5. 1 vol.
6. $100
7. periodic supp.
8. no supp. yet

1. **KANSAS OIL & GAS HANDBOOK, VOL. I**
2. Pierce, David E.
3. Kansas Bar
4. 1986
5. 1 vol.
6. $100
7. periodic supp.
8. no supp. yet
9. 14176672/KFK258.A1P5

1. **KANSAS OIL AND GAS HANDBOOK VOL. II**
2. Pierce, David E.
3. Kansas Bar
4. 1989
5. 1 vol.
6. $115
7. periodic supp.
8. no supp. yet
9. 88-82765/20479961/KFK258.A1K35

1. **KANSAS PERSONAL PROPERTY SECURED TRANSACTIONS**
2. Pearson, Hon. John K.
3. Kansas Bar
4. 1988
5. 1 vol.
6. $90
7. periodic supp.
8. no supp. yet
9. 88-82763/19290376/KFK175.P4

1. **KANSAS REAL ESTATE PRACTICE AND PROCEDURE HANDBOOK**
2. Circo, Heaven, & Goodall, ed.
3. Kansas Bar
4. rev. - 1989
5. 1 vol.
6. $175
7. periodic supp.
8. 1990 - $100
9. 8439173/KFK112.K36

1. **KANSAS STATUTE OF LIMITATIONS AND TIME STANDARDS**
2. McNeil, Chris
3. Kansas Bar
4. 1990
5. 1 vol.
6. $125
7. periodic supp.
8. no supp. yet
9. 22602677/KFK90.T5M36

1. **KANSAS TITLE STANDARDS HANDBOOK**
2. Snapp, Harvey J. & KBA Title Standards Comm.
3. Kansas Bar
4. rev. - 1990
5. 1 vol.
6. $75
7. periodic supp.
8. 1991 - free
9. 23355862/KFK127.K3

1. **KANSAS WORKERS' COMPENSATION PRACTICE MANUAL**
2. King, Shoaf & Hammond, eds.
3. Kansas Bar
4. 1978, rev. - 1990
5. 1 vol.
6. $150
7. periodic supp.
8. 1988 - $10
9. 4836753/KFK342.A6K35

1. **KENOE ON LAND TRUSTS**
2. -
3. Illinois ICLE
4. 1989
5. 1 vol.
6. $91.95
7. periodic supp.
8. no supp. yet
9. 7827574/KFI1339.L3K42

1. **KENTUCKY APPELLATE HANDBOOK**
2. Kentucky Bar Fdtn.
3. Banks

4. 1985
5. 1 vol.
6. $60 incl. 9 mos. supp.
7. periodic supp.
8. 1989 - $21
9. 85-187626/12663313/KFK1755.K46

1. **KENTUCKY COLLECTIONS**
2. Mapother, William R.
3. Lawyers Coop.
4. 1981
5. 1 vol.
6. $115 incl. 6 mos. supp.
7. annual supp.
8. 1990 - $51.50; 1991 - $55
9. 79-91144/8148787/KFK1367.C6M36

1. **KENTUCKY COURT RULES**
2. -
3. Rules
4. 1979
5. 1 vol.
6. $45 incl. 1 yr. supp.
7. periodic supp.
8. renewal fee
9. 79-119069/5989796/KFK1729.A2

1. **KENTUCKY DIVORCE**
2. Revell, Richard A. & Alan T. Slyn
3. Lawyers Coop.
4. 1982
5. 1 vol.
6. $115 incl. 6 mos. supp.
7. annual supp.
8. 1990 - $52; 1991 - $60
9. 79-91145/8624447/KFK1300.R48

1. **KENTUCKY DOMESTIC RELATIONS LAW**
2. Graham, Prof. Louise E. & James E. Keller
3. Banks
4. 1988
5. 1 vol.
6. $110 incl. 9 mos. supp.
7. annual supp.
8. 1990 - $27
9. 18562637/KFK1294.G73

1. **KENTUCKY FINANCIAL INSTITUTION AND SECURITIES LAW**
2. -
3. Banks
4. 1983
5. 1 vol.
6. $85 incl. 9 mos. supp.
7. biennial supp.
8. 1989 - $35
9. 76-352591/2048444/KFK1365.A3

1. **KENTUCKY FORMS & TRANSACTIONS**
2. Wyatt, Tarrant & Combs
3. Banks Baldwin
4. 1991
5. 4 vols.
6. $205
7. annual supp.
9. 24176147/KFK1268.K4

1. **KENTUCKY LAW OF EVIDENCE**
2. Richardson, James R.
3. Anderson
4. 1973
5. 1 vol.
6. $55 incl. 1 yr. supp.
7. annual supp.
8. 1990 - $32.50; 1991 - price NA
9. 73-180314/800212/KFK1740.R5

1. **KENTUCKY MINERAL LAW**
2. Short, David C. & Rich L. Thomas, mng. eds.
3. Banks
4. 1986
5. 3 vols.
6. $295 incl. 9 mos. supp.
7. periodic supp.
9. 87-101433/14696206/KFK1455.K46

1. **KENTUCKY PROBATE**
2. Schmitt, W. Allen
3. Lawyers Coop.
4. 1980
5. 1 vol.
6. $115 incl. 6 mos. supp.
7. annual supp.
8. 1989 - $51; 1990 - $55
9. 79-91146/8051812/KFK1344.S35

1. **KENTUCKY WORKERS' COMPENSATION**
2. Harned, Norman E.
3. Lawyers Coop.
4. 1984
5. 1 vol.
6. $115 incl. 6 mos. supp.
7. annual supp.
8. 1986 - $35; 1990 - $46
9. 83-82000/10654905/KFK1542.H37

1. **THE KNEE AND RELATED STRUCTURES (Courtroom Medicine Series, vols. 9 & 9A)**
2. Kalisch, Jules et al.
3. Bender
4. 1972
5. 2 vols.
6. $240 incl. 3 mos. supp.
7. annual supp.
8. 1989 - $124; 1990 - $180
9. 72-89524/977760/RA1011.C68

1. **LABOR AND EMPLOYMENT ARBITRATION**
2. Bornstein, J., & A. Gosline
3. Bender
4. 1988
5. 3 vols.
6. $325 incl. 3 mos. supp.
7. annual supp.
8. 1989 - $44; 1990 - $100.50
9. 88-71935/19097648/KF3424.L3

1. **LABOR AND EMPLOYMENT IN CONNECTICUT**
2. Hirsch, Jeffrey L.
3. Butterworth-NH
4. 1991
5. 1 vol.
6. $65
7. annual supp.
8. no supp. yet
9. 91-2002/23047924/KFC3931.Z9H57

1. **LABOR AND EMPLOYMENT IN MASSACHUSETTS: A GUIDE TO EMPLOYMENT LAWS, REGULATIONS AND PRACTICES**
2. Hirsch, Jeffrey L.
3. Butterworth-NH
4. 1990
5. 1 vol.
6. $65
7. annual supp.
8. 1991 - $45
9. 89-71324/KFM2731.Z9H57

1. **LABOR AND EMPLOYMENT IN NEW YORK**
2. Liddle, Jeffrey L. & Michael F. Marino III
3. Butterworth-NH
4. 1989
5. 1 vol.
6. $79.50
7. periodic supp.
8. 1991 - $55
9. 88-31054/18715969/KFN5556.L53

1. **LABOR AND EMPLOYMENT LAW: COMPLIANCE AND LITIGATION**
2. Golder, Frederick T.
3. Clark Boardman Callaghan
4. 1985
5. 1 vol.
6. $100 incl. 6 mos. supp.
7. annual supp.
8. 1989 - $78; 1990 - $44
9. 85-26973/12809047/KF3319.G63

1. **LABOR & EMPLOYMENT LAW INSTITUTE 1991**
2. -
3. Minn. CLE
4. 1991
5. 1 vol.
6. $60
7. no supp. planned

1. **LABOR AND EMPLOYMENT LAW PRIVATE SECTOR**
2. Bernstein, Harlan & Richard F. Liebman, eds.
3. Oregon Bar
4. 1990
5. 1 vol.
6. $85
7. periodic supp.
8. no supp. yet
9. 90-62154/23040371/KFO2731.L3Z

1. **LABOR AND EMPLOYMENT LAW PUBLIC SECTOR**
2. Liebman, Richard F. et al., eds.
3. Oregon Bar
4. 1989
5. 1 vol.
6. $65
7. periodic supp.
8. no supp. yet
9. 88-61294/21500777/KF02732.8.P77L33

1. **LABOR ARBITRATION AND DISPUTE SETTLEMENTS**
2. Sedmak, Nancy J.
3. BNA
4. 1946
5. 1 vol. (part of Labor Relations Reporter)
6. $713/yr.
7. weekly supp.
8. renewal - $690/yr.
9. 31639653

1. **LABOR ARBITRATION AWARDS**
2. -
3. CCH
4. 1961
5. 1 vol.
6. $780/yr.; $710/yr. for 2 yrs.
7. weekly supp.
9. 61-2438/4954875/KF3310.5.C618

1. **LABOR ARBITRATION INFORMATION SYSTEM**
2. -
3. LRP
4. 1970
5. 2 vols.
6. $465/yr. (back vols. avail.)
7. monthly supp.
9. 82-159059/8765993/KF3421.5.L3

1. **LABOR LAW (Business Organizations vols. 18-18I)**
2. Kheel, Theodore W. et al.
3. Bender
4. 1973
5. 11 vols.
6. $680/1 yr.; $850 for 2 yrs.
7. quarterly supp. & monthly newsletter
8. 1988 - $695/yr.
9. 64-1242

1. **LABOR LAW AND THE NATIONAL WAGE AGREEMENT; MINERS' RIGHTS & MSHA DISCRIMINATION LAW**
2. -
3. EMLF
4. 1989
5. 1 vol.
6. $80 - members; $100 - nonmembers
7. no supp. planned

1. **LABOR LAW HANDBOOK**
2. -
3. Illinois ICLE
4. 1989
5. 1 vol.
6. $98.95
7. periodic supp.
8. no supp. yet
9. 20615556

1. **LABOR LAW REPORTS**
2. -
3. CCH
4. 1934
5. 16 vols. (incl. Employment Practices Guide)
6. $1995/yr.; $1815/yr. for 2 yrs.
7. weekly supp. & newsletter

1. **LABOR RELATIONS FORMS & AGREEMENTS**
2. WG&L prof. ed. staff
3. WG&L
4. 1987
5. 2 vols.
6. $200/yr.; $190/yr. for 2 yrs.
7. quarterly supp.
8. renewal - $180
9. 16878912

1. **LABOR RELATIONS LAW UPDATE**
2. -
3. Indiana CLE
4. 1989
5. 1 vol.
6. $45
7. no supp. planned

1. **LABOR RELATIONS REPORTER**
2. Sedmak, Nancy J.
3. BNA
4. 1937
5. 17 vols.
6. $2402/yr.
7. weekly supp. & reports
8. renewal - $2260/yr.
9. 40-8499/1643346

1. **LABORATORY REGULATION MANUAL**
2. Halper, H. Robert & Hope S. Foster
3. Aspen
4. 1976
5. 3 vols.
6. $570 incl. 1 yr. supp.
7. quarterly supp.
8. renewal - $495/yr.
9. 76-56666/2733261/KF3826.L3H35

1. **LADNER ON CONVEYANCING IN PENNSYLVANIA, WITH FORMS**
2. Makdisi, J. & R. Stevens
3. Bisel
4. 4th ed. - 1979
5. 2 vols.
6. $100 incl. 3 mos. supp.
7. periodic supp.
8. 1988 - $17.50
9. 79-53058/6446565/KFP127.L3

1. **LAMBERTSON'S AFTERMATH - CIVIL LITIGATION AFTER WORKERS' COMPENSATION**
2. -
3. MILE
4. 1989
5. 1 vol.
6. $58
7. no supp. planned

1. **LAND DEVELOPMENT LAW REPORTER**
2. Bloch, Stuart Marshall & W.B. Ingersoll, eds.
3. Land Dev.
4. rev. - 1979
5. 6 vols.
6. $395 incl. 1 yr. supp.
7. monthly supp. & newsletter
8. renewal - $345/yr.
9. 5466592/KF5698.A4L3

1. **LAND TRUST ADMINISTRATION**
2. -
3. Illinois ICLE
4. 1989
5. 1 vol.
6. $65.95
7. periodic supp.
8. no supp. yet

1. **LAND USE**
2. Mattis, James, et al., eds.
3. Oregon Bar
4. 1975
5. 2 vols.
6. $145
7. no supp. yet
8. 1988 - $55
9. 82-82129/8722645/KFO2858.L36

1. **LAND USE LAW IN THE AGE OF GRIDLOCK**
2. -
3. Wash. Bar
4. 1989
5. 1 vol.
6. $35
7. no supp. planned

1. **LANDLORD'S REMEDIES IN FLORIDA**
2. Boyle, John J.
3. Butterworth-Fla.
4. 1987
5. 1 vol.
6. $80
7. periodic supp.
8. 1989 - $61; 1990 - $35.50
9. 16066695/KFF117.A6B69

1. **LANDMAN'S PRACTICUM**
2. -
3. EMLF
4. 1990
5. 1 vol.
6. $80 - members; $100 - nonmembers
7. no supp. planned

1. **LANE MEDICAL LITIGATION GUIDE**
2. Lane, Fred
3. Clark Boardman Callaghan
4. 1981
5. 4 vols.
6. $340 incl. 6 mos. supp.
7. annual supp.
8. 1989 - $127; 1990 - $137.50
9. 81-10167/7597893/RA1051.L29

1. **LANE'S GOLDSTEIN LITIGATION FORMS**
2. Lane, Fred
3. Clark Boardman Callaghan
4. 1991
5. 3 vols.
6. $325 ($250 without disks) incl. 6 mos. supp.
7. annual supp.
8. no supp. yet
9. 91-17888/23731665/KF8836.L36

1. **LANE'S GOLDSTEIN TRIAL TECHNIQUE**
2. Lane, Fred
3. Clark Boardman Callaghan
4. 1969
5. 3 vols.
6. $250 incl. 6 mos. supp.
7. annual supp.
8. 1989 - $66; 1990 - $69
9. 84-23915/11346109/KF8915.G62

1. **LATIN AMERICA AND THE DEVELOPMENT OF THE LAW OF THE SEA: REGIONAL DOCUMENTS, NATIONAL LEGISLATION**
2. Szekely, Alberto
3. Oceana
4. 1976
5. 2 vols.
6. $200/set
7. periodic supp.
8. 1986 - $150

9. 76-40510/2691635

1. **THE LAW AND BUSINESS OF COMPUTER SOFTWARE**
2. Toedt, D.C. III
3. Clark Boardman Callaghan
4. 1990
5. 1 vol.
6. $95 incl. 3 mos. supp.
7. annual supp.
8. no supp. yet
9. 89-71241/20788968/KF3024.C6L375

1. **THE LAW AND BUSINESS OF LICENSING: LICENSING IN THE 1990s**
2. Bell, Paul B. & Jay Simon, eds. under the auspices of the Licensing Executives Society
3. Clark Boardman Callaghan
4. 1991
5. 1 vol.
6. $95 incl. 3 mos. supp.
7. annual supp.
8. 1991 - $75
9. 90-1961/21522880/K1528.Z9L37

1. **THE LAW AND BUSINESS OF RESORT DEVELOPMENT**
2. Henze, Mark E. and Alan N. Schlaifer
3. Clark Boardman Callaghan
4. 1986
5. 1 vol.
6. $120 incl. 3 mos. supp.
7. annual supp.
8. 1989 - $55; 1990 - $79.50
9. 86-14734/13795061/KF5698.3.H46

1. **THE LAW AND BUSINESS OF TIME-SHARE RESORTS**
2. Henze, Mark E.
3. Clark Boardman Callaghan
4. 1982
5. 2 vols.
6. $240 incl. 3 mos. supp.
7. periodic supp.
8. 1989 - $49.50; 1990 - free ($0)
9. 82-9470/8476383/KF598.H46

1. **LAW AND POLICY OF INTERGOVERNMENTAL PRIMARY COMMODITY AGREEMENTS**
2. Johnston, Charles R., Jr.
3. Oceana
4. 1976
5. 3 vols.
6. $300
7. periodic supp.
8. 1984 - $125; 1985 - $100
9. 76-6559/2091467

1. **THE LAW AND PRACTICE OF INTERNATIONAL FINANCE (International Business and Law Series, vols. 2 & 2A)**
2. Wood, Philip
3. Clark Boardman Callaghan
4. 1981
5. 2 vols.
6. $250 incl. 3 mos. supp.
7. biannual supp.
8. 1986 - $75; 1989 - $79.50
9. 81-10199//r902/7595909/K1005.4.W66

1. **THE LAW AND PRACTICE OF SECURED TRANSACTIONS: WORKING WITH ARTICLE 9**
2. Duncan, Richard F. and Lyons, Williamn H.
3. Law Journal
4. 1987
5. 1 vol.
6. $80
7. periodic supp.
8. 1989 - $37; 1990 - $39
9. 87-3695/15318100/KF1050.D86

1. **LAW AND PRACTICE OF U.S. REGULATION OF INTERNATIONAL TRADE**
2. Johnston, Charles R. Jr.
3. Oceana
4. 1987
5. 1 vol.
6. $175
7. periodic supp.
8. 1988 - $150; 1989 - $150
9. 87-11014

1. **LAW AND PRACTICE UNDER THE GATT**
2. Simmonds, Kenneth R. & Brian H.W. Hill
3. Oceana
4. 1988
5. 4 vols.
6. $575
7. periodic supp.
8. 1990 - $150; 1991 - $150
9. 87-63448/15747096

1. **LAW AND PRACTICE UNDER THE GATT AND OTHER TRADING**

ARRANGEMENTS: THE ASSOCIATION OF SOUTHEAST ASIAN NATIONS
2. Simmonds, Kenneth R. et al., eds.
3. Oceana
4. 1991
5. 1 vol.
6. $150
7. periodic supp.
8. 1991 - $150
9. 24418580/K4602.2

1. **LAW AND PRACTICE UNDER THE GATT AND OTHER TRADING ARRANGEMENTS: EUROPEAN COMMUNITY: THE SINGLE MARKET ACT**
2. Belford, Jane
3. Oceana
4. 1990
5. 1 vol.
6. $150
7. no supp. yet

1. **LAW AND PRACTICE UNDER THE GATT AND OTHER TRADING ARRANGEMENTS: THE EUROPEAN COMMUNITY, THE SOVIET UNION AND THE EASTERN EUROPEAN STATES**
2. Simmonds, Kenneth R., ed.
3. Oceana
4. 1992 projected
5. 1 vol.
6. $150
7. periodic supp.
8. no supp. yet
9. 91-66555/24707198/KJE5105.A23L39

1. **LAW AND PRACTICE UNDER THE GATT AND OTHER TRADING ARRANGEMENTS: EUROPEAN COMMUNITY–TRADING ARRANGEMENTS WITH EFTA COUNTRIES**
2. Fischer, Peter, ed.
3. Oceana
4. 1991
5. 1 vol.
6. $150
7. periodic supp.
8. no supp. yet

1. **LAW AND PRACTICE UNDER THE GATT AND OTHER TRADING ARRANGEMENTS: TRILATERAL TRADE AGREEMENTS: CANADA - U.S. - MEXICO**
2. Battram, Shelly P.
3. Oceana
4. 1992
5. 1 vol.
6. price NA
7. no supp. yet

1. **LAW BOOKS RECOMMENDED FOR LIBRARIES**
2. Association of American Law Schools
3. Rothman
4. 1967
5. 6 basic vols. with 4 vol. supp. publ. in 1967-1970
6. $475
7. no supp. planned
9. 67-30383/862159/K1.B1

1. **LAW DEPARTMENT MANAGEMENT (2nd ed.)**
2. Hancock, W.A.
3. Bus. Laws
4. 1991
5. 1 vol.
6. $95
7. annual supp.
8. renewal - $44/yr.
9. 23671371/KF1425.L39

1. **LAW FIRM MANAGEMENT GUIDE**
2. -
3. Altman Weil Pensa
4. 1989
5. 1 vol.
6. $95
7. no supp. planned
9. 20908775/KF318.A7L38

1. **LAW FIRMS: LATERAL HIRES, BREAK-UPS AND MERGERS**
2. -
3. MILE
4. 1991
5. 1 vol.
6. $68
7. no supp. planned
9. 23667449/KF306.L38

1. **LAW FOR THE HORSEBREEDER**
2. Wood, Kenneth A.
3. Farnam
4. 1979
5. 1 vol.
6. $75 incl. 1 yr. supp.

7. periodic supp.
8. 1989 - $40; 1990 - $40
9. 79-101995/5100618/KF390.5.H6W66

1. **LAW FOR THE LAYMAN: AN ANNOTATED BIBLIOGRAPHY OF SELF-HELP LAW BOOKS**
2. Houdek, Frank G.
3. Rothman
4. 1991
5. 1 vol.
6. $42.50
7. biennial supp.
8. no supp. yet
9. 91-16613/23766463/KF1.H68

1. **THE LAW OF ADVERTISING**
2. Rosden, George E. & Peter E.
3. Bender
4. 1973
5. 4 vols.
6. $525 incl. 3 mos. supp.
7. annual supp.
8. 1989 - $409; 1990 - $500.50
9. 73-90916/897708/KF1614.R68

1. **THE LAW OF ASSOCIATIONS**
2. Webster, George D.
3. Bender
4. rev. 2nd ed. - 1975
5. 1 vol.
6. $130 incl. 3 mos. supp.
7. annual supp.
8. 1989 - $90; 1990 - $123
9. 74-29124/1365936/KF1661.W3

1. **THE LAW OF AUTOMOBILE INSURANCE IN SOUTH CAROLINA**
2. Maybank, Burnet R. et al.
3. S. Carolina Bar
4. 1988
5. 1 vol.
6. $90
7. periodic supp.
8. 1989 - $50
9. 18420410/KFS1991.A4L29

1. **THE LAW OF CHEMICAL REGULATION AND HAZARDOUS WASTE**
2. Stever, Donald W.
3. Clark Boardman Callaghan
4. 1986
5. 3 vols.
6. $297 incl. 3 mos. supp.
7. annual supp.
8. 1989 - $124.50; 1991 - $214
9. 86-2249/13123333/KF3958.S74

1. **THE LAW OF CONDOMINIUM OPERATIONS**
2. Poliakoff, Gary A.
3. Clark Boardman Callaghan
4. 1988
5. 2 vols.
6. $175 incl. 6 mos. supp.
7. annual supp.
8. 1990 - $37.50
9. 88-8150/18464071/KF581.P65

1. **THE LAW OF COPYRIGHT**
2. Abrams, Howard B.
3. Clark Boardman Callaghan
4. 1991
5. 2 vols.
6. $195 incl. 3 mos. supp.
7. annual supp.
8. no supp. yet
9. 91-4402/23015615/KF2994.A72

1. **THE LAW OF CORPORATE OFFICERS AND DIRECTORS: INDEMNIFICATION AND INSURANCE**
2. Bishop, Joseph W., Jr.
3. Clark Boardman Callaghan
4. 1981
5. 1 vol.
6. $100 incl. 6 mos. supp.
7. annual supp.
8. 1989 - $39; 1990 - $78.50
9. 82-4383/8388231/KF1423.B57

1. **LAW OF CORPORATE OFFICERS AND DIRECTORS: RIGHTS, DUTIES, AND LIABILITIES**
2. Brodsky, Edward & M. Patricia Adamski
3. Clark Boardman Callaghan
4. 1984
5. 1 vol.
6. $100 incl. 6 mos. supp.
7. annual supp.
8. 1989 - $78.50; 1990 - $43.50
9. 84-14310/10948715/KF1423.B76

1. **THE LAW OF DAMAGES IN WISCONSIN**
2. -
3. State Bar of Wisc.
4. 1988
5. 2 vols.
6. $165

7. periodic supp.
8. 1990 - $40; 1991 - $57
9. 18434530/KFW2490.D3L38

1. **LAW OF DEFAMATION**
2. Smolla, Rodney A.
3. Clark Boardman Callaghan
4. 1986
5. 1 vol.
6. $125 incl. 3 mos. supp.
7. annual supp.
8. 1989 - $44.50; 1991 - $55
9. 86-14687/13762373/KF1266.S56

1. **THE LAW OF DISTRESSED REAL ESTATE**
2. Dunaway, Baxter
3. Clark Boardman Callaghan
4. 1985
5. 3 vols.
6. $315 incl. 3 mos. supp.
7. annual supp.
8. 1989 - $117.50; 1991 - $174.50
9. 85-4161/11813090/KF1524.D85

1. **THE LAW OF ELECTRONIC SURVEILLANCE**
2. Carr, James G.
3. Clark Boardman Callaghan
4. 1986
5. 1 vol.
6. $110 incl. 3 mos. supp.
7. annual supp.
8. 1989 - $87; 1991 - $102
9. 85-31406/13008817/KF9670.C37

1. **LAW OF ENVIRONMENTAL PROTECTION**
2. Environmental Law Institute
3. Clark Boardman Callaghan
4. 1987
5. 2 vols.
6. $198 incl. 3 mos. supp.
7. periodic supp.
8. 1989 - $75; 1991 - $139
9. 87-725/15163830/KF3775.L39

1. **LAW OF EVIDENCE IN THE DISTRICT OF COLUMBIA**
2. Graae, Judge Steffen W.
3. Bar Assn. of D.C.
4. 2nd ed. - 1989
5. 1 vol.
6. $100
7. periodic supp.
8. 1991 - $25
9. 19454464/KFD1740.G71

1. **THE LAW OF EVIDENCE IN WASHINGTON**
2. Aronson, Robert H.
3. Butterworth-St. Paul
4. 1986
5. 1 vol.
6. $65
7. periodic supp.
8. 1989 - $47.50; 1991 - $55
9. 85-73111/14099558/KFW540.A98

1. **LAW OF FEDERAL ESTATE AND GIFT TAXATION: CODE COMMENTARY**
2. Link, David T. & Larry D. Soderquist
3. Clark Boardman Callaghan
4. 1978
5. 1 vol.
6. $100 incl. 6 mos. supp.
7. annual supp.
8. 1989 - $52.50; 1990 - $39
9. 78-13001/4194427/KF6572.L55

1. **LAW OF FEDERAL OIL AND GAS LEASES**
2. Rocky Mountain Mineral Law Foundation
3. Bender
4. 1964
5. 2 vols.
6. $225 incl. 3 mos. supp.
7. annual supp.
8. 1989 - $110; 1990 - $137.50
9. 64-2251/2474395/KF1865.A6R6

1. **THE LAW OF FINANCIAL SERVICES**
2. Pitt, Harvey L. et al.
3. Prentice Hall Law & Business
4. 1988
5. 7 vols.
6. $595 incl. 4 mos. supp.
7. annual supp.
8. 1990 - $200; 1991 - $220
9. 88-2554/17510128/KF974.P58

1. **LAW OF INDEPENDENT POWER PRODUCTION, COGENERATION AND UTILITY REGULATION**
2. Ferrey, Steven
3. Clark Boardman Callaghan
4. 1989
5. 1 vol.
6. $110 incl. 3 mos. supp.
7. annual supp.

8. 1991 - $49.50
9. 89-34161/19739772/KF2125.F47

1. **THE LAW OF LAWYERING: A HANDBOOK ON THE MODEL RULES OF PROFESSIONAL CONDUCT**
2. Hazard Geoffrey C., Jr. & W. Wm. Hodes
3. Prentice Hall Law & Business
4. 2nd ed. - 1990
5. 2 vols.
6. $175 incl. 4 mos. supp.
7. periodic supp.
8. 1991 - $125
9. 91-49332/22493747/KF306.H33

1. **THE LAW OF LIABILITY INSURANCE**
2. Long, Rowland H.
3. Bender
4. 1976
5. 5 vols.
6. $650 incl. 3 mos. supp.
7. annual supp.
8. 1989 - $531; 1990 - $591
9. 67-4879//r873/2571528/KF1215.A6L6

1. **LAW OF LIFE AND HEALTH INSURANCE**
2. Harnett, Bertram & Irving I. Lesnick
3. Bender
4. 1988
5. 5 vol.
6. $485 incl. 3 mos. supp.
7. annual supp.
8. 1989 - $80; 1990 - $107
9. 88-71096/18403552/KF1173.4.H36

1. **THE LAW OF MERCHANDISING AND CHARACTER LICENSING**
2. Battersby, Gregory J. and Charles W. Grimes
3. Clark Boardman Callaghan
4. 1985
5. 1 vol.
6. $115 incl. 3 mos. supp.
7. annual supp.
8. 1989 - $52.50; 1991 - $75
9. 85-19471/12739855/K1528.B33

1. **THE LAW OF OIL AND GAS LEASES, 2ND ED.**
2. Brown, Earl A.
3. Bender
4. 2nd ed. - 1967
5. 2 vols.
6. $225 incl. 3 mos. supp.
7. annual supp.
8. 1989 - $45; 1990 - $85
9. 73-78949/5222636/KF1865.B72

1. **THE LAW OF POOLING AND UNITIZATION - VOLUNTARY, COMPULSORY**
2. Myers, Raymond L.
3. Bender
4. 2nd ed. - 1967
5. 4 vols. (vol. 1 - bound)
6. $375 incls. 3 mos. supp.
7. annual supp.
8. 1989 - $250; 1990 - $240
9. 68-4550/432810/KF1853.M9

1. **THE LAW OF PROFESSIONAL AND AMATEUR SPORTS**
2. Uberstine, Gary A., ed.
3. Clark Boardman Callaghan
4. 1988
5. 1 vol.
6. $115 incl. 3 mos. supp.
7. periodic supp.
8. 1991 - $100
9. 88-19741/18135334/KF3989.L38

1. **THE LAW OF PURCHASING**
2. Hancock, W.A.
3. Bus. Laws
4. 2nd ed. - 1986
5. 3 vols.
6. $265
7. annual supp.
8. renewal - $74/yr.
9. 17610457

1. **THE LAW OF REAL ESTATE FINANCING**
2. Madison, Michael T. & J.R. Dwyer
3. WG&L
4. 1981
5. 1 vol.
6. $98
7. semiannual supp.
8. 1990 - $112; 1991 - $132.75
9. 80-53430/8042522/KF5698.3.M24

1. **LAW OF REAL PROPERTY**
2. Powell, Richard R. & Patrick J. Rohan
3. Bender
4. rev. ed. - 1973
5. 16 vols.
6. $750 incl. 3 mos. supp.
7. biannual supp.
8. 1989 - $705; 1990 - $775.50
9. 1116641/KF750.P59

1. **LAW OF THE ELDERLY**
2. -
3. MILE
4. 1991
5. 1 vol.
6. $68
7. no supp. planned

1. **THE LAW OF THE EUROPEAN ECONOMIC COMMUNITY - A COMMENTARY ON THE EEC TREATY**
2. Herzog, P.E. et al.
3. Bender
4. 1976
5. 6 vols.
6. $495 incl. 3 mos. supp.
7. periodic supp.
8. 1989 - $198; 1990 - $257.50
9. 76-26843/2459162

1. **LAW OF TOXIC TORTS**
2. Dore, Michael
3. Clark Boardman Callaghan
4. 1987
5. 2 vols.
6. $198 incl. 3 mos. supp.
7. periodic supp.
8. 1989 - $84.50; 1991 - $129
9. 86-31027/14905996/KF1257.D67

1. **THE LAW OF TRANSNATIONAL BUSINESS TRANSACTIONS (International Business & Law Series, vol. 1 & 1A)**
2. Nanda, Ved P.
3. Clark Boardman Callaghan
4. 1981
5. 2 vols.
6. $250 incl. 3 mos. supp.
7. annual supp.
8. 1989 - $99; 1991 - $127.50
9. 81-2392/7671635/K1005.4.L38

1. **LAW OF WATER RIGHTS AND RESOURCES**
2. Tarlock, A. Dan
3. Clark Boardman Callaghan
4. 1988
5. 1 vol.
6. $110 incl. 3 mos. supp.
7. periodic supp.
8. 1989 - $42.50; 1991 - $55
9. 88-16645/18015404/KF5569.T37

1. **LAW OF WETLANDS REGULATION**
2. Want, William L.
3. Clark Boardman Callaghan
4. 1989
5. 1 vol.
6. $110 incl. 3 mos. supp.
7. annual supp.
8. 1991 - $55
9. 89-34160/19739764/KF5624.W36

1. **LAW OF WILLS IN PENNSYLVANIA**
2. Aker, J.B.
3. Bisel
4. 1983
5. 1 vol.
6. $59.50
7. periodic supp.
8. 1989 - $13.75
9. 83-72488/10246555/KFP144.A937

1. **THE LAW OF WORKERS' COMPENSATION**
2. -
3. NH Bar
4. 1989
5. 1 vol.
6. $30
7. no supp. planned
9. 13591628

1. **THE LAW OF ZONING AND PLANNING**
2. Rathkopf, Arden H.
3. Clark Boardman Callaghan
4. 4th ed. - 1977
5. 5 vols.
6. $495 incl. 3 mos. supp.
7. annual supp.
8. 1989 - $277; 1991 - $373.50
9. 56-2013/986672/KF5697.A8R23

1. **LAW OFFICE AUTOMATION AND TECHNOLOGY**
2. Arentowicz, Frank & Ward Bower
3. Bender
4. 1980
5. 1 vol.
6. $115 incl. 3 mos. supp.
7. supp. as needed
8. 1989 - $78; 1990 - $85.50
9. 80-68459/7076271/KF320.A9A73

1. **LAW OFFICE ECONOMICS AND MANAGEMENT MANUAL**
2. Hoffman, Paul S.
3. Clark Boardman Callaghan
4. 1970

5. 2 vols.
6. $145 incl. 6 mos. supp.
7. annual supp.
8. 1988 - $33; 1989 - $37.50
9. 72-121883/142320/KF318.L3

1. **LAW OFFICE GUIDE TO COMPUTER ABBREVIATIONS & ACRONYMS**
2. Greenia, Mark W.
3. Lexikon
4. 1991
5. 1 vol.
6. $25
7. semiannual supp.
8. $15/yr.
9. 19500386/QA76.15.G63

1. **LAW OFFICE MANUAL**
2. -
3. Arkansas Bar
4. 1980
5. 1 vol.
6. $35
7. no supp. yet

1. **LAW OFFICE STAFF MANUAL: MODEL POLICIES AND PROCEDURES FOR LAW OFFICE PERSONNEL**
2. Section of Economics of Law Practice
3. ABA
4. 1982
5. 1 vol.
6. $34.95
7. no supp. yet
9. 82-70934/8727004/KF318.R64

1. **LAWS OF INTERNATIONAL TRADE**
2. Hancock, W.A. ed.
3. Bus. Laws
4. 1986
5. 5 vols.
6. $345
7. periodic supp.
8. renewal - $150/yr.
9. 15996965

1. **LAWS, REGULATIONS, RELATED ACTS**
2. -
3. FDIC
4. 1983
5. 3 vols.
6. $225/yr.
7. semimonthly supp.

1. **LAWYER ADVERTISING**
2. Lee, Tom L.
3. CRI
4. 1987
5. 1 vol.
6. $325 incl. all supp.
7. biennial revision
9. 85-11699/12133002/KF310.A3L44

1. **THE LAWYERS ANNOTATED PRODUCTS LIABILITY CHECKLISTS**
2. -
3. Legal-Med.
4. 1986
5. 1 vol.
6. $95
7. annual editions
8. 1988 - free
9. 15380190/KF8925.P7L34

1. **LAWYER'S BASIC CORPORATE PRACTICE MANUAL**
2. Deer, Richard E.
3. ALI-ABA
4. 3rd ed. - 1984
5. 1 vol.
6. $95
7. periodic supp.
8. 1988 - $26.50
9. 84-72759//r88/11659094/KF1414.D44

1. **THE LAWYER'S DIRECT MAIL HANDBOOK**
2. Lee, Tom L.
3. CRI
4. 1988
5. 1 vol.
6. $69.95
7. biennial revision
8. no supp. yet
9. 23724677

1. **LAWYER'S GUIDE TO ACCOUNTING AND FINANCE ABBREVIATIONS AND ACRONYMS**
2. Greenia, Mark W.
3. Lexikon
4. 1991
5. 1 vol.
6. $10
7. annual supp.
8. $5/yr.
9. 22643931/HF1002.5.G73

1. **LAWYER'S GUIDE TO COMPUTER SECURITY: SOURCEBOOK**

2. Greenia, Mark W.
3. Lexikon
4. 1991
5. 1 vol.
6. $20
7. annual supp.
8. $15/yr.

1. **LAWYER'S GUIDE TO MEDICAL PROOF**
2. Houts, Marshall
3. Bender
4. 1966
5. 5 vols.
6. $540 incl. 3 mos. supp.
7. annual supp.
8. 1989 - $325; 1990 - $392
9. 74-27720/1614116

1. **THE LAWYER'S GUIDE TO THE TEXAS DECEPTIVE TRADE PRACTICES ACT**
2. Alderman, Richard M.
3. Butterworth-Texas
4. 1990
5. 1 vol.
6. $95
7. annual supp.
8. 1990 - $40
9. 89-70883/20758493/KFT1430.A94

1. **LAWYERS' PROFESSIONAL LIABILITY UPDATE**
2. Standing Comm. on Lawyers' Professional Liability
3. ABA
4. 1987
5. 1 vol.
6. $80
7. periodic supp.
8. renewal - $25/yr.
9. 85-646925/9840874/KF313.A15L38

1. **LAWYER'S PUBLICITY HANDBOOK**
2. Lee, Tom L.
3. CRI
4. 1988
5. 1 vol.
6. $69.95
7. biennial revisions
8. no supp. yet
9. 13284931

1. **LEGAL ASPECTS OF AIDS**
2. Hermann, Donald H.J. & William P. Schurgin
3. Clark Boardman Callaghan
4. 1991
5. 1 vol.
6. $95
7. annual supp.
8. no supp. yet
9. 90-19718/22544243/KF3803.A54H47

1. **LEGAL ASPECTS OF DOING BUSINESS IN AFRICA**
2. Campbell, Denis, ed.
3. Kluwer
4. 1991
5. 1 vol.
6. $132 incl. 3 mos. supp.
7. periodic supp.
8. no supp. yet
9. 91-24475/24066437

1. **LEGAL ASPECTS OF DOING BUSINESS IN ASIA & PACIFIC**
2. Campbell, Denis, ed.
3. Kluwer
4. 1991
5. 1 vol.
6. $184 incl. 3 mos. supp.
7. periodic supp.
8. no supp. yet
9. 23719782

1. **LEGAL ASPECTS OF DOING BUSINESS IN EUROPE**
2. Campbell, Dennis
3. Kluwer
4. 1989
5. 1 vol.
6. $237 incl. 3 mos. supp.
7. periodic supp.
9. Z82-17095/22203263/KJC160.B87L43X

1. **LEGAL ASPECTS OF DOING BUSINESS IN NORTH AMERICA**
2. Campbell, Dennis
3. Kluwer
4. 1988
5. 1 vol.
6. $186 incl. 3 mos. supp.
7. periodic supp.
8. 1990 - $148; 1991 - $150

1. **LEGAL ASPECTS OF EXPORTING**
2. -
3. Conn. Bar
4. 1991
5. 1 vol.
6. $53

7. no supp. planned

1. **THE LEGAL ASPECTS OF EXPORTING MANUAL**
2. -
3. FBA
4. 1984
5. 1 vol.
6. $20
7. periodic supp.
8. no supp. yet

1. **THE LEGAL ASPECTS OF INTERNATIONAL SOURCING**
2. Hancock, W.A.
3. Bus. Laws
4. 1986
5. 1 vol.
6. $90
7. annual supp.
8. renewal - $39/yr.
9. 13364172/KF1975.A8L43

1. **THE LEGAL ASPECTS OF SUBSTANCE ABUSE IN THE WORKPLACE**
2. Hancock, W.A., ed.
3. Bus. Laws
4. 1987
5. 1 vol.
6. $90
7. annual supp.
8. renewal - $39/yr.
9. 18573556//KF3540.L44

1. **THE LEGAL AUDIT: CORPORATE INTERNAL INVESTIGATION**
2. Brown, Louis M. & Anne O. Kandel
3. Clark Boardman Callaghan
4. 1990
5. 1 vol.
6. $105 incl. 3 mos. supp.
7. annual supp.
8. no supp. yet
9. 90-36963/21523553/KF1414.B76

1. **LEGAL CHECKLISTS**
2. Becker, Benjamin M., et al.
3. Clark Boardman Callaghan
4. 1968
5. 2 vols.
6. $175 incl. 6 mos. supp.
7. annual supp.
8. 1989 - $124.50; 1990 - $124.50
9. 66-19255/934101/KF386.L44

1. **LEGAL CHECKLISTS - SPECIALLY SELECTED FORMS**
2. Becker, Benjamin M., et al.
3. Clark Boardman Callaghan
4. 1977
5. 1 vol.
6. $90 incl. 6 mos. supp.
7. periodic supp.
8. 1989 - $42.50; 1990 - $44.50
9. 76-56745/2646228/KF170.B43

1. **LEGAL COMPLIANCE CHECKUPS: BUSINESS CLIENTS**
2. Hughes, Robert B.
3. Clark Boardman Callaghan
4. 1985
5. 4 vols.
6. $280 incl. 6 mos. supp.
7. annual supp.
8. 1989 - $85; 1990 - $75
9. 84-15516/10998531/KF889.3.H83

1. **LEGAL DESKBOOK FOR ADMINISTRATORS OF INDEPENDENT COLLEGES AND UNIVERSITIES**
2. Center for Constitutional Studies, Mercer Univ.
3. Baylor Univ. Press
4. 1982
5. 1 vol.
6. $75
7. annual supp.
8. 1985 - $12.50; 1987 - $12.50
9. 85-25901/8759439

1. **LEGAL ETHICS - PROCEDURE & CASE UPDATE**
2. -
3. Okla. Bar CLE
4. 1990
5. 1 vol.
6. $25
7. no supp. planned

1. **LEGAL ETHICS IN ALABAMA**
2. Cohen, Harry & Richard Thigpen
3. ABICLE
4. 1991
5. 1 vol.
6. $45
7. periodic supp.
8. no supp. yet

1. **LEGAL FORM MANUAL FOR REAL ESTATE TRANSACTIONS**

2. State Bar Legal Forms Committee
3. State Bar of Texas
4. rev. - 1986
5. 1 vol.
6. $148
7. periodic supp.
8. 1988 - $18; 1990 - $30
9. 85-62844/11746473/KFT1326.A65L44

1. **LEGAL FORMS AND WORKSHEETS**
2. -
3. Florida Bar
4. 1981
5. 1 vol.
6. $60
7. supp. as needed
8. 1989 - $30; 1991 - $25
9. 8851602/KFF68.L4

1. **LEGAL GUIDE FOR HANDLING TOXIC SUBSTANCES IN THE WORKPLACE**
2. Hancock, W.A., ed.
3. Bus. Laws
4. 1990
5. 1 vol.
6. $95
7. periodic supp.
9. 91-164734/24212376/KF3570.P67

1. **LEGAL GUIDE FOR PHYSICIANS**
2. Taraska, Joseph M.
3. Bender
4. 1987
5. 1 vol.
6. $110 incl. 3 mos. supp.
7. annual supp.
8. 1989 - $59; 1990 - $66.50
9. 87-72445/17433301/KF3821.T37

1. **LEGAL IMPLICATIONS OF THE AIDS CRISES**
2. -
3. MILE
4. 1991
5. 1 vol.
6. $68
7. no supp. planned
9. 24207359/KF3803.A54L34

1. **LEGAL ISSUES, GOVERNMENT PROGRAMS, AND THE ELDERLY (FLORIDA)**
2. Center for Govt. Responsibility
3. Butterworth-Fla.
4. 1987
5. 1 vol.
6. $60
7. periodic supp.
8. no supp. yet
9. 15202241/KF390.A4L434

1. **LEGAL LC SUBJECT HEADINGS WEEKLY LISTS: CUMULATION**
2. Lembke, Melody
3. Rothman
4. 1986
5. 1 vol.
6. $32.50
7. quarterly supp.
8. 1989 - $35; 1990 - $37.50
9. 86-529/13270340/Z695.1.L3L43

1. **LEGAL MALPRACTICE GUIDE**
2. -
3. MILE
4. 1991
5. 1 vol.
6. $68
7. no supp. planned
9. 24576498/KF313.Z9L44

1. **LEGAL OPINIONS IN BUSINESS TRANSACTIONS**
2. Corporations & Other Business Org. Section
3. Conn. Bar
4. 1989
5. 1 vol.
6. $20
7. no supp. planned

1. **LEGAL PERIODICALS IN ENGLISH**
2. Wypyski, Eugene M., ed.
3. Glanville Publishers
4. 1976
5. 5 vols.
6. $525
7. periodic supp.
8. 1991 - $125
9. 75-42308//r823/1974094/K36.W96

1. **LEGAL PLANNING FOR THE ELDERLY IN MASSACHUSETTS**
2. Brisk, William J. & William G. Talis
3. Butterworth-NH
4. 1991
5. 1 vol.
6. $95
7. periodic supp.
8. no supp. yet

9. 90-27041/22909888/KFM2491.A3B75

1. **LEGAL RESEARCH AND LAW LIBRARY MANAGEMENT**
2. Marke, Julius J. & Richard Sloane
3. Law Journal
4. 1990
5. 1 vol.
6. $70
7. supp. as needed
8. no supp. yet
9. 90-19632/22629301/KF240.M24

1. **LEGAL REQUIREMENTS FOR BUSINESS RECORDS - FEDERAL REQUIREMENTS**
2. Skupsky, Donald S.
3. IRC
4. 2nd ed. - 1988
5. 2 vols.
6. $700 incl. 1 yr. supp.
7. quarterly newsletter and annual supp.
8. renewal - $175/yr.
9. 12034132/KF1357.5.L43

1. **LEGAL REQUIREMENTS FOR BUSINESS RECORDS - STATE REQUIREMENTS**
2. Skupsky, Donald S.
3. IRC
4. 2nd ed. - 1989
5. 1 vol.
6. $460 incl. 1 yr. supp.
7. annual supp.
8. renewal - $115/yr.
9. 19681386/KF1357.L431

1. **LEGAL RESEARCH AND WRITING**
2. Merzon, Melvin S.
3. Illinois ICLE
4. 1990
5. 1 vol.
6. $45.95
7. periodic supp.
8. no supp. yet
9. 20427664.KFI1275.M47

1. **LEGAL RIGHTS OF PERSONS WITH DISABILITIES**
2. Tucker, Bonnie P. & Bruce A. Goldstein
3. LRP
4. 1990
5. 1 vol.
6. $98.50
7. periodic supp.
8. 1991 - price NA
9. 90-47698/22421566/KF480.T82

1. **LEGAL SECRETARY BANKRUPTCY**
2. Everett, Pamela I.
3. James
4. 1987
5. 1 vol.
6. $69.97 incl. 3 mos. supp.
7. annual supp.
8. 1990 - $38.91
9. 15362345

1. **LEGAL SECRETARY FEDERAL LITIGATION**
2. Crawford-Hopkins, Lois A.
3. James
4. 3rd ed. -1986
5. 1 vol.
6. $59.97 incl. 3 mos. supp.
7. annual supp.
8. 1989 - $32.99; 1990 - $36.99
9. 13151743/KF319.C73

1. **LEGAL SECRETARY'S HANDBOOK**
2. Legal Secretaries Inc.
3. Rutter
4. 1989
5. 2 vols.
6. $161 incl. 3 mos. supp.
7. annual supp.
8. 1990 - $60; 1991 - price NA
9. 76-52065/21021178/KFC77.B7

1. **LEGAL SECRETARY'S RESOURCE**
2. Education Council of Legal Secretaries, Inc., Calif.
3. Parker
4. 5th ed. - 1988
5. 1 vol.
6. $42 ($32 - bookstores & schools) incl. 3 mos. supp.
7. semiannual supp.
8. 1990 - $20.50; 1991 - $18
9. 88-62127/18500138/KFC77.L44

1. **LEGAL WRITING - FOR EFFECT**
2. -
3. MILE
4. 1991
5. 1 vol.
6. $68
7. no supp. planned

1. **LEGAL YEAR IN REVIEW**
2. -
3. Maine Bar
4. 1990

5. 1 vol.
6. $30
7. no supp. yet

1. **LEGALITY OF MICROFILM**
2. Williams, Robert F., ed.
3. Cohasset
4. 1979
5. 1 vol.
6. $210 incl. 1 yr. supp.
7. 2-4/yr.
8. $55/yr.
9. 80-80848/6430691

1. **LEGALITY OF OPTICAL STORAGE**
2. Williams, Robert F.
3. Cohasset
4. 1986
5. 1 vol.
6. $240 incl. 1 yr. supp.
7. 2-4/yr.
8. $65/yr.
9. 87-24280/16714134/KF8947.Z95L44

1. **LEGISLATIVE DEVELOPMENTS**
2. -
3. NH Bar
4. 1990
5. 1 vol.
6. $35
7. no supp. planned

1. **LEGISLATIVE UPDATE**
2. -
3. Indiana CLE
4. 1991
5. 1 vol.
6. $75
7. no supp. planned

1. **LEGISLATIVE UPDATE**
2. -
3. MILE
4. 1991
5. 1 vol.
6. $68
7. no supp. planned
9. 24081257/KFM5420.N56

1. **LENDER LIABILITY**
2. Cappello, A. Barry & Frances E. Komoroske
3. Parker
4. 1987
5. 1 vol.
6. $80 incl. 3 mos. supp.
7. periodic supp.
8. 1990 -$32.50; 1991 - $20
9. 87-62632/16981811

1. **LENDER LIABILITY: A PRAGMATIC APPROACH**
2. -
3. Indiana CLE
4. 1988
5. 1 vol.
6. $50
7. no supp. planned
9. 1615114/KF1035.A75D48

1. **LENDER LIABILITY: THEORY & PRACTICE**
2. Bucknell, Thomas, Jr. et al.
3. Wiley Law
4. 1988
5. 1 vol.
6. $105
7. annual supp.
8. 1991 - $40; 1992 - price NA
9. 88-207923//r89/18446352/KF1035.B83

1. **LENDER LIABILITY AND BANKING LITIGATION**
2. Mannino, Edward
3. Law Journal
4. 1989
5. 1 vol.
6. $85
7. periodic supp.
8. no supp. yet
9. 89-37089/20561099/KF1301.5.B36M36

1. **LENDER LIABILITY LAW & LITIGATION**
2. Norton, Joseph, ed.
3. Bender
4. 1989
5. 1 vol.
6. $105 incl. 3 mos. supp.
7. annual supp.
8. 1990 - $65.50
9. 89-60359/19913069/KF1301.5.B3N67

1. **LENDER LIABILITY LAW, PRACTICE AND PREVENTION**
2. Blanchard, Gerald L.
3. Clark Boardman Callaghan
4. 1989
5. 2 vols.
6. $180 incl. 6 mos. supp.
7. annual supp.

8. no supp. yet
9. 89-70797/20723017/KF1301.5.B36B575

1. **LESBIAN MOTHER LITIGATION MANUAL**
2. Hitchens, Donna J. and Roberta Achtenberg
3. Natl. Center for Lesbian Rights
4. 2nd ed. - 1990
5. 1 vol.
6. $35 - indiv.; $55 - libraries
7. periodic supp.
9. 83-137043/9645918/KF547.H58

1. **LETTERS OF CREDIT**
2. McCullough, Barton B.
3. Bender
4. 1987
5. 1 vol.
6. $110 incl. 3 mos. supp.
7. periodic supp.
8. 1989 - $49.50; 1990 - $88.50
9. 86-72820/15647108/KF1028.M33

1. **LIABILITY INSURANCE**
2. -
3. Illinois ICLE
4. 1989
5. 1 vol.
6. $65.95
7. periodic supp.
8. no supp. yet

1. **LIABILITY ISSUES IN THE HOSPITAL SETTING**
2. -
3. Indiana CLE
4. 1989
5. 1 vol.
6. $55
7. no supp. planned

1. **LIBEL AND PRIVACY: THE PREVENTION AND DEFENSE OF LITIGATION**
2. Sanford, Bruce W.
3. Prentice Hall Law & Business
4. 2nd ed. - 1991
5. 1 vol.
6. $95 incl. 4 mos. supp.
7. periodic supp.
8. no supp. yet
9. 91-9284/23140387/KF1266.S23

1. **LIBRARY OF CONGRESS CLASSIFICATION CLASS H SUBCLASSES H-HJ - SOCIAL SCIENCES: ECONOMICS - CUMULATIVE SCHEDULE AND INDEX**
2. Dershem, Larry D.
3. Rothman
4. 1989
5. 1 vol.
6. $95
7. quarterly supp.
8. 1989/90 - no charge; 1990/91 - $52.50
9. 89-10441/19981346/Z696.U5H-HJ

1. **LIBRARY OF CONGRESS CLASSIFICATION CLASS H SUBCLASSES HM-HX - SOCIAL SCIENCES: SOCIOLOGY - CUMULATIVE SCHEDULE AND INDEX**
2. Dershem, Larry D.
3. Rothman
4. 1989
5. 1 vol.
6. $75
7. quarterly supp.
8. 1989/90 - $45; 1990/91 - $52.50
9. 88-5916/19325048/Z696.U5HM-HX

1. **LIBRARY OF CONGRESS CLASSIFICATION CLASS J - POLITICAL SCIENCE - CUMULATIVE SCHEDULE AND INDEX**
2. Dershem, Larry D.
3. Rothman
4. 1987
5. 1 vol.
6. $100
7. quarterly supp.
8. 1989/90 - $50; 1990/91 - $47.50
9. 15059680/Z696.U5J

1. **LIBRARY OF CONGRESS CLASSIFICATION CLASS KDZ, KG-KH - LAW OF THE AMERICAS, LATIN AMERICA AND THE WEST INDIES - CUMULATIVE SCHEDULE AND INDEX**
2. Dershem, Larry D.
3. Rothman
4. 1988
5. 1 vol.
6. $85
7. quarterly supp.
8. 1989-1990 - $45; 1990/91 - $47.50
9. 88-18256/18069452/Z696.U5K34

1. **LIBRARY OF CONGRESS CLASSIFICATION CLASS K - SUBCLASS KF - LAW OF THE UNITED STATES - CUMULATIVE INDEX**

2. Dershem, Larry D.
3. Rothman
4. 1982
5. 1 vol.
6. $35
7. quarterly supp.
8. 1989-1990 - $45; 1990/91 - $47.50
9. 82-22987/9044468/Z696.U5K55

1. **LIBRARY OF CONGRESS CLASSIFICATION CLASS K - SUBCLASS KF - LAW OF THE UNITED STATES - CUMULATIVE SCHEDULE**
2. Dershem, Larry D.
3. Rothman
4. 1984
5. 1 vol.
6. $75
7. quarterly supp.
8. 1989/90 - $45; 1990/91 - $47.50
9. 83-22923/10071701/Z696.U5K55

1. **LIBRARY OF CONGRESS CLASSIFICATION CLASS K - SUBCLASS K LAW (GENERAL) - CUMULATIVE SCHEDULE AND INDEX**
2. Dershem, Larry D.
3. Rothman
4. 1985
5. 1 vol.
6. $60
7. quarterly supp.
8. 1989/90 - $45; 1990/91 - $47.50
9. 85-1885/1167745/Z696.U5K23

1. **LIBRARY OF CONGRESS CLASSIFICATION CLASS K - SUBCLASS KD - LAW OF THE UNITED KINGDOM AND IRELAND - CUMULATIVE SCHEDULE AND INDEX**
2. Dershem, Larry D.
3. Rothman
4. 1985
5. 1 vol.
6. $75
7. quarterly supp.
8. 1989/90 - $45; 1990/91 - $47.50
9. 85-25597/12809876/Z696.U5K3

1. **LIBRARY OF CONGRESS CLASSIFICATION CLASS K - SUBCLASS KE - LAW OF CANADA - CUMULATIVE SCHEDULE AND INDEX**
2. Dershem, Larry D.
3. Rothman
4. 1987
5. 1 vol.
6. $75
7. quarterly supp.
8. 1989/90 - $45; 1990/91 - $47.50
9. 87-24147/16685240/Z696.U5K4

1. **LIBRARY OF CONGRESS CLASSIFICATION CLASS KJ-KKZ - LAW OF EUROPE - CUMULATIVE SCHEDULE AND INDEX**
2. Dershem, Larry D.
3. Rothman
4. 1990
5. 1 vol.
6. $95
7. quarterly supp.
8. 1990/91 - free
9. 90-8835/21975655/Z696.U5K64

1. **LIBRARY OF CONGRESS CLASSIFICATION CLASS KJV-KJW - LAW OF FRANCE - CUMULATIVE SCHEDULE AND INDEX**
2. Dershem, Larry D.
3. Rothman
4. 1988
5. 1 vol.
6. $85
7. quarterly supp.
8. 1989/90 - $45; 1990/91 - $47.50
9. 88-37895/18715013/Z696.U5K65

1. **LIBRARY OF CONGRESS CLASSIFICATION CLASS KK-KKC - LAW OF GERMANY - CUMULATIVE SCHEDULE AND INDEX**
2. Dershem, Larry D.
3. Rothman
4. 1989
5. 1 vol.
6. $95
7. quarterly supp.
8. 1990/91 - $52.50
9. 90-8032/20994800/Z696.U5K7

1. **LIBRARY OF CONGRESS CLASSIFICATION CLASS Z - BIBLIOGRAPHY: LIBRARY SCIENCE - CUMULATIVE SCHEDULE AND INDEX**
2. Dershem, Larry D.
3. Rothman
4. 1991
5. 1 vol.

6. price not yet set
7. quarterly supp.
8. 1991 - $52.50

1. **LICENSING IN FOREIGN AND DOMESTIC OPERATIONS**
2. Eckstrom, Lawrence J.
3. Clark Boardman Callaghan
4. 3rd ed. - 1972
5. 3 vols.
6. $345 incl. 3 mos. supp.
7. annual supp.
8. 1989 - $154.50; 1991 - $193
9. 72-189145/408555/KF3147.A6E34

1. **LICENSING IN FOREIGN AND DOMESTIC OPERATIONS: FORMS**
2. Goldscheider, Robert S.
3. Clark Boardman Callaghan
4. 1978-79
5. 4 vols.
6. $435 incl. 3 mos. supp.
7. annual supp.
8. 1989 - $170; 1991 - $264
9. 58-13380/4458977

1. **LIEBER ON PENSIONS**
2. Lieber, William M.
3. Prentice Hall Law & Business
4. 1991
5. 5 vols.
6. $500 incl. 4 mos. supp.
7. periodic supp.
8. no supp. yet
9. 91-230421/23976262/KF3512.L54

1. **LIENS AND CLAIMS – COLORADO**
2. Greenwald, Jack
3. CLE - Colorado
4. 1985
5. 1 vol.
6. $85
7. periodic supp.
8. 1987 - $25; 1991 - $35
9. 12780536/KFC1955.5.G74

1. **LIFE PLANNING IN FLORIDA**
2. Allison, Thomas E. et al.
3. Butterworth-Fla.
4. 1988
5. 1 vol.
6. $19
7. periodic supp.
8. no supp. yet
9. 19407283/KFF91.A3A44

1. **LINDEY ON ENTERTAINMENT, PUBLISHING AND THE ARTS, 2ND ED.**
2. Lindey, Alexander
3. Clark Boardman Callaghan
4. 2nd ed. - 1980-82
5. 4 vols.
6. $450 incl. 3 mos. supp.
7. biannual supp.& annual handbook
8. 1989 - $254.50; 1991 - $297
9. 80-10991/6042938/KF2992.L5

1. **LIQUOR CONTROL LAW REPORTS**
2. -
3. CCH
4. 1934
5. 9 vols (federal & all states)
6. $2255/yr.; $2050/yr. for 2 yrs.
7. monthly supp.
9. 35-96

1. **LIQUOR LIABILITY LAW**
2. Mosher, J.F.
3. Bender
4. 1987
5. 2 vols.
6. $210 incl. 3 mos. supp.
7. periodic supp.
8. 1989 - $55; 1990 - $73
9. 87-171619/17258830/KF1293.5.M67

1. **LITIGATING AGE DISCRIMINATION CASES**
2. Ruzicho, Andrew J. & Louis A. Jacobs
3. Clark Boardman Callaghan
4. 1986
5. 1 vol.
6. $100 incl. 6 mos. supp.
7. annual supp.
8. 1989 - $41; 1990 - $45
9. 86-11736/13582435/KF3465.R89

1. **LITIGATING HEAD TRAUMA CASES**
2. Roberts, Arthur C., M.D., et al.
3. Wiley Law
4. 1989
5. 1 vol.
6. $125
7. annual supp.
8. 1991 - $50; 1992 - price NA
9. 90-167457/21975080/KF8925.P4R63

1. **LITIGATING NECK AND BACK INJURIES**
2. Tarantino, John A. & David J. Oliveira

3. James
4. 1987
5. 1 vol.
6. $79.97 incl. 3 mos. supp.
7. annual supp.
8. 1990 - $39.85; 1991 - $42.96
9. 87-403139/16682064/KF8925.P4T37

1. **LITIGATING WRONGFUL DISCHARGE CLAIMS**
2. Tobias, Paul H., ed.
3. Clark Boardman Callaghan
4. 1987
5. 2 vols.
6. $165 incl. 6 mos. supp.
7. annual supp.
8. 1989 - $43; 1990 - $50
9. 87-13832/15791801/KF3471.T6

1. **LITIGATION AND PRACTICE UNDER RULE 10B-5 (Securities Law Series, vol. 5, 5A, 5B, 5C & 5D)**
2. Jacobs, Arnold S.
3. Clark Boardman Callaghan
4. 2nd ed. - 1981
5. 5 vols.
6. $595 incl. 3 mos. supp.
7. 3 supp./yr.
8. 1989 - $279; 1991 - $329
9. 8l-15493/7837789/KF9369.J3

1. **LITIGATION FORMS AND CHECKLISTS**
2. Schleifer, Nancy
3. Wiley Law
4. 1991
5. 1 vol.
6. $105
7. periodic supp.
8. no supp. yet
9. 91-28621/24376694/KF8836.S35

1. **LITIGATION OF FEDERAL TAX CONTROVERSIES**
2. Burnett & Kafka
3. Shepard's
4. 1986
5. 1 vol.
6. $95
7. semiannual supp.
8. 1989 - $50; 1990 - $28
9. 86-21951/14166820/KF6324.B87

1. **LITIGATION OF INTERNATIONAL DISPUTES IN U.S. COURTS (International Business Law Series vol. 4)**
2. Nanda, Ved P. and David K. Pansius
3. Clark Boardman Callaghan
4. 1986
5. 1 vol.
6. $135 incl. 3 mos. supp.
7. annual supp.
8. 1989 - $62.50; 1991 - $79.50
9. 86-13667/13759714/KF4581.N36

1. **LITIGATION ORGANIZATION AND MANAGEMENT**
2. Dombroff, Mark A
3. Prentice Hall Law & Business
4. 2nd ed. - 1991
5. 2 vols.
6. $170 incl. 4 mos. supp.
7. annual supp.
8. no supp. yet
9. 91-879/24467223/KF8900.D66

1. **LITIGATION PARALEGAL**
2. Signey, Phillip J.
3. James
4. 1990
5. 1 vol.
6. $59.87 incl. 3 mos. supp.
7. annual supp.
8. 1991 - $32.90
9. 90-142565/21223510/KF8841.S58

1. **LIVING AND DYING WITH A REVOCABLE TRUST**
2. -
3. Minn. CLE
4. 1991
5. 1 vol.
6 $60
7. no supp. planned
9. 24679826

1. **LOCAL GOVERNMENT LAW**
2. Antieau, Chester James
3. Bender
4. 1955
5. 7 vols.
6. $650 incl. 3 mos. supp.
7. semiannual supp.
8. 1989 - $574; 1990 - $616
9. 55-3595/4583212/KF5300.A65A5

1. **LOCAL GOVERNMENT LAW**
2. Sands, C. Dallas & Michael E. Libonati
3. Clark Boardman Callaghan
4. 1981
5. 4 vols.

6. $350 incl. 6 mos. supp.
7. annual supp.
8. 1986 - $120; 1989 - $126
9. 81-10259/7672536/KF5300.S26

1. **LOCAL RULES OF KING COUNTY SUPERIOR COURT**
2. -
3. Book Pub.
4. 1985
5. 1 vol.
6. $20
7. annual supp.
8. 1989 - $13.50; 1990 - $10.50

1. **LOCAL RULES OF THE DISTRICT COURTS IN TEXAS**
2. Steves, Sterling W.
3. Butterworth-Texas
4. 1981
5. 1 vol.
6. $135
7. periodic supp.
8. 1990 - $99.50; 1991 - $67.50
9. 14707225/KFT1729.5.D58A2

1. **LOCAL RULES OF THE SUPERIOR COURT: WASHINGTON STATE**
2. Butterworth Staff
3. Butterworth-St. Paul
4. 1981
5. 2 vols.
6. $70
7. periodic supp.
8. 1989 - $155.50; 1990 - $60
9. 80-69436/7659524/KFW529.A2

1. **LONG-TERM CARE ADMINISTRATION: STANDARDS AND GUIDELINES FOR LONG-TERM CARE FACILITIES**
2. Ed. Staff
3. National Health
4. 1989
5. 1 vol.
6. $125 incl. 1 yr. supp.
7. quarterly supp.
8. renewal - $105/yr.
9. 89-217424/20783664/RA997.L657

1. **LONG TERM CARE AND THE LAW**
2. -
3. MILE
4. 1990
5. 1 vol.
6. $79.50
7. no supp. planned

1. **LONG TERM HEALTH CARE**
2. -
3. MILE
4. 1991
5. 1 vol.
6 $85.20
7. no supp. planned
9. 24576581/KF3826.N8L6

1. **THE LONGSHORE NEWSLETTER PROCEDURE MANUAL**
2. Brahm, Robert T.
3. Longshore
4. 1985
5. 1 vol.
6. $325 incl. 1 yr. supp.
7. quarterly supp.
8. renewal - $125/yr.
9. 13148100/KF3628.A6.B7

1. **LOS ANGELES COUNTY ZONING SUBDIVISION CODE**
2. -
3. Book Pub.
4. NA
5. 1 vol.
6. $28
7. quarterly supp.
8. 1989 - $19.50; 1990 - $30

1. **LOUISIANA APPELLATE PRACTICE HANDBOOK**
2. Stetter, Roger A. et al.
3. Lawyers Coop.
4. 1986
5. 1 vol.
6. $105 incl. 6 mos. supp.
7. annual supp.
8. 1989 - $32; 1990 - $34.50
9. 86-81536/14687130/KFL555.L6

1. **LOUISIANA ATTORNEY'S/SECRETARY'S HANDBOOK**
2. -
3. Mariposa
4. 1991
5. 1 vol.
6. $54
7. annual supp.
8. 1990 - $51; 1991 - $45
9. 88-641599/17968035/KFL77.L68

1. **LOUISIANA CORPORATIONS**
2. Holliday, James S. Jr. & Rick Norman
3. Lawyers Coop.
4. 1983
5. 2 vols.
6. $210 incl. 6 mos. supp.
7. annual supp.
8. 1990 - $51.50; 1991 - $55
9. 83-81051/10165376/KFL210.A6H59

1. **LOUISIANA COURTROOM EVIDENCE**
2. Cheatwood, Roy C. et al.
3. Parker
4. 1991
5. 1 vol.
6. price NA incl. 3 mos. supp.
7. annual supp.
8. no supp. yet

1. **LOUISIANA DIVORCE**
2. Lowe, Robert C.
3. Lawyers Coop.
4. 1984
5. 1 vol.
6. $115 incl. 6 mos. supp.
7. annual supp.
8. 1988 - $55; 1991 - $65
9. 83-82099/11398537/KFL100.L68

1. **LOUISIANA LANDLORD & TENANT LAW**
2. Armstrong, George M., Jr.
3. Butterworth-Texas
4. 1987
5. 1 vol.
6. $120
7. annual supp.
8. 1988 - $50; 1989 - $50
9. 15148327

1. **LOUISIANA OIL AND GAS LAW**
2. McDougal, Luther L. III
3. Butterworth-Texas
4. 1988
5. 1 vol.
6. $120
7. periodic supp.
8. 1989 - $57.50; 1990 - $57.50
9. 87-35516/17263138/KFL258.A1M33

1. **LOUISIANA SUCCESSIONS**
2. Carman, Laura Junge
3. Lawyers Coop.
4. 1991
5. 1 vol.
6. $110 incl. 6 mos. supp.
7. annual supp.
8. no supp. yet
9. 90-63601/23244653/KFL142.C37

1. **LOUISIANA WRONGFUL DEATH AND SURVIVOR ACTIONS**
2. Andre, Thomas J. Jr.
3. Butterworth-Texas
4. 1986
5. 1 vol.
6. $120
7. annual supp.
8. 1990 - $66.50
9. 85-26997/KFL197.D25A96

1. **THE LOW BACK (Courtroom Medicine Series, vols. 1, 1A, 1B)**
2. Gelfand, Leo et al.
3. Bender
4. 1962
5. 3 vols.
6. $350 incl. 3 mos. supp.
7. annual supp.
8. 1989 - $208; 1990 - $423
9. 62-6549/11952486/RA1011.C68

1. **LYING, CHEATING AND STEALING**
2. -
3. MILE
4. 1989
5. 1 vol.
6. $58
7. no supp. planned

1. **LYING, CHEATING & STEALING PLUS SECURITIES**
2. -
3. MILE
4. 1991
5. 1 vol.
6. $73.20
7. no supp. planned

1. **MAGISTRATE COURT HANDBOOK, GEORGIA**
2. Warren, Johnny W.
3. Harrison
4. 1984
5. 1 vol.
6. $39.95
7. annual supp.
8. 1989 - $20.95; 1990 - $25.90

1. **MAIL ORDER LEGAL MANUAL**
2. Keup, Erwin J.

3. Oasis
4. 1984
5. 1 vol.
6. $45
7. periodic supp.
8. to be supp. in 1991
9. 81-80335/12230137/KF2028.K48

1. **MAINE ADMINISTRATIVE PROCEDURE**
2. Ferdico, John N.
3. Butterworth-NH
4. 1985
5. 1 vol.
6. $65
7. periodic supp.
8. 1989 - $38.50; 1990 - $45
9. 17250620/KF5402.Z99M22

1. **MAINE BAR DIRECTORY**
2. -
3. Tower
4. 1992
5. 1 vol.
6. $38
7. annual ed.
8. 1991 - $29.50

1. **MAINE CIVIL REMEDIES**
2. Horton, Andrew M. & Peggy L. McGehee
3. Butterworth-NH
4. 1988
5. 1 vol.
6. $90
7. periodic supp.
8. 1989 - $75; 1991 - $15
9. 18462534

1. **MAINE CRIMINAL PRACTICE**
2. Cluchey, David P. & Michael D. Seitzinger
3. Butterworth-NH
4. 1985, 1986
5. 2 vols.
6. $175
7. periodic supp.
8. 1989 - $67.50; 1990 - $57.50
9. 11857567

1. **MAINE EVIDENCE**
2. Field, Richard H. & Peter L. Murray
3. Butterworth-NH
4. 2nd ed. - 1987
5. 1 vol.
6. $85
7. periodic supp.
8. 1991 - $30
9. 16819457

1. **MAINE FAMILY LAW: DIVORCE, SEPARATION AND ANNULMENT**
2. Levy, Jon David
3. Butterworth-NH
4. 1988
5. 1 vol.
6. $85
7. periodic supp.
8. no supp. yet
9. 19087201/KFM100.L48

1. **MAINE JURY INSTRUCTION MANUAL**
2. Alexander, Donald G.
3. Butterworth-NH
4. 1990
5. 1 vol.
6. $75
7. periodic supp.
8. no supp. yet
9. 21681937/KF8984.Z99M22

1. **MAINE MANUAL ON PROFESSIONAL RESPONSIBILITY**
2. Bd. of Overseers of the Bar
3. Butterworth-NH
4. 1986
5. 1 vol.
6. $45
7. periodic supp.
8. 1989 - $27.50; 1990 - $28
9. 91-26756/24172998/KFM76.5.A2M35

1. **MAINE PROBATE: HOW TO SURVIVE YOUR NEXT ESTATE**
2. -
3. Maine Bar
4. 1989
5. 1 vol.
6. $25
7. no supp. planned

1. **MAINE PROBATE FORMS, REV. ED.**
2. Butterworths' Staff
3. Butterworth-NH
4. 1991
5. 1 vol.
6. $40
7. periodic supp.
8. no supp. yet
9. 23719448/KFM144.A433.A2

1. **MAINE PROBATE MANUAL**
2. Mitchell, James E.

3. Butterworth-NH
4. 1988
5. 1 vol.
6. $95 ($40 for forms supp.)
7. periodic supp.
8. 1988 - $75
9. 83-188756/10506747/KFM144.A433A2

1. **MAINE WORKERS COMPENSATION ACT: PRACTICE AND PROCEDURE**
2. Devoe, Charles D.
3. Butterworth-NH
4. 1988
5. 1 vol.
6. $95
7. periodic supp.
8. 1989 - $67.50
9. 10150118/KFM342.A6D48

1. **MAINE WORKERS' COMPENSATION COMMISSION: APPELLATE DIVISION DECISIONS**
2. Devoe, Charles D. and Hull S., eds.
3. Butterworth-NH
4. 1989
5. 1 vol.
6. $55
7. annual vols.

1. **MAKING HEALTH CARE DECISIONS INCLUDING: LIVING WILLS AND DURABLE POWERS OF ATTORNEY**
2. Byrnes, Hon. John Carroll et al.
3. MICPEL
4. 1991
5. 1 vol.
6. $42
7. no supp. planned

1. **MAKING TRIAL OBJECTIONS**
2. McCarthy, James F. Sr., ed.
3. Wiley Law
4. 1986
5. 1 vol.
6. $105
7. annual supp.
8. 1989 - $40; 1991 - $50
9. 86-5488/13270852/KF8935.M25

1. **MANAGER'S MANUAL**
2. -
3. NCSI
4. NA
5. 2 vol.
6. $220 - members; $295 - nonmembers
7. monthly supp.
8. $275/yr. - members; $395/yr. - nonmembers

1. **MANAGING COBRA: THE COMPLETE COMPLIANCE GUIDE**
2. Cowan, Ari & Lee T. Peterson
3. Wiley Law
4. 1990
5. 1 vol.
6. $115 incl. 3 mos. supp.
7. periodic supp.
8. no supp. yet
9. 24583367/KF3515.C68

1. **MANAGING EMPLOYEE BENEFITS**
2. Bennett, Linda, ed.
3. WG&L
4. 1987
5. 1 vol.
6. $229/yr.
7. quarterly supp. & monthly newsletter

1. **MANAGING ENVIRONMENTAL RISK: REAL ESTATE AND BUSINESS TRANSACTIONS**
2. Machlin, Jennifer L. & Tomme R. Young
3. Clark Boardman Callaghan
4. 1988
5. 1 vol.
6. $110 incl. 3 mos. supp.
7. annual supp.
8. 1989 - $49.50; 1991 - $99
9. 88-17497//r89/18051867/KF1298.M32

1. **MANAGING THE FLORIDA CONDOMINIUM**
2. Clark, William D.
3. Butterworth-Fla.
4. 1988
5. 1 vol.
6. $80
7. periodic supp.
8. 1990 - $27
9. 89-122955/18817767/KFF114.C6C55

1. **MANAGING THE SMALL & MEDIUM-SIZED LAW FIRM**
2. -
3. Indiana CLE
4. 1988
5. 1 vol.
6. $40
7. no supp. planned

1. **MANAGING YOUR MEDICAL PRACTICE**
2. Wold, Charles
3. Bender
4. 1986
5. 1 vol.
6. $100 incl. 3 mos. supp.
7. periodic supp.
8. 1989 - $39; 1990 - $49.50
9. 86-70223/14346825/R728.W635

1. **MANITOBA & SASKATCHEWAN TAX REPORTER**
2. -
3. CCH
4. 1973
5. 1 vol.
6. $250/yr.; $225/yr. for 2 yrs.
7. monthly supp.
9. 74-154351/811582

1. **MANUAL FOR COMPLEX LITIGATION**
2. Judicial Panel on Multidistrict Litigation
3. Bender
4. 2nd ed. - 1948
5. 1 vol. (also vol. 1 part 2 - Moore's Federal Practice)
6. $100
7. supp. as needed
8. 1986 - $72; 1987 - $0
9. 48-2333

1. **MANUAL FOR COMPLEX LITIGATION**
2. Federal Judicial Center, ed.
3. Clark Boardman Callaghan
4. 1982
5. 1 vol.
6. $105 incl. 3 mos. supp.
7. periodic supp.
8. no supp. yet
9. 82-9507/8493418/KF8900.M35

1. **THE MANUAL FOR FLORIDA LEGAL SECRETARIES**
2. Florida Assn. of Legal Secretaries
3. Butterworth-Fla.
4. 1984
5. 3 vols.
6. $120
7. periodic supp.
8. 1989 - $40.25; 1990 - $79.40
9. 12367205/KFF77.M35

1. **MANUAL FOR LAWYERS AND LEGAL ASSISTANTS: REAL ESTATE, 2ND ED.**
2. Seward, Peter G. & M. Catherine Cantor
3. ICLE - Michigan
4. 1980
5. 1 vol.
6. $65
7. no supp. planned
9. 79-57456/6143031/KF570.Z9S48

1. **MANUAL FOR PRACTICE BEFORE BOARDS OF CONTRACT APPEALS**
2. -
3. FBA
4. 1984
5. 1 vol.
6. $15
7. periodic supp.
8. no supp. yet
9. 8085715/KF849.F43

1. **MANUAL FOR THE PRACTICE OF U.S. IMPORT LAW**
2. Ince, William & Leslie Glick
3. Kluwer
4. 1990
5. 1 vol.
6. $184 incl. 3 mos. supp.
7. periodic supp.
9. 90-4929/21950394/KF1993.M36

1. **MANUAL OF CLASSIFICATION**
2. U.S. Patent and Trademark Office
3. order from USGPO - stock #903-006-00000-5
4. 1988
5. 1 vol.
6. $66/yr.
7. quarterly supp.
9. 7639764

1. **MANUAL OF CORPORATE FORMS FOR SECURITIES PRACTICE (Securities Law Series, vol. 9 & 9A)**
2. Jacobs, Arnold S.
3. Clark Boardman Callaghan
4. 1981
5. 3 vols.
6. $325 incl. 3 mos. supp.
7. annual supp.
8. 1989 - $59.50; 1991 - $295
9. 81-3857/7462050/KF1437.J3

1. **MANUAL OF PATENT EXAMINING PROCEDURE**
2. U.S. Dept. of Commerce Patent and Trademark Office

3. order from USGPO - stock #903-007-00000-1
4. 1990
5. 1 vol.
6. $78/yr.
7. periodic supp.
9. 7119759/KF3120.A4

1. **MANUAL OF RULES, CLASSIFICATIONS, AND INTERPRETATIONS FOR WORKERS COMPENSATION INSURANCE**
2. Duval, Natalia
3. Intl. Risk Mgmt. Inst.
4. 1990
5. 1 vol.
6. $166 incl. 1 yr. supp. (all state rate pages avail. for $360/yr.)
7. quarterly supp.

1. **MANUAL ON EMPLOYMENT DISCRIMINATION AND CIVIL RIGHTS ACTIONS IN THE FEDERAL COURTS, ATTORNEYS' EDITION**
2. Richey, Charles R.
3. Michie
4. 1988
5. 1 vol.
6. $80 incl. 3 mos. supp.
7. annual supp.
8. no supp. yet
9. 88-9358/KF3464.R53

1. **MANUAL ON THE ADMINISTRATIVE PROCESSING OF FEDERAL SECTOR EEO COMPLAINTS**
2. -
3. FBA
4. 1988
5. 1 vol.
6. $25
7. to be supp. in 1992

1. **MANUFACTURING RISK MANAGEMENT AND INSURANCE**
2. Woodward, Jeffrey et al.
3. Intl. Risk Mgmt. Inst.
4. 1988
5. 2 vols.
6. $196 incl. 1 yr. supp.
7. quarterly supp.
9. 88-127240/18624014/HG9964.W66

1. **MAP PACKAGE: ALTERNATIVE DISPUTE RESOLUTION**
2. Bar Services Div. & Special Comm. on Dispute Resolution
3. ABA
4. 1983
5. 1 vol.
6. $50
7. no supp. planned

1. **MAP PACKAGE: LAW RELATED EDUCATION, TEACHING YOUNG PEOPLE ABOUT THE LAW**
2. Bar Services Div. & Special Comm. on Youth Education for Citizenship
3. ABA
4. 1982
5. 1 vol.
6. $50
7. no supp. planned

1. **MAP PACKAGE: NON-DUES SOURCES OF INCOME**
2. Bar Services Div.
3. ABA
4. 1983
5. 1 vol.
6. $60
7. no supp. planned

1. **MAP PACKAGE #2: LONG RANGE PLANNING**
2. Bar Services Div.
3. ABA
4. 1981
5. 1 vol.
6. $45
7. no supp. planned

1. **MARINE P&I POLICY ANNOTATIONS**
2. Tort & Insurance Practice Section
3. ABA
4. 1982
5. 1 vol.
6. $39.95
7. periodic supp.
8. 1986 - $17
9. 81-71273/8668024/KF1135.A59M37

1. **MARINE POLLUTION AND THE LAW OF THE SEA**
2. Kindt, John Warren
3. Hein
4. 1986
5. 6 vols.
6. $545
7. periodic supp.
8. 1988 - $170
9. 84-814882/12371369/JX4411.K56

1. **MARITAL LAW**
2. -
3. ABICLE
4. 1985
5. 1 vol.
6. $75
7. no supp. yet
8. -
9. 4388632/KFA94.A6A4

1. **MARITAL PROPERTY LAW IN WISCONSIN 2nd ed.**
2. Christiansen, Keith, et al.
3. State Bar of Wisc.
4. 1986
5. 2 vols.
6. $240
7. periodic supp.
8. 1990 - $90; 1991 - $67
9. 85-164611/11791844/KFW2497.M37

1. **MARITIME LAW AND PRACTICE**
2. -
3. Florida Bar
4. 2nd ed. - 1987
5. 1 vol.
6. $65
7. periodic supp.
8. 1989 - $20
9. 87-81291/16369975/KF1104.M37

1. **MARITIME LAW HANDBOOK**
2. Heward, Roger
3. Kluwer
4. 1988
5. 1 vol.
6. $174 incl. 3 mos. supp.
7. periodic supp.
8. 1990 - $130; 1991 - $158
9. 87-17920/16275860/K1155.4.M36

1. **MARITIMES TAX REPORTER**
2. -
3. CCH
4. 1950
5. 1 vol.
6. $260/yr.; $235/yr. for 2 yrs.
7. monthly supp.
9. 82-138413/9829839/KE6190.A6M37

1. **MARKETING FOR LAWYERS AND LAW FIRMS**
2. -
3. Wash. Bar
4. 1989
5. 1 vol.
6. $40
7. no supp. planned

1. **MARSH'S CALIFORNIA CORPORATION LAW**
2. Marsh, Harold, Jr. & R. Roy Finkle
3. Prentice Hall Law & Business
4. 3rd ed. - 1990
5. 4 vols.
6. $395 incl. 4 mos. supp.
7. periodic supp.
8. 1991 - $110
9. 90-48344/22489019/KFC345.M37

1. **MARYLAND APPELLATE PRACTICE: RULES AND COMMENTARY WITH FORMS**
2. Legg, Benson E., et al.
3. MICPEL
4. 1989
5. 1 vol.
6. $60
7. no supp. yet
9. 20475841/KFM1755.L5

1. **MARYLAND CASES ON DISCRIMINATION**
2. Maryland Bar Assn., Section of Labor Law MCHR Digest Subcommittee
3. MICPEL
4. 1986
5. 2 vols.
6. $180
7. periodic supp.
8. no supp. yet
9. 13715958/KFM1534.5.D5M372

1. **MARYLAND CIVIL PROCEDURE FORMS: PRACTICE**
2. Klein, Robert D. & Edward S. Digges
3. Aspen
4. 1984
5. 2 vols.
6. $229 incl. 3 mos. supp.
7. annual supp.
8. 1987 - $89.50; 1988 - $89.95
9. 85-157460/KFM1730.A65D54

1. **MARYLAND COMMERCIAL FINANCING FORMS - PRACTICE**
2. Stalfort, John A. & Michael S. Speas
3. Aspen
4. 1986
5. 1 vol.

6. $159 incl. 3 mos. supp.
7. annual supp.
8. 1987 - $89.50; 1988 - $89.95
9. 86-1173/13126219/KFM1414.A1S73

1. **MARYLAND CONDOMINUM, HOME-OWNER ASSOCIATION, COOPERATIVE AND TIME-SHARING FORMS--PRACTICE**
2. Rottman, S. Leonard
3. Aspen
4. 1986
5. 1 vol.
6. $159 incl. 3 mos. supp.
7. annual supp.
8. 1987 - $80
9. 86-23495/14241563/KFM1314.C6R67

1. **MARYLAND CORPORATE FORMS: PRACTICE**
2. Shapiro, Ronald M. & Alan R. Sachs
3. Aspen
4. 1976
5. 2 vols.
6. $239 incl. 3 mos. supp.
7. annual supp.
8. 1988 - $95; 1989 - $89
9. 76-55157/2968480/KFM1413.A65S5

1. **MARYLAND COURT RULES**
2. -
3. Rules
4. 1966
5. 2 vols.
6. $80 incl. 1 yr. supp.
7. periodic supp.
8. renewal fee

1. **MARYLAND CRIMINAL PATTERN JURY INSTRUCTIONS**
2. Maryland State Bar Assn., Inc. Committee on Criminal Pattern Jury Instructions
3. MICPEL
4. 1991
5. 1 vol.
6. $90
7. periodic supp.
8. -
9. 85-63867/13195100/KFM1783.M39

1. **MARYLAND DIVORCE AND SEPARATION LAW**
2. Thomas, Daniel F.
3. MICPEL
4. 5th ed - 1991
5. 1 vol.
6. $75
7. supp. planned
8. -
9. 85-61567/12432719/KFM1300.M37

1. **MARYLAND DOMESTIC RELATIONS FORMS: PRACTICE**
2. Turnbull, Ann M. & Joseph Wase
3. Aspen
4. 1979
5. 1 vol.
6. $159 incl. 3 mos. supp.
7. annual supp.
8. 1987 - $92.50; 1988 - $85
9. 79-84555/5102026/KFM1294.A65T87

1. **MARYLAND ESTATE PLANNING, WILL DRAFTING AND ESTATE ADMINISTRATION FORMS: PRACTICE**
2. Barr, Albert S., III & A. MacDonough Plant
3. Aspen
4. 1982
5. 1 vol.
6. $159 incl. 3 mos. supp.
7. annual supp.
8. 1988 - $77.95; 1989 - $62
9. 85-29839/8964958/KF1340.A65B37

1. **MARYLAND EVIDENCE CHECKLISTS**
2. Grimm, Paul
3. MICPEL
4. 1989
5. 1 vol.
6. $50
7. no supp. yet
9. 20213216/KFM1740.G744

1. **MARYLAND LICENSING REQUIRE-MENTS: A SOURCEBOOK FOR LAWYERS WHO ADVISE BUSINESSES AND PROFESSIONALS**
2. Johnson, Maureen L., editor
3. MICPEL
4. 1987
5. 1 vol.
6. $85
7. periodic supp.
8. no supp. yet
9. 86-63705/16357439/KFM1525.M37

1. **MARYLAND PRACTICE FORMS**
2. Young Lawyers Section of the Bar Assn. of Baltimore

3. MICPEL
4. 1984
5. 1 vol.
6. $50
7. periodic supp.
8. -
9. 11489470

1. **MARYLAND PUBLIC INFORMATION ACT**
2. -
3. MICPEL
4. 1990
5. 1 vol.
6. $21
7. no supp. yet

1. **MARYLAND REAL ESTATE FORMS: PRACTICE**
2. Reno, Russell R. Jr. & W.E. Simmons, Jr.
3. Aspen
4. 1983
5. 2 vols.
6. $229 incl. 3 mos. supp.
7. annual supp.
8. 1988 - $76.95; 1989 - $89.95
9. 84-149438/10132923/KFM1326.A65R46

1. **MARYLAND REAL ESTATE LEASING FORMS - PRACTICE**
2. Albert, Charles T. & Edward J. Levin
3. Aspen
4. 1988
5. 2 vols.
6. $269 incl. 3 mos. supp.
7. annual supp.
8. $75 - $90/supp.
9. 88-3203/17546764/KFM1317.A65A37

1. **MARYLAND SENTENCING GUIDELINES MANUAL**
2. Admin. Office of the Courts
3. MICPEL
4. 1987
5. 1 vol.
6. $12
7. periodic supp.
8. 1984 - $5
9. 83-622880/10751499/KFM1783.2.A85

1. **MARYLAND STATE BOARD OF CONTRACT APPEALS DECISIONS**
2. Maryland State Board of Contract Appeals
3. MICPEL
4. 1986
5. 3 vols.
6. $315
7. annual supp.
8. 1989 - $90
9. 13673221/KFM1351.5.A8

1. **MARYLAND TAX COURT SERVICE**
2. Eyler, Carl R.
3. Hawkins
4. 1990
5. 1 vol.
6. $375
7. periodic supp.
8. renewal - $250/yr.

1. **MARYLAND TAXES, 2nd Ed.**
2. Rombro, Robert, et al., eds.
3. MICPEL
4. 1990
5. 2 vols.
6. $140
7. periodic supp.
9. 81-83431/8184543/KFM1670.M37

1. **MARYLAND TORT DAMAGES**
2. Shadoan, George W., ed.
3. MICPEL
4. 3rd ed. - 1990
5. 1 vol.
6. $50
7. periodic supp.
8. no supp. yet
9. 90-60858/21530594/KFM1395.M39

1. **MARYLAND TRIAL JUDGES' BENCHBOOK**
2. Administrative Office of the Courts
3. MICPEL
4. 1990
5. 1 vol.
6. $60
7. periodic supp.
8. no supp. yet
9. 14115052/KFM1738.M34

1. **MASSACHUSETTS CIVIL ACTIONS & PROCEDURE**
2. Ed. Staff
3. Gould
4. NA
5. 1 vol.
6. $18
7. annual supp.
8. $5 - $10/supp.

1. **MASSACHUSETTS CIVIL SERVICE REPORTER**
2. -
3. NELP
4. 1989
5. 1 vol./yr.
6. $160/yr.
7. -
9. 19693330/KFM2835.A35M37

1. **MASSACHUSETTS COLLECTION LAW: DEBTOR/CREDITOR PRACTICE, PROCEDURE, REMEDIES**
2. Shapiro, Jordan L. et al.
3. Lawyers Coop.
4. 1984
5. 1 vol.
6. $115 incl. 6 mos. supp.
7. annual supp.
8. 1989 - $47.50; 1990 - $55
9. 84-80874/11362793/KFM2567.C6S5

1. **MASSACHUSETTS COLLECTIONS MANUAL, SECOND EDITION**
2. Kamberg, Berman, Gold & West, PC
3. Butterworth-NH
4. 1990
5. 1 vol.
6. $75
7. periodic supp.
8. no supp. yet
9. 12131679

1. **MASSACHUSETTS CONDOMINIUM LAW**
2. Brown, Barry & Bernard V. Keenan
3. Butterworth-NH
4. 1985
5. 1 vol.
6. $125
7. periodic supp.
8. 1990 - $70; 1991 - $20
9. 85-72503/12841117/KFM2514.C6B76

1. **MASSACHUSETTS CONDOMINIUM LAW**
2. Galvin, Robert J. et al.
3. Mass. CLE
4. NA
5. 2 vols.
6. $75
7. periodic sup.
8. 1991 - $34.50
9. 23935097

1. **MASSACHUSETTS CORPORATE FORMS--PRACTICE**
2. Coggins, Dana C., & Michael J. Bohnen
3. Aspen
4. 1989
5. 2 vols.
6. $280 incl. 3 mos. supp.
7. annual supp.
8. $79-$95/supp.
9. 89-5/19124791/KFM2613.A65C34

1. **MASSACHUSETTS CORPORATE TAX MANUAL, 2ND ED.**
2. Dichele, Ernest Michael and J. Paul Finnegan
3. Butterworth-NH
4. 1986
5. 1 vol.
6. $65
7. periodic supp.
8. no supp. yet
9. 85-73643/14355085/KFM2877.D52

1. **MASSACHUSETTS CORPORATION LAW WITH FEDERAL TAX ANALYSIS**
2. Smith, James W. & Zolman Cavitch
3. Bender
4. 1963
5. 1 vol.
6. $130 incl. 3 mos. supp.
7. annual supp.
8. 1989 - $104; 1990 - $120.50
9. 64-499/9375961/KFM2610.S5

1. **MASSACHUSETTS CORPORATIONS**
2. Muir, Douglas A. & Michael J. Puzo
3. Lawyers Coop.
4. 1981
5. 1 vol.
6. $115 incl. 6 mos. supp.
7. annual supp.
8. 1990 - $61.50; 1991 - $65
9. 79-92872/8598538/KFM2610.A6M953

1. **MASSACHUSETTS DISCRIMINATION LAW REPORTER**
2. -
3. NELP
4. 1979
5. 1 vol./yr.
6. $230/yr.
7. monthly supp.
8. 17718285/KFM2811.A55M32

1. **MASSACHUSETTS DOMESTIC RELATIONS**
2. Harvey, John V. et al.

3. Lawyers Coop.
4. 1982
5. 2 vols.
6. $210 incl. 6 mos. supp.
7. annual supp.
8. 1989 - $62; 1990 - $75
9. 82-82112/9255768/KFM2495.M37

1. **MASSACHUSETTS ENVIRONMENTAL LAW**
2. McGregor, Gregor I. et al.
3. Mass. CLE
4. 1991
5. 2 vols.
6. $125
7. periodic supp.
8. no supp. yet
9. 90-63090/24321881/KFM2754.M37

1. **MASSACHUSETTS ESTATE PLANNING, WILL DRAFTING AND ESTATE ADMINISTRATION FORMS--PRACTICE**
2. Clymer, John H., et al.
3. Aspen
4. 1989
5. 2 vols.
6. $260 incl. 3 mos. supp.
7. annual supp.
8. $79-95/supp.
9. 88-35135/19129989/KFM2540.A65C59

1. **MASSACHUSETTS EVIDENCE: A COURTROOM REFERENCE**
2. McNaught, John J. et al.
3. Mass. CLE
4. 1988
5. 1 vol.
6. $75
7. biennial supp.
8. 1990 - $24.50; 1992 - price NA
9. 87-62743/18590154/KFM2940.M36

1. **MASSACHUSETTS FAMILY LAW MANUAL**
2. Freedman, Hon. Haskell C.
3. Mass. CLE
4. 1986
5. 2 vols.
6. $125
7. periodic supp.
8. 1989 - $27.50; 1992 - price NA
9. 85-62758/15127080/KFM2494.F74

1. **MASSACHUSETTS FORECLOSURES**
2. Vrabel, Joseph P.J. et al.
3. Mass. CLE
4. 1990
5. 1 vol.
6. $75
7. periodic supp.
8. no supp. yet
9. 90-63085/22717249/KFM2530.5.F6V73

1. **MASSACHUSETTS LABOR CASES**
2. -
3. NELP
4. 1974
5. 1 vol./yr.
6. $345/yr.
7. monthly supp.
9. 85-19342/6179029/KFM2731.A555

1. **MASSACHUSETTS LABOR RELATIONS REPORTER**
2.
3. NELP
4. 1974
5. 1 vol./yr.
6. $345/yr.
7. monthly supp.

1. **MASSACHUSETTS PLEADING AND PRACTICE - FORMS AND COMMENTARY**
2. Swartz, Edward M. et al.
3. Bender
4. 1974
5. 7 vols.
6. $545 incl. 3 mos. supp.
7. periodic supp.
8. 1989 - $125; 1990 - $162
9. 74-83487/1287718/KFM2930.S95

1. **MASSACHUSETTS PROBATE MANUAL**
2. Warner, Joseph P. & H.S. Reynolds
3. Mass. CLE
4. 1988
5. 1 vol.
6. $95
7. biennial supp.
8. 1991 - $24.50
9. 87-62744/19613055/KFM2544.M37

1. **MASSACHUSETTS REAL ESTATE**
2. Marzelli, Robert L.
3. Lawyers Coop.
4. 1983
5. 1 vol.
6. $115 incl. 6 mos. supp.
7. annual supp.

8. 1990 - $52; 1991 - $55
9. 83-82338/10996264/KFM2512.M37

1. **MASSACHUSETTS REAL ESTATE LEASING FORMS**
2. Hackett
3. Aspen
4. 1991
5. 2 vols.
6. $159 incl. 3 mos. supp.
7. annual supp. yet
8. no supp. yet
9. 90-45087/23146952/KFM2517.A65H33

1. **MASSACHUSETTS SALES AND USE TAX MANUAL**
2. Donovan, Joseph
3. Butterworth-NH
4. 1987
5. 2 vols.
6. $175
7. periodic supp.
8. 1991 - $155
9. 87-401799/16147833/KFM2884.D66

1. **MASSACHUSETTS STANDARDIZED CIVIL PRACTICE FORMS**
2. Garrity, Paul G. & James A. Frieden
3. Little, Brown
4. 1986
5. 4 vols.
6. $400
7. periodic supp.
8. 1988 - $77
9. 85-80001/14514803/KFM2930.A65G37

1. **MASSACHUSETTS TAXATION AND DOR PRACTICE**
2. Scharaffa, Frank J.
3. Mass. CLE
4. 1989
5. 1 vol.
6. $75
7. periodic supp.
8. 1992 - price NA
9. 88-62783/19787419/KFM2870.M37

1. **MASSACHUSETTS WORKERS' COMPENSATION PRACTICE MANUAL**
2. Gargano, Paul
3. Butterworth-NH
4. 1988
5. 1 vol.
6. $115
7. annual supp.
8. 1991 - $25
9. 88-14505/17876078/KFM2742.G37

1. **MASSACHUSETTS ZONING MANUAL**
2. Healy, Martin R. and Robert W. Mack
3. Mass. CLE
4. 1988
5. 1 vol.
6. $125
7. biennial supp.
8. to be supp. in 1993
9. 87-62745/20702154/KFM2858.M38

1. **MASTER INDEX: CLARK BOARDMAN CALLAGHAN'S ENVIRONMENTAL LAW SERIES**
2. Ilich, Mary Ellen
3. Clark Boardman Callaghan
4. 1990
5. 1 vol.
6. $150 incl. 2 supp.
7. semiannual supp.
8. 1991 - $150

1. **MASTER INDEX--CLARK BOARDMAN CALLAGHAN'S SECURITIES LAW SERIES**
2. -
3. Clark Boardman Callaghan
4. 1989
5. 1 vol.
6. $150/yr.
7. quarterly supp.
9. 89-28499/20564111/KF1431.M37

1. **MATERIALS ON ANTITRUST COMPLIANCE PROGRAMS**
2. Hancock, W.A.
3. Bus. Laws
4. 1982
5. 3 vols.
6. $185
7. quarterly supp.
8. renewal - $88/yr.
9. 8260343/KF1649.A7M38

1. **MATERIALS ON CORPORATE POLITICAL ACTIVITY**
2. Hancock, W.A.
3. Bus. Laws
4. 1981
5. 2 vols.
6. $185
7. quarterly supp.
8. renewal - $88/yr.

9. 10080238/KF4753.C6

1. **MATERIALS ON MINIMIZING MANAGEMENT LIABILITY**
2. Hancock, W.A.
3. Bus. Laws
4. 1979
5. 3 vols.
6. $148
7. quarterly supp.
8. renewal - $67.50/yr.

1. **MATERIALS ON THE AMERICANS WITH DISABILITIES ACT**
2. Hancock, W.A., ed.
3. Bus. Laws
4. 1991
5. 1 vol.
6. $85
7. periodic supp.

1. **MATERIALS ON THE HAZARD COMMUNICATION RULE**
2. Hancock, W.A.
3. Bus. Laws
4. 1986
5. 1 vol.
6. $90
7. quarterly supp.
8. renewal - $39/yr.
9. 13999830

1. **MATRIMONIAL CASELAW, NEW YORK EDITION**
2. Landa, Jay & Willard H. DaSilva
3. Matrimonial CaseLaw
4. 1987
5. 1 vol.
6. $285/yr.
7. monthly & quarterly supp.
9. 16736547

1. **MAXIMIZING DAMAGES IN SMALL PERSONAL INJURY CASES**
2. Rundlett, Ellsworth T.
3. James
4. 1991
5. 1 vol.
6. $59.93 incl. 3 mos. supp.
7. annual supp.
8. no supp. yet
9. 91-180114/24057548/KF8925.P4R86

1. **MAXIMIZING LAW FIRM PROFITABILITY**
2. Henning, Joel
3. Law Journal
4. 1991
5. 1 vol.
6. $75
7. periodic supp.
8. no supp. yet
9. 91-17162/23767297/KF276.5.H46

1. **MCGAFFEY LEGAL FORMS WITH TAX ANALYSIS**
2. McGaffey, Jere D.
3. Clark Boardman Callaghan
4. 1977
5. 6 vols.
6. $400 incl. 6 mos. supp.
7. semiannual supp. & rev. chapters
8. 1989 - $111.50; 1990 - $186
9. 77-12085/3223611/KF6450.A65M33

1. **MCGAFFEY LEGAL FORMS WITH TAX ANALYSIS - ESTATE & PERSONAL PLANNING (VOL. 3)**
2. McGaffey, Jere D.
3. Clark Boardman Callaghan
4. 1982
5. 1 vol.
6. $100 incl. 6 mos. supp.
7. semiannual supp.
8. 1989 - $53; 1990 - $56

1. **MECHANICS AND CONSTRUCTION LIENS IN ALASKA, OREGON AND WASHINGTON**
2. Blum, Brian A.
3. Butterworth-St. Paul
4. 1987
5. 1 vol.
6. $70
7. periodic supp.
8. 1991 - $50
9. 86-73204/KF900.Z95B58

1. **MECHANICS LIENS**
2. -
3. Indiana CLE
4. 1990
5. 1 vol.
6. $70
7. no supp. planned

1. **MECHANICS' LIENS AND MARYLAND'S TRUST FUND LAW**
2. Yumkas, Charles et al.
3. MICPEL
4. 1991

5. 1 vol.
6. $40
7. periodic supp.
8. no supp. yet
9. 13656014/KFM1355.5.Y95

1. **MEDIA LAW REPORTER**
2. Bolbach, Cynthia J.
3. BNA
4. 1977
5. 1 vol.
6. $752/yr.
7. weekly supp.
8. renewal - $696/yr.
9. 77-642176/3264060/KF2750.A513

1. **MEDICAL AND HOSPITAL NEGLIGENCE**
2. Zaremski, Miles J. & Louis S. Goldstein, eds.
3. Clark Boardman Callaghan
4. 1988
5. 4 vols.
6. $350 incl. 6 mos. supp.
7. annual supp.
8. 1990 - $45
9. 88-26231/18413260/KF2905.3.M437

1. **MEDICAL DEVICES REPORTER**
2. -
3. CCH
4. 1976
5. 2 vols.
6. $515/yr.; $470/yr. for 2 yrs.
7. monthly supp.
9. 76-377630/2912982/KF3827.M4C65

1. **MEDICAL EVIDENCE**
2. -
3. Illinois ICLE
4. 1990
5. 1 vol.
6. $79.95
7. periodic supp.
8. no supp. yet

1. **MEDICAL MALPRACTICE**
2. -
3. Illinois ICLE
4. 1989
5. 1 vol.
6. $98.95
7. no supp. planned

1. **MEDICAL MALPRACTICE**
2. Louisell, David W. et al.
3. Bender
4. 1960
5. 4 vols.
6. $475 incl. 3 mos. supp.
7. annual supp.
8. 1989 - $385; 1990 - $593
9. 61-66753/928686/KF2905.3.L68

1. **MEDICAL MALPRACTICE: GUIDE TO MEDICAL ISSUES**
2. Goldsmith, L.S., ed.
3. Bender
4. 1986
5. 7 vols.
6. $630 incl. 3 mos. supp.
7. periodic supp.
8. 1989 - $249; 1990 - $344

1. **MEDICAL MALPRACTICE CLAIMS**
2. -
3. MILE
4. 1990
5. 1 vol.
6. $63
7. no supp. planned

1. **MEDICAL MALPRACTICE CLAIMS IN THE 90's**
2. -
3. MILE
4. 1991
5. 1 vol.
6. $68
7. no supp. planned
9. 23717678/KF2905.3.Z9M455

1. **MEDICAL MALPRACTICE UPDATE**
2. -
3. Indiana CLE
4. 1991
5. 1 vol.
6. $50
7. no supp. planned

1. **MEDICAL TESTING: THE COMPLETE RESOURCE GUIDE TO GOOD LABORATORY PRACTICE AND HCFA COMPLIANCE**
2. -
3. BNA
4. 1989
5. 1 vol.
6. $195
7. no supp. planned
9. 89-15799/19922819/KF3826.L3M43

1. **MEDICARE HOME HEALTH AGENCY MANUAL**
2. U.S. Dept. of Health & Human Services, Health Care Financing Admin.
3. order from USGPO - stock #917-004-00000-5
4. 1986
5. 1 vol.
6. $155/yr.
7. periodic supp.
9. 21172036

1. **MEDICARE HOSPITAL MANUAL**
2. U.S. Dept. of Health & Human Services, Health Care Financing Admin.
3. order from USGPO - stock #917-005-00000-1
4. 1989
5. 1 vol.
6. $299/yr.
7. periodic supp.
9. 20397874

1. **MEDICARE-MEDICAID GUIDE**
2. -
3. CCH
4. 1969
5. 5 vols.
6. $995/yr.; $905/yr. for 2 yrs.
7. semimonthly supp.

1. **MEDICARE SKILLED NURSING FACILITY MANUAL**
2. U.S. Dept. of Health & Human Services, Health Care Financing Admin.
3. order from USGPO - stock #917-008-00000-1
4. 1989
5. 1 vol.
6. $178/yr.
7. periodic supp.
9. 20335171

1. **MEDINA'S BOSTWICK LAWYERS MANUAL**
2. Publisher's Editorial Staff
3. Bender
4. 5th ed. - 1949
5. 5 vols.
6. $490 incl. 3 mos. supp.
7. semiannual supp.
8. 1989 - $350; 1990 - $412
9. 49-3711/3893675/KFN5068.B6

1. **MEETINGS OF STOCKHOLDERS**
2. Balotti, R. Franklin et al.
3. Prentice Hall Law & Business
4. 2nd ed. - 1991
5. 1 vol.
6. $95 incl. 4 mos. supp.
7. periodic supp.
8. no supp. yet
9. 87-25775/24680223/KF1450.B35

1. **MERIT SYSTEMS PROTECTION BOARD SERVICE**
2. -
3. Hawkins
4. 1984
5. 1 vol.
6. $300/yr.
7. monthly supp.

1. **MERRICK-RIPPNER OHIO PROBATE LAW**
2. Carlin, Angela G. & Richard W. Schwartz
3. Banks
4. 4th ed. - 1989
5. 3 vols.
6. $235
7. annual supp.
8. 1990 - $47
9. 19082947/KFO144.M4

1. **MERTENS LAW OF FEDERAL INCOME TAXATION**
2. Weinstein, Martin
3. Clark Boardman Callaghan
4. 1954
5. 37 vols.
6. $1095 incl. 1 yr. supp.
7. monthly supp.
8. 1988 - $840; 1989 - $805
9. 42-22330

1. **MIAMI INSTITUTE ON ESTATE PLANNING**
2. Heckerling, Philip E., ed.
3. Bender
4. 1966
5. vol. 23 - 1989
6. $100
7. annual vol.
8. 1988 - $89.50; 1989 - $95

1. **MICHIGAN ANTITRUST DIGEST**
2. Alterman, Irwin M.
3. ICLE - Michigan
4. 1975
5. 1 vol.
6. $55
7. periodic supp.
9. 2626097/KFM4431.A57A4

1. **MICHIGAN APPELLATE HANDBOOK**
2. Gromek, Carl L., et al.
3. ICLE - Michigan
4. 1985
5. 1 vol.
6. $90
7. periodic supp.
8. 1988 - $30; 1989 - $35
9. 85-80329/13022178/KFM4755.G76

1. **MICHIGAN APPROVED COURT FORMS**
2. -
3. ICLE - Michigan
4. 1987
5. 1 vol.
6. $50/yr.
7. annual supp.
9. 85-60148/17366008/KFM4729.A21

1. **MICHIGAN BASIC PRACTICE HANDBOOK**
2. -
3. ICLE - Michigan
4. 3rd ed. - 1989
5. 2 vols.
6. $125
7. annual supp.
8. 1990 - $45
9. 89-81571/20821570/KFM4277.M5

1. **MICHIGAN BUSINESS FORMBOOK**
2. Kleist, Mark A., et al
3. ICLE - Michigan
4. 1989
5. 3 vols.
6. $195
7. periodic supp.
8. 1990 - $75; 1991 - $60
9. 89-80299//r90/19612186/KFM4352.A65M53

1. **MICHIGAN CIVIL PROCEDURE DURING TRIAL**
2. Young, Robert P., Jr. & Daniel D. Kopka, eds.
3. ICLE - Michigan
4. 1989
5. 1 vol.
6. $95
7. periodic supp.
8. 1990 - $40; 1991 - $32
9. 89-80473/20137950

1. **MICHIGAN CIVIL PROCEDURE FORMS--PRACTICE**
2. Shillman, Jeffrey N., & Richard D. Fox
3. Aspen
4. 1989
5. 2 vols.
6. $159 incl. 3 mos. supp.
7. annual supp.
8. $79-$95/supp.
9. 89-17724/20169991/KFM4730.A65S54

1. **MICHIGAN CORPORATE FORMS--PRACTICE**
2. Borgsdorf, Charles W.
3. Aspen
4. 1989
5. 2 vols.
6. $259 incl. 3 mos. supp.
7. annual supp.
8. $79-$95/supp.
9. 89-6826/19630785/KFM4413.A65M5

1. **MICHIGAN CORPORATION LAW WITH FEDERAL TAX ANALYSIS**
2. Schmidt, Robert M. & Zolman Cavitch
3. Bender
4. 1963
5. 1 vol.
6. $155 incl. 3 mos. supp.
7. annual supp.
8. 1990 - $104; 1991 - $124
9. 63-5035/2043724

1. **MICHIGAN COURTROOM EVIDENCE**
2. Wade, Michael D. & Jennifer J. Strom
3. ICLE - Michigan
4. rev. ed. - 1989
5. 1 vol.
6. $95
7. annual supp.
8. 1990 - $30; 1991 - $40
9. 85-80331/20340820/KFM4740.W34

1. **MICHIGAN CRIMINAL JURY INSTRUCTIONS, 2nd Ed.**
2. Michigan State Bar Special Comm. on Standard Criminal Jury Instructions
3. ICLE - Michigan
4. 1991
5. 3 vols.
6. $185
7. annual supp.
8. 1989 - $110; 1990 - $115
9. 77-71156/2908545/KFM4783.S8

1. **MICHIGAN DRUNK DRIVING LAW AND PRACTICE, REV. ED.**
2. Morgan, Michael V., ed.

3. ICLE - Michigan
4. 1992
5. 1 vol.
6. price NA
7. periodic supp.
8. 1990 - $40
9. 86-80064/13723216/KFM4497.8.M52

1. **MICHIGAN ESTATE PLANNING, WILL DRAFTING AND ESTATE ADMINISTRATION FORMS–PRACTICE**
2. Lower, Joyce Q. & Henry M. Grix
3. Aspen
4. 1989
5. 2 vols.
6. $219 incl. 3 mos. supp.
7. annual supp.
8. $79-$95/supp.
9. 89-14981/19885929/KFM4340.A65L69

1. **MICHIGAN FAMILY LAW**
2. Robbins, Norman N. & Lynn R. Collins eds.
3. ICLE - Michigan
4. 3d ed. - 1988
5. 2 vols.
6. $140
7. annual supp.
8. 1990 - $45; 1991 - $55
9. 87-83702/17408214/KFM4300.M5

1. **MICHIGAN FAMILY LAW SOURCEBOOK**
2. Soper, Katharine B. & Joseph W. Cunningham, eds.
3. ICLE - Michigan
4. 1990
5. 2 vols.
6. $145
7. annual supp.
8. 1991 - $55
9. 90-81123/21914819/KFM4294.6.M5

1. **MICHIGAN LAND TITLE STANDARDS**
2. Land Title Standards Comm., Real Property Law Section
3. State Bar of Mich.
4. 5th ed. - 1989
5. 1 vol.
6. $26
7. as needed
9. 20495426/KFM4326.S84

1. **THE MICHIGAN LAW OF DAMAGES**
2. Stockmeyer, N.O. Jr., ed.
3. ICLE - Michigan
4. 2nd ed. - 1989
5. 1 vol.
6. $125
7. annual supp.
8. 1991 - $45
9. 89-81007/20863742/KFM4395.M5

1. **MICHIGAN LAWYER'S MANUAL**
2. Needham, Roger A.
3. Lawyers Coop.
4. 1964
5. 2 vols.
6. $180 incl. 6 mos. supp.
7. annual supp.
8. 1990 - $69; 1991 - $71.50
9. 64-10719/1846231/KFM4280.N44

1. **MICHIGAN LEGAL FILING DIRECTORY**
2. Mitchell, Shannon and Emma Reardon
3. Shepard's
4. 1990
5. 2 vols.
6. $95
7. annual supp.
8. no supp. yet
9. 90-9112/22422188/KFM4277.M53

1. **MICHIGAN MEDICAL MALPRACTICE CASES ANNOTATED**
2. Dudley, D. Michael, Kitty L. Groh
3. MTLA
4. 1981
5. 2 vols.
6. $175 (member); $225 (nonmember)
7. periodic supp.
8. 1984 - $75; 1988 - $60 (members) - $75 (nonmembers)
9. 8166918/KFM4396.3.M3D835

1. **MICHIGAN NO-FAULT AUTO INSURANCE DECISIONS**
2. Sinas, George T.
3. MTLA
4. 1978
5. 5 vols.
6. $400 (member); $450 (nonmember)
7. quarterly supp.
8. 1990 - $105 (nonmembers); 1991 - $115 (nonmembers)
9. 78-100803/3892087/KFM4391.A46A5

1. **MICHIGAN NO-FAULT AUTOMOBILE CASES: LAW AND PRACTICE**
2. Logeman, Robert E.

3. ICLE - Michigan
4. 1988
5. 1 vol.
6. $95
7. annual supp.
8. $35
9. 88-082096/18768393/KFM4391.A46L63

1. **MICHIGAN PROBATE**
2. Edelman, Leonard
3. Lawyers Coop.
4. 1981
5. 1 vol.
6. $115 incl. 6 mos. supp.
7. annual supp.
8. 1986 - $35; 1990 - $50
9. 79-92366/8169102/KFM4344.A65E33

1. **MICHIGAN PROBATE SOURCEBOOK**
2. Chard, Lynn P. & Anna Headly
3. ICLE - Michigan
4. 2nd ed. - 1991
5. 3 vols.
6. $145
7. annual supp.
8. no supp. yet
9. 91-71293/23448804/KFM4344.M5

1. **MICHIGAN PUBLIC BENEFITS MANUAL**
2. -
3. Mich. Legal
4. 1988
5. 1 vol.
6. $100; $50 for LSC-funded orgs.
7. periodic supp.

1. **MICHIGAN PUBLIC EMPLOYEE REPORTER**
2. -
3. LRP
4. 1988
5. 1 vol.
6. $505/yr.
7. semimonthly supp.
9. 17850798

1. **MICHIGAN REAL ESTATE FORMS–PRACTICE**
2. Cameron, John G., Jr.
3. Aspen
4. 1988
5. 3 vols.
6. $299 incl. 3 mos. supp.
7. annual supp.
8. $79-$95/supp.
9. 88-23465/18322094/KFM4326.A65C36

1. **MICHIGAN REAL ESTATE PRACTICE AND FORMS**
2. Deems, Nyal D. & James M. Tervo
3. ICLE - Michigan
4. 1989
5. 2 vols.
6. $155
7. periodic supp.
8. 1991 - price NA
9. 89-80297/20536068/KFM4326.D44

1. **MICHIGAN RESIDENTIAL LANDLORD TENANT LAW, 2ND ED.**
2. -
3. Mich. Legal
4. 1986
5. 1 vol.
6. $60; $35 for LSC-funded orgs.
7. no supp. yet

1. **MICHIGAN REVOCABLE GRANTOR TRUSTS**
2. Lowe, Richard C. & George F. Bearup, eds.
3. ICLE - Michigan
4. 1991
5. 1 vol.
6. $95
7. periodic supp.
8. no supp. yet
9. 90-85064/23173686/KFM4339.L57M5

1. **MICHIGAN RULES OF PROFESSIONAL CONDUCT AND DISCIPLINARY PROCEDURE**
2. Dubin, Lawrence A. & Michael Alan Schwartz
3. ICLE - Michigan
4. 1989
5. 1 vol.
6. $75
7. periodic supp.
8. 1991 - $45
9. 89-80298/20922656/KFM4276.5.A2D6

1. **MICHIGAN STANDARD JURY INSTRUCTIONS - CIVIL**
2. Michigan Supreme Court Comm. on Standard Jury Instructions
3. ICLE - Michigan
4. 2nd ed. - 1981
5. 2 vols.
6. $130

7. annual supp.
8. 1989 - $35; 1990 - $45
9. 81-80665/7417547/KFM4742.A65S8

1. **MICHIGAN WILL DRAFTING**
2. Irish, Michael W. and John H. Martin
3. ICLE - Michigan
4. 1988
5. 1 vol.
6. $85
7. periodic supp.
8. 1990 - $45; 1991 - $40
9. 87-83699/17927690

1. **MICHIGAN WORKERS' COMPENSATION LAW REPORTER**
2. -
3. LRP
4. 1988
5. 2 vols.
6. $465/yr.
7. semimonthly supp.
9. 88-10459/18012473/KFM4542.A515

1. **MICHIGAN WRONGFUL DISCHARGE AND EMPLOYMENT DISCRIMINATION LAW**
2. Ruga, Barbara A. & Daniel D. Kopka, eds.
3. ICLE - Michigan
4. 1990
5. 1 vol.
6. $95
7. annual supp.
8. 1991 - $35
9. 90-81125/21914071/KFM4739.L32M5

1. **MIDAMERICA COMMODITY EXCHANGE RULES AND REGULATIONS**
2. -
3. MidAmerica
4. NA
5. 1 vol.
6. $30 incl. supp.
7. semiannual supp.
8. renewal - $15/yr.
9. 7990472/KF1087.M52A3

1. **MIDWEST ESTATE, TAX & BUSINESS PLANNING**
2. -
3. Indiana CLE
4. 1991
5. 1 vol.
6. $52
7. no supp. planned

1. **MIDWEST LABOR LAW CONFERENCE**
2. -
3. Ohio CLE
4. annual (1965-)
5. 1987 - 1 vol.
6. $35
7. annual vol.
8. 1989 - $35
9. 11729563/KF3369.A2M5

1. **MIDWEST STOCK EXCHANGE GUIDE**
2. -
3. CCH
4. 1967
5. 1 vol.
6. $340/yr.; $310/yr. for 2 yrs.
7. monthly supp.
9. 68-1482/430422/HG5131.C42M53

1. **MIDWEST TRANSACTION GUIDE**
2. Young, S., et al.
3. Bender
4. 1979
5. 14 vols.
6. $975 incl. 3 mos. supp.
7. supp. as needed
8. 1989 - $548; 1990 - $675
9. 80-6563/6788078/KF385.M5

1. **MILGRIM ON LICENSING**
2. -
3. Bender
4. 1990
5. 1 vol.
6. $105 incl. 3 mos. supp.
7. periodic supp.
8. no supp. yet
9. 90-804842/23030093/KF3145.M5

1. **MILITARY DISCHARGE UPGRADING AND INTRODUCTION TO VETERANS ADMINISTRATION LAW**
2. Addlestone, David F. et al.
3. Natl. Veterans
4. 1990
5. 1 vol.
6. $75
7. bimonthly supp. in newsletter Veterans Advocate
8. supp. planned for 1991
9. 81-53013/8116795/KF7272.M54

1. **MILITARY LAW REPORTER**
2. Alder, Thomas P. and Lawrence M. Baskir, ed.

3. PLEI
4. 1973
5. 1 vol./yr.
6. $350/yr. (set of 17 back vols. avail. - 1974-90 - $260)
7. bimonthly supp.
9. 73-85169/1094745/KF7606.5.P8

1. **MILLER'S STANDARD INSURANCE POLICIES ANNOTATED**
2. Miller, Susan J. & Philip Lefebvre
3. Legal Res. Systems
4. 1986
5. 5 vols.
6. $445
7. semiannual supp.
8. $148/yr.
9. 15318955/KF1160.M54

1. **MINERAL DEVELOPMENT ON INDIAN LANDS**
2. -
3. Rocky Mt.
4. 1989
5. 1 vol.
6. $125
7. no supp. planned

1. **MINERAL FINANCING**
2. -
3. Rocky Mt.
4. 1982
5. 1 vol.
6. $90
7. no supp. planned
9. 10149818/HD9506.AI59

1. **MINERAL LAW**
2. -
3. Illinois ICLE
4. 1986
5. 1 vol.
6. $76.95
7. periodic supp.
8. no supp. yet

1. **MINERAL TITLE EXAMINATION II**
2. -
3. Rocky Mt.
4. 1982
5. 1 vol.
6. $48
7. no supp. planned
9. 10688893

1. **MINERAL TITLE STANDARDS**
2. Real Property Section
3. State Bar of N. Dak.
4. 1990
5. 1 vol.
6. $80
7. no supp. yet

1. **MINING AGREEMENTS**
2. -
3. Rocky Mt.
4. 1979
5. 1 vol.
6. $38.50
7. no supp. planned

1. **MINING AGREEMENTS II**
2. -
3. Rocky Mt.
4. 1981
5. 1 vol.
6. $38.50
7. no supp. planned

1. **MINING AGREEMENTS III**
2. -
3. Rocky Mt.
4. 1991
5. 1 vol.
6. $125
7. no supp. planned

1. **MINING AND PETROLEUM LEGISLATION OF LATIN AMERICA & THE CARIBBEAN**
2. Organization of American States General Legal Division, Dept. of Legal Affairs
3. Oceana
4. 1978
5. 1 vol.
6. $100
7. periodic supp.
8. 1984 - $85; 1986 - $75
9. 78-16150/4056087

1. **MINNESOTA APPELLATE PRACTICE INSTITUTE**
2. -
3. MILE
4. 1991
5. 1 vol.
6. $68
7. no supp. planned
9. 23926681/KFM5955.Z9M555

1. **MINNESOTA ATTORNEY'S/SECRETARY'S HANDBOOK**
2. -
3. Mariposa
4. 1991
5. 1 vol.
6. $49
7. annual supp.
8. 1990 - $45; 1991 - $45

1. **MINNESOTA COLLECTIONS**
2. Zlimen, Allan J.
3. Lawyers Coop.
4. 1980
5. 1 vol.
6. $115 incl. 6 mos. supp.
7. annual supp.
8. 1988 - $35.50; 1991 - $55
9. 79-87463/6148584/KFM5620.Z45

1. **MINNESOTA CONDEMNATION LAW**
2. Lindall, Robert J. et al.
3. Butterworth-St. Paul
4. 1990
5. 1 vol.
6. $95
7. periodic supp.
8. no supp. yet
9. 90-20390/22597493/KFM5850.L56

1. **MINNESOTA CONSERVATORSHIPS & GUARDIANSHIPS**
2. -
3. Minn. CLE
4. 1991
5. 2 vols.
6. $155
7. no supp. planned
9. 24147374

1. **MINNESOTA CORPORATIONS PRACTICE MANUAL**
2. Black, Bert, ed.
3. Butterworth-St. Paul
4. 1986
5. 1 vol.
6. $78
7. periodic supp.
8. 1989 - $32; 1991 - $30
9. 13704662/KFM5613.B43

1. **MINNESOTA CRIMES AND DEFENSES**
2. Forbess, James W.
3. Butterworth-St. Paul
4. 1991
5. 3 vols.
6. $225
7. annual supp.
8. no supp. yet
9. 91-32340/24550279/KFM5961.M56

1. **MINNESOTA CRIMINAL LAW DIGEST**
2. Publisher's Editorial Staff
3. Butterworth-St. Paul
4. 1982
5. 3 vols.
6. $190
7. bimonthly supp.
8. 1989 - $182; 1990 - $240
9. 82-217826/9196718/KFM5961.G44

1. **MINNESOTA DISSOLUTION OF MARRIAGE**
2. Haugh, William E. Jr.
3. Lawyers Coop.
4. 1979
5. 1 vol.
6. $115 incl. 6 mos. supp.
7. annual supp.
8. 1990 - $56.50; 1991 - $60
9. 80-100625/6063661/KFM5500.H38

1. **MINNESOTA EMPLOYMENT AT WILL**
2. -
3. Minn. CLE
4. 1991
5. 1 vol.
6. $50
7. no supp. planned

1. **MINNESOTA EVIDENCE - A PRACTICAL WORKSHOP**
2. -
3. MILE
4. 1991
5. 1 vol.
6. $68
7. no supp. planned

1. **MINNESOTA EVIDENCE TRIALBOOK**
2. Poritsky, Bertrand
3. Butterworth-St. Paul
4. 1987
5. 1 vol.
6. $54
7. periodic supp.
8. 1988 - $20; 1990 - $35
9. 87-406444/17551721/KFM5940.P67

1. **MINNESOTA FAMILY LAW PRACTICE MANUAL, 2nd Ed.**
2. Gorlin, Cathy E.
3. Butterworth-St. Paul
4. 1990
5. 1 vol.
6. $95
7. bimonthly supp.
8. 1991 - $25
9. 12899067

1. **MINNESOTA INSURANCE LAW CONFERENCE**
2. -
3. MILE
4. 1991
5. 1 vol.
6. $79.50
7. no supp. planned
9. 24640804/KFM5585.Z9M527

1. **MINNESOTA LEGAL FORMS--BANKRUPTCY**
2. Wagner, Michael, et al.
3. Butterworth-St. Paul
4. 1981
5. 1 vol.
6. $50; $85 with disk
7. periodic supp.
8. 1987 - $24; 1991 - $30
9. 81-184323/8283709/KFM5621.A65W33

1. **MINNESOTA LEGAL FORMS--COMMERCIAL REAL ESTATE**
2. Miller, John Michael
3. Butterworth-St. Paul
4. 1982
5. 1 vol.
6. $50; $85 with disk
7. periodic supp.
8. 1986 - $17; 1990 - $25
9. 82-239039/9394378/KFM5517.3.A65M54

1. **MINNESOTA LEGAL FORMS--CREDITORS' REMEDIES**
2. Miller, Thomas F.
3. Butterworth-St. Paul
4. 1981
5. 1 vol.
6. $50; $85 with disk
7. periodic supp.
8. 1990 - $25; 1991 - $30
9. 81-184418/7633442/KFM5620.A65M55

1. **MINNESOTA LEGAL FORMS--CRIMINAL LAW**
2. Mattox, Rick E.
3. Butterworth-St. Paul
4. 1981
5. 1 vol.
6. $50; $85 with disk
7. periodic supp.
8. 1990 - $25; 1991 - $25
9. 81-187811/7446960/KFM5975.A65M257

1. **MINNESOTA LEGAL FORMS--FAMILY LAW**
2. McLean, Daniels W.
3. Butterworth-St. Paul
4. 1981
5. 1 vol.
6. $50; $85 with disk
7. periodic supp.
8. 1989 - $20; 1991 - $25
9. 82-223281/9218058/KFM5494.A65M35

1. **MINNESOTA LEGAL FORMS--PERSONAL INJURY**
2. Stoneking, Gary
3. Butterworth-St. Paul
4. 1981
5. 1 vol.
6. $50; $85 with disk
7. periodic supp.
8. 1989 - $20; 1991 - $25
9. 81-184324/8115203/KFM5597.P3S86

1. **MINNESOTA LEGAL FORMS--PROBATE**
2. Hucek, Jeffrey M. & James D. Bates
3. Butterworth-St. Paul
4. 1981
5. 1 vol.
6. $50; $85 with disk
7. periodic supp.
8. 1989 - $20; 1991 - $30

1. **MINNESOTA LEGAL FORMS--RESIDENTIAL REAL ESTATE**
2. Roer, Kathleen
3. Butterworth-St. Paul
4. 1981
5. 1 vol.
6. $50; $85 with disk
7. periodic supp.
8. 1989 - $22; 1991 - $30
9. 82-236359/9441723/KFM5526.A65R63

1. **MINNESOTA LIMITATIONS MANUAL, 2nd ed.**
2. Publ. Ed. Staff
3. Butterworth-St. Paul
4. 1989
5. 1 vol.
6. $50
7. periodic supp.
8. 1989 - $35; 1990 - $40
9. 89-138624/19603152/KFM5936.L5B8

1. **MINNESOTA LIQUOR LIABILITY**
2. -
3. MILE
4. 1990
5. 1 vol.
6. $63
7. no supp. planned

1. **MINNESOTA MECHANIC'S LIENS**
2. -
3. Minn. CLE
4. 1991
5. 1 vol.
6. $25
7. no supp. planned
9. 24147510

1. **MINNESOTA MECHANICS' LIENS PRACTICE MANUAL**
2. Snoxell, James
3. Butterworth-St. Paul
4. 1987
5. 1 vol.
6. $78
7. periodic supp.
8. 1989 - $35; 1990 - $35

1. **MINNESOTA MISDEMEANORS AND MOVING TRAFFIC VIOLATIONS, 3rd ed.**
2. Costello, Martin J., et al.
3. Butterworth-St. Paul
4. 1990
5. 2 vols.
6. $160
7. periodic supp.
8. no supp. yet
9. 13645776/KFM5975.F7

1. **MINNESOTA MOTOR VEHICLE ACCIDENT DESKBOOK**
2. -
3. Minn. CLE
4. 1989
5. 1 vol.
6. $85
7. incl. 6/91 update

1. **THE MINNESOTA MOTOR VEHICLE INSURANCE MANUAL**
2. -
3. MILE
4. 1991
5. 1 vol.
6. $95
7. no supp. planned
9. 23850928/KFM5591.A4S53

1. **MINNESOTA NO-FAULT AUTOMOBILE INSURANCE, 2nd ed.**
2. Steenson, Michael K.
3. Butterworth-St. Paul
4. 1989
5. 2 vols.
6. $140
7. periodic supp.
8. no supp. yet
9. 89-9931/19722418/KFM5591.A46S73

1. **MINNESOTA PROBATE**
2. Helland, Mark D.
3. Lawyers Coop.
4. 1979
5. 1 vol.
6. $115 incl. 6 mos. supp.
7. annual supp.
8. 1990 - $49; 1991 - $55
9. 80-105838/6144999/KFM5544.A65H44

1. **THE MINNESOTA PROBATE AND TRUST LAW DESKBOOK**
2. -
3. Minn. CLE
4. 3rd ed. - 1990
5. 1 vol.
6. $75
7. annual supp.
8. -
9. 13204392/KFM5544.Z9M56

1. **MINNESOTA PROBATE LAW DIGEST**
2. Publisher's Editorial Staff
3. Butterworth-St. Paul
4. 1982
5. 3 vols.
6. $185
7. trimonthly supp.
8. 1989 - $155; 1990 - $230
9. 82-186877/9133386/KFM5544.S63

1. **MINNESOTA PRODUCTS LIABILITY**
2. -
3. MILE
4. 1990
5. 1 vol.
6. $63
7. no supp. planned

1. **MINNESOTA REAL ESTATE**
2. Shumaker, Gordon & Clinton McLagan
3. Lawyers Coop.
4. 1981
5. 1 vol.
6. $115 incl. 6 mos. supp.
7. annual supp.
8. 1990 - $46; 1991 - $55
9. 81-184491/11289422/KFM5526.S55

1. **MINNESOTA SENTENCING GUIDELINES AND COMMENTARY ANNOTATED**
2. Knapp, Kay A.
3. Minn. CLE
4. 1989
5. 1 vol.
6. $55
7. 3 supp./yr.
8. $25/yr.
9. 12036955

1. **MINNESOTA TAX APPEALS**
2. Gustafson, Earl B.
3. Butterworth-St. Paul
4. 1989
5. 1 vol.
6. $65
7. periodic supp.
8. no supp. yet
9. 88-38835/18833993/KFM5871.5.G87

1. **MISSISSIPPI SUPREME COURT PRACTICE**
2. Munford, Luther T.
3. On Point
4. 1987
5. 1 vol.
6. $135
7. biennial supp.
8. $45
9. 87-24834/16755585/KFM7158.M86

1. **MISSOURI ADMINISTRATIVE LAW**
2. -
3. MoBar
4. 2nd ed. - 1990
5. 2 vols.
6. $85
7. periodic supp.
8. no supp. yet
9. 90-170883/21256536

1. **MISSOURI ADVISORY COMMITTEE OPINIONS**
2. -
3. MoBar
4. 1985
5. 1 vol.
6. $40
7. periodic supp.
8. -
9. 85-162418/12552683/KFM7876.5.A2A5

1. **MISSOURI APPELLATE PRACTICE AND EXTRAORDINARY REMEDIES**
2. -
3. MoBar
4. 4th ed. - 1989
5. 2 vols.
6. $80
7. periodic supp.
8. no supp. yet
9. 81-157786/7110177/KFM8355.M57

1. **MISSOURI APPROVED INSTRUCTIONS - CRIMINAL, VOLS. I & II AND MISSOURI APPROVED CHARGES - CRIMINAL**
2. -
3. MoBar
4. 1979
5. 3 vols.
6. $55
7. periodic supp.
8. 1990 - $5; 1991 - $10
9. 79-107819/5100261/KFM8383.M58

1. **MISSOURI ATTORNEY'S/ SECRETARY'S HANDBOOK**
2. -
3. Mariposa
4. 1991
5. 1 vol.
6. $55
7. annual supp.
8. 1990 - $51; 1991 - $46
9. 88-640673/17451944/KFM8308.A19M57

1. **MISSOURI CIVIL ACTIONS I**
2. -
3. MoBar
4. 1980

5. 1 vol.
6. $75
7. periodic supp.
8. 1989 - $20
9. 80-123791/6663778/KFM8333.M57

1. **MISSOURI CIVIL ACTIONS II**
2. -
3. MoBar
4. 1981
5. 1 vol.
6. $75
7. periodic supp.
8. 1989 - $20
9. 80-123791/6663778/KFM8333.M57

1. **MISSOURI CIVIL PROCEDURE**
2. -
3. MoBar
4. 1983
5. 1 vol.
6. $70
7. periodic supp.
8. 1991 - $35
9. 83-168611/10162046/KFM8329.A2

1. **MISSOURI CIVIL PROCEDURE FORMBOOK**
2. -
3. UMKC/CLE
4. 1984 - 1989
5. 2 vols.
6. $85
7. no supp. yet
8. -
9. 13127556/KFM8329.B47

1. **MISSOURI CIVIL PROCEDURE FORMS – PRACTICE**
2. Mooney, Margaret M. & Alan D. Pratzel
3. Aspen
4. 1988
5. 1 vol.
6. $159 incl. 3 mos. supp.
7. annual supp.
8. 1989 - $79.95
9. 87-37346/17300735/KFM8330.A65M66

1. **MISSOURI CIVIL TRIAL PRACTICE**
2. -
3. MoBar
4. 2nd ed. - 1988
5. 2 vols.
6. $85
7. periodic supp.
8. no supp. yet
9. 76-366982/2507659/KFM8338.M5

1. **MISSOURI COMPARATIVE FAULT**
2. Garrison, Gretchen
3. UMKC/CLE
4. 1986
5. 1 vol.
6. $50
7. periodic supp.
8. 1989 supp.
9. 14150410/KFM7995.G37

1. **MISSOURI CONDEMNATION PRACTICE**
2. -
3. MoBar
4. 2nd ed. - 1988
5. 1 vol.
6. $65
7. periodic supp.
8. no supp. yet
9. KFM8250.M5

1. **MISSOURI CONSUMER LAW AND PRACTICE**
2. -
3. MoBar
4. 2nd ed. - 1988
5. 2 vols.
6. $85
7. periodic supp.
8. 1990 - $25
9. 89-103516//r89/18766062

1. **MISSOURI CORPORATE AND PARTNERSHIP FORMS HANDBOOK**
2. -
3. UMKC/CLE
4. 1991
5. 2 vols.
6. $90
7. periodic supp.
8. no supp. yet
9. 24039273

1. **MISSOURI CORPORATE FORMS - PRACTICE**
2. Myers, Charles F. & Edward M. Dolson
3. Aspen
4. 1987
5. 2 vols.
6. $239 incl. 3 mos. supp.
7. annual supp.
8. 1989 - $89.95

9. 87-1254/15549416/KFM8013.A65M94

1. **MISSOURI CORPORATION LAW AND PRACTICE**
2. -
3. MoBar
4. 1985
5. 2 vols.
6. $105
7. periodic supp.
8. 1988 - $20
9. 86-119564/13456583/KFM8013.M58

1. **MISSOURI COURT RULES HANDBOOK**
2. Butterworths Staff
3. Butterworth-Texas
4. 1989
5. 1 vol.
6. $135
7. periodic supp.
8. 1989 - $37.50; 1990 - $148.50
9. 89-782/19322160/KFM8329.A2

1. **MISSOURI CREDITORS'-DEBTORS' REMEDIES**
2. -
3. MoBar
4. 4th ed. - 1985
5. 1 vol.
6. $60
7. periodic supp.
8. 1991 - $30

1. **MISSOURI CRIMINAL PRACTICE**
2. -
3. MoBar
4. 2nd ed. - 1983
5. 2 vols.
6. $105
7. periodic supp.
8. 1989 - $20

1. **MISSOURI DAMAGES**
2. -
3. MoBar
4. 1988
5. 1 vol.
6. $75
7. periodic supp.
8. 1990 - $30
9. 88-138078/17689916/KFM7995.M565

1. **MISSOURI DOMESTIC RELATIONS FORMS - PRACTICE**
2. Turcotte, John A. Jr., & Michael C. Walther
3. Aspen
4. 1987
5. 1 vol.
6. $159 incl. 3 mos. supp.
7. annual supp.
8. 1988 - $56; 1989 - $89
9. 87-1445/15364896/KFM7894.A65T87

1. **MISSOURI EMPLOYER-EMPLOYEE LAW**
2. -
3. MoBar
4. 1985
5. 1 vol.
6. $50
7. periodic supp.
8. 1990 - $25

1. **MISSOURI ESTATE ADMINISTRATION**
2. -
3. MoBar
4. 3rd ed. - 1984
5. 1 vol.
6. $55
7. periodic supp.
8. 1989 - $20
9. 85-129066/11489631/KFM7947.M5

1. **MISSOURI ESTATE PLANNING**
2. -
3. MoBar
4. 1986
5. 2 vols.
6. $80
7. periodic supp.
8. 1988 - $20
9. 86-180479/14166428/KFM7940.M573

1. **MISSOURI ESTATE PLANNING, WILL DRAFTING AND ESTATE ADMINISTRATION FORMS - PRACTICE**
2. Cornfeld, Dave L. & Lawrence Brody
3. Aspen
4. 1987
5. 2 vols.
6. $239 incl. 3 mos. supp.
7. annual supp.
8. 1989 - $86.50
9. 87-27126/16804994/KFM7940.A65C67

1. **MISSOURI EVIDENCE**
2. -
3. MoBar
4. 3rd ed. - 1980
5. 1 vol.

6. $45
7. periodic supp.
8. 1987 - $20
9. 80-133566/7168798/KFM8340.M48

1. **MISSOURI FAMILY LAW**
2. -
3. MoBar
4. 4th ed. - 1988
5. 2 vols.
6. $85
7. periodic supp.
8. 1991 - $30
9. 88-194872/18446938/KFM7894.M57

1. **MISSOURI FAMILY LAW FORMBOOK**
2. Cochran, Jack, ed.
3. UMKC/CLE
4. 1985
5. 1 vol.
6. $80
7. no supp. yet
8. -
9. 13301476/KFM7894.A65M58

1. **MISSOURI FARM LAW**
2. -
3. MoBar
4. 1980
5. 1 vol.
6. $45
7. periodic supp.
8. 1990 - $30
9. 81-153929/7235278/KFM8039.M53

1. **MISSOURI GUARDIANSHIP AND TRUST LAW**
2. -
3. MoBar
4. 1985, 1987
5. 2 vols.
6. $70
7. periodic supp.
8. 1990 - $30
9. 86-125450/12691901/KFM7906.M57

1. **MISSOURI HANDICAPPED, ELDERLY, AND LOW-INCOME PERSONS LAW**
2. -
3. MoBar
4. 1982
5. 1 vol.
6. $50
7. periodic supp.
8. 1990 - $25
9. 83-214019/9151665/KFM7884.5.P6M57

1. **MISSOURI INSURANCE PRACTICE**
2. -
3. MoBar
4. 3rd ed. - 1986
5. 1 vol.
6. $55
7. periodic supp.
8. 1989 - $20
9. 87-146475/16524309/KFM7985.M56

1. **MISSOURI LAWYER'S GUIDE**
2. McCarter, Charles C. & Beverly J. Greenley
3. Lawyers Coop.
4. 1984
5. 2 vols.
6. $180 incl. 6 mos. supp.
7. annual supp.
8. 1990 - $53; 1991 - $55.50
9. 83-15287/9896680/KFM7880.M35

1. **MISSOURI LITIGATION SETTLEMENT**
2. -
3. MoBar
4. 1991
5. 1 vol.
6. price NA
7. periodic supp.
8. no supp. yet

1. **MISSOURI LOCAL GOVERNMENT LAW**
2. -
3. MoBar
4. 2nd ed. - 1986
5. 2 vols.
6. $75
7. periodic supp.
8. 1990 - $25
9. 76-350920/2006227/KFM8230.M5

1. **MISSOURI PROBATE SYSTEM**
2. -
3. MoBar
4. 1990
5. 1 vol.
6. $125
7. periodic supp.
8. no supp. yet

1. **MISSOURI PRODUCTS LIABILITY**
2. -
3. UMKC/CLE

4. 1991
5. 1 vol.
6. $125
7. no supp. yet

1. **MISSOURI REAL ESTATE FORMS - PRACTICE**
2. Scarritt, Richard W,. & Michael C. Kirk
3. Aspen
4. 1988
5. 2 vols.
6. $239 incl. 3 mos. supp.
7. annual supp.
8. $70-95/supp.
9. 88-10406/17766232/KFM7926.A65S29

1. **MISSOURI REAL ESTATE PRACTICE**
2. -
3. MoBar
4. 3rd ed. - 1986
5. 2 vols.
6. $85
7. periodic supp.
8. 1991 - $30
9. 86-216435/13909928/KFM7912.M572

1. **MISSOURI SOURCES OF PROOF**
2. -
3. MoBar
4. 3rd ed. - 1989
5. 1 vol.
6. $75
7. periodic supp.
8. no supp. yet
9. 80-213967/20512276/KFM8340.M582

1. **MISSOURI TAXATION LAW AND PRACTICE**
2. -
3. MoBar
4. 1981
5. 2 vols.
6. $100
7. periodic supp.
8. 1989 - $25
9. 82-104202/7829125/KFM8270.M58

1. **MISSOURI TIME LIMITATIONS**
2. -
3. MoBar
4. 1990
5. 1 vol.
6. $30
7. annual supp.
8. no supp. yet
9. 10642576/KFM7890.L5M5

1. **MISSOURI TORT LAW I & II**
2. -
3. MoBar
4. 2nd ed. - 1990
5. 2 vols.
6. $150
7. periodic supp.
8. no supp. yet
9. 90-63143/22489099/KFM7995.M57

1. **MISSOURI WORKERS' COMPENSATION**
2. -
3. MoBar
4. 1981
5. 1 vol.
6. $50
7. periodic supp.
8. 1991 - $30

1. **MISSOURI WORKERS' COMPENSATION**
2. Kenter, Jerry
3. Lawyers Coop.
4. 1984
5. 2 vols.
6. $210 incl. 6 mos. supp.
7. annual supp.
8. 1990 - $74.50; 1991 - $80
9. 84-80828/11233181/KFM8142.A6K46

1. **MISSOURI WORKERS' COMPENSATION LAW REPORTER**
2. -
3. LRP
4. 1988
5. 2 vols.
6. $465/yr.
7. monthly supp.
9. 18485248/KFM8142.A6M57

1. **MODEL BUSINESS CORPORATION ACT ANNOTATED**
2. -
3. Prentice Hall Law & Business
4. 3rd ed. - 1985
5. 4 vols.
6. $330 incl. 4 mos. supp.
7. periodic supp.
8. 1990 - $150; 1991 - $150
9. 85-13133/12216550/KF1404.52.A65

1. **MODEL INTERROGATORIES: PERSONAL INJURY**
2. Culhane, Kevin R.
3. James
4. 1987
5. 1 vol.
6. $49.78
7. annual supp.
8. 1990 - $39.92

1. **MODEL JURY CHARGES: CIVIL**
2. Supreme Court Committee on Model Jury Charges
3. New Jersey ICLE
4. 3rd ed. - 1990
5. 1 vol.
6. $75
7. periodic supp.
8. 1991 - $39
9. 21942200

1. **MODEL JURY CHARGES: CRIMINAL**
2. Supreme Court Committee on Model Jury Charges
3. New Jersey ICLE
4. 3rd ed. - 1990
5. 1 vol.
6. $75
7. periodic supp.
8. 1991 - $39

1. **MODEL JURY INSTRUCTIONS FOR USE IN THE DISTRICT COURT**
2. District Court Dept. of the Trial Court of the Commonwealth Committee on Juries of Six
3. Mass. CLE
4. 1988
5. 1 vol.
6. $50
7. no supp. yet
8. 1989 - $17.50
9. 17968110

1. **MODEL STANDARDS FOR SPECIALTY AREAS**
2. Standing Comm. on Specialization
3. ABA
4. 1991
5. 1 vol.
6. $10
7. no supp. yet

1. **MODERN ACCOUNTING & AUDITING CHECKLISTS**
2. Loscalzo, Margaret A. & Paul J. Wendell
3. WG&L
4. rev. ed. - 1991
5. 1 vol.
6. $125
7. semiannual supp.
8. 1989 - $100; 1991 - $51.50
9. 81-51905/8002274/KF1357.M63

1. **MODERN BANKING CHECKLISTS**
2. Kusnet, Jack et al.
3. WG&L
4. 3rd ed. - 1981
5. 2 vols.
6. $142
7. semiannual supp.
8. 1989 - $150; 1991 - $82.50
9. 81-50586/7987724/KF975.K87

1. **MODERN BANKING FORMS**
2. Kusnet, Jack, et al.
3. WG&L
4. 3rd ed. - 1981
5. 3 vols.
6. $195
7. semiannual supp.
8. 1989 - $147; 1991 - $164
9. 80-54300/7939200/KF972.M6

1. **MODERN CIVIL DISCOVERY AND DEPOSITIONS**
2. Simpson, Reagan Wm.
3. Wiley Law
4. 1988
5. 1 vol.
6. $105
7. periodic supp. & quarterly newsletter
8. 1991 - $40; 1992 - price NA
9. 88-16331/18052680/KF8900.S55

1. **MODERN CIVIL JURY SELECTION**
2. Werchick, Arne
3. Wiley Law
4. 1988
5. 1 vol.
6. $105
7. periodic supp.
8. 1990 - $25; 1991 - price NA
9. 87-21132/16710637/KF8979.W48

1. **MODERN CONSTRUCTION AND DEVELOPMENT FORMS (Modern Real Estate & Mortgage Forms series)**
2. Douglas, James, et al.
3. WG&L
4. 2nd ed. - 1982

5. 1 vol.
6. $94
7. semiannual supp.
8. 1989 - $118; 1991 - $135.50
9. 82-50345/9102205/KF902.A3D68

1. **MODERN CORPORATION CHECKLISTS**
2. Sardell, William
3. WG&L
4. 2nd ed. - 1982
5. 1 vol.
6. $98
7. semiannual supp.
8. 1989 - $52.75; 1991 - $99.25
9. 82-50343/8972357/KF1414.3.S24

1. **MODERN ESTATE PLANNING**
2. Fiore. E. et al.
3. Bender
4. 1981
5. 7 vols.
6. $660 incl. 3 mos. supp.
7. supp. planned
8. 1989 - $405.50; 1990 - $647.50
9. 80-70546/7596300/KF6584.M63

1. **MODERN FEDERAL JURY INSTRUCTIONS - CRIMINAL & CIVIL**
2. Sand, Leonard
3. Bender
4. 1984
5. 5 vols.
6. $540 incl. 3 mos. supp.
7. annual supp.
8. 1989 - $263; 1990 - $357.50
9. 84-72026/11545922/KF9682.A65M64

1. **MODERN INTELLECTUAL PROPERTY**
2. Epstein, Michael A.
3. Prentice Hall Law & Business
4. 2nd ed. - 1989
5. 1 vol.
6. $85 incl. 4 mos. supp.
7. annual supp.
8. 1990 - $70; 1991 - $75
9. 89-25495/20561732/KF2979.E67

1. **MODERN LAW OF EMPLOYMENT RELATIONSHIPS**
2. Bakaly, Charles G., Jr., & Joel M. Grossman
3. Prentice Hall Law & Business
4. 2nd ed. - 1989
5. 1 vol.
6. $85 incl. 4 mos. supp.
7. periodic supp.
8. 1990 - $55; 1991 - $50
9. 89-32671/19590161/KF3457.B35

1. **MODERN LEGAL SYSTEMS CYCLOPEDIA**
2. Redden, Kenneth R.
3. Hein
4. 1983
5. 10 vols. in 20 books
6. $1920
7. periodic supp.
8. 1989 - $195; 1991 - $195
9. 83-82953/19504664/K530.M62

1. **MODERN REAL ESTATE ACQUISITION AND DISPOSITION FORMS**
2. Kusnet, Jack & Robert Lopatin
3. WG&L
4. 1981
5. 1 vol.
6. $105
7. annual supp.
8. 1989 - $46.75; 1991 - $53.50
9. 80-52970/7530609/KF668.1.K87

1. **MODERN REAL ESTATE AND MORTGAGE FORMS SERIES: VOL. 1 - BASIC FORMS AND AGREEMENTS, 3rd ed.**
2. Arnold, Alvin L. et al.
3. WG&L
4. 3rd ed. - 1987
5. 1 vol.
6. $98
7. semiannual supp.
8. 1989 - $95; 1991 - $111
9. 78-50305/4154340/KF568.1.A77

1. **MODERN REAL ESTATE AND MORTGAGE FORMS SERIES: VOL. 2 - CHECKLISTS**
2. Arnold, Alvin L.
3. WG&L
4. 1979
5. 1 vol.
6. $94
7. semiannual supp.
8. 1989 - $52.75; 1991 - $115.75
9. 79-50553/5266494/KF665.A73

1. **MODERN REAL ESTATE LEASING FORMS**
2. Kusnet, Jack & Robert Lopatin
3. WG&L
4. 1980

5. 1 vol.
6. $98
7. annual supp.
8. 1989 - $46.75; 1991 - $53.50
9. 79-56771/6421340/KF588.1.K87

1. **MODERN TAX PLANNING CHECKLISTS**
2. Bleich, Ronald L.& Hal W. Mandel
3. WG&L
4. 2nd ed. - 1985
5. 1 vol.
6. $88
7. annual supp.
8. 1989 - $108; 1991 - $60.75
9. 84-51762//r85/12345338/KF6297.B62

1. **MODERN TORT LAW, REV. ED.**
2. Lee, J.D. and Barry A. Lindahl
3. Clark Boardman Callaghan
4. 1988
5. 4 vols.
6. $340 incl. 6 mos. supp.
7. annual supp.
8. 1989 - $159.50; 1990 - $179
9. 88-2910/17507064/KF1250.L44

1. **MODERN TRUST FORMS AND CHECKLISTS**
2. Parella, Robert E. & Joel E. Miller
3. WG&L
4. 2nd ed. - 1980
5. 2 vols.
6. $155
7. semiannual supp.
8. 1989 - $154; 1991 - $175.25
9. 79-56181/6294668/KF728.1.P37

1. **MODERN VISUAL EVIDENCE**
2. Joseph, Gregary P.
3. Law Journal
4. 1984
5. 1 vol.
6. $80
7. period supp.
8. 1988 - $74; 1989 - $42
9. 84-19423/11090405/KF8967.J67

1. **MONETARY POLICY AND RESERVE REQUIREMENTS HANDBOOK**
2. -
3. Fed.
4. 1981
5. 1 vol.
6. $75/yr.
7. monthly supp.
9. 7331918/HG2560.M66

1. **MONTANA CRIMINAL JURY INSTRUCTIONS**
2. Montana Supreme Court Criminal Jury Instruction Commission
3. State Bar of Mont.
4. 1990
5. 1 vol.
6. $75
7. periodic supp.
8. no supp. yet
9. 22737989/KFM9583.M77

1. **MONTANA PATTERN JURY INSTRUCTIONS-CIVIL**
2. Montana Supreme Court Commission on Civil Jury Instructions
3. State Bar of Mont.
4. 1987
5. 1 vol.
6. $120
7. periodic supp.
8. 1987 - $10; 1989 - $20
9. 15373683/KFM9542.6.M55

1. **MONTANA PROBATE PROCEDURE**
2. Niklas, David N.
3. State Bar of Mont.
4. 1990
5. 1 vol.
6. $75
7. no supp. planned

1. **MOORE'S FEDERAL PRACTICE, 2ND ED.**
2. Moore, James William et al.
3. Bender
4. 1948
5. 34 vols.
6. $1870 incl. 3 mos. supp.
7. quarterly supp.
8. 1989 - $1342.50; 1990 - $1655.50
9. 48-2333/1560066/KF8820.A313M63

1. **MOORE'S MANUAL - FEDERAL PRACTICE AND PROCEDURE**
2. Moore, James William et al.
3. Bender
4. 1962
5. 3 vols.
6. $410 incl. 3 mos. supp.
7. annual supp.
8. 1989 - $284; 1990 - $339.50
9. 62-51989/1824987/KF8820.A313M64

1. **MOORE'S MANUAL - FORMS**
2. Moore, James William et al.
3. Bender
4. 1964
5. 5 vols.
6. $525 incl. 3 mos. supp.
7. periodic supp.
8. 1989 - $306; 1990 - $387.50
9. 65-1465/5813605/KF8836.M66

1. **MORTGAGE AND REAL ESTATE INVESTMENT GUIDE**
2. Sherman, Alan C.
3. Mortgage
4. 1953
5. 1 vol.
6. $80
7. semiannual supp.
8. 1990 - $70; 1990 - $87.50
9. 6853168/KF696.S53

1. **MORTGAGE FORECLOSURES IN MINNESOTA**
2. -
3. Minn. CLE
4. 1991
5. 1 vol.
6. $60
7. no supp. planned

1. **MORTGAGES AND MORTGAGE FORECLOSURE IN NEW YORK**
2. Publisher's editorial staff
3. Lawyers Coop.
4. rev. ed. - 1982
5. 2 vols.
6. $180 incl. 6 mos. supp.
7. annual supp.
8. 1989 - $89; 1990 - $53
9. 82-20727/8954041/KFN5175.D78

1. **THE MOTION PICTURE AND TELEVISION BUSINESS: CONTRACTS AND PRACTICES**
2. Yeldell, Eric B.
3. EBP
4. 1985
5. 2 vols.
6. $135 incl. 4 mos. supp.
7. periodic supp.
8. no supp. yet
9. 85-4515/11841404/KF4302.Y45

1. **MOTIONS PRACTICE IN INDIANA**
2. -
3. Indiana CLE
4. 1991
5. 1 vol.
6. $40
7. no supp. planned

1. **MOTOR CARRIER - FREIGHT FORWARDER SERVICE**
2. -
3. Hawkins
4. 1937
5. 4 vols.
6. $280/yr.
7. monthly supp.
8. renewal - $260/yr.

1. **MOTOR VEHICLE ADMINISTRATION HEARINGS**
2. -
3. MICPEL
4. 1990
5. 1 vol.
6. $65 (incl. tapes)
7. no supp. yet
9. 15490841/KFM1497.M92

1. **MOUNT LAUREL II AND THE FAIR HOUSING ACT**
2. Surenian, Jeffrey R.
3. New Jersey ICLE
4. 1986
5. 1 vol.
6. $65
7. no supp. planned
9. 14118999/KFN2260.5.D5S97

1. **MULTI-FAMILY GUIDE**
2. -
3. FNMA
4. 1986
5. 1 vol.
6. $300 incl. 2 yr. supp.
7. supp. as needed
8. biennial revisions

1. **MULTIFAMILY HOUSING: FEDERAL PROGRAMS FOR THE PRIVATE SECTOR**
2. Jones, James W.
3. Law Journal
4. 1986
5. 1 vol.
6. $70
7. periodic supp.
8. 1989 - $35; 1990 - $35

9. 86-7243/13396492/KF5735.J66

1. **MULTINATIONAL CORPORATIONS LAW: MEXICO, CENTRAL AMERICA, PANAMA AND THE CENTRAL AMERICAN COMMON MARKET**
2. Gordon, Michael W.
3. Oceana
4. 1980
5. 2 vols. included in MULTINATIONAL CORPORATIONS LAW
6. $200
7. annual supp.
8. 1983 - $50; 1984 - $60
9. 81-420/7204884

1. **MULTINATIONAL CORPORATIONS LAW: THE UNITED NATIONS AND TRANSNATIONAL CORPORATIONS**
2. Simmonds, Kenneth R., ed.
3. Oceana
4. 1979
5. 8 vols. (includes 2 vols. of Bibliography not avail. separately & 2 vols. of Mexico & Central America)
6. $700/set
7. periodic supp.
8. 1988 - $85; 1989 - $85
9. 78-277044/4593114/K1322.U15

1. **MULTISTATE CORPORATE INCOME TAX GUIDE**
2. -
3. CCH
4. 1985
5. 2 vols.
6. $530/yr.; $480/yr. for 2 yrs.
7. monthly supp.
9. 12697815/KF6461.5.M8

1. **MUNICIPAL LAW VIII**
2. -
3. Indiana CLE
4. 1991
5. 1 vol.
6. $75
7. no supp. planned

1. **MUNICIPAL SECURITIES RULEMAKING BOARD MANUAL**
2. -
3. CCH
4. 1977
5. 1 vol.
6. $225/yr.; $205/yr. for 2 yrs.
7. monthly supp.
9. 77-370843/3344289/KF6775.A6M85

1. **MUNICIPAL UTILITY LAW**
2. -
3. Indiana CLE
4. 1988
5. 1 vol.
6. $44
7. no supp. planned

1. **MURPHY'S WILL CLAUSES: ANNOTATIONS AND FORMS WITH TAX EFFECTS (national and N.Y. ed.)**
2. Murphy, Joseph H. et al.
3. Bender
4. 1960
5. 4 vols.
6. $505 incl. 3 mos. supp.
7. biannual supp.
8. 1989 - $491; 1990 - $433
9. 60-4610/2105192/KF755.A65M8

1. **MUTUAL FUNDS GUIDE**
2. -
3. CCH
4. 1969
5. 2 vols.
6. $570/yr.; $520/yr. for 2 yrs.
7. semimonthly supp.
9. 78-5256/19213/KF1078.A6C6

1. **NASD MANUAL**
2. -
3. CCH
4. 1967
5. 1 vol.
6. $275/yr.; $250/yr. for 2 yrs.
7. periodic supp.
9. 4398539/KF1068.4.C67

1. **NATIONAL BACKHAUL GUIDE**
2. -
3. Keller
4. 1976
5. 1 vol.
6. $105
7. semiannual supp.
8. renewal - $90/yr.
9. 76-18485/4006056/KF2268.T7K44

1. **NATIONAL CREDIT UNION ADMINISTRATION RULES AND REGULATIONS**
2. U.S. National Credit Union Admin.

3. order from USGPO - stock #954-004-00000-7
4. 1990
5. 1 vol.
6. $44/yr.
7. periodic supp.
9. 6643532

1. **NATIONAL DIRECTORY FOR THE SERVICE OF CIVIL PROCESS**
2. Lyman, Paul D.
3. Knowles
4. 1991
5. 1 vol.
6. $49.95
7. annual editions
9. KF8700.A19L96

1. **NATIONAL DISABILITY LAW REPORTER**
2. -
3. LRP
4. 1990
5. 3 vols.
6. $655/yr.
7. semimonthly supp.

1. **NATIONAL FIRE CODES SUBSCRIPTION SERVICE**
2. -
3. Natl. Fire Protection Assn.
4. NA
5. 13 vols.
6. $397.50/yr.
7. periodic supp.
9. z38-27236/6753271/TH9111.N375a

1. **NATIONAL FUTURES ASSOCIATION MANUAL**
2. -
3. RIA
4. 1983
5. 1 vol.
6. $254/yr.
7. monthly supp.
9. sn83-636/9365196

1. **NATIONAL LABOR RELATIONS BOARD LAW AND PRACTICE**
2. -
3. Bender
4. 1991
5. 3 vols.
6. $295 incl. 3 mos. supp.
7. annual supp.
8. no supp. yet

1. **NATIONAL LAW LIST**
2. Altman & Weil, eds.
3. Pic's
4. 1986
5. 1 vol.
6. $75 incl. 1 yr. supp.
7. quarterly supp.

1. **NATIONAL PUBLIC EMPLOYMENT REPORTER**
2. -
3. LRP
4. 1979
5. 2 vols.
6. $440/yr. (back vols. and full-text case copy avail.)
7. quarterly supp.
9. 81-649537/4690740/KF3580.G6A496

1. **NATIONAL REPORTER ON LEGAL ETHICS AND PROFESSIONAL RESPONSIBILITY**
2. Luban, David, ed.
3. UPA
4. 1983
5. 4 vols.
6. $695/yr.
7. 10 supp./yr.
9. 12310996/KF308.A6N38

1. **NATIONAL TRANSPORTATION SAFETY BOARD REGULATIONS**
2. -
3. Rules
4. 1973
5. 1 vol.
6. $26 incl. 1 yr. supp.
7. periodic supp.
8. renewal fee

1. **NATIONAL TRANSPORTATION SAFETY BOARD SERVICE**
2. -
3. Hawkins
4. 1972
5. 1 vol.
6. $260/yr.
7. monthly supp.
9. 5214623/KF2172.7.H39

1. **NATIONAL VERDICT SURVEY**
2. Research Dept.
3. Jury Verdict
4. 1983

5. 3 vols.
6. $990/yr. for 2 yr. subscription
7. semimonthly supp.
9. 12566739/KF1256.A8N3

1. **NATURAL GAS CONTRACTS**
2. Munro, Stephen
3. Thompson
4. 1984
5. 1 vol.
6. $513/yr.
7. quarterly supp. & newsletter
8. renewal - $491/yr.
9. 85-643003/10598603

1. **NATURAL GAS HANDBOOK**
2. Munro, Stephen
3. Thompson
4. 1981
5. 2 vols.
6. $400/yr.
7. monthly supp. & newsletter
8. renewal - $389/yr.
9. 82-646880/8466379/KF1870.A15N37

1. **NATURAL GAS MARKETING AND TRANSPORTATION**
2. -
3. Rocky Mt.
4. 1991
5. 1 vol.
6. $125
7. no supp. planned

1. **NATURAL GAS MARKETING II**
2. -
3. Rocky Mt.
4. 1988
5. 1 vol.
6. $125
7. no supp.planned

1. **NATURAL GAS POLICY ACT INFORMATION SERVICE**
2. Munro, Stephen
3. Thompson
4. 1979
5. 24 vols.
6. $1560/yr.
7. semimonthly supp. & newsletter
8. renewal - $1196/yr.

1. **NATURAL GAS TRANSPORTATION INFORMATION SERVICE**
2. Krehbiel, Greg
3. Thompson
4. 1986
5. 1 vol.
6. $569/yr.
7. monthly supp. & newsletter
8. renewal - $555/yr.
9. 13345554

1. **NATURAL RESOURCES AND ENVIRONMENTAL LITIGATION**
2. -
3. Rocky Mt.
4. 1989
5. 1 vol.
6. $105
7. no supp. planned

1. **NEBRASKA LEGAL FORMS– BANKRUPTCY**
2. Minahan, John C. Jr.
3. Butterworth-St. Paul
4. 1982
5. 1 vol.
6. $50; $85 with disk
7. periodic supp.
8. 1990 - $27; 1991 - $30
9. 81-83832/8660488/KFN68.N42x

1. **NEBRASKA LEGAL FORMS– COMMERCIAL REAL ESTATE**
2. Vaughn, Peter J.
3. Butterworth-St. Paul
4. 1981
5. 1 vol.
6. $50; $85 with disk
7. periodic supp.
8. 1989 - $20; 1990 - $30
9. 81-83833/8305559/KFN117.3.A65V38

1. **NEBRASKA LEGAL FORMS– CREDITORS' REMEDIES**
2. Langvardt, Arlen W.
3. Butterworth-St. Paul
4. 1982
5. 1 vol.
6. $50; $85 with disk
7. periodic supp.
8. 1989 - $20; 1990 - $25
9. 81-83829/8589792/KFN220.A65L35

1. **NEBRASKA LEGAL FORMS– CRIMINAL LAW**
2. Fiedler, Donald B. & Deborah Rae Pred
3. Butterworth-St. Paul
4. 1982

5. 1 vol.
6. $50; $85 with disk
7. periodic supp.
8. 1988 - $18; 1990 - $27
9. 81-83830/9255030/KFN561.A65F53

1. **NEBRASKA LEGAL FORMS–FAMILY LAW**
2. Borchers, Elizabeth S.
3. Butterworth-St. Paul
4. 1982
5. 1 vol.
6. $50; $85 with disk
7. periodic supp.
8. 1988 - $25
9. 81-83827/9621264/KFN100.A65B67

1. **NEBRASKA LEGAL FORMS–PERSONAL INJURY**
2. Higgins, John J.
3. Butterworth-St. Paul
4. 1981
5. 1 vol.
6. $50; $85 with disk
7. periodic supp.
8. 1984 - $13; 1991 - $30
9. 81-83831/8283837/KFN197.P3H53

1. **NEBRASKA LEGAL FORMS–RESIDENTIAL REAL ESTATE**
2. Wright, Norman H.
3. Butterworth-St. Paul
4. 1982
5. 1 vol.
6. $50; $85 with disk
7. periodic supp.
8. 1986 - $18; 1989 - $15
9. 81-83834/9621270/KFN126.A65W74

1. **NEBRASKA LEGAL FORMS–WORKER'S COMPENSATION**
2. Cavel, Michael P.
3. Butterworth-St. Paul
4. 1981
5. 1 vol.
6. $50; $85 with disk
7. periodic supp.
8. 1987 - $15; 1988 - $20
9. 81-83828/8283836/KFN342.A65C38

1. **NEBRASKA LIMITATIONS MANUAL, 2nd ed.**
2. Publisher's Ed. Staff
3. Butterworth-St. Paul
4. 1989
5. 1 vol.
6. $50
7. periodic supp.
8. 1990 - $40
9. 89-138503/19920208/KFN90.L5N43

1. **NEBRASKA PROBATE SYSTEM IV**
2. -
3. Nebraska CLE
4. 1991
5. 1 vol.
6. $125
7. periodic supp.
8. no supp. yet

1. **THE NECK (Courtroom Medicine Series, vols. 2, 2A & 2B)**
2. Wolfstone, Leon, et al.
3. Bender
4. 1965
5. 3 vols.
6. $325 incl. 3 mos. supp.
7. annual supp.
8. 1989 - $214; 1990 - $240
9. 66-3050/11952423/RA1011.C68

1. **NECK AND BACK INJURIES**
2. -
3. MILE
4. 1991
5. 1 vol.
6. $68
7. no supp. planned
9. 23098734

1. **NEGOTIATING AND DRAFTING INTERNATIONAL BUSINESS AGREEMENTS**
2. -
3. Wash. Bar
4. 1989
5. 1 vol.
6. $35
7. no supp. planned

1. **NEGOTIATING AND DRAFTING MARITAL AGREEMENTS**
2. -
3. Jt. Comm. Va.
4. 1991
5. 1 vol.
6. $57
7. periodic supp.
8. no supp. yet
9. 87-117754/15550965/KFV2495.N43

1. **NEGOTIATING AND DRAFTING MORTGAGE DOCUMENTS: AN ADVANCED WORKSHOP FOR THE EXPERIENCED LAWYER, BANKER AND MORTGAGE LENDER**
2. -
3. Penn. Bar
4. 1989
5. 1 vol.
6. $60
7. no supp. planned

1. **NEGOTIATING THE SALE, PURCHASE AND FINANCING OF COMMERCIAL REAL ESTATE IN A WORKOUT ENVIRONMENT**
2. Real Property Section
3. Conn. Bar
4. 1990
5. 1 vol.
6. $20
7. no supp. planned

1. **NEPA LAW AND LITIGATION**
2. Mandelker, Daniel R.
3. Clark Boardman Callaghan
4. 1984
5. 1 vol.
6. $110 incl. 6 mos. supp.
7. annual supp.
8. 1989 - $41; 1990 - $43
9. 84-23059/11398492/KF3775.M37

1. **NEW ADMINISTRATIVE PROCEDURES ACT AND MODEL RULES**
2. -
3. Wash. Bar
4. 1989
5. 1 vol.
6. $35
7. no supp. planned

1. **THE NEW CLEAN AIR ACT**
2. -
3. NH Bar
4. 1991
5. 1 vol.
6. $40
7. no supp. planned

1. **NEW DEVELOPMENTS IN REAL ESTATE (7th Annual)**
2. -
3. MILE
4. 1990
5. 1 vol.
6. $63
7. no supp. planned

1. **NEW DEVELOPMENTS IN THE LAW OF DEFAMATION**
2. Abrams, Henry R. et al.
3. MICPEL
4. 1991
5. 1 vol.
6. $40
7. no supp. planned
9. 24235985/KFM1395.A16

1. **NEW DIRECTIONS IN THE LAW OF THE SEA**
2. Simmonds, Kenneth R., gen. ed.
3. Oceana
4. 1983
5. 5 vols.
6. $500
7. periodic supp.
8. 1990 - $110; 1991 - $125
9. 83-13174/9727633/JX4408.N48

1. **NEW ESTATE FREEZING RULES**
2. -
3. Minn. CLE
4. 1991
5. 1 vol.
6. $35
7. no supp. planned

1. **NEW HAMPSHIRE CONSTITUTIONAL LAW**
2. -
3. NH Bar
4. 1988
5. 1 vol.
6. $20
7. no supp. planned

1. **NEW HAMPSHIRE COURT RULES ANNOTATED**
2. -
3. Equity
4. 1979
5. 2 vols.
6. $98
7. semiannual supp.
8. 1990 - $25; 1991 - $46
9. 80-125816/6764147/KFN1729.A2

1. **NEW HAMPSHIRE MUNICIPAL PRACTICE SERIES: LAND USE PLANNING & ZONING**
2. Loughlin, Peter J.
3. Butterworth-NH
4. 1991
5. 2 vols.
6. $140
7. periodic supp.
8. no supp. yet
9. 91-144290/23704153/KFN1658.L68

1. **NEW HAMPSHIRE MUNICIPAL PRACTICE SERIES: MUNICIPAL FINANCE & TAXATION**
2. Loughlin, Peter J.
3. Butterworth-NH
4. 1991
5. 1 vol.
6. $70
7. periodic supp.
8. no supp. yet
9. 23704162

1. **NEW HAMPSHIRE MUNICIPAL PRACTICE SERIES: PUBLIC HEALTH, SAFETY & HIGHWAYS**
2. Loughlin, Peter J.
3. Butterworth-NH
4. 1991
5. 1 vol.
6. $70
7. periodic supp.
8. no supp. yet
9. 23704171

1. **NEW HAMPSHIRE PRACTICE AND PROCEDURE HANDBOOK**
2. -
3. NH Bar
4. 1990
5. 1 vol.
6. $90
7. no supp. planned
9. 10890292/KFN1277.N48

1. **THE NEW IMMIGRATION ACT OF 1990**
2. -
3. MILE
4. 1991
5. 1 vol.
6. $79.50
7. no supp. planned
9. 23271359/KF4819.3.N38

1. **NEW JERSEY APPELLATE PRACTICE HANDBOOK**
2. New Jersey Appellate Practice Study Committee
3. New Jersey ICLE
4. 2nd ed. - 1990
5. 1 vol.
6. $65
7. no supp. planned
9. 21919893/KFN2355.N49

1. **NEW JERSEY CIVIL PRACTICE AND COURT RULES**
2. Ed. Staff
3. Gould
4. NA
5. 1 vol.
6. $15.95
7. annual supp.
8. $5 - $10/supp.

1. **NEW JERSEY CORPORATE FORMS**
2. Pachman, Stuart H. & John L. Conover
3. Aspen
4. 1990
5. 2 vols.
6. $239 incl. 3 mos. supp.
7. annual supp.
8. no supp. yet
9. 90-50//r90/20993095/KFN2013.A65P33

1. **NEW JERSEY COURT RULES**
2. Pressler, Sylvia B., ed.
3. Gann
4. NA
5. 1 vol.
6. $93/yr.
7. supp. 3x/yr.
8. annual editions
9. 19062199/KFN2339.A317A2

1. **NEW JERSEY ENVIRONMENTAL LAW**
2. Goldshore, Lewis & Marsha Wolf
3. New Jersey ICLE
4. 1991
5. 1 vol.
6. $115
7. periodic supp.
8. no supp. yet
9. 23262865/KFN2154.G65

1. **NEW JERSEY ESTATE PLANNING, WILL DRAFTING AND ESTATE ADMINISTRATION FORMS–PRACTICE**

2. Martin, Alvin C., & Robert D. Borteck
3. Aspen
4. 1988
5. 2 vols.
6. $239 incl. 3 mos. supp.
7. annual supp.
8. $79-$95/supp.
9. 88-22165/18191786/KFN1940.A65M37

1. **NEW JERSEY FAMILY LAW PRACTICE**
2. Skoloff, Gary & Lawrence Cutler
3. New Jersey ICLE
4. 6th ed. - 1990
5. 3 vols.
6. $175
7. periodic supp.
8. no supp. yet
9. 22149968/KFN1895.A6S56

1. **NEW JERSEY LAW ENFORCEMENT HANDBOOK**
2. Holtz, Larry E.
3. Gould
4. 1990
5. 1 vol.
6. $34.95
7. annual supp.
8. $5 - $10/supp.
9. 21624997/KFN2362.A65H64

1. **NEW JERSEY LAW WITH FORMS**
2. Seltzer, C. Zachary
3. Bender
4. 1948
5. 9 vols.
6. $575 incl. 3 mos. supp.
7. annual supp.
8. 1989 - $248; 1990 - $214
9. 48-17009/4586873/KFN1865.S4

1. **NEW JERSEY LEGAL SECRETARY'S HANDBOOK**
2. New Jersey Association of Legal Secretaries
3. Michie
4. rev. - 1984
5. 1 vol.
6. $40
7. periodic supp.
8. 1985 - $15; 1987 - $20

1. **NEW JERSEY MORTGAGE FORECLOSURE HANDBOOK**
2. Zucker, Leonard B., et al.
3. New Jersey ICLE
4. rev. ed. - 1991
5. 1 vol.
6. $55
7. no supp. planned

1. **NEW JERSEY PUBLIC EMPLOYEE REPORTER**
2. -
3. LRP
4. 1975
5. 1 vol.
6. $595/yr. (back vols. avail.)
7. semimonthly supp.
9. 12272060/KFN2132.8.P77A48

1. **NEW JERSEY REAL ESTATE FORMS - PRACTICE**
2. Gordon, David S. et al.
3. Aspen
4. 1988
5. 1 vol.
6. $239 incl. 3 mos. supp.
7. annual supp.
8. 1989 - $89
9. 88-3278/17478359/KFN1926.A65G67

1. **NEW JERSEY TAX SERVICE**
2. Publ. Staff
3. Bender
4. 1986
5. 4 vols.
6. $370/1 yr.; $680/2 yrs.
7. periodic supp.
8. 1988 - $280; 1989 - $310
9. 86-71789/15550184/KFN2270.N49

1. **NEW JERSEY TRANSACTION GUIDE**
2. Jennings, E. Judson & C.H. Clancy
3. Bender
4. 1984
5. 14 vols.
6. $1270 incl. 3 mos. supp.
7. annual supp.
8. 1989 - $420; 1990 - $490.50
9. 84-72650/11527195/KFN1880.N43

1. **THE NEW MANUAL OF STANDARD FORMS FOR DECEDENTS' ESTATES**
2. -
3. Ohio State Bar
4. 1991
5. 1 vol.
6. $85
7. periodic supp.
8. no supp. yet

1. **NEW MEXICO APPELLATE PRACTICE MANUAL**
2. Schwarz, Michael
3. Butterworth-Texas
4. 1978
5. 1 vol.
6. $115
7. annual supp.
8. 1989 - $33.75; 1999 - $25

1. **NEW MEXICO CONSTRUCTION LAW**
2. Sheehan, Timothy M.
3. Butterworth-Texas
4. 1987
5. 1 vol.
6. $120
7. periodic supp.
8. 1990 - $85
9. 87-33752/17298835/KFN3755.8.B8S53

1. **NEW MEXICO CREDITOR/DEBTOR LAW**
2. Matthews, Marian and David G. Reynolds
3. Butterworth-Texas
4. 1989
5. 1 vol.
6. $115
7. annual supp.
8. 1991 - $35
9. 89-9750/19670451/KFN3767.C6M38

1. **NEW MEXICO LOCAL & FEDERAL RULES HANDBOOK**
2. Institute of Public Law, Univ. of New Mexico School of Law
3. Butterworth-Texas
4. 1976
5. 2 vols.
6. $135
7. quarterly supp.
8. 1989 - $154; 1990 - $96.50
9. 87-406443/17265194/KFN4129.A2

1. **NEW MEXICO PROBATE MANUAL**
2. Henderson, William N.
3. Butterworth-Texas
4. 1978
5. 1 vol.
6. $120
7. periodic supp.
8. 1990 - $35
9. 87-406442/17201230/KFN3744.A65H46

1. **NEW MEXICO RULES OF EVIDENCE TREATISE (rev. ed.)**
2. Larkin, Murl A.
3. Butterworth-Texas
4. 1983, 1986
5. 1 vol.
6. $125
7. periodic supp.
8. 1988 - $97.50; 1989 - $52.50
9. 13528951/KFN4140.W4

1. **NEW YORK APPELLATE PRACTICE**
2. Newman, Thomas R.
3. Bender
4. 1985
5. 2 vols.
6. $220 incl. 3 mos. supp.
7. periodic supp.
8. 1989 - $84.50; 1990 - $108
9. 85-72457/12988316/KFN6075.A6N4

1. **NEW YORK CANUDO ON EVIDENCE LAWS**
2. Shaw, Gary
3. Gould
4. NA
5. 1 vol.
6. $34.95
7. annual supp.
8. $5 - $10/supp.
9. 73-9968/61062/KFN6030.Z9C3

1. **THE NEW YORK CITY HOUSING COURT REPORTER**
2. Treiman, David M.
3. Lamb's Flight
4. 1983
5. 1 vol.
6. $270/yr.
7. monthly supp.
8. 1989 - $222; 1990 - $95
9. 11742812/KFX2005.H6

1. **NEW YORK CITY HOUSING COURT REPORTER CHRONOLOGICAL ANNOTATOR**
2. Treiman, David
3. Lamb's Flight
4. 1991
5. 1 vol.
6. $84/yr.
7. monthly supp.

1. **THE NEW YORK CITY HOUSING COURT REPORTER DIGEST**
2. Treiman, David M.
3. Lamb's Flight
4. 1990

5. 1 vol.
6. $210
7. monthly supp.
8. 1990 - free

1. **THE NEW YORK CITY HOUSING COURT REPORTER PLAINTIFF-DEFENDANT TABLES**
2. Treiman, David M.
3. Lamb's Flight
4. 1990
5. 1 vol.
6. $150
7. monthly supp.
8. 1990 - free; 1991 - free

1. **NEW YORK CITY LAW DIGEST**
2. Ed. Staff
3. Gould
4. NA
5. 1 vol.
6. $9.95
7. annual supp.
8. $5 - $10/supp.

1. **THE NEW YORK CITY LOFT BOARD REPORTER**
2. Treiman, David M. & Rachel L.
3. Lamb's Flight
4. 1985
5. 1 vol.
6. $150
7. periodic supp.
8. 1990 - $150; 1991 - $150
9. 11874198/KFX2022.A4N4

1. **NEW YORK CIVIL MOTION CITATOR**
2. Adler, Noel D.
3. Nat. Atty.
4. 9th ed. - 1989
5. 1 vol.
6. $175/yr.
7. semiannual supp.
9. 80-80751/6776746/KFN6012.A59A34

1. **NEW YORK CIVIL PRACTICE - CPLR (vols. 1, 2, 2A, 3 3A, 4, 5, 6, 7, 7A, 8 - Table of cases, Table of statutes & Index)**
2. Weinstein, Korn & Miller
3. Bender
4. 1963
5. 14 vols.
6. $1395 incl. 3 mos. supp.
7. biannual supp.
8. 1989 - $820; 1990 - $997
9. 63-5151/212368/KFN5995.N4

1. **NEW YORK CIVIL PRACTICE - ESTATES, POWERS, TRUSTS LAW (vols. 9, 9 pt. 2, 9A, 9A pt. 2, 9B, 9C, 9D)**
2. Rohan, Patrick J.
3. Bender
4. 1969
5. 7 vols.
6. $620 incl. 3 mos. supp.
7. annual supp.
8. 1989 - $455; 1990 - $489.50
9. 73-27761/196097/KFN5995.N4

1. **NEW YORK CIVIL PRACTICE - FAMILY COURT AND FAMILY LAW PROCEEDINGS (vol. 12, 12A, 12B)**
2. Zett, James et al.
3. Bender
4. 1972
5. 4 vols.
6. $460 incl. 3 mos. supp.
7. annual supp.
8. 1989 - $336.50; 1990 - $570
9. 73-156608/610091/KFN5995.N4

1. **NEW YORK CIVIL PRACTICE - MATRIMONIAL ACTIONS (vols. 11, 11A, 11B & 11C)**
2. Zett, James et al.
3. Bender
4. 1971
5. 4 vols.
6. $490 incl. 3 mos. supp.
7. annual supp.
8. 1989 - $597.50; 1990 - $451.50
9. 72-179656/308964/KFN5995.N4

1. **NEW YORK CIVIL PRACTICE - SCPA (vols. 10, 10 pt. 2, 10A, 10B, 10B pt. 2, 10C-10E)**
2. Cox, Joseph A. et al.
3. Bender
4. 1970
5. 8 vols.
6. $620 incl. 3 mos. supp.
7. biannual supp.
8. 1989 - $489; 1990 - $777
9. 77-27762/196564/KFN5995.N4

1. **NEW YORK CIVIL PRACTICE LAW & RULES HANDBOOK**
2. Ed. Staff
3. Gould
4. NA

5. 1 vol.
6. $19.95
7. annual supp.
8. 1990 - $5.50; 1991 - $5.50

1. **NEW YORK CLOSE CORPORATIONS**
2. Kessler, Robert A.
3. Hein
4. 1968 (1983 Reprint)
5. 1 vol.
6. $95
7. periodic supp.
8. 1983 - $47.50
9. 68-16899/439684/KFN5357.C5K4

1. **NEW YORK COLLECTIONS**
2. Rubin, Joseph
3. Lawyers Coop.
4. 1982
5. 1 vol.
6. $115 incl. 6 mos. supp.
7. annual supp.
8. 1990 - $38; 1991 - $45
9. 80-81138/8471118/KFN5256.C65R8

1. **NEW YORK CORPORATION LAW HANDBOOK**
2. Ed. Staff
3. Gould
4. NA
5. 1 vol.
6. $21.95
7. annual supp.
8. 1990 - $12; 1991 - $12

1. **NEW YORK COURT FORMS**
2. Salisbury, Eugene W.
3. Gould
4. NA
5. 1 vol.
6. $34.95
7. periodic supp.
8. $5 - $10/supp.

1. **NEW YORK COURTROOM EVIDENCE**
2. Fuchsberg, Abraham & John E. Durst
3. Parker
4. 1991
5. 1 vol.
6. price NA
7. annual supp.
8. no supp. yet

1. **NEW YORK COURTS MANUAL OF PROCEDURE**
2. Salisbury, Eugene W.
3. Gould
4. NA
5. 1 vol.
6. $28
7. annual supp.
8. $5 - $10/supp.

1. **NEW YORK CRIMINAL CASE CITATOR**
2. Hovani, Steven A.
3. Nat. Atty.
4. 3rd ed. - 1989
5. 1 vol.
6. $150/yr.
7. semiannual supp.
9. 83-62518/10481602/KFN6100.A575N42

1. **NEW YORK CRIMINAL LAW HANDBOOK**
2. Ed. Staff
3. Gould
4. NA
5. 1 vol.
6. $21.95
7. annual supp.
8. $5 - $10/supp.

1. **NEW YORK CRIMINAL PRACTICE**
2. Waxner, Marvin et al.
3. Bender
4. 1973
5. 11 vols.
6. $830 incl. 3 mos. supp.
7. annual supp.
8. 1989 - $679.50; 1990 - $737.50
9. 73-90406/897691/KFN6155.W38

1. **NEW YORK ESTATES - WILLS - TRUSTS**
2. -
3. CCH
4. 1967
5. 1 vol.
6. $870/yr.; $790/yr. for 2 yrs.
7. monthly supp.
9. 67-66280/6962232/KFN5200.A6C6

1. **NEW YORK FAMILY LAW HANDBOOK**
2. Ed Staff
3. Gould
4. NA
5. 1 vol.
6. $19.95
7. annual supp.
8. $5 - $10/supp.

9. 12898565/KFN5116.A31A2

1. **NEW YORK FUTURES EXCHANGE GUIDE**
2. -
3. CCH
4. 1980
5. 1 vol.
6. $270/yr.; $245/yr. for 2 yrs.
7. monthly supp.
9. 80-645199/6699556/HG6024.U6N48a

1. **NEW YORK INSURANCE LAW**
2. Wolcott, B. Dunham, Jr., ed.
3. Bender
4. 1991
5. 4 vols.
6. $420 incl. 3 mos. supp.
7. annual supp.
8. no supp. yet
9. 90-85285/23740568/KFN5290.N49

1. **NEW YORK KASS ON WILLS**
2. Bloom, Judge Bernard
3. Gould
4. NA
5. 1 vol.
6. $24.95
7. annual supp.

1. **NEW YORK LANDLORD & TENANT HANDBOOK**
2. Gallett, Jeffrey L.
3. Gould
5. 1 vol.
6. $34.95
7. periodic supp.
8. $5 - $10/supp.

1. **NEW YORK LAW DIGEST**
2. Ed. Staff
3. Gould
4. NA
5. 1 vol.
6. $12.95
7. annual supp.
8. $5 - $10/supp.

1. **THE NEW YORK LAW OF PRODUCTS LIABILITY**
2. Rheingold, Paul S. & Jeanne Fennell
3. NYSTLA
4. 1991
5. 1 vol.
6. $75
7. biannual supp.
8. no supp. yet
9. 7488208

1. **NEW YORK LAWYER'S DESKBOOK**
2. General Practice Section
3. NYSBA
4. 1990
5. 1 vol.
6. $80
7. annual supp.
8. $45/yr.
9. 21933762/KFN5077.N353

1. **NEW YORK LAWYER'S FORMBOOK**
2. -
3. NYSBA
4. 1990
5. 1 vol.
6. $80
7. annual supp.
8. 1991 - $45
9. 90-50851/23155612/KFN5068.N49

1. **NEW YORK LEGAL FORMS & PROCEDURES HANDBOOK**
2. Ed. Staff
3. Gould
4. 1989
5. 1 vol.
6. $44.95
7. annual supp.
8. no supp. yet
9. 20706165

1. **NEW YORK MAGISTRATES DESK BOOK**
2. Ed. Staff
3. Gould
4. NA
5. 1 vol.
6. $34.95
7. annual supp.
8. $5 - $10/supp.

1. **NEW YORK MATRIMONIAL CASE CITATOR**
2. Sereduke, Peter D.
3. Nat. Atty.
4. 5th ed. - 1989
5. 1 vol.
6. $175/yr.
7. semiannual supp.
9. 82-061851/9252822/KFN5120.A535N42

1. **NEW YORK MATRIMONIAL LAW AND PRACTICE**
2. Tippins, Timothy M.
3. Lawyers Coop.
4. 1986
5. 2 vols.
6. $180 incl. 6 mos. supp.
7. annual supp.
8. 1990 - $45; 1991 - $48
9. 85-25531/12724335/KFN5126.T57

1. **NEW YORK MATRIMONIAL PRACTICE**
2. DaSilva, Willard H.
3. Lawyers Coop.
4. 1980
5. 1 vol.
6. $115 incl. 6 mos. supp.
7. annual supp.
8. 1990 - $64.50; 1991 - $68.50
9. 79-91156/7338117/KFN5120.D38

1. **NEW YORK MEDICAL MALPRACTICE**
2. Bard, Norman
3. NYSTLA
4. 1990
5. 2 vols.
6. $217
7. periodic supp.

1. **NEW YORK MERCANTILE EXCHANGE GUIDE**
2. -
3. CCH
4. 1986
5. 1 vol.
6. $205/yr.; $185/yr. for 2 yrs.
7. monthly supp.
9. 14408097/KF1087.N44A5

1. **NEW YORK PRACTICE GUIDE: BUSINESS AND COMMERCIAL**
2. Lach, E.M.
3. Bender
4. 1987
5. 3 vols.
6. $325 incl. 3 mos. supp.
7. annual supp.
8. 1989 - $98; 1990 - $128.50
9. 87-71818/7253260/KFN5337.N48

1. **NEW YORK PRACTICE GUIDE: DOMESTIC RELATIONS**
2. Sovronsky, R. et al.
3. Bender
4. 1988
5. 3 vols.
6. $325 incl. 3 mos. supp.
7. annual supp.
8. 1989 - $74; 1990 - $97.50
9. 88-70207/17805968/KFN5115.N48

1. **NEW YORK PRACTICE GUIDE: NEGLIGENCE**
2. Miller, Henry G. & Oscar G. Chase
3. Bender
4. 1989
5. 4 vols.
6. $410 incl. 3 mos. supp.
7. annual supp.
8. 1990 - $80.50
9. 21105384/KFN5315.A6N4

1. **NEW YORK PRACTICE GUIDE: PROBATE AND ESTATE ADMINISTRATION**
2. Arenson, Joseph T., et al.
3. Bender
4. 1985
5. 2 vols.
6. $220 incl. 3 mos. supp.
7. periodic supp.
8. 1989 - $119; 1990 - $134.50
9. 85-72835/13391655/KFN5205.P76

1. **NEW YORK PRACTICE GUIDE: REAL ESTATE**
2. Morris, Eugene J., et al.
3. Bender
4. 1986
5. 4 vols.
6. $430 incl. 3 mos. supp.
7. periodic supp.
8. 1989 - $249; 1990 - $286
9. 85-72401/13278594/KFN5140.N48

1. **NEW YORK PROBATE**
2. Schlesinger, Edward S. & Michael M. Mariani
3. Lawyers Coop.
4. 1986
5. 3 vols.
6. $285 incl. 6 mos. supp.
7. annual supp.
8. 1989 - $59.50; 1991 - $84.50
9. 86-82156/14879743/KFN5205.S35

1. **NEW YORK PRODUCTS LIABILITY**
2. Weinberger, Michael
3. Lawyers Coop.
4. 1982

5. 2 vols.
6. $190 incl. 6 mos. supp.
7. annual supp.
8. 1990 - $52.50; 1991 - $54.50
9. 82-9487/8476594/KFN5323.A3W43

1. **NEW YORK REAL PROPERTY LAW HANDBOOK**
2. Ed. Staff
3. Gould
4. NA
5. 1 vol.
6. $21.95
7. annual supp.
9. 89-179332/20671913/KFN5140.A3

1. **NEW YORK REAL PROPERTY SERVICE**
2. -
3. Lawyers Coop.
4. 1987
5. 14 vols.
6. $1470 incl. 1 yr. supp.
7. supp. 3x/yr.
8. 1990 - $270; 1991 - $292.50

1. **NEW YORK SEARCH & SEIZURE**
2. Kamins, Barry
3. Gould
4. NA
5. 1 vol.
6. $34.95
7. periodic supp.

1. **NEW YORK STOCK EXCHANGE GUIDE**
2. -
3. CCH
4. 1957
5. 3 vols.
6. $425/yr.; $385/yr. for 2 yrs.
7. monthly supp.
9. 5898248/HG4572.N417

1. **NEW YORK STOCK EXCHANGE LISTED COMPANY MANUAL**
2. -
3. NYSE
4. 1983
5. 1 vol.
6. $50 incl. 5 yrs. supp.
7. 1-2/yr.
8. supp. incl. in price

1. **NEW YORK SUPPRESSION MANUAL**
2. Katz, Lewis R. & Jay Shapiro
3. Bender
4. 1991
5. 1 vol.
6. $105 incl. 3 mos. supp.
7. annual supp.
8. no supp. yet
9. 90-64156/23348951/KFN1611.K37

1. **NEW YORK TAX CASES**
2. Comeau, Paul R. & Arthur R. Rosen
3. Hein
4. 1988
5. 5 vols.
6. $495
7. monthly supp.
8. 1990 - $425; 1991 - $465
9. 88-658650/17944606/KFN5866.A59N4

1. **NEW YORK TAX SERVICE**
2. Comeau, Paul, et al.
3. Bender
4. 1985
5. 6 vols.
6. $400/1 yr.; $760/2 yrs.
7. monthly supp. & newsletter
8. renewal - $340/yr.
9. 85-71309/12720248/KFN5860.N49

1. **NEW YORK TRIAL GUIDE**
2. Goldberg, Rick
3. Bender
4. 1990
5. 5 vols.
6. $440 incl. 3 mos. supp.
7. periodic supp.
8. no supp. yet
9. 90-83546/22975518/KFN6025.N48

1. **NEW YORK UNCONTESTED DIVORCES AND ANNULMENTS**
2. Gitlitz, James P.
3. Gould
4. NA
5. 1 vol.
6. $34.95
7. annual supp.
8. $5 - $10/supp.

1. **NEW YORK UNIVERSITY ANNUAL INSTITUTE ON FEDERAL TAXATION**
2. Liakas, Nicholas, ed.
3. Bender
4. 1943, looseleaf since 1974
5. 49th annual, - 2 vols.

6. $195
7. annual vols.
8. 1989 - $167; 1990 - $172
9. 44-31413/2825362/KF6289.A2I48

1. **NEW YORK WILLS AND TRUSTS, 3/e**
2. Finger, Bookstaver and McQuaid
3. Shepard's
4. 3rd ed. - 1990
5. 2 vols.
6. $220
7. annual supp.
8. no supp. yet
9. 90-25251/22911267/KFN5201.M38

1. **NEW YORK WORKERS CONPENSATION LAW HANDBOOK**
2. Ed. Staff
3. Gould
4. 1991
5. 1 vol.
6. $21.95
7. annual supp.

1. **NEW YORK WORKER'S COMPENSATION LAW REPORTER**
2. -
3. LRP
4. 1987
5. 2 vols.
6. $575/yr. (back vol. avail.)
7. semimonthly supp.

1. **NICHOLS ON EMINENT DOMAIN**
2. Sackman, Julius L. et al.
3. Bender
4. 3rd 3d. - 1956
5. 18 vols.
6. $1150 incl. 3 mos. supp.
7. biannual supp.
8. 1989 - $913.50; 1990 - $1005.50
9. 50-11264/12878618/KF5599.A6N5

1. **NIMMER ON COPYRIGHT**
2. Nimmer, Melville B.
3. Bender
4. 1963
5. 4 vols.
6. $560 incl. 3 mos. supp.
7. annual supp.
8. 1989 - $474; 1990 - $490.50
9. 78-109488/4514674/KF2991.5.N5

1. **NIMMER ON FREEDOM OF SPEECH**
2. Nimmer, Melville B.
3. Bender
4. 1984
5. 1 vol.
6. $105 incl. 3 mos. supp.
7. annual supp.
8. 1988 - $38; 1989 - $44
9. 84-70559/11129437/KF4772.N55

1. **NINTH ANNUAL BANKRUPTCY INSTITUTE**
2. -
3. Indiana CLE
4. 1991
5. 2 vols.
6. $95
7. no supp. planned
9. 24044719/KFI3221.A75B36

1. **THE 9TH ANNUAL FEDERAL ESTATE PLANNING SYMPOSIUM**
2. -
3. UMKC/CLE
4. 1990
5. 1 vol.
6. $45
7. periodic supp.

1. **NINTH CIRCUIT CT. OF APPEALS - LOCAL RULES**
2. -
3. Book Pub.
4. NA
5. 1 vol.
6. $15
7. supp. as needed
8. 1989 - $7.50

1. **NLRB ADVICE MEMORANDUM REPORTER**
2. -
3. LRP
4. 1976
5. 1 vol.
6. $495/yr. (back vols. avail.)
7. monthly supp.

1. **NLRB CASE HANDLING MANUAL**
2. -
3. CCH
4. 1976
5. 1 vol.
6. $225/yr.; $205/yr. for 2 yrs.
7. periodic supp.
9. 77-152434/3326563/KF3365.C6

1. **NLRB REPRESENTATION ELECTIONS - LAW, PRACTICE & PROCEDURE**
2. Feerick, John et al.
3. Prentice Hall Law & Business
4. 3rd ed. - 1988
5. 2 vols.
6. $85 incl. 4 mos. supp.
7. annual supp.
8. 1990 - $60; 1991 - $60
9. 79-22711/5492613/KF3372.F43

1. **NO-FAULT AND UNINSURED MOTORIST AUTO INSURANCE**
2. Various Contributors
3. Bender
4. 1984
5. 4 vols.
6. $440 incl. 3 mos. supp.
7. annual supp.
8. 1989 - $252; 1990 - $304

1. **THE NO-FAULT HANDBOOK**
2. Weitz, Harvey
3. NYSTLA
4. 1991
5. 1 vol.
6. $80
7. periodic supp.
8. no supp. yet

1. **NONPROFIT AND TAX-EXEMPT ORGANIZATIONS**
2. -
3. Wash. Bar
4. 1988
5. 1 vol.
6. $35
7. no supp. planned

1. **NONPROFIT CORPORATIONS**
2. -
3. Indiana CLE
4. 1991
5. 1 vol.
6. $50
7. no supp. planned

1. **NONPROFIT ENTERPRISES: LAW AND TAXATION**
2. Phelan, Marilyn E.
3. Clark Boardman Callaghan
4. 1985
5. 3 vols.
6. $250 incl. 6 mos. supp.
7. annual supp.
8. 1989 - $95; 1990 - $92
9. 85-7870/11969971/KF1388.P47

1. **NON-QUALIFIED DEFERRED COMPENSATION ARRANGEMENTS**
2. Mancoff, Neal A. & David M. Weiner
3. Clark Boardman Callaghan
4. 1987
5. 1 vol.
6. $130 incl. 6 mos. supp.
7. annual supp.
8. 1989 - $39; 1990 - $46
9. 87-15800/16093129/KF3509.M36

1. **NORTH AMERICA AND ASIA-PACIFIC AND THE DEVELOPMENT OF THE LAW OF THE SEA**
2. Nordquist, Myron H. & Choon H. Park
3. Oceana
4. 1980
5. 2 vols. (set closed)
6. $200/set
7. no supp. planned
8. continued in New Directions in the Law of the Sea Service
9. 81-309/7204584/JX4408.N67

1. **NORTH CAROLINA ESTATE ADMINISTRATION MANUAL**
2. -
3. No. Carolina Bar
4. 1991
5. 1 vol.
6. $127
7. no supp. yet

1. **NORTH CAROLINA PATTERN JURY INSTRUCTIONS FOR CIVIL CASES**
2. -
3. No. Carolina Bar
4. 1970
5. 2 vols.
6. $125
7. annual supp.
8. 1991 - $15
9. 73-156573/610083/KFN7942.A65N67

1. **NORTH CAROLINA PATTERN JURY INSTRUCTIONS FOR CRIMINAL CASES**
2. -
3. No. Carolina Bar
4. 1970
5. 2 vols.
6. $150

7. annual supp.
8. 1991 - $30
9. 77-229632/145074/KFN7983.A65N67

1. **NORTH CAROLINA PATTERN JURY INSTRUCTIONS - MOTOR VEHICLE NEGLIGENCE**
2. -
3. No. Carolina Bar
4. 1973
5. 1 vol.
6. $100
7. annual supp.
8. 1991 - $15
9. 74-177321/1046624/KFN7942.A65N68

1. **NORTH CAROLINA REAL PROPERTY FORMS BOOK**
2. -
3. No. Carolina Bar
4. 1987
5. 3 vols.
6. $265
7. periodic supp.
8. no supp. yet
9. 16463379/KFN7512.A65N67

1. **NORTH DAKOTA PATTERN JURY INSTRUCTIONS - CIVIL**
2. Pattern Jury Instruction Comm.
3. State Bar of N. Dak.
4. 1986
5. 2 vols.
6. $45
7. periodic supp.
8. $15
9. 13775929/KFN9142.6.N67

1. **NORTH DAKOTA PATTERN JURY INSTRUCTIONS - CRIMINAL**
2. Pattern Jury Instruction Comm.
3. State Bar of N. Dak.
4. 1985
5. 1 vol.
6. $40
7. periodic supp.
8. 1986 - $15
9. 3786476/KFN9142.N67x

1. **NORTON BANKRUPTCY LAW AND PRACTICE**
2. Norton, William L., Jr., et al.
3. Clark Boardman Callaghan
4. 1981
5. 6 vols.
6. $495 incl. 1 yr. service
7. quarterly supp. & monthly newsletter
8. 1989 - $350; 1990 - $375
9. 81-10028/7578006/KF1524.N67

1. **NOT-FOR-PROFIT CORPORATIONS**
2. -
3. Illinois ICLE
4. 1987
5. 1 vol.
6. $91.95
7. periodic supp.
8. 1989 - $24.95
9. 16852269/KFI1411.N67

1. **NOT IN MAI: CIVIL JURY INSTRUCTIONS COLLECTED FROM MISSOURI CASES**
2. Knox, William A. & James R. Devine
3. UMC CLE
4. 2nd ed. - 10/91
5. 1 vol.
6. $95
7. biennial supp.
8. no supp. yet
9. 11072575/KFM8342.K56

1. **NOTARY HOME STUDY COURSE**
2. -
3. Nat. Notary
4. 1990
5. 1 vol.
6. $65 - member; $72 - non-members
7. no supp. planned
9. 84-63136/12586400/KF8797.N68

1. **NOTES AND DECISIONS**
2. Pazer, Perry et al.
3. NYSTLA
4. 1991
5. 1 vol.
6. $89
7. annual editions

1. **NTTS FILLED-IN TAX FORMS ENCYCLOPEDIA**
2. -
3. NTTS
4. NA
5. 1 vol.
6. $99.75
7. annual editions

1. **NTTS MASTER TAX FORMS FILE**
2. -

3. NTTS
4. NA
5. 1 vol.
6. $95
7. annual editions

1. **NUCLEAR REGULATION REPORTS**
2. -
3. CCH
4. 1975
5. 2 vols.
6. $2420/yr.; $2200/yr. for 2 yrs.
7. weekly supp.
9. 75-323755/2560673/KF2138.A6C66

1. **NURSING HOME NEGLIGENCE**
2. Barnes, Richard M. et al.
3. MICPEL
4. 1991
5. 1 vol.
6. $42
7. no supp. planned
9. 23949000/KFM1563.N8N8

1. **THE NUTS AND BOLTS OF A BASIC REAL ESTATE DEAL**
2. -
3. Maine Bar
4. 1989
5. 1 vol.
6. $30
7. no supp. planned
9. 22400764/KF570.Z99M213

1. **NUTS & BOLTS OF RAISING STATE CONSTITUTIONAL ISSUES**
2. -
3. Conn. Bar
4. 1990
5. 1 vol.
6. $53
7. no supp. planned

1. **OAKES' CRIMINAL PRACTICE GUIDE**
2. Oakes, Richard T.
3. Wiley Law
4. 1987
5. 1 vol
6. $125
7. periodic supp.
8. 1989 - $25; 1991 - $40
9. 87-17683/16085650/KF9656.025

1. **OBBC REQUIREMENTS ENCYCLOPEDIA**
2. Fencl, Irving and The Preview Group
3. Banks
4. 1990
5. 1 vol.
6. $55
7. periodic supp.
8. 1991 - $19
9. 22164477/KFO459.A3F45

1. **OBJECTIONS TO INTERROGATORIES**
2. Morse, Lawrence A.
3. James
4. 1990
5. 1 vol.
6. $49.92 incl. 3 mos. supp.
7. annual supp.
8. no supp. yet
9. 22502127/KF8900.M67

1. **OBSCENITY LAW REPORTER**
2. -
3. Natl. Obscenity Law Center
4. 1986
5. 2 vols.
6. $240 incl. 1 yr. supp.
7. annual supp.
9. 86-16479/13861422/KF9444.A59O26

1. **OBTAINING IRS PRIVATE LETTER RULINGS: A MANUAL OF FORMS AND PROCEDURES FROM TOUCHE ROSS & CO.**
2. Padwe, Gerald W. et al.
3. Oceana
4. 1983; rev. - 1989
5. 1 vol.
6. $150
7. periodic supp.
8. 1988 - $125; 1989 - $150
9. 82-22311/8976006/KF6301.P33

1. **OCCUPATIONAL SAFETY AND HEALTH ACT**
2. Hogan, Roscoe B. & R. Ben Hogan III
3. Bender
4. 1977
5. 2 vols.
6. $245 incl. 3 mos. supp.
7. annual supp.
8. 1989 - $143; 1990 - $204
9. 77-84163/3682902/KF3570.H63

1. **OCCUPATIONAL SAFETY & HEALTH REPORTER**
2. Pond, Stanley S.

3. BNA
4. 1971
5. 6 vols.
6. $870/yr.
7. weekly supp.
8. renewal - $770/yr.
9. 74-648258/1796421/KF3570.A1O25

1. **OFCCP FEDERAL CONTRACT COMPLIANCE MANUAL**
2. -
3. CCH
4. 1979
5. 1 vol.
6. $220/yr.; $200/yr. for 2 yrs.
7. monthly supp.
9. 79-129120/6091287/KF3464.A856

1. **OFFICIAL DECISIONS, OPINIONS AND RELATED MATTERS OF THE PUBLIC EMPLOYMENT RELATIONS BOARD OF THE STATE OF NEW YORK**
2. -
3. LRP
4. 1968
5. 2 vols.
6. $310/yr. (back vols. avail.)
7. monthly supp.
9. 81-4277/7522552

1. **OFFICIAL FORMS FOR THE SOUTH CAROLINA BUSINESS CORPORATION ACT OF 1988**
2. Haynsworth, Harry J. IV
3. S. Carolina Bar
4. 1989
5. 1 vol.
6. $25
7. no supp. planned
9. 19764008/KFS2013.A65H29

1. **OFFICIAL IRS PUBLICATIONS**
2. RIA prof. editorial staff
3. RIA
4. 1991
5. 3 vols.
6. $260/yr.; $250/yr. for 2 yrs.
7. monthly supp. (April-Oct.); weekly supp. (Nov.-March)
8. renewal - $235/yr.
9. 22934220/KF6289.R53

1. **OHIO ATTORNEY'S/SECRETARY'S HANDBOOK**
2. -
3. Mariposa
4. 1991
5. 1 vol.
6. $59
7. annual supp.
8. 1990 - $51; 1991 - $50
9. 18316653

1. **OHIO BASIC BUILDING CODE AND RELATED CODES**
2. -
3. Banks
4. 1979
5. 2 vols.
6. $135 incl. 9 mos. supp.
7. periodic supp.
8. 1991 - $37.50
9. 79-114726/5407504/KFO459.A1A3

1. **OHIO CORPORATION LAW WITH FEDERAL TAX ANALYSIS**
2. Cavitch, Zolman
3. Bender
4. 1961
5. 1 vol.
6. $120 incl. 3 mos. supp.
7. annual supp.
8. 1989 - $101.50; 1990 - $109.90
9. 61-2478/2025996

1. **OHIO COURTROOM EVIDENCE**
2. Palmer, John
3. Parker
4. 2nd ed. - 1988
5. 1 vol.
6. $85 incl. 3 mos. supp.
7. annual supp.
8. 1990 - $29.50; 1991 - $32
9. 18824203/KFO540.P34

1. **OHIO CRIMINAL PRACTICE & PROCEDURE**
2. Aplin, Kenneth L. et al.
3. Anderson
4. 1989
5. 2 vols. & paperback manual
6. $250 incl. 1 yr. supp.
7. annual supp.
8. 1990 - $87.50; 1991 - $125
9. 89-199889/19570294/KFO561.A95

1. **OHIO FORMS AND TRANSACTIONS**
2. Swisher, Thomas R.

3. Banks
4. 1989
5. 3 vols.
6. $175
7. periodic supp.
9. 20429738/KFO68.S95

1. **OHIO FORMS OF PLEADING AND PRACTICE**
2. Milligan, William W. et al.
3. Bender
4. 1970
5. 18 vols.
6. $980 incl. 3 mos. supp.
7. annual supp.
8. 1989 - $563; 1990 - $535.50
9. 71-129085/106889/KFO530.A65M5

1. **OHIO JURY INSTRUCTIONS**
2. Judicial Conference
3. Anderson
4. 1968
5. 4 vols.
6. $400 incl. 1 yr. supp.
7. periodic supp.
8. 1990 - $80; 1991 - $150
9. 68-2026/430840/KFO542.A65O36

1. **OHIO LEGAL FILING DIRECTORY**
2. Furman, Sandra
3. Shepard's
4. 1991
5. 1 vol.
6. $60
8. no supp. yet

1. **OHIO MANUAL OF PROCEDURE**
2. Leyshon, Frank C.
3. Anderson
4. 3rd ed. - 1976
5. 1 vol.
6. $75 incl. 1 yr. supp.
7. periodic supp.
8. 1988 - $37.50; 1990 - $40
9. 77-360571/3015625/KFO530.L4

1. **OHIO PROBATE**
2. Carmack, Daniel F.
3. Lawyers Coop.
4. 1979
5. 1 vol.
6. $115 incl. 6 mos. supp.
7. annual supp.
8. 1990 - $47; 1991 - $50
9. 79-91159/6143639/KFO144.A64C37

1. **OHIO PUBLIC EMPLOYEE REPORTER**
2. -
3. LRP
4. 1984
5. 1 vol.
6. $475/yr. (back vols. avail)
7. semimonthly supp.
9. 85-14432/10892968/KFO332.8.P77O3

1. **OHIO STATE TAXATION**
2. Belden, Thomas G. and Paul J. Schlather
3. Bender
4. 1985
5. 4 vols.
6. $370/1 yr. service; $680/2 yr. service
7. monthly supp.
8. renewal - $310/yr.
9. 85-72944/13014395/KFO470.A6O3

1. **OHIO TRANSACTION GUIDE - LEGAL FORMS**
2. Cavitch, Zolman et al.
3. Bender
4. 1975
5. 15 vols.
6. $1065 incl. 3 mos. supp.
7. annual supp.
8. 1989 - $610; 1990 - $757
9. 75-330596/1976197/KFO213.A65O39

1. **OHIO WORKERS' COMPENSATION CLAIMS**
2. Nackley, Jeffrey V.
3. Lawyers Coop.
4. 1982
5. 1 vol.
6. $115 incl. 6 mos. supp
7. annual supp.
8. 1990 - $62.50; 1991 - $62.50
9. 82-82437/8751176/KFO342.N3

1. **OIL AND GAS AGREEMENTS**
2. -
3. Rocky Mt.
4. 1983
5. 1 vol.
6. $90
7. no supp. planned
9. 9769972/KF1842.5.I66

1. **OIL AND GAS CONSERVATION LAW AND PRACTICE**
2. -
3. Rocky Mt.
4. 1985

5. 1 vol.
6. $125
7. no supp. planned
9. 13197065/KF1852.A75I5

1. **THE OIL AND GAS JOINT OPERATING AGREEMENT**
2. -
3. Rocky Mt.
4. 1990
5. 1 vol.
6. $125
7. no supp. planned
9. 22225945/KF1865.A75I57

1. **OIL AND GAS LAW**
2. Williams, Howard R. & Charles J. Meyers
3. Bender
4. 1959
5. 8 vols.
6. $875 incl. 3 mos. supp.
7. annual supp.
8. 1989 - $170; 1990 - $240
9. 60-665/1964552/KF1849.W542

1. **OIL AND GAS LAW: ABRIDGED EDITION**
2. Williams, Howard R. & Charles J. Meyers
3. Bender
4. 1973
5. 1 vol.
6. $115 incl. 3 mos. supp.
7. supp. as needed
8. 1987 - $0; 1989 - $0
9. 73-90725/934482/KF1849.W542

1. **OIL AND GAS LAW: THE NORTH SEA EXPLOITATION**
2. Simmonds, Kenneth R. & Brian Hill
3. Oceana
4. 1981
5. 1 vol.
6. $150
7. periodic supp.
8. 1988 - $100; 1989 - $125

1. **OIL AND GAS OPERATIONS IN FEDERAL AND COASTAL WATERS**
2. -
3. Rocky Mt.
4. 1989
5. 1 vol.
6. $105
7. no supp. planned

1. **OIL AND GAS REPORTER**
2. Southwestern Legal Foundation
3. Bender
4. 1952
5. 4 vols./yr.
6. $550/vol.
7. 4 vols./yr.
8. 1988 - $500; 1989 - $510
9. 1606606

1. **OIL SPILL LAW INFORMATION SERVICE**
2. -
3. Thompson
4. 1990
5. 1 vol.
6. $594/yr. (state chapters updated at $104 for quarterly updates)
7. monthly supp.

1. **OKLAHOMA BUSINESS ORGANIZATIONS: FORMATION AND REPRESENTATION**
2. Fraught, Irving L.
3. Aspen
4. 1990
5. 1 vol.
6. $99 incl. 3 mos. supp.
7. periodic supp.
9. 90-34040/21330434/KFO1413.F38

1. **OKLAHOMA CIVIL PROCEDURE FORMS - PRACTICE**
2. Muchmore, Clyde A.
3. Aspen
4. 1987
5. 2 vols.
6. $239 incl. 3 mos. supp.
7. annual supp.
8. 1988- $87.95
9. 87-22331/16647200/KF01730.A65M83

1. **OKLAHOMA CORPORATE FORMS - PRACTICE**
2. Mock, Randall D. and James H. Holloman, Jr.
3. Aspen
4. 1988
5. 2 vols.
6. $239 incl. 3 mos. supp.
7. annual supp.
8. no supp. yet
9. 87-36436/17295685/KF01413.A65M63

1. **OKLAHOMA CRIMINAL PRACTICE MANUAL**

2. Blair, Chris and Charles L. Cantrell
3. Butterworth-Texas
4. 1987
5. 1 vol.
6. $120
7. annual supp.
8. 1990 - $60; 1991 - $77
9. 87-404050/15620377/KFO1775.B55

1. **OKLAHOMA DISCOVERY PRACTICE MANUAL**
2. Adams, Charles W.
3. Butterworth-Texas
4. 1987
5. 1 vol.
6. $120
7. annual supp.
8. 1990 - $85; 1991 - $85
9. 15620408/KFO1737.A93

1. **OKLAHOMA ESTATE PLANNING, WILL DRAFTING AND ESTATE ADMINISTRATION FORMS**
2. Coffman, W. Thomas and C. Robert Jones
3. Aspen
4. 1987
5. 2 vols.
6. $229 incl. 3 mos. supp.
7. annual supp.
8. 1988 - $89.95
9. 87-26977/16753403/KF01340.A65C64

1. **OKLAHOMA LIEN LAWS**
2. Adams, Charles W.
3. Butterworth-Texas
4. 1990
5. 1 vol.
6. $120
7. annual supp.
8. 1991 - $55
9. 89-71194/20826802/KFO1355.5.A93

1. **OKLAHOMA REAL ESTATE FORMS - PRACTICE**
2. Durbin, Alan C. and C. Temple Bixler
3. Aspen
4. 1987
5. 3 vols.
6. $309 incl. 3 mos. supp.
7. annual supp.
8. 1988 - $99: 1989 - $89
9. 87-24189/16581693/KF01326.A65D87

1. **OKLAHOMA WILLS AND INTESTATE SUCCESSION**
2. Kenderdine, Nancy I.
3. Butterworth-Texas
4. 1987
5. 1 vol.
6. $95
7. periodic supp.
8. 1989 - $42.50
9. 87-21732/16525641/KFO1344.K46

1. **O'NEAL CLOSE CORPORATIONS, LAW AND PRACTICE 2ND ED.**
2. O'Neal, F. Hodge & Robert B. Thompson
3. Clark Boardman Callaghan
4. 1971
5. 2 vols.
6. $185 incl. 6 mos. supp.
7. annual supp.
8. 1989 - $50; 1990 - $53
9. 72-145865/213095/KF1466.O52

1. **O'NEAL'S OPPRESSION OF MINORITY SHAREHOLDERS**
2. O'Neal, F. Hodge & Robert B. Thompson
3. Clark Boardman Callaghan
4. 2nd ed. - 1985
5. 2 vols.
6. $185 incl. 6 mos. supp.
7. annual supp.
8. 1989 - $51; 1990 - $54
9. 85-7867/11969968/KF1448.05

1. **ONTARIO CORPORATIONS LAW GUIDE**
2. -
3. CCH
4. 1971
5. 1 vol.
6. $335/yr.; $305/yr. for 2 yrs.
7. monthly supp.

1. **ONTARIO REAL ESTATE LAW GUIDE**
2. -
3. CCH
4. 1975
5. 2 vols.
6. $310/yr.; $280/yr. for 2 yrs.
7. monthly supp.
9. 76-31933/2627563

1. **ONTARIO TAX REPORTER**
2. -
3. CCH
4. 1950
5. 2 vols.
6. $260/yr.; $235/yr. for 2 yrs.

7. monthly supp.

1. **OPENING STATEMENT (Art of Advocacy Series)**
2. Decof, Leonard
3. Bender
4. 1982
5. 1 vol.
6. $110 incl. 3 mos. supp.
7. periodic supp.
8. 1989 - $64; 1990 - $74.50
9. 81-71860/8276571/KF8915.D43

1. **OPENING STATEMENTS**
2. Julien, Alfred S.
3. Clark Boardman Callaghan
4. 1980
5. 1 vol.
6. $98 incl. 6 mos. supp.
7. annual supp.
8. 1989 - $45; 1990 - $47.50
9. 80-15904/6331356/KF8915.J84

1. **OPERATING CIRCULARS OF THE FEDERAL RESERVE BANK OF NEW YORK**
2. -
3. Fed.-NY
4. 1980
5. 1 vol.
6. $28 incl. supp.
7. periodic supp.

1. **OPERATIONS INSTRUCTIONS, REGULATIONS, AND INTERPRETATIONS**
2. U.S. Dept. of Justice, Immigration and Naturalization Service
3. order from USGPO - stock #927-002-00000-1
4. 1988
5. 1 vol.
6. $196/yr.
7. periodic supp.
9. 7583625

1. **OPINION LETTERS IN SECURITIES MATTERS: TEXT-CLAUSES-LAW (Securities Law Series, vol. 8 & 8A)**
2. Jacobs, Arnold S.
3. Clark Boardman Callaghan
4. 1980
5. 2 vols.
6. $215 incl. 3 mos. supp.
7. annual supp.
8. 1989 - $149; 1991 - $85
9. 79-24005/5706497/KF1070.J33

1. **OPINIONS OF THE COMMITTEE ON PROFESSIONAL ETHICS**
2. Association of the Bar of the City of New York Committee on Professional Ethics; Wypyski, Eugene, ed.
3. Oceana
4. 1980
5. 5 vols.
6. $450
7. periodic supp.
8. 1988 - $125; 1990 - $135
9. 80-14204/6223557/KFN5076.5.A2A97

1. **THE OPTIONS CLEARING CORPORATION & THE INTERMARKET CLEARING CORPORATION BY-LAWS AND RULES**
2. -
3. Options Clearing Corp.
4. NA
5. 1 vol.
6. $47
7. semimonthly supp.
9. 21354262/KF1087.O72C6

1. **OREGON APPELLATE MANUAL**
2. Kelly, George W.
3. Butterworth-St. Paul
4. 1986
5. 1 vol.
6. $60
7. periodic supp.
8. 1988 - $22.50; 1990 - $55
9. 85-73110/13570281/KFO2955.K45

1. **OREGON FORMAL ETHICS OPINIONS**
2. Jarvis, Peter R., ed.
3. Oregon Bar
4. 1991
5. 1 vol.
6. $45
7. periodic supp.
8. no supp. yet
9. 91-52945/24233224

1. **THE OREGON STATE BAR DESK REFERENCE - A GUIDE TO THE REGULATORY PROGRAMS OF THE OREGON STATE BAR**
2. Riemer, George A.
3. Oregon Bar
4. 1990
5. 1 vol.
6. $80
7. annual supp.

8. no supp. yet
9. 90-62857/22530463/KFO2477.R53

1. **OREGON UNIFORM TRIAL COURT RULES AND SUPPLEMENTARY LOCAL RULES**
2. Butterworth's Staff
3. Butterworth-St. Paul
4. 1985
5. 1 vol.
6. $50
7. periodic supp.
8. 1989 - $79; 1990 - $40
9. 85-73520/13524377/KFO2929.A2

1. **ORGANIZING A WISCONSIN BUSINESS CORPORATION: ARTICLES, BYLAWS AND OTHER FORMS**
2. Boucher, Joseph W. et al.
3. State Bar of Wisc.
4. 1991
5. 1 vol.
6. $220
7. periodic supp.
8. no supp. yet
9. 91-13483/23382615/KFW2613.5.A65O74

1. **ORGANIZING AND ADVISING ILLINOIS BUSINESSES**
2. -
3. Illinois ICLE
4. 1988
5. 1 vol.
6. $99.95
7. periodic supp.
8. 1991 - $29.95
9. 18555593/KFI1405.073

1. **ORGANIZING CORPORATE AND OTHER BUSINESS ENTERPRISES**
2. Rohrlich, Chester A.
3. Bender
4. rev. 5th ed. - 1975
5. 1 vol.
6. $145 incl. 3 mos. supp.
7. annual supp.
8. 1989 - $112; 1990 - $114
9. 76-357898/3001557/KF1355.R6

1. **ORGANIZING CORPORATIONS IN CALIFORNIA, 2nd ed.**
2. -
3. Calif. CEB
4. 1983
5. 1 vol.
6. $105
7. periodic supp.
8. 1989 - $24; 1990 - $27
9. 82-74145/9522650/KFC345.O7

1. **OSHA COMPLIANCE ENCYCLOPEDIA**
2. -
3. BLR
4. 1990
5. 3 vols.
6. $424/yr.
7. periodic supp. & semimonthly newsletter "OSHA Compliance Advisor"
9. 21437527

1. **OSHA/MOSH 1991**
2. Hemmendinger, Eric et al.
3. MICPEL
4. 1991
5. 1 vol.
6. $40
7. no supp. planned
9. 24236145/KFM1535.O8

1. **OSHA 1910 GUIDE**
2. -
3. Keller
4. 1989
5. 1 vol
6. $125
7. semiannual supp.
8. $95/yr.

1. **OSHA REFERENCE MANUAL**
2. Lollar, Felix A., ed.
3. Merritt
4. 1987
5. 2 vols.
6. $397/yr.
7. periodic supp.
8. renewal - $269/yr.
9. 87-151631/16753786/KF3568.4.083

1. **OTHER REGULATORY MATERIALS**
2. -
3. NILS
4. NA
5. 1 or 2 vols.
6. $75-135 incl. supp. for bal. of calendar yr.
7. periodic supp.

1. **OUTRIGHT CHARITABLE GIFTS - EXPLANATION, SUBSTANTIATING, FORMS**
2. Teitell, Conrad

3. Taxwise
4. 1986
5. 1 vol.
6. $141
7. annual supp.
8. 1990 - $74; 1991 - $74
9. 85-52079/13422533/KF6388.T44

1. **OVERVIEW OF PATENTS, TRADEMARKS, COPYRIGHTS AND TRADE SECRETS FOR THE GENERAL PRACTITIONER**
2. -
3. Wash. Bar
4. 1988
5. 1 vol.
6. $35
7. no supp. planned
9. 20503307

1. **PACIFIC NORTHWEST ADMIRALTY LAW INSTITUTE**
2. -
3. Wash. Bar
4. 1988
5. 1 vol.
6. $35
7. no supp. planned

1. **PACIFIC STOCK EXCHANGE GUIDE**
2. -
3. CCH
4. 1967
5. 1 vol.
6. $325/yr.; $295/yr. for 2 yrs.
7. monthly supp.

1. **PAIN AND SUFFERING (Courtroom Medicine Series, vols. 4, 4A & 4B)**
2. Chapman, Loring F., et al.
3. Bender
4. 1967
5. 4 vols.
6. $420 incl. 3 mos. supp.
7. annual supp.
8. 1989 - $198; 1990 - $239
9. 68-2237/431006/RA1011.C68

1. **PARALEGAL DISCOVERY: ORGANIZATION AND MANAGEMENT**
2. Zalewski, Dianne Dupre
3. James
4. 1987
5. 1 vol.
6. $49.85 incl. 3 mos. supp.
7. annual supp.
8. 1990 - $35.76; 1991 - $38.92
9. 15638294/KF8900.Z3

1. **PARALEGAL DISCOVERY: PROCEDURES AND FORMS**
2. Medina, Pat
3. James
4. 1989
5. 1 vol.
6. $59.90 incl. 3 mos. supp.
7. annual supp.
8. 1991 - $35.93
9. 21487790/KF8900.M36

1. **PARALEGAL LITIGATION FORMS**
2. Fawcett, Marcy Davis
3. James
4. 1987
5. 1 vol.
6. $59.92 incl. 3 mos. supp.
7. annual supp.
8. 1989 - $35.86; 1990 - $39.89
9. 17631623

1. **PARALEGAL MEDICAL RECORDS REVIEW**
2. Appleby, Kristyn S. and Joanne Tarver
3. James
4. 1989
5. 1 vol.
6. $59.89 incl. 3 mos. supp.
7. annual supp.
8. 1990 - $32.94
9. 90-118559/21036155/KF3827.R4A96

1. **PARALEGAL PREPARATION OF PLEADINGS**
2. Monteiro, Cynthia B.
3. James
4. 1988
5. 1 vol.
6. $59.96
7. annual supp.
8. 1990 - $37.93
9. 18756103/KF320.L4M65

1. **PARALEGAL TRIAL HANDBOOK**
2. Hutson, Beverly
3. James
4. 1991
5. 1 vol.
6. $59.91 incl. 3 mos. supp.
7. annual supp.
8. no supp. yet
9. 24178076/KF8915.A7H9

1. **PARTNERSHIP & S CORPORATION COORDINATOR**
2. RIA prof. ed. staff
3. RIA
4. 1987
5. 2 vols.
6. $230/yr.; $215/yr. for 2 yrs.
7. monthly supp.
8. renewal - $200/yr.
9. 16819480

1. **PARTNERSHIP INVESTMENTS: GOING UNDER**
2. -
3. Maine Bar
4. 1990
5. 1 vol.
6. $35
7. no supp.planned

1. **PARTNERSHIP PRACTICE**
2. -
3. Illinois ICLE
4. 1988
5. 1 vol.
6. $99.95
7. periodic supp.
8. 1991 - $29.95
9. 9060132

1. **PARTNERSHIP TAX PRACTICE MANUAL**
2. Brady, Evelyn, et al.
3. Panel
4. 1989
5. 1 vol.
6. $99 incl. 1 yr. supp.
7. semiannual supp.
9. 89-29122/20690972/KF6452.B76

1. **PARTNERSHIP TAX REPORTER**
2. Levun, Charles R.
3. CCH
4. 1987
5. 4 vols.
6. $550/yr.; $500/yr. for 2 yrs.
7. monthly supp.
8. renewal - $79/yr.
9. 89-29122/KF6452.B76

1. **PARTNERSHIP TAXATION**
2. -
3. Wash. Bar
4. 1988
5. 1 vol.
6. $35
7. no supp. planned

1. **PARTNERSHIP TAXATION, 4th ed.**
2. Willis, Arthur B., et al.
3. Shepard's
4. 4th ed. - 1989
5. 4 vols.
6. $195
7. quarterly supp.
8. 1990 - $171; 1991 - $97
9. 89-6397/19630295/KF6452.W55

1. **PARTRIDGE-REMICK, PRACTICE AND PROCEDURE IN ORPHANS COURT IN PENNSYLVANIA**
2. Partridge, R.J. & R. Remick
3. Bender
4. NA
5. 7 vols.
6. $450 incl. 3 mos. supp.
7. annual supp.
8. 1989 - $126.50; 1990 - $135.50

1. **PASS THROUGH ENTITIES: FOURTH ANNUAL STATE AND FEDERAL TAX CONFERENCE**
2. -
3. MILE
4. 1991
5. 1 vol.
6. $68
7. no supp. planned

1. **PASSIVE ACTIVITY LOSSES - THE NEW REGULATION**
2. -
3. MILE
4. 1989
5. 1 vol.
6. $58
7. no supp. planned

1. **PATEL'S IMMIGRATION LAW DIGEST**
2. Patel, P.J.
3. Clark Boardman Callaghan
4. 1985
5. 4 vols.
6. $390 incl. 3 mos. supp.
7. semiannual supp.
8. 1990 - $78; 1991 - $75
9. 84-82185/11837315/KF4814.P38

1. **PATENT AND TRADE SECRETS**
2. -

3. Indiana CLE
4. 1988
5. 1 vol.
6. $30
7. no supp. planned

1. **PATENT AND TRADEMARK STATUTES**
2. -
3. Rules
4. 1985
5. 1 vol.
6. $22 incl. 1 yr. supp.
7. periodic supp.
8. renewal fee

1. **PATENT COOPERATION TREATY AND REGULATIONS**
2. -
3. Rules
4. 1981
5. 1 vol.
6. $32 incl. 1 yr. supp.
7. periodic supp.
8. renewal fee
9. 82-101763/8930891/K1503.3.P37A2

1. **PATENT LAW**
2. Hoxie, Thomas et al.
3. MICPEL
4. 1991
5. 1 vol.
6. $42
7. no supp. planned
9. 23752253/KF3115.H6

1. **PATENT LAW FUNDAMENTALS**
2. Rosenberg, Peter D.
3. Clark Boardman Callaghan
4. 2nd ed. - 1980
5. 3 vols.
6. $345 incl. 3 mos. supp.
7. biannual supp.
8. 1989 - $215; 1991 - $264.50
9. 80-10710/6016374/KF3114.R66

1. **PATENT LAW PERSPECTIVES**
2. Gambrell, James B. et al.
3. Bender
4. 2nd ed. - 1982
5. 6 vols.
6. $650
7. bimonthly supp.
8. renewal - $565/yr.
9. 82-61193/9645662/KF3114.P37

1. **PATENT LAW PRACTICE FORMS**
2. Kramer, Barry and Allen D. Brufsky
3. Clark Boardman Callaghan
4. 1985
5. 3 vols.
6. $345 incl. 3 mos. supp.
7. annual supp.
8. 1989 - $95; 1991 - $145
9. 85-10952/12052010/KF3111.K73

1. **PATENT LICENSING TRANSACTIONS (Patent Law and Practice Series, vols. 1 & 1A & Business Organizations, vols. 14 & 14A)**
2. Einhorn, Harold & Thomas E. Costner
3. Bender
4. 1968
5. 2 vols.
6. $250 incl. 3 mos. supp.
7. annual supp.
8. 1989 - $197; 1990 - $207.50
9. 70-5479/13593/KF3145.C6

1. **PATENT LITIGATION: PROCEDURE AND TACTICS (Patent Law and Practice Series, vol. 3)**
2. White, Robert A.
3. Bender
4. 1971
5. 1 vol.
6. $150 incl. 3 mos. supp.
7. annual supp.
8. 1989 - $147; 1990 - $138.50
9. 70-157551/152411/KF3155.W5

1. **PATENT OFFICE RULES AND PRACTICE**
2. Horwitz, Lester
3. Bender
4. rev. - 1959
5. 9 vols.
6. $980 incl. 3 mos. supp.
7. vols. 1 - 1C semiannual supp. vols 2 - 4 quarterly supp.
8. 1989 - $998.50; 1990 - $867
9. 60-184//r865/5749477/KF3120.A6H6

1. **PATENT, TRADEMARK, AND COPYRIGHT REGULATIONS**
2. Crowne, James D., ed.
3. BNA Books
4. 1991
5. 1 vol.
6. $95

7. periodic supp.
8. no supp. yet
9. 91-19967/23942025/KF2974.6

1. **PATENTS**
2. Chisum, Donald S.
3. Bender
4. 1978
5. 8 vols.
6. $910 incl. 3 mos. supp.
7. semiannual supp.
8. 1989 - $813.50; 1990 - $799.50
9. 78-70641/4386263/KF3114.C47

1. **PATENTS THROUGHOUT THE WORLD**
2. Jacobs, Alan J. ed.
3. Clark Boardman Callaghan
4. 4th ed. - 1989
5. 1 vol.
6. $135 incl. 3 mos. supp.
7. 3 supp./yr.
8. 1989 - $97.50; 1991 - $125
9. 78-978/3627211/K1505.4.P37

1. **PATIENT CARE DECISION-MAKING**
2. Obade, Claire C.
3. Clark Boardman Callaghan
4. 1991
5. 1 vol.
6. $95 incl. 3 mos. supp.
7. annual supp.
9. 91-22470/24107583/KF3825.O2

1. **PATTERN CAPITAL MURDER CHARGES**
2. -
3. ABICLE
4. 1981
5. 2 vols.
6. $20
7. periodic supp.
8. no supp. yet

1. **PATTERN INSTRUCTIONS FOR KANSAS 2D (civil)**
2. Committee on Pattern Jury Instructions
3. Bancroft
4. 1977
5. 1 vol.
6. $95 incl. 6 mos. supp.
7. periodic supp.
8. 1990 - $22; 1992 - $30
9. 77-88793/3785851/KFK542.A65K349

1. **PAYMENT SYSTEM HANDBOOK**
2. -
3. Fed.
4. 1988
5. 1 vol.
6. $75/yr.
7. monthly supp.

1. **PAYROLL ADMINISTRATION GUIDE**
2. Massey, Paul, ed.
3. BNA
4. 1990
5. 4 vols.
6. $449/yr.
7. biweekly supp.
8. renewal - $416/yr.
9. 89-902/19389393/KF6436.A6P392

1. **PAYROLL GUIDE**
2. -
3. WG&L
4. 1943
5. 4 vols.
6. $387/yr.
7. biweekly supp.

1. **PAYROLL MANAGEMENT GUIDE**
2. -
3. CCH
4. 1943
5. 3 vols.
6. $425/yr.; $385/yr. for 2 yrs.
7. weekly supp.
9. 76-26998/157029/KF6436.A6P393

1. **PAYROLL PRACTITIONER'S COMPLIANCE HANDBOOK: YEAR-END AND QUARTERLY REPORTING**
2. Salam, Debera & Howard Freedman
3. WG&L
4. 1991
5. 1 vol.
6. $75/yr.
7. periodic supp.

1. **PCB COMPLIANCE GUIDE FOR ELECTRICAL EQUIPMENT**
2. Youngblood, Phillip L. and Jack E. Cearley
3. BNA Books
4. new ed. - 1991
5. 1 vol.
6. $115
7. annual ed.
9. 18241600/KF3958.Y6

1. **PEACE LAW DOCKET 1945-1990**

2. Ginger, Ann Fagan, ed.
3. Meiklejohn Civil Liberties Institute
4. 3rd ed. - 1990
5. 1 vol.
6. $49
7. no supp. planned
9. sn87-2247/16397755

1. **PENNSYLVANIA ATTORNEY'S/SECRETARY'S HANDBOOK**
2. -
3. Mariposa
4. 1991
5. 1 vol.
6. $54
7. annual supp.
8. 1989 - $49; 1991 - $45
9. 17948650

1. **THE PENNSYLVANIA BUSINESS CORPORATION PRACTICE**
2. Tortorice, Donald A.
3. Penn. Bar
4. 1991
5. 1 vol.
6. $125
7. annual supp.
8. no supp. yet
9. 91-61376/24484705/KFP213.P46

1. **PENNSYLVANIA BUSINESS CORPORATIONS**
2. Sell, W.E. et al.
3. Bisel
4. 1969
5. 3 vols.
6. $157.50 incl. 3 mos. supp.
7. periodic supp.; rev. in prep.
8. 1988 - $22; 1991 - $85
9. 75-7323/47072/KFP213.S4

1. **PENNSYLVANIA CONDOMINIUM LAW AND PRACTICE**
2. Glazer, R.
3. Bisel
4. 2nd ed. - 1981
5. 1 vol.
6. $33.75 incl. 3 mos. supp.
7. periodic supp.
8. 1985-86 - $18.50
9. 81-68874/8106363/KFP114.C6G55

1. **PENNSYLVANIA CONFESSION OF JUDGMENT**
2. Sprenkle, Robert C., Jr.
3. Bisel
4. 1982
5. 2 vols.
6. $42.50 incl. 3 mos. supp.
7. periodic supp.
8. no supp. yet
9. 81-69429/8547186/KFP536.8.S67

1. **PENNSYLVANIA CONSOLIDATED RULES**
2. -
3. Rules
4. 1972
5. 2 vols.
6. $89 incl. 1 yr. supp. (District Justices, civil, criminal & appellate rules avail. separately)
7. periodic supp.
8. renewal fee

1. **PENNSYLVANIA CORPORATION TAX LAW & PRACTICE**
2. Moyer, Sherill T.
3. Banks
4. 1987
5. 2 vols.
6. $195 incl 9 mos. supp.
7. annual supp.
8. 1988 - $26
9. 87-404055/15469756/KFP477.A6M69

1. **PENNSYLVANIA CRIMES CODE AND CRIMINAL LAW**
2. Jarvis, K.
3. Bisel
4. 1974
5. 1 vol
6. $49.50 incl. 3 mos. supp.
7. periodic supp.
8. 1986 - $31.95; rev. in prep.
9. 74-190388/1288029/KFP561.A336J37

1. **PENNSYLVANIA CRIMINAL LAW AND PRACTICE**
2. Ranney, James
3. Bender
4. 1990
5. 3 vols.
6. $310 incl. 3 mos. supp.
7. periodic supp.
8. 1990 - $46
9. 89-81446/21443168/KFP561.R3

1. **PENNSYLVANIA CRIMINAL LAW DIGEST**

2. Ed. Staff
3. Gould
4. NA
5. 1 vol.
6. $17.95
7. periodic supp.
8. $5 - $10/supp.

1. **PENNSYLVANIA CRIMINAL PRACTICE**
2. Wasserbly, Richard S.
3. Lawyers Coop.
4. 1981
5. 3 vols.
6. $285 incl. 6 mos. supp.
7. annual supp.
8. 1990- $60; 1991 - $54
9. 81-10154/7597882/KFP575.W38

1. **PENNSYLVANIA DIVORCE AND DOMESTIC RELATIONS REPORTER**
2. -
3. LRP
4. 1988
5. 1 vol.
6. $480/yr. (back vol. avail.)
7. semimonthly supp.

1. **PENNSYLVANIA DIVORCE CODE**
2. Perlberger, Norman
3. Bisel
4. 1980
5. 1 vol.
6. $50 incl. 3 mos. supp.
7. periodic supp.
8. 1987-88 - $16.50; rev. in prep.
9. 80-68838/7004328/KFP100.P47

1. **PENNSYLVANIA DOMESTIC RELATIONS FORMS–PRACTICE**
2. Levit, Saul
3. Aspen
4. 1989
5. 1 vol.
6. $169 incl. 3 mos. supp.
7. annual supp.
8. $79-$95/supp.
9. 89-6974/19813385/KFP94.A65L48

1. **PENNSYLVANIA EMPLOYMENT LAWS**
2. -
3. LRP
4. 1989
5. 1 vol
6. $125
7. -
9. 19370667/KFP334.P46

1. **PENNSYLVANIA ESTATE PLANNING AND DRAFTING**
2. Aker, J.B.
3. Bisel
4. 1969
5. 2 vols.
6. $90 incl. 3 mos. supp.
7. annual supp.
8. 1989-90 - $45; 1990-91 - $50
9. 71-9185/53347/KFP482.A6A4

1. **PENNSYLVANIA ESTATES PRACTICE**
2. Rothkopf, Nancy & Gilbert M. Cantor
3. Lawyers Coop.
4. 1980
5. 1 vol.
6. $115 incl. 6 mos. supp.
7. annual supp.
8. 1989 - $56; 1990 - $60.50
9. 79-91161/7078152/KFP144.R67

1. **PENNSYLVANIA GUIDE TO CRIMINAL PRACTICE AND PROCEDURE**
2. Reimel, T.
3. Bisel
4. 1969
5. 1 vol.
6. $45 incl. 3 mos. supp.
7. periodic supp.
8. 1985 - $31.50; 1987 - $41.50
9. 77-7720/47280/KFP575.A6R4

1. **PENNSYLVANIA INHERITANCE AND ESTATE TAX**
2. Grossman, R. & M.P. Smith
3. Bisel
4. 2nd ed. - 1986
5. 1 vol.
6. $65 incl. 3 mos. supp.
7. annual supp.
8. 1988 - $7.25; 1989 - $10.50
9. 85-71933/13494326/KFP482.G76

1. **PENNSYLVANIA INSURANCE LAW**
2. Best, Franklin L. Jr.
3. Bisel
4. 1991
5. 1 vol.
6. $79.50 incl. 3 mos. supp.
7. annual supp.
8. no supp. yet
9. 40-84169/24005544/KFP185.B48

1. **PENNSYLVANIA KEYSTONE**
2. Sell, W.E.
3. Bisel
4. 1964-1985
5. 7 vols.
6. $275 incl. 3 mos. supp.
7. annual supp.
8. 1990 - $110; 1991 - $125
9. 64-7197/2731107/KFP81.L38x

1. **PENNSYLVANIA LANDLORD AND TENANT LAW AND PRACTICE WITH FORMS (WITH COMPUTER DISK)**
2. Friedman, Ronald M.
3. Bisel
4. 1988
5. 1 vol.
6. $119 (with disk); $79.50 (without disk)
7. annual supp.
8. 1990 - $12.50; 1991 - $14
9. 88-70977

1. **PENNSYLVANIA LAW ENFORCEMENT HANDBOOK**
2. Holtz, Larry E.
3. Gould
4. NA
5. 1 vol.
6. $34.95
7. periodic supp.
9. 89-184456/20491554/KFP575.H65

1. **PENNSYLVANIA MATRIMONIAL PRACTICE**
2. Rounick, Jack A.
3. Lawyers Coop.
4. 1982
5. 4 vols.
6. $380 incl. 6 mos. supp.
7. annual supp.
8. 1990 - $136; 1991 - $138
9. 81-85429/8664506/KFP95.R68

1. **PENNSYLVANIA MECHANICS' LIENS**
2. Walsh, Michael G.
3. Butterworth-NH
4. 1990
5. 1 vol.
6. $75
7. periodic supp.
8. no supp. yet
9. 89-78356/20931787/KFP155.5.W35

1. **PENNSYLVANIA MUNICIPAL CLAIMS AND TAX LIENS**
2. Hecht, L.
3. Bisel
4. 1967
5. 1 vol.
6. $49.50 incl. 3 mos. supp.
7. periodic supp.
8. 1986 - $17.50; 1988 - $19.25
9. 67-4754/7586306/KFP490.5.H4

1. **PENNSYLVANIA PUBLIC EMPLOYEE REPORTER**
2. -
3. LRP
4. 1970
5. 1 vol.
6. $595/yr. (back vols. avail.)
7. semimonthly supp.

1. **PENNSYLVANIA REAL ESTATE**
2. Iannelli, Emil L. and Lynne P.
3. Lawyers Coop.
4. 1984
5. 1 vol.
6. $115 incl. 6 mos. supp.
7. annual supp.
8. 1990 - $45.50; 1991 - $55
9. 84-80494/11443934/KFP112.I36

1. **PENNSYLVANIA SUGGESTED STANDARD CIVIL JURY INSTRUCTIONS**
2. -
3. Penn. Bar
4. 1984 rev.
5. 1 vol.
6. $85
7. periodic supp.
8. to be rev. in 1992
9. 7729710/KFP542.A6P3

1. **PENNSYLVANIA SUGGESTED STANDARD CRIMINAL JURY INSTRUCTIONS**
2. -
3. Penn. Bar
4. 1979
5. 1 vol.
6. $120
7. periodic supp.
8. 1989 - $40; 1991 - $40

1. **PENNSYLVANIA TAX SERVICE**
2. -
3. Bender
4. 1986

5. 4 vols.
6. $370/1 yr. service; $680 for 2 yrs.
7. ·periodic supp.
8. annual renewal - $310
9. 87-70793/16664450/KFP470.P465

1. **PENNSYLVANIA TAXATION**
2. Bright, Joseph C., Jr.
3. Shepard's
4. 1987
5. 1 vol.
6. $125
7. annual supp.
8. 1989 - $26; 1990 - $35
9. 87-13123/16081776/KFP470.B75

1. **PENNSYLVANIA TRANSACTION GUIDE - LEGAL FORMS**
2. Bongiovanni, Joseph N., Jr.
3. Bender
4. 1974
5. 16 vols.
6. $1025 incl. 3 mos. supp.
7. supp. as needed
8. 1989 - $894; 1990 - $772.50
9. 74-78659/1121284/KFP68.P45

1. **PENNSYLVANIA TRIAL GUIDE (CIVIL)**
2. Feldman, S.
3. Bisel
4. 1991
5. 3 vols.
6. $250 incl. 3 mos. supp.
7. periodic supp.
8. no supp. yet
9. KFP538.L32

1. **PENNSYLVANIA TRIAL GUIDE (CRIMINAL)**
2. Evangelista, Robert L.
3. Bisel
4. 1988
5. 2 vols.
6. $150
7. annual supp.
8. 1991 - $43.50
9. 88-71902/19241810

1. **PENNSYLVANIA VEHICLE CODE, ANNOTATED**
2. Meyer, M.
3. Bisel
4. 1978
5. 1 vol.
6. $55 incl. 3 mos. supp.
7. periodic supp.
8. 1988 - $55; rev. in prep.
9. 77-94199/4037232/KFP297.A34M48

1. **PENNSYLVANIA VEHICLE NEGLIGENCE**
2. Meyer, M.
3. Bisel
4. 1970
5. 2 vols.
6. $85 incl. 3 mos. supp.
7. periodic supp.
8. 1986 - $30.50; 1989 - $42
9. 78-13989/85133/KFP196.A6M4

1. **PENNSYLVANIA WORKER'S COMPENSATION LAW REPORTER**
2. -
3. LRP
4. 1987
5. 2 vols.
6. $575/yr. (back vol. avail.)
7. semimonthly supp.

1. **PENNSYLVANIA WORKMEN'S COMPENSATION, INJURY AND DISEASE LAWS**
2. Barbieri, A.
3. Bisel
4. 1975
5. 3 vols.
6. $157.50 incl. 3 mos. supp.
7. periodic supp.
8. 1991 - $99.50
9. 84-144511/10949052/KFP342.B37

1. **PENNSYLVANIA ZONING LAW AND PRACTICE**
2. Ryan, R.
3. Bisel
4. 2nd ed. - 1982
5. 2 vols.
6. $110 incl. 3 mos. supp.
7. periodic supp.
8. 1986 - $39.50; 1989/90 - $69
9. 76-20107//r843/119284/KFP458.A6R9

1. **PENSION ADMINISTRATOR'S FORMS AND CHECKLISTS**
2. Bildersee, Robert A.
3. WG&L
4. 1987
5. 1 vol.
6. $296/yr.
7. annual supp.

1. **PENSION AND PROFIT SHARING, 2nd ed.**
2. -
3. RIA
4. 1992
5. 7 vols.
6. $730/yr.; $675/yr. for 2 yrs.
7. weekly supp.
8. renewal - $620/yr.

1. **PENSION AND PROFIT SHARING GUIDE**
2. -
3. RIA
4. 1949
5. 2 vols. (also vol. 1 & 1A of Pension & Profit Sharing)
6. $475/yr.
7. weekly supp.

1. **PENSION & PROFIT SHARING PLANS**
2. Scudere, Carmine
3. Bender
4. 1986
5. 5 vols.
6. $425 incl. 1 yr. supp.
7. periodic supp.
8. renewal - $295/yr.
9. 86-70623/14941493/KF3512.S4

1. **PENSION & PROFIT SHARING PLANS (Bus. Orgs. Vols. 19A-E)**
2. Young, Sheldon M.
3. Bender
4. 1977
5. 6 vols.
6. $545 incl. 3 mos. supp.
7. annual supp.
8. 1989 - $358; 1990 - $434.50
9. 77-365431//r885/3273574/KF1355.B87

1. **PENSION & PROFIT SHARING PLANS: FORMS & PRACTICE**
2. Publ. Editorial Staff
3. Bender
4. 1989
5. 3 vols.
6. $315 incl. 3 mos. supp.
7. annual supp.
8. 1989 - $39; 1990- $97.50

1. **PENSION AND WELFARE BENEFITS**
2. -
3. MILE
4. 1991
5. 1 vol.
6. $68
7. no supp. planned

1. **PENSION COORDINATOR**
2. RIA prof. ed. staff
3. RIA
4. 1987
5. 13 vols.
6. $855/yr.; $790/yr. for 2 yrs.
7. weekly supp.
8. renewal - $720/yr.
9. 15503795/KF3512.A6R47

1. **PENSION PLAN FORMS MANUAL**
2. -
3. Corbel
4. 1978
5. 2 vols.
6. $345 incl. 1 yr. supp.
7. semiannual supp.
8. renewal - $160/yr.
9. 79-105388/5051448/KF3512.A65P46

1. **PENSION PLAN GUIDE**
2. -
3. CCH
4. 1953
5. 7 vols.
6. $870/yr.; $790/yr. for 2 yrs.
7. weekly supp. & newsletter
9. 75-313113/1334623/KF3512.A6C64

1. **PENSIONS AND DEFERRED COMPENSATION**
2. -
3. CCH
4. 1987
5. 1 vol.
6. $315/yr.; $285/yr. for 2 yrs.
7. monthly supp.

1. **PERFORMANCE APPRAISALS: THE LATEST LEGAL NIGHTMARE**
2. -
3. Alex. Hamilton Inst.
4. 1986
5. 1 vol.
6. $63.50
7. supp. 3x/yr.
8. $19.50/supp.
9. 86-198525/14412824/HF5549.5.R3P474

1. **PERFORMING ARTS MANAGEMENT AND THE LAW**
2. Taubman, Joseph
3. Law-Arts

4. 1971
5. 7 looseleaf & 2 bound vols.
6. $495
7. periodic supp.

1. **PERSONAL BANKRUPTCY**
2. -
3. Conn. Bar
4. 1990
5. 1 vol.
6. $53
7. no supp. planned

1. **PERSONAL INJURY**
2. -
3. MILE
4. 1991
5. 1 vol.
6. $68
7. no supp. planned
9. 23107392/KFM5597.P3P43

1. **PERSONAL INJURY - ACTIONS, DEFENSES, DAMAGES**
2. Frumer, Louis R. et al.
3. Bender
4. 1957
5. 25 vols.
6. $1300 incl. 3 mos. supp.
7. 3 supp./yr.
8. 1989 - $894; 1990 - $1206
9. 57-2943/10712233/KF8925.P4P38

1. **PERSONAL INJURY: DISCOVERY & TRIAL**
2. Sumpter, Jerry L.
3. James
4. 1986
5. 1 vol.
6. $79.95 incl. 3 mos. supp.
7. annual supp.
8. 1990 - $41.90
9. 86-216374/14231776/KF8925.P4S93

1. **PERSONAL INJURY DEFENSE TECHNIQUES**
2. Dombroff, Mark A., ed.
3. Bender
4. 1987
5. 3 vols.
6. $315 incl. 3 mos. supp.
7. annual supp.
8. 1989 - $92; 1990 - $221.50
9. 87-72160/16937378/KF8925.P4P443

1. **PERSONAL INJURY FORMS: DISCOVERY & SETTLEMENT**
2. Tarantino, John A. & D. J. Oliveira
3. James
4. 1985
5. 1 vol.
6. $79.96 incl. 3 mos. supp.
7. annual supp.
8. 1990 - $42.91
9. 86-100769/2413482/KF1257.A3T37

1. **PERSONAL INJURY HANDBOOK**
2. -
3. James
4. 1991
5. 1 vol.
6. $79.94 incl. 3 mos. supp.
7. annual supp.
8. no supp. yet

1. **PERSONAL INJURY INSTITUTE: 7TH ANNUAL**
2. -
3. MILE
4. 1991
5. 1 vol.
6. $79.50
7. no supp. planned
9. 24681895/KFM5597.P3P47

1. **PERSONAL INJURY PRACTICE**
2. -
3. NH Bar
4. 1989
5. 1 vol.
6. $40
7. no supp. planned
9. 13591849

1. **PERSONAL INJURY VALUATION HANDBOOKS**
2. Research Dept.
3. Jury Verdict
4. 1959
5. 12 vols.
6. $450/yr. for 3 yrs.
7. 3 supp/month
9. 78-29254/200347/KF1256.A8J87

1. **PERSONNEL DOCUMENTATION AUDIT: STEERING CLEAR OF LEGAL PITFALLS**
2. -
3. Alex. Hamilton Inst.

4. 1990
5. 1 vol.
6. $66.50
7. supp. 3x/yr.
8. $19.25/supp.

1. **PERSONNEL FORMS AND EMPLOYMENT CHECKLISTS**
2. Moore, Maureen F.
3. Butterworth-NH
4. 1990
5. 1 vol.
6. $75
7. annual supp.
8. 1991 - $25
9. 22447233/HF5549.2.U5M66

1. **PERSONNEL MANAGEMENT GUIDE**
2. -
3. WG&L
4. 1985
5. 1 vol.
6. $229/yr.
7. quarterly supp. & monthly newsletter
9. 85-233080/12788145/HF5549.2.U5P445

1. **PHARMACY LAW DIGEST**
2. Fink, J.L., et al.
3. Facts
4. 1965
5. 1 vol.
6. $59.50 incl. 1 supp.
7. semiannual supp.
8. 1988-89 - $49.50
9. 72-115322

1. **PHILADELPHIA COUNTY DOMESTIC RELATIONS PRACTICE**
2. -
3. Penn. Bar
4. 1991
5. 1 vol.
6. $75
7. no supp. planned

1. **PHILADELPHIA COURT OF COMMON PLEAS CIVIL PRACTICE MANUAL**
2. Arbittier, Steven A. & David F. Simon
3. Penn. Bar
4. 1989
5. 1 vol.
6. $65
7. periodic supp.
8. 1990 - $57
9. 11441347/KFP516.P4P4

1. **PHILADELPHIA STOCK EXCHANGE GUIDE**
2. -
3. CCH
4. 1965
5. 1 vol.
6. $275/yr.; $250/yr. for 2 yrs.
7. monthly supp.

1. **PHYSICIAN LABORATORY REGULATIONS MANUAL**
2. Grant, David
3. Thompson
4. 1991
5. 1 vol.
6. $285/yr.
7. monthly supp.
8. renewal - $285/yr.

1. **PIERCING THE CORPORATE VEIL**
2. Presser, Stephen B.
3. Clark Boardman Callaghan
4. 1990
5. 1 vol.
6. $95 incl. 3 mos. supp.
7. annual supp.
9. 90-21508/22663056/KF1423.Z95P74

1. **PIMSLEUR'S CHECKLISTS OF BASIC AMERICAN LEGAL PUBLICATIONS**
2. Zubrow, Marcia, ed.
3. Rothman
4. 1962
5. 3 vols.
6. $150
7. biennial supp.
8. 1985 - $65; 1988 - $75
9. 62-18944/12810429/KF1.P54

1. **PLAINTIFF'S PROOF OF A PRIMA FACIE CASE**
2. Publisher's Editorial Staff
3. Clark Boardman Callaghan
4. rev. - 1982
5. 1 vol.
6. $95 incl. 6 mos. supp.
7. annual supp.
8. 1989 - $45; 1990 - $48
9. 81-10261/7652853/KF8940.P7C67

1. **A PLAN FOR LAWYER DEVELOPMENT: A COMPREHENSIVE MANUAL ON ESTABLISHING AND ADMINISTERING CLE PROGRAMS IN THE OFFICE**

2. Prof. Education Div.
3. ABA
4. 1986
5. 1 vol.
6. $50
7. no supp. yet
9. 86-70760/14002872/KF276.5.A96

1. **PLANNED GIVING - STARTING, MARKETING, ADMINISTERING**
2. Teitell, Conrad
3. Taxwise
4. 1986
5. 1 vol.
6. $141
7. supp. as needed
8. 1988 - $74; 1991 - $69

1. **PLANNING AND PAYING FOR LONG TERM CARE**
2. -
3. Maine Bar
4. 1990
5. 1 vol.
6. $20
7. no supp. planned

1. **PLANNING AND ZONING**
2. -
3. Indiana CLE
4. 1989
5. 1 vol
6. $60
7. no supp. planned

1. **PLANNING FOR ESTATE FREEZES UNDER NEW CHAPTER 14**
2. -
3. Conn. Bar
4. 1991
5. 1 vol.
6. $23
7. no supp. planned

1. **PLANNING FOR THE ELDERLY**
2. Barr, Albert S., III et al.
3. MICPEL
4. 1991
5. 1 vol.
6. $42
7. no supp. planned

1. **PLANNING RETIREMENT BENEFITS**
2. -
3. MILE
4. 1989
5. 1 vol.
6. $58
7. no supp. planned

1. **PLANNING TAX-EXEMPT ORGANIZATIONS**
2. Desiderio, Robert J. & Scott A. Taylor
3. Shepard's
4. 1986
5. 2 vols.
6. $195
7. annual supp.
8. 1989 - $38; 1990 - $44
9. 83-16168/9783881/KF6449.D47

1. **A PLANNING WORKBOOK FOR LAW FIRM MANAGEMENT**
2. Economics of Law Practice Section
3. ABA
4. 2nd ed. - 1985
5. 1 vol.
6. $99.95
7. no supp. planned
9. 84-72362/11942849/KF318.C58

1. **PLEADING CAUSES OF ACTION IN MARYLAND**
2. Sandler, Paul Mark & James K. Archibald
3. MICPEL
4. 1991
5. 1 vol.
6. $94.50
7. no supp. planned
9. 90-63338/23126761/KFM1396.S21

1. **PODIATRIC LIABILITY**
2. Rosenblum, James B., ed.
3. Public Reporting Services
4. 1990
5. 1 vol.
6. $128 incl. 6 mos. supp.
7. bimonthly supp. in newsletter "Podiatric Malpractice Reporter"
9. 21833473/WE890.P742L

1. **POLICE CIVIL LIABILITY**
2. Silver, I.
3. Bender
4. 1986
5. 1 vol.
6. $140 incl. 3 mos. supp.
7. periodic supp.
8. 1989 - $93.50; 1990 - $108
9. 86-70621/13712085/KF1307.S55

1. **POLICE INVESTIGATION HANDBOOK**
2. Banzon, Cecilia
3. Bender
4. 1990
5. 1 vol.
6. $115 incl. 3 mos. supp.
7. periodic supp.
8. no supp. yet
9. Z90-81494/22186467/HV8073.I44

1. **POLICE MISCONDUCT: LAW AND LITIGATION**
2. National Lawyers Guild
3. Clark Boardman Callaghan
4. 2nd ed. - 1980
5. 1 vol. & newsletter binder
6. $110 incl. 3 mos. supp.
7. annual supp. & newsletters
8. 1989 - $94.50; 1990 - $104.50
9. 80-23165/6708634/KF9409.A98

1. **POLICY GUIDE OF THE AMERICAN CIVIL LIBERTIES UNION**
2. -
3. ACLU
4. 1986
5. 1 vol.
6. $25 incl. supp.
7. periodic supp.
9. 8434743/KF4749.A74

1. **POLYGRAPH AND THE LAW**
2. Ansley, Norman
3. JKP
4. 1990
5. 3 vols.
6. $100
7. annual supp.

1. **POST-MORTEM ESTATE PLANNING**
2. -
3. MICPEL
4. 1990
5. 1 vol.
6. $40
7. no supp. yet

1. **POST-MORTEM TAX PLANNING**
2. Kasner, Kerry
3. Shepard's
4. 1982
5. 1 vol.
6. $95
7. annual supp.
8. 1990 - $38; 1991 - $44
9. 82-10833/8763150/KF6584.K37

1. **PPC TAX PLANNING GUIDE - CLOSELY HELD CORPORATIONS**
2. Ketter, Linda, et al.
3. Practitioners Publishing
4. 1990
5. 2 vols.
6. $120
7. annual supp.
8. 1991 - $75

1. **PPC TAX PLANNING GUIDE - INDIVIDUALS**
2. DiTommaso, Elizabeth, et al.
3. Practitioners Publishing
4. 1990
5. 2 vols.
6. $120
7. annual supp.
8. 1991 - $75

1. **PPC TAX PLANNING GUIDE - PARTNERSHIPS**
2. Cleveland Grover A., et al.
3. Practitioners Publishing
4. 1990
5. 2 vols.
6. $120
7. annual supp.
8. 1991 - $75

1. **PPC TAX PLANNING GUIDE - S CORPORATIONS**
2. Biebl, Andrew R. & Gregory B. McKeen
3. Practitioners Publishing
4. 1990
5. 2 vols.
6. $120
7. annual supp.
8. 1991 - $75

1. **PPD MASTER PLAN DOCUMENTATION SYSTEM**
2. -
3. PPD
4. 1989
5. 1 vol.
6. $3900
7. supp. as needed

1. **PPD PRACTITIONER REGIONAL PROTOTYPE DOCUMENTATION SYSTEM**

2. -
3. PPD
4. 1989
5. 1 vol.
6. $6500
7. supp. as needed

1. **A PRACTICAL APPROACH TO REAL ESTATE LOAN DEFAULTS AND WORKOUTS**
2. -
3. Wash. Bar
4. 1989
5. 1 vol.
6. $35
7. no supp. planned

1. **PRACTICAL APPROACHES TO EMPLOYMENT DISCRIMINATION PROBLEMS**
2. -
3. Indiana CLE
4. 1988
5. 1 vol.
6. $55
7. no supp. planned

1. **PRACTICAL ESTATE PLANNING: MORE THAN JUST WILLS**
2. -
3. Maine Bar
4. 1991
5. 1 vol.
6. $35
7. no supp. planned
9. 23719303/KF750.Z99M23

1. **A PRACTICAL GUIDE TO BUYING AND SELLING AUTOMOBILE DEALERSHIPS**
2. Pico, John J.
3. Natl. Legal Publishing
4. 1989
5. 2 vols.
6. $295
7. supp. as needed
8. no supp. yet
9. 89-82568/21340635/KF2036.A8P53

1. **A PRACTICAL GUIDE TO DISPUTES BETWEEN ADJOINING LANDOWNERS--EASEMENTS**
2. Thomas, David & James H. Backman
3. Bender
4. 1989
5. 1 vol.
6. $110 incl. 3 mos. supp.
7. annual supp.
8. 1990 - $43
9. 89-51128/20396714/KF657.B3

1. **A PRACTICAL GUIDE TO DOCUMENT AUTHENTICATION: LEGALIZATION OF NOTARIZED AND CERTIFIED DOCUMENTS**
2. Sinnott, John P.
3. Oceana
4. 1984
5. 1 vol.
6. $125
7. periodic supp.
8. 1985 - $100; 1988 - $125
9. 83-22023/10045869/K2380.S56

1. **A PRACTICAL GUIDE TO EQUAL EMPLOYMENT OPPORTUNITY**
2. Connolly, Walter B., Jr. et al.
3. Law Journal
4. 1979
5. 2 vols.
6. $125
7. periodic supp.
8. 1988 - $50; 1989 - $40
9. 79-24064/5706546/KF3464.C66

1. **A PRACTICAL GUIDE TO INTRODUCING EVIDENCE**
2. Potter, Harold W. et al.
3. Mass. CLE
4. 1987
5. 1 vol.
6. $50
7. periodic supp.
8. 1989 - $27.50
9. 86-72608/17264627/KFM2938.P68

1. **A PRACTICAL GUIDE TO OUT-OF-COURT RESTRUCTURINGS AND PREPACKAGED PLANS OF REORGANIZATION**
2. Saggese, Nicholas P. & Alesia Ranney-Marinelli
3. Prentice Hall Law & Business
4. 1991
5. 1 vol.
6. $125 incl. 4 mos. supp.
9. 24682997/KF1544.P72

1. **A PRACTICAL GUIDE TO TAX SHELTER LITIGATION**
2. Brodsky, Edward
3. Law Journal

4. 1982
5. 1 vol.
6. $70
7. periodic supp.
8. 1985 - $34
9. 82-15166/8306636/KF8925.T38B76

1. **A PRACTICAL GUIDE TO THE OCCUPATIONAL SAFETY & HEALTH ACT**
2. Connolly, Walter B., Jr. & Donald R. Crowell II
3. Law Journal
4. 1982
5. 1 vol.
6. $70
7. periodic supp.
8. 1987 - $69; 1988 - $35
9. 82-13006/8629338/KF3570.C66

1. **A PRACTICAL GUIDE TO WINNING LAND USE APPROVAL AND PERMITS**
2. Deems, Nyal D. & N. Stevenson Jennettee
3. Bender
4. 1989
5. 1 vol.
6. $110 incl. 3 mos. supp.
7. annual supp.
8. 1990 - $43
9. 89-61219/20316013/KF5698.D44

1. **PRACTICAL INTERNATIONAL TAX PLANNING**
2. Langer, Marshall J.
3. PLI
4. 1985
5. 1 vol.
6. $155
7. annual supp.
8. 1989 - $55; 1991 - $75
9. 85-62148/12933765/K4464.5.L36

1. **PRACTICE BEFORE FEDERAL MAGISTRATES**
2. Sinclair, Kent, Jr.
3. Bender
4. 1984
5. 1 vol.
6. $120 incl. 3 mos. supp.
7. periodic supp.
8. 1989 - $48; 1990 - $86.50
9. 83-72145/10465605/KF8754.S62

1. **PRACTICE IN THE COURTS OF LIMITED JURISDICTION AND SUPERIOR COURT LOCAL RULES PRACTICE**
2. -
3. Wash. Bar
4. 1989
5. 1 vol.
6. $35
7. no supp. planned

1. **PRACTICE MANUAL FOR THE MARYLAND LAWYER**
2. Young Lawyers Section of Maryland State Bar Assn.
3. MICPEL
4. rev. - 1988
5. 1 vol.
6. $90
7. periodic supp.
8. 1990 - $42
9. 12198163/KFM1738.Z9M3

1. **PRACTICE UNDER FLORIDA USURY LAW**
2. -
3. Florida Bar
4. 2nd ed. - 1989
5. 1 vol.
6. $45
7. supp. as needed
8. no supp. yet
9. 89-80982/2044092/KFF170.P71

1. **PRACTICE UNDER THE FEDERAL SENTENCING GUIDELINES**
2. -
3. Indiana CLE
4. 1989
5. 1 vol.
6. $35
7. no supp. planned

1. **PRACTICE UNDER THE NEW FEDERAL SENTENCING GUIDELINES**
2. Bamberger, Phylis Skloot & David J. Gottlieb, eds.
3. Prentice Hall Law & Business
4. 2nd ed. - 1990
5. 2 vols.
6. $150 incl. 4 mos. supp.
7. periodic supp.
8. 1991 - $90
9. 90-34632/21374103/KF9685.P73

1. **PRACTICING BASIC RESIDENTIAL REAL ESTATE**
2. -
3. MILE

4. 1990
5. 1 vol.
6. $58
7. no supp. planned

1. **PRACTICING IN FEDERAL DISTRICT COURT IN MINNESOTA**
2. -
3. Minn. CLE
4. 1991
5. 1 vol.
6. $40
7. no supp. planned
9. 24681578/KF8821.M6P7

1. **PRACTITIONER'S GUIDE TO THE OKLAHOMA UNIFORM CONSUMER CREDIT CODE**
2. Miller, Frederick H. et al.
3. Butterworth-St. Paul
4. 1990
5. 1 vol.
6. $95
7. periodic supp.
8. no supp. yet
9. 90-2637/22314259/KFO1371.P73

1. **PRACTITIONER'S HANDBOOK FOR APPEALS**
2. -
3. Indiana CLE
4. 1988
5. 1 vol.
6. $10
7. no supp. planned

1. **PRACTITIONERS 1040 DESKBOOK**
2. Biebl, Andrew R., et al.
3. Practitioners Publishing
4. 1991
5. 2 vols.
6. $110
7. annual supp.
8. 1991 - $88

1. **PRACTITIONERS 1065 DESKBOOK**
2. -
3. Practitioners Publishing
4. 1990
5. 2 vols.
6. $110
7. annual supp.
8. 1991 - $88

1. **PREMISES LIABILITY**
2. Landau, N.J., et al.
3. Bender
4. 1987
5. 3 vols.
6. $325 incl. 3 mos. supp.
7. periodic supp.
8. 1989 - $141; 1990 - $199
9. 86-73092/16581340/KF1287.L36

1. **PREMISES LIABILITY**
2. -
3. MILE
4. 1991
5. 1 vol.
6. $68
7. no supp. planned
9. 23825880/KF1325.P3P74

1. **PREMISES LIABILITY**
2. Branton, James L. & James D. Lovett
3. Knowles
4. 1986 (Avail. in Texas and Natl. Eds.)
5. 2 vols.
6. $185 incl. 3 mos. supp.
7. annual supp.
8. 1988 - $30; 1990 - $37

1. **PREPAID LEGAL SERVICES REGULATION REPORTER**
2. Hochstadt, Adrian
3. API
4. 1981
5. 4 vols.
6. $275
7. bimonthly supp.
8. renewal - $155/yr.
9. 8964264

1. **PREPARATION OF THE CASE (Art of Advocacy Series)**
2. Baum, David B.
3. Bender
4. 1981
5. 1 vol.
6. $110 incl. 3 mos. supp.
7. periodic supp.
8. 1989 - $64; 1990 - $74.50
9. 81-69350/7985796/KF8915.B36

1. **PRESENTING AND ATTACKING SCIENTIFIC/DEMONSTRATIVE EVIDENCE IN CIVIL AND CRIMINAL CASES**
2. -
3. Wash. Bar

4. 1988
5. 1 vol.
6. $35
7. no supp. planned

1. **PRESERVATION LAW REPORTER**
2. -
3. NTHP
4. 1982
5. 2 vols.
6. $90/yr. (back vols.avail.)
7. monthly supp.
9. 83-642456/8312620/KF4310.A15P73

1. **PRETRIAL DISCOVERY: STRATEGY AND TACTICS**
2. Imwinkelreid, Edward J. & Theodore Y. Blumoff
3. Clark Boardman Callaghan
4. 1986
5. 1 vol.
6. $95 incl. 6 mos. supp.
7. annual supp.
8. 1989 - $30; 1990 - $32.50
9. 86-26856/14519448/KF8900.I48

1. **PRE-TRIAL HANDBOOK (BASIC CIVIL TRIAL PRACTICE)**
2. Dilloff, Neil J.
3. MICPEL
4. 1984
5. 1 vol.
6. $30
7. supp. planned
9. 11584514/KFM1730.D58

1. **PRE-TRIAL PROCEDURES IN THE FEDERAL COURTS**
2. Cowen, Hon. Robert E., et al.
3. New Jersey ICLE
4. 1987
5. 1 vol.
6. $35
7. no supp. planned
9. 87-141776/17386078/KF8900.S43

1. **PREVENTION AND PROSECUTION OF COMPUTER AND HIGH TECHNOLOGY CRIME**
2. Arkin, Stanley et al.
3. Bender
4. 1988
5. 1 vol.
6. $115 incl. 3 mos. supp.
7. annual supp.
8. 1989 - $35; 1990 - $46
9. 87-73509/17574899/KF9350.P74

1. **PRINCIPLES OF PAYROLL ADMINISTRATION: THE COMPLETE LEARNING AND REFERENCE GUIDE**
2. Salam, Debera & Lucy Key Price
3. WG&L
4. 1986
5. 1 vol.
6. $99
7. annual editions

1. **PRISONERS AND THE LAW**
2. Robbins, Ira P., ed.
3. Clark Boardman Callaghan
4. 1985
5. 2 vols.
6. $295 incl. 3 mos. supp.
7. annual supp.
8. 1988 - $45; 1991 - $85
9. 85-16678/12286602/KF9731.A75P74

1. **PRIVACY LAW AND PRACTICE**
2. Trubow, George B., ed.
3. Bender
4. 1987
5. 3 vols.
6. $325 incl. 3 mos. supp.
7. periodic supp.
8. 1989 - $82; 1990 - $91
9. 87-70369/16900421/KF1262.P753

1. **PRIVATE RADIO RULES SERVICE**
2. Tobias, Jeff, et al.
3. P&F
4. 1987
5. 1 vol.
6. $340
7. bimonthly supp.
8. $245/yr.; $450/2 yrs.
9. 88-416853/17876120/KF2814.A6P55

1. **PRIVATE REAL ESTATE SYNDICATIONS**
2. Constas, Michael & Richard D. Harroch
3. Law Journal
4. 1983
5. 1 vol.
6. $85
7. periodic supp.
8. 1988 - $36; 1989 - $42
9. 83-9417/9532897/KF1079.C66

1. **PRIVATE SECTOR LABOR LAW**
2. -
3. Minn. CLE
4. 1990
5. 1 vol.
6. $60
7. no supp. planned

1. **PRIVATE SECTOR LABOR RELATIONS FOR THE GENERAL PRACTITIONER**
2. Schneider, Mark W.
3. State Bar of Wisc.
4. 1989
5. 1 vol.
6. $65
7. periodic supp.
8. no supp. yet
9. 22248213/KF3369.3.S36

1. **PROBATE ADMINISTRATION IN MICHIGAN: A SYSTEMS APPROACH**
2. Draper, Harold A.
3. ICLE - Michigan
4. 3rd ed. - 1989
5. 1 vol.
6. $95
7. periodic supp.
8. 1991 - $49
9. 84-82232/20148274

1. **PROBATE, ESTATES AND FIDUCIARIES CODE ANNOTATED**
2. Aker, J.B.
3. Bisel
4. 1975
5. 1 vol.
6. $55
7. periodic supp.
8. 1987 - $26.95; 1988 - $26.95
9. 76-355565/2931572/KFP144.A332A44

1. **PROBATE LITIGATION**
2. -
3. Indiana CLE
4. 1990
5. 1 vol.
6. $50
7. no supp. planned

1. **PROBLEMS IN PROBATE**
2. -
3. Ohio CLE
4. 1989
5. 1 vol.
6. $35
7. no supp. planned

1. **PROCEDURES MANUAL FOR LEGAL PERSONNEL**
2. South Carolina Assn. of Legal Secretaries
3. S. Carolina Bar
4. 1989
5. 1 vol.
6. $70
7. no supp. planned
9. 19745126/KFS1877.P76

1. **PRODUCT LIABILITY**
2. Allee, John S.
3. Law Journal
4. 1984
5. 1 vol.
6. $80
7. periodic supp.
8. 1988 - $72; 1989 - $82
9. 84-7928/10725531/KF1296.A95

1. **PRODUCT LIABILITY PRACTICE GUIDE**
2. Vargo, John F.
3. Bender
4. 1988
5. 5 vols.
6. $490 incl. 3 mos. supp.
7. annual supp.
8. 1989 - $93; 1990 - $211
9. 88-161428/18174143/KF1296.V37

1. **PRODUCT SAFETY AND LIABILITY REPORTER**
2. Frank, William Harris
3. BNA
4. 1973
5. 4 vols.
6. $785/yr.
7. weekly supp. & reports
8. renewal - $735/yr.
9. 73-645533/1788141/KF3945.A73P7

1. **PRODUCTS LIABILITY**
2. Frumer, Louis R., et al.
3. Bender
4. 1960
5. 10 vols.
6. $1280 incl. 3 mos. supp.
7. annual supp.
8. 1989 - $943; 1990 - $1097.50
9. 60-52277/1508921

1. **PRODUCTS LIABILITY**
2. -
3. Indiana CLE
4. 1988
5. 1 vol.
6. $50
7. no supp. yet

1. **PRODUCTS LIABILITY**
2. -
3. NH Bar
4. 1990
5. 1 vol.
6. $35
7. no supp. planned
9. KFN1597.P7N7

1. **PRODUCTS LIABILITY: AN INTERNATIONAL MANUAL OF PRACTICE**
2. Freedman, Warren
3. Oceana
4. 1987
5. 2 vols.
6. $250
7. periodic supp.
8. 1988 - $125; 1990 - $95
9. 16955296/K953.P76

1. **PRODUCTS LIABILITY: RECREATION AND SPORTS EQUIPMENT**
2. Wittenberg, Jeffrey D.
3. Law Journal
4. 1985
5. 1 vol.
6. $80
7. periodic supp.
8. 1988 - $35; 1989 - $37
9. 85-209/11757219/KF1297.A77E58

1. **PRODUCTS LIABILITY AND TOXIC TORT LAW IN NEW JERSEY: A PRACTITIONER'S GUIDE**
2. Dreier, Hon. William A. et al.
3. New Jersey ICLE
4. 1988
5. 1 vol.
6. $85
7. periodic supp.
8. 1989 - $5; 1990-91 - $30
9. 18397845/KFN1997.7.D73

1. **PRODUCTS LIABILITY BOOK**
2. Silver, Howard
3. MTLA
4. 1983 - 1986
5. 2 vols.
6. $125 (member); $150 (nonmember)
7. periodic supp.
8. 1989 - $15 (member); $25 (nonmembers)

1. **PRODUCTS LIABILITY LAW IN MINNESOTA**
2. -
3. MILE
4. 1991
5. 1 vol.
6. $68
7. no supp. planned
9. 24207999/KFM5597.7.Z9P78

1. **PRODUCTS LIABILITY LAW IN OKLAHOMA**
2. MacDougall, Vicki Lawrence
3. Butterworth-Texas
4. 1990
5. 1 vol.
6. $120
7. annual supp.
8. no supp. yet
9. 89-23958/20419531/KFO1397.7.M33

1. **PRODUCTS LIABILITY LAW MANUAL**
2. -
3. MICPEL
4. 1990
5. 1 vol.
6. $60
7. no supp. yet

1. **PRODUCTS LIABILITY LITIGATION: CASE EVALUATION**
2. Loggans, Susan E.
3. Clark Boardman Callaghan
4. 1988
5. 1 vol.
6. $85 incl. 6 mos. supp.
7. annual supp.
8. no supp. yet
9. 88-23756//r89/18351041/KF8925.P7L64

1. **PRODUCTS LIABILITY LITIGATION: PRETRIAL PRACTICE**
2. Lowe, James
3. Clark Boardman Callaghan
4. 1988
5. 2 vols.
6. $160 incl. 6 mos. supp.
7. annual supp.
8. no supp. yet

9. 88-19303//r89/18136820/KF8900.L68

1. **PRODUCTS LIABILITY LITIGATION: TRIAL STRATEGY & PROCEDURE**
2. Gibbins, Bob and A. Russell Smith
3. Clark Boardman Callaghan
4. 1988
5. 1 vol.
6. $85 incl. 6 mos. supp.
7. annual supp.
8. no supp. yet
9. 88-30432/18715692/KF8925.97G53

1. **PRODUCTS LIABILITY REPORTS**
2. -
3. CCH
4. 1963
5. 2 vols.
6. $560/yr.; $510/yr. for 2 yrs.
7. semimonthly supp.
9. SN78-864/1564336

1. **PROFESSIONAL CORPORATIONS AND ASSOCIATIONS (Business Organizations, Vols. 17 - 17E)**
2. Eaton, Berrien C., Jr.
3. Bender
4. 1970
5. 7 vols.
6. $495 incl. 6 mos. supp.
7. semiannual supp.
8. 1989 - $302.75; 1990 - $351
9. 77-22636/132253/KF2901.A6E18

1. **PROFESSIONAL CORPORATIONS HANDBOOK**
2. -
3. CCH
4. 1973
5. 2 vols.
6. $425/yr.; $385/yr. for 2 yrs.
7. monthly supp.
9. 73-159457/624473/KF2901.C642

1. **PROFESSIONAL ETHICS OF THE FLORIDA BAR**
2. -
3. Florida Bar
4. 2nd ed. - 1987
5. 1 vol.
6. $40
7. supp. as needed
8. 1988 - $15; 1991 - $15
9. No LC card number/17316755/KFF76.5A2A492

1. **PROFESSIONAL LIABILITY**
2. -
3. Illinois ICLE
4. 1991
5. 1 vol.
6. $99.95
7. periodic supp.
8. no supp. yet

1. **PROFESSIONAL LIABILITY**
2. Branton, James L. and James D. Lovett
3. Knowles
4. 1988
5. 1 vol. (avail. in Texas and national eds.)
6. $135 incl. 3 mos. supp.
7. annual supp.
8. 1990 - $35
9. 17823371/KFT1739.M34B73

1. **PROFESSIONAL LIABILITY: RECOGNIZING, HANDLING, PREVENTING**
2. -
3. NH Bar
4. 1986
5. 1 vol.
6. $35
7. no supp. planned
9. 14177588/KFN1441.2.A75P76

1. **PROFESSIONAL LIABILITY INSURANCE**
2. Bregman, Robert A. & Jack P. Gibson
3. Intl. Risk Mgmt. Inst.
4. 1990
5. 2 vols.
6. $225/yr.
7. periodic supp.
9. 23764933

1. **PROFESSIONAL LIABILITY OF LAWYERS IN FLORIDA**
2. -
3. Florida Bar
4. 1989
5. 1 vol.
6. $60
7. supp. as needed

9. 89-81848/21216497/KF313.Z9P76

1. **PROFESSIONAL NEGLIGENCE: LAW OF MALPRACTICE IN NEW JERSEY**
2. Cohn, Albert L. & Barry A. Knopf
3. New Jersey ICLE

4. 3rd ed. - 1991
5. 1 vol.
6. $85
7. periodic supp.
8. no supp. yet
9. 24350004/KFN2126.3.A59C64

1. **PROFESSIONAL RESPONSIBILITY IN NEW JERSEY**
2. -
3. New Jersey ICLE
4. 1990
5. 1 vol.
6. $85
7. no supp. planned
9. 21920064/KFN1876.5.A2A5

1. **PROFESSIONAL STANDARDS**
2. AICPA
3. CCH
4. 1974
5. 2 vols.
6. $150/yr.; $125/yr. for 2 yrs.
7. periodic supp.
9. 75-303209/1709163/HF5667.A55

1. **PROOF OF DAMAGES**
2. -
3. Illinois ICLE
4. 1987
5. 1 vol.
6. $87.95
7. periodic supp.
8. 1990 - $19.95

1. **PROPERTY INSURANCE**
2. -
3. Illinois ICLE
4. 1986
5. 1 vol.
6. $93.95
7. periodic supp.
8. 1990 - $24.95

1. **PROPERTY INSURANCE ANNOTATIONS: FIRE AND EXTENDED COVERAGES**
2. Tort and Insurance Practice Section
3. ABA
4. 1977
5. 1 vol.
6. $55
7. periodic supp.
8. 1983 - $55; 1988 - $69
9. 83-72659/10907446/KF1190.A59A45

1. **PROPERTY TAXATION**
2. -
3. Inst. of Prop. Tax.
4. 1987
5. 1 vol.
6. $75
7. supp. as needed
8. new ed. due 1993
9. 87-3326/16006288/HJ4120.P6717

1. **PROPERTY TAXES**
2. -
3. RIA
4. 1925
5. 14 vols.
6. $1325/yr.; $1275/yr. for 2 yrs.
7. weekly supp.
8. renewal - $1225/yr.

1. **PROSECUTION AND DEFENSE OF CRIMINAL CONSPIRACY CASES**
2. Marcus, Paul
3. Bender
4. 1978
5. 1 vol.
6. $110 incl. 6 mos. supp.
7. annual supp.
8. 1989 - $77; 1990 - $94.50
9. 78-60134/4207179/KF9479.M37

1. **PROSECUTION AND DEFENSE OF FORFEITURE CASES**
2. Smith, David B.
3. Bender
4. 1985
5. 2 vols.
6. $180 incl. 3 mos. supp.
7. periodic supp.
8. 1989 - $64.50; 1990 - $114
9. 85-72210/12817070/KF9747.S52

1. **PROSECUTION AND DEFENSE OF SEX CRIMES**
2. Morosco, B. Anthony
3. Bender
4. 1976
5. 1 vol.
6. $140 incl. 3 mos. supp.
7. annual supp.
8. 1989 - $67.50; 1990 - $131
9. 76-1371/2414965/KF9325.M67

1. **PROSECUTORIAL MISCONDUCT**
2. Gershman, Bennett L.

3. Clark Boardman Callaghan
4. 1984
5. 1 vol.
6. $110 incl. 3 mos. supp.
7. annual supp.
8. 1989 - $57.50; 1991 - $69.50
9. 84-12399/10824031/KF9640.G46

1. **PROTECTING AGAINST EXPROPRIATION OF RISK IN INVESTING ABROAD**
2. Allison, Richard C.
3. Bender
4. 1988
5. 1 vol.
6. $105 incl. 3 mos. supp.
7. annual supp.
8. no supp. yet
9. 87-72785/17629677/KF1575.A6A55

1. **PROTECTION OF CORPORATE NAMES: A COUNTRY-BY-COUNTRY SURVEY**
2. U.S. Trademark Assn.
3. Clark Boardman Callaghan
4. 1982
5. 1 vol.
6. $125 incl. 3 mos. supp.
7. annual supp.
8. 1989 - $47.50; 1991 - $59.50
9. 82-4235/8306162/K1555.4.P76

1. **PROVING CRIMINAL DEFENSES**
2. Schultz, Gene P.
3. Bender
4. 1991
5. 3 vols.
6. $300 incl. 3 mos. supp.
7. annual supp.
8. no supp. yet
9. 91-73350/24366261/KF9656.P76

1. **PROVING DAMAGES AFTER TORT REFORM**
2. -
3. Ohio CLE
4. 1989
5. 1 vol.
6. $25
7. no supp. planned

1. **PROVING FAULT IN AUTO ACCIDENT CASES**
2. -
3. Illinois ICLE
4. 1988
5. 1 vol.
6. $87.95
7. periodic supp.
8. 1991 - $19.95
9. 5687767

1. **PROVING MEDICAL DIAGNOSIS AND PROGNOSIS**
2. Houts, Marshall & Leonard Marmor
3. Bender
4. 1970
5. 15 vols.
6. $1070 incl. 3 mos. supp.
7. annual supp.
8. 1989 - $690; 1990 - $854.50
9. 78-129084/143240/RA1053.H6

1. **PROXY STATEMENTS: STRATEGY AND FORMS**
2. Deutch, Howard E.
3. Jefren
4. 1985
5. 12 vols.
6. $690/yr.
7. monthly supp.
9. 18243492/KF1451.P7

1. **PSYCHIC INJURIES (Courtroom Medicine Series, Vol. 12)**
2. Lewis, Marvin E. et al.
3. Bender
4. 1975
5. 3 vols.
6. $310 incl. 3 mos. supp.
7. annual supp.
8. 1989 - $175; 1990 - $206
9. 75-18820/1730447/RA1011.C68

1. **PUBLIC EMPLOYEE REPORTER FOR CALIF.**
2. -
3. LRP
4. 1976
5. 1 vol.
6. $595/yr. (back vols. avail.)
7. semimonthly supp.

1. **PUBLIC NATURAL RESOURCES LAW**
2. Coggins, George C.
3. Clark Boardman Callaghan
4. 1990
5. 1 vol.
6. $110 incl. 3 mos. supp.
7. annual supp.
8. 1991 - $102
9. 89-27186/20393234/KF5505.C64

1. **PUBLIC POLICY IN TRANSNATIONAL RELATIONS**
2. Rubino-Sammartano, Mauro
3. Kluwer
4. 1990
5. 1 vol.
6. $87 incl. 3 mos. supp.
7. periodic supp.
9. 90-42340/22006319/K7075.P86

1. **PUBLIC RADIO LEGAL HANDBOOK, 2ND**
2. -
3. NFCB
4. 1986
5. 1 vol.
6. $50 - members; $75 - nonmembers
7. no supp. yet

1. **PUBLIC SECTOR LABOR LAW (7th Annual)**
2. -
3. MILE
4. 1991
5. 1 vol.
6. $68
7. no supp. planned
9. 14706576

1. **PUBLIC SECTOR LABOR RELATIONS IN WISCONSIN**
2. Mulcahy and Wherry, S.C.
3. State Bar of Wisc.
4. 1988
5. 1 vol.
6. $80
7. periodic supp.
8. 1991 - price NA
9. 17978107/KFW2732.8.P77M84

1. **PUBLIC TRUSTEE FORECLOSURE - COLORADO**
2. Bloom, Andrea
3. CLE - Colorado
4. 1985
5. 1 vol.
6. $55
7. periodic supp.
8. 1988 - $20; new ed. due 1992
9. 12780467/KFC1930.5.B62

1. **THE PUBLISHING LAW HANDBOOK**
2. Williams, John Taylor & E. Gabriel Perle
3. Prentice Hall Law & Business
4. 1988
5. 1 vol.
6. $80 incl. 4 mos. supp.
7. annual supp.
8. 1990 - $60; 1991 - $75
9. 88-5819/17618319/KF2750.P43

1. **PUERTO RICO TAX REPORTS**
2. -
3. CCH
4. 1964
5. 2 vol.
6. $385/yr.; $350/yr. for 2 yrs.
7. monthly supp.
9. 64-2670/5855055/KF6736.P87

1. **PUERTO RICO TAXES**
2. Sierra, Ralph J., Jr. & Serapion, Margarita
3. RIA
4. 1983
5. 2 vols.
6. $395/yr.; $375/yr. for 2 yrs.
7. monthly supp.
8. renewal - $350/yr.
9. 82-7811/8996703

1. **PUNITIVE DAMAGES, LAW & PRACTICE**
2. Ghiardi, James D. & John J. Kircher
3. Clark Boardman Callaghan
4. 1981
5. 2 vols.
6. $175 incl. 6 mos. supp.
7. annual supp.
8. 1989 - $87.50; 1990 - $89
9. 81-10088/7578065/KF1250.G55

1. **PURCHASE AND SALE OF A CLOSELY-HELD BUSINESS**
2. -
3. MICPEL
4. 1990
5. 1 vol.
6. $40
7. no supp. yet
9. 22146359/KF1466.P98

1. **PURCHASE AND SALE OF A SMALL BUSINESS**
2. -
3. NH Bar
4. 1988
5. 1 vol.
6. $35
7. no supp. planned

1. **PURCHASE AND SALE OF A SMALL BUSINESS**
2. -
3. Okla. Bar CLE
4. 1990
5. 1 vol.
6. $60
7. no supp. planned

1. **PURCHASE AND SALE OF REAL PROPERTY (REAL ESTATE TRANSACTION SERIES, VOLS. 12, 12A & 12B)**
2. Holtzschue, Karl B.
3. Bender
4. 1987
5. 3 vols.
6. $315 incl. 3 mos. supp.
7. annual supp.
8. 1989 - $109.50; 1990 - $129.50
9. 87-72237/17393084/KF665.H65

1. **PURCHASER'S FORMBOOK OF CONTRACTS AND AGREEMENTS**
2. Hancock, W. A.
3. Bus. Laws
4. 1985
5. 2 vols.
6. $145
7. annual supp.
8. renewal - $48/yr.
9. 11975030/HD52.5.P98

1. **PURCHASING FROM SMALL AND MINORITY BUSINESSES**
2. Hancock, W.A., ed.
3. Bus. Laws
4. 1986
5. 1 vol.
6. $90
7. annual supp.
8. renewal - $39/yr.
9. 88-415783/15039993/KF869.3.P87

1. **Q&A GUIDE TO PERSONNEL DECISIONS**
2. -
3. Alex. Hamilton Inst.
4. 1990
5. 1 vol.
6. $62.95
7. no supp. yet

1. **QUALIFIED DEFERRED COMPENSATION PLANS**
2. Boren, Gary I.
3. Clark Boardman Callaghan
4. 1983
5. 2 vols.
6. $200 incl. 6 mos. supp.
7. semiannual supp.
8. 1989 - $160; 1990 - $140
9. 83-23912/10145784/KF3509.B67

1. **QUALIFIED DEFERRED COMPENSATION PLANS (FORMS)**
2. Mancoff, Neal A. & Allen T. Steinberg
3. Clark Boardman Callaghan
4. 1983
5. 1 vol.
6. $112 incl. 6 mos. supp.
7. semiannual supp.
8. 1989 - $98; 1990 - $100
9. 83-23222/10123467/KF6379.A65M36

1. **QUALIFYING & ATTACKING EXPERT WITNESSES**
2. Clifford, Robert C.
3. James
4. 1988
5. 1 vol.
6. $59.99 incl. 3 mos. supp.
7. annual supp.
8. 1990 - $37.98
9. 18581149/KF8961.C44

1. **QUALITY REVIEW PROGRAM MANUAL**
2. -
3. CCH
4. 1989
5. 1 vol.
6. $160/yr.; $145/yr. for 2 years
7. semiannual supp.

1. **QUEBEC TAX REPORTER**
2. -
3. CCH
4. 1969
5. 2 vols.
6. $260/yr.; $235/yr. for 2 yrs.
7. monthly supp.

1. **QUICK GUIDE FOR THE LEGAL ASSISTANT**
2. -
3. Illinois ICLE
4. 1989
5. 1 vol.
6. $69.95
7. periodic supp.

8. no supp. yet
9. 19409864/KFI1277.Q4

1. **QUINN'S UCC FORMS & PRACTICE**
2. Quinn, Thomas M.
3. WG&L
4. 1986
5. 2 vols.
6. $155
7. periodic supp.
8. 1987 - $47
9. 14555734

1. **RADIO REGULATION, SECOND SERIES**
2. Willis, John W. & R.E. Emeritz
3. P&F
4. 1963
5. 14 vols.
6. $2945 incl. 15 looseleaf & 1 yr. supp. (60 back vols. avail. at $75/vol.).
7. weekly supp.
8. renewal - $1655/yr.; $3050/2 yrs.
9. 70-24229/212471/KF2810.A6P52

1. **RAIL CARRIER SERVICE**
2. -
3. Hawkins
4. 1927
5. 10 vols.
6. $280/yr.
7. monthly supp.
8. renewal - $260/yr.

1. **RAILROAD COMMISSION OF TEXAS RULES**
2. Finklea, Gaylon, ed.
3. RPC
4. 1977
5. 1 vol.
6. $249/yr.
7. periodic supp.

1. **RAISING CAPITAL: PRIVATE PLACEMENT FORMS & TECHNIQUES**
2. Max, Herbert B.
3. Prentice Hall Law & Business
4. 2nd ed. - 1989
5. 1 vol.
6. $95 incl. 4 mos. supp.
7. periodic supp.
8. 1989 - $95; 1990 - $50
9. 80-20409/6626454/KF1439.F76

1. **RAYBURN ON CONDEMNATION/THE TEXAS LAW OF EMINENT DOMAIN**
2. Rayburn, Madison
3. Francis Marion
4. 1960
5. 2 vols.
6. $110 incl. 1 supp.
7. semiannual supp.
8. 1990 - $57; 1991 - $67.50
9. 17858761/KFT1650.R3

1. **RCRA AND SUPERFUND: A PRACTICE GUIDE WITH FORMS**
2. Schraff, Christopher R. & Robert E. Steinberg
3. Shepard's
4. 1990
5. 3 vols.
6. $360
7. semiannual supp.
8. 1989 - $80; 1990 - $35
9. 88-24587/18464373/KF3946.S37

1. **READ'S FLORIDA EVIDENCE**
2. Read, Frank T.
3. Lawyers Coop.
4. 1987
5. 2 vols.
6. $180 incl. 6 mos. supp.
7. annual supp.
8. 1990 - $39.50; 1991 - $42.50
9. 86-31035/14906004/KFF540.R43

1. **REAL ESTATE BROKERAGE LAW AND PRACTICE**
2. Rohan, Patrick, et al.
3. Bender
4. 1985
5. 1 vol.
6. $110 incl. 3 mos. supp.
7. periodic supp.
8. 1989 - $51; 1990 - $65.50
9. 85-72943/12988311/KF2042.R4R6

1. **REAL ESTATE CLOSING**
2. -
3. NH Bar
4. 1987
5. 1 vol.
6. $30
7. no supp. planned

1. **REAL ESTATE COORDINATOR**
2. RIA prof. ed. staff
3. RIA
4. 1985
5. 8 vols.

6. $775/yr.; $715/yr. for 2 yrs.
7. biweekly supp.
8. renewal - $665/yr.
9. 12394463/KF665.A6R42

1. **REAL ESTATE DEVELOPMENT**
2. Morris, Eugene J. ed.
3. Bender
4. 1987
5. 4 vols.
6. $350 incl. 3 mos. supp.
7. annual supp.
8. 1989 - $112; 1990 - $134
9. 87-73405/17842176/KF5698.3.R43

1. **REAL ESTATE DEVELOPMENT: LONG TERM CARE & RETIREMENT FACILITIES**
2. Various Contributing Arthors
3. Bender
4. 1989
5. 1 vol.
6. $95 incl. 3 mos. supp.
7. annual supp.
8. 1990 - $41.50
9. 89-61434/20858328/KF3826.N8R43

1. **REAL ESTATE FINANCING TEXT, FORMS, TAX ANALYSIS (Real Estate Transaction Series, Vol. 4-5)**
2. Rohan, Patrick J.
3. Bender
4. 1973
5. 7 vols.
6. $680 incl. 3 mos. supp.
7. semiannual supp.
8. 1989 - $606.50; 1990 - $621
9. 73-168807/705457/KF695.R6

1. **REAL ESTATE FORMBOOK**
2. McDonald, John
3. State Bar of Mont.
4. 1988
5. 1 vol.
6. $60
7. periodic supp.
8. no supp. yet

1. **REAL ESTATE FORMS FROM ALI-ABA COURSE MATERIALS**
2. -
3. ALI-ABA
4. 2nd ed. - 1991
5. 1 vol.
6. $130
7. periodic supp.
8. no supp. yet

1. **REAL ESTATE LAW: EASEMENTS, ROADS AND WAYS AND LITIGATION**
2. -
3. Maine Bar
4. 1989
5. 1 vol.
6. $30
7. no supp. planned
9. 20969360/KF657.Z99M23

1. **REAL ESTATE LITIGATION**
2. -
3. Maine Bar
4. 1991
5. 1 vol.
6. $20
7. no supp. planned
9. 23893419/KF570.Z99M217

1. **REAL ESTATE LITIGATION**
2. -
3. Illinois ICLE
4. 1988
5. 1 vol.
6. $119.95
7. periodic supp.
8. 1991 - $29.95

1. **REAL ESTATE LOAN WORKOUTS**
2. Real Property & Commercial Law & Bankruptcy Section
3. Conn. Bar
4. 1989
5. 1 vol.
6. $20
7. no supp. yet

1. **REAL ESTATE PRACTITIONER'S TAX GUIDE**
2. Segal, Mark
3. Knowles
4. 1990
5. 1 vol.
6. $135 incl. 3 mos. supp.
7. annual supp.
8. no supp. yet
9. KF6540.S44

1. **REAL ESTATE SYNDICATION MANUAL**
2. Arnold, Alvin L.

3. WG&L
4. 1984
5. 1 vol.
6. $105
7. semiannual supp.
8. 1989 - $115; 1991 - $66
9. 84-51630/11603853/KF1079.A96

1. **REAL ESTATE SYNDICATIONS: LAW, PRACTICE AND FORMS**
2. Rohan, Patrick, et al.
3. Bender
4. 1985
5. 2 vols.
6. $210 incl. 3 mos. supp.
7. periodic supp.
8. 1989 - $102; 1990 - $132.50
9. 85-62786/13108362/KF1079.R64

1. **REAL ESTATE TAX APPEALS**
2. Rohan, Patrick J.
3. Bender
4. 1984
5. 3 vols.
6. $200 incl. 3 mos. supp.
7. annual supp.
8. 1989 - $99.50; 1990 - $121
9. 85-126013/12161457/KF6760.R64

1. **REAL ESTATE TAXATION**
2. -
3. Illinois ICLE
4. 1991
5. 1 vol.
6. $105.95
7. periodic supp.
8. no supp. yet
9. 16850717/KFI1679.R4

1. **REAL ESTATE TRANSACTIONS**
2. Levine, Mark Lee
3. Prof. Pubs.
4. 1991
5. 1 vol.
6. price NA
7. annual supp.

1. **REAL ESTATE TRANSACTIONS: BORROWERS' COUNSELS' OPINION LETTERS**
2. -
3. Conn. Bar
4. 1991
5. 1 vol.
6. $53
7. no supp. planned

1. **REAL ESTATE TRANSACTIONS: STRUCTURE AND ANALYSIS WITH FORMS**
2. Arnold, Alvin
3. WG&L
4. 1990
5. 1 vol.
6. $96 incl. 3 mos. supp.
7. annual supp.
8. 1991 - $49.50
9. 89-51610/21709244/KF665.A82

1. **REAL ESTATE TRANSACTIONS CASEBOOK: CASES & MATERIALS**
2. Raushenbush, Walter B. et al.
3. CLE - Wisc.
4. 1990
5. 1 vol.
6. $40
7. periodic supp.
8. no supp. yet

1. **REAL ESTATE TRANSACTIONS SYSTEM**
2. Harwich, John L.
3. State Bar of Wisc.
4. 1982
5. 1 vol.
6. $105
7. periodic supp.
8. 1988 - $25; 1991 - $60
9. 10069903/KFW2526.H67

1. **REAL PROPERTY**
2. Ball, Robert & David P. Miller eds.
3. Oregon Bar
4. 1975
5. 3 vols.
6. $190
7. periodic supp.
8. 1981 - $75; 1985 - $65
9. 76-370816/2426171/KFO2512.O7

1. **REAL PROPERTY, PROBATE AND TRUST SECTION MID-YEAR MEETING AND SEMINARS - REAL PROPERTY PROGRAM**
2. -
3. Wash. Bar
4. 1991
5. 1 vol.
6. $55
7. annual vol.

1. **REAL PROPERTY TITLE EXAMINATION AND INSURANCE IN FLORIDA**
2. -
3. Florida Bar
4. 2nd ed. - 1988
5. 1 vol.
6. $65
7. supp. as needed
8. 1990 - $20
9. 87-83665/18257980/KFF127.R43

1. **RECALL MANUAL: A GUIDE FOR MANAGEMENT**
2. Holstein, Howard M.
3. HIMA
4. 1981
5. 1 vol.
6. $155-nonmembers; $80-members
7. periodic supp.
8. 1982 - $20
9. 82-136217/8532702/KF3827.M4H64

1. **RECENT DEVELOPMENTS IN MEDICAL MALPRACTICE**
2. -
3. Conn. Bar
4. 1990
5. 1 vol.
6. $43
7. no supp. planned

1. **RECENT ISSUES AND CURRENT DEVELOPMENTS IN LABOR AND EMPLOYMENT LAW**
2. -
3. Maine Bar
4. 1989
5. 1 vol.
6. $30
7. no supp. planned

1. **RECOMMENDED ARIZONA JURY INSTRUCTIONS - CIVIL**
2. Civil Jury Instructions Comm.
3. State Bar of Ariz.
4. 2nd ed. - 1991
5. 1 vol.
6. $35
7. periodic supp.
8. no supp. yet
9. 15136350/KFA2942.6.A65S75

1. **RECORD AND MUSIC PUBLISHING FORMS OF AGREEMENT IN CURRENT USE**
2. Cooper, Jay & Irwin Spiegel
3. Law-Arts
4. 1971
5. 1 vol.
6. $59
7. no supp. planned
9. 72-144789/495524/KF4291.A65S65

1. **REDUCING PERSONAL INCOME TAXES: A GUIDE TO DEDUCTIONS AND CREDITS**
2. Davidian, John and Jacob L. Todres
3. Law Journal
4. 1988
5. 1 vol.
6. $70
7. periodic supp.
8. 1989 - $70
9. 87-37822/17384035/KF6385.D38

1. **REFERENCE GUIDE TO WORKMEN'S COMPENSATION LAW**
2. Blair, Elmer H.
3. Thomas
4. 1974
5. 2 vols.
6. $100
7. annual supp. & midyear alert
8. 1989 - $38.70; 1990 - $40.75
9. 78-1920/220225/KF3615.B53

1. **REGIONAL VERDICT SURVEY**
2. Research Dept.
3. Jury Verdict
4. 1983
5. 3 vols.
6. $390/yr. for 2 yrs.
7. periodic supp.

1. **REGULATION OF BUSINESS ENTERPRISE IN THE U.S.A.**
2. Norton, Joseph J. & H.E. Dobroski
3. Oceana
4. 1983
5. 2 vols.
6. $190/set(closed)
7. no supp. planned
9. 83-2274/9219146/KF1355.N67

1. **THE REGULATION OF CORPORATE DISCLOSURE**
2. Brown, J. Robert, Jr.
3. Prentice Hall Law & Business
4. 1989
5. 1 vol.

6. $95 incl. 4 mos. supp.
7. periodic supp.
8. 1990 - $50; 1991 - $60
9. 89-8376/19556043/KF1449.B76

1. **REGULATION OF FINANCIAL PLANNERS**
2. Moriarity, John D. & Curtlan R. McNeily
3. Clark Boardman Callaghan
4. 1991
5. 1 vol.
6. $110 incl. 3 mos. supp.
7. annual supp.
8. no supp. yet
9. 91-26315/24217903/KF2921.Z95M67

1. **REGULATION OF INTERNATIONAL COMMERCIAL AVIATION: THE INTERNATIONAL REGULATORY STRUCTURE**
2. Fox, James
3. Oceana
4. 1984
5. 2 vols.
6. $170/set
7. periodic supp.
8. 1984 - $85
9. 83-19392

1. **THE REGULATION OF STATELESSNESS UNDER INTERNATIONAL AND NATIONAL LAW: TEXTS AND DOCUMENTS**
2. Mutharika, A. Peter
3. Oceana
4. 1977
5. 2 vols.
6. $170/set
7. periodic supp.
8. 1986 - $85; 1989 - $95
9. 76-45660/11546041/JX4231.S8M87

1. **REGULATION OF THE COMMODITIES FUTURES AND OPTIONS MARKETS**
2. Russo, Thomas A.
3. Shepard's
4. 1983
5. 2 vols.
6. $195
7. annual supp.
8. 1990 - $46; 1991 - $52
9. 83-431/9217043/KF1085.R87

1. **REGULATION OF THE GAS INDUSTRY**
2. Am. Gas Assn., ed.
3. Bender
4. 1981
5. 5 vols.
6. $445 incl. 3 mos. supp.
7. periodic supp.
8. 1989 - $255; 1990 - $295.50
9. 81-68100//r861/8218724/KF1870.R44

1. **REGULATION Z: TRUTH-IN-LENDING COMPREHENSIVE COMPLIANCE MANUAL**
2. Chamness, Robert P.
3. Am. Bankers
4. 1989
5. 2 vols.
6. $95-members; $285-nonmembers
7. supp. planned
8. 1989 - $79
9. 20881966/HG3755.C448

1. **REGULATIONS OF THE BOARD OF GOVERNORS**
2. -
3. Fed.-NY
4. 1980
5. 1 vol.
6. $66 incl. supp.
7. periodic supp.

1. **REGULATORY COMPLIANCE MANUAL**
2. -
3. American Dental
4. 1990
5. 1 vol.
6. $95 incl. supp. to 12/92
7. semiannual supp.
9. 21242841/WC195A512r

1. **REGULATORY COMPLIANCE MANUAL**
2. -
3. MBAA
4. 1986
5. 1 vol.
6. $95-members; $120-nonmembers
7. periodic supp.
8. 1990 - $50; 1991 - $50
9. 9291618/HG2040.5.U5M58

1. **THE REGULATORY EXAMINATION: HOW TO GET BETTER RESULTS**
2. -
3. NCSI
4. 1991
5. 1 vol.
6. $95-members; $150-nonmembers
7. annual edition

1. **REGULATORY MANAGEMENT COMPLIANCE AUDIT DESKBOOK**
2. Naldony, Nancy Z. & William K. Simons
3. Probus
4. 1990
5. 1 vol.
6. $125
7. annual supp.

1. **REINSURANCE LAW**
2. Butler, John S. et al.
3. NILS
4. 1989
5. 1 vol.
6. $240 incl. supp. for bal. of calendar year
7. periodic supp.
8. 1991 - $115
9. 19102156/KF1236.A6R44

1. **RELATED LAWS TO INSURANCE LAWS**
2. -
3. NILS
4. NA
5. 1 vol.
6. $93 (NY and CA, $96) incl. 3 mos. supp.
7. periodic supp.
8. 1989 - $71; 1990 - $86

1. **RELATIVE VALUES: DETERMINING ATTORNEYS' FEES**
2. Fitzgerald, Petri and Painter
3. Shepard's
4. 1985
5. 1 vol.
6. $95
7. annual supp.
8. 1987 - $25; 1989 - $20
9. 84-23578/11398778/KF316.R45

1. **REORGANIZATIONS UNDER CHAPTER 11 OF THE BANKRUPTCY CODE**
2. Broude, Richard F.
3. Law Journal
4. 1986
5. 1 vol.
6. $85
7. periodic supp.
8. 1989 - $80; 1990 - $84
9. 85-23701/13008469/KF1544.B76

1. **REPORTING TO BANK REGULATORS**
2. Mancuso, John & Richard A. Kopek
3. WG&L
4. 1990
5. 1 vol.
6. $165/yr.
7. supp. 3x/yr.
9. 90-71384/22762776/KF974.M35

1. **REPRESENTATION BEFORE THE COLLECTION DIVISION OF IRS**
2. McKenzie, Robert E.
3. Clark Boardman Callaghan
4. 1985
5. 1 vol.
6. $59.95 incl. 3 mos. supp.
7. annual supp.
8. 1989 - $39; 1990 - $30
9. 89-9970/19777397/KF6310.M38

1. **REPRESENTATION OF WITNESSES BEFORE FEDERAL GRAND JURIES**
2. National Lawyers Guild
3. Clark Boardman Callaghan
4. 3rd ed. - 1984
5. 1 vol.
6. $95 incl. 3 mos. supp.
7. annual supp.
8. 1989 - $52.50; 1991 - $104.50
9. 83-15607/11486839/KF9642.R46

1. **REPRESENTING DEBTORS IN CONSUMER BANKRUPTCIES**
2. -
3. Minn. CLE
4. 1990
5. 1 vol.
6. $50
7. no supp. planned

1. **REPRESENTING NONPROFIT ORGANIZATIONS**
2. -
3. MILE
4. 1991
5. 1 vol.
6. $68
7. no supp. planned

1. **REPRESENTING PEOPLE WITH DISABILITIES**
2. Danziger, Peter, ed.
3. NYSBA
4. 1991
5. 1 vol.
6. $80
7. annual supp.
8. 1991 - $45
9. 91-52548/24123178/KF480.A75R47

1. **REPRESENTING RESIDENTIAL TENANTS**
2. -
3. Illinois ICLE
4. 1989
5. 1 vol.
6. $93.95
7. periodic supp.
8. no supp. yet
9. 19961920/KFI1317.R4

1. **REPRESENTING STUDENTS IN PUBLIC SCHOOL DICIPLINARY ACTIONS**
2. Wagonheim, Sylvia Stoler
3. MICPEL
4. 1991
5. 1 vol.
6. $42
7. no supp. planned
9. 23948926/KFM1590.W13

1. **REPRESENTING THE AUDITED TAXPAYER BEFORE THE IRS**
2. McKenzie, Robert, et al.
3. Clark Boardman Callaghan
4. 1990
5. 1 vol.
6. $59.95 incl. 3 mos. service
7. annual supp.
8. no supp. yet
9. 90-1707/21333702/KF6314.M38

1. **REPRESENTING THE CHILD CLIENT**
2. Soler, M.I.
3. Bender
4. 1987
5. 1 vol.
6. $115 incl. 3 mos. supp.
7. annual supp.
8. 1989 - $50; 1990 - $97.50
9. 87-72736/6967431/KF9779.R46

1. **REPRESENTING THE CORPORATE CLIENT: DESIGNS FOR QUALITY**
2. Weise, Richard H.
3. Prentice Hall Law & Business
4. 1991
5. 1 vol.
6. $95 incl. 4 mos. supp.
7. periodic supp.
8. no supp. yet
9. 91-34625/24541187/KF1425.W45

1. **REPRESENTING THE ELDERLY: THE RULES THEY ARE A-CHANGING**
2. -
3. Conn. Bar
4. 1991
5. 1 vol.
6. $53
7. no supp. planned

1. **RESIDENTIAL REAL ESTATE LAW AND PRACTICE IN NEW JERSEY**
2. Horn, Arthur S.
3. New Jersey ICLE
4. 1989
5. 1 vol.
6. $150
7. no supp. planned
9. 20058481/KFN1926.H67

1. **RESIDENTIAL REAL ESTATE PRACTICE**
2. -
3. Minn. CLE
4. 1991
5. 1 vol.
6. $50
7. no supp. planned
9. 24450761

1. **RESIDENTIAL REAL ESTATE SYSTEM**
2. -
3. Illinois ICLE
4. 1990
5. 1 vol.
6. $91.95
7. periodic supp.
8. no supp. yet
9. KFI1326.A65A2

1. **RESIDENTIAL REAL ESTATE TRANSACTIONS**
2. -
3. Minn. CLE
4. 1990
5. 1 vol.
6. $50
7. no supp. planned

1. **RESIDENTIAL REAL ESTATE TRANSACTIONS**
2. Brown, Charles J. & W. Allen Ames, eds.
3. Jt. Comm. Va.
4. 1990
5. 1 vol.
6. $78
7. periodic supp.
8. no supp. yet

9. 7765917/KFV2940.R43

1. **RESIDENTIAL REAL ESTATE TRANSACTIONS**
2. Gordon, Ann C. & S.E. Mitnick, eds.
3. MICPEL
4. 2nd ed. - 1989
5. 1 vol.
6. $75
7. periodic supp.
8. no supp. yet
9. 89-62595/20475932/KFM1326.R47

1. **THE RESOURCE: A PRO BONO MANUAL**
2. Special Comm. on Lawyer's Public Service Responsibility
3. ABA
4. 1983
5. 1 vol.
6. $10
7. no supp. planned
9. 83-72985/12163152/KF336.R47

1. **RESPONSIBILITIES OF INSURANCE AGENTS AND BROKERS**
2. Harnett, Bertram
3. Bender
4. 1974
5. 3 vols.
6. $375 incl. 3 mos. supp.
7. annual supp.
8. 1989 - $280; 1990 - $337.50
9. 73-94100/1120895/KF1167.H35

1. **THE RETENTION BOOK: RETENTION AND PRESERVATION OF RECORDS WITH DESTRUCTION SCHEDULES**
2. Ciura, Jean M. & M. T. Payne
3. Record Controls
4. 1984
5. 1 vol.
6. $75
7. periodic supp.
8. new ed. in 1992
9. 11069159/HF5547.15.R47

1. **RETIREMENT AND BENEFIT PLANNING: STRATEGY AND DESIGN FOR BUSINESSES AND TAX-EXEMPT ORGANIZATIONS**
2. Goodman, Randolph M.
3. Butterworth-NH
4. 1991
5. 1 vol.
6. $95
7. periodic supp.
8. no supp. yet
9. 90-21453/22708072/KF3509.G66

1. **REVOCABLE TRUSTS, 2/e**
2. Turner, George M.
3. Shepard's
4. 1991
5. 1 vol.
6. $95
7. annual supp.
8. no supp. yet
9. 91-7703/23143759/KF734.T87

1. **RHODE ISLAND APPELLATE PRACTICE**
2. Weisberger, Hon. Joseph R.
3. Butterworth-NH
4. 1985
5. 1 vol.
6. $50
7. periodic supp.
8. 1989 - $22.50; 1991 - $25
9. 12300907/KFR558.W44

1. **RHODE ISLAND CRIMINAL PROCEDURE**
2. MacFadyen, John P. and Barbara Hurst
3. Butterworth-NH
4. 1988
5. 1 vol.
6. $125
7. periodic supp.
8. 1989 - $95; 1991 - $40
9. 17933596/KFR575.M32X

1. **RHODE ISLAND RULES OF EVIDENCE**
2. Green, Eric D.
3. Butterworth-NH
4. 1990
5. 1 vol.
6. $85
7. periodic supp.
8. no supp. yet
9. 90-30203/20997228/KFR540.A44G74

1. **RHODE ISLAND SUPREME COURT AND THE LAW OF CRIMES**
2. Pollock, Bruce G.
3. Butterworth-NH
4. 1990
5. 1 vol.
6. $60
7. periodic supp.
8. 1990 - $45; 1991 - $30

9. 10080887/KFR561.A53P6

1. **RICO – RACKETEER INFLUENCED CORRUPT ORGANIZATION**
2. McCormack, David
3. Knowles
4. 1986
5. 2 vols.
6. $185 incl. 3 mos. supp.
7. periodic supp.
8. 1990 - $52; 1991 - $62
9. 89-206656/20894300/KF9375.M35

1. **RICO BUSINESS DISPUTES GUIDE**
2. -
3. CCH
4. 1985
5. 1 vol.
6. $385/yr.; $350/yr. for 2 yrs.
7. monthly supp.
9. 12868400/KF9375.A6R5

1. **RICO – CIVIL AND CRIMINAL, LAW AND STRATEGY**
2. Rakoff, Jed
3. Law Journal
4. 1989
5. 1 vol.
6. $85
7. periodic supp.
9. 89-12394/19920567/KF9375.R5

1. **RICO IN BUSINESS AND COMMERCIAL LITIGATION**
2. Roddy, Kevin P.
3. Shepard's
4. 1991
5. 2 vols.
6. $160
7. annual supp.
8. 1991 - $33
9. 91-8583/23139315/KF9375.R63

1. **RICO LITIGATION**
2. -
3. Indiana CLE
4. 1989
5. 1 vol.
6. $60
7. no supp. planned

1. **RIGHT TO KNOW COMPLIANCE MANUAL**
2. -
3. Keller
4. 1988
5. 1 vol.
6. $75
7. semiannual supp.
8. $60/yr.
9. 88-80010/18589287/KF3570.R54

1. **RIGHT-TO KNOW PLANNING GUIDE**
2. Joseph, Eileen Z.
3. BNA
4. 1987
5. 1 vol.
6. $475/yr.
7. biweekly supp. & biweekly newsletter "Right to know Planning Report"
8. renewal - $425/yr.
9. 17247468/KF5753.A6R5

1. **RIGHTS AND LIABILITIES OF PUBLISHERS, BROADCASTERS AND REPORTERS**
2. Metcalf, Slade R. and Robin Bierstedt
3. Shepard's
4. 1989
5. 2 vols.6.
   $195
7. annual supp.
8. 1989 - $43; 1990 - $56
9. 82-16839/8785235/KF2750.M47

1. **RIGHTS AND REMEDIES OF CONFLICTING MINERAL AND PROPERTY OWNERS**
2. -
3. EMLF
4. 1987
5. 1 vol.
6. $18-members, $23-nonmembers
7. no supp. planned

1. **RIGHTS OF ACCESS AND SURFACE USE**
2. -
3. Rocky Mt.
4. 1984
5. 1 vol.
6. $80
7. no supp. planned
9. 11926312/KF5508.A75I5

1. **RIGHTS OF JUVENILES: THE JUVENILE JUSTICE SYSTEM**
2. Davis, Samuel M.
3. Clark Boardman Callaghan
4. 2nd ed. - 1980

5. 1 vol.
6. $110 incl. 3 mos. supp.
7. annual supp.
8. 1989 - $49.50; 1991 - $65
9. 80-12465/6143266/KF9794.D38

1. **THE RIGHTS OF PUBLICITY AND PRIVACY**
2. McCarthy, Thomas
3. Clark Boardman Callaghan
4. 1987
5. 1 vol.
6. $115 incl. 3 mos. supp.
7. annual supp.
8. 1989 - $57.50; 1991 - $105
9. 86-21543/14164902/KF1262.M4

1. **RIGHTS OF WAY, EASEMENTS AND SURFACE DAMAGES MANUAL**
2. -
3. EMLF
4. 1985
5. 1 vol.
6. $25-nonmembers; $20-members
7. no supp. planned

1. **THE RISK BUSINESS: INSURANCE CONTRACTS, COVERAGES, AND CARRIERS**
2. -
3. MILE
4. 1988
5. 1 vol.
6. $58
7. no supp. planned

1. **RISK FINANCING**
2. -
3. Intl. Risk Mgmt. Inst.
4. 1987
5. 2 vols.
6. $199 incl. 1 yr. supp. & newsletter
7. quarterly supp.
9. 21310283/HG8054.5.R5

1. **RISK MANAGEMENT AND INSURANCE AUDIT TECHNIQUES**
2. Levick, Dwight E.
3. John Liner Org.
4. 1988
5. 1 vol.
6. $137/yr.
7. semiannual supp.
8. renewal - $85/yr.
9. 20533648/KF1164.L482

1. **ROYALTY VALUATION AND MANAGEMENT**
2. -
3. Rocky Mt.
4. 1988
5. 1 vol.
6. $125
7. no supp. planned

1. **THE RTC RESOURCE BOOK**
2. Sullivan, Steve
3. Land Dev.
4. 1991
5. 2 vols.
6. $495/yr.
7. quarterly supp.

1. **THE RULES: A RULES SERVICE FOR MASSACHUSETTS**
2. -
3. Lawyers Weekly
4. 1978
5. 1 vol.
6. $48
7. bimonthly supp.
8. renewal - $38/yr.
9. 8290595/KFM2929.A2R935P451

1. **RULES AND REGULATIONS**
2. U.S. Federal Communications Commission
3. order from USGPO
4. 5 vols. covering various parts - avail. separately priced from $11 - $20 incl. supp.

1. **RULES AND REGULATIONS: TITLE 10, CHAPTER 1, CODE OF FEDERAL REGULATIONS**
2. U.S. Nuclear Regulatory Commission
3. order from USGPO - stock #952-003-00000-3
4. 1989
5. 1 vol.
6. $261/yr.
7. periodic supp.

1. **RULES AND REGULATIONS AND STATEMENTS OF PROCEDURE**
2. U.S. National Labor Relations Board
3. order from USGPO - stock #931-002-00000-7

4. 1987
5. 1 vol.
6. $13/yr.
7. periodic supp.
9. 7031480/KF3372.A6U5x

1. **RULES AND REGULATIONS OF THE CHICAGO BOARD OF TRADE**
2. -
3. Chicago Bd.
4. NA
5. 1 vol.
6. $52
7. monthly supp.
8. $200/yr.

1. **RULES AND REGULATIONS OF THE CHICAGO MERCANTILE EXCHANGE**
2. -
3. CME
4. NA
5. 1 vol.
6. $60
7. periodic supp.
8. renewal - $50/yr.

1. **RULES AND REGULATIONS OF THE LOUISIANA OIL CONSERVATION COMMISSION**
2. -
3. Byram
4. NA
5. 26 vols.
6. $800/yr.
7. monthly supp.
8. renewal - $525/yr.

1. **RULES AND REGULATIONS OF THE MINNEAPOLIS GRAIN EXCHANGE**
2. -
3. Minneap.
4. 1981
5. 1 vol.
6. $25 incl. supp.
7. periodic supp.

1. **RULES AND REGULATIONS OF THE NEW MEXICO OIL CONSERVATION DIVISION**
2. -
3. Byram
4. NA
5. 3 vols.
6. $250/yr.
7. monthly supp.
8. renewal - $200/yr.

1. **RULES AND REGULATIONS OF THE TEXAS RAILROAD COMMISSION**
2. -
3. Byram
4. NA
5. 14 vols.
6. $600/yr.
7. monthly supp.
8. renewal - $400/yr.

1. **RULES OF COURT**
2. -
3. Metropolitan News
4. 1990
5. 1 vol. (avail. for specific counties in California & Federal edition)
6. $35 - $50
7. supp. as needed

1. **RULES OF CRIMINAL PROCEDURE**
2. Cipes, Robert M.
3. Bender
4. 1965
5. 4 vols. (also vols. 8, 8A & 8B Moore's Federal Practice)
6. $555 incl. 3 mos. supp.
7. semiannual supp.
8. 1989 - $424; 1990 - $528
9. 8789790/KF8820.A313M63

1. **RULES OF PRACTICE IN PATENT AND TRADEMARK CASES**
2. -
3. Rules
4. 1978
5. 1 vol.
6. $45 incl. 1 yr. supp.
7. periodic supp.
8. renewal fee
9. 4621291/KF3120.A6R8x

1. **RULES OF THE U.S. COURTS IN NEW YORK**
2. -
3. Clark Boardman Callaghan
4. 2nd ed. - 1978
5. 1 vol.
6. $105 incl. 3 mos. supp.
7. annual supp.
8. 1989 - $47.50; 1991 - $52.50
9. 65-16452/3006728/KF8816.A2

1. **THE S CORPORATION: PLANNING AND OPERATION**
2. Traum, Sydney S.
3. Panel
4. 1983
5. 1 vol.
6. $175 incl. 1 yr. supp.
7. quarterly supp.
9. 83-8303/9557700/KF6491.S36

1. **THE "S" CORPORATION HANDBOOK**
2. Nicholas, Ted
3. Enterprise
4. rev. ed. - 1991
5. 1 vol.
6. $69.95
7. no supp. yet

1. **S CORPORATION TAX GUIDE 1992**
2. Jamison, Robert
3. HBJ Miller
4. 1991
5. 1 vol.
6. $75
7. no supp. planned

1. **S CORPORATION TAX PRACTICE MANUAL**
2. Fox, Ira
3. Panel
4. 1989
5. 1 vol.
6. $99 incl. 1 yr. supp.
7. semiannual supp.
9. 89-26628/KF6491.F68

1. **S CORPORATIONS**
2. -
3. Illinois ICLE
4. 1987
5. 1 vol.
6. $76.95
7. periodic supp.
8. 1989 - $19.95

1. **S CORPORATIONS**
2. Wood, Robert W.
3. WG&L
4. rev. - 1990
5. 1 vol.
6. $350/yr.
7. monthly supp.
9. 83-9219/9549558

1. **S CORPORATIONS: FEDERAL TAXATION**
2. Blau, Richard D. et al.
3. Clark Boardman Callaghan
4. 1989
5. 1 vol.
6. $130 incl. 6 mos. supp.
7. semiannual supp.
8. 1990 - $40
9. 89-25132/20489534/KF6491.B56

1. **S CORPORATIONS: STATE LAW AND TAXATION**
2. Maule, James E.
3. Clark Boardman Callaghan
4. 1989
5. 2 vols.
6. $230 incl. 1 yr. supp.
7. quarterly supp.
8. no supp. yet
9. 89-664/19221933/KF6755.M33

1. **S CORPORATIONS GUIDE**
2. -
3. CCH
4. 1983
5. 1 vol.
6. $415/yr.; $375/yr. for 2 yrs.
7. monthly supp.
9. 12575441/KF6491.A6F6

1. **S CORPORATIONS 1991**
2. Abramson, David M. et al.
3. MICPEL
4. 1991
5. 1 vol.
6. $42
7. no supp. planned

1. **SALE OF A BUSINESS IN MINNESOTA**
2. Gaffaney, George
3. Butterworth-St. Paul
4. 1990
5. 1 vol.
6. $88
7. periodic supp.
8. no supp. yet
9. 90-30825//r91/21043038/KFM5605.G34

1. **SALES AND BULK TRANSFERS UNDER THE UNIFORM COMMERCIAL CODE (Bender's Uniform Commercial Code Service, Vols. 3 & 3A)**
2. Duesenberg, R.W. & L.P. King
3. Bender
4. 1980
5. 2 vols.

6. $230 incl. 3 mos. supp.
7. annual supp.
8. 1989 - $146; 1990 - $180
9. 65-6386

1. **SALES & USE TAX**
2. -
3. RIA
4. 1925
5. 15 vols.
6. $1025/yr.; $975/yr. for 2 yrs.
7. weekly supp.
8. renewal - $950/yr.

1. **SAMPLE ANTITRUST COMPLIANCE PLANS**
2. Hancock, W.A., ed.
3. Bus. Laws
4. 1989
5. 1 vol.
6. $85
7. annual supp.
8. renewal - $38/yr.
9. 17973599

1. **SANCTIONS IN FEDERAL LITIGATION**
2. Solovy, Jerold S. & Laura A. Kaster
3. Butterworth-NH
4. 1991
5. 1 vol.
6. $95
7. periodic supp.
8. no supp. yet
9. 91-6313/23048496/KF8887.S25

1. **SAVINGS INSTITUTIONS: MERGERS, ACQUISITIONS AND CONVERSIONS**
2. Williams, Julie L.
3. Law Journal
4. 1988
5. 1 vol.
6. $90
7. periodic supp.
8. 1989 - $73; 1990 - $92
9. 88-9387/18049800/KF1004.W55

1. **SCHEDULE B COMMODITY CLASSIFICATION AND HARMONIZED SYNOPSIS**
2. -
3. Unz & Co.
4. 1991
5. 1 vol.
6. $275/yr.
7. periodic supp.

1. **SCHROEDER-KATZ, OHIO CRIMINAL LAW AND PRACTICE**
2. Schroeder, Oliver C. & Lewis R. Katz
3. Banks
4. 1974
5. 2 vols.
6. $220 incl. 9 mos. supp.
7. annual supp.
8. 1990 - $75
9. 74-186371/1094427/KFO561.A6S3

1. **SCIENTIFIC AUTOMOBILE ACCIDENT RECONSTRUCTION**
2. Lacy, George W. et al.
3. Bender
4. 1964
5. 6 vols.
6. $500 incl. 3 mos. supp.
7. annual supp.
8. 1989 - $322; 1990 - $376.50
9. 65-1464/10645018

1. **SCOTT ON COMPUTER LAW**
2. Scott, Michael D.
3. Prentice Hall Law & Business
4. 1991
5. 2 vols.
6. $195 incl. 4 mos. supp.
7. periodic supp.
8. no supp. yet
9. 91-31625/24376354/KF390.5.C6538

1. **THE SEARCH AND SEIZURE MANUAL**
2. Reid, Robert et al.
3. OCDLA
4. 1989
5. 1 vol.
6. $125 - nonmembers; $89 - members
7. periodic supp.
8. 1991 supp.

1. **SEARCH WARRANT LAW DESKBOOK**
2. Burkoff, John M.
3. Clark Boardman Callaghan
4. 1987
5. 1 vol.
6. $85 incl. 3 mos. supp.
7. annual supp.
8. 1989 - $70; 1991 - $79
9. 86-26336/14356015/KF9630.B87

1. **SEARCHES & SEIZURES, ARRESTS AND CONFESSIONS**
2. Ringel, William E.

3. Clark Boardman Callaghan
4. 2nd ed. - 1979
5. 3 vols.
6. $295 incl. 3 mos. supp.
7. annual supp.
8. 1989 - $174.50; 1991 - $210
9. 79-22482/5564134/KF9625.R53

1. **SEATTLE ZONING CODE**
2. -
3. Book Pub.
4. rev. - 1984
5. 2 vols.
6. $95
7. quarterly supp.
8. 1989 - $38; 1990 - $110

1. **SEC ACCOUNTING AND REPORTING MANUAL**
2. Badecker, Wm. J. & R.F. Harnek
3. WG&L
4. 1983
5. 1 vol.
6. $295/yr.
7. 3 supp./yr.
8. renewal - $245/yr.
9. 83-60093/10044052/KF1446.B3

1. **SEC ACCOUNTING RULES**
2. -
3. CCH
4. 1968
5. 1 vol.
6. $280/yr.; $255/yr. for 2 yrs.
7. periodic supp.
9. 71-25/37755/KF1446.A6U5

1. **SEC COMPLIANCE - FINANCIAL REPORTING AND FORMS**
2. Walker, Schechtman
3. WG&L
4. 1979
5. 5 vols.
6. $815/yr.
7. monthly supp.
9. 75-39827/2072498/KF1446.A6W4

1. **SEC FINANCIAL REPORTING - ANNUAL REPORTS TO SHAREHOLDERS - FORM 10-K, QUARTERLY FINANCIAL REPORTING, 2ND ED.**
2. Beresford, Dennis R. et al.
3. Bender
4. 2nd ed. - 1983
5. 1 vol.
6. $115 incl. 3 mos. supp.
7. annual supp.
8. 1989 - $70; 1990 - $84.50
9. 83-195088/10123156/KF1446.B47

1. **SEC NO-ACTION LETTERS INDEX & SUMMARIES**
2. -
3. WSB
4. 1971
5. 2 vols. (1971-1987 vols. avail. - $1975)
6. $1145/yr.
7. weekly and monthly supp.

1. **SECONDARY MORTGAGE MARKET GUIDE**
2. Edson, Charles L. & Barry Jacobs
3. Bender
4. 1985
5. 1 vol.
6. $105 incl. 3 mos. supp.
7. periodic supp.
8. 1989 - $72; 1990 - $86.50
9. 84-73156/12216790/KF697.S43E37

1. **SECTION 89 COMPLIANCE MANUAL: THE COMPLETE GUIDE TO THE NEW NON-DISCRIMINATION RULES FOR EMPLOYEE BENEFIT PLANS**
2. -
3. BNA
4. 1988
5. 1 vol.
6. $250
7. no supp. planned
9. 88-37270/18909570/KF3509.S43

1. **SECTION 1983 LITIGATION**
2. -
3. Georgetown
4. 1990
5. 1 vol.
6. $75
7. no supp. planned

1. **SECTION 1983 LITIGATION IN STATE COURTS**
2. Steinglass, Steven H.
3. Clark Boardman Callaghan
4. 1987
5. 1 vol.
6. $105 incl. 3 mos. supp.
7. annual supp.
8. 1989 - $94.50; 1991 - $104.50
9. 87-15496/16092165/KF1325.C58S74

1. **SECTION 16 OF THE SECURITIES EXCHANGE ACT**
2. Jacobs, Arnold S.
3. Clark Boardman Callaghan
4. 1989
5. 1 vol.
6. $125 incl. 3 mos. supp.
7. annual supp.
8. 1991 - $59.59
9. 89-7148//r90/19518701/KF1073.I5J3

1. **SECTION 16 TREATISE AND SERVICE**
2. Romeo, Peter, ed.
3. Exec. Press
4. 1990
5. 1 vol.
6. $390/yr.
7. quarterly supp.
8. renewal - $195/yr.

1. **SECURED LENDING & SECURED FINANCING**
2. -
3. Indiana CLE
4. 1990
5. 1 vol.
6. $55
7. no supp. planned

1. **SECURED TRANSACTIONS**
2. -
3. Illinois ICLE
4. 1990
5. 1 vol.
6. $99.95
7. periodic supp.
8. no supp. yet

1. **SECURED TRANSACTIONS GUIDE**
2. -
3. CCH
4. 1969
5. 5 vols.
6. $775/yr.; $705/yr. for 2 yrs.
7. semimonthly supp.
9. 71-4059/6962112/KF1048.4.C6

1. **SECURED TRANSACTIONS UNDER THE REVISED UNIFORM COMMERCIAL CODE**
2. Dreier, Hon. Wm. A., et al.
3. New Jersey ICLE
4. 3rd ed. - 1989
5. 1 vol.
6. $65
7. no supp. planned
9. 21924605/KFN1975.D73

1. **SECURED TRANSACTIONS UNDER THE UNIFORM COMMERCIAL CODE (Bender's Uniform Commerical Code Service, Vols. 1, 1A, 1B & 1C)**
2. Coogan, Peter F. et al.
3. Bender
4. 1963
5. 5 vols.
6. $520 incl. 3 mos. supp.
7. semiannual supp.
8. 1989 - $340; 1990 - $398.50
9. 64-502/1433426

1. **SECURITIES: PUBLIC & PRIVATE OFFERINGS**
2. Prifti, Wm. M.
3. Clark Boardman Callaghan
4. 1983
5. 1 vol.
6. $98 incl. 6 mos. supp.
7. annual supp.
8. 1989 - $55; 1990 - $55
9. 82-24495/913952/KF1439.P73

1. **SECURITIES AND COMMERCIAL LITIGATION**
2. -
3. MILE
4. 1990
5. 1 vol.
6. $58
7. no supp. planned

1. **SECURITIES AND FEDERAL CORPORATE LAW (Securities Law Series, Vols. 3, 3A, 3B & 3C)**
2. Bloomenthal, Harold S.
3. Clark Boardman Callaghan
4. 1972
5. 5 vols. & newsletter binder
6. $595 incl. 3 mos. supp.
7. biannual supp. & monthly newsletter & annual handbook
8. 1989 - $295; 1991 - $352.50
9. 72-90956/2656235/KF1439.B54

1. **SECURITIES AND PARTNERSHIP LAW FOR MLPs AND OTHER INVESTMENT LIMITED PARTNERSHIPS (Securities Law Series, Vol. 14)**
2. Wertheimer, Linda A.
3. Clark Boardman Callaghan
4. 1987

5. 1 vol.
6. $115 incl. 3 mos. supp.
7. annual supp.
8. 1989 - $52.50; 1991 - $57.50
9. 87-25067/16717825/KF1659.W47

1. **SECURITIES ARBITRATION: PRACTICE AND FORMS**
2. Djinis, Anthony & Joseph A. Post
3. Bender
4. 1991
5. 1 vol.
6. $100 incl. 3 mos. supp.
7. annual supp.
8. no supp. yet

1. **SECURITIES ARBITRATION PROCEDURE MANUAL**
2. Robbins, David E.
3. Butterworth-NH
4. 1990
5. 1 vol.
6. $125
7. annual supp.
8. no supp. yet
9. 89-23997/20420020/KF9085.R6

1. **SECURITIES CREDIT TRANSACTIONS HANDBOOK**
2. -
3. Fed.
4. 1981
5. 1 vol.
6. $75/yr.
7. monthly supp.
9. 7830217/HG2560.S422

1. **SECURITIES FRAUD: LITIGATING UNDER RULE 10B-5**
2. Patton, Thomas Earl, & Terry Rose Saunders
3. Aspen
4. 1989
5. 1 vol.
6. $99 incl. 3 mos. supp.
7. annual supp.
8. $79-$95/supp.
9. 89-17897/20320339/KF9369.P38

1. **SECURITIES FRAUD AND COMMODITIES FRAUD**
2. Bromberg, Alan R. & Lewis D. Lowenfels
3. Shepard's
4. 1980
5. 7 vols.
6. $490
7. annual supp.
8. 1989 - $146; 1990 - $157
9. 67-23473//r917/8101604/KF1070.B76

1. **SECURITIES LAW**
2. -
3. Illinois ICLE
4. 1991
5. 2 vols.
6. $131.95
7. periodic supp.
8. no supp. yet

1. **SECURITIES LAW TECHNIQUES**
2. Sommer, A. A. Jr.
3. Bender
4. 1985
5. 5 vols.
6. $545 incl. 3 mos. supp.
7. periodic supp.
8. 1989 - $353; 1990 - $404.50
9. 84-73249/12937178

1. **SECURITIES LITIGATION: DAMAGES**
2. Kaufman, Michael J.
3. Clark Boardman Callaghan
4. 1989
5. 1 vol.
6. $100 incl. 6 mos. supp.
7. annual supp.
8. 1990 - $35
9. 89-15789/19922784/KF1439.K38

1. **SECURITIES LITIGATION: FORMS & ANALYSIS**
2. Richter, Scott of Popham, Haik, Schnobrich & Kaufman
3. Clark Boardman Callaghan
4. 1989
5. 2 vols.
6. $190 incl. 6 mos supp.
7. annual supp.
8. no supp. yet
9. 89-71217/20826968/KF1437.R35

1. **SECURITIES PRACTICE: FEDERAL AND STATE ENFORCEMENT**
2. Steinberg, Marc I. & Ralph C. Ferrara
3. Clark Boardman Callaghan
4. 1986
5. 2 vols.
6. $190 incl. 6 mos. supp.
7. annual supp.
8. 1989 - $49.50; 1990 - $56
9. 85-25526/12752383/KF9369.S74

1. **SECURITIES REGULATION**
2. -
3. WG&L
4. 1935
5. 5 vols.
6. $843/yr.
7. biweekly supp.
9. 33-19943

1. **SECURITIES REGULATION: LIABILITIES AND REMEDIES**
2. Steinberg, Marc I.
3. Law Journal
4. 1984
5. 1 vol.
6. $80 incl. 3 mos. supp.
7. periodic supp.
8. 1989 - $84; 1990 - $84
9. 83-26840/10300138/KF1439.S737

1. **SECURITIES REGULATION FORMS**
2. Rice, Dennis T. and Charles P. Ortmeyer
3. Clark Boardman Callaghan
4. 1988
5. 2 vols.
6. $215 incl. 3 mos. supp.
7. annual supp.
8. $1989 - $92.50; 1991 - $100
9. 88-17561/18052194/KF1437.R53

1. **SECURITIES TRANSFER GUIDE**
2. -
3. CCH
4. NA
5. 3 vols.
6. $605/yr.; $550/2 yrs.
7. monthly supp.
9. 72-5091/15377/KF1448.C62

1. **SELLERS' & SERVICERS' GUIDE**
2. -
3. Freddie Mac
4. 1984
5. 2 vols.
6. $275/yr.
7. quarterly supp.

1. **SELLING GUIDE**
2. -
3. FNMA
4. 1983
5. 1 vol.
6. $300 incl. 2 yr. supp.
7. supp. as needed
8. biennial revisions

1. **SEMICONDUCTOR CHIP PROTECTION**
2. Stern, Richard H.
3. Prentice Hall Law & Business
4. 1986
5. 1 vol.
6. $75 incl. 4 mos. supp.
7. periodic supp.
8. no supp. yet
9. 86-7141/13358629/KF3065.S74

1. **SENTENCING DEFENSE MANUAL–ADVOCACY/PRACTICE/PROCEDURE**
2. Shein, Marcia G.
3. Clark Boardman Callaghan
4. 1988
5. 1 vol.
6. $110 incl. 3 mos. supp.
7. annual supp.
8. 1989 - $45; 1991 - $75
9. 88-14474/17875289/KF9685.S53

1. **SENTENCING IN WASHINGTON**
2. Boerner, David
3. Butterworth-St. Paul
4. 1985
5. 1 vol.
6. $120
7. periodic supp.
8. new ed. due in 1991
9. 84-72824/12582069/KFW583.2.B64

1. **SENTENCING MANUAL FOR JUDGES**
2. Office of the Courts, Criminal Practice Div.
3. New Jersey ICLE
4. 1988
5. 1 vol.
6. $87
7. periodic supp.
8. 1989 supp.
9. 19119230/KFN2383.2S46

1. **SEPARATION AGREEMENTS AND ANTENUPTIAL CONTRACTS**
2. Lindey, Alexander
3. Bender
4. 2nd ed. - 1964
5. 3 vols.
6. $380 incl. 3 mos. supp.
7. biannual supp.
8. 1989 - $258; 1990 - $305.50
9. 54-2/1541906

1. **SERVICING GUIDE**
2. -

3. FNMA
4. 1983
5. 1 vol.
6. $300 incl. 2 yr. supp.
7. supp. as needed
8. biennial revisions

1. **SETTLEMENT (Art of Advocacy Series)**
2. Miller, Henry G.
3. Bender
4. 1983
5. 1 vol.
6. $110 incl. 3 mos. supp.
7. periodic supp.
8. 1989 - $64; 1990 - $74.50
9. 9588116/KF9084.M5

1. **SEX-BASED DISCRIMINATION: INTERNATIONAL LAW AND ORGANIZATION**
2. Taubenfeld, Howard J. & Rita F. Taubenfeld
3. Oceana
4. 1978
5. 4 vols.
6. $340/set
7. periodic supp.
9. 78-14809/4135377/K644.A56S48

1. **SEX-BASED EMPLOYMENT DISCRIMINATION**
2. Omillian, Susan & Jean Kamp
3. Clark Boardman Callaghan
4. 1990
5. 1 vol.
6. $95 incl. 6 mos. supp.
7. annual supp.
8. no supp. yet
9. 90-21673/22663531/KF3467.O48

1. **THE SEXUAL ABUSE OF CHILDREN**
2. -
3. MILE
4. 1988
5. 1 vol.
6. $58
7. no supp. planned

1. **SEXUAL ORIENTATION AND THE LAW**
2. National Lawyers Guild
3. Clark Boardman Callaghan
4. 1985
5. 1 vol.
6. $110 incl. 3 mos. supp.
7. annual supp.
8. 1989 - $47.50; 1991 - $59.50
9. 84-24213/11316836/KF4754.5.S49

1. **SHAREHOLDER DERIVATIVE ACTIONS**
2. DeMott, Deborah A.
3. Clark Boardman Callaghan
4. 1987
5. 1 vol.
6. $100 incl. 6 mos. supp.
7. annual supp.
8. 1989 - $39; 1990 - $41
9. 86-31029/14905998/KF1448.D46

1. **SHAREHOLDER LITIGATION**
2. Magnuson, Roger J.
3. Clark Boardman Callaghan
4. 1981
5. 3 vols.
6. $265 incl. 6 mos. supp.
7. annual supp.
8. 1989 - $71; 1990 - $112.50
9. 81-6078/7464567/KF8925.S7M33

1. **SHARK REPELLENTS AND GOLDEN PARACHUTES: A HANDBOOK FOR THE PRACTITIONER**
2. Winter, Robert H., et al.
3. Prentice Hall Law & Business
4. 1983
5. 4 vols.
6. $295 incl. 4 mos. supp.
7. periodic supp.
8. 1990 - $85; 1991 - $75
9. 83-13573/9686826/KF1477.S5

1. **SHEPARD'S FEDERAL SECURITIES LAW CITATIONS**
2. -
3. CCH
4. 1991
5. 1 vol.
6. $360/yr.; $325/yr. for 2 yrs.
7. quarterly supp.
9. 90-24449/22860423/KF1435.5.S48

1. **SHIPPING REGULATION**
2. Willis, John W. & David Fialkoff
3. P&F
4. 1961
5. 31 vols.
6. $1980 incl. 7 vols. & 1 yr. supp. (24 back vols. avail. at $55/vol.)
7. biweekly supp.
8. renewal - $1650/yr.; $3050/2 yrs.
9. 61-31808/5105606

1. **SHOPPING CENTER AND STORE LEASES**
2. Halper, Emanuel B.
3. Law Journal
4. 1979
5. 2 vols.
6. $140
7. annual supp.
8. 1989 - $80; 1990 - $42
9. 78-17330/4003882/KF593.C6H3

1. **SHOPPING CENTER LEASES**
2. Garfinkel, Marvin, et al.
3. New Jersey ICLE
4. 1989
5. 1 vol.
6. $40
7. no supp. planned
9. 20820836/KFN1919.3Z9S56

1. **THE SHOULDER AND ELBOW (Courtroom Medicine Series, Vols. 5 & 5A)**
2. Kalisch, Jules et al.
3. Bender
4. 1971
5. 2 vols.
6. $245 incl. 3 mos. supp.
7. annual supp.
8. 1989 - $120; 1990 - $168.50
9. 79-142077/131240/RA1011.C68

1. **SIGNIFICANT SEC FILINGS REPORTER**
2. -
3. WSB
4. 1980
5. 2 vols.
6. $900/yr.
7. monthly supp.

1. **SIMPLE ESTATE PLANNING**
2. -
3. Okla. Bar CLE
4. 1990
5. 1 vol.
6. $40
7. no supp. planned

1. **SIMPLIFIED CONSUMER CREDIT FORMS**
2. Felsenfeld, Carl & Alan Siegel
3. WG&L
4. 1978
5. 1 vol.
6. $88
7. semiannual supp.
8. 1987 - $53.50
9. 78-50301/4078463/KF1040.A3F46

1. **SINGLE AUDIT GUIDE 1992**
2. Harrell, Rhett
3. HBJ Miller
4. 1991
5. 1 vol.
6. $75
7. no supp. planned

1. **SINGLE AUDIT INFORMATION SERVICE**
2. Lamomeaux, Denise
3. Thompson
4. 1985
5. 2 vols.
6. $249/yr.
7. monthly supp.
8. renewal-$221/yr.
9. 12092787/HJ199.S6

1. **SINGLE EUROPEAN MARKET REPORTER**
2. Baker & McKenzie
3. Kluwer
4. 1991
5. 1 vol.
6. $184 incl. 3 mos. supp.
7. periodic supp.

1. **THE SKIN (Courtroom Medicine Series, Vols. 6, 6A & 6B)**
2. Whitmore, Charles W. et al.
3. Bender
4. 1971
5. 3 vols.
6. $380 incl. 3 mos. supp.
7. annual supp.
8. 1989 - $195; 1990 - $257.50
9. 72-142078/149838/RA1011.C68

1. **SLIP AND FALL PRACTICE**
2. Turnbow, Charles E.
3. James
4. 1988
5. 1 vol.
6. $79.99 incl. 3 mos. supp.
7. annual supp.
8. 1990 - $38.90
9. 18662077/KF8925.N4T87

1. **SMALL BUSINESS TAX CONTROL**
2. Witner, Larry H., ed.
3. Corporate Reports
4. 1979
5. 1 vol.
6. $96/yr.

7. monthly supp.

1. **SMALL BUSINESS TAX PLANNER**
2. RIA prof. ed. staff
3. RIA
4. 1983
5. 2 vols.
6. $215/yr.; $200/yr. for 2 yrs.
7. monthly supp.
8. renewal - $185/yr.

1. **SOCIAL SECURITY DISABILITY CLAIMS**
2. Francis, Robert E.
3. Clark Boardman Callaghan
4. 1983
5. 2 vols.
6. $165 incl. 6 mos. supp.
7. annual supp.
8. 1989 - $50; 1990 - $53
9. 82-24286/9083716/KF3649.F7

1. **SOCIAL SECURITY DISABILITY CLAIMS**
2. Gilbert, Ronald R. & J.D. Peters
3. Clark Boardman Callaghan
4. 1983
5. 2 vols.
6. $179 incl. 3 mos. supp.
7. annual supp.
8. 1991 - $59
9. 82-84688/9571847/KF3649.G54

1. **SOCIAL SECURITY DISABILITY PRACTICE**
2. Forrester, Kenneth J.
3. James
4. 1985
5. 1 vol.
6. $49.98 incl. 3 mos. supp.
7. annual supp.
8. 1990 - $41.97
9. 85-205579/12840721/KF3649.F66

1. **SOCIAL SECURITY LAW AND PRACTICE**
2. Publ. Editorial Staff
3. Clark Boardman Callaghan
4. 1987
5. 9 vols.
6. $931.50 incl. 1 yr. supp.
7. quarterly supp. & newsletter 8x/yr.
8. 1991 - $365
9. 86-82947/18742252/KF3646.5.S63

1. **SOCIAL SECURITY PRACTICE GUIDE**
2. National Organization of Social Security Claimants' Representatives
3. Bender
4. 1984
5. 4 vols.
6. $450 incl. 3 mos. supp.
7. periodic supp.
8. 1989 - $229; 1990 - $285.50
9. 83-73412/10587769/KF3649.S63

1. **SOFT-TISSUE INJURY**
2. -
3. MILE
4. 1990
5. 1 vol.
6. $63
7. no supp. planned

1. **THE SOFTWARE LEGAL BOOK**
2. Hoffman, Paul S.
3. Shafer
4. 1981; rev. - 1992
5. 2 vols. - 1 vol. looseleaf & 1 looseleaf forms vol.
6. $180 incl. 3 mos. supp.
7. annual supp.
8. 1990 - $84.50; 1991 - $86.50
9. 85-129108/10704251/KF905.C6H63

1. **SOURCES OF COMPILED LEGISLATIVE HISTORIES: BIBLIOGRAPHY OF GOVERNMENT DOCUMENTS, PERIODICAL ARTICLES AND BOOKS, 1ST CONGRESS-99TH CONGRESS**
2. Johnson, Nancy P., comp.
3. Rothman
4. 1979
5. 1 vol.
6. $35
7. periodic supp.
8. 1988 - $17.50
9. 79-51869/5158039/KF42.2

1. **SOURCES OF PROOF IN PREPARING A LAWSUIT - STATE AND FEDERAL**
2. Moenssens, Andre, ed.
3. Jt. Comm. Va.
4. 1991
5. 1 vol.
6. $62
7. periodic supp.
8. 1985 - $20
9. 8301386/KFV2940.S6

1. **SOUTH CAROLINA ADMINISTRATIVE LAW – 2nd Ed.**
2. Shipley, David E.

3. S. Carolina Bar
4. 2nd ed. - 1988
5. 1 vol.
6. $75
7. -
8. no supp. planned
9. 19904162/KFS2240.S35

1. **THE SOUTH CAROLINA BENCH BOOK FOR MAGISTRATES AND MUNICIPAL COURT JUDGES**
2. -
3. S. Carolina Bar
4. 2nd ed. - 1990
5. 1 vol.
6. $90
7. periodic supp.
8. no supp. yet
9. 21566789/KFS2317.S68

1. **SOUTH CAROLINA CIVIL PROCEDURE**
2. Lightsey, Harry M. Jr. & James Flanagan
3. S. Carolina Bar
4. 1985
5. 1 vol.
6. $80
7. periodic supp.
8. 1988 - $25
9. 12322783

1. **SOUTH CAROLINA CONSUMER LAW AND PRACTICE - Vol. I - SOUTH CAROLINA CONSUMER LAW AND REGULATIONS**
2. Haynsworth, Harry J.
3. S. Carolina Bar
4. 1984
5. 1 vol.
6. $60
7. periodic supp.
8. no supp. yet
9. 18349009/KFS2030.C6

1. **SOUTH CAROLINA CONSUMER LAW AND PRACTICE - Vol. II - TRUTH IN LENDING AND RELATED DISCLOSURE STATUTES**
2. Burke, Lewis W.
3. S. Carolina Bar
4. 1985
5. 1 vol.
6. $60
7. periodic supp.
8. no supp. yet

1. **SOUTH CAROLINA CONSUMER PROTECTION CODE - 1982 TEXT AND COMMENTS – 2nd Ed.**
2. Haynsworth, Harry J.
3. S. Carolina Bar
4. 1990
5. 1 vol.
6. $85
7. periodic supp.
8. -

1. **SOUTH CAROLINA CORPORATE PRACTICE MANUAL**
2. Cleveland, Sherwood M., et al.
3. S. Carolina Bar
4. 1990
5. 2 vols.
6. $225
7. no supp. yet

1. **SOUTH CAROLINA CRIMINAL DEFENSE**
2. Thames, Jon P. et al.
3. S. Carolina Bar
4. 1988
5. 1 vol.
6. $65
7. no supp. yet
9. 18595135/KFS2375.T32

1. **THE SOUTH CAROLINA DUI DEFENSE MANUAL**
2. Cole, Ronnie M.
3. S. Carolina Bar
4. 3rd ed. - 1991
5. 1 vol.
6. price NA
7. no supp. yet
9. 17886083/KFS2097.8.C64

1. **SOUTH CAROLINA INCOME TAXATION**
2. Boyle, Ladson & John C. Von Lehe
3. S. Carolina Bar
4. 3rd. ed. - 1987
5. 1 vol.
6. $80
7. annual supp.
8. no supp. yet
9. 17335136/KFS2275.Z9B69

1. **THE SOUTH CAROLINA PROBATE PRACTICE MANUAL**
2. Moses, Albert L.

3. S. Carolina Bar
4. 1990
5. 1 vol.
6. $125
7. no supp. yet
9. 9598521/KFS1955.Z9M67

1. **SOUTH CAROLINA RADAR DEFENSE MANUAL**
2. Cole, Ronnie M. & Lewis T. Fitch
3. S. Carolina Bar
4. NA
5. 1 vol.
6. $20
7. no supp. planned
9. 18386916/J8987B8.R12

1. **SOUTH CAROLINA RECOMMENDED CIVIL JURY CHARGES**
2. Civil Jury Charge Comm. of the S. Carolina Bar
3. S. Carolina Bar
4. NA
5. 1 vol.
6. $50
7. no supp. yet
9. 20298822/KFS2342.6.S68

1. **SOUTH DAKOTA LEGAL RESEARCH GUIDE**
2. Jorgensen, Delores
3. Hein
4. 1988
5. 1 vol.
6. $27.50
7. periodic supp.
8. no supp. yet
9. 88-4757/17621441/KFS3075.J67

1. **SOUTH DAKOTA PATTERN JURY INSTRUCTIONS-CIVIL**
2. Committee on Pattern Jury Instructions
3. S.D. Bar
4. 1985
5. 1 vol.
6. $75
7. periodic supp.
8. $30/yr.
9. 4250649/KFS3583.S719

1. **SOUTH DAKOTA PATTERN JURY INSTRUCTIONS-CRIMINAL**
2. Committee on Pattern Jury Instructions
3. S.D. Bar
4. 1986
5. 1 vol.
6. $75
7. periodic supp.
8. $30/yr.
9. 13022909/KFS3542.A6S8

1. **SOUTHEAST LITIGATION GUIDE**
2. Colson, Bill et al.
3. Bender
4. 1981
5. 13 vols. projected; 12 currently avail.
6. $925 incl. 3 mos. supp.
7. periodic supp.
8. 1989 - $349; 1990 - $463
9. 81-65964/8174850/KF8840.S67

1. **SOUTHEAST TRANSACTION GUIDE**
2. Parber, Byron L. et al.
3. Bender
4. 1976
5. 20 vols.
6. $975 incl. 3 mos. supp.
7. annual supp.
8. 1989 - $884; 1990 - $776.50
9. 75-45844/2491984/KF1410.S68

1. **SOVIET BUSINESS LAW: INSTITUTIONS, PRINCIPLES AND PROCESSES**
2. Osakwe, Christopher
3. Butterworth-NH
4. 1991
5. 2 vols.
6. $180
7. periodic supp.
8. no supp. yet
9. 90-24741/22767609

1. **SOVIET TAXATION: STATUTES, REGULATIONS AND TREATIES**
2. Newcity, Michael
3. Transnational Juris Publications
4. 1991
5. 1 vol.
6. $185
7. no supp. yet

1. **SPECIAL INSTITUTE INDEX, 1970-1990**
2. -
3. Rocky Mt.
4. 1991
5. 1 vol.
6. $30

7. biennial supp.
9. 7533953

1. **SPECIAL ISSUES IN CRIMINAL LAW**
2. -
3. MICPEL
4. 1991
5. 1 vol.
6. $40
7. no supp. yet
9. 22104958/KFM1737.S74

1. **SPECIALIZATION HANDBOOK**
2. Standing Comm. on Specialization
3. ABA
4. 1990
5. 1 vol.
6. $25
7. no supp. yet

1. **SPECIALIZED LEGAL RESEARCH**
2. Chanin, Leah F., ed.
3. Little, Brown
4. 1987
5. 1 vol.
6. $85
7. periodic supp.
8. 1989 - $15.50
9. 86-80068/1405511

1. **SPENCER'S COMPLIANCE GUIDE FOR HEALTH AND BENEFIT PLANS**
2. Huth, Stephen A. et al.
3. Spencer
4. 1988
5. 1 vol.
6. $420/yr.
7. monthly supp.

1. **SPENCER'S RESEARCH REPORTS ON EMPLOYEE BENEFITS**
2. LaRock, Seymour, et al.
3. Spencer
4. 1953
5. 7 vols.
6. $585 incl. 1 yr. supp.
7. weekly supp.
8. renewal - $525/yr.
9. 5080798/HD7106.U5E553

1. **SPENCER'S RETIREMENT PLAN SERVICE**
2. Spencer, Ross D. et al.
3. Spencer
4. 1959
5. 3 vols.
6. $285/yr.
7. monthly supp.
8. renewal - $260/yr.
9. 11693530/KF3512.A6S630

1. **SPIDELL'S CALIFORNIA TAX FORMS AND INSTRUCTIONS**
2. -
3. Spidell
4. 1975
5. 1 vol.
6. $85/yr; $139/2 yrs.
7. 5-10 supp./yr.
8. renewal - $74/yr.; $119/2 yrs.
9. 78-103221/3934333/KFC860.A65S6

1. **SPILL REPORTING PROCEDURES GUIDE**
2. Leemann, James E.
3. BNA Books
4. new ed. - 1991
5. 1 vol.
6. $155
7. annual editions
9. 16918892/KF3958.L4

1. **SPOUSAL MAINTENANCE**
2. -
3. MILE
4. 1991
5. 1 vol.
6. $68
7. no supp. yet
9. 24510853

1. **THE STACKING OF AUTOMOBILE INSURANCE COVERAGE IN MISSOURI**
2. Ketcherside, John F.
3. UMKC/CLE
4. 1990
5. 1 vol.
6. $29
7. no supp. yet
9. 22917621/KFM7991.A4K47

1. **STANDARD FEDERAL TAX REPORTS (1991 ED.)**
2. -
3. CCH
4. 1913
5. 18 vols. reissued annually
6. $1520/yr,; $1380/2 yrs.
7. weekly supp. & newsletter
9. 30-14274/2848495/KF6285.C67

1. **STANDARDIZED CIVIL JURY INSTRUCTIONS FOR THE DISTRICT OF COLUMBIA, REV. ED.**
2. Young Lawyers Section
3. Bar Assn. of D.C.
4. 1979
5. 1 vol.
6. $75.85
7. no supp. yet
8. new ed. in 1992
9. 81-126612/7838291/KFD1742.6.A65B37

1. **STANDARDS OF TITLE**
2. Title Standards Subcomm. of Real Property, Probate & Trust Section
3. State Bar of N. Dak.
4. 1988
5. 1 vol.
6. $80
7. periodic supp.
8. $25

1. **START-UP COMPANIES: PLANNING, FINANCING AND OPERATING THE SUCCESSFUL BUSINESS**
2. Harroch, Richard D.
3. Law Journal
4. 1985
5. 2 vols.
6. $125
7. periodic supp.
8. 1989 - $50; 1990 - $90
9. 85-10088/12081821/KF1414.S73

1. **STARTING A CASE IN THE 90's: A CURRENT MANUAL OF COMPLAINTS IN MICHIGAN**
2. Christiansen, David W. & David R. Parker
3. MTLA
4. 1991
5. 1 vol.
6. $225-nonmembers; $150-members
7. periodic supp.
8. no supp. yet
9. 24527383/KFM4735.8.C57

1. **STARTING AND OPERATING A BUSINESS IN (STATE SPECIFIC)**
2. Jenkins, Michael et al.
3. Oasis
4. 1987
5. 1 vol.
6. $29.95
7. annual supp.
8. 1990 - $5.95 state supp.; $8.95 - natl. supp.

1. **STATE ADMINISTRATIVE LAW**
2. Johnson, Allen L. & James M. Maltis, eds.
3. Oregon Bar
4. 1985
5. 1 vol.
6. $75
7. periodic supp.
9. 85-63427/13127603/KFO2840.S73

1. **STATE & FEDERAL ADMINISTRATIVE AGENCY PRACTICE**
2. -
3. Indiana CLE
4. 1989
5. 1 vol.
6. $60
7. no supp. planned

1. **STATE & LOCAL GOVERNMENT CIVIL RIGHTS LIABILITY**
2. Bodensteiner, Ivan E. and Rosalie B. Levinson
3. Clark Boardman Callaghan
4. 1987
5. 2 vols.
6. $175 incl. 6 mos. supp.
7. annual supp.
8. 1989 - $37.50; 1990 - $39
9. 87-35231/17261541/KF1325.C58B63

1. **STATE & LOCAL GOVERNMENT DEBT FINANCING**
2. Gelfand, M. David
3. Clark Boardman Callaghan
4. 1986
5. 3 vols.
6. $225 incl. 6 mos. supp.
7. annual supp.
8. 1989 - $89.50; 1990 - $94.50
9. 85-25550/12752397/KF6724.S73

1. **STATE & LOCAL GOVERNMENT SOLID WASTE MANAGEMENT**
2. O'Reilly, James T.
3. Clark Boardman Callaghan
4. 1991
5. 1 vol.
6. $95 incl. 6 mos. supp.
7. annual supp.
8. no supp. yet
9. 91-24474/24108554/TD788.O74

1. **STATE AND LOCAL TAX INSTITUTE**
2. -
3. Georgetown
4. 1990
5. 1 vol.
6. $75
7. no supp. planned

1. **THE STATE & LOCAL TAX PORTFOLIO SERIES**
2. Latcham, Franklin C., ed.
3. Corp. Tax
4. 1989
5. 2 vols.
6. $295/yr.
7. quarterly supp.

1. **STATE AND LOCAL TAXES (vols. available for each state)**
2. -
3. RIA
4. 1925
5. 60 vols. complete plus 1 vol. All States Tax Guide - also avail. for indiv. states at about $325/yr. each
6. $8250/yr.; $8050/yr. for 2 yrs.
7. weekly supp.
8. renewal - $7795/yr.
9. 38-13668

1. **STATE ANTITRUST LAW**
2. Lifland, William T.
3. Law Journal
4. 1984
5. 1 vol.
6. $80
7. periodic supp.
8. 1989 - $39; 1990 - $42
9. 83-27567/10322424/KF1650.L54

1. **STATE CORPORATE INCOME TAX FORMS**
2. -
3. CCH
4. 1974
5. 3 vols.
6. $365/yr.; $330/yr. for 2 yrs.
7. periodic supp.

1. **STATE ENVIRONMENTAL LAW**
2. Selmi, Daniel P. & Kenneth A. Manaster
3. Clark Boardman Callaghan
4. 1989
5. 1 vol.
6. $125 incl. 3 mos. supp.
7. annual supp.
8. 1991 - $59.50
9. 89-37142/20055641/KF3775.Z95S45

1. **STATE HAZARDOUS WASTE REGULATION**
2. Lathrop, Mitchell L.
3. Butterworth-NH
4. 1991
5. 1 vol.
6. $110
7. periodic supp.
8. no supp. yet
9. 91-363/23080085/KF3946.Z95L37

1. **STATE INCOME TAXES**
2. -
3. RIA
4. 1925
5. 20 vols.
6. $1550/yr.; $1495/yr. for 2 yrs.
7. weekly supp.
8. renewal - $1450/yr.

1. **STATE LABOR LAWS**
2. Federigan, Roberto
3. BNA
4. 1954
5. 2 vols. (part of Labor Relations Reporter)
6. $768/yr.
7. weekly supp.
8. renewal - $750/yr.
9. 40-8499/1643346/KF3315.L332

1. **STATE LEGISLATIVE COMPILATIONS: SELECTED SUMMARIES OF REAL ESTATE FINANCE LAWS**
2. -
3. MBAA
4. 1982
5. 1 vol.
6. $150-members; ; $200-nonmembers incl. 1 yr. supp.
7. semiannual supp.
8. renewal - $45/yr.
9. 83-126340/9622108/KF695.Z95S8

1. **STATE LEGISLATIVE SOURCEBOOK**
2. Hellebust, Lynn
3. Govt. Res.
4. 1986
5. 1 vol.
6. $135
7. annual vols.

1. **STATE LIMITED PARTNERSHIP LAWS**
2. Bamberger, Michael A. & Joseph J. Basile, Jr. eds.
3. Prentice Hall Law & Business
4. 1987
5. 6 vols.
6. $350 incl. 4 mos. supp.
7. quarterly supp.
8. 1990 - $95; 1991 - $269

1. **STATE LOBBYING LAWS**
2. Bartz, Elizabeth
3. S&FA
4. 1976
5. 2 vols.
6. $450/yr.
7. 2 supp./yr.
8. renewal - $425/yr.

1. **STATE MOTOR CARRIER GUIDE**
2. -
3. CCH
4. 1940
5. 2 vols.
6. $1650/yr.; $1500/yr. for 2 yrs.
7. semimonthly supp.
9. 8457251/KF2254.C652

1. **STATE PERSONAL INCOME TAX FORMS**
2. -
3. CCH
4. 1974
5. 4 vols.
6. $385/yr.; $350/yr. for 2 yrs.
7. periodic supp.
9. 1423345/KF6752.A65C64x

1. **STATE SPECIALIZATION PLAN BOOK**
2. Standing Comm. on Specialization
3. ABA
4. 1990
5. 1 vol.
6. $40
7. no supp. yet

1. **STATE TAKEOVER LAWS**
2. McGurn, Patrick S. et al.
3. IRRC
4. 1989
5. 1 vol.
6. $200
7. quarterly supp.
8. $150/yr.
9. 20434388/KF1477.Z95M34

1. **STATE TAX ACTION COORDINATOR**
2. RIA prof. ed. staff
3. RIA
4. 1979
5. 6 regional vols. (vols. are available separately)
6. $145/region/yr.; $135/region/yr. for 2 yrs.
7. periodic supp. & monthly newsletter
8. renewal - $125/region/yr.

1. **STATE TAX CASES REPORTS**
2. -
3. CCH
4. 1948
5. 1 vol. (with weekly newsletter - State Tax Review)
6. $355/yr.; $305/yr. for 2 yrs.
7. monthly supp.
9. 49-14096

1. **STATE TAX FORMS: CORPORATION**
2. -
3. Tax Form
4. 1979
5. 2 vols.
6. $175/yr.
7. annual editions
9. 11643437

1. **STATE TAX FORMS: INDIVIDUAL**
2. -
3. Tax Form
4. 1979
5. 2 vols.
6. $175/yr.
7. annual editions
9. 10316520

1. **STATE TAX FORMS: PARTNERSHIP & FIDUCIARY**
2. -
3. Tax Form
4. 1979
5. 1 vol.
6. $95/yr.
7. annual editions
9. 11642863

1. **STATE TAX GUIDE**
2. -
3. CCH
4. 1937
5. 2 vols. (with weekly State Tax Review)
6. $720/yr.; $655/yr. for 2 yrs.

7. semimonthly supp.
9. 37-8086

1. **STATE TAX REPORTS (separate volumes for each state at indiv. price per unit)**
2. -
3. CCH
4. 1917
5. 87 vols. (each state avail. separately)
6. $10,614/yr.; $9,649/yr. for 2 yrs.
7. monthly supp. & weekly State Tax Review

1. **STATE TAXATION OF BANKS AND THRIFT INSTITUTIONS**
2. Taxation Section
3. ABA
4. 2nd ed. - 1983
5. 1 vol.
6. $80
7. periodic supp.
8. no supp. yet
9. 9958927/KF6738.B2S7

1. **STATE TRADEMARK AND UNFAIR COMPETITION LAW**
2. U.S. Trademark Assn.
3. Clark Boardman Callaghan
4. 1987
5. 1 vol.
6. $135 incl. 3 mos. supp.
7. annual supp.
8. 1989 - $99; 1991 - $127.50
9. 87-17637

1. **STATUTE OF LIMITATIONS**
2. -
3. MILE
4. 1990
5. 1 vol.
6. $58
7. no supp. planned
9. 15148151

1. **STATUTORY TIME LIMITATIONS: COLORADO**
2. Butterworth's Staff
3. Butterworth-St. Paul
4. 1981
5. 1 vol.
6. $50
7. periodic supp.
8. 1988 - $14.50; 1990 - $44
9. 81-66550/8613543/KFC1890.T5S73

1. **STATUTORY TIME LIMITATIONS: WASHINGTON STATE**
2. Butterworth's Staff
3. Butterworth-St. Paul
4. 1981
5. 1 vol.
6. $55
7. annual supp.
8. 1989 - $62; 1991 - $55
9. 80-70623/7857251/KFW90.T5L38

1. **STEEL ARBITRATION DIGEST**
2. Willis, John W.
3. P&F
4. 1960
5. 4 vols.
6. $400 incl. 1 yr. supp.
7. periodic supp.
8. renewal - $250/yr.

1. **STEIN ON PROBATE (2d ed.)**
2. Stein, Robert A.
3. Butterworth-St. Paul
4. 1986
5. 2 vols.
6. $225
7. periodic supp.
8. 1989 - $40; 1990 - $95
9. 13705765/KFM5544.S7

1. **STEINMAN'S BERGERMAN & ROTH, NEW YORK REAL PROPERTY FORMS, ANNOTATED**
2. Steinman, Irving I.
3. Bender
4. 2nd ed. - 1948
5. 6 vols.
6. $600 incl. 3 mos. supp.
7. annual supp.
8. 1989 - $471; 1990 - $528
9. 48-1290/12721186/KFN5140.A65S7

1. **STOCKHOLDERS LITIGATION**
2. -
3. NH Bar
4. 1989
5. 1 vol.
6. $20
7. no supp. planned

1. **STORMWATER PERMIT MANUAL**
2. -
3. Thompson

4. 1991
5. 1 vol.
6. $398 incl. 1 yr. supp.
7. monthly supp.
8. renewal - $378/yr.
9. 24137443/KF5571.S76

1. **STRATEGIC FUNDAMENTALS OF PROSECUTING & DEFENDING THE PERSONAL INJURY CASE**
2. -
3. Wash. Bar
4. 1988
5. 1 vol.
6. $35
7. no supp. planned

1. **STRATEGY AND MANAGEMENT OF THE KEY STAGES OF A MATRIMONIAL CASE: THE CORE SKILLS**
2. -
3. Conn. Bar
4. 1990
5. 1 vol.
6. $63
7. no supp. planned

1. **STRUCTURED SETTLEMENTS (Art of Advocacy Series)**
2. Halpern, Richard G.
3. Bender
4. 1991
5. 1 vol.
6. $110 incl. 3 mos. supp.
7. annual supp.
8. no supp. yet
9. 91-72824/24333465/KF1250.H35

1. **STRUCTURED SETTLEMENTS**
2. -
3. MILE
4. 1991
5. 1 vol.
6. $68
7. no supp. planned
9. 24465498/KF1257.Z9S77

1. **STRUCTURED SETTLEMENTS: DESIGN AND EVALUATION**
2. Cooper, Steven, et al.
3. Francis Marion
4. 1991
5. 1 vol.
6. $95
7. annual supp.
8. 1991 - $45; 1992 - $45
9. 83-51695/10954722/KF1257.S77

1. **STRUCTURED SETTLEMENTS AND PERIODIC PAYMENT JUDGMENTS**
2. Hindert, Daniel W. et al.
3. Law Journal
4. 1986
5. 1 vol.
6. $85
7. periodic supp.
8. 1989 - $84; 1990 - $84
9. 85-23205/13008032/KF1250.H55

1. **STRUCTURING COMMERCIAL LOAN AGREEMENTS**
2. Stern, Sandra
3. WG&L
4. 1990
5. 1 vol.
6. $105
7. semiannual supp.
8. 1991 - $103.75
9. 90-70164/21966697/KF1035.S7

1. **STRUCTURING COMMERCIAL REAL ESTATE WORKOUTS: ALTERNATIVES TO FORECLOSURE**
2. Stevens, Stanley M.
3. Prentice Hall Law & Business
4. 1991
5. 1 vol.
6. $95 incl. 4 mos. supp.
7. periodic supp.
8. no supp. yet
9. 91-35571/24467202/KF1535.R43S77

1. **STRUCTURING FOREIGN INVESTMENT IN U.S. REAL ESTATE**
2. Knight, W. Donald, Jr. & Richard L. Doernberg
3. Kluwer
4. 2nd ed. - 1988
5. 1 vol.
6. $171 incl. 3 mos. supp.
7. periodic supp.
8. 1990 - $150; 1991 - $137
9. 88-23253/18321175/KF6441.K55

1. **STRUCTURING SECURED COMMERCIAL LOAN DOCUMENTS**
2. Cunningham, James J. et al.
3. WG&L

4. 1991
5. 1 vol.
6. $105
7. periodic supp.
8. no supp. yet
9. 91-65790/24600411/KF1050.C86

1. **SUBCHAPTER S TAXATION, 3RD ED.**
2. Grant, Irving M.
3. Shepard's
4. 1990
5. 1 vol.
6. $125
7. semiannual supp.
8. 1990 - $24; 1991 - $32
9. 90-8349/21337558/KF6491.G7

1. **SUBDIVISION LAW AND GROWTH MANAGEMENT**
2. Kushner, James A.
3. Clark Boardman Callaghan
4. 1991
5. 1 vol.
6. $110 incl. 3 mos. supp.
7. annual supp.
8. no supp. yet
9. 91-4140/23766498/KF5698.K87

1. **SUBDIVISION REGISTRATION**
2. -
3. NH Bar
4. 1989
5. 1 vol.
6. $35
7. no supp. planned

1. **SUBJECT HEADING INDEX GUIDE FOR OPINIONS AND MEMORANDA OF LAW**
2. Holding, Laura A.
3. Holding
4. 1976 (4th printing - 1988)
5. 1 vol.
6. $57
7. no supp. planned
9. 76-150746/2932652/Z695.1.L3H64

1. **SUCCESSFUL ESTATE PLANNING IDEAS & METHODS**
2. -
3. RIA
4. 1969
5. 2 vols.
6. $470/yr.; $440/yr. for 2 yrs.
7. monthly supp.
8. renewal - $410/yr.

1. **SUCCESSFUL LITIGATION TECHNIQUES**
2. Kelner, Joseph
3. Bender
4. 1964
5. 8 vols.
6. $535 incl. 3 mos. supp.
7. annual supp.
8. 1989 - $357; 1990 - $451
9. 64-7196/1627449/KF8925.P4K42

1. **SUCCESSFUL PAYROLL MANAGEMENT**
2. -
3. WG&L
4. 1986
5. 1 vol.
6. $232/yr.
7. monthly supp.

1. **SUCCESSFULLY LITIGATING TORT INSURANCE ACTIONS**
2. -
3. Indiana CLE
4. 1989
5. 1 vol.
6. $50
7. no supp. planned

1. **SUCCESSFULLY RESOLVING EMPLOYMENT TAX ISSUES WITH THE INTERNAL REVENUE SERVICE**
2. Goldberg, Yale F. & Daniel L. Morgan
3. TSI
4. 1989
5. 1 vol.
6. $63.95
7. periodic supp.
8. no supp. yet

1. **SUGGESTED PATTERN JURY INSTRUCTIONS - VOLUME 1: CIVIL CASES, THIRD ED.**
2. Council of Superior Court Judges of Georgia Committee
3. Institute - Ga.
4. 3rd ed. - 1991
5. 1 vol.
6. $65
7. no supp. yet
9. 84-198175/11023613/KFG542.6.A65C68

1. **SUGGESTED PATTERN JURY INSTRUCTIONS - VOLUME 2: CRIMINAL CASES, SECOND ED.**

2. Council of Superior Court Judges of Georgia Committee
3. Institute - Ga.
4. 1991
5. 1 vol.
6. $65
7. no supp. yet

1. **SUMMARY OF STATE STATUTES AND REGULATIONS FOR OIL AND GAS PRODUCTION**
2. -
3. IOCC
4. 1986
5. 1 vol.
6. $100
7. annual supp.
8. renewal - $25/yr.
9. 5301491/KF1850.Z95I57

1. **SUMMATION (Art of Advocacy Series)**
2. Smith, Lawrence
3. Bender
4. 1978
5. 1 vol.
6. $110 incl. 3 mos. supp.
7. annual supp.
8. 1989 - $64; 1990 - $74.50
9. 78-60620/9121531/KF8915.S58

1. **SUPERFUND: A LEGISLATIVE HISTORY**
2. Needham, Helen Cohn & M. Menefee, eds.
3. ELI
4. 1985
5. 3 vols.
6. $325
7. no supp. planned

1. **SUPERVISORY SERVICE**
2. Wiorski, Robert ed.
3. USLSI
4. 1984
5. 2 vols.
6. $800-nonmembers; $490-members incl. 1 yr. supp.
7. monthly supp.
8. 1991 - $440-nonmembers; $250-members
9. 10468760

1. **SURETY LAW TOPICAL INDEX**
2. Tort & Insurance Practice Section
3. ABA
4. 1987
5. 1 vol.
6. $80
7. no supp. planned
9. 87-62071/16810515/KF1223.A1S87

1. **SURFACE MINING**
2. -
3. EMLF
4. 1986
5. 1 vol.
6. $18-members, $25-nonmembers
7. no supp. planned

1. **SURVEY OF STATE LAWS REGULATING CHARITABLE SOLICITATION**
2. Heckman, Thomas P. Esq. & J. John Stevenson, Esq., eds.
3. Philanthropy Monthly
4. 1976
5. 1 vol.
6. $148/yr.
7. supp. as needed
8. renewal - $124/yr.

1. **SYNOPSIS OF BOILER AND VESSEL PRESSURE LAWS, RULES AND REGULATIONS**
2. Swanson, Raymond P.
3. Uniform Boiler
4. rev. ed. - 1989
5. 1 vol.
6. $50
7. 3 supp./yr.
8. $35/yr.

1. **SYSTEM BOOK FOR FAMILY LAW**
2. Loeb, Leonard L.
3. State Bar of Wisc.
4. 3rd ed. - 1987
5. 2 vols.
6. $165
7. periodic supp.
8. 1988 - $45; 1991 - $76
9. 7312318

1. **TAKEOVER DEFENSE**
2. Fleischer, Arthur Jr. et al.
3. Prentice Hall Law & Business
4. 1990
5. 3 vols.
6. $295 incl. 4 mos. supp.
7. periodic supp.
8. no supp. yet
9. 90-14226/22382381/9946368/KF1477.F443

1. **TAKEOVERS AND FREEZEOUTS**
2. Lipton, Martin and Erica H. Steinberger
3. Law Journal
4. 1978
5. 3 vols.
6. $210
7. periodic supp.
8. 1989 - $185; 1990 - $190
9. 78-26095/4494483/KF1477.L56

1. **TAKING AND DEFENDING DEPOSITIONS**
2. Grimm, Paul W.
3. MICPEL
4. 1991
5. 1 vol.
6. $47.25
7. no supp. planned
9. 24062450/KFM1737.G74

1. **TAKING AND GIVING DEPOSITIONS**
2. -
3. Okla. Bar CLE
4. 1990
5. 1 vol.
6. $40
7. no supp. planned

1. **TANGIBLE EVIDENCE: HOW TO USE EXHIBITS AT TRIAL**
2. Siemer, Deanne C.
3. Prentice Hall Law & Business
4. 2nd ed. - 1989
5. 1 vol.
6. $95 incl. 4 mos. supp.
7. periodic supp.
8. no supp. yet
9. 89-14579/20352136/KF8967.S57

1. **TAX ACCOUNTING**
2. Alkire, Durwood L.
3. Bender
4. 1982
5. 2 vols.
6. $190 incl. 3 mos. supp.
7. annual supp.
8. 1989 - $119; 1990 - $143
9. 82-72350/9225591

1. **TAX ACTION COORDINATOR**
2. RIA prof. ed. staff
3. RIA
4. 1970
5. 10 vols.
6. $580/yr.; $550/yr. for 2 yrs.
7. biweekly supp.
8. renewal - $525/yr.

1. **TAX ASPECTS OF BUYING AND SELLING CORPORATE BUSINESSES**
2. Fleming, Clifton J., Jr.
3. Shepard's
4. 1984
5. 1 vol.
6. $95
7. annual supp.
8. 1989 - $36; 1990 - $38
9. 83-20291/10161761/KF6464.F58

1. **TAX ASPECTS OF DIVORCE AND SEPARATION**
2. Taft, Robert
3. Law Journal
4. 1984
5. 1 vol.
6. $85
7. periodic supp.
8. 1989 - $84; 1990 - $84
9. 83-26825/10300078/KF6428.A4T28

1. **TAX ASPECTS OF INDIANA S CORPORATIONS**
2. -
3. Indiana CLE
4. 1989
5. 1 vol.
6. $40
7. no supp. planned

1. **TAX ASPECTS OF LITIGATION AND SETTLEMENTS**
2. Kasten, Sandy and Brad Seligman
3. Clark Boardman Callaghan
4. 1989
5. 1 vol.
6. $95 incl. 6 mos. supp.
7. annual supp.
8. 1990 - $35
9. 89-9857/19740427/KF6428.D36K37

1. **TAX ASPECTS OF MARITAL DISSOLUTION**
2. Wren, Harold G. et al.
3. Clark Boardman Callaghan
4. 1987
5. 1 vol.
6. $90 incl. 6 mos. supp.
7. annual supp.
8. 1989 - $35; 1990 - $39
9. 86-13005/13670884/KF6333.W74

1. **TAX ASPECTS OF REAL ESTATE INVESTMENTS**
2. Fass, Peter M. et al.
3. Clark Boardman Callaghan
4. 1988
5. 2 vols.
6. $195 incl. 3 mos. supp.
7. annual supp.
8. 1989 - $109; 1990 - $130
9. 87-25617//r88/16682272/KF6535.T38

1. **TAX CONSIDERATIONS IN SELECTING A BUSINESS ENTITY**
2. -
3. Wash. Bar
4. 1988
5. 1 vol.
6. $35
7. no supp. planned

1. **TAX COURT**
2. -
3. RIA
4. 1921
5. 1 vol. (+ 1 annual bound vol.)
6. $525/yr.; $500/yr. for 2 yrs.
7. weekly supp.
8. renewal - $475/yr.

1. **TAX COURT REPORTS**
2. -
3. CCH
4. 1924
5. 3 vols.
6. $775/yr.; $705/yr. for 2 yrs.
7. weekly supp.

1. **TAX, ESTATE AND FINANCIAL PLANNING FOR THE ELDERLY**
2. Reagan, John J.
3. Bender
4. 1985
5. 1 vol.
6. $125 incl. 3 mos. supp.
7. periodic supp.
8. 1989 - $89; 1990 - $108
9. 85-62082/12825029

1. **TAX, ESTATE AND FINANCIAL PLANNING FOR THE ELDERLY – FORMS AND PRACTICE**
2. Reagan, John J.
3. Bender
4. 1991
5. 1 vol.
6. $100 incl. 3 mos. supp.
7. annual supp.
8. no supp. yet

1. **TAX EXEMPT ORGANIZATIONS**
2. -
3. RIA
4. 1971
5. 2 vols.
6. $590/yr.; $545/yr. for 2 yrs.
7. monthly supp.
8. renewal - $500/yr.
9. 74-131012/5630238/KF6449.A6P7

1. **TAX FORUM**
2. -
3. NH Bar
4. 1989
5. 1 vol.
6. $40
7. no supp. planned

1. **TAX FRAUD - AUDITS - INVESTIGATIONS - PROSECUTIONS**
2. Fink, Robert S., et al.
3. Bender
4. 1980
5. 2 vols.
6. $190 incl. 3 mos. supp.
7. annual supp.
8. 1989 - $115; 1990 - $123
9. 80-68458/7049860/KF6334.F55x

1. **TAX-FREE DISPOSITION OF PROPERTY**
2. Ercole, Robert M. et al.
3. MICPEL
4. 1991
5. 1 vol.
6. $42
7. no supp. planned

1. **TAX-FREE TRADE ZONES OF THE WORLD**
2. Diamond, Walter & Dorothy B.
3. Bender
4. 1977
5. 3 vols.
6. $345 incl. 3 mos. supp.
7. quarterly supp.
8. 1989 - $280.50; 1990 - $307
9. 77-76498/3294383/HF1418.D5

1. **TAX GUIDE**
2. RIA prof. ed. staff

3. RIA
4. 1966
5. 2 vols.
6. $340/yr.; $320/yr. for 2 yrs.
7. monthly supp. & weekly newsletter
8. renewal - $290/yr.

1. **TAX HAVENS OF THE WORLD**
2. Diamond, Walter H. & D.B.
3. Bender
4. 1974
5. 3 vols.
6. $290 incl. 1 yr. supp.
7. quarterly supp.
8. 1988 - $173; 1989 - $200
9. 74-78399/1111521

1. **TAX IDEAS**
2. -
3. WG&L
4. 1958
5. 3 vols.
6. $450/yr.
7. monthly supp.

1. **TAX LAWS OF THE WORLD**
2. -
3. Foreign Tax
4. 1947
5. 46 vols. covering 102 countries
6. $1300 incl. 1 yr. supp.
7. weekly supp. & biweekly bulletin
8. renewal - $900/yr.

1. **TAX MANAGEMENT - COMPENSATION PLANNING**
2. Davis, Glenn B.
3. BNA
4. 1982
5. 2 binders & current portfolios
6. $638/yr.
7. quarterly supp. & monthly journal
8. renewal - $615/yr.

1. **TAX MANAGEMENT ESTATES, GIFTS AND TRUSTS REFERENCE FILE**
2. Davis, Glenn B.
3. BNA
4. 1984
5. 4 vols.
6. $451/yr.
7. biweekly supp.
8. renewal - $433/yr.
9. 84-153106/10707391/KF6571.A8T39

1. **TAX MANAGEMENT - ESTATES, GIFTS AND TRUSTS SERIES**
2. Davis, Glenn B.
3. BNA
4. 1967
5. 54+ portfolios (indexed in Master Binder)
6. $676/yr.
7. monthly supp.
8. renewal - $608/yr.

1. **TAX MANAGEMENT FINANCIAL PLANNING**
2. Davis, Glenn B.
3. BNA
4. 1985
5. 4 vols.
6. $661/yr; $615/yr. for 2 yrs.
7. biweekly supp. and monthly "Tax Management Financial Planning Journal"
8. renewal - $591/yr.

1. **TAX MANAGEMENT - FOREIGN INCOME**
2. Davis, Glenn B.
3. BNA
4. 1964
5. 52+ portfolios (indexed in Master Binder)
6. $998/yr.
7. monthly supp.
8. renewal - $898/yr.

1. **TAX MANAGEMENT IRS FORMS**
2. Davis, Glenn B.
3. BNA
4. 1988
5. 4 vols.
6. $265/yr.
7. periodic supp.
8. renewal - $249/yr.
9. 18078223/KF6286.T38X

1. **TAX MANAGEMENT PRIMARY SOURCES SERIES V**
2. Davis, Glenn B.
3. BNA
4. 1987
5. 8 vols.
6. $907/yr.
7. monthly supp.
8. renewal - $664/yr.
9. 16570625/HJ3251.A39T35

1. **TAX MANAGEMENT - REAL ESTATE**
2. Davis, Glenn B.
3. BNA

4. 1984
5. 1 vol. + current portfolios
6. $683/yr.
7. quarterly supp. & bimonthly journal
8. renewal - $615/yr.

1. **TAX MANAGEMENT - U.S. INCOME**
2. Davis, Glenn B.
3. BNA
4. 1959
5. 4 vols. + current portfolios (indexed in Master Binder)
6. $1475/yr.
7. biweekly supp.& weekly report
8. renewal - $1327/yr.

1. **TAX PENALTIES AND INTEREST HANDBOOK**
2. Minars, David & Howard Davidoff
3. Butterworth-NH
4. 1991
5. 1 vol.
6. $80
7. periodic supp.
8. no supp. yet
9. 90-15054/22451721/KF6321.M56

1. **TAX PLANNING FOR CORPORATIONS AND SHAREHOLDERS**
2. Cavitch, Zolman
3. Bender
4. 1974
5. 1 vol.
6. $160/yr.; $285/2 yrs.
7. quarterly supp.
8. 1988 - $109.50; 1989 - $120
9. 74-80468/1104438/KF6464.C38

1. **TAX PLANNING FOR CORPORATIONS AND SHAREHOLDERS - FORMS**
2. Cavitch, Zolman
3. Bender
4. 1985
5. 1 vol.
6. $125 incl. 3 mos. supp.
7. periodic supp.
8. 1989 - $62.50; 1990 - $74
9. 85-226647/12147247/KF6464.C38

1. **TAX PLANNING FOR DISPOSITIONS OF BUSINESS INTERESTS**
2. Ness, Theodore & Wm. F. Indoe
3. WG&L
4. 1984
5. 1 vol.
6. $135
7. semiannual supp.
8. 1989 - $112; 1990 - $100.25
9. 84-51180/11545932/KF6450.N46

1. **TAX PLANNING FOR EXECUTIVE COMPENSATION**
2. Frutkin, Harvey L.
3. Bender
4. 1983
5. 1 vol.
6. $115 incl. 3 mos. supp.
7. periodic supp.
8. 1989 - $78; 1990 - $91.50
9. 82-84732/9568594/KF6289.8.E9F78

1. **TAX PLANNING FOR FAMILY WEALTH TRANSFERS**
2. Zaritsky, Howard M.
3. WG&L
4. 1985
5. 1 vol.
6. $98
7. annual supp.
8. 1988 - $89.25; 1991 - $43.50
9. 85-50929/12627889/KF6572.Z38

1. **TAX PLANNING FOR PARTNERSHIPS**
2. Friedland, Jerold A.
3. Bender
4. 1991
5. 2 vols.
6. $160 incl. 3 mos. supp.
7. annual supp.
8. no supp. yet

1. **TAX PLANNING FOR REAL ESTATE TAXATION**
2. Tucker, Stefan
3. Clark Boardman Callaghan
4. 1989
5. 2 vols.
6. $168 incl. 6 mos. supp.
7. semiannual supp.
8. 1990 - $90
9. 89-9881/19740570/KF6540.T83

1. **TAX PLANNING FOR S CORPORATIONS**
2. Robinson, Richard B. & A. Weiss
3. Bender
4. 1988
5. 1 vol.

6. $115 incl. 3 mos. supp.
7. annual supp.
8. 1989 - $86.50; 1990 - $98
9. 88-71933/19389088/KF6491.R633

1. **TAX PLANNING FOR SMALL BUSINESSES**
2. Wisdom, John C.
3. Clark Boardman Callaghan
4. 1991
5. 1 vol.
6. $59.95 incl. 3 mos.supp.
7. annual supp.
8. no supp. yet
9. 91-34112/24468564/KF6491.W57

1. **TAX PLANNING FOR THE ALTERNATIVE MINIMUM TAX**
2. Rook, Lance W.
3. Bender
4. 1989
5. 1 vol.
6. $105 incl. 3 mos. supp.
7. annual supp.
8. 1990 - $87

1. **TAX PLANNING STRATEGIES**
2. Solomon, Lewis & Susan Flax Posner
3. Clark Boardman Callaghan
4. 1985
5. 2 vols.
6. $160 incl. 6 mos. supp.
7. annual supp. & rev. chapters
8. 1989 - $40; 1990 - $42.50
9. 85-4086/11755827/KF6297.S65

1. **THE TAX PRACTICE DESKBOOK**
2. Freeman, Harrop A. & Norman D.
3. WG&L
4. 1973
5. 1 vol.
6. $105
7. annual supp.
8. 1989 - $69.75; 1990 - $74
9. 78-108034/4468732/KF6320.F74

1. **TAX PRACTICE MANAGEMENT MANUAL**
2. Behrenfeld, William & Robert Ranweiler
3. AICPA
4. 1990
5. 1 vol.
6. $145
7. annual supp.
9. 90-543/21408283/HJ4652.B35

1. **TAX PRACTICE SERIES: THE PROFESSIONAL'S EXPEDITER**
2. -
3. BNA
4. 1989
5. 12 vols.
6. $696/yr.
7. weekly supp. & "Tax Practice Bulletin" newsletter
8. renewal - $636/yr.

1. **TAX SERVICE FOR AFFILIATED GROUPS**
2. Davis, LaVaughn T.
3. Stephens
4. 1988
5. 1 vol.
6. $330/yr.
7. monthly reports & updates
9. 88-92609/19875923/KF6464.D318

1. **TAX SERVICE FOR CORPORATE ACQUISITIONS AND DISPOSITIONS OF BUSINESSES**
2. Davis, LaVaughn T.
3. Stephens
4. 1974
5. 1 vol.
6. $310/yr.
7. monthly report & updates
9. 77-152500/3311569/KF6499.M4D38

1. **TAX SERVICE FOR EMPLOYEE RETIREMENT PLANS**
2. Davis, LaVaughn T.
3. Stephens
4. 1978
5. 2 vols.
6. $390/yr.
7. monthly reports & updates
9. 78-56111/4193265/KF6425.T3

1. **TAX SERVICE FOR SUBCHAPTER "S" CORPORATIONS AND THEIR SHAREHOLDERS**
2. Davis, LaVaughn T.
3. Stephens
4. 1983
5. 1 vol.
6. $310/yr.
7. monthly reports & updates
9. 83-51186/10599324/KF6491.D3

1. **TAX STRATEGIES IN DIVORCE**

2. Mahoney, Dennis C. et al.
3. Wiley Law
4. 1987
5. 1 vol.
6. $105
7. annual supp.
8. 1990 - $35; 1992 - price NA
9. 87-402773/15998265/KF6333.M34

1. **TAX TREATIES**
2. -
3. CCH
4. 1952
5. 3 vols.
6. $425/yr.; $385/yr. for 2 yrs.
7. monthly supp.
9. 7827442

1. **TAX TREATIES**
2. -
3. WG&L
4. 1969
5. 3 vols.
6. $325/yr.
7. monthly supp.

1. **TAXATION FOR THE GENERAL PRACTITIONER**
2. -
3. NH Bar
4. 1989
5. 1 vol.
6. $35
7. no supp. planned

1. **TAXATION OF CORPORATE LIQUIDATIONS**
2. Wood, Robert W.
3. WG&L
4. 1987
5. 1 vol.
6. $135/yr.
7. semiannual supp.
8. $60.50
9. 16637759/KF6499.D5W6

1. **TAXATION OF FINANCIAL INSTITUTIONS**
2. Schmidt, Henry W., et al.
3. Bender
4. 1983
5. 3 vols.
6. $330 incl. 3 mos. supp.
7. periodic supp.
8. 1989 - $224.50; 1990 - $256.50
9. 83-70870/9753684/KF6495.B2T39

1. **TAXATION OF INTELLECTUAL PROPERTY: TAX PLANNING GUIDE**
2. Petry, Marvin
3. Bender
4. 1985
5. 1 vol.
6. $115 incl. 3 mos. supp.
7. periodic supp.
8. 1989 - $75.50; 1990 - $86
9. 85-61901/12734772/KF6428.I5P48

1. **TAXATION OF INVESTMENTS**
2. Solomon, Lewis D.
3. Prentice Hall Law & Business
4. 1987
5. 3 vols.
6. $250 incl. 4 mos. supp.
7. periodic supp.
8. 1990 - $80; 1990 - $80
9. 87-1288/15521318/KF6415.S65

1. **TAXATION OF MINING OPERATIONS**
2. Maxfield, Peter C. & James L. Houghton
3. Bender
4. 1981
5. 1 vol.
6. $125 incl. 3 mos. supp.
7. periodic supp.
8. 1989 - $55; 1990 - $70.50
9. 81-66945/7804936/KF6495.M5M39

1. **TAXATION OF PARTNERSHIPS**
2. Bonn, John R.
3. Clark Boardman Callaghan
4. 1987
5. 2 vols.
6. $175 incl. 6 mos. supp.
7. annual supp.
8. 1989 - $70; 1990 - $77.50
9. 87-15843/16093248/KF6452.B66

1. **TAXATION OF PASSIVE ACTIVITIES**
2. Kimmelfield, Neil D.
3. Prentice Hall Law & Business
4. 1989
5. 2 vols.
6. $250 incl. 4 mos. supp.
7. periodic supp.
8. 1990 - $125; 1991 - $95
9. 89-3592/19221825/KF6396.K56

1. **TAXATION OF REAL ESTATE TRANSACTIONS 2nd ed.**

2. Guerin, Sanford M.
3. Shepard's
4. 1988
5. 2 vols.
6. $195
7. annual supp.
8. 1990 - $36; 1991 - $42
9. 88-15741/17983783/KF6540.G83

1. **TAXATION OF SECURITIES TRANSACTIONS (Business Organizations, vol. 11b)**
2. Fried, Martin L.
3. Bender
4. 1971
5. 1 vol.
6. $135 incl. 3 mos. supp.
7. annual supp.
8. 1989 - $119; 1990 - $124.50
9. 72-178507/286617/KF6415.F75

1. **TAXATION OF THE CLOSELY HELD CORPORATION**
2. Ness, Theodore & Eugene L. Vogel
3. WG&L
4. rev. ed. - 1991
5. 1 vol.
6. $135
7. semiannual supp.
8. 1989 - $120; 1991 - $69.50
9. 91-66206/24727182/KF6464.N4

1. **TAXING CALIFORNIA PROPERTY**
2. Flavin, Sean & Kenneth Ehrman
3. Lawyers Coop.
4. 1988
5. 2 vol.
6. $160 incl. 6 mos. supp.
7. annual supp.
8. 1990 - $39; 1991 - $48
9. 88-24093/18324211/KFC881.E35

1. **TECHNIQUES FOR ALTERNATIVE DISPUTE RESOLUTION**
2. -
3. MILE
4. 1991
5. 1 vol.
6. $68
7. no supp. planned
9. 23613702/KF9084.T43

1. **TECHNIQUES FOR JURY ADVOCACY**
2. -
3. Okla. Bar CLE
4. 1990
5. 1 vol.
6. $60
7. no supp. planned

1. **TECHNIQUES FOR POST MORTEM ESTATE PLANNING**
2. -
3. Maine Bar
4. 1991
5. 1 vol.
6. $20
7. no supp. planned

1. **TECHNOLOGY MANAGEMENT**
2. Goldscheider, Robert
3. Clark Boardman Callaghan
4. 1988
5. 1 vol.
6. $115 incl. 3 mos. supp.
7. annual supp.
8. 1989 - $39.50; 1991 - $52.50
9. 88-4956/17545950/KF3147.G65

1. **TELECOMMUNICATIONS REGULATORY MONITOR**
2. Irwin, David A.
3. Phillips
4. 1985
5. 1 vol.
6. $397/yr.
7. quarterly supp.
8. renewal - $397/yr.
9. 84-203579/11841430/KF2765.I775

1. **TENNESSEE CORPORATIONS**
2. Gilman, Ronald Lee
3. Lawyers Coop.
4. 1980
5. 1 vol.
6. $115 incl. 6 mos. supp.
7. annual supp.
8. 1989 - $48; 1990 - $52
9. 79-91162/6718648/KFT213.G54

1. **TENNESSEE EMPLOYMENT LAW**
2. Phillips, John B. Jr.
3. Smith
4. 1989
5. 1 vol.
6. $89
7. periodic supp.
8. 1989 - $33; 1990 - $33
9. 20185396/KFT334.P54

1. **TENNESSEE LAW OFFICE DESK BOOK**
2. Forrister, Brad
3. Smith
4. 1990
5. 1 vol.
6. $34
7. periodic supp.
8. no supp. yet
9. 22866389

1. **TENNESSEE PROBATE**
2. Secor, Albert W.
3. Lawyers Coop.
4. 1980
5. 2 vols.
6. $210 incl. 6 mos. supp.
7. annual supp.
8. 1990 - $71.50; 1991 - $71.50
9. 79-91164/7625336/KFT144.S4

1. **TERMINATION OF EMPLOYMENT**
2. McCulloch, Kenneth J.
3. WG&L
4. 1984
5. 1 vol.
6. $410/yr.
7. monthly supp.
9. 11256632

1. **TEXAS AIR CONTROL BOARD RULES**
2. Finklea, Gaylon, ed.
3. RPC
4. 1977
5. 1 vol.
6. $249/yr.
7. periodic supp.

1. **TEXAS ATTORNEY'S/SECRETARY'S HANDBOOK**
2. -
3. Mariposa
4. 1991
5. 2 vols.
6. $79
7. annual supp.
8. 1990 - $55; 1991 - $69
9. 88-640131/17792574/KFT1708.A19T47

1. **TEXAS CIVIL TRIAL GUIDE**
2. Various Contributing Authors
3. Bender
4. 1989
5. 5 vols
6. $475 incl. 3 mos. supp.
7. annual supp.
8. 1990 - $81.50
9. 89-60953/20065236/KFT1730.T483

1. **TEXAS CIVIL TRIAL HANDBOOK**
2. Sprouse, Harlow L. & F.M. Misko, eds.
3. State Bar of Texas
4. 1984
5. 2 vols.
6. $150
7. periodic supp.
8. -
9. 84-50268/11831161/KFT1738.T49

1. **TEXAS COLLECTIONS MANUAL**
2. Goldberg, Daniel J. and Roger A. Bartlett, eds.
3. State Bar of Texas
4. 2nd ed.-1987
5. 2 vols.
6. $230
7. periodic supp.
8. 1988 - $55; 1990 - $85
9. 87-60410/6083403

1. **TEXAS COMMERCIAL COLLECTIONS**
2. Baker, Don L.
3. Butterworth-Texas
4. 1989
5. 1 vol.
6. $150
7. annual supp.
8. 1991 - $70
9. 89-15917/20011940/KFT1367.C6B35

1. **TEXAS COMMERCIAL REAL ESTATE FORMS**
2. Bankus, David A.
3. Butterworth-Texas
4. 1990
5. 1 vol.
6. $95
7. annual supp.
8. 1990 - $32.50
9. 89-23961/20419560/KFT1326.A65B36

1. **TEXAS CONDOMINIUM LAW MANUAL**
2. St. Claire, Frank A.
3. Butterworth-Texas
4. 1983
5. 1 vol.
6. $95
7. periodic supp.
8. 1989 - $75; 1991 - $85
9. 84-210625//r872/10182111/ KFT1314.C6T49

1. **TEXAS CORPORATION LAW**
2. Mellett, Jennifer
3. Butterworth-Texas
4. 1981
5. 3 vols.
6. $175
7. periodic supp.
8. 1988 - $125; 1989 - $158.50
9. 83-111130//r872/9441589/KFT1413.T48

1. **TEXAS CORPORATION LAW**
2. Newman, Larry G.
3. Parker
4. 1986
5. 1 vol.
6. $110
7. periodic supp.
8. 1990 - $32.50
9. 88-186527/13767438/KFT1413.N49

1. **TEXAS CORPORATIONS - LAW AND PRACTICE**
2. Aldave, Barbara B., et al.
3. Bender
4. 1984
5. 5 vols.
6. $495 incl. 3 mos. supp.
7. annual supp.
8. 1989 - $189; 1990 - $252
9. 84-71521//r852/11650384/KFT1413.T49

1. **TEXAS COURTROOM EVIDENCE**
2. Hardberger, Philip D.
3. Parker
4. 4th ed. - 1989
5. 1 vol.
6. $85 incl. 3 mos. supp.
7. periodic supp.
8. 1990 - $31.50
9. 89-62492/20348378/KFT140.H37

1. **TEXAS CRIMINAL DEFENSE FORMS ANNOTATED**
2. Dunnam, Bill
3. Knowles
4. 1984
5. 1 vol.
6. $135 incl. 3 mos. supp.
7. annual supp.
8. 1988 - $54; 1990 - $43
9. 11503391/KFT1766.5.A65D86

1. **TEXAS CRIMINAL PRACTICE GUIDE**
2. Teague, Marvin O.
3. Bender
4. 1979
5. 6 vols.
6. $585 incl. 3 mos. supp.
7. supp. as needed
8. 1989 - $360; 1990 - $448.50
9. 79-90356/5940849/KFT1775.B46

1. **TEXAS DEPARTMENT OF HEALTH RULES**
2. Finklea, Gaylon, ed.
3. RPC
4. 1977
5. 1 vol.
6. $249/yr.
7. periodic supp.

1. **TEXAS DISCOVERY FORMS**
2. Robins, Richard C.
3. Butterworth-Texas
4. 1991
5. 1 vol.
6. $95
7. periodic supp.
8. no supp. yet
9. 91-8410/23145512/KFT1737.A65R63

1. **TEXAS DRUNK DRIVING LAW, 2nd Ed.**
2. Trichter, J. Gary & W. Troy McKinney
3. Butterworth-Texas
4. 1991
5. 2 vols.
6. $195
7. periodic supp.
8. no supp. yet
9. 91-8646/23180102/KFT1497.8.T74

1. **TEXAS FAMILY LAW**
2. Dowden, Cheryl, supp. by Butterworths Staff
3. Butterworth-Texas
4. 1982
5. 2 vols.
6. $120
7. periodic supp.
8. 1988 - $50; 1989 - $60
9. 82-234770/9350019/KFT1294.T39

1. **TEXAS FAMILY LAW PRACTICE MANUAL**
2. Council of the Family Law Section
3. State Bar of Texas
4. 1984
5. 4 vols.
6. $325
7. periodic supp.

8. 1990 - $105; 1991 - $85
9. 84-71042/11348742/KFT1294.T38

1. **TEXAS FAMILY LAW SERVICE**
2. -
3. Bancroft
4. 1988
5. 8 vols
6. $802.50/yr.
7. periodic supp.
8. 1991 - $152.50
9. 88-72209//r89/19457405/KFT1294.T393

1. **TEXAS FAMILY LAW TRIAL GUIDE**
2. -
3. Bender
4. 1983
5. 1 vol.
6. $225 incl. 1 yr. supp.
7. 3 supp./yr.
8. renewal - $95/yr.
9. 81-70957/10321737

1. **TEXAS FIRE & POLICE CIVIL SERVICE LAW**
2. Miller, Richard
3. Francis Marion
4. 1985
5. 1 vol.
6. $65 incl. 1 supp.
7. semiannual supp.
8. 1990 - 45; 1991 - $45

1. **TEXAS GENERAL LAND OFFICE/SCHOOL LAND BOARD RULES**
2. Finklea, Gaylon, ed.
3. RPC
4. 1977
5. 1 vol.
6. $249/yr.
7. periodic supp.

1. **TEXAS GUARDIANSHIP MANUAL**
2. Goode, John W., Jr. & S.S. Barrows, eds.
3. State Bar of Texas
4. 1983
5. 1 vol.
6. $65
7. periodic supp.
8. no supp. yet
9. 82-61569/9222391/KFT1306.T49

1. **TEXAS HOSPITAL LAW**
2. Griffith, Richard L. and Dewey W. Johnston, M.D.
3. Butterworth-Texas
4. 1988
5. 1 vol.
6. $115
7. annual supp.
8. 1989 - $47.50; 1990 - $85
9. 88-24106/18324300/KFT1561.G75

1. **TEXAS LAND USE LAW**
2. Anderson, Arthur J.
3. Wiley Law
4. 1989
5. 1 vol.
6. $105
7. annual supp.
8. 1990 - $40
9. 21056933/KFT1658.A6A5

1. **TEXAS LAW OF OIL AND GAS**
2. Smith, Ernest E.
3. Butterworth-Texas
4. 1989
5. 3 vols.
6. $350
7. annual supp.
8. 1990 - $110
9. 89-7370/19623990/KFT1458.A1S64

1. **TEXAS LAW OFFICE HANDBOOK**
2. Texas Assn. of Legal Secretaries
3. Parker
4. 1990
5. 1 vol.
6. $75
7. supp. as needed
8. 1991 - $31
9. 90-61966/22146513/KFT1277.T44

1. **TEXAS LAWYERS' PROFESSIONAL ETHICS**
2. Young Lawyers Assn. Committee on Professional Ethics
3. State Bar of Texas
4. 2nd ed. - 1986
5. 1 vol.
6. $63
7. periodic supp.
8. no supp. yet
9. 86-61559/5791185/KFT1276.5.A2T49

1. **TEXAS LEGAL PRACTICE FORMS**
2. Taylor, Dennis H. & S. Lee Stevenson
3. Lawyers Coop.
4. 1982
5. 4 vols.

6. $295 incl. 6 mos. supp.
7. annual supp.
8. 1989 - $51; 1990 - $58
9. 82-20673/8930311/KFT1268.S85

1. **TEXAS LIMITATIONS MANUAL**
2. Mellett, Jennifer Nosler
3. Butterworth-Texas
4. 1987
5. 1 vol.
6. $85
7. periodic supp.
8. 1988 - $35; 1990 - $85
9. 16314639/KFT1290.T5M44

1. **TEXAS LITIGATION GUIDE**
2. Dorsaneo, William V., III et al.
3. Bender
4. 1977
5. 21 vols.
6. $1500 incl. 3 mos. supp.
7. annual supp.
8. 1989 - $1159.50; 1990 - $1110.50
9. 77-71200/3205370/KFT1730.T4

1. **TEXAS LITIGATOR'S HANDBOOK**
2. Butler, Edward F.
3. Butterworth-Texas
4. 1989
5. 1 vol.
6. $95
7. periodic supp.
8. 1990 - $65
9. 89-448/19125590/KFT1738.B88

1. **TEXAS MUNICIPAL ZONING LAW**
2. Mixon, John
3. Butterworth-Texas
4. 1985
5. 1 vol.
6. $110
7. periodic supp.
8. 1989 - $117.50; 1990 - $45
9. 85-389/11623749/KFT1658.M58

1. **TEXAS PATTERN JURY CHARGES, VOL. 1 (GENERAL; MOTOR VEHICLES; DAMAGES)**
2. State Bar Comm. on Pattern Jury Charges
3. State Bar of Texas
4. 2nd ed. - 1987
5. 1 vol.
6. $85
7. periodic supp.
8. 1989 - $30
9. 87-62226/16945647/KFT1742.6.A65T49

1. **TEXAS PATTERN JURY CHARGES, VOL. 4 (BUSINESS, COMMERCIAL, DECEPTIVE TRADE PRACTICES, INSURANCE CODE & DAMAGES)**
2. State Bar Comm. on Pattern Jury Charges
3. State Bar of Texas
4. 1990
5. 1 vol.
6. $100
7. periodic supp.
8. no supp. yet

1. **TEXAS PATTERN JURY CHARGES, VOL. 5 (FAMILY LAW)**
2. State Bar Comm, on Pattern Jury Charges
3. State Bar of Texas
4. 1989
5. 1 vol.
6. $105
7. periodic supp.
8. no supp. yet
9. 87-62226/16945647/KFT1742.6.A65T49

1. **TEXAS PATTERN JURY CHARGES, VOL. 3 (PROFESSIONALS; PREMISES; PRODUCTS; DAMAGES)**
2. State Bar Committee on Pattern Jury Charges
3. State Bar of Texas
4. 2nd ed. - 1990
5. 1 vol.
6. $110
7. periodic supp.
8. 1991 - free
9. 87-62226/16945647/KFT1742.6.A65T49

1. **TEXAS PATTERN JURY CHARGES, VOL. 2 (WORKERS' COMPENSATION)**
2. State Bar Comm. on Pattern Jury Charges
3. State Bar of Texas
4. 3rd ed. - 1989
5. 1 vol.
6. $115
7. periodic supp.
8. no supp. yet
9. 87-62226/16945647/KFT1742.6.A65T49

1. **TEXAS PERSONAL INJURY FORMS**
2. Tone, Ruth
3. Butterworth-Texas

4. 1984
5. 1 vol.
6. $65
7. periodic supp.
8. 1990 - $40; 1991 - $32.50
9. 84-208474/11517467/KFT1739.P4T66

1. **TEXAS PERSONAL INJURY LAW**
2. Mellett, Jennifer Nosler
3. Butterworth-Texas
4. 1981
5. 3 vols.
6. $185
7. periodic supp.
8. 1990 - $57.50; 1991 - $55
9. 82-234758//r87/8071555/ KFT1397.P3T49

1. **TEXAS PRACTICE GUIDE - PERSONAL INJURY**
2. Hebdon, Jack et al.
3. Lawyers Coop.
4. 1987
5. 2 vols.
6. $160 incl. 6 mos. supp.
7. annual supp.
8. 1990 - $70; 1991 - $75
9. 87-30925/16924409/KFT1739.P4G44

1. **TEXAS PROBATE CODE MANUAL**
2. Mellett, Jennifer Nosler
3. Butterworth-Texas
4. 1984
5. 2 vols.
6. $125
7. periodic supp.
8. 1990 - $57.50; 1991 - $41.50
9. 11024311/KFT1344.A6T49

1. **TEXAS PROBATE SYSTEM**
2. Brill, James E. & L.D. Woodall, eds.
3. State Bar of Texas
4. 1983
5. 2 vols.
6. $135
7. periodic supp.
8. new ed. in 1992
9. 83-50453/10237251/KFT1344.T49

1. **TEXAS PRODUCTS LIABILITY LAW**
2. Powers, William C. Jr.
3. Butterworth-Texas
4. 1986
5. 1 vol.
6. $110
7. annual supp.
8. 1990 - $55; 1991 - $57.50
9. 85-30941/KFT1397.7.P69

1. **TEXAS PROPERTY TAX–PROTEST & APPEALS**
2. Myers, Robert
3. Francis Marion
4. 1991
5. 1 vol.
6. $65
7. semiannual supp.
8. 1992 - $45

1. **TEXAS PUBLIC UTILITY COMMISSION RULES**
2. Finklea, Gaylon, ed.
3. RPC
4. 1977
5. 1 vol.
6. $249/yr.
7. periodic supp.

1. **TEXAS RESIDENTIAL LANDLORD-TENANT LAW**
2. Hauser, James, et al.
3. Butterworth-Texas
4. 1986
5. 1 vol.
6. $125
7. periodic supp.
8. 1990 - $60; 1991 - $67.50
9. 87-405713/15256067/KFT1317.H38

1. **TEXAS RULES OF APPELLATE PROCEDURE**
2. Butterworths staff
3. Butterworth-Texas
4. 1986
5. 1 vol.
6. $40
7. periodic supp.
8. 1989 - $16; 1990 - no charge
9. 87-405735/16240823/KFT1755.A433A2

1. **TEXAS RULES OF CIVIL PROCEDURE**
2. Butterworths staff
3. Butterworth-Texas
4. 1984
5. 1 vol.
6. $38.50
7. periodic supp.
8. 1989 - $15; 1990 - no charge
9. 84-1870/10459117/KFT1729.A313A2

1. **TEXAS RULES OF CRIMINAL EVIDENCE**
2. Acherman, John
3. Francis Marion
4. 1988
5. 1 vol.
6. $65 incl. 1 supp.
7. semiannual supp.
8. 1990 - $55; 1991 - $55
9. 20458746/KFT1740.A4A34

1. **TEXAS RULES OF EVIDENCE MANUAL**
2. Wendorf, Hulen D. et al.
3. Bender
4. 1991
5. 1 vol.
6. $95 incl. 3 mos. supp.
7. annual supp.
8. no supp. yet
9. 91-72825/24281284/KFT1740.W46

1. **TEXAS SPECIAL ISSUES FORMS**
2. Robins, Richard C.
3. Butterworth-Texas
4. 1988
5. 1 vol.
6. $110
7. annual supp.
8. 1989 - $48.50; 1990 - $60
9. 88-2589/17441649/KFT1742.4.A65

1. **TEXAS TAX SERVICE**
2. Bishop, D.M. et al.
3. Bender
4. 1985
5. 5 vols.
6. $370 incl. 1 yr. service; $680 for 2 yrs.
7. monthly supp.
8. renewal - $310/yr.
9. 85-70632/12128401/KFT1670.T49

1. **TEXAS TITLE INSURANCE**
2. Ellis, Billie, Jr. et al.
3. Wiley Law
4. 1987
5. 1 vol.
6. $105
7. annual supp.
8. 1991 - $45; 1992 - price NA
9. 88-416849/18442547/KFT1393.T5E45

1. **TEXAS TORTS AND REMEDIES**
2. Edgar, J. Hadley Jr. & James B. Sales, editorial consultants
3. Bender
4. 1987
5. 5 vols.
6. $595 incl. 3 mos. supp.
7. annual supp.
8. 1989 - $225; 1990 - $291
9. 87-62320/17359113/KFT1395.T49

1. **TEXAS TRANSACTION GUIDE - LEGAL FORMS**
2. Kendrick, Herbert S. et al.
3. Bender
4. 1972
5. 19 vols.
6. $1325 incl. 3 mos. supp.
7. annual supp.
8. 1989 - $870; 1990 - $1060
9. 72-86337/570577/KFT1268.K45

1. **TEXAS WATER COMMISSION/TEXAS WATER DEVELOPMENT BOARD RULES**
2. Finklea, Gaylon, ed.
3. RPC
4. 1977
5. 1 vol.
6. $275/yr.
7. periodic supp.

1. **TEXAS WORKER'S COMPENSATION LAW**
2. -
3. Bender
4. 1990
5. 3 vols.
6. $300 incl. 3 mos. supp.
7. periodic supp.
8. no supp. yet
9. 90-81932/22437670/KFT1542.A6T45

1. **TEXAS WORKERS' COMPENSATION TRIAL MANUAL**
2. Hardberger, Phillip D.
3. Parker
4. 1991
5. 1 vol.
6. $90 incl. 3 mos. supp.
7. periodic supp.
8. 1987 - $28.75; 1990 - $32
9. 91-61266/24112735/KFT1542.A59H37

1. **THIRD PARTY PRACTICE**
2. -
3. Illinois ICLE
4. rev. - 1987
5. 1 vol.
6. $90.95

7. periodic supp.
8. 1990 - $24.95
9. 11286317/KFI1736.6.J6T45

1. **TITLE TO REAL ESTATE**
2. -
3. Ohio CLE
4. 1990
5. 1 vol. & formbook
6. $35
7. no supp. planned
9. KFO126.T5

1. **TITLES TO REAL ESTATE**
2. Vance, James J.
3. CLE - Wisc.
4. 1977
5. 1 vol.
6. $55
7. periodic supp.
8. 1983 - $30; 1986 - $30
9. 77-82631/3480580/KFW2527.V3

1. **TOBACCO PRODUCTS LITIGATION REPORTER**
2. Daynard, Richard A., ed.
3. TPLR
4. 1985
5. 4 vols.
6. $725/yr.
7. quarterly supp. & special alerts
9. 12872258

1. **TORT LAW**
2. -
3. Indiana CLE
4. 1989
5. 1 vol.
6. $50
7. no supp. planned

1. **TORT REFORM II: A PRACTICAL DEMONSTRATION**
2. -
3. Conn. Bar
4. 1989
5. 1 vol.
6. $20
7. no supp. planned

1. **TORTS**
2. Calkins, Win, ed.
3. Oregon Bar
4. 1981
5. 2 vols.
6. $145
7. periodic supp.
8. 1988 - $45; to be rev. in 1992
9. 81-85577/8029435/KFO2595.T67

1. **TORTS: MICHIGAN LAW & PRACTICE**
2. Atkinson, Linda Miller & Katharine B. Soper, eds.
3. ICLE - Michigan
4. 1991
5. 2 vols.
6. $155
7. annual supp.
8. no supp. yet

1. **THE TOUCHE ROSS INTERNATIONAL BUSINESS INVESTMENT AND TAXATION HANDBOOK**
2. Touche Ross International
3. Probus
4. 1989
5. 3 vols.
6. $425/yr.
7. periodic supp.
8. 1990 - $125

1. **TOXIC SUBSTANCES CONTROL ACT–COMPLIANCE GUIDE AND SERVICE**
2. Wheeler, John R.
3. Environment Books
4. 1988
5. 3 vols.
6. $345 incl. 1 yr. supp.
7. quarterly supp.
8. renewal - $90/yr.
9. 88-80678/18268643/KF3958.W47

1. **TOXIC TORTS**
2. -
3. MILE
4. 1988
5. 1 vol.
6. $58
7. no supp. planned

1. **TOXIC TORTS AND HAZARDOUS WASTE**
2. -
3. NH Bar
4. 1987
5. 1 vol.
6. $35
7. no supp. planned

1. **TRADE REGULATION REPORTS**

2. -
3. CCH
4. 1914
5. 7 vols.
6. $1433/yr.; $1300/yr. for 2 yrs.
7. weekly supp.
9. 36-33431/1564342/HD2877.C58

1. **TRADE SECRETS (Business Organizations, Vols. 12 & 12a)**
2. Milgrim, Roger M.
3. Bender
4. 1967
5. 4 vols.
6. $450 incl. 3 mos. supp.
7. annual supp.
8. 1989 - $544; 1990 - $660.50
9. 67-3921/1169547/KF3197.A6M5

1. **TRADE SECRETS LAW**
2. Jager, Melvin F.
3. Clark Boardman Callaghan
4. 1985
5. 3 vols.
6. $345 incl. 3 mos. supp.
7. annual supp.
8. 1989 - $142; 1991 - $180
9. 85-16654/12262272/KF3197.J34

1. **TRADEMARK LAW PRACTICE FORMS**
2. Kramer, Barry and Allen D. Brufsky
3. Clark Boardman Callaghan
4. 1986
5. 2 vols.
6. $215 incl. 3 mos. supp.
7. annual supp.
8. 1989 - $95; 1991 - $127.50
9. 85-30913/13004292/KF3178.5.T7

1. **THE TRADEMARK LAW REVISION ACT OF 1988**
2. Intellectual Property Section
3. Conn. Bar
4. 1989
5. 1 vol.
6. $20
7. no supp. planned

1. **TRADEMARK MANUAL OF EXAMINING PROCEDURE**
2. U.S. Dept. of Commerce Patent Office
3. order from USGPO - stock #903-010-00000-2
4. 1986
5. 1 vol.
6. $14/yr.
7. semiannual supp.
9. 21001793/T223.V1U58

1. **TRADEMARK PROTECTION AND PRACTICE**
2. Gilson, Jerome
3. Bender
4. 1974
5. 6 vols.
6. $535 incl. 3 mos. supp.
7. annual supp.
8. 1989 - $445; 1990 - $430
9. 74-25023/1323786/KF3180.G54

1. **TRADEMARK REGISTRATION PRACTICE**
2. Hawes, James E.
3. Clark Boardman Callaghan
4. 1987
5. 1 vol.
6. $120 incl. 3 mos. supp.
7. periodic supp.
8. 1989 - $55; 1991 - $114.50
9. 86-29896/14716314/KF3181.H39

1. **TRADEMARKS THROUGHOUT THE WORLD**
2. Jacobs, Alan J. ed.
3. Clark Boardman Callaghan
4. 4th ed. - 1987-89
5. 1 vol.
6. $135 incl. 3 mos. supp.
7. 3 supp./yr.
8. 1989 - $97.50; 1991 - $125
9. 79-137/4591463/K1555.4.T7

1. **TRAFFIC LAW AND PRACTICE IN WISCONSIN**
2. Hammer, Thomas J. et al.
3. State Bar of Wisc.
4. 1989
5. 2 vols.
6. $135
7. periodic supp.
8. 1989 - $58
9. 16322330/KFW2696.T72

1. **TRANSNATIONAL CONTRACTS: APPLICABLE LAW AND SETTLEMENT OF DISPUTES – A STUDY IN CONFLICT AVOIDANCE LAW AND PRACTICE**
2. Delaume, Georges R.
3. Oceana
4. 1979

5. 6 vols.
6. $600/set
7. 1-2 supp./yr.
8. 1990 - $150; 1991 - $150
9. 74-30028/1111422/K7265.D44

1. **TRANSNATIONAL ECONOMIC AND MONETARY LAW: TRANSACTIONS AND CONTRACTS.**
2. Lazar, Leonard
3. Oceana
4. 1978
5. 10 vols.
6. $850/set
7. periodic supp.
8. 1989 - $100; 1990 - $100
9. 77-8398/3003077/K3823.L37

1. **TRANSNATIONAL JOINT VENTURES**
2. Fitzpatrick, Peter B., ed.
3. Bus. Laws
4. 1989
5. 1 vol.
6. $185
7. annual supp.
8. renewal - $44/yr.
9. 89-164967/20222890/K1309.T73

1. **TRANSPORT LAWS OF THE WORLD**
2. Evans, Malcolm and Martin Stanford
3. Oceana
4. 1978
5. 7 vols.
6. $600
7. periodic supp.
8. 1990 - $150; 1991 - $150
9. 77-8397/3003078/K4025.4.T7

1. **TRANSPORTATION LAW INSTITUTE PAPERS AND PROCEEDINGS**
2. Jones, E. Dale, exec. ed.
3. ATP
4. 1989
5. 1 vol.
6. $50
7. annual supp.
8. 1990 - $50; 1991 - $50
9. 20300892

1. **TRANSPORTATION LAW STUDY GUIDE**
2. Bromley, James F.
3. ATP
4. new ed. due 1992
5. 1 vol.
6. price NA
7. no supp. yet

1. **TRANSPORTATION SAFETY LAW PRACTICE MANUAL**
2. Kenworthy, William E.
3. Butterworth-NH
4. 1989
5. 2 vols.
6. $165
7. periodic supp.
8. 1991 - $65
9. 89-644/19221713/KF2251.K46

1. **TRAVEL LAW**
2. Dickerson, Thomas A.
3. Law Journal
4. 1981
5. 1 vol.
6. $80
7. periodic supp.
8. 1989 - $84; 1990 - $84
9. 81-2056/7276385/KF2042.T75D53

1. **TREATISE ON ENVIRONMENTAL LAW**
2. Grad, Frank P.
3. Bender
4. 1973
5. 5 vols.
6. $510 incl. 3 mos. supp.
7. annual supp.
8. 1989 - $420; 1990 - $484.50
9. 73-87337/805188/KF3775.G7

1. **TREATISE ON HEALTH CARE LAW**
2. MacDonald, Michael B. et al.
3. Bender
4. 1991
5. 4 vols.
6. $395 incl. 3 mos. supp.
7. annual supp.
8. no supp. yet
9. 91-70558/24326156/KF3821.T74

1. **TREIMAN'S LANDLORD & TENANT ENCYCLOPEDIA & REVIEW**
2. Treiman, David M.
3. Lamb's Flight
4. 1991
5. 1 vol.
6. $180 incl. 2 supps.
7. quarterly supp.

1. **TREIMAN'S NEW YORK LANDLORD TENANT STATUTES, ANNOTATED**

2. Treiman, David M.
3. Lamb's Flight
4. 1990
5. 1 vol.
6. $225
7. monthly supp.
9. 20727302

1. **TREIMAN'S RENT STABILIZATION CODE, ANNOTATED**
2. Treiman, David M., ed.
3. Lamb's Flight
4. 1990
5. 1 vol.
6. $150
7. monthly supp.
8. 1991 - $60
9. 19880564/KFX2085.R3T74

1. **TRENDS IN DIVORCE STATEGY**
2. -
3. Maine Bar
4. 1991
5. 1 vol.
6. $35
7. no supp. planned
9. 23893437/KF535.Z99M245

1. **TRESPASS TO TRY TITLE (TEXAS)**
2. Thurow, Harold F.
3. Butterworth-Texas
4. 1988
5. 1 vol.
6. $95
7. periodic supp.
8. 1989 - $38.50; 1990 - $38.50
9. 88-15475/17982568/KFT1397.T73T48

1. **TRIAL ADVOCACY: THE AUTOMOBILE ACCIDENT**
2. -
3. Maine Bar
4. 1990
5. 1 vol.
6. $30
7. no supp. planned

1. **TRIAL ATTORNEY'S EVIDENCE CODE NOTEBOOK, 3rd ed.**
2. -
3. Calif. CEB
4. 3rd ed. - 1982
5. 1 vol.
6. $60
7. periodic supp.
8. 1990 - $45; 1991 - $45
9. 82-73213/9049665/KFC1030.T74

1. **TRIAL BY NOTEBOOK**
2. Vesper, Tom
3. ATLA
4. 1988
5. 1 vol.
6. $110 - nonmembers; $85 - members
7. new ed. planned in 1992

1. **TRIAL EVIDENCE FOUNDATIONS**
2. Tarantino, John A.
3. James
4. 1986
5. 1 vol.
6. $69.93 incl. 3 mos. supp.
7. annual supp.
8. 1990 - $40.99
9. 86-216436/14960010/KF8935.T26

1. **TRIAL HANDBOOK**
2. Sinclair, Kent
3. PLI
4. 2nd. ed. - 1990
5. 1 vol.
6. $95
7. periodic supp.
8. 1991 - $40
9. 85-61114/12368705/KF8915.S56

1. **TRIAL HEARSAY: OBJECTIONS & EXCEPTIONS**
2. Dombroff, Mark A.
3. James
4. 2nd ed. - 1991
5. 1 vol.
6. $49.88 incl. 3 mos. supp.
7. annual supp.
8. 1990 - $37.95; 1991 - $39.91
9. 84-218048/11398708/KF8969.D65

1. **TRIAL MANUAL FOR DEFENSE ATTORNEYS IN JUVENILE COURT**
2. Hertz, Randy, et al.
3. ALI-ABA
4. 1990
5. 2 vols.
6. $250
7. periodic supp.
8. no supp. yet

1. **THE TRIAL NOTEBOOK**
2. DeMuniz, Paul J., et al.
3. OCDLA

4. 1984
5. 1 vol.
6. $65-nonmembers; $45-members
7. periodic supp.
8. no supp. yet
9. 85-143016/12344765/KFO2979.T75

1. **TRIAL OBJECTIONS**
2. Dombroff, Mark A.
3. James
4. 1985
5. 1 vol.
6. $69.94 incl. 3 mos. supp.
7. annual supp.
8. 1989 - $37.85; 1990 - $41.53
9. 85-204987/12057007/KF8935.D65

1. **TRIAL OF ACCIDENT CASES**
2. Schwartz, Louis E.
3. Bender
4. 3rd ed. - 1958
5. 8 vols.
6. $830 incl. 3 mos. supp.
7. annual supp.
8. 1989 - $719; 1990 - $786
9. 59-320/3773776/KF1290.A8S253

1. **TRIAL PREPARATION OF A COMMERCIAL LITIGATION CASE**
2. -
3. Okla. Bar CLE
4. 1990
5. 1 vol.
6. $60
7. no supp. planned

1. **TRIAL SKILLS FOR YOUNG LAWYERS – 3RD ANNUAL**
2. -
3. Minn. CLE
4. 1991
5. 1 vol.
6. $35
7. no supp. planned

1. **THE TRIALBOOK: A TOTAL SYSTEM FOR THE PREPARATION AND PRESENTATION OF A CASE**
2. Sonsteng, John O., et al.
3. West
4. 1985
5. 1 vol.
6. $52.50
7. no supp. yet
9. 85-3273/11754876/KF8915.S66

1. **TROUBLED REAL ESTATE PROJECTS**
2. -
3. Maine Bar
4. 1989
5. 1 vol.
6. $27.50
7. no supp. planned
9. 20905772/KF570.Z99M221

1. **TROUTMAN'S PENNSYLVANIA DAMAGES, PERSONAL INJURY VERDICTS**
2. Hankin, A.
3. Bisel
4. 1969
5. 1 vol.
6. $45 incl. 3 mos. supp.
7. periodic supp.
8. 1990 - $32.50
9. 77-20587/121365/KFP539.P4T72

1. **TROUTMAN'S PENNSYLVANIA NEGLIGENCE INSTANT CASE FINDER**
2. Hankin, A.
3. Bisel
4. 1967
5. 3 vols.
6. $125 incl. 3 mos. supp.
7. periodic supp.
8. 1990 - $46.50
9. 68-2235/431004/KFP196.A53T7

1. **TRUCKING PERMIT GUIDE**
2. -
3. Keller
4. 1974
5. 1 vol.
6. $145
7. quarterly supp.
8. $112/yr.
9. 74-31865

1. **TRUCKING SAFETY GUIDE**
2. Weiland, Betty Bartel
3. Keller
4. 1974
5. 1 vol.
6. $145
7. quarterly supp.
8. $112/yr.
9. 74-31865/3242701/KF2265.K4

1. **TRUST ACTIVITIES HANDBOOK**
2. -
3. Office of Thrift Supervision

4. 1990
5. 1 vol.
6. $50 - regulated instits.; $75 - others
7. periodic supp.

1. **TRUST ADMINISTRATION AND TAXATION**
2. Nossaman, Walter L. & Joseph L. Wyatt, Jr.
3. Bender
4. rev. 2nd ed. - 1966
5. 4 vols.
6. $370 incl. 3 mos. supp.
7. annual supp.
8. 1980 - $220.25; 1990 - $291
9. 8466610/KF6443.A6T7

1. **TRUST ADMINISTRATION IN ILLINOIS**
2. -
3. Illinois ICLE
4. 1987
5. 1 vol.
6. $109.95
7. periodic supp.
8. 1989 - $29.95

1. **TRUST AND WILL PROVISIONS**
2. -
3. U.S. Trust
4. rev. ed. - 1986
5. 1 vol.
6. $255/yr. incl. quarterly "Practical Drafting"
7. revised editions

1. **TRUST DEPARTMENT ADMINISTRATION AND OPERATIONS**
2. Whitney, Victor P.
3. Bender
4. 1981
5. 2 vols.
6. $170 incl. 3 mos. supp.
7. periodic supp.
8. 1989 - $71.50; 1990 - $93.50
9. 81-65436/7707034/KF744.W49

1. **TRUSTEE & DIRECTORS HANDBOOK**
2. Williams, Harding Dec
3. NCSI
4. 1990
5. 1 vol.
6. $115 - members; $170 - nonmembers
7. quarterly supp.
8. $80 - members; $125 - nonmbers

1. **TRUSTMASTER™ – TRUST DRAFTING SYSTEM**
2. Stork, Philip C.
3. Calif. CEB
4. 1986
5. 1 vol. (diskettes avail.)
6. $95 (with disks $395)
7. periodic supp.
8. 1989 - $30

1. **TRUSTS AND TRUSTEES**
2. -
3. Indiana CLE
4. 1989
5. 1 vol.
6. $60
7. no supp. planned

1. **TRUTH IN LENDING: A COMPREHENSIVE GUIDE**
2. Brandel, Roland E., et al.
3. Prentice Hall Law & Business
4. 2nd ed. - 1991
5. 1 vol.
6. $125 incl. 4 mos. supp.
7. periodic supp.
8. no supp. yet
9. 84-22423/11291093/KF1040.B73

1. **TRUTH IN LENDING FOR THE COMMUNITY BANK: A PRACTICAL APPROACH TO REGULATION Z**
2. Stevenson, T. Herbert
3. Probus
4. 1989
5. 1 vol.
6. $75
7. periodic supp.
8. no supp. yet
9. 89-61853/20747003/KF1030.S87

1. **TULANE TAX INSTITUTE**
2. -
3. Claitor's
4. 40th annual - 1990
5. 1 vol.
6. $47.50
7. annual institutes

1. **THE 12TH ANNUAL FRANCHISE LAW INSTITUTE**
2. -
3. UMKC/CLE
4. 1990
5. 1 vol.
6. $50
7. annual institutes

1. **U.C.C. STATE VARIATIONS**
2. Ed. Staff
3. Gould
4. NA
5. 1 vol.
6. $25.95
7. annual supp.
8. $5 - $10/supp.

1. **UNCHARGED MISCONDUCT EVIDENCE**
2. Imwinkelreid, Edward J.
3. Clark Boardman Callaghan
4. 1984
5. 1 vol.
6. $98 incl. 6 mos. supp.
7. annual supp.
8. 1989 - $41.50; 1990 - $45
9. 84-7619/10695855/KF8935.I455

1. **UNCITRAL MODEL LAW OF INTERNATIONAL COMMERCIAL ARBITRATION: A DOCUMENTARY HISTORY**
2. Kavass, Igor I. & Arno Liivak
3. Hein
4. 1985
5. 2 vols.
6. $125
7. periodic supp.
8. 1988 - $67.50; 1989 - $17.50
9. 85-81187/13153488/K2400.U523

1. **UNCLAIMED PROPERTY LAW**
2. Epstein, David J.
3. Bender
4. 1984
5. 5 vols.
6. $565 incl. 3 mos. supp.
7. periodic supp.
8. 1989 - $380; 1990 - $453
9. 83-73619/10692385KF780.Z95E67

1. **UNDERGROUND STORAGE TANK GUIDE**
2. Leiter, Jeffrey, ed.
3. Thompson
4. 1988
5. 2 vols.
6. $350/yr.
7. monthly supp.
8. renewal - $283/yr.
9. 19073210/TD811.5.U57

1. **UNDERGROUND STORAGE TANK LAW**
2. Farer, David B.
3. New Jersey ICLE
4. 2nd ed. - 1990
5. 1 vol.
6. $65
7. periodic supp.
8. no supp. yet

1. **UNDERSTANDING EMPLOYEE BENEFITS**
2. -
3. Ohio CLE
4. 1990
5. 1 vol.
6. $20
7. no supp. planned

1. **UNDERSTANDING FIRREA: A PRACTICAL GUIDE TO PLANNING AND COMPLIANCE**
2. Arnold & Porter, Secura Group, & Arthur Andersen & Co.
3. Prentice Hall Law & Business
4. 1989
5. 1 vol.
6. $95 incl. 4 mos. supp.
7. periodic supp.
8. no supp. yet
9. 89-25564/20595493/KF1009.I85

1. **UNDERSTANDING MINNESOTA WORKERS' COMPENSATION**
2. -
3. MILE
4. 1991
5. 1 vol.
6. $73
7. no supp. planned

1. **UNDERSTANDING THE ALTA TITLE INSURANCE POLICY FORMS**
2. -
3. ALTA
4. 1988
5. 1 vol.
6. $30-members; $40-nonmembers
7. periodic supp.

1. **UNEMPLOYMENT INSURANCE REPORTS**
2. -
3. CCH
4. 1934
5. 16 vols. (federal & all states)
6. $1750/yr.; $1590/yr. for 2 yrs.
7. weekly supp.
9. 7810611/KF3673.4.C6

1. **UNEMPLOYMENT LAW AND PROCEDURE IN S.C.**
2. Garner, Everett Hope
3. S. Carolina Bar
4. 1981
5. 1 vol.
6. $25
7. no supp. yet
9. 13877225/KFS2145.G27

1. **UNIFORM BUILDING CODE**
2. -
3. ICBO
4. 1991
5. 1 vol., new ed. every 3 yrs.
6. $72.50
7. periodic supp.
8. -
9. 81-86610/8649765/KF5701.I525

1. **UNIFORM CIVIL JURY INSTRUCTIONS 1990**
2. -
3. Oregon Bar
4. 1990
5. 1 vol.
6. $82.50
7. annual supp.
8. 1991 - $20
9. KFO2942.A65O711

1. **UNIFORM COMMERCIAL CODE: SELECTED ISSUES**
2. -
3. NH Bar
4. 1987
5. 1 vol.
6. $35
7. no supp. planned

1. **UNIFORM COMMERCIAL CODE CASE DIGEST – NORTHEAST REGION**
2. Pike & Fischer
3. Clark Boardman Callaghan
4. 1991
5. 6 vols.
6. $375. incl. 6 mos. supp.
7. supp. 3x/yr.
8. no supp. yet
9. 91-125021/23255462

1. **UNIFORM COMMERCIAL CODE – CODE SERVICE**
2. Pike & Fischer, ed.
3. Clark Boardman Callaghan
4. 1965
5. 3 vols.
6. $150 incl. 1 yr. supp. & 1 bound vol.
7. quarterly supp.
8. 1988 - $95; 1990 - $105

1. **THE UNIFORM COMMERCIAL CODE FILING GUIDE**
2. Lee, Jacqueline A., ed.
3. Prentice Hall Legal & Financial Services
4. 1991
5. 5 vols.
6. $595/yr.
7. quarterly supp.
9. 91-52948/23988689/KF890.U5

1. **UNIFORM COMMERCIAL CODE REPORTER - DIGEST (Bender's Uniform Commercial Code Service Vols. 6 - 6G)**
2. Hart, Frederick M. & Wm. F. Willier
3. Bender
4. 1965
5. 12 looseleaf vols.
6. $1060 incl. 3 mos. supp.
7. quarterly supp.
8. 1989 - $805.50; 1990 - $935.50
9. 65-6386/10837301/KF890.U5

1. **UNIFORM COMMERCIAL CODE REPORTING SERVICE**
2. Pike & Fischer, ed.
3. Clark Boardman Callaghan
4. 1964
5. 55 vols.
6. $1100 incl. 52 bound vols. & 1 yr. service
7. monthly supp.
8. 1989 - $832.50; 1990 - $882.50
9. 65-3329/14069842/KF885.A45

1. **UNIFORM COMMERCIAL CODE SERIES**
2. Hawkland, William D. et al.
3. Clark Boardman Callaghan
4. 1982
5. 9 vols.
6. $580 incl. 6 mos. supp.
7. annual supp.
8. 1989 - $125; 1990 - $230
9. 82-9735/12745327/KF879.527.H38

1. **UNIFORM COMMERCIAL CODE SERIES–SECURED TRANSACTIONS**
2. Hawkland, William D.
3. Clark Boardman Callaghan
4. 1986

5. 2 vols.
6. $190 incl. 6 mos. supp.
7. annual supp.
8. 1989 - $37.50; 1990 - $39.50

1. **UNIFORM COMMERCIAL CODE TRANSACTION GUIDE: ANALYSIS AND FORMS**
2. Alces, Peter et al.
3. Clark Boardman Callaghan
4. 1988
5. 4 vols.
6. $350 incl. 6 mos. supp.
7. annual supp.
8. 1990 - $49
9. 88-26223/18413205/KF890.U53

1. **UNIFORM CRIMINAL JURY INSTRUCTIONS 1990**
2. -
3. Oregon Bar
4. 1990
5. 1 vol.
6. $82.50
7. annual supp.
8. 1991 - $20
9. KFO2983.A65O71

1. **UNIFORM FIRE CODE**
2. -
3. ICBO
4. 1991
5. 1 vol. new ed. every 3 yrs.
6. $51.25
7. periodic supp.

1. **UNIFORM PRACTICES FOR THE CLEARANCE AND SETTLEMENT OF MORTGAGE–BACKED SECURITIES AND OTHER RELATED SECURITIES**
2. -
3. PSA
4. 1988
5. 1 vol.
6. $400 incl. 1 yr supp.
7. periodic supp.
8. renewal - $300/yr.
9. 18336163/HG4631.U52

1. **UNINSURED AND UNDERINSURED MOTORIST INSURANCE, 2ND ED.**
2. Widiss, Alan I.
3. Anderson
4. 1985; 1986
5. 3 vols.
6. $275 incl. 1 yr. supp.
7. periodic supp.
8. 1990 - $125
9. 84-29772/11621837/KF1218.8.W5

1. **UNINSURED MOTORIST**
2. Blakeslee, Wes et al.
3. MICPEL
4. 1991
5. 1 vol.
6. $73.50 (with audio tapes)
7. no supp. planned

1. **UNINSURED MOTORIST**
2. -
3. NH Bar
4. 1987
5. 1 vol.
6. $20
7. no supp. planned

1. **UNINSURED/UNDERINSURED MOTORIST COVERAGE**
2. -
3. MILE
4. 1991
5. 1 vol.
6. $68
7. no supp. planned

1. **UNION LABOR REPORT**
2. Manville, Bill L.
3. BNA
4. 1947
5. 2 vols.
6. $572/yr.
7. biweekly supp. & weekly newsletter
8. renewal - $548/yr.
9. 73-643590/1786751/KF3365.U5

1. **UNION LIST OF LEGISLATIVE HISTORIES, 47TH CONGRESS, 1881 - 101st CONGRESS, 1990**
2. Law Librarian's Society of D.C.
3. Rothman
4. 6th ed. - 1991
5. 1 vol.
6. $95
7. periodic supp.
9. 91-31271/KF4.U55

1. **UNITED STATES ATTORNEYS' MANUAL**
2. U.S. Justice Dept. Executive Office for U.S. Attorneys

3. order from USGPO - stock #927-004-00000-3 (Titles 1-8) #927-005-00000-0 (Title 9)
4. 1988
5. 9 vols.
6. $937/yr.
7. periodic supp.
9. 7222662

1. **U.S.–CANADA FREE TRADE AGREEMENT: THE COMPLETE RESOURCE GUIDE**
2. -
3. BNA
4. 1988
5. 3 vols.
6. $260
7. no supp. planned
9. 18151633/HF1480.5.U55

1. **UNITED STATES, COMMON MARKET AND INTERNATIONAL ANTITRUST: A COMPARATIVE GUIDE**
2. Hawk, Barry E.
3. Prentice Hall Law & Business
4. 2nd ed. - 1984
5. 4 vols.
6. $360 incl. 4 mos. supp.
7. periodic supp.
8. 1990 - $95; 1991 - $95
9. 84-27790//r902/11523683/K3856.H39

1. **U.S. CORPORATE HANDBOOK**
2. Schneemann, Angela
3. Mariposa
4. 1990
5. 2 vols.
6. $150
7. periodic supp.

1. **UNITED STATES COURT OF INTERNATIONAL TRADE - RULES**
2. -
3. Invictus
4. 1980
5. 1 vol.
6. $32 incl. 1 yr. supp.
7. supp. as required
9. 7903736/KF6698.A4

1. **U.S. COURT OF INTERNATIONAL TRADE RULES AND ANNOTATION SERVICE**
2. -
3. Rules
4. 1984
5. 1 vol.
6. $45 incl. 1 yr. supp.
7. periodic supp.
8. renewal fee

1. **U.S. CUSTOMS AND INTERNATIONAL TRADE GUIDE**
2. Feller, Peter Buck
3. Bender
4. 1979
5. 4 vols.
6. $405 incl. 3 mos. supp.
7. semiannual supp.
8. 1989 - $105; 1990 - $385
9. 79-56008/6707816/KF6659.F44

1. **U.S. CUSTOMS REGULATIONS**
2. -
3. Unz & Co.
4. 1991
5. 1 vol.
6. $275/yr.
7. periodic supp.

1. **UNITED STATES DISTRICT COURT RULES FOR THE DISTRICT OF ALASKA**
2. -
3. Book Pub.
4. NA
5. 1 vol.
6. $23
7. supp. as needed
8. 1990 - $7.50; 1991 - free
9. 9897965

1. **UNITED STATES EXPORT CONTROLS**
2. Liebman, John R. & William A. Root
3. Prentice Hall Law & Business
4. 3rd ed. - 1991
5. 1 vol.
6. $95 incl. 4 mos. supp.
7. periodic supp.
8. no supp.yet
9. 91-37498/24590062/KF1987.L54

1. **UNITED STATES FEDERAL ELECTION LAW: FEDERAL REGULATION OF POLITICAL CAMPAIGN FINANCE AND PARTICIPATION**
2. Bauer, Robert F. & Doris M. Kafka
3. Oceana
4. 1982
5. 1 vol.
6. $125
7. periodic supp.

8. 1984 - $100
9. 82-12455/8589271/KF4920.B35

1. **UNITED STATES INCOME TAX TREATIES**
2. Shannon, Harry
3. Kluwer
4. 1989
5. 1 vol.
6. $138 incl. 3 mos. supp.
7. periodic supp.
8. 1990 - $76; 1991 - $100
9. 89-8104/19627489/KF6306.S53

1. **U.S. INTELLECTUAL PROPERTY LEGISLATIVE REVIEW**
2. Lver, Jack Q., ed.
3. Clark Boardman Callaghan
4. 1991
5. 1 vol.
6. $95 incl. 5 mos. supp.
7. annual supp.
8. no supp. yet
9. 24244015/KF2973.99.U85

1. **U.S. INTERNATIONAL TAXATION**
2. Kuntz, Joel & Robert Peroni
3. WG&L
4. 1991
5. 2 vols.
6. $295
7. supp. 3x/yr.
8. no supp. yet

1. **UNITED STATES INTERNATIONAL TRADE REPORTS**
2. Newman, Edwin S. & Eugene M. Wypyski
3. Oceana
4. 1981-86
5. 7 vols.
6. $525
7. set closed
8. continued by U.S. International Trade Reports - New Series
9. 81-11181/7653247/KF6655.A52U54

1. **U.S. INTERNATIONAL TRADE REPORTS, NEW SERIES**
2. Newman, Edwin S. & Eugene M. Wypyski
3. Oceana
4. 1986
5. 5 vols.
6. $400
7. periodic supp.
8. 1990 - $125; 1991 - $125
9. 81-11181/14181623/KF6655.A52U54

1. **U.S. - ISRAEL FREE TRADE AGREEMENT**
2. Samet, Andrew James & Moshe Goldberg, eds.
3. Bus. Laws
4. 1989
5. 1 vol.
6. $75
7. no supp. planned

1. **UNITED STATES LAW WEEK**
2. Pease, Gregory R.
3. BNA
4. 1932
5. 2 vols.
6. $668/yr.
7. weekly supp.; daily when court is in session
8. renewal - $632/yr.
9. 34-436/1768758

1. **UNITED STATES LEGISLATION ON FOREIGN RELATIONS AND INTERNATIONAL COMMERCE**
2. Kavass, Igor I. & Michael J. Blake
3. Hein
4. rev. ed. - 1991-92
5. 5 vols.
6. $625
7. periodic supp.
8. no supp. yet
9. 10244732/KF4650.A3

1. **U.S. POSTAL SERVICE PROCUREMENT MANUAL**
2. U.S. Postal Service
3. order from USGPO
   - stock #939-006-00000-1
4. 1987
5. 1 vol.
6. $103 incl. all supp.
7. periodic supp.
9. 16874800

1. **UNITED STATES SPACE LAW – NATIONAL AND INTERNATIONAL REGULATIONS**
2. Gorove, Stephen
3. Oceana
4. 1982
5. 3 vols.
6. $300/set
7. periodic supp.
8. 1990 - $125; 1991 - $125
9. 81-22465

1. **U.S. SUPREME COURT BULLETIN**
2. -
3. CCH
4. 1936
5. 1 vol.
6. $580/yr.; $525/yr. for 2 yrs.
7. daily supp. when court in session
9. 78-6453/4170787/KF101.C64

1. **U.S. SUPREME COURT CASES AND COMMENTS**
2. Erickson, Hon. William H., et al.
3. Bender
4. 1985
5. 2 vols.
6. $210 incl. 3 mos. supp.
7. periodic supp.
8. 1989 - $105; 1990 - $129.50
9. 85-72658/12905828/KF9218.E75

1. **UNITED STATES TAX CONVENTIONS. (Roberts & Holland Collection)**
2. Roberts, Sydney I, ed.
3. Hein
4. 1986
5. 16 vols.
6. $1395
7. annual supp.
8. 1988 - $185

1. **U.S. TAXATION OF INTERNATIONAL OPERATIONS**
2. -
3. WG&L
4. 1973
5. 1 vol.
6. $475/yr.
7. semimonthly supp.
9. 83-9560/9541478

1. **U.S. TRADEMARK LAW - RULES OF PRACTICE, FORMS & FEDERAL STATUTES**
2. -
3. USTA
4. 1989
5. 1 vol.
6. $89.95
7. periodic supp.
8. 1988 - $16.95; 1990 - free
9. 84-50807/10854576/KF3181.A3

1. **UNJUST DISMISSAL**
2. Larson, Lex R.
3. Bender
4. 1985
5. 2 vols.
6. $250 incl. 3 mos. supp.
7. annual supp.
8. 1989 - $175; 1990 - $196
9. 84-73553/11882326/KF3471.Z95L37

1. **USE OF EXPERTS FOR ACCIDENT RECONSTRUCTION**
2. Baldwin, Rignal W., Jr. et al.
3. MICPEL
4. 1991
5. 1 vol.
6. $42
7. no supp. planned

1. **USE OF STATISTICS IN EQUAL EMPLOYMENT OPPORTUNITY**
2. Connolly, Walter B. Jr. & David Peterson
3. Law Journal
4. 1979
5. 1 vol.
6. $75
7. periodic supp.
8. 1988 - $74; 1989 - $40
9. 79-28419/5887677/KF3464.C67

1. **A USER'S GUIDE TO COMPUTER CONTRACTING: FORMS, TECHNIQUES AND STRATEGIES**
2. Davis, Lanny J., et al.
3. Prentice Hall Law & Business
4. 1984
5. 1 vol.
6. $75 incl. 4 mos. supp.
7. periodic supp.
8. 1988 - $45; 1989 - $45
9. 84-9667/10752880/KF905.C6U84

1. **USSR, EASTERN EUROPE AND THE DEVELOPMENT OF THE LAW OF THE SEA**
2. Butler, William E.
3. Oceana
4. 1983
5. 2 vols.
6. $200/set
7. periodic supp.
8. 1986 - $65; 1987 - $65
9. 85-132907/10807790/JX4422.E852U77

1. **UTAH ENVIRONMENTAL LAND USE PERMIT MANUAL**
2. -
3. Utah Bar

4. 1986
5. 1 vol.
6. $40
7. no supp. yet

1. **UTILITIES LAW REPORTS**
2. -
3. CCH
4. 1928
5. 3 vols.
6. $1845/yr.; $1675/yr. for 2 yrs.
7. weekly supp.
9. 78-6452/4170780

1. **UTILITY HOLDING COMPANIES**
2. Hawes, Douglas W.
3. Clark Boardman Callaghan
4. 1984
5. 1 vol.
6. $120 incl. 3 mos. supp.
7. annual supp.
8. 1986 - $40; 1987 - $47.50
9. 84-292/10349874/KF2099.H38

1. **VALENTINE-BINNS JUSTICE**
2. Valentine, W.
3. Bisel
4. 1966
5. 1 vol.
6. $49.50 incl. 3 mos. supp.
7. periodic supp.
8. 1984 - $28
9. 7864601/KFP520.B55

1. **VALUATION AND DISTRIBUTION OF MARITAL PROPERTY**
2. Publ. Ed. Staff
3. Bender
4. 1984
5. 3 vols.
6. $335 incl. 3 mos. supp.
7. periodic supp.
8. 1989 - $247; 1990 - $277.50
9. 83-73628/10646874/KF524.V35

1. **VALUATION OF A CLOSELY HELD BUSINESS & USE OF FINANCIAL EXPERTS IN LITIGATION**
2. -
3. Minn. CLE
4. 1991
5. 1 vol.
6. $35
7. no supp. planned

1. **VEHICLE SIZES AND WEIGHTS MANUAL**
2. Weiland, Betty Bartel
3. Keller
4. 1974
5. 1 vol.
6. $95
7. semiannual supp.
8. $85/yr.
9. 74-31863/1818060/KF2212.A6K44

1. **VENTURE CAPITAL AND PUBLIC OFFERING NEGOTIATION**
2. Halloran, Michael J., ed.
3. Prentice Hall Law & Business
4. 1983
5. 2 vols.
6. $160 incl. 4 mos. supp.
7. annual supp.
8. 1990 - $60; 1991 - $60
9. 82-23943/9083289/KF1366.V46

1. **VENTURE CAPITAL AND SMALL BUSINESS FINANCINGS (Securities Law Series, Vol. 2, 2A & 2B)**
2. Haft, Robert J.
3. Clark Boardman Callaghan
4. 1984
5. 4 vols.
6. $435 incl. 3 mos. supp.
7. annual supp.
8. 1989 - $217.50; 1991 - $265
9. 84-14514/10996242/KF1659.H33

1. **VERMONT COURT RULES ANNOTATED**
2. -
3. Equity
4. 1981
5. 2 vols.
6. $85
7. semiannual supp.
8. 1990 - $45; 1991 - $38
9. 84-189009/11188343/KFV529.A2

1. **VICTIMS' RIGHTS: LAW AND LITIGATION**
2. Rapp, J. and F. Carrington
3. Bender
4. 1989
5. 1 vol.
6. $115 incl. 3 mos. supp.
7. annual supp.
8. 1990 - $50
9. 88-63258/19275420/KF9763.C37

1. **VIRGINIA ADMINISTRATIVE LAW AND PRACTICE**
2. Midkiff, Charles J. & Michael Maupin, eds.
3. Jt. Comm. Va.
4. 2nd ed. - 1986
5. 1 vol.
6. $52
7. periodic supp.
8. no supp. yet
9. 1326095//KFV2840.V57

1. **VIRGINIA CIRCUIT COURT JUDGES BENCHBOOK – CIVIL**
2. Circuit Court Benchbook Comm. of the Supreme Court of Va.
3. Michie
4. 1991
5. 1 vol.
6. $90 incl. 3 mos. supp.
7. periodic supp.
9. 91-60479/24247232/KFV2975.V57

1. **VIRGINIA CIRCUIT COURT JUDGES BENCHBOOK – CRIMINAL**
2. Circuit Court Benchbook Comm. of the Supreme Court of Va.
3. Michie
4. 1991
5. 1 vol.
6. $90 incl. 3 mos. supp.
7. periodic supp.
9. 91-60480/24430560/KFV2928.V57

1. **VIRGINIA CONDOMINIUM LAW**
2. MacGregor, Douglas S.
3. Butterworth-Fla.
4. 1987
5. 1 vol.
6. $50
7. periodic supp.
8. 1990 - $27.75
9. 87-402185/16471429/KFV2514.C6M33

1. **VIRGINIA CORPORATIONS**
2. Lefcoe, Vann H.
3. Lawyers Coop.
4. 1982
5. 1 vol.
6. $115 incl. 6 mos. supp.
7. annual supp.
8. 1990 - $54; 1991 - $57.50
9. 81-85751/8570684/KFV2613.L43

1. **VIRGINIA COURT RULES SERVICE**
2. -
3. Rules
4. 1991
5. 2 vols.
6. $75 incl. 1 yr. supp.
7. periodic supp.
8. no supp. yet

1. **THE VIRGINIA LAWYER: A BASIC PRACTICE HANDBOOK**
2. Mayes, Joseph R.
3. Michie
4. 1979
5. 2 vols.
6. $100
7. periodic supp.
8. 1989 - $40; 1991 - $50
9. 5691605/KFV2477.V5

1. **VIRGINIA MODEL JURY INSTRUCTIONS - CIVIL**
2. Model Jury Instructions Committee
3. Michie
4. 1988
5. 2 vols.
6. $180
7. periodic supp.
8. 1990 - $60
9. 88-63947/19342402/KFV2983.A65V5

1. **VIRGINIA MODEL JURY INSTRUCTIONS - CRIMINAL**
2. Model Jury Instructions Committee
3. Michie
4. 1989
5. 2 vols.
6. $180
7. periodic supp.
8. 1990 - $60
9. 13052675/KFV2983.A65M63

1. **VIRGINIA PROBATE LAW**
2. Hapner, Elisabeth
3. Butterworth-Fla.
4. 1987
5. 2 vols.
6. $80
7. periodic supp.
8. 1991 - $24
9. 19101286/KFV2544.A6H3

1. **VOIR DIRE: LEARN TO USE IT OR LOSE IT**
2. -
3. Wash. Bar
4. 1988

5. 1 vol.
6. $35
7. no supp. planned

1. **VOLUNTARY TERMINATION OF PARENTAL RIGHTS AND ADOPTION**
2. Newton, Judith Sperling
3. State Bar of Wisc.
4. 1990
5. 1 vol.
6. $95
7. periodic supp.
8. no supp. yet
9. 89-71245//r90/20827153/ KFW2504.6.N49

1. **WAGES AND HOURS: LAW AND PRACTICE**
2. Leader, Laurie E.
3. Bender
4. 1990
5. 1 vol.
6. $100 incl. 3 mos. supp.
7. periodic supp.
8. no supp. yet
9. 89-82392/21347155/KF3489.L4

1. **WARD ON TITLE EXAMINATIONS**
2. -
3. Illinois ICLE
4. 1986
5. 1 vol.
6. $90.95
7. periodic supp.
8. no supp. yet
9. 75-32865/2090861/KFI1327.W36

1. **WARRANTLESS SEARCH LAW DESKBOOK**
2. Joseph, Paul R.
3. Clark Boardman Callaghan
4. 1991
5. 1 vol.
6. $75 incl. 3 mos. supp.
7. annual supp.
9. 91-12047/23355593/KF9630.J67

1. **WARREN'S FORMS OF AGREEMENTS**
2. Warren, Oscar Leroy, et al.
3. Bender
4. 1954
5. 4 vols.
6. $500 incl. 3 mos. supp.
7. annual supp.
8. 1989 - $542; 1990 - $471.50
9. 64-1863/615144/KF886.W36

1. **WARREN'S FORMS OF AGREEMENTS - BUSINESS FORMS: DESK EDITION**
2. Greenhill, Amelia C.
3. Bender
4. 1975
5. 1 vol.
6. $145 incl. 3 mos. supp.
7. annual supp.
8. 1989 - $114; 1990 - $134
9. 75-27334/13989337/R346.73

1. **WARREN'S HEATON SURROGATE'S COURT PRACTICE**
2. Warren, Oscar L. et al.
3. Bender
4. 6th ed. - 1940
5. 22 vols.
6. $1250 incl. 3 mos. supp.
7. biannual supp.
8. 1989 - $853; 1990 - $1099
9. 40-3521/2400230/KFN5205.H47

1. **WARREN'S NEGLIGENCE IN NEW YORK COURTS**
2. Warren, O.L.
3. Bender
4. 1966
5. 23 vols.
6. $790 incl. 3 mos. supp.
7. semiannual supp.
8. 1989 - $497; 1990 - $638
9. 67-9319//r892/3176352/KFN5315.W33

1. **WARREN'S WEED NEW YORK REAL PROPERTY**
2. Warren, Oscar L. et al.
3. Bender
4. 4th ed. - 1950
5. 14 vols.
6. $1100 incl. 3 mos. supp.
7. annual supp.
8. 1989 - $902; 1990 - $977
9. 50-3981/1737559/KFN5140.W4

1. **WASHINGTON ADMINISTRATIVE LAW PRACTICE MANUAL**
2. Finnigan, Richard A. et al.
3. Butterworth-St. Paul
4. 1991
5. 1 vol.
6. $85
7. periodic supp.
8. no supp. yet

9. 91-1974/23015365//KFW440.W36

1. **WASHINGTON CIVIL PROCEDURE BEFORE TRIAL DESKBOOK**
2. McKintry, Ronald E. Ed.
3. Wash. Bar
4. 1981, 1986
5. 2 vols.
6. $125
7. periodic supp.
8. 1986 - $45
9. 80-620013/7128518/KFW537.W37

1. **WASHINGTON COMMERCIAL LAW DESKBOOK**
2. Daheim, Warren J,. ed.
3. Wash. Bar
4. 1983
5. 3 vols.
6. $125
7. periodic supp.
7. 1987 - $45

1. **WASHINGTON COMMUNITY PROPERTY DESKBOOK**
2. Shields, Hon. George T., ed.
3. Wash. Bar
4. 2nd ed. - 1989
5. 1 vol.
6. $95
7. periodic supp.
8. no supp. yet
9. 86-51044/20363856/KFW97.W38

1. **WASHINGTON CORPORATE FORMS**
2. Hoff, David D. & Morris G. Kremin
3. Aspen
4. 1991
5. 2 vols.
6. $160 incl. 3 mos. supp.
7. annual supp.
8. no supp. yet

1. **WASHINGTON COURT RULES ANNOTATED WITH FORMS**
2. Hall, Glenna S.
3. Bancroft
4. 1977
5. 3 vols.
6. $225 incl. 6 mos. supp.
7. annual supp.
8. 1990 - $45; 1991 - $50
9. 77-82260//r872/3343641/KFW529.A2

1. **WASHINGTON FAMILY LAW DESKBOOK**
2. Halverson, Lowell K., ed.
3. Wash. Bar
4. 1989
5. 2 vols.
6. $145
7. periodic supp.
8. no supp. yet
9. 88-51799//r89/20297646/KFW94.W37

1. **WASHINGTON GUARDIANSHIP LAW: ADMINISTRATION AND LITIGATION**
2. Treacy, Gerald B. Jr.
3. Butterworth-St. Paul
4. 1988
5. 1 vol.
6. $75
7. biennial supp.
8. 1991 - $50
9. 88-14593/KFW106.T74

1. **WASHINGTON MOTOR VEHICLE ACCIDENT DESKBOOK**
2. Creatura, J. Richard
3. Wash. Bar
4. 1988
5. 1 vol.
6. $120
7. periodic supp.
8. no supp. yet
9. 87-51491/18380730/KFW196.3.A8W37

1. **WASHINGTON MOTOR VEHICLE ACCIDENT INSURANCE DESKBOOK**
2. Taylor, Robert & Karen Weaver, eds.
3. Wash. Bar
4. 1989
5. 1 vol.
6. $80
7. periodic supp.
8. no supp. yet
9. 88-51553/20394239/KFW191.A4W37

1. **WASHINGTON MOTOR VEHICLE ACCIDENT LITIGATION DESKBOOK**
2. -
3. Wash. Bar
4. 1990
5. 1 vol.
6. $120
7. periodic supp.
8. no supp. yet

1. **WASHINGTON PARTNERSHIP LAW AND PRACTICE HANDBOOK**
2. -

3. Wash. Bar
4. 1984
5. 1 vol.
6. $95
7. no supp. planned

1. **WASHINGTON PROBATE PRACTICE, PROCEDURE AND TAX MANUALS**
2. Mucklestone, Robert S.
3. Book Pub.
4. 1983
5. 3 vols.
6. $200
7. annual supp.
8. 1990 - $45; 1991 - $45
9. 84-233218/11573698/KFW144.W28

1. **WASHINGTON PUBLIC EMPLOYMENT RELATIONS REPORTER**
2. -
3. Book Pub.
4. 1976
5. 7 vols.
6. $250 incl. 3 mos. supp.
7. monthly supp.
8. renewal - $600/yr.
9. 6984172/KF3409.P77W38

1. **WASHINGTON REAL PROPERTY DESKBOOK, 2ND ED.**
2. Kuhrau, Edward W. ed.
3. Wash. Bar
4. 1986
5. 4 vols.
6. $265
7. periodic supp.
8. 1989 - $85
9. 86-50423//r87/15161921/KFW112.W37

1. **WASHINGTON RULES OF COURT ANNOTATED**
2. -
3. Book Pub.
4. 1974
5. 3 vols.
6. $157
7. semiannual supp.
8. 1989 - $101; 1990 - $100
9. 10917994/KFW529.A2

1. **THE WASHINGTON STATE ENVIRONMENTAL POLICY ACT: A LEGAL AND POLICY ANALYSIS (SEPA)**
2. Settle, Richard L.
3. Butterworth-St. Paul
4. 1987
5. 1 vol.
6. $75
7. periodic supp.
8. 1990 - $30
9. 86-72033/15577829/KFW354.S47

1. **WASHINGTON WILLS & TRUST FORMS**
2. Mucklestone, Robert S.
3. Book Pub.
4. 1987
5. 1 vol.
6. $75
7. periodic supp.
8. no supp. yet
9. 16119555

1. **WATER POLLUTION CONTROL**
2. Joseph, Eileen L.
3. BNA
4. 1979
5. 2 vols.
6. $545 incl. 1 yr. supp.
7. biweekly supp. & biweekly newsletter - "Air and Water Pollution Control"
8. renewal - $495/yr.
9. 79-9433/5319928

1. **WEINSTEIN, KORN AND MILLER CPLR MANUAL**
2. Chase, Oscar G.
3. Bender
4. 2nd ed. - 1980
5. 1 vol.
6. $125 incl. 3 mos. supp.
7. annual supp.
8. 1989 - $97.50; 1990 - $86.50
9. 80-69176/6776763/KFN5995.W4

1. **WEINSTEIN'S EVIDENCE MANUAL**
2. Weinstein J.B. and M.A. Berger
3. Bender
4. 1987
5. 1 vol.
6. $125 incl. 3 mos. supp.
7. periodic supp.
8. 1989 - $59.50; 1990 - $70
9. 87-070538/15649870/KF8935.W4

1. **WEINSTEIN'S EVIDENCE, UNITED STATES COURT RULES**
2. Weinstein, Hon. Jack B. & Margaret A. Berger
3. Bender

4. 1975
5. 7 vols.
6. $1015 incl. 3 mos. supp.
7. semiannual supp.
8. 1989 - $676; 1990 - $899.50
9. 72-97503/2656287/KF8935.W39

1. **WELFARE BENEFITS GUIDE 91-92**
2. Routh, Paul J. & Ronald A. Kladder
3. Clark Boardman Callaghan
4. 1990
5. 1 vol.
6. $75 incl. 3 mos. supp.
7. annual supp.
8. no supp. yet
9. Z90-2624/24705452/KF3509.R68

1. **WEST COAST CONSTRUCTION LIENS & CLAIMS MANUAL**
2. Keyes, Michael
3. Book Pub.
4. 1979
5. 1 vol.
6. $55
7. supp. as needed
8. 1988 - $35; 1989 - $13.50

1. **WEST VIRGINIA PRACTICE HANDBOOK, 3rd ed.**
2. West Va. State Bar, Young Lawyers Section
3. Michie
4. 1988
5. 2 vols.
6. $160
7. periodic supp.
9. 88-60640/18559423/KFW1730.W47

1. **WESTERN EUROPE AND THE DEVELOPMENT OF LAW OF THE SEA; NATIONAL LEGISLATION**
2. Durante, Francesco
3. Oceana
4. 1979
5. 4 vols. (set closed)
6. $300/set
7. no supp. planned
8. continued in New Directions in the Law of the Sea
9. 79-55008/5540350/K1150.D87

1. **WESTERN WATER LAW**
2. Musick, John
3. Francis Marion
4. 1991
5. 2 vols.
6. $150
7. semiannual supp.
8. 1992 - $65

1. **WG&L ESTATE PLANNING AND ADMINISTRATION**
2. Whitman, Robert, ed.
3. WG&L
4. 1988
5. 1 vol.
6. $175/yr.
7. periodic supp.

1. **WG&L HUMAN RESOURCES FORMS WITH COMMENTARY**
2. Asquith, Nancy
3. WG&L
4. 1976
5. 1 vol.
6. $98
7. semiannual supp.
8. 1988 - $80; 1991 - $87.50
9. 76-26207/2644190/HF5549.5.P4M63

1. **WG&L TAX PLANNING CHECKLISTS**
2. Stanislaw, James & Daniel E. Feld
3. WG&L
4. 1991
5. 1 vol.
6. $98
7. annual editions

1. **WHAT EVERYONE NEEDS TO KNOW ABOUT ENVIRONMENTAL LAW**
2. -
3. Indiana CLE
4. 1988
5. 1 vol.
6. $40
7. no supp. planned

1. **WHAT THE WASHINGTON PRACTITIONER NEEDS TO KNOW ABOUT BASIC REAL ESTATE**
2. -
3. Wash. Bar
4. 1988
5. 1 vol.
6. $35
7. no supp. planned

1. **WHAT TO DO ABOUT PERSONNEL PROBLEMS IN [YOUR STATE]**
2. -
3. BLR

4. 1987 -
5. 2 vols.
6. $216/yr.
7. 2 monthly newsletters

1. **WHAT YOU NEED TO KNOW TO SETTLE WITH INSURANCE COMPANIES**
2. Veitch, Thomas
3. James
4. 1991
5. 1 vol.
6. $69.98 incl. 3 mos. supp.
7. annual supp.
8. no supp. yet
9. 24200335/KF1146.V44W52

1. **WHEN YOU NEED TO KNOW: FAMILY LAW**
2. -
3. Wash. Bar
4. 1989
5. 1 vol.
6. $35
7. no supp. planned

1. **WHITE COLLAR CRIME**
2. -
3. NH Bar
4. 1988
5. 1 vol.
6. $35
7. no supp. planned

1. **WHITE COLLAR CRIME: BUSINESS AND REGULATORY OFFENSES**
2. Obermaier, Otto G. & Robert G. Morvillo, eds.
3. Law Journal
4. 1989
5. 1 vol.
6. $85
7. periodic supp.
8. no supp. yet
9. 90-5425/21036673/KF9350.W43

1. **WHITE COLLAR LITIGATION: CIVIL AND CRIMINAL**
2. -
3. MILE
4. 1991
5. 1 vol.
6. $68
7. no supp. planned
9. 24207327/KF9350.Z9W55

1. **WHITE, NEW YORK CORPORATIONS**
2. Kantrowitz, Isidore
3. Bender
4. 13th ed. - 1963
5. 8 vols.
6. $555 incl. 3 mos. supp.
7. annual supp.
8. 1989 - $462; 1990 - $525
9. 78-643378/4407049/KFN5340.A29B46

1. **WILL DRAFTING – "BEYOND THE BASICS"**
2. Counts, Richard L., III, et al.
3. MICPEL
4. 1990
5. 1 vol.
6. $40
7. periodic supp.
8. no supp. yet
9. 18965736/KFM1342.W68

1. **WILL DRAFTING: PLANNING IN LESS CERTAIN TIMES**
2. -
3. Conn. Bar
4. 1991
5. 1 vol.
6. $53
7. no supp. planned

1. **WILL DRAFTING AND BASIC ESTATE PLANNING**
2. -
3. MILE
4. 1990
5. 1 vol.
6. $63
7. no supp. planned

1. **WILL FORMS AND CLAUSES**
2. Lynn, Robert J.
3. Anderson
4. 1984
5. 1 vol.
6. $49.50 incl. 1 yr. supp.
7. annual supp.
8. 1990 - $25; 1991 - $30
9. 11963493/KF755.A65A52

1. **WILLS TRUSTS FORMS**
2. -
3. RIA
4. 1961
5. 1 vol.

6. $400/yr.; $375/yr. for 2 yrs.
7. monthly supp.
8. renewal - $350/yr.

1. **WINNING ATTORNEY'S FEES FROM THE U.S. GOVERNMENT**
2. Bennett, Joel P.
3. Law Journal
4. 1984
5. 1 vol.
6. $70 incl. 3 mos. supp.
7. periodic supp.
8. 1989 - $39; 1990 - $40
9. 84-4363/10505854/KF8995.B46

1. **WINNING FINAL ARGUMENTS**
2. Linkner, Monica Farris
3. MTLA
4. 1985
5. 1 vol.
6. $60 (member); $75 (nonmember)
7. no supp. planned

1. **WINNING ON APPEAL: GOOD APPELLATE PRACTICE**
2. -
3. Indiana CLE
4. 1990
5. 1 vol.
6. $50
7. no supp. planned

1. **WINNING YOUR CASE THROUGH EFFECTIVE PRETRIAL DISCOVERY**
2. -
3. Indiana CLE
4. 1990
5. 1 vol.
6. $60
7. no supp. planned

1. **WISCONSIN ATTORNEY'S DESK REFERENCE**
2. -
3. State Bar of Wisc.
4. 1986
5. 1 vol.
6. $105
7. periodic supp.
8. 1990 - $64; 1991 - $57
9. 15172687/KFW2481.W57

1. **WISCONSIN ATTORNEY'S/ SECRETARY'S HANDBOOK**
2. -
3. Mariposa
4. 1991
5. 1 vol.
6. $51
7. annual supp.
8. 1990 - $49; 1991 - $42
9. 20476870

1. **WISCONSIN CIVIL PRACTICE FORMS**
2. -
3. Lawyers Coop.
4. 1970
5. 4 vols.
6. $340 incl. 6 mos. supp.
7. annual supp.
8. 1989 - $92; 1990 - $98.50
9. 79-102900/133702/KFW2930.A65K4

1. **WISCONSIN CORPORATIONS**
2. Postlewaite, Jack A.
3. Lawyers Coop.
4. 1980
5. 1 vol.
6. $115 incl. 6 mos. supp.
7. annual supp.
8. 1990 - $54; 1991 - $65
9. 79-91166/6598836/KFW2613.P655

1. **WISCONSIN DISCOVERY LAW AND PRACTICE**
2. Bolton, Richard L., et al.
3. State Bar of Wisc.
4. 1990
5. 1 vol.
6. $120
7. periodic supp.
8. no supp. yet
9. 90-20815/22624180/KFW2937.W57

1. **WISCONSIN ETHICS OPINIONS**
2. -
3. State Bar of Wisc.
4. 1990
5. 1 vol.
6. $70
7. annual supp.
8. 1991 - $32

1. **THE WISCONSIN FAIR DEALERSHIP LAW**
2. Butler, Brian E. & Michael A. Bowen
3. State Bar of Wisc.
4. 1988
5. 1 vol.
6. $115

7. periodic supp.
8. 1990 - $30; 1991 - $48.50
9. 88-20076/18191352/KFW2681.F7B69

1. **WISCONSIN INHERITANCE, ESTATE AND GIFT TAX HANDBOOK**
2. Schmidt, Neal E.
3. CLE - Wisc.
4. 1982
5. 1 vol.
6. $60
7. annual supp.
8. 1990 - $40; 1991 - $40
9. 8502469/KFW2882.Z9S35

1. **WISCONSIN JUDICIAL BENCHBOOK: VOL. 1 - CRIMINAL AND TRAFFIC**
2. -
3. State Bar of Wisc.
4. 1982
5. 1 vol.
6. $95 ($250/set of 4 vols.)
7. periodic supp.
8. 1988 - $17
9. 82-620023/8938914/KFW2930.W57

1. **WISCONSIN JUDICIAL BENCHBOOK: VOL. 2 - CIVIL**
2. -
3. State Bar of Wisc.
4. 1982
5. 1 vol.
6. $95 ($250/set of 4 vols.)
7. periodic supp.
8. 1984 - $30; 1989 - $55
9. 82-620023/8938914/KFW2930.W57

1. **WISCONSIN JUDICIAL BENCHBOOK: VOL. 3 - FAMILY**
2. -
3. State Bar of Wisc.
4. 1982
5. 1 vol.
6. $80 ($250/set of 4 vols.)
7. annual supp.
8. 1990 - $60
9. 82-620023/8938914/KFW2930.W57

1. **WISCONSIN JUDICIAL BENCHBOOK: VOL. 4 - PROBATE, JUVENILE AND MENTAL**
2. -
3. State Bar of Wisc.
4. 1988
5. 1 vol.
6. $95 ($250/set of 4 vols.)
7. annual supp.
8. 1989 - $40; 1991 - $43.50

1. **WISCONSIN JURY INSTRUCTIONS - CIVIL**
2. Committee
3. CLE - Wisc.
4. 1981
5. 3 vols.
6. $150
7. annual supp.
8. 1990 - $60; 1991 - $60
9. 81-50689/7478213/KFW2942.A6W5

1. **WISCONSIN JURY INSTRUCTIONS - CRIMINAL**
2. Committee
3. CLE - Wisc.
4. 1980
5. 4 vols.
6. $150
7. quarterly supp.
8. renewal - $50/yr.

1. **WISCONSIN MISDEMEANORS AND MOVING TRAFFIC VIOLATIONS, 2ND ED.**
2. Steele, Clifford R.
3. Butterworth-St. Paul
4. 2nd ed. - 1989
5. 1 vol.
6. $88
7. periodic supp.
8. no supp. yet
9. 88-37495/18983773/KFW2975.W57

1. **THE WISCONSIN PROBATE SYSTEM BOOK**
2. -
3. State Bar of Wisc.
4. 1989
5. 1 vol.
6. $125
7. periodic supp.
8. 1991 - Milwaukee supp. - $28

1. **WISCONSIN REAL ESTATE**
2. Greenberg, Martin J.
3. Lawyers Coop.
4. 1982
5. 2 vols.
6. $210 incl. 6 mos. supp.
7. annual supp.
8. 1990 - $83.50; 1991 - $83.50

9. 79-92516/8678246/KFW2526.G73

1. **WISCONSIN RULES OF EVIDENCE: A COURTROOM HANDBOOK**
2. Bell, Thomas D. and Thomas H. Barland
3. State Bar of Wisc.
4. 1982
5. 1 vol.
6. $85
7. periodic supp.
8. 1989 - $35; 1991 - price NA
9. 8359411/KFW2940.B37

1. **WOMEN AND THE LAW**
2. Lefcourt, Carol H.
3. Clark Boardman Callaghan
4. 1984
5. 1 vol.
6. $110 incl. 3 mos. supp.
7. annual supp.
8. 1989 - $55; 1991 - $69.50
9. 84-11150/10799614/KF478.W65

1. **WORDPERFECT FOR LAWYERS (Version 5.1)**
2. Silver, Don
3. Adams-Hall
4. 1990
5. 1 vol. (incl. 3 tutorial diskettes)
6. $149
7. supp. as needed

1. **WORKERS' COMPENSATION**
2. Workers Comp. Section
3. Conn. Bar
4. 1991
5. 1 vol.
6. $35
7. no supp. planned

1. **WORKERS' COMPENSATION**
2. -
3. MILE
4. 1991
5. 1 vol.
6. $68
7. no supp. planned
9. 24034171/KFM5742.Z9W685

1. **WORKER'S COMPENSATION**
2. -
3. Indiana CLE
4. 1990
5. 1 vol.
6. $40
7. no supp. planned

1. **WORKERS' COMPENSATION: A PRACTICAL GUIDE**
2. -
3. MILE
4. 1991
5. 1 vol.
6. $68
7. no supp. planned
9. 24439878/KFM5742.Z9W624

1. **WORKERS' COMPENSATION DESKBOOK**
2. -
3. Arkansas Bar
4. 1986
5. 1 vol.
6. $75
7. periodic supp.

1. **WORKER'S COMPENSATION FOR THE EMPLOYER'S ATTORNEY & CLAIMANT'S ATTORNEY**
2. -
3. Jt. Comm. Va.
4. 1987
5. 1 vol.
6. $47
7. periodic supp.
8. 1990 - $26
9. 87-402751/16471484/KFV2742.W67

1. **WORKER'S COMPENSATION HANDBOOK**
2. Neal, John D.
3. State Bar of Wisc.
4. 1990
5. 1 vol.
6. $85
7. biennial supp.
8. no supp. yet
9. 10198048/KFW2742.N42

1. **WORKERS' COMPENSATION HANDBOOK**
2. -
3. Nebraska CLE
4. 1992
5. 1 vol.
6. $125
7. no supp. planned

1. **WORKER'S COMPENSATION IN MICHIGAN: LAW & PRACTICE, Rev. Ed.**
2. Welch, Edward M.
3. ICLE - Michigan
4. 1991
5. 1 vol.
6. $95
7. periodic supp.
8. no supp. yet
9. 91-71292/11124461/KFM4542.W45

1. **WORKERS' COMPENSATION INDEX**
2. -
3. Minn. CLE
4. 1979
5. 1 vol.
6. $60
7. semiannual supp.
8. $30/yr.

1. **WORKERS' COMPENSATION LAW REPORTS**
2. -
3. CCH
4. 1939
5. 1 vol.
6. $825/yr.; $750/yr. for 2 yrs.
7. semimonthly supp.
9. 82-2159/7534634/KF3613.4.W67

1. **WORKERS' COMPENSATION MANUAL**
2. Saltviet, Noreen & Sidney Galton, eds.
3. Oregon Bar
4. 1990
5. 1 vol.
6. $95
7. periodic supp.
8. 1990 - $35
9. 90-622753/22310923/KFO2742.W64

1. **WORKERS' COMPENSATION MANUAL, 6th ed.**
2. Cornblatt, Theodore B. et al.
3. MICPEL
4. rev. - 1989
5. 2 vols.
6. $50
7. periodic supp.
8. 1991 - $25; new ed. due in 1992
9. 7450163/KFM1542.W68

1. **WORKERS COMPENSATION PRACTICE IN MINNESOTA**
2. -
3. Minn. CLE
4. 1991
5. 1 vol.
6. $50
7. no supp. planned

1. **WORKERS COMPENSATION PRACTICE MANUAL**
2. May, Eric M.
3. D.C. Bar
4. 1988
5. 1 vol.
6. $35
7. periodic supp.
8. 1990 - $15
9. 17782930

1. **WORKING GUIDE TO THE TENNESSEE BUSINESS CORPORATION ACT**
2. Youngquist, Eric V.
3. Smith
4. 1988
5. 1 vol.
6. $34
7. periodic supp.
8. 1989 - $34
9. 88-92456/23525494/KFT213.A6W6

1. **WORKMEN'S COMPENSATION FOR OCCUPATIONAL INJURIES AND DEATH (desk ed.)**
2. Larson, Arthur
3. Bender
4. 1972
5. 3 vols.
6. $350 incl. 3 mos. supp.
7. annual supp.
8. 1989 - $292; 1990 - $330.50
9. 72-91866/613759/KF3613.4.L33

1. **WORKMEN'S COMPENSATION LAW**
2. Larson, Arthur
3. Bender
4. 1952
5. 11 vols.
6. $1305 incl. 3 mos. supp.
7. semmiannual supp.
8. 1989 - $973; 1990 - $1117
9. 52-3034/13822001/KF3613.4.L3

1. **WORKPLACE LITERACY: THE COMPLETE RESOURCE GUIDE**
2. -
3. BNA
4. 1988

5. 1 vol.
6. $95
7. no supp. planned
9. 18903261

1. **WORLD ACCOUNTING SERVICE**
2. Orfini, L.L., et. al.
3. Bender
4. 1986
5. 3 vols.
6. $290 incl. 3 mos. supp.
7. periodic supp.
8. 1989 - $95; 1990 - $208.50
9. 11685867

1. **WORLD PATENT LAW: PATENT STATUTES, REGULATIONS AND TREATIES (Patent Law and Practice Series, vols. 2B - 2L)**
2. Sinnott, John P.
3. Bender
4. 1974
5. 13 vols.
6. $570 incl. 3 mos. supp.
7. quarterly supp.
8. 1989 - $511; 1990 - $379
9. 75-15004

1. **WORLD PATENT LAW AND PRACTICE (Patent Law and Practice Series, vols. 2, 2A & 2A pt. 2)**
2. Baxter, J.W.
3. Bender
4. 1968
5. 3 vols.
6. $345/yr.
7. quarterly supp.
8. renewal - $295/yr.
9. 76-384756/18205

1. **WORLD SHIPPING LAWS: INTERNATIONAL CONVENTIONS**
2. Jackson, David C., ed.
3. Oceana
4. 1979
5. 6 vols. and Finding Tools
6. $675
7. periodic supp.
8. 1989 - $125; 1991 - $125
9. 79-18789/5239393/K1150.W67

1. **WORLD TAX SERIES - GERMANY**
2. Gumpel, Henry J.
3. CCH
4. 1969
5. 2 vols.
6. $585/yr.; $530/yr. for 2 yrs.
7. monthly supp.
9. 70-4743/13501

1. **WORLD TRADEMARK LAW AND PRACTICE**
2. Horwitz, Ethan
3. Bender
4. 1982
5. 3 vols.
6. $360 incl. 3 mos. supp.
7. periodic supp.
8. 1989 - $319; 1990 - $343
9. 82-74276/9532072/K1555.4.467

1. **WRITE YOUR OWN BUSINESSS CONTRACTS: WHAT YOUR ATTORNEY WON'T TELL YOU**
2. Barrett, E.T.
3. Oasis
4. 1990
5. 1 vol.
6. $39.95
7. no supp. yet
9. 22194431

1. **WRITTEN DISCOVERY**
2. -
3. Minn. CLE
4. 1990
5. 1 vol.
6. $40
7. no supp. planned

1. **WRONGFUL TERMINATION LITIGATION**
2. Gasiorek and Golden
3. MTLA
4. 1986
5. 1 vol.
6. $60 (member); $85 (nonmember)
7. no supp. planned

1. **WYOMING COURT RULES**
2. Supreme Court of Wyoming
3. Michie
4. rev. ed. - 1991
5. 1 vol.
6. $80
7. annual supp.
8. 1989 - $88; 1991 - $15

1. **YUDES FAMILY LAW CITATOR**
2. -

3. New Jersey ICLE
4. 1989
5. 1 vol.
6. $60
7. periodic supp.
8. 1991 - $39
9. 21863418/KFN1900.A53Y82

1. **ZONING: RULES, PROCEDURES & PROBLEMS**
2. -
3. Indiana CLE
4. 1988
5. 1 vol.
6. $65
7. no supp. planned

1. **ZONING AND LAND USE CONTROLS**
2. Rohan, Patrick J.
3. Bender
4. 1977
5. 10 vols.
6. $580 incl. 3 mos. supp.
7. annual supp.
8. 1989 - $476; 1990 - $670
9. 77-85275/3712763/KF5698.R63

1. **ZONING AND PLANNING DESKBOOK**
2. Kmiec, Douglas W.
3. Clark Boardman Callaghan
4. 1986
5. 1 vol.
6. $110 incl. 3 mos. supp.
7. annual supp.
8. 1989 - $49.50; 1991 - $62.50
9. 85-16833/12312867/KF5698.K59

1. **ZONING LAW MANUAL**
2. Blumenthal, Harry C. et al.
3. MICPEL
4. 1990
5. 1 vol.
6. $75
7. periodic supp.
8. no supp. yet
9. 9252241/KFM1658.Z66

1. **ZONING RESOLUTION**
2. -
3. NYC
4. 1985
5. 3 vols.
6. $435.94 incl. 2 yrs. supp.
7. periodic supp.
9. 8796585/KFX2080.A2X

LIST OF CESSATIONS AND DELETIONS

The following is a list of titles that appeared in the 1991 edition and have been deleted.

ABA sales & use tax handbook (ABA)
Accountant's law, tax, accounting & business management manual with forms (Garland)
Actions and remedies (Callaghan)
Adoption, surrogate mothers, and other legal and medical remedies (MICPEL)
ADR: the promise of arbitration and summary jury trials (NH Bar)
Advising Minnesota corporations (Minn. CLE)
Agricultural biotechnology (Hamline Univ.)
AIDS and the law (Minn. CLE)
AIDS and the law (NH Bar)
Alaska rules of court (Book Pub.)
Annotations to the homeowners' policy (ABA)
Annual meeting papers and proceedings (ATP)
Antitrust developments (Minn. CLE)
Appellate advocacy (Maine Bar)
Appellate advocacy (No. Carolina Bar)
Arizona probate (Bancroft)
Assessment and valuation legal reporter (IAAO)
Attorney marketing and advertising (NH Bar)
Attorneys' fees (NH Bar)
Attorney's guide to engineering (Bender)

Back to the basics--a new look at fundamental oil & gas issues (Okla. Bar CLE)
Banking law (Nebraska CLE)
Bankruptcy law (NH Bar)
Bankruptcy practice (Nebraska CLE)
Barclays United States Federal Circuit service (Barclays)
Basic introduction to auto insurance (Ohio LCI)
Basic real estate (Maine Bar)
Basic trial advocacy: the automobile accident (Maine Bar)
Basics of commercial real estate (Ohio LCI)
Basics of real estate development (Indiana CLE)
Basics of workers' compensation (Ohio LCI)
Blackford, Ohio corporation law (Banks)
Buying, selling and dissolving the professional practice (Illinois ICLE)

Calculating & proving damages in personal injury & wrongful death cases (Okla. Bar CLE)
California corporations code annotated to CEB publications (Calif. CEB)
California will drafting Willmaster System (Calif. CEB)
Capital adjustments (Maxwell Macmillan)
Charitable gifts (Garland)
Child custody and visitation (Ohio LCI)
Child sexual abuse: civil litigation (NH Bar)
Child support and maintenance in Missouri (UMKC/CLE)
Children & the courts (Okla. Bar CLE)
Citator (Maxwell Macmillan)
Civil commitment (Hamline Univ.)
Client counseling competition: explanation and consultation situations (ABA)
Commercial real estate (Hamline Univ.)
Commercial real estate (Indiana CLE)

Common competitive problems of small and growing businesses (MILE)
Compensating U.S. employees abroad (Bender)
The complete book of corporate benefits (Enterprise)
Complete book of employee forms (Enterprise)
The complete credit & collection system (Enterprise)
Completing the internal market of the European Community: 1992 legislation (Kluwer)
Compliance activities handbook (Office of Thrift Supervision)
Compliance update: federal regulations for loss prevention (Bank Admin. Inst.)
Comptroller's handbook for National Trust examiners (U.S. Compt.)
Comptroller's manual for national banks (U.S. Compt.)
Computer law (Indiana CLE)
Computer law (Wiley Law)
Computers and estate planning: how to draft wills, trust and probate documents using WordPerfect (Adams-Hall)
Computers for non-users (Nebraska CLE)
Computers in the law office (Okla. Bar CLE)
Condominium law (NH Bar)
Condominiums, cooperatives and cluster developments (Butterworth-Fla.)
Connecticut jury instructions (Atlantic)
Construction claims: the business and liability of it all (MILE)
Consumer and commercial credit - installment sales (Maxwell Macmillan)
Consumer law for the low & moderate income client (NH Bar)
Consumer protection and trade regulations (NH Bar)
Control of banking (Maxwell Macmillan)
Copyright protection in the Americas (Oceana)
Corporate capital restructuring: liquidations, redemptions and recapitalization (Garland)
Corporate capital transactions coordinator (RIA)
Corporate law update (Ohio LCI)
Corporate practice (Nebraska CLE)
Corporate taxation (Maxwell Macmillan)
Corpsystem--California corporations system (Calif. CEB)
Counseling the non-profit organization (Nebraska CLE)
Countertrade update (Bus. Intern.)
Creditors' remedies (MILE)
Creditors' rights (Hamline Univ.)
Criminal appeals in Minnesota (Butterworth-St. Paul)
Criminal evidence in Minnesota (Butterworth-St. Paul)
Criminal rules--Maryland (Hanford)
Criminal trial manual (avail. separately for Pa.; N.J.; Md.; Tx.; N.Y.) (Hanford)
Critical issues in today's banking (Okla. Bar CLE)
Current concerns in corporate practice (Okla. Bar CLE)
Current employment law issues (Nebraska CLE)
Current guide to federal taxes (Maxwell Macmillan)
Current issues for employer & employee clients (Indiana CLE)
Current issues in real estate development (Indiana CLE)

Defending criminal law cases (Okla. Bar CLE)
Discovery--winning before trial (Okla. Bar CLE)
Domestic relations: the basics (MICPEL)
Drafting wills and trusts (Indiana CLE)
Drafting wills and trusts (Ohio LCI)
The drunk driving case: from municipal court to supreme court (New Jersey ICLE)
DUI (MILE)

Eastern transportation law seminar papers and proceedings (ATP)
Effective family law (Hamline Univ.)
Efficient workers comp practice (Minn. CLE)
Emergency planning & community right-to-know (Bus. Laws)
The employee benefits institute (UMKC/CLE)
Employer's guide to Equal Employment Opportunity Law (Bus. Laws)
Employment discrimination (Indiana CLE)
Employment discrimination coordinator--primary source material (RIA)
Employment law (Nebraska CLE)
Employment law (NH Bar)
Employment law: a preventive law approach to successful management (Hamline Univ.)
Environmental hazards, employees' claims, and business costs (Hamline Univ.)
Environmental issues in the oil & gas industry (EMLF)
Environmental law (Nebraska CLE)
Environmental law (Okla. Bar CLE)
Estate planning and probate (Nebraska CLE)
Evidence problems (Indiana CLE)
Executive's handbook on political contributions (S&FA)
Expert witnesses--medical experts & economists (Okla. Bar CLE)

Family law (Nebraska CLE)
Family law (Okla. Bar CLE)
Family law 1989 (Indiana CLE)
Family law manual (avail. separately for Md.; Pa.) (Hanford)
Family law symposium (New Jersey ICLE)
Family litigation manual (avail. for Texas, N.Y., North Carolina, Mass.) (Hanford)
Federal appellate practice (MILE)
Federal government subcontract forms (Callaghan)
Federal laws affecting newspapers (NNA)
Federal lawyer's manual (Callaghan)
Federal Onshore Oil and Gas Leasing Amendments Act of 1987 (Rocky Mt.)
Federal practice in New Hampshire--current issues and trends (NH Bar)
Federal regulations of employee welfare plans: ERISA, internal revenue codes, and other delights (Conn. Bar)
Federal revenue forms (Maxwell Macmillan)
Felony sentencing in Minnesota (Butterworth-St. Paul)
Financial institutions 1988 (MILE)
FIRREA--its impact on financial institutions (Minn. CLE)
Florida condominium law and practice (Bender)
Florida criminal procedure (Lawyers Coop.)
Florida state & local taxes (Florida Bar)
Forms of commercial agreements (Garland)
Franchising (Nebraska CLE)
Freight claims manual: prevention, handling, settlement (Keller)
Fundamentals of bankruptcy practice (Nebraska CLE)

Georgia corporations (Lawyers Coop.)
Georgia probate (Lawyers Coop.)
Government contract fraud (Fed. Publ.)
Government practice (Nebraska CLE)
Guardianship (MICPEL)
Guide to veterans benefits (Natl. Veteran)

Handbook on buying and selling a business (Enterprise)

Handling a product liability case (Okla. Bar CLE)
Hot topics in corporate practice (Indiana CLE)

Illinois legal research manual (Butterworth-St. Paul)
Illinois school law (Illinois ICLE)
Immigration law (MILE)
Income tax for general practitioners (MICPEL)
Indiana family law (Indiana CLE)
Inheritance tax law & the estate tax law (Indiana CLE)
Insurance code/related laws to insurance code/official regulations (NILS)
Insurance contracts, real estate contracts (MILE)
Insurance law in the 80's (Okla. Bar CLE)
Insurance: employee benefits and estate planning in the new tax era (MILE)
Introduction to personal injury (MILE)
Iowa legal forms--law office systems (Butterworth-St. Paul)
IRS memoranda & letter rulings (Maxwell Macmillan)

Judgments & appeals in Oklahoma (Okla. Bar CLE)

Kentucky legal forms (Banks)

Labor and employment law update (Maine Bar)
Landlord-tenant relationship (MILE)
Law and aging (NH Bar)
Law of the workplace (Okla. Bar CLE)
Law office management & technology (Okla. Bar CLE)
Legal research practicum (Daniel)
Legislative history: Worker Adjustment and Retraining Notification Act (PL100-379) (BNA Plus)
The lemon file: an auto warranty litigation case reference service (Center)
Life insurance planning (Maxwell Macmillan)
Liquor liability 1988 (MILE)
Litigating eminent domain (MILE)
Litigation and trial of air crash cases (Callaghan)
Local government (Oregon Bar)

Manual for presenting a case before Maryland Commission on Human Relations (MICPEL)
Manual for the practice of international trade law (FBA)
Map package: lawyer referral and information service (ABA)
Marine operations reporter (MAS)
The Maryland employer's guide to labor and employment law (Michie)
Massachusetts health law (Butterworth-NH)
Massachusetts Right to Know Law compliance manual (Butterworth-NH)
Measure of damages (Nebraska CLE)
Mechanic's liens in Minnesota (Minn. CLE)
Mediation in family law (MILE)
Medical malpractice (Conn. Bar)
Medical malpractice 1986: from case evaluation through discovery and at trial (UMKC/CLE)
Medical/legal aspects of workers' compensation--a look at the new AMA guidelines (Okla. Bar CLE)
Meeting the EEO challenge (Alex. Hamilton Inst.)
Michigan collections (Lawyers Coop.)
Michigan divorce (Lawyers Coop.)
Midwestern corporate counsel (UMKC/CLE)
Mine to market: the legal issues (Rocky Mt.)
Mineral resources permitting (Rocky Mt.)

Mineral taxes (EMLF)
Minnesota civil trial practice (Minn. CLE)
Minnesota civil trial practice II (Minn. CLE)
Minnesota criminal jury trial handbook (Butterworth-St. Paul)
Minnesota criminal pretrial practice & procedure (Butterworth-St. Paul)
Minnesota legal forms--law office systems (Butterworth-St. Paul)
Minnesota new trust law (Minn. CLE)
Minnesota practice handbooks I & II (Minn. CLE)
Minnesota real estate law (Butterworth-St. Paul)
Minnesota real estate law practice manual (Butterworth-St. Paul)
Missouri trial tactics (UMKC/CLE)
Missouri's new medical malpractice law--a practice guidebook with forms (UMKC/CLE)
Modern Pennsylvania civil practice (Bisel)
Montana administrative procedures handbook (State Bar of Mont.)
Mortgage foreclosure (Okla. Bar CLE)
Mortgages, liens and foreclosures (NH Bar)

1990 civil trial practice institute (MILE)
1990 Minnesota evidence (MILE)
NABE bar executives handbook (ABA)
National conference on legal clinics notebook (ABA)
The national corporation law series (P-H Law & Bus.)
Natural resources administrative law and procedure (Rocky Mt.)
Nebraska legal forms--law office systems (Butterworth-St. Paul)
Nebraska probate system III (Nebraska CLE)
Nebraska probate system updates (Nebraska CLE)
Nebraska rules of evidence (Nebraska CLE)
Negotiations (Nebraska CLE)
New developments in consumer mortgage lending (Conn. Bar)
New Hampshire district court practice (NH Bar)
New Jersey close corporations (Callaghan)
New York attorney's/secretary's handbook (Mariposa)

Obtaining maximum benefits from structured settlement (UMKC/CLE)
Ohio civil discovery (Ohio LCI)
Ohio corporations (Lawyers Coop.)
Ohio Environmental Protection Agency, laws and regulations (Anderson)
Oil and gas lease payments and administration (EMLF)
Oil and gas litigation issues in the 1990's (Okla. Bar CLE)
Oregon probate system manual (Oregon Bar)
Organizing and summarizing dispositions for paralegals (James)
OSHA (Illinois ICLE)
Overthrust belt--oil and gas legal and land issues (Rocky Mt.)
Owens California forms & procedure (Parker)

Partnerships (MICPEL)
Pennsylvania school law (Banks)
Pension administrator's form book (Panel)
Pension and profit sharing/docuprep (Maxwell Macmillan)
Pension and welfare benefits for the insurance professional (MILE)
Permanent spousal maintenance--until death do us part? (MILE)
Personal injury litigation (Okla. Bar CLE)
A personal injury primer (Hamline Univ.)
Personnel policies workbook (Maxwell Macmillan)

Plan administrator's compliance manual (Maxwell Macmillan)
Planning benefits for the employee and the employer (MILE)
Practical ethics (NH Bar)
Practice in municipal court and collateral consequences (UMKC/CLE)
Practice in the federal courts (MICPEL)
The practitioner's guide to residential real estate transactions (Smith)
Preparing accurate settlement documentation (UMKC/CLE)
Preparing and trying a divorce/custody case (NH Bar)
A preventive approach to employment law (Hamline Univ.)
Principles of bankruptcy and reorganization (CLE-Colorado)
Private placement oil and gas programs (EMLF)
Probate system IV (Nebraska CLE)
Problems and opportunities during hard times in the minerals industry (Rocky Mt.)
Product liability litigation (MILE)
Professional liability (Nebraska CLE)
Prosecution of a criminal case (Illinois ICLE)
Proving business damages (PESI)
Public employee bargaining (CCH)
Publications of the IRS (Maxwell Macmillan)

Real estate development (MILE)
Real estate development: current issues (NH Bar)
Real estate financing forms manual (WG&L)
Real estate investment checklists/forms (Maxwell Macmillan)
Real estate investment planning (Maxwell Macmillan)
Real estate investment trusts (Maxwell Macmillan)
Real estate law developments (MILE)
Real estate securities after tax reform (UMKC/CLE)
Real estate title problems (NH Bar)
Real estate transactions (Okla. Bar CLE)
Recent developments in Oklahoma law (Okla. Bar CLE)
Recent developments in tort law (Okla. Bar CLE)
Remedies (NH Bar)
Reporter on the legal profession (Legal-Med.)
Resolution and avoidance of disputes (Rocky Mt.)
RICO (Knowles)
Rights of borrowers with the FDIC & FSLIC (Okla. Bar CLE)
Rules of the district and municipal courts in Washington (Butterworth-Wash.)

S corporations (MILE)
School law (Nebraska CLE)
Search & seizure (Okla. Bar CLE)
SEC guidelines (Maxwell Macmillan)
Secured lending transactions (Okla. Bar CLE)
Securities and blue sky law (NH Bar)
Securities arbitration (NYIF)
Selected topics in estate planning (Okla. Bar CLE)
Self insurance alternative (MILE)
Sexual harassment (Minn. CLE)
Sixth annual review of professional ethics (Conn. Bar)
Some select problems in complex litigation (Okla. Bar CLE)
South Carolina condominium law manual (Butterworth-Fla.)
State and federal tax conference (MILE)

State regulations for private truck operators (NPTC)
Steps in administering a decedent's estate (Ohio LCI)
Strategies and techniques in criminal defense (2nd ed.) (Butterworth-Wash.)
Substantive criminal law in Wisconsin (PESI)

Tax aspects of not-for-profit corporations (Indiana CLE)
Tax law for the general practitioner (Nebraska CLE)
Tax planning for individuals, estates & trusts (MILE)
Tax planning forms for businesses and individuals (WG&L)
Tax preparers liability service (RIA)
The Tax Reform Act of 1986 (UMKC/CLE)
Tenant-landlord practice (New Jersey ICLE)
Texas firemen's and policemen's civil service law (Butterworth-Texas)
Texas lawyer's guide (Callaghan)
Texas tort reform: legislative history 1987 (Butterworth-Texas)
Texas torts: forms, concepts and trends (Butterworth-Texas)
Timesharing in the U.S. (Butterworth-NH)
Title insurance (Indiana CLE)
Title insurance in Minnesota (Minn. CLE)
Tort reform I: a practical demonstration (Conn. Bar)
Trial evidence--making & meeting objections (Okla. Bar CLE)
Trial practice in Oklahoma (Okla. Bar CLE)
Trusts for the young and elderly (NH Bar)

U.S. Court of Veterans Appeals rules (Rules)
Underground tank leak insurance--maximizing your coverage (PMAA)
Uniform jury instructions, civil and criminal (Oregon Bar)
United States Court of International Trade procedural handbook (Rules)
The use of expert witnesses (UMKC/CLE)
User's guide to software licenses (Bus. Laws)
UST cumulative index service. 1976 (Hein)

Veterans' law reporter (Veterans Education)

Washington appellate practice handbook (Wash. Bar)
Western transportation law seminar papers and proceedings (ATP)
Whiteside, Ohio appellate practice (MICPEL)
Wills, estate and trusts (Maxwell Macmillan)
Winning jury trials (Conn. Bar)
Winning motor vehicle accident cases (CRI)
Wisconsin collections 1 & 2 (Lawyers Coop.)
Wisconsin divorce (Lawyers Coop.)
Worker's compensation (Nebraska CLE)
Workers' compensation (Okla. Bar CLE)
Writing for effect (MILE)

Zoning, planning and the regulation of land use (NH Bar)

PUBLISHER INDEX

ACLU
POLICY GUIDE OF THE AMERICAN CIVIL LIBERTIES UNION

Adams-Hall
WORDPERFECT FOR LAWYERS (Version 5.1)

AHC
HORSE OWNERS AND BREEDERS TAX MANUAL

AIA
AIA BUILDING CONSTRUCTION LEGAL CITATOR
THE ARCHITECT'S HANDBOOK OF PROFESSIONAL PRACTICE, 11TH ED.

AICPA
THE ACCOUNTANT'S BUSINESS MANUAL
TAX PRACTICE MANAGEMENT MANUAL

Alex. Hamilton Inst.
DESIGNING EFFECTIVE COMPANY POLICIES: PLUG LEGAL LOOPHOLES AND PUMP UP PRODUCTIVITY
EMPLOYEE DISCIPLINE PRACTICES AND PROBLEMS: AVOIDING THE MENACE OF LEGAL LIABILITY
THE EMPLOYEE HANDBOOK AUDIT: REDUCING THE RISKS OF UNJUST CLAIMS
THE EMPLOYEE PROBLEM SOLVER
"FIRE ME & I'LL SUE" - A MANAGER'S SURVIVAL GUIDE TO EMPLOYEE RIGHTS
PERFORMANCE APPRAISALS: THE LATEST LEGAL NIGHTMARE
PERSONNEL DOCUMENTATION AUDIT: STEERING CLEAR OF LEGAL PITFALLS
Q&A GUIDE TO PERSONNEL DECISIONS

ALI-ABA
BUSINESS FORMS FROM ALI-ABA COURSE MATERIALS
CIVIL TRIAL MANUAL II
LAWYER'S BASIC CORPORATE PRACTICE MANUAL
REAL ESTATE FORMS FROM ALI-ABA COURSE MATERIALS
TRIAL MANUAL FOR DEFENSE ATTORNEYS IN JUVENILE COURT

ALTA
UNDERSTANDING THE ALTA TITLE INSURANCE POLICY FORMS

Altman Weil Pensa
COMPLETE PERSONNEL ADMINISTRATION HANDBOOK FOR LAW FIRMS
LAW FIRM MANAGEMENT GUIDE

Am. Bankers
ABA'S COMPLIANCE SOURCEBOOK
EFT REGULATION E COMPREHENSIVE COMPLIANCE MANUAL
ESTATE PLANNING MANUAL FOR TRUST OFFICERS
REGULATION Z: TRUTH-IN-LENDING COMPREHENSIVE COMPLIANCE MANUAL

Am. Lawyer
THE AMERICAN LAWYER MANAGEMENT SERVICE

American Dental
REGULATORY COMPLIANCE MANUAL

American Immigration Lawyers Assn.
IMMIGRATION JUDGE BENCHBOOK

Anderson
ANDERSON'S OHIO CIVIL PRACTICE WITH FORMS
ANDERSON'S OHIO EVIDENCE: CIVIL & CRIMINAL
ANDERSON'S OHIO PROBATE PRACTICE AND PROCEDURE
BAKER'S OHIO SCHOOL LAW GUIDE
KENTUCKY LAW OF EVIDENCE
OHIO CRIMINAL PRACTICE & PROCEDURE

OHIO JURY INSTRUCTIONS
OHIO MANUAL OF PROCEDURE
UNINSURED AND UNDERINSURED MOTORIST INSURANCE, 2ND ED.
WILL FORMS AND CLAUSES

<u>API</u>
PREPAID LEGAL SERVICES REGULATION REPORTER

<u>Arkansas Bar</u>
AGRICULTURAL LAW SYSTEM
ARKANSAS CORPORATION SYSTEM
ARKANSAS DOMESTIC RELATIONS SYSTEM
ARKANSAS FORMBOOK
CRIMINAL LAW HANDBOOK
DEBTORS-CREDITORS SYSTEM
LAW OFFICE MANUAL
WORKERS' COMPENSATION DESKBOOK

<u>Arlen</u>
THE ARLEN MUTUAL FUND HANDBOOK

<u>ASCS</u>
CHECKLISTS OF FEDERAL AND STATE STATUTES ON INTERLOCKING DIRECTORSHIPS
ESCHEAT AND ABANDONED PROPERTY LAWS

<u>ASE</u>
AMERICAN STOCK EXCHANGE COMPANY GUIDE

<u>Aspen</u>
COLORADO CORPORATE FORMS - PRACTICE
COLORADO DOMESTIC RELATIONS FORMS - PRACTICE
COLORADO ESTATE PLANNING, WILL DRAFTING AND ESTATE ADMINISTRATION FORMS - PRACTICE
COLORADO REAL ESTATE FORMS - PRACTICE
GEORGIA CIVIL PROCEDURE FORMS -- PRACTICE
GEORGIA COMMERCIAL FINANCING FORMS
GEORGIA CORPORATE FORMS-PRACTICE
GEORGIA DOMESTIC RELATIONS FORMS - PRACTICE
GEORGIA ESTATE PLANNING, WILL DRAFTING AND ESTATE ADMINISTRATION FORMS--PRACTICE
GEORGIA REAL ESTATE FORMS-PRACTICE
HEALTH CARE LABOR MANUAL
HOSPITAL CONTRACTS MANUAL
HOSPITAL LAW MANUAL, ATTORNEY'S VOLUMES
HOSPITAL LEGAL FORMS, CHECKLISTS & GUIDELINES
ILLINOIS COMMERCIAL FINANCING
ILLINOIS CORPORATE FORMS--PRACTICE
ILLINOIS DOMESTIC RELATIONS FORMS--PRACTICE
ILLINOIS ESTATE PLANNING, WILL DRAFTING AND ESTATE ADMINISTRATION FORMS--PRACTICE
ILLINOIS REAL ESTATE FORMS--PRACTICE
LABORATORY REGULATION MANUAL
MARYLAND CIVIL PROCEDURE FORMS: PRACTICE
MARYLAND COMMERCIAL FINANCING FORMS - PRACTICE
MARYLAND CONDOMINUM, HOMEOWNER ASSOCIATION, COOPERATIVE AND TIME-SHARING FORMS--PRACTICE
MARYLAND CORPORATE FORMS: PRACTICE
MARYLAND DOMESTIC RELATIONS FORMS: PRACTICE
MARYLAND ESTATE PLANNING, WILL DRAFTING AND ESTATE ADMINISTRATION FORMS: PRACTICE
MARYLAND REAL ESTATE FORMS: PRACTICE
MARYLAND REAL ESTATE LEASING FORMS - PRACTICE
MASSACHUSETTS CORPORATE FORMS--PRACTICE
MASSACHUSETTS ESTATE PLANNING, WILL DRAFTING AND ESTATE ADMINISTRATION FORMS--PRACTICE

MASSACHUSETTS REAL ESTATE LEASING FORMS
MICHIGAN CIVIL PROCEDURE FORMS--PRACTICE
MICHIGAN CORPORATE FORMS--PRACTICE
MICHIGAN ESTATE PLANNING, WILL DRAFTING AND ESTATE ADMINISTRATION FORMS--PRACTICE
MICHIGAN REAL ESTATE FORMS--PRACTICE
MISSOURI CIVIL PROCEDURE FORMS -- PRACTICE
MISSOURI CORPORATE FORMS - PRACTICE
MISSOURI DOMESTIC RELATIONS FORMS - PRACTICE
MISSOURI ESTATE PLANNING, WILL DRAFTING AND ESTATE ADMINISTRATION FORMS - PRACTICE
MISSOURI REAL ESTATE FORMS - PRACTICE
NEW JERSEY CORPORATE FORMS
NEW JERSEY ESTATE PLANNING, WILL DRAFTING AND ESTATE ADMINISTRATION FORMS--PRACTICE
NEW JERSEY REAL ESTATE FORMS - PRACTICE
OKLAHOMA BUSINESS ORGANIZATIONS: FORMATION AND REPRESENTATION
OKLAHOMA CIVIL PROCEDURE FORMS - PRACTICE
OKLAHOMA CORPORATE FORMS - PRACTICE
OKLAHOMA ESTATE PLANNING, WILL DRAFTING AND ESTATE ADMINISTRATION FORMS
OKLAHOMA REAL ESTATE FORMS - PRACTICE
PENNSYLVANIA DOMESTIC RELATIONS FORMS--PRACTICE
SECURITIES FRAUD: LITIGATING UNDER RULE 10B-5
WASHINGTON CORPORATE FORMS

ATLA
COMPUTERS AND THE TRIAL LAWYER
TRIAL BY NOTEBOOK

Atlantic
CONNECTICUT CRIMINAL PROCEDURE
CONNECTICUT EVIDENCE
CONNECTICUT LAW OF REAL PROPERTY
CONNECTICUT PRACTICE BOOK

Atlantic Info.
AIDS REFERENCE GUIDE

ATP
TRANSPORTATION LAW INSTITUTE PAPERS AND PROCEEDINGS
TRANSPORTATION LAW STUDY GUIDE

Bancroft
COLORADO JURY INSTRUCTIONS 3D - CIVIL
COLORADO REAL ESTATE TRANSACTIONS
KANSAS CODE OF CIVIL PROCEDURE 2D ANNOTATED
PATTERN INSTRUCTIONS FOR KANSAS 2D (civil)
TEXAS FAMILY LAW SERVICE
WASHINGTON COURT RULES ANNOTATED WITH FORMS

Banks
BALDWIN'S KENTUCKY PRACTICE
BALDWIN'S OHIO CIVIL PRACTICE
BALDWIN'S OHIO DOMESTIC RELATIONS LAW
BALDWIN'S OHIO SCHOOL LAW
BALDWIN'S OHIO TAX LAW AND RULES
BALDWIN'S OHIO TOWNSHIP LAW
BLETZACKER'S OBBC STUDY GUIDE
FRIEDMAN, OHIO SECURITIES LAW AND PRACTICE
GIANNELLI, OHIO EVIDENCE MANUAL
GOTHERMAN & BABBIT, OHIO MUNICIPAL LAW
HAUSSER & VAN AKEN, OHIO REAL ESTATE LAW & PRACTICE
KENTUCKY APPELLATE HANDBOOK
KENTUCKY DOMESTIC RELATIONS LAW
KENTUCKY FINANCIAL INSTITUTION AND SECURITIES LAW

KENTUCKY MINERAL LAW
MERRICK-RIPPNER OHIO PROBATE LAW
OBBC REQUIREMENTS ENCYCLOPEDIA
OHIO BASIC BUILDING CODE AND RELATED CODES
OHIO FORMS AND TRANSACTIONS
PENNSYLVANIA CORPORATION TAX LAW & PRACTICE
SCHROEDER-KATZ, OHIO CRIMINAL LAW AND PRACTICE

Banks Baldwin
KENTUCKY FORMS & TRANSACTIONS

Bar Assn. of D.C.
ADMINISTRATIVE LAW MANUAL
CRIMINAL JURY INSTRUCTIONS FOR THE DISTRICT OF COLUMBIA
LAW OF EVIDENCE IN THE DISTRICT OF COLUMBIA
STANDARDIZED CIVIL JURY INSTRUCTIONS FOR THE DISTRICT OF COLUMBIA, REV. ED.

Barclays
BARCLAYS CALIFORNIA SUPREME COURT SERVICE
BARCLAYS UNITED STATES D.C. CIRCUIT SERVICE
BARCLAYS UNITED STATES EIGHTH CIRCUIT SERVICE
BARCLAYS UNITED STATES ELEVENTH CIRCUIT SERVICE
BARCLAYS UNITED STATES FIFTH CIRCUIT SERVICE
BARCLAYS UNITED STATES FIRST CIRCUIT SERVICE
BARCLAYS UNITED STATES FOURTH CIRCUIT SERVICE
BARCLAYS UNITED STATES NINTH CIRCUIT SERVICE
BARCLAYS UNITED STATES SECOND CIRCUIT SERVICE
BARCLAYS UNITED STATES SEVENTH CIRCUIT SERVICE
BARCLAYS UNITED STATES SIXTH CIRCUIT SERVICE
BARCLAYS UNITED STATES TENTH CIRCUIT SERVICE
BARCLAYS UNITED STATES THIRD CIRCUIT SERVICE

Baylor Univ. Press
LEGAL DESKBOOK FOR ADMINISTRATORS OF INDEPENDENT COLLEGES AND UNIVERSITIES

Bender
ABDOMINAL INJURIES (Courtroom Medicine Series vol. 10 & 10A)
ACCOUNTANT'S WORKBOOK SERIES
ACCOUNTING FOR BANKS
ACCOUNTING FOR GOVERNMENT CONTRACTS - COST ACCOUNTING STANDARDS
ACCOUNTING FOR GOVERNMENT CONTRACTS - FEDERAL ACQUISITION REGULATION
ACCOUNTING FOR PUBLIC UTILITIES
ACCOUNTING SYSTEMS FOR LAW OFFICES
ADMINISTRATIVE LAW
ADOPTION LAW AND PRACTICE
AGRICULTURAL LAW
AGRICULTURAL LAW MANUAL
ALIMONY, CHILD SUPPORT AND COUNSEL FEES
THE AMERICAN LAW OF MINING
AMERICAN LAW OF REAL PROPERTY
ANTITRUST AND TRADE REGULATION (Business Organizations vols. 16-16N & Index)
ANTITRUST AND TRADE REGULATION: DESK ED.
ANTITRUST COUNSELING AND LITIGATION TECHNIQUES
APPEALS (Art of Advocacy Series)
APPLYING GAAP AND GAAS
APPLYING GOVERNMENT ACCOUNTING PRINCIPLES
APPLYING GOVERNMENT AUDITING STANDARDS
ASSET-BASED FINANCING
ATTORNEY'S DICTIONARY OF MEDICINE, 16TH ED.
ATTORNEY'S DICTIONARY OF PATENT CLAIMS
ATTORNEY'S HANDBOOK OF ACCOUNTING
ATTORNEY'S TEXTBOOK OF MEDICINE, 3RD ED.
ATTORNEYS' TEXTBOOK OF MEDICINE: MANUAL OF TRAUMATIC INJURIES
AUTOMOBILE ACCIDENT LAW AND PRACTICE

AVIATION ACCIDENT LAW
BANK HOLDING COMPANY COMPLIANCE MANUAL
BANKING LAW
BANKING LAW MANUAL
BANKS AND THRIFTS: GOVERNMENT ENFORCEMENT AND RECEIVERSHIP
BENDER'S FEDERAL PRACTICE FORMS
BENDER'S FEDERAL PRACTICE MANUAL
BENDER'S FEDERAL TAX FORMS
BENDER'S FEDERAL TAX SERVICE
BENDER'S FLORIDA FORMS OF PLEADING
BENDER'S FORMS FOR THE CIVIL PRACTICE
BENDER'S FORMS OF DISCOVERY
BENDER'S FORMS OF PLEADING
BENDER'S I.N.S. REGULATION SERVICE
BENDER'S MODERN UCC LITIGATION FORMS (Bender's Uniform Commercial Code Service vols. 4 & 4A)
BENDER'S NEW YORK EVIDENCE - CPLR
BENEDICT ON ADMIRALTY, 7TH ED.
BENEFITS REVIEW BOARD - BLACK LUNG REPORTER
BENEFITS REVIEW BOARD - LONGSHORE REPORTER
BERGMAN ON NEW YORK MORTGAGE FORECLOSURES
BLUE SKY REGULATIONS (Business Organiz. vols. 11c, pt. 1 & 2)
BUSINESS CRIME
BUSINESS INSURANCE LAW & PRACTICE GUIDE
BUSINESS LAW MONOGRAPHS
BUSINESS ORGANIZATIONS WITH TAX PLANNING
BUSINESS TORTS
BUSINESS TRANSACTIONS IN GERMANY (FRG)
CABLE TELEVISION LAW: A VIDEO COMMUNICATIONS PRACTICE GUIDE
CALIFORNIA ATTORNEY PRACTICE
CALIFORNIA CIVIL ACTIONS - PLEADING AND PRACTICE
CALIFORNIA CLOSELY HELD CORPORATIONS
CALIFORNIA COMMUNITY PROPERTY WITH TAX ANALYSIS
CALIFORNIA CORPORATE SECURITIES LAW OF 1968
CALIFORNIA CRIMINAL DEFENSE PRACTICE
CALIFORNIA DEPOSITION AND DISCOVERY PRACTICE
CALIFORNIA EMPLOYERS GUIDE TO EMPLOYEE HANDBOOKS & PERSONNEL POLICY MANUALS
CALIFORNIA EMPLOYMENT LAW
CALIFORNIA ENVIRONMENTAL LAW & LAND USE PRACTICE
CALIFORNIA FAMILY LAW - PRACTICE AND PROCEDURE
CALIFORNIA FAMILY TAX PLANNING
CALIFORNIA FORMS OF JURY INSTRUCTION
CALIFORNIA FORMS OF PLEADING AND PRACTICE-ANNOTATED
CALIFORNIA INSURANCE LAW & PRACTICE
CALIFORNIA LAW OF EMPLOYEE INJURIES AND WORKMEN'S COMPENSATION
CALIFORNIA LEGAL FORMS - TRANSACTION GUIDE
CALIFORNIA POINTS AND AUTHORITIES
CALIFORNIA PROBATE PRACTICE
CALIFORNIA PRODUCTS LIABILITY ACTIONS
CALIFORNIA PUBLIC AGENCY PRACTICE
CALIFORNIA PUBLIC SECTOR LABOR RELATIONS
CALIFORNIA REAL ESTATE LAW AND PRACTICE
CALIFORNIA TAXATION
CALIFORNIA TORTS
CALIFORNIA TRIAL GUIDE
CALIFORNIA WILLS & TRUSTS
CALIFORNIA WILLS & TRUSTS - FORMS
CANCER (Courtroom Medicine Series vol. 13)
CAPITAL FORMATION AND INVESTMENT INCENTIVES AROUND THE WORLD
CHECKS, DRAFTS & NOTES
CHEST, HEART & LUNGS (Courtroom Medicine Series vol. 11)
CHILD CUSTODY AND VISITATION LAW AND PRACTICE
CIVIL RICO
CIVIL RIGHTS ACTIONS
COAL LAW AND REGULATION

COLLIER BANKRUPTCY CASES, 2ND SERIES
COLLIER BANKRUPTCY COMPENSATION GUIDE
COLLIER BANKRUPTCY EXEMPTION GUIDE
COLLIER BANKRUPTCY FORMS MANUAL, 3RD ED.
COLLIER BANKRUPTCY MANUAL, 3RD DESK ED.
COLLIER BANKRUPTCY PRACTICE GUIDE
COLLIER FAMILY LAW AND THE BANKRUPTCY CODE
COLLIER FARM BANKRUPTCY GUIDE
COLLIER HANDBOOK FOR CREDITOR'S COMMITTEES
COLLIER LABOR LAW AND THE BANKRUPTCY CODE
COLLIER ON BANKRUPTCY, 15TH ED.
COLLIER REAL ESTATE TRANSACTION AND BANKRUPTCY CODE
COLLIER'S LENDING INSTITUTIONS AND THE BANKRUPTCY CODE
COMMERCIAL AND CONSUMER WARRANTIES
COMMERCIAL DAMAGES: A GUIDE TO REMEDIES IN BUSINESS LITIGATION
COMMERCIAL FINANCE GUIDE
COMMERCIAL LAW AND PRACTICE GUIDE
COMMERCIAL LOAN DOCUMENTATION GUIDE
COMMERCIAL PAPER UNDER THE UNIFORM COMMERCIAL CODE (Bender Uniform Commercial Code Service, vol. 2 series)
COMPARATIVE NEGLIGENCE
COMPETITION LAW OF CANADA
COMPETITION LAW OF THE EEC
COMPETITION LAW OF THE UNITED KINGDOM/REPUBLIC OF IRELAND
COMPETITION LAWS OF THE PACIFIC RIM COUNTRIES
COMPLYING WITH INTERNATIONAL ANTITRUST REGULATIONS
COMPUTER CONTRACTS
COMPUTER LAW: EVIDENCE AND PROCEDURE
CONDEMNATION PROCEDURES AND TECHNIQUES - FORMS (Real Estate Transaction Series, vols. 3 pts. 1 & 2, 3A, 3A pt. 2, 3B, 3B pt. 2)
CONDOMINIUM LAW AND PRACTICE - FORMS (Real Estate Transaction Series, vols. 1, 1 pt. 2 & 3, 1A, 1B, 1C)
CONSTRUCTION LAW
CONSUMER CREDIT
COOPERATIVE HOUSING LAW AND PRACTICE FORMS (Real Estate Transactions Series, vols. 2, 2A, 2B)
CORPORATE ACQUISITIONS AND MERGERS (Business Organizations vols. 13, 13A & 13B)
COURT AWARDED ATTORNEY FEES
COURT OF APPEALS FOR THE FEDERAL CIRCUIT: PRACTICE AND PROCEDURE
COURT OF APPEALS FOR THE FEDERAL CIRCUIT: REVIEW OF PATENT AND TRADEMARK CASES
COURTROOM TOXICOLOGY
CREDIT UNION LAW SERVICE
CRIMINAL CONSTITUTIONAL LAW
CRIMINAL DEFENSE TECHNIQUES
CRIMINAL LAW ADVOCACY
CRIMINAL LAW DESKBOOK
CROSS-EXAMINATION OF LAY WITNESSES (Art of Advocacy Series)
CROSS-EXAMINATION OF MEDICAL EXPERTS
CROSS-EXAMINATION OF NON-MEDICAL EXPERTS (Art of Advocacy Series)
CURRENT LEASING LAW AND TECHNIQUES - FORMS (Real Estate Transaction Series, vols. 7, 7A, & 7B)
CURRENT LEGAL FORMS WITH TAX ANALYSIS
DAMAGES IN TORT ACTIONS
DEATH (Courtroom Medicine Series vols. 3, 3A & 3B)
DEBTOR-CREDITOR LAW
DEFENSE OF DRUNK DRIVING CASES: CRIMINAL - CIVIL
DEFENSE OF NARCOTICS CASES
DEFENSE OF SPEEDING, RECKLESS DRIVING, VEHICULAR HOMICIDE
DELAWARE CORPORATION LAW & PRACTICE
DEMONSTRATIVE EVIDENCE (Art of Advocacy Series)
DEPOSITION - STRATEGY, LAW AND FORMS
DEPRECIATION HANDBOOK
DIRECT EXAMINATION (Art of Advocacy Series)

DISCOVERY (Art of Advocacy Series)
DISPUTED PATERNITY PROCEEDINGS
DISTRIBUTING FOREIGN PRODUCED PRODUCTS IN THE U.S.
DOCUMENTARY EVIDENCE (Art of Advocacy Series)
DOING BUSINESS IN CANADA
DOING BUSINESS IN CHINA
DOING BUSINESS IN FRANCE
DOING BUSINESS IN IRELAND
DOING BUSINESS IN JAPAN
DOING BUSINESS IN MEXICO
DOING BUSINESS IN SPAIN
DOING BUSINESS IN THE UNITED KINGDOM
DOING BUSINESS IN THE UNITED STATES
DRAFTING NEW YORK WILLS
DRAFTING THE UNION CONTRACT
DRUG PRODUCT LIABILITY
DUNLAP-HANNA, PENNSYLVANIA FORMS
EDUCATION LAW
EMPLOYEE BENEFITS GUIDE
EMPLOYEE, BUSINESS AND PROFESSIONAL DEFAMATION
EMPLOYEE RIGHTS LITIGATION: PLEADING AND PRACTICE
EMPLOYER'S IMMIGRATION COMPLIANCE GUIDE
EMPLOYMENT DISCRIMINATION
EMPLOYMENT LAW DESKBOOK
EMPLOYMENT SCREENING
ENERGY LAW & TRANSACTIONS
ENFORCEMENT OF MONEY JUDGMENTS ABROAD
ENGINEERING FOR THE PERSONAL INJURY ATTORNEY: THEORY, EXPERTS, EVIDENCE
ENTERTAINMENT INDUSTRY CONTRACTS: NEGOTIATIONS & DRAFTING GUIDE
ENVIRONMENTAL IMPACT REVIEW IN NEW YORK
ESTABLISHING A TRANSNATIONAL FRANCHISE
ESTABLISHING A U.S. JOINT VENTURE WITH A FOREIGN PARTNER
ESTATE TAX FREEZE
ESTATE TAX TECHNIQUES
THE EYE (Courtroom Medicine Series, vol. 14)
FAMILY LAW AND PRACTICE
FAMILY LAW LITIGATION GUIDE: DISCOVERY, EVIDENCE AND TRIAL PRACTICE
FAMILY LAW: TEXAS PRACTICE AND PROCEDURE
FAMILY TAX PLANNING
FEDERAL CONTRACT MANAGEMENT - A MANUAL FOR THE CONTRACT PROFESSIONAL
FEDERAL EVIDENCE PRACTICE GUIDE
FEDERAL INCOME, GIFT AND ESTATE TAXATION
FEDERAL INCOME TAXATION OF CORPORATIONS FILING CONSOLIDATED RETURNS
FEDERAL INCOME TAXATION OF INVENTORIES
FEDERAL INCOME TAXATION OF LIFE INSURANCE COMPANIES
FEDERAL LITIGATION GUIDE
FEDERAL SECURITIES ACT -- ANALYSIS, PROCEDURES AND FORMS (Business Organizations vol. 11, 11 pt. 1, 1A, 2, 2A)
FEDERAL SECURITIES EXCHANGE ACT OF 1934 (Business Organizations vols. 11A parts 1-2D)
FEDERAL SENTENCING MANUAL
FEDERAL TAX GUIDEBOOK
FEDERAL TAXATION OF OIL AND GAS TRANSACTIONS
FEDERAL TAXES AFFECTING REAL ESTATE
FINANCIAL AND ESTATE PLANNING RESOURCE GUIDE
FINANCIAL MANAGEMENT AND ACCOUNTING FOR THE CONSTRUCTION INDUSTRY
FINANCING TRANSNATIONAL PROJECTS
FLORIDA CORPORATIONS -- LAWS AND PRACTICE
FLORIDA ESTATES PRACTICE GUIDE
FLORIDA FAMILY LAW
FLORIDA FORMS OF JURY INSTRUCTIONS
FLORIDA REAL ESTATE TRANSACTIONS
FLORIDA TAX SERVICE - 2nd ed.
FLORIDA TORTS
FLORIDA TRIAL GUIDE

FOREIGN TAX AND TRADE BRIEFS
FORENSIC SCIENCE
FORMS AND PROCEDURES UNDER THE UNIFORM COMMERCIAL CODE (Bender's Uniform Commercial Code service vols. 5, 5A, 5B, 5C, 5D)
FRANCHISING (Business Organizations vols. 15, 15A, 15B & 15C)
GILBERT CRIMINAL LAW AND PROCEDURE OF NEW YORK
GOODS IN TRANSIT
GOVERNMENT CONTRACTS: CYCLOPEDIC GUIDE TO LAW, ADMINISTRATION AND PROCEDURE
A GUIDE TO REHABILITATION
GUIDE TO TOXIC TORTS
HANDBOOK FOR INTERNAL AUDITORS
HANDLING FEDERAL TORT CLAIMS: ADMINISTRATIVE AND JUDICIAL REMEDIES
HAZARDOUS WASTE
HEAD AND BRAIN (Courtroom Medicine Series vol. 8, 8A & 8B)
HEALTH CARE LAW SOURCEBOOK
HEALTH CARE LAW: A PRACTICAL GUIDE
HIP AND THIGH (Courtroom Medicine Series, vols. 7 & 7A)
HISTORIC PRESERVATION LAW (Real Estate Transaction Series, vols. 11, 11A & 11B)
HOMEOWNERS ASSOCIATIONS AND PLANNED UNIT DEVELOPMENTS - LAW AND PRACTICE (Real Estate Transactions series, vols. 6 & 6A)
HONG KONG REVENUE LAW
HOW TO MANAGE YOUR LAW OFFICE
HOW TO SAVE TIME AND TAXES IN HANDLING ESTATES (How to Save Time and Taxes Series vol.1)
HOW TO SAVE TIME AND TAXES PREPARING FIDUCIARY INCOME TAX RETURNS - FEDERAL AND STATE (How to Save Time and Taxes Series vol. 2)
HOW TO SAVE TIME AND TAXES PREPARING THE FEDERAL PARTNERSHIP RETURN
ILLINOIS CIVIL TRIAL GUIDE
ILLINOIS FORMS OF JURY INSTRUCTIONS
ILLINOIS TAX SERVICE
IMMIGRATION LAW AND PROCEDURE REPORTER
IMMIGRATION LAW AND PROCEDURE, REV. ED.
IMMIGRATION LAW AND PROCEDURE: DESK ED.
INCOME TAXATION OF FOREIGN-RELATED TRANSACTIONS
INDIANA ESTATE PLANNING AND PROBATE PRACTICE
INDIANA FORMS OF PLEADING AND PRACTICE
INNOVATIONS IN HEAD INJURY REHABILITATION
INSURANCE AND RISK MANAGEMENT FOR STATE AND LOCAL GOVERNMENTS
INSURANCE BAD FAITH LITIGATION
INSURING REAL PROPERTY
INTELLECTUAL PROPERTY COUNSELING AND LITIGATION
INTERNATIONAL BUSINESS PLANNING: LAW AND TAXATION - UNITED STATES
INTERNATIONAL BUSINESS PORTFOLIOS
INTERNATIONAL COMPUTER LAW
INTERNATIONAL COPYRIGHT LAW AND PRACTICE
INTERNATIONAL EXPORTING AGREEMENTS
INTERNATIONAL WITHHOLDING TAX TREATY GUIDE
IRAs, SEPs AND SELF-EMPLOYED PLANS COMPLIANCE GUIDE
JAPANESE INTERNATIONAL TAXATION
JURY INSTRUCTIONS (Art of Advocacy Series)
JURY SELECTION (Art of Advocacy Series)
THE KNEE AND RELATED STRUCTURES (Courtroom Medicine Series, vols. 9 & 9A)
LABOR AND EMPLOYMENT ARBITRATION
LABOR LAW (Business Organizations vols. 18-18I)
THE LAW OF ADVERTISING
THE LAW OF ASSOCIATIONS
LAW OF FEDERAL OIL AND GAS LEASES
THE LAW OF LIABILITY INSURANCE
LAW OF LIFE AND HEALTH INSURANCE
THE LAW OF OIL AND GAS LEASES, 2ND ED.
THE LAW OF POOLING AND UNITIZATION - VOLUNTARY, COMPULSORY
LAW OF REAL PROPERTY
THE LAW OF THE EUROPEAN ECONOMIC COMMUNITY - A COMMENTARY ON THE EEC TREATY
LAW OFFICE AUTOMATION AND TECHNOLOGY

LAWYER'S GUIDE TO MEDICAL PROOF
LEGAL GUIDE FOR PHYSICIANS
LENDER LIABILITY LAW & LITIGATION
LETTERS OF CREDIT
LIQUOR LIABILITY LAW
LOCAL GOVERNMENT LAW
THE LOW BACK (Courtroom Medicine Series, vols. 1, 1A, 1B)
MANAGING YOUR MEDICAL PRACTICE
MANUAL FOR COMPLEX LITIGATION
MASSACHUSETTS CORPORATION LAW WITH FEDERAL TAX ANALYSIS
MASSACHUSETTS PLEADING AND PRACTICE - FORMS AND COMMENTARY
MEDICAL MALPRACTICE
MEDICAL MALPRACTICE: GUIDE TO MEDICAL ISSUES
MEDINA'S BOSTWICK LAWYERS MANUAL
MIAMI INSTITUTE ON ESTATE PLANNING
MICHIGAN CORPORATION LAW WITH FEDERAL TAX ANALYSIS
MIDWEST TRANSACTION GUIDE
MILGRIM ON LICENSING
MODERN ESTATE PLANNING
MODERN FEDERAL JURY INSTRUCTIONS - CRIMINAL & CIVIL
MOORE'S FEDERAL PRACTICE, 2ND ED.
MOORE'S MANUAL - FEDERAL PRACTICE AND PROCEDURE
MOORE'S MANUAL - FORMS
MURPHY'S WILL CLAUSES: ANNOTATIONS AND FORMS WITH TAX EFFECTS (national and N.Y. ed.)
NATIONAL LABOR RELATIONS BOARD LAW AND PRACTICE
THE NECK (Courtroom Medicine Series, vols. 2, 2A & 2B)
NEW JERSEY LAW WITH FORMS
NEW JERSEY TAX SERVICE
NEW JERSEY TRANSACTION GUIDE
NEW YORK APPELLATE PRACTICE
NEW YORK CIVIL PRACTICE - CPLR (vols. 1, 2, 2A, 3 3A, 4, 5, 6, 7, 7A, 8 - Table of cases, Table of statutes & Index)
NEW YORK CIVIL PRACTICE - ESTATES, POWERS, TRUSTS LAW (vols. 9, 9 pt. 2, 9A, 9A pt. 2, 9B, 9C, 9D)
NEW YORK CIVIL PRACTICE - FAMILY COURT AND FAMILY LAW PROCEEDINGS (vol. 12, 12A, 12B)
NEW YORK CIVIL PRACTICE - MATRIMONIAL ACTIONS (vols. 11, 11A, 11B & 11C)
NEW YORK CIVIL PRACTICE - SCPA (vols. 10, 10 pt. 2, 10A, 10B, 10B pt. 2, 10C-10E)
NEW YORK CRIMINAL PRACTICE
NEW YORK INSURANCE LAW
NEW YORK PRACTICE GUIDE: BUSINESS AND COMMERCIAL
NEW YORK PRACTICE GUIDE: DOMESTIC RELATIONS
NEW YORK PRACTICE GUIDE: NEGLIGENCE
NEW YORK PRACTICE GUIDE: PROBATE AND ESTATE ADMINISTRATION
NEW YORK PRACTICE GUIDE: REAL ESTATE
NEW YORK SUPPRESSION MANUAL
NEW YORK TAX SERVICE
NEW YORK TRIAL GUIDE
NEW YORK UNIVERSITY ANNUAL INSTITUTE ON FEDERAL TAXATION
NICHOLS ON EMINENT DOMAIN
NIMMER ON COPYRIGHT
NIMMER ON FREEDOM OF SPEECH
NO-FAULT AND UNINSURED MOTORIST AUTO INSURANCE
OCCUPATIONAL SAFETY AND HEALTH ACT
OHIO CORPORATION LAW WITH FEDERAL TAX ANALYSIS
OHIO FORMS OF PLEADING AND PRACTICE
OHIO STATE TAXATION
OHIO TRANSACTION GUIDE - LEGAL FORMS
OIL AND GAS LAW
OIL AND GAS LAW: ABRIDGED EDITION
OIL AND GAS REPORTER
OPENING STATEMENT (Art of Advocacy Series)
ORGANIZING CORPORATE AND OTHER BUSINESS ENTERPRISES

PAIN AND SUFFERING (Courtroom Medicine Series, vols. 4, 4A & 4B)
PARTRIDGE-REMICK, PRACTICE AND PROCEDURE IN ORPHANS COURT IN PENNSYLVANIA
PATENT LAW PERSPECTIVES
PATENT LICENSING TRANSACTIONS (Patent Law and Practice Series, vols. 1 & 1A & Business Organizations, vols. 14 & 14A)
PATENT LITIGATION: PROCEDURE AND TACTICS (Patent Law and Practice Series, vol. 3)
PATENT OFFICE RULES AND PRACTICE
PATENTS
PENNSYLVANIA CRIMINAL LAW AND PRACTICE
PENNSYLVANIA TAX SERVICE
PENNSYLVANIA TRANSACTION GUIDE - LEGAL FORMS
PENSION & PROFIT SHARING PLANS (Bus. Orgs. Vols. 19A-E)
PENSION & PROFIT SHARING PLANS
PENSION & PROFIT SHARING PLANS: FORMS & PRACTICE
PERSONAL INJURY - ACTIONS, DEFENSES, DAMAGES
PERSONAL INJURY DEFENSE TECHNIQUES
POLICE CIVIL LIABILITY
POLICE INVESTIGATION HANDBOOK
A PRACTICAL GUIDE TO DISPUTES BETWEEN ADJOINING LANDOWNERS--EASEMENTS
A PRACTICAL GUIDE TO WINNING LAND USE APPROVAL AND PERMITS
PRACTICE BEFORE FEDERAL MAGISTRATES
PREMISES LIABILITY
PREPARATION OF THE CASE (Art of Advocacy Series)
PREVENTION AND PROSECUTION OF COMPUTER AND HIGH TECHNOLOGY CRIME
PRIVACY LAW AND PRACTICE
PRODUCT LIABILITY PRACTICE GUIDE
PRODUCTS LIABILITY
PROFESSIONAL CORPORATIONS AND ASSOCIATIONS (Business Organizations, Vols. 17 - 17E)
PROSECUTION AND DEFENSE OF CRIMINAL CONSPIRACY CASES
PROSECUTION AND DEFENSE OF FORFEITURE CASES
PROSECUTION AND DEFENSE OF SEX CRIMES
PROTECTING AGAINST EXPROPRIATION OF RISK IN INVESTING ABROAD
PROVING CRIMINAL DEFENSES
PROVING MEDICAL DIAGNOSIS AND PROGNOSIS
PSYCHIC INJURIES (Courtroom Medicine Series, Vol. 12)
PURCHASE AND SALE OF REAL PROPERTY (REAL ESTATE TRANSACTION SERIES, VOLS. 12, 12A & 12B)
REAL ESTATE BROKERAGE LAW AND PRACTICE
REAL ESTATE DEVELOPMENT
REAL ESTATE DEVELOPMENT: LONG TERM CARE & RETIREMENT FACILITIES
REAL ESTATE FINANCING TEXT, FORMS, TAX ANALYSIS (Real Estate Transaction Series, Vol. 4-5)
REAL ESTATE SYNDICATIONS: LAW, PRACTICE AND FORMS
REAL ESTATE TAX APPEALS
REGULATION OF THE GAS INDUSTRY
REPRESENTING THE CHILD CLIENT
RESPONSIBILITIES OF INSURANCE AGENTS AND BROKERS
RULES OF CRIMINAL PROCEDURE
SALES AND BULK TRANSFERS UNDER THE UNIFORM COMMERCIAL CODE (Bender's Uniform Commercial Code Service, Vols. 3 & 3A)
SCIENTIFIC AUTOMOBILE ACCIDENT RECONSTRUCTION
SEC FINANCIAL REPORTING - ANNUAL REPORTS TO SHAREHOLDERS - FORM 10-K, QUARTERLY FINANCIAL REPORTING, 2ND ED.
SECONDARY MORTGAGE MARKET GUIDE
SECURED TRANSACTIONS UNDER THE UNIFORM COMMERCIAL CODE (Bender's Uniform Commerical Code Service, Vols. 1, 1A, 1B & 1C)
SECURITIES ARBITRATION: PRACTICE AND FORMS
SECURITIES LAW TECHNIQUES
SEPARATION AGREEMENTS AND ANTENUPTIAL CONTRACTS
SETTLEMENT (Art of Advocacy Series)
THE SHOULDER AND ELBOW (Courtroom Medicine Series, Vols. 5 & 5A)
THE SKIN (Courtroom Medicine Series, Vols. 6, 6A & 6B)
SOCIAL SECURITY PRACTICE GUIDE

SOUTHEAST LITIGATION GUIDE
SOUTHEAST TRANSACTION GUIDE
STEINMAN'S BERGERMAN & ROTH, NEW YORK REAL PROPERTY FORMS, ANNOTATED
STRUCTURED SETTLEMENTS (Art of Advocacy Series)
SUCCESSFUL LITIGATION TECHNIQUES
SUMMATION (Art of Advocacy Series)
TAX ACCOUNTING
TAX, ESTATE AND FINANCIAL PLANNING FOR THE ELDERLY -- FORMS AND PRACTICE
TAX, ESTATE AND FINANCIAL PLANNING FOR THE ELDERLY
TAX FRAUD - AUDITS - INVESTIGATIONS - PROSECUTIONS
TAX HAVENS OF THE WORLD
TAX PLANNING FOR CORPORATIONS AND SHAREHOLDERS
TAX PLANNING FOR CORPORATIONS AND SHAREHOLDERS - FORMS
TAX PLANNING FOR EXECUTIVE COMPENSATION
TAX PLANNING FOR PARTNERSHIPS
TAX PLANNING FOR S CORPORATIONS
TAX PLANNING FOR THE ALTERNATIVE MINIMUM TAX
TAX-FREE TRADE ZONES OF THE WORLD
TAXATION OF FINANCIAL INSTITUTIONS
TAXATION OF INTELLECTUAL PROPERTY: TAX PLANNING GUIDE
TAXATION OF MINING OPERATIONS
TAXATION OF SECURITIES TRANSACTIONS (Business Organizations, vol. 11b)
TEXAS CIVIL TRIAL GUIDE
TEXAS CORPORATIONS - LAW AND PRACTICE
TEXAS CRIMINAL PRACTICE GUIDE
TEXAS FAMILY LAW TRIAL GUIDE
TEXAS LITIGATION GUIDE
TEXAS RULES OF EVIDENCE MANUAL
TEXAS TAX SERVICE
TEXAS TORTS AND REMEDIES
TEXAS TRANSACTION GUIDE - LEGAL FORMS
TEXAS WORKER'S COMPENSATION LAW
TRADE SECRETS (Business Organizations, Vols. 12 & 12a)
TRADEMARK PROTECTION AND PRACTICE
TREATISE ON ENVIRONMENTAL LAW
TREATISE ON HEALTH CARE LAW
TRIAL OF ACCIDENT CASES
TRUST ADMINISTRATION AND TAXATION
TRUST DEPARTMENT ADMINISTRATION AND OPERATIONS
U.S. CUSTOMS AND INTERNATIONAL TRADE GUIDE
U.S. SUPREME COURT CASES AND COMMENTS
UNCLAIMED PROPERTY LAW
UNIFORM COMMERCIAL CODE REPORTER - DIGEST (Bender's Uniform Commercial Code Service Vols. 6 - 6G)
UNJUST DISMISSAL
VALUATION AND DISTRIBUTION OF MARITAL PROPERTY
VICTIMS' RIGHTS: LAW AND LITIGATION
WAGES AND HOURS: LAW AND PRACTICE
WARREN'S FORMS OF AGREEMENTS
WARREN'S FORMS OF AGREEMENTS - BUSINESS FORMS: DESK EDITION
WARREN'S HEATON SURROGATE'S COURT PRACTICE
WARREN'S NEGLIGENCE IN NEW YORK COURTS
WARREN'S WEED NEW YORK REAL PROPERTY
WEINSTEIN, KORN AND MILLER CPLR MANUAL
WEINSTEIN'S EVIDENCE MANUAL
WEINSTEIN'S EVIDENCE, UNITED STATES COURT RULES
WHITE, NEW YORK CORPORATIONS
WORKMEN'S COMPENSATION FOR OCCUPATIONAL INJURIES AND DEATH (desk ed.)
WORKMEN'S COMPENSATION LAW
WORLD ACCOUNTING SERVICE
WORLD PATENT LAW AND PRACTICE (Patent Law and Practice Series, vols. 2, 2A & 2A pt. 2)
WORLD PATENT LAW: PATENT STATUTES, REGULATIONS AND TREATIES (Patent Law and Practice Series, vols. 2B - 2L)

WORLD TRADEMARK LAW AND PRACTICE
ZONING AND LAND USE CONTROLS

Bender & Oyez
DOING BUSINESS IN BRAZIL
EUROPEAN PATENTS HANDBOOK, 2nd ed.

Bender & Parker
BALLANTINE AND STERLING CALIFORNIA CORPORATION LAWS

Big Foot
JURY INSTRUCTIONS IN INTELLECTUAL PROPERTY CASES

Bisel
BRÉGY: SELECTED SECTIONS OF PENNSYLVANIA PROBATE, ESTATES AND FIDUCIARIES CODE
FLORIDA KEYSTONE, LAWYER'S DESK LIBRARY OF PRACTICE
LADNER ON CONVEYANCING IN PENNSYLVANIA, WITH FORMS
LAW OF WILLS IN PENNSYLVANIA
PENNSYLVANIA BUSINESS CORPORATIONS
PENNSYLVANIA CONDOMINIUM LAW AND PRACTICE
PENNSYLVANIA CONFESSION OF JUDGMENT
PENNSYLVANIA CRIMES CODE AND CRIMINAL LAW
PENNSYLVANIA DIVORCE CODE
PENNSYLVANIA ESTATE PLANNING AND DRAFTING
PENNSYLVANIA GUIDE TO CRIMINAL PRACTICE AND PROCEDURE
PENNSYLVANIA INHERITANCE AND ESTATE TAX
PENNSYLVANIA INSURANCE LAW
PENNSYLVANIA KEYSTONE
PENNSYLVANIA LANDLORD AND TENANT LAW AND PRACTICE WITH FORMS (WITH COMPUTER DISK)
PENNSYLVANIA MUNICIPAL CLAIMS AND TAX LIENS
PENNSYLVANIA TRIAL GUIDE (CIVIL)
PENNSYLVANIA TRIAL GUIDE (CRIMINAL)
PENNSYLVANIA VEHICLE CODE, ANNOTATED
PENNSYLVANIA VEHICLE NEGLIGENCE
PENNSYLVANIA WORKMEN'S COMPENSATION, INJURY AND DISEASE LAWS
PENNSYLVANIA ZONING LAW AND PRACTICE
PROBATE, ESTATES AND FIDUCIARIES CODE ANNOTATED
TROUTMAN'S PENNSYLVANIA DAMAGES, PERSONAL INJURY VERDICTS
TROUTMAN'S PENNSYLVANIA NEGLIGENCE INSTANT CASE FINDER
VALENTINE-BINNS JUSTICE

Blais
FREE TRADE AGREEMENT ANNOTATED

BLR
EMPLOYEE BENEFITS COMPLIANCE MADE SIMPLE
EMPLOYEE COMPENSATION IN [YOUR STATE]
EMPLOYER'S GUIDE TO THE IMMIGRATION REFORM AND CONTROL ACT OF 1986
HOW TO COMPLY WITH THE DRUG-FREE WORKPLACE ACT
OSHA COMPLIANCE ENCYCLOPEDIA
WHAT TO DO ABOUT PERSONNEL PROBLEMS IN [YOUR STATE]

BNA
ABA/BNA LAWYER'S MANUAL ON PROFESSIONAL CONDUCT
AFFIRMATIVE ACTION COMPLIANCE MANUAL FOR FEDERAL CONTRACTORS
AIDS IN THE WORKPLACE: RESOURCE MATERIAL
AIR POLLUTION CONTROL
ALCOHOL AND DRUG ABUSE IN THE WORKPLACE: THE COMPLETE RESOURCE GUIDE
ASBESTOS ABATEMENT RESOURCE GUIDE, 2ND ED.
ASBESTOS ABATEMENT RULES: THE COMPLETE RESOURCE GUIDE
BNA CIVIL TRIAL MANUAL
BNA CRIMINAL PRACTICE MANUAL
BNA PENSION REPORTER

BNA POLICY AND PRACTICE SERIES
BNA'S PATENT, TRADEMARK & COPYRIGHT JOURNAL
CHEMICAL REGULATION REPORTER
CHEMICAL SUBSTANCES CONTROL
COLLECTIVE BARGAINING NEGOTIATIONS AND CONTRACTS
CORPORATE PRACTICE SERIES
THE CRIMINAL LAW REPORTER
EEOC COMPLIANCE MANUAL
EMPLOYEE BENEFITS CASES
EMPLOYEE TESTING: THE COMPLETE RESOURCE GUIDE
EMPLOYMENT GUIDE
ENVIRONMENT REPORTER
FAIR EMPLOYMENT PRACTICES
FALSE CLAIMS, ANTI-KICKBACK AND PROGRAM FRAUD CIVIL REMEDIES
THE FAMILY LAW REPORTER
FUNDING WASTEWATER TREATMENT FACILITIES: THE COMPLETE RESOURCE GUIDE TO THE NEW STATE REVOLVING FUND PROGRAM
GOVERNMENT EMPLOYEE RELATIONS REPORT
HAZARD COMMUNICATION COMPLIANCE MANUAL: THE COMPLETE GUIDE FOR WORKER RIGHT-TO-KNOW
HAZARDOUS MATERIALS TRANSPORTATION
INDEX TO CHEMICAL REGULATION
INDIVIDUAL EMPLOYMENT RIGHTS
INFECTIOUS WASTE: THE COMPLETE RESOURCE GUIDE
INTERNATIONAL ENVIRONMENT REPORTER
INTERNATIONAL TRADE REPORTER CURRENT REPORTS
INTERNATIONAL TRADE REPORTER DECISIONS
INTERNATIONAL TRADE REPORTER EXPORT REFERENCE MANUAL
INTERNATIONAL TRADE REPORTER IMPORT REFERENCE MANUAL
JOB SAFETY AND HEALTH
LABOR ARBITRATION AND DISPUTE SETTLEMENTS
LABOR RELATIONS REPORTER
MEDIA LAW REPORTER
MEDICAL TESTING: THE COMPLETE RESOURCE GUIDE TO GOOD LABORATORY PRACTICE AND HCFA COMPLIANCE
OCCUPATIONAL SAFETY & HEALTH REPORTER
PAYROLL ADMINISTRATION GUIDE
PRODUCT SAFETY AND LIABILITY REPORTER
RIGHT-TO KNOW PLANNING GUIDE
SECTION 89 COMPLIANCE MANUAL: THE COMPLETE GUIDE TO THE NEW NON-DISCRIMINATION RULES FOR EMPLOYEE BENEFIT PLANS
STATE LABOR LAWS
TAX MANAGEMENT - COMPENSATION PLANNING
TAX MANAGEMENT ESTATES, GIFTS AND TRUSTS REFERENCE FILE
TAX MANAGEMENT - ESTATES, GIFTS AND TRUSTS SERIES
TAX MANAGEMENT FINANCIAL PLANNING
TAX MANAGEMENT - FOREIGN INCOME
TAX MANAGEMENT IRS FORMS
TAX MANAGEMENT PRIMARY SOURCES SERIES V
TAX MANAGEMENT - REAL ESTATE
TAX MANAGEMENT - U.S. INCOME
TAX PRACTICE SERIES: THE PROFESSIONAL'S EXPEDITER
U.S.--CANADA FREE TRADE AGREEMENT: THE COMPLETE RESOURCE GUIDE
UNION LABOR REPORT
UNITED STATES LAW WEEK
WATER POLLUTION CONTROL
WORKPLACE LITERACY: THE COMPLETE RESOURCE GUIDE

<u>BNA Books</u>

BNA ADMINISTRATIVE PRACTICE MANUAL
COMPUTER SOFTWARE PROTECTION LAW
COPYRIGHT LAWS AND TREATIES OF THE WORLD
INTERNATIONAL PATENT LITIGATION: A COUNTRY-BY-COUNTRY ANALYSIS
PATENT, TRADEMARK, AND COPYRIGHT REGULATIONS

PCB COMPLIANCE GUIDE FOR ELECTRICAL EQUIPMENT
SPILL REPORTING PROCEDURES GUIDE

<u>Book Pub.</u>
ALASKA BANKRUPTCY RULES
ALASKA DIRECTORY OF PERMITS
ALASKA TIME LIMITS: STATUTES AND COURT RULES
BANKRUPTCY STAY MANUAL
DIGEST OF UNEMPLOYMENT COMMISSION DECISIONS
LOCAL RULES OF KING COUNTY SUPERIOR COURT
LOS ANGELES COUNTY ZONING SUBDIVISION CODE
NINTH CIRCUIT CT. OF APPEALS - LOCAL RULES
SEATTLE ZONING CODE
UNITED STATES DISTRICT COURT RULES FOR THE DISTRICT OF ALASKA
WASHINGTON PROBATE PRACTICE, PROCEDURE AND TAX MANUALS
WASHINGTON PUBLIC EMPLOYMENT RELATIONS REPORTER
WASHINGTON RULES OF COURT ANNOTATED
WASHINGTON WILLS & TRUST FORMS
WEST COAST CONSTRUCTION LIENS & CLAIMS MANUAL

<u>Bowne</u>
APPEAL SECURITIES ACT HANDBOOK

<u>Bus. Intern.</u>
CHINA HAND: INVESTING, LICENSING & TRADING CONDITIONS TODAY
DOING BUSINESS WITH EASTERN EUROPE
FINANCING FOREIGN OPERATIONS (FFO)
FINANCING FOREIGN OPERATIONS/LATIN AMERICA
INVESTING, LICENSING AND TRADING CONDITIONS ABROAD (ILT)

<u>Bus. Laws</u>
ALTERNATIVE DISPUTE RESOLUTION TECHNIQUES
COMPANY POLICY STATEMENTS
CORPORATE COUNSEL'S GUIDE TO BUSINESS ETHICS POLICIES
CORPORATE COUNSEL'S GUIDE TO BUSINESS-RELATED IMMIGRATION
CORPORATE COUNSEL'S GUIDE TO CONSTRUCTION CONTRACTS
CORPORATE COUNSEL'S GUIDE TO CONSULTING AGREEMENTS
CORPORATE COUNSEL'S GUIDE TO DISTRIBUTION COUNSELING
CORPORATE COUNSEL'S GUIDE TO EMPLOYEE RELATIONS LAW
CORPORATE COUNSEL'S GUIDE TO EMPLOYMENT CONTRACTS
CORPORATE COUNSEL'S GUIDE TO ENVIRONMENTAL LAW
CORPORATE COUNSEL'S GUIDE TO EUROPEAN ECONOMIC COMMUNITY LAW
CORPORATE COUNSEL'S GUIDE TO GOVERNMENT CONTRACTING & SUBCONTRACTING
CORPORATE COUNSEL'S GUIDE TO INTERNATIONAL ANTITRUST LAWS
CORPORATE COUNSEL'S GUIDE TO LITIGATION MANAGEMENT
CORPORATE COUNSEL'S GUIDE TO PROTECTING TRADE SECRETS
CORPORATE COUNSEL'S GUIDE TO THE ROBINSON-PATMAN ACT
CORPORATE COUNSEL'S GUIDE TO UNFAIR COMPETITION
CORPORATE COUNSEL'S MANAGERIAL GUIDE
DATA PROCESSING AGREEMENTS (2nd ed.)
DEALING WITH FINANCIALLY TROUBLED COMPANIES
DIRECTOR & OFFICER LIABILITY: INSURANCE & INDEMNIFICATION
EMPLOYER'S GUIDE TO AUDITING PERSONNEL & EMPLOYMENT PRACTICES
FEDERAL BUSINESS LAWS
FOREIGN CORRUPT PRACTICES ACT REPORTER
GUIDE TO ACQUISITIONS AND DIVESTITURES
GUIDE TO COUNTERTRADE
GUIDE TO EXPORT CONTROLS
GUIDE TO PURCHASE & SALES FORMS
GUIDE TO RECORDS RETENTION
GUIDE TO THE INTERNATIONAL SALES OF GOODS CONVENTION
HANDLING GOVERNMENT INVESTIGATIONS
INTERNATIONAL BOYCOTTS
LAW DEPARTMENT MANAGEMENT (2nd ed.)
THE LAW OF PURCHASING

LAWS OF INTERNATIONAL TRADE
THE LEGAL ASPECTS OF INTERNATIONAL SOURCING
THE LEGAL ASPECTS OF SUBSTANCE ABUSE IN THE WORKPLACE
LEGAL GUIDE FOR HANDLING TOXIC SUBSTANCES IN THE WORKPLACE
MATERIALS ON ANTITRUST COMPLIANCE PROGRAMS
MATERIALS ON CORPORATE POLITICAL ACTIVITY
MATERIALS ON MINIMIZING MANAGEMENT LIABILITY
MATERIALS ON THE AMERICANS WITH DISABILITIES ACT
MATERIALS ON THE HAZARD COMMUNICATION RULE
PURCHASER'S FORMBOOK OF CONTRACTS AND AGREEMENTS
PURCHASING FROM SMALL AND MINORITY BUSINESSES
SAMPLE ANTITRUST COMPLIANCE PLANS
TRANSNATIONAL JOINT VENTURES
U.S. - ISRAEL FREE TRADE AGREEMENT

Butterworth-Fla.

AIDS AND FLORIDA LAW
APPEALS TO THE ELEVENTH CIRCUIT
ATTORNEY'S FEES IN FLORIDA
CLA STUDY GUIDE
FLORIDA ADMINISTRATIVE PRACTICE MANUAL
FLORIDA APPELLATE PRACTICE MANUAL
FLORIDA CIVIL DISCOVERY MANUAL
FLORIDA CIVIL PROCEDURE
FLORIDA COMMERCIAL LANDLORD-TENANT LAW
FLORIDA CONDOMINIUM LAW MANUAL
FLORIDA CONSUMER LAW MANUAL
FLORIDA CORPORATIONS MANUAL
FLORIDA CREDITORS' RIGHTS MANUAL
FLORIDA CRIMINAL DEFENSE TRIAL MANUAL
FLORIDA CRIMINAL DISCOVERY AND PRE-TRIAL MOTIONS MANUAL
FLORIDA CRIMINAL PROCEDURE SERVICE
FLORIDA CRIMINAL SENTENCING LAW
FLORIDA EVIDENCE MANUAL
FLORIDA FAMILY LAW PRACTICE
FLORIDA JUVENILE PROCEDURE
FLORIDA LAND USE RESTRICTIONS
FLORIDA LAW OF SECURED TRANSACTIONS IN PERSONAL PROPERTY
FLORIDA LEGAL RESEARCH AND SOURCEBOOK
FLORIDA MECHANICS' LIEN MANUAL
FLORIDA MOTOR VEHICLE LIABILITY LAW
FLORIDA NEGLIGENCE LAW MANUAL
FLORIDA PARALEGAL SERIES: WILLS, TRUSTS, ESTATES
FLORIDA PREMISES LIABILITY
FLORIDA PROBATE CODE MANUAL
FLORIDA REAL ESTATE CLOSINGS
FLORIDA REAL ESTATE CONTRACTS
FLORIDA REAL ESTATE TRANSACTIONS
FLORIDA RESIDENTIAL LANDLORD TENANT LAW MANUAL
FLORIDA RULES OF COURT SERVICE
FLORIDA SECURITIES LAW
FLORIDA STATE & LOCAL TAXATION
FLORIDA SUMMARY CLAIMS HANDBOOK
FLORIDA TRAFFIC AND D.U.I. PRACTICE MANUAL
FLORIDA WORKERS' COMPENSATION MANUAL
FLORIDA ZONING LAW MANUAL
FRANCHISING AND LICENSING OF PUBLIC SERVICES IN FLORIDA
GEORGIA ARREST SEARCH AND SEIZURE
GEORGIA CONDOMINIUM LAW MANUAL
GEORGIA CREDITORS' RIGHTS MANUAL
GEORGIA FAMILY LAW MANUAL
GEORGIA LANDLORD-TENANT LAW
GEORGIA PROBATE MANUAL
GEORGIA STATE RULES OF COURT
LANDLORD'S REMEDIES IN FLORIDA

LEGAL ISSUES, GOVERNMENT PROGRAMS, AND THE ELDERLY (FLORIDA)
LIFE PLANNING IN FLORIDA
MANAGING THE FLORIDA CONDOMINIUM
THE MANUAL FOR FLORIDA LEGAL SECRETARIES
VIRGINIA CONDOMINIUM LAW
VIRGINIA PROBATE LAW

Butterworth-NH

ADMINISTRATIVE INTERPRETATIONS OF THE UNIFORM CONSUMER CREDIT CODE
APPEALS TO THE THIRD CIRCUIT
BANKRUPTCY PRACTICE DESKBOOK, Rev. Ed.
BLUE SKY COMPLIANCE MANUAL
THE BUSINESS TORT OF FRAUD AND MISREPRESENTATION
COMMERCIAL PAPER AND PAYMENT SYSTEMS
CONNECTICUT APPELLATE PRACTICE AND PROCEDURE
CONNECTICUT REAL PROPERTY STATUTES
CONNECTICUT TIME LIMITATIONS
DOMESTIC RELATIONS (MASSACHUSETTS): THE SUBSTANTIVE LAW
DRUG AND ALCOHOL TESTING: ADVISING EMPLOYERS
EMPLOYMENT DISCRIMINATION
ENTERTAINMENT LAW AND BUSINESS
ENVIRONMENTAL CITIZEN SUITS
ENVIRONMENTAL INSURANCE COVERAGE: STATE LAW & REGULATION
ENVIRONMENTAL LIABILITY -- LAW AND STRATEGY FOR BUSINESSES AND CORPORATIONS
ESTATE ADMINISTRATION (MASSACHUSETTS): A HANDBOOK WITH FORMS
EXECUTIVE AND PROFESSIONAL EMPLOYMENT CONTRACTS
FAMILY LAW GUIDEBOOK (MASSACHUSETTS): A HANDBOOK WITH FORMS
FEDERAL ENVIRONMENTAL REGULATION
FEDERAL TRIAL EVIDENCE
FOREIGN STATE IMMUNITY IN COMMERCIAL TRANSACTIONS
FOREIGN TRADE AND INVESTMENT
GUARDIANSHIP AND CONSERVATORSHIP IN MASSACHUSETTS
INTELLECTUAL PROPERTY PROTECTION IN ASIA
INTERNATIONAL AGENCY AND DISTRIBUTION AGREEMENTS
INTERNATIONAL INCOME TAX RULES OF THE UNITED STATES
INTERNATIONAL LOAN WORKOUTS AND BANKRUPTCIES
INTERNATIONAL PERSONAL TAX PLANNING ENCYCLOPEDIA
INTERROGATORIES, DOCUMENTS AND ADMISSIONS
JOINT VENTURES WITH INTERNATIONAL PARTNERS
JOINT VENTURES WITH THE SOVIET UNION
LABOR AND EMPLOYMENT IN CONNECTICUT
LABOR AND EMPLOYMENT IN MASSACHUSETTS: A GUIDE TO EMPLOYMENT LAWS, REGULATIONS AND PRACTICES
LABOR AND EMPLOYMENT IN NEW YORK
LEGAL PLANNING FOR THE ELDERLY IN MASSACHUSETTS
MAINE ADMINISTRATIVE PROCEDURE
MAINE CIVIL REMEDIES
MAINE CRIMINAL PRACTICE
MAINE EVIDENCE
MAINE FAMILY LAW: DIVORCE, SEPARATION AND ANNULMENT
MAINE JURY INSTRUCTION MANUAL
MAINE MANUAL ON PROFESSIONAL RESPONSIBILITY
MAINE PROBATE FORMS, REV. ED.
MAINE PROBATE MANUAL
MAINE WORKERS COMPENSATION ACT: PRACTICE AND PROCEDURE
MAINE WORKERS' COMPENSATION COMMISSION: APPELLATE DIVISION DECISIONS
MASSACHUSETTS COLLECTIONS MANUAL, SECOND EDITION
MASSACHUSETTS CONDOMINIUM LAW
MASSACHUSETTS CORPORATE TAX MANUAL, 2ND ED.
MASSACHUSETTS SALES AND USE TAX MANUAL
MASSACHUSETTS WORKERS' COMPENSATION PRACTICE MANUAL
NEW HAMPSHIRE MUNICIPAL PRACTICE SERIES: MUNICIPAL FINANCE & TAXATION
NEW HAMPSHIRE MUNICIPAL PRACTICE SERIES: PUBLIC HEALTH, SAFETY & HIGHWAYS
NEW HAMPSHIRE MUNICIPAL PRACTICE SERIES: LAND USE PLANNING & ZONING
PENNSYLVANIA MECHANICS' LIENS

PERSONNEL FORMS AND EMPLOYMENT CHECKLISTS
RETIREMENT AND BENEFIT PLANNING: STRATEGY AND DESIGN FOR BUSINESSES AND TAX-EXEMPT ORGANIZATIONS
RHODE ISLAND APPELLATE PRACTICE
RHODE ISLAND CRIMINAL PROCEDURE
RHODE ISLAND RULES OF EVIDENCE
RHODE ISLAND SUPREME COURT AND THE LAW OF CRIMES
SANCTIONS IN FEDERAL LITIGATION
SECURITIES ARBITRATION PROCEDURE MANUAL
SOVIET BUSINESS LAW: INSTITUTIONS, PRINCIPLES AND PROCESSES
STATE HAZARDOUS WASTE REGULATION
TAX PENALTIES AND INTEREST HANDBOOK
TRANSPORTATION SAFETY LAW PRACTICE MANUAL

Butterworth-St. Paul

ATTORNEY FEES IN WASHINGTON
CIVIL COMMITMENT IN MINNESOTA, 2nd Ed.
CLOSING OFFICER'S GUIDE (WASHINGTON)
DEFENDING DWIs IN WASHINGTON
THE DRINKING DRIVER IN MINNESOTA, 2nd Ed.
EMPLOYMENT IN ILLINOIS
EMPLOYMENT IN IOWA
EMPLOYMENT IN MINNESOTA
EMPLOYMENT IN OHIO
EMPLOYMENT IN OREGON
EMPLOYMENT IN WASHINGTON STATE: REV. ED.
EMPLOYMENT IN WISCONSIN
FINE'S WISCONSIN EVIDENCE
GITLIN ON DIVORCE: A GUIDE TO ILLINOIS MATRIMONIAL LAW
ILLINOIS LIMITATIONS MANUAL, 2ND ED.
ILLINOIS TRIALS: LAW AND STRATEGY
IOWA BANKRUPTCY
IOWA LEGAL FORMS -- COMMERCIAL REAL ESTATE
IOWA LEGAL FORMS -- CORPORATIONS
IOWA LEGAL FORMS -- CREDITORS' REMEDIES
IOWA LEGAL FORMS -- CRIMINAL LAW
IOWA LEGAL FORMS -- FAMILY LAW
IOWA LEGAL FORMS -- PERSONAL INJURY
IOWA LEGAL FORMS -- PROBATE
IOWA LEGAL FORMS -- RESIDENTIAL REAL ESTATE
IOWA LEGAL FORMS -- WORKERS' COMPENSATION
IOWA LIMITATIONS MANUAL, 2ND ED.
IOWA MATRIMONIAL LAW
IOWA PLEADING AND CAUSES OF ACTION
JURISDICTION AND SUMMONS IN OREGON
JUVENILE COURT HANDBOOK FOR MINNESOTA
THE LAW OF EVIDENCE IN WASHINGTON
LOCAL RULES OF THE SUPERIOR COURT: WASHINGTON STATE
MECHANICS AND CONSTRUCTION LIENS IN ALASKA, OREGON AND WASHINGTON
MINNESOTA CONDEMNATION LAW
MINNESOTA CORPORATIONS PRACTICE MANUAL
MINNESOTA CRIMES AND DEFENSES
MINNESOTA CRIMINAL LAW DIGEST
MINNESOTA EVIDENCE TRIALBOOK
MINNESOTA FAMILY LAW PRACTICE MANUAL, 2nd Ed.
MINNESOTA LEGAL FORMS--BANKRUPTCY
MINNESOTA LEGAL FORMS--COMMERCIAL REAL ESTATE
MINNESOTA LEGAL FORMS--CREDITORS' REMEDIES
MINNESOTA LEGAL FORMS--CRIMINAL LAW
MINNESOTA LEGAL FORMS--FAMILY LAW
MINNESOTA LEGAL FORMS--PERSONAL INJURY
MINNESOTA LEGAL FORMS--PROBATE
MINNESOTA LEGAL FORMS--RESIDENTIAL REAL ESTATE
MINNESOTA LIMITATIONS MANUAL, 2nd ed.
MINNESOTA MECHANICS' LIENS PRACTICE MANUAL

MINNESOTA MISDEMEANORS AND MOVING TRAFFIC VIOLATIONS, 3rd ed.
MINNESOTA NO-FAULT AUTOMOBILE INSURANCE, 2nd ed.
MINNESOTA PROBATE LAW DIGEST
MINNESOTA TAX APPEALS
NEBRASKA LEGAL FORMS--BANKRUPTCY
NEBRASKA LEGAL FORMS--COMMERCIAL REAL ESTATE
NEBRASKA LEGAL FORMS--CREDITORS' REMEDIES
NEBRASKA LEGAL FORMS--CRIMINAL LAW
NEBRASKA LEGAL FORMS--FAMILY LAW
NEBRASKA LEGAL FORMS--PERSONAL INJURY
NEBRASKA LEGAL FORMS--RESIDENTIAL REAL ESTATE
NEBRASKA LEGAL FORMS--WORKER'S COMPENSATION
NEBRASKA LIMITATIONS MANUAL, 2nd ed.
OREGON APPELLATE MANUAL
OREGON UNIFORM TRIAL COURT RULES AND SUPPLEMENTARY LOCAL RULES
PRACTITIONER'S GUIDE TO THE OKLAHOMA UNIFORM CONSUMER CREDIT CODE
SALE OF A BUSINESS IN MINNESOTA
SENTENCING IN WASHINGTON
STATUTORY TIME LIMITATIONS: COLORADO
STATUTORY TIME LIMITATIONS: WASHINGTON STATE
STEIN ON PROBATE (2d ed.)
WASHINGTON ADMINISTRATIVE LAW PRACTICE MANUAL
WASHINGTON GUARDIANSHIP LAW: ADMINISTRATION AND LITIGATION
THE WASHINGTON STATE ENVIRONMENTAL POLICY ACT: A LEGAL AND POLICY ANALYSIS (SEPA)
WISCONSIN MISDEMEANORS AND MOVING TRAFFIC VIOLATIONS, 2ND ED.

<u>Butterworth-Texas</u>

APPEALS TO THE FIFTH CIRCUIT
BOHANNON'S NEW MEXICO ENVIRONMENTAL LAW HANDBOOK
CIVIL EVIDENCE TRIAL MANUAL FOR TEXAS LAWYERS
THE COMPLETE GUIDE TO MECHANIC'S AND MATERIALMAN'S LIEN LAWS OF TEXAS, 3RD ED.
CRIMINAL EVIDENCE TRIAL MANUAL FOR TEXAS LAWYERS
EMPLOYMENT IN MISSOURI, 2nd Ed.
EMPLOYMENT IN TEXAS, 3rd Ed.
FEDERAL EVIDENCE FOUNDATIONS
A GUIDE TO TEXAS WORKERS' COMPENSATION REFORM
THE LAWYER'S GUIDE TO THE TEXAS DECEPTIVE TRADE PRACTICES ACT
LOCAL RULES OF THE DISTRICT COURTS IN TEXAS
LOUISIANA LANDLORD & TENANT LAW
LOUISIANA OIL AND GAS LAW
LOUISIANA WRONGFUL DEATH AND SURVIVOR ACTIONS
MISSOURI COURT RULES HANDBOOK
NEW MEXICO APPELLATE PRACTICE MANUAL
NEW MEXICO CONSTRUCTION LAW
NEW MEXICO CREDITOR/DEBTOR LAW
NEW MEXICO LOCAL & FEDERAL RULES HANDBOOK
NEW MEXICO PROBATE MANUAL
NEW MEXICO RULES OF EVIDENCE TREATISE (rev. ed.)
OKLAHOMA CRIMINAL PRACTICE MANUAL
OKLAHOMA DISCOVERY PRACTICE MANUAL
OKLAHOMA LIEN LAWS
OKLAHOMA WILLS AND INTESTATE SUCCESSION
PRODUCTS LIABILITY LAW IN OKLAHOMA
TEXAS COMMERCIAL COLLECTIONS
TEXAS COMMERCIAL REAL ESTATE FORMS
TEXAS CONDOMINIUM LAW MANUAL
TEXAS CORPORATION LAW
TEXAS DISCOVERY FORMS
TEXAS DRUNK DRIVING LAW, 2nd Ed.
TEXAS FAMILY LAW
TEXAS HOSPITAL LAW
TEXAS LAW OF OIL AND GAS
TEXAS LIMITATIONS MANUAL

TEXAS LITIGATOR'S HANDBOOK
TEXAS MUNICIPAL ZONING LAW
TEXAS PERSONAL INJURY FORMS
TEXAS PERSONAL INJURY LAW
TEXAS PROBATE CODE MANUAL
TEXAS PRODUCTS LIABILITY LAW
TEXAS RESIDENTIAL LANDLORD-TENANT LAW
TEXAS RULES OF APPELLATE PROCEDURE
TEXAS RULES OF CIVIL PROCEDURE
TEXAS SPECIAL ISSUES FORMS
TRESPASS TO TRY TITLE (TEXAS)

Byram

RULES AND REGULATIONS OF THE LOUISIANA OIL CONSERVATION COMMISSION
RULES AND REGULATIONS OF THE NEW MEXICO OIL CONSERVATION DIVISION
RULES AND REGULATIONS OF THE TEXAS RAILROAD COMMISSION

Calif. CEB

ATTORNEY'S GUIDE TO CALIFORNIA PROFESSIONAL CORPORATIONS, 4th ed.
ATTORNEY'S GUIDE TO PENSION AND PROFIT-SHARING PLANS
BUSINESS BUY-SELL AGREEMENTS
CALIFORNIA CIVIL LITIGATION FORMS MANUAL
CALIFORNIA CIVIL PROCEDURE BEFORE TRIAL
CALIFORNIA COMMISSION OF CORPORATIONS OFFICIAL OPINIONS
CALIFORNIA CONSERVATORSHIPS AND GUARDIANSHIPS
CALIFORNIA CORPORATE SECURITIES LAW NOTEBOOK
CALIFORNIA DECEDENT ESTATE PRACTICE
CALIFORNIA EXPERT WITNESS GUIDE, 2nd ed.
CALIFORNIA JUDICIAL COUNCIL FORMS MANUAL
CALIFORNIA LIABILITY INSURANCE PRACTICE: CLAIMS AND LITIGATION
CALIFORNIA MARITAL TERMINATION AGREEMENTS
CALIFORNIA PROBATE WORKFLOW MANUAL, REVISED
CALIFORNIA REAL PROPERTY PRACTICE FORMS MANUAL
CALIFORNIA TAXES, 2nd ed.
CALIFORNIA WILL DRAFTING, THIRD EDITION
DRAFTING CALIFORNIA IRREVOCABLE LIVING TRUSTS, 2nd ed.
EFFECTIVE INTRODUCTION OF EVIDENCE IN CALIFORNIA
ESTATE PLANNING PRACTICE
FAIR EMPLOYMENT & HOUSING COMMISSION PRECEDENTIAL DECISIONS SERVICE
FAIR POLITICAL PRACTICES COMMISSION NOTEBOOK SERVICE
FAIR POLITICAL PRACTICES COMMISSION'S ENFORCEMENT DECISIONS
FEE AGREEMENT FORMS MANUAL
ORGANIZING CORPORATIONS IN CALIFORNIA, 2nd ed.
TRIAL ATTORNEY'S EVIDENCE CODE NOTEBOOK, 3rd ed.
TRUSTMASTER™ -- TRUST DRAFTING SYSTEM

Calif. Jnl. Press

THE CALIFORNIA STATE GOVERNMENT DIRECTORY
FIFTY-STATE LEGISLATIVE DIRECTORY

Carroll

FEDERAL ORGANIZATION SERVICE CIVIL
FEDERAL ORGANIZATION SERVICE MILITARY

CCH

ACCOUNTANCY LAW REPORTS
ACCOUNTANTS SEC PRACTICE MANUAL
ACCOUNTING ARTICLES
AICPA AUDIT AND ACCOUNTING MANUAL
AICPA TECHNICAL PRACTICE AIDS
ALBERTA-NORTHWEST TERRITORY & YUKON TAX REPORTER
ALL-STATE SALES TAX REPORTS
AMERICAN STOCK EXCHANGE GUIDE
AUDIT & ACCOUNTING GUIDES
AUSTRALIAN FEDERAL TAX REPORTS

AUSTRALIAN INCOME TAX GUIDE - (without legislation)
AUSTRALIAN INCOME TAX GUIDE & INCOME TAX LEGISLATION
AUSTRALIAN SECURITIES LAW REPORTS
AUSTRALIAN TAX CASES
AUSTRALIAN TAX LIBRARY
AUSTRALIAN TRADE PRACTICES REPORTS
AUTOMOBILE LAW REPORTS (insurance cases)
AVIATION LAW REPORTS
BANKRUPTCY LAW REPORTS
BLUE SKY LAW REPORTS
BOSTON STOCK EXCHANGE GUIDE
BRITISH COLUMBIA CORPORATIONS LAW GUIDE
BRITISH COLUMBIA REAL ESTATE LAW GUIDE
BRITISH COLUMBIA TAX REPORTER
BRITISH TAX CASES
BRITISH TAX GUIDE
BRITISH TAX LEGISLATION
BUSINESS FRANCHISE GUIDE
BUSINESS STRATEGIES
CALIFORNIA ELIGIBLE SECURITIES LIST
CALIFORNIA MEDI-CAL GUIDE
CANADA CORPORATE SECRETARY'S GUIDE
CANADA CORPORATIONS LAW REPORTS
CANADA INCOME TAX GUIDE
CANADIAN COMMERCIAL LAW GUIDE
CANADIAN EMPLOYMENT BENEFITS AND PENSION GUIDE
CANADIAN EMPLOYMENT SAFETY AND HEALTH GUIDE
CANADIAN ENERGY NEWS
CANADIAN ENERGY PROGRAM REPORTER
CANADIAN ESTATE PLANNING AND ADMINISTRATION REPORTER
CANADIAN FAMILY LAW GUIDE
CANADIAN GOVERNMENT PROGRAMS AND SERVICES GUIDE
CANADIAN INCOME TAX ACT, REGULATIONS AND RULINGS
CANADIAN INDUSTRIAL RELATIONS & PERSONNEL DEVELOPMENT
CANADIAN INSURANCE LAW REPORTS
CANADIAN LABOUR LAW REPORTS
CANADIAN PRODUCT SAFETY GUIDE
CANADIAN SALES TAX REPORTS
CANADIAN SECURITIES LAW REPORTS
CANADIAN SMALL BUSINESS GUIDE
CANADIAN TAX REPORTS
CAPITAL CHANGES REPORTER
CCH NASAA REPORTS
CCH TAX TRANSACTIONS LIBRARY
CHICAGO BOARD OPTIONS EXCHANGE GUIDE
CHINA LAWS FOR FOREIGN BUSINESS
CODE AND REGULATIONS
COFFEE, SUGAR AND COCOA EXCHANGE INC. GUIDE
COMMODITY FUTURES LAW REPORTS
COMMON MARKET REPORTS
COMPLIANCE GUIDE FOR PLAN ADMINISTRATORS
CONGRESSIONAL INDEX
CONSUMER CREDIT GUIDE
CONSUMER PRODUCT SAFETY GUIDE
CONTRACT APPEALS DECISIONS
COPYRIGHT LAW REPORTS
CORPORATE SECRETARY'S GUIDE
COST ACCOUNTING STANDARDS GUIDE
DOING BUSINESS IN EUROPE
DOMINION TAX CASES
EEOC COMPLIANCE MANUAL
EMPLOYEE BENEFITS MANAGEMENT
EMPLOYMENT PRACTICES GUIDE
EMPLOYMENT SAFETY AND HEALTH GUIDE
ENERGY MANAGEMENT AND FEDERAL ENERGY GUIDELINES

ENERGY RESOURCES TAX REPORTER
EXEMPT ORGANIZATIONS REPORTS
FAMILY LAW TAX GUIDE
FCC RULEMAKING REPORTS
FEDERAL AUDIT GUIDES
FEDERAL BANKING LAW REPORTS
FEDERAL CARRIERS REPORTS
FEDERAL ELECTION CAMPAIGN FINANCING GUIDE
FEDERAL ENERGY REGULATORY COMMISSION REPORTS
FEDERAL ESTATE AND GIFT TAX REPORTS
FEDERAL EXCISE TAX REPORTS
FEDERAL SECURITIES LAW REPORTS
FEDERAL SECURITIES LAWS - REGULATIONS - FORMS
FEDERAL TAX ADVISOR
FEDERAL TAX ADVISOR -- CONTROL EDITION
FEDERAL TAX ARTICLES
FEDERAL TAX FORMS
FEDERAL TAX GUIDE
FEDERAL TAX GUIDE REPORTS (Control Edition)
FEDERAL TAX MANUAL (with monthly reports)
FIDUCIARY TAX GUIDE
FINANCIAL AND ESTATE PLANNING
FINANCIAL STATEMENT PREPARATION MANUAL
FOOD DRUG COSMETIC LAW REPORTS
FREE TRADE LAW REPORTS
FRINGE BENEFITS TAX GUIDE
GOVERNMENT CONTRACTS REPORTS
GUIDE TO COMPUTER LAW
GUIDE TO GOVERNMENT CONTRACTING
HEALTH CARE FACILITY MANAGEMENT
HUMAN RESOURCES MANAGEMENT
HUMAN RESOURCES MANAGEMENT -- OSHA COMPLIANCE
INDIVIDUAL RETIREMENT PLANS GUIDE - IRA, SEP, KEOGH
INFORMATION RETURNS GUIDE
INHERITANCE, ESTATE AND GIFT TAX REPORTS
INSURANCE LAW REPORTS - FIRE AND CASUALTY
INSURANCE LAW REPORTS - LIFE, HEALTH & ACCIDENT
INTERNAL REVENUE MANUAL - ADMINISTRATION
INTERNAL REVENUE MANUAL - AUDIT
INTERNATIONAL OFFSHORE FINANCIAL CENTRES
INTERNATIONAL TAX PLANNING MANUAL
IRS LETTER RULINGS
IRS POSITIONS
IRS PUBLICATIONS
LABOR ARBITRATION AWARDS
LABOR LAW REPORTS
LIQUOR CONTROL LAW REPORTS
MANITOBA & SASKATCHEWAN TAX REPORTER
MARITIMES TAX REPORTER
MEDICAL DEVICES REPORTER
MEDICARE-MEDICAID GUIDE
MIDWEST STOCK EXCHANGE GUIDE
MULTISTATE CORPORATE INCOME TAX GUIDE
MUNICIPAL SECURITIES RULEMAKING BOARD MANUAL
MUTUAL FUNDS GUIDE
NASD MANUAL
NEW YORK ESTATES - WILLS - TRUSTS
NEW YORK FUTURES EXCHANGE GUIDE
NEW YORK MERCANTILE EXCHANGE GUIDE
NEW YORK STOCK EXCHANGE GUIDE
NLRB CASE HANDLING MANUAL
NUCLEAR REGULATION REPORTS
OFCCP FEDERAL CONTRACT COMPLIANCE MANUAL
ONTARIO CORPORATIONS LAW GUIDE
ONTARIO REAL ESTATE LAW GUIDE

ONTARIO TAX REPORTER
PACIFIC STOCK EXCHANGE GUIDE
PARTNERSHIP TAX REPORTER
PAYROLL MANAGEMENT GUIDE
PENSION PLAN GUIDE
PENSIONS AND DEFERRED COMPENSATION
PHILADELPHIA STOCK EXCHANGE GUIDE
PRODUCTS LIABILITY REPORTS
PROFESSIONAL CORPORATIONS HANDBOOK
PROFESSIONAL STANDARDS
PUERTO RICO TAX REPORTS
QUALITY REVIEW PROGRAM MANUAL
QUEBEC TAX REPORTER
RICO BUSINESS DISPUTES GUIDE
S CORPORATIONS GUIDE
SEC ACCOUNTING RULES
SECURED TRANSACTIONS GUIDE
SECURITIES TRANSFER GUIDE
SHEPARD'S FEDERAL SECURITIES LAW CITATIONS
STANDARD FEDERAL TAX REPORTS (1991 ED.)
STATE CORPORATE INCOME TAX FORMS
STATE MOTOR CARRIER GUIDE
STATE PERSONAL INCOME TAX FORMS
STATE TAX CASES REPORTS
STATE TAX GUIDE
STATE TAX REPORTS (separate volumes for each state at indiv. price per unit)
TAX COURT REPORTS
TAX TREATIES
TRADE REGULATION REPORTS
U.S. SUPREME COURT BULLETIN
UNEMPLOYMENT INSURANCE REPORTS
UTILITIES LAW REPORTS
WORKERS' COMPENSATION LAW REPORTS
WORLD TAX SERIES - GERMANY

Center for Immig. Rights
THE GUIDE TO IMMIGRATION COUNSELING: A STEP-BY-STEP LEGAL HANDBOOK

Central
THE AGENDA OF REGULATIONS

CFLR
CALIFORNIA FAMILY LAW PRACTICE

CGL
CGL REPORTER - TRIAL AND INSURANCE COUNSEL'S HANDBOOK

Chase Manhattan
THE CHASE WILL & TRUST FORMS MANUAL

Chicago Bd.
RULES AND REGULATIONS OF THE CHICAGO BOARD OF TRADE

Cincinnati
BY-LAWS AND RULES OF THE CINCINNATI STOCK EXCHANGE

Claitor's
TULANE TAX INSTITUTE

Clark Boardman Callaghan
ACQUISITIONS AND MERGERS: NEGOTIATED AND CONTESTED TRANSACTIONS (Securities Law Series Vol. II)
ADVISING SMALL BUSINESSES
AIR POLLUTION: FEDERAL LAW AND ANALYSIS

ANTIDUMPING AND COUNTERVAILING DUTY LAWS (International Business and Law Series, vol. 3)
AUTOMOBILE LIABILITY INSURANCE
AVOIDING AND DEFENDING WRONGFUL DISCHARGE CLAIMS
BAD FAITH ACTIONS: LIABILITY AND DAMAGES
BANKING CRIMES
BANKRUPTCY
BANKRUPTCY LAW FUNDAMENTALS
BANKRUPTCY LOCAL COURT RULES
BANKRUPTCY PRACTICE HANDBOOK
BIOTECHNOLOGY AND THE LAW
BLUE SKY LAW (Securities Law Series; Vol. 12 & 12A)
BROKER-DEALER REGULATION (Securities Law Series, Vol. 15)
CABLE TELEVISION AND OTHER NONBROADCAST VIDEO
CALLAGHAN'S APPELLATE ADVOCACY MANUAL
CALLMANN UNFAIR COMPETITION, TRADEMARKS AND MONOPOLIES, 4TH ED.
CASE ASSESSMENT AND EVALUATION
CASEY FEDERAL TAX PRACTICE
CIVIL LIABILITIES: ENFORCEMENT AND LITIGATION UNDER THE 1933 ACT
CLASS ACTIONS: LAW & PRACTICE WITH FORMS
CLOSING ARGUMENTS
COMMERCIAL ASSET-BASED FINANCING
COMMERCIAL LAW ANNUAL
COMMODITIES REGULATION: FRAUD, MANIPULATION & OTHER CLAIMS
COMPARATIVE NEGLIGENCE MANUAL
COMPUTER SOFTWARE: PROTECTION, LIABILITY, LAW, FORMS
CONDOMINUM DEVELOPMENT: FORMS WITH COMMENTARY
CONSOLIDATED TAX RETURNS: A TREATISE ON THE LAW OF CONSOLIDATED FEDERAL INCOME TAX RETURNS
CONSUMER PROTECTION AND THE LAW
CONTEMPORARY FAMILY LAW
COPYRIGHT REGISTRATION PRACTICE
CORPORATE CRIMINAL LIABILITY
CRIMINAL DEFENSE ETHICS: LAW & LIABILITY
DAMAGES UNDER THE UNIFORM COMMERCIAL CODE
DEFENSE AGAINST A PRIMA FACIE CASE
DESIGN AND UTILITY MODELS THROUGHOUT THE WORLD
DETERMINING CHILD & SPOUSAL SUPPORT
DISABILITY DISCRIMINATION IN EMPLOYMENT
DOMKE LAW AND PRACTICE OF COMMERCIAL ARBITRATION
DRINKING/DRIVING LITIGATION TRIAL NOTEBOOK
DRINKING/DRIVING LITIGATION: CRIMINAL AND CIVIL
DRUG ABUSE AND THE LAW SOURCEBOOK
DRUG TESTING LAW, TECHNOLOGY & PRACTICE
DRUG TESTING LEGAL MANUAL
EMPLOYEE AND UNION MEMBER GUIDE TO LABOR LAW
EMPLOYEE NONCOMPETITION LAW
EMPLOYMENT DISCRIMINATION AND CIVIL RIGHTS ACTIONS
EMPLOYMENT LAW CHECKLISTS & FORMS
ENVIRONMENTAL REGULATION OF LAND USE
EQUAL EMPLOYMENT COMPLIANCE MANUAL
ESTATE & PERSONAL FINANCIAL PLANNING
EXAMINATION OF WITNESSES
EXCESS LIABILITY: DUTIES & RESPONSIBILITIES OF THE INSURER
EXEMPTED TRANSACTIONS UNDER THE SECURITIES ACT OF 1933 (Securities Law Series, vol. 7, 7A, 7B, 7C & 7D)
EYE-WITNESS IDENTIFICATION
FAMILY LAW CHECKLISTS
FEDERAL CIRCUIT PATENT CASE DIGESTS
FEDERAL CRIMINAL APPEALS
FEDERAL LAND USE LAW
FEDERAL RULES OF BANKRUPTCY
FEDERAL RULES OF CIVIL PROCEDURE
FEDERAL RULES OF CRIMINAL PROCEDURE
FEDERAL RULES OF EVIDENCE

FEDERAL TAXATION OF BUSINESS ENTERPRISES
FEDERAL TAXATION OF CLOSE CORPORATIONS
FEDERAL TESTIMONIAL PRIVILEGES
FEDERAL UNFAIR COMPETITION: LANHAM ACT 43(a)
FLETCHER CORPORATE PRACTICE DESKBOOK
FORMS AND AGREEMENTS FOR ARCHITECTS, ENGINEERS AND CONTRACTORS
FORMS AND AGREEMENTS ON INTELLECTUAL PROPERTY AND INTERNATIONAL LICENSING
FRANCHISE & DISTRIBUTION LAW & PRACTICE
GOING PUBLIC AND THE PUBLIC CORPORATION (Securities Law Series vols. 1 & 1A)
GOVERNMENT DISCRIMINATION
GRAND JURY LAW AND PRACTICE
GUIDEBOOK TO SECURITY INTERESTS IN PERSONAL PROPERTY
GUIDEBOOK TO THE FREEDOM OF INFORMATION AND PRIVACY ACTS
HANDLING MOTOR VEHICLE ACCIDENT CASES: TREATISE
HANDLING MOTOR VEHICLE ACCIDENT CASES: FORMS
HANDLING OCCUPATIONAL DISEASE CASES
HEALTH CARE FRAUD AND ABUSE: A GUIDE TO FEDERAL SANCTIONS
HERZOG'S BANKRUPTCY FORMS AND PRACTICE
HOUSING DISCRIMINATION: LAW AND LITIGATION
IMMIGRATION LAW AND BUSINESS
IMMIGRATION LAW AND CRIMES
IMMIGRATION LAW AND DEFENSE, 3rd ED.
INSIDER TRADING REGULATION
INTELLECTUAL PROPERTY AND ANTITRUST LAW
INTERNAL REVENUE MANUAL: ABRIDGED & ANNOTATED
INTERNATIONAL CAPITAL MARKETS AND SECURITIES REGULATION (Securities Law Series, vol. 10, 10A. 10B & 10C)
INTERNATIONAL TAX GUIDE: U.S. INCOME TAXATION
INVESTIGATING EMPLOYEE CONDUCT
INVESTMENT LIMITED PARTNERSHIPS AND OTHER PASS-THROUGH VEHICLES (Securities Law Series, Vols. 4, 4A, 4B, 4C)
JOINT VENTURES
JURISDICTION AND FORUM SELECTION
JUROR MISCONDUCT
JURY SELECTION: STRATEGY AND SCIENCE
JURYWORK - SYSTEMATIC TECHNIQUES
LABOR AND EMPLOYMENT LAW: COMPLIANCE AND LITIGATION
LANE MEDICAL LITIGATION GUIDE
LANE'S GOLDSTEIN LITIGATION FORMS
LANE'S GOLDSTEIN TRIAL TECHNIQUE
THE LAW AND BUSINESS OF COMPUTER SOFTWARE
THE LAW AND BUSINESS OF LICENSING: LICENSING IN THE 1990s
THE LAW AND BUSINESS OF RESORT DEVELOPMENT
THE LAW AND BUSINESS OF TIME-SHARE RESORTS
THE LAW AND PRACTICE OF INTERNATIONAL FINANCE (International Business and Law Series, vols. 2 & 2A)
THE LAW OF CHEMICAL REGULATION AND HAZARDOUS WASTE
THE LAW OF CONDOMINIUM OPERATIONS
THE LAW OF COPYRIGHT
LAW OF CORPORATE OFFICERS AND DIRECTORS: RIGHTS, DUTIES, AND LIABILITIES
THE LAW OF CORPORATE OFFICERS AND DIRECTORS: INDEMNIFICATION AND INSURANCE
LAW OF DEFAMATION
THE LAW OF DISTRESSED REAL ESTATE
THE LAW OF ELECTRONIC SURVEILLANCE
LAW OF ENVIRONMENTAL PROTECTION
LAW OF FEDERAL ESTATE AND GIFT TAXATION: CODE COMMENTARY
LAW OF INDEPENDENT POWER PRODUCTION, COGENERATION AND UTILITY REGULATION
THE LAW OF MERCHANDISING AND CHARACTER LICENSING
THE LAW OF PROFESSIONAL AND AMATEUR SPORTS
LAW OF TOXIC TORTS
THE LAW OF TRANSNATIONAL BUSINESS TRANSACTIONS (International Business & Law Series, vol. 1 & 1A)
LAW OF WATER RIGHTS AND RESOURCES
LAW OF WETLANDS REGULATION

THE LAW OF ZONING AND PLANNING
LAW OFFICE ECONOMICS AND MANAGEMENT MANUAL
LEGAL ASPECTS OF AIDS
THE LEGAL AUDIT: CORPORATE INTERNAL INVESTIGATION
LEGAL CHECKLISTS
LEGAL CHECKLISTS - SPECIALLY SELECTED FORMS
LEGAL COMPLIANCE CHECKUPS: BUSINESS CLIENTS
LENDER LIABILITY LAW, PRACTICE AND PREVENTION
LICENSING IN FOREIGN AND DOMESTIC OPERATIONS: FORMS
LICENSING IN FOREIGN AND DOMESTIC OPERATIONS
LINDEY ON ENTERTAINMENT, PUBLISHING AND THE ARTS, 2ND ED.
LITIGATING AGE DISCRIMINATION CASES
LITIGATING WRONGFUL DISCHARGE CLAIMS
LITIGATION AND PRACTICE UNDER RULE 10B-5 (Securities Law Series, vol. 5, 5A, 5B, 5C & 5D)
LITIGATION OF INTERNATIONAL DISPUTES IN U.S. COURTS (International Business Law Series vol. 4)
LOCAL GOVERNMENT LAW
MANAGING ENVIRONMENTAL RISK: REAL ESTATE AND BUSINESS TRANSACTIONS
MANUAL FOR COMPLEX LITIGATION
MANUAL OF CORPORATE FORMS FOR SECURITIES PRACTICE (Securities Law Series, vol. 9 & 9A)
MASTER INDEX: CLARK BOARDMAN CALLAGHAN'S ENVIRONMENTAL LAW SERIES
MASTER INDEX--CLARK BOARDMAN CALLAGHAN'S SECURITIES LAW SERIES
MCGAFFEY LEGAL FORMS WITH TAX ANALYSIS - ESTATE & PERSONAL PLANNING (VOL. 3)
MCGAFFEY LEGAL FORMS WITH TAX ANALYSIS
MEDICAL AND HOSPITAL NEGLIGENCE
MERTENS LAW OF FEDERAL INCOME TAXATION
MODERN TORT LAW, REV. ED.
NEPA LAW AND LITIGATION
NON-QUALIFIED DEFERRED COMPENSATION ARRANGEMENTS
NONPROFIT ENTERPRISES: LAW AND TAXATION
NORTON BANKRUPTCY LAW AND PRACTICE
O'NEAL CLOSE CORPORATIONS, LAW AND PRACTICE 2ND ED.
O'NEAL'S OPPRESSION OF MINORITY SHAREHOLDERS
OPENING STATEMENTS
OPINION LETTERS IN SECURITIES MATTERS: TEXT-CLAUSES-LAW (Securities Law Series, vol. 8 & 8A)
PATEL'S IMMIGRATION LAW DIGEST
PATENT LAW FUNDAMENTALS
PATENT LAW PRACTICE FORMS
PATENTS THROUGHOUT THE WORLD
PATIENT CARE DECISION-MAKING
PIERCING THE CORPORATE VEIL
PLAINTIFF'S PROOF OF A PRIMA FACIE CASE
POLICE MISCONDUCT: LAW AND LITIGATION
PRETRIAL DISCOVERY: STRATEGY AND TACTICS
PRISONERS AND THE LAW
PRODUCTS LIABILITY LITIGATION: CASE EVALUATION
PRODUCTS LIABILITY LITIGATION: PRETRIAL PRACTICE
PRODUCTS LIABILITY LITIGATION: TRIAL STRATEGY & PROCEDURE
PROSECUTORIAL MISCONDUCT
PROTECTION OF CORPORATE NAMES: A COUNTRY-BY-COUNTRY SURVEY
PUBLIC NATURAL RESOURCES LAW
PUNITIVE DAMAGES, LAW & PRACTICE
QUALIFIED DEFERRED COMPENSATION PLANS
QUALIFIED DEFERRED COMPENSATION PLANS (FORMS)
REGULATION OF FINANCIAL PLANNERS
REPRESENTATION BEFORE THE COLLECTION DIVISION OF IRS
REPRESENTATION OF WITNESSES BEFORE FEDERAL GRAND JURIES
REPRESENTING THE AUDITED TAXPAYER BEFORE THE IRS
RIGHTS OF JUVENILES: THE JUVENILE JUSTICE SYSTEM
THE RIGHTS OF PUBLICITY AND PRIVACY
RULES OF THE U.S. COURTS IN NEW YORK

S CORPORATIONS: FEDERAL TAXATION
S CORPORATIONS: STATE LAW AND TAXATION
SEARCH WARRANT LAW DESKBOOK
SEARCHES & SEIZURES, ARRESTS AND CONFESSIONS
SECTION 16 OF THE SECURITIES EXCHANGE ACT
SECTION 1983 LITIGATION IN STATE COURTS
SECURITIES: PUBLIC & PRIVATE OFFERINGS
SECURITIES AND FEDERAL CORPORATE LAW (Securities Law Series, Vols. 3, 3A, 3B & 3C)
SECURITIES AND PARTNERSHIP LAW FOR MLPs AND OTHER INVESTMENT LIMITED PARTNERSHIPS (Securities Law Series, Vol. 14)
SECURITIES LITIGATION: DAMAGES
SECURITIES LITIGATION: FORMS & ANALYSIS
SECURITIES PRACTICE: FEDERAL AND STATE ENFORCEMENT
SECURITIES REGULATION FORMS
SENTENCING DEFENSE MANUAL--ADVOCACY/PRACTICE/PROCEDURE
SEX-BASED EMPLOYMENT DISCRIMINATION
SEXUAL ORIENTATION AND THE LAW
SHAREHOLDER DERIVATIVE ACTIONS
SHAREHOLDER LITIGATION
SOCIAL SECURITY DISABILITY CLAIMS
SOCIAL SECURITY DISABILITY CLAIMS
SOCIAL SECURITY LAW AND PRACTICE
STATE & LOCAL GOVERNMENT CIVIL RIGHTS LIABILITY
STATE & LOCAL GOVERNMENT DEBT FINANCING
STATE & LOCAL GOVERNMENT SOLID WASTE MANAGEMENT
STATE ENVIRONMENTAL LAW
STATE TRADEMARK AND UNFAIR COMPETITION LAW
SUBDIVISION LAW AND GROWTH MANAGEMENT
TAX ASPECTS OF LITIGATION AND SETTLEMENTS
TAX ASPECTS OF MARITAL DISSOLUTION
TAX ASPECTS OF REAL ESTATE INVESTMENTS
TAX PLANNING FOR REAL ESTATE TAXATION
TAX PLANNING FOR SMALL BUSINESSES
TAX PLANNING STRATEGIES
TAXATION OF PARTNERSHIPS
TECHNOLOGY MANAGEMENT
TRADE SECRETS LAW
TRADEMARK LAW PRACTICE FORMS
TRADEMARK REGISTRATION PRACTICE
TRADEMARKS THROUGHOUT THE WORLD
U.S. INTELLECTUAL PROPERTY LEGISLATIVE REVIEW
UNCHARGED MISCONDUCT EVIDENCE
UNIFORM COMMERCIAL CODE -- CODE SERVICE
UNIFORM COMMERCIAL CODE CASE DIGEST -- NORTHEAST REGION
UNIFORM COMMERCIAL CODE REPORTING SERVICE
UNIFORM COMMERCIAL CODE SERIES
UNIFORM COMMERCIAL CODE SERIES--SECURED TRANSACTIONS
UNIFORM COMMERCIAL CODE TRANSACTION GUIDE: ANALYSIS AND FORMS
UTILITY HOLDING COMPANIES
VENTURE CAPITAL AND SMALL BUSINESS FINANCINGS (Securities Law Series, Vol. 2, 2A & 2B)
WARRANTLESS SEARCH LAW DESKBOOK
WELFARE BENEFITS GUIDE 91-92
WOMEN AND THE LAW
ZONING AND PLANNING DESKBOOK

CLE - Colorado

COLORADO APPELLATE HANDBOOK
COLORADO ESTATE PLANNING FORMS BOOK
COLORADO ESTATE PLANNING HANDBOOK
COLORADO ETHICS OPINIONS HANDBOOK
COLORADO PROBATE SYSTEM
COLORADO REAL ESTATE PRACTICE
COLORADO TITLE INSURANCE PRACTICE

CORPORATIONS MANUAL - COLORADO
THE GREENBOOK-SELECTED COLORADO MATERIALS ON WILLS, ESTATES, TRUSTS AND TAXES
HANDBOOK OF COLORADO FAMILY LAW
LIENS AND CLAIMS -- COLORADO
PUBLIC TRUSTEE FORECLOSURE - COLORADO

<u>CLE - Wisc.</u>
REAL ESTATE TRANSACTIONS CASEBOOK: CASES & MATERIALS
TITLES TO REAL ESTATE
WISCONSIN INHERITANCE, ESTATE AND GIFT TAX HANDBOOK
WISCONSIN JURY INSTRUCTIONS - CIVIL
WISCONSIN JURY INSTRUCTIONS - CRIMINAL

<u>CLP</u>
COLORADO LOCAL COURT RULES
COLORADO RULES OF EVIDENCE (ANNOTATED)
COLORADO WORKERS' COMPENSATION LAW AND PRACTICE

<u>CME</u>
RULES AND REGULATIONS OF THE CHICAGO MERCANTILE EXCHANGE

<u>Cohasset</u>
LEGALITY OF MICROFILM
LEGALITY OF OPTICAL STORAGE

<u>COMEX</u>
COMEX BY-LAWS, RULES AND REGULATIONS

<u>Commonwealth</u>
GUIDE TO UNCLAIMED PROPERTY AND ESCHEAT LAWS

<u>Conn. Bar</u>
ADMINISTRATIVE LAW
ADVANCED PLANNING & ZONING
ADVANCED WORKERS' COMPENSATION LAW
ANNUAL SURVEY OF CONNECTICUT BUSINESS LAW
ANNUAL TAX PLANNING INSTITUTE
ASSET BASED LOAN TRANSACTION
AVOIDING LEGAL PITFALLS IN LAND USE AND REAL ESTATE DEVELOPMENT; WATER RESOURCES & REGULATIONS
BANKRUPTCY FOR THE CORPORATE LAWYER
BASIC CORPORATE PRACTICE
BASIC RESIDENTIAL REAL ESTATE CLOSINGS
THE CHANGING SCENE FOR ALIENS: THE IMMIGRATION ACT OF 1990
CHILD CUSTODY & CHILD PROTECTION
COMMERCIAL LEASE LITIGATION
CONDOMINIUMS AND COMMUNITY ASSOCIATIONS IN THE 1990'S: HOW TO REPRESENT THEM AND THOSE WHO DEAL WITH THEM
THE CONNECTICUT CHILD SUPPORT GUIDELINES
CONNECTICUT SUMMARY PROCESS LAW
THE CONNECTICUT UNFAIR TRADE PRACTICES ACT
CONTEMPORARY ISSUES IN FORECLOSURES
CURRENT DEVELOPMENTS IN INTELLECTUAL PROPERTY LAW
DAMAGES IN EMPLOYMENT CASES
DEBT COLLECTION
DRUG TESTING IN THE WORKPLACE: COMPLYING WITH THE LAW
EMPLOYMENT DISCRIMINATION COMPLAINTS
EXAMINING EYEWITNESSES AND INTERVIEWING WITNESSES
FUNDAMENTALS OF FEDERAL CRIMINAL PRACTICE & FEDERAL SENTENCING GUIDELINES
GOING TO TRIAL
HOW TO HAVE A MILLION DOLLAR PRACTICE
IMMIGRATION LAW FOR GENERAL PRACTITIONERS AND HUMAN RESOURCE PERSONNEL
INTRODUCTION TO CONNECTICUT ENVIRONMENTAL LAW
INTRODUCTION TO CONNECTICUT ENVIRONMENTAL LAW - PART I: POLLUTION CONTROL

LEGAL ASPECTS OF EXPORTING
LEGAL OPINIONS IN BUSINESS TRANSACTIONS
NEGOTIATING THE SALE, PURCHASE AND FINANCING OF COMMERCIAL REAL ESTATE IN A WORKOUT ENVIRONMENT
NUTS & BOLTS OF RAISING STATE CONSTITUTIONAL ISSUES
PERSONAL BANKRUPTCY
PLANNING FOR ESTATE FREEZES UNDER NEW CHAPTER 14
REAL ESTATE LOAN WORKOUTS
REAL ESTATE TRANSACTIONS: BORROWERS' COUNSELS' OPINION LETTERS
RECENT DEVELOPMENTS IN MEDICAL MALPRACTICE
REPRESENTING THE ELDERLY: THE RULES THEY ARE A-CHANGING
STRATEGY AND MANAGEMENT OF THE KEY STAGES OF A MATRIMONIAL CASE: THE CORE SKILLS
TORT REFORM II: A PRACTICAL DEMONSTRATION
THE TRADEMARK LAW REVISION ACT OF 1988
WILL DRAFTING: PLANNING IN LESS CERTAIN TIMES
WORKERS' COMPENSATION

Conn. Law Tribune
THE CONNECTICUT SUMMARY PROCESS MANUAL
HANDBOOK OF FORMS FOR THE CONNECTICUT FAMILY LAWYER

Corbel
ESOP FORMS MANUAL
GUIDE TO CAFETERIA PLAN DESIGN, ADMINISTRATION & COMMUNICATION
PENSION PLAN FORMS MANUAL

Corp. Tax
THE STATE & LOCAL TAX PORTFOLIO SERIES

Corporate Reports
SMALL BUSINESS TAX CONTROL

Council of Mich. Fdtns.
ESTABLISHING A CHARITABLE FOUNDATION IN MICHIGAN

Court Info.
COURT RULES UPDATE

CRI
HOW TO MARKET AND ADVERTISE YOUR LAW PRACTICE
LAWYER ADVERTISING
THE LAWYER'S DIRECT MAIL HANDBOOK
LAWYER'S PUBLICITY HANDBOOK

CRS
DETENTION AND CORRECTIONS CASELAW CATALOG

D.C. Bar
D.C. CODE OF PROFESSIONAL RESPONSIBILITY AND OPINIONS OF THE D.C. BAR LEGAL ETHICS COMMITTEE
D.C. RULES OF PROFESSIONAL RESPONSIBILITY
THE DISTRICT OF COLUMBIA ESTATES, TRUSTS AND PROBATE LAW DIGEST
THE DISTRICT OF COLUMBIA PRACTICE MANUAL
JUVENILE LAW AND PRACTICE IN THE DISTRICT OF COLUMBIA
WORKERS COMPENSATION PRACTICE MANUAL

Daniel
HANDLING YOUR OWN DIVORCE WITHOUT A LAWYER: A GUIDE TO SELF- REPRESENTATION IN INDIANA
INDIANA ANIMAL AND WILDLIFE LAW

Dearborn
ADVANCED UNDERWRITING SERVICE (AUS)

EBP
THE MOTION PICTURE AND TELEVISION BUSINESS: CONTRACTS AND PRACTICES

EFRC
CHAPTER 1 HANDBOOK
GUIDE TO FEDERAL FUNDING FOR EDUCATION

ELI
ENVIRONMENTAL LAW REPORTER
SUPERFUND: A LEGISLATIVE HISTORY

EMLF
ACQUISITIONS AND DISPOSITIONS OF OIL AND GAS PROPERTIES
BANKRUPTCY & WORKOUTS IN THE TROUBLED OIL & GAS INDUSTRY
BASIC COAL, OIL & GAS LAW
BASIC TAXATION OF NATURAL RESOURCES
COALBED METHANE LEGAL ISSUES
LABOR LAW AND THE NATIONAL WAGE AGREEMENT; MINERS' RIGHTS & MSHA DISCRIMINATION LAW
LANDMAN'S PRACTICUM
RIGHTS AND REMEDIES OF CONFLICTING MINERAL AND PROPERTY OWNERS
RIGHTS OF WAY, EASEMENTS AND SURFACE DAMAGES MANUAL
SURFACE MINING

Enterprise
THE "S" CORPORATION HANDBOOK
BASIC BOOK OF BUSINESS AGREEMENTS
THE COMPLETE BOOK OF CORPORATE FORMS
COMPLETE NON-PROFIT CORPORATION HANDBOOK
DIRECTOR'S PORTFOLIO

Environment Books
TOXIC SUBSTANCES CONTROL ACT--COMPLIANCE GUIDE AND SERVICE

Equity
NEW HAMPSHIRE COURT RULES ANNOTATED
VERMONT COURT RULES ANNOTATED

Exec. Press
SECTION 16 TREATISE AND SERVICE

Facts
PHARMACY LAW DIGEST

Farnam
HORSE SYNDICATION MANUAL
LAW FOR THE HORSEBREEDER

FASB
ACCOUNTING STANDARDS - ORIGINAL PRONOUNCEMENTS
EITF ABSTRACTS (A SUMMARY OF PROCEEDINGS OF THE FASB EMERGING ISSUES TASK FORCE)
FASB ACCOUNTING STANDARDS - CURRENT TEXT

Fast Eddie
CALIFORNIA DRUNK DRIVING LAW

FBA
THE LEGAL ASPECTS OF EXPORTING MANUAL
MANUAL FOR PRACTICE BEFORE BOARDS OF CONTRACT APPEALS
MANUAL ON THE ADMINISTRATIVE PROCESSING OF FEDERAL SECTOR EEO COMPLAINTS

FDIC
LAWS, REGULATIONS, RELATED ACTS

Fed.

BANK HOLDING COMPANY SUPERVISION MANUAL
CONSUMER AND COMMUNITY AFFAIRS HANDBOOK
FEDERAL RESERVE REGULATORY SERVICE
FEDERAL RESERVE SYSTEM COMPLIANCE HANDBOOK
MONETARY POLICY AND RESERVE REQUIREMENTS HANDBOOK
PAYMENT SYSTEM HANDBOOK
SECURITIES CREDIT TRANSACTIONS HANDBOOK

Fed. Publ.

BOARD OF CONTRACT APPEALS BID PROTEST DECISIONS
COMPTROLLER GENERAL'S PROCUREMENT DECISIONS
EXTRAORDINARY CONTRACTUAL RELIEF REPORTER
FEDERAL COURT PROCUREMENT DECISIONS
GOVERNMENT CONTRACT ACCOUNTING 2ND ED.
GOVERNMENT CONTRACT BIDDING
GOVERNMENT CONTRACT DISPUTES, 2ND ED.
GOVERNMENT CONTRACT GUIDEBOOK

Fed.-NY

OPERATING CIRCULARS OF THE FEDERAL RESERVE BANK OF NEW YORK
REGULATIONS OF THE BOARD OF GOVERNORS

Fed-Track

FED-TRACK GUIDE TO ANTIDUMPING FINDINGS AND ORDERS
FED-TRACK GUIDE TO COUNTERVAILING DUTY CASES
FED-TRACK GUIDE TO INVESTIGATION OF UNFAIR TRADE PRACTICES

Finan. Pub.

THE COST OF PERSONAL BORROWING IN THE UNITED STATES

Florida Bar

ADOPTION, PATERNITY AND OTHER FLORIDA FAMILY PRACTICE
ALTERNATE DISPUTE RESOLUTION
BUSINESS LITIGATION IN FLORIDA
CASES AND MATERIALS ON FLORIDA DOMESTIC RELATIONS
CRIMINAL TRIAL PRACTICE IN FLORIDA
DRAFTING MARRIAGE CONTRACTS IN FLORIDA
DUI AND OTHER TRAFFIC OFFENSES IN FLORIDA
EVIDENCE IN FLORIDA
FLORIDA ADMINISTRATIVE PRACTICE
THE FLORIDA BAR PROBATE SYSTEM
FLORIDA CIVIL TRIAL PRACTICE
FLORIDA CONDOMINIUM LAW AND PRACTICE
FLORIDA CONSTRUCTION LAW & PRACTICE
FLORIDA CORPORATE PRACTICE
FLORIDA CRIMINAL RULES AND PRACTICE
FLORIDA DISSOLUTION OF MARRIAGE
FLORIDA ENVIRONMENTAL AND LAND USE LAW
FLORIDA JUVENILE LAW AND PRACTICE
FLORIDA PRETRIAL PRACTICE IN CRIMINAL CASES
FLORIDA PROCEEDINGS AFTER DISSOLUTION OF MARRIAGE
FLORIDA SMALL BUSINESS PRACTICE
FLORIDA STANDARD JURY INSTRUCTIONS IN CIVIL CASES
FLORIDA STANDARD JURY INSTRUCTIONS IN CRIMINAL CASES
FLORIDA WILL AND TRUST DRAFTING
IMMIGRATION LAW AND PRACTICE IN FLORIDA
INTERNATIONAL TRANSACTIONS
LEGAL FORMS AND WORKSHEETS
MARITIME LAW AND PRACTICE
PRACTICE UNDER FLORIDA USURY LAW
PROFESSIONAL ETHICS OF THE FLORIDA BAR
PROFESSIONAL LIABILITY OF LAWYERS IN FLORIDA
REAL PROPERTY TITLE EXAMINATION AND INSURANCE IN FLORIDA

FNMA
MULTI-FAMILY GUIDE
SELLING GUIDE
SERVICING GUIDE

Foreign Tax
COMMERCIAL LAWS OF THE WORLD
TAX LAWS OF THE WORLD

Francis Marion
ARKANSAS RULES OF EVIDENCE
FLORIDA RULES OF CRIMINAL EVIDENCE
HAWAII RULES OF EVIDENCE
RAYBURN ON CONDEMNATION/THE TEXAS LAW OF EMINENT DOMAIN
STRUCTURED SETTLEMENTS: DESIGN AND EVALUATION
TEXAS FIRE & POLICE CIVIL SERVICE LAW
TEXAS PROPERTY TAX--PROTEST & APPEALS
TEXAS RULES OF CRIMINAL EVIDENCE
WESTERN WATER LAW

Freddie Mac
SELLERS' & SERVICERS' GUIDE

Gann
NEW JERSEY COURT RULES

Georgetown
ADVANCED BANKRUPTCY INSTITUTE
ADVANCED ESTATE PLANNING INSTITUTE
COMMERCIAL LEASE NEGOTIATIONS
CORPORATE TAXATION
DEVELOPMENTS IN SEC DISCLOSURE
EEO UPDATE 1990
ENVIRONMENTAL LAW AFFECTING REAL ESTATE DEVELOPMENTS
FEDERAL ENFORCEMENT
HANDLING COMPLEX CRIMINAL CASES
SECTION 1983 LITIGATION
STATE AND LOCAL TAX INSTITUTE

GIS
GUIDE TO FEDERAL FUNDING FOR ANTI-DRUG PROGRAMS
GUIDE TO FEDERAL FUNDING FOR GOVERNMENTS AND NON-PROFITS

Glanville Publishers
LEGAL PERIODICALS IN ENGLISH

Gould
BILINGUAL DICTIONARY OF CRIMINAL JUSTICE TERMS (ENGLISH/SPANISH)
CONNECTICUT LAW ENFORCEMENT HANDBOOK
CONTEMPORARY CRIMINAL PROCEDURE
FEDERAL BANKRUPTCY HANDBOOK
FEDERAL CIVIL PRACTICE HANDBOOK
ILLINOIS CRIMINAL LAW & PROCEDURE
MASSACHUSETTS CIVIL ACTIONS & PROCEDURE
NEW JERSEY CIVIL PRACTICE AND COURT RULES
NEW JERSEY LAW ENFORCEMENT HANDBOOK
NEW YORK CANUDO ON EVIDENCE LAWS
NEW YORK CITY LAW DIGEST
NEW YORK CIVIL PRACTICE LAW & RULES HANDBOOK
NEW YORK CORPORATION LAW HANDBOOK
NEW YORK COURT FORMS
NEW YORK COURTS MANUAL OF PROCEDURE
NEW YORK CRIMINAL LAW HANDBOOK
NEW YORK FAMILY LAW HANDBOOK
NEW YORK KASS ON WILLS

NEW YORK LANDLORD & TENANT HANDBOOK
NEW YORK LAW DIGEST
NEW YORK LEGAL FORMS & PROCEDURES HANDBOOK
NEW YORK MAGISTRATES DESK BOOK
NEW YORK REAL PROPERTY LAW HANDBOOK
NEW YORK SEARCH & SEIZURE
NEW YORK UNCONTESTED DIVORCES AND ANNULMENTS
NEW YORK WORKERS CONPENSATION LAW HANDBOOK
PENNSYLVANIA CRIMINAL LAW DIGEST
PENNSYLVANIA LAW ENFORCEMENT HANDBOOK
U.C.C. STATE VARIATIONS

<u>Govt. Inst.</u>
EVALUATING THE FLUIDIZED BED COMBUSTION (FBC) OPTION, 6th Ed.

<u>Govt. Res.</u>
STATE LEGISLATIVE SOURCEBOOK

<u>Greenwood</u>
ADVERTISING COMPLIANCE SERVICE

<u>Griffin</u>
THE ATTORNEY'S UMBRELLA BOOK

<u>Gulf</u>
HOW TO AVOID OSHA

<u>Harrison</u>
CIVIL PLEADING AND PRACTICE FORMS, GEORGIA
HARRISON'S SAPP. FLORIDA PLEADINGS, PRACTICE & LEGAL FORMS ANNOTATED, 2D ED.
MAGISTRATE COURT HANDBOOK, GEORGIA

<u>Hawkins</u>
AVIATION REGULATORY DIGEST SERVICE
FEDERAL MARITIME COMMISSION SERVICE
MARYLAND TAX COURT SERVICE
MERIT SYSTEMS PROTECTION BOARD SERVICE
MOTOR CARRIER - FREIGHT FORWARDER SERVICE
NATIONAL TRANSPORTATION SAFETY BOARD SERVICE
RAIL CARRIER SERVICE

<u>HBJ Miller</u>
S CORPORATION TAX GUIDE 1992
SINGLE AUDIT GUIDE 1992

<u>Hein</u>
BANKRUPTCY FORMS MANUAL
CONGRESSIONAL HEARINGS CALENDAR
CONSTITUTIONS OF AMERICAN DENOMINATIONS
EXTRADITION LAWS AND TREATIES OF THE UNITED STATES
FEDERAL REGULATION OF INTERNATIONAL BUSINESS
HEIN'S INTERIM DECISION SERVICE
HEIN'S LEGAL PERIODICAL CHECKLIST
HEIN'S STATE REPORT CHECKLIST
INTERNATIONAL HUMAN RIGHTS INSTRUMENTS
MARINE POLLUTION AND THE LAW OF THE SEA
MODERN LEGAL SYSTEMS CYCLOPEDIA
NEW YORK CLOSE CORPORATIONS
NEW YORK TAX CASES
SOUTH DAKOTA LEGAL RESEARCH GUIDE
UNCITRAL MODEL LAW OF INTERNATIONAL COMMERCIAL ARBITRATION: A DOCUMENTARY HISTORY
UNITED STATES LEGISLATION ON FOREIGN RELATIONS AND INTERNATIONAL COMMERCE
UNITED STATES TAX CONVENTIONS. (Roberts & Holland Collection)

HICLE

ENCYCLOPEDIA OF FINANCIAL AND ESTATE PLANNING
FINANCIAL AND ESTATE PLANNING FORMS MANUAL
HAWAII ADOPTION MANUAL
HAWAII APPELLATE HANDBOOK
HAWAII COMMERCIAL REAL ESTATE MANUAL
HAWAII CONVEYANCE MANUAL
HAWAII CRIMINAL LAW AND PROCEDURE DIGEST
HAWAII DIVORCE MANUAL: A COOPERATIVE EFFORT
HAWAII LEGAL PRACTICE MANUAL - CORPORATIONS & REAL ESTATE
HAWAII LEGAL PRACTICE MANUAL - LITIGATION
HAWAII REAL ESTATE FINANCING
HAWAII SURROGATE COURTS FILING PROCEDURES MANUAL
IT'S THE LAW: WHAT NONPROFITS NEED TO KNOW

HIMA

HIMA REGULATORY MANUAL
RECALL MANUAL: A GUIDE FOR MANAGEMENT

Holding

SUBJECT HEADING INDEX GUIDE FOR OPINIONS AND MEMORANDA OF LAW

IBL

EMPLOYMENT REGULATIONS IN [STATE]: A SURVIVAL KIT FOR [STATE] EMPLOYERS: PROCEEDINGS
ENVIRONMENTAL COMPLIANCE MANAGEMENT IN [STATE]
ENVIRONMENTAL REGULATIONS FOR [STATE]

ICBO

UNIFORM BUILDING CODE
UNIFORM FIRE CODE

ICI

BLUE SKY GUIDE
INVESTMENT ADVISERS GUIDE

ICLE - Michigan

ADVISING THE OLDER CLIENT
BANKRUPTCY LAW AND PRACTICE IN MICHIGAN
COURT RULES OF MICHIGAN ANNOTATED
GILMORE ON MICHIGAN CIVIL PROCEDURE BEFORE TRIAL
GOVERNMENTAL IMMUNITY IN MICHIGAN
A GUIDE TO MICHIGAN TORT REFORM
HANDLING THE AUTOMOBILE NEGLIGENCE CASE: A SYSTEMS APPROACH
HANDLING THE MEDICAL MALPRACTICE CASE: A SYSTEMS APPROACH
INTRODUCING EVIDENCE: A PRACTICAL GUIDE FOR MICHIGAN LAWYERS
MANUAL FOR LAWYERS AND LEGAL ASSISTANTS: REAL ESTATE, 2ND ED.
MICHIGAN ANTITRUST DIGEST
MICHIGAN APPELLATE HANDBOOK
MICHIGAN APPROVED COURT FORMS
MICHIGAN BASIC PRACTICE HANDBOOK
MICHIGAN BUSINESS FORMBOOK
MICHIGAN CIVIL PROCEDURE DURING TRIAL
MICHIGAN COURTROOM EVIDENCE
MICHIGAN CRIMINAL JURY INSTRUCTIONS, 2nd Ed.
MICHIGAN DRUNK DRIVING LAW AND PRACTICE, REV. ED.
MICHIGAN FAMILY LAW
MICHIGAN FAMILY LAW SOURCEBOOK
THE MICHIGAN LAW OF DAMAGES
MICHIGAN NO-FAULT AUTOMOBILE CASES: LAW AND PRACTICE
MICHIGAN PROBATE SOURCEBOOK
MICHIGAN REAL ESTATE PRACTICE AND FORMS
MICHIGAN REVOCABLE GRANTOR TRUSTS
MICHIGAN RULES OF PROFESSIONAL CONDUCT AND DISCIPLINARY PROCEDURE
MICHIGAN STANDARD JURY INSTRUCTIONS - CIVIL

MICHIGAN WILL DRAFTING
MICHIGAN WRONGFUL DISCHARGE AND EMPLOYMENT DISCRIMINATION LAW
PROBATE ADMINISTRATION IN MICHIGAN: A SYSTEMS APPROACH
TORTS: MICHIGAN LAW & PRACTICE
WORKER'S COMPENSATION IN MICHIGAN: LAW & PRACTICE, Rev. Ed.

<u>Idaho Law</u>
IDAHO APPELLATE HANDBOOK
IDAHO CIVIL JURY INSTRUCTIONS
IDAHO PRE-TRIAL CIVIL PROCEDURE
IDAHO REAL ESTATE PRACTICE HANDBOOK

<u>IDDS</u>
ARMS CONTROL REPORTER

<u>IFA</u>
FTC FRANCHISING RULE: THE IFA COMPLIANCE KIT

<u>Illinois ICLE</u>
ADVISING ELDERLY CLIENTS AND THEIR FAMILIES
ADVISING FARMERS
ADVISING ILLINOIS FINANCIAL INSTITUTIONS
ANNOTATED GUIDE TO THE ILLINOIS RULES OF PROFESSIONAL CONDUCT
ARBITRATION PRACTICE
ARREST, SEARCH AND SEIZURE
BANKRUPTCY PRACTICE
BASIC ESTATE PLANNING
BASIC REAL ESTATE PRACTICE, VOL. 1
BASIC REAL ESTATE PRACTICE, VOL. 2
BUSINESS AND COMMERCIAL LITIGATION
BUSINESS INTERESTS IN ESTATES
BUYING AND SELLING BUSINESSES
CHANCERY AND SPECIAL REMEDIES
CIVIL APPEALS
CLASS ACTIONS
CLOSELY HELD CORPORATIONS
COMMERCIAL LANDLORD/TENANT PRACTICE
CONSTRUCTION LITIGATION
CONTESTED ESTATES
CONTRACTS AND SALES OF GOODS
CREDITORS' RIGHTS IN ILLINOIS
DEEDS IN LIEU OF FORECLOSURE
DEFENDING DUI AND TRAFFIC CASES
DEFENDING ILLINOIS CRIMINAL CASES
DRAFTING WILLS AND TRUST AGREEMENTS
EMPLOYEE BENEFITS LAW
EMPLOYMENT DISCRIMINATION
EMPLOYMENT TERMINATION
ENVIRONMENTAL LAW FOR TRANSACTIONAL ATTORNEYS
FEDERAL CIVIL PRACTICE
FEDERAL CRIMINAL PRACTICE
FEDERAL TAX ASPECTS OF REAL ESTATE TRANSACTIONS
FEDERAL TAX PRACTICE AND PROCEDURE
FINANCING REAL ESTATE TRANSACTIONS
HEALTH CARE LAW
ILLINOIS ADMINISTRATIVE LAW
ILLINOIS CIVIL DISCOVERY PRACTICE
ILLINOIS CIVIL PRACTICE
ILLINOIS CIVIL TRIAL EVIDENCE
ILLINOIS CONDOMINIUM LAW
ILLINOIS DRAM SHOP ACT PRACTICE
ILLINOIS EMINENT DOMAIN PRACTICE
ILLINOIS ESTATE ADMINISTRATION
ILLINOIS FAMILY LAW
ILLINOIS JUVENILE LAW AND PRACTICE

ILLINOIS LAND USE LAW
ILLINOIS MECHANICS' LIENS PRACTICE
ILLINOIS MUNICIPAL LAW
ILLINOIS PRODUCT LIABILITY PRACTICE
ILLINOIS STATE AND LOCAL TAXATION
ILLINOIS STRUCTURAL WORK ACT PRACTICE
ILLINOIS WORKERS' COMPENSATION PRACTICE
IMMIGRATION AND NATURALIZATION PRACTICE
KENOE ON LAND TRUSTS
LABOR LAW HANDBOOK
LAND TRUST ADMINISTRATION
LEGAL RESEARCH AND WRITING
LIABILITY INSURANCE
MEDICAL EVIDENCE
MEDICAL MALPRACTICE
MINERAL LAW
NOT-FOR-PROFIT CORPORATIONS
ORGANIZING AND ADVISING ILLINOIS BUSINESSES
PARTNERSHIP PRACTICE
PROFESSIONAL LIABILITY
PROOF OF DAMAGES
PROPERTY INSURANCE
PROVING FAULT IN AUTO ACCIDENT CASES
QUICK GUIDE FOR THE LEGAL ASSISTANT
REAL ESTATE LITIGATION
REAL ESTATE TAXATION
REPRESENTING RESIDENTIAL TENANTS
RESIDENTIAL REAL ESTATE SYSTEM
S CORPORATIONS
SECURED TRANSACTIONS
SECURITIES LAW
THIRD PARTY PRACTICE
TRUST ADMINISTRATION IN ILLINOIS
WARD ON TITLE EXAMINATIONS

<u>Indiana CLE</u>

ACCELERATED DISPUTE RESOLUTIONS
ADOPTION LAW
ADVISING THE SMALL BUSINESS CLIENT
AMERICAN DISABILITY ACT
ANNUAL FEDERAL CIVIL PRACTICE
APPELLATE PRACTICE
BANKRUPTCY "A BASIC REVIEW"
BANKRUPTCY--CHAPTER 13
BASIC CORPORATE PRACTICE
BASIC ESTATE PLANNING
BASIC INSURANCE LAW
BASIC INSURANCE LAW II
BASIC PROBATE
BECOMING EXPERT WITH WORDPERFECT IN YOUR LAW OFFICE
BUSINESS, BANKS, BORROWERS & THE ENVIRONMENT
CLEAN AIR ACT
COLLECTIONS
CONSUMER LAW
CONTRACT LAW
CRIMINAL DEFENSE
CRIMINAL LAW
DAMAGES IN CONSTRUCTION LITIGATION
DEFENSE TECHNIQUES FOR DWI CLIENTS
DEMONSTRATIVE EVIDENCE
DISCOVERY TOOLS: HOW TO WIN YOUR CASE BEFORE TRIAL
DIVORCE
DIVORCE TAXATION
DIVORCE: COMMON & COMPLEX ISSUES
DWI - DRAM SHOP

EFFECTIVE LEGAL WRITING
ELDER LAW
EMINENT DOMAIN
EMPLOYEE BENEFITS UPDATE: INCLUDING SECTION 89
ENVIRONMENTAL LAW FOR ENVIRONMENTAL LAWYERS
ENVIRONMENTAL LAW FOR THE GENERAL PRACTITIONER
ENVIRONMENTAL LAW SYMPOSIUM
ESTATE & GUARDIANSHIP ADMINISTRATION
ESTATE PLANNING
ESTATE PLANNING & ADMINISTRATION IN INDIANA
EVERYTHING ELSE YOU NEEDED TO KNOW ABOUT FAMILY LAW
EVIDENCE: KEEPING IT OUT
FINANCIAL INSTITUTIONS REFORM, RECOVERY & ENFORCEMENT ACT OF 1989
FRAUDULENT CONVEYANCES
FUNDAMENTALS OF HEALTH CARE LAW
GUARDIANSHIP
HOT ISSUES IN EMPLOYMENT LITIGATION
INDIANA LAW UPDATE
INDIANA'S NEW GUARDIANSHIP LAW--AN UPDATE
INTELLECTUAL PROPERTY LAW
INTERNATIONAL LAW
LABOR RELATIONS LAW UPDATE
LEGISLATIVE UPDATE
LENDER LIABILITY: A PRAGMATIC APPROACH
LIABILITY ISSUES IN THE HOSPITAL SETTING
MANAGING THE SMALL & MEDIUM-SIZED LAW FIRM
MECHANICS LIENS
MEDICAL MALPRACTICE UPDATE
MIDWEST ESTATE, TAX & BUSINESS PLANNING
MOTIONS PRACTICE IN INDIANA
MUNICIPAL LAW VIII
MUNICIPAL UTILITY LAW
NINTH ANNUAL BANKRUPTCY INSTITUTE
NONPROFIT CORPORATIONS
PATENT AND TRADE SECRETS
PLANNING AND ZONING
PRACTICAL APPROACHES TO EMPLOYMENT DISCRIMINATION PROBLEMS
PRACTICE UNDER THE FEDERAL SENTENCING GUIDELINES
PRACTITIONER'S HANDBOOK FOR APPEALS
PROBATE LITIGATION
PRODUCTS LIABILITY
RICO LITIGATION
SECURED LENDING & SECURED FINANCING
STATE & FEDERAL ADMINISTRATIVE AGENCY PRACTICE
SUCCESSFULLY LITIGATING TORT INSURANCE ACTIONS
TAX ASPECTS OF INDIANA S CORPORATIONS
TORT LAW
TRUSTS AND TRUSTEES
WHAT EVERYONE NEEDS TO KNOW ABOUT ENVIRONMENTAL LAW
WINNING ON APPEAL: GOOD APPELLATE PRACTICE
WINNING YOUR CASE THROUGH EFFECTIVE PRETRIAL DISCOVERY
WORKER'S COMPENSATION
ZONING: RULES, PROCEDURES & PROBLEMS

Inst. of Prop. Tax.
PROPERTY TAXATION

Institute - Ga.
SUGGESTED PATTERN JURY INSTRUCTIONS - VOLUME 1: CIVIL CASES, THIRD ED.
SUGGESTED PATTERN JURY INSTRUCTIONS - VOLUME 2: CRIMINAL CASES, SECOND ED.

Intl. Law Inst.
CHINESE FOREIGN ECONOMIC LAW
INTERNATIONAL JUDICIAL ASSISTANCE (CIVIL AND COMMERCIAL)
INTERNATIONAL JUDICIAL ASSISTANCE (CRIMINAL)

Intl. Risk Mgmt. Inst.

COMMERCIAL LIABILITY INSURANCE
COMMERCIAL PROPERTY INSURANCE
CONSTRUCTION RISK MANAGEMENT
MANUAL OF RULES, CLASSIFICATIONS, AND INTERPRETATIONS FOR WORKERS COMPENSATION INSURANCE
MANUFACTURING RISK MANAGEMENT AND INSURANCE
PROFESSIONAL LIABILITY INSURANCE
RISK FINANCING

Invictus

UNITED STATES COURT OF INTERNATIONAL TRADE - RULES

IOCC

SUMMARY OF STATE STATUTES AND REGULATIONS FOR OIL AND GAS PRODUCTION

Iowa Bar

IOWA CIVIL JURY INSTRUCTIONS
IOWA FAMILY LAW MANUAL
IOWA LAND TITLE EXAMINATION STANDARDS
IOWA PROBATE MANUAL
IOWA REAL ESTATE MANUAL
IOWA UNIFORM JURY INSTRUCTIONS - CRIMINAL

IRC

LEGAL REQUIREMENTS FOR BUSINESS RECORDS - FEDERAL REQUIREMENTS
LEGAL REQUIREMENTS FOR BUSINESS RECORDS - STATE REQUIREMENTS

IRRC

STATE TAKEOVER LAWS

James

CALIFORNIA LEGAL SECRETARY
DEFENDING DRINKING DRIVERS
DETERMINING ECONOMIC DAMAGES
DWI DEFENSE FORMS
ESTIMATING AND PROVING PERSONAL INJURY DAMAGES
FEDERAL TRIAL EVIDENCE
FLORIDA LEGAL SECRETARY
HOW INSURANCE COMPANIES SETTLE CASES
HOW TO PREPARE FOR, TAKE, AND USE A DEPOSITION
ILLINOIS TRIAL EVIDENCE
INSURANCE SETTLEMENT HANDBOOK
LEGAL SECRETARY BANKRUPTCY
LEGAL SECRETARY FEDERAL LITIGATION
LITIGATING NECK AND BACK INJURIES
LITIGATION PARALEGAL
MAXIMIZING DAMAGES IN SMALL PERSONAL INJURY CASES
MODEL INTERROGATORIES: PERSONAL INJURY
OBJECTIONS TO INTERROGATORIES
PARALEGAL DISCOVERY: ORGANIZATION AND MANAGEMENT
PARALEGAL DISCOVERY: PROCEDURES AND FORMS
PARALEGAL LITIGATION FORMS
PARALEGAL MEDICAL RECORDS REVIEW
PARALEGAL PREPARATION OF PLEADINGS
PARALEGAL TRIAL HANDBOOK
PERSONAL INJURY FORMS: DISCOVERY & SETTLEMENT
PERSONAL INJURY HANDBOOK
PERSONAL INJURY: DISCOVERY & TRIAL
QUALIFYING & ATTACKING EXPERT WITNESSES
SLIP AND FALL PRACTICE
SOCIAL SECURITY DISABILITY PRACTICE
TRIAL EVIDENCE FOUNDATIONS
TRIAL HEARSAY: OBJECTIONS & EXCEPTIONS

TRIAL OBJECTIONS
WHAT YOU NEED TO KNOW TO SETTLE WITH INSURANCE COMPANIES

Jefren
PROXY STATEMENTS: STRATEGY AND FORMS

JKP
POLYGRAPH AND THE LAW

John Liner Org.
RISK MANAGEMENT AND INSURANCE AUDIT TECHNIQUES

Jt. Comm. Va.
ADVISING SMALL BUSINESS CLIENTS, VOL. 1
ADVISING SMALL BUSINESS CLIENTS, VOL. 2
APPELLATE PRACTICE - VIRGINIA AND FEDERAL COURTS
BASIC ESTATE PLANNING AND ADMINISTRATION
DEFENDING CRIMINAL CASES IN VIRGINIA
EMINENT DOMAIN--STATE AND FEDERAL
ENFORCEMENT OF LIENS AND JUDGMENTS
FAMILY LAW AND PRACTICE IN VIRGINIA
NEGOTIATING AND DRAFTING MARITAL AGREEMENTS
RESIDENTIAL REAL ESTATE TRANSACTIONS
SOURCES OF PROOF IN PREPARING A LAWSUIT - STATE AND FEDERAL
VIRGINIA ADMINISTRATIVE LAW AND PRACTICE
WORKER'S COMPENSATION FOR THE EMPLOYER'S ATTORNEY & CLAIMANT'S ATTORNEY

Jury Verdict
BETTER, EARLIER SETTLEMENTS THROUGH ECONOMIC LEVERAGE
CASE EVALUATOR'S MANUAL
NATIONAL VERDICT SURVEY
PERSONAL INJURY VALUATION HANDBOOKS
REGIONAL VERDICT SURVEY

Kansas Bar
KANSAS ADMINISTRATIVE LAW WITH FEDERAL REFERENCES
KANSAS APPELLATE PRACTICE
KANSAS BANKRUPTCY HANDBOOK
KANSAS CORPORATION LAW AND PRACTICE
KANSAS CRIMINAL LAW HANDBOOK
KANSAS EMPLOYMENT LAW
KANSAS ESTATE ADMINISTRATION
KANSAS EVIDENCE OBJECTIONS WITH EVIDENTIARY FOUNDATIONS
KANSAS FAMILY LAW HANDBOOK
KANSAS LAW OF SALES UNDER THE UNIFORM COMMERCIAL CODE
KANSAS LOCAL GOVERNMENT LAW
KANSAS OIL & GAS HANDBOOK, VOL. I
KANSAS OIL AND GAS HANDBOOK VOL. II
KANSAS PERSONAL PROPERTY SECURED TRANSACTIONS
KANSAS REAL ESTATE PRACTICE AND PROCEDURE HANDBOOK
KANSAS STATUTE OF LIMITATIONS AND TIME STANDARDS
KANSAS TITLE STANDARDS HANDBOOK
KANSAS WORKERS' COMPENSATION PRACTICE MANUAL

Keller
CHEMICAL CRISIS MANAGEMENT GUIDE
DRUG TESTING MANUAL
FLEET SAFETY COMPLIANCE MANUAL
HAZARD COMMUNICATION GUIDE
HAZARDOUS MATERIALS GUIDE
HAZARDOUS WASTE MANAGEMENT GUIDE: IDENTIFICATION, MONITORING, TREATMENT AND DISPOSAL
HAZARDOUS WASTE OPERATIONS & EMERGENCY RESPONSE COMPLIANCE MANUAL
HAZARDOUS WASTE REGULATORY GUIDE
INTERSTATE COMMERCE GUIDE

INTERSTATE MOTOR CARRIER FORMS MANUAL
NATIONAL BACKHAUL GUIDE
OSHA 1910 GUIDE
RIGHT TO KNOW COMPLIANCE MANUAL
TRUCKING PERMIT GUIDE
TRUCKING SAFETY GUIDE
VEHICLE SIZES AND WEIGHTS MANUAL

<u>Kluwer</u>

BUSINESS LAW IN EUROPE
COMPANIES AND OTHER LEGAL PERSONS UNDER NETHERLANDS LAW
COMPETITION LAW IN WESTERN EUROPE & THE USA
CONTRACT CHECKLISTS
COUNTRY HANDBOOKS
CROSS BORDER PRACTICE COMPENDIUM
DUTCH BUSINESS LAW
EEC MERGER CONTROL REPORTER
FINANCIAL SERVICES AND EEC LAW
GUIDE TO PRACTICAL APPLICATIONS OF THE UN CONVENTION ON CONTRACTS FOR THE INTERNATIONAL SALE OF GOODS
HANDBOOK ON EUROPEAN EMPLOYEE CO-MANAGEMENT
INTERNATIONAL BUSINESS TRANSACTIONS
INTERNATIONAL ENCYCLOPEDIA FOR LABOUR LAW AND INDUSTRIAL RELATIONS
INTERNATIONAL HANDBOOK ON COMMERCIAL ARBITRATION -- NATIONAL REPORTS AND BASIC LEGAL TEXTS
INTERNATIONAL HANDBOOK ON CONTRACTS OF EMPLOYMENT
INTERNATIONAL TRANSPORT TREATIES
LEGAL ASPECTS OF DOING BUSINESS IN ASIA & PACIFIC
LEGAL ASPECTS OF DOING BUSINESS IN AFRICA
LEGAL ASPECTS OF DOING BUSINESS IN EUROPE
LEGAL ASPECTS OF DOING BUSINESS IN NORTH AMERICA
MANUAL FOR THE PRACTICE OF U.S. IMPORT LAW
MARITIME LAW HANDBOOK
PUBLIC POLICY IN TRANSNATIONAL RELATIONS
SINGLE EUROPEAN MARKET REPORTER
STRUCTURING FOREIGN INVESTMENT IN U.S. REAL ESTATE
UNITED STATES INCOME TAX TREATIES

<u>Knowles</u>

AUTOMOBILES
CALIFORNIA DEPOSITIONS
CRIMINAL DEFENSE JURY INSTRUCTIONS
DAMAGES
DEPOSITIONS
DISCOVERY
ERISMAN'S REVERSIBLE ERRORS
ERISMAN'S REVERSIBLE ERRORS IN ILLINOIS CRIMINAL CASES
EVIDENCE (TEXAS & NATIONAL EDITIONS)
EXTRANEOUS OFFENSES & UNCHARGED CONDUCT
FAMILY LAW
NATIONAL DIRECTORY FOR THE SERVICE OF CIVIL PROCESS
PREMISES LIABILITY
PROFESSIONAL LIABILITY
REAL ESTATE PRACTITIONER'S TAX GUIDE
RICO -- RACKETEER INFLUENCED CORRUPT ORGANIZATION
TEXAS CRIMINAL DEFENSE FORMS ANNOTATED

<u>LADJ</u>

COURT RULES FOR NORTHERN CALIFORNIA
COURT RULES FOR SOUTHERN CALIFORNIA
JUDICIAL PROFILES

<u>Lamb's Flight</u>

NEW YORK CITY HOUSING COURT REPORTER CHRONOLOGICAL ANNOTATOR
THE NEW YORK CITY HOUSING COURT REPORTER DIGEST

THE NEW YORK CITY HOUSING COURT REPORTER PLAINTIFF-DEFENDANT TABLES
THE NEW YORK CITY HOUSING COURT REPORTER
THE NEW YORK CITY LOFT BOARD REPORTER
TREIMAN'S LANDLORD & TENANT ENCYCLOPEDIA & REVIEW
TREIMAN'S NEW YORK LANDLORD TENANT STATUTES, ANNOTATED
TREIMAN'S RENT STABILIZATION CODE, ANNOTATED

Lambda
AIDS LEGAL GUIDE: A PROFESSIONAL RESOURCE ON AIDS-RELATED ISSUES & DISCRIMINATION

Lame
ATTORNEY'S GUIDE TO CONDUCTING DEPOSITIONS - AUTOMOBILE NEGLIGENCE CASES

Land Dev.
DIGEST OF STATE LAND SALES REGULATIONS
LAND DEVELOPMENT LAW REPORTER
THE RTC RESOURCE BOOK

Law Bulletin
ILLINOIS COURTS RULE BOOK

Law Journal
ACQUISITIONS UNDER THE HART-SCOTT-RODINO ANTITRUST IMPROVEMENTS ACT
ALL ABOUT CABLE
ANTITRUST: AN ECONOMIC APPROACH
ANTITRUST BASICS
CHANGING THE SITUS OF A TRUST
CLASS ACTIONS: THE LAW OF 50 STATES
COMPUTER LAW - DRAFTING AND NEGOTIATING FORMS AND AGREEMENTS
DIVORCE, SEPARATION AND THE DISTRIBUTION OF PROPERTY
EMPLOYEE BENEFITS LAW, ERISA AND BEYOND
ENVIRONMENTAL REGULATION OF REAL PROPERTY
ESTATE PLANNING
FEDERAL BANK HOLDING COMPANY LAW
FEDERAL TAXATION OF INTELLECTUAL PROPERTY TRANSFERS
FEDERAL TAXATION OF REAL ESTATE
FEDERAL TAXATION OF S CORPORATIONS
FEDERAL TRADE COMMISSION: LAW, PRACTICE AND PROCEDURE
FRANCHISING: REALITIES AND REMEDIES
FRANCHISING: REALITIES AND REMEDIES FORMS VOLUME
GOING PRIVATE
GROUND LEASES AND LAND ACQUISITION CONTRACTS
HOSPITAL LIABILITY
THE LAW AND PRACTICE OF SECURED TRANSACTIONS: WORKING WITH ARTICLE 9
LEGAL RESEARCH AND LAW LIBRARY MANAGEMENT
LENDER LIABILITY AND BANKING LITIGATION
MAXIMIZING LAW FIRM PROFITABILITY
MODERN VISUAL EVIDENCE
MULTIFAMILY HOUSING: FEDERAL PROGRAMS FOR THE PRIVATE SECTOR
A PRACTICAL GUIDE TO EQUAL EMPLOYMENT OPPORTUNITY
A PRACTICAL GUIDE TO TAX SHELTER LITIGATION
A PRACTICAL GUIDE TO THE OCCUPATIONAL SAFETY & HEALTH ACT
PRIVATE REAL ESTATE SYNDICATIONS
PRODUCT LIABILITY
PRODUCTS LIABILITY: RECREATION AND SPORTS EQUIPMENT
REDUCING PERSONAL INCOME TAXES: A GUIDE TO DEDUCTIONS AND CREDITS
REORGANIZATIONS UNDER CHAPTER 11 OF THE BANKRUPTCY CODE
RICO -- CIVIL AND CRIMINAL, LAW AND STRATEGY
SAVINGS INSTITUTIONS: MERGERS, ACQUISITIONS AND CONVERSIONS
SECURITIES REGULATION: LIABILITIES AND REMEDIES
SHOPPING CENTER AND STORE LEASES
START-UP COMPANIES: PLANNING, FINANCING AND OPERATING THE SUCCESSFUL BUSINESS
STATE ANTITRUST LAW

STRUCTURED SETTLEMENTS AND PERIODIC PAYMENT JUDGMENTS
TAKEOVERS AND FREEZEOUTS
TAX ASPECTS OF DIVORCE AND SEPARATION
TRAVEL LAW
USE OF STATISTICS IN EQUAL EMPLOYMENT OPPORTUNITY
WHITE COLLAR CRIME: BUSINESS AND REGULATORY OFFENSES
WINNING ATTORNEY'S FEES FROM THE U.S. GOVERNMENT

Law-Arts

PERFORMING ARTS MANAGEMENT AND THE LAW
RECORD AND MUSIC PUBLISHING FORMS OF AGREEMENT IN CURRENT USE

Lawpress

CALIFORNIA ARBITRATION PRACTICE GUIDE 2D
CALIFORNIA CORPORATE PRACTICE GUIDE 2D

Lawyers Coop.

BANKRUPTCY DESK GUIDE
BENCH BOOK FOR TRIAL JUDGES - NEW YORK
BILLS OF PARTICULARS IN NEW YORK
BLACK'S TEXAS EVIDENCE
CALIFORNIA DRUNK DRIVING DEFENSE
CALIFORNIA PERSONAL INJURY FORMS
CALIFORNIA PLEADING AND PRACTICE FORMS
CALLAGHAN'S CRIMINAL LAW IN NY
CALLAGHAN'S FAMILY COURT LAW AND PRACTICE IN NEW YORK
CHARGES TO THE JURY AND REQUESTS TO CHARGE IN A CRIMINAL CASE IN NEW YORK
COLORADO CORPORATE FORMS
CONNECTICUT PROBATE DESKBOOK
COUNSELING THE ELDERLY CLIENT IN MICHIGAN
CRIMINAL PROCEDURE IN NEW YORK PART 1 & PART 2
CRITICAL ISSUES: TRADEMARKS
ENVIRONMENTAL LAW: ALR ANNOTATIONS
ESTATE PLANNING IN LOUISIANA
ESTATE TAXATION IN MASSACHUSETTS, WITH FORMS
EVIDENCE -- A TRIAL MANUAL FOR MICHIGAN LAWYERS
EXAMINATION BEFORE TRIAL AND OTHER DISCLOSURE DEVICES
FEDERAL CRIMINAL LAW AND PROCEDURE: ALR ANNOTATIONS
FEDERAL LOCAL COURT FORMS
FEDERAL LOCAL COURT RULES
FEDERAL RULES OF EVIDENCE SERVICE
FLORIDA CORPORATIONS
FLORIDA LAWYER'S GUIDE
FLORIDA PRACTICE GUIDE: PERSONAL INJURY
FLORIDA REAL ESTATE
FORM DRAFTING CHECKLISTS - AM JUR PRACTICE GUIDE
GEORGIA DIVORCE
ILLINOIS LAWYER'S MANUAL, 3RD ED.
ILLINOIS NON-PATTERN JURY INSTRUCTIONS
ILLINOIS PRACTICE GUIDE - PERSONAL INJURY
ILLINOIS REAL ESTATE
ILLINOIS REAL PROPERTY SERVICE
IOWA PRACTICE
KENTUCKY COLLECTIONS
KENTUCKY DIVORCE
KENTUCKY PROBATE
KENTUCKY WORKERS' COMPENSATION
LOUISIANA APPELLATE PRACTICE HANDBOOK
LOUISIANA CORPORATIONS
LOUISIANA DIVORCE
LOUISIANA SUCCESSIONS
MASSACHUSETTS COLLECTION LAW: DEBTOR/CREDITOR PRACTICE, PROCEDURE, REMEDIES
MASSACHUSETTS CORPORATIONS
MASSACHUSETTS DOMESTIC RELATIONS
MASSACHUSETTS REAL ESTATE

MICHIGAN LAWYER'S MANUAL
MICHIGAN PROBATE
MINNESOTA COLLECTIONS
MINNESOTA DISSOLUTION OF MARRIAGE
MINNESOTA PROBATE
MINNESOTA REAL ESTATE
MISSOURI LAWYER'S GUIDE
MISSOURI WORKERS' COMPENSATION
MORTGAGES AND MORTGAGE FORECLOSURE IN NEW YORK
NEW YORK COLLECTIONS
NEW YORK MATRIMONIAL LAW AND PRACTICE
NEW YORK MATRIMONIAL PRACTICE
NEW YORK PROBATE
NEW YORK PRODUCTS LIABILITY
NEW YORK REAL PROPERTY SERVICE
OHIO PROBATE
OHIO WORKERS' COMPENSATION CLAIMS
PENNSYLVANIA CRIMINAL PRACTICE
PENNSYLVANIA ESTATES PRACTICE
PENNSYLVANIA MATRIMONIAL PRACTICE
PENNSYLVANIA REAL ESTATE
READ'S FLORIDA EVIDENCE
TAXING CALIFORNIA PROPERTY
TENNESSEE CORPORATIONS
TENNESSEE PROBATE
TEXAS LEGAL PRACTICE FORMS
TEXAS PRACTICE GUIDE - PERSONAL INJURY
VIRGINIA CORPORATIONS
WISCONSIN CIVIL PRACTICE FORMS
WISCONSIN CORPORATIONS
WISCONSIN REAL ESTATE

Lawyers Coop. & Bancroft
AMERICAN LAW OF PRODUCTS LIABILITY 3D
BANKRUPTCY SERVICE, LAWYERS EDITION
IMMIGRATION LAW SERVICE

Lawyers Weekly
THE RULES: A RULES SERVICE FOR MASSACHUSETTS

Legal Res. Systems
MILLER'S STANDARD INSURANCE POLICIES ANNOTATED

Legal-Med.
EUROPEAN COMMUNITY LAW & BUSINESS REPORTER
THE FAMILY LAW PRACTICE MANUAL
THE LAWYERS ANNOTATED PRODUCTS LIABILITY CHECKLISTS

Lexikon
LAW OFFICE GUIDE TO COMPUTER ABBREVIATIONS & ACRONYMS
LAWYER'S GUIDE TO ACCOUNTING AND FINANCE ABBREVIATIONS AND ACRONYMS
LAWYER'S GUIDE TO COMPUTER SECURITY: SOURCEBOOK

Little, Brown
BERNACCHI ON COMPUTER LAW - A GUIDE TO THE LEGAL AND MANAGEMENT ASPECTS OF COMPUTER TECHNOLOGY
BROMBERG AND RIBSTEIN ON PARTNERSHIP
ESTATE PLANNING, 5TH ED.
FOLK ON THE DELAWARE GENERAL CORPORATION LAW: A COMMENTARY AND ANALYSIS, 2nd ed.
MASSACHUSETTS STANDARDIZED CIVIL PRACTICE FORMS
SPECIALIZED LEGAL RESEARCH

Longshore
- THE BRAHM COURT INDEX
- THE LONGSHORE NEWSLETTER PROCEDURE MANUAL

LRP
- BANKRUPTCY COURT DECISIONS
- FEDERAL EQUAL OPPORTUNITY REPORTER
- FEDERAL LABOR RELATIONS REPORTER
- FEDERAL MERIT SYSTEMS REPORTER
- FEDERAL PAY AND BENEFITS REPORTER
- FLORIDA PUBLIC EMPLOYEE REPORTER
- ILLINOIS PUBLIC EMPLOYEE REPORTER
- INDIANA PUBLIC EMPLOYEE REPORTER
- INDIVIDUALS WITH DISABILITIES EDUCATION LAW REPORTER
- LABOR ARBITRATION INFORMATION SYSTEM
- LEGAL RIGHTS OF PERSONS WITH DISABILITIES
- MICHIGAN PUBLIC EMPLOYEE REPORTER
- MICHIGAN WORKERS' COMPENSATION LAW REPORTER
- MISSOURI WORKERS' COMPENSATION LAW REPORTER
- NATIONAL DISABILITY LAW REPORTER
- NATIONAL PUBLIC EMPLOYMENT REPORTER
- NEW JERSEY PUBLIC EMPLOYEE REPORTER
- NEW YORK WORKER'S COMPENSATION LAW REPORTER
- NLRB ADVICE MEMORANDUM REPORTER
- OFFICIAL DECISIONS, OPINIONS AND RELATED MATTERS OF THE PUBLIC EMPLOYMENT RELATIONS BOARD OF THE STATE OF NEW YORK
- OHIO PUBLIC EMPLOYEE REPORTER
- PENNSYLVANIA DIVORCE AND DOMESTIC RELATIONS REPORTER
- PENNSYLVANIA EMPLOYMENT LAWS
- PENNSYLVANIA PUBLIC EMPLOYEE REPORTER
- PENNSYLVANIA WORKER'S COMPENSATION LAW REPORTER
- PUBLIC EMPLOYEE REPORTER FOR CALIF.

M & M Resources
- CALIFORNIA EMPLOYMENT LAW: A GUIDE TO CALIFORNIA LAWS REGULATING EMPLOYMENT IN THE PRIVATE SECTOR
- CALIFORNIA WAGE AND HOUR GUIDE

Maine Bar
- BANKRUPTCY LAW FOR THE GENERAL PRACTITIONER
- BUSINESS TORTS
- CHOICE OF BUSINESS ENTITY AND PURCHASE AND SALE OF A BUSINESS
- COMMERCIAL BANKRUPTCY
- COPING WITH FORECLOSURES
- DEFENSE OF DRUNK DRIVING CASES: A GUIDE FOR THE GENERAL PRACTITIONER
- DEFINITION OF SUBDIVISION IN MAINE LAW
- ECONOMIC ISSUES IN DIVORCE
- EFFECTIVE STATE AND MUNICIPAL HEARINGS PRACTICE
- ELDER LAW
- ENVIRONMENTAL LAW
- FORGOING LIFE SUPPORT: LIVING WILLS AND HEALTH CARE POWERS OF ATTORNEY
- HOW TO HANDLE PROBLEM CRIMINAL CASES, AND A LOOK AT NEW CRIMES
- LEGAL YEAR IN REVIEW
- MAINE PROBATE: HOW TO SURVIVE YOUR NEXT ESTATE
- THE NUTS AND BOLTS OF A BASIC REAL ESTATE DEAL
- PARTNERSHIP INVESTMENTS: GOING UNDER
- PLANNING AND PAYING FOR LONG TERM CARE
- PRACTICAL ESTATE PLANNING: MORE THAN JUST WILLS
- REAL ESTATE LAW: EASEMENTS, ROADS AND WAYS AND LITIGATION
- REAL ESTATE LITIGATION
- RECENT ISSUES AND CURRENT DEVELOPMENTS IN LABOR AND EMPLOYMENT LAW
- TECHNIQUES FOR POST MORTEM ESTATE PLANNING
- TRENDS IN DIVORCE STATEGY
- TRIAL ADVOCACY: THE AUTOMOBILE ACCIDENT
- TROUBLED REAL ESTATE PROJECTS

Manak
THE ILLINOIS LAW OF CRIMINAL INVESTIGATION

Mariposa
FLORIDA ATTORNEY'S/SECRETARY'S HANDBOOK
GEORGIA ATTORNEY'S/SECRETARY'S HANDBOOK
ILLINOIS ATTORNEY'S/SECRETARY'S HANDBOOK
IOWA ATTORNEY'S/SECRETARY'S HANDBOOK
LOUISIANA ATTORNEY'S/SECRETARY'S HANDBOOK
MINNESOTA ATTORNEY'S/SECRETARY'S HANDBOOK
MISSOURI ATTORNEY'S/SECRETARY'S HANDBOOK
OHIO ATTORNEY'S/SECRETARY'S HANDBOOK
PENNSYLVANIA ATTORNEY'S/SECRETARY'S HANDBOOK
TEXAS ATTORNEY'S/SECRETARY'S HANDBOOK
U.S. CORPORATE HANDBOOK
WISCONSIN ATTORNEY'S/SECRETARY'S HANDBOOK

Mass. CLE
CHAPTER 93A RIGHTS AND REMEDIES
COMPENDIUM OF MASSACHUSETTS FAMILY LAW
DRAFTING WILLS AND TRUSTS IN MASSACHUSETTS
ESTATE PLANNING FOR THE AGING OR INCAPACITATED CLIENT IN MASSACHUSETTS
FEDERAL CRIMINAL PRACTICE
HANDBOOK OF LEGAL RESEARCH IN MASSACHUSETTS
JURY TRIAL MANUAL FOR CRIMINAL OFFENSES TRIED IN THE DISTRICT COURT
MASSACHUSETTS CONDOMINIUM LAW
MASSACHUSETTS ENVIRONMENTAL LAW
MASSACHUSETTS EVIDENCE: A COURTROOM REFERENCE
MASSACHUSETTS FAMILY LAW MANUAL
MASSACHUSETTS FORECLOSURES
MASSACHUSETTS PROBATE MANUAL
MASSACHUSETTS TAXATION AND DOR PRACTICE
MASSACHUSETTS ZONING MANUAL
MODEL JURY INSTRUCTIONS FOR USE IN THE DISTRICT COURT
A PRACTICAL GUIDE TO INTRODUCING EVIDENCE

Matrimonial CaseLaw
MATRIMONIAL CASELAW, NEW YORK EDITION

MBAA
REGULATORY COMPLIANCE MANUAL
STATE LEGISLATIVE COMPILATIONS: SELECTED SUMMARIES OF REAL ESTATE FINANCE LAWS

Medilex
THE ARIZONA LAW OF MEDICAL MALPRACTICE

Meiklejohn Civil Liberties Institute
HUMAN RIGHTS ORGANIZATIONS AND PERIODICALS DIRECTORY
PEACE LAW DOCKET 1945-1990

Merritt
OSHA REFERENCE MANUAL

Metropolitan News
RULES OF COURT

Mich. Legal
MICHIGAN PUBLIC BENEFITS MANUAL
MICHIGAN RESIDENTIAL LANDLORD TENANT LAW, 2ND ED.

Michie
COLORADO COURT RULES
CONSTRUCTION AND DESIGN LAW
FEDERAL CRIMINAL JURY INSTRUCTIONS

HANDBOOK FOR LEGAL SECRETARIES IN VIRGINIA 2ND ED.
INDIANA PATTERN JURY INSTRUCTIONS - CIVIL
INDIANA PATTERN JURY INSTRUCTIONS - CRIMINAL
MANUAL ON EMPLOYMENT DISCRIMINATION AND CIVIL RIGHTS ACTIONS IN THE FEDERAL COURTS, ATTORNEYS' EDITION
NEW JERSEY LEGAL SECRETARY'S HANDBOOK
VIRGINIA CIRCUIT COURT JUDGES BENCHBOOK -- CIVIL
VIRGINIA CIRCUIT COURT JUDGES BENCHBOOK -- CRIMINAL
THE VIRGINIA LAWYER: A BASIC PRACTICE HANDBOOK
VIRGINIA MODEL JURY INSTRUCTIONS - CIVIL
VIRGINIA MODEL JURY INSTRUCTIONS - CRIMINAL
WEST VIRGINIA PRACTICE HANDBOOK, 3rd ed.
WYOMING COURT RULES

<u>MICPEL</u>
ADMINISTRATIVE HEARINGS
ADVANCED BANKRUPTCY INSTITUTE
ADVANCED ESTATE PLANNING
ADVANCED REAL PROPERTY INSTITUTE
ADVISING FINANCIAL INSTITUTIONS
ADVOCATING FOR CHILDREN AND FAMILIES IN CINA PROCEEDING
AIDS AND THE LAW
AMERICANS WITH DISABILITIES ACT
BANKRUPTCY TAX
BUSINESS, TAX & ESTATE PLANNING FOR THE CLOSELY-HELD BUSINESS
CLEAN AIR ACT
CONDEMNATION AND EMINENT DOMAIN
CRIMINAL PRACTICE AND PROCEDURE IN THE DISTRICT COURT OF MARYLAND
DIGEST OF MARYLAND CASES ON DISCRIMINATION
DIGEST OF MARYLAND UNEMPLOYMENT INSURANCE DECISIONS
DISCOVERY UNDER THE MARYLAND RULES
DISTRICT COURT FORMS
DISTRICT COURT PRACTICE MANUAL- CIVIL
DIVORCE ORGANIZATION SYSTEM: A SYSTEM FOR MANAGING A DIVORCE PRACTICE IN MARYLAND 2ND ED.
DOMESTIC VIOLENCE TRAINING MANUAL
EDUCATION LAW
EMPLOYMENT LAW INSTITUTE
FAMILY LAW INSTITUTE
FEDERAL SENTENCING GUIDELINES 1991
FIDUCIARY INCOME TAXES
FRANCHISES
FUNDAMENTALS OF ESTATE PLANNING
FUNDAMENTALS OF FAMILY LAW
GIBBER ON ADMINISTERING ESTATES IN MARYLAND
GORDON ON MARYLAND FORECLOSURES
HANDLING DWI CASES, 1991 Ed.
HUD AND CDA FINANCING TECHNIQUES
IMMIGRATION LAW UPDATE
INTELLECTUAL PROPERTY AND COPYRIGHT LAW
ISSUES ON ENVIRONMENTAL LAW
MAKING HEALTH CARE DECISIONS INCLUDING: LIVING WILLS AND DURABLE POWERS OF ATTORNEY
MARYLAND APPELLATE PRACTICE: RULES AND COMMENTARY WITH FORMS
MARYLAND CASES ON DISCRIMINATION
MARYLAND CRIMINAL PATTERN JURY INSTRUCTIONS
MARYLAND DIVORCE AND SEPARATION LAW
MARYLAND EVIDENCE CHECKLISTS
MARYLAND LICENSING REQUIREMENTS: A SOURCEBOOK FOR LAWYERS WHO ADVISE BUSINESSES AND PROFESSIONALS
MARYLAND PRACTICE FORMS
MARYLAND PUBLIC INFORMATION ACT
MARYLAND SENTENCING GUIDELINES MANUAL
MARYLAND STATE BOARD OF CONTRACT APPEALS DECISIONS
MARYLAND TAXES, 2nd Ed.

MARYLAND TORT DAMAGES
MARYLAND TRIAL JUDGES' BENCHBOOK
MECHANICS' LIENS AND MARYLAND'S TRUST FUND LAW
MOTOR VEHICLE ADMINISTRATION HEARINGS
NEW DEVELOPMENTS IN THE LAW OF DEFAMATION
NURSING HOME NEGLIGENCE
OSHA/MOSH 1991
PATENT LAW
PLANNING FOR THE ELDERLY
PLEADING CAUSES OF ACTION IN MARYLAND
POST-MORTEM ESTATE PLANNING
PRACTICE MANUAL FOR THE MARYLAND LAWYER
PRE-TRIAL HANDBOOK (BASIC CIVIL TRIAL PRACTICE)
PRODUCTS LIABILITY LAW MANUAL
PURCHASE AND SALE OF A CLOSELY-HELD BUSINESS
REPRESENTING STUDENTS IN PUBLIC SCHOOL DICIPLINARY ACTIONS
RESIDENTIAL REAL ESTATE TRANSACTIONS
S CORPORATIONS 1991
SPECIAL ISSUES IN CRIMINAL LAW
TAKING AND DEFENDING DEPOSITIONS
TAX-FREE DISPOSITION OF PROPERTY
UNINSURED MOTORIST
USE OF EXPERTS FOR ACCIDENT RECONSTRUCTION
WILL DRAFTING -- "BEYOND THE BASICS"
WORKERS' COMPENSATION MANUAL, 6th ed.
ZONING LAW MANUAL

<u>MidAmerica</u>
MIDAMERICA COMMODITY EXCHANGE RULES AND REGULATIONS

<u>MII</u>
EMPLOYMENT AND TRAINING REPORTER

<u>MILE</u>
ACCOUNTING MALPRACTICE
ADR IN BUSINESS DISPUTES
ADVERTISING LIABILITY
ADVISING THE EMPLOYER
AIDS, HERPES & INFECTIOUS DISEASES
AMERICANS WITH DISABILITIES ACT
ARBITRATION OF COMMERCIAL AND CONSTRUCTION DISPUTES
ASSET VALUATION IN DIVORCE
AUTOMOBILE ACCIDENT RECONSTRUCTION
BANKING AND FINANCE
BANKING AND THRIFT: AN INDUSTRY IN TRANSITION
BANKRUPTCY LITIGATION CONFERENCE
CIVIL PRETRIAL PRACTICE
CLOSELY HELD CORPORATIONS: BUYING - SELLING - MERGING
COMMERCIAL PRACTICE INSTITUTE
THE CONSTRUCTION INSTITUTE
CONSTRUCTION INSTITUTE 1991
CONSTRUCTION LITIGATION
CONSUMER CREDITORS' REMEDIES
CONTROLLING TOXICS
CORPORATE PRACTICE INSTITUTE
CRASH LITIGATION
CREDITOR'S REMEDIES AND BANKRUPTCY
CRIME 1991
DIRECTOR & OFFICER INSURANCE COVERAGE
DIRECTORS IN THE HOT SEAT
DRUG & MEDICAL DEVICE LIABILITY
DRUNK DRIVING 1991
EMINENT DOMAIN
EMPLOYEE STOCK OWNERSHIP PLANS
EMPLOYMENT LAW - 7th ANNUAL

EMPLOYMENT LAW UPDATE
ENVIRONMENTAL ISSUES CONCERNING FINANCIAL INSTITUTIONS
ENVIRONMENTAL LAW INSTITUTE
FEDERAL CIVIL LITIGATION
FINANCIAL INSTITUTIONS LAW
FRAUD -- CIVIL FRAUD & WHITE COLLAR CRIME
GLOBAL MARKETS
GOVERNMENT CONTRACT AND PROGRAM FRAUD
GUARDIANS & CONSERVATORS
HARASSMENT IN THE WORKPLACE
HAZARDOUS WASTE LIABILITY
HEALTH CARE 1991
HOSTILE TAKEOVERS: 1988 UPPER MIDWEST UPDATE
INTELLECTUAL PROPERTY LAW
INTERNAL REVENUE SERVICE
LAMBERTSON'S AFTERMATH - CIVIL LITIGATION AFTER WORKERS' COMPENSATION
LAW FIRMS: LATERAL HIRES, BREAK-UPS AND MERGERS
LAW OF THE ELDERLY
LEGAL IMPLICATIONS OF THE AIDS CRISES
LEGAL MALPRACTICE GUIDE
LEGAL WRITING - FOR EFFECT
LEGISLATIVE UPDATE
LONG TERM CARE AND THE LAW
LONG TERM HEALTH CARE
LYING, CHEATING AND STEALING
LYING, CHEATING & STEALING PLUS SECURITIES
MEDICAL MALPRACTICE CLAIMS
MEDICAL MALPRACTICE CLAIMS IN THE 90's
MINNESOTA APPELLATE PRACTICE INSTITUTE
MINNESOTA EVIDENCE - A PRACTICAL WORKSHOP
MINNESOTA INSURANCE LAW CONFERENCE
MINNESOTA LIQUOR LIABILITY
THE MINNESOTA MOTOR VEHICLE INSURANCE MANUAL
MINNESOTA PRODUCTS LIABILITY
NECK AND BACK INJURIES
NEW DEVELOPMENTS IN REAL ESTATE (7th Annual)
THE NEW IMMIGRATION ACT OF 1990
PASS THROUGH ENTITIES: FOURTH ANNUAL STATE AND FEDERAL TAX CONFERENCE
PASSIVE ACTIVITY LOSSES - THE NEW REGULATION
PENSION AND WELFARE BENEFITS
PERSONAL INJURY
PERSONAL INJURY INSTITUTE: 7TH ANNUAL
PLANNING RETIREMENT BENEFITS
PRACTICING BASIC RESIDENTIAL REAL ESTATE
PREMISES LIABILITY
PRODUCTS LIABILITY LAW IN MINNESOTA
PUBLIC SECTOR LABOR LAW (7th Annual)
REPRESENTING NONPROFIT ORGANIZATIONS
THE RISK BUSINESS: INSURANCE CONTRACTS, COVERAGES, AND CARRIERS
SECURITIES AND COMMERCIAL LITIGATION
THE SEXUAL ABUSE OF CHILDREN
SOFT-TISSUE INJURY
SPOUSAL MAINTENANCE
STATUTE OF LIMITATIONS
STRUCTURED SETTLEMENTS
TECHNIQUES FOR ALTERNATIVE DISPUTE RESOLUTION
TOXIC TORTS
UNDERSTANDING MINNESOTA WORKERS' COMPENSATION
UNINSURED/UNDERINSURED MOTORIST COVERAGE
WHITE COLLAR LITIGATION: CIVIL AND CRIMINAL
WILL DRAFTING AND BASIC ESTATE PLANNING
WORKERS' COMPENSATION
WORKERS' COMPENSATION: A PRACTICAL GUIDE

Minn. CLE

ADVISING CLIENTS ABOUT RETIREMENT PLANS
ADVISING CLIENTS ABOUT WELFARE BENEFITS
ADVISING SMALL BUSINESS
ANNUAL EMPLOYEE BENEFITS
ANNUAL TAX INSTITUTE MANUAL
BANKRUPTCY INSTITUTE
CHARITABLE TRUSTS IN ESTATE PLANNING
COMMERCIAL REAL ESTATE TRANSACTIONS
CONTRACTS FOR DEED: USE AND REMEDIES
EFFICIENT MARITAL DISSOLUTION
EMPLOYMENT LAW HANDBOOK
ENVIRONMENTAL LIABILITY IN REAL ESTATE MATTERS
ERISA CLAIMS AND LITIGATION
ESTATE PLANNING FOR THE SINGLE PARENT
EXAMINATION OF TITLE
FAMILY LAW UPDATE
FEDERAL RULE BOOK
FORECLOSURES IN MINNESOTA
FUNDAMENTALS OF ESTATE PLANNING PRACTICE
FUNDAMENTALS OF ORGANIZING MINNESOTA CORPORATIONS
FUNDAMENTALS OF PROBATE PRACTICE
HANDLING CLAIMS IN PROBATE MATTERS
INFORMAL PROBATE
INSURANCE COVERAGE FOR EMPLOYMENT CLAIMS
INSURANCE LAW
INTELLECTUAL PROPERTY LITIGATION
JUDGES CRIMINAL BENCHBOOK
LABOR & EMPLOYMENT LAW INSTITUTE 1991
LIVING AND DYING WITH A REVOCABLE TRUST
MINNESOTA CONSERVATORSHIPS & GUARDIANSHIPS
MINNESOTA EMPLOYMENT AT WILL
MINNESOTA MECHANIC'S LIENS
MINNESOTA MOTOR VEHICLE ACCIDENT DESKBOOK
THE MINNESOTA PROBATE AND TRUST LAW DESKBOOK
MINNESOTA SENTENCING GUIDELINES AND COMMENTARY ANNOTATED
MORTGAGE FORECLOSURES IN MINNESOTA
NEW ESTATE FREEZING RULES
PRACTICING IN FEDERAL DISTRICT COURT IN MINNESOTA
PRIVATE SECTOR LABOR LAW
REPRESENTING DEBTORS IN CONSUMER BANKRUPTCIES
RESIDENTIAL REAL ESTATE PRACTICE
RESIDENTIAL REAL ESTATE TRANSACTIONS
TRIAL SKILLS FOR YOUNG LAWYERS -- 3RD ANNUAL
VALUATION OF A CLOSELY HELD BUSINESS & USE OF FINANCIAL EXPERTS IN LITIGATION
WORKERS' COMPENSATION INDEX
WORKERS COMPENSATION PRACTICE IN MINNESOTA
WRITTEN DISCOVERY

Minneap.

RULES AND REGULATIONS OF THE MINNEAPOLIS GRAIN EXCHANGE

MoBar

ENVIRONMENTAL LAW
JUVENILE LAW
MISSOURI ADMINISTRATIVE LAW
MISSOURI ADVISORY COMMITTEE OPINIONS
MISSOURI APPELLATE PRACTICE AND EXTRAORDINARY REMEDIES
MISSOURI APPROVED INSTRUCTIONS - CRIMINAL, VOLS. I & II AND MISSOURI APPROVED CHARGES - CRIMINAL
MISSOURI CIVIL ACTIONS I
MISSOURI CIVIL ACTIONS II
MISSOURI CIVIL PROCEDURE
MISSOURI CIVIL TRIAL PRACTICE

MISSOURI CONDEMNATION PRACTICE
MISSOURI CONSUMER LAW AND PRACTICE
MISSOURI CORPORATION LAW AND PRACTICE
MISSOURI CREDITORS'-DEBTORS' REMEDIES
MISSOURI CRIMINAL PRACTICE
MISSOURI DAMAGES
MISSOURI EMPLOYER-EMPLOYEE LAW
MISSOURI ESTATE ADMINISTRATION
MISSOURI ESTATE PLANNING
MISSOURI EVIDENCE
MISSOURI FAMILY LAW
MISSOURI FARM LAW
MISSOURI GUARDIANSHIP AND TRUST LAW
MISSOURI HANDICAPPED, ELDERLY, AND LOW-INCOME PERSONS LAW
MISSOURI INSURANCE PRACTICE
MISSOURI LITIGATION SETTLEMENT
MISSOURI LOCAL GOVERNMENT LAW
MISSOURI PROBATE SYSTEM
MISSOURI REAL ESTATE PRACTICE
MISSOURI SOURCES OF PROOF
MISSOURI TAXATION LAW AND PRACTICE
MISSOURI TIME LIMITATIONS
MISSOURI TORT LAW I & II
MISSOURI WORKERS' COMPENSATION

Mortgage
MORTGAGE AND REAL ESTATE INVESTMENT GUIDE

MTLA
COMPLAINT BOOK
EMPLOYMENT DISCRIMINATION LAW
EMPLOYMENT DISCRIMINATION LAW, VOL. II
MICHIGAN MEDICAL MALPRACTICE CASES ANNOTATED
MICHIGAN NO-FAULT AUTO INSURANCE DECISIONS
PRODUCTS LIABILITY BOOK
STARTING A CASE IN THE 90's: A CURRENT MANUAL OF COMPLAINTS IN MICHIGAN
WINNING FINAL ARGUMENTS
WRONGFUL TERMINATION LITIGATION

Nat. Atty.
NEW YORK CIVIL MOTION CITATOR
NEW YORK CRIMINAL CASE CITATOR
NEW YORK MATRIMONIAL CASE CITATOR

Nat. Notary
NOTARY HOME STUDY COURSE

National Health
DIRECTOR OF NURSING MANUAL: FEDERAL REGULATIONS AND GUIDELINES
HEALTH ADMINISTRATION: LAWS, REGULATIONS AND GUIDELINES
HOME HEALTH AND HOSPICE MANUAL: REGULATIONS AND GUIDELINES
LONG-TERM CARE ADMINISTRATION: STANDARDS AND GUIDELINES FOR LONG-TERM CARE FACILITIES

Natl. Asbestos
ASBESTOS REGULATORY DIRECTORY

Natl. Center for Lesbian Rights
LESBIAN MOTHER LITIGATION MANUAL

Natl. Fire Protection Assn.
NATIONAL FIRE CODES SUBSCRIPTION SERVICE

Natl. Lawyers Guild AIDS Network
AIDS PRACTICE MANUAL

<u>Natl. Legal Publishing</u>
A PRACTICAL GUIDE TO BUYING AND SELLING AUTOMOBILE DEALERSHIPS

<u>Natl. Obscenity Law Center</u>
OBSCENITY LAW REPORTER

<u>Natl. Underwriter</u>
ADVANCED SALES REFERENCE SERVICE
FIRE, CASUALTY & SURETY BULLETINS

<u>Natl. Veterans</u>
MILITARY DISCHARGE UPGRADING AND INTRODUCTION TO VETERANS ADMINISTRATION LAW

<u>NCCCD</u>
COMPUTER CRIME LAW REPORTER

<u>NCFA</u>
COMPENDIUM OF COMMERCIAL FINANCE LAW

<u>NCSI</u>
MANAGER'S MANUAL
THE REGULATORY EXAMINATION: HOW TO GET BETTER RESULTS
TRUSTEE & DIRECTORS HANDBOOK

<u>Nebraska CLE</u>
CORPORATE FORMS
NEBRASKA PROBATE SYSTEM IV
WORKERS' COMPENSATION HANDBOOK

<u>NELI</u>
AFFIRMATIVE ACTION BRIEFING WORKBOOK
AMERICANS WITH DISABILITIES ACT
DRUG TESTING PROGRAM MATERIALS
EEO IN FEDERAL, STATE AND LOCAL GOVERNMENT CONFERENCE MANUAL
EMPLOYMENT DISCRIMINATION LAW UPDATE
EMPLOYMENT LAW BRIEFING MANUAL
EMPLOYMENT LAW CONFERENCE MANUAL
EMPLOYMENT LITIGATION IN THE NINETIES

<u>NELP</u>
EMPLOYMENT-AT-WILL REPORTER
MASSACHUSETTS CIVIL SERVICE REPORTER
MASSACHUSETTS DISCRIMINATION LAW REPORTER
MASSACHUSETTS LABOR CASES
MASSACHUSETTS LABOR RELATIONS REPORTER

<u>New Jersey ICLE</u>
THE ABCs OF LOCAL GOVERNMENT LAW
ALTERNATIVE DISPUTE RESOLUTION
AUTOMOBILE INSURANCE HANDBOOK
CONDEMNATION: TRIAL TECHNIQUES AND RECENT DEVELOPMENTS
CORPORATE TAX PLANNING
CRIMINAL TRIAL PRACTICE
ECRA COMPLIANCE
ESTATE PLANNING AND BUSINESS TAX SYMPOSIUM
FORMS FOR HANDLING CONDOMINUM AND COOPERATIVE CONVERSIONS
FORMS FOR NEW JERSEY DIVORCE PRACTICE
GUARDIANSHIPS
GUIDEBOOK TO CHANCERY PRACTICE IN NEW JERSEY
MODEL JURY CHARGES: CIVIL
MODEL JURY CHARGES: CRIMINAL
MOUNT LAUREL II AND THE FAIR HOUSING ACT
NEW JERSEY APPELLATE PRACTICE HANDBOOK
NEW JERSEY ENVIRONMENTAL LAW

NEW JERSEY FAMILY LAW PRACTICE
NEW JERSEY MORTGAGE FORECLOSURE HANDBOOK
PRE-TRIAL PROCEDURES IN THE FEDERAL COURTS
PRODUCTS LIABILITY AND TOXIC TORT LAW IN NEW JERSEY: A PRACTITIONER'S GUIDE
PROFESSIONAL NEGLIGENCE: LAW OF MALPRACTICE IN NEW JERSEY
PROFESSIONAL RESPONSIBILITY IN NEW JERSEY
RESIDENTIAL REAL ESTATE LAW AND PRACTICE IN NEW JERSEY
SECURED TRANSACTIONS UNDER THE REVISED UNIFORM COMMERCIAL CODE
SENTENCING MANUAL FOR JUDGES
SHOPPING CENTER LEASES
UNDERGROUND STORAGE TANK LAW
YUDES FAMILY LAW CITATOR

NFCB
PUBLIC RADIO LEGAL HANDBOOK, 2ND

NH Bar
ABC'S OF PRO BONO DIVORCE
ADMINISTRATIVE LAW
APPELLATE ADVOCACY HANDBOOK
THE ART OF DISCOVERY
BANKRUPTCY AND LENDER LIABILITY LITIGATION
BIRTH LAW/ADOPTION
BUSINESS LITIGATION: CURRENT ISSUES
COMPLEXITIES OF DIVORCE PRACTICE IN THE 1990's
CONSTRUCTION LAW
CORPORATE LAW: ROLE OF THE LAWYER
CRIMINAL DEFENSE PRACTICE
THE DWI CASE: STRATEGIES AND TECHNICAL CONSIDERATIONS FOR DEFENSE AND PROSECUTION
EMPLOYMENT DISPUTES
ESTATE PLANNING -- BASICS
EVIDENCE: SELECTED PROBLEMS
FEDERAL SENTENCING GUIDELINES
FUNDAMENTALS OF PROBATE ADMINISTRATION
HOUSING LAW
INSURANCE LAW
JUVENILE LAW
THE LAW OF WORKERS' COMPENSATION
LEGISLATIVE DEVELOPMENTS
THE NEW CLEAN AIR ACT
NEW HAMPSHIRE CONSTITUTIONAL LAW
NEW HAMPSHIRE PRACTICE AND PROCEDURE HANDBOOK
PERSONAL INJURY PRACTICE
PRODUCTS LIABILITY
PROFESSIONAL LIABILITY: RECOGNIZING, HANDLING, PREVENTING
PURCHASE AND SALE OF A SMALL BUSINESS
REAL ESTATE CLOSING
STOCKHOLDERS LITIGATION
SUBDIVISION REGISTRATION
TAX FORUM
TAXATION FOR THE GENERAL PRACTITIONER
TOXIC TORTS AND HAZARDOUS WASTE
UNIFORM COMMERCIAL CODE: SELECTED ISSUES
UNINSURED MOTORIST
WHITE COLLAR CRIME

NILS
CALIFORNIA CONSUMER CREDIT LAW & REGULATIONS
THE CAPTIVE INSURANCE MANUAL
FEDERAL CONSUMER CREDIT LAWS & REGULATIONS
FEDERAL INSURANCE LAWS
FEDERAL INSURANCE REGULATIONS
INSURANCE LAWS (FOR THE 50 U.S. STATES, THE DISTRICT OF COLUMBIA, PUERTO RICO, AND THE VIRGIN ISLANDS)

INSURANCE REGULATIONS
INSURANCE RELATED REGULATIONS
OTHER REGULATORY MATERIALS
REINSURANCE LAW
RELATED LAWS TO INSURANCE LAWS

No. Carolina Bar
ANNUAL BANKRUPTCY LAW INSTITUTE
BANKRUPTCY PRACTICE MANUAL
NORTH CAROLINA ESTATE ADMINISTRATION MANUAL
NORTH CAROLINA PATTERN JURY INSTRUCTIONS FOR CRIMINAL CASES
NORTH CAROLINA PATTERN JURY INSTRUCTIONS - MOTOR VEHICLE NEGLIGENCE
NORTH CAROLINA PATTERN JURY INSTRUCTIONS FOR CIVIL CASES
NORTH CAROLINA REAL PROPERTY FORMS BOOK

NPTC
FEDERAL REGULATIONS FOR PRIVATE TRUCK OPERATIONS

NTHP
PRESERVATION LAW REPORTER

NTIS
FDA COMPLIANCE POLICY GUIDES MANUAL

NTTS
ALLSTATE PERSONAL INCOME TAX FORMS FILE
NTTS FILLED-IN TAX FORMS ENCYCLOPEDIA
NTTS MASTER TAX FORMS FILE

NYC
ZONING RESOLUTION

NYPER
A CONCISE GUIDE TO DISCIPLINE IN THE PUBLIC SERVICE

NYS OCA
CRIMINAL JURY INSTRUCTIONS - NEW YORK

NYSBA
HANDLING THE BASIC WORKER'S COMPENSATION CASE IN NEW YORK
INDIVIDUAL JUDGES' RULES
NEW YORK LAWYER'S DESKBOOK
NEW YORK LAWYER'S FORMBOOK
REPRESENTING PEOPLE WITH DISABILITIES

NYSE
INTERPRETATION HANDBOOK
NEW YORK STOCK EXCHANGE LISTED COMPANY MANUAL

NYSTLA
ATTORNEY GUIDE TO CONDUCTING A DEPOSITION
THE NEW YORK LAW OF PRODUCTS LIABILITY
NEW YORK MEDICAL MALPRACTICE
THE NO-FAULT HANDBOOK
NOTES AND DECISIONS

Oasis
COMPANY POLICY AND PERSONNEL WORKBOOK
CORPORATE PACKAGE & MINUTE BOOK (CA, FL, TX)
MAIL ORDER LEGAL MANUAL
STARTING AND OPERATING A BUSINESS IN (STATE SPECIFIC)
WRITE YOUR OWN BUSINESS CONTRACTS: WHAT YOUR ATTORNEY WON'T TELL YOU

OCDLA

CRIMINAL LAW FORMBOOK
DUII TRIAL NOTEBOOK
THE SEARCH AND SEIZURE MANUAL
THE TRIAL NOTEBOOK

Oceana

AIR AND AVIATION TREATIES OF THE WORLD
THE ALIEN UNDER AMERICAN LAW: TEXT, MATERIALS, CASES
ANTITRUST AND RESTRICTIVE BUSINESS PRACTICES: INTERNATIONAL, REGIONAL & NATIONAL REGULATION
CLIVE SCHMITTHOFF'S INTERNATIONAL COMMERCIAL ARBITRATION
COLLECTED LEGISLATION OF THE USSR AND THE CONSTITUENT UNION REPUBLICS: LEGISLATION AND CONSTITUTIONS
A COLLECTION OF BIBLIOGRAPHIC & RESEARCH RESOURCES
COMMERCIAL, BUSINESS AND TRADE LAWS AND COMMERCIAL LAWS OF THE MIDDLE EAST (COMPLETE SERVICE)
COMMERCIAL BUSINESS & TRADE LAWS OF THE WORLD
COMMERCIAL LAWS OF THE MIDDLE EAST
CONSTITUTIONS OF CANADA: FEDERAL AND PROVINCIAL (English/French)
CONSTITUTIONS OF DEPENDENCIES AND SPECIAL SOVEREIGNTIES
CONSTITUTIONS OF THE COUNTRIES OF THE WORLD: A SERIES OF UPDATED TEXTS, CONSTITUTIONAL CHRONOLOGIES AND ANNOTATED BIBLIOGRAPHIES
CONSTITUTIONS OF THE UNITED STATES: NATIONAL AND STATE, 2nd ed.
CUSTOMS LAW AND ADMINISTRATION (INCLUDING CUSTOMS SERVICE DECISIONS)
DIGEST OF COMMERCIAL LAWS OF THE WORLD -- (INCLUDING FORMS OF COMMERCIAL AGREEMENTS AND STATE VARIATIONS OF COMMERCIAL LAW)
DIGEST OF COMMERCIAL LAWS OF THE WORLD -- FORMS OF COMMERCIAL AGREEMENTS OF THE WORLD
DIGEST OF COMMERCIAL LAWS OF THE WORLD -- STATE VARIATIONS OF COMMERCIAL LAW
DIGEST OF INTELLECTUAL PROPERTY LAWS OF THE WORLD
DIGEST OF LEGAL ACTIVITIES OF INTERNATIONAL ORGANIZATIONS AND OTHER INSTITUTIONS
EASTERN EUROPEAN STATES AND THE DEVELOPMENT OF THE LAW OF THE SEA: REGIONAL DOCUMENTS, NATIONAL LEGISLATION
ENCYCLOPEDIC DICTIONARY OF CONTRACT AND PROCUREMENT LAW
EUROPEAN COMMUNITY COMPANY LAW
FEDERAL CONSUMER PROTECTION: LAWS, RULES AND REGULATIONS
HUMAN RIGHTS: THE INTER-AMERICAN SYSTEM
HUMAN RIGHTS: THE INTERNATIONAL PETITION SYSTEM: A REPERTOIRE OF PRACTICE
INTERNATIONAL COMMERCIAL ARBITRATION -- INTER-AMERICAN COMMERCIAL ARBITRATION
INTERNATIONAL COMMERCIAL ARBITRATION -- INTERNATIONAL CHAMBER OF COMMERCE ARBITRATION
INTERNATIONAL COMMERCIAL ARBITRATION -- SOVIET COMMERCIAL AND MARITIME ARBITRATION
INTERNATIONAL COMMERCIAL ARBITRATION: CASES UNDER THE NEW YORK CONVENTION
INTERNATIONAL COMMERCIAL ARBITRATION: COMMERCIAL ARBITRATION LAW IN ASIA AND THE PACIFIC
INTERNATIONAL EXTRADITION: U.S. LAW AND PRACTICE
INTERNATIONAL PROTECTION OF THE ENVIRONMENT: TREATIES AND RELATED DOCUMENTS 2d Series
INTERNATIONAL SECURITIES REGULATION
INTERNATIONAL TELECOMMUNICATIONS AGREEMENTS
INVESTMENT LAWS OF THE WORLD: THE DEVELOPING NATIONS
INVESTMENT PROMOTION AND PROTECTION TREATIES
THE ITALIAN CIVIL CODE AND COMPLEMENTARY LEGISLATION
LATIN AMERICA AND THE DEVELOPMENT OF THE LAW OF THE SEA: REGIONAL DOCUMENTS, NATIONAL LEGISLATION
LAW AND POLICY OF INTERGOVERNMENTAL PRIMARY COMMODITY AGREEMENTS
LAW AND PRACTICE OF U.S. REGULATION OF INTERNATIONAL TRADE
LAW AND PRACTICE UNDER THE GATT
LAW AND PRACTICE UNDER THE GATT AND OTHER TRADING ARRANGEMENTS: THE ASSOCIATION OF SOUTHEAST ASIAN NATIONS

LAW AND PRACTICE UNDER THE GATT AND OTHER TRADING ARRANGEMENTS: EUROPEAN COMMUNITY: THE SINGLE MARKET ACT
LAW AND PRACTICE UNDER THE GATT AND OTHER TRADING ARRANGEMENTS: EUROPEAN COMMUNITY--TRADING ARRANGEMENTS WITH EFTA COUNTRIES
LAW AND PRACTICE UNDER THE GATT AND OTHER TRADING ARRANGEMENTS: TRILATERAL TRADE AGREEMENTS: CANADA - U.S. - MEXICO
LAW AND PRACTICE UNDER THE GATT AND OTHER TRADING ARRANGEMENTS: THE EUROPEAN COMMUNITY, THE SOVIET UNION AND THE EASTERN EUROPEAN STATES
MINING AND PETROLEUM LEGISLATION OF LATIN AMERICA & THE CARIBBEAN
MULTINATIONAL CORPORATIONS LAW: MEXICO, CENTRAL AMERICA, PANAMA AND THE CENTRAL AMERICAN COMMON MARKET
MULTINATIONAL CORPORATIONS LAW: THE UNITED NATIONS AND TRANSNATIONAL CORPORATIONS
NEW DIRECTIONS IN THE LAW OF THE SEA
NORTH AMERICA AND ASIA-PACIFIC AND THE DEVELOPMENT OF THE LAW OF THE SEA
OBTAINING IRS PRIVATE LETTER RULINGS: A MANUAL OF FORMS AND PROCEDURES FROM TOUCHE ROSS & CO.
OIL AND GAS LAW: THE NORTH SEA EXPLOITATION
OPINIONS OF THE COMMITTEE ON PROFESSIONAL ETHICS
A PRACTICAL GUIDE TO DOCUMENT AUTHENTICATION: LEGALIZATION OF NOTARIZED AND CERTIFIED DOCUMENTS
PRODUCTS LIABILITY: AN INTERNATIONAL MANUAL OF PRACTICE
REGULATION OF BUSINESS ENTERPRISE IN THE U.S.A.
REGULATION OF INTERNATIONAL COMMERCIAL AVIATION: THE INTERNATIONAL REGULATORY STRUCTURE
THE REGULATION OF STATELESSNESS UNDER INTERNATIONAL AND NATIONAL LAW: TEXTS AND DOCUMENTS
SEX-BASED DISCRIMINATION: INTERNATIONAL LAW AND ORGANIZATION
TRANSNATIONAL CONTRACTS: APPLICABLE LAW AND SETTLEMENT OF DISPUTES -- A STUDY IN CONFLICT AVOIDANCE LAW AND PRACTICE
TRANSNATIONAL ECONOMIC AND MONETARY LAW: TRANSACTIONS AND CONTRACTS.
TRANSPORT LAWS OF THE WORLD
U.S. INTERNATIONAL TRADE REPORTS, NEW SERIES
UNITED STATES FEDERAL ELECTION LAW: FEDERAL REGULATION OF POLITICAL CAMPAIGN FINANCE AND PARTICIPATION
UNITED STATES INTERNATIONAL TRADE REPORTS
UNITED STATES SPACE LAW -- NATIONAL AND INTERNATIONAL REGULATIONS
USSR, EASTERN EUROPE AND THE DEVELOPMENT OF THE LAW OF THE SEA
WESTERN EUROPE AND THE DEVELOPMENT OF LAW OF THE SEA; NATIONAL LEGISLATION
WORLD SHIPPING LAWS: INTERNATIONAL CONVENTIONS

Office of Thrift Supervision
CAPITAL REGULATIONS TRAINING MANUAL
HOLDING COMPANIES HANDBOOK
TRUST ACTIVITIES HANDBOOK

Ohio CLE
ADVANCED PROBATE LAW
ADVANCED WORKERS' COMPENSATION LAW
APPELLATE ADVOCACY
BASICS OF BUSINESS LAW
ENVIRONMENTAL LAW
EUROPE 1992
GUARDIANSHIP
INTRODUCTION TO BANKRUPTCY
MIDWEST LABOR LAW CONFERENCE
PROBLEMS IN PROBATE
PROVING DAMAGES AFTER TORT REFORM
TITLE TO REAL ESTATE
UNDERSTANDING EMPLOYEE BENEFITS

Ohio State Bar
THE NEW MANUAL OF STANDARD FORMS FOR DECEDENTS' ESTATES

Okla. Bar CLE
- BASIC BANKRUPTCY
- BASIC PROBATE
- COUNSELING LANDLORDS AND TENANTS
- CREDITOR/DEBTOR RIGHTS
- DRAFTING ESTATE PLANNING DOCUMENTS
- ENVIRONMENTAL LAW UPDATE FROM VARIOUS PERSPECTIVES
- HOW TO HANDLE A MOTOR VEHICLE ACCIDENT CASE
- LEGAL ETHICS - PROCEDURE & CASE UPDATE
- PURCHASE AND SALE OF A SMALL BUSINESS
- SIMPLE ESTATE PLANNING
- TAKING AND GIVING DEPOSITIONS
- TECHNIQUES FOR JURY ADVOCACY
- TRIAL PREPARATION OF A COMMERCIAL LITIGATION CASE

On Point
- MISSISSIPPI SUPREME COURT PRACTICE

Options Clearing Corp.
- THE OPTIONS CLEARING CORPORATION & THE INTERMARKET CLEARING CORPORATION BY-LAWS AND RULES

Oregon Bar
- ADMINISTERING OREGON ESTATES
- ADVISING OREGON BUSINESS FORMS VOLUME
- ADVISING OREGON BUSINESSES
- APPEAL AND REVIEW
- ARBITRATION AND MEDIATION
- BANKRUPTCY LAW
- CIVIL LITIGATION
- CIVIL PLEADING AND PRACTICE
- CONSTRUCTION LAW
- CONTRACT LAW IN OREGON
- CREDITOR'S RIGHTS AND REMEDIES
- CRIMINAL LAW
- DAMAGES
- DOCUMENTATION OF REAL ESTATE TRANSACTIONS
- THE ETHICAL OREGON LAWYER
- EVIDENCE
- FAMILY LAW
- FORECLOSING SECURITY INTERESTS
- FUNDAMENTALS OF REAL ESTATE TRANSACTIONS
- JUVENILE LAW
- LABOR AND EMPLOYMENT LAW PRIVATE SECTOR
- LABOR AND EMPLOYMENT LAW PUBLIC SECTOR
- LAND USE
- OREGON FORMAL ETHICS OPINIONS
- THE OREGON STATE BAR DESK REFERENCE - A GUIDE TO THE REGULATORY PROGRAMS OF THE OREGON STATE BAR
- REAL PROPERTY
- STATE ADMINISTRATIVE LAW
- TORTS
- UNIFORM CIVIL JURY INSTRUCTIONS 1990
- UNIFORM CRIMINAL JURY INSTRUCTIONS 1990
- WORKERS' COMPENSATION MANUAL

P&F
- ADMINISTRATIVE LAW, THIRD SERIES
- BROADCAST RULES SERVICE
- CABLE TV RULES SERVICE
- EQUIPMENT RULES SERVICE
- FCC RULES CURRENT SERVICE
- PRIVATE RADIO RULES SERVICE
- RADIO REGULATION, SECOND SERIES

SHIPPING REGULATION
STEEL ARBITRATION DIGEST

Pacific Law Inst.
HAWAII ARBITRATION SOURCEBOOK
HAWAII COLLECTION SOURCEBOOK
HAWAII CORPORATION SOURCEBOOK
HAWAII GUARDIANSHIP SOURCEBOOK (vol. I - Property)
HAWAII LEGISLATIVE SOURCEBOOK
HAWAII PRACTICE GUIDE: NO FAULT LAW
HAWAII PROBATE SOURCEBOOK
HAWAII WILLS AND TRUSTS SOURCEBOOK

Panel
AUTOMATIC TAX PLANNER
CORPORATE TAX PRACTICE MANUAL
PARTNERSHIP TAX PRACTICE MANUAL
S CORPORATION TAX PRACTICE MANUAL
THE S CORPORATION: PLANNING AND OPERATION

Pantagraph
ILLINOIS FAMILY LAW
ILLINOIS RULES & PRACTICE HANDBOOK, 2ND ED.

Parker
ATTORNEY'S MEDICAL REFFERENCE
BANKRUPTCY PRACTICE HANDBOOK
BUSINESS LITIGATORS INSURANCE GUIDE
CALIFORNIA ARBITRATION HANDBOOK
CALIFORNIA COMPLEX LITIGATION
CALIFORNIA COURTROOM EVIDENCE
CALIFORNIA DAMAGES: LAW AND PROOF
CALIFORNIA INSURANCE DISPUTES
CALIFORNIA MECHANICS' LIEN LAW AND CONSTRUCTION INDUSTRY PRACTICE
CALIFORNIA PARALEGAL'S GUIDE
CALIFORNIA PROBATE PROCEDURE
CALIFORNIA TRIAL TECHNIQUES
CALIFORNIA UNEMPLOYMENT AND DISABILITY PROGRAMS
CALIFORNIA UNINSURED MOTORIST LAW
CALIFORNIA WHITE COLLAR CRIME
CALIFORNIA WORKERS' COMPENSATION CLAIMS & BENEFITS
CALIFORNIA WORKERS' COMPENSATION LAW
COLORADO ESTATE PLANNING
COLORADO LAW OFFICE HANDBOOK
COMMERCIAL ARBITRATION HANDBOOK
FEDERAL CIVIL PROCEDURE
FEDERAL COURTROOM EVIDENCE
GUIDE TO CALIFORNIA EVIDENCE
LEGAL SECRETARY'S RESOURCE
LENDER LIABILITY
LOUISIANA COURTROOM EVIDENCE
NEW YORK COURTROOM EVIDENCE
OHIO COURTROOM EVIDENCE
TEXAS CORPORATION LAW
TEXAS COURTROOM EVIDENCE
TEXAS LAW OFFICE HANDBOOK
TEXAS WORKERS' COMPENSATION TRIAL MANUAL

Pearson
COMPUTER FUNDAMENTALS FOR LEGAL PROFESSIONALS

Penn. Bar
BUYING AND SELLING A BUSINESS
CHECKLISTS FOR TRANSACTIONS IN PENNSYLVANIA RESIDENTIAL REAL ESTATE
FOUR COUNTY DOMESTIC PRACTICE

NEGOTIATING AND DRAFTING MORTGAGE DOCUMENTS: AN ADVANCED WORKSHOP FOR THE EXPERIENCED LAWYER, BANKER AND MORTGAGE LENDER
THE PENNSYLVANIA BUSINESS CORPORATION PRACTICE
PENNSYLVANIA SUGGESTED STANDARD CIVIL JURY INSTRUCTIONS
PENNSYLVANIA SUGGESTED STANDARD CRIMINAL JURY INSTRUCTIONS
PHILADELPHIA COUNTY DOMESTIC RELATIONS PRACTICE
PHILADELPHIA COURT OF COMMON PLEAS CIVIL PRACTICE MANUAL

Philanthropy Monthly
SURVEY OF STATE LAWS REGULATING CHARITABLE SOLICITATION

Phillips
TELECOMMUNICATIONS REGULATORY MONITOR

Pic's
NATIONAL LAW LIST

PLEI
MILITARY LAW REPORTER

PLI
DOCUMENTING SECURED TRANSACTIONS: PROBLEM AVOIDANCE AND EFFECTIVE DRAFTING
FEDERAL BAIL & DETENTION HANDBOOK
FEDERAL TAXATION OF S CORPORATIONS AND SHAREHOLDERS
INFORMATION LAW: FREEDOM OF INFORMATION, PRIVACY, OPEN MEETINGS, OTHER ACCESS LAWS
PRACTICAL INTERNATIONAL TAX PLANNING
TRIAL HANDBOOK

PPD
ERISA QUALIFIED PLAN GUIDE
FUNDAMENTALS OF QUALIFIED PENSION AND PROFIT SHARING PLANS OUTLINE
PPD MASTER PLAN DOCUMENTATION SYSTEM
PPD PRACTITIONER REGIONAL PROTOTYPE DOCUMENTATION SYSTEM

Practitioners Publishing
GUIDE TO HOMEOWNERS' ASSOCIATIONS AND OTHER COMMON INTEREST REALTY ASSOCIATIONS
PPC TAX PLANNING GUIDE - CLOSELY HELD CORPORATIONS
PPC TAX PLANNING GUIDE - INDIVIDUALS
PPC TAX PLANNING GUIDE - PARTNERSHIPS
PPC TAX PLANNING GUIDE - S CORPORATIONS
PRACTITIONERS 1040 DESKBOOK
PRACTITIONERS 1065 DESKBOOK

Pratt
BANK WAGE-HOUR AND PERSONNEL SERVICE
FEDERAL BANKING LAW SERVICE

Prentice Hall Law & Business
ALMANAC OF THE FEDERAL JUDICIARY, VOL. I (District Judges)
ALMANAC OF THE FEDERAL JUDICIARY, VOL. II (Circuit Judges)
THE AUTOMATED LAW FIRM: A COMPLETE GUIDE TO SOFTWARE AND SYSTEMS
BANKRUPTCY: ANNOTATED FORMS
BANKRUPTCY: TEXT, STATUTES, RULES
BANKRUPTCY LITIGATION MANUAL
THE BUSINESS JUDGMENT RULE
THE BUSINESS OF LAW - A HANDBOOK ON HOW TO MANAGE LAW FIRMS
BUSINESS VENTURES IN EASTERN EUROPE AND THE SOVIET UNION: THE EMERGING LEGAL FRAMEWORK FOR FOREIGN INVESTMENT
CALIFORNIA REAL ESTATE FORMS AND COMMENTARIES
CIVIL DISCOVERY: A GUIDE TO EFFICIENT PRACTICE
THE COMMUNITY REINVESTMENT ACT MANUAL: POLICIES AND COMPLIANCE
CONGRESSIONAL INVESTIGATIONS: LAW AND PRACTICE

CONTEMPORARY FEDERAL CRIMINAL PRACTICE: A PRACTICAL GUIDE TO THE COMPREHENSIVE CRIME CONTROL ACT OF 1984
CONTRACTING WITH THE RTC AND FDIC
THE CORPORATE COUNSELLOR'S DESKBOOK
CURRENT PATENT INTERFERENCE PRACTICE
D.C. FEDERAL COURTS HANDBOOK
THE DELAWARE LAW OF CORPORATIONS AND BUSINESS ORGANIZATIONS
THE DEPARTMENT OF JUSTICE MANUAL
THE DISABILITY LAW REPORTER SERVICE
DRAFTING EFFECTIVE CONTRACTS
DRAFTING LICENSE AGREEMENTS
EMERGENCY REPORTING REQUIREMENTS FOR ENVIRONMENTAL SPILLS AND RELEASES
ENCYCLOPEDIA OF MATRIMONIAL PRACTICE
EXECUTIVE COMPENSATION
FAIR HOUSING - FAIR LENDING
FDIC ENFORCEMENT DECISIONS AND ORDERS
FEDERAL INCOME TAXATION OF DEBT INSTRUMENTS
FEDERAL REGULATORY PROCESS: AGENCY PRACTICES & PROCEDURES
GENERIC DRUGS: A GUIDE TO FDA APPROVAL REQUIREMENTS
A GUIDE TO MUNICIPAL OFFICIAL STATEMENTS
A GUIDE TO THE FEDERAL LAW OF BANKING AND INSURANCE
HANDBOOK OF INSURANCE COVERAGE DISPUTES
HANDBOOK ON INSURANCE COVERAGE DISPUTES
THE LAW OF FINANCIAL SERVICES
THE LAW OF LAWYERING: A HANDBOOK ON THE MODEL RULES OF PROFESSIONAL CONDUCT
LIBEL AND PRIVACY: THE PREVENTION AND DEFENSE OF LITIGATION
LIEBER ON PENSIONS
LITIGATION ORGANIZATION AND MANAGEMENT
MARSH'S CALIFORNIA CORPORATION LAW
MEETINGS OF STOCKHOLDERS
MODEL BUSINESS CORPORATION ACT ANNOTATED
MODERN INTELLECTUAL PROPERTY
MODERN LAW OF EMPLOYMENT RELATIONSHIPS
NLRB REPRESENTATION ELECTIONS - LAW, PRACTICE & PROCEDURE
A PRACTICAL GUIDE TO OUT-OF-COURT RESTRUCTURINGS AND PREPACKAGED PLANS OF REORGANIZATION
PRACTICE UNDER THE NEW FEDERAL SENTENCING GUIDELINES
THE PUBLISHING LAW HANDBOOK
RAISING CAPITAL: PRIVATE PLACEMENT FORMS & TECHNIQUES
THE REGULATION OF CORPORATE DISCLOSURE
REPRESENTING THE CORPORATE CLIENT: DESIGNS FOR QUALITY
SCOTT ON COMPUTER LAW
SEMICONDUCTOR CHIP PROTECTION
SHARK REPELLENTS AND GOLDEN PARACHUTES: A HANDBOOK FOR THE PRACTITIONER
STATE LIMITED PARTNERSHIP LAWS
STRUCTURING COMMERCIAL REAL ESTATE WORKOUTS: ALTERNATIVES TO FORECLOSURE
TAKEOVER DEFENSE
TANGIBLE EVIDENCE: HOW TO USE EXHIBITS AT TRIAL
TAXATION OF INVESTMENTS
TAXATION OF PASSIVE ACTIVITIES
TRUTH IN LENDING: A COMPREHENSIVE GUIDE
UNDERSTANDING FIRREA: A PRACTICAL GUIDE TO PLANNING AND COMPLIANCE
UNITED STATES, COMMON MARKET AND INTERNATIONAL ANTITRUST: A COMPARATIVE GUIDE
UNITED STATES EXPORT CONTROLS
A USER'S GUIDE TO COMPUTER CONTRACTING: FORMS, TECHNIQUES AND STRATEGIES
VENTURE CAPITAL AND PUBLIC OFFERING NEGOTIATION

Prentice Hall Legal & Financial Services
THE UNIFORM COMMERCIAL CODE FILING GUIDE

Privatization Council
COMPENDIUM OF STATE PRIVATIZATION LAWS

Probus
    BANK REGULATORY REPORTING REQUIREMENTS: A GUIDE TO MEASURING COMPLIANCE
    THE COMMUNITY REINVESTMENT ACT
    HOME MORTGAGE DISCLOSURE ACT: A PRACTICAL APPROACH TO MANAGING COMPLIANCE
    REGULATORY MANAGEMENT COMPLIANCE AUDIT DESKBOOK
    THE TOUCHE ROSS INTERNATIONAL BUSINESS INVESTMENT AND TAXATION HANDBOOK
    TRUTH IN LENDING FOR THE COMMUNITY BANK: A PRACTICAL APPROACH TO REGULATION Z

Prof. Dev. Fdtn.
    THE FEDERAL ESTATE TAX PREPARATION OF THE 706

Prof. Pubs.
    APPRAISERS' LIABILITY
    EXCHANGING REAL ESTATE
    REAL ESTATE TRANSACTIONS

PSA
    THE GOVERNMENT SECURITIES MANUAL
    UNIFORM PRACTICES FOR THE CLEARANCE AND SETTLEMENT OF MORTGAGE--BACKED SECURITIES AND OTHER RELATED SECURITIES

Public Reporting Services
    PODIATRIC LIABILITY

Record Controls
    THE RETENTION BOOK: RETENTION AND PRESERVATION OF RECORDS WITH DESTRUCTION SCHEDULES

RIA
    ALL STATES TAX GUIDE
    ANALYSIS OF FEDERAL TAXES: INCOME
    ANALYSIS OF FEDERAL TAXES: INCOME, ESTATE & GIFT
    ANNOTATED TAX FORMS
    BUSINESS TRANSACTIONS: TAX PLANNING AND ANALYSIS
    COMPLETE FEDERAL TAX FORMS
    CUMULATIVE CHANGES
    ESTATE PLANNING
    ESTATE PLANNING AND TAXATION COORDINATOR
    ESTATE PLANNING CHECKLISTS/FORMS
    EXECUTIVE COMPENSATION AND TAXATION COORDINATOR
    FEDERAL ESTATE AND GIFT TAXES
    FEDERAL EXCISE TAXES
    FEDERAL TAX COORDINATOR 2D
    FEDERAL TAX GUIDE
    FEDERAL TAX REGULATIONS
    FEDERAL TAXATION OF INSURANCE COMPANIES
    FEDERAL TAXES, 2ND
    INCOME TAXATION OF NATURAL RESOURCES
    INTERNAL REVENUE CODE & REGULATIONS
    INTERNAL REVENUE CODE OF 1986 AS AMENDED
    IRA COMPLIANCE MANUAL
    NATIONAL FUTURES ASSOCIATION MANUAL
    OFFICIAL IRS PUBLICATIONS
    PARTNERSHIP & S CORPORATION COORDINATOR
    PENSION AND PROFIT SHARING, 2nd ed.
    PENSION AND PROFIT SHARING GUIDE
    PENSION COORDINATOR
    PROPERTY TAXES
    PUERTO RICO TAXES
    REAL ESTATE COORDINATOR
    SALES & USE TAX
    SMALL BUSINESS TAX PLANNER
    STATE AND LOCAL TAXES (vols. available for each state)
    STATE INCOME TAXES

STATE TAX ACTION COORDINATOR
SUCCESSFUL ESTATE PLANNING IDEAS & METHODS
TAX ACTION COORDINATOR
TAX COURT
TAX EXEMPT ORGANIZATIONS
TAX GUIDE
WILLS TRUSTS FORMS

<u>Rocky Mt.</u>

ENVIRONMENTAL CONSIDERATIONS IN NATURAL RESOURCE AND REAL PROPERTY TRANSACTIONS
ENVIRONMENTAL LAW: AN UPDATE FOR THE BUSY NATURAL RESOURCES PRACTITIONER
FEDERAL ONSHORE OIL AND GAS POOLING AND UNITIZATION II
GOLD MINE FINANCING
GOWER FEDERAL SERVICE - MINING
GOWER FEDERAL SERVICE - MISCELLANEOUS LAND DECISIONS
GOWER FEDERAL SERVICE - OIL AND GAS
GOWER FEDERAL SERVICE - OUTER CONTINENTAL SHELF LANDS
GOWER FEDERAL SERVICE - ROYALTY VALUATION AND MANAGEMENT
GROUND WATER CONTAMINATION
INTERNATIONAL RESOURCES LAW: A BLUEPRINT FOR MINERAL DEVELOPMENT
MINERAL DEVELOPMENT ON INDIAN LANDS
MINERAL FINANCING
MINERAL TITLE EXAMINATION II
MINING AGREEMENTS
MINING AGREEMENTS II
MINING AGREEMENTS III
NATURAL GAS MARKETING AND TRANSPORTATION
NATURAL GAS MARKETING II
NATURAL RESOURCES AND ENVIRONMENTAL LITIGATION
OIL AND GAS AGREEMENTS
OIL AND GAS CONSERVATION LAW AND PRACTICE
THE OIL AND GAS JOINT OPERATING AGREEMENT
OIL AND GAS OPERATIONS IN FEDERAL AND COASTAL WATERS
RIGHTS OF ACCESS AND SURFACE USE
ROYALTY VALUATION AND MANAGEMENT
SPECIAL INSTITUTE INDEX, 1970-1990

<u>Ronin</u>

CONTROLLED SUBSTANCES: A LEGAL AND CHEMICAL GUIDE TO THE FEDERAL DRUG LAWS

<u>Rothman</u>

AALL ANNUAL MEETINGS: AN ANNOTATED INDEX OF THE RECORDINGS
ANNUALS AND SURVEYS APPEARING IN LEGAL PERIODICALS: AN ANNOTATED LISTING
CATALOGING LEGAL LITERATURE: A MANUAL ON AACR2 AND LIBRARY OF CONGRESS SUBJECT HEADINGS FOR LEGAL MATERIALS, WITH ILLUSTRATIONS
FEDERAL JUDGES AND JUSTICES : A CURRENT LISTING OF NOMINATIONS, CONFIRMATIONS, ELEVATIONS, RESIGNATIONS AND RETIREMENTS
FOREIGN LAW: CURRENT SOURCES OF CODES AND BASIC LEGISLATION IN JURISDICTIONS OF THE WORLD (vol. I: The Western Hemisphere; vol. II: Western & Eastern Europe; vol. III: Africa, Asia, Australia)
GUIDE TO STATE LEGISLATIVE AND ADMINISTRATIVE MATERIALS
INDEX TO LAW SCHOOL ALUMNI PUBLICATIONS
LAW BOOKS RECOMMENDED FOR LIBRARIES
LAW FOR THE LAYMAN: AN ANNOTATED BIBLIOGRAPHY OF SELF-HELP LAW BOOKS
LEGAL LC SUBJECT HEADINGS WEEKLY LISTS: CUMULATION
LIBRARY OF CONGRESS CLASSIFICATION CLASS H SUBCLASSES HM-HX - SOCIAL SCIENCES: SOCIOLOGY - CUMULATIVE SCHEDULE AND INDEX
LIBRARY OF CONGRESS CLASSIFICATION CLASS Z - BIBLIOGRAPHY: LIBRARY SCIENCE - CUMULATIVE SCHEDULE AND INDEX
LIBRARY OF CONGRESS CLASSIFICATION CLASS KDZ, KG-KH - LAW OF THE AMERICAS, LATIN AMERICA AND THE WEST INDIES - CUMULATIVE SCHEDULE AND INDEX
LIBRARY OF CONGRESS CLASSIFICATION CLASS H SUBCLASSES H-HJ - SOCIAL SCIENCES: ECONOMICS - CUMULATIVE SCHEDULE AND INDEX

LIBRARY OF CONGRESS CLASSIFICATION CLASS J - POLITICAL SCIENCE - CUMULATIVE SCHEDULE AND INDEX
LIBRARY OF CONGRESS CLASSIFICATION CLASS K - SUBCLASS KE - LAW OF CANADA - CUMULATIVE SCHEDULE AND INDEX
LIBRARY OF CONGRESS CLASSIFICATION CLASS KJ-KKZ - LAW OF EUROPE - CUMULATIVE SCHEDULE AND INDEX
LIBRARY OF CONGRESS CLASSIFICATION CLASS KJV-KJW - LAW OF FRANCE - CUMULATIVE SCHEDULE AND INDEX
LIBRARY OF CONGRESS CLASSIFICATION CLASS KK-KKC - LAW OF GERMANY - CUMULATIVE SCHEDULE AND INDEX
LIBRARY OF CONGRESS CLASSIFICATION CLASS K - SUBCLASS KF - LAW OF THE UNITED STATES - CUMULATIVE INDEX
LIBRARY OF CONGRESS CLASSIFICATION CLASS K - SUBCLASS KD - LAW OF THE UNITED KINGDOM AND IRELAND - CUMULATIVE SCHEDULE AND INDEX
LIBRARY OF CONGRESS CLASSIFICATION CLASS K - SUBCLASS K LAW (GENERAL) - CUMULATIVE SCHEDULE AND INDEX
LIBRARY OF CONGRESS CLASSIFICATION CLASS K - SUBCLASS KF - LAW OF THE UNITED STATES - CUMULATIVE SCHEDULE
PIMSLEUR'S CHECKLISTS OF BASIC AMERICAN LEGAL PUBLICATIONS
SOURCES OF COMPILED LEGISLATIVE HISTORIES: BIBLIOGRAPHY OF GOVERNMENT DOCUMENTS, PERIODICAL ARTICLES AND BOOKS, 1ST CONGRESS-99TH CONGRESS
UNION LIST OF LEGISLATIVE HISTORIES, 47TH CONGRESS, 1881 - 101st CONGRESS, 1990

<u>Roytech</u>
THE CONSOLIDATED CHEMICAL REGULATION GUIDEBOOK

<u>RPC</u>
RAILROAD COMMISSION OF TEXAS RULES
TEXAS AIR CONTROL BOARD RULES
TEXAS DEPARTMENT OF HEALTH RULES
TEXAS GENERAL LAND OFFICE/SCHOOL LAND BOARD RULES
TEXAS PUBLIC UTILITY COMMISSION RULES
TEXAS WATER COMMISSION/TEXAS WATER DEVELOPMENT BOARD RULES

<u>Rules</u>
CITATION SERVICE - MARYLAND RULES OF PROCEDURE
DISTRICT OF COLUMBIA CITATION SERVICE
DISTRICT OF COLUMBIA COURT RULES
FEDERAL AVIATION ADMINISTRATION - CODIFIED REGULATIONS
FEDERAL CIRCUIT COURT RULES SERVICE
FEDERAL COMMUNICATIONS COMMISSION RULES AND REGULATIONS
INTERSTATE COMMERCE COMMISSION - RULES OF PRACTICE
KENTUCKY COURT RULES
MARYLAND COURT RULES
NATIONAL TRANSPORTATION SAFETY BOARD REGULATIONS
PATENT AND TRADEMARK STATUTES
PATENT COOPERATION TREATY AND REGULATIONS
PENNSYLVANIA CONSOLIDATED RULES
RULES OF PRACTICE IN PATENT AND TRADEMARK CASES
U.S. COURT OF INTERNATIONAL TRADE RULES AND ANNOTATION SERVICE
VIRGINIA COURT RULES SERVICE

<u>Rutter</u>
CALIFORNIA PRACTICE GUIDE - BAD FAITH
CALIFORNIA PRACTICE GUIDE - CIVIL APPEALS AND WRITS
CALIFORNIA PRACTICE GUIDE - CIVIL PROCEDURE BEFORE TRIAL
CALIFORNIA PRACTICE GUIDE - CORPORATIONS
CALIFORNIA PRACTICE GUIDE - ENFORCING JUDGMENTS AND DEBTS
CALIFORNIA PRACTICE GUIDE - FAMILY LAW
CALIFORNIA PRACTICE GUIDE - FEDERAL CIVIL PROCEDURE BEFORE TRIAL
CALIFORNIA PRACTICE GUIDE - LANDLORD-TENANT
CALIFORNIA PRACTICE GUIDE - PERSONAL INJURY
CALIFORNIA PRACTICE GUIDE - PROBATE
LEGAL SECRETARY'S HANDBOOK

S. Carolina Bar

HANDBOOK ON LEGAL ETHICS FOR SOUTH CAROLINA LAWYERS - 2nd ed.
INSURANCE COVERAGE ISSUES RELATIVE TO NATURAL DISASTERS
THE LAW OF AUTOMOBILE INSURANCE IN SOUTH CAROLINA
OFFICIAL FORMS FOR THE SOUTH CAROLINA BUSINESS CORPORATION ACT OF 1988
PROCEDURES MANUAL FOR LEGAL PERSONNEL
SOUTH CAROLINA ADMINISTRATIVE LAW -- 2nd Ed.
THE SOUTH CAROLINA BENCH BOOK FOR MAGISTRATES AND MUNICIPAL COURT JUDGES
SOUTH CAROLINA CIVIL PROCEDURE
SOUTH CAROLINA CONSUMER LAW AND PRACTICE - Vol. I - SOUTH CAROLINA CONSUMER LAW AND REGULATIONS
SOUTH CAROLINA CONSUMER LAW AND PRACTICE - Vol. II - TRUTH IN LENDING AND RELATED DISCLOSURE STATUTES
SOUTH CAROLINA CONSUMER PROTECTION CODE - 1982 TEXT AND COMMENTS -- 2nd Ed.
SOUTH CAROLINA CORPORATE PRACTICE MANUAL
SOUTH CAROLINA CRIMINAL DEFENSE
THE SOUTH CAROLINA DUI DEFENSE MANUAL
SOUTH CAROLINA INCOME TAXATION
THE SOUTH CAROLINA PROBATE PRACTICE MANUAL
SOUTH CAROLINA RADAR DEFENSE MANUAL
SOUTH CAROLINA RECOMMENDED CIVIL JURY CHARGES
UNEMPLOYMENT LAW AND PROCEDURE IN S.C.

S.D. Bar

SOUTH DAKOTA PATTERN JURY INSTRUCTIONS-CIVIL
SOUTH DAKOTA PATTERN JURY INSTRUCTIONS-CRIMINAL

S&FA

STATE LOBBYING LAWS

Shafer

THE SOFTWARE LEGAL BOOK

Shepard's

AGE DISCRIMINATION
BANKRUPTCY PRACTICE FOR THE GENERAL PRACTITIONER, 2/E
CABLE TELEVISION: HANDBOOK AND FORMS
CALIFORNIA FORECLOSURE: LAW AND PRACTICE
CALIFORNIA LAND USE PROCEDURE
CALIFORNIA LEGAL FILING DIRECTORY
CHAPTER 11 REORGANIZATIONS
CHAPTER 12: FARM REORGANIZATIONS
CHAPTER 13 PRACTICE AND PROCEDURE
COMMERCIAL REAL ESTATE FORMS
CONSTRUCTION LAW DIGESTS
CREDITOR'S RIGHTS IN BANKRUPTCY
DIVORCE TAX PLANNING STRATEGIES
DRAFTING THE DURABLE POWER OF ATTORNEY: A SYSTEMS APPROACH, 2nd ed.
DRAFTING WILLS AND TRUST AGREEMENTS: A SYSTEMS APPROACH, 2nd ed.
ENTERTAINMENT LAW
ENVIRONMENTAL LAW FORMS GUIDE
ERISA PRACTICE AND PROCEDURE
ESTATE PLANNING FOR FARMERS & RANCHERS, 2nd ed.
FAMILY BUSINESS ORGANIZATION
FEDERAL INCOME TAXATION OF CORPORATE LIQUIDATIONS
FEDERAL INFORMATION DISCLOSURE
FEDERAL REGULATION OF THE CHEMICAL INDUSTRY
FEDERAL TAX ASPECTS OF BANKRUPTCY
FEDERAL TAX ASPECTS OF CORPORATE REORGANIZATIONS
FEDERAL TAX PLANNING
FEDERAL TRADE COMMISSION REGULATORY MANUAL
FIRREA: A LEGISLATIVE HISTORY AND SECTION-BY-SECTION ANALYSIS
FLORIDA LEGAL FILING DIRECTORY
FLORIDA TAXATION
FOOD AND DRUG ADMINISTRATION REGULATORY MANUAL

FRAUD, WINDOW DRESSING, AND NEGLIGENCE IN FINANCIAL STATEMENTS
GUIDE TO EFFECTIVE BANKRUPTCY LITIGATION
GUIDE TO INTERNATIONAL COMMERCE LAW
GUIDE TO PENSION AND PROFIT SHARING PLANS: TAXATION, SELECTION AND DESIGN
ILLINOIS LEGAL FILING DIRECTORY
INCOME TAXATION: ACCOUNTING METHODS AND PERIODS
INTERNATIONAL ESTATE PLANNING
INTERNATIONAL TRADE PRACTICE
JOINT VENTURES: STRUCTURING ALTERNATIVES
LITIGATION OF FEDERAL TAX CONTROVERSIES
MICHIGAN LEGAL FILING DIRECTORY
NEW YORK WILLS AND TRUSTS, 3/e
OHIO LEGAL FILING DIRECTORY
PARTNERSHIP TAXATION, 4th ed.
PENNSYLVANIA TAXATION
PLANNING TAX-EXEMPT ORGANIZATIONS
POST-MORTEM TAX PLANNING
RCRA AND SUPERFUND: A PRACTICE GUIDE WITH FORMS
REGULATION OF THE COMMODITIES FUTURES AND OPTIONS MARKETS
RELATIVE VALUES: DETERMINING ATTORNEYS' FEES
REVOCABLE TRUSTS, 2/e
RICO IN BUSINESS AND COMMERCIAL LITIGATION
RIGHTS AND LIABILITIES OF PUBLISHERS, BROADCASTERS AND REPORTERS
SECURITIES FRAUD AND COMMODITIES FRAUD
SUBCHAPTER S TAXATION, 3RD ED.
TAX ASPECTS OF BUYING AND SELLING CORPORATE BUSINESSES
TAXATION OF REAL ESTATE TRANSACTIONS 2nd ed.

Sheshunoff
BANK ACCOUNTING AND AUDITING SERVICE
BANK CAPITAL SERVICE
GUIDE TO COMMERCIAL LENDING LAW
GUIDE TO CONSUMER LENDING LAW

Simpson
ARBITRATOR'S QUALIFICATIONS REPORTS

Smith
EMPLOYMENT LAW DESK BOOK FOR TENNESSEE EMPLOYERS
TENNESSEE EMPLOYMENT LAW
TENNESSEE LAW OFFICE DESK BOOK
WORKING GUIDE TO THE TENNESSEE BUSINESS CORPORATION ACT

Spencer
INTERNATIONAL BENEFITS INFORMATION SERVICE
SPENCER'S COMPLIANCE GUIDE FOR HEALTH AND BENEFIT PLANS
SPENCER'S RESEARCH REPORTS ON EMPLOYEE BENEFITS
SPENCER'S RETIREMENT PLAN SERVICE

Spidell
SPIDELL'S CALIFORNIA TAX FORMS AND INSTRUCTIONS

Staffort
THE DEMONSTRATIVE EVIDENCE SOURCEBOOK

State Bar of Ariz.
ARIZONA APPELLATE HANDBOOK
ARIZONA ATTORNEY'S FEES MANUAL
ARIZONA COURTROOM EVIDENCE MANUAL
ARIZONA COURTS MANUAL
ARIZONA LAND USE LAW
ARIZONA LEGAL SERVICES PRACTICE MANUAL, VOL. I
ARIZONA PROBATE CODE PRACTICE MANUAL
COMMERCIAL REAL ESTATE TRANSACTIONS PRACTICE MANUAL
EMINENT DOMAIN IN ARIZONA

INS AND OUTS OF FORECLOSURES
RECOMMENDED ARIZONA JURY INSTRUCTIONS - CIVIL

State Bar of Calif.
CALIFORNIA COMPENDIUM ON PROFESSIONAL RESPONSIBILITY
FORECLOSURE LAW MANUAL

State Bar of Mich.
MICHIGAN LAND TITLE STANDARDS

State Bar of Mont.
FAMILY LAW FORMBOOK
MONTANA CRIMINAL JURY INSTRUCTIONS
MONTANA PATTERN JURY INSTRUCTIONS-CIVIL
MONTANA PROBATE PROCEDURE
REAL ESTATE FORMBOOK

State Bar of N. Dak.
MINERAL TITLE STANDARDS
NORTH DAKOTA PATTERN JURY INSTRUCTIONS - CIVIL
NORTH DAKOTA PATTERN JURY INSTRUCTIONS - CRIMINAL
STANDARDS OF TITLE

State Bar of Texas
LEGAL FORM MANUAL FOR REAL ESTATE TRANSACTIONS
TEXAS CIVIL TRIAL HANDBOOK
TEXAS COLLECTIONS MANUAL
TEXAS FAMILY LAW PRACTICE MANUAL
TEXAS GUARDIANSHIP MANUAL
TEXAS LAWYERS' PROFESSIONAL ETHICS
TEXAS PATTERN JURY CHARGES, VOL. 1 (GENERAL; MOTOR VEHICLES; DAMAGES)
TEXAS PATTERN JURY CHARGES, VOL. 2 (WORKERS' COMPENSATION)
TEXAS PATTERN JURY CHARGES, VOL. 3 (PROFESSIONALS; PREMISES; PRODUCTS; DAMAGES)
TEXAS PATTERN JURY CHARGES, VOL. 4 (BUSINESS, COMMERCIAL, DECEPTIVE TRADE PRACTICES, INSURANCE CODE & DAMAGES)
TEXAS PATTERN JURY CHARGES, VOL. 5 (FAMILY LAW)
TEXAS PROBATE SYSTEM

State Bar of Wisc.
APPELLATE PRACTICE & PROCEDURE HANDBOOK
THE ATTORNEY'S GUIDE TO THE SEVENTH CIRCUIT COURT OF APPEALS
CONSTRUCTION LIEN LAW HANDBOOK
ECKHARDT'S WORKBOOK FOR WISCONSIN ESTATE PLANNERS
ETHICS & PROFESSIONAL RESPONSIBILITY: A HANDBOOK FOR WISCONSIN LAWYERS
FAMILY LAW CASENOTES AND QUOTES
FEDERAL CRIMINAL PRACTICE HANDBOOK
THE GUARDIAN AD ITEM HANDBOOK
A GUIDE FOR WISCONSIN NONPROFIT ORGANIZATIONS
THE LAW OF DAMAGES IN WISCONSIN
MARITAL PROPERTY LAW IN WISCONSIN 2nd ed.
ORGANIZING A WISCONSIN BUSINESS CORPORATION: ARTICLES, BYLAWS AND OTHER FORMS
PRIVATE SECTOR LABOR RELATIONS FOR THE GENERAL PRACTITIONER
PUBLIC SECTOR LABOR RELATIONS IN WISCONSIN
REAL ESTATE TRANSACTIONS SYSTEM
SYSTEM BOOK FOR FAMILY LAW
TRAFFIC LAW AND PRACTICE IN WISCONSIN
VOLUNTARY TERMINATION OF PARENTAL RIGHTS AND ADOPTION
WISCONSIN ATTORNEY'S DESK REFERENCE
WISCONSIN DISCOVERY LAW AND PRACTICE
WISCONSIN ETHICS OPINIONS
THE WISCONSIN FAIR DEALERSHIP LAW
WISCONSIN JUDICIAL BENCHBOOK: VOL. 1 - CRIMINAL AND TRAFFIC
WISCONSIN JUDICIAL BENCHBOOK: VOL. 2 - CIVIL

WISCONSIN JUDICIAL BENCHBOOK: VOL. 3 - FAMILY
WISCONSIN JUDICIAL BENCHBOOK: VOL. 4 - PROBATE, JUVENILE AND MENTAL
THE WISCONSIN PROBATE SYSTEM BOOK
WISCONSIN RULES OF EVIDENCE: A COURTROOM HANDBOOK
WORKER'S COMPENSATION HANDBOOK

Sten-O-Press
CAL-OSHA REPORTER

Stephens
IRS PRACTICE AND PROCEDURES TAX PACKAGE
TAX SERVICE FOR AFFILIATED GROUPS
TAX SERVICE FOR CORPORATE ACQUISITIONS AND DISPOSITIONS OF BUSINESSES
TAX SERVICE FOR EMPLOYEE RETIREMENT PLANS
TAX SERVICE FOR SUBCHAPTER "S" CORPORATIONS AND THEIR SHAREHOLDERS

Tax Form
FEDERAL TAX AND RELATED FORMS
STATE TAX FORMS: CORPORATION
STATE TAX FORMS: INDIVIDUAL
STATE TAX FORMS: PARTNERSHIP & FIDUCIARY

Taxwise
CHARITABLE LEAD TRUSTS - EXPLANATION, SPECIMEN AGREEMENTS, FORMS
DEFERRED GIVING - EXPLANATION, SPECIMEN AGREEMENTS, FORMS
OUTRIGHT CHARITABLE GIFTS - EXPLANATION, SUBSTANTIATING, FORMS
PLANNED GIVING - STARTING, MARKETING, ADMINISTERING

Thomas
REFERENCE GUIDE TO WORKMEN'S COMPENSATION LAW

Thompson
ABOVEGROUND STORAGE TANK GUIDE
ADA COMPLIANCE GUIDE
CHEMICAL PROCESS SAFETY REPORT
CLEAN AIR PERMITS: MANAGER'S GUIDE TO THE 1990 CLEAN AIR ACT
COMMUNITY RIGHT-TO-KNOW MANUAL: GUIDE TO SARA TITLE III
EMPLOYER'S GUIDE TO MANDATED HEALTH BENEFITS - THE COBRA HANDBOOK
EMPLOYER'S HANDBOOK - COMPLYING WITH IRS EMPLOYEE BENEFIT RULES
FAIR LABOR STANDARDS HANDBOOK FOR STATES, LOCAL GOVERNMENTS AND SCHOOLS
THE FDA ENFORCEMENT MANUAL
FEDERAL GRANTS MANAGEMENT HANDBOOK
FERC PRACTICE AND PROCEDURE MANUAL
THE FLEX PLAN HANDBOOK
THE 401(K) HANDBOOK
GAS TRANSPORTATION MARKETING SERVICE
GUIDE TO ASSIGNING AND LOANING BENEFIT PLAN MONEY
GUIDE TO CONTRACTING WITH THE RESOLUTION TRUST CORPORATION
GUIDE TO ENVIRONMENTAL LIABILITY IN REAL ESTATE TRANSACTIONS
GUIDE TO U.S. FOOD LABELING LAW
HANDICAPPED REQUIREMENTS HANDBOOK
NATURAL GAS CONTRACTS
NATURAL GAS HANDBOOK
NATURAL GAS POLICY ACT INFORMATION SERVICE
NATURAL GAS TRANSPORTATION INFORMATION SERVICE
OIL SPILL LAW INFORMATION SERVICE
PHYSICIAN LABORATORY REGULATIONS MANUAL
SINGLE AUDIT INFORMATION SERVICE
STORMWATER PERMIT MANUAL
UNDERGROUND STORAGE TANK GUIDE

Tower
MAINE BAR DIRECTORY

TPLR
  TOBACCO PRODUCTS LITIGATION REPORTER

Transnational Juris Publications
  BUSINESS IN CZECHOSLOVAKIA: A PRIMER AND OVERVIEW
  BUSINESS IN HUNGARY: A PRIMER AND OVERVIEW
  BUSINESS IN POLAND: A PRIMER AND OVERVIEW
  BUSINESS IN THE SOVIET UNION: A PRIMER AND OVERVIEW
  BUSINESS IN YUGOSLAVIA: A PRIMER AND OVERVIEW
  GERMAIN'S TRANSNATIONAL LAW RESEARCH
  SOVIET TAXATION: STATUTES, REGULATIONS AND TREATIES

TSI
  SUCCESSFULLY RESOLVING EMPLOYMENT TAX ISSUES WITH THE INTERNAL REVENUE SERVICE

U.S. Compt.
  COMPTROLLER'S HANDBOOK FOR CONSUMER EXAMINATIONS
  COMPTROLLER'S HANDBOOK FOR NATIONAL BANK EXAMINERS
  COMPTROLLER'S MANUAL FOR CORPORATE ACTIVITIES

U.S. Trust
  TRUST AND WILL PROVISIONS

UMC CLE
  NOT IN MAI: CIVIL JURY INSTRUCTIONS COLLECTED FROM MISSOURI CASES

UMKC/CLE
  ATTORNEY'S DESKBOOK FOR TAKING AND DEFENDING DEPOSITIONS
  AUTOMOBILE ACCIDENT HANDBOOK
  MISSOURI CIVIL PROCEDURE FORMBOOK
  MISSOURI COMPARATIVE FAULT
  MISSOURI CORPORATE AND PARTNERSHIP FORMS HANDBOOK
  MISSOURI FAMILY LAW FORMBOOK
  MISSOURI PRODUCTS LIABILITY
  THE 9TH ANNUAL FEDERAL ESTATE PLANNING SYMPOSIUM
  THE STACKING OF AUTOMOBILE INSURANCE COVERAGE IN MISSOURI
  THE 12TH ANNUAL FRANCHISE LAW INSTITUTE

Uniform Boiler
  SYNOPSIS OF BOILER AND VESSEL PRESSURE LAWS, RULES AND REGULATIONS

United Communications Group
  THE ATTORNEY'S GUIDE TO THE HANLESTER EXCLUSION CASE

Univ. Publ.
  AIDS LAW & LITIGATION REPORTER
  AIDS REFERENCE & RESEARCH COLLECTION

Unz & Co.
  EXPORT ADMINISTRATION REGULATIONS AND EXPORT RESOURCES
  HARMONIZED TARIFF OF THE U.S.
  SCHEDULE B COMMODITY CLASSIFICATION AND HARMONIZED SYNOPSIS
  U.S. CUSTOMS REGULATIONS

UPA
  BIOLAW
  EMPLOYMENT TESTING: A NATIONAL REPORTER ON DRUG, POLYGRAPH, AIDS AND GENETIC TESTING
  NATIONAL REPORTER ON LEGAL ETHICS AND PROFESSIONAL RESPONSIBILITY

USGPO
  ANTITRUST DIVISION MANUAL
  CASEHANDLING MANUAL
  COMPARISON OF STATE UNEMPLOYMENT INSURANCE LAWS

CONSTRUCTION INDUSTRY STANDARDS AND INTERPRETATIONS
CONTRACT AUDIT MANUAL
CUSTOMS REGULATIONS OF THE UNITED STATES
DOMESTIC MAIL MANUAL
EXPORT ADMINISTRATION REGULATIONS
FEDERAL ACQUISITION REGULATIONS
FEDERAL AVIATION REGULATIONS
FEDERAL MOTOR VEHICLE SAFETY STANDARDS AND REGULATIONS
GENERAL INDUSTRY STANDARDS AND INTERPRETATIONS
HARMONIZED TARIFF SCHEDULES OF THE UNITED STATES ANNOTATED
HART-SCOTT-RODINO ANTITRUST IMPROVEMENTS ACT OF 1976: REMERGER NOTIFICATION SOURCE BOOK
HISTORY OF THE TARIFF SCHEDULES OF THE UNITED STATES ANNOTATED
INDEX OF FEDERAL SPECIFICATIONS, STANDARDS AND COMMERCIAL ITEM DESCRIPTIONS
MANUAL OF CLASSIFICATION
MANUAL OF PATENT EXAMINING PROCEDURE
MEDICARE HOME HEALTH AGENCY MANUAL
MEDICARE HOSPITAL MANUAL
MEDICARE SKILLED NURSING FACILITY MANUAL
NATIONAL CREDIT UNION ADMINISTRATION RULES AND REGULATIONS
OPERATIONS INSTRUCTIONS, REGULATIONS, AND INTERPRETATIONS
RULES AND REGULATIONS
RULES AND REGULATIONS: TITLE 10, CHAPTER 1, CODE OF FEDERAL REGULATIONS
RULES AND REGULATIONS AND STATEMENTS OF PROCEDURE
TRADEMARK MANUAL OF EXAMINING PROCEDURE
UNITED STATES ATTORNEYS' MANUAL
U.S. POSTAL SERVICE PROCUREMENT MANUAL

USLSI
FEDERAL GUIDE
SUPERVISORY SERVICE

USTA
U.S. TRADEMARK LAW - RULES OF PRACTICE, FORMS & FEDERAL STATUTES

Utah Bar
UTAH ENVIRONMENTAL LAND USE PERMIT MANUAL

Wash. Bar
ADVISING THE SMALL BUSINESS CLIENT
ALTERNATIVE DISPUTE RESOLUTION DESKBOOK: ARBITRATION & MEDIATION IN WASHINGTON
ANNUAL ESTATE PLANNING SEMINAR
ANNUAL NORTHWEST SECURITIES INSTITUTE
ATTORNEY ASSISTANCE MANUAL FOR PERSONS WITH AIDS/ARC
ATTORNEYS' FEES: BEYOND THE DOLLARS
THE BASICS OF BANKRUPTCIES: CHAPTERS 7 AND 13
COMPUTER LAW INSTITUTE
CONFLICTS OF INTEREST IN BUSINESS TRANSACTIONS
CONSTRUCTION BANKRUPTCY
CONSUMER PROTECTION, ANTITRUST & UNFAIR BUSINESS PRACTICES
CORPORATION BUSINESS AND BANKING MID-YEAR
CREDITOR-DEBTOR RIGHTS SECTION MID-YEAR MEETING
DISCOVERY -- HOW TO MAKE IT WORK FOR YOU
EMPLOYMENT LAW FOR THE GENERAL PRACTITIONER
EMPLOYMENT LAW UPDATE
ENVIRONMENTAL AND LAND USE LAW MID-YEAR MEETING
ESSENTIALS OF EVIDENCE
FAMILY LAW SECTION MID-YEAR MEETING & SEMINARS
FOOTING THE BILL: THE PRICE OF LAND USE REGULATION
GETTING PAID: EFFECTIVELY USING STATUTORY LIEN AND BOND RIGHTS
HAZARDOUS SUBSTANCES AND THE LAW AT A COMPLEX AQUATIC SITE
HOW TO PROBATE AN ESTATE AND HANDLE POST-MORTEM MATTERS
LAND USE LAW IN THE AGE OF GRIDLOCK
MARKETING FOR LAWYERS AND LAW FIRMS

NEGOTIATING AND DRAFTING INTERNATIONAL BUSINESS AGREEMENTS
NEW ADMINISTRATIVE PROCEDURES ACT AND MODEL RULES
NONPROFIT AND TAX-EXEMPT ORGANIZATIONS
OVERVIEW OF PATENTS, TRADEMARKS, COPYRIGHTS AND TRADE SECRETS FOR THE GENERAL PRACTITIONER
PACIFIC NORTHWEST ADMIRALTY LAW INSTITUTE
PARTNERSHIP TAXATION
A PRACTICAL APPROACH TO REAL ESTATE LOAN DEFAULTS AND WORKOUTS
PRACTICE IN THE COURTS OF LIMITED JURISDICTION AND SUPERIOR COURT LOCAL RULES PRACTICE
PRESENTING AND ATTACKING SCIENTIFIC/DEMONSTRATIVE EVIDENCE IN CIVIL AND CRIMINAL CASES
REAL PROPERTY, PROBATE AND TRUST SECTION MID-YEAR MEETING AND SEMINARS - REAL PROPERTY PROGRAM
STRATEGIC FUNDAMENTALS OF PROSECUTING & DEFENDING THE PERSONAL INJURY CASE
TAX CONSIDERATIONS IN SELECTING A BUSINESS ENTITY
VOIR DIRE: LEARN TO USE IT OR LOSE IT
WASHINGTON CIVIL PROCEDURE BEFORE TRIAL DESKBOOK
WASHINGTON COMMERCIAL LAW DESKBOOK
WASHINGTON COMMUNITY PROPERTY DESKBOOK
WASHINGTON FAMILY LAW DESKBOOK
WASHINGTON MOTOR VEHICLE ACCIDENT DESKBOOK
WASHINGTON MOTOR VEHICLE ACCIDENT INSURANCE DESKBOOK
WASHINGTON MOTOR VEHICLE ACCIDENT LITIGATION DESKBOOK
WASHINGTON PARTNERSHIP LAW AND PRACTICE HANDBOOK
WASHINGTON REAL PROPERTY DESKBOOK, 2ND ED.
WHAT THE WASHINGTON PRACTITIONER NEEDS TO KNOW ABOUT BASIC REAL ESTATE
WHEN YOU NEED TO KNOW: FAMILY LAW

West

CALIFORNIA CIVIL TRIALBOOK
CALIFORNIA CRIMINAL TRIALBOOK
CALIFORNIA JURY INSTRUCTIONS - CIVIL (BAJI)
CALIFORNIA JURY INSTRUCTIONS - CRIMINAL (CALJIC)
DEPOSITIONS: PROCEDURE, STRATEGY AND TECHNIQUE
FEDERAL CIVIL TRIALBOOK
THE TRIALBOOK: A TOTAL SYSTEM FOR THE PREPARATION AND PRESENTATION OF A CASE

WG&L

BASIC LEGAL FORMS
BASIC LEGAL TRANSACTIONS
BENEFITS AND RETIREMENT PLAN GUIDE
BENEFITS COORDINATOR
CHARITABLE GIVING AND SOLICITATION
CLOSELY HELD CORPORATIONS: FORMS AND CHECKLISTS
COMPENSATION STRATEGY AND MANAGEMENT
COMPLIANCE EXAMINATIONS UPDATE FOR FINANCIAL INSTITUTIONS
COMPUTER SOFTWARE AGREEMENTS: FORMS AND COMMENTARY
THE CONSOLIDATED TAX RETURN
CORPORATE ACQUISITIONS, MERGERS AND DIVESTITURES
CORPORATION FORMS
DEPRECIATION AND CAPITAL PLANNING
DISABILITIES IN THE WORKPLACE: A GUIDE TO FEDERAL AND STATE LAWS
DIVORCE TAXATION
EEO COMPLIANCE MANUAL
EMPLOYEE BENEFITS COMPLIANCE COORDINATOR
EMPLOYEE COMMUNICATIONS GUIDE
EMPLOYMENT COORDINATOR
EMPLOYMENT DISCRIMINATION COORDINATOR
ESTATE PLANNING LAW AND TAXATION
FARM PRODUCTS FINANCING AND FILING SERVICE
FEDERAL INCOME TAXATION OF BANKS AND FINANCIAL INSTITUTIONS
FEDERAL INCOME TAXATION OF CORPORATIONS AND SHAREHOLDERS: FORMS
FEDERAL INCOME TAXATION OF INDIVIDUALS

FEDERAL INCOME TAXATION OF OIL AND GAS INVESTMENTS
FEDERAL INCOME TAXATION OF PASSIVE ACTIVITIES
FEDERAL INCOME TAXATION OF REAL ESTATE: FORMS AND CHECKLISTS
FEDERAL INCOME TAXATION OF REAL ESTATE
FEDERAL INCOME TAXATION OF S CORPORATIONS
FEDERAL REGULATION OF DEPOSITORY INSTITUTIONS
FEDERAL TAX DEDUCTIONS
FEDERAL TAXATION OF PARTNERSHIPS AND PARTNERS
FEDERAL TAXATION OF PARTNERSHIPS AND PARTNERS: STRUCTURING AND DRAFTING AGREEMENTS
FEDERAL TAXATION OF TRUSTS, GRANTORS AND BENEFICIARIES
FORMS OF BUSINESS AGREEMENTS, VOL. 3 (Commercial Transactions)
FORMS OF BUSINESS AGREEMENTS, VOLS. 1 & 2
GAAP PRACTICE MANUAL
GOVERNMENTAL ACCOUNTING AND AUDITING DISCLOSURE MANUAL
GUIDE TO EMPLOYMENT LAW AND REGULATION
HOUSING AND DEVELOPMENT REPORTER
HR POLICY AND PROCEDURE
HUMAN RESOURCE MANAGEMENT IN CANADA
LABOR RELATIONS FORMS & AGREEMENTS
THE LAW OF REAL ESTATE FINANCING
MANAGING EMPLOYEE BENEFITS
MODERN ACCOUNTING & AUDITING CHECKLISTS
MODERN BANKING CHECKLISTS
MODERN BANKING FORMS
MODERN CONSTRUCTION AND DEVELOPMENT FORMS (Modern Real Estate & Mortgage Forms series)
MODERN CORPORATION CHECKLISTS
MODERN REAL ESTATE ACQUISITION AND DISPOSITION FORMS
MODERN REAL ESTATE AND MORTGAGE FORMS SERIES: VOL. 2 - CHECKLISTS
MODERN REAL ESTATE AND MORTGAGE FORMS SERIES: VOL. 1 - BASIC FORMS AND AGREEMENTS, 3rd ed.
MODERN REAL ESTATE LEASING FORMS
MODERN TAX PLANNING CHECKLISTS
MODERN TRUST FORMS AND CHECKLISTS
PAYROLL GUIDE
PAYROLL PRACTITIONER'S COMPLIANCE HANDBOOK: YEAR-END AND QUARTERLY REPORTING
PENSION ADMINISTRATOR'S FORMS AND CHECKLISTS
PERSONNEL MANAGEMENT GUIDE
PRINCIPLES OF PAYROLL ADMINISTRATION: THE COMPLETE LEARNING AND REFERENCE GUIDE
QUINN'S UCC FORMS & PRACTICE
REAL ESTATE SYNDICATION MANUAL
REAL ESTATE TRANSACTIONS: STRUCTURE AND ANALYSIS WITH FORMS
REPORTING TO BANK REGULATORS
S CORPORATIONS
SEC ACCOUNTING AND REPORTING MANUAL
SEC COMPLIANCE - FINANCIAL REPORTING AND FORMS
SECURITIES REGULATION
SIMPLIFIED CONSUMER CREDIT FORMS
STRUCTURING COMMERCIAL LOAN AGREEMENTS
STRUCTURING SECURED COMMERCIAL LOAN DOCUMENTS
SUCCESSFUL PAYROLL MANAGEMENT
TAX IDEAS
TAX PLANNING FOR DISPOSITIONS OF BUSINESS INTERESTS
TAX PLANNING FOR FAMILY WEALTH TRANSFERS
THE TAX PRACTICE DESKBOOK
TAX TREATIES
TAXATION OF CORPORATE LIQUIDATIONS
TAXATION OF THE CLOSELY HELD CORPORATION
TERMINATION OF EMPLOYMENT
U.S. INTERNATIONAL TAXATION
U.S. TAXATION OF INTERNATIONAL OPERATIONS
WG&L ESTATE PLANNING AND ADMINISTRATION

WG&L HUMAN RESOURCES FORMS WITH COMMENTARY
WG&L TAX PLANNING CHECKLISTS

Wiley
HAZARDOUS WASTE LAW AND PRACTICE

Wiley Law
ADVANCED CHAPTER 11 BANKRUPTCY PRACTICE
BANKRUPTCY LAW & PROCEDURE: A FUNDAMENTAL GUIDE FOR LAW OFFICE PROFESSIONALS
BANKRUPTCY LITIGATION AND PRACTICE: A PRACTITIONER'S GUIDE
BANKRUPTCY STRATEGIES FOR LENDERS
CHAPTER 13 BANKRUPTCY
CONSUMER CREDIT REGULATIONS
DRAFTING BANKRUPTCY REORGANIZATION PLANS
ESTATE PLANNING SIMPLIFIED
FIRE LITIGATION SOURCEBOOK
FLORIDA TRIAL EVIDENCE
HANDBOOK OF ANNOTATED FORMS FOR THE SURVEYING PRACTICE
LENDER LIABILITY: THEORY & PRACTICE
LITIGATING HEAD TRAUMA CASES
LITIGATION FORMS AND CHECKLISTS
MAKING TRIAL OBJECTIONS
MANAGING COBRA: THE COMPLETE COMPLIANCE GUIDE
MODERN CIVIL DISCOVERY AND DEPOSITIONS
MODERN CIVIL JURY SELECTION
OAKES' CRIMINAL PRACTICE GUIDE
TAX STRATEGIES IN DIVORCE
TEXAS LAND USE LAW
TEXAS TITLE INSURANCE

WSB
CFTC ADMINISTRATIVE REPORTER
ERISA CITATOR
ERISA UPDATE
ETHICS IN GOVERNMENT REPORTER
SEC NO-ACTION LETTERS INDEX & SUMMARIES
SIGNIFICANT SEC FILINGS REPORTER

SUBJECT INDEX

COMMERCIAL DAMAGES: A GUIDE TO REMEDIES IN BUSINESS LITIGATION (Bender)
DEFENDING DRINKING DRIVERS (James)
DEFENSE AGAINST A PRIMA FACIE CASE (Clark Boardman Callaghan)
DEFENSE OF SPEEDING, RECKLESS DRIVING, VEHICULAR HOMICIDE (Bender)
DRINKING/DRIVING LITIGATION: CRIMINAL AND CIVIL (Clark Boardman Callaghan)
DRINKING/DRIVING LITIGATION TRIAL NOTEBOOK (Clark Boardman Callaghan)
EMPLOYEE RIGHTS LITIGATION: PLEADING AND PRACTICE (Bender)
EMPLOYMENT LITIGATION IN THE NINETIES (NELI)
FAMILY LAW LITIGATION GUIDE: DISCOVERY, EVIDENCE AND TRIAL PRACTICE (Bender)
FEDERAL LITIGATION GUIDE (Bender)
FIRE LITIGATION SOURCEBOOK (Wiley Law)
GOVERNMENT DISCRIMINATION (Clark Boardman Callaghan)
GUIDE TO EFFECTIVE BANKRUPTCY LITIGATION (Shepard's)
HANDBOOK OF INSURANCE COVERAGE DISPUTES (Prentice Hall Law & Business)
HANDLING COMPLEX CRIMINAL CASES (Georgetown)
IMMIGRATION LAW AND DEFENSE, 3rd ED. (Clark Boardman Callaghan)
INSURANCE BAD FAITH LITIGATION (Bender)
INTELLECTUAL PROPERTY COUNSELING AND LITIGATION (Bender)
INTERNATIONAL PATENT LITIGATION: A COUNTRY-BY-COUNTRY ANALYSIS (BNA Books)
LENDER LIABILITY AND BANKING LITIGATION (Law Journal)
LESBIAN MOTHER LITIGATION MANUAL (Natl. Center for Lesbian Rights)
LIBEL AND PRIVACY: THE PREVENTION AND DEFENSE OF LITIGATION (Prentice Hall Law & Business)
LITIGATING AGE DISCRIMINATION CASES (Clark Boardman Callaghan)
LITIGATING HEAD TRAUMA CASES (Wiley Law)
LITIGATING NECK AND BACK INJURIES (James)
LITIGATING WRONGFUL DISCHARGE CLAIMS (Clark Boardman Callaghan)
LITIGATION AND PRACTICE UNDER RULE 10B-5 (Securities Law Series, vol. 5, 5A, 5B, 5C & 5D) (Clark Boardman Callaghan)
LITIGATION OF FEDERAL TAX CONTROVERSIES (Shepard's)
LITIGATION OF INTERNATIONAL DISPUTES IN U.S. COURTS (International Business Law Series vol. 4) (Clark Boardman Callaghan)
LITIGATION ORGANIZATION AND MANAGEMENT (Prentice Hall Law & Business)
MEDICAL AND HOSPITAL NEGLIGENCE (Clark Boardman Callaghan)
NATURAL RESOURCES AND ENVIRONMENTAL LITIGATION (Rocky Mt.)
PERSONAL INJURY - ACTIONS, DEFENSES, DAMAGES (Bender)
PERSONAL INJURY DEFENSE TECHNIQUES (Bender)
A PRACTICAL GUIDE TO TAX SHELTER LITIGATION (Law Journal)
PROSECUTION AND DEFENSE OF FORFEITURE CASES (Bender)
PROVING CRIMINAL DEFENSES (Bender)
SECURITIES LITIGATION: DAMAGES (Clark Boardman Callaghan)
SECURITIES LITIGATION: FORMS & ANALYSIS (Clark Boardman Callaghan)
SETTLEMENT (Art of Advocacy Series) (Bender)
SHAREHOLDER LITIGATION (Clark Boardman Callaghan)
SOUTHEAST LITIGATION GUIDE (Bender)
USE OF STATISTICS IN EQUAL EMPLOYMENT OPPORTUNITY (Law Journal)
VICTIMS' RIGHTS: LAW AND LITIGATION (Bender)

ACTIONS AND DEFENSES--CALIFORNIA

CALIFORNIA CIVIL ACTIONS - PLEADING AND PRACTICE (Bender)
CALIFORNIA CIVIL LITIGATION FORMS MANUAL (Calif. CEB)
CALIFORNIA COMPLEX LITIGATION (Parker)
CALIFORNIA CRIMINAL DEFENSE PRACTICE (Bender)
CALIFORNIA DRUNK DRIVING DEFENSE (Lawyers Coop.)
CALIFORNIA FORMS OF PLEADING AND PRACTICE-ANNOTATED (Bender)
CALIFORNIA INSURANCE DISPUTES (Parker)
CALIFORNIA LIABILITY INSURANCE PRACTICE: CLAIMS AND LITIGATION (Calif. CEB)
CALIFORNIA PRODUCTS LIABILITY ACTIONS (Bender)

ACTIONS AND DEFENSES--FLORIDA

BENDER'S FLORIDA FORMS OF PLEADING (Bender)
BUSINESS LITIGATION IN FLORIDA (Florida Bar)

ACTIONS AND DEFENSES--FORMS

LITIGATION FORMS AND CHECKLISTS (Wiley Law)
PARALEGAL LITIGATION FORMS (James)

ACTIONS AND DEFENSES--ILLINOIS

BUSINESS AND COMMERCIAL LITIGATION (Illinois ICLE)
CHANCERY AND SPECIAL REMEDIES (Illinois ICLE)
CONSTRUCTION LITIGATION (Illinois ICLE)
DEFENDING ILLINOIS CRIMINAL CASES (Illinois ICLE)
REAL ESTATE LITIGATION (Illinois ICLE)

ACTIONS AND DEFENSES--INDIANA

CRIMINAL DEFENSE (Indiana CLE)
DEFENSE TECHNIQUES FOR DWI CLIENTS (Indiana CLE)
INDIANA FORMS OF PLEADING AND PRACTICE (Bender)
RICO LITIGATION (Indiana CLE)
SUCCESSFULLY LITIGATING TORT INSURANCE ACTIONS (Indiana CLE)

ACTIONS AND DEFENSES--IOWA

IOWA PLEADING AND CAUSES OF ACTION (Butterworth-St. Paul)

ACTIONS AND DEFENSES--MAINE

MAINE CIVIL REMEDIES (Butterworth-NH)

ACTIONS AND DEFENSES--MARYLAND

PLEADING CAUSES OF ACTION IN MARYLAND (MICPEL)

ACTIONS AND DEFENSES--MASSACHUSETTS

MASSACHUSETTS CIVIL ACTIONS & PROCEDURE (Gould)
MASSACHUSETTS PLEADING AND PRACTICE - FORMS AND COMMENTARY (Bender)

ACTIONS AND DEFENSES--MICHIGAN

COMPLAINT BOOK (MTLA)
HANDLING THE MEDICAL MALPRACTICE CASE: A SYSTEMS APPROACH (ICLE - Michigan)
STARTING A CASE IN THE 90's: A CURRENT MANUAL OF COMPLAINTS IN MICHIGAN (MTLA)
WRONGFUL TERMINATION LITIGATION (MTLA)

ACTIONS AND DEFENSES--MINNESOTA

CRASH LITIGATION (MILE)
SECURITIES AND COMMERCIAL LITIGATION (MILE)
WHITE COLLAR LITIGATION: CIVIL AND CRIMINAL (MILE)

ACTIONS AND DEFENSES--NEW HAMPSHIRE

BUSINESS LITIGATION: CURRENT ISSUES (NH Bar)
STOCKHOLDERS LITIGATION (NH Bar)

ACTIONS AND DEFENSES--NEW YORK

BENDER'S FORMS OF PLEADING (Bender)
BILLS OF PARTICULARS IN NEW YORK (Lawyers Coop.)
PLAINTIFF'S PROOF OF A PRIMA FACIE CASE (Clark Boardman Callaghan)

ACTIONS AND DEFENSES--OHIO

OHIO FORMS OF PLEADING AND PRACTICE (Bender)

ACTIONS AND DEFENSES--OKLAHOMA

TRIAL PREPARATION OF A COMMERCIAL LITIGATION CASE (Okla. Bar CLE)

ACTIONS AND DEFENSES--OREGON

CIVIL LITIGATION (Oregon Bar)

ACTIONS AND DEFENSES--PENNSYLVANIA

VALENTINE-BINNS JUSTICE (Bisel)

ACTIONS AND DEFENSES--TEXAS

TEXAS CRIMINAL DEFENSE FORMS ANNOTATED (Knowles)
TEXAS LITIGATION GUIDE (Bender)

ACTIONS AND DEFENSES--WASHINGTON

STRATEGIC FUNDAMENTALS OF PROSECUTING & DEFENDING THE PERSONAL INJURY CASE (Wash. Bar)

ADMINISTRATIVE LAW AND PROCEDURE
ADMINISTRATIVE LAW (Bender)
ADMINISTRATIVE LAW, THIRD SERIES (P&F)
BNA ADMINISTRATIVE PRACTICE MANUAL (BNA Books)
FEDERAL REGULATORY PROCESS: AGENCY PRACTICES & PROCEDURES (Prentice Hall Law & Business)

ADMINISTRATIVE LAW AND PROCEDURE--CONNECTICUT
ADMINISTRATIVE LAW (Conn. Bar)

ADMINISTRATIVE LAW AND PROCEDURE--DISTRICT OF COLUMBIA
ADMINISTRATIVE LAW MANUAL (Bar Assn. of D.C.)

ADMINISTRATIVE LAW AND PROCEDURE--FLORIDA
FLORIDA ADMINISTRATIVE PRACTICE (Florida Bar)
FLORIDA ADMINISTRATIVE PRACTICE MANUAL (Butterworth-Fla.)

ADMINISTRATIVE LAW AND PROCEDURE--ILLINOIS
ILLINOIS ADMINISTRATIVE LAW (Illinois ICLE)

ADMINISTRATIVE LAW AND PROCEDURE--INDIANA
STATE & FEDERAL ADMINISTRATIVE AGENCY PRACTICE (Indiana CLE)

ADMINISTRATIVE LAW AND PROCEDURE--KANSAS
KANSAS ADMINISTRATIVE LAW WITH FEDERAL REFERENCES (Kansas Bar)

ADMINISTRATIVE LAW AND PROCEDURE--MAINE
EFFECTIVE STATE AND MUNICIPAL HEARINGS PRACTICE (Maine Bar)
MAINE ADMINISTRATIVE PROCEDURE (Butterworth-NH)

ADMINISTRATIVE LAW AND PROCEDURE--MARYLAND
ADMINISTRATIVE HEARINGS (MICPEL)
MOTOR VEHICLE ADMINISTRATION HEARINGS (MICPEL)

ADMINISTRATIVE LAW AND PROCEDURE--MISSOURI
MISSOURI ADMINISTRATIVE LAW (MoBar)

ADMINISTRATIVE LAW AND PROCEDURE--NEW HAMPSHIRE
ADMINISTRATIVE LAW (NH Bar)

ADMINISTRATIVE LAW AND PROCEDURE--OREGON
STATE ADMINISTRATIVE LAW (Oregon Bar)

ADMINISTRATIVE LAW AND PROCEDURE--SOUTH CAROLINA
SOUTH CAROLINA ADMINISTRATIVE LAW -- 2nd Ed. (S. Carolina Bar)

ADMINISTRATIVE LAW AND PROCEDURE--VIRGINIA
VIRGINIA ADMINISTRATIVE LAW AND PRACTICE (Jt. Comm. Va.)

ADMINISTRATIVE LAW AND PROCEDURE--WASHINGTON
NEW ADMINISTRATIVE PROCEDURES ACT AND MODEL RULES (Wash. Bar)
WASHINGTON ADMINISTRATIVE LAW PRACTICE MANUAL (Butterworth-St. Paul)

ADMIRALTY
see also Law of the sea; Ships and shipping

BENEDICT ON ADMIRALTY, 7TH ED. (Bender)
MARINE POLLUTION AND THE LAW OF THE SEA (Hein)
MARITIME LAW HANDBOOK (Kluwer)
PACIFIC NORTHWEST ADMIRALTY LAW INSTITUTE (Wash. Bar)

ADOPTION
see Domestic relations

ADVERTISING LAWS
ADVERTISING COMPLIANCE SERVICE (Greenwood)
THE LAW OF ADVERTISING (Bender)

ANTITRUST LAW
see also Competition, unfair; Trade regulation

ACQUISITIONS UNDER THE HART-SCOTT-RODINO ANTITRUST IMPROVEMENTS ACT (Law Journal)
ANTITRUST: AN ECONOMIC APPROACH (Law Journal)
ANTITRUST AND TRADE REGULATION (Business Organizations vols. 16-16N & Index) (Bender)
ANTITRUST AND TRADE REGULATION: DESK ED. (Bender)
ANTITRUST BASICS (Law Journal)
ANTITRUST CIVIL JURY INSTRUCTIONS (ABA)
ANTITRUST CONSENT DECREE MANUAL (ABA)
ANTITRUST COUNSELING AND LITIGATION TECHNIQUES (Bender)
ANTITRUST DISCOVERY HANDBOOK (ABA)
ANTITRUST DIVISION MANUAL (USGPO)
COMPETITION LAW IN WESTERN EUROPE & THE USA (Kluwer)
COMPETITION LAW OF THE EEC (Bender)
COMPETITION LAWS OF THE PACIFIC RIM COUNTRIES (Bender)
CORPORATE COUNSEL'S GUIDE TO THE ROBINSON-PATMAN ACT (Bus. Laws)
EMPLOYEE NONCOMPETITION LAW (Clark Boardman Callaghan)
JURY INSTRUCTIONS IN CRIMINAL ANTITRUST CASES 1964-1976 (ABA)
MATERIALS ON ANTITRUST COMPLIANCE PROGRAMS (Bus. Laws)
SAMPLE ANTITRUST COMPLIANCE PLANS (Bus. Laws)
TRADE REGULATION REPORTS (CCH)

ANTITRUST LAW--CANADA
COMPETITION LAW OF CANADA (Bender)

ANTITRUST LAW--INTERNATIONAL
ANTITRUST AND RESTRICTIVE BUSINESS PRACTICES: INTERNATIONAL, REGIONAL & NATIONAL REGULATION (Oceana)
COMPLYING WITH INTERNATIONAL ANTITRUST REGULATIONS (Bender)
CORPORATE COUNSEL'S GUIDE TO INTERNATIONAL ANTITRUST LAWS (Bus. Laws)
UNITED STATES, COMMON MARKET AND INTERNATIONAL ANTITRUST: A COMPARATIVE GUIDE (Prentice Hall Law & Business)

ANTITRUST LAW--MICHIGAN
MICHIGAN ANTITRUST DIGEST (ICLE - Michigan)

ANTITRUST LAW--STATES
STATE ANTITRUST LAW (Law Journal)

ANTITRUST LAW--UNITED KINGDOM
COMPETITION LAW OF THE UNITED KINGDOM/REPUBLIC OF IRELAND (Bender)

APPELLATE PROCEDURE
see also Civil procedure; Criminal procedure; Trial practice

APPEALS (Art of Advocacy Series) (Bender)
APPEALS TO THE ELEVENTH CIRCUIT (Butterworth-Fla.)
APPEALS TO THE FIFTH CIRCUIT (Butterworth-Texas)
APPEALS TO THE THIRD CIRCUIT (Butterworth-NH)
CALLAGHAN'S APPELLATE ADVOCACY MANUAL (Clark Boardman Callaghan)
EFFICIENCY AND JUSTICE IN APPEALS: METHODS AND SELECTED MATERIALS (ABA)
FEDERAL CRIMINAL APPEALS (Clark Boardman Callaghan)

APPELLATE PROCEDURE--ALABAMA
ALABAMA APPELLATE PRACTICE (ABICLE)

APPELLATE PROCEDURE--ARIZONA
ARIZONA APPELLATE HANDBOOK (State Bar of Ariz.)

APPELLATE PROCEDURE--COLORADO
COLORADO APPELLATE HANDBOOK (CLE - Colorado)

APPELLATE PROCEDURE--CONNECTICUT
CONNECTICUT APPELLATE PRACTICE AND PROCEDURE (Butterworth-NH)

APPELLATE PROCEDURE--FLORIDA
FLORIDA APPELLATE PRACTICE MANUAL (Butterworth-Fla.)

APPELLATE PROCEDURE--HAWAII
HAWAII APPELLATE HANDBOOK (HICLE)

APPELLATE PROCEDURE--IDAHO
IDAHO APPELLATE HANDBOOK (Idaho Law)

APPELLATE PROCEDURE--ILLINOIS
CIVIL APPEALS (Illinois ICLE)

APPELLATE PROCEDURE--INDIANA
APPELLATE PRACTICE (Indiana CLE)
THE ATTORNEY'S GUIDE TO THE SEVENTH CIRCUIT COURT OF APPEALS (State Bar of Wisc.)
PRACTITIONER'S HANDBOOK FOR APPEALS (Indiana CLE)
WINNING ON APPEAL: GOOD APPELLATE PRACTICE (Indiana CLE)

APPELLATE PROCEDURE--KANSAS
KANSAS APPELLATE PRACTICE (Kansas Bar)

APPELLATE PROCEDURE--KENTUCKY
BALDWIN'S KENTUCKY PRACTICE (Banks)
KENTUCKY APPELLATE HANDBOOK (Banks)

APPELLATE PROCEDURE--LOUISIANA
LOUISIANA APPELLATE PRACTICE HANDBOOK (Lawyers Coop.)

APPELLATE PROCEDURE--MARYLAND
MARYLAND APPELLATE PRACTICE: RULES AND COMMENTARY WITH FORMS (MICPEL)

APPELLATE PROCEDURE--MICHIGAN
MICHIGAN APPELLATE HANDBOOK (ICLE - Michigan)

APPELLATE PROCEDURE--MINNESOTA
MINNESOTA APPELLATE PRACTICE INSTITUTE (MILE)

APPELLATE PROCEDURE--MISSISSIPPI
MISSISSIPPI SUPREME COURT PRACTICE (On Point)

APPELLATE PROCEDURE--MISSOURI
MISSOURI APPELLATE PRACTICE AND EXTRAORDINARY REMEDIES (MoBar)

APPELLATE PROCEDURE--NEW HAMPSHIRE
APPELLATE ADVOCACY HANDBOOK (NH Bar)

APPELLATE PROCEDURE--NEW JERSEY
NEW JERSEY APPELLATE PRACTICE HANDBOOK (New Jersey ICLE)

APPELLATE PROCEDURE--NEW MEXICO
NEW MEXICO APPELLATE PRACTICE MANUAL (Butterworth-Texas)

APPELLATE PROCEDURE--NEW YORK
NEW YORK APPELLATE PRACTICE (Bender)

APPELLATE PROCEDURE--OHIO
APPELLATE ADVOCACY (Ohio CLE)

APPELLATE PROCEDURE--OREGON
APPEAL AND REVIEW (Oregon Bar)
OREGON APPELLATE MANUAL (Butterworth-St. Paul)

APPELLATE PROCEDURE--RHODE ISLAND
RHODE ISLAND APPELLATE PRACTICE (Butterworth-NH)

APPELLATE PROCEDURE--TEXAS
TEXAS RULES OF APPELLATE PROCEDURE (Butterworth-Texas)

APPELLATE PROCEDURE--VIRGINIA
APPELLATE PRACTICE - VIRGINIA AND FEDERAL COURTS (Jt. Comm. Va.)

APPELLATE PROCEDURE--WISCONSIN
APPELLATE PRACTICE & PROCEDURE HANDBOOK (State Bar of Wisc.)
THE ATTORNEY'S GUIDE TO THE SEVENTH CIRCUIT COURT OF APPEALS (State Bar of Wisc.)

ARBITRATION
see also Labor arbitration

COMMERCIAL ARBITRATION HANDBOOK (Parker)
DOMKE LAW AND PRACTICE OF COMMERCIAL ARBITRATION (Clark Boardman Callaghan)
INTERNATIONAL HANDBOOK ON COMMERCIAL ARBITRATION -- NATIONAL REPORTS AND BASIC LEGAL TEXTS (Kluwer)
SECURITIES ARBITRATION PROCEDURE MANUAL (Butterworth-NH)
STATE LABOR LAWS (BNA)

ARBITRATION--CALIFORNIA
CALIFORNIA ARBITRATION HANDBOOK (Parker)
CALIFORNIA ARBITRATION PRACTICE GUIDE 2D (Lawpress)

ARBITRATION--HAWAII
HAWAII ARBITRATION SOURCEBOOK (Pacific Law Inst.)

ARBITRATION--ILLINOIS
ARBITRATION PRACTICE (Illinois ICLE)

ARBITRATION--MINNESOTA
ARBITRATION OF COMMERCIAL AND CONSTRUCTION DISPUTES (MILE)

ARBITRATION--OREGON
ARBITRATION AND MEDIATION (Oregon Bar)

ARBITRATION--USSR
INTERNATIONAL COMMERCIAL ARBITRATION -- SOVIET COMMERCIAL AND MARITIME ARBITRATION (Oceana)

ARBITRATION--WASHINGTON
ALTERNATIVE DISPUTE RESOLUTION DESKBOOK: ARBITRATION & MEDIATION IN WASHINGTON (Wash. Bar)

ARBITRATION, INTERNATIONAL
CLIVE SCHMITTHOFF'S INTERNATIONAL COMMERCIAL ARBITRATION (Oceana)
INTERNATIONAL COMMERCIAL ARBITRATION -- INTER-AMERICAN COMMERCIAL ARBITRATION (Oceana)
INTERNATIONAL COMMERCIAL ARBITRATION -- INTERNATIONAL CHAMBER OF COMMERCE ARBITRATION (Oceana)
INTERNATIONAL COMMERCIAL ARBITRATION: COMMERCIAL ARBITRATION LAW IN ASIA AND THE PACIFIC (Oceana)
INTERNATIONAL COMMERCIAL ARBITRATION: CASES UNDER THE NEW YORK CONVENTION (Oceana)
UNCITRAL MODEL LAW OF INTERNATIONAL COMMERCIAL ARBITRATION: A DOCUMENTARY HISTORY (Hein)

ARCHITECTS AND ENGINEERS
see Building contracts

ARMS CONTROL
ARMS CONTROL REPORTER (IDDS)

ARREST
see also Criminal procedure; Police

SEARCHES & SEIZURES, ARRESTS AND CONFESSIONS (Clark Boardman Callaghan)

ARREST--GEORGIA
GEORGIA ARREST SEARCH AND SEIZURE (Butterworth-Fla.)

ARREST--ILLINOIS
ARREST, SEARCH AND SEIZURE (Illinois ICLE)

ARSON
ARSON LEGISLATION REFERENCE MANUAL (ABA)
FIRE LITIGATION SOURCEBOOK (Wiley Law)

ASBESTOS
see also Environmental law

ASBESTOS ABATEMENT RESOURCE GUIDE, 2ND ED. (BNA)
ASBESTOS ABATEMENT RULES: THE COMPLETE RESOURCE GUIDE (BNA)
ASBESTOS REGULATORY DIRECTORY (Natl. Asbestos)

ASSOCIATIONS
see Nonprofit associations

ATOMIC ENERGY
see Nuclear energy

ATTORNEY'S FEES
see Lawyer's fees

AUDITING
see also Accounting; Tax auditing

AICPA AUDIT AND ACCOUNTING MANUAL (CCH)
APPLYING GOVERNMENT AUDITING STANDARDS (Bender)
AUDIT & ACCOUNTING GUIDES (CCH)
EMPLOYER'S GUIDE TO AUDITING PERSONNEL & EMPLOYMENT PRACTICES (Bus. Laws)
FEDERAL AUDIT GUIDES (CCH)
GOVERNMENTAL ACCOUNTING AND AUDITING DISCLOSURE MANUAL (WG&L)
HANDBOOK FOR INTERNAL AUDITORS (Bender)
MODERN ACCOUNTING & AUDITING CHECKLISTS (WG&L)
SINGLE AUDIT GUIDE 1992 (HBJ Miller)

AUTOMOBILE ACCIDENTS
see also Negligence; Personal injuries

ATTORNEY'S GUIDE TO CONDUCTING DEPOSITIONS - AUTOMOBILE NEGLIGENCE CASES (Lame)
AUTOMOBILE ACCIDENT LAW AND PRACTICE (Bender)
AUTOMOBILES (Knowles)
DEFENSE OF SPEEDING, RECKLESS DRIVING, VEHICULAR HOMICIDE (Bender)
HANDLING MOTOR VEHICLE ACCIDENT CASES: FORMS (Clark Boardman Callaghan)
HANDLING MOTOR VEHICLE ACCIDENT CASES: TREATISE (Clark Boardman Callaghan)
PROVING FAULT IN AUTO ACCIDENT CASES (Illinois ICLE)
SCIENTIFIC AUTOMOBILE ACCIDENT RECONSTRUCTION (Bender)

AUTOMOBILE ACCIDENTS--MAINE
TRIAL ADVOCACY: THE AUTOMOBILE ACCIDENT (Maine Bar)

AUTOMOBILE ACCIDENTS--MICHIGAN
HANDLING THE AUTOMOBILE NEGLIGENCE CASE: A SYSTEMS APPROACH (ICLE - Michigan)

AUTOMOBILE ACCIDENTS--MINNESOTA
AUTOMOBILE ACCIDENT RECONSTRUCTION (MILE)
MINNESOTA MOTOR VEHICLE ACCIDENT DESKBOOK (Minn. CLE)

<u>AUTOMOBILE ACCIDENTS--MISSOURI</u>
AUTOMOBILE ACCIDENT HANDBOOK (UMKC/CLE)

<u>AUTOMOBILE ACCIDENTS--OKLAHOMA</u>
HOW TO HANDLE A MOTOR VEHICLE ACCIDENT CASE (Okla. Bar CLE)

<u>AUTOMOBILE ACCIDENTS--WASHINGTON</u>
WASHINGTON MOTOR VEHICLE ACCIDENT INSURANCE DESKBOOK (Wash. Bar)
WASHINGTON MOTOR VEHICLE ACCIDENT LITIGATION DESKBOOK (Wash. Bar)

<u>AUTOMOBILE ACCIDENTS--WISCONSIN</u>
WASHINGTON MOTOR VEHICLE ACCIDENT DESKBOOK (Wash. Bar)

<u>AUTOMOBILE INSURANCE</u>
see Insurance, automobile

<u>AUTOMOBILES</u>
see Vehicles

<u>AVIATION</u>
see also Space law

AIR AND AVIATION TREATIES OF THE WORLD (Oceana)
AVIATION ACCIDENT LAW (Bender)
AVIATION LAW REPORTS (CCH)
AVIATION REGULATORY DIGEST SERVICE (Hawkins)
FEDERAL AVIATION ADMINISTRATION - CODIFIED REGULATIONS (Rules)
FEDERAL AVIATION REGULATIONS (USGPO)

<u>AVIATION--INTERNATIONAL</u>
REGULATION OF INTERNATIONAL COMMERCIAL AVIATION: THE INTERNATIONAL REGULATORY STRUCTURE (Oceana)

<u>BANKRUPTCY</u>
see also Debtor and creditor

ADVANCED BANKRUPTCY INSTITUTE (Georgetown)
ADVANCED CHAPTER 11 BANKRUPTCY PRACTICE (Wiley Law)
BANKRUPTCY (Clark Boardman Callaghan)
BANKRUPTCY: TEXT, STATUTES, RULES (Prentice Hall Law & Business)
BANKRUPTCY & WORKOUTS IN THE TROUBLED OIL & GAS INDUSTRY (EMLF)
BANKRUPTCY COURT DECISIONS (LRP)
BANKRUPTCY DESK GUIDE (Lawyers Coop.)
BANKRUPTCY FOR THE CORPORATE LAWYER (Conn. Bar)
BANKRUPTCY LAW & PROCEDURE: A FUNDAMENTAL GUIDE FOR LAW OFFICE PROFESSIONALS (Wiley Law)
BANKRUPTCY LAW FUNDAMENTALS (Clark Boardman Callaghan)
BANKRUPTCY LAW REPORTS (CCH)
BANKRUPTCY LITIGATION AND PRACTICE: A PRACTITIONER'S GUIDE (Wiley Law)
BANKRUPTCY LITIGATION MANUAL (Prentice Hall Law & Business)
BANKRUPTCY LOCAL COURT RULES (Clark Boardman Callaghan)
BANKRUPTCY PRACTICE DESKBOOK, Rev. Ed. (Butterworth-NH)
BANKRUPTCY PRACTICE FOR THE GENERAL PRACTITIONER, 2/E (Shepard's)
BANKRUPTCY PRACTICE HANDBOOK (Clark Boardman Callaghan)
BANKRUPTCY PRACTICE HANDBOOK (Parker)
BANKRUPTCY PRACTICE MANUAL (No. Carolina Bar)
BANKRUPTCY SERVICE, LAWYERS EDITION (Lawyers Coop. & Bancroft)
BANKRUPTCY STAY MANUAL (Book Pub.)
BANKRUPTCY STRATEGIES FOR LENDERS (Wiley Law)
BANKRUPTCY--CHAPTER 13 (Indiana CLE)
CHAPTER 11 REORGANIZATIONS (Shepard's)
CHAPTER 12: FARM REORGANIZATIONS (Shepard's)
CHAPTER 13 BANKRUPTCY (Wiley Law)
CHAPTER 13 PRACTICE AND PROCEDURE (Shepard's)
COLLIER BANKRUPTCY CASES, 2ND SERIES (Bender)
COLLIER BANKRUPTCY COMPENSATION GUIDE (Bender)
COLLIER BANKRUPTCY MANUAL, 3RD DESK ED. (Bender)

COLLIER BANKRUPTCY PRACTICE GUIDE (Bender)
COLLIER FAMILY LAW AND THE BANKRUPTCY CODE (Bender)
COLLIER FARM BANKRUPTCY GUIDE (Bender)
COLLIER HANDBOOK FOR CREDITOR'S COMMITTEES (Bender)
COLLIER LABOR LAW AND THE BANKRUPTCY CODE (Bender)
COLLIER ON BANKRUPTCY, 15TH ED. (Bender)
COLLIER REAL ESTATE TRANSACTION AND BANKRUPTCY CODE (Bender)
COLLIER'S LENDING INSTITUTIONS AND THE BANKRUPTCY CODE (Bender)
CONSTRUCTION BANKRUPTCY (Wash. Bar)
CREDITOR'S RIGHTS IN BANKRUPTCY (Shepard's)
DEALING WITH FINANCIALLY TROUBLED COMPANIES (Bus. Laws)
DRAFTING BANKRUPTCY REORGANIZATION PLANS (Wiley Law)
FEDERAL BANKRUPTCY HANDBOOK (Gould)
FEDERAL RULES OF BANKRUPTCY (Clark Boardman Callaghan)
FEDERAL TAX ASPECTS OF BANKRUPTCY (Shepard's)
GUIDE TO EFFECTIVE BANKRUPTCY LITIGATION (Shepard's)
HERZOG'S BANKRUPTCY FORMS AND PRACTICE (Clark Boardman Callaghan)
INTERNATIONAL LOAN WORKOUTS AND BANKRUPTCIES (Butterworth-NH)
INTRODUCTION TO BANKRUPTCY (Ohio CLE)
LEGAL SECRETARY BANKRUPTCY (James)
NORTON BANKRUPTCY LAW AND PRACTICE (Clark Boardman Callaghan)
A PRACTICAL GUIDE TO OUT-OF-COURT RESTRUCTURINGS AND PREPACKAGED PLANS OF REORGANIZATION (Prentice Hall Law & Business)
REORGANIZATIONS UNDER CHAPTER 11 OF THE BANKRUPTCY CODE (Law Journal)
STRUCTURING COMMERCIAL REAL ESTATE WORKOUTS: ALTERNATIVES TO FORECLOSURE (Prentice Hall Law & Business)

BANKRUPTCY--ALASKA
ALASKA BANKRUPTCY RULES (Book Pub.)

BANKRUPTCY--CONNECTICUT
PERSONAL BANKRUPTCY (Conn. Bar)
REAL ESTATE LOAN WORKOUTS (Conn. Bar)

BANKRUPTCY--FORMS
BANKRUPTCY: ANNOTATED FORMS (Prentice Hall Law & Business)
BANKRUPTCY FORMS MANUAL (Hein)
COLLIER BANKRUPTCY FORMS MANUAL, 3RD ED. (Bender)

BANKRUPTCY--ILLINOIS
BANKRUPTCY PRACTICE (Illinois ICLE)

BANKRUPTCY--INDIANA
BANKRUPTCY "A BASIC REVIEW" (Indiana CLE)
NINTH ANNUAL BANKRUPTCY INSTITUTE (Indiana CLE)

BANKRUPTCY--IOWA
IOWA BANKRUPTCY (Butterworth-St. Paul)

BANKRUPTCY--KANSAS
KANSAS BANKRUPTCY HANDBOOK (Kansas Bar)

BANKRUPTCY--MAINE
BANKRUPTCY LAW FOR THE GENERAL PRACTITIONER (Maine Bar)
COMMERCIAL BANKRUPTCY (Maine Bar)

BANKRUPTCY--MARYLAND
ADVANCED BANKRUPTCY INSTITUTE (MICPEL)
BANKRUPTCY TAX (MICPEL)

BANKRUPTCY--MICHIGAN
BANKRUPTCY LAW AND PRACTICE IN MICHIGAN (ICLE - Michigan)

BANKRUPTCY--MINNESOTA
BANKRUPTCY INSTITUTE (Minn. CLE)
BANKRUPTCY LITIGATION CONFERENCE (MILE)
CREDITOR'S REMEDIES AND BANKRUPTCY (MILE)

MINNESOTA LEGAL FORMS--BANKRUPTCY (Butterworth-St. Paul)
REPRESENTING DEBTORS IN CONSUMER BANKRUPTCIES (Minn. CLE)

BANKRUPTCY--NEBRASKA
NEBRASKA LEGAL FORMS--BANKRUPTCY (Butterworth-St. Paul)

BANKRUPTCY--NEW HAMPSHIRE
BANKRUPTCY AND LENDER LIABILITY LITIGATION (NH Bar)

BANKRUPTCY--NORTH CAROLINA
ANNUAL BANKRUPTCY LAW INSTITUTE (No. Carolina Bar)

BANKRUPTCY--OKLAHOMA
BASIC BANKRUPTCY (Okla. Bar CLE)

BANKRUPTCY--OREGON
BANKRUPTCY LAW (Oregon Bar)

BANKRUPTCY--STATES
THE BASICS OF BANKRUPTCIES: CHAPTERS 7 AND 13 (Wash. Bar)
COLLIER BANKRUPTCY EXEMPTION GUIDE (Bender)

BANKRUPTCY--WASHINGTON
A PRACTICAL APPROACH TO REAL ESTATE LOAN DEFAULTS AND WORKOUTS (Wash. Bar)

BANKS AND BANKING
see also Consumer credit; Interest and usury; Money

ABA'S COMPLIANCE SOURCEBOOK (Am. Bankers)
ACCOUNTING FOR BANKS (Bender)
BANK ACCOUNTING AND AUDITING SERVICE (Sheshunoff)
BANK CAPITAL SERVICE (Sheshunoff)
BANK HOLDING COMPANY COMPLIANCE MANUAL (Bender)
BANK HOLDING COMPANY SUPERVISION MANUAL (Fed.)
BANK REGULATORY REPORTING REQUIREMENTS: A GUIDE TO MEASURING COMPLIANCE (Probus)
BANK WAGE-HOUR AND PERSONNEL SERVICE (Pratt)
BANKING CRIMES (Clark Boardman Callaghan)
BANKING LAW (Bender)
BANKING LAW MANUAL (Bender)
BANKS AND THRIFTS: GOVERNMENT ENFORCEMENT AND RECEIVERSHIP (Bender)
CAPITAL REGULATIONS TRAINING MANUAL (Office of Thrift Supervision)
CHECKS, DRAFTS & NOTES (Bender)
COMMERCIAL ASSET-BASED FINANCING (Clark Boardman Callaghan)
THE COMMUNITY REINVESTMENT ACT (Probus)
THE COMMUNITY REINVESTMENT ACT MANUAL: POLICIES AND COMPLIANCE (Prentice Hall Law & Business)
COMPLIANCE EXAMINATIONS UPDATE FOR FINANCIAL INSTITUTIONS (WG&L)
COMPTROLLER'S HANDBOOK FOR CONSUMER EXAMINATIONS (U.S. Compt.)
COMPTROLLER'S HANDBOOK FOR NATIONAL BANK EXAMINERS (U.S. Compt.)
COMPTROLLER'S MANUAL FOR CORPORATE ACTIVITIES (U.S. Compt.)
CONTRACTING WITH THE RTC AND FDIC (Prentice Hall Law & Business)
EFT REGULATION E COMPREHENSIVE COMPLIANCE MANUAL (Am. Bankers)
FDIC ENFORCEMENT DECISIONS AND ORDERS (Prentice Hall Law & Business)
FEDERAL BANK HOLDING COMPANY LAW (Law Journal)
FEDERAL BANKING LAW REPORTS (CCH)
FEDERAL BANKING LAW SERVICE (Pratt)
FEDERAL GUIDE (USLSI)
FEDERAL REGULATION OF DEPOSITORY INSTITUTIONS (WG&L)
FEDERAL RESERVE REGULATORY SERVICE (Fed.)
FINANCIAL INSTITUTIONS REFORM, RECOVERY & ENFORCEMENT ACT OF 1989 (Indiana CLE)
FIRREA: A LEGISLATIVE HISTORY AND SECTION-BY-SECTION ANALYSIS (Shepard's)
GUIDE TO CONTRACTING WITH THE RESOLUTION TRUST CORPORATION (Thompson)
A GUIDE TO THE FEDERAL LAW OF BANKING AND INSURANCE (Prentice Hall Law & Business)
HOLDING COMPANIES HANDBOOK (Office of Thrift Supervision)

THE LAW OF FINANCIAL SERVICES (Prentice Hall Law & Business)
LAWS, REGULATIONS, RELATED ACTS (FDIC)
LAWYER'S GUIDE TO ACCOUNTING AND FINANCE ABBREVIATIONS AND ACRONYMS (Lexikon)
LENDER LIABILITY (Parker)
LENDER LIABILITY: THEORY & PRACTICE (Wiley Law)
LENDER LIABILITY AND BANKING LITIGATION (Law Journal)
LENDER LIABILITY LAW & LITIGATION (Bender)
LENDER LIABILITY LAW, PRACTICE AND PREVENTION (Clark Boardman Callaghan)
LETTERS OF CREDIT (Bender)
MANAGER'S MANUAL (NCSI)
MODERN BANKING CHECKLISTS (WG&L)
MONETARY POLICY AND RESERVE REQUIREMENTS HANDBOOK (Fed.)
OPERATING CIRCULARS OF THE FEDERAL RESERVE BANK OF NEW YORK (Fed.-NY)
PAYMENT SYSTEM HANDBOOK (Fed.)
REGULATIONS OF THE BOARD OF GOVERNORS (Fed.-NY)
REGULATORY COMPLIANCE MANUAL (MBAA)
THE REGULATORY EXAMINATION: HOW TO GET BETTER RESULTS (NCSI)
REGULATORY MANAGEMENT COMPLIANCE AUDIT DESKBOOK (Probus)
REPORTING TO BANK REGULATORS (WG&L)
THE RTC RESOURCE BOOK (Land Dev.)
SAVINGS INSTITUTIONS: MERGERS, ACQUISITIONS AND CONVERSIONS (Law Journal)
SUPERVISORY SERVICE (USLSI)
TRUST ACTIVITIES HANDBOOK (Office of Thrift Supervision)
TRUST DEPARTMENT ADMINISTRATION AND OPERATIONS (Bender)
TRUSTEE & DIRECTORS HANDBOOK (NCSI)
TRUTH IN LENDING: A COMPREHENSIVE GUIDE (Prentice Hall Law & Business)
TRUTH IN LENDING FOR THE COMMUNITY BANK: A PRACTICAL APPROACH TO REGULATION Z (Probus)
UNDERSTANDING FIRREA: A PRACTICAL GUIDE TO PLANNING AND COMPLIANCE (Prentice Hall Law & Business)

BANKS AND BANKING--FORMS
MODERN BANKING FORMS (WG&L)

BANKS AND BANKING--ILLINOIS
ADVISING ILLINOIS FINANCIAL INSTITUTIONS (Illinois ICLE)

BANKS AND BANKING--INDIANA
BUSINESS, BANKS, BORROWERS & THE ENVIRONMENT (Indiana CLE)
LENDER LIABILITY: A PRAGMATIC APPROACH (Indiana CLE)

BANKS AND BANKING--INTERNATIONAL
INTERNATIONAL OFFSHORE FINANCIAL CENTRES (CCH)

BANKS AND BANKING--KENTUCKY
KENTUCKY FINANCIAL INSTITUTION AND SECURITIES LAW (Banks)

BANKS AND BANKING--MARYLAND
ADVISING FINANCIAL INSTITUTIONS (MICPEL)

BANKS AND BANKING--MINNESOTA
BANKING AND FINANCE (MILE)
BANKING AND THRIFT: AN INDUSTRY IN TRANSITION (MILE)
ENVIRONMENTAL ISSUES CONCERNING FINANCIAL INSTITUTIONS (MILE)
FINANCIAL INSTITUTIONS LAW (MILE)

BANKS AND BANKING--STATES
STATE TAXATION OF BANKS AND THRIFT INSTITUTIONS (ABA)

BANKS AND BANKING--TAXATION
FEDERAL INCOME TAXATION OF BANKS AND FINANCIAL INSTITUTIONS (WG&L)
TAXATION OF FINANCIAL INSTITUTIONS (Bender)

BANKS AND BANKING--WASHINGTON
CORPORATION BUSINESS AND BANKING MID-YEAR (Wash. Bar)

BUILDING LAW--FORMS
HANDBOOK OF ANNOTATED FORMS FOR THE SURVEYING PRACTICE (Wiley Law)

BUILDING LAW--ILLINOIS
CONSTRUCTION LITIGATION (Illinois ICLE)
ILLINOIS STRUCTURAL WORK ACT PRACTICE (Illinois ICLE)

BUILDING LAW--INDIANA
DAMAGES IN CONSTRUCTION LITIGATION (Indiana CLE)

BUILDING LAW--MINNESOTA
THE CONSTRUCTION INSTITUTE (MILE)
CONSTRUCTION INSTITUTE 1991 (MILE)
CONSTRUCTION LITIGATION (MILE)

BUILDING LAW--NEW HAMPSHIRE
CONSTRUCTION LAW (NH Bar)

BUILDING LAW--NEW MEXICO
NEW MEXICO CONSTRUCTION LAW (Butterworth-Texas)

BUILDING LAW--OHIO
BLETZACKER'S OBBC STUDY GUIDE (Banks)
OHIO BASIC BUILDING CODE AND RELATED CODES (Banks)

BUILDING LAW--OREGON
CONSTRUCTION LAW (Oregon Bar)

BUILDING LAW--WASHINGTON
CONSTRUCTION BANKRUPTCY (Wash. Bar)

BUILDING LAW--WISCONSIN
CONSTRUCTION LIEN LAW HANDBOOK (State Bar of Wisc.)

BUSINESS ENTERPRISES
see also Close corporations; Corporation law

ADVISING SMALL BUSINESSES (Clark Boardman Callaghan)
BUSINESS ORGANIZATIONS WITH TAX PLANNING (Bender)
BUSINESS STRATEGIES (CCH)
COMPANY POLICY STATEMENTS (Bus. Laws)
DESIGNING EFFECTIVE COMPANY POLICIES: PLUG LEGAL LOOPHOLES AND PUMP UP PRODUCTIVITY (Alex. Hamilton Inst.)
DOING BUSINESS IN IRELAND (Bender)
FAMILY BUSINESS ORGANIZATION (Shepard's)
LEGAL COMPLIANCE CHECKUPS: BUSINESS CLIENTS (Clark Boardman Callaghan)
ORGANIZING CORPORATE AND OTHER BUSINESS ENTERPRISES (Bender)
REGULATION OF BUSINESS ENTERPRISE IN THE U.S.A. (Oceana)
SMALL BUSINESS TAX CONTROL (Corporate Reports)
SMALL BUSINESS TAX PLANNER (RIA)
START-UP COMPANIES: PLANNING, FINANCING AND OPERATING THE SUCCESSFUL BUSINESS (Law Journal)
STARTING AND OPERATING A BUSINESS IN (STATE SPECIFIC) (Oasis)
TAX PLANNING FOR DISPOSITIONS OF BUSINESS INTERESTS (WG&L)
TAX PLANNING FOR SMALL BUSINESSES (Clark Boardman Callaghan)

BUSINESS ENTERPRISES--AFRICA
LEGAL ASPECTS OF DOING BUSINESS IN AFRICA (Kluwer)

BUSINESS ENTERPRISES--ASIA
LEGAL ASPECTS OF DOING BUSINESS IN ASIA & PACIFIC (Kluwer)

BUSINESS ENTERPRISES--CALIFORNIA
BUSINESS BUY-SELL AGREEMENTS (Calif. CEB)

BUSINESS ENTERPRISES--CANADA
CANADIAN SMALL BUSINESS GUIDE (CCH)
DOING BUSINESS IN CANADA (Bender)

BUSINESS ENTERPRISES--CONNECTICUT
ANNUAL SURVEY OF CONNECTICUT BUSINESS LAW (Conn. Bar)

BUSINESS ENTERPRISES--CZECHOSLOVAKIA
BUSINESS IN CZECHOSLOVAKIA: A PRIMER AND OVERVIEW (Transnational Juris Publications)

BUSINESS ENTERPRISES--EASTERN EUROPE
BUSINESS VENTURES IN EASTERN EUROPE AND THE SOVIET UNION: THE EMERGING LEGAL FRAMEWORK FOR FOREIGN INVESTMENT (Prentice Hall Law & Business)

BUSINESS ENTERPRISES--EUROPE
BUSINESS LAW IN EUROPE (Kluwer)

BUSINESS ENTERPRISES--FLORIDA
BUSINESS LITIGATION IN FLORIDA (Florida Bar)
FLORIDA SMALL BUSINESS PRACTICE (Florida Bar)

BUSINESS ENTERPRISES--HUNGARY
BUSINESS IN HUNGARY: A PRIMER AND OVERVIEW (Transnational Juris Publications)

BUSINESS ENTERPRISES--ILLINOIS
BUYING AND SELLING BUSINESSES (Illinois ICLE)
ORGANIZING AND ADVISING ILLINOIS BUSINESSES (Illinois ICLE)

BUSINESS ENTERPRISES--INDIANA
ADVISING THE SMALL BUSINESS CLIENT (Indiana CLE)

BUSINESS ENTERPRISES--MAINE
CHOICE OF BUSINESS ENTITY AND PURCHASE AND SALE OF A BUSINESS (Maine Bar)

BUSINESS ENTERPRISES--MICHIGAN
MICHIGAN BUSINESS FORMBOOK (ICLE - Michigan)

BUSINESS ENTERPRISES--MINNESOTA
ADVISING SMALL BUSINESS (Minn. CLE)
SALE OF A BUSINESS IN MINNESOTA (Butterworth-St. Paul)

BUSINESS ENTERPRISES--NEW HAMPSHIRE
PURCHASE AND SALE OF A SMALL BUSINESS (NH Bar)

BUSINESS ENTERPRISES--NEW YORK
NEW YORK PRACTICE GUIDE: BUSINESS AND COMMERCIAL (Bender)

BUSINESS ENTERPRISES--OKLAHOMA
OKLAHOMA BUSINESS ORGANIZATIONS: FORMATION AND REPRESENTATION (Aspen)
PURCHASE AND SALE OF A SMALL BUSINESS (Okla. Bar CLE)

BUSINESS ENTERPRISES--OREGON
ADVISING OREGON BUSINESSES (Oregon Bar)

BUSINESS ENTERPRISES--PENNSYLVANIA
BUYING AND SELLING A BUSINESS (Penn. Bar)

BUSINESS ENTERPRISES--POLAND
BUSINESS IN POLAND: A PRIMER AND OVERVIEW (Transnational Juris Publications)

BUSINESS ENTERPRISES--TAXATION
FEDERAL TAXATION OF BUSINESS ENTERPRISES (Clark Boardman Callaghan)

BUSINESS ENTERPRISES--USSR
BUSINESS IN THE SOVIET UNION: A PRIMER AND OVERVIEW (Transnational Juris Publications)

BUSINESS ENTERPRISES--VIRGINIA
ADVISING SMALL BUSINESS CLIENTS, VOL. 2 (Jt. Comm. Va.)
ADVISING SMALL BUSINESS CLIENTS, VOL. 1 (Jt. Comm. Va.)

BUSINESS ENTERPRISES--WASHINGTON
CONFLICTS OF INTEREST IN BUSINESS TRANSACTIONS (Wash. Bar)
TAX CONSIDERATIONS IN SELECTING A BUSINESS ENTITY (Wash. Bar)

BUSINESS ENTERPRISES--YUGOSLAVIA
BUSINESS IN YUGOSLAVIA: A PRIMER AND OVERVIEW (Transnational Juris Publications)

BUSINESS LAW
THE BUSINESS JUDGMENT RULE (Prentice Hall Law & Business)
A GUIDE TO MUNICIPAL OFFICIAL STATEMENTS (Prentice Hall Law & Business)

BUSINESS LAW--CZECHOSLOVAKIA
BUSINESS IN CZECHOSLOVAKIA: A PRIMER AND OVERVIEW (Transnational Juris Publications)

CABLE
see Community antenna television

CARRIERS
see also Transportation; U.S. Interstate Commerce Commission

FEDERAL CARRIERS REPORTS (CCH)
FEDERAL REGULATIONS FOR PRIVATE TRUCK OPERATIONS (NPTC)
FLEET SAFETY COMPLIANCE MANUAL (Keller)
GOODS IN TRANSIT (Bender)
MOTOR CARRIER - FREIGHT FORWARDER SERVICE (Hawkins)
NATIONAL BACKHAUL GUIDE (Keller)
RAIL CARRIER SERVICE (Hawkins)
STATE MOTOR CARRIER GUIDE (CCH)
TRAVEL LAW (Law Journal)
TRUCKING PERMIT GUIDE (Keller)
TRUCKING SAFETY GUIDE (Keller)
VEHICLE SIZES AND WEIGHTS MANUAL (Keller)

CARRIERS--FORMS
INTERSTATE MOTOR CARRIER FORMS MANUAL (Keller)

CARRIERS--TEXAS
RULES AND REGULATIONS OF THE TEXAS RAILROAD COMMISSION (Byram)

CHARITABLE USES
see also Foundations

CHARITABLE GIVING AND SOLICITATION (WG&L)
CHARITABLE LEAD TRUSTS - EXPLANATION, SPECIMEN AGREEMENTS, FORMS (Taxwise)
DEFERRED GIVING - EXPLANATION, SPECIMEN AGREEMENTS, FORMS (Taxwise)
OUTRIGHT CHARITABLE GIFTS - EXPLANATION, SUBSTANTIATING, FORMS (Taxwise)
PLANNED GIVING - STARTING, MARKETING, ADMINISTERING (Taxwise)
SURVEY OF STATE LAWS REGULATING CHARITABLE SOLICITATION (Philanthropy Monthly)

CHEMICALS
see also Hazardous substances

CHEMICAL PROCESS SAFETY REPORT (Thompson)
CHEMICAL REGULATION REPORTER (BNA)
CHEMICAL SUBSTANCES CONTROL (BNA)
THE CONSOLIDATED CHEMICAL REGULATION GUIDEBOOK (Roytech)

CIVIL PROCEDURE--ILLINOIS
ILLINOIS CIVIL DISCOVERY PRACTICE (Illinois ICLE)
ILLINOIS CIVIL PRACTICE (Illinois ICLE)
ILLINOIS CIVIL TRIAL GUIDE (Bender)
ILLINOIS RULES & PRACTICE HANDBOOK, 2ND ED. (Pantagraph)

CIVIL PROCEDURE--INDIANA
INDIANA FORMS OF PLEADING AND PRACTICE (Bender)

CIVIL PROCEDURE--IOWA
IOWA PRACTICE (Lawyers Coop.)

CIVIL PROCEDURE--ITALY
THE ITALIAN CIVIL CODE AND COMPLEMENTARY LEGISLATION (Oceana)

CIVIL PROCEDURE--KENTUCKY
BALDWIN'S KENTUCKY PRACTICE (Banks)
KANSAS CODE OF CIVIL PROCEDURE 2D ANNOTATED (Bancroft)

CIVIL PROCEDURE--MARYLAND
MARYLAND CIVIL PROCEDURE FORMS: PRACTICE (Aspen)

CIVIL PROCEDURE--MASSACHUSETTS
MASSACHUSETTS CIVIL ACTIONS & PROCEDURE (Gould)
MASSACHUSETTS PLEADING AND PRACTICE - FORMS AND COMMENTARY (Bender)
MASSACHUSETTS STANDARDIZED CIVIL PRACTICE FORMS (Little, Brown)

CIVIL PROCEDURE--MICHIGAN
COMPLAINT BOOK (MTLA)
GILMORE ON MICHIGAN CIVIL PROCEDURE BEFORE TRIAL (ICLE - Michigan)
MICHIGAN CIVIL PROCEDURE DURING TRIAL (ICLE - Michigan)

CIVIL PROCEDURE--MICHIGAN-FORMS
MICHIGAN CIVIL PROCEDURE FORMS--PRACTICE (Aspen)

CIVIL PROCEDURE--MINNESOTA
FEDERAL CIVIL LITIGATION (MILE)
PRACTICING IN FEDERAL DISTRICT COURT IN MINNESOTA (Minn. CLE)

CIVIL PROCEDURE--MISSOURI
MISSOURI CIVIL ACTIONS I (MoBar)
MISSOURI CIVIL ACTIONS II (MoBar)
MISSOURI CIVIL PROCEDURE (MoBar)
MISSOURI CIVIL PROCEDURE FORMBOOK (UMKC/CLE)

CIVIL PROCEDURE--MISSOURI-FORMS
MISSOURI CIVIL PROCEDURE FORMS -- PRACTICE (Aspen)

CIVIL PROCEDURE--NEW JERSEY
NEW JERSEY CIVIL PRACTICE AND COURT RULES (Gould)

CIVIL PROCEDURE--NEW MEXICO
NEW MEXICO LOCAL & FEDERAL RULES HANDBOOK (Butterworth-Texas)

CIVIL PROCEDURE--NEW YORK
BENDER'S FORMS FOR THE CIVIL PRACTICE (Bender)
BENDER'S FORMS OF PLEADING (Bender)
NEW YORK CITY LAW DIGEST (Gould)
NEW YORK CIVIL MOTION CITATOR (Nat. Atty.)
NEW YORK CIVIL PRACTICE LAW & RULES HANDBOOK (Gould)
NEW YORK CIVIL PRACTICE - CPLR (vols. 1, 2, 2A, 3 3A, 4, 5, 6, 7, 7A, 8 - Table of cases, Table of statutes & Index) (Bender)
NEW YORK COURTS MANUAL OF PROCEDURE (Gould)
NEW YORK LAW DIGEST (Gould)
WEINSTEIN, KORN AND MILLER CPLR MANUAL (Bender)

CIVIL PROCEDURE--OHIO
ANDERSON'S OHIO CIVIL PRACTICE WITH FORMS (Anderson)
BALDWIN'S OHIO CIVIL PRACTICE (Banks)
OHIO FORMS OF PLEADING AND PRACTICE (Bender)
OHIO MANUAL OF PROCEDURE (Anderson)

CIVIL PROCEDURE--OKLAHOMA-FORMS
OKLAHOMA CIVIL PROCEDURE FORMS - PRACTICE (Aspen)

CIVIL PROCEDURE--OREGON
CIVIL PLEADING AND PRACTICE (Oregon Bar)
JURISDICTION AND SUMMONS IN OREGON (Butterworth-St. Paul)

CIVIL PROCEDURE--PENNSYLVANIA
PHILADELPHIA COURT OF COMMON PLEAS CIVIL PRACTICE MANUAL (Penn. Bar)
VALENTINE-BINNS JUSTICE (Bisel)

CIVIL PROCEDURE--SOUTH CAROLINA
SOUTH CAROLINA CIVIL PROCEDURE (S. Carolina Bar)

CIVIL PROCEDURE--TEXAS
TEXAS CIVIL TRIAL GUIDE (Bender)
TEXAS CIVIL TRIAL HANDBOOK (State Bar of Texas)
TEXAS RULES OF CIVIL PROCEDURE (Butterworth-Texas)
TEXAS SPECIAL ISSUES FORMS (Butterworth-Texas)

CIVIL PROCEDURE--WASHINGTON
PRACTICE IN THE COURTS OF LIMITED JURISDICTION AND SUPERIOR COURT LOCAL RULES PRACTICE (Wash. Bar)
WASHINGTON CIVIL PROCEDURE BEFORE TRIAL DESKBOOK (Wash. Bar)

CIVIL PROCEDURE--WEST VIRGINIA
WEST VIRGINIA PRACTICE HANDBOOK, 3rd ed. (Michie)

CIVIL PROCEDURE--WISCONSIN
WISCONSIN CIVIL PRACTICE FORMS (Lawyers Coop.)
WISCONSIN JUDICIAL BENCHBOOK: VOL. 2 - CIVIL (State Bar of Wisc.)

CIVIL RIGHTS
see also Discrimination

CIVIL RIGHTS ACTIONS (Bender)
GOVERNMENT DISCRIMINATION (Clark Boardman Callaghan)
PEACE LAW DOCKET 1945-1990 (Meiklejohn Civil Liberties Institute)
POLICY GUIDE OF THE AMERICAN CIVIL LIBERTIES UNION (ACLU)
SECTION 1983 LITIGATION (Georgetown)
SECTION 1983 LITIGATION IN STATE COURTS (Clark Boardman Callaghan)
STATE & LOCAL GOVERNMENT CIVIL RIGHTS LIABILITY (Clark Boardman Callaghan)

CIVIL RIGHTS--CALIFORNIA
FAIR EMPLOYMENT & HOUSING COMMISSION PRECEDENTIAL DECISIONS SERVICE (Calif. CEB)

CIVIL SERVICE--MASSACHUSETTS
MASSACHUSETTS CIVIL SERVICE REPORTER (NELP)

CIVIL SERVICE--TEXAS
TEXAS FIRE & POLICE CIVIL SERVICE LAW (Francis Marion)

CLASS ACTIONS
CLASS ACTIONS: LAW & PRACTICE WITH FORMS (Clark Boardman Callaghan)
CLASS ACTIONS: THE LAW OF 50 STATES (Law Journal)

CLASS ACTIONS--ILLINOIS
CLASS ACTIONS (Illinois ICLE)

CLASS ACTIONS--NEW HAMPSHIRE
STOCKHOLDERS LITIGATION (NH Bar)

CLOSE CORPORATIONS
CLOSELY HELD CORPORATIONS: FORMS AND CHECKLISTS (WG&L)
GOING PRIVATE (Law Journal)
O'NEAL CLOSE CORPORATIONS, LAW AND PRACTICE 2ND ED. (Clark Boardman Callaghan)
O'NEAL'S OPPRESSION OF MINORITY SHAREHOLDERS (Clark Boardman Callaghan)
PARTNERSHIP & S CORPORATION COORDINATOR (RIA)
THE S CORPORATION: PLANNING AND OPERATION (Panel)
THE "S" CORPORATION HANDBOOK (Enterprise)
S CORPORATIONS: STATE LAW AND TAXATION (Clark Boardman Callaghan)
S CORPORATIONS (WG&L)
S CORPORATIONS GUIDE (CCH)
TAX PLANNING FOR S CORPORATIONS (Bender)

CLOSE CORPORATIONS--CALIFORNIA
CALIFORNIA CLOSELY HELD CORPORATIONS (Bender)

CLOSE CORPORATIONS--ILLINOIS
CLOSELY HELD CORPORATIONS (Illinois ICLE)
S CORPORATIONS (Illinois ICLE)

CLOSE CORPORATIONS--INDIANA
TAX ASPECTS OF INDIANA S CORPORATIONS (Indiana CLE)

CLOSE CORPORATIONS--MARYLAND
BUSINESS, TAX & ESTATE PLANNING FOR THE CLOSELY-HELD BUSINESS (MICPEL)
PURCHASE AND SALE OF A CLOSELY-HELD BUSINESS (MICPEL)
S CORPORATIONS 1991 (MICPEL)

CLOSE CORPORATIONS--MINNESOTA
CLOSELY HELD CORPORATIONS: BUYING - SELLING - MERGING (MILE)
VALUATION OF A CLOSELY HELD BUSINESS & USE OF FINANCIAL EXPERTS IN LITIGATION (Minn. CLE)

CLOSE CORPORATIONS--NEW YORK
NEW YORK CLOSE CORPORATIONS (Hein)

CLOSE CORPORATIONS--TAXATION
FEDERAL INCOME TAXATION OF S CORPORATIONS (WG&L)
FEDERAL TAXATION OF CLOSE CORPORATIONS (Clark Boardman Callaghan)
FEDERAL TAXATION OF S CORPORATIONS (Law Journal)
FEDERAL TAXATION OF S CORPORATIONS AND SHAREHOLDERS (PLI)
PPC TAX PLANNING GUIDE - CLOSELY HELD CORPORATIONS (Practitioners Publishing)
S CORPORATION TAX GUIDE 1992 (HBJ Miller)
S CORPORATION TAX PRACTICE MANUAL (Panel)
S CORPORATIONS: FEDERAL TAXATION (Clark Boardman Callaghan)
SUBCHAPTER S TAXATION, 3RD ED. (Shepard's)
TAX SERVICE FOR SUBCHAPTER "S" CORPORATIONS AND THEIR SHAREHOLDERS (Stephens)
TAXATION OF THE CLOSELY HELD CORPORATION (WG&L)

COLLECTION LAWS
see also Debtor and creditor

COLLECTION LAWS--CALIFORNIA
CALIFORNIA PRACTICE GUIDE - ENFORCING JUDGMENTS AND DEBTS (Rutter)

COLLECTION LAWS--CONNECTICUT
DEBT COLLECTION (Conn. Bar)

COLLECTION LAWS--HAWAII
HAWAII COLLECTION SOURCEBOOK (Pacific Law Inst.)

COLLECTION LAWS--INDIANA
COLLECTIONS (Indiana CLE)

COLLECTION LAWS--KENTUCKY
KENTUCKY COLLECTIONS (Lawyers Coop.)

COLLECTION LAWS--MASSACHUSETTS
MASSACHUSETTS COLLECTION LAW: DEBTOR/CREDITOR PRACTICE, PROCEDURE, REMEDIES (Lawyers Coop.)
MASSACHUSETTS COLLECTIONS MANUAL, SECOND EDITION (Butterworth-NH)

COLLECTION LAWS--MINNESOTA
MINNESOTA COLLECTIONS (Lawyers Coop.)

COLLECTION LAWS--NEW YORK
NEW YORK COLLECTIONS (Lawyers Coop.)

COLLECTION LAWS--TEXAS
TEXAS COLLECTIONS MANUAL (State Bar of Texas)
TEXAS COMMERCIAL COLLECTIONS (Butterworth-Texas)

COLLECTION LAWS--VIRGINIA
ENFORCEMENT OF LIENS AND JUDGMENTS (Jt. Comm. Va.)

COLLECTION LAWS--WASHINGTON
GETTING PAID: EFFECTIVELY USING STATUTORY LIEN AND BOND RIGHTS (Wash. Bar)

COLLECTIVE BARGAINING
see also Labor and labor relations

COLLECTIVE BARGAINING NEGOTIATIONS AND CONTRACTS (BNA)

COLLECTIVE BARGAINING--WASHINGTON
WASHINGTON PUBLIC EMPLOYMENT RELATIONS REPORTER (Book Pub.)

COLLEGES
see Universities and colleges

COMMERCIAL CRIMES
see also Fraud

BANKING CRIMES (Clark Boardman Callaghan)
BUSINESS CRIME (Bender)
CORPORATE CRIMINAL LIABILITY (Clark Boardman Callaghan)
WHITE COLLAR CRIME (NH Bar)

COMMERCIAL LAW
ADMINISTRATIVE INTERPRETATIONS OF THE UNIFORM CONSUMER CREDIT CODE (Butterworth-NH)
BUSINESS LAW MONOGRAPHS (Bender)
COMMERCIAL AND CONSUMER WARRANTIES (Bender)
COMMERCIAL FINANCE GUIDE (Bender)
COMMERCIAL LAW AND PRACTICE GUIDE (Bender)
COMMERCIAL LAW ANNUAL (Clark Boardman Callaghan)
COMMERCIAL LOAN DOCUMENTATION GUIDE (Bender)
COMMERCIAL PAPER AND PAYMENT SYSTEMS (Butterworth-NH)
COMMERCIAL PAPER UNDER THE UNIFORM COMMERCIAL CODE (Bender Uniform Commercial Code Service, vol. 2 series) (Bender)
COMPENDIUM OF COMMERCIAL FINANCE LAW (NCFA)
CORPORATE COUNSEL'S GUIDE TO DISTRIBUTION COUNSELING (Bus. Laws)
COUNTRY HANDBOOKS (Kluwer)
DAMAGES UNDER THE UNIFORM COMMERCIAL CODE (Clark Boardman Callaghan)
DOING BUSINESS IN THE UNITED STATES (Bender)
FEDERAL BUSINESS LAWS (Bus. Laws)
FOREIGN STATE IMMUNITY IN COMMERCIAL TRANSACTIONS (Butterworth-NH)
FORMS AND PROCEDURES UNDER THE UNIFORM COMMERCIAL CODE (Bender's Uniform Commercial Code service vols. 5, 5A, 5B, 5C, 5D) (Bender)

GUIDE TO COMMERCIAL LENDING LAW (Sheshunoff)
GUIDE TO PRACTICAL APPLICATIONS OF THE UN CONVENTION ON CONTRACTS FOR THE INTERNATIONAL SALE OF GOODS (Kluwer)
GUIDE TO THE INTERNATIONAL SALES OF GOODS CONVENTION (Bus. Laws)
INTERNATIONAL BUSINESS TRANSACTIONS (Kluwer)
THE LAW AND PRACTICE OF SECURED TRANSACTIONS: WORKING WITH ARTICLE 9 (Law Journal)
THE LAW OF PURCHASING (Bus. Laws)
LEGAL ASPECTS OF DOING BUSINESS IN NORTH AMERICA (Kluwer)
A PRACTICAL GUIDE TO BUYING AND SELLING AUTOMOBILE DEALERSHIPS (Natl. Legal Publishing)
PURCHASER'S FORMBOOK OF CONTRACTS AND AGREEMENTS (Bus. Laws)
SALES AND BULK TRANSFERS UNDER THE UNIFORM COMMERCIAL CODE (Bender's Uniform Commercial Code Service, Vols. 3 & 3A) (Bender)
SECURED TRANSACTIONS GUIDE (CCH)
SECURED TRANSACTIONS UNDER THE UNIFORM COMMERCIAL CODE (Bender's Uniform Commerical Code Service, Vols. 1, 1A, 1B & 1C) (Bender)
STRUCTURING COMMERCIAL LOAN AGREEMENTS (WG&L)
U.C.C. STATE VARIATIONS (Gould)
UNIFORM COMMERCIAL CODE TRANSACTION GUIDE: ANALYSIS AND FORMS (Clark Boardman Callaghan)
UNIFORM COMMERCIAL CODE -- CODE SERVICE (Clark Boardman Callaghan)
UNIFORM COMMERCIAL CODE CASE DIGEST -- NORTHEAST REGION (Clark Boardman Callaghan)
THE UNIFORM COMMERCIAL CODE FILING GUIDE (Prentice Hall Legal & Financial Services)
UNIFORM COMMERCIAL CODE REPORTER - DIGEST (Bender's Uniform Commercial Code Service Vols. 6 - 6G) (Bender)
UNIFORM COMMERCIAL CODE REPORTING SERVICE (Clark Boardman Callaghan)
UNIFORM COMMERCIAL CODE SERIES (Clark Boardman Callaghan)
UNIFORM COMMERCIAL CODE SERIES--SECURED TRANSACTIONS (Clark Boardman Callaghan)

<u>COMMERCIAL LAW--AFRICA</u>
LEGAL ASPECTS OF DOING BUSINESS IN AFRICA (Kluwer)

<u>COMMERCIAL LAW--ASIA</u>
LEGAL ASPECTS OF DOING BUSINESS IN ASIA & PACIFIC (Kluwer)

<u>COMMERCIAL LAW--BRAZIL</u>
DOING BUSINESS IN BRAZIL (Bender & Oyez)

<u>COMMERCIAL LAW--CANADA</u>
CANADIAN COMMERCIAL LAW GUIDE (CCH)
DOING BUSINESS IN CANADA (Bender)

<u>COMMERCIAL LAW--CHINA</u>
CHINESE FOREIGN ECONOMIC LAW (Intl. Law Inst.)
DOING BUSINESS IN CHINA (Bender)

<u>COMMERCIAL LAW--EASTERN EUROPE</u>
DOING BUSINESS WITH EASTERN EUROPE (Bus. Intern.)

<u>COMMERCIAL LAW--EUROPE</u>
DOING BUSINESS IN EUROPE (CCH)
LEGAL ASPECTS OF DOING BUSINESS IN EUROPE (Kluwer)

<u>COMMERCIAL LAW--FLORIDA</u>
FLORIDA CONSUMER LAW MANUAL (Butterworth-Fla.)
FLORIDA LAW OF SECURED TRANSACTIONS IN PERSONAL PROPERTY (Butterworth-Fla.)

<u>COMMERCIAL LAW--FOREIGN</u>
COMMERCIAL BUSINESS & TRADE LAWS OF THE WORLD (Oceana)
COMMERCIAL LAWS OF THE WORLD (Foreign Tax)
DIGEST OF COMMERCIAL LAWS OF THE WORLD -- (INCLUDING FORMS OF COMMERCIAL AGREEMENTS AND STATE VARIATIONS OF COMMERCIAL LAW) (Oceana)

COMMERCIAL LAW--FORMS
BENDER'S MODERN UCC LITIGATION FORMS (Bender's Uniform Commercial Code Service vols. 4 & 4A) (Bender)
DIGEST OF COMMERCIAL LAWS OF THE WORLD -- FORMS OF COMMERCIAL AGREEMENTS OF THE WORLD (Oceana)
FORMS OF BUSINESS AGREEMENTS, VOL. 3 (Commercial Transactions) (WG&L)
QUINN'S UCC FORMS & PRACTICE (WG&L)

COMMERCIAL LAW--FRANCE
DOING BUSINESS IN FRANCE (Bender)

COMMERCIAL LAW--GEORGIA
GEORGIA COMMERCIAL FINANCING FORMS (Aspen)

COMMERCIAL LAW--GERMANY
BUSINESS TRANSACTIONS IN GERMANY (FRG) (Bender)

COMMERCIAL LAW--HUNGARY
BUSINESS IN HUNGARY: A PRIMER AND OVERVIEW (Transnational Juris Publications)

COMMERCIAL LAW--ILLINOIS
BUSINESS AND COMMERCIAL LITIGATION (Illinois ICLE)
ILLINOIS COMMERCIAL FINANCING (Aspen)

COMMERCIAL LAW--INDIANA
CONSUMER LAW (Indiana CLE)

COMMERCIAL LAW--IRELAND
DOING BUSINESS IN IRELAND (Bender)

COMMERCIAL LAW--JAPAN
DOING BUSINESS IN JAPAN (Bender)

COMMERCIAL LAW--KANSAS
KANSAS LAW OF SALES UNDER THE UNIFORM COMMERCIAL CODE (Kansas Bar)

COMMERCIAL LAW--KENTUCKY
KENTUCKY FINANCIAL INSTITUTION AND SECURITIES LAW (Banks)

COMMERCIAL LAW--MEXICO
DOING BUSINESS IN MEXICO (Bender)

COMMERCIAL LAW--MIDDLE EAST
COMMERCIAL, BUSINESS AND TRADE LAWS AND COMMERCIAL LAWS OF THE MIDDLE EAST (COMPLETE SERVICE) (Oceana)
COMMERCIAL LAWS OF THE MIDDLE EAST (Oceana)

COMMERCIAL LAW--MINNESOTA
COMMERCIAL PRACTICE INSTITUTE (MILE)

COMMERCIAL LAW--NETHERLANDS
DUTCH BUSINESS LAW (Kluwer)

COMMERCIAL LAW--NEW HAMPSHIRE
UNIFORM COMMERCIAL CODE: SELECTED ISSUES (NH Bar)

COMMERCIAL LAW--NEW JERSEY
NEW JERSEY TRANSACTION GUIDE (Bender)
SECURED TRANSACTIONS UNDER THE REVISED UNIFORM COMMERCIAL CODE (New Jersey ICLE)

COMMERCIAL LAW--NEW YORK
NEW YORK PRACTICE GUIDE: BUSINESS AND COMMERCIAL (Bender)

COMMERCIAL LAW--OHIO
BASICS OF BUSINESS LAW (Ohio CLE)

COMMERCIAL LAW--POLAND

BUSINESS IN POLAND: A PRIMER AND OVERVIEW (Transnational Juris Publications)

COMMERCIAL LAW--SOUTH CAROLINA

SOUTH CAROLINA CONSUMER LAW AND PRACTICE - Vol. I - SOUTH CAROLINA CONSUMER LAW AND REGULATIONS (S. Carolina Bar)

COMMERCIAL LAW--SPAIN

DOING BUSINESS IN SPAIN (Bender)

COMMERCIAL LAW--STATES

DIGEST OF COMMERCIAL LAWS OF THE WORLD -- STATE VARIATIONS OF COMMERCIAL LAW (Oceana)

COMMERCIAL LAW--TEXAS

THE LAWYER'S GUIDE TO THE TEXAS DECEPTIVE TRADE PRACTICES ACT (Butterworth-Texas)
TEXAS COMMERCIAL COLLECTIONS (Butterworth-Texas)

COMMERCIAL LAW--UNITED KINDGOM

DOING BUSINESS IN THE UNITED KINGDOM (Bender)

COMMERCIAL LAW--USSR

BUSINESS IN THE SOVIET UNION: A PRIMER AND OVERVIEW (Transnational Juris Publications)
SOVIET BUSINESS LAW: INSTITUTIONS, PRINCIPLES AND PROCESSES (Butterworth-NH)

COMMERCIAL LAW--WASHINGTON

WASHINGTON COMMERCIAL LAW DESKBOOK (Wash. Bar)

COMMERCIAL LAW--YUGOSLAVIA

BUSINESS IN YUGOSLAVIA: A PRIMER AND OVERVIEW (Transnational Juris Publications)

COMMODITIES

CFTC ADMINISTRATIVE REPORTER (WSB)
COMMODITIES REGULATION: FRAUD, MANIPULATION & OTHER CLAIMS (Clark Boardman Callaghan)
COMMODITY FUTURES LAW REPORTS (CCH)
REGULATION OF THE COMMODITIES FUTURES AND OPTIONS MARKETS (Shepard's)
SECURITIES FRAUD AND COMMODITIES FRAUD (Shepard's)

COMMODITIES--INTERNATIONAL

LAW AND POLICY OF INTERGOVERNMENTAL PRIMARY COMMODITY AGREEMENTS (Oceana)

COMMODITY EXCHANGES

COFFEE, SUGAR AND COCOA EXCHANGE INC. GUIDE (CCH)
COMEX BY-LAWS, RULES AND REGULATIONS (COMEX)
MIDAMERICA COMMODITY EXCHANGE RULES AND REGULATIONS (MidAmerica)
NEW YORK MERCANTILE EXCHANGE GUIDE (CCH)
RULES AND REGULATIONS OF THE CHICAGO BOARD OF TRADE (Chicago Bd.)
RULES AND REGULATIONS OF THE CHICAGO MERCANTILE EXCHANGE (CME)
RULES AND REGULATIONS OF THE MINNEAPOLIS GRAIN EXCHANGE (Minneap.)

COMMON MARKET

see European Community

COMMUNITY ANTENNA TELEVISION

see also Telecommunications; U.S. Federal Communications Commission

ALL ABOUT CABLE (Law Journal)
CABLE TELEVISION: HANDBOOK AND FORMS (Shepard's)
CABLE TELEVISION AND OTHER NONBROADCAST VIDEO (Clark Boardman Callaghan)
CABLE TELEVISION LAW: A VIDEO COMMUNICATIONS PRACTICE GUIDE (Bender)
CABLE TV RULES SERVICE (P&F)

COMMUNITY PROPERTY
see also Marriage and divorce

COMMUNITY PROPERTY--CALIFORNIA
CALIFORNIA COMMUNITY PROPERTY WITH TAX ANALYSIS (Bender)

COMMUNITY PROPERTY--WASHINGTON
WASHINGTON COMMUNITY PROPERTY DESKBOOK (Wash. Bar)

COMPETITION, UNFAIR
see also Trade regulation; Trade secrets; Trademarks

CALLMANN UNFAIR COMPETITION, TRADEMARKS AND MONOPOLIES, 4TH ED. (Clark Boardman Callaghan)
CORPORATE COUNSEL'S GUIDE TO UNFAIR COMPETITION (Bus. Laws)
FEDERAL UNFAIR COMPETITION: LANHAM ACT 43(a) (Clark Boardman Callaghan)
UNITED STATES, COMMON MARKET AND INTERNATIONAL ANTITRUST: A COMPARATIVE GUIDE (Prentice Hall Law & Business)

COMPUTERS
THE AUTOMATED LAW FIRM: A COMPLETE GUIDE TO SOFTWARE AND SYSTEMS (Prentice Hall Law & Business)
BECOMING EXPERT WITH WORDPERFECT IN YOUR LAW OFFICE (Indiana CLE)
BERNACCHI ON COMPUTER LAW - A GUIDE TO THE LEGAL AND MANAGEMENT ASPECTS OF COMPUTER TECHNOLOGY (Little, Brown)
COMPUTER CONTRACTS (Bender)
COMPUTER CRIME LAW REPORTER (NCCCD)
COMPUTER FUNDAMENTALS FOR LEGAL PROFESSIONALS (Pearson)
COMPUTER LAW: EVIDENCE AND PROCEDURE (Bender)
COMPUTER LAW - DRAFTING AND NEGOTIATING FORMS AND AGREEMENTS (Law Journal)
COMPUTER LAW INSTITUTE (Wash. Bar)
COMPUTER SOFTWARE: PROTECTION, LIABILITY, LAW, FORMS (Clark Boardman Callaghan)
COMPUTER SOFTWARE AGREEMENTS: FORMS AND COMMENTARY (WG&L)
COMPUTER SOFTWARE PROTECTION LAW (BNA Books)
COMPUTERS AND THE TRIAL LAWYER (ATLA)
DATA PROCESSING AGREEMENTS (2nd ed.) (Bus. Laws)
GUIDE TO COMPUTER LAW (CCH)
INTERNATIONAL COMPUTER LAW (Bender)
THE LAW AND BUSINESS OF COMPUTER SOFTWARE (Clark Boardman Callaghan)
LAW OFFICE GUIDE TO COMPUTER ABBREVIATIONS & ACRONYMS (Lexikon)
LAWYER'S GUIDE TO COMPUTER SECURITY: SOURCEBOOK (Lexikon)
LEGALITY OF OPTICAL STORAGE (Cohasset)
MODERN VISUAL EVIDENCE (Law Journal)
PREVENTION AND PROSECUTION OF COMPUTER AND HIGH TECHNOLOGY CRIME (Bender)
SCOTT ON COMPUTER LAW (Prentice Hall Law & Business)
SEMICONDUCTOR CHIP PROTECTION (Prentice Hall Law & Business)
THE SOFTWARE LEGAL BOOK (Shafer)
A USER'S GUIDE TO COMPUTER CONTRACTING: FORMS, TECHNIQUES AND STRATEGIES (Prentice Hall Law & Business)
WORDPERFECT FOR LAWYERS (Version 5.1) (Adams-Hall)

CONDEMNATION
see Eminent domain

CONDOMINIUMS
see also Cooperative housing; Timesharing

CONDOMINUM DEVELOPMENT: FORMS WITH COMMENTARY (Clark Boardman Callaghan)
CONDOMINIUM LAW AND PRACTICE - FORMS (Real Estate Transaction Series, vols. 1, 1 pt. 2 & 3, 1A, 1B, 1C) (Bender)
THE LAW OF CONDOMINIUM OPERATIONS (Clark Boardman Callaghan)

CONDOMINIUMS--CONNECTICUT
CONDOMINIUMS AND COMMUNITY ASSOCIATIONS IN THE 1990'S: HOW TO REPRESENT THEM AND THOSE WHO DEAL WITH THEM (Conn. Bar)

CONDOMINIUMS--FLORIDA
FLORIDA CONDOMINIUM LAW AND PRACTICE (Florida Bar)
FLORIDA CONDOMINIUM LAW MANUAL (Butterworth-Fla.)
MANAGING THE FLORIDA CONDOMINIUM (Butterworth-Fla.)

CONDOMINIUMS--GEORGIA
GEORGIA CONDOMINIUM LAW MANUAL (Butterworth-Fla.)

CONDOMINIUMS--ILLINOIS
ILLINOIS CONDOMINIUM LAW (Illinois ICLE)

CONDOMINIUMS--MARYLAND-FORMS
MARYLAND CONDOMINUM, HOMEOWNER ASSOCIATION, COOPERATIVE AND TIME-SHARING FORMS--PRACTICE (Aspen)

CONDOMINIUMS--MASSACHUSETTS
MASSACHUSETTS CONDOMINIUM LAW (Butterworth-NH)
MASSACHUSETTS CONDOMINIUM LAW (Mass. CLE)

CONDOMINIUMS--NEW HAMPSHIRE
NEW HAMPSHIRE CONSTITUTIONAL LAW (NH Bar)

CONDOMINIUMS--NEW JERSEY-FORMS
FORMS FOR HANDLING CONDOMINUM AND COOPERATIVE CONVERSIONS (New Jersey ICLE)

CONDOMINIUMS--PENNSYLVANIA
PENNSYLVANIA CONDOMINIUM LAW AND PRACTICE (Bisel)

CONDOMINIUMS--TEXAS
TEXAS CONDOMINIUM LAW MANUAL (Butterworth-Texas)

CONDOMINIUMS--VIRGINIA
VIRGINIA CONDOMINIUM LAW (Butterworth-Fla.)

CONFESSION OF JUDGMENT--PENNSYLVANIA
PENNSYLVANIA CONFESSION OF JUDGMENT (Bisel)

CONFIDENTIAL COMMUNICATIONS
FEDERAL TESTIMONIAL PRIVILEGES (Clark Boardman Callaghan)

CONFLICT OF LAWS
see also Antitrust law

PUBLIC POLICY IN TRANSNATIONAL RELATIONS (Kluwer)
TRANSNATIONAL CONTRACTS: APPLICABLE LAW AND SETTLEMENT OF DISPUTES -- A STUDY IN CONFLICT AVOIDANCE LAW AND PRACTICE (Oceana)

CONSENT DECREES
ANTITRUST CONSENT DECREE MANUAL (ABA)

CONSOLIDATION AND MERGER OF CORPORATIONS
ACQUISITIONS AND MERGERS: NEGOTIATED AND CONTESTED TRANSACTIONS (Securities Law Series Vol. II) (Clark Boardman Callaghan)
ACQUISITIONS UNDER THE HART-SCOTT-RODINO ANTITRUST IMPROVEMENTS ACT (Law Journal)
CORPORATE ACQUISITIONS AND MERGERS (Business Organizations vols. 13, 13A & 13B) (Bender)
CORPORATE ACQUISITIONS, MERGERS AND DIVESTITURES (WG&L)
CORPORATE PRACTICE SERIES (BNA)
EEC MERGER CONTROL REPORTER (Kluwer)
GUIDE TO ACQUISITIONS AND DIVESTITURES (Bus. Laws)
SHARK REPELLENTS AND GOLDEN PARACHUTES: A HANDBOOK FOR THE PRACTITIONER (Prentice Hall Law & Business)
STATE TAKEOVER LAWS (IRRC)
TAKEOVER DEFENSE (Prentice Hall Law & Business)
TAKEOVERS AND FREEZEOUTS (Law Journal)

CONSOLIDATION AND MERGER OF CORPORATIONS--TAXATION
TAX ASPECTS OF BUYING AND SELLING CORPORATE BUSINESSES (Shepard's)
TAX SERVICE FOR CORPORATE ACQUISITIONS AND DISPOSITIONS OF BUSINESSES (Stephens)

CONSTITUTIONAL LAW
CRIMINAL CONSTITUTIONAL LAW (Bender)

CONSTITUTIONAL LAW--CONNECTICUT
NUTS & BOLTS OF RAISING STATE CONSTITUTIONAL ISSUES (Conn. Bar)

CONSTITUTIONS
CONSTITUTIONS OF AMERICAN DENOMINATIONS (Hein)
CONSTITUTIONS OF CANADA: FEDERAL AND PROVINCIAL (English/French) (Oceana)
CONSTITUTIONS OF DEPENDENCIES AND SPECIAL SOVEREIGNTIES (Oceana)
CONSTITUTIONS OF THE COUNTRIES OF THE WORLD: A SERIES OF UPDATED TEXTS, CONSTITUTIONAL CHRONOLOGIES AND ANNOTATED BIBLIOGRAPHIES (Oceana)
CONSTITUTIONS OF THE UNITED STATES: NATIONAL AND STATE, 2nd ed. (Oceana)

CONSTRUCTION LAW
see Building law

CONSUMER FINANCE
see also Interest and usury; Credit unions

COMPENDIUM OF COMMERCIAL FINANCE LAW (NCFA)
COMPLIANCE EXAMINATIONS UPDATE FOR FINANCIAL INSTITUTIONS (WG&L)
CONSUMER AND COMMUNITY AFFAIRS HANDBOOK (Fed.)
CONSUMER CREDIT (Bender)
CONSUMER CREDIT GUIDE (CCH)
CONSUMER CREDIT REGULATIONS (Wiley Law)
THE COST OF PERSONAL BORROWING IN THE UNITED STATES (Finan. Pub.)
FAIR HOUSING - FAIR LENDING (Prentice Hall Law & Business)
FEDERAL CONSUMER CREDIT LAWS & REGULATIONS (NILS)
GUIDE TO CONSUMER LENDING LAW (Sheshunoff)
REGULATION Z: TRUTH-IN-LENDING COMPREHENSIVE COMPLIANCE MANUAL (Am. Bankers)
TRUTH IN LENDING: A COMPREHENSIVE GUIDE (Prentice Hall Law & Business)
TRUTH IN LENDING FOR THE COMMUNITY BANK: A PRACTICAL APPROACH TO REGULATION Z (Probus)

CONSUMER FINANCE--CALIFORNIA
CALIFORNIA CONSUMER CREDIT LAW & REGULATIONS (NILS)

CONSUMER FINANCE--FORMS
SIMPLIFIED CONSUMER CREDIT FORMS (WG&L)

CONSUMER FINANCE--OKLAHOMA
PRACTITIONER'S GUIDE TO THE OKLAHOMA UNIFORM CONSUMER CREDIT CODE (Butterworth-St. Paul)

CONSUMER FINANCE--SOUTH CAROLINA
SOUTH CAROLINA CONSUMER LAW AND PRACTICE - Vol. II - TRUTH IN LENDING AND RELATED DISCLOSURE STATUTES (S. Carolina Bar)

CONSUMER PROTECTION
CONSUMER PROTECTION AND THE LAW (Clark Boardman Callaghan)
FEDERAL CONSUMER PROTECTION: LAWS, RULES AND REGULATIONS (Oceana)
FEDERAL RESERVE SYSTEM COMPLIANCE HANDBOOK (Fed.)

CONSUMER PROTECTION--CONNECTICUT
THE CONNECTICUT UNFAIR TRADE PRACTICES ACT (Conn. Bar)

CONSUMER PROTECTION--MASSACHUSETTS
CHAPTER 93A RIGHTS AND REMEDIES (Mass. CLE)

CONSUMER PROTECTION--MISSOURI
MISSOURI CONSUMER LAW AND PRACTICE (MoBar)

CONSUMER PROTECTION--SOUTH CAROLINA
SOUTH CAROLINA CONSUMER PROTECTION CODE - 1982 TEXT AND COMMENTS -- 2nd Ed. (S. Carolina Bar)

CONSUMER PROTECTION--WASHINGTON
CONSUMER PROTECTION, ANTITRUST & UNFAIR BUSINESS PRACTICES (Wash. Bar)

CONTRACTS
COMPUTER CONTRACTS (Bender)
COMPUTER SOFTWARE AGREEMENTS: FORMS AND COMMENTARY (WG&L)
CONTRACT CHECKLISTS (Kluwer)
CORPORATE COUNSEL'S GUIDE TO CONSULTING AGREEMENTS (Bus. Laws)
CORPORATE COUNSEL'S GUIDE TO EMPLOYMENT CONTRACTS (Bus. Laws)
DRAFTING EFFECTIVE CONTRACTS (Prentice Hall Law & Business)
DRAFTING THE UNION CONTRACT (Bender)
ENTERTAINMENT INDUSTRY CONTRACTS: NEGOTIATIONS & DRAFTING GUIDE (Bender)
EXECUTIVE AND PROFESSIONAL EMPLOYMENT CONTRACTS (Butterworth-NH)
GUIDE TO PRACTICAL APPLICATIONS OF THE UN CONVENTION ON CONTRACTS FOR THE INTERNATIONAL SALE OF GOODS (Kluwer)
HOSPITAL CONTRACTS MANUAL (Aspen)
INTERNATIONAL HANDBOOK ON CONTRACTS OF EMPLOYMENT (Kluwer)
LINDEY ON ENTERTAINMENT, PUBLISHING AND THE ARTS, 2ND ED. (Clark Boardman Callaghan)
MODERN LAW OF EMPLOYMENT RELATIONSHIPS (Prentice Hall Law & Business)
NATURAL GAS CONTRACTS (Thompson)
RECORD AND MUSIC PUBLISHING FORMS OF AGREEMENT IN CURRENT USE (Law-Arts)
WARREN'S FORMS OF AGREEMENTS - BUSINESS FORMS: DESK EDITION (Bender)
WRITE YOUR OWN BUSINESSS CONTRACTS: WHAT YOUR ATTORNEY WON'T TELL YOU (Oasis)

CONTRACTS--ILLINOIS
CONTRACTS AND SALES OF GOODS (Illinois ICLE)

CONTRACTS--INDIANA
CONTRACT LAW (Indiana CLE)

CONTRACTS--MINNESOTA
CONTRACTS FOR DEED: USE AND REMEDIES (Minn. CLE)

CONTRACTS--OREGON
CONTRACT LAW IN OREGON (Oregon Bar)

CONVEYANCING
see Real property

COOPERATIVE HOUSING
see also Condominiums; Timesharing

COOPERATIVE HOUSING LAW AND PRACTICE FORMS (Real Estate Transactions Series, vols. 2, 2A, 2B) (Bender)

COOPERATIVE HOUSING--MARYLAND-FORMS
MARYLAND CONDOMINUM, HOMEOWNER ASSOCIATION, COOPERATIVE AND TIME-SHARING FORMS--PRACTICE (Aspen)

COOPERATIVE HOUSING--NEW JERSEY-FORMS
FORMS FOR HANDLING CONDOMINUM AND COOPERATIVE CONVERSIONS (New Jersey ICLE)

COPYRIGHT
see also Intellectual property; Patents; Trademarks

BNA'S PATENT, TRADEMARK & COPYRIGHT JOURNAL (BNA)
COMPUTER SOFTWARE PROTECTION LAW (BNA Books)
COPYRIGHT LAW REPORTS (CCH)

COPYRIGHT LAWS AND TREATIES OF THE WORLD (BNA Books)
COPYRIGHT REGISTRATION PRACTICE (Clark Boardman Callaghan)
INTELLECTUAL PROPERTY AND COPYRIGHT LAW (MICPEL)
INTERNATIONAL COMPUTER LAW (Bender)
INTERNATIONAL COPYRIGHT LAW AND PRACTICE (Bender)
THE LAW OF COPYRIGHT (Clark Boardman Callaghan)
LINDEY ON ENTERTAINMENT, PUBLISHING AND THE ARTS, 2ND ED. (Clark Boardman Callaghan)
NIMMER ON COPYRIGHT (Bender)
PATENT, TRADEMARK, AND COPYRIGHT REGULATIONS (BNA Books)
PERFORMING ARTS MANAGEMENT AND THE LAW (Law-Arts)
RECORD AND MUSIC PUBLISHING FORMS OF AGREEMENT IN CURRENT USE (Law-Arts)
SEMICONDUCTOR CHIP PROTECTION (Prentice Hall Law & Business)

CORPORATION LAW

see also Close corporations; Consolidation and merger of corporations; Professional corporations

BUSINESS ORGANIZATIONS WITH TAX PLANNING (Bender)
CHECKLISTS OF FEDERAL AND STATE STATUTES ON INTERLOCKING DIRECTORSHIPS (ASCS)
CORPORATE COUNSEL'S MANAGERIAL GUIDE (Bus. Laws)
THE CORPORATE COUNSELLOR'S DESKBOOK (Prentice Hall Law & Business)
CORPORATE CRIMINAL LIABILITY (Clark Boardman Callaghan)
CORPORATE PACKAGE & MINUTE BOOK (CA, FL, TX) (Oasis)
CORPORATE PRACTICE SERIES (BNA)
CORPORATE SECRETARY'S GUIDE (CCH (in coop. with Am. Society of Corp. Secretaries))
DIRECTOR & OFFICER LIABILITY: INSURANCE & INDEMNIFICATION (Bus. Laws)
DIRECTOR'S PORTFOLIO (Enterprise)
FEDERAL INCOME TAXATION OF CORPORATE LIQUIDATIONS (Shepard's)
FLETCHER CORPORATE PRACTICE DESKBOOK (Clark Boardman Callaghan)
GOING PUBLIC AND THE PUBLIC CORPORATION (Securities Law Series vols. 1 & 1A) (Clark Boardman Callaghan)
HANDLING GOVERNMENT INVESTIGATIONS (Bus. Laws)
THE LAW OF CORPORATE OFFICERS AND DIRECTORS: INDEMNIFICATION AND INSURANCE (Clark Boardman Callaghan)
LAW OF CORPORATE OFFICERS AND DIRECTORS: RIGHTS, DUTIES, AND LIABILITIES (Clark Boardman Callaghan)
LAWYER'S BASIC CORPORATE PRACTICE MANUAL (ALI-ABA)
THE LEGAL AUDIT: CORPORATE INTERNAL INVESTIGATION (Clark Boardman Callaghan)
LEGAL COMPLIANCE CHECKUPS: BUSINESS CLIENTS (Clark Boardman Callaghan)
LEGAL OPINIONS IN BUSINESS TRANSACTIONS (Conn. Bar)
MATERIALS ON CORPORATE POLITICAL ACTIVITY (Bus. Laws)
MATERIALS ON MINIMIZING MANAGEMENT LIABILITY (Bus. Laws)
MODEL BUSINESS CORPORATION ACT ANNOTATED (Prentice Hall Law & Business)
MODERN CORPORATION CHECKLISTS (WG&L)
O'NEAL'S OPPRESSION OF MINORITY SHAREHOLDERS (Clark Boardman Callaghan)
ORGANIZING CORPORATE AND OTHER BUSINESS ENTERPRISES (Bender)
PIERCING THE CORPORATE VEIL (Clark Boardman Callaghan)
THE REGULATION OF CORPORATE DISCLOSURE (Prentice Hall Law & Business)
SECTION 16 TREATISE AND SERVICE (Exec. Press)
SECURITIES AND FEDERAL CORPORATE LAW (Securities Law Series, Vols. 3, 3A, 3B & 3C) (Clark Boardman Callaghan)
SHAREHOLDER DERIVATIVE ACTIONS (Clark Boardman Callaghan)
SHAREHOLDER LITIGATION (Clark Boardman Callaghan)
TAX PLANNING FOR DISPOSITIONS OF BUSINESS INTERESTS (WG&L)
U.S. CORPORATE HANDBOOK (Mariposa)

CORPORATION LAW--CONNECTICUT

BASIC CORPORATE PRACTICE (Conn. Bar)

CORPORATION LAW--MINNESOTA

DIRECTOR & OFFICER INSURANCE COVERAGE (MILE)

CORPORATIONS
MEETINGS OF STOCKHOLDERS (Prentice Hall Law & Business)

CORPORATIONS--ACCOUNTING
see Financial statements

CORPORATIONS--ALABAMA
ALABAMA BUSINESS CORPORATION LAW (ABICLE)

CORPORATIONS--ARKANSAS
ARKANSAS CORPORATION SYSTEM (Arkansas Bar)

CORPORATIONS--BRITISH COLUMBIA
BRITISH COLUMBIA CORPORATIONS LAW GUIDE (CCH)

CORPORATIONS--CALIFORNIA
BALLANTINE AND STERLING CALIFORNIA CORPORATION LAWS (Bender & Parker)
CALIFORNIA COMMISSION OF CORPORATIONS OFFICIAL OPINIONS (Calif. CEB)
CALIFORNIA CORPORATE PRACTICE GUIDE 2D (Lawpress)
CALIFORNIA PRACTICE GUIDE - CORPORATIONS (Rutter)
MARSH'S CALIFORNIA CORPORATION LAW (Prentice Hall Law & Business)
ORGANIZING CORPORATIONS IN CALIFORNIA, 2nd ed. (Calif. CEB)

CORPORATIONS--CANADA
CANADA CORPORATE SECRETARY'S GUIDE (CCH)
CANADA CORPORATIONS LAW REPORTS (CCH)

CORPORATIONS--CHINA
CHINA LAWS FOR FOREIGN BUSINESS (CCH)

CORPORATIONS--COLORADO
COLORADO CORPORATE FORMS (Lawyers Coop.)
COLORADO CORPORATE FORMS - PRACTICE (Aspen)
CORPORATIONS MANUAL - COLORADO (CLE - Colorado)

CORPORATIONS--CONNECTICUT
BASIC CORPORATE PRACTICE (Conn. Bar)

CORPORATIONS--DELAWARE
DELAWARE CORPORATION LAW & PRACTICE (Bender)
THE DELAWARE LAW OF CORPORATIONS AND BUSINESS ORGANIZATIONS (Prentice Hall Law & Business)
FOLK ON THE DELAWARE GENERAL CORPORATION LAW: A COMMENTARY AND ANALYSIS, 2nd ed. (Little, Brown)

CORPORATIONS--FINANCE
see Venture capital

CORPORATIONS--FLORIDA
FLORIDA CORPORATE PRACTICE (Florida Bar)
FLORIDA CORPORATIONS (Lawyers Coop.)
FLORIDA CORPORATIONS -- LAWS AND PRACTICE (Bender)
FLORIDA CORPORATIONS MANUAL (Butterworth-Fla.)

CORPORATIONS--FORMS
THE COMPLETE BOOK OF CORPORATE FORMS (Enterprise)
CORPORATION FORMS (WG&L)
PROXY STATEMENTS: STRATEGY AND FORMS (Jefren)

CORPORATIONS--GEORGIA-FORMS
GEORGIA CORPORATE FORMS-PRACTICE (Aspen)

CORPORATIONS--HAWAII
HAWAII CORPORATION SOURCEBOOK (Pacific Law Inst.)
HAWAII LEGAL PRACTICE MANUAL - CORPORATIONS & REAL ESTATE (HICLE)

CORPORATIONS--ILLINOIS-FORMS
ILLINOIS CORPORATE FORMS--PRACTICE (Aspen)

CORPORATIONS--INDIANA
BASIC CORPORATE PRACTICE (Indiana CLE)

CORPORATIONS--IOWA
IOWA LEGAL FORMS -- CORPORATIONS (Butterworth-St. Paul)

CORPORATIONS--KANSAS
KANSAS CORPORATION LAW AND PRACTICE (Kansas Bar)

CORPORATIONS--LOUISIANA
LOUISIANA CORPORATIONS (Lawyers Coop.)

CORPORATIONS--MARYLAND-FORMS
MARYLAND COMMERCIAL FINANCING FORMS - PRACTICE (Aspen)
MARYLAND CORPORATE FORMS: PRACTICE (Aspen)

CORPORATIONS--MASSACHUSETTS
MASSACHUSETTS CORPORATION LAW WITH FEDERAL TAX ANALYSIS (Bender)
MASSACHUSETTS CORPORATIONS (Lawyers Coop.)

CORPORATIONS--MASSACHUSETTS-FORMS
MASSACHUSETTS CORPORATE FORMS--PRACTICE (Aspen)

CORPORATIONS--MASSACHUSETTS-TAXATION
MASSACHUSETTS CORPORATE TAX MANUAL, 2ND ED. (Butterworth-NH)

CORPORATIONS--MICHIGAN
MICHIGAN CORPORATION LAW WITH FEDERAL TAX ANALYSIS (Bender)

CORPORATIONS--MICHIGAN-FORMS
MICHIGAN CORPORATE FORMS--PRACTICE (Aspen)

CORPORATIONS--MINNESOTA
CORPORATE PRACTICE INSTITUTE (MILE)
DIRECTORS IN THE HOT SEAT (MILE)
FUNDAMENTALS OF ORGANIZING MINNESOTA CORPORATIONS (Minn. CLE)
MINNESOTA CORPORATIONS PRACTICE MANUAL (Butterworth-St. Paul)

CORPORATIONS--MISSOURI
MISSOURI CORPORATE AND PARTNERSHIP FORMS HANDBOOK (UMKC/CLE)
MISSOURI CORPORATION LAW AND PRACTICE (MoBar)

CORPORATIONS--MISSOURI-FORMS
MISSOURI CORPORATE FORMS - PRACTICE (Aspen)

CORPORATIONS--NEBRASKA
CORPORATE FORMS (Nebraska CLE)

CORPORATIONS--NETHERLANDS
COMPANIES AND OTHER LEGAL PERSONS UNDER NETHERLANDS LAW (Kluwer)

CORPORATIONS--NEW HAMPSHIRE
CORPORATE LAW: ROLE OF THE LAWYER (NH Bar)
STOCKHOLDERS LITIGATION (NH Bar)

CORPORATIONS--NEW JERSEY
CORPORATE TAX PLANNING (New Jersey ICLE)

CORPORATIONS--NEW JERSEY-FORMS
NEW JERSEY CORPORATE FORMS (Aspen)

CORPORATIONS--NEW YORK
NEW YORK CORPORATION LAW HANDBOOK (Gould)
WHITE, NEW YORK CORPORATIONS (Bender)

CORPORATIONS--OHIO
OHIO CORPORATION LAW WITH FEDERAL TAX ANALYSIS (Bender)

CORPORATIONS--OKLAHOMA
OKLAHOMA BUSINESS ORGANIZATIONS: FORMATION AND REPRESENTATION (Aspen)

CORPORATIONS--OKLAHOMA-FORMS
OKLAHOMA CORPORATE FORMS - PRACTICE (Aspen)

CORPORATIONS--ONTARIO
ONTARIO CORPORATIONS LAW GUIDE (CCH)

CORPORATIONS--OREGON
ADVISING OREGON BUSINESSES (Oregon Bar)

CORPORATIONS--OREGON-FORMS
ADVISING OREGON BUSINESS FORMS VOLUME (Oregon Bar)

CORPORATIONS--PENNSYLVANIA
THE PENNSYLVANIA BUSINESS CORPORATION PRACTICE (Penn. Bar)
PENNSYLVANIA BUSINESS CORPORATIONS (Bisel)
PENNSYLVANIA CORPORATION TAX LAW & PRACTICE (Banks)

CORPORATIONS--SOUTH CAROLINA
SOUTH CAROLINA CORPORATE PRACTICE MANUAL (S. Carolina Bar)

CORPORATIONS--SOUTH CAROLINA-FORMS
OFFICIAL FORMS FOR THE SOUTH CAROLINA BUSINESS CORPORATION ACT OF 1988 (S. Carolina Bar)

CORPORATIONS--TAXATION
BUSINESS TRANSACTIONS: TAX PLANNING AND ANALYSIS (RIA)
THE CONSOLIDATED TAX RETURN (WG&L)
CONSOLIDATED TAX RETURNS: A TREATISE ON THE LAW OF CONSOLIDATED FEDERAL INCOME TAX RETURNS (Clark Boardman Callaghan)
CORPORATE TAX PRACTICE MANUAL (Panel)
CORPORATE TAXATION (Georgetown)
FEDERAL INCOME TAXATION OF CORPORATIONS AND SHAREHOLDERS: FORMS (WG&L)
FEDERAL INCOME TAXATION OF CORPORATIONS FILING CONSOLIDATED RETURNS (Bender)
FEDERAL TAX ASPECTS OF CORPORATE REORGANIZATIONS (Shepard's)
MULTISTATE CORPORATE INCOME TAX GUIDE (CCH)
PPC TAX PLANNING GUIDE - S CORPORATIONS (Practitioners Publishing)
STATE TAX FORMS: CORPORATION (Tax Form)
TAX PLANNING FOR CORPORATIONS AND SHAREHOLDERS (Bender)
TAX SERVICE FOR AFFILIATED GROUPS (Stephens)
TAX SERVICE FOR CORPORATE ACQUISITIONS AND DISPOSITIONS OF BUSINESSES (Stephens)
TAXATION OF CORPORATE LIQUIDATIONS (WG&L)

CORPORATIONS--TENNESSEE
TENNESSEE CORPORATIONS (Lawyers Coop.)
WORKING GUIDE TO THE TENNESSEE BUSINESS CORPORATION ACT (Smith)

CORPORATIONS--TEXAS
TEXAS CORPORATION LAW (Parker)
TEXAS CORPORATION LAW (Butterworth-Texas)
TEXAS CORPORATIONS - LAW AND PRACTICE (Bender)

CORPORATIONS--VIRGINIA
VIRGINIA CORPORATIONS (Lawyers Coop.)

CORPORATIONS--WASHINGTON
ADVISING THE SMALL BUSINESS CLIENT (Wash. Bar)
CORPORATION BUSINESS AND BANKING MID-YEAR (Wash. Bar)

CORPORATIONS--WASHINGTON-FORMS
WASHINGTON CORPORATE FORMS (Aspen)

CORPORATIONS--WISCONSIN
ORGANIZING A WISCONSIN BUSINESS CORPORATION: ARTICLES, BYLAWS AND OTHER FORMS (State Bar of Wisc.)
WISCONSIN CORPORATIONS (Lawyers Coop.)

CORPORATIONS, INTERNATIONAL
CAPITAL FORMATION AND INVESTMENT INCENTIVES AROUND THE WORLD (Bender)
MULTINATIONAL CORPORATIONS LAW: MEXICO, CENTRAL AMERICA, PANAMA AND THE CENTRAL AMERICAN COMMON MARKET (Oceana)
MULTINATIONAL CORPORATIONS LAW: THE UNITED NATIONS AND TRANSNATIONAL CORPORATIONS (Oceana)

CORRUPT PRACTICES
FOREIGN CORRUPT PRACTICES ACT REPORTER (Bus. Laws)

COSMETICS
see Food, drugs, cosmetics

COURT RULES
THE ATTORNEY'S GUIDE TO THE SEVENTH CIRCUIT COURT OF APPEALS (State Bar of Wisc.)
BANKRUPTCY LOCAL COURT RULES (Clark Boardman Callaghan)
BARCLAYS UNITED STATES D.C. CIRCUIT SERVICE (Barclays)
BARCLAYS UNITED STATES EIGHTH CIRCUIT SERVICE (Barclays)
BARCLAYS UNITED STATES ELEVENTH CIRCUIT SERVICE (Barclays)
BARCLAYS UNITED STATES FIFTH CIRCUIT SERVICE (Barclays)
BARCLAYS UNITED STATES FIRST CIRCUIT SERVICE (Barclays)
BARCLAYS UNITED STATES FOURTH CIRCUIT SERVICE (Barclays)
BARCLAYS UNITED STATES NINTH CIRCUIT SERVICE (Barclays)
BARCLAYS UNITED STATES SECOND CIRCUIT SERVICE (Barclays)
BARCLAYS UNITED STATES SEVENTH CIRCUIT SERVICE (Barclays)
BARCLAYS UNITED STATES SIXTH CIRCUIT SERVICE (Barclays)
BARCLAYS UNITED STATES TENTH CIRCUIT SERVICE (Barclays)
BARCLAYS UNITED STATES THIRD CIRCUIT SERVICE (Barclays)
FEDERAL CIRCUIT COURT RULES SERVICE (Rules)
FEDERAL LOCAL COURT RULES (Lawyers Coop.)
NINTH CIRCUIT CT. OF APPEALS - LOCAL RULES (Book Pub.)
RULES OF THE U.S. COURTS IN NEW YORK (Clark Boardman Callaghan)
U.S. COURT OF INTERNATIONAL TRADE RULES AND ANNOTATION SERVICE (Rules)
UNITED STATES COURT OF INTERNATIONAL TRADE - RULES (Invictus)

COURT RULES--ALASKA
UNITED STATES DISTRICT COURT RULES FOR THE DISTRICT OF ALASKA (Book Pub.)

COURT RULES--CALIFORNIA
COURT RULES FOR NORTHERN CALIFORNIA (LADJ)
COURT RULES FOR SOUTHERN CALIFORNIA (LADJ)
RULES OF COURT (Metropolitan News)

COURT RULES--COLORADO
COLORADO COURT RULES (Michie)
COLORADO LOCAL COURT RULES (CLP)

COURT RULES--DISTRICT OF COLUMBIA
DISTRICT OF COLUMBIA CITATION SERVICE (Rules)
DISTRICT OF COLUMBIA COURT RULES (Rules)

COURT RULES--FLORIDA
FLORIDA RULES OF COURT SERVICE (Butterworth-Fla.)

COURT RULES--GEORGIA
GEORGIA STATE RULES OF COURT (Butterworth-Fla.)

BARCLAYS UNITED STATES FIFTH CIRCUIT SERVICE (Barclays)
BARCLAYS UNITED STATES FIRST CIRCUIT SERVICE (Barclays)
BARCLAYS UNITED STATES FOURTH CIRCUIT SERVICE (Barclays)
BARCLAYS UNITED STATES NINTH CIRCUIT SERVICE (Barclays)
BARCLAYS UNITED STATES SECOND CIRCUIT SERVICE (Barclays)
BARCLAYS UNITED STATES SEVENTH CIRCUIT SERVICE (Barclays)
BARCLAYS UNITED STATES SIXTH CIRCUIT SERVICE (Barclays)
BARCLAYS UNITED STATES TENTH CIRCUIT SERVICE (Barclays)
BARCLAYS UNITED STATES THIRD CIRCUIT SERVICE (Barclays)
JURISDICTION AND FORUM SELECTION (Clark Boardman Callaghan)
LEGAL SECRETARY FEDERAL LITIGATION (James)
LEGAL SECRETARY'S RESOURCE (Parker)
U.S. SUPREME COURT BULLETIN (CCH)
UNITED STATES LAW WEEK (BNA)

<u>COURTS--ARIZONA</u>
ARIZONA COURTS MANUAL (State Bar of Ariz.)

<u>COURTS--CALIFORNIA</u>
BARCLAYS CALIFORNIA SUPREME COURT SERVICE (Barclays)
CALIFORNIA LEGAL SECRETARY (James)

<u>COURTS--DISTRICT OF COLUMBIA</u>
D.C. FEDERAL COURTS HANDBOOK (Prentice Hall Law & Business)

<u>COURTS--FLORIDA</u>
THE MANUAL FOR FLORIDA LEGAL SECRETARIES (Butterworth-Fla.)

<u>COURTS--FORMS</u>
FEDERAL LOCAL COURT FORMS (Lawyers Coop.)

<u>COURTS--ILLINOIS</u>
ILLINOIS LEGAL FILING DIRECTORY (Shepard's)

<u>COURTS--MARYLAND</u>
DISTRICT COURT FORMS (MICPEL)
MARYLAND TAX COURT SERVICE (Hawkins)

<u>COURTS--MICHIGAN</u>
MICHIGAN LEGAL FILING DIRECTORY (Shepard's)

<u>COURTS--MICHIGAN-FORMS</u>
MICHIGAN APPROVED COURT FORMS (ICLE - Michigan)

<u>COURTS--MINNESOTA</u>
JUVENILE COURT HANDBOOK FOR MINNESOTA (Butterworth-St. Paul)
PRACTICING IN FEDERAL DISTRICT COURT IN MINNESOTA (Minn. CLE)

<u>COURTS--NEW JERSEY</u>
GUIDEBOOK TO CHANCERY PRACTICE IN NEW JERSEY (New Jersey ICLE)

<u>COURTS--NEW YORK</u>
NEW YORK COURT FORMS (Gould)
NEW YORK COURTS MANUAL OF PROCEDURE (Gould)

<u>COURTS--NEW YORK CITY</u>
COURT RULES UPDATE (Court Info.)

<u>COURTS--OHIO</u>
OHIO LEGAL FILING DIRECTORY (Shepard's)

<u>COURTS--PENNSYLVANIA</u>
PHILADELPHIA COURT OF COMMON PLEAS CIVIL PRACTICE MANUAL (Penn. Bar)

<u>COURTS--TEXAS</u>
TEXAS SPECIAL ISSUES FORMS (Butterworth-Texas)

CREDIT
see Consumer finance

CREDIT UNIONS
CREDIT UNION LAW SERVICE (Bender)
NATIONAL CREDIT UNION ADMINISTRATION RULES AND REGULATIONS (USGPO)

CREDITORS
see Debtor and creditor

CRIMINAL INVESTIGATION
FORENSIC SCIENCE (Bender)

CRIMINAL JUSTICE, ADMINISTRATION OF
ABA STANDARDS FOR CRIMINAL JUSTICE, 2nd ed. (ABA)

CRIMINAL LAW
BILINGUAL DICTIONARY OF CRIMINAL JUSTICE TERMS (ENGLISH/SPANISH) (Gould)
CONTEMPORARY FEDERAL CRIMINAL PRACTICE: A PRACTICAL GUIDE TO THE COMPREHENSIVE CRIME CONTROL ACT OF 1984 (Prentice Hall Law & Business)
CRIMINAL LAW DESKBOOK (Bender)
THE CRIMINAL LAW REPORTER (BNA)
DRUG ABUSE AND THE LAW SOURCEBOOK (Clark Boardman Callaghan)
FEDERAL CRIMINAL LAW AND PROCEDURE: ALR ANNOTATIONS (Lawyers Coop.)
FEDERAL ENFORCEMENT (Georgetown)
THE LAW OF ELECTRONIC SURVEILLANCE (Clark Boardman Callaghan)
PRISONERS AND THE LAW (Clark Boardman Callaghan)
PROSECUTION AND DEFENSE OF CRIMINAL CONSPIRACY CASES (Bender)
U.S. SUPREME COURT CASES AND COMMENTS (Bender)
WHITE COLLAR CRIME: BUSINESS AND REGULATORY OFFENSES (Law Journal)

CRIMINAL LAW--ALABAMA
PATTERN CAPITAL MURDER CHARGES (ABICLE)

CRIMINAL LAW--ARKANSAS
CRIMINAL LAW HANDBOOK (Arkansas Bar)

CRIMINAL LAW--CALIFORNIA
CALIFORNIA WHITE COLLAR CRIME (Parker)

CRIMINAL LAW--FLORIDA
FLORIDA CRIMINAL DEFENSE TRIAL MANUAL (Butterworth-Fla.)

CRIMINAL LAW--HAWAII
HAWAII CRIMINAL LAW AND PROCEDURE DIGEST (HICLE)

CRIMINAL LAW--ILLINOIS
DEFENDING ILLINOIS CRIMINAL CASES (Illinois ICLE)
ILLINOIS CRIMINAL LAW & PROCEDURE (Gould)

CRIMINAL LAW--INDIANA
CRIMINAL LAW (Indiana CLE)

CRIMINAL LAW--IOWA
IOWA LEGAL FORMS -- CRIMINAL LAW (Butterworth-St. Paul)

CRIMINAL LAW--KANSAS
KANSAS CRIMINAL LAW HANDBOOK (Kansas Bar)

CRIMINAL LAW--MAINE
HOW TO HANDLE PROBLEM CRIMINAL CASES, AND A LOOK AT NEW CRIMES (Maine Bar)

CRIMINAL LAW--MARYLAND
SPECIAL ISSUES IN CRIMINAL LAW (MICPEL)

CRIMINAL LAW--MINNESOTA
CRIME 1991 (MILE)

LYING, CHEATING & STEALING PLUS SECURITIES (MILE)
MINNESOTA CRIMES AND DEFENSES (Butterworth-St. Paul)
MINNESOTA CRIMINAL LAW DIGEST (Butterworth-St. Paul)
MINNESOTA LEGAL FORMS--CRIMINAL LAW (Butterworth-St. Paul)

<u>CRIMINAL LAW--NEBRASKA</u>
NEBRASKA LEGAL FORMS--CRIMINAL LAW (Butterworth-St. Paul)

<u>CRIMINAL LAW--NEW YORK</u>
CALLAGHAN'S CRIMINAL LAW IN NY (Lawyers Coop.)
GILBERT CRIMINAL LAW AND PROCEDURE OF NEW YORK (Bender)
NEW YORK CRIMINAL CASE CITATOR (Nat. Atty.)
NEW YORK CRIMINAL LAW HANDBOOK (Gould)

<u>CRIMINAL LAW--OHIO</u>
SCHROEDER-KATZ, OHIO CRIMINAL LAW AND PRACTICE (Banks)

<u>CRIMINAL LAW--OREGON</u>
CRIMINAL LAW FORMBOOK (OCDLA)
PENNSYLVANIA CRIMES CODE AND CRIMINAL LAW (Bisel)

<u>CRIMINAL LAW--PENNSYLVANIA</u>
PENNSYLVANIA CRIMINAL LAW DIGEST (Gould)

<u>CRIMINAL LAW--RHODE ISLAND</u>
RHODE ISLAND SUPREME COURT AND THE LAW OF CRIMES (Butterworth-NH)

<u>CRIMINAL PROCEDURE</u>
see also Appellate procedure; Criminal law; Evidence; Trial practice

BNA CRIMINAL PRACTICE MANUAL (BNA)
CONTEMPORARY CRIMINAL PROCEDURE (Gould)
CRIMINAL DEFENSE ETHICS: LAW & LIABILITY (Clark Boardman Callaghan)
CRIMINAL DEFENSE TECHNIQUES (Bender)
CRIMINAL LAW ADVOCACY (Bender)
DETENTION AND CORRECTIONS CASELAW CATALOG (CRS)
EYE-WITNESS IDENTIFICATION (Clark Boardman Callaghan)
FEDERAL BAIL & DETENTION HANDBOOK (PLI)
FEDERAL CRIMINAL APPEALS (Clark Boardman Callaghan)
FEDERAL CRIMINAL LAW AND PROCEDURE: ALR ANNOTATIONS (Lawyers Corp.)
FEDERAL CRIMINAL PRACTICE (Illinois ICLE)
FEDERAL CRIMINAL PRACTICE (Mass. CLE)
FEDERAL RULES OF CRIMINAL PROCEDURE (Clark Boardman Callaghan)
FEDERAL SENTENCING GUIDELINES 1991 (MICPEL)
FEDERAL SENTENCING MANUAL (Bender)
HANDLING COMPLEX CRIMINAL CASES (Georgetown)
OAKES' CRIMINAL PRACTICE GUIDE (Wiley Law)
PRACTICE UNDER THE FEDERAL SENTENCING GUIDELINES (Indiana CLE)
PRACTICE UNDER THE NEW FEDERAL SENTENCING GUIDELINES (Prentice Hall Law & Business)
PREVENTION AND PROSECUTION OF COMPUTER AND HIGH TECHNOLOGY CRIME (Bender)
PROSECUTORIAL MISCONDUCT (Clark Boardman Callaghan)
PROVING CRIMINAL DEFENSES (Bender)
RULES OF CRIMINAL PROCEDURE (Bender)
SEARCHES & SEIZURES, ARRESTS AND CONFESSIONS (Clark Boardman Callaghan)
SENTENCING DEFENSE MANUAL--ADVOCACY/PRACTICE/PROCEDURE (Clark Boardman Callaghan)
VICTIMS' RIGHTS: LAW AND LITIGATION (Bender)

<u>CRIMINAL PROCEDURE--CALIFORNIA</u>
CALIFORNIA CRIMINAL DEFENSE PRACTICE (Bender)
CALIFORNIA CRIMINAL TRIALBOOK (West)
CALIFORNIA FORMS OF PLEADING AND PRACTICE-ANNOTATED (Bender)

<u>CRIMINAL PROCEDURE--CONNECTICUT</u>
CONNECTICUT CRIMINAL PROCEDURE (Atlantic)

CONNECTICUT LAW ENFORCEMENT HANDBOOK (Gould)
FUNDAMENTALS OF FEDERAL CRIMINAL PRACTICE & FEDERAL SENTENCING GUIDELINES (Conn. Bar)

CRIMINAL PROCEDURE--FLORIDA
CRIMINAL TRIAL PRACTICE IN FLORIDA (Florida Bar)
FLORIDA CRIMINAL DISCOVERY AND PRE-TRIAL MOTIONS MANUAL (Butterworth-Fla.)
FLORIDA CRIMINAL PROCEDURE SERVICE (Butterworth-Fla.)
FLORIDA CRIMINAL RULES AND PRACTICE (Florida Bar)
FLORIDA CRIMINAL SENTENCING LAW (Butterworth-Fla.)
FLORIDA PRETRIAL PRACTICE IN CRIMINAL CASES (Florida Bar)

CRIMINAL PROCEDURE--ILLINOIS
ARREST, SEARCH AND SEIZURE (Illinois ICLE)
ERISMAN'S REVERSIBLE ERRORS IN ILLINOIS CRIMINAL CASES (Knowles)
THE ILLINOIS LAW OF CRIMINAL INVESTIGATION (Manak)

CRIMINAL PROCEDURE--INDIANA
CRIMINAL DEFENSE (Indiana CLE)

CRIMINAL PROCEDURE--KENTUCKY
BALDWIN'S KENTUCKY PRACTICE (Banks)

CRIMINAL PROCEDURE--MAINE
MAINE CRIMINAL PRACTICE (Butterworth-NH)

CRIMINAL PROCEDURE--MARYLAND
CRIMINAL PRACTICE AND PROCEDURE IN THE DISTRICT COURT OF MARYLAND (MICPEL)
MARYLAND SENTENCING GUIDELINES MANUAL (MICPEL)

CRIMINAL PROCEDURE--MASSACHUSETTS
JURY TRIAL MANUAL FOR CRIMINAL OFFENSES TRIED IN THE DISTRICT COURT (Mass. CLE)

CRIMINAL PROCEDURE--MINNESOTA
MINNESOTA SENTENCING GUIDELINES AND COMMENTARY ANNOTATED (Minn. CLE)

CRIMINAL PROCEDURE--MISSOURI
MISSOURI CRIMINAL PRACTICE (MoBar)

CRIMINAL PROCEDURE--NEW HAMPSHIRE
CRIMINAL DEFENSE PRACTICE (NH Bar)
FEDERAL SENTENCING GUIDELINES (NH Bar)

CRIMINAL PROCEDURE--NEW JERSEY
CRIMINAL TRIAL PRACTICE (New Jersey ICLE)
NEW JERSEY LAW ENFORCEMENT HANDBOOK (Gould)

CRIMINAL PROCEDURE--NEW YORK
CRIMINAL PROCEDURE IN NEW YORK PART 1 & PART 2 (Lawyers Coop.)
NEW YORK COURTS MANUAL OF PROCEDURE (Gould)
NEW YORK CRIMINAL PRACTICE (Bender)
NEW YORK SUPPRESSION MANUAL (Bender)
SENTENCING MANUAL FOR JUDGES (New Jersey ICLE)

CRIMINAL PROCEDURE--OHIO
OHIO CRIMINAL PRACTICE & PROCEDURE (Anderson)
OHIO MANUAL OF PROCEDURE (Anderson)

CRIMINAL PROCEDURE--OKLAHOMA
OKLAHOMA CRIMINAL PRACTICE MANUAL (Butterworth-Texas)

CRIMINAL PROCEDURE--OREGON
CRIMINAL LAW (Oregon Bar)

CRIMINAL PROCEDURE--PENNSYLVANIA
PENNSYLVANIA CRIMINAL LAW AND PRACTICE (Bender)

PENNSYLVANIA CRIMINAL PRACTICE (Lawyers Coop.)
PENNSYLVANIA GUIDE TO CRIMINAL PRACTICE AND PROCEDURE (Bisel)
PENNSYLVANIA LAW ENFORCEMENT HANDBOOK (Gould)
VALENTINE-BINNS JUSTICE (Bisel)

<u>CRIMINAL PROCEDURE--RHODE ISLAND</u>
RHODE ISLAND CRIMINAL PROCEDURE (Butterworth-NH)

<u>CRIMINAL PROCEDURE--SOUTH CAROLINA</u>
SOUTH CAROLINA CRIMINAL DEFENSE (S. Carolina Bar)

<u>CRIMINAL PROCEDURE--TEXAS</u>
TEXAS CRIMINAL DEFENSE FORMS ANNOTATED (Knowles)
TEXAS CRIMINAL PRACTICE GUIDE (Bender)

<u>CRIMINAL PROCEDURE--VIRGINIA</u>
DEFENDING CRIMINAL CASES IN VIRGINIA (Jt. Comm. Va.)

<u>CRIMINAL PROCEDURE--WASHINGTON</u>
SENTENCING IN WASHINGTON (Butterworth-St. Paul)

<u>CRIMINAL PROCEDURE--WISCONSIN</u>
FEDERAL CRIMINAL PRACTICE HANDBOOK (State Bar of Wisc.)
WISCONSIN JUDICIAL BENCHBOOK: VOL. 1 - CRIMINAL AND TRAFFIC (State Bar of Wisc.)
WISCONSIN MISDEMEANORS AND MOVING TRAFFIC VIOLATIONS, 2ND ED. (Butterworth-St. Paul)

<u>CROSS-EXAMINATION</u>
CROSS-EXAMINATION OF MEDICAL EXPERTS (Bender)
CROSS-EXAMINATION OF NON-MEDICAL EXPERTS (Art of Advocacy Series) (Bender)

<u>CUSTOMS</u>
see International Trade

<u>DAMAGES</u>
see also Accidents; Negligence; Personal injuries; Torts

BAD FAITH ACTIONS: LIABILITY AND DAMAGES (Clark Boardman Callaghan)
COMMERCIAL DAMAGES: A GUIDE TO REMEDIES IN BUSINESS LITIGATION (Bender)
DAMAGES (Knowles)
DAMAGES IN TORT ACTIONS (Bender)
DAMAGES UNDER THE UNIFORM COMMERCIAL CODE (Clark Boardman Callaghan)
DETERMINING ECONOMIC DAMAGES (James)
ESTIMATING AND PROVING PERSONAL INJURY DAMAGES (James)
GOODS IN TRANSIT (Bender)
MAXIMIZING DAMAGES IN SMALL PERSONAL INJURY CASES (James)
PERSONAL INJURY - ACTIONS, DEFENSES, DAMAGES (Bender)
PUNITIVE DAMAGES, LAW & PRACTICE (Clark Boardman Callaghan)
SECURITIES LITIGATION: DAMAGES (Clark Boardman Callaghan)
TAX ASPECTS OF LITIGATION AND SETTLEMENTS (Clark Boardman Callaghan)

<u>DAMAGES--CALIFORNIA</u>
CALIFORNIA DAMAGES: LAW AND PROOF (Parker)
CALIFORNIA PRACTICE GUIDE - BAD FAITH (Rutter)
PROOF OF DAMAGES (Illinois ICLE)

<u>DAMAGES--CONNECTICUT</u>
DAMAGES IN EMPLOYMENT CASES (Conn. Bar)

<u>DAMAGES--INDIANA</u>
DAMAGES IN CONSTRUCTION LITIGATION (Indiana CLE)

<u>DAMAGES--MICHIGAN</u>
THE MICHIGAN LAW OF DAMAGES (ICLE - Michigan)

ATTORNEY'S GUIDE TO CONDUCTING DEPOSITIONS - AUTOMOBILE NEGLIGENCE CASES (Lame)
DEPOSITION - STRATEGY, LAW AND FORMS (Bender)
DEPOSITIONS (Knowles)
DEPOSITIONS: PROCEDURE, STRATEGY AND TECHNIQUE (West)
HOW TO PREPARE FOR, TAKE, AND USE A DEPOSITION (James)
MODERN CIVIL DISCOVERY AND DEPOSITIONS (Wiley Law)

<u>DEPOSITIONS--CALIFORNIA</u>
CALIFORNIA DEPOSITION AND DISCOVERY PRACTICE (Bender)
CALIFORNIA DEPOSITIONS (Knowles)

<u>DEPOSITIONS--MARYLAND</u>
TAKING AND DEFENDING DEPOSITIONS (MICPEL)

<u>DEPOSITIONS--OKLAHOMA</u>
TAKING AND GIVING DEPOSITIONS (Okla. Bar CLE)

<u>DICTIONARIES</u>
ATTORNEY'S DICTIONARY OF MEDICINE, 16TH ED. (Bender)
ATTORNEY'S DICTIONARY OF PATENT CLAIMS (Bender)
BILINGUAL DICTIONARY OF CRIMINAL JUSTICE TERMS (ENGLISH/SPANISH) (Gould)

<u>DIRECTORIES</u>
FEDERAL ORGANIZATION SERVICE CIVIL (Carroll)
FEDERAL ORGANIZATION SERVICE MILITARY (Carroll)
FIFTY-STATE LEGISLATIVE DIRECTORY (Calif. Jnl. Press)
HUMAN RIGHTS ORGANIZATIONS AND PERIODICALS DIRECTORY (Meiklejohn Civil Liberties Institute)
NATIONAL DIRECTORY FOR THE SERVICE OF CIVIL PROCESS (Knowles)
NATIONAL LAW LIST (Pic's)
STATE LEGISLATIVE SOURCEBOOK (Govt. Res.)

<u>DIRECTORIES--ALASKA</u>
ALASKA DIRECTORY OF PERMITS (Book Pub.)

<u>DIRECTORIES--MAINE</u>
MAINE BAR DIRECTORY (Tower)

<u>DISCOVERY</u>
see also Pre-trial procedure

ANTITRUST DISCOVERY HANDBOOK (ABA)
BENDER'S FORMS OF DISCOVERY (Bender)
CIVIL DISCOVERY: A GUIDE TO EFFICIENT PRACTICE (Prentice Hall Law & Business)
DISCOVERY (Art of Advocacy Series) (Bender)
DISCOVERY -- HOW TO MAKE IT WORK FOR YOU (Wash. Bar)
MODERN CIVIL DISCOVERY AND DEPOSITIONS (Wiley Law)
OBJECTIONS TO INTERROGATORIES (James)
PARALEGAL DISCOVERY: ORGANIZATION AND MANAGEMENT (James)
PARALEGAL DISCOVERY: PROCEDURES AND FORMS (James)

<u>DISCOVERY--CALIFORNIA</u>
CALIFORNIA DEPOSITION AND DISCOVERY PRACTICE (Bender)

<u>DISCOVERY--FLORIDA</u>
FLORIDA CIVIL DISCOVERY MANUAL (Butterworth-Fla.)
FLORIDA CRIMINAL DISCOVERY AND PRE-TRIAL MOTIONS MANUAL (Butterworth-Fla.)

<u>DISCOVERY--ILLINOIS</u>
ILLINOIS CIVIL DISCOVERY PRACTICE (Illinois ICLE)

<u>DISCOVERY--INDIANA</u>
DISCOVERY TOOLS: HOW TO WIN YOUR CASE BEFORE TRIAL (Indiana CLE)
WINNING YOUR CASE THROUGH EFFECTIVE PRETRIAL DISCOVERY (Indiana CLE)

DISCOVERY--MARYLAND
DISCOVERY UNDER THE MARYLAND RULES (MICPEL)

DISCOVERY--MINNESOTA
WRITTEN DISCOVERY (Minn. CLE)

DISCOVERY--NEW HAMPSHIRE
THE ART OF DISCOVERY (NH Bar)

DISCOVERY--OKLAHOMA
OKLAHOMA DISCOVERY PRACTICE MANUAL (Butterworth-Texas)

DISCOVERY--TEXAS
DISCOVERY (Knowles)

DISCOVERY--TEXAS--FORMS
TEXAS DISCOVERY FORMS (Butterworth-Texas)

DISCOVERY--WISCONSIN
WISCONSIN DISCOVERY LAW AND PRACTICE (State Bar of Wisc.)

DISCRIMINATION
see also Civil rights

THE DISABILITY LAW REPORTER SERVICE (Prentice Hall Law & Business)
SEX-BASED DISCRIMINATION: INTERNATIONAL LAW AND ORGANIZATION (Oceana)
SEXUAL ORIENTATION AND THE LAW (Clark Boardman Callaghan)
WOMEN AND THE LAW (Clark Boardman Callaghan)

DISCRIMINATION--MARYLAND
DIGEST OF MARYLAND CASES ON DISCRIMINATION (MICPEL)
MARYLAND CASES ON DISCRIMINATION (MICPEL)

DISCRIMINATION--MASSACHUSETTS
MASSACHUSETTS DISCRIMINATION LAW REPORTER (NELP)

DISCRIMINATION IN EMPLOYMENT
AGE DISCRIMINATION (Shepard's)
DISABILITY DISCRIMINATION IN EMPLOYMENT (Clark Boardman Callaghan)
EEO COMPLIANCE MANUAL (WG&L)
EEO UPDATE 1990 (Georgetown)
EEOC COMPLIANCE MANUAL (BNA)
EEOC COMPLIANCE MANUAL (CCH)
EMPLOYMENT DISCRIMINATION (Bender)
EMPLOYMENT DISCRIMINATION (Butterworth-NH)
EMPLOYMENT DISCRIMINATION AND CIVIL RIGHTS ACTIONS (Clark Boardman Callaghan)
EMPLOYMENT DISCRIMINATION COORDINATOR (WG&L)
EMPLOYMENT DISCRIMINATION LAW UPDATE (NELI)
EMPLOYMENT PRACTICES GUIDE (CCH)
EQUAL EMPLOYMENT COMPLIANCE MANUAL (Clark Boardman Callaghan)
FAIR EMPLOYMENT PRACTICES (BNA)
HOT ISSUES IN EMPLOYMENT LITIGATION (Indiana CLE)
LITIGATING AGE DISCRIMINATION CASES (Clark Boardman Callaghan)
LITIGATING WRONGFUL DISCHARGE CLAIMS (Clark Boardman Callaghan)
MANUAL ON EMPLOYMENT DISCRIMINATION AND CIVIL RIGHTS ACTIONS IN THE FEDERAL COURTS, ATTORNEYS' EDITION (Michie)
OFCCP FEDERAL CONTRACT COMPLIANCE MANUAL (CCH)
A PRACTICAL GUIDE TO EQUAL EMPLOYMENT OPPORTUNITY (Law Journal)
SECTION 89 COMPLIANCE MANUAL: THE COMPLETE GUIDE TO THE NEW NON-DISCRIMINATION RULES FOR EMPLOYEE BENEFIT PLANS (BNA)
SEX-BASED EMPLOYMENT DISCRIMINATION (Clark Boardman Callaghan)
USE OF STATISTICS IN EQUAL EMPLOYMENT OPPORTUNITY (Law Journal)

DISCRIMINATION IN EMPLOYMENT--CALIFORNIA
FAIR EMPLOYMENT & HOUSING COMMISSION PRECEDENTIAL DECISIONS SERVICE (Calif. CEB)

DISCRIMINATION IN EMPLOYMENT--CONNECTICUT
EMPLOYMENT DISCRIMINATION COMPLAINTS (Conn. Bar)
EMPLOYMENT DISCRIMINATION COMPLAINTS (Conn. Bar)

DISCRIMINATION IN EMPLOYMENT--ILLINOIS
EMPLOYMENT DISCRIMINATION (Illinois ICLE)

DISCRIMINATION IN EMPLOYMENT--INDIANA
PRACTICAL APPROACHES TO EMPLOYMENT DISCRIMINATION PROBLEMS (Indiana CLE)

DISCRIMINATION IN EMPLOYMENT--MICHIGAN
EMPLOYMENT DISCRIMINATION LAW (MTLA)
EMPLOYMENT DISCRIMINATION LAW, VOL. II (MTLA)
MICHIGAN WRONGFUL DISCHARGE AND EMPLOYMENT DISCRIMINATION LAW (ICLE - Michigan)

DISCRIMINATION IN HOUSING
FAIR HOUSING - FAIR LENDING (Prentice Hall Law & Business)
HOUSING DISCRIMINATION: LAW AND LITIGATION (Clark Boardman Callaghan)

DISCRIMINATION IN HOUSING--CALIFORNIA
FAIR EMPLOYMENT & HOUSING COMMISSION PRECEDENTIAL DECISIONS SERVICE (Calif. CEB)

DISPUTE RESOLUTION
ALTERNATIVE DISPUTE RESOLUTION (New Jersey ICLE)
ALTERNATIVE DISPUTE RESOLUTION TECHNIQUES (Bus. Laws)
MAP PACKAGE: ALTERNATIVE DISPUTE RESOLUTION (ABA)

DISPUTE RESOLUTION--FLORIDA
ALTERNATE DISPUTE RESOLUTION (Florida Bar)

DISPUTE RESOLUTION--INDIANA
ACCELERATED DISPUTE RESOLUTIONS (Indiana CLE)

DISPUTE RESOLUTION--MINNESOTA
ADR IN BUSINESS DISPUTES (MILE)
TECHNIQUES FOR ALTERNATIVE DISPUTE RESOLUTION (MILE)

DISPUTE RESOLUTION--WASHINGTON
ALTERNATIVE DISPUTE RESOLUTION DESKBOOK: ARBITRATION & MEDIATION IN WASHINGTON (Wash. Bar)

DIVORCE
see Marriage and divorce

DOCUMENTS
A PRACTICAL GUIDE TO DOCUMENT AUTHENTICATION: LEGALIZATION OF NOTARIZED AND CERTIFIED DOCUMENTS (Oceana)

DOMESTIC LAW--MASSACHUSETTS
COMPENDIUM OF MASSACHUSETTS FAMILY LAW (Mass. CLE)

DOMESTIC RELATIONS
see also Marriage and divorce

CHILD CUSTODY AND VISITATION LAW AND PRACTICE (Bender)
COLLIER FAMILY LAW AND THE BANKRUPTCY CODE (Bender)
CONTEMPORARY FAMILY LAW (Clark Boardman Callaghan)
DETERMINING CHILD & SPOUSAL SUPPORT (Clark Boardman Callaghan)
DISPUTED PATERNITY PROCEEDINGS (Bender)
FAMILY LAW (Knowles)
FAMILY LAW AND PRACTICE (Bender)
FAMILY LAW CHECKLISTS (Clark Boardman Callaghan)
FAMILY LAW LITIGATION GUIDE: DISCOVERY, EVIDENCE AND TRIAL PRACTICE (Bender)
THE FAMILY LAW PRACTICE MANUAL (Legal-Med.)

THE FAMILY LAW REPORTER (BNA)
FAMILY LAW TAX GUIDE (CCH)
IMPROVING CHILD SUPPORT PRACTICE (ABA)
LESBIAN MOTHER LITIGATION MANUAL (Natl. Center for Lesbian Rights)

DOMESTIC RELATIONS--ARKANSAS
ARKANSAS DOMESTIC RELATIONS SYSTEM (Arkansas Bar)

DOMESTIC RELATIONS--CALIFORNIA
CALIFORNIA FAMILY LAW - PRACTICE AND PROCEDURE (Bender)
CALIFORNIA FAMILY LAW PRACTICE (CFLR)
CALIFORNIA PRACTICE GUIDE - FAMILY LAW (Rutter)

DOMESTIC RELATIONS--CANADA
CANADIAN FAMILY LAW GUIDE (CCH)

DOMESTIC RELATIONS--COLORADO
HANDBOOK OF COLORADO FAMILY LAW (CLE - Colorado)

DOMESTIC RELATIONS--COLORADO-FORMS
COLORADO DOMESTIC RELATIONS FORMS - PRACTICE (Aspen)

DOMESTIC RELATIONS--CONNECTICUT
THE CONNECTICUT CHILD SUPPORT GUIDELINES (Conn. Bar)
HANDBOOK OF FORMS FOR THE CONNECTICUT FAMILY LAWYER (Conn. Law Tribune)

DOMESTIC RELATIONS--FLORIDA
ADOPTION, PATERNITY AND OTHER FLORIDA FAMILY PRACTICE (Florida Bar)
CASES AND MATERIALS ON FLORIDA DOMESTIC RELATIONS (Florida Bar)
FLORIDA FAMILY LAW (Bender)
FLORIDA FAMILY LAW PRACTICE (Butterworth-Fla.)

DOMESTIC RELATIONS--GEORGIA
GEORGIA FAMILY LAW MANUAL (Butterworth-Fla.)

DOMESTIC RELATIONS--GEORGIA-FORMS
GEORGIA DOMESTIC RELATIONS FORMS - PRACTICE (Aspen)

DOMESTIC RELATIONS--HAWAII
HAWAII ADOPTION MANUAL (HICLE)
HAWAII SURROGATE COURTS FILING PROCEDURES MANUAL (HICLE)

DOMESTIC RELATIONS--ILLINOIS
ILLINOIS FAMILY LAW (Illinois ICLE)
ILLINOIS FAMILY LAW (Pantagraph)

DOMESTIC RELATIONS--ILLINOIS-FORMS
ILLINOIS DOMESTIC RELATIONS FORMS--PRACTICE (Aspen)

DOMESTIC RELATIONS--INDIANA
ADOPTION LAW (Indiana CLE)
EVERYTHING ELSE YOU NEEDED TO KNOW ABOUT FAMILY LAW (Indiana CLE)

DOMESTIC RELATIONS--IOWA
IOWA FAMILY LAW MANUAL (Iowa Bar)
IOWA LEGAL FORMS -- FAMILY LAW (Butterworth-St. Paul)

DOMESTIC RELATIONS--KANSAS
KANSAS FAMILY LAW HANDBOOK (Kansas Bar)

DOMESTIC RELATIONS--KENTUCKY
KENTUCKY DOMESTIC RELATIONS LAW (Banks)

DOMESTIC RELATIONS--MARYLAND
ADVOCATING FOR CHILDREN AND FAMILIES IN CINA PROCEEDING (MICPEL)
DOMESTIC VIOLENCE TRAINING MANUAL (MICPEL)

FAMILY LAW INSTITUTE (MICPEL)
FUNDAMENTALS OF FAMILY LAW (MICPEL)

DOMESTIC RELATIONS--MARYLAND-FORMS
MARYLAND DOMESTIC RELATIONS FORMS: PRACTICE (Aspen)

DOMESTIC RELATIONS--MASSACHUSETTS
COMPENDIUM OF MASSACHUSETTS FAMILY LAW (Mass. CLE)
DOMESTIC RELATIONS (MASSACHUSETTS): THE SUBSTANTIVE LAW (Butterworth-NH)
FAMILY LAW GUIDEBOOK (MASSACHUSETTS): A HANDBOOK WITH FORMS (Butterworth-NH)
MASSACHUSETTS DOMESTIC RELATIONS (Lawyers Coop.)
MASSACHUSETTS FAMILY LAW MANUAL (Mass. CLE)

DOMESTIC RELATIONS--MICHIGAN
MICHIGAN FAMILY LAW (ICLE - Michigan)
MICHIGAN FAMILY LAW SOURCEBOOK (ICLE - Michigan)

DOMESTIC RELATIONS--MINNESOTA
FAMILY LAW UPDATE (Minn. CLE)
MINNESOTA FAMILY LAW PRACTICE MANUAL, 2nd Ed. (Butterworth-St. Paul)
MINNESOTA LEGAL FORMS--FAMILY LAW (Butterworth-St. Paul)

DOMESTIC RELATIONS--MISSOURI
MISSOURI FAMILY LAW FORMBOOK (UMKC/CLE)
MISSOURI FAMILY LAW (MoBar)

DOMESTIC RELATIONS--MISSOURI-FORMS
MISSOURI DOMESTIC RELATIONS FORMS - PRACTICE (Aspen)

DOMESTIC RELATIONS--MONTANA
FAMILY LAW FORMBOOK (State Bar of Mont.)

DOMESTIC RELATIONS--NEBRASKA
NEBRASKA LEGAL FORMS--FAMILY LAW (Butterworth-St. Paul)

DOMESTIC RELATIONS--NEW HAMPSHIRE
BIRTH LAW/ADOPTION (NH Bar)

DOMESTIC RELATIONS--NEW JERSEY
NEW JERSEY FAMILY LAW PRACTICE (New Jersey ICLE)
YUDES FAMILY LAW CITATOR (New Jersey ICLE)

DOMESTIC RELATIONS--NEW YORK
CALLAGHAN'S FAMILY COURT LAW AND PRACTICE IN NEW YORK (Lawyers Coop.)
NEW YORK CIVIL PRACTICE - FAMILY COURT AND FAMILY LAW PROCEEDINGS (vol. 12, 12A, 12B) (Bender)
NEW YORK CIVIL PRACTICE - SCPA (vols. 10, 10 pt. 2, 10A, 10B, 10B pt. 2, 10C-10E) (Bender)
NEW YORK FAMILY LAW HANDBOOK (Gould)
NEW YORK PRACTICE GUIDE: DOMESTIC RELATIONS (Bender)

DOMESTIC RELATIONS--OHIO
BALDWIN'S OHIO DOMESTIC RELATIONS LAW (Banks)

DOMESTIC RELATIONS--OREGON
FAMILY LAW (Oregon Bar)

DOMESTIC RELATIONS--PENNSYLVANIA
FOUR COUNTY DOMESTIC PRACTICE (Penn. Bar)
PENNSYLVANIA DIVORCE AND DOMESTIC RELATIONS REPORTER (LRP)
PHILADELPHIA COUNTY DOMESTIC RELATIONS PRACTICE (Penn. Bar)

DOMESTIC RELATIONS--PENNSYLVANIA--FORMS
PENNSYLVANIA DOMESTIC RELATIONS FORMS--PRACTICE (Aspen)

DOMESTIC RELATIONS--TEXAS
FAMILY LAW: TEXAS PRACTICE AND PROCEDURE (Bender)
TEXAS FAMILY LAW (Butterworth-Texas)
TEXAS FAMILY LAW PRACTICE MANUAL (State Bar of Texas)
TEXAS FAMILY LAW SERVICE (Bancroft)
TEXAS FAMILY LAW TRIAL GUIDE (Bender)

DOMESTIC RELATIONS--VIRGINIA
FAMILY LAW AND PRACTICE IN VIRGINIA (Jt. Comm. Va.)
NEGOTIATING AND DRAFTING MARITAL AGREEMENTS (Jt. Comm. Va.)

DOMESTIC RELATIONS--WASHINGTON
FAMILY LAW SECTION MID-YEAR MEETING & SEMINARS (Wash. Bar)
WASHINGTON FAMILY LAW DESKBOOK (Wash. Bar)
WHEN YOU NEED TO KNOW: FAMILY LAW (Wash. Bar)

DOMESTIC RELATIONS--WISCONSIN
FAMILY LAW CASENOTES AND QUOTES (State Bar of Wisc.)
VOLUNTARY TERMINATION OF PARENTAL RIGHTS AND ADOPTION (State Bar of Wisc.)
WISCONSIN JUDICIAL BENCHBOOK: VOL. 3 - FAMILY (State Bar of Wisc.)

DRUG ABUSE
ALCOHOL AND DRUG ABUSE IN THE WORKPLACE: THE COMPLETE RESOURCE GUIDE (BNA)
DRUG ABUSE AND THE LAW SOURCEBOOK (Clark Boardman Callaghan)
GUIDE TO FEDERAL FUNDING FOR ANTI-DRUG PROGRAMS (GIS)

DRUG TESTING
DRUG AND ALCOHOL TESTING: ADVISING EMPLOYERS (Butterworth-NH)
DRUG TESTING LAW, TECHNOLOGY & PRACTICE (Clark Boardman Callaghan)
DRUG TESTING LEGAL MANUAL (Clark Boardman Callaghan)
DRUG TESTING MANUAL (Keller)
DRUG TESTING PROGRAM MATERIALS (NELI)
EMPLOYMENT SCREENING (Bender)
THE LEGAL ASPECTS OF SUBSTANCE ABUSE IN THE WORKPLACE (Bus. Laws)

DRUG TESTING--CONNECTICUT
DRUG TESTING IN THE WORKPLACE: COMPLYING WITH THE LAW (Conn. Bar)

DRUGS
see Food, drugs, cosmetics

DRUNK DRIVING
see also Automobile accidents; Traffic violations

DEFENDING DRINKING DRIVERS (James)
DEFENSE OF DRUNK DRIVING CASES: CRIMINAL - CIVIL (Bender)
DRINKING/DRIVING LITIGATION: CRIMINAL AND CIVIL (Clark Boardman Callaghan)
DRINKING/DRIVING LITIGATION TRIAL NOTEBOOK (Clark Boardman Callaghan)
LIQUOR LIABILITY LAW (Bender)

DRUNK DRIVING--CALIFORNIA
CALIFORNIA DRUNK DRIVING DEFENSE (Lawyers Coop.)
CALIFORNIA DRUNK DRIVING LAW (Fast Eddie)

DRUNK DRIVING--FLORIDA
DUI AND OTHER TRAFFIC OFFENSES IN FLORIDA (Florida Bar)
FLORIDA TRAFFIC AND D.U.I. PRACTICE MANUAL (Butterworth-Fla.)

DRUNK DRIVING--FORMS
DWI DEFENSE FORMS (James)

DRUNK DRIVING--ILLINOIS
DEFENDING DUI AND TRAFFIC CASES (Illinois ICLE)

DRUNK DRIVING--INDIANA
DEFENSE TECHNIQUES FOR DWI CLIENTS (Indiana CLE)
DWI - DRAM SHOP (Indiana CLE)

DRUNK DRIVING--MAINE
DEFENSE OF DRUNK DRIVING CASES: A GUIDE FOR THE GENERAL PRACTITIONER (Maine Bar)

DRUNK DRIVING--MARYLAND
HANDLING DWI CASES, 1991 Ed. (MICPEL)

DRUNK DRIVING--MICHIGAN
MICHIGAN DRUNK DRIVING LAW AND PRACTICE, REV. ED. (ICLE - Michigan)

DRUNK DRIVING--MINNESOTA
THE DRINKING DRIVER IN MINNESOTA, 2nd Ed. (Butterworth-St. Paul)
DRUNK DRIVING 1991 (MILE)
MINNESOTA LIQUOR LIABILITY (MILE)

DRUNK DRIVING--NEW HAMPSHIRE
THE DWI CASE: STRATEGIES AND TECHNICAL CONSIDERATIONS FOR DEFENSE AND PROSECUTION (NH Bar)

DRUNK DRIVING--OREGON
DUII TRIAL NOTEBOOK (OCDLA)

DRUNK DRIVING--SOUTH CAROLINA
THE SOUTH CAROLINA DUI DEFENSE MANUAL (S. Carolina Bar)

DRUNK DRIVING--TEXAS
TEXAS DRUNK DRIVING LAW, 2nd Ed. (Butterworth-Texas)

DRUNK DRIVING--WASHINGTON
DEFENDING DWIs IN WASHINGTON (Butterworth-St. Paul)

EDUCATION
see also Schools

EDUCATION LAW (Bender)
GUIDE TO FEDERAL FUNDING FOR EDUCATION (EFRC)
INDIVIDUALS WITH DISABILITIES EDUCATION LAW REPORTER (LRP)
LEGAL DESKBOOK FOR ADMINISTRATORS OF INDEPENDENT COLLEGES AND UNIVERSITIES (Baylor Univ. Press)

EDUCATION--MARYLAND
EDUCATION LAW (MICPEL)

ELECTION LAW
FEDERAL ELECTION CAMPAIGN FINANCING GUIDE (CCH)
MATERIALS ON CORPORATE POLITICAL ACTIVITY (Bus. Laws)
UNITED STATES FEDERAL ELECTION LAW: FEDERAL REGULATION OF POLITICAL CAMPAIGN FINANCE AND PARTICIPATION (Oceana)

ELECTION LAW--CALIFORNIA
FAIR POLITICAL PRACTICES COMMISSION NOTEBOOK SERVICE (Calif. CEB)
FAIR POLITICAL PRACTICES COMMISSION'S ENFORCEMENT DECISIONS (Calif. CEB)

ELECTRONIC FUNDS TRANSFER
see Banks and banking

EMINENT DOMAIN
CONDEMNATION PROCEDURES AND TECHNIQUES - FORMS (Real Estate Transaction Series, vols. 3 pts. 1 & 2, 3A, 3A pt. 2, 3B, 3B pt. 2) (Bender)
NICHOLS ON EMINENT DOMAIN (Bender)
PROTECTING AGAINST EXPROPRIATION OF RISK IN INVESTING ABROAD (Bender)

EMINENT DOMAIN--ARIZONA
EMINENT DOMAIN IN ARIZONA (State Bar of Ariz.)

EMINENT DOMAIN--ILLINOIS
ILLINOIS EMINENT DOMAIN PRACTICE (Illinois ICLE)

EMINENT DOMAIN--INDIANA
EMINENT DOMAIN (Indiana CLE)

EMINENT DOMAIN--MARYLAND
CONDEMNATION AND EMINENT DOMAIN (MICPEL)

EMINENT DOMAIN--MINNESOTA
EMINENT DOMAIN (MILE)
MINNESOTA CONDEMNATION LAW (Butterworth-St. Paul)

EMINENT DOMAIN--MISSOURI
MISSOURI CONDEMNATION PRACTICE (MoBar)

EMINENT DOMAIN--NEW JERSEY
CONDEMNATION: TRIAL TECHNIQUES AND RECENT DEVELOPMENTS (New Jersey ICLE)

EMINENT DOMAIN--TEXAS
RAYBURN ON CONDEMNATION/THE TEXAS LAW OF EMINENT DOMAIN (Francis Marion)

EMINENT DOMAIN--VIRGINIA
EMINENT DOMAIN--STATE AND FEDERAL (Jt. Comm. Va.)

EMPLOYEE BENEFITS
see also Pension plans; Profit sharing

ADVISING CLIENTS ABOUT WELFARE BENEFITS (Minn. CLE)
BENEFITS AND RETIREMENT PLAN GUIDE (WG&L)
BENEFITS COORDINATOR (WG&L)
COMPLETE PERSONNEL ADMINISTRATION HANDBOOK FOR LAW FIRMS (Altman Weil Pensa)
EMPLOYEE BENEFITS CASES (BNA)
EMPLOYEE BENEFITS COMPLIANCE COORDINATOR (WG&L)
EMPLOYEE BENEFITS COMPLIANCE MADE SIMPLE (BLR)
EMPLOYEE BENEFITS GUIDE (Bender)
EMPLOYEE BENEFITS LAW (Illinois ICLE)
EMPLOYEE BENEFITS LAW, ERISA AND BEYOND (Law Journal)
EMPLOYEE BENEFITS MANAGEMENT (CCH)
EMPLOYEE BENEFITS UPDATE: INCLUDING SECTION 89 (Indiana CLE)
EMPLOYEE COMPENSATION IN [YOUR STATE] (BLR)
EMPLOYEE STOCK OWNERSHIP PLANS (MILE)
EMPLOYER'S GUIDE TO MANDATED HEALTH BENEFITS - THE COBRA HANDBOOK (Thompson)
EMPLOYER'S HANDBOOK - COMPLYING WITH IRS EMPLOYEE BENEFIT RULES (Thompson)
EXECUTIVE COMPENSATION (Prentice Hall Law & Business)
EXECUTIVE COMPENSATION AND TAXATION COORDINATOR (RIA)
FEDERAL PAY AND BENEFITS REPORTER (LRP)
THE 401(K) HANDBOOK (Thompson)
THE FLEX PLAN HANDBOOK (Thompson)
FRINGE BENEFITS TAX GUIDE (CCH)
GUIDE TO ASSIGNING AND LOANING BENEFIT PLAN MONEY (Thompson)
GUIDE TO CAFETERIA PLAN DESIGN, ADMINISTRATION & COMMUNICATION (Corbel)
INTERNATIONAL BENEFITS INFORMATION SERVICE (Spencer)
MANAGING EMPLOYEE BENEFITS (WG&L)
NON-QUALIFIED DEFERRED COMPENSATION ARRANGEMENTS (Clark Boardman Callaghan)
QUALIFIED DEFERRED COMPENSATION PLANS (Clark Boardman Callaghan)
QUALIFIED DEFERRED COMPENSATION PLANS (FORMS) (Clark Boardman Callaghan)
RETIREMENT AND BENEFIT PLANNING: STRATEGY AND DESIGN FOR BUSINESSES AND TAX-EXEMPT ORGANIZATIONS (Butterworth-NH)
SECTION 89 COMPLIANCE MANUAL: THE COMPLETE GUIDE TO THE NEW NON-DISCRIMINATION RULES FOR EMPLOYEE BENEFIT PLANS (BNA)
SPENCER'S COMPLIANCE GUIDE FOR HEALTH AND BENEFIT PLANS (Spencer)
SPENCER'S RESEARCH REPORTS ON EMPLOYEE BENEFITS (Spencer)
SPENCER'S RETIREMENT PLAN SERVICE (Spencer)
TAX MANAGEMENT - COMPENSATION PLANNING (BNA)
TAX SERVICE FOR EMPLOYEE RETIREMENT PLANS (Stephens)
UNDERSTANDING EMPLOYEE BENEFITS (Ohio CLE)
WELFARE BENEFITS GUIDE 91-92 (Clark Boardman Callaghan)

MANAGING ENVIRONMENTAL RISK: REAL ESTATE AND BUSINESS TRANSACTIONS (Clark Boardman Callaghan)
MARINE POLLUTION AND THE LAW OF THE SEA (Hein)
MASTER INDEX: CLARK BOARDMAN CALLAGHAN'S ENVIRONMENTAL LAW SERIES (Clark Boardman Callaghan)
NEPA LAW AND LITIGATION (Clark Boardman Callaghan)
OIL SPILL LAW INFORMATION SERVICE (Thompson)
SPILL REPORTING PROCEDURES GUIDE (BNA Books)
STATE ENVIRONMENTAL LAW (Clark Boardman Callaghan)
STORMWATER PERMIT MANUAL (Thompson)
SUPERFUND: A LEGISLATIVE HISTORY (ELI)
TOXIC SUBSTANCES CONTROL ACT--COMPLIANCE GUIDE AND SERVICE (Environment Books)
TREATISE ON ENVIRONMENTAL LAW (Bender)
WATER POLLUTION CONTROL (BNA)

ENVIRONMENTAL LAW--CALIFORNIA
CALIFORNIA ENVIRONMENTAL LAW & LAND USE PRACTICE (Bender)

ENVIRONMENTAL LAW--CONNECTICUT
INTRODUCTION TO CONNECTICUT ENVIRONMENTAL LAW (Conn. Bar)

ENVIRONMENTAL LAW--FLORIDA
FLORIDA ENVIRONMENTAL AND LAND USE LAW (Florida Bar)

ENVIRONMENTAL LAW--FOREIGN
INTERNATIONAL ENVIRONMENT REPORTER (BNA)
INTERNATIONAL PROTECTION OF THE ENVIRONMENT: TREATIES AND RELATED DOCUMENTS 2d Series (Oceana)

ENVIRONMENTAL LAW--FORMS
ENVIRONMENTAL LAW FORMS GUIDE (Shepard's)

ENVIRONMENTAL LAW--ILLINOIS
ENVIRONMENTAL LAW FOR TRANSACTIONAL ATTORNEYS (Illinois ICLE)

ENVIRONMENTAL LAW--INDIANA
ENVIRONMENTAL LAW FOR ENVIRONMENTAL LAWYERS (Indiana CLE)
ENVIRONMENTAL LAW FOR THE GENERAL PRACTITIONER (Indiana CLE)
ENVIRONMENTAL LAW SYMPOSIUM (Indiana CLE)
WHAT EVERYONE NEEDS TO KNOW ABOUT ENVIRONMENTAL LAW (Indiana CLE)

ENVIRONMENTAL LAW--MAINE
ENVIRONMENTAL LAW (Maine Bar)

ENVIRONMENTAL LAW--MARYLAND
ISSUES ON ENVIRONMENTAL LAW (MICPEL)

ENVIRONMENTAL LAW--MASSACHUSETTS
MASSACHUSETTS ENVIRONMENTAL LAW (Mass. CLE)

ENVIRONMENTAL LAW--MINNESOTA
ENVIRONMENTAL LAW INSTITUTE (MILE)
ENVIRONMENTAL LIABILITY IN REAL ESTATE MATTERS (Minn. CLE)

ENVIRONMENTAL LAW--MISSOURI
ENVIRONMENTAL LAW (MoBar)

ENVIRONMENTAL LAW--NEW HAMPHIRE
THE NEW CLEAN AIR ACT (NH Bar)

ENVIRONMENTAL LAW--NEW JERSEY
ECRA COMPLIANCE (New Jersey ICLE)
NEW JERSEY ENVIRONMENTAL LAW (New Jersey ICLE)

ENVIRONMENTAL LAW--NEW MEXICO
BOHANNON'S NEW MEXICO ENVIRONMENTAL LAW HANDBOOK (Butterworth-Texas)

ENVIRONMENTAL LAW--NEW YORK
ENVIRONMENTAL IMPACT REVIEW IN NEW YORK (Bender)

ENVIRONMENTAL LAW--OHIO
ENVIRONMENTAL LAW (Ohio CLE)

ENVIRONMENTAL LAW--OKLAHOMA
ENVIRONMENTAL LAW UPDATE FROM VARIOUS PERSPECTIVES (Okla. Bar CLE)

ENVIRONMENTAL LAW--STATES
ENVIRONMENTAL COMPLIANCE MANAGEMENT IN [STATE] (IBL)
ENVIRONMENTAL REGULATIONS FOR [STATE] (IBL)

ENVIRONMENTAL LAW--TEXAS
TEXAS AIR CONTROL BOARD RULES (RPC)

ENVIRONMENTAL LAW--WASHINGTON
THE WASHINGTON STATE ENVIRONMENTAL POLICY ACT: A LEGAL AND POLICY ANALYSIS (SEPA) (Butterworth-St. Paul)

EQUAL EMPLOYMENT
see Affirmative action programs; Discrimination in employment; Labor and labor relations

EQUITABLE DISCRIMINATION
see Marriage and divorce

ESCHEAT
see Estates, unclaimed

ESTATE AND GIFT TAXES
ANALYSIS OF FEDERAL TAXES: INCOME, ESTATE & GIFT (RIA)
CHARITABLE LEAD TRUSTS - EXPLANATION, SPECIMEN AGREEMENTS, FORMS (Taxwise)
ESTATE PLANNING AND TAXATION COORDINATOR (RIA)
ESTATE TAX FREEZE (Bender)
ESTATE TAX TECHNIQUES (Bender)
FEDERAL ESTATE AND GIFT TAX REPORTS (CCH)
FEDERAL ESTATE AND GIFT TAXES (RIA)
THE FEDERAL ESTATE TAX PREPARATION OF THE 706 (Prof. Dev. Fdtn.)
FEDERAL INCOME, GIFT AND ESTATE TAXATION (Bender)
FIDUCIARY TAX GUIDE (CCH)
HOW TO SAVE TIME AND TAXES IN HANDLING ESTATES (How to Save Time and Taxes Series vol.1) (Bender)
HOW TO SAVE TIME AND TAXES PREPARING FIDUCIARY INCOME TAX RETURNS - FEDERAL AND STATE (How to Save Time and Taxes Series vol. 2) (Bender)
INHERITANCE, ESTATE AND GIFT TAX REPORTS (CCH)
LAW OF FEDERAL ESTATE AND GIFT TAXATION: CODE COMMENTARY (Clark Boardman Callaghan)
TAX MANAGEMENT ESTATES, GIFTS AND TRUSTS REFERENCE FILE (BNA)
TAX MANAGEMENT - ESTATES, GIFTS AND TRUSTS SERIES (BNA)

ESTATE AND GIFT TAXES--HONG KONG
HONG KONG REVENUE LAW (Bender)

ESTATE AND GIFT TAXES--MASSACHUSETTS
ESTATE TAXATION IN MASSACHUSETTS, WITH FORMS (Lawyers Coop.)

ESTATE AND GIFT TAXES--PENNSYLVANIA
PENNSYLVANIA INHERITANCE AND ESTATE TAX (Bisel)

ESTATE AND GIFTS TAXES--WISCONSIN
WISCONSIN INHERITANCE, ESTATE AND GIFT TAX HANDBOOK (CLE - Wisc.)

ESTATE PLANNING
ADVANCED ESTATE PLANNING INSTITUTE (Georgetown)
ESTATE & PERSONAL FINANCIAL PLANNING (Clark Boardman Callaghan)
ESTATE PLANNING (Law Journal)

ESTATE PLANNING (RIA)
ESTATE PLANNING, 5TH ED. (Little, Brown)
ESTATE PLANNING AND TAXATION COORDINATOR (RIA)
ESTATE PLANNING CHECKLISTS/FORMS (RIA)
ESTATE PLANNING FOR FARMERS & RANCHERS, 2nd ed. (Shepard's)
ESTATE PLANNING LAW AND TAXATION (WG&L)
ESTATE PLANNING MANUAL FOR TRUST OFFICERS (Am. Bankers)
ESTATE PLANNING SIMPLIFIED (Wiley Law)
ESTATE TAX TECHNIQUES (Bender)
FEDERAL TAXATION OF TRUSTS, GRANTORS AND BENEFICIARIES (WG&L)
FINANCIAL AND ESTATE PLANNING (CCH)
FINANCIAL AND ESTATE PLANNING RESOURCE GUIDE (Bender)
MCGAFFEY LEGAL FORMS WITH TAX ANALYSIS - ESTATE & PERSONAL PLANNING (VOL. 3) (Clark Boardman Callaghan)
MIAMI INSTITUTE ON ESTATE PLANNING (Bender)
MIDWEST ESTATE, TAX & BUSINESS PLANNING (Indiana CLE)
MODERN ESTATE PLANNING (Bender)
THE 9TH ANNUAL FEDERAL ESTATE PLANNING SYMPOSIUM (UMKC/CLE)
SUCCESSFUL ESTATE PLANNING IDEAS & METHODS (RIA)
TAX, ESTATE AND FINANCIAL PLANNING FOR THE ELDERLY -- FORMS AND PRACTICE (Bender)
WG&L ESTATE PLANNING AND ADMINISTRATION (WG&L)

ESTATE PLANNING--CALIFORNIA
CALIFORNIA WILL DRAFTING, THIRD EDITION (Calif. CEB)
ESTATE PLANNING PRACTICE (Calif. CEB)

ESTATE PLANNING--CANADA
CANADIAN ESTATE PLANNING AND ADMINISTRATION REPORTER (CCH)

ESTATE PLANNING--COLORADO
COLORADO ESTATE PLANNING (Parker)
COLORADO ESTATE PLANNING FORMS BOOK (CLE - Colorado)
COLORADO ESTATE PLANNING HANDBOOK (CLE - Colorado)
COLORADO ESTATE PLANNING, WILL DRAFTING AND ESTATE ADMINISTRATION FORMS - PRACTICE (Aspen)

ESTATE PLANNING--FLORIDA
LIFE PLANNING IN FLORIDA (Butterworth-Fla.)

ESTATE PLANNING--GEORGIA-FORMS
GEORGIA ESTATE PLANNING, WILL DRAFTING AND ESTATE ADMINISTRATION FORMS--PRACTICE (Aspen)

ESTATE PLANNING--HAWAII
ENCYCLOPEDIA OF FINANCIAL AND ESTATE PLANNING (HICLE)
FINANCIAL AND ESTATE PLANNING FORMS MANUAL (HICLE)

ESTATE PLANNING--ILLINOIS
BASIC ESTATE PLANNING (Illinois ICLE)

ESTATE PLANNING--ILLINOIS-FORMS
ILLINOIS ESTATE PLANNING, WILL DRAFTING AND ESTATE ADMINISTRATION FORMS--PRACTICE (Aspen)

ESTATE PLANNING--INDIANA
BASIC ESTATE PLANNING (Indiana CLE)
ESTATE PLANNING (Indiana CLE)
ESTATE PLANNING & ADMINISTRATION IN INDIANA (Indiana CLE)
INDIANA ESTATE PLANNING AND PROBATE PRACTICE (Bender)

ESTATE PLANNING--INTERNATIONAL
INTERNATIONAL ESTATE PLANNING (Shepard's)

ESTATE PLANNING--LOUISIANA
ESTATE PLANNING IN LOUISIANA (Lawyers Coop.)

ESTATE PLANNING--MAINE
PRACTICAL ESTATE PLANNING: MORE THAN JUST WILLS (Maine Bar)
TECHNIQUES FOR POST MORTEM ESTATE PLANNING (Maine Bar)

ESTATE PLANNING--MARYLAND
ADVANCED ESTATE PLANNING (MICPEL)
BUSINESS, TAX & ESTATE PLANNING FOR THE CLOSELY-HELD BUSINESS (MICPEL)
FUNDAMENTALS OF ESTATE PLANNING (MICPEL)
POST-MORTEM ESTATE PLANNING (MICPEL)

ESTATE PLANNING--MARYLAND-FORMS
MASSACHUSETTS ESTATE PLANNING, WILL DRAFTING AND ESTATE ADMINISTRATION FORMS--PRACTICE (Aspen)

ESTATE PLANNING--MASSACHUSETTS
ESTATE PLANNING FOR THE AGING OR INCAPACITATED CLIENT IN MASSACHUSETTS (Mass. CLE)

ESTATE PLANNING--MICHIGAN-FORMS
MICHIGAN ESTATE PLANNING, WILL DRAFTING AND ESTATE ADMINISTRATION FORMS--PRACTICE (Aspen)

ESTATE PLANNING--MINNESOTA
CHARITABLE TRUSTS IN ESTATE PLANNING (Minn. CLE)
ESTATE PLANNING FOR THE SINGLE PARENT (Minn. CLE)
FUNDAMENTALS OF ESTATE PLANNING PRACTICE (Minn. CLE)
WILL DRAFTING AND BASIC ESTATE PLANNING (MILE)

ESTATE PLANNING--MISSOURI
MISSOURI ESTATE PLANNING (MoBar)

ESTATE PLANNING--MISSOURI-FORMS
MISSOURI ESTATE PLANNING, WILL DRAFTING AND ESTATE ADMINISTRATION FORMS - PRACTICE (Aspen)

ESTATE PLANNING--NEW HAMPSHIRE
ESTATE PLANNING -- BASICS (NH Bar)

ESTATE PLANNING--NEW JERSEY
ESTATE PLANNING AND BUSINESS TAX SYMPOSIUM (New Jersey ICLE)

ESTATE PLANNING--NEW JERSEY-FORMS
NEW JERSEY ESTATE PLANNING, WILL DRAFTING AND ESTATE ADMINISTRATION FORMS--PRACTICE (Aspen)

ESTATE PLANNING--NEW YORK
NEW YORK ESTATES - WILLS - TRUSTS (CCH)

ESTATE PLANNING--OKLAHOMA
DRAFTING ESTATE PLANNING DOCUMENTS (Okla. Bar CLE)
SIMPLE ESTATE PLANNING (Okla. Bar CLE)

ESTATE PLANNING--OKLAHOMA-FORMS
OKLAHOMA ESTATE PLANNING, WILL DRAFTING AND ESTATE ADMINISTRATION FORMS (Aspen)

ESTATE PLANNING--PENNSYLVANIA
PENNSYLVANIA ESTATE PLANNING AND DRAFTING (Bisel)

ESTATE PLANNING--VIRGINIA
BASIC ESTATE PLANNING AND ADMINISTRATION (Jt. Comm. Va.)

ESTATE PLANNING--WASHINGTON
ANNUAL ESTATE PLANNING SEMINAR (Wash. Bar)

ESTATE PLANNING--WISCONSIN
ECKHARDT'S WORKBOOK FOR WISCONSIN ESTATE PLANNERS (State Bar of Wisc.)

ESTATES--ALABAMA
HOW TO ADMINISTER ESTATES IN ALABAMA (ABICLE)

ESTATES--CALIFORNIA
CALIFORNIA DECEDENT ESTATE PRACTICE (Calif. CEB)

ESTATES--CONNECTICUT
PLANNING FOR ESTATE FREEZES UNDER NEW CHAPTER 14 (Conn. Bar)

ESTATES--FLORIDA
FLORIDA ESTATES PRACTICE GUIDE (Bender)

ESTATES--ILLINOIS
BUSINESS INTERESTS IN ESTATES (Illinois ICLE)
CONTESTED ESTATES (Illinois ICLE)
ILLINOIS ESTATE ADMINISTRATION (Illinois ICLE)

ESTATES--INDIANA
ESTATE & GUARDIANSHIP ADMINISTRATION (Indiana CLE)

ESTATES--KANSAS
KANSAS ESTATE ADMINISTRATION (Kansas Bar)

ESTATES--LOUISIANA
LOUISIANA SUCCESSIONS (Lawyers Coop.)

ESTATES--MARYLAND
FIDUCIARY INCOME TAXES (MICPEL)
GIBBER ON ADMINISTERING ESTATES IN MARYLAND (MICPEL)
MARYLAND ESTATE PLANNING, WILL DRAFTING AND ESTATE ADMINISTRATION FORMS: PRACTICE (Aspen)

ESTATES--MASSACHUSETTS
ESTATE ADMINISTRATION (MASSACHUSETTS): A HANDBOOK WITH FORMS (Butterworth-NH)

ESTATES--MICHIGAN
PROBATE ADMINISTRATION IN MICHIGAN: A SYSTEMS APPROACH (ICLE - Michigan)

ESTATES--MINNESOTA
NEW ESTATE FREEZING RULES (Minn. CLE)

ESTATES--MISSOURI
MISSOURI ESTATE ADMINISTRATION (MoBar)

ESTATES--NEW YORK
NEW YORK CIVIL PRACTICE - ESTATES, POWERS, TRUSTS LAW (vols. 9, 9 pt. 2, 9A, 9A pt. 2, 9B, 9C, 9D) (Bender)

ESTATES--NORTH CAROLINA
NORTH CAROLINA ESTATE ADMINISTRATION MANUAL (No. Carolina Bar)

ESTATES--OHIO-FORMS
THE NEW MANUAL OF STANDARD FORMS FOR DECEDENTS' ESTATES (Ohio State Bar)

ESTATES--OREGON
ADMINISTERING OREGON ESTATES (Oregon Bar)

ESTATES--PENNSYLVANIA
PENNSYLVANIA ESTATES PRACTICE (Lawyers Coop.)

ESTATES--WASHINGTON
WASHINGTON PROBATE PRACTICE, PROCEDURE AND TAX MANUALS (Book Pub.)

ESTATES, UNCLAIMED
ESCHEAT AND ABANDONED PROPERTY LAWS (ASCS)

GUIDE TO UNCLAIMED PROPERTY AND ESCHEAT LAWS (Commonwealth)
UNCLAIMED PROPERTY LAW (Bender)

ETHICS
see also Legal ethics

CORPORATE COUNSEL'S GUIDE TO BUSINESS ETHICS POLICIES (Bus. Laws)
ETHICS IN GOVERNMENT REPORTER (WSB)

EUROPEAN COMMUNITY
BUSINESS LAW IN EUROPE (Kluwer)
COMMON MARKET REPORTS (CCH)
COMPETITION LAW OF THE EEC (Bender)
CORPORATE COUNSEL'S GUIDE TO EUROPEAN ECONOMIC COMMUNITY LAW (Bus. Laws)
EEC MERGER CONTROL REPORTER (Kluwer)
EUROPE 1992 (Ohio CLE)
EUROPEAN COMMUNITY COMPANY LAW (Oceana)
EUROPEAN COMMUNITY LAW & BUSINESS REPORTER (Legal-Med.)
FINANCIAL SERVICES AND EEC LAW (Kluwer)
LAW AND PRACTICE UNDER THE GATT AND OTHER TRADING ARRANGEMENTS: EUROPEAN COMMUNITY: THE SINGLE MARKET ACT (Oceana)
THE LAW OF THE EUROPEAN ECONOMIC COMMUNITY - A COMMENTARY ON THE EEC TREATY (Bender)
SINGLE EUROPEAN MARKET REPORTER (Kluwer)
UNITED STATES, COMMON MARKET AND INTERNATIONAL ANTITRUST: A COMPARATIVE GUIDE (Prentice Hall Law & Business)

EVIDENCE
DEMONSTRATIVE EVIDENCE (Art of Advocacy Series) (Bender)
THE DEMONSTRATIVE EVIDENCE SOURCEBOOK (Staffort)
DOCUMENTARY EVIDENCE (Art of Advocacy Series) (Bender)
EVIDENCE (TEXAS & NATIONAL EDITIONS) (Knowles)
EVIDENCE: SELECTED PROBLEMS (NH Bar)
FEDERAL COURTROOM EVIDENCE (Parker)
FEDERAL EVIDENCE FOUNDATIONS (Butterworth-Texas)
FEDERAL EVIDENCE PRACTICE GUIDE (Bender)
FEDERAL RULES OF EVIDENCE (Clark Boardman Callaghan)
FEDERAL RULES OF EVIDENCE SERVICE (Lawyers Coop.)
FEDERAL TRIAL EVIDENCE (James)
FEDERAL TRIAL EVIDENCE (Butterworth-NH)
LEGALITY OF MICROFILM (Cohasset)
MODERN VISUAL EVIDENCE (Law Journal)
QUALIFYING & ATTACKING EXPERT WITNESSES (James)
TANGIBLE EVIDENCE: HOW TO USE EXHIBITS AT TRIAL (Prentice Hall Law & Business)
TRIAL EVIDENCE FOUNDATIONS (James)
TRIAL OBJECTIONS (James)
UNCHARGED MISCONDUCT EVIDENCE (Clark Boardman Callaghan)
WEINSTEIN'S EVIDENCE MANUAL (Bender)
WEINSTEIN'S EVIDENCE, UNITED STATES COURT RULES (Bender)

EVIDENCE--ARIZONA
ARIZONA COURTROOM EVIDENCE MANUAL (State Bar of Ariz.)

EVIDENCE--ARKANSAS
ARKANSAS RULES OF EVIDENCE (Francis Marion)

EVIDENCE--CALIFORNIA
CALIFORNIA COURTROOM EVIDENCE (Parker)
EFFECTIVE INTRODUCTION OF EVIDENCE IN CALIFORNIA (Calif. CEB)
GUIDE TO CALIFORNIA EVIDENCE (Parker)
TRIAL ATTORNEY'S EVIDENCE CODE NOTEBOOK, 3rd ed. (Calif. CEB)

EVIDENCE--COLORADO
COLORADO RULES OF EVIDENCE (ANNOTATED) (CLP)

EVIDENCE--CONNECTICUT
CONNECTICUT EVIDENCE (Atlantic)

EVIDENCE--DISTRICT OF COLUMBIA
LAW OF EVIDENCE IN THE DISTRICT OF COLUMBIA (Bar Assn. of D.C.)

EVIDENCE--FLORIDA
EVIDENCE IN FLORIDA (Florida Bar)
FLORIDA EVIDENCE MANUAL (Butterworth-Fla.)
FLORIDA RULES OF CRIMINAL EVIDENCE (Francis Marion)
FLORIDA TRIAL EVIDENCE (Wiley Law)
READ'S FLORIDA EVIDENCE (Lawyers Coop.)

EVIDENCE--HAWAII
HAWAII RULES OF EVIDENCE (Francis Marion)

EVIDENCE--ILLINOIS
ILLINOIS CIVIL TRIAL EVIDENCE (Illinois ICLE)
ILLINOIS TRIAL EVIDENCE (James)

EVIDENCE--INDIANA
DEMONSTRATIVE EVIDENCE (Indiana CLE)
EVIDENCE: KEEPING IT OUT (Indiana CLE)

EVIDENCE--KANSAS
KANSAS EVIDENCE OBJECTIONS WITH EVIDENTIARY FOUNDATIONS (Kansas Bar)

EVIDENCE--KENTUCKY
KENTUCKY LAW OF EVIDENCE (Anderson)

EVIDENCE--LOUISIANA
LOUISIANA COURTROOM EVIDENCE (Parker)

EVIDENCE--MAINE
MAINE EVIDENCE (Butterworth-NH)

EVIDENCE--MARYLAND
MARYLAND EVIDENCE CHECKLISTS (MICPEL)

EVIDENCE--MASSACHUSETTS
MASSACHUSETTS EVIDENCE: A COURTROOM REFERENCE (Mass. CLE)
A PRACTICAL GUIDE TO INTRODUCING EVIDENCE (Mass. CLE)

EVIDENCE--MICHIGAN
EVIDENCE -- A TRIAL MANUAL FOR MICHIGAN LAWYERS (Lawyers Coop.)
INTRODUCING EVIDENCE: A PRACTICAL GUIDE FOR MICHIGAN LAWYERS (ICLE - Michigan)
MICHIGAN COURTROOM EVIDENCE (ICLE - Michigan)

EVIDENCE--MINNESOTA
MINNESOTA EVIDENCE - A PRACTICAL WORKSHOP (MILE)
MINNESOTA EVIDENCE TRIALBOOK (Butterworth-St. Paul)

EVIDENCE--MISSOURI
MISSOURI EVIDENCE (MoBar)
MISSOURI SOURCES OF PROOF (MoBar)

EVIDENCE--NEW MEXICO
NEW MEXICO RULES OF EVIDENCE TREATISE (rev. ed.) (Butterworth-Texas)

EVIDENCE--NEW YORK
BENDER'S NEW YORK EVIDENCE - CPLR (Bender)
NEW YORK CANUDO ON EVIDENCE LAWS (Gould)
NEW YORK COURTROOM EVIDENCE (Parker)
NEW YORK SUPPRESSION MANUAL (Bender)

<u>FARMERS--MISSOURI</u>
MISSOURI FARM LAW (MoBar)

<u>FEDERAL AID</u>
see Grants

<u>FINANCE, PERSONAL</u>
see also Consumer finance

ADVANCED UNDERWRITING SERVICE (AUS) (Dearborn)
FINANCIAL AND ESTATE PLANNING RESOURCE GUIDE (Bender)
TAX MANAGEMENT FINANCIAL PLANNING (BNA)

<u>FINANCIAL STATEMENTS</u>
see also Accounting; Securities

ACCOUNTANTS SEC PRACTICE MANUAL (CCH)
FINANCIAL STATEMENT PREPARATION MANUAL (CCH)
FRAUD, WINDOW DRESSING, AND NEGLIGENCE IN FINANCIAL STATEMENTS (Shepard's)
SEC ACCOUNTING AND REPORTING MANUAL (WG&L)
SEC COMPLIANCE - FINANCIAL REPORTING AND FORMS (WG&L)
SEC FINANCIAL REPORTING - ANNUAL REPORTS TO SHAREHOLDERS - FORM 10-K, QUARTERLY FINANCIAL REPORTING, 2ND ED. (Bender)

<u>FINANCING</u>
ASSET-BASED FINANCING (Bender)
COMMERCIAL ASSET-BASED FINANCING (Clark Boardman Callaghan)
FINANCING FOREIGN OPERATIONS (FFO) (Bus. Intern.)
FINANCING FOREIGN OPERATIONS/LATIN AMERICA (Bus. Intern.)
FUNDING WASTEWATER TREATMENT FACILITIES: THE COMPLETE RESOURCE GUIDE TO THE NEW STATE REVOLVING FUND PROGRAM (BNA)
THE LAW OF REAL ESTATE FINANCING (WG&L)
REAL ESTATE FINANCING TEXT, FORMS, TAX ANALYSIS (Real Estate Transaction Series, Vol. 4-5) (Bender)
STATE & LOCAL GOVERNMENT DEBT FINANCING (Clark Boardman Callaghan)
VENTURE CAPITAL AND SMALL BUSINESS FINANCINGS (Securities Law Series, Vol. 2, 2A & 2B) (Clark Boardman Callaghan)

<u>FINANCING--ILLINOIS</u>
FINANCING REAL ESTATE TRANSACTIONS (Illinois ICLE)
ILLINOIS COMMERCIAL FINANCING (Aspen)

<u>FINANCING--MARYLAND</u>
HUD AND CDA FINANCING TECHNIQUES (MICPEL)

<u>FINANCING--STATES</u>
STATE LEGISLATIVE COMPILATIONS: SELECTED SUMMARIES OF REAL ESTATE FINANCE LAWS (MBAA)

<u>FIRE INSURANCE</u>
see Insurance, fire

<u>FIRES</u>
NATIONAL FIRE CODES SUBSCRIPTION SERVICE (Natl. Fire Protection Assn.)
UNIFORM FIRE CODE (ICBO)

<u>FOOD, DRUGS, COSMETICS</u>
CONTROLLED SUBSTANCES: A LEGAL AND CHEMICAL GUIDE TO THE FEDERAL DRUG LAWS (Ronin)
DRUG & MEDICAL DEVICE LIABILITY (MILE)
DRUG PRODUCT LIABILITY (Bender)
FDA COMPLIANCE POLICY GUIDES MANUAL (NTIS - order # PB91-915499/CAU (manual); PB91-915400/CAU (updates))
THE FDA ENFORCEMENT MANUAL (Thompson)
FOOD AND DRUG ADMINISTRATION REGULATORY MANUAL (Shepard's)
FOOD DRUG COSMETIC LAW REPORTS (CCH)

GENERIC DRUGS: A GUIDE TO FDA APPROVAL REQUIREMENTS (Prentice Hall Law & Business)
GUIDE TO U.S. FOOD LABELING LAW (Thompson)
HIMA REGULATORY MANUAL (HIMA)
MEDICAL DEVICES REPORTER (CCH)
PHARMACY LAW DIGEST (Facts)
RECALL MANUAL: A GUIDE FOR MANAGEMENT (HIMA)

FORECLOSURES--ARIZONA
INS AND OUTS OF FORECLOSURES (State Bar of Ariz.)

FORECLOSURES--CALIFORNIA
CALIFORNIA FORECLOSURE: LAW AND PRACTICE (Shepard's)
FORECLOSURE LAW MANUAL (State Bar of Calif.)

FORECLOSURES--COLORADO
PUBLIC TRUSTEE FORECLOSURE - COLORADO (CLE - Colorado)

FORECLOSURES--CONNECTICUT
CONTEMPORARY ISSUES IN FORECLOSURES (Conn. Bar)

FORECLOSURES--ILLINOIS
DEEDS IN LIEU OF FORECLOSURE (Illinois ICLE)

FORECLOSURES--MAINE
COPING WITH FORECLOSURES (Maine Bar)

FORECLOSURES--MARYLAND
GORDON ON MARYLAND FORECLOSURES (MICPEL)

FORECLOSURES--MASSACHUSETTS
MASSACHUSETTS FORECLOSURES (Mass. CLE)

FORECLOSURES--MINNESOTA
FORECLOSURES IN MINNESOTA (Minn. CLE)
MORTGAGE FORECLOSURES IN MINNESOTA (Minn. CLE)

FORECLOSURES--NEW JERSEY
NEW JERSEY MORTGAGE FORECLOSURE HANDBOOK (New Jersey ICLE)

FORECLOSURES--NEW YORK
BERGMAN ON NEW YORK MORTGAGE FORECLOSURES (Bender)
MORTGAGES AND MORTGAGE FORECLOSURE IN NEW YORK (Lawyers Coop.)

FORECLOSURES--OREGON
FORECLOSING SECURITY INTERESTS (Oregon Bar)

FORECLOSURES--WASHINGTON
A PRACTICAL APPROACH TO REAL ESTATE LOAN DEFAULTS AND WORKOUTS (Wash. Bar)

FOREIGN INVESTMENTS
see Investments, foreign

FOREIGN LICENSING AGREEMENTS
CHINA HAND: INVESTING, LICENSING & TRADING CONDITIONS TODAY (Bus. Intern.)
ESTABLISHING A U.S. JOINT VENTURE WITH A FOREIGN PARTNER (Bender)
INVESTING, LICENSING AND TRADING CONDITIONS ABROAD (ILT) (Bus. Intern.)
JOINT VENTURES (Clark Boardman Callaghan)
JOINT VENTURES: STRUCTURING ALTERNATIVES (Shepard's)
LICENSING IN FOREIGN AND DOMESTIC OPERATIONS (Clark Boardman Callaghan)
TRANSNATIONAL JOINT VENTURES (Bus. Laws)
UNITED STATES, COMMON MARKET AND INTERNATIONAL ANTITRUST: A COMPARATIVE GUIDE (Prentice Hall Law & Business)

FOREIGN LICENSING AGREEMENTS--FORMS
LICENSING IN FOREIGN AND DOMESTIC OPERATIONS: FORMS (Clark Boardman Callaghan)

FORENSIC SCIENCE
see Criminal investigation

FORENSIC TOXICOLOGY
COURTROOM TOXICOLOGY (Bender)

FORMS
BASIC BOOK OF BUSINESS AGREEMENTS (Enterprise)
BASIC LEGAL FORMS (WG&L)
BENDER'S FEDERAL PRACTICE FORMS (Bender)
BENDER'S FORMS OF DISCOVERY (Bender)
BUSINESS FORMS FROM ALI-ABA COURSE MATERIALS (ALI-ABA)
THE COMPLETE BOOK OF CORPORATE FORMS (Enterprise)
CURRENT LEGAL FORMS WITH TAX ANALYSIS (Bender)
DATA PROCESSING AGREEMENTS (2nd ed.) (Bus. Laws)
DIGEST OF COMMERCIAL LAWS OF THE WORLD -- FORMS OF COMMERCIAL AGREEMENTS OF THE WORLD (Oceana)
DRAFTING THE DURABLE POWER OF ATTORNEY: A SYSTEMS APPROACH, 2nd ed. (Shepard's)
FORM DRAFTING CHECKLISTS - AM JUR PRACTICE GUIDE (Lawyers Coop.)
FORMS AND PROCEDURES UNDER THE UNIFORM COMMERCIAL CODE (Bender's Uniform Commercial Code service vols. 5, 5A, 5B, 5C, 5D) (Bender)
FORMS OF BUSINESS AGREEMENTS, VOLS. 1 & 2 (WG&L)
FORMS OF BUSINESS AGREEMENTS, VOL. 3 (Commercial Transactions) (WG&L)
GUIDE TO PURCHASE & SALES FORMS (Bus. Laws)
LANE'S GOLDSTEIN LITIGATION FORMS (Clark Boardman Callaghan)
LEGAL CHECKLISTS - SPECIALLY SELECTED FORMS (Clark Boardman Callaghan)
LITIGATION FORMS AND CHECKLISTS (Wiley Law)
MCGAFFEY LEGAL FORMS WITH TAX ANALYSIS (Clark Boardman Callaghan)
MCGAFFEY LEGAL FORMS WITH TAX ANALYSIS - ESTATE & PERSONAL PLANNING (VOL. 3) (Clark Boardman Callaghan)
PURCHASER'S FORMBOOK OF CONTRACTS AND AGREEMENTS (Bus. Laws)
SIMPLIFIED CONSUMER CREDIT FORMS (WG&L)
WARREN'S FORMS OF AGREEMENTS (Bender)
WARREN'S FORMS OF AGREEMENTS - BUSINESS FORMS: DESK EDITION (Bender)

FORMS--ARKANSAS
ARKANSAS FORMBOOK (Arkansas Bar)

FORMS--CALIFORNIA
CALIFORNIA CIVIL LITIGATION FORMS MANUAL (Calif. CEB)
CALIFORNIA FORMS OF PLEADING AND PRACTICE-ANNOTATED (Bender)
CALIFORNIA JUDICIAL COUNCIL FORMS MANUAL (Calif. CEB)
CALIFORNIA LEGAL FORMS - TRANSACTION GUIDE (Bender)
CALIFORNIA PLEADING AND PRACTICE FORMS (Lawyers Coop.)
CALIFORNIA REAL ESTATE FORMS AND COMMENTARIES (Prentice Hall Law & Business)
LEGAL SECRETARY'S HANDBOOK (Rutter)

FORMS--COLORADO
COLORADO LAW OFFICE HANDBOOK (Parker)

FORMS--FLORIDA
BENDER'S FLORIDA FORMS OF PLEADING (Bender)
HARRISON'S SAPP. FLORIDA PLEADINGS, PRACTICE & LEGAL FORMS ANNOTATED, 2D ED. (Harrison)
LEGAL FORMS AND WORKSHEETS (Florida Bar)

FORMS--GEORGIA
CIVIL PLEADING AND PRACTICE FORMS, GEORGIA (Harrison)

FORMS--INDIANA
INDIANA FORMS OF PLEADING AND PRACTICE (Bender)

<u>FORMS--KENTUCKY</u>
KENTUCKY FORMS & TRANSACTIONS (Banks Baldwin)

<u>FORMS--MARYLAND</u>
DISTRICT COURT FORMS (MICPEL)
MARYLAND PRACTICE FORMS (MICPEL)

<u>FORMS--MASSACHUSETTS</u>
MASSACHUSETTS PLEADING AND PRACTICE - FORMS AND COMMENTARY (Bender)
MASSACHUSETTS STANDARDIZED CIVIL PRACTICE FORMS (Little, Brown)

<u>FORMS--MICHIGAN</u>
MICHIGAN BUSINESS FORMBOOK (ICLE - Michigan)

<u>FORMS--MISSOURI</u>
MISSOURI CIVIL PROCEDURE FORMBOOK (UMKC/CLE)
MISSOURI CORPORATE AND PARTNERSHIP FORMS HANDBOOK (UMKC/CLE)
MISSOURI FAMILY LAW FORMBOOK (UMKC/CLE)

<u>FORMS--NEW JERSEY</u>
NEW JERSEY CORPORATE FORMS (Aspen)
NEW JERSEY LAW WITH FORMS (Bender)

<u>FORMS--NEW YORK</u>
BENDER'S FORMS FOR THE CIVIL PRACTICE (Bender)
BENDER'S FORMS OF PLEADING (Bender)
BILLS OF PARTICULARS IN NEW YORK (Lawyers Coop.)
MEDINA'S BOSTWICK LAWYERS MANUAL (Bender)
NEW YORK COURT FORMS (Gould)
NEW YORK LAWYER'S FORMBOOK (NYSBA)
NEW YORK LEGAL FORMS & PROCEDURES HANDBOOK (Gould)

<u>FORMS--OHIO</u>
OHIO FORMS AND TRANSACTIONS (Banks)
OHIO FORMS OF PLEADING AND PRACTICE (Bender)
OHIO LEGAL FILING DIRECTORY (Shepard's)
OHIO TRANSACTION GUIDE - LEGAL FORMS (Bender)

<u>FORMS--PENNSYLVANIA</u>
DUNLAP-HANNA, PENNSYLVANIA FORMS (Bender)
PENNSYLVANIA TRANSACTION GUIDE - LEGAL FORMS (Bender)

<u>FORMS--TEXAS</u>
TEXAS LAW OFFICE HANDBOOK (Parker)
TEXAS LEGAL PRACTICE FORMS (Lawyers Coop.)
TEXAS PERSONAL INJURY FORMS (Butterworth-Texas)
TEXAS TRANSACTION GUIDE - LEGAL FORMS (Bender)

<u>FORMS--WISCONSIN</u>
WISCONSIN CIVIL PRACTICE FORMS (Lawyers Coop.)

<u>FOUNDATIONS</u>
ESTABLISHING A CHARITABLE FOUNDATION IN MICHIGAN (Council of Mich. Fdtns.)
EXEMPT ORGANIZATIONS REPORTS (CCH)

<u>FRANCHISES</u>
BUSINESS FRANCHISE GUIDE (CCH)
ESTABLISHING A TRANSNATIONAL FRANCHISE (Bender)
FRANCHISE & DISTRIBUTION LAW & PRACTICE (Clark Boardman Callaghan)
FRANCHISING (Business Organizations vols. 15, 15A, 15B & 15C) (Bender)
FRANCHISING: REALITIES AND REMEDIES (Law Journal)
FRANCHISING: REALITIES AND REMEDIES FORMS VOLUME (Law Journal)
FTC FRANCHISING RULE: THE IFA COMPLIANCE KIT (IFA)
THE 12TH ANNUAL FRANCHISE LAW INSTITUTE (UMKC/CLE)

<u>FRANCHISES--FLORIDA</u>
FRANCHISING AND LICENSING OF PUBLIC SERVICES IN FLORIDA (Butterworth-Fla.)

FRANCHISES--MARYLAND
FRANCHISES (MICPEL)

FRANCHISES--WISCONSIN
THE WISCONSIN FAIR DEALERSHIP LAW (State Bar of Wisc.)

FRAUD
BUSINESS CRIME (Bender)
THE BUSINESS TORT OF FRAUD AND MISREPRESENTATION (Butterworth-NH)
FALSE CLAIMS, ANTI-KICKBACK AND PROGRAM FRAUD CIVIL REMEDIES (BNA)
FRAUD, WINDOW DRESSING, AND NEGLIGENCE IN FINANCIAL STATEMENTS (Shepard's)
LITIGATION AND PRACTICE UNDER RULE 10B-5 (Securities Law Series, vol. 5, 5A, 5B, 5C & 5D) (Clark Boardman Callaghan)
LYING, CHEATING AND STEALING (MILE)
SECURITIES FRAUD: LITIGATING UNDER RULE 10B-5 (Aspen)
SECURITIES FRAUD AND COMMODITIES FRAUD (Shepard's)
WHITE COLLAR CRIME: BUSINESS AND REGULATORY OFFENSES (Law Journal)

FRAUD--CALIFORNIA
CALIFORNIA WHITE COLLAR CRIME (Parker)

FRAUD--INDIANA
FRAUDULENT CONVEYANCES (Indiana CLE)

FRAUD--MINNESOTA
FRAUD -- CIVIL FRAUD & WHITE COLLAR CRIME (MILE)

FREE PORTS AND ZONES
see International trade

FREEDOM OF INFORMATION
ACCESS REPORTS/FREEDOM OF INFORMATION NEWSLETTER AND REFERENCE FILE (Access Reports)
FEDERAL INFORMATION DISCLOSURE (Shepard's)
GUIDEBOOK TO THE FREEDOM OF INFORMATION AND PRIVACY ACTS (Clark Boardman Callaghan)
INFORMATION LAW: FREEDOM OF INFORMATION, PRIVACY, OPEN MEETINGS, OTHER ACCESS LAWS (PLI)
PRIVACY LAW AND PRACTICE (Bender)

FREEDOM OF INFORMATION--MARYLAND
MARYLAND PUBLIC INFORMATION ACT (MICPEL)

FREEDOM OF SPEECH
NIMMER ON FREEDOM OF SPEECH (Bender)

GAS
see Oil and Gas

GIFT TAXES
see Estate and Gift Taxes

GOVERNMENT
see also Local government; Municipal government

THE CALIFORNIA STATE GOVERNMENT DIRECTORY (Calif. Jnl. Press)
CONGRESSIONAL INVESTIGATIONS: LAW AND PRACTICE (Prentice Hall Law & Business)
FEDERAL ORGANIZATION SERVICE CIVIL (Carroll)
FEDERAL ORGANIZATION SERVICE MILITARY (Carroll)
FEDERAL REGULATORY PROCESS: AGENCY PRACTICES & PROCEDURES (Prentice Hall Law & Business)
FIFTY-STATE LEGISLATIVE DIRECTORY (Calif. Jnl. Press)
THE GOVERNMENT SECURITIES MANUAL (PSA)
GOVERNMENTAL ACCOUNTING AND AUDITING DISCLOSURE MANUAL (WG&L)
GUIDE TO FEDERAL FUNDING FOR GOVERNMENTS AND NON-PROFITS (GIS)

INSURANCE AND RISK MANAGEMENT FOR STATE AND LOCAL GOVERNMENTS (Bender)
STATE & LOCAL GOVERNMENT DEBT FINANCING (Clark Boardman Callaghan)

<u>GOVERNMENT--CALIFORNIA</u>
CALIFORNIA PUBLIC AGENCY PRACTICE (Bender)

<u>GOVERNMENT--CANADA</u>
CANADIAN GOVERNMENT PROGRAMS AND SERVICES GUIDE (CCH)

<u>GOVERNMENT--MICHIGAN</u>
MICHIGAN PUBLIC BENEFITS MANUAL (Mich. Legal)

<u>GOVERNMENT CONTRACTS</u>
ACCOUNTING FOR GOVERNMENT CONTRACTS - COST ACCOUNTING STANDARDS (Bender)
ACCOUNTING FOR GOVERNMENT CONTRACTS - FEDERAL ACQUISITION REGULATION (Bender)
BOARD OF CONTRACT APPEALS BID PROTEST DECISIONS (Fed. Publ.)
COMPTROLLER GENERAL'S PROCUREMENT DECISIONS (Fed. Publ.)
CONTRACT APPEALS DECISIONS (CCH)
CONTRACT AUDIT MANUAL (USGPO)
CORPORATE COUNSEL'S GUIDE TO GOVERNMENT CONTRACTING & SUBCONTRACTING (Bus. Laws)
COST ACCOUNTING STANDARDS GUIDE (CCH)
ENCYCLOPEDIC DICTIONARY OF CONTRACT AND PROCUREMENT LAW (Oceana)
EXTRAORDINARY CONTRACTUAL RELIEF REPORTER (Fed. Publ.)
FALSE CLAIMS, ANTI-KICKBACK AND PROGRAM FRAUD CIVIL REMEDIES (BNA)
FEDERAL ACQUISITION REGULATIONS (USGPO)
FEDERAL CONTRACT MANAGEMENT - A MANUAL FOR THE CONTRACT PROFESSIONAL (Bender)
FEDERAL COURT PROCUREMENT DECISIONS (Fed. Publ.)
GOVERNMENT CONTRACT ACCOUNTING 2ND ED. (Fed. Publ.)
GOVERNMENT CONTRACT BIDDING (Fed. Publ.)
GOVERNMENT CONTRACT DISPUTES, 2ND ED. (Fed. Publ.)
GOVERNMENT CONTRACT GUIDEBOOK (Fed. Publ.)
GOVERNMENT CONTRACTS: CYCLOPEDIC GUIDE TO LAW, ADMINISTRATION AND PROCEDURE (Bender)
GOVERNMENT CONTRACTS REPORTS (CCH)
GUIDE TO GOVERNMENT CONTRACTING (CCH)
INDEX OF FEDERAL SPECIFICATIONS, STANDARDS AND COMMERCIAL ITEM DESCRIPTIONS (USGPO)
MANUAL FOR PRACTICE BEFORE BOARDS OF CONTRACT APPEALS (FBA)
OFCCP FEDERAL CONTRACT COMPLIANCE MANUAL (CCH)
PURCHASING FROM SMALL AND MINORITY BUSINESSES (Bus. Laws)
U.S. POSTAL SERVICE PROCUREMENT MANUAL (USGPO)

<u>GOVERNMENT CONTRACTS--MARYLAND</u>
MARYLAND STATE BOARD OF CONTRACT APPEALS DECISIONS (MICPEL)

<u>GOVERNMENT CONTRACTS--MINNESOTA</u>
GOVERNMENT CONTRACT AND PROGRAM FRAUD (MILE)

<u>GOVERNMENT INFORMATION</u>
ACCESS REPORTS/FREEDOM OF INFORMATION NEWSLETTER AND REFERENCE FILE (Access Reports)
FEDERAL INFORMATION DISCLOSURE (Shepard's)
GUIDEBOOK TO THE FREEDOM OF INFORMATION AND PRIVACY ACTS (Clark Boardman Callaghan)
INFORMATION LAW: FREEDOM OF INFORMATION, PRIVACY, OPEN MEETINGS, OTHER ACCESS LAWS (PLI)

<u>GOVERNMENT LIABILITY</u>
HANDLING FEDERAL TORT CLAIMS: ADMINISTRATIVE AND JUDICIAL REMEDIES (Bender)
STATE & LOCAL GOVERNMENT CIVIL RIGHTS LIABILITY (Clark Boardman Callaghan)

<u>GOVERNMENT LIABILITY--MICHIGAN</u>
GOVERNMENTAL IMMUNITY IN MICHIGAN (ICLE - Michigan)

GRAND JURY
- GRAND JURY LAW AND PRACTICE (Clark Boardman Callaghan)
- REPRESENTATION OF WITNESSES BEFORE FEDERAL GRAND JURIES (Clark Boardman Callaghan)

GRANTS
- CHAPTER 1 HANDBOOK (EFRC)
- FEDERAL GRANTS MANAGEMENT HANDBOOK (Thompson)
- GUIDE TO FEDERAL FUNDING FOR ANTI-DRUG PROGRAMS (GIS)
- GUIDE TO FEDERAL FUNDING FOR EDUCATION (EFRC)
- GUIDE TO FEDERAL FUNDING FOR GOVERNMENTS AND NON-PROFITS (GIS)
- SINGLE AUDIT INFORMATION SERVICE (Thompson)

GUARDIAN AND WARD--CALIFORNIA
- CALIFORNIA CONSERVATORSHIPS AND GUARDIANSHIPS (Calif. CEB)

GUARDIAN AND WARD--HAWAII
- HAWAII GUARDIANSHIP SOURCEBOOK (vol. I - Property) (Pacific Law Inst.)

GUARDIAN AND WARD--INDIANA
- GUARDIANSHIP (Indiana CLE)
- INDIANA'S NEW GUARDIANSHIP LAW--AN UPDATE (Indiana CLE)

GUARDIAN AND WARD--MASSACHUSETTS
- GUARDIANSHIP AND CONSERVATORSHIP IN MASSACHUSETTS (Butterworth-NH)

GUARDIAN AND WARD--MINNESOTA
- CIVIL COMMITMENT IN MINNESOTA, 2nd Ed. (Butterworth-St. Paul)
- GUARDIANS & CONSERVATORS (MILE)
- MINNESOTA CONSERVATORSHIPS & GUARDIANSHIPS (Minn. CLE)

GUARDIAN AND WARD--MISSOURI
- MISSOURI GUARDIANSHIP AND TRUST LAW (MoBar)

GUARDIAN AND WARD--NEW JERSEY
- GUARDIANSHIPS (New Jersey ICLE)

GUARDIAN AND WARD--OHIO
- GUARDIANSHIP (Ohio CLE)

GUARDIAN AND WARD--TEXAS
- TEXAS GUARDIANSHIP MANUAL (State Bar of Texas)

GUARDIAN AND WARD--WASHINGTON
- WASHINGTON GUARDIANSHIP LAW: ADMINISTRATION AND LITIGATION (Butterworth-St. Paul)

GUARDIAN AND WARD--WISCONSIN
- THE GUARDIAN AD ITEM HANDBOOK (State Bar of Wisc.)

HANDICAPPED PERSONS
- ADA COMPLIANCE GUIDE (Thompson)
- AMERICAN DISABILITY ACT (Indiana CLE)
- AMERICANS WITH DISABILITIES ACT (MICPEL)
- AMERICANS WITH DISABILITIES ACT (MILE)
- AMERICANS WITH DISABILITIES ACT (NELI)
- DISABILITIES IN THE WORKPLACE: A GUIDE TO FEDERAL AND STATE LAWS (WG&L)
- DISABILITY DISCRIMINATION IN EMPLOYMENT (Clark Boardman Callaghan)
- THE DISABILITY LAW REPORTER SERVICE (Prentice Hall Law & Business)
- HANDICAPPED REQUIREMENTS HANDBOOK (Thompson)
- INDIVIDUALS WITH DISABILITIES EDUCATION LAW REPORTER (LRP)
- LEGAL RIGHTS OF PERSONS WITH DISABILITIES (LRP)
- MATERIALS ON THE AMERICANS WITH DISABILITIES ACT (Bus. Laws)
- NATIONAL DISABILITY LAW REPORTER (LRP)
- REPRESENTING PEOPLE WITH DISABILITIES (NYSBA)

DIRECTOR OF NURSING MANUAL: FEDERAL REGULATIONS AND GUIDELINES (National Health)
GENERIC DRUGS: A GUIDE TO FDA APPROVAL REQUIREMENTS (Prentice Hall Law & Business)
A GUIDE TO REHABILITATION (Bender)
HEALTH ADMINISTRATION: LAWS, REGULATIONS AND GUIDELINES (National Health)
HEALTH CARE FACILITY MANAGEMENT (CCH)
HEALTH CARE FRAUD AND ABUSE: A GUIDE TO FEDERAL SANCTIONS (Clark Boardman Callaghan)
HEALTH CARE LABOR MANUAL (Aspen)
HEALTH CARE LAW: A PRACTICAL GUIDE (Bender)
HEALTH CARE LAW SOURCEBOOK (Bender)
HOME HEALTH AND HOSPICE MANUAL: REGULATIONS AND GUIDELINES (National Health)
LABORATORY REGULATION MANUAL (Aspen)
LEGAL GUIDE FOR PHYSICIANS (Bender)
LONG-TERM CARE ADMINISTRATION: STANDARDS AND GUIDELINES FOR LONG-TERM CARE FACILITIES (National Health)
MANAGING YOUR MEDICAL PRACTICE (Bender)
MEDICAL TESTING: THE COMPLETE RESOURCE GUIDE TO GOOD LABORATORY PRACTICE AND HCFA COMPLIANCE (BNA)
MEDICARE HOME HEALTH AGENCY MANUAL (USGPO)
MEDICARE SKILLED NURSING FACILITY MANUAL (USGPO)
PATIENT CARE DECISION-MAKING (Clark Boardman Callaghan)
PHYSICIAN LABORATORY REGULATIONS MANUAL (Thompson)
REGULATORY COMPLIANCE MANUAL (American Dental)
TREATISE ON HEALTH CARE LAW (Bender)

HEALTH CARE--CALIFORNIA
CALIFORNIA MEDI-CAL GUIDE (CCH)

HEALTH CARE--CONNECTICUT
RECENT DEVELOPMENTS IN MEDICAL MALPRACTICE (Conn. Bar)

HEALTH CARE--ILLINOIS
HEALTH CARE LAW (Illinois ICLE)

HEALTH CARE--INDIANA
FUNDAMENTALS OF HEALTH CARE LAW (Indiana CLE)
MEDICAL MALPRACTICE UPDATE (Indiana CLE)

HEALTH CARE--MAINE
FORGOING LIFE SUPPORT: LIVING WILLS AND HEALTH CARE POWERS OF ATTORNEY (Maine Bar)
PLANNING AND PAYING FOR LONG TERM CARE (Maine Bar)

HEALTH CARE--MARYLAND
MAKING HEALTH CARE DECISIONS INCLUDING: LIVING WILLS AND DURABLE POWERS OF ATTORNEY (MICPEL)

HEALTH CARE--MINNESOTA
HEALTH CARE 1991 (MILE)
LONG TERM CARE AND THE LAW (MILE)
LONG TERM HEALTH CARE (MILE)
MEDICAL MALPRACTICE CLAIMS IN THE 90's (MILE)

HEALTH CARE--TEXAS
TEXAS DEPARTMENT OF HEALTH RULES (RPC)

HISTORIC PRESERVATION
HISTORIC PRESERVATION LAW (Real Estate Transaction Series, vols. 11, 11A & 11B) (Bender)
PRESERVATION LAW REPORTER (NTHP)

HORSES
HORSE SYNDICATION MANUAL (Farnam)
LAW FOR THE HORSEBREEDER (Farnam)

HORSES--TAXATION
HORSE OWNERS AND BREEDERS TAX MANUAL (AHC)

HOSPITALS
HOSPITAL CONTRACTS MANUAL (Aspen)
HOSPITAL LAW MANUAL, ATTORNEY'S VOLUMES (Aspen)
HOSPITAL LIABILITY (Law Journal)
INFECTIOUS WASTE: THE COMPLETE RESOURCE GUIDE (BNA)
MEDICARE HOSPITAL MANUAL (USGPO)

HOSPITALS--FORMS
HOSPITAL LEGAL FORMS, CHECKLISTS & GUIDELINES (Aspen)

HOSPITALS--INDIANA
LIABILITY ISSUES IN THE HOSPITAL SETTING (Indiana CLE)

HOSPITALS--TEXAS
TEXAS HOSPITAL LAW (Butterworth-Texas)

HOUSING
see also Condominiums; Cooperative housing; Discrimination in housing; Real Property

FAIR HOUSING - FAIR LENDING (Prentice Hall Law & Business)
HOMEOWNERS ASSOCIATIONS AND PLANNED UNIT DEVELOPMENTS - LAW AND PRACTICE (Real Estate Transactions series, vols. 6 & 6A) (Bender)
HOUSING AND DEVELOPMENT REPORTER (WG&L)
MULTIFAMILY HOUSING: FEDERAL PROGRAMS FOR THE PRIVATE SECTOR (Law Journal)

HOUSING--CALIFORNIA
CALIFORNIA REAL ESTATE FORMS AND COMMENTARIES (Prentice Hall Law & Business)

HOUSING--CONNECTICUT
BASIC RESIDENTIAL REAL ESTATE CLOSINGS (Conn. Bar)

HOUSING--MARYLAND
HUD AND CDA FINANCING TECHNIQUES (MICPEL)

HOUSING--MINNESOTA
PRACTICING BASIC RESIDENTIAL REAL ESTATE (MILE)

HOUSING--NEW YORK CITY
NEW YORK CITY HOUSING COURT REPORTER CHRONOLOGICAL ANNOTATOR (Lamb's Flight)

HUMAN RIGHTS
see also Discrimination

HUMAN RIGHTS ORGANIZATIONS AND PERIODICALS DIRECTORY (Meiklejohn Civil Liberties Institute)
PEACE LAW DOCKET 1945-1990 (Meiklejohn Civil Liberties Institute)

HUMAN RIGHTS--INTERNATIONAL
HUMAN RIGHTS: THE INTER-AMERICAN SYSTEM (Oceana)
HUMAN RIGHTS: THE INTERNATIONAL PETITION SYSTEM: A REPERTOIRE OF PRACTICE (Oceana)
INTERNATIONAL HUMAN RIGHTS INSTRUMENTS (Hein)
THE REGULATION OF STATELESSNESS UNDER INTERNATIONAL AND NATIONAL LAW: TEXTS AND DOCUMENTS (Oceana)
SEX-BASED DISCRIMINATION: INTERNATIONAL LAW AND ORGANIZATION (Oceana)

IMMIGRATION LAW
see also Aliens

BENDER'S I.N.S. REGULATION SERVICE (Bender)
THE CHANGING SCENE FOR ALIENS: THE IMMIGRATION ACT OF 1990 (Conn. Bar)

CORPORATE COUNSEL'S GUIDE TO BUSINESS-RELATED IMMIGRATION (Bus. Laws)
EMPLOYER'S GUIDE TO THE IMMIGRATION REFORM AND CONTROL ACT OF 1986 (BLR)
EMPLOYER'S IMMIGRATION COMPLIANCE GUIDE (Bender)
THE GUIDE TO IMMIGRATION COUNSELING: A STEP-BY-STEP LEGAL HANDBOOK (Center for Immig. Rights)
HEIN'S INTERIM DECISION SERVICE (Hein)
IMMIGRATION JUDGE BENCHBOOK (American Immigration Lawyers Assn.)
IMMIGRATION LAW AND BUSINESS (Clark Boardman Callaghan)
IMMIGRATION LAW AND CRIMES (Clark Boardman Callaghan)
IMMIGRATION LAW AND DEFENSE, 3rd ED. (Clark Boardman Callaghan)
IMMIGRATION LAW AND PROCEDURE, REV. ED. (Bender)
IMMIGRATION LAW AND PROCEDURE: DESK ED. (Bender)
IMMIGRATION LAW AND PROCEDURE REPORTER (Bender)
IMMIGRATION LAW FOR GENERAL PRACTITIONERS AND HUMAN RESOURCE PERSONNEL (Conn. Bar)
IMMIGRATION LAW SERVICE (Lawyers Coop. & Bancroft)
THE NEW IMMIGRATION ACT OF 1990 (MILE)
OPERATIONS INSTRUCTIONS, REGULATIONS, AND INTERPRETATIONS (USGPO)
PATEL'S IMMIGRATION LAW DIGEST (Clark Boardman Callaghan)

IMMIGRATION LAW--FLORIDA
IMMIGRATION LAW AND PRACTICE IN FLORIDA (Florida Bar)

IMMIGRATION LAW--ILLINOIS
IMMIGRATION AND NATURALIZATION PRACTICE (Illinois ICLE)

IMMIGRATION LAW--MARYLAND
IMMIGRATION LAW UPDATE (MICPEL)

IMPORTS
see International trade

INCOME TAX
see also Taxation

ANALYSIS OF FEDERAL TAXES: INCOME (RIA)
ANALYSIS OF FEDERAL TAXES: INCOME, ESTATE & GIFT (RIA)
FEDERAL INCOME, GIFT AND ESTATE TAXATION (Bender)
FEDERAL INCOME TAXATION OF BANKS AND FINANCIAL INSTITUTIONS (WG&L)
FEDERAL INCOME TAXATION OF CORPORATE LIQUIDATIONS (Shepard's)
FEDERAL INCOME TAXATION OF CORPORATIONS FILING CONSOLIDATED RETURNS (Bender)
FEDERAL INCOME TAXATION OF INDIVIDUALS (WG&L)
FEDERAL INCOME TAXATION OF INVENTORIES (Bender)
FEDERAL INCOME TAXATION OF LIFE INSURANCE COMPANIES (Bender)
FEDERAL INCOME TAXATION OF OIL AND GAS INVESTMENTS (WG&L)
FEDERAL INCOME TAXATION OF PASSIVE ACTIVITIES (WG&L)
FEDERAL INCOME TAXATION OF REAL ESTATE (WG&L)
FEDERAL TAX DEDUCTIONS (WG&L)
FEDERAL TAX MANUAL (with monthly reports) (CCH)
FEDERAL TAX REGULATIONS (RIA)
HOW TO SAVE TIME AND TAXES PREPARING THE FEDERAL PARTNERSHIP RETURN (Bender)
INCOME TAXATION: ACCOUNTING METHODS AND PERIODS (Shepard's)
INCOME TAXATION OF FOREIGN-RELATED TRANSACTIONS (Bender)
INTERNATIONAL INCOME TAX RULES OF THE UNITED STATES (Butterworth-NH)
INTERNATIONAL TAX GUIDE: U.S. INCOME TAXATION (Clark Boardman Callaghan)
MERTENS LAW OF FEDERAL INCOME TAXATION (Clark Boardman Callaghan)
PPC TAX PLANNING GUIDE - INDIVIDUALS (Practitioners Publishing)
PRACTITIONERS 1040 DESKBOOK (Practitioners Publishing)
REDUCING PERSONAL INCOME TAXES: A GUIDE TO DEDUCTIONS AND CREDITS (Law Journal)
TAX MANAGEMENT - FOREIGN INCOME (BNA)
TAX MANAGEMENT - U.S. INCOME (BNA)

INCOME TAX--AUSTRALIA
AUSTRALIAN FEDERAL TAX REPORTS (CCH)

AUSTRALIAN INCOME TAX GUIDE - (without legislation) (CCH)
AUSTRALIAN INCOME TAX GUIDE & INCOME TAX LEGISLATION (CCH)

<u>INCOME TAX--CANADA</u>
CANADA INCOME TAX GUIDE (CCH)
CANADIAN INCOME TAX ACT, REGULATIONS AND RULINGS (CCH)

<u>INCOME TAX--FORMS</u>
ALLSTATE PERSONAL INCOME TAX FORMS FILE (NTTS)
COMPLETE FEDERAL TAX FORMS (RIA)
FEDERAL INCOME TAXATION OF CORPORATIONS AND SHAREHOLDERS: FORMS (WG&L)
STATE CORPORATE INCOME TAX FORMS (CCH)
STATE PERSONAL INCOME TAX FORMS (CCH)
STATE TAX FORMS: INDIVIDUAL (Tax Form)

<u>INCOME TAX--MARYLAND</u>
FIDUCIARY INCOME TAXES (MICPEL)

<u>INCOME TAX--SOUTH CAROLINA</u>
SOUTH CAROLINA INCOME TAXATION (S. Carolina Bar)

<u>INCOME TAX--STATES</u>
STATE INCOME TAXES (RIA)

<u>INCORPORATION</u>
see Corporation law

<u>INDIANS</u>
MINERAL DEVELOPMENT ON INDIAN LANDS (Rocky Mt.)

<u>INDUSTRIAL RELATIONS</u>
see Labor and labor relations

<u>INDUSTRIAL REVENUE BONDS</u>
see Financing

<u>INHERITANCE TAX</u>
see Estate and gift taxes

<u>INJURIES</u>
see Accidents; Damages; Medical jurisprudence; Personal injuries; Torts

<u>INSTALLMENT SALES</u>
see Sales

<u>INSTRUCTIONS TO JURIES</u>
see Jury instructions

<u>INSURANCE</u>
see also Reinsurance

ADVANCED SALES REFERENCE SERVICE (Natl. Underwriter)
ADVANCED UNDERWRITING SERVICE (AUS) (Dearborn)
ANNOTATIONS TO SURPLUS LINES STATUTES (ABA)
BAD FAITH & PUNITIVE DAMAGES: ANNOTATIONS TO FIRST PARTY INSURANCE CASES, STATUTES, AND REGULATIONS (ABA)
BUSINESS INSURANCE LAW & PRACTICE GUIDE (Bender)
BUSINESS LITIGATORS INSURANCE GUIDE (Parker)
THE CAPTIVE INSURANCE MANUAL (NILS)
COMMERCIAL BLANKET BOND ANNOTATED (ABA)
CONSTRUCTION RISK MANAGEMENT (Intl. Risk Mgmt. Inst.)
DIRECTOR & OFFICER LIABILITY: INSURANCE & INDEMNIFICATION (Bus. Laws)
ENVIRONMENTAL INSURANCE COVERAGE: STATE LAW & REGULATION (Butterworth-NH)
EXCESS LIABILITY: DUTIES & RESPONSIBILITIES OF THE INSURER (Clark Boardman Callaghan)
FEDERAL INSURANCE LAWS (NILS)
FEDERAL INSURANCE REGULATIONS (NILS)

FEDERAL TAXATION OF INSURANCE COMPANIES (RIA)
FIDELITY LAW TOPICAL OUTLINE & BIBLIOGRAPHY (ABA)
A GUIDE TO THE FEDERAL LAW OF BANKING AND INSURANCE (Prentice Hall Law & Business)
HANDBOOK OF INSURANCE COVERAGE DISPUTES (Prentice Hall Law & Business)
HOW INSURANCE COMPANIES SETTLE CASES (James)
INSURANCE AND RISK MANAGEMENT FOR STATE AND LOCAL GOVERNMENTS (Bender)
INSURANCE BAD FAITH LITIGATION (Bender)
INSURANCE COVERAGE ISSUES RELATIVE TO NATURAL DISASTERS (S. Carolina Bar)
INSURANCE LAWS (FOR THE 50 U.S. STATES, THE DISTRICT OF COLUMBIA, PUERTO RICO, AND THE VIRGIN ISLANDS) (NILS)
INSURANCE REGULATIONS (NILS)
INSURANCE RELATED REGULATIONS (NILS)
INSURANCE SETTLEMENT HANDBOOK (James)
INSURING REAL PROPERTY (Bender)
MANUFACTURING RISK MANAGEMENT AND INSURANCE (Intl. Risk Mgmt. Inst.)
MILLER'S STANDARD INSURANCE POLICIES ANNOTATED (Legal Res. Systems)
OTHER REGULATORY MATERIALS (NILS)
PROFESSIONAL LIABILITY INSURANCE (Intl. Risk Mgmt. Inst.)
RELATED LAWS TO INSURANCE LAWS (NILS)
RISK FINANCING (Intl. Risk Mgmt. Inst.)
RISK MANAGEMENT AND INSURANCE AUDIT TECHNIQUES (John Liner Org.)
SURETY LAW TOPICAL INDEX (ABA)

INSURANCE--CALIFORNIA
CALIFORNIA INSURANCE DISPUTES (Parker)
CALIFORNIA INSURANCE LAW & PRACTICE (Bender)
CALIFORNIA UNINSURED MOTORIST LAW (Parker)

INSURANCE--CANADA
CANADIAN INSURANCE LAW REPORTS (CCH)

INSURANCE--HAWAII
HAWAII PRACTICE GUIDE: NO FAULT LAW (Pacific Law Inst.)

INSURANCE--INDIANA
BASIC INSURANCE LAW II (Indiana CLE)
BASIC INSURANCE LAW (Indiana CLE)
SUCCESSFULLY LITIGATING TORT INSURANCE ACTIONS (Indiana CLE)

INSURANCE--MINNESOTA
DIRECTOR & OFFICER INSURANCE COVERAGE (MILE)
INSURANCE COVERAGE FOR EMPLOYMENT CLAIMS (Minn. CLE)
INSURANCE LAW (Minn. CLE)
MINNESOTA INSURANCE LAW CONFERENCE (MILE)
THE RISK BUSINESS: INSURANCE CONTRACTS, COVERAGES, AND CARRIERS (MILE)

INSURANCE--MISSOURI
MISSOURI INSURANCE PRACTICE (MoBar)

INSURANCE--NEW HAMPSHIRE
INSURANCE LAW (NH Bar)

INSURANCE--NEW YORK
NEW YORK INSURANCE LAW (Bender)
THE NO-FAULT HANDBOOK (NYSTLA)

INSURANCE--PENNSYLVANIA
PENNSYLVANIA INSURANCE LAW (Bisel)

INSURANCE--STATES
INSURANCE LAWS (FOR THE 50 U.S. STATES, THE DISTRICT OF COLUMBIA, PUERTO RICO, AND THE VIRGIN ISLANDS) (NILS)
INSURANCE REGULATIONS (NILS)
INSURANCE RELATED REGULATIONS (NILS)
OTHER REGULATORY MATERIALS (NILS)
RELATED LAWS TO INSURANCE LAWS (NILS)

INSURANCE, AUTOMOBILE

AUTOMOBILE LAW REPORTS (insurance cases) (CCH)
AUTOMOBILE LIABILITY INSURANCE (Clark Boardman Callaghan)
FEDERAL INCOME TAXATION OF LIFE INSURANCE COMPANIES (Bender)
NO-FAULT AND UNINSURED MOTORIST AUTO INSURANCE (Bender)
UNINSURED AND UNDERINSURED MOTORIST INSURANCE, 2ND ED. (Anderson)

INSURANCE, AUTOMOBILE--MARYLAND

UNINSURED MOTORIST (MICPEL)

INSURANCE, AUTOMOBILE--MICHIGAN

MICHIGAN NO-FAULT AUTO INSURANCE DECISIONS (MTLA)
MICHIGAN NO-FAULT AUTOMOBILE CASES: LAW AND PRACTICE (ICLE - Michigan)

INSURANCE, AUTOMOBILE--MINNESOTA

THE MINNESOTA MOTOR VEHICLE INSURANCE MANUAL (MILE)
MINNESOTA NO-FAULT AUTOMOBILE INSURANCE, 2nd ed. (Butterworth-St. Paul)
UNINSURED/UNDERINSURED MOTORIST COVERAGE (MILE)

INSURANCE, AUTOMOBILE--MISSOURI

THE STACKING OF AUTOMOBILE INSURANCE COVERAGE IN MISSOURI (UMKC/CLE)

INSURANCE, AUTOMOBILE--NEW HAMPSHIRE

UNINSURED MOTORIST (NH Bar)

INSURANCE, AUTOMOBILE--NEW JERSEY

AUTOMOBILE INSURANCE HANDBOOK (New Jersey ICLE)

INSURANCE, AUTOMOBILE--NEW YORK

AUTOMOBILE INSURANCE HANDBOOK (New Jersey ICLE)

INSURANCE, AUTOMOBILE--SOUTH CAROLINA

THE LAW OF AUTOMOBILE INSURANCE IN SOUTH CAROLINA (S. Carolina Bar)

INSURANCE, AUTOMOBILE--WASHINGTON

WASHINGTON MOTOR VEHICLE ACCIDENT INSURANCE DESKBOOK (Wash. Bar)

INSURANCE, CASUALTY

ANNOTATED FINANCIAL INSTITUTION BOND (ABA)
INSURANCE LAW REPORTS - FIRE AND CASUALTY (CCH)

INSURANCE, FIRE

FIRE, CASUALTY & SURETY BULLETINS (Natl. Underwriter)
INSURANCE LAW REPORTS - FIRE AND CASUALTY (CCH)

INSURANCE, HEALTH

HEALTH CARE FRAUD AND ABUSE: A GUIDE TO FEDERAL SANCTIONS (Clark Boardman Callaghan)
INSURANCE LAW REPORTS - LIFE, HEALTH & ACCIDENT (CCH)
LAW OF LIFE AND HEALTH INSURANCE (Bender)
MANAGING COBRA: THE COMPLETE COMPLIANCE GUIDE (Wiley Law)
MEDICARE HOME HEALTH AGENCY MANUAL (USGPO)
MEDICARE HOSPITAL MANUAL (USGPO)
MEDICARE SKILLED NURSING FACILITY MANUAL (USGPO)
MEDICARE-MEDICAID GUIDE (CCH)

INSURANCE, LIABILITY

THE ATTORNEY'S UMBRELLA BOOK (Griffin)
CGL REPORTER - TRIAL AND INSURANCE COUNSEL'S HANDBOOK (CGL)
COMMERCIAL LIABILITY INSURANCE (Intl. Risk Mgmt. Inst.)
THE LAW OF LIABILITY INSURANCE (Bender)
PODIATRIC LIABILITY (Public Reporting Services)

INSURANCE, LIABILITY--CALIFORNIA

CALIFORNIA LIABILITY INSURANCE PRACTICE: CLAIMS AND LITIGATION (Calif. CEB)

INSURANCE, LIABILITY--ILLINOIS
LIABILITY INSURANCE (Illinois ICLE)

INSURANCE, LIFE
INSURANCE LAW REPORTS - LIFE, HEALTH & ACCIDENT (CCH)
LAW OF LIFE AND HEALTH INSURANCE (Bender)

INSURANCE, MARINE
MARINE P&I POLICY ANNOTATIONS (ABA)

INSURANCE, PROPERTY
COMMERCIAL PROPERTY INSURANCE (Intl. Risk Mgmt. Inst.)
PROPERTY INSURANCE ANNOTATIONS: FIRE AND EXTENDED COVERAGES (ABA)

INSURANCE, PROPERTY--ILLINOIS
PROPERTY INSURANCE (Illinois ICLE)

INSURANCE, TITLE--COLORADO
COLORADO TITLE INSURANCE PRACTICE (CLE - Colorado)

INSURANCE, TITLE--FORMS
UNDERSTANDING THE ALTA TITLE INSURANCE POLICY FORMS (ALTA)

INSURANCE, TITLE--TEXAS
TEXAS TITLE INSURANCE (Wiley Law)

INSURANCE, UNEMPLOYMENT
COMPARISON OF STATE UNEMPLOYMENT INSURANCE LAWS (USGPO)
UNEMPLOYMENT INSURANCE REPORTS (CCH)

INSURANCE, UNEMPLOYMENT--MARYLAND
DIGEST OF MARYLAND UNEMPLOYMENT INSURANCE DECISIONS (MICPEL)

INSURANCE, UNEMPLOYMENT--SOUTH CAROLINA
UNEMPLOYMENT LAW AND PROCEDURE IN S.C. (S. Carolina Bar)

INSURANCE AGENTS
RESPONSIBILITIES OF INSURANCE AGENTS AND BROKERS (Bender)

INSURANCE COMPANIES
WHAT YOU NEED TO KNOW TO SETTLE WITH INSURANCE COMPANIES (James)

INTELLECTUAL PROPERTY
see also Copyright; Patents; Trademarks

CURRENT PATENT INTERFERENCE PRACTICE (Prentice Hall Law & Business)
FEDERAL TAXATION OF INTELLECTUAL PROPERTY TRANSFERS (Law Journal)
INTELLECTUAL PROPERTY AND COPYRIGHT LAW (MICPEL)
INTELLECTUAL PROPERTY AND ANTITRUST LAW (Clark Boardman Callaghan)
INTELLECTUAL PROPERTY COUNSELING AND LITIGATION (Bender)
INTELLECTUAL PROPERTY LAW (Indiana CLE)
INTELLECTUAL PROPERTY LITIGATION (Minn. CLE)
JURY INSTRUCTIONS IN INTELLECTUAL PROPERTY CASES (Big Foot)
MODERN INTELLECTUAL PROPERTY (Prentice Hall Law & Business)
OVERVIEW OF PATENTS, TRADEMARKS, COPYRIGHTS AND TRADE SECRETS FOR THE GENERAL PRACTITIONER (Wash. Bar)
SCOTT ON COMPUTER LAW (Prentice Hall Law & Business)
TAXATION OF INTELLECTUAL PROPERTY: TAX PLANNING GUIDE (Bender)
U.S. INTELLECTUAL PROPERTY LEGISLATIVE REVIEW (Clark Boardman Callaghan)

INTELLECTUAL PROPERTY--ASIA
INTELLECTUAL PROPERTY PROTECTION IN ASIA (Butterworth-NH)

INTELLECTUAL PROPERTY--CONNECTICUT
CURRENT DEVELOPMENTS IN INTELLECTUAL PROPERTY LAW (Conn. Bar)

INTELLECTUAL PROPERTY--FORMS
FORMS AND AGREEMENTS ON INTELLECTUAL PROPERTY AND INTERNATIONAL LICENSING (Clark Boardman Callaghan)

INTELLECTUAL PROPERTY--MINNESOTA
INTELLECTUAL PROPERTY LAW (MILE)

INTEREST AND USURY
see also Banks and Banking; Consumer finance

INTEREST AND USURY--FLORIDA
PRACTICE UNDER FLORIDA USURY LAW (Florida Bar)

INTERGOVERNMENTAL RELATIONS
LAW AND POLICY OF INTERGOVERNMENTAL PRIMARY COMMODITY AGREEMENTS (Oceana)

INTERNATIONAL ARBITRATION
see Arbitration, international

INTERNATIONAL CORPORATIONS
see Corporations, international

INTERNATIONAL COURT OF JUSTICE
INTERNATIONAL COURT OF JUSTICE OPINION BRIEFS (ABA)

INTERNATIONAL FINANCE
INTERNATIONAL BUSINESS PLANNING: LAW AND TAXATION - UNITED STATES (Bender)
THE LAW AND PRACTICE OF INTERNATIONAL FINANCE (International Business and Law Series, vols. 2 & 2A) (Clark Boardman Callaghan)
THE TOUCHE ROSS INTERNATIONAL BUSINESS INVESTMENT AND TAXATION HANDBOOK (Probus)

INTERNATIONAL LAW
ARMS CONTROL REPORTER (IDDS)
CROSS BORDER PRACTICE COMPENDIUM (Kluwer)
ENFORCEMENT OF MONEY JUDGMENTS ABROAD (Bender)
GERMAIN'S TRANSNATIONAL LAW RESEARCH (Transnational Juris Publications)
INTERNATIONAL BUSINESS TRANSACTIONS (Kluwer)
INTERNATIONAL JUDICIAL ASSISTANCE (CIVIL AND COMMERCIAL) (Intl. Law Inst.)
INTERNATIONAL JUDICIAL ASSISTANCE (CRIMINAL) (Intl. Law Inst.)
INTERNATIONAL LAW (Indiana CLE)
JOINT VENTURES WITH INTERNATIONAL PARTNERS (Butterworth-NH)
JOINT VENTURES WITH THE SOVIET UNION (Butterworth-NH)
LITIGATION OF INTERNATIONAL DISPUTES IN U.S. COURTS (International Business Law Series vol. 4) (Clark Boardman Callaghan)

INTERNATIONAL ORGANIZATIONS
DIGEST OF LEGAL ACTIVITIES OF INTERNATIONAL ORGANIZATIONS AND OTHER INSTITUTIONS (Oceana)

INTERNATIONAL TRADE
ANTIDUMPING AND COUNTERVAILING DUTY LAWS (International Business and Law Series, vol. 3) (Clark Boardman Callaghan)
CHINA HAND: INVESTING, LICENSING & TRADING CONDITIONS TODAY (Bus. Intern.)
COMMERCIAL BUSINESS & TRADE LAWS OF THE WORLD (Oceana)
CUSTOMS LAW AND ADMINISTRATION (INCLUDING CUSTOMS SERVICE DECISIONS) (Oceana)
CUSTOMS REGULATIONS OF THE UNITED STATES (USGPO)
EXPORT ADMINISTRATION REGULATIONS (USGPO)
EXPORT ADMINISTRATION REGULATIONS AND EXPORT RESOURCES (Unz & Co.)
FED-TRACK GUIDE TO ANTIDUMPING FINDINGS AND ORDERS (Fed-Track)
FED-TRACK GUIDE TO COUNTERVAILING DUTY CASES (Fed-Track)
FED-TRACK GUIDE TO INVESTIGATION OF UNFAIR TRADE PRACTICES (Fed-Track)
FEDERAL REGULATION OF INTERNATIONAL BUSINESS (Hein)
FINANCING FOREIGN OPERATIONS (FFO) (Bus. Intern.)
FINANCING FOREIGN OPERATIONS/LATIN AMERICA (Bus. Intern.)
FOREIGN TRADE AND INVESTMENT (Butterworth-NH)

FREE TRADE AGREEMENT ANNOTATED (Blais)
FREE TRADE LAW REPORTS (CCH)
GLOBAL MARKETS (MILE)
GUIDE TO COUNTERTRADE (Bus. Laws)
GUIDE TO EXPORT CONTROLS (Bus. Laws)
GUIDE TO INTERNATIONAL COMMERCE LAW (Shepard's)
GUIDE TO THE INTERNATIONAL SALES OF GOODS CONVENTION (Bus. Laws)
HARMONIZED TARIFF OF THE U.S. (Unz & Co.)
HARMONIZED TARIFF SCHEDULES OF THE UNITED STATES ANNOTATED (USGPO)
HISTORY OF THE TARIFF SCHEDULES OF THE UNITED STATES ANNOTATED (USGPO)
INTERNATIONAL AGENCY AND DISTRIBUTION AGREEMENTS (Butterworth-NH)
INTERNATIONAL BOYCOTTS (Bus. Laws)
INTERNATIONAL BUSINESS PLANNING: LAW AND TAXATION - UNITED STATES (Bender)
INTERNATIONAL BUSINESS PORTFOLIOS (Bender)
INTERNATIONAL EXPORTING AGREEMENTS (Bender)
INTERNATIONAL TRADE PRACTICE (Shepard's)
INTERNATIONAL TRADE REPORTER CURRENT REPORTS (BNA)
INTERNATIONAL TRADE REPORTER DECISIONS (BNA)
INTERNATIONAL TRADE REPORTER IMPORT REFERENCE MANUAL (BNA)
INVESTING, LICENSING AND TRADING CONDITIONS ABROAD (ILT) (Bus. Intern.)
INVESTMENT LAWS OF THE WORLD: THE DEVELOPING NATIONS (Oceana)
LAW AND PRACTICE UNDER THE GATT (Oceana)
LAW AND PRACTICE UNDER THE GATT AND OTHER TRADING ARRANGEMENTS: THE ASSOCIATION OF SOUTHEAST ASIAN NATIONS (Oceana)
LAW AND PRACTICE UNDER THE GATT AND OTHER TRADING ARRANGEMENTS: EUROPEAN COMMUNITY--TRADING ARRANGEMENTS WITH EFTA COUNTRIES (Oceana)
LAW AND PRACTICE UNDER THE GATT AND OTHER TRADING ARRANGEMENTS: THE EUROPEAN COMMUNITY, THE SOVIET UNION AND THE EASTERN EUROPEAN STATES (Oceana)
LAW AND PRACTICE UNDER THE GATT AND OTHER TRADING ARRANGEMENTS: TRILATERAL TRADE AGREEMENTS: CANADA - U.S. - MEXICO (Oceana)
LAW AND PRACTICE OF U.S. REGULATION OF INTERNATIONAL TRADE (Oceana)
THE LAW OF TRANSNATIONAL BUSINESS TRANSACTIONS (International Business & Law Series, vol. 1 & 1A) (Clark Boardman Callaghan)
LAWS OF INTERNATIONAL TRADE (Bus. Laws)
LEGAL ASPECTS OF EXPORTING (Conn. Bar)
THE LEGAL ASPECTS OF EXPORTING MANUAL (FBA)
THE LEGAL ASPECTS OF INTERNATIONAL SOURCING (Bus. Laws)
MANUAL FOR THE PRACTICE OF U.S. IMPORT LAW (Kluwer)
NEGOTIATING AND DRAFTING INTERNATIONAL BUSINESS AGREEMENTS (Wash. Bar)
SCHEDULE B COMMODITY CLASSIFICATION AND HARMONIZED SYNOPSIS (Unz & Co.)
TAX-FREE TRADE ZONES OF THE WORLD (Bender)
TRANSNATIONAL ECONOMIC AND MONETARY LAW: TRANSACTIONS AND CONTRACTS. (Oceana)
U.S. COURT OF INTERNATIONAL TRADE RULES AND ANNOTATION SERVICE (Rules)
U.S. CUSTOMS AND INTERNATIONAL TRADE GUIDE (Bender)
U.S. CUSTOMS REGULATIONS (Unz & Co.)
U.S. INTERNATIONAL TRADE REPORTS, NEW SERIES (Oceana)
U.S.--CANADA FREE TRADE AGREEMENT: THE COMPLETE RESOURCE GUIDE (BNA)
U.S. - ISRAEL FREE TRADE AGREEMENT (Bus. Laws)
UNITED STATES COURT OF INTERNATIONAL TRADE - RULES (Invictus)
UNITED STATES EXPORT CONTROLS (Prentice Hall Law & Business)
UNITED STATES INTERNATIONAL TRADE REPORTS (Oceana)
UNITED STATES LEGISLATION ON FOREIGN RELATIONS AND INTERNATIONAL COMMERCE (Hein)

INTERNATIONAL TRADE--CHINA
CHINA LAWS FOR FOREIGN BUSINESS (CCH)
CHINESE FOREIGN ECONOMIC LAW (Intl. Law Inst.)

INTERSTATE COMMERCE
see U.S. Interstate Commerce Commission; Carriers

INVENTORIES--TAXATION
FEDERAL INCOME TAXATION OF INVENTORIES (Bender)

JUDGES--SOUTH CAROLINA
THE SOUTH CAROLINA BENCH BOOK FOR MAGISTRATES AND MUNICIPAL COURT JUDGES (S. Carolina Bar)

JUDGES--VIRGINIA
VIRGINIA CIRCUIT COURT JUDGES BENCHBOOK -- CIVIL (Michie)
VIRGINIA CIRCUIT COURT JUDGES BENCHBOOK -- CRIMINAL (Michie)

JUDGES--WISCONSIN
WISCONSIN JUDICIAL BENCHBOOK: VOL. 4 - PROBATE, JUVENILE AND MENTAL (State Bar of Wisc.)

JUDGMENTS
see Collection laws

JURY
see also Grand Jury; Jury Instructions

JUROR MISCONDUCT (Clark Boardman Callaghan)
JURY SELECTION (Art of Advocacy Series) (Bender)
JURY SELECTION: STRATEGY AND SCIENCE (Clark Boardman Callaghan)
JURYWORK - SYSTEMATIC TECHNIQUES (Clark Boardman Callaghan)
MODERN CIVIL JURY SELECTION (Wiley Law)
NATIONAL VERDICT SURVEY (Jury Verdict)

JURY--OKLAHOMA
TECHNIQUES FOR JURY ADVOCACY (Okla. Bar CLE)

JURY--WASHINGTON
VOIR DIRE: LEARN TO USE IT OR LOSE IT (Wash. Bar)

JURY INSTRUCTIONS
ANTITRUST CIVIL JURY INSTRUCTIONS (ABA)
FEDERAL CRIMINAL JURY INSTRUCTIONS (Michie)
JURY INSTRUCTIONS (Art of Advocacy Series) (Bender)
JURY INSTRUCTIONS IN CRIMINAL ANTITRUST CASES 1964-1976 (ABA)
JURY INSTRUCTIONS IN INTELLECTUAL PROPERTY CASES (Big Foot)
MODERN FEDERAL JURY INSTRUCTIONS - CRIMINAL & CIVIL (Bender)

JURY INSTRUCTIONS--ALABAMA
CRIMINAL PATTERN JURY INSTRUCTIONS (ABICLE)
PATTERN CAPITAL MURDER CHARGES (ABICLE)

JURY INSTRUCTIONS--ARIZONA
RECOMMENDED ARIZONA JURY INSTRUCTIONS - CIVIL (State Bar of Ariz.)

JURY INSTRUCTIONS--CALIFORNIA
CALIFORNIA FORMS OF JURY INSTRUCTION (Bender)
CALIFORNIA JURY INSTRUCTIONS - CIVIL (BAJI) (West)
CALIFORNIA JURY INSTRUCTIONS - CRIMINAL (CALJIC) (West)
CRIMINAL DEFENSE JURY INSTRUCTIONS (Knowles)

JURY INSTRUCTIONS--COLORADO
COLORADO JURY INSTRUCTIONS 3D - CIVIL (Bancroft)

JURY INSTRUCTIONS--DISTRICT OF COLUMBIA
CRIMINAL JURY INSTRUCTIONS FOR THE DISTRICT OF COLUMBIA (Bar Assn. of D.C.)
STANDARDIZED CIVIL JURY INSTRUCTIONS FOR THE DISTRICT OF COLUMBIA, REV. ED. (Bar Assn. of D.C.)

JURY INSTRUCTIONS--FLORIDA
FLORIDA FORMS OF JURY INSTRUCTIONS (Bender)
FLORIDA STANDARD JURY INSTRUCTIONS IN CIVIL CASES (Florida Bar)
FLORIDA STANDARD JURY INSTRUCTIONS IN CRIMINAL CASES (Florida Bar)

JURY INSTRUCTIONS--GEORGIA

SUGGESTED PATTERN JURY INSTRUCTIONS - VOLUME 1: CIVIL CASES, THIRD ED. (Institute - Ga.)

SUGGESTED PATTERN JURY INSTRUCTIONS - VOLUME 2: CRIMINAL CASES, SECOND ED. (Institute - Ga.)

JURY INSTRUCTIONS--IDAHO

IDAHO CIVIL JURY INSTRUCTIONS (Idaho Law)

JURY INSTRUCTIONS--ILLINOIS

ILLINOIS FORMS OF JURY INSTRUCTIONS (Bender)

ILLINOIS NON-PATTERN JURY INSTRUCTIONS (Lawyers Coop.)

JURY INSTRUCTIONS--INDIANA

INDIANA PATTERN JURY INSTRUCTIONS - CIVIL (Michie)

INDIANA PATTERN JURY INSTRUCTIONS - CRIMINAL (Michie)

JURY INSTRUCTIONS--IOWA

IOWA CIVIL JURY INSTRUCTIONS (Iowa Bar)

IOWA UNIFORM JURY INSTRUCTIONS - CRIMINAL (Iowa Bar)

JURY INSTRUCTIONS--KANSAS

PATTERN INSTRUCTIONS FOR KANSAS 2D (civil) (Bancroft)

JURY INSTRUCTIONS--MAINE

MAINE JURY INSTRUCTION MANUAL (Butterworth-NH)

JURY INSTRUCTIONS--MARYLAND

MARYLAND CRIMINAL PATTERN JURY INSTRUCTIONS (MICPEL)

JURY INSTRUCTIONS--MASSACHUSETTS

MODEL JURY INSTRUCTIONS FOR USE IN THE DISTRICT COURT (Mass. CLE)

JURY INSTRUCTIONS--MICHIGAN

MICHIGAN CRIMINAL JURY INSTRUCTIONS, 2nd Ed. (ICLE - Michigan)

MICHIGAN STANDARD JURY INSTRUCTIONS - CIVIL (ICLE - Michigan)

JURY INSTRUCTIONS--MISSOURI

MISSOURI APPROVED INSTRUCTIONS - CRIMINAL, VOLS. I & II AND MISSOURI APPROVED CHARGES - CRIMINAL (MoBar)

NOT IN MAI: CIVIL JURY INSTRUCTIONS COLLECTED FROM MISSOURI CASES (UMC CLE)

JURY INSTRUCTIONS--MONTANA

MONTANA CRIMINAL JURY INSTRUCTIONS (State Bar of Mont.)

MONTANA PATTERN JURY INSTRUCTIONS-CIVIL (State Bar of Mont.)

JURY INSTRUCTIONS--NEW JERSEY

MODEL JURY CHARGES: CIVIL (New Jersey ICLE)

MODEL JURY CHARGES: CRIMINAL (New Jersey ICLE)

JURY INSTRUCTIONS--NEW YORK

CHARGES TO THE JURY AND REQUESTS TO CHARGE IN A CRIMINAL CASE IN NEW YORK (Lawyers Coop.)

CRIMINAL JURY INSTRUCTIONS - NEW YORK (NYS OCA)

JURY INSTRUCTIONS--NORTH CAROLINA

NORTH CAROLINA PATTERN JURY INSTRUCTIONS FOR CIVIL CASES (No. Carolina Bar)

NORTH CAROLINA PATTERN JURY INSTRUCTIONS FOR CRIMINAL CASES (No. Carolina Bar)

NORTH CAROLINA PATTERN JURY INSTRUCTIONS - MOTOR VEHICLE NEGLIGENCE (No. Carolina Bar)

JURY INSTRUCTIONS--NORTH DAKOTA

NORTH DAKOTA PATTERN JURY INSTRUCTIONS - CIVIL (State Bar of N. Dak.)

NORTH DAKOTA PATTERN JURY INSTRUCTIONS - CRIMINAL (State Bar of N. Dak.)

JURY INSTRUCTIONS--OHIO
OHIO JURY INSTRUCTIONS (Anderson)

JURY INSTRUCTIONS--OREGON
UNIFORM CIVIL JURY INSTRUCTIONS 1990 (Oregon Bar)
UNIFORM CRIMINAL JURY INSTRUCTIONS 1990 (Oregon Bar)

JURY INSTRUCTIONS--PENNSYLVANIA
PENNSYLVANIA SUGGESTED STANDARD CIVIL JURY INSTRUCTIONS (Penn. Bar)
PENNSYLVANIA SUGGESTED STANDARD CRIMINAL JURY INSTRUCTIONS (Penn. Bar)

JURY INSTRUCTIONS--SOUTH CAROLINA
SOUTH CAROLINA RECOMMENDED CIVIL JURY CHARGES (S. Carolina Bar)

JURY INSTRUCTIONS--SOUTH DAKOTA
SOUTH DAKOTA PATTERN JURY INSTRUCTIONS-CIVIL (S.D. Bar)
SOUTH DAKOTA PATTERN JURY INSTRUCTIONS-CRIMINAL (S.D. Bar)

JURY INSTRUCTIONS--TEXAS
TEXAS PATTERN JURY CHARGES, VOL. 5 (FAMILY LAW) (State Bar of Texas)
TEXAS PATTERN JURY CHARGES, VOL. 4 (BUSINESS, COMMERCIAL, DECEPTIVE TRADE PRACTICES, INSURANCE CODE & DAMAGES) (State Bar of Texas)
TEXAS PATTERN JURY CHARGES, VOL. 1 (GENERAL; MOTOR VEHICLES; DAMAGES) (State Bar of Texas)
TEXAS PATTERN JURY CHARGES, VOL. 3 (PROFESSIONALS; PREMISES; PRODUCTS; DAMAGES) (State Bar of Texas)
TEXAS PATTERN JURY CHARGES, VOL. 2 (WORKERS' COMPENSATION) (State Bar of Texas)

JURY INSTRUCTIONS--VIRGINIA
VIRGINIA MODEL JURY INSTRUCTIONS - CIVIL (Michie)
VIRGINIA MODEL JURY INSTRUCTIONS - CRIMINAL (Michie)

JURY INSTRUCTIONS--WISCONSIN
WISCONSIN JURY INSTRUCTIONS - CIVIL (CLE - Wisc.)
WISCONSIN JURY INSTRUCTIONS - CRIMINAL (CLE - Wisc.)

JURY VERDICTS
REGIONAL VERDICT SURVEY (Jury Verdict)

JUVENILE LAW
ADOPTION LAW AND PRACTICE (Bender)
CHILD SUPPORT REFERENCE MANUAL (ABA)
IMPROVING CHILD SUPPORT PRACTICE (ABA)
REPRESENTING THE CHILD CLIENT (Bender)
RIGHTS OF JUVENILES: THE JUVENILE JUSTICE SYSTEM (Clark Boardman Callaghan)
TRIAL MANUAL FOR DEFENSE ATTORNEYS IN JUVENILE COURT (ALI-ABA)

JUVENILE LAW--ALABAMA
JUVENILE JUSTICE PROCEDURES MANUAL (ABICLE)

JUVENILE LAW--CONNECTICUT
CHILD CUSTODY & CHILD PROTECTION (Conn. Bar)
THE CONNECTICUT CHILD SUPPORT GUIDELINES (Conn. Bar)

JUVENILE LAW--DISTRICT OF COLUMBIA
JUVENILE LAW AND PRACTICE IN THE DISTRICT OF COLUMBIA (D.C. Bar)

JUVENILE LAW--FLORIDA
FLORIDA JUVENILE LAW AND PRACTICE (Florida Bar)
FLORIDA JUVENILE PROCEDURE (Butterworth-Fla.)

JUVENILE LAW--ILLINOIS
ILLINOIS JUVENILE LAW AND PRACTICE (Illinois ICLE)

JUVENILE LAW--MARYLAND

ADVOCATING FOR CHILDREN AND FAMILIES IN CINA PROCEEDING (MICPEL)
REPRESENTING STUDENTS IN PUBLIC SCHOOL DICIPLINARY ACTIONS (MICPEL)

JUVENILE LAW--MINNESOTA

JUVENILE COURT HANDBOOK FOR MINNESOTA (Butterworth-St. Paul)

JUVENILE LAW--MISSOURI

JUVENILE LAW (MoBar)

JUVENILE LAW--NEW HAMPSHIRE

JUVENILE LAW (NH Bar)

JUVENILE LAW--OREGON

JUVENILE LAW (Oregon Bar)

JUVENILE LAW--PENNSYLVANIA

PARTRIDGE-REMICK, PRACTICE AND PROCEDURE IN ORPHANS COURT IN PENNSYLVANIA (Bender)

JUVENILE LAW--WISCONSIN

VOLUNTARY TERMINATION OF PARENTAL RIGHTS AND ADOPTION (State Bar of Wisc.)
WISCONSIN JUDICIAL BENCHBOOK: VOL. 3 - FAMILY (State Bar of Wisc.)

LABOR AND LABOR RELATIONS

see also Affirmative action programs; Collective bargaining; Discrimination in employment: Public employees; Wages

AIDS IN THE WORKPLACE: RESOURCE MATERIAL (BNA)
ALCOHOL AND DRUG ABUSE IN THE WORKPLACE: THE COMPLETE RESOURCE GUIDE (BNA)
AVOIDING AND DEFENDING WRONGFUL DISCHARGE CLAIMS (Clark Boardman Callaghan)
BANK WAGE-HOUR AND PERSONNEL SERVICE (Pratt)
BNA POLICY AND PRACTICE SERIES (BNA)
CASEHANDLING MANUAL (USGPO)
COLLIER LABOR LAW AND THE BANKRUPTCY CODE (Bender)
COMPANY POLICY AND PERSONNEL WORKBOOK (Oasis)
CORPORATE COUNSEL'S GUIDE TO EMPLOYEE RELATIONS LAW (Bus. Laws)
CORPORATE COUNSEL'S GUIDE TO EMPLOYMENT CONTRACTS (Bus. Laws)
DRAFTING THE UNION CONTRACT (Bender)
EEO IN FEDERAL, STATE AND LOCAL GOVERNMENT CONFERENCE MANUAL (NELI)
EMPLOYEE AND UNION MEMBER GUIDE TO LABOR LAW (Clark Boardman Callaghan)
EMPLOYEE COMMUNICATIONS GUIDE (WG&L)
EMPLOYEE DISCIPLINE PRACTICES AND PROBLEMS: AVOIDING THE MENACE OF LEGAL LIABILITY (Alex. Hamilton Inst.)
THE EMPLOYEE HANDBOOK AUDIT: REDUCING THE RISKS OF UNJUST CLAIMS (Alex. Hamilton Inst.)
EMPLOYEE NONCOMPETITION LAW (Clark Boardman Callaghan)
THE EMPLOYEE PROBLEM SOLVER (Alex. Hamilton Inst.)
EMPLOYEE RIGHTS LITIGATION: PLEADING AND PRACTICE (Bender)
EMPLOYEE TESTING: THE COMPLETE RESOURCE GUIDE (BNA)
EMPLOYER'S GUIDE TO AUDITING PERSONNEL & EMPLOYMENT PRACTICES (Bus. Laws)
EMPLOYMENT AND TRAINING REPORTER (MII)
EMPLOYMENT COORDINATOR (WG&L)
EMPLOYMENT GUIDE (BNA)
EMPLOYMENT LAW BRIEFING MANUAL (NELI)
EMPLOYMENT LAW CONFERENCE MANUAL (NELI)
EMPLOYMENT LAW DESKBOOK (Bender)
EMPLOYMENT LITIGATION IN THE NINETIES (NELI)
EMPLOYMENT SCREENING (Bender)
EMPLOYMENT TESTING: A NATIONAL REPORTER ON DRUG, POLYGRAPH, AIDS AND GENETIC TESTING (UPA)
EMPLOYMENT-AT-WILL REPORTER (NELP)
FAIR LABOR STANDARDS HANDBOOK FOR STATES, LOCAL GOVERNMENTS AND SCHOOLS (Thompson)
FEDERAL EQUAL OPPORTUNITY REPORTER (LRP)
FEDERAL LABOR RELATIONS REPORTER (LRP)
FEDERAL MERIT SYSTEMS REPORTER (LRP)

"FIRE ME & I'LL SUE" - A MANAGER'S SURVIVAL GUIDE TO EMPLOYEE RIGHTS (Alex. Hamilton Inst.)
GUIDE TO EMPLOYMENT LAW AND REGULATION (WG&L)
HANDBOOK ON EUROPEAN EMPLOYEE CO-MANAGEMENT (Kluwer)
HOW TO COMPLY WITH THE DRUG-FREE WORKPLACE ACT (BLR)
HR POLICY AND PROCEDURE (WG&L)
HUMAN RESOURCES MANAGEMENT (CCH)
HUMAN RESOURCES MANAGEMENT -- OSHA COMPLIANCE (CCH)
INDIVIDUAL EMPLOYMENT RIGHTS (BNA)
INTERNATIONAL ENCYCLOPEDIA FOR LABOUR LAW AND INDUSTRIAL RELATIONS (Kluwer)
INTERNATIONAL HANDBOOK ON CONTRACTS OF EMPLOYMENT (Kluwer)
INVESTIGATING EMPLOYEE CONDUCT (Clark Boardman Callaghan)
LABOR AND EMPLOYMENT LAW: COMPLIANCE AND LITIGATION (Clark Boardman Callaghan)
LABOR LAW (Business Organizations vols. 18-18I) (Bender)
LABOR LAW AND THE NATIONAL WAGE AGREEMENT; MINERS' RIGHTS & MSHA DISCRIMINATION LAW (EMLF)
LABOR LAW REPORTS (CCH)
LABOR RELATIONS REPORTER (BNA)
THE LEGAL ASPECTS OF SUBSTANCE ABUSE IN THE WORKPLACE (Bus. Laws)
LITIGATING WRONGFUL DISCHARGE CLAIMS (Clark Boardman Callaghan)
MERIT SYSTEMS PROTECTION BOARD SERVICE (Hawkins)
MIDWEST LABOR LAW CONFERENCE (Ohio CLE)
MODERN LAW OF EMPLOYMENT RELATIONSHIPS (Prentice Hall Law & Business)
NATIONAL LABOR RELATIONS BOARD LAW AND PRACTICE (Bender)
NLRB ADVICE MEMORANDUM REPORTER (LRP)
NLRB CASE HANDLING MANUAL (CCH)
NLRB REPRESENTATION ELECTIONS - LAW, PRACTICE & PROCEDURE (Prentice Hall Law & Business)
PERFORMANCE APPRAISALS: THE LATEST LEGAL NIGHTMARE (Alex. Hamilton Inst.)
PERSONNEL DOCUMENTATION AUDIT: STEERING CLEAR OF LEGAL PITFALLS (Alex. Hamilton Inst.)
PERSONNEL FORMS AND EMPLOYMENT CHECKLISTS (Butterworth-NH)
PERSONNEL MANAGEMENT GUIDE (WG&L)
Q&A GUIDE TO PERSONNEL DECISIONS (Alex. Hamilton Inst.)
RULES AND REGULATIONS AND STATEMENTS OF PROCEDURE (USGPO)
STATE LABOR LAWS (BNA)
TERMINATION OF EMPLOYMENT (WG&L)
UNION LABOR REPORT (BNA)
UNJUST DISMISSAL (Bender)
WAGES AND HOURS: LAW AND PRACTICE (Bender)
WHAT TO DO ABOUT PERSONNEL PROBLEMS IN [YOUR STATE] (BLR)
WORKPLACE LITERACY: THE COMPLETE RESOURCE GUIDE (BNA)

LABOR AND LABOR RELATIONS--CALIFORNIA

CALIFORNIA EMPLOYERS GUIDE TO EMPLOYEE HANDBOOKS & PERSONNEL POLICY MANUALS (Bender)
CALIFORNIA EMPLOYMENT LAW (Bender)
CALIFORNIA EMPLOYMENT LAW: A GUIDE TO CALIFORNIA LAWS REGULATING EMPLOYMENT IN THE PRIVATE SECTOR (M & M Resources)
CALIFORNIA WAGE AND HOUR GUIDE (M & M Resources)

LABOR AND LABOR RELATIONS--CANADA

CANADIAN INDUSTRIAL RELATIONS & PERSONNEL DEVELOPMENT (CCH)
CANADIAN LABOUR LAW REPORTS (CCH)
HUMAN RESOURCE MANAGEMENT IN CANADA (WG&L)

LABOR AND LABOR RELATIONS--CONNECTICUT

DAMAGES IN EMPLOYMENT CASES (Conn. Bar)
LABOR AND EMPLOYMENT IN CONNECTICUT (Butterworth-NH)

LABOR AND LABOR RELATIONS--FORMS

EMPLOYMENT LAW CHECKLISTS & FORMS (Clark Boardman Callaghan)
LABOR RELATIONS FORMS & AGREEMENTS (WG&L)
WG&L HUMAN RESOURCES FORMS WITH COMMENTARY (WG&L)

LABOR AND LABOR RELATIONS--ILLINOIS
EMPLOYMENT IN ILLINOIS (Butterworth-St. Paul)
EMPLOYMENT TERMINATION (Illinois ICLE)
LABOR LAW HANDBOOK (Illinois ICLE)

LABOR AND LABOR RELATIONS--INDIANA
LABOR RELATIONS LAW UPDATE (Indiana CLE)

LABOR AND LABOR RELATIONS--IOWA
EMPLOYMENT IN IOWA (Butterworth-St. Paul)

LABOR AND LABOR RELATIONS--KANSAS
KANSAS EMPLOYMENT LAW (Kansas Bar)

LABOR AND LABOR RELATIONS--MAINE
RECENT ISSUES AND CURRENT DEVELOPMENTS IN LABOR AND EMPLOYMENT LAW (Maine Bar)

LABOR AND LABOR RELATIONS--MARYLAND
EMPLOYMENT LAW INSTITUTE (MICPEL)

LABOR AND LABOR RELATIONS--MASSACHUSETTS
LABOR AND EMPLOYMENT IN MASSACHUSETTS: A GUIDE TO EMPLOYMENT LAWS, REGULATIONS AND PRACTICES (Butterworth-NH)
MASSACHUSETTS LABOR CASES (NELP)
MASSACHUSETTS LABOR RELATIONS REPORTER (NELP)

LABOR AND LABOR RELATIONS--MICHIGAN
MICHIGAN WRONGFUL DISCHARGE AND EMPLOYMENT DISCRIMINATION LAW (ICLE - Michigan)
WRONGFUL TERMINATION LITIGATION (MTLA)

LABOR AND LABOR RELATIONS--MINNESOTA
ADVISING THE EMPLOYER (MILE)
EMPLOYMENT IN MINNESOTA (Butterworth-St. Paul)
EMPLOYMENT LAW - 7th ANNUAL (MILE)
EMPLOYMENT LAW HANDBOOK (Minn. CLE)
EMPLOYMENT LAW UPDATE (MILE)
HARASSMENT IN THE WORKPLACE (MILE)
LABOR & EMPLOYMENT LAW INSTITUTE 1991 (Minn. CLE)
MINNESOTA EMPLOYMENT AT WILL (Minn. CLE)
PRIVATE SECTOR LABOR LAW (Minn. CLE)

LABOR AND LABOR RELATIONS--MISSOURI
EMPLOYMENT IN MISSOURI, 2nd Ed. (Butterworth-Texas)
MISSOURI EMPLOYER-EMPLOYEE LAW (MoBar)

LABOR AND LABOR RELATIONS--NEW HAMPSHIRE
EMPLOYMENT DISPUTES (NH Bar)

LABOR AND LABOR RELATIONS--NEW YORK
LABOR AND EMPLOYMENT IN NEW YORK (Butterworth-NH)

LABOR AND LABOR RELATIONS--OHIO
EMPLOYMENT IN OHIO (Butterworth-St. Paul)

LABOR AND LABOR RELATIONS--OREGON
EMPLOYMENT IN OREGON (Butterworth-St. Paul)
LABOR AND EMPLOYMENT LAW PRIVATE SECTOR (Oregon Bar)

LABOR AND LABOR RELATIONS--PENNSYLVANIA
PENNSYLVANIA EMPLOYMENT LAWS (LRP)

LABOR AND LABOR RELATIONS--STATES
EMPLOYMENT REGULATIONS IN [STATE]: A SURVIVAL KIT FOR [STATE] EMPLOYERS: PROCEEDINGS (IBL)

<u>LABOR AND LABOR RELATIONS--TENNESSEE</u>
EMPLOYMENT LAW DESK BOOK FOR TENNESSEE EMPLOYERS (Smith)
TENNESSEE EMPLOYMENT LAW (Smith)

<u>LABOR AND LABOR RELATIONS--TEXAS</u>
EMPLOYMENT IN TEXAS, 3rd Ed. (Butterworth-Texas)

<u>LABOR AND LABOR RELATIONS--WASHINGTON</u>
DIGEST OF UNEMPLOYMENT COMMISSION DECISIONS (Book Pub.)
EMPLOYMENT IN WASHINGTON STATE: REV. ED. (Butterworth-St. Paul)
EMPLOYMENT LAW FOR THE GENERAL PRACTITIONER (Wash. Bar)
EMPLOYMENT LAW UPDATE (Wash. Bar)

<u>LABOR AND LABOR RELATIONS--WISCONSIN</u>
EMPLOYMENT IN WISCONSIN (Butterworth-St. Paul)
PRIVATE SECTOR LABOR RELATIONS FOR THE GENERAL PRACTITIONER (State Bar of Wisc.)

<u>LABOR ARBITRATION</u>
ARBITRATOR'S QUALIFICATIONS REPORTS (Simpson)
LABOR AND EMPLOYMENT ARBITRATION (Bender)
LABOR ARBITRATION AND DISPUTE SETTLEMENTS (BNA)
LABOR ARBITRATION AWARDS (CCH)
LABOR ARBITRATION INFORMATION SYSTEM (LRP)

<u>LAND SALES</u>
DIGEST OF STATE LAND SALES REGULATIONS (Land Dev.)
RIGHTS OF ACCESS AND SURFACE USE (Rocky Mt.)
RIGHTS OF WAY, EASEMENTS AND SURFACE DAMAGES MANUAL (EMLF)

<u>LAND SALES--NEW HAMPSHIRE</u>
SUBDIVISION REGISTRATION (NH Bar)

<u>LAND TRUSTS--ILLINOIS</u>
KENOE ON LAND TRUSTS (Illinois ICLE)
LAND TRUST ADMINISTRATION (Illinois ICLE)

<u>LAND USE</u>
see also Zoning law

ENVIRONMENTAL REGULATION OF LAND USE (Clark Boardman Callaghan)
ENVIRONMENTAL REGULATION OF REAL PROPERTY (Law Journal)
FEDERAL LAND USE LAW (Clark Boardman Callaghan)
GOWER FEDERAL SERVICE - MISCELLANEOUS LAND DECISIONS (Rocky Mt.)
LAND DEVELOPMENT LAW REPORTER (Land Dev.)
A PRACTICAL GUIDE TO WINNING LAND USE APPROVAL AND PERMITS (Bender)
ZONING AND LAND USE CONTROLS (Bender)

<u>LAND USE--ARIZONA</u>
ARIZONA LAND USE LAW (State Bar of Ariz.)

<u>LAND USE--CALIFORNIA</u>
CALIFORNIA ENVIRONMENTAL LAW & LAND USE PRACTICE (Bender)
CALIFORNIA LAND USE PROCEDURE (Shepard's)

<u>LAND USE--CONNECTICUT</u>
AVOIDING LEGAL PITFALLS IN LAND USE AND REAL ESTATE DEVELOPMENT; WATER RESOURCES & REGULATIONS (Conn. Bar)

<u>LAND USE--FLORIDA</u>
FLORIDA ENVIRONMENTAL AND LAND USE LAW (Florida Bar)
FLORIDA LAND USE RESTRICTIONS (Butterworth-Fla.)

<u>LAND USE--ILLINOIS</u>
ILLINOIS LAND USE LAW (Illinois ICLE)

<u>LAND USE--MARYLAND</u>
ZONING LAW MANUAL (MICPEL)

<u>LAND USE--NEW HAMPSHIRE</u>
NEW HAMPSHIRE MUNICIPAL PRACTICE SERIES: LAND USE PLANNING & ZONING (Butterworth-NH)

<u>LAND USE--NEW JERSEY</u>
MOUNT LAUREL II AND THE FAIR HOUSING ACT (New Jersey ICLE)

<u>LAND USE--OREGON</u>
LAND USE (Oregon Bar)

<u>LAND USE--TEXAS</u>
TEXAS LAND USE LAW (Wiley Law)

<u>LAND USE--UTAH</u>
UTAH ENVIRONMENTAL LAND USE PERMIT MANUAL (Utah Bar)

<u>LAND USE--WASHINGTON</u>
ENVIRONMENTAL AND LAND USE LAW MID-YEAR MEETING (Wash. Bar)
FOOTING THE BILL: THE PRICE OF LAND USE REGULATION (Wash. Bar)
LAND USE LAW IN THE AGE OF GRIDLOCK (Wash. Bar)

<u>LANDLORD AND TENANT</u>
see also Leases; Real property

<u>LANDLORD AND TENANT--CALIFORNIA</u>
CALIFORNIA PRACTICE GUIDE - LANDLORD-TENANT (Rutter)

<u>LANDLORD AND TENANT--CONNECTICUT</u>
CONNECTICUT SUMMARY PROCESS LAW (Conn. Bar)

<u>LANDLORD AND TENANT--FLORIDA</u>
FLORIDA COMMERCIAL LANDLORD-TENANT LAW (Butterworth-Fla.)
FLORIDA RESIDENTIAL LANDLORD TENANT LAW MANUAL (Butterworth-Fla.)
LANDLORD'S REMEDIES IN FLORIDA (Butterworth-Fla.)

<u>LANDLORD AND TENANT--GEORGIA</u>
GEORGIA LANDLORD-TENANT LAW (Butterworth-Fla.)

<u>LANDLORD AND TENANT--ILLINOIS</u>
COMMERCIAL LANDLORD/TENANT PRACTICE (Illinois ICLE)
REPRESENTING RESIDENTIAL TENANTS (Illinois ICLE)

<u>LANDLORD AND TENANT--LOUISIANA</u>
LOUISIANA LANDLORD & TENANT LAW (Butterworth-Texas)

<u>LANDLORD AND TENANT--MARYLAND-FORMS</u>
MARYLAND REAL ESTATE LEASING FORMS - PRACTICE (Aspen)

<u>LANDLORD AND TENANT--MICHIGAN</u>
MICHIGAN RESIDENTIAL LANDLORD TENANT LAW, 2ND ED. (Mich. Legal)

<u>LANDLORD AND TENANT--NEW HAMPSHIRE</u>
HOUSING LAW (NH Bar)

<u>LANDLORD AND TENANT--NEW YORK</u>
THE NEW YORK CITY HOUSING COURT REPORTER (Lamb's Flight)
THE NEW YORK CITY HOUSING COURT REPORTER PLAINTIFF-DEFENDANT TABLES (Lamb's Flight)
THE NEW YORK CITY LOFT BOARD REPORTER (Lamb's Flight)
THE NEW YORK CITY HOUSING COURT REPORTER DIGEST (Lamb's Flight)
NEW YORK LANDLORD & TENANT HANDBOOK (Gould)
TREIMAN'S LANDLORD & TENANT ENCYCLOPEDIA & REVIEW (Lamb's Flight)
TREIMAN'S NEW YORK LANDLORD TENANT STATUTES, ANNOTATED (Lamb's Flight)
TREIMAN'S RENT STABILIZATION CODE, ANNOTATED (Lamb's Flight)

LANDLORD AND TENANT--OKLAHOMA

COUNSELING LANDLORDS AND TENANTS (Okla. Bar CLE)

LANDLORD AND TENANT--PENNSYLVANIA

PENNSYLVANIA LANDLORD AND TENANT LAW AND PRACTICE WITH FORMS (WITH COMPUTER DISK) (Bisel)

LANDLORD AND TENANT--TEXAS

TEXAS RESIDENTIAL LANDLORD-TENANT LAW (Butterworth-Texas)

LAW OF THE SEA

EASTERN EUROPEAN STATES AND THE DEVELOPMENT OF THE LAW OF THE SEA: REGIONAL DOCUMENTS, NATIONAL LEGISLATION (Oceana)
NEW DIRECTIONS IN THE LAW OF THE SEA (Oceana)
NORTH AMERICA AND ASIA-PACIFIC AND THE DEVELOPMENT OF THE LAW OF THE SEA (Oceana)

LAW OF THE SEA--EASTERN EUROPE

USSR, EASTERN EUROPE AND THE DEVELOPMENT OF THE LAW OF THE SEA (Oceana)

LAW OF THE SEA--LATIN AMERICA

LATIN AMERICA AND THE DEVELOPMENT OF THE LAW OF THE SEA: REGIONAL DOCUMENTS, NATIONAL LEGISLATION (Oceana)

LAW OF THE SEA--WESTERN EUROPE

WESTERN EUROPE AND THE DEVELOPMENT OF LAW OF THE SEA; NATIONAL LEGISLATION (Oceana)

LAW OFFICE MANAGEMENT

ACCOUNTING SYSTEMS FOR LAW OFFICES (Bender)
THE AMERICAN LAWYER MANAGEMENT SERVICE (Am. Lawyer)
THE AUTOMATED LAW FIRM: A COMPLETE GUIDE TO SOFTWARE AND SYSTEMS (Prentice Hall Law & Business)
THE BUSINESS OF LAW - A HANDBOOK ON HOW TO MANAGE LAW FIRMS (Prentice Hall Law & Business)
COMPLETE PERSONNEL ADMINISTRATION HANDBOOK FOR LAW FIRMS (Altman Weil Pensa)
HOW TO MANAGE YOUR LAW OFFICE (Bender)
HOW TO MARKET AND ADVERTISE YOUR LAW PRACTICE (CRI)
INITIATIVE: A RESOURCE GUIDE TO DEVELOPING SUCCESSFUL MINORITY PROGRAMS (ABA)
LAW DEPARTMENT MANAGEMENT (2nd ed.) (Bus. Laws)
LAW FIRM MANAGEMENT GUIDE (Altman Weil Pensa)
LAW OFFICE AUTOMATION AND TECHNOLOGY (Bender)
LAW OFFICE ECONOMICS AND MANAGEMENT MANUAL (Clark Boardman Callaghan)
LAW OFFICE MANUAL (Arkansas Bar)
LAW OFFICE STAFF MANUAL: MODEL POLICIES AND PROCEDURES FOR LAW OFFICE PERSONNEL (ABA)
MANAGING THE SMALL & MEDIUM-SIZED LAW FIRM (Indiana CLE)
MARKETING FOR LAWYERS AND LAW FIRMS (Wash. Bar)
MAXIMIZING LAW FIRM PROFITABILITY (Law Journal)
A PLANNING WORKBOOK FOR LAW FIRM MANAGEMENT (ABA)
TENNESSEE LAW OFFICE DESK BOOK (Smith)

LAW OFFICE MANAGEMENT--SOUTH CAROLINA

PROCEDURES MANUAL FOR LEGAL PERSONNEL (S. Carolina Bar)

LAW OFFICE MANAGEMENT--TEXAS

TEXAS LAW OFFICE HANDBOOK (Parker)

LAW SCHOOLS

INDEX TO LAW SCHOOL ALUMNI PUBLICATIONS (Rothman)

LAW-RELATED EDUCATION

MAP PACKAGE: LAW RELATED EDUCATION, TEACHING YOUNG PEOPLE ABOUT THE LAW (ABA)

LAWYER'S FEES

COURT AWARDED ATTORNEY FEES (Bender)
RELATIVE VALUES: DETERMINING ATTORNEYS' FEES (Shepard's)
SECTION 1983 LITIGATION IN STATE COURTS (Clark Boardman Callaghan)
WINNING ATTORNEY'S FEES FROM THE U.S. GOVERNMENT (Law Journal)

LAWYER'S FEES--ARIZONA

ARIZONA ATTORNEY'S FEES MANUAL (State Bar of Ariz.)

LAWYER'S FEES--CALIFORNIA

FEE AGREEMENT FORMS MANUAL (Calif. CEB)

LAWYER'S FEES--FLORIDA

ATTORNEY'S FEES IN FLORIDA (Butterworth-Fla.)

LAWYER'S FEES--WASHINGTON

ATTORNEY FEES IN WASHINGTON (Butterworth-St. Paul)
ATTORNEYS' FEES: BEYOND THE DOLLARS (Wash. Bar)

LEASES

see also Landlord and tenant; Real Property

COMMERCIAL LEASE NEGOTIATIONS (Georgetown)
CURRENT LEASING LAW AND TECHNIQUES - FORMS (Real Estate Transaction Series, vols. 7, 7A, & 7B) (Bender)
GROUND LEASES AND LAND ACQUISITION CONTRACTS (Law Journal)
MODERN REAL ESTATE LEASING FORMS (WG&L)
SHOPPING CENTER AND STORE LEASES (Law Journal)

LEASES--CONNECTICUT

COMMERCIAL LEASE LITIGATION (Conn. Bar)

LEASES--MARYLAND-FORMS

MARYLAND REAL ESTATE LEASING FORMS - PRACTICE (Aspen)

LEASES--NEW JERSEY

SHOPPING CENTER LEASES (New Jersey ICLE)

LEGAL ASSISTANTS

CLA STUDY GUIDE (Butterworth-Fla.)
LITIGATION PARALEGAL (James)
PARALEGAL TRIAL HANDBOOK (James)

LEGAL ASSISTANTS--ILLINOIS

QUICK GUIDE FOR THE LEGAL ASSISTANT (Illinois ICLE)

LEGAL BIBLIOGRAPHY

ANNUALS AND SURVEYS APPEARING IN LEGAL PERIODICALS: AN ANNOTATED LISTING (Rothman)
A COLLECTION OF BIBLIOGRAPHIC & RESEARCH RESOURCES (Oceana)
HEIN'S LEGAL PERIODICAL CHECKLIST (Hein)
HEIN'S STATE REPORT CHECKLIST (Hein)
INDEX TO LAW SCHOOL ALUMNI PUBLICATIONS (Rothman)
LAW BOOKS RECOMMENDED FOR LIBRARIES (Rothman)
LAW FOR THE LAYMAN: AN ANNOTATED BIBLIOGRAPHY OF SELF-HELP LAW BOOKS (Rothman)
LEGAL PERIODICALS IN ENGLISH (Glanville Publishers)
PIMSLEUR'S CHECKLISTS OF BASIC AMERICAN LEGAL PUBLICATIONS (Rothman)
SOURCES OF COMPILED LEGISLATIVE HISTORIES: BIBLIOGRAPHY OF GOVERNMENT DOCUMENTS, PERIODICAL ARTICLES AND BOOKS, 1ST CONGRESS-99TH CONGRESS (Rothman)

LEGAL EDUCATION

A PLAN FOR LAWYER DEVELOPMENT: A COMPREHENSIVE MANUAL ON ESTABLISHING AND ADMINISTERING CLE PROGRAMS IN THE OFFICE (ABA)

LEGAL ETHICS

ABA/BNA LAWYER'S MANUAL ON PROFESSIONAL CONDUCT (BNA)
THE JUDICIAL RESPONSE TO LAWYER MISCONDUCT (ABA)
THE LAW OF LAWYERING: A HANDBOOK ON THE MODEL RULES OF PROFESSIONAL CONDUCT (Prentice Hall Law & Business)
NATIONAL REPORTER ON LEGAL ETHICS AND PROFESSIONAL RESPONSIBILITY (UPA)

LEGAL ETHICS--ALABAMA

LEGAL ETHICS IN ALABAMA (ABICLE)

LEGAL ETHICS--CALIFORNIA

CALIFORNIA COMPENDIUM ON PROFESSIONAL RESPONSIBILITY (State Bar of Calif.)

LEGAL ETHICS--COLORADO

COLORADO ETHICS OPINIONS HANDBOOK (CLE - Colorado)

LEGAL ETHICS--DISTRICT OF COLUMBIA

D.C. CODE OF PROFESSIONAL RESPONSIBILITY AND OPINIONS OF THE D.C. BAR LEGAL ETHICS COMMITTEE (D.C. Bar)
D.C. RULES OF PROFESSIONAL RESPONSIBILITY (D.C. Bar)

LEGAL ETHICS--FLORIDA

PROFESSIONAL ETHICS OF THE FLORIDA BAR (Florida Bar)
PROFESSIONAL LIABILITY OF LAWYERS IN FLORIDA (Florida Bar)

LEGAL ETHICS--ILLINOIS

ANNOTATED GUIDE TO THE ILLINOIS RULES OF PROFESSIONAL CONDUCT (Illinois ICLE)

LEGAL ETHICS--MAINE

MAINE MANUAL ON PROFESSIONAL RESPONSIBILITY (Butterworth-NH)

LEGAL ETHICS--MICHIGAN

MICHIGAN RULES OF PROFESSIONAL CONDUCT AND DISCIPLINARY PROCEDURE (ICLE - Michigan)

LEGAL ETHICS--MISSOURI

MISSOURI ADVISORY COMMITTEE OPINIONS (MoBar)

LEGAL ETHICS--NEW JERSEY

PROFESSIONAL RESPONSIBILITY IN NEW JERSEY (New Jersey ICLE)

LEGAL ETHICS--NEW YORK CITY

OPINIONS OF THE COMMITTEE ON PROFESSIONAL ETHICS (Oceana)

LEGAL ETHICS--NEW YORK STATE

OPINIONS OF THE COMMITTEE ON PROFESSIONAL ETHICS (Oceana)

LEGAL ETHICS--OKLAHOMA

LEGAL ETHICS - PROCEDURE & CASE UPDATE (Okla. Bar CLE)

LEGAL ETHICS--OREGON

THE ETHICAL OREGON LAWYER (Oregon Bar)
OREGON FORMAL ETHICS OPINIONS (Oregon Bar)
THE OREGON STATE BAR DESK REFERENCE - A GUIDE TO THE REGULATORY PROGRAMS OF THE OREGON STATE BAR (Oregon Bar)

LEGAL ETHICS--SOUTH CAROLINA

HANDBOOK ON LEGAL ETHICS FOR SOUTH CAROLINA LAWYERS - 2nd ed. (S. Carolina Bar)

LEGAL ETHICS--TEXAS

TEXAS LAWYERS' PROFESSIONAL ETHICS (State Bar of Texas)

LEGAL ETHICS--WASHINGTON

CONFLICTS OF INTEREST IN BUSINESS TRANSACTIONS (Wash. Bar)

LEGAL ETHICS--WISCONSIN
ETHICS & PROFESSIONAL RESPONSIBILITY: A HANDBOOK FOR WISCONSIN LAWYERS (State Bar of Wisc.)
WISCONSIN ETHICS OPINIONS (State Bar of Wisc.)

LEGAL RESEARCH
A COLLECTION OF BIBLIOGRAPHIC & RESEARCH RESOURCES (Oceana)
FOREIGN LAW: CURRENT SOURCES OF CODES AND BASIC LEGISLATION IN JURISDICTIONS OF THE WORLD (vol. I: The Western Hemisphere; vol. II: Western & Eastern Europe; vol. III: Africa, Asia, Australia) (Rothman)
GERMAIN'S TRANSNATIONAL LAW RESEARCH (Transnational Juris Publications)
GUIDE TO STATE LEGISLATIVE AND ADMINISTRATIVE MATERIALS (Rothman)
LEGAL PERIODICALS IN ENGLISH (Glanville Publishers)
LEGAL RESEARCH AND LAW LIBRARY MANAGEMENT (Law Journal)
LEGAL RESEARCH AND WRITING (Illinois ICLE)
SPECIALIZED LEGAL RESEARCH (Little, Brown)
SUBJECT HEADING INDEX GUIDE FOR OPINIONS AND MEMORANDA OF LAW (Holding)

LEGAL RESEARCH--FLORIDA
FLORIDA LEGAL RESEARCH AND SOURCEBOOK (Butterworth-Fla.)

LEGAL RESEARCH--MASSACHUSETTS
HANDBOOK OF LEGAL RESEARCH IN MASSACHUSETTS (Mass. CLE)

LEGAL RESEARCH--NEW YORK
NEW YORK LAWYER'S DESKBOOK (NYSBA)

LEGAL RESEARCH--SOUTH DAKOTA
SOUTH DAKOTA LEGAL RESEARCH GUIDE (Hein)

LEGAL SECRETARIES
LEGAL SECRETARY FEDERAL LITIGATION (James)

LEGAL SECRETARIES--CALIFORNIA
CALIFORNIA LEGAL FILING DIRECTORY (Shepard's)
LEGAL SECRETARY'S HANDBOOK (Rutter)

LEGAL SECRETARIES--COLORADO
COLORADO LAW OFFICE HANDBOOK (Parker)

LEGAL SECRETARIES--FLORIDA
FLORIDA ATTORNEY'S/SECRETARY'S HANDBOOK (Mariposa)
FLORIDA LEGAL FILING DIRECTORY (Shepard's)
THE MANUAL FOR FLORIDA LEGAL SECRETARIES (Butterworth-Fla.)

LEGAL SECRETARIES--GEORGIA
GEORGIA ATTORNEY'S/SECRETARY'S HANDBOOK (Mariposa)

LEGAL SECRETARIES--ILLINOIS
ILLINOIS ATTORNEY'S/SECRETARY'S HANDBOOK (Mariposa)
ILLINOIS LEGAL FILING DIRECTORY (Shepard's)

LEGAL SECRETARIES--IOWA
IOWA ATTORNEY'S/SECRETARY'S HANDBOOK (Mariposa)

LEGAL SECRETARIES--LOUISIANA
LOUISIANA ATTORNEY'S/SECRETARY'S HANDBOOK (Mariposa)

LEGAL SECRETARIES--MICHIGAN
MICHIGAN LEGAL FILING DIRECTORY (Shepard's)

LEGAL SECRETARIES--MINNESOTA
MINNESOTA ATTORNEY'S/SECRETARY'S HANDBOOK (Mariposa)

LEGAL SECRETARIES--MISSOURI
MISSOURI ATTORNEY'S/SECRETARY'S HANDBOOK (Mariposa)

LEGAL SECRETARIES--NEW JERSEY
NEW JERSEY LEGAL SECRETARY'S HANDBOOK (Michie)

LEGAL SECRETARIES--OHIO
OHIO ATTORNEY'S/SECRETARY'S HANDBOOK (Mariposa)

LEGAL SECRETARIES--PENNSYLVANIA
PENNSYLVANIA ATTORNEY'S/SECRETARY'S HANDBOOK (Mariposa)

LEGAL SECRETARIES--SOUTH CAROLINA
PROCEDURES MANUAL FOR LEGAL PERSONNEL (S. Carolina Bar)

LEGAL SECRETARIES--TEXAS
TEXAS ATTORNEY'S/SECRETARY'S HANDBOOK (Mariposa)
TEXAS LAW OFFICE HANDBOOK (Parker)

LEGAL SECRETARIES--VIRGINIA
HANDBOOK FOR LEGAL SECRETARIES IN VIRGINIA 2ND ED. (Michie)

LEGAL SECRETARIES--WISCONSIN
WISCONSIN ATTORNEY'S/SECRETARY'S HANDBOOK (Mariposa)

LEGAL SERVICES
PREPAID LEGAL SERVICES REGULATION REPORTER (API)
THE RESOURCE: A PRO BONO MANUAL (ABA)

LEGAL SERVICES--ARIZONA
ARIZONA LEGAL SERVICES PRACTICE MANUAL, VOL. I (State Bar of Ariz.)

LEGAL WRITING
EFFECTIVE LEGAL WRITING (Indiana CLE)
LEGAL WRITING - FOR EFFECT (MILE)

LEGISLATION
CONGRESSIONAL HEARINGS CALENDAR (Hein)
CONGRESSIONAL INDEX (CCH)
U.S. INTELLECTUAL PROPERTY LEGISLATIVE REVIEW (Clark Boardman Callaghan)
UNITED STATES LEGISLATION ON FOREIGN RELATIONS AND INTERNATIONAL COMMERCE (Hein)

LEGISLATION--HAWAII
HAWAII LEGISLATIVE SOURCEBOOK (Pacific Law Inst.)

LEGISLATION--INDIANA
LEGISLATIVE UPDATE (Indiana CLE)

LEGISLATION--ITALY
THE ITALIAN CIVIL CODE AND COMPLEMENTARY LEGISLATION (Oceana)

LEGISLATION--MINNESOTA
LEGISLATIVE UPDATE (MILE)

LEGISLATION--NEW HAMPSHIRE
LEGISLATIVE DEVELOPMENTS (NH Bar)

LEGISLATION--STATES
GUIDE TO STATE LEGISLATIVE AND ADMINISTRATIVE MATERIALS (Rothman)
STATE LEGISLATIVE SOURCEBOOK (Govt. Res.)

LEGISLATION--USSR
COLLECTED LEGISLATION OF THE USSR AND THE CONSTITUENT UNION REPUBLICS: LEGISLATION AND CONSTITUTIONS (Oceana)

LEGISLATIVE HISTORIES
SOURCES OF COMPILED LEGISLATIVE HISTORIES: BIBLIOGRAPHY OF GOVERNMENT DOCUMENTS, PERIODICAL ARTICLES AND BOOKS, 1ST CONGRESS-99TH CONGRESS (Rothman)

UNION LIST OF LEGISLATIVE HISTORIES, 47TH CONGRESS, 1881 - 101st CONGRESS, 1990 (Rothman)

LEGISLATIVE HISTORIES--TAXATION
TAX MANAGEMENT PRIMARY SOURCES SERIES V (BNA)

LIABILITY
see also Government liability; Insurance, liability; Malpractice; Products liability, Torts

APPRAISERS' LIABILITY (Prof. Pubs.)
GUIDE TO ENVIRONMENTAL LIABILITY IN REAL ESTATE TRANSACTIONS (Thompson)
LAWYERS' PROFESSIONAL LIABILITY UPDATE (ABA)
LENDER LIABILITY: A PRAGMATIC APPROACH (Indiana CLE)
LENDER LIABILITY LAW & LITIGATION (Bender)
LIQUOR LIABILITY LAW (Bender)
MATERIALS ON MINIMIZING MANAGEMENT LIABILITY (Bus. Laws)
PREMISES LIABILITY (Bender)
PROFESSIONAL LIABILITY (Knowles)
PROFESSIONAL LIABILITY INSURANCE (Intl. Risk Mgmt. Inst.)
RCRA AND SUPERFUND: A PRACTICE GUIDE WITH FORMS (Shepard's)
RESPONSIBILITIES OF INSURANCE AGENTS AND BROKERS (Bender)

LIABILITY--FLORIDA
FLORIDA PREMISES LIABILITY (Butterworth-Fla.)
PROFESSIONAL LIABILITY OF LAWYERS IN FLORIDA (Florida Bar)

LIABILITY--ILLINOIS
PROFESSIONAL LIABILITY (Illinois ICLE)

LIABILITY--INDIANA
LIABILITY ISSUES IN THE HOSPITAL SETTING (Indiana CLE)

LIABILITY--MINNESOTA
PREMISES LIABILITY (MILE)

LIABILITY--NEW HAMPSHIRE
PROFESSIONAL LIABILITY: RECOGNIZING, HANDLING, PREVENTING (NH Bar)

LIABILITY--TEXAS
PREMISES LIABILITY (Knowles)

LIBEL
EMPLOYEE, BUSINESS AND PROFESSIONAL DEFAMATION (Bender)
LAW OF DEFAMATION (Clark Boardman Callaghan)
LIBEL AND PRIVACY: THE PREVENTION AND DEFENSE OF LITIGATION (Prentice Hall Law & Business)

LIBEL AND SLANDER--MARYLAND
NEW DEVELOPMENTS IN THE LAW OF DEFAMATION (MICPEL)

LIBRARIES
AALL ANNUAL MEETINGS: AN ANNOTATED INDEX OF THE RECORDINGS (Rothman)
CATALOGING LEGAL LITERATURE: A MANUAL ON AACR2 AND LIBRARY OF CONGRESS SUBJECT HEADINGS FOR LEGAL MATERIALS, WITH ILLUSTRATIONS (Rothman)
LEGAL LC SUBJECT HEADINGS WEEKLY LISTS: CUMULATION (Rothman)
LEGAL RESEARCH AND LAW LIBRARY MANAGEMENT (Law Journal)
LIBRARY OF CONGRESS CLASSIFICATION CLASS H SUBCLASSES H-HJ - SOCIAL SCIENCES: ECONOMICS - CUMULATIVE SCHEDULE AND INDEX (Rothman)
LIBRARY OF CONGRESS CLASSIFICATION CLASS H SUBCLASSES HM-HX - SOCIAL SCIENCES: SOCIOLOGY - CUMULATIVE SCHEDULE AND INDEX (Rothman)
LIBRARY OF CONGRESS CLASSIFICATION CLASS J - POLITICAL SCIENCE - CUMULATIVE SCHEDULE AND INDEX (Rothman)
LIBRARY OF CONGRESS CLASSIFICATION CLASS K - SUBCLASS K LAW (GENERAL) - CUMULATIVE SCHEDULE AND INDEX (Rothman)
LIBRARY OF CONGRESS CLASSIFICATION CLASS K - SUBCLASS KD - LAW OF THE UNITED KINGDOM AND IRELAND - CUMULATIVE SCHEDULE AND INDEX (Rothman)

LIBRARY OF CONGRESS CLASSIFICATION CLASS KDZ, KG-KH - LAW OF THE AMERICAS, LATIN AMERICA AND THE WEST INDIES - CUMULATIVE SCHEDULE AND INDEX (Rothman)
LIBRARY OF CONGRESS CLASSIFICATION CLASS K - SUBCLASS KE - LAW OF CANADA - CUMULATIVE SCHEDULE AND INDEX (Rothman)
LIBRARY OF CONGRESS CLASSIFICATION CLASS K - SUBCLASS KF - LAW OF THE UNITED STATES - CUMULATIVE INDEX (Rothman)
LIBRARY OF CONGRESS CLASSIFICATION CLASS K - SUBCLASS KF - LAW OF THE UNITED STATES - CUMULATIVE SCHEDULE (Rothman)
LIBRARY OF CONGRESS CLASSIFICATION CLASS KJ-KKZ - LAW OF EUROPE - CUMULATIVE SCHEDULE AND INDEX (Rothman)
LIBRARY OF CONGRESS CLASSIFICATION CLASS KJV-KJW - LAW OF FRANCE - CUMULATIVE SCHEDULE AND INDEX (Rothman)
LIBRARY OF CONGRESS CLASSIFICATION CLASS KK-KKC - LAW OF GERMANY - CUMULATIVE SCHEDULE AND INDEX (Rothman)
LIBRARY OF CONGRESS CLASSIFICATION CLASS Z - BIBLIOGRAPHY: LIBRARY SCIENCE - CUMULATIVE SCHEDULE AND INDEX (Rothman)

LICENSES
see also Foreign licensing agreements; Patent licenses

DISTRIBUTING FOREIGN PRODUCED PRODUCTS IN THE U.S. (Bender)
DRAFTING LICENSE AGREEMENTS (Prentice Hall Law & Business)
THE LAW AND BUSINESS OF LICENSING: LICENSING IN THE 1990s (Clark Boardman Callaghan)
LICENSING IN FOREIGN AND DOMESTIC OPERATIONS: FORMS (Clark Boardman Callaghan)
MILGRIM ON LICENSING (Bender)
TECHNOLOGY MANAGEMENT (Clark Boardman Callaghan)

LICENSES--ALASKA
ALASKA DIRECTORY OF PERMITS (Book Pub.)

LICENSES--MARYLAND
MARYLAND LICENSING REQUIREMENTS: A SOURCEBOOK FOR LAWYERS WHO ADVISE BUSINESSES AND PROFESSIONALS (MICPEL)

LIE DETECTORS
POLYGRAPH AND THE LAW (JKP)

LIENS
see Mechanics' liens; Tax liens

LIFE INSURANCE
see Insurance, life

LIMITATION OF ACTIONS--ALASKA
ALASKA TIME LIMITS: STATUTES AND COURT RULES (Book Pub.)

LIMITATION OF ACTIONS--COLORADO
STATUTORY TIME LIMITATIONS: COLORADO (Butterworth-St. Paul)

LIMITATION OF ACTIONS--CONNECTICUT
CONNECTICUT TIME LIMITATIONS (Butterworth-NH)

LIMITATION OF ACTIONS--ILLINOIS
ILLINOIS LIMITATIONS MANUAL, 2ND ED. (Butterworth-St. Paul)

LIMITATION OF ACTIONS--IOWA
IOWA LIMITATIONS MANUAL, 2ND ED. (Butterworth-St. Paul)

LIMITATION OF ACTIONS--KANSAS
KANSAS STATUTE OF LIMITATIONS AND TIME STANDARDS (Kansas Bar)

LIMITATION OF ACTIONS--MINNESOTA
MINNESOTA LIMITATIONS MANUAL, 2nd ed. (Butterworth-St. Paul)
STATUTE OF LIMITATIONS (MILE)

LIMITATION OF ACTIONS--MISSOURI
MISSOURI TIME LIMITATIONS (MoBar)

LIMITATION OF ACTIONS--NEBRASKA
NEBRASKA LIMITATIONS MANUAL, 2nd ed. (Butterworth-St. Paul)

LIMITATION OF ACTIONS--TEXAS
TEXAS LIMITATIONS MANUAL (Butterworth-Texas)

LIMITATION OF ACTIONS--WASHINGTON
STATUTORY TIME LIMITATIONS: WASHINGTON STATE (Butterworth-St. Paul)

LIMITED PARTNERSHIP
see also Partnership

INVESTMENT LIMITED PARTNERSHIPS AND OTHER PASS-THROUGH VEHICLES (Securities Law Series, Vols. 4, 4A, 4B, 4C) (Clark Boardman Callaghan)
TAX ASPECTS OF REAL ESTATE INVESTMENTS (Clark Boardman Callaghan)

LIMITED PARTNERSHIP--MAINE
PARTNERSHIP INVESTMENTS: GOING UNDER (Maine Bar)

LIMITED PARTNERSHIP--STATES
STATE LIMITED PARTNERSHIP LAWS (Prentice Hall Law & Business)

LIQUOR LAWS
LIQUOR CONTROL LAW REPORTS (CCH)
LIQUOR LIABILITY LAW (Bender)

LIQUOR LAWS--ILLINOIS
ILLINOIS DRAM SHOP ACT PRACTICE (Illinois ICLE)

LITIGATION
see Actions and defenses

LOANS
see also Banks and banking; Interest and usury; Mortgages

ASSET-BASED FINANCING (Bender)
COLLIER'S LENDING INSTITUTIONS AND THE BANKRUPTCY CODE (Bender)
COMMERCIAL LOAN DOCUMENTATION GUIDE (Bender)
GUIDE TO COMMERCIAL LENDING LAW (Sheshunoff)
GUIDE TO CONSUMER LENDING LAW (Sheshunoff)
LENDER LIABILITY: THEORY & PRACTICE (Wiley Law)
LENDER LIABILITY AND BANKING LITIGATION (Law Journal)
STRUCTURING COMMERCIAL LOAN AGREEMENTS (WG&L)
STRUCTURING SECURED COMMERCIAL LOAN DOCUMENTS (WG&L)

LOANS--CONNECTICUT
ASSET BASED LOAN TRANSACTION (Conn. Bar)

LOBBYING--STATES
STATE LOBBYING LAWS (S&FA)

LOCAL GOVERNMENT
see also Municipal government

LOCAL GOVERNMENT LAW (Bender)
LOCAL GOVERNMENT LAW (Clark Boardman Callaghan)

LOCAL GOVERNMENT--KANSAS
KANSAS LOCAL GOVERNMENT LAW (Kansas Bar)

LOCAL GOVERNMENT--MISSOURI
MISSOURI LOCAL GOVERNMENT LAW (MoBar)

LOCAL GOVERNMENT--NEW JERSEY
THE ABCs OF LOCAL GOVERNMENT LAW (New Jersey ICLE)

LOCAL GOVERNMENT--OHIO
BALDWIN'S OHIO TOWNSHIP LAW (Banks)

MALPRACTICE
LAWYERS' PROFESSIONAL LIABILITY UPDATE (ABA)
MEDICAL AND HOSPITAL NEGLIGENCE (Clark Boardman Callaghan)
MEDICAL MALPRACTICE (Bender)
MEDICAL MALPRACTICE: GUIDE TO MEDICAL ISSUES (Bender)
PODIATRIC LIABILITY (Public Reporting Services)

MALPRACTICE--ARIZONA
THE ARIZONA LAW OF MEDICAL MALPRACTICE (Medilex)

MALPRACTICE--CONNECTICUT
RECENT DEVELOPMENTS IN MEDICAL MALPRACTICE (Conn. Bar)

MALPRACTICE--ILLINOIS
MEDICAL MALPRACTICE (Illinois ICLE)

MALPRACTICE--MICHIGAN
HANDLING THE MEDICAL MALPRACTICE CASE: A SYSTEMS APPROACH (ICLE - Michigan)
MICHIGAN MEDICAL MALPRACTICE CASES ANNOTATED (MTLA)

MALPRACTICE--MINNESOTA
ACCOUNTING MALPRACTICE (MILE)
LEGAL MALPRACTICE GUIDE (MILE)
MEDICAL MALPRACTICE CLAIMS (MILE)
MEDICAL MALPRACTICE CLAIMS IN THE 90's (MILE)

MALPRACTICE--NEW JERSEY
PROFESSIONAL NEGLIGENCE: LAW OF MALPRACTICE IN NEW JERSEY (New Jersey ICLE)

MALPRACTICE--NEW YORK
NEW YORK MEDICAL MALPRACTICE (NYSTLA)

MARITIME LAW
see Admiralty; Ships and shipping

MARRIAGE AND DIVORCE
ALIMONY, CHILD SUPPORT AND COUNSEL FEES (Bender)
DIVORCE, SEPARATION AND THE DISTRIBUTION OF PROPERTY (Law Journal)
DIVORCE TAX PLANNING STRATEGIES (Shepard's)
ENCYCLOPEDIA OF MATRIMONIAL PRACTICE (Prentice Hall Law & Business)
THE FAMILY LAW REPORTER (BNA)
SEPARATION AGREEMENTS AND ANTENUPTIAL CONTRACTS (Bender)
TAX ASPECTS OF DIVORCE AND SEPARATION (Law Journal)
TAX ASPECTS OF MARITAL DISSOLUTION (Clark Boardman Callaghan)
TAX STRATEGIES IN DIVORCE (Wiley Law)
VALUATION AND DISTRIBUTION OF MARITAL PROPERTY (Bender)

MARRIAGE AND DIVORCE--ALABAMA
ALABAMA DIVORCE SYSTEMS MANUAL (ABICLE)
MARITAL LAW (ABICLE)

MARRIAGE AND DIVORCE--CALIFORNIA
CALIFORNIA FAMILY LAW - PRACTICE AND PROCEDURE (Bender)
CALIFORNIA MARITAL TERMINATION AGREEMENTS (Calif. CEB)
CALIFORNIA PRACTICE GUIDE - FAMILY LAW (Rutter)

MARRIAGE AND DIVORCE--CONNECTICUT
STRATEGY AND MANAGEMENT OF THE KEY STAGES OF A MATRIMONIAL CASE: THE CORE SKILLS (Conn. Bar)

<u>MARRIAGE AND DIVORCE--FLORIDA</u>
DRAFTING MARRIAGE CONTRACTS IN FLORIDA (Florida Bar)
FLORIDA DISSOLUTION OF MARRIAGE (Florida Bar)
FLORIDA FAMILY LAW PRACTICE (Butterworth-Fla.)
FLORIDA PROCEEDINGS AFTER DISSOLUTION OF MARRIAGE (Florida Bar)

<u>MARRIAGE AND DIVORCE--GEORGIA</u>
GEORGIA DIVORCE (Lawyers Coop.)

<u>MARRIAGE AND DIVORCE--HAWAII</u>
HAWAII DIVORCE MANUAL: A COOPERATIVE EFFORT (HICLE)

<u>MARRIAGE AND DIVORCE--ILLINOIS</u>
GITLIN ON DIVORCE: A GUIDE TO ILLINOIS MATRIMONIAL LAW (Butterworth-St. Paul)
ILLINOIS FAMILY LAW (Illinois ICLE)

<u>MARRIAGE AND DIVORCE--INDIANA</u>
DIVORCE (Indiana CLE)
DIVORCE: COMMON & COMPLEX ISSUES (Indiana CLE)
DIVORCE TAXATION (Indiana CLE)
HANDLING YOUR OWN DIVORCE WITHOUT A LAWYER: A GUIDE TO SELF- REPRESENTATION IN INDIANA (Daniel)

<u>MARRIAGE AND DIVORCE--IOWA</u>
IOWA MATRIMONIAL LAW (Butterworth-St. Paul)

<u>MARRIAGE AND DIVORCE--KENTUCKY</u>
KENTUCKY DIVORCE (Lawyers Coop.)

<u>MARRIAGE AND DIVORCE--LOUISIANA</u>
LOUISIANA DIVORCE (Lawyers Coop.)

<u>MARRIAGE AND DIVORCE--MAINE</u>
ECONOMIC ISSUES IN DIVORCE (Maine Bar)
MAINE FAMILY LAW: DIVORCE, SEPARATION AND ANNULMENT (Butterworth-NH)
TRENDS IN DIVORCE STATEGY (Maine Bar)

<u>MARRIAGE AND DIVORCE--MARYLAND</u>
DIVORCE ORGANIZATION SYSTEM: A SYSTEM FOR MANAGING A DIVORCE PRACTICE IN MARYLAND 2ND ED. (MICPEL)
MARYLAND DIVORCE AND SEPARATION LAW (MICPEL)

<u>MARRIAGE AND DIVORCE--MICHIGAN</u>
MICHIGAN FAMILY LAW (ICLE - Michigan)

<u>MARRIAGE AND DIVORCE--MINNESOTA</u>
ASSET VALUATION IN DIVORCE (MILE)
EFFICIENT MARITAL DISSOLUTION (Minn. CLE)
MINNESOTA DISSOLUTION OF MARRIAGE (Lawyers Coop.)
SPOUSAL MAINTENANCE (MILE)

<u>MARRIAGE AND DIVORCE--NEW HAMPSHIRE</u>
ABC'S OF PRO BONO DIVORCE (NH Bar)
COMPLEXITIES OF DIVORCE PRACTICE IN THE 1990's (NH Bar)

<u>MARRIAGE AND DIVORCE--NEW JERSEY</u>
FORMS FOR NEW JERSEY DIVORCE PRACTICE (New Jersey ICLE)

<u>MARRIAGE AND DIVORCE--NEW YORK</u>
MATRIMONIAL CASELAW, NEW YORK EDITION (Matrimonial CaseLaw)
NEW YORK CIVIL PRACTICE - MATRIMONIAL ACTIONS (vols. 11, 11A, 11B & 11C) (Bender)
NEW YORK MATRIMONIAL CASE CITATOR (Nat. Atty.)
NEW YORK MATRIMONIAL LAW AND PRACTICE (Lawyers Coop.)
NEW YORK MATRIMONIAL PRACTICE (Lawyers Coop.)
NEW YORK UNCONTESTED DIVORCES AND ANNULMENTS (Gould)

MARRIAGE AND DIVORCE--PENNSYLVANIA
PENNSYLVANIA DIVORCE CODE (Bisel)
PENNSYLVANIA MATRIMONIAL PRACTICE (Lawyers Coop.)

MARRIAGE AND DIVORCE--TAXATION
DIVORCE TAXATION (WG&L)

MARRIAGE AND DIVORCE--TEXAS
FAMILY LAW: TEXAS PRACTICE AND PROCEDURE (Bender)

MARRIAGE AND DIVORCE--WASHINGTON
WASHINGTON COMMUNITY PROPERTY DESKBOOK (Wash. Bar)

MARRIAGE AND DIVORCE--WISCONSIN
MARITAL PROPERTY LAW IN WISCONSIN 2nd ed. (State Bar of Wisc.)
SYSTEM BOOK FOR FAMILY LAW (State Bar of Wisc.)

MECHANICS' LIENS
see also Foreclosures

MECHANICS AND CONSTRUCTION LIENS IN ALASKA, OREGON AND WASHINGTON (Butterworth-St. Paul)
WEST COAST CONSTRUCTION LIENS & CLAIMS MANUAL (Book Pub.)

MECHANICS' LIENS--CALIFORNIA
CALIFORNIA MECHANICS' LIEN LAW AND CONSTRUCTION INDUSTRY PRACTICE (Parker)

MECHANICS' LIENS--COLORADO
LIENS AND CLAIMS -- COLORADO (CLE - Colorado)

MECHANICS' LIENS--FLORIDA
FLORIDA MECHANICS' LIEN MANUAL (Butterworth-Fla.)
ILLINOIS MECHANICS' LIENS PRACTICE (Illinois ICLE)

MECHANICS' LIENS--INDIANA
MECHANICS LIENS (Indiana CLE)

MECHANICS' LIENS--MARYLAND
MECHANICS' LIENS AND MARYLAND'S TRUST FUND LAW (MICPEL)

MECHANICS' LIENS--MINNESOTA
MINNESOTA MECHANIC'S LIENS (Minn. CLE)
MINNESOTA MECHANICS' LIENS PRACTICE MANUAL (Butterworth-St. Paul)

MECHANICS' LIENS--OKLAHOMA
OKLAHOMA LIEN LAWS (Butterworth-Texas)

MECHANICS' LIENS--PENNSYLVANIA
PENNSYLVANIA MECHANICS' LIENS (Butterworth-NH)

MECHANICS' LIENS--TEXAS
THE COMPLETE GUIDE TO MECHANIC'S AND MATERIALMAN'S LIEN LAWS OF TEXAS, 3RD ED. (Butterworth-Texas)

MECHANICS' LIENS--VIRGINIA
ENFORCEMENT OF LIENS AND JUDGMENTS (Jt. Comm. Va.)

MEDIA LAW
MEDIA LAW REPORTER (BNA)

MEDICAL JURISPRUDENCE
see also Health care; Hospitals

ABDOMINAL INJURIES (Courtroom Medicine Series vol. 10 & 10A) (Bender)
ATTORNEY'S MEDICAL REFFERENCE (Parker)
ATTORNEY'S TEXTBOOK OF MEDICINE, 3RD ED. (Bender)
CANCER (Courtroom Medicine Series vol. 13) (Bender)

CHEST, HEART & LUNGS (Courtroom Medicine Series vol. 11) (Bender)
CROSS-EXAMINATION OF MEDICAL EXPERTS (Bender)
DEATH (Courtroom Medicine Series vols. 3, 3A & 3B) (Bender)
DIRECTOR OF NURSING MANUAL: FEDERAL REGULATIONS AND GUIDELINES (National Health)
THE EYE (Courtroom Medicine Series, vol. 14) (Bender)
HEAD AND BRAIN (Courtroom Medicine Series vol. 8, 8A & 8B) (Bender)
HIP AND THIGH (Courtroom Medicine Series, vols. 7 & 7A) (Bender)
THE KNEE AND RELATED STRUCTURES (Courtroom Medicine Series, vols. 9 & 9A) (Bender)
LANE MEDICAL LITIGATION GUIDE (Clark Boardman Callaghan)
LAWYER'S GUIDE TO MEDICAL PROOF (Bender)
THE LOW BACK (Courtroom Medicine Series, vols. 1, 1A, 1B) (Bender)
MEDICAL EVIDENCE (Illinois ICLE)
THE NECK (Courtroom Medicine Series, vols. 2, 2A & 2B) (Bender)
PAIN AND SUFFERING (Courtroom Medicine Series, vols. 4, 4A & 4B) (Bender)
PATIENT CARE DECISION-MAKING (Clark Boardman Callaghan)
PROVING MEDICAL DIAGNOSIS AND PROGNOSIS (Bender)
PSYCHIC INJURIES (Courtroom Medicine Series, Vol. 12) (Bender)
THE SHOULDER AND ELBOW (Courtroom Medicine Series, Vols. 5 & 5A) (Bender)
THE SKIN (Courtroom Medicine Series, Vols. 6, 6A & 6B) (Bender)

MEDICAL MALPRACTICE
see Malpractice

MEDICAL PERSONNEL
LEGAL GUIDE FOR PHYSICIANS (Bender)
PHYSICIAN LABORATORY REGULATIONS MANUAL (Thompson)

MEDICAL PERSONNEL--ARIZONA
THE ARIZONA LAW OF MEDICAL MALPRACTICE (Medilex)

MEDICAL PERSONNEL--MARYLAND
NURSING HOME NEGLIGENCE (MICPEL)

MEDICARE
see Insurance, Health

MEDICINE
ATTORNEYS' TEXTBOOK OF MEDICINE: MANUAL OF TRAUMATIC INJURIES (Bender)
BIOLAW (UPA)
MEDICAL TESTING: THE COMPLETE RESOURCE GUIDE TO GOOD LABORATORY PRACTICE AND HCFA COMPLIANCE (BNA)
PARALEGAL MEDICAL RECORDS REVIEW (James)

MEDICINE--DICTIONARIES
ATTORNEY'S DICTIONARY OF MEDICINE, 16TH ED. (Bender)

MENTAL HEALTH--MINNESOTA
CIVIL COMMITMENT IN MINNESOTA, 2nd Ed. (Butterworth-St. Paul)

MERGERS
see Consolidation and merger of corporations

MICROFILM
LEGALITY OF MICROFILM (Cohasset)

MILITARY
FEDERAL ORGANIZATION SERVICE MILITARY (Carroll)
MILITARY DISCHARGE UPGRADING AND INTRODUCTION TO VETERANS ADMINISTRATION LAW (Natl. Veterans)
MILITARY LAW REPORTER (PLEI)

MINES AND MINING
see also Oil and gas

THE AMERICAN LAW OF MINING (Bender)

BASIC COAL, OIL & GAS LAW (EMLF)
COAL LAW AND REGULATION (Bender)
GOLD MINE FINANCING (Rocky Mt.)
GOWER FEDERAL SERVICE - MINING (Rocky Mt.)
GOWER FEDERAL SERVICE - ROYALTY VALUATION AND MANAGEMENT (Rocky Mt.)
LABOR LAW AND THE NATIONAL WAGE AGREEMENT; MINERS' RIGHTS & MSHA DISCRIMINATION LAW (EMLF)
MINERAL DEVELOPMENT ON INDIAN LANDS (Rocky Mt.)
MINERAL FINANCING (Rocky Mt.)
MINING AGREEMENTS (Rocky Mt.)
MINING AGREEMENTS II (Rocky Mt.)
MINING AGREEMENTS III (Rocky Mt.)
RIGHTS AND REMEDIES OF CONFLICTING MINERAL AND PROPERTY OWNERS (EMLF)
SURFACE MINING (EMLF)

<u>MINES AND MINING--ILLINOIS</u>
MINERAL LAW (Illinois ICLE)

<u>MINES AND MINING--KENTUCKY</u>
KENTUCKY MINERAL LAW (Banks)

<u>MINES AND MINING--LATIN AMERICA</u>
MINING AND PETROLEUM LEGISLATION OF LATIN AMERICA & THE CARIBBEAN (Oceana)

<u>MINES AND MINING--NORTH DAKOTA</u>
MINERAL TITLE STANDARDS (State Bar of N. Dak.)

<u>MONEY</u>
see also Banks and banking; Interest and usury

<u>MORTGAGES</u>
see also Foreclosures; Financing

THE COMMUNITY REINVESTMENT ACT MANUAL: POLICIES AND COMPLIANCE (Prentice Hall Law & Business)
HOME MORTGAGE DISCLOSURE ACT: A PRACTICAL APPROACH TO MANAGING COMPLIANCE (Probus)
MORTGAGE AND REAL ESTATE INVESTMENT GUIDE (Mortgage)
MULTI-FAMILY GUIDE (FNMA)
NEGOTIATING AND DRAFTING MORTGAGE DOCUMENTS: AN ADVANCED WORKSHOP FOR THE EXPERIENCED LAWYER, BANKER AND MORTGAGE LENDER (Penn. Bar)
REGULATORY COMPLIANCE MANUAL (MBAA)
SECONDARY MORTGAGE MARKET GUIDE (Bender)
SELLERS' & SERVICERS' GUIDE (Freddie Mac)
SELLING GUIDE (FNMA)
SERVICING GUIDE (FNMA)

<u>MORTGAGES--COLORADO--FORMS</u>
COLORADO REAL ESTATE FORMS - PRACTICE (Aspen)

<u>MORTGAGES--FORMS</u>
MODERN CONSTRUCTION AND DEVELOPMENT FORMS (Modern Real Estate & Mortgage Forms series) (WG&L)
MODERN REAL ESTATE AND MORTGAGE FORMS SERIES: VOL. 1 - BASIC FORMS AND AGREEMENTS, 3rd ed. (WG&L)
MODERN REAL ESTATE AND MORTGAGE FORMS SERIES: VOL. 2 - CHECKLISTS (WG&L)

<u>MORTGAGES--GEORGIA-FORMS</u>
GEORGIA REAL ESTATE FORMS-PRACTICE (Aspen)

<u>MORTGAGES--ILLINOIS-FORMS</u>
ILLINOIS REAL ESTATE FORMS--PRACTICE (Aspen)

<u>MORTGAGES--MICHIGAN-FORMS</u>
MICHIGAN REAL ESTATE FORMS--PRACTICE (Aspen)

MORTGAGES--MISSOURI-FORMS
MISSOURI REAL ESTATE FORMS - PRACTICE (Aspen)

MORTGAGES--NEW JERSEY-FORMS
NEW JERSEY REAL ESTATE FORMS - PRACTICE (Aspen)

MORTGAGES--NEW YORK
BERGMAN ON NEW YORK MORTGAGE FORECLOSURES (Bender)
MORTGAGES AND MORTGAGE FORECLOSURE IN NEW YORK (Lawyers Coop.)

MOTOR VEHICLES
see Vehicles

MULTINATIONAL CORPORATIONS
see Corporations, international

MUNICIPAL BONDS
see also Securities

A GUIDE TO MUNICIPAL OFFICIAL STATEMENTS (Prentice Hall Law & Business)
MUNICIPAL SECURITIES RULEMAKING BOARD MANUAL (CCH)

MUNICIPAL GOVERNMENT--ILLINOIS
ILLINOIS MUNICIPAL LAW (Illinois ICLE)

MUNICIPAL GOVERNMENT--INDIANA
MUNICIPAL LAW VIII (Indiana CLE)

MUNICIPAL GOVERNMENT--NEW HAMPSHIRE
NEW HAMPSHIRE MUNICIPAL PRACTICE SERIES: MUNICIPAL FINANCE & TAXATION (Butterworth-NH)
NEW HAMPSHIRE MUNICIPAL PRACTICE SERIES: PUBLIC HEALTH, SAFETY & HIGHWAYS (Butterworth-NH)

MUNICIPAL GOVERNMENT--OHIO
GOTHERMAN & BABBIT, OHIO MUNICIPAL LAW (Banks)

MUTUAL FUNDS
see Securities

NARCOTICS
DEFENSE OF NARCOTICS CASES (Bender)

NATURAL RESOURCES
see also Environmental law; Mines and mining; Oil and gas

BASIC TAXATION OF NATURAL RESOURCES (EMLF)
GROUND WATER CONTAMINATION (Rocky Mt.)
LAW OF WATER RIGHTS AND RESOURCES (Clark Boardman Callaghan)
NATURAL RESOURCES AND ENVIRONMENTAL LITIGATION (Rocky Mt.)
PUBLIC NATURAL RESOURCES LAW (Clark Boardman Callaghan)
WESTERN WATER LAW (Francis Marion)

NATURAL RESOURCES--INTERNATIONAL
INTERNATIONAL RESOURCES LAW: A BLUEPRINT FOR MINERAL DEVELOPMENT (Rocky Mt.)

NATURAL RESOURCES--TAXATION
INCOME TAXATION OF NATURAL RESOURCES (RIA)

NATURAL RESOURCES--TEXAS
TEXAS WATER COMMISSION/TEXAS WATER DEVELOPMENT BOARD RULES (RPC)

NATURALIZATION
see Immigration law

NEGLIGENCE
see also Accidents; Automobile accidents; Damages; Products liability; Torts

FRAUD, WINDOW DRESSING, AND NEGLIGENCE IN FINANCIAL STATEMENTS (Shepard's)

NEGLIGENCE--CALIFORNIA
CALIFORNIA UNINSURED MOTORIST LAW (Parker)

NEGLIGENCE--FLORIDA
FLORIDA NEGLIGENCE LAW MANUAL (Butterworth-Fla.)

NEGLIGENCE--MARYLAND
NURSING HOME NEGLIGENCE (MICPEL)

NEGLIGENCE--NEW JERSEY
PROFESSIONAL NEGLIGENCE: LAW OF MALPRACTICE IN NEW JERSEY (New Jersey ICLE)

NEGLIGENCE--NEW YORK
NEW YORK PRACTICE GUIDE: NEGLIGENCE (Bender)
WARREN'S NEGLIGENCE IN NEW YORK COURTS (Bender)

NEGLIGENCE, COMPARATIVE
COMPARATIVE NEGLIGENCE (Bender)
COMPARATIVE NEGLIGENCE MANUAL (Clark Boardman Callaghan)

NEGLIGENCE, COMPARATIVE--MISSOURI
MISSOURI COMPARATIVE FAULT (UMKC/CLE)

NEGOTIABLE INSTRUMENTS
see also Commercial law

COMMERCIAL PAPER UNDER THE UNIFORM COMMERCIAL CODE (Bender Uniform Commercial Code Service, vol. 2 series) (Bender)

NONPROFIT ASSOCIATIONS
COMPLETE NON-PROFIT CORPORATION HANDBOOK (Enterprise)
GUIDE TO FEDERAL FUNDING FOR GOVERNMENTS AND NON-PROFITS (GIS)
THE LAW OF ASSOCIATIONS (Bender)
NONPROFIT ENTERPRISES: LAW AND TAXATION (Clark Boardman Callaghan)
PLANNING TAX-EXEMPT ORGANIZATIONS (Shepard's)
TAX-EXEMPT ORGANIZATIONS (RIA)

NONPROFIT ASSOCIATIONS--HAWAII
IT'S THE LAW: WHAT NONPROFITS NEED TO KNOW (HICLE)

NONPROFIT ASSOCIATIONS--ILLINOIS
NOT-FOR-PROFIT CORPORATIONS (Illinois ICLE)

NONPROFIT ASSOCIATIONS--INDIANA
NONPROFIT CORPORATIONS (Indiana CLE)

NONPROFIT ASSOCIATIONS--MINNESOTA
REPRESENTING NONPROFIT ORGANIZATIONS (MILE)

NONPROFIT ASSOCIATIONS--WASHINGTON
NONPROFIT AND TAX-EXEMPT ORGANIZATIONS (Wash. Bar)

NONPROFIT ASSOCIATIONS--WISCONSIN
A GUIDE FOR WISCONSIN NONPROFIT ORGANIZATIONS (State Bar of Wisc.)

NOTARIES
NOTARY HOME STUDY COURSE (Nat. Notary)

NUCLEAR ENERGY
RULES AND REGULATIONS: TITLE 10, CHAPTER 1, CODE OF FEDERAL REGULATIONS (USGPO)

NURSING
see Health care

OCCUPATIONAL SAFETY
EMPLOYMENT SAFETY AND HEALTH GUIDE (CCH)
GENERAL INDUSTRY STANDARDS AND INTERPRETATIONS (USGPO)
HANDLING OCCUPATIONAL DISEASE CASES (Clark Boardman Callaghan)
HOW TO AVOID OSHA (Gulf)
HUMAN RESOURCES MANAGEMENT -- OSHA COMPLIANCE (CCH)
JOB SAFETY AND HEALTH (BNA)
OCCUPATIONAL SAFETY AND HEALTH ACT (Bender)
OCCUPATIONAL SAFETY & HEALTH REPORTER (BNA)
OSHA COMPLIANCE ENCYCLOPEDIA (BLR)
OSHA 1910 GUIDE (Keller)
OSHA REFERENCE MANUAL (Merritt)
A PRACTICAL GUIDE TO THE OCCUPATIONAL SAFETY & HEALTH ACT (Law Journal)
REGULATORY COMPLIANCE MANUAL (American Dental)

OCCUPATIONAL SAFETY--CALIFORNIA
CAL-OSHA REPORTER (Sten-O-Press)

OCCUPATIONAL SAFETY--CANADA
CANADIAN EMPLOYMENT SAFETY AND HEALTH GUIDE (CCH)

OCCUPATIONAL SAFETY--MARYLAND
OSHA/MOSH 1991 (MICPEL)

OFFICERS AND DIRECTORS
see Corporation law

OIL AND GAS
ACQUISITIONS AND DISPOSITIONS OF OIL AND GAS PROPERTIES (EMLF)
BANKRUPTCY & WORKOUTS IN THE TROUBLED OIL & GAS INDUSTRY (EMLF)
BASIC COAL, OIL & GAS LAW (EMLF)
FEDERAL ONSHORE OIL AND GAS POOLING AND UNITIZATION II (Rocky Mt.)
GAS TRANSPORTATION MARKETING SERVICE (Thompson)
LANDMAN'S PRACTICUM (EMLF)
THE LAW OF POOLING AND UNITIZATION - VOLUNTARY, COMPULSORY (Bender)
MINERAL TITLE EXAMINATION II (Rocky Mt.)
NATURAL GAS CONTRACTS (Thompson)
NATURAL GAS HANDBOOK (Thompson)
NATURAL GAS MARKETING AND TRANSPORTATION (Rocky Mt.)
NATURAL GAS MARKETING II (Rocky Mt.)
NATURAL GAS POLICY ACT INFORMATION SERVICE (Thompson)
NATURAL GAS TRANSPORTATION INFORMATION SERVICE (Thompson)
OIL AND GAS AGREEMENTS (Rocky Mt.)
OIL AND GAS CONSERVATION LAW AND PRACTICE (Rocky Mt.)
THE OIL AND GAS JOINT OPERATING AGREEMENT (Rocky Mt.)
OIL AND GAS LAW (Bender)
OIL AND GAS LAW: ABRIDGED EDITION (Bender)
OIL AND GAS LAW: THE NORTH SEA EXPLOITATION (Oceana)
OIL AND GAS OPERATIONS IN FEDERAL AND COASTAL WATERS (Rocky Mt.)
OIL AND GAS REPORTER (Bender)
REGULATION OF THE GAS INDUSTRY (Bender)
ROYALTY VALUATION AND MANAGEMENT (Rocky Mt.)
SPECIAL INSTITUTE INDEX, 1970-1990 (Rocky Mt.)
UNDERGROUND STORAGE TANK GUIDE (Thompson)

OIL AND GAS--KANSAS
KANSAS OIL & GAS HANDBOOK, VOL. I (Kansas Bar)
KANSAS OIL AND GAS HANDBOOK VOL. II (Kansas Bar)

OIL AND GAS--LATIN AMERICA
MINING AND PETROLEUM LEGISLATION OF LATIN AMERICA & THE CARIBBEAN (Oceana)

OIL AND GAS--LOUISIANA
LOUISIANA OIL AND GAS LAW (Butterworth-Texas)
RULES AND REGULATIONS OF THE LOUISIANA OIL CONSERVATION COMMISSION (Byram)

OIL AND GAS--NEW JERSEY
UNDERGROUND STORAGE TANK LAW (New Jersey ICLE)

OIL AND GAS--NEW MEXICO
RULES AND REGULATIONS OF THE NEW MEXICO OIL CONSERVATION DIVISION (Byram)

OIL AND GAS--STATES
SUMMARY OF STATE STATUTES AND REGULATIONS FOR OIL AND GAS PRODUCTION (IOCC)

OIL AND GAS--TAXATION
FEDERAL TAXATION OF OIL AND GAS TRANSACTIONS (Bender)
TAXATION OF MINING OPERATIONS (Bender)

OIL AND GAS--TEXAS
TEXAS LAW OF OIL AND GAS (Butterworth-Texas)

OIL AND GAS LEASES
GOWER FEDERAL SERVICE - OIL AND GAS (Rocky Mt.)
GOWER FEDERAL SERVICE - OUTER CONTINENTAL SHELF LANDS (Rocky Mt.)
GOWER FEDERAL SERVICE - ROYALTY VALUATION AND MANAGEMENT (Rocky Mt.)
LAW OF FEDERAL OIL AND GAS LEASES (Bender)
THE LAW OF OIL AND GAS LEASES, 2ND ED. (Bender)

PARTNERSHIP
see also Limited partnership

BROMBERG AND RIBSTEIN ON PARTNERSHIP (Little, Brown)
BUSINESS ORGANIZATIONS WITH TAX PLANNING (Bender)
ESTABLISHING A U.S. JOINT VENTURE WITH A FOREIGN PARTNER (Bender)
PARTNERSHIP & S CORPORATION COORDINATOR (RIA)
SECURITIES AND PARTNERSHIP LAW FOR MLPs AND OTHER INVESTMENT LIMITED PARTNERSHIPS (Securities Law Series, Vol. 14) (Clark Boardman Callaghan)

PARTNERSHIP--ILLINOIS
PARTNERSHIP PRACTICE (Illinois ICLE)

PARTNERSHIP--MISSOURI
MISSOURI CORPORATE AND PARTNERSHIP FORMS HANDBOOK (UMKC/CLE)

PARTNERSHIP--TAXATION
FEDERAL TAXATION OF PARTNERSHIPS AND PARTNERS (WG&L)
FEDERAL TAXATION OF PARTNERSHIPS AND PARTNERS: STRUCTURING AND DRAFTING AGREEMENTS (WG&L)
HOW TO SAVE TIME AND TAXES PREPARING THE FEDERAL PARTNERSHIP RETURN (Bender)
PARTNERSHIP TAX PRACTICE MANUAL (Panel)
PARTNERSHIP TAX REPORTER (CCH)
PARTNERSHIP TAXATION, 4th ed. (Shepard's)
PPC TAX PLANNING GUIDE - PARTNERSHIPS (Practitioners Publishing)
STATE TAX FORMS: PARTNERSHIP & FIDUCIARY (Tax Form)
TAX PLANNING FOR PARTNERSHIPS (Bender)
TAXATION OF PARTNERSHIPS (Clark Boardman Callaghan)

PARTNERSHIP--WASHINGTON
PARTNERSHIP TAXATION (Wash. Bar)
WASHINGTON PARTNERSHIP LAW AND PRACTICE HANDBOOK (Wash. Bar)

PATENT LICENSES
THE LAW OF MERCHANDISING AND CHARACTER LICENSING (Clark Boardman Callaghan)
PATENT LICENSING TRANSACTIONS (Patent Law and Practice Series, vols. 1 & 1A & Business Organizations, vols. 14 & 14A) (Bender)

PATENT PRACTICE
CURRENT PATENT INTERFERENCE PRACTICE (Prentice Hall Law & Business)
MANUAL OF PATENT EXAMINING PROCEDURE (USGPO)
PATENT OFFICE RULES AND PRACTICE (Bender)

PATENT SUITS
ATTORNEY'S DICTIONARY OF PATENT CLAIMS (Bender)
PATENT LITIGATION: PROCEDURE AND TACTICS (Patent Law and Practice Series, vol. 3) (Bender)

PATENTS
see also Intellectual property; Trademarks

BIOTECHNOLOGY AND THE LAW (Clark Boardman Callaghan)
BNA'S PATENT, TRADEMARK & COPYRIGHT JOURNAL (BNA)
COURT OF APPEALS FOR THE FEDERAL CIRCUIT: REVIEW OF PATENT AND TRADEMARK CASES (Bender)
DIGEST OF INTELLECTUAL PROPERTY LAWS OF THE WORLD (Oceana)
FEDERAL CIRCUIT PATENT CASE DIGESTS (Clark Boardman Callaghan)
MANUAL OF CLASSIFICATION (USGPO)
PATENT AND TRADEMARK STATUTES (Rules)
PATENT COOPERATION TREATY AND REGULATIONS (Rules)
PATENT LAW FUNDAMENTALS (Clark Boardman Callaghan)
PATENT LAW PERSPECTIVES (Bender)
PATENT, TRADEMARK, AND COPYRIGHT REGULATIONS (BNA Books)
PATENTS (Bender)
RULES OF PRACTICE IN PATENT AND TRADEMARK CASES (Rules)

PATENTS--EUROPE
EUROPEAN PATENTS HANDBOOK, 2nd ed. (Bender & Oyez)

PATENTS--FOREIGN
INTERNATIONAL PATENT LITIGATION: A COUNTRY-BY-COUNTRY ANALYSIS (BNA Books)
PATENTS THROUGHOUT THE WORLD (Clark Boardman Callaghan)
WORLD PATENT LAW: PATENT STATUTES, REGULATIONS AND TREATIES (Patent Law and Practice Series, vols. 2B - 2L) (Bender)
WORLD PATENT LAW AND PRACTICE (Patent Law and Practice Series, vols. 2, 2A & 2A pt. 2) (Bender)

PATENTS--FORMS
PATENT LAW PRACTICE FORMS (Clark Boardman Callaghan)

PATENTS--INDIANA
PATENT AND TRADE SECRETS (Indiana CLE)

PATENTS--MARYLAND
PATENT LAW (MICPEL)

PATERNITY
see Domestic relations

PAYROLL
PAYROLL ADMINISTRATION GUIDE (BNA)
PAYROLL GUIDE (WG&L)
PAYROLL MANAGEMENT GUIDE (CCH)
PAYROLL PRACTITIONER'S COMPLIANCE HANDBOOK: YEAR-END AND QUARTERLY REPORTING (WG&L)
PRINCIPLES OF PAYROLL ADMINISTRATION: THE COMPLETE LEARNING AND REFERENCE GUIDE (WG&L)
SUCCESSFUL PAYROLL MANAGEMENT (WG&L)

PENSION PLANS
see also Employee benefits; Profit sharing

ADVISING CLIENTS ABOUT RETIREMENT PLANS (Minn. CLE)
ATTORNEY'S GUIDE TO PENSION AND PROFIT-SHARING PLANS (Calif. CEB)
BENEFITS AND RETIREMENT PLAN GUIDE (WG&L)

BENEFITS COORDINATOR (WG&L)
BNA PENSION REPORTER (BNA)
COMPLIANCE GUIDE FOR PLAN ADMINISTRATORS (CCH)
ERISA CITATOR (WSB)
ERISA CLAIMS AND LITIGATION (Minn. CLE)
ERISA PRACTICE AND PROCEDURE (Shepard's)
ERISA QUALIFIED PLAN GUIDE (PPD)
ERISA UPDATE (WSB)
ESOP FORMS MANUAL (Corbel)
THE 401(K) HANDBOOK (Thompson)
FUNDAMENTALS OF QUALIFIED PENSION AND PROFIT SHARING PLANS OUTLINE (PPD)
GUIDE TO ASSIGNING AND LOANING BENEFIT PLAN MONEY (Thompson)
GUIDE TO PENSION AND PROFIT SHARING PLANS: TAXATION, SELECTION AND DESIGN (Shepard's)
INDIVIDUAL RETIREMENT PLANS GUIDE - IRA, SEP, KEOGH (CCH)
IRA COMPLIANCE MANUAL (RIA)
IRAs, SEPs AND SELF-EMPLOYED PLANS COMPLIANCE GUIDE (Bender)
PENSION AND PROFIT SHARING, 2nd ed. (RIA)
PENSION AND PROFIT SHARING GUIDE (RIA)
PENSION & PROFIT SHARING PLANS (Bender)
PENSION & PROFIT SHARING PLANS (Bus. Orgs. Vols. 19A-E) (Bender)
PENSION & PROFIT SHARING PLANS: FORMS & PRACTICE (Bender)
PENSION ADMINISTRATOR'S FORMS AND CHECKLISTS (WG&L)
PENSION COORDINATOR (RIA)
PENSION PLAN FORMS MANUAL (Corbel)
PENSION PLAN GUIDE (CCH)
PENSIONS AND DEFERRED COMPENSATION (CCH)
PPD MASTER PLAN DOCUMENTATION SYSTEM (PPD)
PPD PRACTITIONER REGIONAL PROTOTYPE DOCUMENTATION SYSTEM (PPD)
RETIREMENT AND BENEFIT PLANNING: STRATEGY AND DESIGN FOR BUSINESSES AND TAX-EXEMPT ORGANIZATIONS (Butterworth-NH)
SPENCER'S RETIREMENT PLAN SERVICE (Spencer)
TAX MANAGEMENT - COMPENSATION PLANNING (BNA)
TAX SERVICE FOR EMPLOYEE RETIREMENT PLANS (Stephens)

<u>PENSION PLANS--CANADA</u>
CANADIAN EMPLOYMENT BENEFITS AND PENSION GUIDE (CCH)

<u>PENSION PLANS--MINNESOTA</u>
PENSION AND WELFARE BENEFITS (MILE)
PLANNING RETIREMENT BENEFITS (MILE)

<u>PERFORMING ARTS</u>
PERFORMING ARTS MANAGEMENT AND THE LAW (Law-Arts)

<u>PERSONAL INJURIES</u>
see also Accidents; Damages; Workmen's compensation

ABDOMINAL INJURIES (Courtroom Medicine Series vol. 10 & 10A) (Bender)
ATTORNEYS' TEXTBOOK OF MEDICINE: MANUAL OF TRAUMATIC INJURIES (Bender)
BETTER, EARLIER SETTLEMENTS THROUGH ECONOMIC LEVERAGE (Jury Verdict Research, Inc.)
CANCER (Courtroom Medicine Series vol. 13) (Bender)
CASE EVALUATOR'S MANUAL (Jury Verdict)
CHEST, HEART & LUNGS (Courtroom Medicine Series vol. 11) (Bender)
DEATH (Courtroom Medicine Series vols. 3, 3A & 3B) (Bender)
ENGINEERING FOR THE PERSONAL INJURY ATTORNEY: THEORY, EXPERTS, EVIDENCE (Bender)
ESTIMATING AND PROVING PERSONAL INJURY DAMAGES (James)
THE EYE (Courtroom Medicine Series, vol. 14) (Bender)
HANDLING MOTOR VEHICLE ACCIDENT CASES: FORMS (Clark Boardman Callaghan)
HEAD AND BRAIN (Courtroom Medicine Series vol. 8, 8A & 8B) (Bender)
HIP AND THIGH (Courtroom Medicine Series, vols. 7 & 7A) (Bender)
INNOVATIONS IN HEAD INJURY REHABILITATION (Bender)
THE KNEE AND RELATED STRUCTURES (Courtroom Medicine Series, vols. 9 & 9A) (Bender)
LITIGATING HEAD TRAUMA CASES (Wiley Law)

LITIGATING NECK AND BACK INJURIES (James)
THE LOW BACK (Courtroom Medicine Series, vols. 1, 1A, 1B) (Bender)
MAXIMIZING DAMAGES IN SMALL PERSONAL INJURY CASES (James)
MODEL INTERROGATORIES: PERSONAL INJURY (James)
NATIONAL VERDICT SURVEY (Jury Verdict)
THE NECK (Courtroom Medicine Series, vols. 2, 2A & 2B) (Bender)
PAIN AND SUFFERING (Courtroom Medicine Series, vols. 4, 4A & 4B) (Bender)
PERSONAL INJURY: DISCOVERY & TRIAL (James)
PERSONAL INJURY - ACTIONS, DEFENSES, DAMAGES (Bender)
PERSONAL INJURY DEFENSE TECHNIQUES (Bender)
PERSONAL INJURY HANDBOOK (James)
PERSONAL INJURY VALUATION HANDBOOKS (Jury Verdict)
PSYCHIC INJURIES (Courtroom Medicine Series, Vol. 12) (Bender)
REGIONAL VERDICT SURVEY (Jury Verdict)
SCIENTIFIC AUTOMOBILE ACCIDENT RECONSTRUCTION (Bender)
THE SHOULDER AND ELBOW (Courtroom Medicine Series, Vols. 5 & 5A) (Bender)
THE SKIN (Courtroom Medicine Series, Vols. 6, 6A & 6B) (Bender)
SLIP AND FALL PRACTICE (James)
STRUCTURED SETTLEMENTS: DESIGN AND EVALUATION (Francis Marion)
TRIAL OF ACCIDENT CASES (Bender)

PERSONAL INJURIES--CALIFORNIA
CALIFORNIA PERSONAL INJURY FORMS (Lawyers Coop.)
CALIFORNIA PRACTICE GUIDE - PERSONAL INJURY (Rutter)

PERSONAL INJURIES--FLORIDA
FLORIDA PRACTICE GUIDE: PERSONAL INJURY (Lawyers Coop.)

PERSONAL INJURIES--FORMS
PERSONAL INJURY FORMS: DISCOVERY & SETTLEMENT (James)

PERSONAL INJURIES--ILLINOIS
ILLINOIS PRACTICE GUIDE - PERSONAL INJURY (Lawyers Coop.)
ILLINOIS STRUCTURAL WORK ACT PRACTICE (Illinois ICLE)

PERSONAL INJURIES--IOWA
IOWA LEGAL FORMS -- PERSONAL INJURY (Butterworth-St. Paul)

PERSONAL INJURIES--MINNESOTA
MINNESOTA LEGAL FORMS--PERSONAL INJURY (Butterworth-St. Paul)
NECK AND BACK INJURIES (MILE)
PERSONAL INJURY (MILE)
PERSONAL INJURY INSTITUTE: 7TH ANNUAL (MILE)
PREMISES LIABILITY (MILE)
SOFT-TISSUE INJURY (MILE)

PERSONAL INJURIES--NEBRASKA
NEBRASKA LEGAL FORMS--PERSONAL INJURY (Butterworth-St. Paul)

PERSONAL INJURIES--NEW HAMPSHIRE
PERSONAL INJURY PRACTICE (NH Bar)

PERSONAL INJURIES--PENNSYLVANIA
TROUTMAN'S PENNSYLVANIA DAMAGES, PERSONAL INJURY VERDICTS (Bisel)

PERSONAL INJURIES--TEXAS
PREMISES LIABILITY (Knowles)
TEXAS PERSONAL INJURY FORMS (Butterworth-Texas)
TEXAS PERSONAL INJURY LAW (Butterworth-Texas)
TEXAS PRACTICE GUIDE - PERSONAL INJURY (Lawyers Coop.)

PERSONAL INJURIES--WASHINGTON
STRATEGIC FUNDAMENTALS OF PROSECUTING & DEFENDING THE PERSONAL INJURY CASE (Wash. Bar)

PERSONNEL
see Labor and labor relations

REPRESENTING THE CORPORATE CLIENT: DESIGNS FOR QUALITY (Prentice Hall Law & Business)
SOUTHEAST TRANSACTION GUIDE (Bender)
SPECIALIZATION HANDBOOK (ABA)
STATE SPECIALIZATION PLAN BOOK (ABA)

PRACTICE OF LAW--CALIFORNIA
CALIFORNIA ATTORNEY PRACTICE (Bender)
CALIFORNIA LEGAL FORMS - TRANSACTION GUIDE (Bender)
CALIFORNIA PARALEGAL'S GUIDE (Parker)

PRACTICE OF LAW--CONNECTICUT
HOW TO HAVE A MILLION DOLLAR PRACTICE (Conn. Bar)

PRACTICE OF LAW--DISTRICT OF COLUMBIA
THE DISTRICT OF COLUMBIA PRACTICE MANUAL (D.C. Bar)

PRACTICE OF LAW--EUROPE
CROSS BORDER PRACTICE COMPENDIUM (Kluwer)

PRACTICE OF LAW--FLORIDA
FLORIDA ATTORNEY'S/SECRETARY'S HANDBOOK (Mariposa)
FLORIDA KEYSTONE, LAWYER'S DESK LIBRARY OF PRACTICE (Bisel)
FLORIDA LAWYER'S GUIDE (Lawyers Coop.)

PRACTICE OF LAW--GEORGIA
GEORGIA ATTORNEY'S/SECRETARY'S HANDBOOK (Mariposa)

PRACTICE OF LAW--ILLINOIS
ILLINOIS ATTORNEY'S/SECRETARY'S HANDBOOK (Mariposa)
ILLINOIS LAWYER'S MANUAL, 3RD ED. (Lawyers Coop.)

PRACTICE OF LAW--INDIANA
INDIANA LAW UPDATE (Indiana CLE)

PRACTICE OF LAW--IOWA
IOWA ATTORNEY'S/SECRETARY'S HANDBOOK (Mariposa)

PRACTICE OF LAW--LOUISIANA
LOUISIANA ATTORNEY'S/SECRETARY'S HANDBOOK (Mariposa)

PRACTICE OF LAW--MAINE
LEGAL YEAR IN REVIEW (Maine Bar)

PRACTICE OF LAW--MARYLAND
PRACTICE MANUAL FOR THE MARYLAND LAWYER (MICPEL)

PRACTICE OF LAW--MICHIGAN
MICHIGAN BASIC PRACTICE HANDBOOK (ICLE - Michigan)
MICHIGAN LAWYER'S MANUAL (Lawyers Coop.)

PRACTICE OF LAW--MINNESOTA
MINNESOTA ATTORNEY'S/SECRETARY'S HANDBOOK (Mariposa)

PRACTICE OF LAW--MISSOURI
MISSOURI ATTORNEY'S/SECRETARY'S HANDBOOK (Mariposa)
MISSOURI LAWYER'S GUIDE (Lawyers Coop.)

PRACTICE OF LAW--NEW HAMPSHIRE
NEW HAMPSHIRE PRACTICE AND PROCEDURE HANDBOOK (NH Bar)

PRACTICE OF LAW--NEW JERSEY
NEW JERSEY LAW WITH FORMS (Bender)
NEW JERSEY TRANSACTION GUIDE (Bender)

<u>PRACTICE OF LAW--NEW YORK</u>
NEW YORK LAWYER'S DESKBOOK (NYSBA)
NEW YORK LAWYER'S FORMBOOK (NYSBA)

<u>PRACTICE OF LAW--OHIO</u>
OHIO ATTORNEY'S/SECRETARY'S HANDBOOK (Mariposa)

<u>PRACTICE OF LAW--OREGON</u>
THE OREGON STATE BAR DESK REFERENCE - A GUIDE TO THE REGULATORY PROGRAMS OF THE OREGON STATE BAR (Oregon Bar)

<u>PRACTICE OF LAW--PENNSYLVANIA</u>
PENNSYLVANIA ATTORNEY'S/SECRETARY'S HANDBOOK (Mariposa)
PENNSYLVANIA KEYSTONE (Bisel)
PENNSYLVANIA TRANSACTION GUIDE - LEGAL FORMS (Bender)

<u>PRACTICE OF LAW--TENNESSEE</u>
TENNESSEE LAW OFFICE DESK BOOK (Smith)

<u>PRACTICE OF LAW--TEXAS</u>
TEXAS ATTORNEY'S/SECRETARY'S HANDBOOK (Mariposa)
TEXAS TRANSACTION GUIDE - LEGAL FORMS (Bender)

<u>PRACTICE OF LAW--VIRGINIA</u>
THE VIRGINIA LAWYER: A BASIC PRACTICE HANDBOOK (Michie)

<u>PRACTICE OF LAW--WASHINGTON</u>
CLOSING OFFICER'S GUIDE (WASHINGTON) (Butterworth-St. Paul)

<u>PRACTICE OF LAW--WEST VIRGINIA</u>
WEST VIRGINIA PRACTICE HANDBOOK, 3rd ed. (Michie)

<u>PRACTICE OF LAW--WISCONSIN</u>
WISCONSIN ATTORNEY'S DESK REFERENCE (State Bar of Wisc.)
WISCONSIN ATTORNEY'S/SECRETARY'S HANDBOOK (Mariposa)

<u>PRE-TRIAL PROCEDURE</u>
BENDER'S FORMS OF DISCOVERY (Bender)
DEPOSITION - STRATEGY, LAW AND FORMS (Bender)
EXAMINATION BEFORE TRIAL AND OTHER DISCLOSURE DEVICES (Lawyers Coop.)
FEDERAL BAIL & DETENTION HANDBOOK (PLI)
INTERROGATORIES, DOCUMENTS AND ADMISSIONS (Butterworth-NH)
MANUAL FOR COMPLEX LITIGATION (Bender)
MANUAL FOR COMPLEX LITIGATION (Clark Boardman Callaghan)
OBJECTIONS TO INTERROGATORIES (James)
PREPARATION OF THE CASE (Art of Advocacy Series) (Bender)
PRETRIAL DISCOVERY: STRATEGY AND TACTICS (Clark Boardman Callaghan)
PRODUCTS LIABILITY LITIGATION: CASE EVALUATION (Clark Boardman Callaghan)
PRODUCTS LIABILITY LITIGATION: PRETRIAL PRACTICE (Clark Boardman Callaghan)

<u>PRE-TRIAL PROCEDURE--CALIFORNIA</u>
CALIFORNIA CIVIL PROCEDURE BEFORE TRIAL (Calif. CEB)
CALIFORNIA DEPOSITION AND DISCOVERY PRACTICE (Bender)
CALIFORNIA PRACTICE GUIDE - CIVIL PROCEDURE BEFORE TRIAL (Rutter)
CALIFORNIA PRACTICE GUIDE - FEDERAL CIVIL PROCEDURE BEFORE TRIAL (Rutter)
CALIFORNIA PRACTICE GUIDE - LANDLORD-TENANT (Rutter)

<u>PRE-TRIAL PROCEDURE--FLORIDA</u>
FLORIDA CRIMINAL DISCOVERY AND PRE-TRIAL MOTIONS MANUAL (Butterworth-Fla.)
FLORIDA PRETRIAL PRACTICE IN CRIMINAL CASES (Florida Bar)

<u>PRE-TRIAL PROCEDURE--IDAHO</u>
IDAHO PRE-TRIAL CIVIL PROCEDURE (Idaho Law)

<u>PRE-TRIAL PROCEDURE--MARYLAND</u>
PRE-TRIAL HANDBOOK (BASIC CIVIL TRIAL PRACTICE) (MICPEL)

PROBATE LAW AND PRACTICE--IOWA
IOWA LEGAL FORMS -- PROBATE (Butterworth-St. Paul)
IOWA PROBATE MANUAL (Iowa Bar)

PROBATE LAW AND PRACTICE--KENTUCKY
BALDWIN'S KENTUCKY PRACTICE (Banks)
KENTUCKY PROBATE (Lawyers Coop.)

PROBATE LAW AND PRACTICE--MAINE
MAINE PROBATE: HOW TO SURVIVE YOUR NEXT ESTATE (Maine Bar)
MAINE PROBATE MANUAL (Butterworth-NH)

PROBATE LAW AND PRACTICE--MAINE--FORMS
MAINE PROBATE FORMS, REV. ED. (Butterworth-NH)

PROBATE LAW AND PRACTICE--MASSACHUSETTS
MASSACHUSETTS PROBATE MANUAL (Mass. CLE)

PROBATE LAW AND PRACTICE--MICHIGAN
MICHIGAN PROBATE (Lawyers Coop.)
MICHIGAN PROBATE SOURCEBOOK (ICLE - Michigan)
PROBATE ADMINISTRATION IN MICHIGAN: A SYSTEMS APPROACH (ICLE - Michigan)

PROBATE LAW AND PRACTICE--MINNESOTA
FUNDAMENTALS OF PROBATE PRACTICE (Minn. CLE)
HANDLING CLAIMS IN PROBATE MATTERS (Minn. CLE)
INFORMAL PROBATE (Minn. CLE)
MINNESOTA LEGAL FORMS--PROBATE (Butterworth-St. Paul)
MINNESOTA PROBATE (Lawyers Coop.)
THE MINNESOTA PROBATE AND TRUST LAW DESKBOOK (Minn. CLE)
MINNESOTA PROBATE LAW DIGEST (Butterworth-St. Paul)
STEIN ON PROBATE (2d ed.) (Butterworth-St. Paul)

PROBATE LAW AND PRACTICE--MISSOURI
MISSOURI PROBATE SYSTEM (MoBar)

PROBATE LAW AND PRACTICE--MONTANA
MONTANA PROBATE PROCEDURE (State Bar of Mont.)

PROBATE LAW AND PRACTICE--NEBRASKA
NEBRASKA PROBATE SYSTEM IV (Nebraska CLE)

PROBATE LAW AND PRACTICE--NEW HAMPSHIRE
FUNDAMENTALS OF PROBATE ADMINISTRATION (NH Bar)

PROBATE LAW AND PRACTICE--NEW MEXICO
NEW MEXICO PROBATE MANUAL (Butterworth-Texas)

PROBATE LAW AND PRACTICE--NEW YORK
NEW YORK PRACTICE GUIDE: PROBATE AND ESTATE ADMINISTRATION (Bender)
NEW YORK PROBATE (Lawyers Coop.)
WARREN'S HEATON SURROGATE'S COURT PRACTICE (Bender)

PROBATE LAW AND PRACTICE--OHIO
ADVANCED PROBATE LAW (Ohio CLE)
ANDERSON'S OHIO PROBATE PRACTICE AND PROCEDURE (Anderson)
MERRICK-RIPPNER OHIO PROBATE LAW (Banks)
OHIO PROBATE (Lawyers Coop.)
PROBLEMS IN PROBATE (Ohio CLE)

PROBATE LAW AND PRACTICE--OKLAHOMA
BASIC PROBATE (Okla. Bar CLE)

PROBATE LAW AND PRACTICE--PENNSYLVANIA
BRÉGY: SELECTED SECTIONS OF PENNSYLVANIA PROBATE, ESTATES AND FIDUCIARIES CODE (Bisel)
PROBATE, ESTATES AND FIDUCIARIES CODE ANNOTATED (Bisel)

PROBATE LAW AND PRACTICE--SOUTH CAROLINA
THE SOUTH CAROLINA PROBATE PRACTICE MANUAL (S. Carolina Bar)

PROBATE LAW AND PRACTICE--TENNESSEE
TENNESSEE PROBATE (Lawyers Coop.)

PROBATE LAW AND PRACTICE--TEXAS
TEXAS PROBATE CODE MANUAL (Butterworth-Texas)
TEXAS PROBATE SYSTEM (State Bar of Texas)

PROBATE LAW AND PRACTICE--VIRGINIA
VIRGINIA PROBATE LAW (Butterworth-Fla.)

PROBATE LAW AND PRACTICE--WASHINGTON
HOW TO PROBATE AN ESTATE AND HANDLE POST-MORTEM MATTERS (Wash. Bar)
WASHINGTON PROBATE PRACTICE, PROCEDURE AND TAX MANUALS (Book Pub.)

PROBATE LAW AND PRACTICE--WISCONSIN
WISCONSIN JUDICIAL BENCHBOOK: VOL. 4 - PROBATE, JUVENILE AND MENTAL (State Bar of Wisc.)
THE WISCONSIN PROBATE SYSTEM BOOK (State Bar of Wisc.)

PROBATE LAW AND PROCEDURE--HAWAII
HAWAII PROBATE SOURCEBOOK (Pacific Law Inst.)

PRODUCT SAFETY
CONSUMER PRODUCT SAFETY GUIDE (CCH)
PRODUCT SAFETY AND LIABILITY REPORTER (BNA)

PRODUCT SAFETY--CANADA
CANADIAN PRODUCT SAFETY GUIDE (CCH)

PRODUCTS LIABILITY
AMERICAN LAW OF PRODUCTS LIABILITY 3D (Lawyers Coop. & Bancroft)
ASBESTOS ABATEMENT RULES: THE COMPLETE RESOURCE GUIDE (BNA)
DRUG PRODUCT LIABILITY (Bender)
THE LAWYERS ANNOTATED PRODUCTS LIABILITY CHECKLISTS (Legal-Med.)
PRODUCT LIABILITY (Law Journal)
PRODUCT LIABILITY PRACTICE GUIDE (Bender)
PRODUCTS LIABILITY (Bender)
PRODUCTS LIABILITY: AN INTERNATIONAL MANUAL OF PRACTICE (Oceana)
PRODUCTS LIABILITY: RECREATION AND SPORTS EQUIPMENT (Law Journal)
PRODUCTS LIABILITY LITIGATION: CASE EVALUATION (Clark Boardman Callaghan)
PRODUCTS LIABILITY LITIGATION: PRETRIAL PRACTICE (Clark Boardman Callaghan)
PRODUCTS LIABILITY LITIGATION: TRIAL STRATEGY & PROCEDURE (Clark Boardman Callaghan)
PRODUCTS LIABILITY REPORTS (CCH)
SCIENTIFIC AUTOMOBILE ACCIDENT RECONSTRUCTION (Bender)
TOBACCO PRODUCTS LITIGATION REPORTER (TPLR)

PRODUCTS LIABILITY--CALIFORNIA
CALIFORNIA PRODUCTS LIABILITY ACTIONS (Bender)

PRODUCTS LIABILITY--ILLINOIS
ILLINOIS PRODUCT LIABILITY PRACTICE (Illinois ICLE)

PRODUCTS LIABILITY--INDIANA
PRODUCTS LIABILITY (Indiana CLE)

PRODUCTS LIABILITY--MARYLAND
PRODUCTS LIABILITY LAW MANUAL (MICPEL)

PRODUCTS LIABILITY--MICHIGAN
PRODUCTS LIABILITY BOOK (MTLA)

PUBLIC EMPLOYEES
- A CONCISE GUIDE TO DISCIPLINE IN THE PUBLIC SERVICE (NYPER)
- FEDERAL PAY AND BENEFITS REPORTER (LRP)
- GOVERNMENT EMPLOYEE RELATIONS REPORT (BNA)
- MANUAL ON THE ADMINISTRATIVE PROCESSING OF FEDERAL SECTOR EEO COMPLAINTS (FBA)
- MERIT SYSTEMS PROTECTION BOARD SERVICE (Hawkins)
- NATIONAL PUBLIC EMPLOYMENT REPORTER (LRP)

PUBLIC EMPLOYEES--CALIFORNIA
- CALIFORNIA PUBLIC SECTOR LABOR RELATIONS (Bender)
- PUBLIC EMPLOYEE REPORTER FOR CALIF. (LRP)

PUBLIC EMPLOYEES--FLORIDA
- FLORIDA PUBLIC EMPLOYEE REPORTER (LRP)

PUBLIC EMPLOYEES--ILLINOIS
- ILLINOIS PUBLIC EMPLOYEE REPORTER (LRP)

PUBLIC EMPLOYEES--INDIANA
- INDIANA PUBLIC EMPLOYEE REPORTER (LRP)

PUBLIC EMPLOYEES--MICHIGAN
- MICHIGAN PUBLIC EMPLOYEE REPORTER (LRP)

PUBLIC EMPLOYEES--MINNESOTA
- PUBLIC SECTOR LABOR LAW (7th Annual) (MILE)

PUBLIC EMPLOYEES--NEW JERSEY
- NEW JERSEY PUBLIC EMPLOYEE REPORTER (LRP)

PUBLIC EMPLOYEES--NEW YORK
- OFFICIAL DECISIONS, OPINIONS AND RELATED MATTERS OF THE PUBLIC EMPLOYMENT RELATIONS BOARD OF THE STATE OF NEW YORK (LRP)

PUBLIC EMPLOYEES--OHIO
- OHIO PUBLIC EMPLOYEE REPORTER (LRP)

PUBLIC EMPLOYEES--OREGON
- LABOR AND EMPLOYMENT LAW PUBLIC SECTOR (Oregon Bar)

PUBLIC EMPLOYEES--PENNSYLVANIA
- PENNSYLVANIA PUBLIC EMPLOYEE REPORTER (LRP)

PUBLIC EMPLOYEES--WASHINGTON
- WASHINGTON PUBLIC EMPLOYMENT RELATIONS REPORTER (Book Pub.)

PUBLIC EMPLOYEES--WISCONSIN
- PUBLIC SECTOR LABOR RELATIONS IN WISCONSIN (State Bar of Wisc.)

PUBLIC PROSECUTORS
- PROSECUTORIAL MISCONDUCT (Clark Boardman Callaghan)

PUBLIC UTILITIES
- ACCOUNTING FOR PUBLIC UTILITIES (Bender)
- LAW OF INDEPENDENT POWER PRODUCTION, COGENERATION AND UTILITY REGULATION (Clark Boardman Callaghan)
- UTILITIES LAW REPORTS (CCH)
- UTILITY HOLDING COMPANIES (Clark Boardman Callaghan)

PUBLIC UTILITIES--INDIANA
- MUNICIPAL UTILITY LAW (Indiana CLE)

PUBLIC UTILITIES--TEXAS
- TEXAS PUBLIC UTILITY COMMISSION RULES (RPC)

PUBLISHERS AND PUBLISHING
THE PUBLISHING LAW HANDBOOK (Prentice Hall Law & Business)
RIGHTS AND LIABILITIES OF PUBLISHERS, BROADCASTERS AND REPORTERS (Shepard's)

PUBLISHERS AND PUBLISHING--FORMS
RECORD AND MUSIC PUBLISHING FORMS OF AGREEMENT IN CURRENT USE (Law-Arts)

RADAR
SOUTH CAROLINA RADAR DEFENSE MANUAL (S. Carolina Bar)

RADIO
see Broadcasting

RAILROADS
see Carriers; Transportation; U.S. Interstate Commerce Commission

REAL ESTATE
see Real property

REAL ESTATE INVESTMENT
see also Syndicates

MORTGAGE AND REAL ESTATE INVESTMENT GUIDE (Mortgage)
STRUCTURING COMMERCIAL REAL ESTATE WORKOUTS: ALTERNATIVES TO FORECLOSURE (Prentice Hall Law & Business)
STRUCTURING FOREIGN INVESTMENT IN U.S. REAL ESTATE (Kluwer)
TAX ASPECTS OF REAL ESTATE INVESTMENTS (Clark Boardman Callaghan)

REAL ESTATE INVESTMENT--TAXATION
TAX PLANNING FOR REAL ESTATE TAXATION (Clark Boardman Callaghan)

REAL PROPERTY
see also Financing; Leases; Landlord and tenant; Mortgages

AMERICAN LAW OF REAL PROPERTY (Bender)
APPRAISERS' LIABILITY (Prof. Pubs.)
COLLIER REAL ESTATE TRANSACTION AND BANKRUPTCY CODE (Bender)
CURRENT LEASING LAW AND TECHNIQUES - FORMS (Real Estate Transaction Series, vols. 7, 7A, & 7B) (Bender)
ENVIRONMENTAL CONSIDERATIONS IN NATURAL RESOURCE AND REAL PROPERTY TRANSACTIONS (Rocky Mt.)
ENVIRONMENTAL LAW AFFECTING REAL ESTATE DEVELOPMENTS (Georgetown)
ENVIRONMENTAL REGULATION OF REAL PROPERTY (Law Journal)
EXCHANGING REAL ESTATE (Prof. Pubs.)
GUIDE TO CONTRACTING WITH THE RESOLUTION TRUST CORPORATION (Thompson)
GUIDE TO ENVIRONMENTAL LIABILITY IN REAL ESTATE TRANSACTIONS (Thompson)
GUIDE TO HOMEOWNERS' ASSOCIATIONS AND OTHER COMMON INTEREST REALTY ASSOCIATIONS (Practitioners Publishing)
INSURING REAL PROPERTY (Bender)
THE LAW AND BUSINESS OF RESORT DEVELOPMENT (Clark Boardman Callaghan)
THE LAW OF DISTRESSED REAL ESTATE (Clark Boardman Callaghan)
THE LAW OF REAL ESTATE FINANCING (WG&L)
LAW OF REAL PROPERTY (Bender)
MANAGING ENVIRONMENTAL RISK: REAL ESTATE AND BUSINESS TRANSACTIONS (Clark Boardman Callaghan)
A PRACTICAL GUIDE TO DISPUTES BETWEEN ADJOINING LANDOWNERS--EASEMENTS (Bender)
PRIVATE REAL ESTATE SYNDICATIONS (Law Journal)
PURCHASE AND SALE OF REAL PROPERTY (REAL ESTATE TRANSACTION SERIES, VOLS. 12, 12A & 12B) (Bender)
REAL ESTATE BROKERAGE LAW AND PRACTICE (Bender)
REAL ESTATE COORDINATOR (RIA)
REAL ESTATE DEVELOPMENT: LONG TERM CARE & RETIREMENT FACILITIES (Bender)
REAL ESTATE FINANCING TEXT, FORMS, TAX ANALYSIS (Real Estate Transaction Series, Vol. 4-5) (Bender)
REAL ESTATE SYNDICATION MANUAL (WG&L)

REAL ESTATE SYNDICATIONS: LAW, PRACTICE AND FORMS (Bender)
REAL ESTATE TAX APPEALS (Bender)
REAL ESTATE TRANSACTIONS (Prof. Pubs.)
REAL ESTATE TRANSACTIONS: STRUCTURE AND ANALYSIS WITH FORMS (WG&L)
THE RTC RESOURCE BOOK (Land Dev.)
STRUCTURING FOREIGN INVESTMENT IN U.S. REAL ESTATE (Kluwer)
SUBDIVISION LAW AND GROWTH MANAGEMENT (Clark Boardman Callaghan)
TAX MANAGEMENT - REAL ESTATE (BNA)

REAL PROPERTY--ARIZONA
COMMERCIAL REAL ESTATE TRANSACTIONS PRACTICE MANUAL (State Bar of Ariz.)

REAL PROPERTY--BRITISH COLOMBIA
BRITISH COLUMBIA REAL ESTATE LAW GUIDE (CCH)
CALIFORNIA REAL ESTATE LAW AND PRACTICE (Bender)

REAL PROPERTY--CALIFORNIA-FORMS
CALIFORNIA REAL PROPERTY PRACTICE FORMS MANUAL (Calif. CEB)

REAL PROPERTY--COLORADO
COLORADO REAL ESTATE PRACTICE (CLE - Colorado)
COLORADO REAL ESTATE TRANSACTIONS (Bancroft)

REAL PROPERTY--CONNECTICUT
BASIC RESIDENTIAL REAL ESTATE CLOSINGS (Conn. Bar)
CONNECTICUT LAW OF REAL PROPERTY (Atlantic)
CONNECTICUT REAL PROPERTY STATUTES (Butterworth-NH)
NEGOTIATING THE SALE, PURCHASE AND FINANCING OF COMMERCIAL REAL ESTATE IN A WORKOUT ENVIRONMENT (Conn. Bar)
REAL ESTATE LOAN WORKOUTS (Conn. Bar)
REAL ESTATE TRANSACTIONS: BORROWERS' COUNSELS' OPINION LETTERS (Conn. Bar)

REAL PROPERTY--FLORIDA
FLORIDA PREMISES LIABILITY (Butterworth-Fla.)
FLORIDA REAL ESTATE (Lawyers Coop.)
FLORIDA REAL ESTATE CLOSINGS (Butterworth-Fla.)
FLORIDA REAL ESTATE CONTRACTS (Butterworth-Fla.)
FLORIDA REAL ESTATE TRANSACTIONS (Butterworth-Fla.)
FLORIDA REAL ESTATE TRANSACTIONS (Bender)
REAL PROPERTY TITLE EXAMINATION AND INSURANCE IN FLORIDA (Florida Bar)

REAL PROPERTY--FORMS
COMMERCIAL REAL ESTATE FORMS (Shepard's)
HANDBOOK OF ANNOTATED FORMS FOR THE SURVEYING PRACTICE (Wiley Law)
MODERN CONSTRUCTION AND DEVELOPMENT FORMS (Modern Real Estate & Mortgage Forms series) (WG&L)
MODERN REAL ESTATE ACQUISITION AND DISPOSITION FORMS (WG&L)
MODERN REAL ESTATE LEASING FORMS (WG&L)
REAL ESTATE FORMS FROM ALI-ABA COURSE MATERIALS (ALI-ABA)

REAL PROPERTY--HAWAII
HAWAII COMMERCIAL REAL ESTATE MANUAL (HICLE)
HAWAII CONVEYANCE MANUAL (HICLE)
HAWAII REAL ESTATE FINANCING (HICLE)

REAL PROPERTY--IDAHO
IDAHO REAL ESTATE PRACTICE HANDBOOK (Idaho Law)

REAL PROPERTY--ILLINOIS
BASIC REAL ESTATE PRACTICE, VOL. 1 (Illinois ICLE)
BASIC REAL ESTATE PRACTICE, VOL. 2 (Illinois ICLE)
FINANCING REAL ESTATE TRANSACTIONS (Illinois ICLE)
ILLINOIS REAL ESTATE (Lawyers Coop.)
ILLINOIS REAL PROPERTY SERVICE (Lawyers Coop.)
REAL ESTATE LITIGATION (Illinois ICLE)
RESIDENTIAL REAL ESTATE SYSTEM (Illinois ICLE)

REAL PROPERTY--ILLINOIS-FORMS
ILLINOIS REAL ESTATE FORMS--PRACTICE (Aspen)

REAL PROPERTY--INDIANA
FRAUDULENT CONVEYANCES (Indiana CLE)

REAL PROPERTY--IOWA
IOWA LEGAL FORMS -- COMMERCIAL REAL ESTATE (Butterworth-St. Paul)
IOWA LEGAL FORMS -- RESIDENTIAL REAL ESTATE (Butterworth-St. Paul)
IOWA REAL ESTATE MANUAL (Iowa Bar)

REAL PROPERTY--KANSAS
KANSAS REAL ESTATE PRACTICE AND PROCEDURE HANDBOOK (Kansas Bar)

REAL PROPERTY--MAINE
DEFINITION OF SUBDIVISION IN MAINE LAW (Maine Bar)
THE NUTS AND BOLTS OF A BASIC REAL ESTATE DEAL (Maine Bar)
REAL ESTATE LAW: EASEMENTS, ROADS AND WAYS AND LITIGATION (Maine Bar)
REAL ESTATE LITIGATION (Maine Bar)
TROUBLED REAL ESTATE PROJECTS (Maine Bar)

REAL PROPERTY--MARYLAND
ADVANCED REAL PROPERTY INSTITUTE (MICPEL)
RESIDENTIAL REAL ESTATE TRANSACTIONS (MICPEL)

REAL PROPERTY--MARYLAND--FORMS
MARYLAND REAL ESTATE FORMS: PRACTICE (Aspen)

REAL PROPERTY--MASSACHUSETTS
MASSACHUSETTS REAL ESTATE (Lawyers Coop.)
MASSACHUSETTS REAL ESTATE LEASING FORMS (Aspen)

REAL PROPERTY--MICHIGAN
MANUAL FOR LAWYERS AND LEGAL ASSISTANTS: REAL ESTATE, 2ND ED. (ICLE - Michigan)
MICHIGAN REAL ESTATE PRACTICE AND FORMS (ICLE - Michigan)

REAL PROPERTY--MICHIGAN-FORMS
MICHIGAN REAL ESTATE FORMS--PRACTICE (Aspen)

REAL PROPERTY--MINNESOTA
COMMERCIAL REAL ESTATE TRANSACTIONS (Minn. CLE)
ENVIRONMENTAL LIABILITY IN REAL ESTATE MATTERS (Minn. CLE)
MINNESOTA LEGAL FORMS--COMMERCIAL REAL ESTATE (Butterworth-St. Paul)
MINNESOTA LEGAL FORMS--RESIDENTIAL REAL ESTATE (Butterworth-St. Paul)
MINNESOTA REAL ESTATE (Lawyers Coop.)
NEW DEVELOPMENTS IN REAL ESTATE (7th Annual) (MILE)
RESIDENTIAL REAL ESTATE PRACTICE (Minn. CLE)
RESIDENTIAL REAL ESTATE TRANSACTIONS (Minn. CLE)

REAL PROPERTY--MISSOURI
MISSOURI REAL ESTATE PRACTICE (MoBar)

REAL PROPERTY--MONTANA-FORMS
REAL ESTATE FORMBOOK (State Bar of Mont.)

REAL PROPERTY--NEBRASKA
NEBRASKA LEGAL FORMS--COMMERCIAL REAL ESTATE (Butterworth-St. Paul)
NEBRASKA LEGAL FORMS--RESIDENTIAL REAL ESTATE (Butterworth-St. Paul)

REAL PROPERTY--NEW HAMPSHIRE
REAL ESTATE CLOSING (NH Bar)

REAL PROPERTY--NEW JERSEY
NEW JERSEY REAL ESTATE FORMS - PRACTICE (Aspen)
RESIDENTIAL REAL ESTATE LAW AND PRACTICE IN NEW JERSEY (New Jersey ICLE)

REAL PROPERTY--NEW YORK
NEW YORK PRACTICE GUIDE: REAL ESTATE (Bender)
NEW YORK REAL PROPERTY LAW HANDBOOK (Gould)
NEW YORK REAL PROPERTY SERVICE (Lawyers Coop.)
WARREN'S WEED NEW YORK REAL PROPERTY (Bender)

REAL PROPERTY--NEW YORK--FORMS
STEINMAN'S BERGERMAN & ROTH, NEW YORK REAL PROPERTY FORMS, ANNOTATED (Bender)

REAL PROPERTY--NORTH CAROLINA-FORMS
NORTH CAROLINA REAL PROPERTY FORMS BOOK (No. Carolina Bar)

REAL PROPERTY--OHIO
HAUSSER & VAN AKEN, OHIO REAL ESTATE LAW & PRACTICE (Banks)

REAL PROPERTY--OKLAHOMA
OKLAHOMA LIEN LAWS (Butterworth-Texas)

REAL PROPERTY--OKLAHOMA-FORMS
OKLAHOMA REAL ESTATE FORMS - PRACTICE (Aspen)

REAL PROPERTY--ONTARIO
ONTARIO REAL ESTATE LAW GUIDE (CCH)

REAL PROPERTY--OREGON
DOCUMENTATION OF REAL ESTATE TRANSACTIONS (Oregon Bar)
FUNDAMENTALS OF REAL ESTATE TRANSACTIONS (Oregon Bar)
REAL PROPERTY (Oregon Bar)

REAL PROPERTY--PENNSYLVANIA
CHECKLISTS FOR TRANSACTIONS IN PENNSYLVANIA RESIDENTIAL REAL ESTATE (Penn. Bar)
LADNER ON CONVEYANCING IN PENNSYLVANIA, WITH FORMS (Bisel)
PENNSYLVANIA REAL ESTATE (Lawyers Coop.)

REAL PROPERTY--STATES
STATE LEGISLATIVE COMPILATIONS: SELECTED SUMMARIES OF REAL ESTATE FINANCE LAWS (MBAA)

REAL PROPERTY--TAXATION
FEDERAL INCOME TAXATION OF OIL AND GAS INVESTMENTS (WG&L)
FEDERAL INCOME TAXATION OF REAL ESTATE (WG&L)
FEDERAL INCOME TAXATION OF S CORPORATIONS (WG&L)
FEDERAL TAX ASPECTS OF REAL ESTATE TRANSACTIONS (Illinois ICLE)
FEDERAL TAXATION OF REAL ESTATE (Law Journal)
PROPERTY TAXATION (Inst. of Prop. Tax.)
PROPERTY TAXES (RIA)
REAL ESTATE PRACTITIONER'S TAX GUIDE (Knowles)
TAX PLANNING FOR REAL ESTATE TAXATION (Clark Boardman Callaghan)
TAXATION OF REAL ESTATE TRANSACTIONS 2nd ed. (Shepard's)

REAL PROPERTY--TAXATION--CALIFORNIA
TAXING CALIFORNIA PROPERTY (Lawyers Coop.)

REAL PROPERTY--TAXATION--FORMS
FEDERAL INCOME TAXATION OF REAL ESTATE: FORMS AND CHECKLISTS (WG&L)

REAL PROPERTY--TAXATION--ILLINOIS
REAL ESTATE TAXATION (Illinois ICLE)

REAL PROPERTY--TAXATION--MARYLAND
TAX-FREE DISPOSITION OF PROPERTY (MICPEL)

REAL PROPERTY--TAXATION--TEXAS
TEXAS PROPERTY TAX--PROTEST & APPEALS (Francis Marion)

SALES TAX
see also Taxation

ALL-STATE SALES TAX REPORTS (CCH)
SALES & USE TAX (RIA)

SALES TAX--CANADA
CANADIAN SALES TAX REPORTS (CCH)

SALES TAX--MASSACHUSETTS
MASSACHUSETTS SALES AND USE TAX MANUAL (Butterworth-NH)

SAVINGS BANKS
see Banks and banking

SCHOOLS
see also Education; Universities and colleges

SCHOOLS--MARYLAND
REPRESENTING STUDENTS IN PUBLIC SCHOOL DICIPLINARY ACTIONS (MICPEL)

SCHOOLS--OHIO
BAKER'S OHIO SCHOOL LAW GUIDE (Anderson)
BALDWIN'S OHIO SCHOOL LAW (Banks)

SCHOOLS--TEXAS
TEXAS GENERAL LAND OFFICE/SCHOOL LAND BOARD RULES (RPC)

SEARCHES AND SEIZURES
see also Criminal procedure

SEARCH WARRANT LAW DESKBOOK (Clark Boardman Callaghan)
SEARCHES & SEIZURES, ARRESTS AND CONFESSIONS (Clark Boardman Callaghan)
WARRANTLESS SEARCH LAW DESKBOOK (Clark Boardman Callaghan)

SEARCHES AND SEIZURES--GEORGIA
GEORGIA ARREST SEARCH AND SEIZURE (Butterworth-Fla.)

SEARCHES AND SEIZURES--ILLINOIS
ARREST, SEARCH AND SEIZURE (Illinois ICLE)

SEARCHES AND SEIZURES--NEW YORK
NEW YORK SEARCH & SEIZURE (Gould)

SEARCHES AND SEIZURES--OREGON
THE SEARCH AND SEIZURE MANUAL (OCDLA)

SECURED TRANSACTIONS
see Security

SECURITIES
see also Stock exchanges

ACCOUNTANTS SEC PRACTICE MANUAL (CCH)
ANNUAL NORTHWEST SECURITIES INSTITUTE (Wash. Bar)
APPEAL SECURITIES ACT HANDBOOK (Bowne)
THE ARLEN MUTUAL FUND HANDBOOK (Arlen)
BROKER-DEALER REGULATION (Securities Law Series, Vol. 15) (Clark Boardman Callaghan)
CIVIL LIABILITIES: ENFORCEMENT AND LITIGATION UNDER THE 1933 ACT (Clark Boardman Callaghan)
DEVELOPMENTS IN SEC DISCLOSURE (Georgetown)
EXEMPTED TRANSACTIONS UNDER THE SECURITIES ACT OF 1933 (Securities Law Series, vol. 7, 7A, 7B, 7C & 7D) (Clark Boardman Callaghan)
FEDERAL SECURITIES ACT -- ANALYSIS, PROCEDURES AND FORMS (Business Organizations vol. 11, 11 pt. 1, 1A, 2, 2A) (Bender)

FEDERAL SECURITIES EXCHANGE ACT OF 1934 (Business Organizations vols. 11A parts 1-2D) (Bender)
FEDERAL SECURITIES LAW REPORTS (CCH)
FEDERAL SECURITIES LAWS - REGULATIONS - FORMS (CCH)
GOING PRIVATE (Law Journal)
THE GOVERNMENT SECURITIES MANUAL (PSA)
A GUIDE TO MUNICIPAL OFFICIAL STATEMENTS (Prentice Hall Law & Business)
INSIDER TRADING REGULATION (Clark Boardman Callaghan)
INTERNATIONAL CAPITAL MARKETS AND SECURITIES REGULATION (Securities Law Series, vol. 10, 10A. 10B & 10C) (Clark Boardman Callaghan)
INVESTMENT ADVISERS GUIDE (ICI)
LITIGATION AND PRACTICE UNDER RULE 10B-5 (Securities Law Series, vol. 5, 5A, 5B, 5C & 5D) (Clark Boardman Callaghan)
MASTER INDEX--CLARK BOARDMAN CALLAGHAN'S SECURITIES LAW SERIES (Clark Boardman Callaghan)
MUNICIPAL SECURITIES RULEMAKING BOARD MANUAL (CCH)
MUTUAL FUNDS GUIDE (CCH)
NASD MANUAL (CCH)
NATIONAL FUTURES ASSOCIATION MANUAL (RIA)
OPINION LETTERS IN SECURITIES MATTERS: TEXT-CLAUSES-LAW (Securities Law Series, vol. 8 & 8A) (Clark Boardman Callaghan)
THE OPTIONS CLEARING CORPORATION & THE INTERMARKET CLEARING CORPORATION BY-LAWS AND RULES (Options Clearing Corp.)
RAISING CAPITAL: PRIVATE PLACEMENT FORMS & TECHNIQUES (Prentice Hall Law & Business)
THE REGULATION OF CORPORATE DISCLOSURE (Prentice Hall Law & Business)
REGULATION OF FINANCIAL PLANNERS (Clark Boardman Callaghan)
SEC ACCOUNTING AND REPORTING MANUAL (WG&L)
SEC COMPLIANCE - FINANCIAL REPORTING AND FORMS (WG&L)
SEC FINANCIAL REPORTING - ANNUAL REPORTS TO SHAREHOLDERS - FORM 10-K, QUARTERLY FINANCIAL REPORTING, 2ND ED. (Bender)
SEC NO-ACTION LETTERS INDEX & SUMMARIES (WSB)
SECTION 16 OF THE SECURITIES EXCHANGE ACT (Clark Boardman Callaghan)
SECURITIES: PUBLIC & PRIVATE OFFERINGS (Clark Boardman Callaghan)
SECURITIES AND PARTNERSHIP LAW FOR MLPs AND OTHER INVESTMENT LIMITED PARTNERSHIPS (Securities Law Series, Vol. 14) (Clark Boardman Callaghan)
SECURITIES ARBITRATION: PRACTICE AND FORMS (Bender)
SECURITIES ARBITRATION PROCEDURE MANUAL (Butterworth-NH)
SECURITIES CREDIT TRANSACTIONS HANDBOOK (Fed.)
SECURITIES FRAUD AND COMMODITIES FRAUD (Shepard's)
SECURITIES FRAUD: LITIGATING UNDER RULE 10B-5 (Aspen)
SECURITIES LAW TECHNIQUES (Bender)
SECURITIES LITIGATION: DAMAGES (Clark Boardman Callaghan)
SECURITIES LITIGATION: FORMS & ANALYSIS (Clark Boardman Callaghan)
SECURITIES PRACTICE: FEDERAL AND STATE ENFORCEMENT (Clark Boardman Callaghan)
SECURITIES REGULATION (WG&L)
SECURITIES REGULATION: LIABILITIES AND REMEDIES (Law Journal)
SHEPARD'S FEDERAL SECURITIES LAW CITATIONS (CCH)
SIGNIFICANT SEC FILINGS REPORTER (WSB)
UNIFORM PRACTICES FOR THE CLEARANCE AND SETTLEMENT OF MORTGAGE--BACKED SECURITIES AND OTHER RELATED SECURITIES (PSA)
UTILITY HOLDING COMPANIES (Clark Boardman Callaghan)
VENTURE CAPITAL AND PUBLIC OFFERING NEGOTIATION (Prentice Hall Law & Business)

SECURITIES--AUSTRALIA

AUSTRALIAN SECURITIES LAW REPORTS (CCH)

SECURITIES--CALIFORNIA

CALIFORNIA CORPORATE SECURITIES LAW NOTEBOOK (Calif. CEB)
CALIFORNIA CORPORATE SECURITIES LAW OF 1968 (Bender)
CALIFORNIA ELIGIBLE SECURITIES LIST (CCH)

SECURITIES--CANADA

CANADIAN SECURITIES LAW REPORTS (CCH)

SECURITIES--FLORIDA
FLORIDA SECURITIES LAW (Butterworth-Fla.)

SECURITIES--FORMS
MANUAL OF CORPORATE FORMS FOR SECURITIES PRACTICE (Securities Law Series, vol. 9 & 9A) (Clark Boardman Callaghan)
PROXY STATEMENTS: STRATEGY AND FORMS (Jefren)
SECURITIES REGULATION FORMS (Clark Boardman Callaghan)

SECURITIES--ILLINOIS
SECURITIES LAW (Illinois ICLE)

SECURITIES--INTERNATIONAL
INTERNATIONAL SECURITIES REGULATION (Oceana)

SECURITIES--KENTUCKY
KENTUCKY FINANCIAL INSTITUTION AND SECURITIES LAW (Banks)

SECURITIES--MINNESOTA
LYING, CHEATING & STEALING PLUS SECURITIES (MILE)
SECURITIES AND COMMERCIAL LITIGATION (MILE)

SECURITIES--OHIO
FRIEDMAN, OHIO SECURITIES LAW AND PRACTICE (Banks)

SECURITIES--STATES
BLUE SKY COMPLIANCE MANUAL (Butterworth-NH)
BLUE SKY GUIDE (ICI)
BLUE SKY LAW (Securities Law Series; Vol. 12 & 12A) (Clark Boardman Callaghan)
BLUE SKY LAW REPORTS (CCH)
BLUE SKY REGULATIONS (Business Organiz. vols. 11c, pt. 1 & 2) (Bender)
CCH NASAA REPORTS (CCH)

SECURITIES--TAXATION
CAPITAL CHANGES REPORTER (CCH)
TAXATION OF SECURITIES TRANSACTIONS (Business Organizations, vol. 11b) (Bender)

SECURITY
see also Commercial law

DOCUMENTING SECURED TRANSACTIONS: PROBLEM AVOIDANCE AND EFFECTIVE DRAFTING (PLI)
GUIDEBOOK TO SECURITY INTERESTS IN PERSONAL PROPERTY (Clark Boardman Callaghan)
THE LAW AND PRACTICE OF SECURED TRANSACTIONS: WORKING WITH ARTICLE 9 (Law Journal)
SECURED TRANSACTIONS GUIDE (CCH)
SECURED TRANSACTIONS UNDER THE UNIFORM COMMERCIAL CODE (Bender's Uniform Commerical Code Service, Vols. 1, 1A, 1B & 1C) (Bender)
STRUCTURING SECURED COMMERCIAL LOAN DOCUMENTS (WG&L)
UNIFORM COMMERCIAL CODE SERIES--SECURED TRANSACTIONS (Clark Boardman Callaghan)

SECURITY--FLORIDA
FLORIDA LAW OF SECURED TRANSACTIONS IN PERSONAL PROPERTY (Butterworth-Fla.)

SECURITY--GEORGIA
GEORGIA COMMERCIAL FINANCING FORMS (Aspen)

SECURITY--ILLINOIS
SECURED TRANSACTIONS (Illinois ICLE)

SECURITY--INDIANA
SECURED LENDING & SECURED FINANCING (Indiana CLE)

SECURITY--KANSAS
KANSAS PERSONAL PROPERTY SECURED TRANSACTIONS (Kansas Bar)

SECURITY--MARYLAND-FORMS
MARYLAND COMMERCIAL FINANCING FORMS - PRACTICE (Aspen)

SECURITY--NEW JERSEY
SECURED TRANSACTIONS UNDER THE REVISED UNIFORM COMMERCIAL CODE (New Jersey ICLE)

SECURITY--OREGON
FORECLOSING SECURITY INTERESTS (Oregon Bar)

SENIOR CITIZENS
ADVISING THE OLDER CLIENT (ICLE - Michigan)
AGE DISCRIMINATION (Shepard's)
ELDER LAW (Maine Bar)
TAX, ESTATE AND FINANCIAL PLANNING FOR THE ELDERLY (Bender)
TAX, ESTATE AND FINANCIAL PLANNING FOR THE ELDERLY -- FORMS AND PRACTICE (Bender)

SENIOR CITIZENS--CONNECTICUT
REPRESENTING THE ELDERLY: THE RULES THEY ARE A-CHANGING (Conn. Bar)

SENIOR CITIZENS--FLORIDA
LEGAL ISSUES, GOVERNMENT PROGRAMS, AND THE ELDERLY (FLORIDA) (Butterworth-Fla.)
LIFE PLANNING IN FLORIDA (Butterworth-Fla.)

SENIOR CITIZENS--ILLINOIS
ADVISING ELDERLY CLIENTS AND THEIR FAMILIES (Illinois ICLE)

SENIOR CITIZENS--INDIANA
ELDER LAW (Indiana CLE)

SENIOR CITIZENS--MARYLAND
PLANNING FOR THE ELDERLY (MICPEL)

SENIOR CITIZENS--MASSACHUSETTS
LEGAL PLANNING FOR THE ELDERLY IN MASSACHUSETTS (Butterworth-NH)

SENIOR CITIZENS--MICHIGAN
COUNSELING THE ELDERLY CLIENT IN MICHIGAN (Lawyers Coop.)

SENIOR CITIZENS--MINNESOTA
LAW OF THE ELDERLY (MILE)

SENIOR CITIZENS--MISSOURI
MISSOURI HANDICAPPED, ELDERLY, AND LOW-INCOME PERSONS LAW (MoBar)

SENTENCING
see Criminal procedure

SETTLEMENTS
see also Structured settlements

SETTLEMENT (Art of Advocacy Series) (Bender)

SEX CRIMES
PROSECUTION AND DEFENSE OF SEX CRIMES (Bender)

SEX CRIMES--MINNESOTA
THE SEXUAL ABUSE OF CHILDREN (MILE)

SHIPS AND SHIPPING
see also Admiralty; Law of the sea

THE BRAHM COURT INDEX (Longshore)
FEDERAL MARITIME COMMISSION SERVICE (Hawkins)
INTERNATIONAL TRADE REPORTER EXPORT REFERENCE MANUAL (BNA)
THE LONGSHORE NEWSLETTER PROCEDURE MANUAL (Longshore)
MARITIME LAW AND PRACTICE (Florida Bar)
SHIPPING REGULATION (P&F)

SHIPS AND SHIPPING--INTERNATIONAL
WORLD SHIPPING LAWS: INTERNATIONAL CONVENTIONS (Oceana)

SHOPPING CENTERS
SHOPPING CENTER AND STORE LEASES (Law Journal)

SHOPPING CENTERS--NEW JERSEY
SHOPPING CENTER LEASES (New Jersey ICLE)

SMALL CLAIMS--FLORIDA
FLORIDA SUMMARY CLAIMS HANDBOOK (Butterworth-Fla.)

SOCIAL SECURITY
SOCIAL SECURITY DISABILITY CLAIMS (Clark Boardman Callaghan)
SOCIAL SECURITY DISABILITY PRACTICE (James)
SOCIAL SECURITY LAW AND PRACTICE (Clark Boardman Callaghan)
SOCIAL SECURITY PRACTICE GUIDE (Bender)
UNEMPLOYMENT INSURANCE REPORTS (CCH)

SOFTWARE
see Computers

SPACE LAW
see also Aviation

UNITED STATES SPACE LAW -- NATIONAL AND INTERNATIONAL REGULATIONS (Oceana)

SPORTS
THE LAW OF PROFESSIONAL AND AMATEUR SPORTS (Clark Boardman Callaghan)

STATE TAXATION
see Taxation--states

STATISTICS
USE OF STATISTICS IN EQUAL EMPLOYMENT OPPORTUNITY (Law Journal)

STATUTE OF LIMITATIONS
see Limitation of actions

STEEL INDUSTRY
STEEL ARBITRATION DIGEST (P&F)

STOCK EXCHANGES
AMERICAN STOCK EXCHANGE COMPANY GUIDE (ASE)
AMERICAN STOCK EXCHANGE GUIDE (CCH)
BOSTON STOCK EXCHANGE GUIDE (CCH)
BY-LAWS AND RULES OF THE CINCINNATI STOCK EXCHANGE (Cincinnati)
CHICAGO BOARD OPTIONS EXCHANGE GUIDE (CCH)
INTERNATIONAL CAPITAL MARKETS AND SECURITIES REGULATION (Securities Law Series, vol. 10, 10A. 10B & 10C) (Clark Boardman Callaghan)
INTERPRETATION HANDBOOK (NYSE)
MIDWEST STOCK EXCHANGE GUIDE (CCH)
NEW YORK FUTURES EXCHANGE GUIDE (CCH)
NEW YORK STOCK EXCHANGE GUIDE (CCH)
NEW YORK STOCK EXCHANGE LISTED COMPANY MANUAL (NYSE)
PACIFIC STOCK EXCHANGE GUIDE (CCH)
PHILADELPHIA STOCK EXCHANGE GUIDE (CCH)

<u>STOCK TRANSFERS</u>
see also Securities

SECURITIES TRANSFER GUIDE (CCH)

<u>STRIKES</u>
see Labor and labor relations

<u>STRUCTURED SETTLEMENTS</u>
STRUCTURED SETTLEMENTS (Art of Advocacy Series) (Bender)
STRUCTURED SETTLEMENTS: DESIGN AND EVALUATION (Francis Marion)
STRUCTURED SETTLEMENTS AND PERIODIC PAYMENT JUDGMENTS (Law Journal)

<u>STRUCTURED SETTLEMENTS--MINNESOTA</u>
STRUCTURED SETTLEMENTS (MILE)

<u>SYNDICATES</u>
HORSE SYNDICATION MANUAL (Farnam)
REAL ESTATE SYNDICATION MANUAL (WG&L)
REAL ESTATE SYNDICATIONS: LAW, PRACTICE AND FORMS (Bender)

<u>TAKEOVERS</u>
see Consolidation and merger of corporations; Tender offers

<u>TARIFF</u>
see International trade

<u>TAX AUDITING</u>
TAX FRAUD - AUDITS - INVESTIGATIONS - PROSECUTIONS (Bender)

<u>TAX EVASION</u>
TAX FRAUD - AUDITS - INVESTIGATIONS - PROSECUTIONS (Bender)

<u>TAX HAVENS</u>
INTERNATIONAL OFFSHORE FINANCIAL CENTRES (CCH)
TAX HAVENS OF THE WORLD (Bender)

<u>TAX LIENS--PENNSYLVANIA</u>
PENNSYLVANIA MUNICIPAL CLAIMS AND TAX LIENS (Bisel)

<u>TAX PLANNING</u>
see also Estate planning

AUTOMATIC TAX PLANNER (Panel)
BUSINESS STRATEGIES (CCH)
BUSINESS TRANSACTIONS: TAX PLANNING AND ANALYSIS (RIA)
DIVORCE TAX PLANNING STRATEGIES (Shepard's)
ESTATE & PERSONAL FINANCIAL PLANNING (Clark Boardman Callaghan)
FAMILY TAX PLANNING (Bender)
FEDERAL TAX GUIDE (CCH)
FEDERAL TAX GUIDE REPORTS (Control Edition) (CCH)
FEDERAL TAX PLANNING (Shepard's)
MCGAFFEY LEGAL FORMS WITH TAX ANALYSIS (Clark Boardman Callaghan)
MODERN TAX PLANNING CHECKLISTS (WG&L)
POST-MORTEM TAX PLANNING (Shepard's)
PPC TAX PLANNING GUIDE - CLOSELY HELD CORPORATIONS (Practitioners Publishing)
PPC TAX PLANNING GUIDE - INDIVIDUALS (Practitioners Publishing)
PPC TAX PLANNING GUIDE - PARTNERSHIPS (Practitioners Publishing)
PPC TAX PLANNING GUIDE - S CORPORATIONS (Practitioners Publishing)
SMALL BUSINESS TAX CONTROL (Corporate Reports)
SMALL BUSINESS TAX PLANNER (RIA)
TAX GUIDE (RIA)
TAX IDEAS (WG&L)
TAX MANAGEMENT FINANCIAL PLANNING (BNA)
TAX PLANNING FOR CORPORATIONS AND SHAREHOLDERS (Bender)
TAX PLANNING FOR DISPOSITIONS OF BUSINESS INTERESTS (WG&L)

TAX PLANNING FOR EXECUTIVE COMPENSATION (Bender)
TAX PLANNING FOR FAMILY WEALTH TRANSFERS (WG&L)
TAX PLANNING FOR PARTNERSHIPS (Bender)
TAX PLANNING FOR SMALL BUSINESSES (Clark Boardman Callaghan)
TAX PLANNING FOR THE ALTERNATIVE MINIMUM TAX (Bender)
TAX PLANNING STRATEGIES (Clark Boardman Callaghan)
TAXATION OF INVESTMENTS (Prentice Hall Law & Business)
WG&L TAX PLANNING CHECKLISTS (WG&L)

<u>TAX PLANNING--CALIFORNIA</u>
CALIFORNIA FAMILY TAX PLANNING (Bender)

<u>TAX PLANNING--CONNECTICUT</u>
ANNUAL TAX PLANNING INSTITUTE (Conn. Bar)

<u>TAX PLANNING--FORMS</u>
TAX PLANNING FOR CORPORATIONS AND SHAREHOLDERS - FORMS (Bender)

<u>TAX PLANNING--INTERNATIONAL</u>
INTERNATIONAL PERSONAL TAX PLANNING ENCYCLOPEDIA (Butterworth-NH)
INTERNATIONAL TAX PLANNING MANUAL (CCH)
PRACTICAL INTERNATIONAL TAX PLANNING (PLI)

<u>TAX SHELTERS</u>
INVESTMENT LIMITED PARTNERSHIPS AND OTHER PASS-THROUGH VEHICLES (Securities Law Series, Vols. 4, 4A, 4B, 4C) (Clark Boardman Callaghan)
A PRACTICAL GUIDE TO TAX SHELTER LITIGATION (Law Journal)
TAXATION OF PASSIVE ACTIVITIES (Prentice Hall Law & Business)

<u>TAX TREATIES</u>
INTERNATIONAL WITHHOLDING TAX TREATY GUIDE (Bender)
TAX TREATIES (CCH)
TAX TREATIES (WG&L)
UNITED STATES INCOME TAX TREATIES (Kluwer)
UNITED STATES TAX CONVENTIONS. (Roberts & Holland Collection) (Hein)

<u>TAX-EXEMPT ORGANIZATIONS</u>
see Nonprofit associations

<u>TAXATION</u>
see also Estate and gift taxes; Income tax; Sales tax; "Taxation" subdivision under various headings

BASIC TAXATION OF NATURAL RESOURCES (EMLF)
BENDER'S FEDERAL TAX SERVICE (Bender)
CASEY FEDERAL TAX PRACTICE (Clark Boardman Callaghan)
CCH TAX TRANSACTIONS LIBRARY (CCH)
CODE AND REGULATIONS (CCH)
CONSOLIDATED TAX RETURNS: A TREATISE ON THE LAW OF CONSOLIDATED FEDERAL INCOME TAX RETURNS (Clark Boardman Callaghan)
CORPORATE TAX PLANNING (New Jersey ICLE)
CUMULATIVE CHANGES (RIA)
DEPRECIATION AND CAPITAL PLANNING (WG&L)
DEPRECIATION HANDBOOK (Bender)
FAMILY LAW TAX GUIDE (CCH)
FEDERAL EXCISE TAX REPORTS (CCH)
FEDERAL EXCISE TAXES (RIA)
FEDERAL INCOME TAXATION OF DEBT INSTRUMENTS (Prentice Hall Law & Business)
FEDERAL TAX ADVISOR (CCH)
FEDERAL TAX ADVISOR -- CONTROL EDITION (CCH)
FEDERAL TAX ARTICLES (CCH)
FEDERAL TAX ASPECTS OF BANKRUPTCY (Shepard's)
FEDERAL TAX COORDINATOR 2D (RIA)
FEDERAL TAX GUIDE (CCH)
FEDERAL TAX GUIDE (RIA)
FEDERAL TAX GUIDEBOOK (Bender)
FEDERAL TAX PRACTICE AND PROCEDURE (Illinois ICLE)

FEDERAL TAXATION OF INSURANCE COMPANIES (RIA)
FEDERAL TAXES, 2ND (RIA)
FEDERAL TAXES AFFECTING REAL ESTATE (Bender)
FIDUCIARY TAX GUIDE (CCH)
INCOME TAXATION OF FOREIGN-RELATED TRANSACTIONS (Bender)
INFORMATION RETURNS GUIDE (CCH)
INTERNAL REVENUE CODE & REGULATIONS (RIA)
INTERNAL REVENUE CODE OF 1986 AS AMENDED (RIA)
INTERNAL REVENUE MANUAL - ADMINISTRATION (CCH)
INTERNAL REVENUE MANUAL - AUDIT (CCH)
INTERNATIONAL BUSINESS PLANNING: LAW AND TAXATION - UNITED STATES (Bender)
INTERNATIONAL INCOME TAX RULES OF THE UNITED STATES (Butterworth-NH)
IRS LETTER RULINGS (CCH)
IRS PRACTICE AND PROCEDURES TAX PACKAGE (Stephens)
IRS PUBLICATIONS (CCH)
LITIGATION OF FEDERAL TAX CONTROVERSIES (Shepard's)
MERTENS LAW OF FEDERAL INCOME TAXATION (Clark Boardman Callaghan)
NEW YORK UNIVERSITY ANNUAL INSTITUTE ON FEDERAL TAXATION (Bender)
OBTAINING IRS PRIVATE LETTER RULINGS: A MANUAL OF FORMS AND PROCEDURES FROM TOUCHE ROSS & CO. (Oceana)
OFFICIAL IRS PUBLICATIONS (RIA)
PRACTITIONERS 1065 DESKBOOK (Practitioners Publishing)
REPRESENTING THE AUDITED TAXPAYER BEFORE THE IRS (Clark Boardman Callaghan)
STANDARD FEDERAL TAX REPORTS (1991 ED.) (CCH)
STATE AND LOCAL TAX INSTITUTE (Georgetown)
THE STATE & LOCAL TAX PORTFOLIO SERIES (Corp. Tax)
SUCCESSFULLY RESOLVING EMPLOYMENT TAX ISSUES WITH THE INTERNAL REVENUE SERVICE (TSI)
TAX ACCOUNTING (Bender)
TAX ACTION COORDINATOR (RIA)
TAX ASPECTS OF BUYING AND SELLING CORPORATE BUSINESSES (Shepard's)
TAX COURT (RIA)
TAX COURT REPORTS (CCH)
TAX IDEAS (WG&L)
TAX MANAGEMENT - ESTATES, GIFTS AND TRUSTS SERIES (BNA)
TAX MANAGEMENT - FOREIGN INCOME (BNA)
TAX MANAGEMENT PRIMARY SOURCES SERIES V (BNA)
TAX MANAGEMENT - U.S. INCOME (BNA)
TAX PENALTIES AND INTEREST HANDBOOK (Butterworth-NH)
THE TAX PRACTICE DESKBOOK (WG&L)
TAX PRACTICE MANAGEMENT MANUAL (AICPA)
TAX PRACTICE SERIES: THE PROFESSIONAL'S EXPEDITER (BNA)
TAX SERVICE FOR SUBCHAPTER "S" CORPORATIONS AND THEIR SHAREHOLDERS (Stephens)
TAXATION FOR THE GENERAL PRACTITIONER (NH Bar)
TAXATION OF SECURITIES TRANSACTIONS (Business Organizations, vol. 11b) (Bender)
THE TOUCHE ROSS INTERNATIONAL BUSINESS INVESTMENT AND TAXATION HANDBOOK (Probus)
TRUST ADMINISTRATION AND TAXATION (Bender)
TULANE TAX INSTITUTE (Claitor's)
U.S. TAXATION OF INTERNATIONAL OPERATIONS (WG&L)

TAXATION--AUSTRALIA
AUSTRALIAN FEDERAL TAX REPORTS (CCH)
AUSTRALIAN TAX CASES (CCH)
AUSTRALIAN TAX LIBRARY (CCH)

TAXATION--CALIFORNIA
CALIFORNIA TAXATION (Bender)
CALIFORNIA TAXES, 2nd ed. (Calif. CEB)

TAXATION--CALIFORNIA--FORMS
SPIDELL'S CALIFORNIA TAX FORMS AND INSTRUCTIONS (Spidell)

TAXATION--CANADA
ALBERTA-NORTHWEST TERRITORY & YUKON TAX REPORTER (CCH)

BRITISH COLUMBIA TAX REPORTER (CCH)
CANADIAN TAX REPORTS (CCH)
DOMINION TAX CASES (CCH)
MANITOBA & SASKATCHEWAN TAX REPORTER (CCH)
MARITIMES TAX REPORTER (CCH)
ONTARIO TAX REPORTER (CCH)
QUEBEC TAX REPORTER (CCH)

TAXATION--FLORIDA
FLORIDA STATE & LOCAL TAXATION (Butterworth-Fla.)
FLORIDA TAX SERVICE - 2nd ed. (Bender)
FLORIDA TAXATION (Shepard's)
FOREIGN TAX AND TRADE BRIEFS (Bender)

TAXATION--FOREIGN
TAX LAWS OF THE WORLD (Foreign Tax)

TAXATION--FORMS
ANNOTATED TAX FORMS (RIA)
BENDER'S FEDERAL TAX FORMS (Bender)
COMPLETE FEDERAL TAX FORMS (RIA)
FEDERAL TAX AND RELATED FORMS (Tax Form)
FEDERAL TAX FORMS (CCH)
NTTS FILLED-IN TAX FORMS ENCYCLOPEDIA (NTTS)
NTTS MASTER TAX FORMS FILE (NTTS)

TAXATION--GERMANY
WORLD TAX SERIES - GERMANY (CCH)

TAXATION--GREAT BRITAIN
BRITISH TAX CASES (CCH)
BRITISH TAX GUIDE (CCH)
BRITISH TAX LEGISLATION (CCH)

TAXATION--HONG KONG
HONG KONG REVENUE LAW (Bender)

TAXATION--ILLINOIS
ILLINOIS STATE AND LOCAL TAXATION (Illinois ICLE)
ILLINOIS TAX SERVICE (Bender)

TAXATION--INTERNATIONAL
INTERNATIONAL TAX GUIDE: U.S. INCOME TAXATION (Clark Boardman Callaghan)
U.S. INTERNATIONAL TAXATION (WG&L)

TAXATION--JAPAN
JAPANESE INTERNATIONAL TAXATION (Bender)

TAXATION--MARYLAND
MARYLAND TAX COURT SERVICE (Hawkins)
MARYLAND TAXES, 2nd Ed. (MICPEL)

TAXATION--MASSACHUSETTS
MASSACHUSETTS CORPORATE TAX MANUAL, 2ND ED. (Butterworth-NH)
MASSACHUSETTS TAXATION AND DOR PRACTICE (Mass. CLE)

TAXATION--MINNESOTA
ANNUAL TAX INSTITUTE MANUAL (Minn. CLE)
MINNESOTA TAX APPEALS (Butterworth-St. Paul)
PASS THROUGH ENTITIES: FOURTH ANNUAL STATE AND FEDERAL TAX CONFERENCE (MILE)
PASSIVE ACTIVITY LOSSES - THE NEW REGULATION (MILE)

TAXATION--MISSOURI
MISSOURI TAXATION LAW AND PRACTICE (MoBar)

TAXATION--NEW HAMPSHIRE
NEW HAMPSHIRE MUNICIPAL PRACTICE SERIES: MUNICIPAL FINANCE & TAXATION (Butterworth-NH)
TAX FORUM (NH Bar)

TAXATION--NEW JERSEY
NEW JERSEY TAX SERVICE (Bender)

TAXATION--NEW YORK
NEW YORK TAX CASES (Hein)
NEW YORK TAX SERVICE (Bender)

TAXATION--OHIO
BALDWIN'S OHIO TAX LAW AND RULES (Banks)
OHIO STATE TAXATION (Bender)

TAXATION--PENNSYLVANIA
PENNSYLVANIA TAX SERVICE (Bender)
PENNSYLVANIA TAXATION (Shepard's)

TAXATION--PUERTO RICO
PUERTO RICO TAX REPORTS (CCH)
PUERTO RICO TAXES (RIA)

TAXATION--STATES
ALL STATES TAX GUIDE (RIA)
STATE AND LOCAL TAXES (vols. available for each state) (RIA)
STATE TAX CASES REPORTS (CCH)
STATE TAX GUIDE (CCH)
STATE TAX REPORTS (separate volumes for each state at indiv. price per unit) (CCH)
STATE TAXATION OF BANKS AND THRIFT INSTITUTIONS (ABA)

TAXATION--STATES--FORMS
STATE TAX ACTION COORDINATOR (RIA)
STATE TAX FORMS: CORPORATION (Tax Form)
STATE TAX FORMS: INDIVIDUAL (Tax Form)
STATE TAX FORMS: PARTNERSHIP & FIDUCIARY (Tax Form)

TAXATION--TEXAS
TEXAS TAX SERVICE (Bender)

TAXATION--USSR
SOVIET TAXATION: STATUTES, REGULATIONS AND TREATIES (Transnational Juris Publications)

TAXATION--WASHINGTON
PARTNERSHIP TAXATION (Wash. Bar)

TECHNOLOGY
COMPUTER LAW INSTITUTE (Wash. Bar)
TECHNOLOGY MANAGEMENT (Clark Boardman Callaghan)

TELECOMMUNICATIONS
FEDERAL COMMUNICATIONS COMMISSION RULES AND REGULATIONS (Rules)
INTERNATIONAL TELECOMMUNICATIONS AGREEMENTS (Oceana)
RADIO REGULATION, SECOND SERIES (P&F)
RULES AND REGULATIONS (USGPO)
TELECOMMUNICATIONS REGULATORY MONITOR (Phillips)

TENANT
see Landlord and tenant

TENDER OFFERS
see also Securities

ACQUISITIONS AND MERGERS: NEGOTIATED AND CONTESTED TRANSACTIONS (Securities Law Series Vol. II) (Clark Boardman Callaghan)
HART-SCOTT-RODINO ANTITRUST IMPROVEMENTS ACT OF 1976: REMERGER NOTIFICATION SOURCE BOOK (USGPO)
HOSTILE TAKEOVERS: 1988 UPPER MIDWEST UPDATE (MILE)
SHARK REPELLENTS AND GOLDEN PARACHUTES: A HANDBOOK FOR THE PRACTITIONER (Prentice Hall Law & Business)
TAKEOVER DEFENSE (Prentice Hall Law & Business)
TAKEOVERS AND FREEZEOUTS (Law Journal)

TIMESHARING
THE LAW AND BUSINESS OF TIME-SHARE RESORTS (Clark Boardman Callaghan)

TITLE EXAMINATION
MINERAL TITLE EXAMINATION II (Rocky Mt.)

TITLE EXAMINATION--FLORIDA
REAL PROPERTY TITLE EXAMINATION AND INSURANCE IN FLORIDA (Florida Bar)

TITLE EXAMINATION--ILLINOIS
WARD ON TITLE EXAMINATIONS (Illinois ICLE)

TITLE EXAMINATION--IOWA
IOWA LAND TITLE EXAMINATION STANDARDS (Iowa Bar)

TITLE EXAMINATION--MINNESOTA
EXAMINATION OF TITLE (Minn. CLE)

TITLES--KANSAS
KANSAS TITLE STANDARDS HANDBOOK (Kansas Bar)

TITLES--MICHIGAN
MICHIGAN LAND TITLE STANDARDS (State Bar of Mich.)

TITLES--NORTH DAKOTA
STANDARDS OF TITLE (State Bar of N. Dak.)

TITLES--OHIO
TITLE TO REAL ESTATE (Ohio CLE)

TITLES--TEXAS
TRESPASS TO TRY TITLE (TEXAS) (Butterworth-Texas)

TITLES-WISCONSIN
TITLES TO REAL ESTATE (CLE - Wisc.)

TORTS
see also Accidents; Damages; Negligence; Personal injuries

BAD FAITH ACTIONS: LIABILITY AND DAMAGES (Clark Boardman Callaghan)
BAD FAITH & PUNITIVE DAMAGES: ANNOTATIONS TO FIRST PARTY INSURANCE CASES, STATUTES, AND REGULATIONS (ABA)
THE BUSINESS TORT OF FRAUD AND MISREPRESENTATION (Butterworth-NH)
BUSINESS TORTS (Bender)
DAMAGES IN TORT ACTIONS (Bender)
EMPLOYEE, BUSINESS AND PROFESSIONAL DEFAMATION (Bender)
GUIDE TO TOXIC TORTS (Bender)
HANDLING FEDERAL TORT CLAIMS: ADMINISTRATIVE AND JUDICIAL REMEDIES (Bender)
LAW OF TOXIC TORTS (Clark Boardman Callaghan)
MODERN TORT LAW, REV. ED. (Clark Boardman Callaghan)
NOTES AND DECISIONS (NYSTLA)
REGIONAL VERDICT SURVEY (Jury Verdict)

NATIONAL TRANSPORTATION SAFETY BOARD SERVICE (Hawkins)
NATURAL GAS TRANSPORTATION INFORMATION SERVICE (Thompson)
TRANSPORTATION LAW INSTITUTE PAPERS AND PROCEEDINGS (ATP)
TRANSPORTATION LAW STUDY GUIDE (ATP)
TRANSPORTATION SAFETY LAW PRACTICE MANUAL (Butterworth-NH)
TRUCKING PERMIT GUIDE (Keller)
TRUCKING SAFETY GUIDE (Keller)

TRANSPORTATION--INTERNATIONAL
TRANSPORT LAWS OF THE WORLD (Oceana)

TRANSPORTATION--TEXAS
RAILROAD COMMISSION OF TEXAS RULES (RPC)

TRAVEL LAW
TRAVEL LAW (Law Journal)

TREATIES
see also Tax treaties

AIR AND AVIATION TREATIES OF THE WORLD (Oceana)
ARMS CONTROL REPORTER (IDDS)
COPYRIGHT LAWS AND TREATIES OF THE WORLD (BNA Books)
EXTRADITION LAWS AND TREATIES OF THE UNITED STATES (Hein)
INTERNATIONAL PROTECTION OF THE ENVIRONMENT: TREATIES AND RELATED DOCUMENTS 2d Series (Oceana)
INTERNATIONAL TRANSPORT TREATIES (Kluwer)
INVESTMENT PROMOTION AND PROTECTION TREATIES (Oceana)
LAW AND PRACTICE UNDER THE GATT AND OTHER TRADING ARRANGEMENTS: TRILATERAL TRADE AGREEMENTS: CANADA - U.S. - MEXICO (Oceana)

TRIAL PRACTICE
see also Actions and defenses; Appellate procedure; Civil procedure; Criminal procedure; Evidence; Jury; Jury instructions; Probate law and practice

ABA LAWYERING SKILLS: COURSE MATERIALS, CLIENT INSTRUCTIONS (ABA)
ABA LAWYERING SKILLS: COURSE MATERIALS, PARTICIPANTS' COPY (group A & group B) (ABA)
ABA LAWYERING SKILLS: INSTRUCTOR'S MANUAL (ABA)
BNA CIVIL TRIAL MANUAL (BNA)
CALLAGHAN'S APPELLATE ADVOCACY MANUAL (Clark Boardman Callaghan)
CIVIL TRIAL MANUAL II (ALI-ABA)
CLOSING ARGUMENTS (Clark Boardman Callaghan)
COMPUTERS AND THE TRIAL LAWYER (ATLA)
DEFENSE OF DRUNK DRIVING CASES: CRIMINAL - CIVIL (Bender)
DEFENSE OF NARCOTICS CASES (Bender)
DIRECT EXAMINATION (Art of Advocacy Series) (Bender)
FEDERAL CIVIL TRIALBOOK (West)
FEDERAL RULE BOOK (Minn. CLE)
GOING TO TRIAL - A STEP-BY STEP GUIDE TO TRIAL PRACTICE AND PROCEDURE (ABA)
HANDLING MOTOR VEHICLE ACCIDENT CASES: TREATISE (Clark Boardman Callaghan)
LANE MEDICAL LITIGATION GUIDE (Clark Boardman Callaghan)
LANE'S GOLDSTEIN LITIGATION FORMS (Clark Boardman Callaghan)
LANE'S GOLDSTEIN TRIAL TECHNIQUE (Clark Boardman Callaghan)
LITIGATION ORGANIZATION AND MANAGEMENT (Prentice Hall Law & Business)
MAKING TRIAL OBJECTIONS (Wiley Law)
MANUAL FOR COMPLEX LITIGATION (Clark Boardman Callaghan)
MANUAL FOR COMPLEX LITIGATION (Bender)
OAKES' CRIMINAL PRACTICE GUIDE (Wiley Law)
OPENING STATEMENT (Art of Advocacy Series) (Bender)
OPENING STATEMENTS (Clark Boardman Callaghan)
PARALEGAL TRIAL HANDBOOK (James)
PRODUCTS LIABILITY LITIGATION: TRIAL STRATEGY & PROCEDURE (Clark Boardman Callaghan)
PROSECUTION AND DEFENSE OF CRIMINAL CONSPIRACY CASES (Bender)
PROSECUTION AND DEFENSE OF SEX CRIMES (Bender)

SOUTHEAST LITIGATION GUIDE (Bender)
SUCCESSFUL LITIGATION TECHNIQUES (Bender)
SUMMATION (Art of Advocacy Series) (Bender)
TRIAL BY NOTEBOOK (ATLA)
TRIAL HANDBOOK (PLI)
TRIAL HEARSAY: OBJECTIONS & EXCEPTIONS (James)
TRIAL MANUAL FOR DEFENSE ATTORNEYS IN JUVENILE COURT (ALI-ABA)
TRIAL OBJECTIONS (James)
TRIAL OF ACCIDENT CASES (Bender)
THE TRIALBOOK: A TOTAL SYSTEM FOR THE PREPARATION AND PRESENTATION OF A CASE (West)
UNCHARGED MISCONDUCT EVIDENCE (Clark Boardman Callaghan)

TRIAL PRACTICE--CALIFORNIA
CALIFORNIA CIVIL LITIGATION FORMS MANUAL (Calif. CEB)
CALIFORNIA CIVIL TRIALBOOK (West)
CALIFORNIA COMPLEX LITIGATION (Parker)
CALIFORNIA CRIMINAL DEFENSE PRACTICE (Bender)
CALIFORNIA CRIMINAL TRIALBOOK (West)
CALIFORNIA POINTS AND AUTHORITIES (Bender)
CALIFORNIA PRACTICE GUIDE - FEDERAL CIVIL PROCEDURE BEFORE TRIAL (Rutter)
CALIFORNIA TRIAL GUIDE (Bender)
CALIFORNIA TRIAL TECHNIQUES (Parker)

TRIAL PRACTICE--CONNECTICUT
GOING TO TRIAL (Conn. Bar)

TRIAL PRACTICE--FLORIDA
FLORIDA CIVIL TRIAL PRACTICE (Florida Bar)
FLORIDA CRIMINAL DEFENSE TRIAL MANUAL (Butterworth-Fla.)
FLORIDA PRACTICE GUIDE: PERSONAL INJURY (Lawyers Coop.)
FLORIDA TRIAL GUIDE (Bender)

TRIAL PRACTICE--HAWAII
HAWAII LEGAL PRACTICE MANUAL - LITIGATION (HICLE)

TRIAL PRACTICE--ILLINOIS
ILLINOIS CIVIL TRIAL GUIDE (Bender)
ILLINOIS TRIALS: LAW AND STRATEGY (Butterworth-St. Paul)
THIRD PARTY PRACTICE (Illinois ICLE)

TRIAL PRACTICE--INDIANA
MOTIONS PRACTICE IN INDIANA (Indiana CLE)

TRIAL PRACTICE--IOWA
IOWA PLEADING AND CAUSES OF ACTION (Butterworth-St. Paul)

TRIAL PRACTICE--MAINE
TRIAL ADVOCACY: THE AUTOMOBILE ACCIDENT (Maine Bar)

TRIAL PRACTICE--MASSACHUSETTS
A PRACTICAL GUIDE TO INTRODUCING EVIDENCE (Mass. CLE)

TRIAL PRACTICE--MICHIGAN
HANDLING THE AUTOMOBILE NEGLIGENCE CASE: A SYSTEMS APPROACH (ICLE - Michigan)
MICHIGAN CIVIL PROCEDURE DURING TRIAL (ICLE - Michigan)
STARTING A CASE IN THE 90's: A CURRENT MANUAL OF COMPLAINTS IN MICHIGAN (MTLA)
WINNING FINAL ARGUMENTS (MTLA)

TRIAL PRACTICE--MINNESOTA
TRIAL SKILLS FOR YOUNG LAWYERS -- 3RD ANNUAL (Minn. CLE)

TRIAL PRACTICE--MISSOURI
MISSOURI CIVIL TRIAL PRACTICE (MoBar)
MISSOURI LITIGATION SETTLEMENT (MoBar)

TRIAL PRACTICE--NEW JERSEY
CRIMINAL TRIAL PRACTICE (New Jersey ICLE)

TRIAL PRACTICE--NEW YORK
NEW YORK TRIAL GUIDE (Bender)
PLAINTIFF'S PROOF OF A PRIMA FACIE CASE (Clark Boardman Callaghan)

TRIAL PRACTICE--OREGON
CIVIL LITIGATION (Oregon Bar)
THE TRIAL NOTEBOOK (OCDLA)

TRIAL PRACTICE--PENNSYLVANIA
PENNSYLVANIA TRIAL GUIDE (CIVIL) (Bisel)
PENNSYLVANIA TRIAL GUIDE (CRIMINAL) (Bisel)

TRIAL PRACTICE--TEXAS
ERISMAN'S REVERSIBLE ERRORS (Knowles)
TEXAS CIVIL TRIAL GUIDE (Bender)
TEXAS CIVIL TRIAL HANDBOOK (State Bar of Texas)
TEXAS LITIGATION GUIDE (Bender)
TEXAS LITIGATOR'S HANDBOOK (Butterworth-Texas)

TRUSTS AND TRUSTEES
CHANGING THE SITUS OF A TRUST (Law Journal)
CHARITABLE LEAD TRUSTS - EXPLANATION, SPECIMEN AGREEMENTS, FORMS (Taxwise)
THE CHASE WILL & TRUST FORMS MANUAL (Chase Manhattan)
DEFERRED GIVING - EXPLANATION, SPECIMEN AGREEMENTS, FORMS (Taxwise)
DRAFTING WILLS AND TRUST AGREEMENTS: A SYSTEMS APPROACH, 2nd ed. (Shepard's)
REVOCABLE TRUSTS, 2/e (Shepard's)
TRUST ACTIVITIES HANDBOOK (Office of Thrift Supervision)
TRUST ADMINISTRATION AND TAXATION (Bender)
TRUST DEPARTMENT ADMINISTRATION AND OPERATIONS (Bender)

TRUSTS AND TRUSTEES--CALIFORNIA
DRAFTING CALIFORNIA IRREVOCABLE LIVING TRUSTS, 2nd ed. (Calif. CEB)
TRUSTMASTER™ -- TRUST DRAFTING SYSTEM (Calif. CEB)

TRUSTS AND TRUSTEES--FORMS
MODERN TRUST FORMS AND CHECKLISTS (WG&L)
WILLS TRUSTS FORMS (RIA)

TRUSTS AND TRUSTEES--HAWAII
HAWAII WILLS AND TRUSTS SOURCEBOOK (Pacific Law Inst.)

TRUSTS AND TRUSTEES--ILLINOIS
DRAFTING WILLS AND TRUST AGREEMENTS (Illinois ICLE)
TRUST ADMINISTRATION IN ILLINOIS (Illinois ICLE)

TRUSTS AND TRUSTEES--INDIANA
TRUSTS AND TRUSTEES (Indiana CLE)

TRUSTS AND TRUSTEES--MASSACHUSETTS
DRAFTING WILLS AND TRUSTS IN MASSACHUSETTS (Mass. CLE)

TRUSTS AND TRUSTEES--MICHIGAN
MICHIGAN REVOCABLE GRANTOR TRUSTS (ICLE - Michigan)

TRUSTS AND TRUSTEES--MINNESOTA
LIVING AND DYING WITH A REVOCABLE TRUST (Minn. CLE)

TRUSTS AND TRUSTEES--NEW YORK
NEW YORK CIVIL PRACTICE - ESTATES, POWERS, TRUSTS LAW (vols. 9, 9 pt. 2, 9A, 9A pt. 2, 9B, 9C, 9D) (Bender)
NEW YORK WILLS AND TRUSTS, 3/e (Shepard's)
TRUST AND WILL PROVISIONS (U.S. Trust)

TRUSTS AND TRUSTEES--TAXATION
FEDERAL TAXATION OF TRUSTS, GRANTORS AND BENEFICIARIES (WG&L)

TRUSTS AND TRUSTEES--WASHINGTON
ANNUAL ESTATE PLANNING SEMINAR (Wash. Bar)
WASHINGTON WILLS & TRUST FORMS (Book Pub.)

U.S. DEPARTMENT OF JUSTICE
THE DEPARTMENT OF JUSTICE MANUAL (Prentice Hall Law & Business)
UNITED STATES ATTORNEYS' MANUAL (USGPO)

U.S. FEDERAL AVIATION ADMINISTRATION
FEDERAL AVIATION ADMINISTRATION - CODIFIED REGULATIONS (Rules)
FEDERAL AVIATION REGULATIONS (USGPO)

U.S. FEDERAL COMMUNICATIONS COMMISSION
see also Broadcasting

FCC RULEMAKING REPORTS (CCH)
FCC RULES CURRENT SERVICE (P&F)
FEDERAL COMMUNICATIONS COMMISSION RULES AND REGULATIONS (Rules)
RADIO REGULATION, SECOND SERIES (P&F)
RULES AND REGULATIONS (USGPO)

U.S. FEDERAL ENERGY REGULATORY COMMISSION
FEDERAL ENERGY REGULATORY COMMISSION REPORTS (CCH)

U.S. FEDERAL MARITIME COMMISSION
FEDERAL MARITIME COMMISSION SERVICE (Hawkins)
SHIPPING REGULATION (P&F)

U.S. FEDERAL NATIONAL MORTGAGE ASSOCIATION
MULTI-FAMILY GUIDE (FNMA)
SELLING GUIDE (FNMA)
SERVICING GUIDE (FNMA)

U.S. FEDERAL TRADE COMMISSION
FEDERAL TRADE COMMISSION: LAW, PRACTICE AND PROCEDURE (Law Journal)
FEDERAL TRADE COMMISSION REGULATORY MANUAL (Shepard's)

U.S. FOOD AND DRUG ADMINISTRATION
FDA COMPLIANCE POLICY GUIDES MANUAL (NTIS - order # PB91-915499/CAU (manual); PB91-915400/CAU (updates))
THE FDA ENFORCEMENT MANUAL (Thompson)
FOOD AND DRUG ADMINISTRATION REGULATORY MANUAL (Shepard's)

U.S. INTERNAL REVENUE MANUAL
INTERNAL REVENUE MANUAL: ABRIDGED & ANNOTATED (Clark Boardman Callaghan)

U.S. INTERNAL REVENUE SERVICE
INTERNAL REVENUE CODE & REGULATIONS (RIA)
INTERNAL REVENUE MANUAL - ADMINISTRATION (CCH)
INTERNAL REVENUE MANUAL - AUDIT (CCH)
INTERNAL REVENUE SERVICE (MILE)
IRS LETTER RULINGS (CCH)
IRS POSITIONS (CCH)
IRS PRACTICE AND PROCEDURES TAX PACKAGE (Stephens)
IRS PUBLICATIONS (CCH)
OBTAINING IRS PRIVATE LETTER RULINGS: A MANUAL OF FORMS AND PROCEDURES FROM TOUCHE ROSS & CO. (Oceana)
OFFICIAL IRS PUBLICATIONS (RIA)
REPRESENTATION BEFORE THE COLLECTION DIVISION OF IRS (Clark Boardman Callaghan)
REPRESENTING THE AUDITED TAXPAYER BEFORE THE IRS (Clark Boardman Callaghan)
SUCCESSFULLY RESOLVING EMPLOYMENT TAX ISSUES WITH THE INTERNAL REVENUE SERVICE (TSI)
TAX MANAGEMENT IRS FORMS (BNA)

<u>VEHICLES--PENNSYLVANIA</u>
PENNSYLVANIA VEHICLE CODE, ANNOTATED (Bisel)
PENNSYLVANIA VEHICLE NEGLIGENCE (Bisel)

<u>VENDORS AND PURCHASERS</u>
see Real property; Sales

<u>VENTURE CAPITAL</u>
RAISING CAPITAL: PRIVATE PLACEMENT FORMS & TECHNIQUES (Prentice Hall Law & Business)
VENTURE CAPITAL AND PUBLIC OFFERING NEGOTIATION (Prentice Hall Law & Business)
VENTURE CAPITAL AND SMALL BUSINESS FINANCINGS (Securities Law Series, Vol. 2, 2A & 2B) (Clark Boardman Callaghan)

<u>VETERANS</u>
MILITARY DISCHARGE UPGRADING AND INTRODUCTION TO VETERANS ADMINISTRATION LAW (Natl. Veterans)

<u>WAGES</u>
see also Executive compensation; Labor and labor relations; Payroll

COMPENSATION STRATEGY AND MANAGEMENT (WG&L)
EMPLOYEE COMPENSATION IN [YOUR STATE] (BLR)
WAGES AND HOURS: LAW AND PRACTICE (Bender)

<u>WAGES--CALIFORNIA</u>
CALIFORNIA WAGE AND HOUR GUIDE (M & M Resources)

<u>WARRANTY</u>
see Commercial law; Products liability

<u>WHITE COLLAR CRIMES</u>
see Corrupt practices; Commercial crimes; Fraud; Tax evasion

<u>WILLS</u>
see also Estate planning; Estates; Probate law and practice; Trusts and trustees

THE CHASE WILL & TRUST FORMS MANUAL (Chase Manhattan)
DRAFTING WILLS AND TRUST AGREEMENTS: A SYSTEMS APPROACH, 2nd ed. (Shepard's)
MURPHY'S WILL CLAUSES: ANNOTATIONS AND FORMS WITH TAX EFFECTS (national and N.Y. ed.) (Bender)
WILL FORMS AND CLAUSES (Anderson)

<u>WILLS--CALIFORNIA</u>
CALIFORNIA WILLS & TRUSTS (Bender)
CALIFORNIA WILLS & TRUSTS - FORMS (Bender)

<u>WILLS--COLORADO-FORMS</u>
COLORADO ESTATE PLANNING, WILL DRAFTING AND ESTATE ADMINISTRATION FORMS - PRACTICE (Aspen)

<u>WILLS--CONNECTICUT</u>
WILL DRAFTING: PLANNING IN LESS CERTAIN TIMES (Conn. Bar)

<u>WILLS--FLORIDA</u>
FLORIDA PARALEGAL SERIES: WILLS, TRUSTS, ESTATES (Butterworth-Fla.)
FLORIDA WILL AND TRUST DRAFTING (Florida Bar)

<u>WILLS--FORMS</u>
WILLS TRUSTS FORMS (RIA)

<u>WILLS--GEORGIA-FORMS</u>
GEORGIA ESTATE PLANNING, WILL DRAFTING AND ESTATE ADMINISTRATION FORMS--PRACTICE (Aspen)

WILLS--HAWAII
HAWAII WILLS AND TRUSTS SOURCEBOOK (Pacific Law Inst.)

WILLS--ILLINOIS
DRAFTING WILLS AND TRUST AGREEMENTS (Illinois ICLE)

WILLS--ILLINOIS-FORMS
ILLINOIS ESTATE PLANNING, WILL DRAFTING AND ESTATE ADMINISTRATION FORMS--PRACTICE (Aspen)

WILLS--MARYLAND
MARYLAND ESTATE PLANNING, WILL DRAFTING AND ESTATE ADMINISTRATION FORMS: PRACTICE (Aspen)
WILL DRAFTING -- "BEYOND THE BASICS" (MICPEL)

WILLS--MARYLAND-FORMS
MASSACHUSETTS ESTATE PLANNING, WILL DRAFTING AND ESTATE ADMINISTRATION FORMS--PRACTICE (Aspen)

WILLS--MASSACHUSETTS
DRAFTING WILLS AND TRUSTS IN MASSACHUSETTS (Mass. CLE)

WILLS--MICHIGAN
MICHIGAN WILL DRAFTING (ICLE - Michigan)

WILLS--MICHIGAN-FORMS
MICHIGAN ESTATE PLANNING, WILL DRAFTING AND ESTATE ADMINISTRATION FORMS--PRACTICE (Aspen)

WILLS--MISSOURI-FORMS
MISSOURI ESTATE PLANNING, WILL DRAFTING AND ESTATE ADMINISTRATION FORMS - PRACTICE (Aspen)

WILLS--NEW JERSEY
NEW JERSEY ESTATE PLANNING, WILL DRAFTING AND ESTATE ADMINISTRATION FORMS--PRACTICE (Aspen)

WILLS--NEW YORK
DRAFTING NEW YORK WILLS (Bender)
MURPHY'S WILL CLAUSES: ANNOTATIONS AND FORMS WITH TAX EFFECTS (national and N.Y. ed.) (Bender)
NEW YORK KASS ON WILLS (Gould)
NEW YORK WILLS AND TRUSTS, 3/e (Shepard's)

WILLS--OKLAHOMA
OKLAHOMA WILLS AND INTESTATE SUCCESSION (Butterworth-Texas)

WILLS--OKLAHOMA-FORMS
OKLAHOMA ESTATE PLANNING, WILL DRAFTING AND ESTATE ADMINISTRATION FORMS (Aspen)

WILLS--PENSYLVANIA
LAW OF WILLS IN PENNSYLVANIA (Bisel)

WILLS--WASHINGTON
WASHINGTON WILLS & TRUST FORMS (Book Pub.)

WITNESSES
see also Depositions; Evidence

CALIFORNIA EXPERT WITNESS GUIDE, 2nd ed. (Calif. CEB)
CROSS-EXAMINATION OF LAY WITNESSES (Art of Advocacy Series) (Bender)
CROSS-EXAMINATION OF MEDICAL EXPERTS (Bender)
CROSS-EXAMINATION OF NON-MEDICAL EXPERTS (Art of Advocacy Series) (Bender)
DIRECT EXAMINATION (Art of Advocacy Series) (Bender)
EXAMINATION OF WITNESSES (Clark Boardman Callaghan)
QUALIFYING & ATTACKING EXPERT WITNESSES (James)

REPRESENTATION OF WITNESSES BEFORE FEDERAL GRAND JURIES (Clark Boardman Callaghan)

<u>WITNESSES--CONNECTICUT</u>
EXAMINING EYEWITNESSES AND INTERVIEWING WITNESSES (Conn. Bar)

<u>WITNESSES--MARYLAND</u>
EYE-WITNESS IDENTIFICATION (Clark Boardman Callaghan)

<u>WOMEN'S RIGHTS</u>
WOMEN AND THE LAW (Clark Boardman Callaghan)

<u>WORKMEN'S COMPENSATION</u>
BENEFITS REVIEW BOARD - BLACK LUNG REPORTER (Bender)
BENEFITS REVIEW BOARD - LONGSHORE REPORTER (Bender)
HANDLING OCCUPATIONAL DISEASE CASES (Clark Boardman Callaghan)
MANUAL OF RULES, CLASSIFICATIONS, AND INTERPRETATIONS FOR WORKERS COMPENSATION INSURANCE (Intl. Risk Mgmt. Inst.)
MANUFACTURING RISK MANAGEMENT AND INSURANCE (Intl. Risk Mgmt. Inst.)
WORKERS' COMPENSATION LAW REPORTS (CCH)
WORKMEN'S COMPENSATION FOR OCCUPATIONAL INJURIES AND DEATH (desk ed.) (Bender)
WORKMEN'S COMPENSATION LAW (Bender)

<u>WORKMEN'S COMPENSATION--ARKANSAS</u>
WORKERS' COMPENSATION DESKBOOK (Arkansas Bar)

<u>WORKMEN'S COMPENSATION--CALIFORNIA</u>
CALIFORNIA LAW OF EMPLOYEE INJURIES AND WORKMEN'S COMPENSATION (Bender)
CALIFORNIA UNEMPLOYMENT AND DISABILITY PROGRAMS (Parker)
CALIFORNIA WORKERS' COMPENSATION CLAIMS & BENEFITS (Parker)
CALIFORNIA WORKERS' COMPENSATION LAW (Parker)

<u>WORKMEN'S COMPENSATION--COLORADO</u>
COLORADO WORKERS' COMPENSATION LAW AND PRACTICE (CLP)

<u>WORKMEN'S COMPENSATION--CONNECTICUT</u>
ADVANCED WORKERS' COMPENSATION LAW (Conn. Bar)
WORKERS' COMPENSATION (Conn. Bar)

<u>WORKMEN'S COMPENSATION--DISTRICT OF COLUMBIA</u>
WORKERS COMPENSATION PRACTICE MANUAL (D.C. Bar)

<u>WORKMEN'S COMPENSATION--FLORIDA</u>
FLORIDA WORKERS' COMPENSATION MANUAL (Butterworth-Fla.)

<u>WORKMEN'S COMPENSATION--ILLINOIS</u>
ILLINOIS WORKERS' COMPENSATION PRACTICE (Illinois ICLE)

<u>WORKMEN'S COMPENSATION--INDIANA</u>
WORKER'S COMPENSATION (Indiana CLE)

<u>WORKMEN'S COMPENSATION--IOWA</u>
IOWA LEGAL FORMS -- WORKERS' COMPENSATION (Butterworth-St. Paul)

<u>WORKMEN'S COMPENSATION--KANSAS</u>
KANSAS WORKERS' COMPENSATION PRACTICE MANUAL (Kansas Bar)

<u>WORKMEN'S COMPENSATION--KENTUCKY</u>
KENTUCKY WORKERS' COMPENSATION (Lawyers Coop.)

<u>WORKMEN'S COMPENSATION--MAINE</u>
MAINE WORKERS COMPENSATION ACT: PRACTICE AND PROCEDURE (Butterworth-NH)
MAINE WORKERS' COMPENSATION COMMISSION: APPELLATE DIVISION DECISIONS (Butterworth-NH)

WORKMEN'S COMPENSATION--MARYLAND
WORKERS' COMPENSATION MANUAL, 6th ed. (MICPEL)

WORKMEN'S COMPENSATION--MASSACHUSETTS
MASSACHUSETTS WORKERS' COMPENSATION PRACTICE MANUAL (Butterworth-NH)

WORKMEN'S COMPENSATION--MICHIGAN
MICHIGAN WORKERS' COMPENSATION LAW REPORTER (LRP)
WORKER'S COMPENSATION IN MICHIGAN: LAW & PRACTICE, Rev. Ed. (ICLE - Michigan)

WORKMEN'S COMPENSATION--MINNESOTA
LAMBERTSON'S AFTERMATH - CIVIL LITIGATION AFTER WORKERS' COMPENSATION (MILE)
UNDERSTANDING MINNESOTA WORKERS' COMPENSATION (MILE)
WORKERS COMPENSATION PRACTICE IN MINNESOTA (Minn. CLE)
WORKERS' COMPENSATION (MILE)
WORKERS' COMPENSATION: A PRACTICAL GUIDE (MILE)
WORKERS' COMPENSATION INDEX (Minn. CLE)

WORKMEN'S COMPENSATION--MISSOURI
MISSOURI WORKERS' COMPENSATION (MoBar)
MISSOURI WORKERS' COMPENSATION (Lawyers Coop.)
MISSOURI WORKERS' COMPENSATION LAW REPORTER (LRP)
REFERENCE GUIDE TO WORKMEN'S COMPENSATION LAW (Thomas)

WORKMEN'S COMPENSATION--NEBRASKA
NEBRASKA LEGAL FORMS--WORKER'S COMPENSATION (Butterworth-St. Paul)
WORKERS' COMPENSATION HANDBOOK (Nebraska CLE)

WORKMEN'S COMPENSATION--NEW HAMPSHIRE
THE LAW OF WORKERS' COMPENSATION (NH Bar)

WORKMEN'S COMPENSATION--NEW YORK
HANDLING THE BASIC WORKER'S COMPENSATION CASE IN NEW YORK (NYSBA)
NEW YORK WORKER'S COMPENSATION LAW REPORTER (LRP)
NEW YORK WORKERS CONPENSATION LAW HANDBOOK (Gould)

WORKMEN'S COMPENSATION--OHIO
ADVANCED WORKERS' COMPENSATION LAW (Ohio CLE)
OHIO WORKERS' COMPENSATION CLAIMS (Lawyers Coop.)

WORKMEN'S COMPENSATION--OREGON
WORKERS' COMPENSATION MANUAL (Oregon Bar)

WORKMEN'S COMPENSATION--PENNSYLVANIA
PENNSYLVANIA WORKER'S COMPENSATION LAW REPORTER (LRP)
PENNSYLVANIA WORKMEN'S COMPENSATION, INJURY AND DISEASE LAWS (Bisel)

WORKMEN'S COMPENSATION--TEXAS
A GUIDE TO TEXAS WORKERS' COMPENSATION REFORM (Butterworth-Texas)
TEXAS WORKER'S COMPENSATION LAW (Bender)
TEXAS WORKERS' COMPENSATION TRIAL MANUAL (Parker)

WORKMEN'S COMPENSATION--VIRGINIA
WORKER'S COMPENSATION FOR THE EMPLOYER'S ATTORNEY & CLAIMANT'S ATTORNEY (Jt. Comm. Va.)

WORKMEN'S COMPENSATION--WISCONSIN
WORKER'S COMPENSATION HANDBOOK (State Bar of Wisc.)

WRONGFUL DEATH
see Torts

ZONING LAW
THE LAW OF ZONING AND PLANNING (Clark Boardman Callaghan)
A PRACTICAL GUIDE TO WINNING LAND USE APPROVAL AND PERMITS (Bender)

ZONING AND LAND USE CONTROLS (Bender)
ZONING AND PLANNING DESKBOOK (Clark Boardman Callaghan)

<u>ZONING LAW--CALIFORNIA</u>
LOS ANGELES COUNTY ZONING SUBDIVISION CODE (Book Pub.)

<u>ZONING LAW--CONNECTICUT</u>
ADVANCED PLANNING & ZONING (Conn. Bar)

<u>ZONING LAW--FLORIDA</u>
FLORIDA ZONING LAW MANUAL (Butterworth-Fla.)

<u>ZONING LAW--INDIANA</u>
PLANNING AND ZONING (Indiana CLE)
ZONING: RULES, PROCEDURES & PROBLEMS (Indiana CLE)

<u>ZONING LAW--MARYLAND</u>
ZONING LAW MANUAL (MICPEL)

<u>ZONING LAW--MASSACHUSETTS</u>
MASSACHUSETTS ZONING MANUAL (Mass. CLE)

<u>ZONING LAW--NEW HAMPSHIRE</u>
NEW HAMPSHIRE MUNICIPAL PRACTICE SERIES: LAND USE PLANNING & ZONING (Butterworth-NH)

<u>ZONING LAW--NEW YORK CITY</u>
ZONING RESOLUTION (NYC)

<u>ZONING LAW--PENNSYLVANIA</u>
PENNSYLVANIA ZONING LAW AND PRACTICE (Bisel)

<u>ZONING LAW--TEXAS</u>
TEXAS MUNICIPAL ZONING LAW (Butterworth-Texas)

<u>ZONING LAW--WASHINGTON</u>
SEATTLE ZONING CODE (Book Pub.)